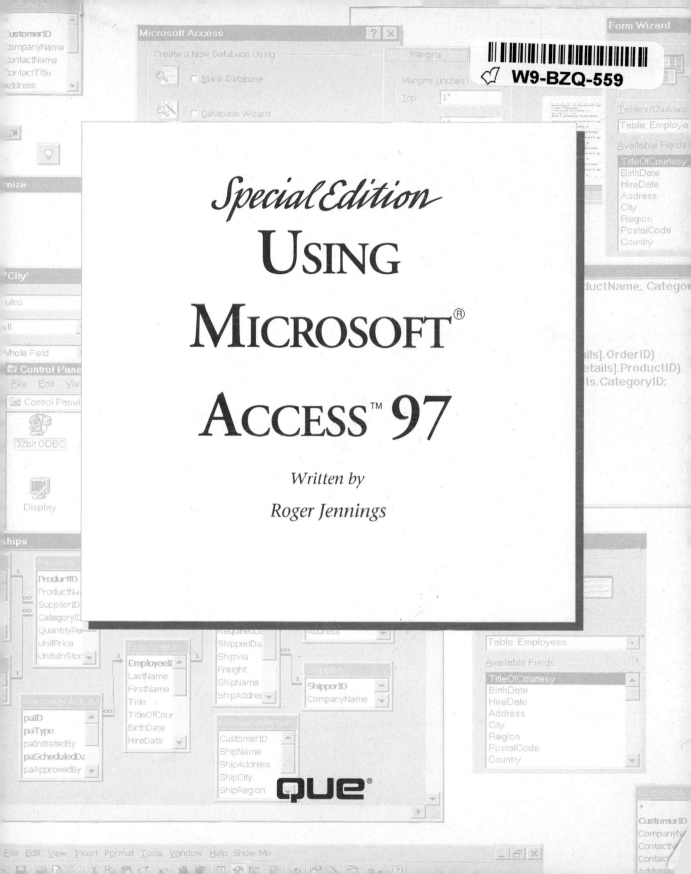

*Special Edition*
# USING
# MICROSOFT®
# ACCESS™ 97

*Written by*

*Roger Jennings*

**que®**

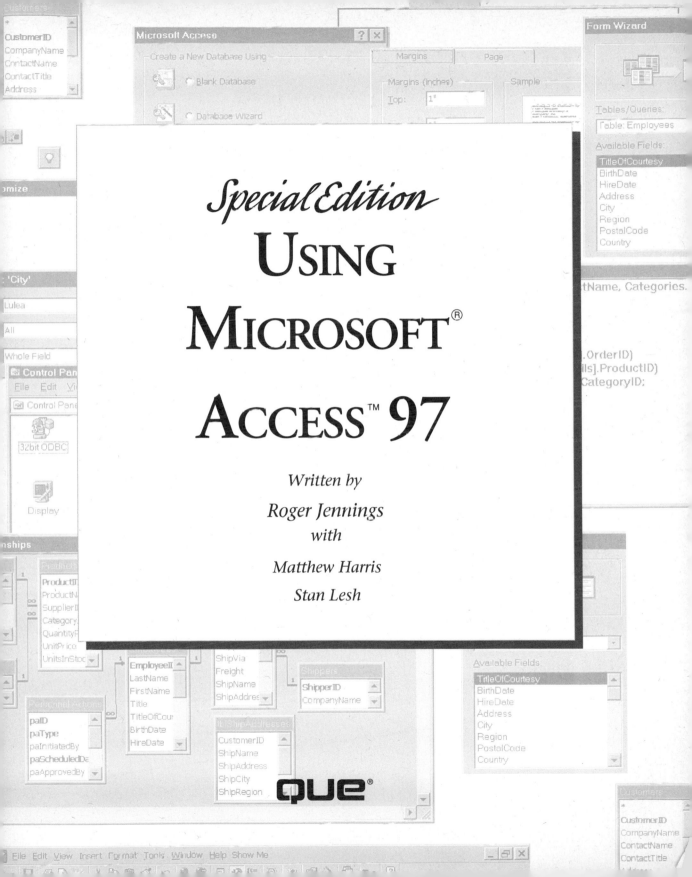

*Special Edition*

# USING

# MICROSOFT®

# ACCESS™ 97

*Written by*

*Roger Jennings*

*with*

*Matthew Harris*

*Stan Lesh*

que®

# Special Edition Using Microsoft® Access™ 97

Library of Congress Catalog No.: 96-71443

ISBN: 0-7897-0916-3

99 98 97    6  5  4  3  2  1

Interpretation of the printing code: the rightmost double-digit number is the year of the book's printing; the rightmost single-digit number, the number of the book's printing. For example, a printing code of 96-1 shows that the first printing of the book occurred in 1996.

Composed in *Stone Serif* and *MCPdigital* by Que Corporation

# Contents at a Glance

Learning Fundamentals

for Information

Creating Forms and Reports

Publishing Data

Integrating Access

Using Advanced Techniques

# Contents

## 7 Linking, Importing, and Exporting Tables    203

## 26  Connecting to Client/Server Databases             913

## 27  Replicating Access Databases                        955

## 30 Responding to Events with VBA 5.0          1049

## 31 Exchanging Data with Automation and ActiveX Controls          1095

# Credits

*This book is dedicated to my wife, Alexandra.*

# About the Author

**Roger Jennings** is a consultant and author specializing in Windows database and digital video applications. He was a member of the Microsoft beta-test team for Microsoft Access 1.0, 1.1, 2.0, 95, and 97; Windows 3.1 and 95; Windows NT 3.5, 3.51, and 4.0; Visual Basic 2.0, 3.0, 4.0, and 5.0; SQL Server 6.0 and 6.5; Internet Information Server 3.0 (code-named Denali); and ActiveMovie. In addition to writing the four preceding editions of this book, he is the author of Que's *Special Edition Using Windows NT Server 4*, *Unveiling Windows 95*, *Discover Windows 3.1 Multimedia*, and *Access for Windows Hot Tips*. Roger was a contributing author to Que's *Special Edition Using Windows 95*, *The Official VBPJ Guide to Visual Basic*, *Excel Professional Techniques*, *Killer Windows Utilities*, and *Using Visual Basic*. He has written two other books about creating database applications with Access and Visual Basic, co-authored a book on using Microsoft Visual C++ for database development, is a contributing editor of *Visual Basic Programmer's Journal*, and has written articles for the *Microsoft Developer Network News* and the MSDN CD-ROMs.

Roger has more than 25 years of computer-related experience and has presented technical papers on computer hardware and software to the Academy of Sciences of the former USSR, the Society of Automotive Engineers, the American Chemical Society, and a variety of other scientific and technical organizations. He is a principal of OakLeaf Systems, a Northern California software development and consulting firm. You may contact him via CompuServe (**70233,2161**) or on the Internet (**70233.2161@compuserve. com**).

# Acknowledgments

Matthew Harris, a consultant and author living in Oakland, California, updated Chapters 2 through 15, 19 through 22, 27, and 28 from the fourth edition of this book, *Special Edition Using Access 95*. Matthew has been involved with the microcomputer industry since 1980. He has provided programming technical support, training, and consulting services to the 6th international Conference on AIDS, the University of California at San Francisco, and many private firms. Matthew began programming applications for IBM PCs and compatibles in 1983 and has written commercially-distributed applications and in-house programs for a variety of clients. He also has taught classes on using MS-DOS and on programming in BASIC and Pascal. Matthew is the author of *The Disk Compression Book*, and the co-author of *Using FileMaker Pro 2.0 for Windows* (both published by Que). He was a contributing author for Que's *Special Edition Using Word for Windows 6*, *Special Edition Using Excel 5*, *Excel Professional Techniques*, *Using Paradox 4.5 for DOS*, *Special Edition Using Paradox for Windows 5.0*, *The Paradox Developer's Guide*, *Using MS-DOS 6*, and *Unveiling Windows 95*. Reach Matthew on CompuServe at **74017,766**.

Stan Leszynski is the author of the *Leszynski Naming Conventions for MicroSoft Access*, an abridged version of which appears in Appendix B, "Naming Conventions for Access Objects and Variables." He also is the author of *Access Expert Solutions* published by Que. Stan founded Leszynski Company, Inc., in 1982 to create custom PC database applications, and since that time the firm has created solutions for hundreds of clients, including Microsoft Corporation. The company also has written retail products sold by Microsoft, Microrim, Qualitas, and Kwery, which have a user base of more than two million people. Successful products include the OLE Calender control shipped with Access 2.0 and Access 95, the 386MAX memory manager, and four R:BASE developer tools. Stan's company currently specializes in Access, Visual Basic, SQL Server, and Visual C++ applications. Stan's second company, Kwery Corporation, shipped the first Access add-in, Access to Word, and the first OLE Controls for Access 2.0, Kwery Control Pak 1. Stan is a columnist on developer issues for *Access/Visual Basic Advisor* magazine and speaks regularly at Access conferences in the U.S., Canada, and Europe. Contact Stan on CompuServe (**71151,1114**).

Thanks to Jim Sturms, Monte Slichter, Richard Dickinson, and all of the other members of Microsoft Corporation's product support and product management staff during the beta-testing period for Access 97. Their prompt replies to questions concerning the pre-release versions of Access are especially appreciated. Thanks also to Access Insiders and other members of Access 97 beta program for aiding in the resolution of many prerelease issues.

Kevin Kloss, development editor, provided valuable insight and suggestions for the development of this book's content and organization. Angela Wethington, acquisitions editor, made sure that I did not fall too far behind the manuscript submission schedule. Lisa Gebken, production editor, put in long hours to add last-minute changes incorporated in the final release candidate of Access 97 and still met a very tight publication schedule. Technical editing was done by Jim O'Connor, Tim Schubach, and Sara Strock. Their contributions to this book are gratefully acknowledged. The responsibility for any errors or omissions, however, rests solely on my shoulders.

## We'd Like to Hear from You!

As part of our continuing effort to produce books of the highest possible quality, Que would like to hear your comments. To stay competitive, we *really* want you, as a computer book reader and user, to let us know what you like or dislike most about this book or other Que products.

You can mail comments, ideas, or suggestions for improving future editions to the address below, or send us a fax at (317) 581-4663. For the online inclined, Macmillan Computer Publishing has a forum on CompuServe (type **GO QUEBOOKS** at any prompt) through which our staff and authors are available for questions and comments. The address of our Internet site is **http://www.mcp.com** (World Wide Web).

In addition to exploring our forum, please feel free to contact me personally to discuss your opinions of this book: I'm **74201,1064** on CompuServe, and I'm **kkloss@que.mcp.com** on the Internet.

Thanks in advance—your comments will help us to continue publishing the best books available on computer topics in today's market.

Kevin Kloss
Product Development Specialist
Que Corporation
201 W. 103rd Street
Indianapolis, Indiana 46290
USA

# Introduction

Microsoft Access 97, Version 8.0 (called Access 97 in this book) is a powerful and robust 32-bit relational database management system (RDBMS) for creating desktop and client/ server database applications that run under Windows 95 and Windows NT 3.51 and 4.0. As a component of the Professional and Developer Editions of the Microsoft Office 97 suite, Access 97 has an upgraded user interface that is consistent with Microsoft Excel 97 and Word 97, as well as Windows 95 common controls, such as an Explorer-style Database window and common file open and save dialogs.

Like all members of Office 97, Access 97 offers a variety of new Internet-related features for creating HTML documents used by the World Wide Web. The upgraded Jet 3.5 database engine speeds queries against client/server databases with ODBCDirect. Aside from Internet enhancements and ODBCDirect, Access 97 does not differ dramatically from Access 95. Improved performance was Microsoft's first priority for the developers of Access 97, because Access 95 had gained a well-deserved reputation for slow operation. Ease of use was the second priority; Access 97 includes many new or improved wizards and other aids designed for first-time database users.

If you're a new Access user, a brief history of Microsoft Access is useful to put Access 97 in perspective. Version 1.0 of Access revolutionized the Windows database market and achieved a new record for sales of a Windows application—Microsoft Corporation received orders for more than 750,000 copies of Access 1.0 between its release data in mid-November 1992, and January 31, 1993. Access 1.1, introduced in May 1993, solved some of the shortcomings in Access 1.0, and the Access 1.1 Distribution Kit (ADK) gave developers the ability to release royalty-free, runtime versions of their Access applications.

Access 2.0, released about a year after Access 1.1, added OLE 2.0 client capability and was the first Microsoft application to use 16-bit OLE Controls, prepackaged objects that extended the already rich set of control objects of Access. Access 2.0 was a member of the Professional Edition of the phenomenally successful Microsoft Office 4.x software suite. Office 4.x gained almost 90 percent of the Windows productivity software suite market. By far, the majority of Access 2.0's multimillion-copy sales resulted from the product's inclusion in Office 4.x.

Microsoft introduced Access 95, the first 32-bit version of Access, in late 1995 as a component of Microsoft Office 95. Access 95 adopted VBA as its programming language and was the first multithreaded member of the Office suite. The success of Office 95, and thus Access 95, was dependent on adoption of Windows 95 and, to a lesser extent, Windows NT Workstation 3.5+, by major corporate accounts. Windows 95 was installed on more than 80 percent of all new PCs shipped, but the rate of migration from 16-bit to 32-bit Windows on existing PCs turned out to be much slower than anticipated by Microsoft and other software publishers. In many cases, moving to Access 95 required additional RAM. Even with 16M of RAM, however, many 32-bit Access applications ran slower than their 16-bit predecessors in 8M of RAM. Fortunately, the trend toward upgrading 80486DX PCs to 133-MHz and faster Pentium models accelerated during 1996, and 16M became the standard for all but the most parsimonious organizations. Use of Access 95 began to really take off in mid-1996. In the fall of 1996, Microsoft announced that the firm had sold a cumulative total of 10 million copies of Access.

One of the primary reasons for Access's success is that Access duplicates on the PC desktop many of the features of client/server relational database systems, also called *SQL databases*. Client/server RDBMSs are leading the way in transferring database applications from minicomputers and mainframes to networked PCs—a process called *downsizing*. Despite Access's power, this desktop RDBMS is easy for nonprogrammers to use. Buttons on upgraded multiple toolbars, which are almost identical across the Office 97 members, offer shortcuts for menu commands. An extensive collection of wizards and add-ins handle most of the mundane chores involved in creating and modifying tables, queries, forms, graphs, and reports. Builders aid you in creating complex controls on forms and reports, as well as in writing expressions. Last, and in this case least, an animated Office Assistant attempts to anticipate users' questions about Access 97.

Microsoft Access 1.0 introduced a new approach to writing macros that automate repetitive database operations. Access 95's 40+ macro instructions were remarkably powerful; you could create quite sophisticated database applications using only Access macros. Access 97 relegates macros to the "for backward compatibility only" category. Office 97 brings a common version 5.0 of 32-bit Visual Basic for Applications (VBA) to Access, Excel, Word, and even PowerPoint. Visual Basic 5.0 shares the same VBA engine with members of Office 97. VBA's syntax is easy to learn, yet VBA provides a vocabulary rich enough to satisfy veteran xBase and Paradox application developers. Making the transition from Access macros to VBA is important, because there's no guarantee that the next version of Access will continue to support macro programming.

Access 97 supports 32-bit Object Linking and Embedding (OLE) 2.1 as both a container (client) and as an ActiveX component (formerly OLE Automation server) application, giving you the benefits of in-place activation of objects, such as Excel 97 worksheets and Word 97 documents stored in Access databases. (Access 2.0 was an OLE 2.0 container application only.) Conversely, you can manipulate Access objects within an Excel 97, Word 97, Project 97, or 32-bit Visual Basic 4+ application. Access 97 also lets you manipulate ActiveX components created with Visual Basic 4+. *LOBjects* (Line of Business Objects) built with Visual Basic 4+ and shared with other VBA-enabled applications promise to make a major change in the methodology of creating enterprise-scale database applications.

Access 97 and Visual Basic 4+ share the ability to take advantage of the new ActiveX Controls (formerly OLE Controls) that Microsoft, third-party add-in software publishers, and you create. (The Control Creation Edition of Visual Basic 5.0 lets you design your own ActiveX controls that are compatible with Access 97.) ActiveX Controls provide Access 97 with the extensibility that VBX custom controls brought to Visual Basic. Access 97 can accommodate almost every 32-bit OLE Control included with the Professional and Enterprise editions of Visual Basic 4.0. The new, lightweight ActiveX controls for Internet applications, many of which are available for downloading from **http://www. microsoft.com**, carry much less overhead. Other members of Office 97 also can take advantage of ActiveX controls in dialogs created with Microsoft's new Forms 2.0 technology.

Access is specifically designed for creating multiuser applications where database files are shared on networks, and Access incorporates a sophisticated security system to prevent unauthorized persons from viewing or modifying the databases you create. Access's security system is modeled on that of Microsoft SQL Server 4+. Access 2.0 simplified the labyrinthine security employed by versions 1.x and made creating secure Access applications much easier. No substantial changes have been made to the Access security system in Access 97, but the User-Level Security Wizard introduced with Access 95 makes secure applications easier to implement.

Access has a unique database structure that is capable of combining all related data tables and their indexes, forms, reports, macros, and VBA code within a single .mdb database file. It is now a generally-accepted database design practice (GADBDP) to use separate .mdb files to contain data and application objects; your application .mdb links tables contained in the data .mdb. (The term *link* replaced *attach* beginning with Access 95.) Access 97 introduces a new file format, .mde, so you can distribute Access applications without including your original VBA source code.

Access has the capability to import data from and export data to the more popular PC database and spreadsheet files, as well as text files. Access also can attach dBASE, FoxPro, and Paradox table files to databases and manipulate these files in their native formats. You also can use Access on workstations that act as clients of networked file and database servers in client/server database systems. Access, therefore, fulfills all the requirements of a professional relational database management system, as well as a front-end development tool for use with client/server databases. Microsoft has made several improvements to these features in Access 97. The most important new features of Access 97 are discussed in Chapter 1, "Access 97 for Access 95 and 2.0 Users: What's New."

Several chapters of this book are devoted to using Access 97 with other members of Office 97, such as Microsoft Excel 97 and Microsoft Word 97, plus Microsoft Graph 8.0 and the Paint applet supplied with Windows 95. Applets are small but useful applications supplied as components of major applications; Graph 8.0, for example, is an OLE 2.1 applet.

# Who Should Read This Book?

*Special Edition Using Microsoft Access 97* takes an approach that is different from most books about database management applications. This book doesn't begin with the creation of a database for Widgets, Inc., nor does it require you to type a list of fictional customers for their new Widget II product line to learn the basics of Access. Instead, this book makes the following basic assumptions about your interest in Microsoft's relational database management system:

- You have one or more PCs operating in a business, professional, institutional, or government agency setting.

- You are using or have decided to use Microsoft Windows 95 or Windows NT Workstation 4.0 as the operating environment for at least some, if not all, of your PCs. (Applications you create with Access 97 run only under Windows 95 or Windows NT 3.51+.)

- You are able to navigate Microsoft Windows 95 using the mouse and keyboard. Books about DOS database managers no longer attempt to teach you DOS, nor does *Special Edition Using Microsoft Access 97* try to teach you Windows fundamentals.

- You aren't starting from "ground zero." You now have or will have access via your PC to data that you want to process with a Windows database manager. You already may have acquired Access and want to learn to use it more quickly and effectively. Or, you may be considering using Access as the database manager for yourself, your department or division, or your entire organization.

- Your existing data is in the form of one or more database, spreadsheet, or even plain text files that you want to manipulate with a relational database management system. Access can process the most common varieties of all three types of files.

- If you're planning to use Access 97 as a front-end to a client/server RDBMS, you have SQL Server 6.5 installed or have a 32-bit ODBC driver and the required client license for your SQL database.

- If your data is on a mini- or mainframe computer, you are connected to that computer by a local area network and a database gateway or through terminal emulation software and an adapter card. Otherwise, you are able to obtain the data on PC-compatible disks; some people call this method *SneakerNet* or *FootWare*.

If some or all of your data is in the form of ASCII or ANSI text files, or files from a spreadsheet application, you need to know how to create an Access database from the beginning and import the data into Access's own .mdb file structure. If your data is in the form of dBASE, FoxPro, or Paradox files, you can link the files as tables and continue to use them in the format native to your prior database manager. Access 97 lets you link Excel and text files to Access databases. (Access 2.0 required the Microsoft ODBC Desktop Database Driver kit to attach Excel and text files. Office 97 includes the required ODBC drivers.) The capability to link files in their native format is an important advantage to have during conversion from one database management system to another. Each of these subjects receives thorough coverage in this book.

*Special Edition Using Microsoft Access 97* is designed to accommodate readers who are new to database management; who are occasional or frequent users of dBASE, FoxPro, or Paradox for DOS or Windows; or who are seasoned Windows database application developers who are migrating to Microsoft Access.

# How This Book Is Organized

*Special Edition Using Microsoft Access 97* is divided into eight parts that are arranged in increasing levels of detail and complexity. Each division after Part I draws on the knowledge and experience you have gained in the prior parts, so use of the book in a linear, front-to-back manner through Part IV, "Publishing Data on Intranets and the Internet," is recommended during the initial learning process. After you've absorbed the basics, *Special Edition Using Microsoft Access 97* becomes a valuable reference tool for the advanced topics.

As you progress through the chapters in this book, you create a model of an Access application called *Personnel Actions*. In Chapter 4, "Working with Access Databases and Tables," you create the Personnel Actions table. In the following chapters, you add new features to the Personnel Actions application. Make sure to perform the example exercises for the Personnel Actions application each time you encounter them, because succeeding examples build on your prior work.

The eight parts of *Special Edition Using Microsoft Access 97*, and the topics they cover are described in the following sections.

### Part I, "Learning Access Fundamentals"

Part I introduces you to Access and many of the unique features that make Access the easiest to use of all database managers. The chapters in Part I deal almost exclusively with tables, the basic elements of Access databases.

Chapter 1, "Access 97 for Access 95 and 2.0 Users: What's New" provides a summary of the most important new features of Access 97 and a detailed description of each of these additions and improvements. Much of the content of this chapter is of interest primarily to readers who now use Access 2.0, because most of the changes from Access 95 to Access 97 are incremental in nature. Readers new to Access, however, benefit from the explanations of why many of these features are significant in everyday use of Access 97.

In Chapter 2, "Up and Running with Access 97," you learn how to open an Access database, view a table, use a typical query, add a few new data items, view the results of your work, and finally print a formatted report. Chapter 2 shows you how to use the Database Wizard, introduced by Access 95, to create a database from the standard database templates included with Access 97.

Chapter 3, "Navigating Within Access," shows you how to navigate Access by explaining its toolbar and menu choices and how they relate to the structure of Access.

Chapter 4, "Working with Access Databases and Tables," delves into the details of Access tables and shows you how to create tables, and choose the optimum data types from the many new types Access offers.

Chapter 5, "Entering, Editing, and Validating Data in Tables," shows you how to arrange the data in tables to suit your needs and limit the data displayed to only that information you want. Finding and replacing data in the fields of tables also is covered here.

Chapter 6, "Sorting, Finding, and Filtering Data in Tables," describes how to add new records to tables, enter data in the new records, and edit data in existing records. Chapter 6 describes how to make best use of the Filter by Form and Filter by Selection features of Access 97.

Chapter 7, "Linking, Importing, and Exporting Tables," explains how you import and export files of other database managers, spreadsheet applications, and even ASCII files you may download from the Internet or information utilities such as The Microsoft Network, CompuServe, America Online, Dow Jones News Service, or government-sponsored databases. Chapter 7 explains the Table Analyzer Wizard that aids in creating a relational database structure from "flat files" in ASCII and spreadsheet formats.

### Part II, "Querying for Information"

Part II explains how to create Access queries to select the way you view data contained in tables and how you take advantage of Access's relational database structure to link multiple tables with joins.

Chapter 8, "Using Query by Example," starts you off with simple queries created with Access's graphic query-by-example (QBE) design window. You learn how to choose the fields of the tables that are included in your query and return query result sets from these tables. Chapter 8 shows you how to use the Select Query Wizard to simplify the QBE process.

Chapter 9, "Understanding Operators and Expressions in Access," introduces you to the operators and expressions that you need to create queries that provide a meaningful result. You use the improved Debug window of the VBA 5.0 code editor to evaluate the expressions you write.

In Chapter 10, "Creating Multitable and Crosstab Queries," you create relations between tables, called *joins*, and learn how to add criteria to queries so that the query result set includes only those records you want. Chapter 10 also takes you through the process of designing powerful crosstab queries to summarize data and to present information in a format similar to that of worksheets.

Chapter 11, "Using Action Queries," shows you how to develop action queries that update the tables underlying append, delete, update, and make-table queries. Chapter 11 also covers Access 95's referential integrity features, including cascading updates and cascading deletions.

### Part III, "Creating Forms and Reports"

Part III is your introduction to the primary application objects of Access. (Tables and queries are considered database objects.) Forms make your Access applications come alive with the control objects you add using Access 97's toolbox. Access's full-featured report generator lets you print fully formatted reports or save reports to files that you can process in Excel 97 or Word 97.

Chapter 12, "Creating and Using Forms," shows you how to use Access's Form Wizards to create simple forms and subforms that you can modify to suit your particular needs. Chapter 12 introduces you to the Subform Builder Wizard that uses drag-and-drop techniques to automatically create subforms for you.

Chapter 13, "Designing Custom Multitable Forms," shows you how to design custom forms for viewing and entering your own data with Access's advanced form design tools.

Chapter 14, "Printing Basic Reports and Mailing Labels," describes how to design and print simple reports with Access's Report Wizard and how to print preformatted mailing labels using the Mailing Label Wizard.

Chapter 15, "Preparing Advanced Reports," describes how to use more sophisticated sorting and grouping techniques, as well as subreports, to obtain a result that exactly meets your detail and summary data reporting requirements.

### Part IV, "Publishing Data on Intranets and the Internet"

Part IV describes the new Internet enhancements of Access 97.

Chapter 16, "Working with Hyperlinks and HTML," describes Microsoft's Internet strategy and introduces you to Access 97's new Hyperlink field data type. The chapter shows you how to use hyperlinks to connect to Word documents and Excel worksheets, as well as open Access form and report objects.

Chapter 17, "Exporting Data to World Wide Web Pages," describes how to export formatted static Web pages from table and query datasheets. You also learn how to use HTML templates and the Publish to the Web Wizard to create multipage Web documents from Access reports.

Chapter 18, "Creating Dynamic Web Pages," describes Internet Information Server 2+'s Internet Database Connector (IDC) for creating dynamic Web pages from Open Database Connectivity (ODBC) data sources. The chapter explains how to set up an Access ODBC data source and leads you through exporting Access datasheets to the .idc/.htx file combination required by IDC.

### Part V, "Integrating Access with Other Office 97 Applications"

Part V shows you how to use the new 32-bit Object Linking and Embedding (OLE) 2.1 features of Access 97 with Microsoft Graph 8.0, plus OfficeLinks to Excel 97 and Word 97.

Chapter 19, "Using 32-Bit OLE Components," explains Object Linking and Embedding, the principles that make OLE 2.1 useful in Windows application development, how these principles apply to your Access database applications, and how you use 32-bit ActiveX server applications with Access 95. Chapter 19 also explains Windows 95's Registry that replaces the registration database (REG.DAT) and .INI files of Windows 3.x.

Chapter 20, "Adding Graphics to Forms and Reports," describes how to best take advantage of Access OLE Object field data type and bound object frames to display graphics and play multimedia objects stored in your Access tables. Adding static graphics to forms and reports with unbound object frames is also covered.

Chapter 21, "Using Access with Microsoft Excel," gives you detailed examples of exchanging data between Access and Excel 97 workbooks by using Access as an OLE 2.1 client and server, without the need to write VBA code. The "Analyze It with MS Excel" OfficeLink feature of Access 97 also is covered.

Chapter 22, "Using Access with Microsoft Word and Mail Merge," shows you how to store documents in OLE Object fields, explains the OfficeLink "Publish It with MS Word" option for database publishing, and how to use Access 97's "Merge It" OfficeLink feature to interactively create form letters and envelopes addressed with data from your Access applications.

### Part VI, "Using Advanced Access Techniques"

Part VI covers the theoretical and practical aspects of relational database design and Structured Query Language (SQL), and then goes on to describe how to set up and use secure Access applications on a local area network. Part VI also describes how you use the ODBC Application Programming Interface (API) to create Access front-ends for client/ server databases.

Chapter 23, "Exploring Relational Database Design and Implementation," describes the process you use to create relational database tables from real-world data—a technique called *normalizing the database structure*. This chapter explains how to use the Database Documentor tool included with Access 97 to create a data dictionary that fully identifies each object in your database.

Chapter 24, "Working with Structured Query Language," explains how Access uses the Jet dialect of SQL to create queries and how to write your own SQL statements. Special emphasis is given to the newer Jet SQL extensions, such as UNION queries and subqueries, as well as Jet 3.5's implementation of SQL's Data Definition Language (DDL).

Chapter 25, "Securing Multiuser Network Applications," explains how to set up Access to share database files on a network and how to use the security features of Access to prevent unauthorized viewing of or tampering with your database files.

Chapter 26, "Connecting to Client/Server Databases," introduces you to the 32-bit ODBC 2.5 API and shows you how to create ODBC data sources from client/server databases, as well as the basics of designing Access front-ends for client/server databases.

Chapter 27, "Replicating Access Databases," shows you how to create independent replicas of Access databases on network servers or disks. Users update the replica databases, and the updated replicas later are merged with the design master database. The chapter briefly describes Access 97's new partial replication features.

### Part VII, "Programming, Distributing, and Converting Access Applications"

Part VII assumes that you have no programming experience in any language. Part VII explains the principles of writing programming code in object-enabled VBA and applies these principles to using Automation to exchange data with Excel 97 worksheets and Word 97 documents. Part VII also describes the Office 97 Developer Edition's Setup Wizard and supplies tips for converting Access 2.0 and 95 applications to Access 97.

Chapter 28, "Writing Visual Basic for Applications Code," describes how to use VBA to create user-defined functions stored in modules and to write simple procedures that you activate with macros or directly from events. Access's class modules (called *Code Behind Forms* in Access 2.0), which let you store event-handling code in Form and Report objects, also are described.

Chapter 29, "Understanding the Data Access Object Class," shows you how to declare and use members of the Jet 3.5 database engine's object collections, such as `TableDefs`, to create new tables and modify the properties of tables with VBA code.

Chapter 30, "Responding to Events with VBA 5.0," describes how to use VBA event-handling subprocedures in class modules to replace the macros used by earlier versions of Access. Chapter 30 explains the events triggered by Access form, report, and control object, and how to use methods of the `DoCmd` object to respond to events, such as clicking a command button.

Chapter 31, "Exchanging Data with Automation and ActiveX Controls," gives you a complete, working application that uses VBA and Automation (formerly OLE Automation) to transfer data to and from an Excel 97 worksheet. Using ActiveX controls, which replace the OLE Controls of prior Access versions, also is covered in this chapter.

Chapter 32, "Using the Office 97 Developer Edition," describes the content of the ODE, the distributable 32-bit ActiveX Controls included in the ODE, and how to use the Setup Wizard to create distribution disks for your runtime Access applications.

Chapter 33, "Migrating Access 2.0 and Access 95 Applications to Access 97," tells you what changes you need to make when you convert your current Access 2.0 and Access 95 database applications to Access 97. This chapter also describes how to use 32-bit Access 97 front-end applications with 16-bit Access 2.0 databases.

**Part VIII: "Appendixes"**
Appendix A, "Glossary," presents a glossary of the terms, abbreviations, and acronyms used in this book that may not be familiar to you and cannot be found in commonly used dictionaries.

Appendix B, "Naming Conventions for Access Objects and Variables," incorporates the most commonly used set of standardized rules for naming Access objects and Access VBA variables, the *Leszynski Naming Conventions for Microsoft Access*.

Appendix C, "Data Dictionary for the Personnel Actions Table," shows you how to implement the Personnel Actions table that is used for many of the examples in this book.

# How This Book Is Designed

The following special features are included in this book to assist readers.

 Readers who have never used a database management application are provided with quick-start examples to gain confidence and experience while using Access with the Northwind Traders sample database. Like Access, this book uses the *tabula rasa* approach: each major topic begins with the assumption that the reader has no prior experience with the subject. Therefore, when a button from the toolbar or control object toolbox is used, its icon is displayed in the margin.

> **Note**
>
> Notes offer advice to aid you in using Access, describe differences between Access 2 and 1.x, and explain the few remaining anomalies you find in version 2.0 of Access. In a few instances, notes explain similarities or differences between Access and other database management applications.

> **Tip**
>
> Tips describe shortcuts and alternative approaches to gaining an objective. These tips are based on the experience the authors gained during more than two years of testing successive alpha and beta versions of Access and the Access Distribution Kit.

> **Caution**
>
> Cautions are provided when an action can lead to an unexpected or unpredictable result, including loss of data; the text provides an explanation of how you can avoid such a result.

 Features that are new or have been modified in Access 97 are indicated by the Best of 97 icon in the margin, unless the change is only cosmetic. Where the changes are extensive and apply to an entire section of a chapter, the icon appears to the left or right of the section head.

All sample databases and associated queries, forms, reports, and the like, used in this book are posted to a page accessible from the Que Microsoft Office page of the Macmillan Superlibrary on the Internet (**http://www.mcp.com/que/MSoffice**).

Most software manuals require you to wade through all the details relating to a particular function of an application in a single chapter or part, before you progress to the next topic. In contrast, *Special Edition Using Microsoft Access 97* first takes you through the most frequently used steps to manipulate database tables and then concentrates on using your existing files with Access. Advanced features and nuances of Access are covered in later chapters. This type of structure requires cross-referencing so that you can easily locate more detailed or advanced coverage of the topic. Cross-references to specific sections in other chapters occur in the margins next to the material they pertain to, such as in the sample reference next to this paragraph:

▶▶ See "Opening a Database During Access Startup," p. 48

### Troubleshooting

*Troubleshooting boxes provide commonly asked questions about problems or challenges typically encountered by users.*

These troubleshooting tips are presented in the form of a commonly asked question and its answer.

# Typographic Conventions Used in This Book

This book uses various typesetting styles to distinguish between explanatory and instructional text, text you enter in dialogs, and text you enter in code-editing windows.

### Key Combinations and Menu Choices

Key combinations that you use to perform Windows operations are indicated by joining the keys with a plus sign: Alt+F4, for example. This indicates that you press and hold the Alt key while pressing the function key F4. In the rare cases when you must press and release a control key, and then enter another key, the keys are separated by a comma without an intervening space: Alt,F4, for example. Key combinations that perform menu operations that require more than one keystroke are called *shortcut keys*. An example of such a shortcut is the Windows 95 key combination, Ctrl+C, which substitutes for the Copy choice of the Edit menu in almost all Windows applications.

To select a menu option with the keyboard instead of the mouse, you press the letter that appears with an underscore (_) in the menu option. Sequences of individual menu items are separated by a comma: Edit, Cut, for example. The Alt key required to activate a choice from the main menu with an accelerator key is assumed and not shown.

Successive entries in dialogs follow the tab order of the dialog. Tab order is the sequence in which the caret moves when you press the Tab key to move from one entry or control option to another, a process known as *changing the focus*. The entry or control option that has the focus is the one that receives keystrokes or mouse clicks. Command buttons, option buttons, and check box choices are treated similarly to menu choices, but their accelerator key letters in the text don't include the underscore attribute.

File and folder names are initial-letter-capitalized in the text and headings of this book, in conformity to Windows 95 and Windows NT 4.0 filenaming conventions and the appearance of file names in Windows Explorer.

### SQL Statements and Keywords in Other Languages

SQL statements and code examples, including macro commands, are set in a monospace font. Keywords of SQL statements, such as SELECT, are set in all uppercase, as are the keywords of foreign database programming languages when they are used in comparative examples, such as xBase's DO WHILE ... ENDDO structure. Ellipses indicate intervening programming code that isn't shown in the text or examples.

Square brackets in **monospace boldface** type (**[]**) that appear within Jet SQL statements don't indicate optional items as they do in syntax descriptions. In this case, the square brackets are used in lieu of quotation marks to frame a literal string or to allow use of a table and field names, such as [Personnel Actions], that include embedded spaces or special punctuation, or field names that are identical to reserved words in VBA.

### Typographic Conventions Used for VBA

This book uses a special set of typographic conventions for references to Visual Basic for Applications keywords in the presentation of VBA examples:

- Monospace (MCPdigital) type is used for all examples of VBA code, as in the following statement:

  ```
  Dim NewArray ( ) As Long
  ReDim NewArray (9, 9, 9)
  ```

- Monospace type also is used when referring to names of properties of Access database objects, such as FormName.Width. The captions for text boxes and drop-down lists in which you enter values of properties, such as Source Connect String, are set in the proportionally spaced font (Stone Serif) of this book.

- **Bold monospace** type is used for all VBA reserved words and type-declaration symbols (which are not used in the code examples in this book), as shown in the preceding example. Standard function names in VBA also are set in bold type so that reserved words, standard function names, and reserved symbols stand out from variable and function names and values you assign to variables.

- *Italic monospace* type indicates a replaceable item. For example,

  ```
  Dim DataItem As String
  ```

- ***Bold italic monospace*** type indicates a replaceable reserved word, such as a data type, as in

  ```
  Dim DataItem As DataType
  ```

  ***DataType*** is replaced by a keyword corresponding to the desired VBA data type, such as **String** or **Variant**.

- An ellipsis (...) substitutes for code not shown in syntax and code examples, as in

  ```
  If...Then...Else...End If
  ```

- French braces ({}) surrounding two or more identifiers separated by the pipe symbol ( ¦ ) indicate that you must choose one of these identifiers, as in

  ```
  Do {While¦Until}...Loop
  ```

In this case, you must use either the **While** or the **Until** reserved word in your statement.

■ Square brackets ([], not in bold type) surrounding an identifier indicate that the identifier is optional, as in

```
Set tblName = dbName.OpenTable(strTableName[, fExclusive])
```

Here, the fExclusive flag, if set **True**, opens the table specified by strTableName for exclusive use. fExclusive is an optional argument.

# System Requirements for Access 97

Access 97 is a very resource-intensive application. Access must be installed on an 80486DX33 or better PC running Windows 95, Windows NT 3.51, or Windows NT 4.0. Although it's possible to install Windows 95 and Access 97 on an 80386 PC, you will find execution of Access on computers using the 80386-series CPUs to be very slow, and operation may be glacial with large tables. Access 97 requires 12M of RAM for adequate performance under Windows 95. If you plan to use Access 97 for extensive handling of graphic images or run it often with other applications using Object Linking and Embedding (OLE), 16M to 20M of RAM should be installed for use under Windows 95 and 24M of RAM or more for Windows NT 3.51+. Using OLE 2.1 to manipulate complex objects, such as large bitmaps, requires substantial amounts of memory. As a rule, adding more RAM is more cost-effective than increasing processor speed or power if you're using an 80486DX-based PC.

Most users of Access 97 install the product in conjunction with Office 97. A complete installation of Office 97 requires approximately 170M of disk space. A complete installation of the stand-alone version of Access 97 requires a total of about 70M of free disk space, and you should reserve at least 10M to store the new databases you create. (The incremental disk space requirement of Access 97 is somewhat less if you've already installed Office 97; Access 97 and the other members of Office 97 share a variety of files.) Installing the Office 97 Developer Edition requires another 20M of disk space. You also should have at least 25M of space available for a Windows 95 swap file or a dedicated Windows NT paging file of at least 50M. Access also makes use of numerous temporary files when processing large client/server database tables or storing large amounts of data returned from queries against client/server databases.

Access 97 and Windows 95 have been tested under Microsoft's DriveSpace disk data compression system included with Microsoft Plus! for Windows 95. DriveSpace reduces the physical fixed disk space required to install Access 95 by a factor of about 1.5 to 1.7. Bear in mind that DriveSpace compression is not compatible with the file compression system included with Windows NT 3.51 and Windows NT 4.0, so you cannot share compressed disk volumes between Windows 95 and Windows NT in dual-boot mode.

---

**Note**

Fixed disk compression utilities such as DriveSpace do not compress encrypted Access .mdb files significantly. Compression utilities rely on creating tokens that represent repeating groups of bytes in files. The utility stores the tokens and a single copy of the translation of each token. Encryption removes most, if not all, of the repeating groups of bytes in the file.

---

A mouse or trackball isn't a requirement for using the Access applications you create, but you need one of these two pointing devices to select and size the objects that you add to forms and reports using Access's toolbox. Because a pointing device is required to create Access applications, this book dispenses with the traditional "Here's how you do it with the mouse..." and "If you want to use the keyboard..." duplicate methodology in step-by-step examples. Designing your Access applications with accelerator keys to eliminate mouse operations speeds keyboard-oriented data entry by enabling the operator to keep his or her fingers on the keyboard during the entire process. Users accustomed to mouseless DOS database applications will appreciate your thoughtfulness.

# Other Sources of Information for Access

SQL and relational database design, which are discussed in Chapters 19 and 20, are the subject of myriad guides and texts covering one or both of these topics. Articles in database-related periodicals and files you read on the Internet or download from online information utilities, such as CompuServe, provide up-to-date assistance in using Access 97. The following sections provide a bibliography of database-related books and periodicals, as well as a brief description of Internet Web sites and CompuServe forums of interest to Access users.

### Books

The following books published by Que complement the content of this book by providing detailed coverage of Access programming techniques, application design, Structured Query Language, client/server databases, and the Windows 95 and Windows NT operating systems:

- *Access 97 Power Programming,* by F. Scott Barker, shows you how to get the most out of the Access flavor of VBA 5.0 and complements the VBA programming chapters of Part VII of this book. (Que, ISBN 0-7897-0915-5.)

- *Access 97 Expert Solutions,* by Stan Leszynzki, describes the Access 97 application design and implementation techniques employed by one of North America's top database developers. Stan is the author of the *Leszynski Naming Conventions for Microsoft Access*, Appendix B of this book. (Que, ISBN 0-7897-0367-X.)

- *Introduction to Databases*, by James J. Townsend, gives a thorough explanation of personal computer databases and their design. This book is especially recommended if the subject of PC databases is new to you. (Que, ISBN 0-88022-840-7.)

- *Understanding the New SQL: A Complete Guide*, by Jim Melton and Alan R. Simpson, describes the history and implementation of the American National Standards Institute's X3.135.1-1992 standard for the latest official version of Structured Query Language, SQL-92, on which Jet SQL is based. Jim Melton of Digital Equipment Corp. was the editor of the ANSI SQL-92 standard, which consists of more than 500 pages of fine print. (Morgan Kaufmann Publishers, ISBN 1-55860-245-3.)

- *Special Edition Using Microsoft SQL Server 6.5,* by Bob Branchek, Peter Hazelhurst, Stephen Wynkoop, and Scott Warner is designed to bring system and database administrators, as well as developers, up-to-date on the latest version of Microsoft SQL Server. (Que, ISBN 07897-0097-2.)

- *Special Edition Using Microsoft Internet Information Server* supplies detailed instructions for setting up an Internet or intranet Web site using IIS 2.0. This book extends the coverage of Part IV, "Publishing Data on Intranets and the Internet." (Que, ISBN 07897-0850-7.)

- *Special Edition Using Windows NT Server 4*, by Roger Jennings, provides all of the information you need to set up Windows NT Server 4.0 for sharing Access databases, install and run SQL Server 6.5, and create your own intranet Web site with Internet Information Server. (Que, ISBN 07897-0251-7.)

- *Special Edition Using Windows NT Workstation 4.0* by Paul Sanna, et al., complements this book by providing coverage of the client-side features of Windows NT 4.0 that are beyond the scope of this book. (Que, ISBN 07897-0673-3.)

- *Platinum Edition Using Windows 95* by Ron Person, et al., is a 1,300+ page book that covers all aspects of Windows 95 in detail and is especially useful as a reference for Windows 95 client networking and user/policy management. (Que, ISBN 07897-0797-7.)

### Periodicals

The following are a few of the magazines and newsletters that cover Access exclusively or in which articles on Microsoft Access appear on a regular basis:

- *Access/Visual Basic Advisor,* published by Advisor Communications International, Inc., is a full-color, bimonthly magazine intended to serve Access users and developers. You can supplement your subscription with an accompanying disk that includes sample databases, utilities, and other software tools for Access.

- *Data Based Advisor* is published by Data Based Solutions, Inc., a firm related to the publishers of Access Advisor. Data Based Advisor covers the gamut of desktop databases, with emphasis on xBase products, but Access receives its share of coverage, too.

- *DBMS* magazine, published by M&T, a Miller-Freeman company, is devoted to database technology as a whole, but DBMS concentrates on the growing field of client/server RDBMS. DBMS covers subjects, such as SQL and relational database design, that are of interest to all developers, not just those who use Access.

- *Inside Microsoft Access* is a monthly newsletter of Access tips and techniques of the Cobb Group, which publishes a variety of newsletters on products such as Visual Basic and Paradox.

- *Microsoft Interactive Developer,* published by Fawcette Technical Publications, Inc., covers Internet- and intranet-related topics, with emphasis on Internet Information Server and Visual Basic, Scripting Edition (VBScript).

- *Smart Access* is a monthly newsletter of Pinnacle Publishing, Inc., which publishes several other database-related newsletters. Smart Access is directed primarily to developers and Access power users. This newsletter tends toward advanced topics, such as creating libraries and using the Windows API with VBA. A disk is included with each issue. Like other publications directed to Access users, much of the content of Smart Access is of equal interest to Visual Basic database developers.

■ *Visual Basic Programmer's Journal* is a monthly magazine from Fawcette Technical Publications that covers all of the dialects of VBA. *Visual Basic Programmer's Journal* has a monthly column devoted to database topics of interest to Access and Visual Basic developers.

## Online Sources

The following sections describe the primary online sources of information of interest to users of Access 97. Prior to 1996, Microsoft provided end-user technical support for its products through a large number of CompuServe Information Services forums. Microsoft's Web site now is the primary source of new and updated information for Access users and developers. The former Microsoft CompuServe forums now are run by independent organizations, such as the Windows Users Group Network (WUGNET).

**The Internet.**   Internet Web sites and newsgroups rapidly are replacing commercial online services as the principal source of information of interest to all users of Windows and its applications. Following are the primary Web sites and news groups for Access 97 users and developers:

■ Microsoft's Access home page, **http://www.microsoft.com/msaccess/**, is the jumping-off point for Access users and includes links to all related home pages on the Microsoft Web site.

■ Microsoft's Access Developer home page, **http://www.microsoft.com/ accessdev/**, provides a variety of links to information of particular interest to the Access developer community. This home page provides a link for downloading the Access 97 Upsizing Wizard for automating the migration of Access multiuser applications to SQL Server 6.5 databases.

■ Microsoft's AnswerPoint home page, **http://www.microsoft.com/ supportnet/answerpoint/**, provides information about Microsoft's no-fee and low-fee support services for all its products. For other support options, go to **http://www.microsoft.com/Support/**.

■ *DevX*, Fawcette Technical Publications' new Web site for Windows developers at **http://www.windx.com/**, offers a wide range of news, features, and product reviews of ActiveX controls.

■ *Avatar Magazine*, an online service of Fawcette Technical Publications, Inc., complements *Microsoft Interactive Developer* as "an interactive publication for creators of interactive media...from Web sites to digital video." Check out the Avatar site at **http://www.avatarmag.com/**.

■ Microsoft's **msnews.microsoft.com** news server offers a variety of Access-related newsgroups at **microsoft.public.access.*subject***. When this book was written, there were more than 20 Access subject areas. A list of Microsoft Access newsgroups is available at **http://www.microsoft.com/support/news/Access.htm**.

■ The Access Developer Network site at **http://www.wji.com/access/homepage.html** provides a forum for Access developers with tips and source code, Access User Group meeting announcements, and links to other sites with Access content.

■ The UseNet **comp.databases.ms-access** newsgroup is an active community of Access users and developers.

**CompuServe.** CompuServe offers the following forums of interest to Access 97 users and developers:

■ The Microsoft Access forum (**GO MSACCESS**) provides peer-to-peer technical support for all versions of Access. The MSACCESS forum is one of the most active application forums on CompuServe. Many authors of books about Access and contributors to publications that feature Access, as well as professional Access developers, participate regularly in this forum. A variety of useful utility and sample applications written by third-party developers also are available for no charge other than the cost of connection time to CompuServe.

■ The Microsoft Knowledge Base (**GO MSKB**) contains text files of technical tips, workarounds for bugs, and other useful information about Microsoft applications. Use **Access** as the search term, but remember to turn on your communication software's capture-to-file feature because the information is in the form of messages that scroll down your screen, not in the form files. You also can search the Knowledge Base on America Online; use the keyword **Microsoft**.

■ Fawcette Technical Publications operates the *Visual Basic Programmers Journal and Discussion* forum (**GO VBPJFO**) and two Windows Components forums (**GO COMPA** and **GO COMPB**). VBPJFO offers message and library sections devoted to OLE, VBA/Office, Database, and Client/Server topics. Now that Access 97 has adopted the VBA programming language and shares 32-bit ActiveX Controls with Visual Basic 4+, Access and Visual Basic developers have many areas of common interest. As publishers of Visual Basic .vbxcustom controls migrate their products to ActiveX Controls, you'll find the Windows Components forums to be an excellent source of information and product support for extensions to Access 97.

■ *Data Based Advisor* magazine operates a forum on CompuServe (**GO DBA**) that covers a wide range of database topics, including client/server systems. One section of the DBA forum is devoted to Microsoft Access and Visual Basic.

■ *DBMS* magazine runs a forum (**GO DBMS**) on CompuServe primarily devoted to client/server database issues.

# Part I

# Learning Access Fundamentals

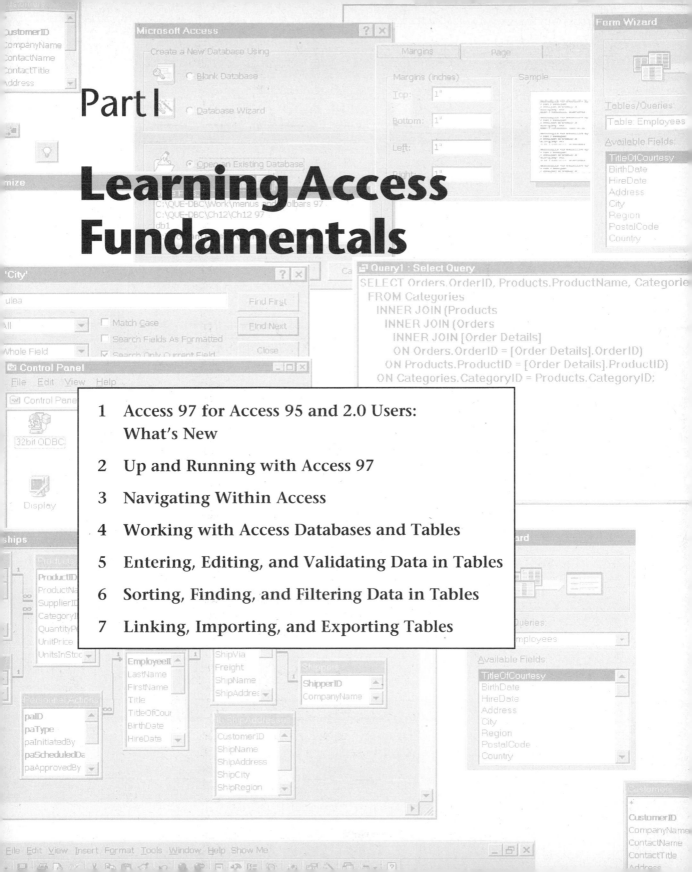

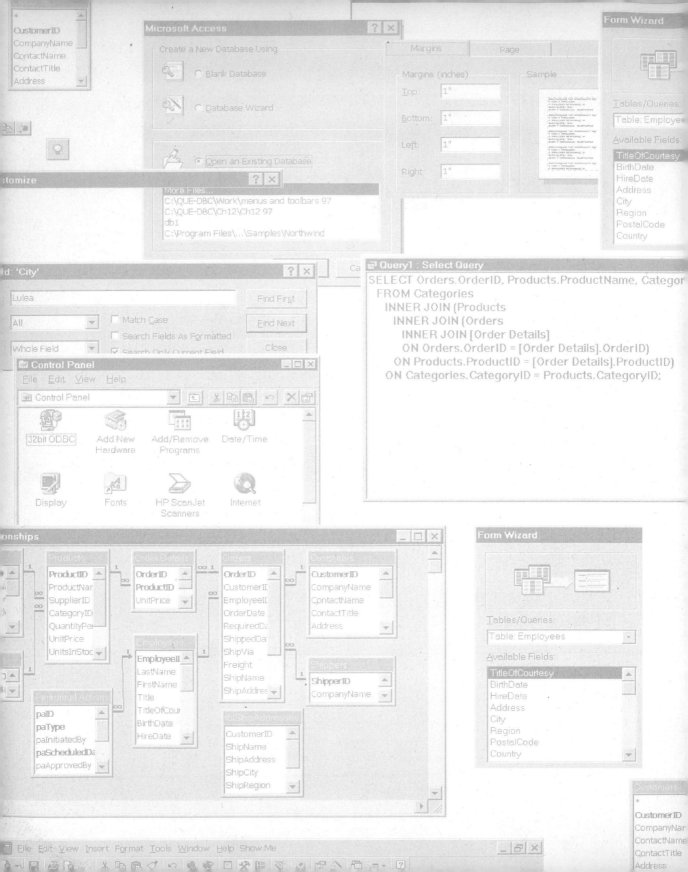

# Chapter 1

# Access 97 for Access 95 and 2.0 Users: What's New

Access 97 is a member of the Microsoft Office 97 Professional software suite that consists of second-generation, 32-bit versions of Microsoft Word, Excel, PowerPoint, and Binder, plus the first iteration of Microsoft Outlook. Most users acquire Access 97 by upgrading from Office 4.x or Office 95, or through purchase of Office 97 Professional licenses. The Office 97 Professional CD-ROM includes the Office 97 ValuPack, a collection of supplemental files for each of the Office members. The Office 97 Developer Edition (ODE), which replaces the Access Developer's Toolkit (ADT) of Access 95 and 2.0, lets you distribute run-time versions of your Access 97 applications. The ODE includes all of the components of the Professional Edition; if you already have Office 97 Professional Edition, you can buy an ODE upgrade. You also can purchase a stand-alone version of Access 97.

This chapter begins with a capsule summary of what's new in Access 97 and the features that Microsoft introduced in Access 95. The reason for discussion of Access 95 in a book about Access 97 is that many Access 2.0 (and even 1.x) users skipped the Access 95 release. The chapter concludes with sections devoted to installing Access 97 with the newly revised Setup application of the Office 97 Professional CD-ROM, installing ValuPack components, and installing the Office Developer Edition files from the Office 97 Resource Kit and Office 97 Developer Tools CD-ROM. In all of the following chapters of this book, the "Best of 97" icon, shown here in the margin, indicates a new or altered feature. Because this chapter is devoted primarily to the new features of and improvements to Access 97, the icon appears only once in this chapter.

> **Note**
>
> This chapter assumes familiarity with Access 2.0 and, to a lesser extent, with Access 95. If you're a new Access user, consider skipping to the section "Installing Access 97" near the end of this chapter. After you've worked your way through the first four parts of this book (Chapters 2 through 18), you're likely to find most of the "What's New" information presented here to be much more meaningful.

# Analyzing Access 97's Enhancements and Changes

Microsoft is determined to move all users of 16-bit Windows 3.1+ to 32-bit Windows 95 or, better yet, Windows NT Workstation 4.0. Press reports from the July 31, 1996, Microsoft briefing for security analysts quote Bill Gates as saying that the software market is an "annuity business," which explains (at least in part) the almost-annual updates to Microsoft Office and thus to Microsoft Access. Many large organizations, especially those with thousands of PCs, decided not to pay the 1995-96 annuity premium for the Windows 95 upgrade, opting to stay with "tried-and-true" Windows 3.1+ and Microsoft Office 4.x.

PC vendors installed Windows 95 on about 80 percent of all new PCs delivered after August 1995, but sales of Windows 95 and its 32-bit applications to corporations and other large organizations did not meet distributors' expectations. According to Computer Intelligence, a well-respected market research firm, corporate sales of Windows 3.1+ applications still were outpacing Windows 95 versions by better than 2:1 as of August 1996, and retail 16-bit and 32-bit application sales were about neck and neck.

1997 promises to be the year for corporate adoption of Windows 95 and Windows NT 4.0, changing the ratio of application sales in favor of 32-bit versions. Web-based corporate intranets provide much of the impetus for moving to 32-bit Windows operating systems; today's 32-bit Web browsers offer better performance and more features than the 16-bit variety. Rapidly declining prices of Pentium-based PCs and dynamic RAM during 1996 reduced the cost of upgrading to "Designed for Windows 95" PCs. Replacing 80486 and slower processors with Pentiums disguises the slower operating speed of many large 32-bit Windows applications. A continuing trend toward the use of laptop PCs in the corporate environment makes the Plug and Play, energy management, and PCMCIA card support features of Windows 95 compelling reasons for upgrading to 32-bits.

### Major Access 97 Enhancements

Continuing enhancement of the members of the 32-bit Office software suite are intended to accelerate the trend toward 32-bit Windows operating systems. Access 97 is an incremental upgrade to Access 95, not the major upgrade represented by the transition from Access 2.0 to Access 95. Following is a list of the most significant new features of Access 97:

■ *Internet features* are the primary addition to Access 97, as well as to other members of Office 97. You can export datasheets to static or active HTML pages for the World Wide Web, publish multipage reports in a series of static Web pages, and use the Publish to the Web Wizard to create the HTML 3.2 equivalent of Access forms (see Figure 1.1). Access now sports an HTML field data type to store Web URLs (Uniform Resource Locators), as well as pointers to content stored within Office documents. You also can synchronize Briefcase replicas over the Internet. Chapters 16, 17, and 18 show you how to take advantage of Access 97's new features for private intranets and the public Internet.

▶▶ See "Putting Microsoft's Internet Program in Perspective," p. 575

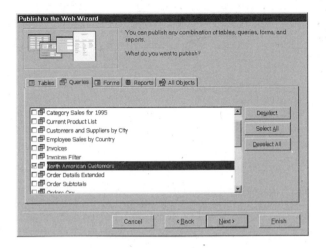

**FIG. 1.1**  The second dialog of the Publish to the Web Wizard.

- *Performance is enhanced* compared with Access 95, which many Access 95 users might consider damnation by faint praise. The major complaint among Access developers was that most Access 95 applications ran slower than their Access 2.0 counterparts. Forms that don't include event-handling code load faster. Microsoft has fine-tuned the Jet 3.5 database engine and Access 97 for increased operating speed. The new lightweight ActiveX controls also are faster than Access 95's OLE Controls.

▶▶ See "Adding ActiveX Controls to Your Application," p. 1122

- *CommandBar objects* let you customize menus and create toolbars with the ability to show or hide, customize, resize, dock, or move the toolbar. You also use CommandBar objects to create custom popup menus. You can program CommandBar objects with VBA, eliminating the need for the menu macros of Access 95 and prior versions.

▶▶ See "Replacing AddMenu Macro Actions with CommandBar Objects," p. 1075

- *The Tab control* is an Access native control, included in the toolbox, instead of the add-on 32-bit OLE Control for Access 95. Tab controls let you create forms that emulate the tabbed dialogs of Windows 95 properties sheets. Figure 1.2 shows the tabbed SolutionsHyperForm of the Solutions.mdb database included with Office 97.

▶▶ See "Creating a Tab Control," p. 489

**Learning Fundamentals**

**I**

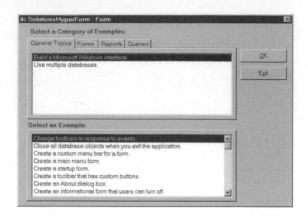

**FIG. 1.2** The Solutions example database's SolutionsHyperForm, which uses Access 97's built-in Tab control.

■ *Jet 3.5* lets you limit the number of records returned by queries. This feature prevents *runaway queries*, which can return thousands of rows when users specify inappropriate criteria. All members of Office 97 now can use the Jet 3.5 Data Access Object for database connectivity.

 ▶▶ See "Creating a Reference to the Data Access Object," p. 1025

■ *Open Database Connectivity (ODBC) 3.0* brings you the new tabbed 32-bit ODBC Data Source Administrator control panel tool shown in Figure 1.3. You now can create system-wide data sources (System DSN page) that aren't specific to a single user (User DSN page), and you can share *Datasource*.dsn files (File DSN page) that specify ODBC connections to simplify deployment of Access client/server front ends. ODBC 3.0 provides enhanced tracing capability (Tracing page) and now displays of the version numbers of all ODBC-related files (ODBC Drivers and About pages). You also can create ODBC 3.0 data sources from within Access 97. ODBC 3.0 is required to use Microsoft's new OLE DB technology and ActiveX Data Objects with Internet Information Server 3.0's Active Server Pages (ASPs).

 ▶▶ See "Using the ODBC Data Source Administrator to Create a SQL Server Data Source," p. 924
▶▶ See "Creating a File Data Source Within Access 97," p. 931

■ *ODBCDirect* speeds client/server queries by using the Remote Data Object (RDO) of Visual Basic's Enterprise Edition to bypass the Jet 3.5 database engine. ODBCDirect, which is of primary interest to Access developers, also lets you execute asynchronous queries and batch updates of changes to Recordset objects.

 ▶▶ See "Using ODBCDirect and the Remote Data Object," p. 1044

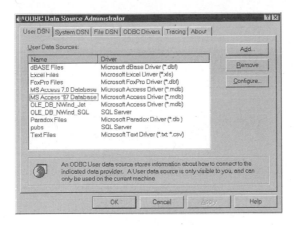

**FIG. 1.3**  ODBC 3.0's enhanced ODBC Data Source Administrator.

- *Microsoft Graph 8.0* represents a considerable improvement over version 5.0 included with Access 95. Graph 8.0 includes new chart types, such as Bubble, Cylinder, and Cone. Graph 8.0 is a 32-bit OLE applet used by all of the members of Office 97. Figure 1.4 shows most of the graph and chart types provided by the Graph 8.0.

▶▶ See "Using the Chart Wizard to Create an Unlinked Graph," p. 711

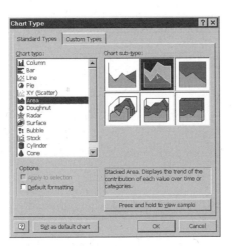

**FIG. 1.4**  Some of the graph and chart types you can create with Microsoft Graph 8.0.

- *Visual Basic for Applications 5.0* now is common to the Office 97 product line, including Word 97 but not Outlook. (Outlook uses Visual Basic, Scripting Edition, a subset of VBA 5.0, as its programming language). Visual Basic 5.0 also uses VBA 5.0. Access 97 makes extensive use of the Access DoCmd object, so this book uses the term *Access VBA* to identify code that relies on Access-specific objects.

Learning Fundamentals

▶▶ See "Introducing Access VBA," p. 978

■ *The .mde file format* lets you save .mdb files without including readable VBA source code. This feature lets developers protect their intellectual property when creating Access 97 applications, libraries, and wizards.

■ *Auto List Members* in the Module window displays a list of possible values for completion of statements. Typing the first letter of an object type, property, or method automatically positions the list (see Figure 1.5). Auto Quick Info provides syntax information for VBA. Auto Parameter provides parameter information for object methods. You can turn these features on and off with menu commands.

▶▶ See "Printing to the Debug Window with the **Debug** Object," p. 1018

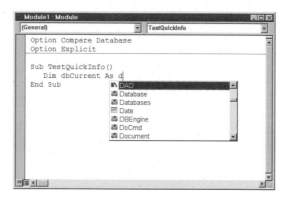

**FIG. 1.5** The automatic Quick Info feature listing possible objects for completion of a variable declaration statement.

■ *Programmatic references* to object libraries is an important new feature for Access developers. Access 97 provides the `References` collection, which you can manipulate with VBA 5.0.

■ *Improvements to the Debug window* include a change from a modal dialog to a non-modal window. You also can specify that the Debug window remain on top of other windows. The Expression pane of the Debug window shows you the current value of variables during execution of VBA code (see Figure 1.6).

▶▶ See "Using the Debug Window," p. 1016

■ *A redesigned Object Browser* is shared by all Office 97 members (see Figure 1.7). You can display all of the objects to which you've created references, only the member objects of a specific reference, or search for an object by name. When you select a member object, such as a property or method, the syntax for the member object automatically appears in the lower pane of the Object Browser. Clicking the Help button opens the help topic for the object or member object, if a help topic is available.

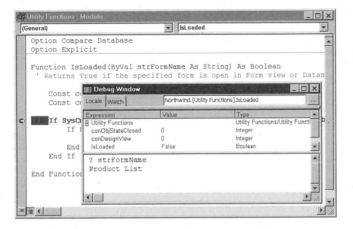

**FIG. 1.6**   Obtaining the value of a variable in the Debug window opened by a breakpoint placed in VBA code.

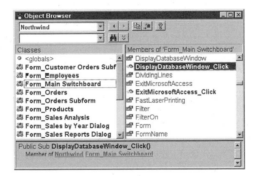

**FIG. 1.7**   Object Browser displaying objects in the Northwind project (Northwind.mdb).

To navigate through Microsoft's entire list of new Access 97 features, use Explorer to open the Acnew80.hlp file or choose Help, Contents and Index from Access 97's window, then click the Welcome to Microsoft Access 97—What's New txVic. Each of the individual help windows includes what's new in both Access 97 and Access 95.

▶▶ See "Examining Project Class Module Members in the Object Browser," p. 1054

### Important Access 97 Changes

Changes primarily are of interest to users of prior versions of Access upgrading to Access 97. Following is a list of the principal differences between Access 95 and Access 97 that don't qualify as enhancements:

■ *The Jet .mdb file structure has changed* for the fourth time. Access 97's Jet 3.5 .mdb file structure is not backwardly compatible with Access 95 or 2.0. You can open an Access 1.x, 2.0, or 95 database in Access 97, but you cannot open an Access 97 database in any prior version of Access. You cannot change in Access 97 the properties of database objects created with prior versions of Access; you must convert the file to Jet 3.5 format to make design-mode changes. Fortunately, you can link (the new term for *attach*) Access 1.x, 2.0, or 95 tables to Access 97 applications. Thus, you can accommodate simultaneous links to tables in Access 1.x, 2.0, and 95 .mdb files by database front-end applications created with Access 97 and its predecessors.

 ▶▶ See "Using Access 2.0 Application .mdb Files with Access 97," p. 1151

■ *Access executable and support files are installed in a common default Office folder,* \Program Files\Microsoft Office\Office, together with the other members of Office 97. Example files, such as Northwind.mdb, are stored in \Program Files\Microsoft Office\Office\Samples.

■ *System.mdw has moved.* Setup now installs the workgroup information file (previously called the *system file* or *system database*) in the \\*Windows*\System folder of Windows 95 or the \\*WinNT*\System32 folder of Windows NT 3.51+. Previously, System.mda (Access 2.0 and earlier) or System.mdw (Access 95+) was installed in the same folder as Msaccess.exe. According to Microsoft, the relocation of System.mdw is necessary to support the run-from-network and run-from-CD-ROM versions of Office 97.

 ▶▶ See "Creating a Folder and System File for File Sharing," p. 868

■ *Wrkgadm.exe has moved,* apparently following System.mdw. Like System.mdw, the Workgroup Administrator application has moved from the …\Access folder of prior versions to the \\*Windows*\System folder of Windows 95 or the \\*WinNT*\System32 folder of Windows NT 3.51+. Setup doesn't create a Start menu choice for Wrkgadm.exe; you should create a desktop shortcut to Wrkgadm.exe to expedite connection to multiuser Access applications.

■ *Macro support is for backward compatibility only.* Now that all of the members of Office 97, except Outlook, support VBA 5.0, Microsoft wants you to substitute VBA event-handling code for macros. Access 95 required you to write custom menu macros; you program `CommandBar` objects to create custom menus and toolbars with Access 97. There's no assurance that future versions of Access will support macros, so Access macros are obsolescent, at best.

 ▶▶ See "Converting Access Macros to VBA Code," p. 1080

■ *Some files you need are part of the Office 97 ValuPack.* As an example, the help files for programming Graph 8.0 are located in the \ValuPack\MoreHelp folder of the Office 97 CD-ROM. You must copy the .hlp (help) and .cnt (content) files you need to your ...\Office folder, then delete the existing .gid file to create a new search index for the help file.

■ *Class modules replace code-behind-forms (CBF) modules* of Access 2.0 and Access 95. Class modules, which originated in Visual Basic 4.0, also let you write VBA code in the form of reusable components, each with its own set of custom properties and methods.

Many of the changes in the preceding list are the result of Microsoft's desire to fully integrate Access with the other members of the Office software suite. Microsoft's Office program management group is responsible for assuring "look and feel" consistency across all members of Office 97 and its successors.

# Summarizing Access 95's Improvements to Access 2.0

Access 95 was a major upgrade from Access 2.0 and incorporated more than 100 significant changes to the last 16-bit version of Access. As mentioned at the beginning of this chapter, the "New in Access 95" features are included for the benefit of new Access users and those who skipped the Access 95 upgrade. Access 95's features and improvements, all of which are incorporated in Access 97, fell into the 10 categories of the following list:

■ *User interface (UI) modifications* made Access 95 conform to the "look and feel" of the other members of Microsoft Office 95. The primary changes to the Access 95 UI included a tabbed Database window that features the Explorer look, new File Open common dialogs that also support import and link operations, and many relocated menu commands. Access 95's toolbars conformed to the Office 95 model. Tabbed dialogs used to set Access 95's operating environment options and set database file properties emulated Windows 95's property sheets. Windows 95 proportional scroll bars sized the scroll button to indicate the percentage of the data being displayed. When you clicked the scroll button, Access 95 displayed a "scroll tip" with the current record number and the total number of records. The primary change to Access 97's UI is the move to dynamic from 3-D toolbar buttons and addition of the optional Web toolbar (see Figure 1.8).

▶▶ See "Starting Access and Opening Databases," p. 47

■ *Multithreaded preemptive multitasking* improved the performance of large Access 95 applications. Access and Visual Basic for Applications (VBA) each gained their own thread of execution and the Jet 3.0 Data Access Object became multithreaded. Very large Access 95 applications could take advantage of Windows NT's Symmetrical Multiprocessing (SMP) when running on a Windows NT workstation having two or more Intel processors. There are no significant changes to the Access 95 and Jet 3.0 threading model in Access 95 and Jet 3.5.

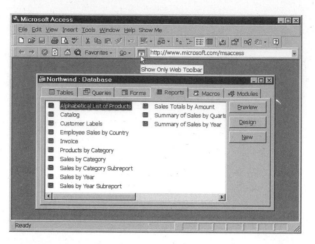

**FIG. 1.8**   Access 97 displaying the new optional Web toolbar.

- *New and improved add-ins and wizards* aided Access users by automating a wider variety of tasks. The Database Splitter Add-In automated the process of separating data objects and application objects into individual .mdb files. The Table Analyzer Wizard found repeated data in tables imported from flat ASCII or spreadsheet files and automatically creates a related lookup table to eliminate the redundancy. The Performance Analyzer Wizard made suggestions for improving your application's operating speed. The User-Level Security Wizard automatically created a new secure database file from a conventional, unsecured database. Only minor changes have been made to Access 97's wizard collection; the new Publish to the World Wide Web Wizard is discussed in the section "Major Access 97 Enhancements" earlier in the chapter.

- *Data import and export operations* were enhanced. The Import/Export Wizard made setting up import and export specifications a snap. Exporting reports to other applications in .xls, .rtf, and .txt file formats included data in subreports, and data pasted into Excel worksheets included text formatting. Dragging selected data from an Access datasheet into an Excel worksheet also preserved formatting. Access 97 adds the ability to import and export HTML tables.

- *Lookup fields* let you make selections in table datasheets from a drop-down combo box or list box populated by a field of a related table or from a list of fixed values. Lookup fields generated controversy among relational database purists because the foreign key value stored in a column of the Lookup data type is replaced in Datasheet view by a value returned from another table. There is no change to the lookup field feature in Access 97.

- *Filter by Form and Filter by Selection* aided searches for the data. Filter by Form let you enter a value in a control of a form or a field of a datasheet, then let you limit by applying the filter the underlying data set to records that match the entered value. Filter by Selection let you select a value in a form or datasheet and limit the underlying data set to records containing the selected value. Access 97 lets you type a filter criterion in the Filter For text box (see Figure 1.9).

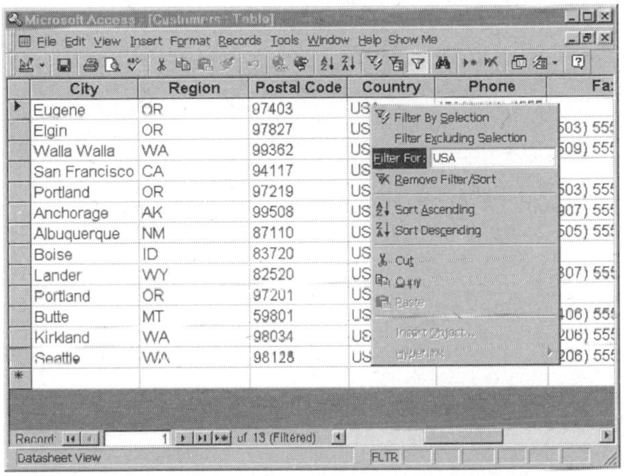

**FIG. 1.9**   Filtering by a criterion typed in the new Filter For text box on the popup menu for a table field.

- *Startup properties* eliminated the need for AutoExec macros and let you assign an opening form, customize the title bar caption, and control a variety of other application properties without writing macros or Access VBA code. There is no change to the Startup dialog in Access 97.

- *Briefcase replication* made easy the process of synchronizing changes to Access tables by users without network access to shared databases. You also can distribute updated versions of your application .mdbs with Windows 95 Briefcases. Access 97 adds the ability to create partial replicas, either with VBA code or by using the Partial Replica Wizard. The advantage of a partial replica is that you only include a subset of the records of a design-master replica table in the partial replica.

▶▶ See "Obtaining and Installing the Partial Replica Wizard," p. 972

The Partial Replica Wizard isn't included with Office 97 Professional Edition, Developer Edition, or the stand-alone version of Access 97. You can download the Partial Replica Wizard from

On the Web

**http://www.microsoft.com/msaccess**

- *Full support for 32-bit OLE 2.1* let you extend your repertoire of Access control objects with 32-bit OLE Controls (.ocxs) included with Visual Basic 4.0 and from third-party OLE Control publishers. Access 95 became an (OLE) Automation client and server. In addition to 32-bit OLE Controls, which are now obsolete, Access 97 is a container for ActiveX Controls. An ActiveX version of Access 95's Calendar control is included with Access 97 (see Figure 1.10).

▶▶ See "Using the Calendar Control," p. 1124

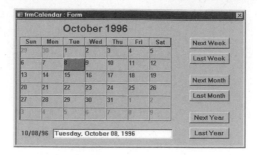

**FIG. 1.10**   A form containing the Calendar ActiveX Control, a date display text box, and command buttons to change the displayed date.

# Installing Access 97

Office 97 Professional Edition includes a redesigned Setup program for installing the individual members of Office 97, as well as common files used by all of the member applications. If you choose the Typical Setup option, many of the files you need to take full advantage of Access 97's features aren't installed. The sections that follow describe the Setup process for a new installation and how to modify an existing Office 97 Typical installation to copy the added files required to gain maximum benefit from this book.

### Making an Initial Installation of Access 97

The following steps describe how to install the Access 97 and Data Access components of Office 97 from the distribution CD-ROM, either as a new installation or as an upgrade to a prior version of Office, using the Custom Setup option:

1. Close all running applications and insert the distribution CD-ROM in your CD-ROM drive. Alternatively, you can use a CD-ROM drive shared by a server or another PC in your workgroup.

2. From the Windows 95 or Windows NT 4.0 Start menu, choose Run to open the Run dialog. Click the Browse button, select your CD-ROM drive, and double-click the Setup.exe item to close the Browse dialog.

3. Click OK to close the Run dialog and start the Setup program. After a few seconds, depending on the speed of your CD-ROM, Setup's opening dialog appears (see Figure 1.11).

4. Click continue to open the Name and Organization dialog. Setup obtains the default entries for the Name and Organization text boxes that came from the entries you made when installing Windows 95 or Windows NT (see Figure 1.12). Edit the entries, if necessary, and click OK to open the Confirm Name and Organization dialog. Click OK again to continue.

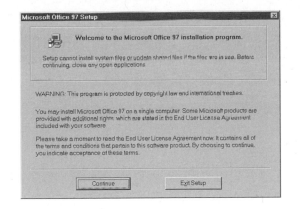

**FIG. 1.11**   Office 97's opening Setup dialog for a new installation.

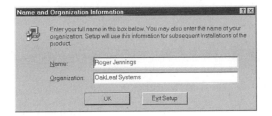

**FIG. 1.12**   Specifying your name and optional organization name for registering Office 97.

**5.** Type the CD Key number from the sticker on the Office 97 distribution CD-ROM cover in the two CD Key text boxes and click OK (see Figure 1.13).

**FIG. 1.13**   Providing the CD Key number to verify your Office 97 license.

**6.** Click OK in the Setup dialog that displays the Product ID for Office 97 to open the folder location dialog. Microsoft proposes to install most of the Office 97 files in subfolders of C:\Program Files\Microsoft Office (see Figure 1.14).

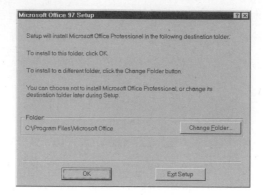

**FIG. 1.14** The Setup dialog displaying the default folder for installation of most Office 97 files.

If you want to change to a different drive or folder, click Change Folder to display the Change Folder dialog (see Figure 1.15). Type the drive and path for the Office 97 files or select an existing folder, either on the C: drive or on another different logical drive, then click OK to close the Change Folder dialog. After selecting the location for the files, click OK to continue.

**FIG. 1.15** The Change Folder dialog for specifying a non-default location for Office 97 files.

> **Note**
>
> The installation process also installs a substantial number of files in your \Windows\System or \WinNT\System32 folder, and into subfolders of the \Program Files\Common Files\ Microsoft Shared folder. The location of these files is not determined by the folder you choose for installing Office 97.

7. Click the Custom button to specify user-selected options for all Office 97 applications (see Figure 1.16). By selecting optional components carefully, you can install Office 97 and consume substantially less disk space than selecting the Typical option.

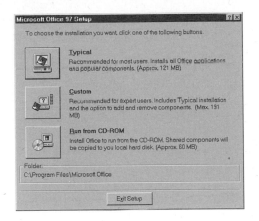

**FIG. 1.16**  The three installation options for Office 97.

**8.** In the Microsoft Office—Custom dialog, select Microsoft Access (see Figure 1.17). You can click the Select All button to install all Access files on the CD-ROM or the Change Option button to choose what files to install. To follow this procedure, click the Change Option button.

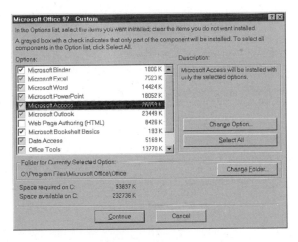

**FIG. 1.17**  The opening version of the Microsoft Office 97—Custom dialog.

> **Note**
>
> Boxes with a check mark and a white background indicate that all files in the category will be installed unless you change the option. Boxes with a gray check mark and light gray background indicate that only those files that correspond to the Typical Setup option will be installed.

9. Figure 1.18 shows the default settings for the Microsoft Office 97—Microsoft Access dialog. There are no options for installing Microsoft Access Program Files. All of the Help Topics files are not installed, so click to select the Help Topics item, then click the Change Option button.

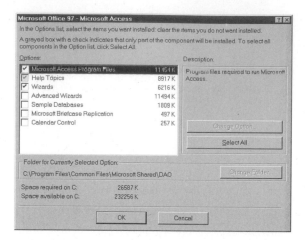

**FIG. 1.18**   The opening version of the Microsoft Office 97—Microsoft Access options dialog.

10. In the Microsoft Office 97—Help Topics dialog, click the Select All button or click the Programming Help item to specify installation of the help file (Acvba80.hlp) for Access VBA (see Figure 1.19). Click OK to return to the Microsoft Office 97— Microsoft Access dialog.

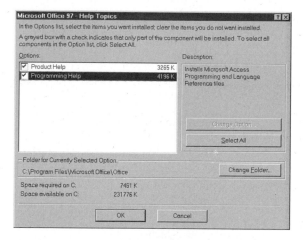

**FIG. 1.19**   Specifying installation of the Programming Help file for Access.

11. In the Microsoft Office 97—Microsoft Access dialog, click the Advanced Wizards item of the Options list to install all of the Access 97 wizards.

12. Select Sample databases to open the Microsoft Office 97—Sample Databases dialog. Click Select All to install all three of the sample databases: Northwind.mdb, Orders.mdb, and Solutions.mdb (see Figure 1.20). Click OK to return to the Microsoft Office 97—Microsoft Access dialog.

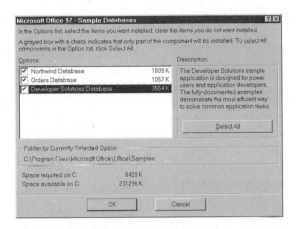

**FIG. 1.20**  Selecting all of the sample databases for installation.

> **Note**
>
> Northwind.mdb is used for most of the examples in this book. Orders.mdb demonstrates how to create a simple order entry application. Solutions.mdb offers a variety of interesting examples of the use of new features of Access 97, including VBA programming techniques.

13. In the Microsoft Office 97—Microsoft Access dialog, click to select the Microsoft Briefcase Replication and Calendar Control items. The dialog appears as shown in Figure 1.21.

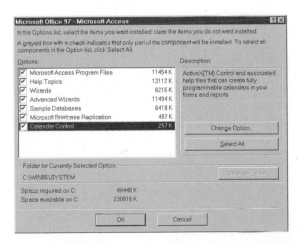

**FIG. 1.21**  Adding Briefcase Replication and the Calendar Control to the installation options.

---

**Note**

Figure 1.21 shows that all of the components of Access 97 options are selected. It's faster to simply click the Select All button, as noted in preceding step 8, but going through the Access 97 option selection process prepares you for choosing installation options for other members of Office 97.

---

**14.** Click OK to return to the Microsoft Office 97—Custom dialog and select Data Access. Click the Change Option button to open the Microsoft Office 97—Data Access dialog (see Figure 1.22). The Data Access choices you make apply to all members of Office 97 that use the Jet 3.5 Data Access Object (DAO), including Access 97.

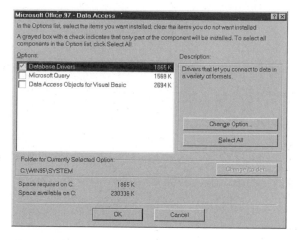

**FIG. 1.22**  The default option selections of the Microsoft Office 97—Data Access dialog.

**15.** Select the Database Drivers item in the Options list and click the Change Option button to open the Microsoft Office 97—Database Drivers dialog. All of the drivers except the Microsoft SQL Server Driver are selected by default.

---

**Note**

The Access, dBASE and FoxPro, Excel, and Text drivers formerly were called the *Desktop Database Drivers*. All drivers are 32-bit ODBC drivers. The HTML driver is a new Office 97 driver.

---

**16.** If you intend to use Access 97 as a front-end to SQL Server 6.x, click to select the SQL Server driver (see Figure 1.23). Click OK to return to the Microsoft Office 97—Data Access dialog.

You can save some disk space by deselecting the dBASE and Microsoft FoxPro Drivers, if you don't intend to import, export, or link xBase files. The Microsoft Access

Driver is required for other Office applications to import, export, or link Access databases.

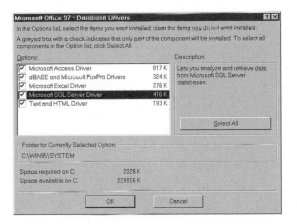

**FIG. 1.23**  Specifying installation of the 32-bit ODBC 3.0 driver for Microsoft SQL Server 6.x.

   **17.** Click to select the Data Access Objects for Visual Basic item of the Options list. Each of the members of Office 97 can create a reference to the Jet 3.5 DAO. If you selected all of the database drivers in the preceding step, your Microsoft Office 97— Data Access dialog appears as shown in Figure 1.24. Click OK to return to the Office 97—Custom dialog.

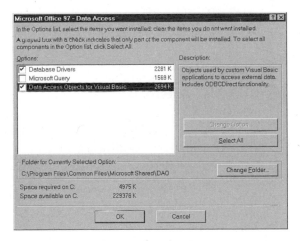

**FIG. 1.24**  Adding the Jet 3.5 DAO for installation.

   **18.** Choose the options you want to install for the other members of Office 97, as well as for files that are common to Office 97. When you've completed the specification process, click Continue in the Microsoft Office 97—Custom dialog to begin copying files.

> **Note**
>
> Once you click Continue in the Microsoft Office 97—Custom dialog, there's no way to change the options you selected. If you forgot to specify options for other applications, you can click Cancel in the Copy Progress dialog to terminate the Setup program and start over. Alternatively, you can let Setup run its course, then modify the installation as described in the next section.

Setup checks for available disk space, then copies files from the CD-ROM to your fixed disk. During the copying process, the dialog shown in Figure 1.25 displays installation progress.

**FIG. 1.25**   The Progress Monitor dialog during the file copying process.

19. When installation is complete, the dialog shown in Figure 1.26 appears. You can elect to use the Registration Wizard to register your copy of Office 97 online; otherwise, click OK to complete the Setup process. Depending on the installation, you may be requested to reboot Windows at this point.

**FIG. 1.26**   The Setup dialog indicating completion of Office 97 installation.

> **Note**
>
> The installation of the stand-alone version of Access 97 is similar to that for the Office 97 Professional Edition, except that you complete only the Access 97 and Data Access option steps. The stand-alone version of Access 97 primarily is of interest to purchasers of the standard Office 97 or Small Business editions.

### Customizing a Typical Installation

If you installed Office 97 with the Typical option or want to install or remove options from an existing Typical or Custom Office 97 installation, follow these steps:

1. Close all running applications and insert the distribution CD-ROM in your CD-ROM drive. Alternatively, you can use a CD-ROM drive shared by a server or another PC in your workgroup. The CD-ROM is required even if you intend only to delete previously selected options.

2. From the Windows 95 or Windows NT 4.0 Start menu, choose Run to open the Run dialog. Click the Browse button, select your CD-ROM drive, and double-click the Setup.exe item to close the Browse dialog.

3. Click OK to close the Run dialog and start the Setup program. After a few seconds, depending on the speed of your CD-ROM, Setup's maintenance dialog appears (see Figure 1.27).

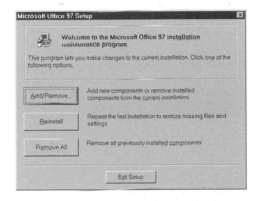

**FIG. 1.27**  The opening dialog of the maintenance version of the Setup program.

4. Click the Add/Remove button to open the Microsoft Office 97—Maintenance dialog. Select Microsoft Access (see Figure 1.28) or any other component whose setup options you want to change, and click the Change Options dialog.

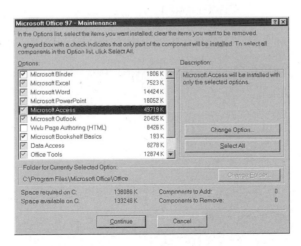

**FIG. 1.28**  The Office 97—Maintenance dialog that lets you add or remove options for all members of Office 97.

**5.** If you're changing the options for a Typical installation of Access 97, follow steps 9–18 of the preceding selection to add the features you need to take full advantage of Access 97 and the examples of this book.

# Installing ValuPack Components

The Microsoft Office 97 ValuPack, which is included only on the CD-ROM version of Office 97, includes a variety of useful utilities and accessories for Office 97 users and developers. To check out the ValuPack's contents, follow these steps:

**1.** With the Office 97 Professional Edition CD-ROM in an accessible CD-ROM drive, open Explorer and navigate to the \ValuPack folder of the CD-ROM.

**2.** Double-click the Valupack.hlp file to open the main help topic, Welcome to the Microsoft Office 97 ValuPack (see Figure 1.29).

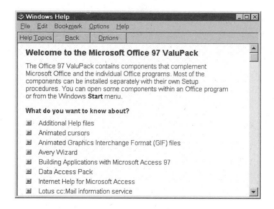

**FIG. 1.29**  The opening help topic of the Valupack.hlp file.

**3.** Click the button associated with the ValuPack topic you want to examine. Figure 1.30 shows the topic for the HTML version of the book *Building Applications with Microsoft Access 97*, the printed version of which is included with the Office 97 Developer Edition. Many of the ValuPack utilities have their own setup file to install the required files on your local fixed disk.

**4.** For a more graphic-intensive view of the content of the ValuPack folder of the CD-ROM, double-click the Overview.ppt file to launch PowerPoint 97. Figure 1.31 shows the first slide of the Overview.

**FIG. 1.30**  A description of the HTML version of *Building Applications with Microsoft Access 97*.

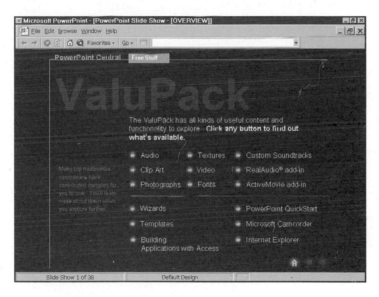

**FIG. 1.31**  The first PowerPoint 97 slide for the Overview of the ValuPack.

# Installing the Office Developer Edition Components

The Office 97 Developer Edition CD-ROM consists of two components: the Office 97 Resource Kit (ORK) and Office 97 Developer Edition (ODE) Tools. Following are the steps you take to install the Access 97 Setup Wizard and other tools included with the Developer edition:

1. With the ODE CD-ROM in an accessible CD-ROM drive, from the Windows 95 or Windows NT 4.0 Start menu, choose Run to open the Run dialog. Click the Browse button, select your CD-ROM drive, and navigate to the \ODE folder. Double-click the Setup.exe item to close the Browse dialog and open the first Setup dialog (see Figure 1.32).

**FIG. 1.32**    The opening dialog of the Microsoft Office 97 Developer Edition ODE Tools Setup program.

2. Click Continue to enter and confirm your name and organization. When you click OK in the Product ID dialog, the dialog to select the installation folder appears (see Figure 1.33). Unless you have a good reason to do otherwise, select the default location for the ODETools folder.

3. Click OK to open the Installation Options dialog (see Figure 1.34). Most Access developers are likely to install all of the ODE tools, so click the Complete button to install the Setup Wizard, Replication Manager, and other ODE tools. The Setup application installs the files in the folder specified in the preceding step.

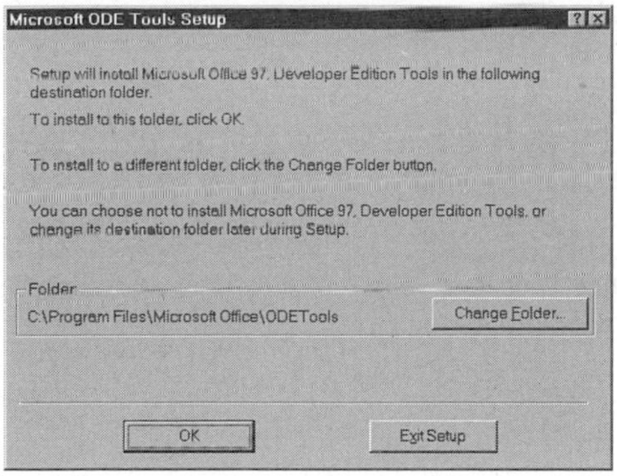

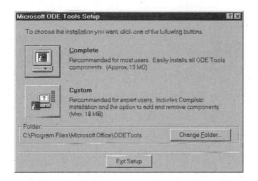

**FIG. 1.33** Accepting the default location for the ODETools folder.

**FIG. 1.34** Choosing between Complete and Custom installation of the ODE Tools.

## Chapter 2

# Up and Running with Access 97

This chapter is designed to give you an overview of Access's two most important database objects: databases and tables. Even if you're well acquainted with previous versions of Access, you might want to browse this chapter for the Access 97 icon in the margin that indicates a description of a new feature or an improvement over Access 95. You see the Access 97 icon at each location in this book where a new or improved feature is discussed except in Chapter 1, which is devoted to the novel elements of Access 97.

The examples in this chapter, like most other examples in this book, use the Northwind Traders sample database, Northwind.mdb, that is supplied with Access 97. Northwind Traders is a fictitious wholesaler of specialty food products whose accounting system is an Access database application created by Microsoft. The sample database includes tables, forms, and reports that a small firm might use to automate its invoicing, inventory control, ordering, and personnel operations.

The remainder of Part I (Chapters 3 – 7) expands on the subjects you learn in this chapter using Northwind.mdb and describes in detail how you create and use Access database tables.

---

**Note**

This chapter assumes that you have already installed Access. If you haven't installed Access, refer to your Access documentation for instructions on setting up Access on your computer.

---

## Starting Access and Opening Databases

Before you can open any database in Access, you must start Access itself. You can open a database at the same time you start Access, or you can open a database any time after you've started Access. You also can run multiple instances of Access, if you have enough system resources. Access allows you to have only one database per instance open at a time, however.

The next two sets of instructions first explain how to open a database at the same time you start Access 97, and then explain how to open a database after Access is already running.

### Opening a Database During Access Startup

To simultaneously start Access and open the Northwind Traders database, Northwind.mdb, perform the following steps:

1. Choose Microsoft Access from Windows 95's or Windows NT 4.0's Start, Programs menu. (Access is installed on this menu by default.)

   As Access is loading, a copyright notice (called a *splash screen*) appears with the name and organization that was entered at the time Access was installed. After Access has loaded, it displays the database opening dialog shown in Figure 2.1.

   Notice the list of previously opened databases at the bottom of the dialog; if this is the first time you've ever run Access, this list does not appear.

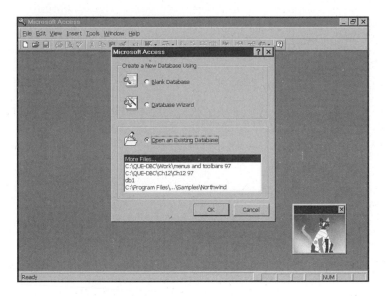

**FIG. 2.1**   The Access 97 startup dialog for opening a database.

2. Select the Open an Existing Database option.

3. Select the More Files choice in the list at the bottom of the dialog, and then click OK. (If this is the first time Access has been run, the list at the bottom of the dialog doesn't appear; in this case, just click OK.) Access displays a standard Windows 95 Open dialog, shown in Figure 2.2.

**4.** Select the \Program Files\Microsoft Office\Office\Samples folder in the Open dialog. (The Northwind.mdb files are located in the Samples subfolder of whatever folder in which you installed Access 97; the default location is \Program Files\ Microsoft Office\Office.) Figure 2.2 shows the Open dialog with the contents of the Samples folder displayed.

**FIG. 2.2** Displaying the sample database in the Open dialog.

**5.** Double-click Northwind.mdb to open the Northwind Traders sample database. Access opens the Northwind Traders database.

If this is the first time you've opened the Northwind Traders sample database, the Access Visual Basic for Applications (VBA) program code in the sample database displays a special splash screen for the Northwind Traders database (see Figure 2.3). If you don't want to see this splash screen again, mark the Don't Show This Screen Again check box.

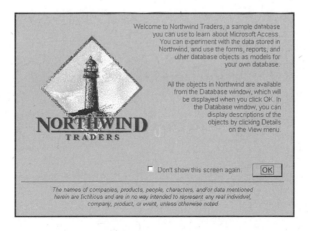

**FIG. 2.3** The splash screen of the Northwind Traders sample database.

6. Click OK to close the Northwind Traders splash screen. After closing the Northwind Traders splash screen, Access displays the Database window shown in Figure 2.4.

**FIG. 2.4** The Database window, Access's "home base."

> **Note**
>
> You can use several other methods to open a database in the common Open dialog. You can click Northwind.mdb to select it and then click Open. Or you can type **Northwind** in the File Name text box and click OK. Access adds the default .mdb extension for you. However, double-clicking is the fastest and most mistake-proof method of opening a database.

### Opening a Database When Access Is Already Running

As you'd expect, it's also possible to open a database after you start Access. You can have only one database open at a time in an instance of Access, so opening a database causes Access to close any currently open database, and replaces the contents of the Database window with the newly opened database's information. (The Database window is explained in the next section of this chapter.)

To open the Northwind Traders database, Northwind.mdb, when Access is already running, follow these steps:

1. Click the Open Database button of the toolbar, or choose File from the main menubar. If you use the menu to open a database, the File menu appears (see Figure 2.5); if you click the Open Database toolbar button, the file Open dialog appears immediately.

   If you have run Access previously, the file names of up to four Access database files you have opened may appear above Exit.

2. Choose File, Open Database to display the Open dialog (refer to Figure 2.2).

3. Finish opening the Northwind Traders database by following the procedures in steps 4–6 of the preceding section ("Opening a Database During Access Startup").

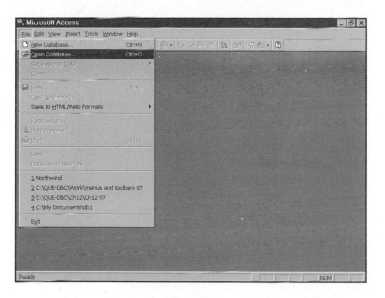

**FIG. 2.5**   Choosing File, Open Database to open an Access database.

Learning Fundamentals

---

**Note**

Access's toolbar buttons provide ScreenTips (called ToolTips in earlier versions of Access). *Screen-Tips* are small captions that appear under a button after the mouse pointer has rested on a button for more than about 0.5 seconds. If you find ScreenTips to be distracting, you can turn them off by choosing View, Toolbars, Customize to display the Customize dialog for toolbars. Click the Options tab to display the Options sheet, and then click the Show ScreenTips on Toolbars check box to remove the check mark; click the Close button to close the Customize dialog. If you're using SVGA mode (800×600 pixels) or UVGA mode (1,024×768 pixels), you may want to try clicking the Large Buttons check box of the Toolbars dialog. The icons of larger buttons are easier to discern in SVGA mode and especially UVGA mode.

---

**Note**

You can close any open database by clicking the close button at the top right corner of the Database window, or by choosing File, Close. When there is no open database, Access displays an empty window; only the New Database, Open Database, and Office Assistant toolbar buttons are enabled; and the File, Close command is disabled.

---

### Understanding the Database Window

The Database window is your "home base" for all operations with the sample database or databases you create. Almost every operation you perform with Access begins with a choice you make from the Database window.

After you open a database file, the 20 buttons to the right of the New Database and Open Database buttons of the Database toolbar (under the main menubar) are enabled or disabled, depending on Access 97's current status. *Toolbar buttons*, a common feature of contemporary Windows applications (and of Windows 95 itself), are shortcuts for menu choices.

Any operation you can perform by clicking a toolbar button can be performed by making two or more menu choices. Access 97 has 20 standard toolbars; Access displays the appropriate toolbar for the database object in the active window. You can customize the standard toolbars or create your own special-purpose toolbars. Using the toolbar buttons is much quicker and, once you learn what the symbols mean, more intuitive than using the standard menu structure. Chapter 3, "Navigating Within Access," describes the use of Access 97's new toolbars in detail.

 ▶▶ See "The Toolbars in Table View," p. 71

> **Note**
>
> Access 97 and the other members of the Microsoft Office 97 software suite use the term *command bars* to refer collectively to menubars and toolbars. Menubars and toolbars perform identical functions; they differ only in appearance. Toolbars, however, offer more flexibility than menubars. For instance, toolbars can include drop-down lists.

# Using Database Tables

This chapter is devoted to exploring tables, which are the basic elements of all databases and the portion of the Access database file where data is stored.

 ▶▶ See "Understanding Access's Table Display," p. 67

### Viewing Data in Tables

To display the contents of the Categories table, which describes the types of products in which Northwind trades, double-click Categories in the Database window's list of tables. The Categories table appears, as shown in Figure 2.6.

> **Tip**
>
> You also can display the Categories table by clicking Categories and then clicking the Open button or pressing Enter. The double-clicking method is quicker, however.

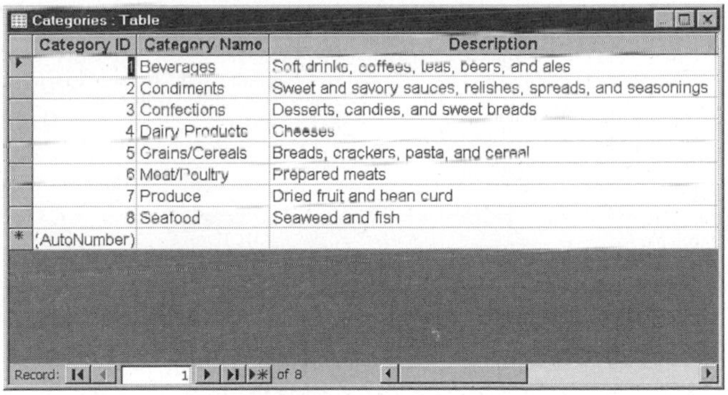

| Category ID | Category Name | Description |
|---|---|---|
| 1 | Beverages | Soft drinks, coffees, teas, beers, and ales |
| 2 | Condiments | Sweet and savory sauces, relishes, spreads, and seasonings |
| 3 | Confections | Desserts, candies, and sweet breads |
| 4 | Dairy Products | Cheeses |
| 5 | Grains/Cereals | Breads, crackers, pasta, and cereal |
| 6 | Meat/Poultry | Prepared meats |
| 7 | Produce | Dried fruit and bean curd |
| 8 | Seafood | Seaweed and fish |
| (AutoNumber) | | |

Record: |◄ ◄   1   ► ►| ►* of 8

**FIG. 2.6**   The Datasheet display of the records in the Categories table.

The normal method of displaying the information contained in relational database tables is the familiar row-column technique used by spreadsheet applications. Every widely used PC RDBMS (relational database management system) uses row-column presentation for data contained in tables. The rows of a table are known as *records*, and the columns are referred to as *fields*. A record contains information on a single item, such as one class of product or a particular invoice. A field contains the same type of information, such as a product code, for all records in a table. In this book, the intersection between a row and a column—a single field of a single record—is called a *data cell*. A data cell contains a single piece of information. The terms *data item* and *data entity* often are used as synonyms for data cell.

Figure 2.6 shows the data in the Categories table in what Access calls *Datasheet view*—the default method of displaying a table. You select Datasheet view, if another type of view is active, by clicking the Datasheet button, which resembles a spreadsheet, on the toolbar (the Datasheet button only appears when the table is *not* in Datasheet view). You also can choose <u>V</u>iew, Data<u>s</u>heet. Datasheet view also is the default for viewing the results of queries; you can see a Datasheet view of the table or query when you are creating an Access form.

### Selecting and Editing Data Records

To change the data contained in any cell of the table (other than in OLE Object fields used to display pictures or hyperlink fields), select the cell by clicking it with the mouse or by using the arrow keys. Selected content is indicated by the white on black (reverse) appearance of the cell. The default selected cell is the first field of the first record of the table. All contents of that cell are selected when you first display the table.

---

**Caution**

If you type a character into a cell when its entire content is selected, the character you type replaces what was in that cell. You can recover from an accidental replacement by pressing Esc; this action restores the original content, but only if you have not yet selected a different cell. When you

*(continues)*

(continued)

make a change in a data cell and then move to a new data cell, the change is made to the content of the table. Click the selected data cell to deselect the entire contents of the cell. You can choose Edit, Undo Saved Record or press Ctrl+Z to reverse the changes you made after saving a record.

---

**Note**

See Chapter 5, "Entering, Editing, and Validating Data in Tables," for detailed information on editing data records.

---

You can select any cell to edit by positioning the mouse pointer at the point within a cell where you want to make the change and then clicking your left mouse button. The mouse pointer resembles an I-beam when it is located within the contents of data cells. The editing cursor, a thin vertical line called the *caret* by Windows and this book (often referred to as the *insertion point* in other texts), appears.

The conventional text-editing functions of Windows applications apply to Access. At this point, you shouldn't change the data, called *values*, of the data cells. Changes to values may affect the appearance of examples in later chapters. If you do make a change, a pencil symbol appears in the gray box at the left of the window corresponding to the record whose value you have changed. You can return to the original value by pressing Esc.

If you click an OLE Object field, the cell has a gray border and the caret does not appear. (The Categories table contains an OLE Object field, although it isn't visible in Figure 2.6; the field stores a bitmap picture, and contains the words `Bitmap Image` to let you know that this is an OLE Object field containing picture data.) You cannot edit the text of an OLE Object field. If you click a hyperlink field, Access invokes your default Internet World Wide Web browsing application, and attempts to connect to the URL or UNC address specified by the hyperlink. (The Categories table doesn't contain a hyperlink field; the Suppliers table of Northwind.mdb does contain a hyperlink field.) To select a hyperlink field without starting your Web browser, move the caret into the field using the keyboard instead of the mouse. (A *URL* is a Universal Resource Link address and is used primarily to specify Web addresses; UNC stands for Universal Naming Convention, and is used primarily for addresses in a local or wide-area network.)

▶▶ See "Understanding Access 97's Hyperlink Field Data Type," p. 585

You use the empty record at the bottom of the table, indicated by the asterisk (*) in the selection button column for the record, to add a new record to the table. If you enter any data into a cell of this record, a new record containing the data you entered is added to the table. If you accidentally add data in this *tentative append* record, click the Record Selection button to select the record, and then press Delete. A dialog appears, requesting confirmation of your deletion. Click Yes. (A record's *selection button* is the gray square that appears at the left of each row in Datasheet view; refer to Figure 2.6.)

If you use the arrow keys to select a data cell, all contents of the cell are selected. You cannot click the corner of a cell and drag the mouse pointer to a cell in the opposite corner of an imaginary rectangle to select a group of cells, as you do with Excel. You can, however, select an entire record by clicking the selection button for that record, or you can select a group of records by dragging the mouse down the selection button column. Records and groups of records most often are selected to copy the records to the Windows Clipboard. Notice that when you select a cell with the keyboard or the mouse, the triangular arrow moves to the selected record. The button with the triangular arrow is called the *current record pointer*, or sometimes the *active record pointer*. (The first record in Figure 2.6 is the current record; notice the triangular arrow in the record selection button at the left edge of the record.)

You use the left set of buttons in the bar at the bottom of the datasheet window to position the current record pointer within the bounds of the table. Click the button with a left-arrow and vertical bar to position the current record pointer at the first record in the table. Click the button with a right arrow and vertical bar to move to the last or bottom record of the table. The left- and right-arrow buttons move the pointer one record at a time in the direction indicated. You can enter a record number in the Record text box or use the vertical scroll bar to position the active record pointer. The vertical scroll bar appears only if more records are present than can fit in the vertical dimension of the Datasheet window.

The horizontal scroll bar enables you to view fields that lie to the right of the far right visible field. Use the left and right arrows for small movements, or use the scroll box to make large moves to the left or right. You also can traverse several fields by clicking the region of the scroll bar between the scroll box and the arrow. If you click the right scroll arrow in the Categories table two or three times, you'll be able to see the column for the Picture field, which is an OLE Object field containing Windows Paint bitmap pictures.

To select all data cells in a field column, click the button containing the field name at the top of the datasheet; as an example, Figure 2.7 shows the Description column selected. When the mouse pointer is over a field name, the pointer changes to a down arrow. You can search for cells within the selected field that contain a particular group of characters by clicking the toolbar's Find button—a pair of binoculars. The Find dialog appears (see Figure 2.7).

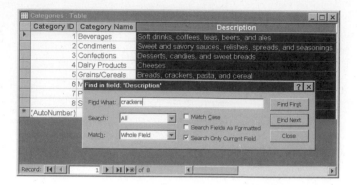

**FIG. 2.7** Locating records whose fields contain particular words or phrases with the Find dialog.

Enter the characters you want to find in the Find What text box. Then open the Match drop-down list box by clicking the down arrow, and select Any Part of Field. You can search up, down, or in both directions from the position of the current record by selecting Up, Down, or All in the Search drop-down list box. If you select All, Access searches down from the current record until it reaches the end of the database, and then continues from the beginning until the current record position is reached. When searching Up or Down, Access searches in the specified direction and stops when it reaches the beginning or end of the database records. Click the Find First button to search for the first occurrence of a match, and then click the Find Next button to locate other matches. After you find all matching records or no matching records, a dialog appears stating that you have reached the end of the table. Click the Close button to return to the Table window.

### Viewing and Editing Graphics

One of the reasons for choosing the Categories table for this chapter is that it includes bitmapped graphic images stored in an OLE Object field. If you double-click one of the Bitmap Image data cells, Windows 95's Paint window appears with the bitmapped image displayed, as shown in Figure 2.8. (You may need to scroll to the right to make the Picture field column visible in the window.)

You can use Paint to display the image or to edit it. Because Windows 95's Paint is an ActiveX component (referred to in earlier versions of Microsoft Office as an OLE server), all of Paint's bitmapped image display and editing capabilities are available to you while you are using Access. (In-place editing isn't suitable in Datasheet view, so Access invokes Paint in a separate window if you edit a Bitmap Image field when the table is in Datasheet view.)

When you're finished viewing an image, click the Close Window button in the upper-right corner of Paint's window to close the image. You also can exit an ActiveX component by choosing File, Exit & Return.

**FIG. 2.8** A bitmapped image displayed using Windows 95 Paint.

> ## Caution
>
> If you make changes to a Bitmap Image OLE Object field, Access automatically stores your changes when you exit Paint; your changes cannot be undone.

### Using Design Mode

Design mode for tables displays the characteristics of each field in the table in a grid format similar to a spreadsheet. To view the design of the Categories table, click the Design View button, which appears as an architect's triangle and pencil, at the left end of the toolbar. Design mode appears, as shown in Figure 2.9. Alternatively, you can choose View, Table Design or select the table name in the Database window and click the Design button.

▶▶ See "Defining Access Operating Modes," p. 66

You can view and edit the properties that apply to the table object as a whole in the Table Properties window, as shown in Figure 2.10. Click the Properties button on the toolbar (a hand pointing to a window) or choose View, Properties to display t he Table Properties window. The Table Properties window enables you to enter a text description of the table and assign a value to the Validation Rule property of the table. Table-level validation rules can contain a rule that applies to more than one field in a table. The Validation Text text property is the message that appears if you attempt to violate the validation rule.

▶▶ See "Validating Data Entry," p. 170

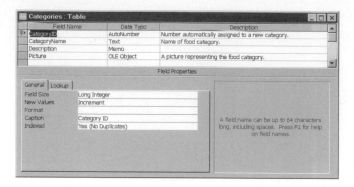

**FIG. 2.9** Displaying Field Name, Data Type, and Description properties in Design view.

**FIG. 2.10** Adding validation rules and messages that appear when the rules are violated in the Table Properties window.

 Click the Indexes button or choose View, Indexes to display the Indexes window. The Indexes window, shown in Figure 2.11, displays each of the fields of the table and identifies the *primary-key field*, which is the field with the symbol of the key in its selection button column. The primary-key field is the field or combination of fields that is used to uniquely identify each record in the table. Most tables are indexed on a single primary-key field, and primary-key field indexes do not permit duplicate keys. *Indexes* are internal tables that speed the creation of query result tables by simulating the sorting of the table on the value of the key field. Key fields establish the relations by which multiple tables of a database are linked when you create a query. The term *relational database* indicates database management applications that are capable of linking tables by key fields.

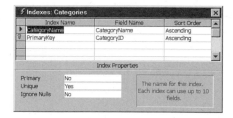

**FIG. 2.11** Displaying the Index Name, Field Name, and Sort Order for each index of a table in the Indexes window.

▶▶ See "Using Access Indexes," p. 823

Each field in a table requires a unique name and must be assigned a field data type. Field names, data types, and an optional text description of the field are entered in the design grid. (Click the Indexes button or click the Close Window button of the Indexes window to close it so that the entire design grid is visible. Do the same to close the Properties window.) Text is the most common type of data in tables; therefore, Text is the default data type.

Many other field data types are available in Access; you already have been introduced to the OLE Object field data type. Click one of the Data Type cells, and then click the down arrow to open the Data Type drop-down list box to display the Data Type choices offered by Access. Click the arrow again to close the list. Field data types in Access include various numeric formats, date and time, and other types that you learn about in later chapters of this book. Now click the Datasheet View button to display the Datasheet view of the Categories table in Run mode.

# Printing the Contents of a Table

Access enables you to print the contents of your table without creating a fully formatted report. You may want to print raw table data to proofread the new records you have created or the old ones you have edited. The Print Preview window is much like the one offered by Microsoft Word and Excel. The Print Preview window enables you to see how tables, forms, and reports will appear if printed.

To see how the Categories table will appear if printed, click the toolbar's Preview button (the page symbol with the magnifying glass). The Print Preview window appears, as shown in Figure 2.12. The title bar of the Print Preview window reflects what you're preparing to print. In this example, the title bar shows Categories:Table. You also can choose File, Print Preview to display the Print Preview window.

To see a magnified view of how the printed version of your table will appear, click the surface of the simulated sheet of paper in the Print Preview window. When the mouse pointer is on the paper, the pointer turns into the shape of a magnifying glass, as shown in Figure 2.12. Place the magnifying glass over the image; otherwise, when the window is magnified, the view is of a blank page and you wonder where the table went. Figure 2.13 shows the magnified (zoomed) view of the Categories table. Click again to restore the original, unreadable version of the report. The Zoom button has an effect similar to clicking the mouse on the surface of the preview image.

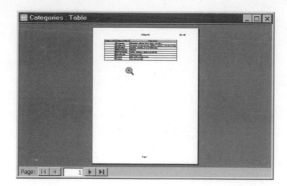

**FIG. 2.12**    Displaying the eight records of the Categories table in the Print Preview window.

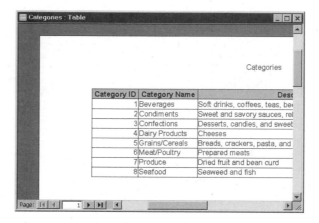

**FIG. 2.13**    Clicking the print preview image to show a magnified view of the Categories table.

 When you are ready to print, click the Print button (with the symbol of a printer) on the toolbar—Access immediately begins printing the table, using the current printer settings for your computer.

 To print in Landscape mode with your laser printer or to otherwise change your printer's settings, you must choose File, Print to display the Print dialog, shown in Figure 2.14. To change the printer settings, click the Properties button and make the appropriate changes in the *PrinterName* properties sheet for your printer, as shown in Figure 2.15 (the exact appearance of your printer's Properties sheet depends on your specific printer). Click the OK button to close the printer properties sheet, then click OK in the Print dialog to begin printing the table.

 If you want to change the printing margins, choose File, Page Setup to display the Page Setup dialog shown in Figure 2.16. Click the Margins tab to display the page margin settings, and change the print margins by entering different values in the Margins text boxes. Click OK to close the Page Setup dialog and return to the Print Preview windows. Click the Print button on the toolbar to print the table with the new margin settings.

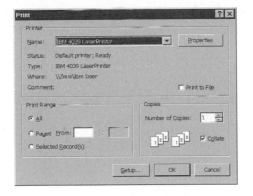

**FIG. 2.14** The Print dialog for reports.

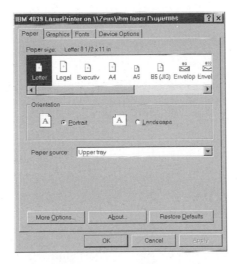

**FIG. 2.15** Setting printer-specific options in the printer properties sheet.

### Tip

You can also change the page orientation (portrait or landscape) on the Page sheet of the Page Setup dialog. If you only want to change printing margins or the page orientation, using the Page Setup dialog is easiest.

Now that you have run the gamut of the basic operations available for Access tables, double-click the Document Control menu box to close the Print Preview window and return to the Database window.

Now, you may open one or more of the other tables that comprise the Northwind Traders database to learn a bit more about their contents. The Employees table includes scanned images of photographs of the fictional staff of Northwind Traders. The Suppliers table lists an eclectic group of food-processing firms from many points on the globe; the suppliers table also contains a Hyperlink field to connect you to a simulated Web page for some suppliers.

**FIG. 2.16**  Changing printing margins and paper orientation in the Page Setup dialog.

You can see most of the international characters, such as umlauts and tildes, in Windows' ANSI character set in the supplier name and address fields. Both Access 97 and Windows 95 are available in a wide range of languages in addition to British, Canadian, and U.S. English. Access 97 replaces 8-bit ANSI with 16-bit Unicode characters to accommodate Asian and other languages that use more than the about 200 characters accommodated by ANSI. Use of Unicode in Access 97 is transparent to the user, but requires modification of specific string operations performed with Access VBA.

To see a brief description of each table listed in the Database window, click the Details button on the toolbar. Access displays the text entered in the Description text box of the table's Table Properties dialog to the right of the table's name, along with date and time the table was last modified, and the date and time of the table's creation. You can display the contents of the Database window in any of the viewing formats available in any Windows 95 folder window: large icons, small icons, list, and details.

# Chapter 3

# Navigating Within Access

This chapter describes how Microsoft has structured and organized Access to expedite the design and use of the database objects that it offers. A substantial portion of this chapter consists of tables that list the functions of window Control-menu boxes, toolbar buttons, and an array of function-key combinations. Many function and key assignments derive from other Microsoft applications, such as Excel (F2 for editing) and Word for Windows (Shift+F4 to find the next occurrence of a match).

This chapter is a reference to which you can return when you conclude that a keystroke combination might be a better choice for an action than a mouse click, but you cannot remember the required combination. (Refer to Chapter 5, "Entering, Editing, and Validating Data in Tables," for details of the key combinations that you use to edit data in tables and queries.) This chapter also explains the structure and content of Access's Help system.

## Understanding Access's Functions and Modes

Access, unlike word processing and spreadsheet applications, is a truly multi-functional program. Although word processing applications, for example, have many sophisticated capabilities, their basic purpose is to support text entry, page layout, and formatted printing. All word-processing application's primary functions and supporting features are directed to these ends. You perform all word processing operations using views that represent a sheet of paper—usually 8 1/2×11 inches. Most spreadsheet applications use the row-column metaphor for all their functions—even for writing highly sophisti-cated programs in the applications' macro languages. The sections that follow describe Access's basic functions and operating modes.

### Defining Access Functions

To qualify as a full-fledged relational database management system, an appli-cation must perform the following four basic but distinct functions, each with its own presentation (or view) to the user:

- *Data organization* involves creating and manipulating tables that contain data in conventional tabular (row-column or spreadsheet) format, called *Datasheet View* by Access.

- *Table linking and data extraction* links multiple tables by data relationships to create temporary tables, stored in your computer's memory or temporary disk files, that contain the data that you choose. Access uses *queries* to link tables and to choose the data to be stored in a temporary table called a Recordset object. (For backward compatibility, Access 97 supports Access 1.x's Dynaset and Snapshot objects, which are both Recordset objects.) A Recordset object consists of the data that results from running the query; Recordset objects are called *virtual tables* because they are stored in your computer's memory rather than in database files. The capability to link tables by relations distinguishes relational database systems from simple list-processing applications, called *flat-file* managers. Data extraction limits the presentation of Recordsets to specific groups of data that meet criteria that you establish. *Expressions* are used to calculate values from data (for example, you can calculate an extended amount by multiplying unit price and quantity), and to display the calculated values as if they were a field in one of the tables.

- *Data entry and editing* require design and implementation of data viewing, entry, and editing forms as an alternative to tabular presentation. A form enables you, rather than the application, to control how the data is presented. For most users, forms are much easier to use for data entry than are Recordsets in tabular format, especially when many fields are involved. The capability to print forms, such as sales orders and invoices, is definitely a benefit to the user.

- *Data presentation* requires the creation of reports that can summarize the information in Recordsets that you can view and print (this is the last step in the process). The capability to provide meaningful reports is the ultimate purpose of any database management application. Also, the management of an enterprise usually lends more credence to reports that are attractively formatted and contain charts or graphs. Charts and graphs summarize the data for those officials who take the "broad brush" approach.

The four basic functions of Access that are implemented as views are organized into the application structure shown in Figure 3.1. If you are creating a new database, you use the basic functions of Access in the top-down sequence shown in Figure 3.1. You choose a function by clicking a button in the Datasheet window (except for security and printing operations, which are menu choices). In most views, you can display the Print Preview window that leads to printing operations by clicking the Print Preview button of the toolbar.

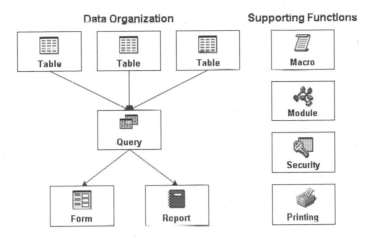

**FIG. 3.1** The basic and supporting functions of Access.

Four supporting functions apply to all the basic functions of Access:

■ *Macros* are sequences of actions that automate repetitive database operations. You create a macro in Access by choosing from a list of available actions, in the order in which you want Access to perform them. You can use a macro, for example, to open a report, print the report, and then close the report. Later, this section defines *open* and *close* as they are used in Access terminology. In prior versions of Access, macros were the primary means of automating database operations. In Access 97, macros are supported primarily for purposes of compatibility with databases created in earlier versions of Access. For Access 97 databases, you use the Access version of Visual Basic for Applications to automate database actions.

■ *Modules* are functions and procedures written in Access's dialect of the Visual Basic for Applications (VBA) programming language. (Access's dialect of VBA was formerly known as Access Basic, and is still frequently referred to by that name.) You use Access VBA functions to make calculations that are more complex than those that can be expressed easily by a series of conventional mathematical symbols, or to make calculations that require decisions to be made. Access VBA procedures are written to perform operations that exceed the capabilities of standard macro actions—one of the reasons why macro support is gradually being dropped from Access. You run Access VBA procedures by attaching the procedure to particular events, such as clicking a command button with the mouse, that occur when a form or report is the active object. In Access 97, you can also execute Access VBA procedures directly from their module.

■ *Security* consists of functions available as menu choices only. With security functions in a multiuser environment, you can let other people use your database. You can grant access to user groups and individuals, and you can restrict their ability to view or modify all or a portion of the tables in the database.

■ *Printing* enables you to print virtually anything you can view in Access's Run mode. From the toolbar, you can print your Access VBA code, but not the macros that you write. (You can use the Documenter add-in to print the content of your macros.)

The terms *open* and *close* have the same basic usage in Access as in other Windows applications, but usually involve more than one basic function:

■ Opening a database makes its content available to the application through the Database window described in Chapter 2, "Up and Running with Access 97." You can open only one database at a time during ordinary use of Access. Writing Access VBA code enables you to operate with tables from more than one database. You can achieve the equivalent of multiple open Access databases by *linking* (Access 97's term for *attaching*) tables from other databases.

■ Opening a table displays a Datasheet view of its contents.

■ Opening a query opens the tables involved but does not display them. Access then runs the query on these tables to create a tabular `Recordset`. Changes made to data in the `Recordset` cause corresponding changes to be made to the data in the tables associated with the query, if the `Recordset` is updatable. (Access 1.x's `Table` and `Dynaset` objects usually are updatable, but `Snapshot` objects are never updatable. The same rules apply to `Recordset` objects of the `Table`, `Dynaset`, and `Snapshot` type.)

■ Opening a form or report automatically opens the table or query with which it is associated. Both forms and reports usually are associated with queries, but a query also can employ a single table.

■ Closing a query closes the associated tables.

■ Closing a form or report closes the associated query and its tables.

### Defining Access Operating Modes

Access has three basic operating modes:

■ *Startup mode* enables you to compress, convert, encrypt, decrypt, and repair a database by choosing commands from the Tools, Database Utilities and Tools, Security menu before opening a database. These commands, some of which are discussed at the end of this chapter, are available only when you *don't* have a database open.

■ *Design mode* enables you to create and modify the structure of tables and queries, develop forms to display and edit your data, and format reports for printing. Access calls Design mode *Design view*.

■ *Run mode* displays your table, form, and report designs in individual document windows (Run is the default mode). You execute macros by choosing one and then selecting run mode. Run mode does not apply to Access VBA modules, because functions are executed when encountered as elements of queries, forms, and reports. Procedures in modules are run by macro commands, or directly from events of forms and reports. Run mode is called *Datasheet view* for tables and queries, *Form view* for forms, and *Print Preview* for reports.

You can select design or run mode by choosing command buttons in the Datasheet window, buttons on the toolbar, or commands from the <u>V</u>iew menu.

You can change the default conditions under which Access displays and prints your tables, queries, forms, and reports by choosing <u>T</u>ools, <u>O</u>ptions. The section "Setting Default Options" near the end of this chapter, describes options that apply to Access as a whole and those that apply only to tables.

# Understanding Access's Table Display

You're probably familiar with the basic terms for many of the components that comprise the basic window in which all conventional Windows 95 applications run (these controls, although similar in function, have a somewhat different appearance and location than those used in Windows 3.x). The presentation of Access windows differs with each of the basic functions that Access performs. Because Part I of this book deals almost exclusively with tables, the examples that follow use Table view. Figure 3.2 shows Access for Windows's basic display for operations with tables. Table 3.1 describes the window's individual components.

| Table 3.1 Components of the Access Display for Tables | |
|---|---|
| **Term** | **Description** |
| Active window | The window to which all mouse and keyboard actions are directed. When an application or document is active, its title bar appears in color (dark blue, unless you have changed your Windows color scheme). If both the application title bar and a document title bar are active, the document title bar receives the mouse and keyboard actions. |
| Application Control-menu box | The icon for the Application Control menu that controls the presentation of the Application window. You display the Application Control menu by clicking the box or pressing Alt+space bar. |
| Application title bar | A bar at the top of the application's window that displays its name. You can move the entire application, if it isn't maximized, by clicking the application title bar and dragging it to a new position. |
| Application window | The window within which Windows displays Access. Each application that you launch runs within its own application window. (Figure 3.2 shows the maximized Access 97 application window.) |
| Caret | A vertical flashing line that indicates the insertion point for keyboard entry in areas of a window that accept text. (The caret isn't visible in Figure 3.2.) |
| Current Record button | A button that indicates a single selected record in the table. When you are editing the current record, the button icon becomes a pencil rather than a triangular arrow. The Current Record button also is called the *record pointer*. |

(continues)

**Table 3.1  Continued**

| Term | Description |
| --- | --- |
| Current Record selection | Buttons that position the record pointer to the first, next, preceding, and last record number in the table, and show the number of the currently selected record. If the table has a key field, the record number reflects the sequence of records in the primary key's sorting order; if there is no primary key in the table, the record number corresponds to the order in which records were physically added to the table. |
| Database window | The window that controls the operating mode of Access and selects the active document window's current function. From the database components displayed in the Database window, you select the component (such as a particular table) to display in the document window. |
| Document Control-menu box | The icon for the Document Control menu that controls a document window's presentation. To access the Document Control menu, click the box or press Alt+- (hyphen). |
| Document title bar | At the top of each document's window, a bar that displays the document's name. You can move the document, if it isn't maximized, by clicking the application title bar and dragging the document to a new position. |
| Document window | The window that displays an Access database component. Tables, queries, forms, reports, macros, and modules are referred to as *documents* in Windows terminology. You can have multiple Access documents of any type open simultaneously. These windows are called *multiple document interface (MDI) child windows*, because the Access application window is their *parent*. |
| Field scroll bar | The scroll bar that enables you to view fields of tables that are outside the bounds of the document window. Record scroll bars provide access to records located outside the document window. |
| Function tabs | Six tabs with which you can choose whether the active document window displays tables, queries, forms, reports, macros, or modules. |
| Inactive window | A window in the background, usually with a grayed title bar. Clicking the surface of an inactive window makes it the active window and brings it to the front. If an inactive window is not visible because other windows obscure it, you can make the window active by choosing the window's name from the Window menu. |
| Maximize button | Clicking the application's Maximize button causes Access to occupy your entire display. Clicking the document's Maximize button causes the document to take over the entire display. When a window is maximized, as shown in Figure 3.2, this button's icon changes to the Restore button. Figure 3.3 shows a maximized table document. |
| Menubar | A horizontal bar containing the main menu choices. The specific main menu choices, and the choices in the drop-down menus corresponding to the main menu selections change, depending on Access's status. Menubars and toolbars collectively are called *command bars*. |
| Minimize button | A button that enables you to collapse the application or document window to an icon at the bottom of your display. |
| Mode buttons | Three buttons that determine the operating mode of Access. *Open* places Access in Run mode. *New* or *Design* puts Access in Design mode, where you can create or edit tables. |

| Term | Description |
|------|-------------|
| New Record button | A button with an asterisk that indicates the location of the next record to be added to a table. Entering data in the new record appends the record to the table and creates another new record. |
| Restore button | A double set of boxes that, when clicked, returns the window from full display to its normal size, with movable borders. When displayed, the Restore button takes the place of the Maximize button in the window's upper-right corner. |
| Status bar | A bar, located at the bottom of the application window, that displays prompts and indicators, such as the status of the Num Lock key. |
| Toolbar | A bar containing command buttons that duplicate the more commonly used menu choices. The number and type of toolbar buttons change depending on which basic function of Access you are using. |

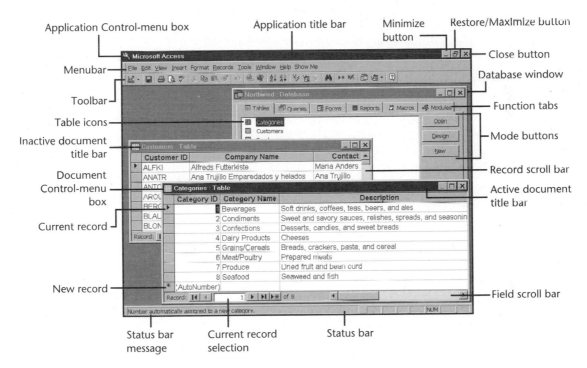

**FIG. 3.2**  Access 97's basic display for tables.

### Maximized Document Windows

Access uses a windowing technique that you should know about; otherwise, you might accidentally minimize or close Access when you intended to minimize or close a maximized document. After you click a document window's Maximize button, the document window takes the place of the application window and occupies the entire display, except for the menu bar and toolbar (see Figure 3.3). Most other Windows applications that display multiple documents, such as Word for Windows and Excel, have a similar capability to expand a document to occupy the entire window.

**FIG. 3.3**   An Access table in a maximized document window.

The Document Control-menu box and the Document Minimize, Restore, and Close buttons move to the menu bar's extreme left and right, respectively. The title of the document is added to the application title in the title bar at the top of the display. To return the document window to its original size, established when the application window was first active, click the Document Restore button; alternatively, click the Document Control-menu box and then choose Restore from the Document Control menu. You can close the document window by clicking the Document Close button, or by double-clicking the Document Control-menu box. If you accidentally click the Application Close button (or double-click the Application Control-menu box just above the Document Control-menu box), however, you close Access 97. You receive no warning that you are about to exit Access unless you have changed the design of an object.

### Document Windows Minimized to Icons

Working with several overlapping windows limits each to a size that enables you to select another by clicking its surface. This overlapping might overly restrict your view of the data that the windows contain. You can minimize Access document windows and the Database window to icons that remain within the application window, as shown at the bottom of Figure 3.4. If you minimize a document window to an icon instead of closing it, you can quickly return the window to its original size by double-clicking the icon. If you single-click the icon, you can choose how the window reappears by using the Document Control menu, as shown for the Database window in Figure 3.4. You can also restore, maximize, or close a minimized icon by clicking the corresponding button within the icon.

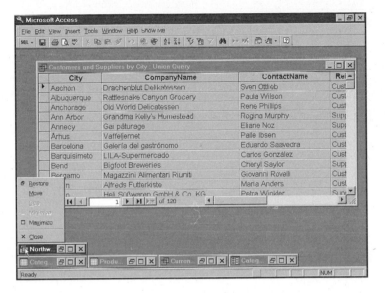

**FIG. 3.4** Tables, a query, a form, and the Database window minimized to icons within the application window.

If you choose to display your document window in maximized form by choosing Maximize from the Document Control menu that appears when you click the icon, the document hides the icons at the bottom of the application window. In this case, open the Window menu and choose the document that you want. If you size your document windows (like the window in Figure 3.4) by dragging their borders, you can avoid the substantial mouse movement and two-step menu-selection process to select the active document.

### The Toolbars in Table View

The buttons that appear in Access's toolbar, and the number of toolbars displayed, changes according to the function that Access is currently performing. When you are working with tables in Run mode, Access 97 displays the Table Datasheet and the Datasheet Formatting toolbars, shown in Figures 3.5 and 3.6, respectively. The next two sections of this chapter describe the toolbars that appear in Table Run mode (Datasheet view).

---

**Note**

Even if you have some experience with previous versions of Access, you should note Tables 3.2 and 3.3. Access 97 adds many new shortcut buttons to the toolbars and has also moved or restructured several menu commands. For example, the View, Toolbars command now leads to a submenu, instead of to a dialog. The View, Toolbars submenu lists only those toolbars most pertinent to Access's current operating mode, making it easier for you to select an appropriate assortment of toolbars; a Customize menu choice leads to the Toolbars dialog, which is familiar to users of Access 95.

---

**The Table Datasheet Toolbar.** The Table Datasheet toolbar appears whenever you open an Access table in Datasheet view. Figure 3.5 shows the Table Datasheet toolbar, and Table 3.2 describes the buttons that appear on the toolbar.

---

**Note**

Toolbar buttons provide shortcuts to traditional selection methods, such as choosing menu commands or choosing command or option buttons in a particular sequence. The Alternate Method columns of Tables 3.2 and 3.3 list how you can achieve the same effect as clicking a toolbar button by using the menus or the command buttons in the Database window.

---

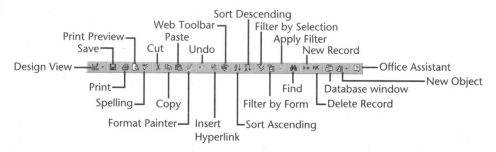

**FIG. 3.5** Access's Table Datasheet toolbar displayed when a table is open in Datasheet view.

**Table 3.2 Appearance and Functions of Buttons and Other Elements of the Table Datasheet Toolbar**

| Icon | Button | Alternate Method | Function |
|------|--------|------------------|----------|
| | Design View | View, Design View | Design mode. In Design mode, you specify the properties of the table. |
| | Datasheet View | View, Datasheet View | Returns the table display to Run mode (Datasheet view) from Design mode. (You cannot see this button in Figure 3.5; it appears only when the table is in Design view.) |
| | Save | File, Save | Saves the database. |
| | Print | File, Print | Prints the table. |
| | Print Preview | File, Print Preview | Displays the contents of a table in report format and enables you to print the table's contents. |
| | Spelling | Tools, Spelling | Starts the spelling checker. |
| | Cut | Edit, Cut | Cuts the selected information and puts it in the Windows Clipboard. |

| Icon | Button | Alternate Method | Function |
|------|--------|------------------|----------|
| | Copy | Edit, Copy | Copies selected information to the Windows Clipboard. |
| | Paste | Edit, Paste | Pastes information from the Windows Clipboard into Access at the current location of the caret. |
| | Format Painter | | Copies a control's format to another control. Used only in Design view; it is enabled only when you select a control. |
| | Undo | Edit, Undo | Returns you to the status immediately preceding the last action that you took. The Undo button is inactive if there is no action to undo. Access provides a single-level Undo feature that repeals only one action. |
| | Insert Hyperlink | Insert, Hyperlink | Opens the Insert Hyperlink dialog, which lets you add a URL or UNC address to a hyperlink field in a table. Chapter 16, "Working with Hyperlinks and HTML," describes hyperlink fields in more detail. |
| | Web Toolbar | | Displays or hides the Web toolbar. The Web toolbar lets you activate your Web browser to view HTML pages stored locally on your computer or network, or on the Internet. The Web Toolbar button is a toggle button—when in its "up" position, the Web toolbar is hidden; when in its "down" position, the Web toolbar is displayed. |
| | Sort Ascending | Records, Sort, Ascending | Sorts the records in ascending order, based on the current field. |
| | Sort Descending | Records, Sort, Descending | Sorts the records in descending order, based on the current field. |
| | Filter by Selection | Records, Filter, Filter by Selection | Filters records based on the selected text in a field. |
| | Filter by Form | Records, Filter, Filter by Form | Enables you to enter criteria in a table datasheet to establish how records are filtered. |

*(continues)*

**Table 3.2    Continued**

| Icon | Button | Alternate Method | Function |
|------|--------|------------------|----------|
| ▽ | Apply/ Remove Filter | Records, Apply Filter/Sort | Applies or removes a filter. |
| 🔍 | Find | Edit, Find | Displays the Find dialog that locates records with specific characters in a single field or all fields. |
| ▶＊ | New Record | Edit, Go To, New | Selects the tentative append record. |
| ✕ | Delete Record | Edit, Delete Record | Deletes the active record. |
| ▤ | Database Window | Window, 1 | Displays the Database window. |
| ▤▼ | New Object | | Displays a drop-down list from which you choose the type of new object that you want to create: tables, forms, reports, queries, macros, or modules. |
| ⁇ | Office Assistant | F1 | Activates the Microsoft Office Assistant described in the "Using the Office Assistant" section later in this chapter. |

---

**Note**

In Access 97, and in other applications in Microsoft Office 97, the toolbar buttons appear as flat icons on the toolbar. The toolbar buttons only have a raised button-like appearance when the mouse pointer is over the button. The exception to this rule is "toggle" buttons—that is, buttons that represent the on/off status of a feature, like the Web Toolbar button (refer to Table 3.2 and Figure 3.5). When a toggle button is "up," it appears as a flat icon on the toolbar until you move the mouse pointer over it; the button's "up" appearance indicates that the feature controlled by that button is off. Toggle buttons in the "down" positions are shaded so that they look as if they are sunken below the surface of the toolbar; the "down" appearance indicates that the feature controlled by that button is on.

---

**The Datasheet Formatting Toolbar.** In addition to the Table Datasheet toolbar, you can display the Datasheet Formatting toolbar whenever you view a table in Datasheet View. Choose View, Toolbars, Formatting (Datasheet) to add the toolbar. The buttons in the Datasheet Formatting toolbar provide shortcuts to various text-formatting commands. In Datasheet view, the text-formatting commands apply to the entire table; you cannot format individual cells in Datasheet view. Figure 3.6 shows the Datasheet Formatting toolbar, and Table 3.3 summarizes the action of each button on the toolbar.

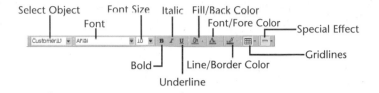

**FIG. 3.6** The Datasheet Formatting toolbar in Datasheet view.

**Table 3.3 Appearance and Functions of Buttons and Other Elements of the Datasheet Formatting Toolbar**

| Icon | Button | Alternate Method | Function |
|---|---|---|---|
| CustomerID | Select Object | | Displays a drop-down list from which you can jump quickly to any field in the table. |
| Arial | Font | Format, Font | Enables you to select the font (typeface) for text in a table. |
| 10 | Font Size | Format, Font | Enables you to select the size of the text in a table. |
| B | Bold | Format, Font | Turns bold text formatting on and off for the text in a table. |
| I | Italic | Format, Font | Turns italic text formatting on and off for text in a table. |
| U | Underline | Format, Font | Turns underlining on and off for text in a table. |
| | Fill/Back Color | Format, Cells | Displays a palette of colors from which to choose the background color for the table's data cells. |
| | Font/Fore Color | Format, Font | Displays a palette of colors from which to choose the color of the text in the table. |
| | Line/Border Color | Format, Cells | Displays a color palette from which to choose the color of the gridlines that indicate rows and columns in the table. |
| | Gridlines | Format, Cells | Displays four buttons that enable you to choose which gridlines are shown: horizontal and vertical, vertical only, horizontal only, or none. |
| | Special Effect | Format, Cells | Displays three buttons that enable you to choose the cell display style: flat, raised, or sunken. |

### Manipulating Access's Toolbars

Access 97 uses the resizable, customizable, floating toolbars that have become standard in Microsoft applications such as Excel and Microsoft Word. In Microsoft Office 97, menubars and toolbars have been combined into a single object, called a *command bar*, and now share many features in common. The primary characteristic that distinguishes a menubar from a toolbar in Access 97 (and other Office 97 applications) is that every application has at least one menu bar, and the menubar may not be hidden. In all other respects, menubars and toolbars are now the same.

Access 97's View, Toolbars menu choice enables you to select which toolbars are currently visible. The View, Toolbars menu lists those toolbars pertinent to Access's current operating mode. Figure 3.7 shows the View, Toolbars menu for Table Datasheet view. The currently displayed toolbars are indicated on the menu by a check mark at the left of the menu choice for that specific toolbar. To display or hide a toolbar, click its name in the submenu.

**FIG. 3.7**   Displaying or hiding toolbars with the View, Toolbars menu choice.

---

### Note

In Figure 3.7, and other figures throughout this book, you may notice a menu choice that isn't discussed in the text—Show Me. The Show Me choice only appears on the menu bar when the Northwind.mdb database is open, and only if you also chose to install the Show Me help files when you installed Access 97. The Show Me menu isn't part of Access 97; instead, it is displayed by Northwind.mdb. If you're interested in viewing help topics relating to the Access VBA code that is part of the Northwind.mdb sample database, click the Show Me menu choice.

---

The Customize choice on the View, Toolbars menu opens the Customize dialog (see Figure 3.8) that lets you display as many toolbars at once as will fit in your display—or hide toolbars that Access would otherwise display automatically. To display a toolbar, click the Toolbars tab to display the Toolbars page (if necessary), then click the box to the left of the toolbar name in the Toolbars dialog so that the check box is selected. To hide a toolbar, click the box again to clear the check box selection. For help using the Customize dialog, click the Office Assistant button at the lower-left area of the Customize dialog to activate the Office Assistant, if it isn't already active (see "Using the Office Assistant" later in this chapter).

---

### Note

When an Access toolbar is in its docked position, it has a fixed width, anchored at its left edge. If you reduce the width of Access's application window by dragging either vertical border inward, the buttons at the docked toolbar's extreme right begin to disappear beyond the application window's right edge. Operating Access in a maximized window with docked toolbars is usually best, because you can then easily access all the toolbar buttons when you use the default in-line horizontal toolbar.

---

**FIG. 3.8**   Selecting the toolbars to be displayed in the Customize dialog.

You also can use the Customize dialog to change the viewing options for toolbars. Click the Options tab of the Customize dialog to display the Options page shown in Figure 3.9; the Options page enables you to select various toolbar viewing options. If you're using SVGA 1024×768 screen resolution, you may want to select the Large Icons option, which causes the toolbar button icons to approximately double in size; this makes the icons easier to discern, and easier to click with the mouse. The Show ScreenTips on toolbars option governs whether Access displays the ScreenTips (formerly known as ToolTips) hints on the mouse cursor for toolbar buttons. The Show Shortcut Keys in ScreenTips option determines whether Access displays the keyboard shortcut (if there is one) as part of the ScreenTip text. Finally, the Menu Animations drop-down list lets you choose how Access draws menus on-screen. You may choose None (for no special effects when drawing menus), Random (Access randomly chooses an animation effect each time you open a menu), Unfold (the menu unfolds like a fan), or Slide (the menu opens like a roller-shade) as the technique for displaying Access's menus.

**FIG. 3.9**   Selecting viewing options for toolbars and menus in the Options page of the Customize dialog.

In addition to displaying multiple toolbars, you can reshape or reposition the toolbars to suit your own taste. Click a blank area of the toolbar and hold down the left mouse button to drag the toolbar to a new location. The toolbar turns into a popup floating toolbar, similar to the toolbox that you use to add control objects to forms and reports. Popup toolbars always appear on top of any other windows open in your application.

Figure 3.10 shows three floating command bars: the Table Datasheet toolbar, the Formatting Datasheet toolbar, and the Menu Bar. (These are the same toolbars—discussed in the preceding section of this chapter—that Access displays in Datasheet View mode. The Menu Bar—which is Access's main menubar—was moved from its position at the top of the Access application window to demonstrate its new features as a command bar.) Command bars in their fixed position are called *docked* command bars, while command bars in their popup window are referred to as *floating* command bars. After you change a command bar to a floating command bar (or dock it), Access always displays the command bar in that location until you again reposition the command bar.

> **Tip**
>
> You can also dock command bars (both menubars and toolbars) at the bottom of the Access application window, or at either the left or right edge of the application window.

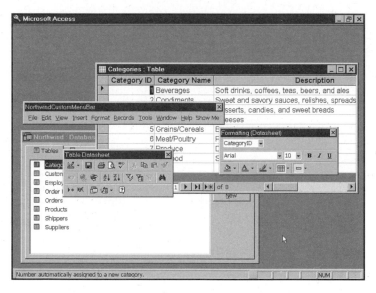

**FIG. 3.10**   Access's Table Datasheet toolbar, Datasheet Formatting toolbar, and main menubar dragged from their default positions at the top of the application window.

### Right Mouse Button Shortcut Menus

Another feature that Access 97 shares with other Microsoft applications, plus Windows 95 and Windows NT 4.0, is the shortcut menu that appears when you right-click the surface of an Access database object. Shortcut menus (also called *popup* or *context* menus) present choices that vary depending on the type of object that you click. Figure 3.11 shows the shortcut menu for a field of a table selected by clicking the field name header.

---

**Tip**

Shortcut menus are quite useful, and provide shortcuts to many common tasks. If you're not sure what you can do with an object on-screen, try right-clicking it to see what shortcut menu commands are available.

---

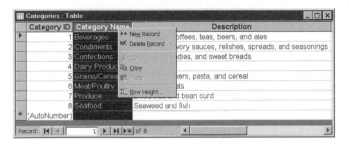

**FIG. 3.11**   The shortcut menu for selected column of a table.

# Using the Function Keys

Access assigns specific purposes to all 12 function keys of the 101-key extended keyboard. Some keys, such as Shift+F4 (which you press to find the next occurrence of a match with the Find dialog), derive from other Microsoft applications—in this case, Word for Windows. You use function keys with the Shift, Alt, and Ctrl keys to enable users to perform as many as 96 functions with the 12 function keys.

### Global Function Keys

Windows, rather than Access, uses global function-key assignments, except for F11 and Alt+F1, to perform functions that are identical in all Windows applications. Table 3.4 lists the global function-key assignments.

| Table 3.4 | Global Function-Key Assignments |
|---|---|
| **Key** | **Function** |
| F1 | Displays context-sensitive help related to the present basic function and status of Access. If a context-sensitive help topic isn't available, F1 starts the Office Assistant (described in the next section of this chapter). |
| Shift+F1 | Adds a question mark to the mouse pointer. Place the mouse pointer with the question mark over an object on-screen for which you want help and then click. |
| Ctrl+F4 | Closes the active window. |
| Alt+F4 | Exits Access or closes a dialog if one is open. |
| Ctrl+F6 | Selects each open window in sequence as the active window. |
| F11 or Alt+F1 | Selects the Database window as the active window. |
| F12 or Alt+F2 | Opens the File Save As dialog. |
| Shift+F12 or Alt+Shift+F2 | Saves your open database; the equivalent of the File, Save menu choice. |

### Function-Key Assignments for Fields, Grids, and Text Boxes

Access assigns function-key combinations that aren't reserved for global operations to actions that are specific to the basic function that you are performing at the moment. Table 3.5 lists the function-key combinations that apply to fields, grids, and text boxes. (To present complete information, this table repeats some information that appears in the previous tables.)

▶▶ See "Using Keyboard Operations for Entering and Editing Data," p. 162

**Table 3.5    Function Keys for Fields, Grids, and Text Boxes**

| Key | Function |
| --- | --- |
| F2 | Toggles between displaying the caret for editing and selecting the entire field. |
| Shift+F2 | Opens the Zoom box for entering expressions and other text. |
| F4 | Opens a drop-down combo list or list box. |
| Shift+F4 | Finds the next occurrence of a match of the text entered in the Find or Replace dialog, if the dialog is closed. |
| F5 | Moves the caret to the record-number box. Enter the number of the record that you want to display and press Enter. |
| F6 | In Table Design view, cycles between upper and lower parts of the window. In Form Design view, cycles through the header, body (detail section), and footer. |
| Shift+F6 | In Form Design view, cycles through the footer, body (detail section), and header, moving backward. |
| F7 | Starts the spelling checker. |
| F8 | Turns on Extend mode. Press F8 again to extend the selection to a word, the entire field, the whole record, and then all records. |
| Shift+F8 | Reverses the F8 selection process. |
| Ctrl+F | Opens the Find dialog. |
| Ctrl+H | Opens the Replace dialog. |
| Ctrl++ (plus sign) | Adds a new record to the database. |
| Ctrl+- (minus sign) | Deletes the current record. |
| Shift+Enter | Saves changes to the active record in the database. |
| Esc | Undoes changes in the current record or field. By pressing Esc twice, you can undo changes in both the current field and record. Also cancels extend mode. |

### Function Keys in the Module Window

You use the Module window when writing Access VBA code, which is the subject of this book's Part VII, "Programming, Distributing, and Converting Access." Table 3.6 lists the purposes of the Module window's function keys. The Module window shares many of the characteristics of Windows's Notepad applet, including the F3 key, which you use for searching.

▶▶ See "Exploring the Module Window," p. 1007

| Table 3.6    **Function Keys in the Module Window** | |
|---|---|
| **Key** | **Function** |
| F1 | Displays context-sensitive help about the currently selected Access VBA keyword, dialog, or menu command. |
| F2 | Opens the Object Browser dialog, which enables you to view Access objects and move among them and other applications that support VBA, including the applications' properties, controls, procedures, and methods. |
| Shift+F2 | Goes to the procedure selected in the Module window. |
| F3 | Finds the next occurrence of text specified in the Find or Replace dialog. |
| Shift+F3 | Finds the preceding occurrence of text specified in the Find or Replace dialog. |
| F5 | Continues executing code after a break condition. |
| Shift+F5 | Resets the VBA interpreter, utilizing all variables. |
| F6 | Cycles between upper and lower panes (if you have split the window). |
| F8 | Traces execution one step at a time (single step or Step Into mode). |
| Shift+F8 | Traces execution by procedure (procedure step or Step Over mode). |
| F9 | Toggles a breakpoint at the selected line. |
| Shift+F9 | Creates an Instant Watch for the selected variable or expression. |
| Ctrl+Shift+F9 | Clears all breakpoints. |
| Ctrl+F | Opens the Find dialog. |
| Ctrl+G | Displays the Debug window. |
| Ctrl+H | Opens the Replace dialog. |
| Ctrl+L | Displays the Calls dialog. |
| Ctrl+M | Indents selected lines. |
| Ctrl+Shift+M | Removes indentation. |
| Ctrl+Y | Cuts the current line and copies it to the Clipboard. |
| Ctrl+Break | Halts macro execution. |
| Ctrl+↑ | Displays the previous procedure. |
| Ctrl+↓ | Displays the next procedure. |

# Setting Default Options

You can set about 100 options that establish the default settings for the system as a whole, and also those for the six functions defined by the Database window's tabs. You aren't likely to change default options until you are more familiar with Access. However, because this book is a reference as well as a tutorial guide, and options are a basic element of Access's overall structure, this section explains how to change these settings.

You set defaults by choosing Tools, Options. The Options dialog appears as shown in Figure 3.12. View, General, Keyboard, and Edit/Find Category options apply to the system as a whole. Datasheet, Tables/Queries, and Forms/Reports options all apply to table views in Datasheet view, forms, and queries. The remainder of the option categories are specific to other basic functions.

**FIG. 3.12** The Options dialog displaying the View Options sheet.

You select an Options category by clicking the tab near the top of the Options dialog. When you change a category, the dialog displays the Options sheet for that category. Most of the settings are option buttons and check boxes, although many other items require multiple-choice entries that you select from drop-down lists. In some cases, you must enter a specific value from the keyboard. After you complete your changes, click OK to close the dialog. If you decide not to implement your changes, click Cancel to exit the Options dialog without making any changes. The next few sections and their tables summarize options that affect Access as a whole, and those options that affect viewing and printing data in Datasheet view.

### System Defaults

Access uses a special Access database, System.mdw, to store all default properties for displaying and printing the contents of tables, queries, forms, reports, and modules for each user of Access. The .mdw extension for workgroup system files was new with Access 95, replacing the .MDA extension shared by libraries, wizards, and System.mda in Access 1.x and 2.0. Access 97, like Access 95, stores user default properties in system tables, along with other tables that determine the behavior of Access, in System.mdw. System.mdw also stores user names and passwords when you secure your Access database or use Access in a multiuser (workgroup) environment.

 ▶▶ See "Sharing Your Access Database Files with Other Users," p. 868

> **Note**
>
> System.mdw is vital to the proper operation of Access. You should keep a backup copy of System.mdw on a floppy disk. If you make changes to any options or implement Access's security features, you should create an updated backup after completing your changes or additions.

**View Options.** The View options, as described in Table 3.7, enable you to customize the appearance of Access's application window.

### Table 3.7   View Options for the Access System

| Option | Group | Function |
| --- | --- | --- |
| Status Bar | Show | If checked, displays the status bar at the bottom of the Access application window. |
| Startup Dialog Box | Show | If checked, displays the startup dialog whenever you start Access. This dialog prompts you to open an existing database or to create a new one. |
| Hidden Objects | Show | When checked, displays hidden objects in the Database window. |
| System Objects | Show | If checked, displays system objects in the Database window. |
| Names Column | Macro Design | If checked, displays the Names column in new macros. |
| Conditions | Macro Design | If checked, displays the Conditions Column column in new macros. |

**General Options.** General options, described in Table 3.8, apply to Access as a whole. The settings that you make in the General options apply to any new objects that you create (tables, forms, and reports), but don't retroactively affect existing objects. For example, changing the print margins in General options affects only any reports that you create subsequently, but not any existing reports. To change the print margins of existing objects, you must change each object's individual printing settings in Design view.

Margins usually are expressed in inches. If you are using an international version of Access, margin settings are in centimeters. You also can specify margin settings in twips, the default measurement of Windows. A *twip* is 1/20 of a printer's point. A point is 1/72 inch, so a twip is 1/1,440 inch.

The one-inch default margins are arbitrary; you might want to reset them to your preference before creating any forms or reports of your own. If you are using a laser printer, refer to its manual to determine the maximum printable area. The printable area determines the minimum margins that you can use.

Apart from the printing margins, the General option you're most likely to want to change is the default database directory. When you create your own databases, you should store them in a folder dedicated to databases, to simplify backup operations. A dedicated database folder also is a good place to keep a backup copy of System.mdw.

## Table 3.8  General Options for the Access System

| Option | Group | Function |
|---|---|---|
| Left Margin | Print Margins | Establishes the default left margin. |
| Top Margin | Print Margins | Establishes the default top margin. |
| Right Margin | Print Margins | Establishes the default right margin. |
| Bottom Margin | Print Margins | Establishes the default bottom margin. |
| Default Database Folder | | Changes the default folder for the Open Database dialog. The default folder is the Access working folder, indicated by a period. |
| New Database Sort Order | | Sets the alphabetical sort order used for new databases. You can change the sort order for an existing database by selecting a different sort-order setting and then compacting the database by choosing Tools, Database Utilities, Compact Database. |
| Already Followed | Hyperlink | Selects the color for hyperlink text which has been followed in this session. |
| Not Yet Followed | Hyperlink | Selects color for hyperlink text which hasn't yet been clicked this session. |
| Underline Hyperlinks | Hyperlink | If selected, Access displays hyperlink text with an underline. |
| Show Hyperlink Addresses in Status Bar | Hyperlink | If selected, Access displays the full hyperlink address in the status bar at the bottom of the application window. |

**Edit/Find Options.** The Edit/Find options all affect the behavior of Access's Find feature for both tables in Form or Datasheet view and when working with Access VBA code in a module. Table 3.9 summarizes the Edit/Find options and their effects. The options in the Default Find/Replace Behavior group all determine the default searching method for the Edit, Find and Edit, Replace commands. Options in the Confirm group all determine which actions Access asks the user to confirm. The final option group in the Find/Replace options sheet is the Filter by Form Defaults for the current database. These options don't actually affect Access itself, but affect the defaults for the particular database that is open.

## Table 3.9  Edit/Find Options for the Access System

| Option | Group | Function |
|---|---|---|
| Fast Search | Default Find/Replace Behavior | Sets the default search method to search in the current field, and to match the whole field. |
| General Search | Default Find/Replace Behavior | Sets the default search method to search in all fields, and matches any part of a field. |

| Option | Group | Function |
|---|---|---|
| Start of Field Search | Default Find/Replace Behavior | Causes the default search method to search the current field, matching only the beginning of the field. |
| Record Changes | Confirm | Causes Access to confirm any changes that you make to a record. |
| Document Deletions | Confirm | Causes Access to confirm document (table, form, or report) deletions. |
| Action Queries | Confirm | Causes Access to confirm an action query (such as adding or deleting records) before carrying out the query. |
| Local Indexed Fields | Filter by Form Defaults | Includes local indexed fields in the list of values that you can use criteria. |
| Local Non-Indexed Fields | Filter by Form Defaults | Includes nonindexed fields in the list of values that you can use when entering filter criteria. |
| ODBC Fields | Filter by Form Defaults | Includes fields from remote ODBC tables in the lists of values that you can use when entering filter criteria. |
| Don't Display Lists Where More Than This Number Of Records Read | | Prohibits the display of filter values whenever the number of items in the list exceeds the specified number. |

**Keyboard Options.** Keyboard options, listed in Table 3.10, are especially important if you are accustomed to a particular type of arrow-key behavior. You probably will want to change keyboard options more than any of the other categories. For example, you can make the arrow keys behave as if you are editing xBase fields, instead of using the keys' default behavior, which duplicates that of Excel. The options in the Move After Enter group affect what Access does when you press Enter after editing or entering data. The options in the Arrow Key Behavior group affect how the left- and right-arrow keys work, while the options in the Behavior Entering Field group determine what happens when the caret enters a field.

▶▶ See "Using Data Entry and Editing Keys," p. 163

**Table 3.10  Keyboard Options for the Access System**

| Option | Group | Function |
|---|---|---|
| Don't Move | Move After Enter | When selected, the caret remains in the current field when you press Enter. |
| Next Field | Move After Enter | When selected, the caret moves to the next or previous field when you press Enter. This is the Move After Enter group's default option. |

(continues)

| Table 3.10 Continued | | |
|---|---|---|
| **Option** | **Group** | **Function** |
| Next Record | Move After Enter | When selected, the caret moves down the column to the next or previous record when you press Enter. |
| Next Field | Arrow Key Behavior | If selected, pressing the right- or left-arrow keys moves the caret to the next or previous field. This is the Arrow Key Behavior group's default option. |
| Next Character | Arrow Key Behavior | If selected, pressing the right- or left-arrow keys moves the caret to the next or previous character in the same field. |
| Select Entire Field | Behavior Entering Field | When this option is selected, the entire field's contents are selected when you use the arrow keys to move the caret into the field. This is the Behavior Entering Field group's default option. |
| Go to Start of Field | Behavior Entering Field | If selected, causes the caret to move to the beginning of the field when you use the the arrow keys to move the caret into the field. |
| Go to End of Field | Behavior Entering Field | If selected, causes the caret to move to the end of the field when you use the arrow keys to move the caret into the field. |
| Cursor Stops at First/Last Field | | If selected, keeps the caret from moving to another record when the left- or right-arrow keys are pressed, and the caret is in the first or last field of the record. |

**Advanced Options.** Access has several advanced system options that affect multiuser operations, OLE updates, DDE linking and updating, and tables attached by the Open Database Connectivity (ODBC) feature of the Jet 3.5 database engine. Table 3.11 describes the Advanced options that you can set. Options in the Default Record Locking group affect how Access locks records in a multiuser environment, and the Default Open Mode option group controls whether Access shares opened databases. The DDE Operation options group controls how Access handles DDE requests from other applications; other options control OLE updating and query updating. The Current Database Only group contains options that relate to any Access VBA code that may be stored in your database. Usually you won't need to change the Advanced options much, unless you're working in a multiuser environment with several users sharing the same database, or the database contains Access VBA code that uses command arguments and conditional compiler directives.

**Table 3.11  Advanced Options for the Access System**

| Option | Group | Function |
|---|---|---|
| No Locks | Default Record Locking | When selected, leaves all records unlocked in the open database tables, so that other networked users can update the records. This is the group's default option. |
| All Records | Default Record Locking | When selected, locks all records in the open database tables. No other networked users can update the records. |
| Edited Records | Default Record Locking | When selected, locks only edited records. When the changes to the record are saved, Access unlocks the record. |
| Ignore DDE Request | DDE Operations | If enabled, ignores all Dynamic Data Exchange (DDE) requests from other Windows applications. |
| Enable DDE Refresh | DDE Operations | If enabled, lets Access dynamically update linked DDE data. This is the group's default option. |
| OLE/DDE Timeout (sec) | | Specifies how long Access waits for a response from a DDE or OLE server. If the specified interval passes without a response, Access reports an error. Access's default value for this option is 30 seconds. |
| Shared | Default Open Mode | When selected, enables other networked users to use the open database simultaneously. This is the group's default option. |
| Exclusive | Default Open Mode | When selected, opens the database in an exclusive mode so that other network users cannot open the database. |
| Number of Update Retries | | Specifies how many times that Access tries to update a query, OLE object, or DDE link before giving up. The default number of tries is 2. |
| ODBC Refresh Interval (sec) | | Specifies how many seconds that Access waits before refreshing records that you view through an ODBC connection. The default interval is 1,500 seconds. |
| Refresh Interval (sec) | | Specifies how many seconds that Access waits before refreshing remote data. The default Refresh Interval is 60 seconds. |
| Update Retry Interval (msec) | | Specifies how many milliseconds (thousandths of a second) that Access waits in between attempts at updating an OLE, DDE, ODBC, or other link. The default is 25 ms. |

(continues)

**Table 3.11   Continued**

| Option | Group | Function |
|--------|-------|----------|
| Command-Line Arguments | Current Database Only | Use this text box to enter any arguments that you want returnedby the Command() function. |
| Conditional Compilation | Current Database Only | Use this text box to specify values for conditional compilation directives. |
| Project Name | Current Database Only | Enter a name for your Access VBA project in this text box; this is the name by which code in your Access database is known to other applications. |

### Defaults for Datasheet View

You use Datasheet View options to customize the display of all query datasheets and new table and form datasheets (see Table 3.12). As with printing options, to change the display format of existing table and form datasheets, you must edit the appropriate properties of the table or form in Design view. The Datasheet View options that you set don't apply to forms and reports created with Access wizards. Each wizard has its own set of default values. The options in the Default Colors group set the background and foreground colors for text displayed in Datasheet view, while the Default Font group's options determine the typeface and text size. The Default Gridlines Showing options determine which gridlines (if any) Access displays in Datasheet view. Finally, the Default Cell Effect options enable you to select a default style for datasheet cells.

**Table 3.12   Options for Datasheet Views**

| Option | Group | Function |
|--------|-------|----------|
| Font | Default Colors | Displays a drop-down list from which you can select the color of the text in new tables, queries, and forms. Access's default Font color selection is black. |
| Background | Default Colors | Enables you to select the background color of cells in Datasheet view. Access's default Background color is white. |
| Gridlines | Default Colors | Enables you to select the color of the gridlines displayed in Datasheet view. Access's default gridline color is silver. |
| Font | Default Font | Displays a drop-down list from which you can select the typeface that Access uses to display text in Datasheet view. Access's default font is Arial. |
| Weight | Default Font | Displays a drop-down list from which you can select the weight of the text characters displayed in Datasheet view. You can select Normal (the default), Thin, Extra Light, Medium, Semi-bold, Bold, Extra Bold, or Heavy. |

| Option | Group | Function |
|---|---|---|
| Size | Default Font | Enables you to select the default font size, in points. Access's default font size is 10 points. |
| Italic | Default Font | If selected, displays all datasheet text in italics. |
| Underline | Default Font | If selected, displays all datasheet text with a single underline. |
| Horizontal | Default Gridlines Showing | If selected, displays horizontal gridlines (that is, gridlines between rows) in Datasheet view. By default, this option and the Vertical Gridlines option are turned on. |
| Vertical | Default Gridlines Showing | If selected, displays vertical gridlines (that is, gridlines between columns) in Datasheet view. You can display both vertical and horizontal gridlines by combining the Vertical Gridlines option with the Horizontal Gridlines option. |
| Default Column Width | | Specifies the default column width in inches. Access's default value for this text box setting is one inch. |
| Flat | Default Cell Effect | When selected, displays a data cell as a "flat" cell—that is, the cell has no special shading. This is the group's default option. |
| Raised | Default Cell Effect | When selected, adds shadow effects to each data cell so that the cell appears to be raised above the surface of the screen, like a command button. |
| Sunken | Default Cell Effect | When selected, adds shadow effects to each data cell so that the cell appears to be sunken below the surface of the screen. |
| Show Animations | | If selected, displays animated cursors and other animation effects. If you have a slow computer, you'll probably want to turn this option off to improve Access's operating speed slightly. |

### Note

The remaining option categories—Tables/Queries, Forms/Reports, and Module—are discussed in the chapter(s) of this book that cover the subject of the particular option category. Also, options related to multiuser, DDE, and ODBC features are described in more detail in the chapter(s) devoted to those special topics.

# Using Access Help

The Access help system is extensive and easy to use. All the new help functions incorporated in Windows 95's 32-bit WinHelp engine are used by Access's Help system.

### Context-Sensitive Help

*Context-sensitive help* tries to anticipate your need for information by displaying help windows related to the operating mode, function, and operation in which you are involved or attempting to perform. You can get context-sensitive help in any of the following ways:

■ By using the help mouse pointer that appears after you click the What's This button (located near the top-right corner of the dialog window) in the active dialog. Move the help mouse pointer over the dialog option for which you want help, and click again to display a popup help window with information about that dialog option.

■ By using the help mouse pointer that appears after you press Shift+F1 or choose Help, What's This?. Move the help mouse pointer over the item for which you want help, and click again to display a popup help window.

■ By pressing the F1 key. Access displays a help window with information about the active area (dialog control, window, menu command, and so on), or displays the Office Assistant, described later in this section.

■ By clicking the Help button in a dialog. Use this method, or press the F1 key, for dialogs that don't have a What's This button.

To get context-sensitive help in an open dialog, click the What's This button; the mouse pointer changes to a question mark. Move the help mouse pointer over the dialog control that you want help with, and click. You can also get context-sensitive help on the active dialog control by pressing F1 or clicking the control with the right mouse button. For example, you might want more information about the effects of the Find dialog's Match Case option. To find such information, click the What's This button, and then click the Find dialog's Match Case option. Figure 3.13 shows the resulting popup help window explaining the Match Case option.

**FIG. 3.13**   The context-sensitive help for the Find dialog's Match Case option.

Another method for getting context-sensitive help is to press Shift+F1 (or choose Help, What's This?) and then place the mouse pointer with the question mark on the item with which you need help. When you click the mouse button, the topic related to the object appears. Figure 3.14 shows an example that explains the purpose of the Table Datasheet toolbar's Find button.

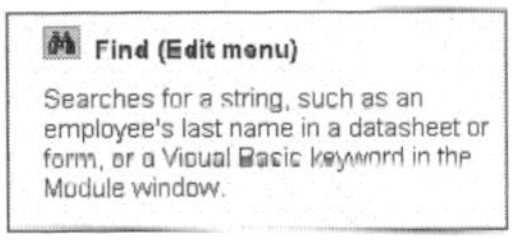

Find (Edit menu)

Searches for a string, such as an employee's last name in a datasheet or form, or a Visual Basic keyword in the Module window.

**FIG. 3.14**  The popup help window explaining the purpose of the toolbar's Find button.

### The Help Menu

Access's Help menu provides an alternative to using context-sensitive help. Table 3.13 lists the options that the Help menu presents.

| Table 3.13 | Access's Help Menu Options |
| --- | --- |
| **Option** | **Function** |
| Microsoft Access Help | Activates the Office Assistant, described later in this section. |
| Contents and Index | Displays the Help Topics dialog, which enables you to select or search for help topics either through a table of contents, an index, or a Find utility. |
| What's This? | Changes the mouse pointer to the Help pointer for obtaining context-sensitive help. Move the Help mouse pointer over the object or menu choice for which you want help, and click to display a popup help window. |
| Microsoft on the Web | Displays a submenu list of Web sites related to Microsoft, Microsoft Access, frequently asked questions, free software, and other topics. |
| About Microsoft Access | Displays the copyright notice for Microsoft Access, and the name and organization that you entered during setup. The About dialog also contains two command buttons: one that displays sources of technical support for Access in North America and throughout the world, and another that displays information about your computer system, such as how much memory you have installed, whether you have a math coprocessor, and the amount of remaining disk space. |

### Using the Help Topics Dialog

You can get a more general form of help by choosing Help, Contents and Index. In this case, you always start from square one—the Help Topics dialog for the entire help system, shown in Figure 3.15. The Help Topics dialog contains three tabbed sheets: Contents, Index, and Find; each of these options is described in the following paragraphs.

> **Note**
>
> The Answer Wizard of Access 95 has been incorporated in the new Office Assistant feature of Access 97; the Office Assistant is described at the end of this section.

**The Contents Tab.** Figure 3.15 shows the Help Topics Contents tab (you might have to click the Contents tab to bring the table of contents to the front of the dialog). The Contents tab is like the table of contents in a book; it shows the structure of the topics in the Help system, based on the topic's title.

Each table of contents entry that has subheadings is indicated by a book icon to its left. To see subheadings for a topic, double-click the closed book icon. The Help system expands the topic list and changes the icon to an open book. (To hide the list of subheadings, double-click the open book icon; this hides the expanded subheading branch and changes the icon back to a closed book.)

Table of contents headings that lack subheadings have to their left an icon resembling a sheet of paper with a question mark on it. Figure 3.15 shows the "Finding and Sorting Data" heading expanded to show its subheadings; the "Sorting Data in Tables, Queries, and Forms" subheading, in turn, has been expanded, revealing a list of three help topics. To display a topic, double-click it. Figure 3.16 shows the displayed help topic for "Sort records in a table, query, form, or subform."

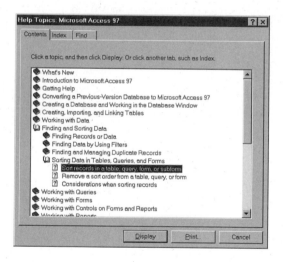

**FIG. 3.15**  The Contents tab of the Help Topics dialog, showing expanded headings and subheadings.

**Understanding the Help Window.** You can reposition and resize the help window by dragging its borders with your mouse. To reposition the help window, click and drag the Help title bar. If the help file on the topic that you selected has more information than can fit in the window, a vertical scroll bar appears at the right of the window. Drag the scroll box down to display additional text.

**FIG. 3.16** You display a help topic by double-clicking a topic in the Help Topics dialog's Contents list.

> **Tip**
>
> You can copy text from any help window. Simply drag the mouse over the text that you want to copy to select it, and then press Ctrl+C or choose Edit, Copy. You can then paste the copied help text into any Windows application from the Clipboard.

Most of Access's help windows include hotspots that provide additional information about a topic. Hotspots with dotted underlines, such as "Form view" and "Datasheet view" in Figure 3.16, display popup windows that usually contain a definition of the term or contain more detailed information about that topic. Figure 3.17 shows the window that pops up when you click the "Datasheet view" hotspot. To close the popup window, click anywhere on the screen outside the popup window.

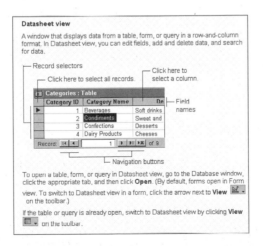

**FIG. 3.17** The popup window displayed by the "Datasheet view" hotspot.

> **Note**
>
> When you click hotspot text, which usually is highlighted in green, you receive an explanation of the hotspot topic. Hotspots in green, underlined, and bold text are links to additional windows in the help file related to the hotspot's topic.

Some hotspots lead to additional help topics. These hotspots are usually shown in bold text with a solid underline (like all hotspots, they're typically displayed in green text). You click the hotspot that represents the subject about which you want to learn. This action causes a jump to the subject's first help window, which often provides several additional choices for more detailed help on a specific topic.

> **Tip**
>
> You can return to the Help Topics dialog at any time by clicking the Help Topics button in the Help window.

Most help windows, in addition to providing information about a particular topic, also have tutorial, step-by-step instructions for the task about which you are inquiring. In Figure 3.16, notice that the help topic has a section titled "What do you want to do?" (visible near the bottom of the window). This section lists a variety of tasks that you might be trying to accomplish if you're looking for help on sorting records (the list extends beyond the bottom edge of the dialog in Figure 3.16). Each item in the list has a button to its left. After you click this button, Access displays a help screen with step-by-step instructions for accomplishing the indicated task.

For example, Figure 3.18 shows the step-by-step tutorial help window that Access displays if you click the button next to Sort Records on Demand in Datasheet View or Form View at the bottom of the dialog in Figure 3.16.

**FIG. 3.18**   A step-by-step help window opened by clicking the first button in the "What do you want to do?" list from the Sort records help topic shown in Figure 3.16.

> **Tip**
>
> To return to the previously displayed topic, choose the Back button in the Help window. To move backward through more than one topic, choose the same button repeatedly. When there are no previous topics to return to, Access disables the Back button.

Notice the icon near the bottom of the step-by-step help window shown in Figure 3.18. This icon, which depicts the Sort Ascending toolbar button described earlier in this chapter, is also a hotspot. Clicking this hot spot displays a popup window describing the action of the Sort Ascending toolbar button. Many help topics throughout the Access Help system contain graphic hotspots like this one.

> **Tip**
>
> Whenever you place the mouse pointer over a help hotspot, the pointer turns into a pointing-hand shape.

**The Index Tab.** You can also look up help topics in an index much like that which is at the end of this book. Click the Index tab in the Help Topics dialog to bring the Index sheet to the front of the dialog. Figure 3.19 shows the Index sheet as it appears after you type the topic **help** in the text box.

**FIG. 3.19** The Index sheet of the Help Topics dialog.

Using the Help Topics Index is simple—just type in the text box at the top of the dialog the name of the topic on which you want help. As you type, the Help system adjusts the topic list in the bottom of the dialog to show the topic that most closely matches the text that you've typed so far. In Figure 3.19, the user has typed **help** in the text box at the top of the dialog, and the help topics list shows the first matching entry: "Help

Authoring kit." To display a topic from the list, double-click it (or click once to select it and then choose the Display button). If you want, you can also use the scroll bar to view the list of available help topics.

**The Find Tab.** The Help Topics Index is only an alphabetical listing of the help topics available. The Find tab provides you with a way to search quickly through the actual text in the available help topics so that you can quickly find topics even if you don't know the name of the topic.

Click the Find tab in the Help Topics dialog to display the Find sheet. Figure 3.20 shows the Find sheet, after searching for the words **getting help**.

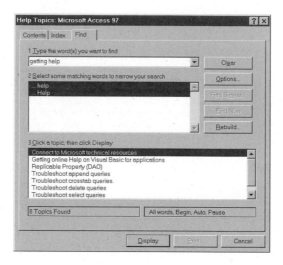

**FIG. 3.20**   The Find sheet of the Help Topics dialog.

---

**Note**

The first time that you use the Help Topics Find option, the Windows 95 WinHelp engine must build a word list to use for searching. The Help system needs to build this word list only once; thereafter, the system loads that list each time that you display the Find sheet.

---

The Help Topics Find sheet works essentially the same as the Index sheet. In the text box at the top of the dialog, you type words related to the topics that you want help on. Find uses its word list to locate all the topics that contain the words that you type. The list in the center of the dialog displays additional matching words, and a list at the bottom of the dialog displays matching help topics. Unfortunately, explaining all the options available in the Find sheet is beyond the scope of this book. For most searches, the default settings work just fine. To get more help about the specific controls in the Find sheet, click the What's This button.

**The Help Window Options.** The Help system provides you with several options that you can take advantage of to print, copy, or annotate the displayed help topic, or that enable you to change the help window's style or appearance. To display a menu of options, click the help window's Options button or right-click the dialog. Table 3.14 summarizes each menu choice and its effect.

| Table 3.14 | Help Window Options |
| --- | --- |
| **Option** | **Function** |
| Annotate | Enables you to add your own comments to the current help topic. |
| Copy | Copies selected text from the help window to the Windows Clipboard. |
| Print Topic | Prints the currently visible help topic on your printer. |
| Font | Enables you to select one of three predetermined font sizes for text displayed in the help window: Small, Normal, and Large. |
| Keep Help on Top | Enables you to choose whether the help window always displays on top of other windows, never displays on top of other windows, or displays with the default setting. (The Help system determines whether the window should be on top or not.) |
| Use System Colors | Tells the Help system to use the window border and background colors defined for the Windows 95 system as a whole. By default, the Help system uses its own color scheme for its windows. |

### Using the Office Assistant

An important new feature in Access (and all the Microsoft Office 97 applications) is the Office Assistant. The Office Assistant integrates several features found in previous versions of Access, Word, and Excel; in particular, the Office Assistant is the new embodiment of the Tip Wizard and the Answer Wizard. When the Office Assistant is on, it displays tips related to activities that you are currently performing, and provides a means for you to search for help on specific tasks.

The Office Assistant appears as an animated character in its own floating window, and displays its messages in a "speech" balloon. You may choose one of several available office assistant characters. Figure 3.21 shows Clippit, the default Office Assistant character (an animated paper clip) as it appears while asking if the user wants to save changes to a table's layout. In this case, the Office Assistant takes the place of Windows' standard message box.

**FIG. 3.21**   The Office Assistant's version of a conventional message box.

> **Note**
>
> All cautions, warnings, requests for confirmation, and other Access messages are displayed in a text balloon by the Office Assistant, whenever the Office Assistant is turned on. Figure 3.22 shows the same message displayed by the Office Assistant in Figure 3.21—and, generated under the exact same circumstances—as it appears when the Office Assistant is off.

**FIG. 3.22**  The standard message box for warnings, cautions, and requests for information.

By default, the Office Assistant is activated. You might find the Office Assistant distracting or prefer to use the Office Assistant only when you specifically want help. You can turn the Office Assistant off by either clicking the Close button on the Office Assistant's floating window, or by right-clicking the Office Assistant and then choosing Hide Office Assistant from the popup menu.

If you hide the Office Assistant, it remains hidden until you turn it on again, or until you use a wizard or some other feature of Access which automatically invokes the Office Assistant. Access "remembers" the status of the Office Assistant whenever you close Access; if the Office Assistant was hidden at the time you last exited Access, then the Office Assistant remains hidden the next time you start Access.

You can activate the Office Assistant by clicking the Office Assistant button on the toolbar, or by choosing Help, Microsoft Access Help. Access also starts the Office Assistant if you press F1 for context-sensitive help, but Access can't determine the precise context in which you're working.

To use the Office Assistant to search for help on any topic, click anywhere on the Office Assistant window; the Office Assistant displays the text balloon shown in Figure 3.23. Type a question about what you want to do in the text box, and then click Search. Figure 3.24 shows the Office Assistant's text balloon after searching for help topics that answer the question "How do I find text in a field?" The Office Assistant displays a list of topics that answer your question, and lead to step-by-step instructions on carrying out various tasks. To initiate a new search, type another question in the text box, and click Search again.

> **Tip**
>
> If you can't find help any other way, use the Search feature of the Office Assistant.

If the Office Assistant has a tip for you, a light bulb icon appears in the Office Assistant window. Click the Office Assistant window to view the tip. You may also view tips related to recent activities you have performed, by clicking the Office Assistant and then clicking the Tips button (refer to Figure 3.23); the Office Assistant displays a speech balloon similar to the one shown in Figure 3.25. Click Back and Next to move to the previous or next available tip. When you're done with the Office Assistant, click Close to close the text balloon; the Office Assistant remains on-screen.

**FIG. 3.23**   The Office Assistant enables you to search for help on any task.

**FIG. 3.24**   The Office Assistant, after searching for help related to finding text in a field.

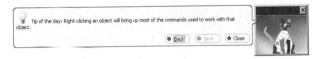

**FIG. 3.25**   The Office Assistant can also display tips related to activities you have performed recently.

As mentioned previously, you can select one of several Office Assistant characters. You can also modify the Office Assistant's behavior. To change the Office Assistant character, or to change the Office Assistant's behavior, click the Options button in the Office Assistant's text balloon, or right-click the Office Assistant window and then select Options from the popup menu. The Office Assistant dialog appears, as shown in Figure 3.26.

**Learning Fundamentals**

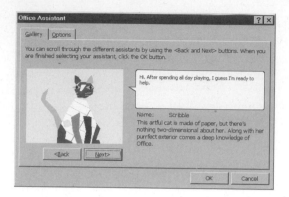

**FIG. 3.26**   The Office Assistant offers several animated characters.

To select a different Office Assistant character, click the Gallery tab to display the Gallery sheet. Click the Back and Next buttons to view the available Office Assistant characters; click OK to select the character you want. If the animation data files for the Office Assistant character you select weren't installed on your hard disk at the time Microsoft Office 97 was installed, you'll be prompted to insert your distribution disk so that Office Assistant can load the required animation data files onto your computer's hard disk.

To alter the Office Assistant's behavior, click the Options tab to display the Options sheet, shown in Figure 3.27. The options in the Assistant capabilities group affect how much help the Office Assistant provides when it is active. The Show Tips About options group contains settings that affect what kinds of tips the Office Assistant shows you, as does the Other Tip Options group. Table 3.15 lists the available Office Assistant option settings, and summarizes their effect.

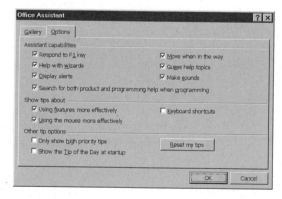

**FIG. 3.27**   The Office Assistant's behavior is controlled by the settings on the Options sheet.

**Table 3.15   Office Assistant Options**

| Option | Group | Function |
|---|---|---|
| Respond to F1 Key | Assistant Capabilities | When selected, causes the Office Assistant to respond to the F1 key. If This check box is cleared, then the Help Topics dialog appears when you press F1. |
| Help with Wizards | Assistant Capabilities | When selected, causes the Access wizards to provide help through the Office Assistant. |
| Display Alerts | Assistant Capabilities | When selected, causes all Access alert messages to be displayed by the Office Assistant; if cleared, Access alert messages appear in a standard dialog, whether or not the Office Assistant is active. |
| Search for Both Product and Programming Help When Programming | Assistant Capabilities | If selected, causes Access to search for help topics in both the VBA programming reference and in the Access application help when you are programming in VBA. |
| Move When in the Way | Assistant Capabilities | If selected, causes the Office Assistant window to move out of the way on-screen if it would otherwise obscure a dialog, table view, or other on-screen object. Also causes the Office Assistant window to shrink to a smaller size if the Office Assistant isn't used in five minutes. |
| Guess Help Topics | Assistant Capabilities | If selected, the Office Assistant offers help based on your current activities. |
| Make Sounds | Assistant Capabilities | If selected, the Office Assistant plays various sound effects as you use it. You must have a sound card and speakers installed in your computer to hear sounds; this option may be selected even if your computer isn't capable of playing sounds. |
| Using Features More Effectively | Show Tips About | When selected, this option causes the Office Assistant to display tips to help you learn about Access features you don't know, and to more effectively use features you do know. |
| Using the Mouse More Effectively | Show Tips About | When selected, the Office Assistant also shows tips related to using the mouse more efficiently in Access. |
| Keyboard Shortcuts | Show Tips About | When selected, the Office Assistant shows tips related to using keyboard shortcuts. |

(continues)

| Table 3.15 Continued | | |
| --- | --- | --- |
| **Option** | **Group** | **Function** |
| Only Show High Priority Tips | Other Tip Options | If selected, limits the tips displayed by the Office Assistant to only those with a high priority, such as time-saving alternatives. |
| Show the Tip of the Day At Startup | Other tip options | When selected, the Office Assistant starts each time you start an Office program, and displays a tip of the day. |
| Reset my Tips | Other tip options | Clicking this command button resets the Office Assistant's internal record of tips you have already seen; click this button if you want the Office Assistant to display tips you have seen previously. |

# Using the Database Utilities

Access 97 offers four utility functions, which you access from the Tools, Database Utilities menu. Three of these functions (Compact a Database, Repair a Database, and Make an MDE File) you may perform with or without a database open; the fourth utility function (Convert a database) can only be performed when there is no open database. If you have a large database, these operations take a considerable amount of time. If you select one of the utility operations described in the following sections when you do *not* already have a database open, the operation involves two dialogs. In the first dialog, you select the database in which Access is to perform the operation; in the second dialog, you enter the name of the file that the operation is to create. Default file names for new files are Db#.mdb, where # is a sequential number, beginning with 1, assigned by Access. For the three utility operations you can perform with an open database, only the Make MDE File option displays a dialog. When compacting or repairing an open database, Access assumes that you want to operate on the open database, and that you want the resulting compacted or repaired database to replace the currently open database.

## Compacting Databases

After you make numerous additions and changes to objects within a database file, especially additions and deletions of data in tables, the database file can become disorganized. When you delete a record, you don't automatically regain the space in the file that the deleted data occupied. You must compact the database to optimize both its file size and the organization of data within the tables that the file contains. When you pack an Access file, you regain space only in 32K increments.

To compact a database, perform the following steps:

1. Open the database you want to compact.

2. Choose Tools, Database Utilities, Compact Database. Access immediately begins compacting the open database. When Access finishes compacting the database, it returns you to the Database Window. Your compacted database is stored with the same name it had before you compacted it.

If you want, you may also compact a database and save the compacted database in a different database file by following these steps:

**1.** Close any open database.

**2.** Choose Tools, Database Utilities, Compact Database. The Database to Compact From dialog appears, as shown in Figure 3.28.

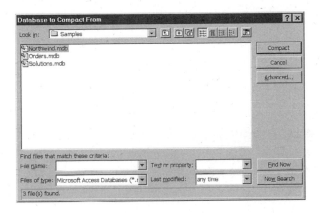

**FIG. 3.28**    The Database to Compact From dialog.

**3.** Double-click the name of the database file that you want to compact, or click the name and then click Compact. The Compact Database Into dialog appears, as shown in Figure 3.29.

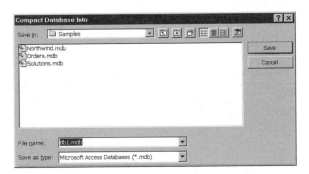

**FIG. 3.29**    The Compact Database Into dialog.

**4.** In the File Name text box, enter the name of the new file that is to result from the compaction process. If you choose to replace the existing file with the compacted version, you see a message box requesting that you confirm your choice. Click Save.

---

**Caution**

If the compaction process fails, your database might be damaged. Databases damaged in the compaction process are unlikely to be repairable (see the "Repairing Databases" section that follows). Thus, you should not compact the database into a new database with the same name. Do so only after backing up your database with a different name, in a different folder, or on a floppy disk.

---

Access then creates a compacted version of the file. The progress of the compaction is shown in a blue bar in the status bar. If you decide to use the same file name, the new file replaces the preceding file after compaction.

Periodically compacting files usually is the duty of the database administrator in a multiuser environment, typically in relation to backup operations. You should back up your existing file on disk or tape before creating a compacted version. When you're developing an Access 97 database, you should compact the database frequently. Uncompacted Access 97 databases grow in size much more rapidly during modification than with prior versions of Access.

### Converting Databases to Access 97 Format

To convert Access .mdb database files, .MDA library files created with Access 1.x or Access 2.0, and .mde library files created with Access 95 to the new database format of Access 97, first close any open database, then choose Tools, Database Utilities, Convert Database. The process of converting database files from earlier versions of Access database formats to that of Access 97 is almost identical to the second file-compaction process described in the preceding section. The only difference that you'll notice is that the names of the dialogs are Database to Convert From and Database to Convert Into. (Chapter 33, "Migrating Access 2.0 and Access 95 Applications to Access 97," covers this conversion process in detail.)

---

**Caution**

Although you can convert databases created with earlier versions of Access into Access 97 format, Access 97 does not enable you to convert the databases back from Access 97 format to a prior Access database format. If you attempt to open an Access 97 database or library file with the Convert Database menu choice, you receive the following message: `The database you tried to convert was either created in or was already converted to the current version of Microsoft Access`. Thus, if you want to support users of Access database applications who do not have Access 97, you must maintain two separate sets of database files. Therefore, you must have the retail versions of any earlier Access versions and Access 97 available to maintain your application.

---

### Repairing Databases

A database can become corrupted as the result of the following problems:

- Hardware problems in writing to your database file, either locally or on a network server.

- Accidental restarting of the computer while Access databases are open.

- A power failure that occurs after you have made modifications to an Access object, but have not saved the object.

Access includes a database repair facility that you can use to recover a usable database file from the majority of files corrupted by one of the preceding causes. The process is the same as that for creating compacted and encrypted versions of the file.

Occasionally, a file might become corrupted without Access detecting the problem. This lack of detection occurs most frequently with corrupted indexes. If Access or your application behaves strangely when you open an existing database and display its contents, try repairing the database. Choose Tools, Database Utilities, Repair Database, and then follow the same steps as described for compacting the database.

### Creating MDE Files

An .mde file is a special version of an Access .mdb file. In an .mde file, all VBA code is stored only in compiled format, and the program source code for that database is unavailable. (The file extension .mde stands for Microkernel Development Environment.) Also, users are no longer able to modify forms, reports, queries, or tables stored in that database, although those object may be exported to other databases. Typically, .mde databases are used to create libraries of add-in wizards, custom database applications intended for commercial or in-house distribution, and to provide templates for forms, reports, queries, and other objects for use in other databases.

You can convert any .mdb database to an .mde file by choosing Tools, Database Utilities, Make MDE File. If you have a database open at the time you select this command, Access assumes you want to save the current open database as an .mde file, and immediately displays a Save MDE As dialog; this dialog functions essentially the same way as any Save As dialog. If you choose Tools, Database Utilities, Make MDE File when there is no database open, Access first displays a Database to Save as MDE dialog; use this dialog to select the .mdb database file you want to convert to an .mde file. Part VIII of this book, "Programming, Distributing, and Converting Access Applications," discusses .mde files in more detail.

# Chapter 4

# Working with Access Databases and Tables

The traditional definition of a database is *a collection of related data items that are stored in an organized manner.* Access is unique among desktop database development applications for the PC because of its all-encompassing database file structure. A single Access .mdb file can contain data objects—tables, indexes, and queries—as well as application objects—forms, reports, macros, and Access Visual Basic for Applications (VBA) code modules. Thus, you can create a complete Access database application stored in a single .mdb file. Most Access developers use two .mdb files: one to contain data objects and the other to hold application objects.

This chapter and Chapter 25, "Securing Multiuser Network Applications," explain why developers use two .mdb files. Regardless of the approach that you choose, Access's all-encompassing .mdb file structure makes creating and distributing database applications simpler.

## Defining the Elements of Access Databases

Access databases include the following elements in a single .mdb database file:

- *Tables* store data items in a row-column format similar to that used by spreadsheet applications. An Access database can include as many as 32,768 objects (the combination of tables, forms, reports, queries, and so on), and as many as 1,024 tables can be open at one time if you have sufficient resources available. You can import tables from other database applications (such as xBase and Paradox), client/server databases (such as Microsoft SQL Server), and spreadsheet applications (such as Microsoft Excel and Lotus 1-2-3). In addition, you can link to Access databases other types of database tables (dBASE, FoxPro, and Paradox tables, for example), formatted files (Excel worksheet and ASCII text), and other Access databases. Chapter 7 discusses linking, importing, and exporting tables.

⊞ Tables

■ *Queries* display selected data contained in as many as 16 tables. With queries, you can specify how to present data by choosing the tables that comprise the query and as many as 255 specific fields (columns) of the chosen tables. You determine the records (rows) to display by specifying the criteria that the data items in the query data must meet to be included in the display. Part II, "Querying for Specific Information," explains how to create queries.

■ *Forms* display data contained in tables or queries and enable you to add new data and update or delete existing data. You can incorporate pictures and graphs in your forms, and, if you have a sound card, include narration and music in your form. You learn how to create forms in Chapters 12 and 13, and you learn how to add graphics to forms in Chapter 20. Access 97 forms also can incorporate Access VBA code in class models to provide event-handling subprocedures for forms and the controls that appear on forms.

■ *Reports* print data from tables or queries in virtually any format that you want. Access enables you to add graphics to your reports so that you can print a complete, illustrated catalog of products from an Access database. Access's report capabilities are much more flexible than those of most other relational database management applications, including those designed for mini- and mainframe computers. Like forms, you can include Access VBA event-handling subprocedures in Access 97 reports. Chapters 14 and 15 cover creating reports.

■ *Macros* automate Access operations. In prior versions of Access, macros took the place of the programming code required by other database applications, such as xBase, to perform specific actions in response to user-initiated events, such as clicking a command button. Access 97 supports macros primarily for compatibility with database applications created with earlier versions of Access. Microsoft recommends that you use Access VBA program code for any automation or event-handling procedures you create in Access 97 databases; future versions of Access are likely to phase out macro support in favor of VBA programming.

■ *Modules* contain Access VBA code that you write to handle events such as clicking a command button in a form, to create customized functions for use in forms, reports, and queries, and to otherwise automate database operations. By judiciously adding Access VBA code to your database, you can create complete database applications with customized menus, toolbars, and other features. Access VBA code enables you to programmatically control many database options and operations you can't control with a macro. Chapter 28 describes how to write Access VBA code in general. Chapter 30 describes the specifics of writing event-handling VBA code stored behind forms and reports.

▶▶ See "Defining the Client/Server Environment," p. 915

A better definition of an Access database is *a collection of related data items and, optionally, the methods necessary to select, display, update, and report the data*. This definition emphasizes an important distinction between Access and other database management applications. Even client/server database systems, such as Microsoft SQL Server, that include all related tables within a single database do not include the equivalent of forms and reports within the database. You must use another application, called a *front-end*, to display, edit, and report data stored in client/server databases. You can use Access to create front-ends for client/server databases by linking tables from the client/server database to your Access database. Creating front-ends for client/server databases is one of the major applications for Access in medium- to large-sized firms.

> **Note**
>
> It is a good database application development practice to maintain tables that store your application's data in one Access database (.mdb) file and the remainder of your application's objects, such as forms and reports, in a separate .mdb file. This chapter uses the Northwind Traders sample database, which is a self-contained application with a single .mdb file. Chapter 7, "Linking, Importing, and Exporting Tables," describes how to use or create separate .mdb files to store data and application objects.

This chapter introduces you to Access databases and tables—the fundamental elements of an Access application. You will see many references in this book to the term *Access application*. An Access application is an Access database that has the following characteristics:

- It contains the queries, forms, reports, and macros necessary to display the data in a meaningful way and to update the data as necessary. This book calls these elements *application objects*. A self-contained (single-user) Access application includes tables in the application database. Multiuser Access applications usually consist of two .mdb files, one containing the tables shared by users (*database objects*) and the other consisting of the Access application that manipulates the data. (Most Access developers use separate application and data .mdb files even for single-user applications.) If you are creating a front-end application, you usually link tables from the client/server database. Some front-end applications, however, also use local tables stored in the application database file.

- It does not require the database's users to know how to design any of its elements. All elements of the database are fully predefined during the application's design stage. In most cases, you want to restrict other users from intentionally or unintentionally changing the application's design.

- It is automated by Access VBA code (and/or Access macros for applications created prior to Access 97) so that users make choices from command buttons or custom-designed menus rather than from the lists in the Database window that you used in Chapter 2, "Up and Running with Access 97."

As you progress through the chapters in this book, you create a model of an Access application called Personnel Actions. Later in this chapter, you create the Personnel Actions table. In the following chapters, you add new features to the Personnel Actions application until you have a complete, automated method of adding and editing Personnel

Actions data. Therefore, you should read this book sequentially, at least to Chapter 15, "Preparing Advanced Reports." Make sure to perform the example exercises for the Personnel Actions application each time that you encounter them, because succeeding examples build on your prior work.

# Understanding Relational Databases

All desktop database managers enable you to enter, edit, view, and print information contained in one or more tables divided into rows and columns. At this point, the definition of a database manager doesn't differ from that of a spreadsheet application—most spreadsheets can emulate database functions. Three principal characteristics distinguish relational database management systems (RDBMS) from spreadsheet applications:

- All RDBMS are designed to deal efficiently with very large amounts of data—much more than spreadsheets can handle conveniently.

- RDBMS easily link two or more tables so that they appear to the user as if they are one table. This process is difficult or impossible to accomplish with spreadsheets.

- RDBMS minimize information duplication by requiring repetition of only those data items, such as product or customer codes, by which multiple tables are linked.

Database managers that cannot link multiple tables are called *flat-file managers* and are used primarily to compile simple lists such as names, addresses, and telephone numbers.

Because relational databases eliminate most duplicate information, they minimize data storage and application memory requirements. Figure 4.1 shows a typical relational database that a manufacturing or distributing firm might use. This database structure is similar to that of the Northwind Traders sample database provided with Access.

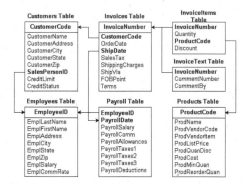

**FIG. 4.1**    A portion of a typical database for a manufacturing or distributing firm.

 ▶▶ See "The Process of Database Design," p. 790

If your job is to create an invoice-entry database, you don't need to enter a customer's name and address more than once. Just assign each customer a unique number or code and add to the Customers table a record containing this information. Similarly, you don't need to enter the names and prices of the standard products for each invoice. You assign unique codes to products, and then add records for them to the Products table. When you want to create a new invoice for an existing customer, you enter the customer code and type the codes and quantities for the products ordered. This process adds one record (identified by an automatically assigned sequential numeric code) to the Invoices table and one record for each different item purchased to the InvoiceItems table.

▶▶ See "Joining Tables to Create Multitable Queries," p. 322

Each table is related to the other by the customer, invoice, and product codes and numbers, shown by the connecting lines between the tables in Figure 4.1. The codes and numbers shown in boxes are unique; only one customer corresponds to a particular code, and one invoice or product corresponds to a given number. When you display or print an invoice, the Invoices table is linked (called a *join*) with both the Customers and InvoiceItems tables by their codes. In turn, the InvoiceItems table is joined with the Products table by the common value of a ProductCode in the InvoiceItems table and a ProductNumber in the Products table. Your query (view) of the desired sales orders displays the appropriate customer, invoice, items, and product information from the linked records. (The following section explains queries.) You can calculate quantity-price extensions, including discounts, by multiplying the appropriate values stored in the tables. You can add the extended items, sales taxes, and freight charges; you also can calculate the total invoice amount. These calculated values need not be included (and in a properly designed database never are included) in the database tables.

# Using Access Database Files and Tables

Access has its own database file structure, similar to that used by client/server RDBMS, and uses the .mdb extension. As discussed in this chapter's introduction, Access differs from traditional PC databases in that a single file contains all the related tables, indexes, forms, and report definitions. The .mdb file even includes the programming code that you write in Access VBA. You don't need to be concerned with the intricacies of the .mdb file structure because Access handles all the details of file management for you.

All the field data types familiar to xBase and Paradox users are available in Access, as well as some new and useful field data types, such as Currency for monetary transactions. dBASE users need to learn to use the term *table* for file and *database* to indicate a group of related tables or files, the equivalent of dBASE's CATALOG. Records commonly are called *rows*, and fields often are called *columns*. This book uses the terms *records* and *fields* when referring to database tables, rows, and columns for sets of records returned by queries. Users with Paradox, Excel, or 1-2-3 experience should find the terminology of Access quite familiar. Paradox and FoxPro users will appreciate dealing with only one .mdb file rather than the myriad of files that make up a multitable Paradox or FoxPro database.

### The Access System Database

In addition to including database files with the .mdb extension, Access includes a master database file, called a *workgroup file*, named System.mdw. (System.mdw is the equivalent of Access 2.0's SYSTEM.MDA.) This file contains information about the following:

◄◄ See "Setting Default Options," p. 81

- Names of users and groups of users who can open Access

- User passwords and a unique binary code, called a System ID (SID), that identifies the current user to Access

- Operating preferences that you establish by choosing Tools, Options

- Definitions of customized Access 97 toolbars that each user creates

Chapter 25, "Securing Networked Multiuser Applications," covers sharing database files and granting permission for others to use the files.

### Access Library Databases

Another category of Access database files is *add-ins*, also called *libraries*. Add-ins are Access library databases, usually with an .mde or .mda extension to distinguish them from user databases, that you can link to Access by choosing Tools, References in the Module window, or through the Add-In Manager (which you can access by choosing Tools, Add-Ins).

►► See "Creating a Transaction-Processing Form with the Form Wizard," p. 397
►► See "Access's Integrated Data Dictionary System," p. 819

When you link to an Access library, all the elements of the library database are available to you after you open Access. The Access 97 wizards—which you use to create forms, reports, and graphs—are stored in a series of Access library database files: Wzlib80.mde, Wztool80.mde, and Wzmain80.mde. Another wizard enables you to create data dictionaries for Access databases. A *data dictionary* is a detailed written description of each of a database's elements. Add-in library databases are an important and unique feature of Access. Microsoft and other third-party firms provide a wide range of Access libraries to add new features and capabilities to Access.

# Creating a New Database

If you have experience with relational database management systems, you might want to start building your own database as you progress through this book. In this case, you need to create a new database file at this point. If database management systems are new to you, however, you should instead explore the sample databases supplied with Access as you progress through the chapters of this book, and design your first database using the principles outlined in Chapter 23, "Exploring Relational Database Design and Implementation." Then return to this section and create your new database file.

To create a new database, follow these steps:

1. If you aren't already running Access, launch it and skip to step 3.

2. If Access is running and the Database window is visible, click its title bar to make the Database window the active window. If the Database window is not visible, click the Show Database Window button of the toolbar, choose <u>W</u>indow, <u>1</u> Database, or press the F11 key.

   This action is called giving the Database window the *focus*. When a window has the focus, the background of its title bar is usually blue; when a window does not have the focus, it is inactive and its title bar is usually gray. If you have changed from the default Windows color scheme by altering the Windows 95 desktop's properties, these colors are different.

3. Click the New Database button of the toolbar, or choose <u>F</u>ile, <u>N</u>ew Database. For the Database toolbar to be visible and the New Database and other database file options to be present when you open the <u>F</u>ile menu, the Access application window must be empty or the Database window must be active. The New dialog appears as shown in Figure 4.2.

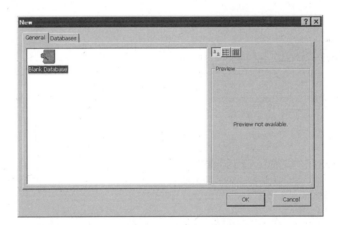

**FIG. 4.2**   The New dialog, in which you select the type of database to create.

The General page of the New dialog enables you to choose to create a blank database, and the Database page lets you use any one of 22 new database templates. Access 97 comes with database templates for asset tracking, book and video collections, contact management, and many other typical business and personal database uses. You choose a template that suits the purpose for which you want to create the database.

4. For this example, click the General tab, select Blank Database, and then click OK to display the File New Database dialog shown in Figure 4.3.

   Access supplies the default file name, db1.mdb, for new databases. (If you have previously saved a database file as db1.mdb, Access proposes db2.mdb as the default.)

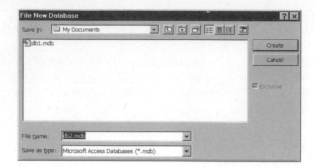

**FIG. 4.3**   The File New Database dialog, in which you enter the new database's name.

**5.** In the File Name text box, enter a file name for the new database. Use conventional Windows 95 file-naming rules (you can use spaces and punctuation in the name). Don't include an extension in the file name; Access automatically supplies the .mdb extension.

**6.** Click Create or press Enter to create the new database.

If a database was open when you created the new database, Access closes any windows associated with the database and the Database window. During the process of creating the database, the following message appears in the status bar:

```
Verifying system objects
```

Whenever you open a new or existing database, Access checks whether all the database's elements are intact. Access's main window and the Database window for the new database (named new.mdb for this example) appear as shown in Figure 4.4.

**FIG. 4.4**   The Database window for a newly created database.

Each new Access 97 database occupies approximately 60K of disk space when you create it—a reduction in size from the approximately 80K databases created by Access 95. Most of the 60K is space consumed by hidden system tables for adding the information necessary to specify the names and locations of other database elements that the database file contains. Because of the way that data is stored in Access tables, what appears to be an excessive amount of reserved space quickly is compensated for by Access's more efficient data storage methods.

# Understanding the Properties of Tables and Fields

Before you add a table to a database that you have created, or to one of the sample databases supplied with Access, you need to know the terms and conventions that Access uses to describe the structure of a table and the fields that contain the data items that comprise the information stored in the table. With Access, you specify properties of tables and fields.

▶▶ See "Working with Data Dictionaries," p. 818

Properties of Access tables apply to the table as a whole. Entering table properties is optional. You enter properties of tables in text boxes of the Table Properties window (see Figure 4.5), which you display by clicking the toolbar's Properties button in Table Design view. The five basic properties of Access tables follow:

- *Description* allows you to enter an optional explanation of the table's purpose. If you choose View, Details, the Database window displays this description. This description also is useful with a data dictionary. You use data dictionaries to document databases and database applications.

- *Validation Rule* allows you to enter an optional Validation Rule property value that lets you establish domain integrity rules with expressions that refer to more than one field of the table. The validation rule that you enter here applies to the table as a whole, rather than to a single field.

- *Validation Text* allows you to enter an optional Validation Text property value that specifies the text of the message box that appears if you violate a table's Validation Rule expression.

- *Filter* allows you to enter an optional property value that specifies a filter to apply to the table whenever it is opened. Chapter 6, "Sorting, Finding, and Filtering Data in Tables," discusses filters.

- *Order By* allows you to enter an optional property value that specifies a sorting order to apply to the table whenever it is opened. Chapter 6 also explains sorting orders.

▶▶ See "Using Access Indexes," p. 823

Access 97 provides an Indexes window to specify the primary key and all table indexes. The section "Adding Indexes to Tables" later in this chapter describes how to use the Indexes window.

You assign each field of an Access table a set of properties. The first three field properties are assigned within the Table Design grid, the upper pane of the Table Design window shown in Figure 4.6. To assign the Primary Key property, select the field and click the

Primary Key button on the toolbar (the Order Details table shown in Figure 4.6 has two primary keys). You set the remaining property values in the Table Design window's lower pane, Field Properties.

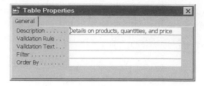

**FIG. 4.5** The Table Properties window for the Northwind Traders sample database's Order Details table.

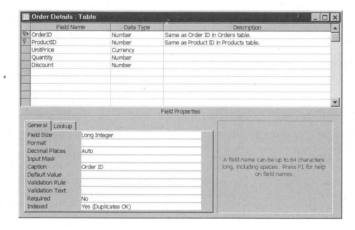

**FIG. 4.6** The Table Design window for the Northwind Traders sample database's Order Details table.

The following list summarizes the properties that you set in the Table Design grid:

- *Field Name.* You enter the name of the field in the Table Design grid's first column. Field names can be as long as 64 characters and can include embedded (but not leading) spaces and punctuation—except periods (.), exclamation marks (!), and square brackets ([ ]). Field names are mandatory, and you cannot assign the same field name to more than one field. It is a good database programming practice not to include spaces in field names. (Substitute an underscore (_) for spaces or use upper- and lowercase letters to improve the readability of field names.) Minimizing the length of field names conserves resources and saves typing when you refer to the field name in macros or Access VBA code.

- *Data Type.* You select data types from a drop-down list in the Table Design grid's second column. Data types include Text, Memo, Number, Date/Time, Currency, AutoNumber, Yes/No, OLE Object, Hyperlink, and Lookup Wizard. (AutoNumber replaces the Counter data type of Access 1.x and 2.0; Hyperlink data types are a new feature of Access 97.) Choosing a data type is the subject of the next section of this chapter.

- *Description.* You can enter an optional description of the field in the text box in the Table Design grid's third column. If you add a description, it appears in the status bar at the lower left of Access's window when you select the field for data entry or editing.

- *Primary Key.* To choose a field as the primary-key field, select the field by clicking the field-selection button to the left of the Field Name column, and then click the Primary Key button on the toolbar. The Order Details table has a composite primary key, consisting of the OrderID and ProductID fields. (See "Selecting a Primary Key" later in this chapter for instructions on how to create a composite primary key.)

Depending on the specific data type that you choose for a field, there are additional properties that you can set for a table field. You set these additional properties in the General tab of the Table Design window's Field Properties pane by selecting from drop-down or combo lists or by typing values in text boxes. (You use the Field Properties pane's Lookup tab to set the control type for lookup fields on forms—list box, combo list, and so on. Chapter 13, "Designing Custom Multitable Forms," describes how to use lookup fields.) The following list summarizes the General field properties:

- *Field Size.* You enter the field size for the Text data type in this text box. (See "Text Fields" later in this chapter to learn how to choose a text field size.) For Numeric data types, you choose the field size by selecting from a drop-down list. Field size does not apply to the Date/Time, Yes/No, Currency, Memo, Hyperlink, or OLE Object data type.

- *Format.* You can select a standard, predefined format in which to display the values in the field from the drop-down combo list applicable to the data type that you chose (except Text). Alternatively, you can enter a custom format in the text box (see "Custom Display Formats" later in this chapter). The Format property does not affect the data values; it affects only how these values are displayed. The Format property does not apply to OLE Object fields.

- *Decimal Places.* You can select Auto or a specific number of decimal places from the drop-down combo list, or you can enter a number in the text box. The Decimal Places property applies only to Number and Currency fields. Like the Format property, the Decimal Places property affects only the display, not the data values, of the field.

- *Input Mask.* Input masks are character strings, similar to the character strings used for the Format property, that determine how to display data during data entry and editing. If you click the Ellipsis button for a field of the Text, Currency, Number, or Date/Time field data type, Access starts the Input Mask Wizard to provide you with a predetermined selection of standard input masks, such as telephone numbers with optional area codes.

■ *Caption*. If you want a name (other than the field name) to appear in the field name header button in Table Datasheet View, you can enter in the Caption list box an alias for the field name. The restrictions on punctuation symbols do not apply to the Caption property. (You can use periods, exclamation points, and square brackets.)

■ *Default Value*. By entering a value in the Default Value text box, you specify a default value that Access automatically enters in the field when a new record is added to the table. The current date is a common default value for a Date/Time field. (See "Setting Default Values of Fields" later in this chapter for more information.) Default values do not apply to fields with AutoNumber or OLE Object field data types.

■ *Validation Rule*. Validation rules test the value entered in a field against criteria that you supply in the form of an Access expression. Chapter 9, "Understanding Operators and Expressions in Access," explains expressions. The Validation Rule property is not available for fields with AutoNumber, Memo, or OLE Object field data types. Adding validation rules to table fields is one of the subjects in Chapter 5, "Entering, Editing, and Validating Data in Tables."

■ *Validation Text*. You enter the text that is to appear in the status bar if the value entered does not meet the Validation Rule criteria.

■ *Required*. If you set the value of the Required property to Yes, you must enter a value in the field. Setting the Required property to Yes is the equivalent of typing **Is Not Null** as a field validation rule. (You do not need to set the value of the Required property to Yes for fields included in the primary key because Access does not permit `Null` values in primary-key fields.)

■ *Allow Zero Length*. If you set the value of the Allow Zero Length property to Yes, and the Required property is also Yes, the field must contain at least one character. The Allow Zero Length property applies to the Text, Memo, and Hyperlink field data types only. A zero-length string (`""`) and the `Null` value are not the same.

■ *Indexed*. From the drop-down list, you can select between an index that allows duplicate values or one that requires each value of the field to be unique. You remove an existing index (except from a field that is a single primary-key field) by choosing No. The Indexed property is not available for Memo, OLE Object, or Hyperlink fields. (See "Adding Indexes to Tables" later in this chapter for more information on indexes.)

■ *New Values*. This property applies only to AutoNumber fields. You select either Increment or Random from a drop-down list. If you set the New Values property to Increment, Access generates new values for the AutoNumber field by adding 1 to the highest existing AutoNumber field value. If you set the property to Random, Access generates new values for the AutoNumber field by producing a pseudo-random-long integer. Typically, Access uses randomly generated AutoNumber values for replicated databases to ensure that it assigns unique values to records in the database replicas.

To add your first table, Personnel Actions, to the Northwind Traders database, you must choose appropriate data types, sizes, and formats for your table's fields.

# Choosing Field Data Types, Sizes, and Formats

You must assign a field data type to each field of a table, unless you want to use the Text data type that Access assigns as the default. One of the principles of relational database design is that all the data in a single field consists of one type of data. Access provides a much wider variety of data types and formats from which to choose than most PC database managers. Besides setting the data type, you can set other field properties that determine the format, size, and other characteristics of the data that affect its appearance and the accuracy with which numerical values are stored. Table 4.1 lists the field data types that you can select for data contained in Access tables.

| Table 4.1    Field Data Types Available in Access | | |
|---|---|---|
| **Information** | **Data Type** | **Description of Data Type** |
| Characters | Text | Text fields are most common, so Access assigns Text as the default data type. A Text field can contain as many as 255 characters, and you can designate a maximum length less than or equal to 255. Access assigns a default length of 50 characters. A fixed-length Text data type is similar to xBase's Character field and Paradox's Alphanumeric field. |
| | Memo | Memo fields can contain as many as 64,000 characters. You use them to provide descriptive comments. Memo fields are similar to those of xBase, except that the Memo field's data is included in the table rather than in a separate file. Access displays the contents of Memo fields in Datasheet view. A Memo field cannot be a key field, and you cannot index a Memo field. |
| Numeric Values | Number | A variety of numeric data subtypes are available. You choose the appropriate data subtype by selecting one of the Field Size property settings listed in Table 4.2. You specify how to display the number by setting its Format property to one of the formats listed in Table 4.4. |
| | AutoNumber | An AutoNumber field is a numeric (Long Integer) value that Access automatically fills in for each new record that you add to a table. Access can increment the AutoNumber field by one for each new record, or fill in the field with a randomly generated number, depending on the New Values property setting that you choose. An AutoNumber field creates a value similar to xBase's and Paradox's record number. The maximum number of records in a table that can use the AutoNumber field is slightly more than two billion. |

(continues)

| Table 4.1 Continued | | |
| --- | --- | --- |
| **Information** | **Data Type** | **Description of Data Type** |
| | Yes/No | Logical (Boolean) fields in Access use numeric (Logical Fields) values: –1 for Yes (**True**) and 0 for No (**False**). You use the Format property to display Yes/No fields as Yes or No, True or False, On or Off, or –1 or 0. (You also can use any nonzero number to represent **True**.) Logical fields cannot be key fields, but they can be indexed. Currency is a special fixed format with four decimal places designed to prevent rounding errors that would affect accounting operations where the value must match to the penny (similar to the Paradox Currency data type). |
| Dates and Times | Date/Time | Dates and times are stored in a special fixed format. The date is represented by the whole number portion of the Date/Time value, and the time is represented by its decimal fraction. You control how Access displays dates by selecting one of the Date/Time Format properties listed in Table 4.4. |
| Large Objects | OLE Object (BLOBs, binary, large objects) | Includes bitmapped graphics, vector-type drawings, waveform audio files and other types of data that can be created by an ActiveX component application (formerly known as an OLE server application), some of which are listed in Table 4.3. You cannot assign an OLE Object as a key field, and you cannot include an OLE Object field in an index. |
| Web and other HTML document addresses | Hyperlink | Hyperlink fields store Web page addresses. A Web address stored in the Hyperlink field may refer to a Web page on the Internet, or a Web page stored locally on your computer or network. Clicking a Hyperlink field causes Access to start your Web browser and display the referenced Web page; choose Insert, Hyperlink to add a new hyperlink address. |

Regardless of the length that you set for Text fields in Access, the database file stores them in variable-length records. All trailing spaces are removed. This technique conserves the space wasted in xBase files, for example, which store text in fixed-length character fields. Fixed-length character fields in conventional PC RDBMS waste the bytes used to pad short text entries in long fields.

### Choosing Field Sizes for Numeric and Text Data

The Field Size property of a field determines which data type a Number field uses or how many characters fixed-length text fields can accept. Field Size properties are called *subtypes* to distinguish them from the *data types* listed in Table 4.2. For numbers, you select a Field Size property value from the Field Size drop-down list in the Table Design window's lower pane, Field Properties (refer to Figure 4.6).

**Subtypes for Numeric Data.** The Number data type of Table 4.2 isn't a fully specified data type. You must select one of the subtypes from those listed in Table 4.3 for the Field

Size property to define the numeric data type properly. To select a data subtype for a Number field, follow these steps:

1. Select the Data Type cell of the Number field for which you want to select the subtype.

2. Click the Field Size text box in the Field Properties window. You also can press F6 to switch windows, and then use the arrow keys to position the caret within the Field Size text box.

3. Click the drop-down arrow to open the list of choices shown in Figure 4.7. You can also press the F4 key to open the list.

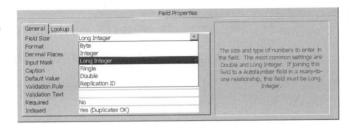

**FIG. 4.7** Selecting from the Field Size list a subtype for the Number data type.

4. Select the data subtype. Table 4.3 describes data subtypes. When you make a selection, the list closes.

After you select a Field Size property, you select a Format property from those listed in Table 4.4 to determine how to display the data. Table 4.4 includes the Currency data type because it also can be considered a subtype of the Numeric data type.

Regardless of how you format your data for display, the number of decimal digits, the range, and the storage requirement remains that specified by the Field Size property. Except for the Byte and Boolean data types, these data types are available in most dialects of BASIC, including Visual Basic for Applications and Visual Basic 4.0. Access VBA includes all the data types listed in Table 4.2 as reserved words. You cannot use a reserved data type word for any purpose in Access VBA functions and procedures other than to specify a data type.

**Table 4.2  Subtypes of the Number Data Type Determined by the Field Size Property**

| Field Size | Decimals | Range of Values | Bytes | xBase | Paradox |
|---|---|---|---|---|---|
| Double | 15 places | $-1.797 * 10^{308}$ to $+1.797 * 10^{308}$ | 8 | Numeric | Numeric |
| Single | 7 places | $-3.4 * 10^{38}$ to $+3.4 * 10^{38}$ | 4 | N/A | N/A |

(continues)

| Table 4.2 | Continued | | | | |
|---|---|---|---|---|---|
| **Field Size** | **Decimals** | **Range of Values** | **Bytes** | **xBase** | **Paradox** |
| Long Integer | None | −2,147,483,648 to +2,147,483,647 | 4 | N/A | N/A |
| Integer | None | −32,768 to 32,767 | 2 | N/A | Short Number |
| Byte | None | 0 to 255 | 1 | N/A | N/A |
| Currency (a data type, not a subtype) | 4 places | −922337203685477.5808 to +922337203685477.5808 | 4 | N/A | N/A |

Table 4.2's xBase and Paradox columns indicate the Access data types that correspond to data types commonly used with these two types of Windows and DOS RDBMSs.

Both xBase RDBMSs and Paradox store numbers with 15 significant-digit precision. Neither xBase nor Paradox, however, offers the full range of values of numbers having Access's Double Field Size property. All references to Paradox in this book apply to DOS 4.5 and Paradox for Windows 5. Access is compatible only with Paradox 3.5 (and later) tables.

As a rule, you select the Field Size property that results in the smallest number of bytes that encompasses the range of values you expect and that expresses the value in sufficient precision for your needs. Mathematical operations with Integer and Long Integer proceed more quickly than those with Single and Double data types (called *floating-point numbers*) or the Currency and Date/Time data types (*fixed-point numbers*).

**Fixed-Width Text Fields.** You can create a fixed-width Text field by setting the value of the Field Size property. By default, Access creates a 50-character-wide Text field. Enter the number, from 1 to 255, in the Field Size cell corresponding to the fixed length that you want. If you import to the field data that is longer than the selected field size, Access truncates the data; thus, you lose the far right characters that exceed your specified limit. You therefore enter a field length value that accommodates the maximum number of characters that you expect to enter in the field. Fixed-width Text fields behave identically to the Character and Alphanumeric field data types of xBase and Paradox applications.

> **Note**
>
> The terms *fixed-width* and *fixed-length* have two different meanings in Access. Even if you specify a fixed-width for a field of the Text field data type, Access stores the data in the field in variable-length format.

**Subtypes for the OLE Object Data Type.** Fields that have data types other than characters and numbers must use the OLE (object linking and embedding) Object data type. Chapter 19, "Using 32-Bit OLE Components," describes object linking and embedding, and Chapter 20, "Adding Graphics to Forms and Reports," explains the OLE Object field data type. Because many subtypes of OLE data exist, this data type enables you to violate the rule of database design that requires all data in a field to be of a single data type. Table 4.3 lists typical OLE Object subtypes. To avoid breaking the rule, you should create separate OLE Object fields for different OLE data subtypes. For example, if your table stores both sound and images, use one OLE Object field for OLE sound objects, and a second OLE Object field for OLE images.

| **Table 4.3** | **Subtypes of the OLE Object Data Type and the OLE Servers that Create Them** | |
|---|---|---|
| **OLE Subtype** | **File Format** | **OLE Server(s) that Create the Subtype** |
| Bitmapped graphics | .bmp, .dib, .tif | Paint (supplied with Windows 95 and Windows NT 4.0), Adobe Photoshop |
| Vector-based drawings | .wmf | CorelDRAW!, PowerPoint |
| Diagrams | .vsd | Visio 3 and higher |
| Formatted text | .rtf | Wordpad (supplied with Windows 95 and Windows NT 4.0), Word for Windows, Lotus WordPro |
| Unformatted text | .txt | Object Packager (with Windows Notepad as the application); Memo fields are a better choice |
| Spreadsheet | .xls, .dif | Microsoft Excel 3.0 and later |
| Waveform audio | .wav | Windows 95/NT 4.0 Sound Recorder, Windows 95/NT 4.0 Media Player |
| MIDI music | .mid | Windows 95/NT 4.0 Media Player |
| Digital video | .avi | Windows 95/NT 4.0 Media Player |

In the case of OLE Object fields, the data subtype is determined by the OLE server used to create the data, rather than by an entry in a text box or a selection from a list box. Windows 95's and Windows NT's Object Packager OLE server enables you to embed files created by applications that aren't OLE servers. You can, for example, embed .txt and .mid files with Object Packager.

### Selecting a Display Format

You establish the Format property for the data types that you select so that Access displays them appropriately for your application. You select a format by selecting the field and then clicking the Format text box in the Field Properties window. Figure 4.8 shows the choices that Access offers for formatting the Long Integer data type. You format Number, Date/Time, and Yes/No data types by selecting a standard format or creating your own custom format. The following sections describe these two methods.

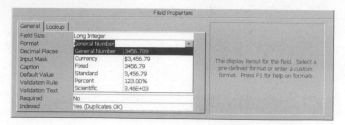

**FIG. 4.8** Assigning a standard format to a Long Integer field.

**Standard Formats for Number, Date/Time, and Yes/No Data Types.** Access provides 17 standard formats that apply to the numeric values in fields of the Number, Date/Time, and Yes/No data types. The standard formats shown in Table 4.4 probably will meet most of your needs.

**Table 4.4   Standard Display Formats for Access Number, Date/Time, and Yes/No Data Types**

| Data Type | Format | Appearance |
|---|---|---|
| Number | General Number | 1234.5 |
| | Currency | $1,234.50 |
| | Fixed | 12345 |
| | Standard | 1,234.50 |
| | Percent | 0.1234 = 12.34% |
| | Scientific | 1.23E+03 |
| Date/Time | General Date | 10/1/97 4:00:00 PM |
| | Long Date | Thursday, October 1, 1997 |
| | Medium Date | 1-Oct-97 |
| | Short Date | 10/1/97 |
| | Long Time | 4:00:00 PM |
| | Medium Time | 04:00 PM |
| | Short Time | 16:00 |
| Yes/No | Yes/No | Yes or No |
| | True/False | True or False |
| | On/Off | On or Off |
| | None | –1 or 0 |

The Short Date format is similar to the Date data type in xBase and Paradox, except that leading zeros for months and days having a value less than 10 aren't displayed. The four date formats are included in the 11 date formats offered by Paradox; you can create the other Paradox formats by using custom formats described in the next section. The Short Time format is equivalent to what you obtain from an xBase SUBSTR(TIME(),5) expression. A Double data type with Currency format appears identical to Paradox's Currency data type.

**The *Null* Value in Access Tables.** Fields in Access tables can have a special value, **Null**, which is a new term for most users of PC-based database management systems. The **Null** value indicates that the field contains no data at all. **Null** isn't the same as a numeric value of zero, nor is it equivalent to blank text that consists of one or more spaces. **Null** is similar but not equivalent to an empty string (a string of zero length, often called a *null string*). For now, the best synonym for **Null** is *no entry*. (**Null** is set in monospace bold type because it is a reserved word in Access VBA.)

The **Null** value is useful for determining whether a value has been entered in a field, especially a numeric field in which zero values are valid. Until the advent of Access, the capability to use **Null** values in database managers running on PCs was limited to fields in the tables of client/server database systems, such as Microsoft SQL Server. Later in this chapter, the sections "Custom Display Formats" and "Setting Default Values of Fields" use the **Null** value.

**Custom Display Formats.** To duplicate precisely the format of xBase's Date data type, or one of the date formats offered by Paradox that is not a standard format in Access, you must create a custom format. You also want or need to create custom display formats if you have some special format in which you want data to appear. You can set a custom display format for any field type, except OLE Object. You do so by creating an image of the format using combinations of a special set of characters called *placeholders*, listed in Table 4.5. Figure 4.9 shows an example of a custom format for date and time. If you enter **mmmm dd", "yyyy - hh:nn** as the format, the date 03/01/97 displays as March 1, 1997 - 00:00.

Except as noted, the example numeric value that Table 4.5 uses is 1234.5. Bold type distinguishes the placeholders that you type from the surrounding text. The resulting display is shown in monospace type.

**FIG. 4.9**    A custom date and time format entry in the Format text box.

### Table 4.5    Placeholders for Creating Custom Display Formats

| Placeholder | Function |
| --- | --- |
| Empty string | Displays the number with no formatting. Enter an empty string by deleting the value in the Format Text field of the Field Properties window. |
| 0 | Displays a digit if one exists in the position, or a zero if not. You can use the 0 placeholder to display leading zeros for whole numbers and trailing zeros in decimal fractions. **00000.000** displays 01234.500. |
| # | Displays a digit, if one exists in the position; otherwise, displays zeros. The # placeholder is equivalent to 0, except that leading and trailing zeros aren't displayed. **#####.###** displays 1234.5. |

*(continues)*

**Table 4.5   Continued**

| Placeholder | Function |
|---|---|
| $ | Displays a dollar sign in the position. **$###,###.00** displays $1,234.50. |
| . | Displays a decimal point at the indicated position in a string of 0 and # placeholders. **##.##** displays 1234.5. |
| % | Multiplies the value by 100 and adds a percent sign in the position shown with 0 and # placeholders. **#0.00%** displays 0.12345 as 12.35% (12.345 is rounded to 12.35). |
| , (comma) | Adds commas as thousands separators in strings of 0 and # placeholders. **###,###,###.00** displays 1,234.50. |
| E– e– | Displays values in scientific format with the sign of exponent for negative values only. **#.####E–00** displays 1.2345E03. 0.12345 is displayed as 1.2345E–01. |
| E+ e+ | Displays values in scientific format with the sign of exponent for positive and negative values. **#.####E+00** displays 1.2345E+03. |
| / | Separates the day, month, and year to format date values. **mm/dd/yy** displays 06/06/97. You can substitute hyphens to display 06-06-97. |
| m | Specifies how to display months for dates. **m** displays 1, **mm** displays 01, **mmm** displays Jan, and **mmmm** displays January. |
| d | Specifies how to display days for dates. **d** displays 1, **dd** displays 01, **ddd** displays Mon, and **dddd** displays Monday. |
| y | Specifies how to display years for dates. **yy** displays 97, and **yyyy** displays 1997. |
| : (colon) | Separates hours, minutes, and seconds in format time values. **hh:mm:ss** displays 02:02:02. |
| h | Specifies how to display hours for time. **h** displays 2, and **hh** displays 02. If you use an AM/PM placeholder, **h** or **hh** displays 4 PM for 16:00 hours. |
| n | Minutes placeholder for time. **n** displays 1, and **nn** displays 01. **hhnn "hours"** displays 1600 hours. |
| s | Seconds placeholder for time. **s** displays 1, and **ss** displays 01. |
| AM/PM | Displays time in 12-hour time with AM or PM appended. **h:nn AM/PM** displays 4:00 PM. Alternative formats include am/pm, A/P, and a/p. |
| @ | Indicates that a character is required in the position in a Text or Memo field. You can use @ to format telephone numbers in a Text field, as in **@@@-@@@-@@@@** or **(@@@) @@@-@@@@**. |
| & | Indicates that a character in a Text or Memo field is optional. |

| Placeholder | Function |
|---|---|
| > | Changes all text characters in the field to uppercase. |
| < | Changes all text characters in the field to lowercase. |
| * | Displays the character following the asterisk as a fill character for empty spaces in a field. **"ABCD"*x** in an eight-character field appears as ABCDxxxx. |

The Format drop-down combo list is one of the few examples in Access where you can select from a list of options or type your own entry. Format is a true drop-down combo list; lists that only enable you to select from the listed options are *drop-down lists*. You don't need to enter the quotation marks shown in Figure 4.9 surrounding the comma and space in the Format text box (**mmmm dd", "yyyy - hh:nn**) because Access does this for you. The comma is a nonstandard formatting symbol for dates (but is standard for number fields). When you create nonstandard formatting characters in the Field Properties window, Access automatically encloses them in double quotation marks.

When you change Format or any other property of a field, and then change to Datasheet view in Run mode to view the result of your work, you first must save the updated table design. The confirmation dialog shown in Figure 4.10 asks you to confirm any design changes.

**FIG. 4.10** The confirmation dialog for changes to a field's format.

If you apply the custom format string **mmmm dd", "yyyy - hh:nn** (refer to Figure 4.9) to the Birth Date field of the Employees table, the Birth Date field entries appear as shown in Figure 4.11. For example, Nancy Davolio's birth date appears as December 08, 1948 - 00:00. The original format of the Birth Date field was Medium Date, the format also used for the Hire Date field.

You need to expand the width of the Birth Date field to accommodate the additional characters in the Long Date format. You increase the field's width by dragging the field name header's right vertical bar to the right to display the entire field. Access left-justifies date fields.

Access displays the time of birth as 00:00 because the decimal fraction that determines time is 0 for all entries in the Birth Date field.

The following is an example that formats negative numbers enclosed in parentheses and replaces a **Null** entry with text:

```
$###,###,##0.00;$(###,###,##0.00);0.00;"No Entry Here"
```

The entries 1234567.89, –1234567.89, 0, and a **Null** default value appear as follows:

```
$1,234,567.89
$(1,234,567.89)
0.00
No Entry Here
```

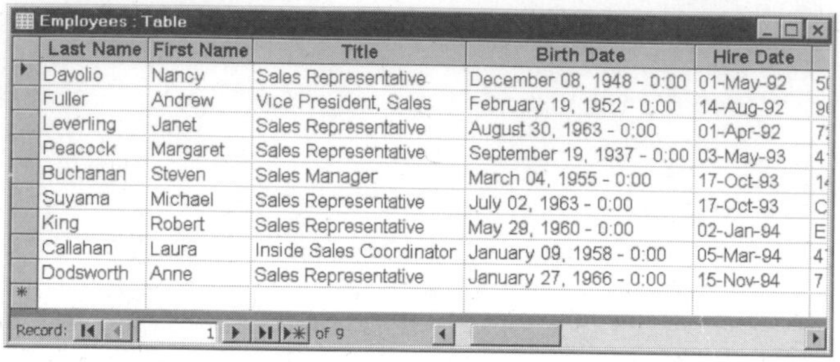


| Last Name | First Name | Title | Birth Date | Hire Date |
|---|---|---|---|---|
| Davolio | Nancy | Sales Representative | December 08, 1948 - 0:00 | 01-May-92 |
| Fuller | Andrew | Vice President, Sales | February 19, 1952 - 0:00 | 14-Aug-92 |
| Leverling | Janet | Sales Representative | August 30, 1963 - 0:00 | 01-Apr-92 |
| Peacock | Margaret | Sales Representative | September 19, 1937 - 0:00 | 03-May-93 |
| Buchanan | Steven | Sales Manager | March 04, 1955 - 0:00 | 17-Oct-93 |
| Suyama | Michael | Sales Representative | July 02, 1963 - 0:00 | 17-Oct-93 |
| King | Robert | Sales Representative | May 29, 1960 - 0:00 | 02-Jan-94 |
| Callahan | Laura | Inside Sales Coordinator | January 09, 1958 - 0:00 | 05-Mar-94 |
| Dodsworth | Anne | Sales Representative | January 27, 1966 - 0:00 | 15-Nov-94 |

**FIG. 4.11** Comparing date formats.

### Using Input Masks

Access 97 enables you to restrict entries in Text fields to numbers or to otherwise control the formatting of entered data. Access 97's Input Mask property is used to format telephone numbers, Social Security numbers, ZIP codes, and similar data. Table 4.6 lists the placeholders that you can use in character strings for input masks in fields of the Text field data type.

**Table 4.6 Placeholders for Creating Input Masks**

| Placeholder | Function |
|---|---|
| Empty string | No input mask. |
| `0` | Number (0–9) or sign (+/–) required. |
| `9` | Number (0–9) optional (a space if nothing is entered). |
| `#` | Number (0–9) or space optional (a space if nothing is entered). |
| `L` | Letter (A–Z) required. |
| `?` | Letter (A–Z) not required (a space if nothing is entered). |
| `A` | Letter (A–Z) or number (0–9) required. |
| `a` | Letter (A–Z) or number (0–9) optional. |
| `&` | Any character or a space required. |
| `C` | Any character or a space optional. |

| Placeholder | Function |
| --- | --- |
| . , : ;  / ( ) | Literal decimal, thousands, date, time, and special separators. |
| > | All characters to the right are converted to uppercase. |
| < | All characters to the right are converted to lowercase. |
| ! | Fills the mask from right to left. |
| \ | Precedes the other placeholders to include the literal character in a format string. |

For example, typing **\(000") "000\-0000** as the value of the Input Mask property causes results in the appearance of (___) ___-____ for a blank telephone number cell of a table. Typing **000\ 00\ 000** creates a mask for Social Security numbers, ___-__-____. When you type the telephone number or Social Security number, the digits that you type replace the underscores.

Access 97 includes an Input Mask Wizard that appears when you place the caret in the Input Mask text box for a field of the Text or Date/Time field data type and click the Ellipsis button at the extreme right of the text box. Figure 4.12 shows the opening dialog of the Input Mask Wizard, which provides 10 common input mask formats from which you can choose.

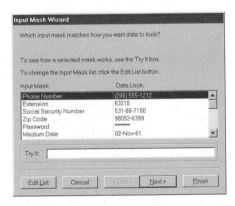

**FIG. 4.12**   The Input Mask Wizard for Text and Date/Time field data types.

# Using the Northwind Traders Sample Database

One of the fundamental problems with books about database management applications is the usual method of demonstrating how to create a "typical" database. You are asked to type fictitious names, addresses, and telephone numbers into a Customers table. Next, you must create additional tables that relate these fictitious customers to their purchases of various widgets in assorted sizes and quantities. This process is unrewarding for readers and authors, and few readers ever complete the exercises.

Therefore, this book takes a different tack. Access includes a comprehensive and interesting sample database, Northwind Traders. Instead of creating a new database at this point, you create a new table as an addition to the Northwind Traders database. Adding a new table minimizes the amount of typing required and requires just a few entries to make the table functional. The new Personnel Actions table demonstrates many of the elements of relational database design. Before you proceed to create the Personnel Actions table, try the quick example of adding a new table to the Northwind Traders sample database that is given in the following section.

## Using the Table Wizard to Create New Tables

Access includes a variety of wizards that provide services that simplify the creation of new database objects. Wizards lead you through a predetermined set of steps that determine the characteristics of the object that you want to create. Access 97 includes a Table Wizard that you can use to create new tables based on prefabricated designs for 77 business-oriented and 44 personal-type tables. Many of the business-oriented table designs are based on tables contained in Northwind.mdb.

The Table Wizard serves as an excellent introduction to the use of Access wizards in general. Follow these steps to create a new Access table that catalogs a video collection:

1. If the Employees table is open, close it by clicking the Close Window button to make the Database window active. Alternatively, click the Show Database Window button of the toolbar.

2. Click the Tables button of the Database window if it isn't selected, and then click the New button to display the New Table dialog shown in Figure 4.13.

**FIG. 4.13**    The New Table dialog.

3. Select Table Wizard in the list, and click OK to display the opening dialog of the Table Wizard. (If you select Datasheet view, Access creates a blank table with default fields; Design view creates a blank table and displays it in design mode ready for you to add fields. The Import Table Wizard and Link Table Wizard import databases and link external tables to a database, respectively.)

4. Click the Personal option button to display a list of tables for personal use in the Sample Tables list, and then use the vertical scroll bar to display the Video Collection entry in the list.

5. In the Sample Tables list, click the Video Collection entry to display the predetermined set of field names for the new table in the Sample Fields list.

6. Click the >> button to add all the fields from the Sample Fields list to the Fields in My New Table list. (The > button adds a single selected field from the Sample Fields list, the < button removes a single selected field from the My New Table list, and the << button deletes all the fields in the My New Table list.) The Table Wizard's dialog now appears as in Figure 4.14.

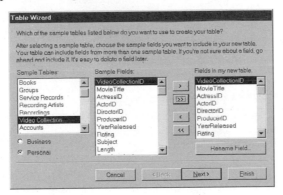

**FIG. 4.14**   Adding fields to the new Video Collection table.

7. Choose the Next button to display the second Table Wizard dialog in which you select the name for your new table, and select how to determine the table's primary-key field. Accept the default table name or enter a name of your choice, and then click the option button No, I'll Set the Primary Key. The Table Wizard's second dialog now appears (see Figure 4.15).

8. Choose the Next button to display the dialog shown in Figure 4.16. This dialog enables you to select the primary-key field and its data type. The VideoCollectionID field is the logical choice for a primary key, and the AutoNumber field data type, which automatically creates a sequential number for the VideoCollectionID, is appropriate in this case. (The Table Wizard's Consecutive Numbers Microsoft Access Assigns Automatically to New Records option creates an AutoNumber type field.) Thus, you can accept the default values determined by the Table Wizard.

Learning Fundamentals

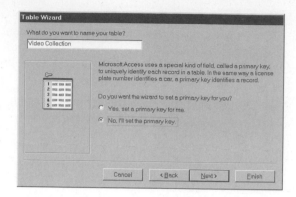

**FIG. 4.15**   Choosing a table name and how to determine the table's primary key.

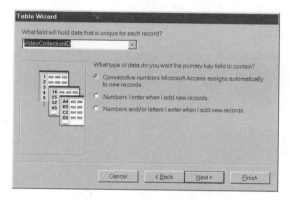

**FIG. 4.16**   The Table Wizard's primary-key dialog.

9.  Choose the Next button to continue with the next stage of the table design definition process. The Table Wizard's relationships dialog (see Figure 4.17) appears only if other tables already exist in the database in which you're creating the new table. Because almost every database consists of two or more related tables, the Table Wizard gives you an opportunity to define the relationships between tables. By default, the new table has no relationship to other tables in the database. In this exercise, you don't add any table relationships to the new Video Collection table.

10.  Choose the Next button to finish designing the table. Access displays the final step of the Table Wizard, shown in Figure 4.18.

11.  Click the Modify the Table Design option, and then choose the Finish button to display your new table in Design mode, as shown in Figure 4.19.

12.  When you have finished reviewing the design of your new table, click the Close Window button to close the table.

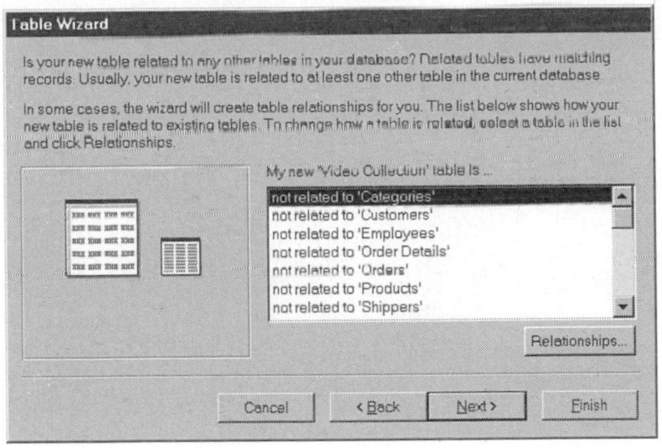

**FIG. 4.17**    Specifying relationships between fields in the new table and other tables.

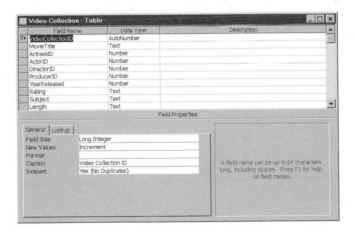

**FIG. 4.18**    The final Table Wizard dialog.

**FIG. 4.19**    The new Video Collection table in Design mode.

---

**Tip**

In any wizard, you can always redo a step by choosing the Back button until you return to the step that you want to redo.

---

If you want to delete the Video Collection table from Northwind.mdb, click the Show Database Window button of the toolbar, click the Table button if the Tables list is not open, and then click the Video Collection entry (or whatever you named your table) in the Table list to select (highlight) it. Press Delete, and click OK when the message box asks you to confirm the deletion. (You must close a table before you can delete it.)

---

**Note**

Creating tables based on the sample tables provided by the Table Wizard has limited usefulness in real-life business applications. In most cases, you import data from another database or spreadsheet application to create your Access tables. If you can't import the data, you probably need to define the fields of the tables to suit particular business needs. Thus, in the remainder of this chapter, you design a new database table by using the traditional method of manually adding fields to a blank table design and then specifying the properties of each field.

---

### Creating a Table Directly in Datasheet View

If you're a complete database novice, and you're under pressure to create database tables immediately, Access enables you to create tables directly in Datasheet view. When you create a table in Datasheet view, Access creates an empty table with a default structure of 20 fields and 30 empty records. You then enter data directly into the table. When you save the table, Access analyzes the data you have entered and chooses a field type for each field that best matches the data you have entered. To create a table in Datasheet view, follow these steps:

1. Close any open tables to make the Database window active. Alternatively, click the Show Database Window button of the toolbar.

2. Click the Tables button of the Database window if it isn't selected, and then click the New button to display the New Table dialog (refer to Figure 4.13).

3. Select Datasheet View in the list, and click OK. Access displays an empty table, shown in Figure 4.20. By default, the new table contains 20 fields and 30 records.

4. Type your data into the table, pressing Enter to move to the next field. To see how creating a table in Datasheet view works, type in the following mailing address (taken from the Employees table of Northwind.mdb) for Nancy Davolio in the first record of the new table:

> **Ms. Nancy Davolio**
> **Sales Representative**
> **507 20th Ave. E.**
> **Seattle WA 98122**
> **USA**

As you enter this address, divide the information into several fields. For example, type **Ms.**, then press Enter to move to the next field; type **Nancy**, then press Enter to move to the next field, and so on, until you have entered the complete address. The complete address should occupy nine fields when you are finished: title of respect, first name, last name, job title, street, city, state, ZIP code, and country.

5. When you have finished entering records into the table, click the Design View button on the toolbar to review the table's structure. Access displays the Save As dialog (shown in Figure 4.21) prompting you to enter a name for the new table. Alternatively, you can click the Close button to close the new table; in this case, Access first asks you to confirm saving changes to the table, and then asks if you want to create a primary key for the table, before prompting you for the table's name. For this exercise, answer No if asked to create a primary key; you learn more about primary keys later in this chapter.

**FIG. 4.20**   Creating a new table in Datasheet view.

**FIG. 4.21**   The Save As dialog.

6. Enter a suitable name for your table in the Table Name text box of the Save As dialog, and then click OK to save the table. Access saves the table, including only fields in which you have entered data, and including only those records you entered. If you entered only one record with nine fields, then Access saves a table with nine fields and one record. After saving the table, Access displays the new table in Design view, as shown in Figure 4.22.

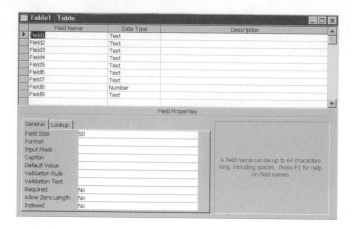

**FIG. 4.22**  The new table in Design view.

When you first save a table created in Datasheet view, Access analyzes the records you entered on a field-by-field basis. If all of the fields in a particular column of the table contain only numbers, then Access assigns a Number Data Type to that field column. If none of the numbers contain a decimal fraction, Access gives the Number field a Long Integer subtype, otherwise it assigns the field a Double subtype. If the fields in a single column of the table contain text, or a mixture of numbers and text (either in the same field or different fields of the same column), then Access assigns that field a Text Data Type. Text fields in the new table have the default Field Size setting of 50.

In Figure 4.22, notice that the fields are named in the format Field*N*, where *N* corresponds to the order of the field in the table from left to right. Although Access provided a default of 20 fields, only those fields in which you actually entered data are saved. Pay attention to the Data Type of Field8; this is the field in which the mailing address's ZIP code was entered. Because this field contained only digits, Access has assigned it the Number Data Type. Because the number entered in this field contained no decimal fraction, it has the Long Integer subtype.

If you want to delete the table you just created from Northwind.mdb, click the Show Database Window button of the toolbar, click the Tables tab if the Tables list isn't open, and then click the name of the table you just created (the name you entered in step 6 of the preceding instructions) to select it. Press Delete, and click OK when the message box asks you to confirm the deletion. (You must close a table before you can delete it.)

> **Note**
>
> Creating tables in Datasheet view has limited use. The table fields don't have meaningful names, so you'll almost always need to edit the table's structure to rename its fields. Further, as seen in the ZIP code example, Access may not always make the best determination for a field's Data Type—ZIP or postal code fields should almost always be of the Text type. Also, tables you create in Datasheet view cannot include OLE Object or Memo fields—if you want such fields in your table,

> you need to alter its design. Because of the amount of additional field name and Data Type property editing you'll almost always need to perform for tables created in Datasheet view, you won't necessarily save much time over creating tables by using the traditional method of manually adding fields and setting their properties in a blank table design.

### Adding a New Table to an Existing Database

The Northwind Traders database includes an Employees table that provides most of the information about the employees of the firm that is typical of personnel tables. This chapter explains how to add a table called Personnel Actions to the database. The Personnel Actions table is a record of hire date, salary, commission rate, bonuses, performance reviews, and other compensation-related events for employees. Because Personnel Actions is based on information in the Employees table, the first step of this process is to review the structure of the Employees table to see how you can use it with your new table. The structure of tables is displayed in Design mode. In the next chapter, "Entering, Editing, and Validating Data in Tables," you add validation rules to the Personnel Actions table and enter records in the table.

To open the Employees table in design mode, follow these steps:

1. Close any Access document windows that you have open, and then click the Tables tab button in the Database window to display the list of tables in the Northwind.mdb database.

   Tables

2. Click Employees in the Database window, and then click the Design button. You also can open the Employees table by double-clicking the Database window entry and then clicking the Tables toolbar's Design View button.

   Design

3. The Design grid for the Employees table appears. Maximize the document window to the size of your Access window by clicking the document's Maximize button.

4. Close the Properties window, if it appears, by clicking its Close Window button. Alternatively, you can choose View, Properties.

   The View, Properties command toggles the visibility of the Table Properties window. The Properties icon to the left of the Properties menu choice has a sunken appearance to indicate that the Properties window is always visible in Table Design view.

At this point, your display resembles that shown in Figure 4.23.

The Table Design window displays the field names and the field data types and provides a third column for an optional description of each field in the table. This display is called a *grid* rather than a *datasheet* because the display doesn't contain data from a table. A scroll bar is provided, regardless of whether more fields exist in the table than the window can display. The Field Properties pane enables you to set additional properties of individual fields and briefly describes the purpose of each column of the grid and of the Field Properties entries as you select them. You cannot resize this pane.

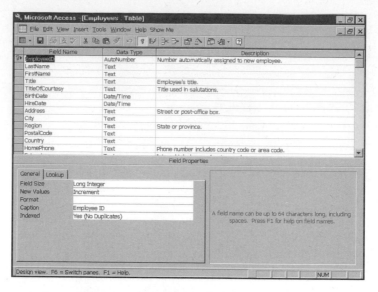

**FIG. 4.23**   The Table Design view of the Employees table.

One field is conspicuous by its absence: the Social Security number that most firms use in databases to identify their personnel. The EmployeeID field is an adequate substitute for the Social Security number for an example table because a unique sequential number (the AutoNumber field data type) is assigned to each employee. Click the Datasheet View button to display the data in the EmployeeID field, and then return to Design mode by clicking the Design View button.

### Designing the Personnel Actions Table

Instead of adding fields for entries (such as salary, commission rate, and bonuses) to the Employees table, you should place employee remuneration data in a table of its own, for the following reasons:

- Multiple personnel actions are taken for individual employees over time. If you add these actions to records in the Employees table, you have to create many additional fields to hold an arbitrary number of personnel actions. If, for example, quarterly performance reviews are entered, you have to add a new field for every quarter to hold the review information. In this situation, flat-file managers encounter difficulties.

- You can categorize personnel actions by type so that any action taken can use a common set of field names and field data types. This feature makes the design of the Personnel Actions table simple.

- You can identify employees uniquely by their EmployeeID numbers. Therefore, records for entries of personnel actions can be related to the Employees table by an EmployeeID field. This feature eliminates the necessity of adding employee names and other information to the records in the Personnel Action table. You link the Employees table to the Personnel table by the EmployeeID field, and the two tables are joined; they act as if they are a single table. Minimizing information duplication to only what is required to link the tables is your reward for choosing a relational, rather than a flat-file, database management system. (In an actual business's employee database, you would probably use the employee's Social Security number as the unique identifier for each employee, and as the link to the Personnel Actions table.)

■ Personnel actions usually are considered confidential information and are made accessible only to a limited number of people. Although Access enables you to grant permission for others to view specific fields, restricting permission to view an entire table is simpler.

The next step is to design the Personnel Actions table. Chapter 23, "Exploring Relational Database Design and Implementation," discusses the theory of database design and the tables that make up databases. Because the Personnel Actions table has an easily discernible relationship to the Employees table, the theoretical background isn't necessary for this example.

**Determining What Information the Table Should Include.** Designing a table requires that you identify the type of information that the table should contain. Information associated with typical personnel actions might consist of the following items:

■ *Important dates*. The date of hire and termination, if applicable, are important dates, but so are the dates when the employer adjusts salaries, changes commission rates, and grants bonuses. You should accompany each action with the date when it was scheduled to occur and the date when it actually occurred.

■ *Types of actions*. Less typing is required if personnel actions are identified by a code character rather than a full-text description of the action. This feature saves valuable disk space, too. First-letter abbreviations used as codes, such as *H* for *hired*, *T* for *terminated*, and *Q* for *quarterly review*, are easy to remember.

■ *Initiation and approval of actions*. As a rule, the employee's supervisor initiates a personnel action, and the supervisor's manager approves it. Therefore, the table should include the supervisor's and manager's EmployeeID number.

■ *Amounts involved*. Salaries are assumed to be based on monthly payment, bonuses are paid quarterly with quarterly performance reviews, and commissions are paid on a percentage of sales made by the employee.

■ *Performance rating*. Rating employee performance by a numerical value is a universal, but somewhat arbitrary, practice. Scales of 1 to 9 are common, with exceptional performance ranked as 9 and candidacy for termination as 1.

■ *Summaries and comments*. The table should provide for a summary of performance, explanation of exceptionally high or low ratings, and reasons for adjusting salaries or bonuses.

If you are involved in personnel management, you probably can think of additional information that the table might include, such as accruable sick leave and vacation hours per pay period. The Personnel Actions table is just an example; it isn't meant to add full-scale human resources development capabilities to the database. The limited amount of data described serves to demonstrate several uses of the new table in this and subsequent chapters.

**Assigning Information to Fields.** After you determine the types of information, called *data entities* or *entities*, to include in the table, you must assign each data entity to a field of the table. This process involves choosing a field name that must be unique within the table. Table 4.7 lists the candidate fields for the Personnel Actions table. Candidate fields are written descriptions of the fields proposed for the table. Data types have been assigned from those listed in Table 4.8 in the following section.

> **Note**
>
> Although the table name contains a space, the field names of the Personnel Actions table do not contain spaces (as shown in Table 4.8). As mentioned earlier in this book, including spaces in table names or field names is not a good database design practice. In this case, the table names include a space to demonstrate the special rule (enclosing the name within square brackets) that you must observe when referring to object names that include spaces. The Northwind Traders sample database includes spaces in many of its table names, so the use of spaces here is consistent with the other tables in the database.

**Table 4.7   Candidate Fields for the Personnel Actions Table**

| Field Name | Data Type | Description |
| --- | --- | --- |
| paID | Number | The employee to whom the action applies. paID numbers are assigned based on the EmployeeID field of the Employee table (to which the Personnel Actions table is linked). |
| paType | Text | Code for the type of action taken: H is for hired; C, commission rate adjustment; Q, quarterly review; Y, yearly review; S, salary adjustment; B, bonus adjustment; and T, terminated. |
| paInitiatedBy | Number | The EmployeeID number of the supervisor who initiates or is responsible for recommending the action. |
| paScheduledDate | Date/Time | The date when the action is scheduled to occur. |
| paApprovedBy | Number | The EmployeeID number of the manager who approves the action proposed by the supervisor. |
| paEffectiveDate | Date/Time | The date when the action occurred. The effective date remains blank if the action has not occurred. |
| paRating | Number | Performance on a scale of 1–9, with higher numbers indicating better performance. A blank indicates no rating; 0 is reserved for terminated employees. |

| Field Name | Data Type | Description |
|---|---|---|
| paAmount | Currency | The salary per month, the bonus per quarter, or commission rate as a percent of the amount of the order, expressed as a decimal fraction. |
| paComments | Memo | Abstracts of performance reviews and comments on actions proposed or taken. The comments can be of unlimited length. The supervisor and manager can contribute to the comments. |

**Note**

Use distinctive names for each field. This example precedes each field name with the abbreviation *pa* to identify the field with the Personnel Actions table. A common practice is to use similar names for fields that contain identical data but are located in different tables. Because of the way that Access uses field names in expressions for validating data entry and calculating field values (discussed later in this chapter and in Chapter 9, "Understanding Operators and Expressions in Access"), the best practice is to assign related, but distinctive, names to such fields.

### Creating the Personnel Actions Table

Now you can put to work what you have learned about field names, data types, and formats by adding the Personnel Actions table to the Northwind Traders database. Table 4.8 shows the field names, taken from Table 4.7, and the set of properties that you assign to the fields. The text in the Caption property column substitutes for the Field Name property that is otherwise displayed in the field header buttons.

**Table 4.8  Field Properties for the Personnel Actions Table**

| Field Name | Caption | Data Type | Field Size | Format |
|---|---|---|---|---|
| paID | ID | Number | Long Integer | General Number |
| paType | Type | Text | 1 | >@ (all uppercase) |
| paInitiatedBy | Initiated By | Number | Long Integer | General Number |
| paScheduledDate | Scheduled | Date/Time | N/A | Short Date |
| paApprovedBy | Approved By | Number | Long Integer | General Number |
| paEffectiveDate | Effective | Date/Time | N/A | Short Date |
| paRating | Rating | Number | Integer | General Number |
| paAmount | Amount | Currency | N/A | #,##0.00# |
| paComments | Comments | Memo | N/A | (None) |

You must set the paID field's Field Size property to the Long Integer data type, although you might not expect Northwind Traders to have more than the 32,767 employees that an integer allows. You must use the Long Integer data type because the AutoNumber field data type of the Employees table's EmployeeID field is a Long Integer. The section "Enforcing Referential Integrity" later in this chapter explains why paID's data type must match that of the Employees table's EmployeeID number field.

To add the new Personnel Actions table to the Northwind Traders database, complete the following steps:

1. Close the Employees table, if it is open, by clicking the Close Window button to make the Database window active.

2. Click the Tables tab of the Database window, if it isn't selected, and then click the New button. Select Design View in the New Table dialog and click OK. Access enters Design mode and opens a blank grid where you enter field names, data types, and optional comments. By default, Access selects the grid's first cell.

3. Enter **paID** as the first field name. Press Enter to accept the field name. The caret moves to the Data Type column; Access adds the default field type, Text.

4. Press F4 to open the Data Type list. You use the function keys rather than the mouse because your entries are from the keyboard.

5. Use the arrow keys to select the Number data type, and press Enter to accept your selection (see Figure 4.24).

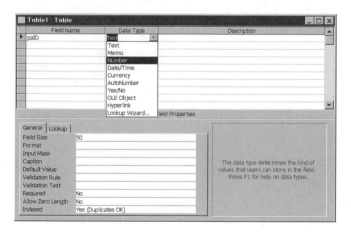

**FIG. 4.24** Entering the paID field's Data Type.

6. Press F6 to move to the Field Properties window's Field Size text box. Access has already entered Long Integer as the value of the default Field Size property. To learn more about the Field Size property, press F1 for help.

   Whenever you create a new Number type field, Access enters Long Integer in the Field Size property as the default. Because the paID field should be a Long Integer, you don't need to set the Field Size property for this field, and can skip to step 8; continue with step 7 when you enter the other fields from Table 4.8.

7. For Number data types, press F4 to open the Field Size list. Select from the list the appropriate field size value for the field, and press Enter.

8. Press the down arrow to select the Format text box. You can press F1 for context-sensitive help on the Format property.

9. Press F4 to open the Format list, select General Number from the list, and press Enter (see Figure 4.25).

10. Press the down-arrow key three times, bypassing the Decimal Places and Input Mask properties, and select the Caption text box. You skip the Decimal Places property; Long Integers cannot have decimal fractions, so Decimal Places can remain set to Auto. You skip the Input Mask property because this field doesn't need an input mask.

11. Enter **ID** as the caption and press Enter. ID is used as the Caption property to minimize the column width necessary to display the paID number.

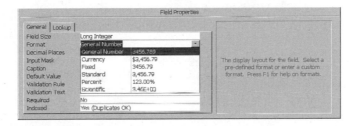

**FIG. 4.25**　Assigning the General Number format to the paID field.

12. Press F6 to return to the Table Design grid. The caret is located in the Description column. You complete the remaining properties for each field after completing the basic properties shown in Table 4.8.

13. You use descriptions to create prompts that appear in the status bar when you are adding or editing records in Run mode's Datasheet view. Although descriptions are optional, a good database design practice is to enter the field's purpose if its use isn't obvious from its Field Name or Caption property. You can skip the Caption property entries for now. After completing the basic steps described here, refer to Table 4.8 and enter the captions as a group.

14. Press Enter to move the caret to the first cell of the next row of the grid.

15. Repeat steps 3–13, entering the values shown in Table 4.8 for each of the eight remaining fields of the Personnel Action table. N/A (not applicable) means that the entry in Table 4.8 doesn't apply to the field's data type.

Your Table Design grid should now look similar to the one shown in Figure 4.26. You can double-check your properties entries by selecting each field name with the arrow keys and reading the values shown in the properties text boxes of the Field Properties window.

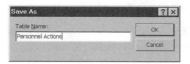

| Field Name | Data Type | Description |
|---|---|---|
| paID | Number | |
| paType | Text | |
| paInitiatedBy | Number | |
| paScheduledDate | Date/Time | |
| paApprovedBy | Number | |
| paEffectiveDate | Date/Time | |
| paRating | Number | |
| paAmount | Currency | |
| paComments | Memo | |

**FIG. 4.26**   The initial design of the Personnel Actions table.

 Click the Datasheet toolbar button to return to Datasheet view in Run mode to view the results of your work. You receive the Must save table first. Save now? message. Click OK, and a Save As dialog appears requesting that you give your table a name and suggesting the default table name, Table1. Type **Personnel Actions**, as shown in Figure 4.27, and press Enter or click OK.

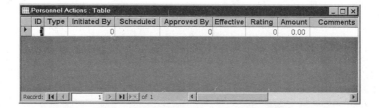

**FIG. 4.27**   The Save As dialog for naming the Personnel Actions table.

At this point, Access displays a dialog informing you that the new table does not have a primary key. You add primary keys to the Personnel Actions table later in this chapter, so click No in this dialog.

Your table appears in Datasheet view, with its first default record. To view all the fields of your new table, narrow the field name header buttons by dragging to the left the right vertical bar that separates each of the headers. When you finish adjusting your fields' display widths, the Personnel Actions table appears in Datasheet view as shown in Figure 4.28. Only the empty tentative append record (a new record that Access will add to your table if you enter values in the cells) is present. You have more property values to add to your Personnel Actions table, so don't enter data in the tentative append record at this point.

**FIG. 4.28**   The tentative append record of the Personnel Actions table.

# Setting Default Values of Fields

Access 1.x assigned your fields' default values, such as 0 for Number and Currency fields and No for Yes/No fields. Access 2.0 did not assign default values to Number and Yes/No fields automatically. Access 95 and Access 97 cover the middle ground by assigning Number and Currency fields a default value of 0; all other field types are empty by default. (Notice that the tentative append record in Figure 4.28 has zeros entered in all the Number and Currency fields.) In all versions of Access, Text, Memo, and Date fields are empty by default. You can save data-entry time by establishing your own default values for fields; in some cases, Access 97's default values for Number and Currency fields may be inappropriate, and you'll need to change them. Table 4.9 lists the default values for the Personnel Actions table's fields.

**Table 4.9   Default Field Values for the Personnel Actions Table**

| Field Name | Default Value | Comments |
| --- | --- | --- |
| paID | No entry | 0 is not a valid Employee ID number, so you should remove Access's default. |
| paType | Q | Quarterly performance reviews are the most common personnel action. |
| paInitiatedBy | No entry | 0 is not a valid Employee ID number. |
| paScheduledDate | Date() | The expression to enter today's (DOS) date. |
| paApprovedBy | No entry | 0 is not a valid Employee ID. |
| paEffectiveDate | Date()+28 | Today's date plus 28 days. (The date is obtained from your computer's system clock.) |
| paRating | No entry | In many cases, a rating does not apply. A 0 rating is reserved for terminated employees. |
| paAmount | No entry | If a salary, bonus, or commission has no change, no entry should appear. 0 would indicate no salary, for example. |
| paComments | No change | For now, Access's default is adequate. |

If you don't enter anything in the Default Value text box, you create a **Null** default value. You can use **Null** values for testing whether a value has been entered into a field. Such a test can ensure that the user has entered required data. (The following section discusses this subject.) The Date()+28 default is an *expression* that returns the date (according to your computer's clock) plus four weeks. You use expressions to enter values in fields, make calculations, and perform other useful duties, such as validating data entries. Expressions are discussed briefly in the next section and in greater detail in Chapter 9, "Understanding Operators and Expressions in Access." Expressions that establish default values always are preceded by an equal sign.

To assign the new default values from those of Table 4.9 to the fields of the Personnel Actions table, complete these steps:

1. Change to design mode by choosing View, Design View. Select the paID field.

2. Press F6 to switch to the Field Properties window, and then move the caret to the Default Value text box. Press Delete to clear the text box.

3. Press F6 to switch back to the Table Design grid. Move to the next field and press F6 again.

4. Create the default values for the eight remaining fields from the entries shown in Table 4.9, repeating steps 2–4. For example, after selecting the Default Value text box for the paType field, you would type **Q** to set the default value. Enter **=Date( )** for the paScheduledDate field and **=Date( )+28** for the paEffectiveDate Date field. Delete any default values that might appear in the other fields that call for no entry in Table 4.9.

5. After completing your default entries, choose View, Datasheet View to return to Run mode. A dialog appears requesting that you confirm your changes. Click OK. The Personnel Actions table now appears in Datasheet view with the new default entries that you have assigned, as shown in Figure 4.29.

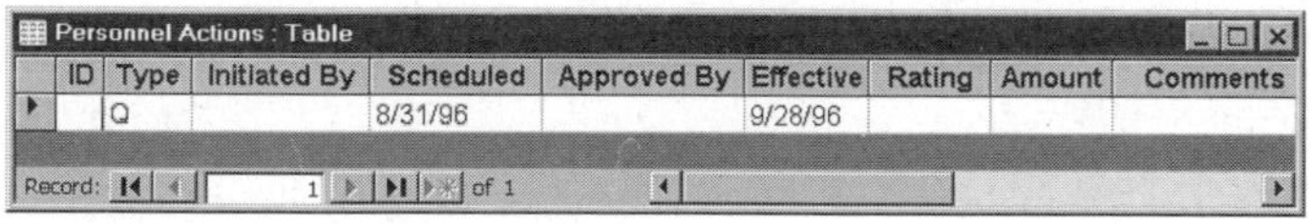

**FIG. 4.29**   The first record of the Personnel Actions table with the new default values.

# Working with Relations, Key Fields, and Indexes

Your final tasks before adding records to the Personnel Actions table are to determine the relationship between Personnel Actions and an existing table in the database, assign a primary-key field, and add indexes to your table.

### Establishing Relationships Between Tables

Relationships between existing tables and your new table determine the field used as the new table's primary key. The following four possibilities exist for relationships between tables:

- *One-to-one* relationships require that the key field's value in only one record in your new table matches a single corresponding value of the related field in the existing table. In this case, the key field in your new table must be unique; duplicate values aren't allowed in the key field. A key field that refers to another table's primary-key field is called a *foreign-key field*. A one-to-one relationship is the equivalent of a table that contains all the fields of the existing table and the new table. Tables with one-to-one relationships are uncommon.

- *Many-to-one* relationships allow your new table to have more than one value in the key field corresponding to a single value in the related field of the existing table. In this case, duplicate key field values are allowed because the field is a foreign-key field. Many-to-one relationships are the most common type; the capability to create many-to-one relationships is the principal reason for choosing a relational system, rather than a flat-file application, to manage your databases.

- *One-to-many* relationships require that your new table's primary-key field be unique, but the values in the foreign-key field of the new table can match many entries in the related field of the existing database. In this case, the related field of the existing database has a many-to-one relationship with the primary-key field of the new database.

- *Many-to-many* relationships are free-for-alls in which no unique relationship exists between the key fields in the existing table or the new table, and both of the tables' foreign-key fields contain duplicate values. Many-to-many relationships are created through *relation tables* that contain only foreign-key fields.

Keep in mind that the many-to-one and one-to-many relationships apply to how your new table relates to an existing table. When viewed from the existing table's standpoint, the relationships to your new table are one-to-many and many-to-one, respectively. Chapter 23, "Exploring Relational Database Design and Implementation," explains the four types of relations more comprehensively.

▶▶ See "Types of Relationships," p. 809

Many entries in the Personnel Actions table may apply to a single employee whose record appears in the Employees table. A record is created in Personnel Actions when the employee is hired, and a record is created for each quarterly and yearly performance review. Also, any changes made to bonuses or commissions other than as the result of a performance review are entered, and employees may be terminated. Over time, the number of records in the Personnel Actions table is likely to be greater by a factor of 10 or more than the number of records in the Employees table. Thus, the records in the new Personnel table have a many-to-one relationship with the records in the Employees table. Establishing the relationships between the new and existing tables when you create the new table enables Access to reestablish the relationship automatically when you use the tables in queries, forms, and reports.

Access requires that the two fields participating in the relationship have exactly the same data type. In the case of the Number field data type, the Field Size property of the two fields must be identical. You cannot, for example, create a relationship between an AutoNumber type field (which uses a Long Integer data type) and a field containing Byte, Integer, Single, Double, or Currency data. On the other hand, Access enables you to relate two tables by text fields of different lengths. Such a relationship, if created, can lead to strange behavior when you create queries, which is the subject of Part II, "Querying for Specific Information." As a rule, the relationships between text fields should use fields of the same length.

Access 97 uses a graphical Relationships window to display and create the relationships among tables in a database. To establish the relationships between two tables using Access's Relationships dialog, follow these steps:

1. Close the Personnel Actions table by clicking the Close Window button. If the Employees table is open, close it. You cannot create or modify relationships between open tables.

2. If the Database window isn't the active window (indicated by a colored title bar), click the Database window, click the Show Database Window button of the toolbar, or choose <u>W</u>indow, <u>1</u> Northwind : Database. As many as nine of the windows for database objects that you have opened appear as numbered choices in the <u>W</u>indows menu. (The Database window is always number 1.) Before you can establish relationships, the Database window must be active.

3. Click the Relationships button of the toolbar or choose <u>T</u>ools, <u>R</u>elationships. The Relationships window for the Northwind Traders database appears (see Figure 4.30). This window displays all the tables for which relationships are defined.

4. Click the Show Table button of the toolbar or choose <u>R</u>elationships, <u>S</u>how Table. The Show Table dialog shown in Figure 4.31 appears.

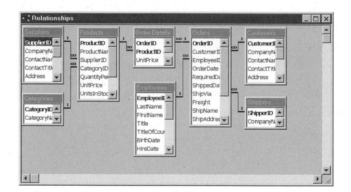

**FIG. 4.30**  The Relationships window.

**FIG. 4.31**  The Show Table dialog, used to add tables to the Relationships window.

5. Add the Personnel Actions table to the Relationships window by double-clicking the Personnel Actions entry in the Tables list or by clicking the entry to select it and then choosing the Add button. Choose the Close button to close the Show Table dialog.

6. The relationship of the Personnel Actions table with the Employees table is based on the Personnel Actions table's paID field and the Employees table's EmployeeID field. Click the Employees table's EmployeeID field and, holding the left mouse button down, drag the field to the Personnel Actions table's paID field. Release the left mouse button to drop the field symbol on the paID field. When you drag-and-drop a new relationship, the Relationships dialog appears (see Figure 4.32).

> **Note**
>
> The sequence of the drag-and-drop operation to create a new relationship is important. Drag the field from the *one* side of a one-to-many relationship and drop it on the *many* side. This sequence ensures that the primary (or base) table for the *one* side of the relationship appears in the Table/Query list and that the table for the *many* side appears in the Related Table/ Query list. If you reverse the relationships (creating a many-to-one relationship) and attempt to enforce referential integrity, you receive an error message in the final step of the process when you attempt to create the relationship.

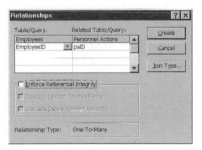

**FIG. 4.32**  Defining a relationship with the Relationships dialog.

7. Choose the Join Type button to display the Join Properties dialog shown in Figure 4.33. You want to create a one-to-many join between the Employees table's EmployeeID field (the *one* side) and the Personnel Actions table's paID field (the *many* side). Thus, you want to include *all* Personnel Actions records for a single employee. To do so, choose option 3 in the Join Properties dialog. Click OK to close the dialog and return to the Relationships dialog.

8. The Relationships dialog offers the Enforce Referential Integrity check box so that you can specify that Access perform validation testing and accept entries in the paID field that correspond to values for the Employees table's EmployeeID field. This process is called *enforcing* (or maintaining) referential integrity. The following section discusses referential integrity. The relationship between these two tables requires enforced referential integrity, so make sure that you select this check box. The Relationships dialog now appears as shown in Figure 4.34.

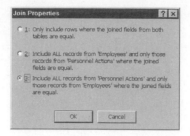

**FIG. 4.33** Choosing the type of join for the Personnel Actions and Employees tables.

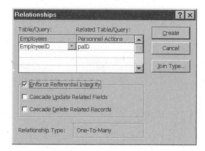

**FIG. 4.34** The Relationships dialog entries for a one-to-many relationship with referential integrity enforced.

> **Note**
>
> Access 97 automatically maintains referential integrity of tables by providing check boxes that you can select to cause cascading updates to, and cascade deletions of, related records when the primary table changes. The following section discusses cascading updates and deletions. Access enables the cascade check boxes only if you elect to enforce referential integrity.

9. Click the Create button to accept the new relationship and display it in the Relationships window as shown in Figure 4.35.

10. Click the Close Window button to close the Relationships window and return to the Database window. Click Yes when asked to confirm that you want to save the layout changes to the Relationships diagram.

Access uses the relationship that you have created when you create queries and design forms and reports that require data in the Personnel Actions table. Access does not require that the related table be indexed.

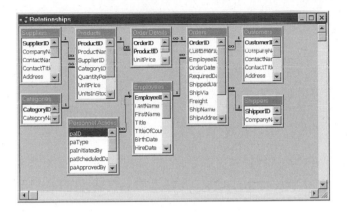

**FIG. 4.35** The Relationships window with the new Personnel Actions relationship added.

**Enforcing Referential Integrity.** The capability to enforce referential integrity automatically is an important feature of Access; few other PC relational database managers include this feature. Referential integrity prevents the creation of orphan records that have no connection to a primary table. An example of an orphan record is a record for a personnel action for paID 10 when you have records in the Employees file for employees numbered only 1 through 9. You could not know who employee 10 is until you enter the next employee hired. Then the orphan record, intended for some other employee, is linked, improperly, to the new employee's record.

**How Referential Integrity Is Enforced.** Referential integrity enforcement prevents you from deleting or modifying values of a primary table's record on which related records depend. If you terminate an employee and then try to delete the employee's record from the Employees table, Access prevents you from doing so. Access displays a message box informing you that you must delete all records related to the primary table's record before you can delete the primary record. You can't change a value in the Employees table's EmployeeID field because the field data type is AutoNumber. If the data types are such that you can change the value of an EmployeeID on which related records depend, however, Access also displays a warning message.

Similarly, if you attempt to change an employee ID value in the paID field of the Personnel Actions table to a value that does not exist in the Employees table's EmployeeID field, you also incur an error message. Thus, enforcing referential integrity eliminates the need to validate entries in the paID field using the Validation Rule property. With referential integrity enforced, Access automatically ensures that the value you enter corresponds to a valid EmployeeID value when you save the new or edited record.

**Cascading Updates and Deletions.** Prior to Access 2.0, you had to write macros or Access VBA code to implement the series of actions required to maintain referential integrity. For example, to delete a record in the Employees table, you had to run a test to determine whether related records existed in any other table that depended on the EmployeeID field, and then delete the dependent records. If you wanted to change the CustomerID of a record in the Customers table, the situation became more complex:

You couldn't change the related records to a new CustomerID that wasn't yet in the table, nor could you change the CustomerID in the primary table because it had dependent records. You could resolve this dichotomy by a variety of methods, none of which were simple.

With Access 97's cascading deletion and cascading update options for tables with enforced referential integrity, maintaining referential integrity is a simple process: Just check the Cascade Update Related Fields and Cascade Delete Related Records check boxes. Access 97 does all the work for you.

---

**Note**

Automatically enforcing referential integrity is usually, but not always, a good database design practice. An example of where you would *not* want to employ cascade deletions is between the EmployeeID fields of the Orders and Employee tables. If you terminate an employee and then attempt to delete the employee's record, you might accidentally choose to delete the dependent records in the Orders table. Deleting records in the Orders table could have serious consequences from a marketing and accounting standpoint. (In the real world, however, you probably would not delete a terminated employee's record.)

---

### Selecting a Primary Key

You do not need to designate a primary-key field for a table that is never used as a primary table. A *primary table* contains information representing a real-world object, such as a person or an invoice, and only one record uniquely associated with that object. The Personnel Actions table can qualify as a primary table because it identifies an object—in this case, the equivalent of a paper form representing the outcome of two actions: initiation and approval. Personnel Actions, however, probably would not be used as a primary table in a relationship with another table.

Using a key field is a simple method of preventing the duplication of records in a table. Access requires that you specify a primary key if you want to create a one-to-one relationship or to update two or more tables at the same time. Chapter 10, "Creating Multitable and Crosstab Queries," covers this subject.

The primary table participating in relations that you set with the Relationships dialog must have a primary key. Access considers a table without a primary-key field to be an oddity; therefore, when you make changes to the table and return to Design view, you might see a message stating that you haven't created a key field. (Access 97 asks you only once whether you want to add a primary-key field.) Related tables can have primary-key fields and often do. A primary-key field is useful to prevent the accidental addition of duplicate records.

You can create primary keys on more than one field. In the case of the Personnel Actions table, a primary key that prevents duplicate records must consist of more than one field, because more than one personnel action for an employee can be scheduled or approved on the same date. If you establish the rule that no more than one type of personnel action for an employee can be scheduled for the same date, you can create a primary key that consists of the paID, paType, and paScheduledDate fields. When you create a primary key, Access creates an index based on the primary key. The next section and Chapter 23, "Exploring Relational Database Design and Implementation," discuss indexes in detail.

To create a multiple-field primary key and index for the Personnel Actions table, follow these steps:

1.  Open the Personnel Actions table from the Database window in Design view.

2.  Click the selection button for the paID field.

3.  Hold down the Ctrl key and click the selection button for the paType field. In most instances, when you hold down Ctrl and click a selection button, you can make multiple selections.

4.  Hold down Ctrl and click the selection button for the paScheduledDate field.

    If you accidentally select one of the other fields, click the field's selection button again to deselect it.

5.  Click the Primary Key button on the toolbar. Symbols of keys appear in each of the selected fields, indicating their inclusion in the primary key (see Figure 4.36).

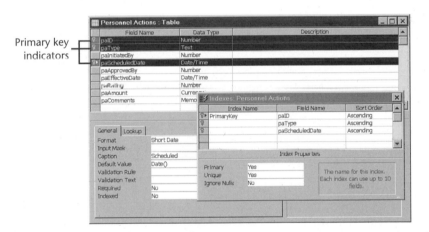

**FIG. 4.36**   Setting a multiple-field primary key for the Personnel Actions table.

6.  To determine the sequence of the fields in the primary key, click the toolbar's Index button to display the Indexes window as shown in Figure 4.36.

    In Access, you can create multiple-field primary keys and indexes with fields of different data types. The capability to concatenate different data types to form an index instruction or a string is the result of Access's Variant data type, which is discussed in Chapter 28, "Writing Visual Basic for Applications Code."

You now have a multiple-field primary key and a corresponding index to the Personnel Actions table that precludes the addition of records that duplicate records with the same primary key.

## Adding Indexes to Tables

Although Access creates an index on the primary key, you might want to create an index on some other field or fields in the table. Indexes speed searches for records that contain specific types of data. You might want to find all personnel actions that occurred in a given period and all quarterly reviews for all employees in paScheduledDate sequence, for example. If you have many records in the table, an index speeds up the searching process. A disadvantage of multiple indexes is that data entry operations are slowed by the time that it takes to update the additional indexes. You can create as many as 32 indexes for each Access table, and five of those can be of the multiple-field type. Each multiple-field index can include as many as 10 fields.

To create a single-field index for the Personnel Actions table based on the paEffectiveDate field, and a multiple-field index based on the paType and the paScheduledDate fields, follow these steps:

**1.** Select the paEffectiveDate field by clicking its selection button.

**2.** Select the Indexed text box in the Field Properties window.

**3.** Open the Indexed drop-down list by clicking the arrow button or pressing F4. The list appears as shown in Figure 4.37.

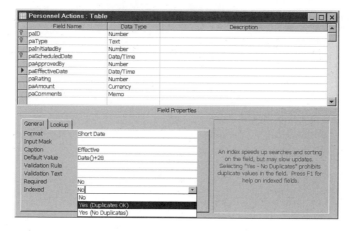

**FIG. 4.37**   Creating a single-field index on the paEffectiveDate field.

**4.** In this case, duplicate entries are acceptable, so click Yes (Duplicates OK) and close the list. You can create only a single-field index by using this method.

**5.** Click the Indexes button if the Indexes window is not open. The Primary Key and paEffectiveDate indexes already created appear in the list boxes. Enter **paType/ Date** as the name of the composite index, and then select **paType** in the Field Name drop-down list; move the caret to the next row of the Field Name column and select **paScheduledDate** to create a multiple-field index on these two fields, as shown in Figure 4.38.

6. Click the Datasheet View button to return to Run mode. Click OK when the message box asks whether you want to save your design changes. A message in the status bar indicates that Access is creating the new indexes as you leave Design mode.

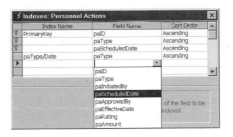

**FIG. 4.38**   Creating a multiple-field index.

You now have three indexes for the Primary Key table: the index automatically created for the primary key, the single-key index on paEffectiveDate, and the multiple-key index on paType and paScheduledDate.

# Altering Fields and Relationships

When you are designing your own database, you often discover that you must alter the original choices that you made for the sequence of fields in a table, data types, or relationships between tables. One of the reasons for adding substantial numbers of records to tables during the testing process is to discover any changes that are necessary before putting the database into daily use.

You can change formats, change validation rules and text, change lengths of Text fields, and make other minor modifications to the table by changing to Design mode, selecting the field to modify, and making the changes in the Properties boxes. Changing data types can cause a loss of data, however, so be sure to read the section "Changing Field Data Types and Sizes" later in this chapter before you attempt to make such changes. Changing relationships between tables is considered a drastic action if you have entered a substantial amount of data, so this subject also is covered in a later section, "Changing Relationships Between Tables."

> **Note**
>
> Avoid changing a field name if you have created data entry forms or reports that use the data in the field. Although Access performs many operations automatically, it does not change the field names that you have assigned to text boxes and other objects in forms or to the groups in reports. The time to finalize field names is while creating your tables; a bit of extra thought at this point saves hours of modification after you are well into creation of a complex application.

### Rearranging the Sequence of Fields in a Table

If you are manually entering historical data in Datasheet view, you might find that the sequence of entries isn't optimum. You might, for example, be entering data from a printed form with a top-to-bottom, left-to-right sequence that doesn't correspond to the left-to-right sequence of the corresponding fields in your table. Access makes rearranging the order of fields in tables a matter of dragging and dropping fields where you want them. You can choose whether to make the revised layout temporary or permanent when you close the table.

To rearrange the fields of the Personnel Actions table, follow these steps:

1. Click the Datasheet View button. This is the only table design change that you can implement in Access's Datasheet view.

2. Click the field name button of the field that you want to move. This action selects the field name button and all the field's data cells.

3. Hold down the left mouse button while over the field name button. The mouse pointer turns into the drag-and-drop symbol, and a heavy vertical bar marks the field's far-left position. Figure 4.39 shows the paScheduledDate field being moved to a position immediately to the left of the paEffectiveDate field.

| ID | Type | Initiated B | Scheduled | Approved By | Effective | Rating | Amount | Comments |
|----|------|-------------|-----------|-------------|-----------|--------|--------|----------|
| 1 | H | 1 | 5/1/95 | | 5/28/95 | | 2,000.00 | Hired |
| 2 | H | 1 | 8/14/95 | | 9/11/95 | | 3,500.00 | Hired |
| 3 | H | 1 | 4/1/95 | | 4/29/95 | | 2,250.00 | Hired |
| 4 | H | 2 | 5/2/96 | | 2 5/30/96 | | 2,250.00 | Hired |
| 5 | H | 2 | 10/16/96 | | 2 11/13/96 | | 2,500.00 | Hired |
| 5 | Q | 2 | 1/1/97 | | 2 2/11/97 | 8 | 2,750.00 | First quarterl |
| 5 | Q | 2 | 3/31/97 | | 2 5/12/97 | 7 | 3,000.00 | Steven could |
| 5 | Q | 2 | 6/30/97 | | 2 8/11/97 | 8 | 3,500.00 | Steven's sale: |
| 5 | Q | 2 | 9/30/97 | | 2 11/11/97 | 8 | 4,000.00 | Steven contir |
| 5 | Y | 7 | 1/1/98 | | 7 2/11/98 | 9 | 4,250.00 | Despite Steve |
| 6 | H | 5 | 10/16/96 | | 2 11/13/96 | 8 | 4,000.00 | Hired |
| 7 | H | 5 | 1/1/97 | | 2 1/29/97 | | 3,000.00 | Hired |
| 8 | H | 2 | 3/4/97 | | 2 4/1/97 | | 2,500.00 | Hired |
| 9 | H | 5 | 11/14/97 | | 2 12/12/97 | | 3,000.00 | Hired |
| * | Q | | 8/31/96 | | 9/28/96 | | | |

**FIG. 4.39** Dragging a field to a new position in Datasheet view.

4. Move the mouse pointer and vertical bar combination to the new position for the selected field and release the mouse button. The field assumes the new position shown in Figure 4.40.

5. When you close the Personnel Actions table, you see the familiar Save Changes message box. To make the modification permanent, click OK; otherwise, click No.

You can reposition fields in Design View by clicking the select button of the row of the field that you want to move and then dragging the row vertically to a new location. Changing the position of a table's field doesn't change any of the field's other properties.

### Changing Field Data Types and Sizes

You might have to change a field data type as the design of your database develops, or if you import tables from another database, a spreadsheet, or a text file. If you import tables, the data type automatically chosen by Access during the importation process probably won't be what you want, especially with Number fields. Chapter 7, "Linking, Importing, and Exporting Tables," discusses importing and exporting tables and data from other applications. Another example of altering field properties is changing the number of characters in fixed-length Text fields to accommodate entries that are longer than expected, or converting variable-length Text fields to fixed-length fields.

| | ID | Type | Initiated B | Approved By | Scheduled | Effective | Rating | Amount | Comments |
|---|---|---|---|---|---|---|---|---|---|
| ▶ | 1 | H | 1 | | 5/1/95 | 5/29/95 | | 2,000.00 | Hired |
| | 2 | H | 1 | | 8/14/95 | 9/11/95 | | 3,500.00 | Hired |
| | 3 | H | 1 | | 4/1/95 | 4/29/95 | | 2,250.00 | Hired |
| | 4 | H | 2 | 2 | 5/2/96 | 5/30/96 | | 2,250.00 | Hired |
| | 5 | H | 2 | 2 | 10/16/96 | 11/13/96 | | 2,500.00 | Hired |
| | 5 | Q | 2 | 2 | 1/1/97 | 2/11/97 | 8 | 2,750.00 | First quarterly |
| | 5 | Q | 2 | 2 | 3/31/97 | 5/12/97 | 7 | 3,000.00 | Steven could |
| | 5 | Q | 2 | 2 | 6/30/97 | 8/11/97 | 8 | 3,500.00 | Steven's sale: |
| | 5 | Q | 2 | 2 | 9/30/97 | 11/11/97 | 8 | 4,000.00 | Steven contir |
| | 5 | Y | 7 | 7 | 1/1/98 | 2/11/98 | 0 | 1,260.00 | Despite Steve |
| | 6 | H | 5 | 2 | 10/16/96 | 11/13/96 | 8 | 4,000.00 | Hired |
| | 7 | H | 5 | 2 | 1/1/97 | 1/29/97 | | 3,000.00 | Hired |
| | 8 | H | 2 | 2 | 3/4/97 | 4/1/97 | | 2,500.00 | Hired |
| | 9 | H | 5 | 2 | 11/14/97 | 12/12/97 | | 3,000.00 | Hired |
| * | | Q | | | 8/31/96 | 9/28/96 | | | |

**FIG. 4.40**  The paScheduledDate field dropped into a new position.

> **Caution**
>
> Before making changes to the field data types of a table that contains substantial amounts of data, back up the table by copying or exporting it to a backup Access database. If you accidentally lose parts of the data contained in the table, such as decimal fractions, while changing the field data type, you can import the backup table to your current database. Chapter 7, "Linking, Importing, and Exporting Tables," covers the simple and quick process of exporting Access tables. After creating a backup database file, you can copy a table to Windows Clipboard and then paste the table to the backup database. The section "Copying and Pasting Tables" later in this chapter discusses copying and pasting tables to and from the Clipboard.

**Numeric Fields.** Changing a data type to one that requires more bytes of storage is, in almost all circumstances, safe. You do not sacrifice your data's accuracy. Changing a numeric data type from Byte to Integer to Long Integer to Single and, finally, to Double does not affect your data's value because each change, except for Long Integer to Single, requires more bytes of storage for a data value. Changing from Long Integer to Single and Single to Currency involves the same number of bytes and decreases the accuracy of the data only in exceptional circumstances. The exceptions can occur when you are using very high numbers or extremely small decimal fractions, such as in some scientific and engineering calculations.

On the other hand, if you change to a data type with fewer data bytes required to store it, Access might truncate your data. If you change from a fixed-point format (Currency) or floating-point format (Single or Double) to Byte, Integer, or Long Integer, any decimal fractions in your data are truncated. *Truncation* means reducing the number of digits in a number to fit the new Field Size property that you choose. If you change a numeric data type from Single to Currency, for example, you might lose your Single data in the fifth, sixth, and seventh decimal places (if any exists) because Single provides as many as seven decimal places and Currency provides only four.

You cannot convert any type of field to an AutoNumber-type field. You can use the AutoNumber field only as a record counter; the only way that you can enter a new value in an AutoNumber field is by appending new records. You cannot edit an AutoNumber field. When you delete a record in Access, the AutoNumber values of the higher-numbered records are *not* reduced by 1. Sequential Access AutoNumber field values are assigned to records in the order in which the records were entered, not the order of the primary key. Access also provides a random assignment of AutoNumber field values, primarily for use with replicated databases. The randomly assigned AutoNumber values help ensure that, when replicated database copies are reconciled, there will be no duplication of values in AutoNumber fields.

**Text Fields.** You can convert Text fields to Memo fields without Access truncating your text. Converting a Memo field to a Text field, however, truncates characters beyond the 255-character limit of Text fields. Similarly, if you convert a variable-length Text field to a fixed-length field, and some records contain character strings that exceed the length that you chose, Access truncates these strings.

**Conversion Between Number, Date, and Text Field Data Types.** Access makes many conversions between Number, Date, and Text field data types for you. Conversion from Number or Date to Text field data types does not follow the Format property that you assigned to the original data type. Numbers are converted using the General Number format, and dates use the Short Date format. Access is quite intelligent in the methods it uses to convert suitable Text fields to Number data types. For example, it accepts dollar signs, commas, and decimals during the conversion, but ignores trailing spaces. Access converts dates and times in the following Text formats to internal Date/Time values that you then can format the way that you want:

```
1/4/97 10:00 AM

04-Jan-97

January 4

10:00

10:00:00
```

### Changing Relationships Between Tables

Adding new relationships between tables is a straightforward process, but changing relationships might require you to change data types so that the related fields have the same data type. To change a relationship between two tables, complete the following steps:

1. Close the tables that are involved in the relationship.

2. If the Database window is not active, click the Show Database Window button, or choose <u>W</u>indow, <u>1</u> Database.

3. Display the Relationships window by clicking the Relationships button of the toolbar or choosing <u>T</u>ools, <u>R</u>elationships.

4. Click the join line that connects to the field whose data type you want to change. When you select the join line, the line becomes darker (wider) as shown in Figure 4.41.

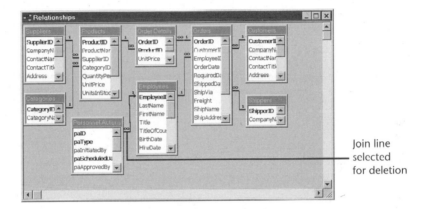

Join line
selected
for deletion

**FIG. 4.41**    Selecting a relationship to delete or modify.

5. Press Delete to clear the existing relationship. Click Yes when the message box asks you to confirm your deletion.

6. If you are changing the data type of a field that constitutes or is a member field of the primary table's primary key, delete all other relationships that exist between the primary table and every other table to which it is related.

7. Change the data types of the fields in the tables so that the data types match in the new relationships.

8. Re-create the relationships, using the procedure described in the earlier section, "Establishing Relationships Between Tables."

# Copying and Pasting Tables

You can copy a complete table or records of a table to the Windows Clipboard by using the same methods that apply to most other Windows applications. (Using the Clipboard to paste individual records or sets of records into a table is one of the subjects of the next chapter.) You use Clipboard operations extensively when you reach Part V of this book, "Integrating Access with Other Office 97 Applications." You can copy tables into other databases, such as a general-purpose backup database, by using the Clipboard; however, exporting a table to a temporary database file, described in Chapter 7, "Linking, Importing, and Exporting Tables," is a more expeditious method.

To copy a table to another Access database, a destination database must exist. To create a backup database and copy the contents of the Personnel Actions table to the database, follow these steps:

1. Make the Database window active by clicking it, if it is accessible, or by choosing Window, 1 Database.

2. Click the Tables Tab, if necessary, to display the list of tables.

3. Select the table that you want to copy to the new database.

4. Click the Copy button on the toolbar, press Ctrl+C, or choose Edit, Copy.

   If you plan to copy the table to your current database, skip to step 7.

5. If you have created a destination backup database, choose File, Open Database to open the database; then skip to step 7.

6. To create a backup database, choose File, New Database; choose a blank database and name it backup.mdb or another appropriate file name. Access creates your Backup.mdb database, which occupies approximately 60K without any tables (this is called 60K of *overhead*). Your new database is now active.

7. Click the Paste button on the toolbar, press Ctrl+V, or choose Edit, Paste. The Paste Table As dialog shown in Figure 4.42 appears.

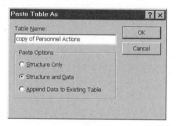

**FIG. 4.42**   The Paste Table As dialog.

8. You have three options for pasting the backup table to the destination database. You can create a new table or replace the data in a table of the name that you enter in the Table Name text box by selecting Structure and Data. This is the most common choice. You also can paste the structure only and then append data to the table later by selecting Structure Only, or append the records to an existing table of the name that you enter. For this example, accept the default: Structure and Data.

9. Your current or backup database now has a copy of the table that you selected, and the name that you entered appears in the backup's Database window. You can save multiple copies of the same table under different names if you are making a series of changes to the table that might affect the integrity of the data that it contains.

To delete a table from a database, select the table name in the Database window and then press Delete. A confirmation message box appears. Click Yes to delete the table forever. You cannot choose Edit, Undo after deleting a table.

# Chapter 5

# Entering, Editing, and Validating Data in Tables

Ease of data entry is a primary criterion for an effective database development environment. Most of your Access database applications probably use forms for data entry. In many instances, however, entering data in Table Datasheet view is more expeditious than using a form, especially during the database development cycle. For example, it is a good idea to test your proposed database structure before you commit to designing the forms and reports because changing table and field names or altering relationships between tables after you create a collection of forms and reports, involves a substantial amount of work.

In order to test the database design, you often need to enter test data. In this instance, using Table Datasheet view to enter data makes more sense than using a form. Even if you import data from another database type or from a worksheet, you will likely need to edit the data to make it compatible with your new application. The first part of this chapter concentrates on data entry and editing methods.

Another important factor in a database development environment is the capability to maintain the domain integrity of your data. *Domain integrity rules* limit the values you enter in fields to a range or set

Like Access 95, Access 97 enables you to enforce domain integrity rules (often called *business rules*) at the field and table levels. You enforce domain integrity by entering expressions as the value of the Validation Rule property of fields and tables. This chapter teaches you how to use simple expressions for domain integrity validation rules. After you master Access operators and expressions (the subject of Chapter 9, "Understanding Operators and Expressions in Access"), you can write complex validation rules that minimize the possibility of erroneous data in your tables.

# Using Keyboard Operations for Entering and Editing Data

Although Access is oriented to using a mouse to make selections, keyboard equivalents are provided for the most common actions. One reason for providing keyboard commands is that constant shifting of the hand from a keyboard to mouse and back can reduce data entry rates by more than half. Shifting between a keyboard and mouse also can lead to or aggravate repetitive stress injury (RSI), of which the most common type is carpal tunnel syndrome (CTS).

Keyboard operations are as important in a data entry environment as they are in word processing applications. Consequently, the information concerning key combinations for data entry appears here rather than being relegated to fine print in an appendix. The data entry procedures you learn in the sections that follow prove quite useful when you come to the "Entering Personnel Actions Table Data and Testing Validation Rules" section near the end of the chapter.

### Creating an Experimental Copy of Northwind.mdb

If you want to experiment with the various keyboard operations described in the following sections, you are wise to work with a copy of the Northwind.mdb database. When you use a copy, you don't need to worry about making changes that affect the sample database. Experimenting also gives you the opportunity to try the Access database-compacting operation described in Chapter 3, "Navigating Within Access."

> **Tip**
>
> If you're not short on fixed disk space, open a new database and copy the Northwind.mdb Customers and Orders tables to your new database as described in the "Copying and Pasting Tables" section of Chapter 4, "Working with Access Databases and Tables."

To compact Northwind.mdb to a new copy of Northwind.mdb, follow these steps:

1. Close all open document windows.

2. Choose File, Close, or click the Close Window button on the Database window to close the database. Access reverts to a blank window.

3. Choose Tools, Database Utilities, Compact Database to open the Database to Compact From dialog. In this case, the file is compacted to make a copy of the Northwind.mdb file.

4. Double-click the Northwind.mdb item in the Database to Compact From dialog's list box. The Compact Into dialog appears.

5. You can accept the default filename, db1.mdb, in the Filename text box, or you can enter a more creative name, such as **Illwind.mdb**, in the Filename text box, then click Save. Compacting a database file with a new name creates a new, compacted database that you can use for testing.

**6.** Choose File, Open Database, and double-click db1.mdb or the name of your file from step 5.

**7.** Open the Customers table by double-clicking its entry in the Database window.

---

**Note**

Most keyboard operations described in this section apply to tables and updatable queries in Datasheet view, text boxes on forms, and text boxes used for entering property values in Properties windows and in the Field Properties grid of Table Design view. In the examples in this section, the Arrow Key Behavior property is set to the Next Character value rather than the Next Field value (the default). See the "Setting Data Entry Options" section that follows for instructions on how to change the value of the Arrow Key Behavior property. When the Arrow Key Behavior property is set to Next Field, the arrow keys move the caret from field to field. Data entry operators accustomed to DOS or mainframe database applications usually prefer the Next Character approach.

---

### Using Data Entry and Editing Keys

Arrow keys and key combinations in Access are, for the most part, identical to those used in other Windows applications. Little resemblance exists between these combinations and the key combinations used by DOS database managers, however. The F2 key, used for editing cell contents in Excel, has a different function in Access—it toggles between editing and select mode. *Toggle* means to alternate between two states. In the editing state, the caret indicates the insertion point in the field; the key combinations shown in Table 5.1 are active. If the field is selected (indicated by a black background with white type), the editing keys behave as indicated in Table 5.2.

---

**Note**

In the tables that follow, the term *field* is used in place of the more specific description, *data cell* or *cell*, to maintain consistency with Access's documentation and the Help windows. A *field*, in conventional database terminology, indicates the collection of data consisting of the contents of a certain category of information in every record of the table.

The term *grid* in the tables that follow indicates a display in tabular form that doesn't represent fields and records. The list of fields and their descriptions in Table Design mode is an example of a grid.

---

### Table 5.1    Keys for Editing Fields, Grids, and Text Boxes

| Key | Function |
| --- | --- |
| F2 | Toggles between displaying the caret for editing and selecting the entire field. The field must be deselected (black type on a white background), and the caret must be visible for the keys in this table to operate as described. |
| Ctrl+End | Moves the caret to the end of the line. |

(continues)

| Table 5.1 | Continued |
|-----------|-----------|
| **Key** | **Function** |
| Ctrl+End | Moves the caret to the end of a multiple-line field. |
| ← | Moves the caret one character to the left until you reach the first character in the line. |
| Ctrl+← | Moves the caret one word to the left until you reach the first word in the line. |
| Home | Moves the caret to the beginning of the line. |
| Ctrl+Home | Moves the caret to the beginning of the field in multiple-line fields. |
| Backspace | Deletes the entire selection or the character to the left of the caret. |
| Delete | Deletes the entire selection or the character to the right of the caret. |
| Ctrl+Z | Undoes typing, a replace operation, or any other change to the record since the last time it was saved. An edited record is saved to the database when you move to a new record or close the editing window. |
| Alt+Backspace | Same as Ctrl+Z. |
| Esc | Undoes changes to the current field. Press Esc twice to undo changes to the current field and to the entire current record, if you edited other fields. |

| Table 5.2 | Keys for Selecting Text in Fields, Grids, and Text Boxes | |
|-----------|-----|----------|
| **Selection** | **Key** | **Function** |
| Text within a field | F2 | Toggles between displaying the caret for editing and selecting the entire field. The field must be selected (white type on a black background) for the keys in this table to operate as described. |
| | Shift+→ | Selects or deselects one character to the right. |
| | Ctrl+Shift+→ | Selects or deselects one word to the right. Includes trailing spaces. |
| | Shift+← | Selects or deselects one character to the left. |
| | Ctrl+Shift+← | Selects or deselects one word to the left. |
| Next field | Tab or Enter | Selects the next field. The "Setting Default Data Entry Options" section later in this chapter tells you how to change the effect of the Enter key. |
| Record | Shift+spacebar | Selects or deselects the entire current record. |

| Selection | Key | Function |
|---|---|---|
| | ↑ | Selects the preceding record when a record is selected. |
| | ↓ | Selects the next record when a record is selected. |
| Column | Ctrl+spacebar | Toggles selection of the current column. |
| | ← | Selects the column to the left (if a column is selected and there is a column to the left). |
| Fields and records | F8 | Turns on Extend mode. You see EXT in the status bar. In Extend mode, pressing F8 extends the selection to the word, field, record, and all records. |
| | Shift+F8 | Reverses the last F8. |
| | Esc | Cancels Extend mode. |

Operations that select the entire field or a portion of the field, as listed in Table 5.2, generally are used with the Windows Clipboard operations. Selecting an entire field and then pressing Delete or typing a character is a quick way of ridding the field of its original contents.

### Using Key Combinations for Windows Clipboard Operations

In Table Datasheet view, the Windows Clipboard is used primarily for transferring Access data between applications. However, you also can use the Clipboard for repetitive data entry. Access 97 enables you to select a rectangular block of data cells in a table and copy the block to the Clipboard. To select a block of cells, follow these steps:

1. Position the mouse pointer at the left edge of the top left cell of the block you want to select. The mouse pointer (shaped like an I-beam until this point) turns into a cross similar to the mouse pointer for Excel worksheets.

2. Hold the left mouse button down and drag the mouse pointer to the right edge of the bottom right cell of the desired block.

3. The selected block appears in reverse video (white on black). Release the left mouse button when the selection meets your requirement.

A selected block of data in the Customers table appears in Figure 5.1. You can copy data blocks but cannot cut them.

Table 5.3 lists the key combinations for copying or cutting data to and pasting data from the Clipboard. When you paste data from the Clipboard, all the data in the Clipboard is pasted to a single cell if the Clipboard data is of the correct data type and fits within the size of the field. You also can use the Cut, Copy, and Paste buttons on the toolbar as a substitute for the key combinations. Another alternative is to choose Edit, Cut, Copy, or Paste.

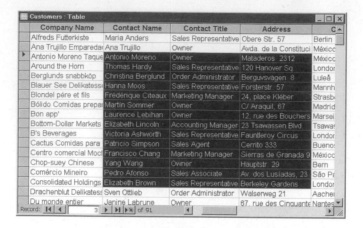

**FIG. 5.1** Selecting a rectangular data block in Table Datasheet view.

| Table 5.3 | Key Combinations for Windows Clipboard Operations |
|---|---|
| **Key** | **Function** |
| Ctrl+C | Copies the selection to the Clipboard. |
| Ctrl+Insert | Copies the selection to the Clipboard. |
| Ctrl+V | Pastes the contents of the Clipboard at the location of the caret. |
| Shift+Insert | Pastes the contents of the Clipboard at the location of the caret. |
| Ctrl+X | Copies the selection to the Clipboard, and then deletes it. This operation also is called a *cut*. You can cut only the content of a single cell you select with the caret. |
| Shift+Delete | Copies the selection to the Clipboard, and then deletes it. This operation also is called a *cut*. You can cut only the content of a single cell you select with the caret. |
| Ctrl+Z | Undoes your last Cut, Delete, or Paste operation. |
| Alt+Backspace | Undoes your last Cut, Delete, or Paste operation. |

**Note**

If you attempt to paste a rectangular block into a cell, you receive a `Data too long for field` error message. Access then creates a Paste Errors table that contains the contents of the rectangular block. This is a quick way of creating a new table from a block selection. If you create a table this way, rename it immediately, or Access overwrites the table with a new Paste Errors table the next time a paste error occurs.

### Using Shortcut Keys for Fields and Text Boxes

You use shortcut keys to minimize the number of keystrokes required to accomplish common data entry tasks. Most shortcut key combinations use the Ctrl key with other keys. Ctrl+C, Ctrl+V, and Ctrl+X for Clipboard operations are examples of global shortcut keys in Windows 95. Table 5.4 lists shortcut keys applicable to field and text box entries.

| Table 5.4 Shortcut Keys for Text Boxes and Fields in Tables | |
| --- | --- |
| **Key** | **Function** |
| Ctrl+; (semicolon) | Inserts the current date. |
| Ctrl+: (colon) | Inserts the current time. |
| Ctrl+' (apostrophe) or Ctrl+" (quote) | Inserts the value from the same field in the preceding record. |
| Ctrl+Enter | Inserts a newline character (carriage return plus line feed) in a text box. |
| Ctrl++ (plus) | Adds a new record to the table. |
| Ctrl+– (minus) | Deletes the current record from the table. |
| Shift+Enter | Saves all changes to the current record. |

### Tip

Emulating the data entry key behavior of DOS or mainframe RDBMS can make a major difference in the acceptance of your database applications by data entry operators who have years of experience with DOS or mainframe database applications.

### Setting Data Entry Options

You can modify the behavior of the arrow keys and the Tab and Enter keys by choosing Tools, Options and clicking the Keyboard tab to display the keyboard options settings. Table 5.5 lists the available options with the default values shown in bold type. (This table also appears in Chapter 3, "Navigating Within Access.") These keyboard options enable you to make the behavior of the data entry keys similar to that of DOS database managers, such as dBASE and Paradox.

◀◀ See "Keyboard Options," p. 85

| Table 5.5 Keyboard Options for the Access System | | |
|---|---|---|
| **Option** | **Group** | **Function** |
| Don't Move | Move After Enter | When this option is selected, the caret remains in the current field when you press Enter. |
| Next Field | Move After Enter | When this option is selected, the caret moves to the next field when you press Enter. Use this setting to duplicate xBase behavior. |
| Next Record | Move After Enter | When this option is selected, the caret moves down the column to the next record when you press Enter. |
| Next Field | Arrow Key Behavior | If this option is selected, pressing the right or left arrow keys moves the caret to the next field. |
| Next Character | Arrow Key Behavior | If this option is selected, pressing the right or left arrow keys moves the caret to the previous or next character in the same field. Use this setting if you want to duplicate the behavior of xBase or mainframe databases. |
| Select Entire Field | Behavior Entering Field | When this option is selected, the entire field's contents are selected when you use the arrow keys to move the caret into the field. |
| Go to Start of Field | Behavior Entering Field | Selecting this option causes the caret to move to the beginning of the field when you use the arrow keys to move the caret into the field. |
| Go to End of Field | Behavior Entering Field | Selecting this option causes the caret to move to the end of the field when you use the arrow keys to move the caret into the field. Use this setting to duplicate xBase and mainframe database behavior. |
| Cursor Stops at First/Last | None | If this option is selected, it keeps the caret from moving to Field another record when the left or right arrow keys are pressed,and the caret is in the first or last field of the record. |

# Adding Records to a Table

 When you create a new table in Datasheet view, it contains 30 empty records with an asterisk (*) in the record selection button of the last (31st) row. Record selection buttons are the gray buttons in the leftmost column of Table Datasheet view. A similar blank record also appears at the end of an existing table if the table is updatable. (An *updatable table* is one whose data you can add to or edit.) If you open a database for read-only access by marking the Exclusive check box of the Open dialog, this blank record does not appear. Tables attached from other databases also can be read-only; the updatability of attached tables is discussed in Chapter 7, "Linking, Importing, and Exporting Tables."

▶▶ See "Modifying Linked and Imported Tables," p. 251

This book refers to the blank record as the *tentative append record*. The term *tentative* is used because the record is appended to the table only after you enter data in one of the fields and then save the changes you make to the record. You can save changes to a record by moving the record pointer to a different record or by choosing <u>R</u>ecords, Save Recor<u>d</u>. The location of the record pointer is indicated by an arrow symbol in the record selection button. The record with the arrow symbol is called the *selected record*.

### Tip

To go to the tentative append record quickly, click the New Record button on the toolbar.

◀◀ See "Using Input Masks," p. 128

When you place the caret in a field of the tentative append record, the record selection button's asterisk symbol turns into the selected record symbol. When you add data to a field of the selected tentative append record, the selected record symbol changes to the edit symbol (a pencil), and a new tentative append record appears in the row after your addition. Figure 5.2 shows a new record in the process of being added to the Customers table. The CustomerID field has an input mask that requires you to enter five letters, which are capitalized automatically as you enter them. The input mask changes the caret from an I-beam to a reverse-video block.

| Customer ID | Company Name | Contact Name | Contact Title | Addres ▲ |
|---|---|---|---|---|
| VAFFE | Vaffeljernet | Palle Ibsen | Sales Manager | Smagsløget 45 |
| VICTE | Victuailles en stock | Mary Saveley | Sales Agent | 2, rue du Com |
| VINET | Vins et alcools Chevali | Paul Henriot | Accounting Manager | 59 rue de l'Abl |
| WANDK | Die Wandernde Kuh | Rita Müller | Sales Representative | Adenauerallee |
| WARTH | Wartian Herkku | Pirkko Koskitalo | Accounting Manager | Torikatu 38 |
| WELLI | Wellington Importadora | Paula Parente | Sales Manager | Rua do Merca |
| WHITC | White Clover Markets | Karl Jablonski | Owner | 305 - 14th Ave |
| WILMK | Wilman Kala | Matti Karttunen | Owner/Marketing Ass | Keskuskatu 45 |
| WOLZA | Wolski  Zajazd | Zbyszek Piestrzenie | Owner | ul. Filtrowa 68 |
| YYZ | | | | |

Record: ◀◀ ◀  92  ▶ ▶I ▶✳ of 92

**FIG. 5.2**   Adding a new record to the Customer table.

You can cancel the addition of a new record by deleting all the entries you made in the record before moving the record pointer. If you edited only the first field and did not move the record pointer, you can press the Esc button to cancel the addition.

# Selecting, Appending, Replacing, and Deleting Table Records

You can select a single record or a group of records to copy or cut to the Clipboard, or to delete from the table, by the following methods:

- To select a single record, click its record selection button.

- To select a contiguous group of records, click the first record's selection button and then drag the mouse pointer along the record selection buttons to the last record of the group.

- Alternatively, to select a group of records, click the first record's selection button, hold down the Shift key, and then click the last record to include in the group. Alternatively, you can hold down the Shift key and press the down arrow to select a group of records.

> **Note**
>
> You can cut groups of records to the Clipboard, deleting them from the table, but you cannot cut data blocks. A *group of records* includes all fields of one or more selected records. A *data block* consists of a selection in a table datasheet that does not include all fields of the selected rows. The Edit, Cut menu choice is enabled for groups of records and disabled for data blocks.

You can cut or copy and append duplicate records to the same table (if appending the duplicate records does not cause a primary-key violation) or to another table. You cannot cut records from a primary table that have dependent records in a related table if you enforce referential integrity. The following methods are applicable to appending or re-placing the content of records with records stored in the Clipboard:

- To append records from the Clipboard to a table, choose Edit, Paste Append. (No shortcut key exists for Paste Append.)

- To replace the content of a record(s) with data from the Clipboard, select the record(s) whose content you want to replace and then press Ctrl+V or choose Edit, Paste or click the Paste button on the toolbar. Only the number of records you select or the number of records stored in the Clipboard, whichever is fewer, is replaced.

To delete one or more records, select the records you want to delete and press Delete. If deletion is allowed, a message box asks you to confirm your deletion. You cannot undo deletions of records.

# Validating Data Entry

The data entered in tables must be accurate if the database is to be valuable to you or your organization. Even the most experienced data entry operators occasionally enter incorrect information. You can add simple tests for the reasonableness of entries by adding short expressions to the Validation Rule text box. If the data entered fails to conform to your validation rule, a message box informs the operator that a violation occurred. Validating data maintains the domain integrity of your tables.

*Expressions* are the core element of computer programming. Access enables you to create expressions without requiring that you be a programmer, although some familiarity with a programming language is helpful. Expressions are statements used to calculate values using the familiar arithmetic symbols, **+**, **–** , **\*** (multiply), and **/** (divide). These symbols are called *operators* because they operate on (use) the values that precede and follow them. The symbols are printed in bold monospace type because they are reserved symbols in Access VBA. The values operated on by operators are called *operands*.

You can also use operators to compare two values; the < (less than) and > (greater than) symbols are examples of *comparison operators*. **And**, **Or**, **Is**, **Not**, Between, and Like are called *logical operators*. Comparison and logical operators return only **True**, **False**, and unknown (the **Null** value). The **&** operator combines two text entries (*character strings* or just *strings*) into a single string. (You can use + in Access to concatenate strings, but **&** is the preferred symbol because it leaves no doubt as to the intended operation; using the + operator with numbers and strings may be ambiguous to both Access and users as to whether string concatenation or arithmetic addition is intended.) To qualify as an expression, at least one operator must be included. You can construct complex expressions by combining the different operators according to rules that apply to each of the operators involved. The collection of these rules is called *operator syntax*.

▶▶ See "Understanding the Elements in Expressions," p. 288

Data validation rules use expressions that result in one of two values: **True** or **False**. Entries in a data cell are accepted if the result of the validation is true and rejected if it is false. If the data is rejected by the validation rule, the text you enter in the Validation Text text box appears in a message box. Chapter 9, "Understanding Operators and Expressions in Access," explains the syntax of Access validation expressions.

### Adding Field-Level Validation Rules

Validation rules that restrict the values entered in a field based on only one field are called *field-level validation rules*. Table 5.6 lists the simple field-level validation rules used for some of the fields of the Personnel Actions table you created in Chapter 4, "Working with Access Databases and Tables."

| Table 5.6    Validation Criteria for the Fields of the Personnel Actions Table | | |
|---|---|---|
| **Field Name** | **Validation Rule** | **Validation Text** |
| paID | >0 | Please enter a valid employee ID number. |
| paType | "H" **Or** "S" **Or** "Q" **Or** "Y" **Or** "B" **Or** "C" | Only H, S, Q, Y, B, and C codes can be entered. |
| paInitiated By | >0 | Please enter a valid supervisor ID number. |
| paScheduledDate | Between **Date**() -3650 **And** **Date**() + 365 | Scheduled dates cannot be more than 10 years ago or more than one year from now. |
| paApprovedBy | >0 **Or Is Null** | Enter a valid manager ID number or leave blank if not approved. |
| paRating | Between 0 **And** 9 **Or Is Null** | Rating range is 0 for terminated employees, 1 to 9, or blank. |
| paAmount | No rule | No text |
| paComments | No rule | No text |

The validation rules for fields that require employee ID numbers are not, in their present form, capable of ensuring that a valid ID number is entered. You could enter a number greater than the total number of employees in the firm. The validation rule for the paID field tests the EmployeeID number field of the Employees table to determine whether the paID number is present. You don't need to create this test because the rules of referential integrity, discussed in the "Enforcing Referential Integrity" section in Chapter 4, "Working with Access Databases and Tables," perform this validation for you. Validation rules for paInitiatedBy and paApprovedBy require tests based on entries in the Employees table.

To add the validation rules to the Personnel Actions table, follow these steps:

1. Open the Personnel Actions table, if it isn't already open, by double-clicking the table name in the Database window.

2. Return to Design mode by clicking the Design View button. The paID field is selected.

3. Press F6 to switch to the Field Properties window, and then move to the Validation Rule text box.

4. Enter **>0**. Press Enter to accept the entry and move to the Validation Text text box.

5. Type **Please enter a valid employee ID number** in the Validation Text text box. The text scrolls to the left when it becomes longer than can be displayed in the text box. To display the beginning of the text, press Home. Press End to position the caret at the last character. Press Enter to complete the operation.

6. Move to the Required text box and enter **Yes**, or open the drop-down list and click Yes. Figure 5.3 shows your entries in the Field Properties text boxes.

7. Press F6 to switch back to the Table Design grid. Move to the next field, and press F6.

8. Enter the validation rule and validation text for the six remaining fields listed in Table 5.6 that use data entry validation, repeating steps 2 through 5. Square brackets ([ ]) enclose field names that include punctuation or spaces. Enter **Yes** in the Required text box for the paType, paInitiatedBy, and paScheduledDate fields.

| Field Properties | | |
| --- | --- | --- |
| General | Lookup | |
| Field Size | Long Integer | |
| Format | General Number | |
| Decimal Places | Auto | |
| Input Mask | | |
| Caption | ID | |
| Default Value | | |
| Validation Rule | >0 | |
| Validation Text | Please enter a valid employee ID number | |
| Required | Yes | |
| Indexed | No | |

(Require data entry in this field?)

**FIG. 5.3**    The Field Properties text boxes, showing your first validation entries.

You test your validation rule entries in the "Entering Personnel Actions Table Data and Testing Validation Rules" section later in this chapter.

### Adding Table-Level Validation Rules and Using the Expression Builder

One of the fields, paEffectiveDate, requires a validation rule that depends on the value of paScheduledDate. The effective date of the personnel department's action should not be prior to the scheduled date for the review that results in the action. Access 1.x enabled you to refer to one or more field names when creating a field-level validation rule expression. Like Access 2.0 and Access 95, however, you cannot refer to other field names in a validation rule expression in Access 97; instead, you enter the validation rule in the Table Properties window. Validation rules in which the value of one field depends on a previously entered value in another field of the current record are called *table-level validation rules*.

The following steps create a table-level validation rule for the paEffectiveDate field:

1. Click the Properties button on the toolbar to display the Table Properties window (see Figure 5.4).

2. Enter **Personnel Department Actions** in the Description text box, as shown in Figure 5.4.

3. Move the caret to the Validation Rule text box. Click the ellipsis button (...) that appears to right of the Validation Rule text box (see Figure 5.5) to display the Expression Builder dialog. The current table, Personnel Actions, is selected in the left list, and the fields of the table appear in the center list.

4. Double-click paEffectiveDate in the center list to place [paEffectiveDate] in the Expression text box at the top of the dialog.

5. Enter **>=** in the expression text box and double-click paScheduledDate in the center list to add [paScheduledDate] to the expression.

6. You also want to accept a blank entry if the effective date of the personnel action is not scheduled, so add **Or [paEffectiveDate] Is Null** to the expression. Your expression appears as shown in Figure 5.5.

7. Click OK to add the table-level validation rule and close the Expression Builder dialog.

8. Move to the Validation Text text box and enter **Effective date must be on or after scheduled date**. Your Table Properties dialog appears as shown in Figure 5.6.

9. Click the Close Window button of the Table Properties window or click the Properties button on the toolbar to close the window.

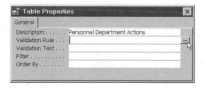

**FIG. 5.4** Adding a table description in the Table Properties dialog.

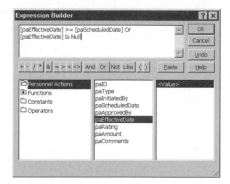

**FIG. 5.5** Creating a validation rule with the Expression Builder.

**FIG. 5.6** Adding Validation Text to a table-level validation rule.

> **Note**
>
> You can create more than one table-level validation rule by using the And reserved word and then adding another expression that involves the relationship between other fields of the table. However, Access only provides a single Validation Text message that appears when you violate any of the table-level validation rules. You can also use an Access VBA function procedure to supply a table- or field-level validation rule. By using an Access VBA function procedure, you can display different validation text messages—in this case, your validation messages are generated by your VBA function procedure, rather than the Validation Text property. Chapter 28, "Writing Visual Basic for Applications Code," describes how to use Access VBA.

# Adding Records to the Personnel Actions Table

Now you have a chance to test your work in creating the Personnel Actions table and to check whether Access is enforcing referential integrity. The initial entries for each of the nine employees of Northwind Trading are shown in Table 5.7. The entries for paScheduledDate and paEffectiveDate are taken from the HireDate field of the Employees table. The HireDate field of the Employees table now is superfluous because it duplicates the data in the Personnel Actions table. You delete the HireDate field in a later chapter. Feel free to be as generous or as parsimonious as you want with the monthly salaries shown in the paAmount field.

**Table 5.7   First Nine Entries for the Personnel Actions Table**

| ID | Type | Initiated By | Scheduled | Approved By | Effective Date | New Amount | Comments |
|----|------|--------------|-----------|-------------|----------------|------------|----------|
| 1 | H | 1 | 01-May-92 |   | 01-May-92 | 2,000 | Hired |
| 2 | H | 1 | 14-Aug-92 |   | 14-Aug-92 | 3,500 | Hired |
| 3 | H | 1 | 01-Apr-92 |   | 01-Apr-92 | 2,250 | Hired |
| 4 | H | 2 | 03-May-93 | 2 | 03-May-93 | 2,250 | Hired |
| 5 | H | 2 | 17-Oct-93 | 2 | 17-Oct-93 | 2,500 | Hired |
| 6 | H | 5 | 17-Oct-93 | 2 | 17-Oct-93 | 4,000 | Hired |
| 7 | H | 5 | 02-Jan-94 | 2 | 02-Jan-94 | 3,000 | Hired |
| 8 | H | 2 | 05-Mar-94 | 2 | 05-Mar-94 | 2,500 | Hired |
| 9 | H | 5 | 15-Nov-94 | 2 | 15-Nov-94 | 3,000 | Hired |

Entering historical information in a table in Datasheet view is a relatively fast process for an experienced data entry operator. This process also gives you a chance to test your default entries and Format properties for each field. You can enter bogus values that don't comply with your validation rules to verify that your rules are operational. To add the first nine historical records to the Personnel Actions table using the data from Table 5.7, follow these steps:

1. Click the Datasheet button on the toolbar to return to Datasheet view in Run mode, if necessary. The caret is positioned in the paID field of the default first record.

2. Enter the paID of the employee. Press Enter, Tab, or the right-arrow key to move to the next field. When you do this, a new default blank record is added to the view but not to the content of the table. A new record is added to the table only when a value is entered in one of the fields of the default blank record.

3. Type **H** in the Type field, and then press Enter, Tab, or the right-arrow key to move to the next field.

4. Type the numeric value for the paInitiatedBy field. (You need a value in this field for each employee because of the field's validation rule.) Press Enter, Tab, or the right-arrow key to move to the next field.

5. Type the paScheduledDate entry. You don't need to delete the default date value. When you type a new date, it replaces the default value. Then press Enter, Tab, or the right-arrow key.

6. If a value is in the table for paApprovedBy, type the value. Then press Enter, Tab, or the right-arrow key.

7. Type the paEffectiveDate entry. Press Enter, Tab, or the right-arrow key twice to skip the Rating field, which is inapplicable to newly hired employees.

8. Enter the paAmount of the monthly salary at the time of hiring. Press Enter, Tab, or the right-arrow key.

9. Type **Hired** in the paComments field, or any other comment you care to make. Press Enter, Tab, or the right-arrow key. The caret moves to the paID field of the next default blank record.

10. Repeat steps 2–9 for eight more employees in Table 5.7. (You can add similar records for employees 10–15 if you want.)

When you complete your entries, the Personnel Actions table appears as shown in Figure 5.7.

## Troubleshooting

*Error messages appear when I attempt to enter data in fields with validation rules.*

Edit or reenter the data to conform to the data types and validation rules for the field. Error messages that appear when you enter the data correctly indicate that something is amiss with your validation rules. In this case, change to design mode and review your validation rules for the offending fields against those listed in Table 5.6. You may want to remove the validation rule temporarily by selecting the entire expression and cutting the rule to the Clipboard. (You can paste the expression back into the text box later.) Return to Run mode to continue with your entries.

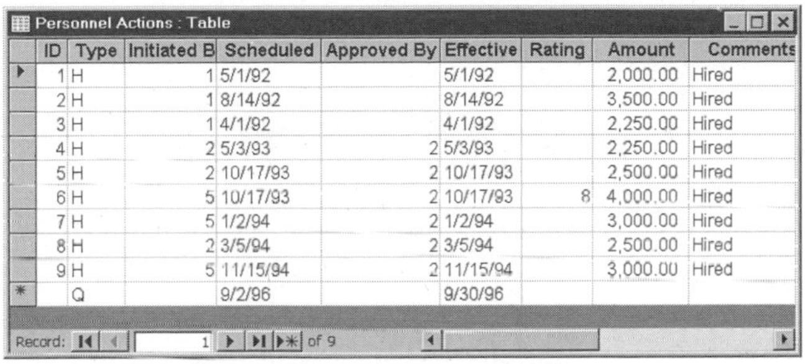

| ID | Type | Initiated B | Scheduled | Approved By | Effective | Rating | Amount | Comments |
|---|---|---|---|---|---|---|---|---|
| 1 | H | 1 | 5/1/92 | | 5/1/92 | | 2,000.00 | Hired |
| 2 | H | 1 | 8/14/92 | | 8/14/92 | | 3,500.00 | Hired |
| 3 | H | 1 | 4/1/92 | | 4/1/92 | | 2,250.00 | Hired |
| 4 | H | 2 | 5/3/93 | 2 | 5/3/93 | | 2,250.00 | Hired |
| 5 | H | 2 | 10/17/93 | 2 | 10/17/93 | | 2,500.00 | Hired |
| 6 | H | 5 | 10/17/93 | 2 | 10/17/93 | 8 | 4,000.00 | Hired |
| 7 | H | 5 | 1/2/94 | 2 | 1/2/94 | | 3,000.00 | Hired |
| 8 | H | 2 | 3/5/94 | 2 | 3/5/94 | | 2,500.00 | Hired |
| 9 | H | 5 | 11/15/94 | 2 | 11/15/94 | | 3,000.00 | Hired |
| * | Q | | 9/2/96 | | 9/30/96 | | | |

Record: 1 of 9

**FIG. 5.7**   The first nine records of the Personnel Actions table.

# Entering Personnel Actions Table Data and Testing Validation Rules

You can experiment with entering table data and testing your validation rules at the same time. Testing database applications often requires much more time and effort than creating them. The following basic tests are required to confirm your validation rules:

- *Referential integrity.* Type **25** in the paID field and **2** in the paInitiatedBy field of the default blank record, record number 10, and then press the up-arrow key. Pressing the up-arrow key tells Access that you are finished with the current record and to move up to the preceding record with the caret in the same field. Access then tests the primary-key integrity before enabling you to leave the current record. The message box shown in Figure 5.8 appears. Click OK, or press Enter.

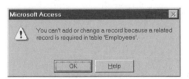

**FIG. 5.8**   The message box indicating an entry that violates referential integrity rules.

- *No duplicates restriction for primary key.* In the record just added, attempt to duplicate exactly the entries for record number 9, and then press the up-arrow key. You see the message box shown in Figure 5.9. Click OK, or press Enter.

- *paType validation.* Type **x** and press the right-arrow key to display the message box with the validation text you entered for the paType field, shown in Figure 5.10. Click OK, or press Enter.

**FIG. 5.9**  The message box alerting you that a record has a duplicate key.

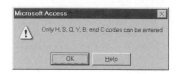

**FIG. 5.10**  The message box displayed when an entry violates a validation rule.

Type **q**, and move to the paInitiatedBy field. When the caret leaves the paType field, the **q** changes to Q because of the > format character used. Type **0** (an invalid employee ID number), and press the right-arrow key to display the message box shown in Figure 5.11. Click OK, or press Enter.

**FIG. 5.11**  The message box that appears in response to an invalid employee ID number entry.

Continue with the testing. Type a date, such as **1/31/97**, for the paScheduledDate, and type a date one day earlier (such as **1/30/97**) for the paEffectiveDate to display the error message boxes with the validation text you entered. (You must move the caret to a different record to cause the table-level validation rule to be applied.) Enter a valid date after the test. To edit a field rather than retype it, press F2 to deselect the entire field and display the caret for editing. F2 toggles selection and editing operations.

When you finish your testing, click the selection button of the last record you added, and then press Delete. The confirmation message box shown in Figure 5.12 appears.

**FIG. 5.12**  The confirmation dialog for deleting one or more records.

# Chapter 6

# Sorting, Finding, and Filtering Data in Tables

Microsoft Access provides a variety of sorting and filtering features that make customizing the display data in Table Datasheet view a quick and simple process. Sorting and filtering records in tables is quite useful when you use data in a table to create a mailing list or print a particular set of records.

Access also includes versatile search (find) and replace facilities that enable you to locate every record that matches a value you specify, and then, optionally, change that value. If you have a large table, Access's find facility enables you to quickly locate the needles in the haystacks. Search and replace often is needed when you import data from another database or a worksheet, which is the subject of the next chapter.

The sorting, filtering, searching, and replacing features of Access actually are implemented by behind-the-scenes queries that Access creates for you. When you reach Part II of this book, which deals exclusively with queries, you'll probably choose to implement these features with Access's graphical query-by-example (QBE) methods. Learning the fundamentals of these operations with tables, however, makes understanding queries easier. You also can apply filters to query result sets, use the find feature with queries in Datasheet view, and use search and replace on the result sets of updatable queries. For readers who are xBase users or know SQL, statements in these two languages equivalent to the operation being performed are given where applicable.

## Sorting Table Data

A fundamental requirement of a database development environment is the capability to sort records quickly so that they appear in the desired sequence. Early desktop database managers, such as dBASE II and III/III+, required that you create a new copy of a table if you physically wanted to sort the table's records in a new order. Creating and specifying an index on a field table enabled you to display or print the table in the order of the index. If you wanted to sort the data by two or more fields, however, you either had to create a composite index on the fields, or presort the data in the order of one or more fields, and then apply the single-field index.

Modern desktop database development systems, such as Access, never require that you physically sort the table. Instead, the physical location of the records in the file is the order in which the records were entered. By default, Access displays records in the order of the primary key. This behavior is similar to that of Borland's Paradox. If your table doesn't have a primary key, the records display in the order you enter them. Unlike dBASE and its clones, you cannot choose a specific Access index to alter the order in which the records display in Table Datasheet view of the user interface (UI). You can, however, specify an index to order records of tables you manipulate with Access VBA code. Access uses sorting methods to display records in the desired order. If an index exists on the field in which you sort the records, the sorting process is much quicker. Access automatically uses indexes, if indexes exist, to speed the sort. This process is called *query optimization*. Access's indexes and query optimization methods are discussed in Chapter 23, "Exploring Relational Database Design and Implementation."

The following sections show you how to use Access's sorting methods to display records in the sequence you want. The Customers table of Northwind.mdb is used for the majority of the examples in this chapter because it is typical of a table whose data you can use for a variety of purposes.

### Freezing Display of a Table Field

If the table you are sorting contains more fields than you can display in Access's Table Datasheet View, you can freeze one or more fields to make viewing the sorted data easier. Freezing a field makes the field visible at all times, regardless of which other fields you display by manipulating the horizontal scroll bar. To freeze the Customer ID and Company Name fields of the Customers table, follow these steps:

1. Open the Customers table in Datasheet view.

2. Click the field header button of the Customer ID field to select the first column.

3. Hold the Shift key down and click the Company Name field header button. Alternatively, you can drag the mouse from the Customer ID field to the Company Name field to select the first and second columns.

4. Choose Format, Freeze Columns.

When you scroll to fields to the right of the frozen columns, your Datasheet view of the Customers table appears as illustrated in Figure 6.1. A solid vertical line replaces the half-tone grid line between the frozen and thawed (selectable) field columns.

> **Note**
>
> If you frequently freeze columns, you can add the Freeze Columns button from the Datasheet collection to your Datasheet toolbar. See Chapter 13, "Designing Custom Multitable Forms," to learn how to customize your toolbars.

Customers : Table

| Customer ID | Company Name | Region | Postal Code | Country |
|---|---|---|---|---|
| ALFKI | Alfreds Futterkiste | | 12200 | Germany |
| ANATR | Ana Trujillo Emparedados y helados | | 05021 | Mexico |
| ANTON | Antonio Moreno Taquería | | 05023 | Mexico |
| AROUT | Around the Horn | | WA1 1DP | UK |
| BERGS | Berglunds snabbköp | | S-958 22 | Sweden |
| BLAUS | Blauer See Delikatessen | | 68306 | Germany |
| BLONP | Blondel père et fils | | 67000 | France |
| BOLID | Bólido Comidas preparadas | | 28023 | Spain |
| BONAP | Bon app' | | 13008 | France |
| BOTTM | Bottom-Dollar Markets | BC | T2F 8M4 | Canada |
| BSBEV | B's Beverages | | EC2 5NT | UK |
| CACTU | Cactus Comidas para llevar | | 1010 | Argentina |
| CENTC | Centro comercial Moctezuma | | 05022 | Mexico |
| CHOPS | Chop-suey Chinese | | 3012 | Switzerland |
| COMMI | Comércio Mineiro | SP | 05432-043 | Brazil |

Record: 1 of 91

**FIG. 6.1** The Northwind.mdb Customers table with the CustomerID and CompanyName columns frozen.

### Sorting Data on a Single Field

When creating a mailing list, a standard practice in the United States is to sort the records in ascending ZIP Code order. This practice often is observed in other countries that use postal codes, also. To sort the Customers table in the order of the Postal Code field, follow these steps:

1. Select the Postal Code field by clicking the field header button of the Postal Code field.

2. Click the Sort Ascending (A-Z) button of the toolbar or choose Records, Sort, Ascending.

▸▸ See "Writing Select Queries in SQL," p. 847

Your Customers table quickly is sorted into the order shown in Figure 6.2. Sorting a table is equivalent to specifying the selected field as the table name of the `ORDER BY` clause of an SQL statement, as in:

```
SELECT * FROM Customers ORDER BY [Postal Code]
```

Customers : Table

| Customer ID | Company Name | Region | Postal Code | Country |
|---|---|---|---|---|
| HUNGO | Hungry Owl All-Night Grocers | Co. Cork | | Ireland |
| WOLZA | Wolski Zajazd | | 01-012 | Poland |
| QUICK | QUICK-Stop | | 01307 | Germany |
| QUEDE | Que Delícia | RJ | 02389-673 | Brazil |
| RICAR | Ricardo Adocicados | RJ | 02389-890 | Brazil |
| MORGK | Morgenstern Gesundkost | | 04179 | Germany |
| GOURL | Gourmet Lanchonetes | SP | 04876-786 | Brazil |
| ANATR | Ana Trujillo Emparedados y helados | | 05021 | Mexico |
| CENTC | Centro comercial Moctezuma | | 05022 | Mexico |
| ANTON | Antonio Moreno Taquería | | 05023 | Mexico |
| PERIC | Pericles Comidas clásicas | | 05033 | Mexico |
| TORTU | Tortuga Restaurante | | 05033 | Mexico |
| COMMI | Comércio Mineiro | SP | 05432-043 | Brazil |
| FAMIA | Familia Arquibaldo | SP | 05442-030 | Brazil |
| HANAR | Hanari Carnes | RJ | 05454-876 | Brazil |

Record: 1 of 91

**FIG. 6.2** Applying an ascending sort order to the Postal Code field.

## Sorting Data on Multiple Fields

Although the sort operation in the preceding section accomplishes exactly what you specify, the result is less than useful because of the vagaries of postal code formats used in different countries. What's needed here is a multiple-field sort on the Country field first and then the Postal Code field. Thus, you might select both the Country and the Postal Code fields to perform the multi-column sort. The Quick Sort technique, however, automatically applies the sorting priority to the leftmost field you select, Postal Code. Access offers two methods of handling this problem: reorder the field display or specify the sort order in a Filter window. Filters are discussed in the "Filtering Table Data" section later in this chapter, so follow these steps to use the reordering process:

1. Select the Country field by clicking its field header button.

2. Hold the left mouse button down and drag the Country field to the left of the Postal Code field. Release the left mouse button to drop the field in its new location.

3. Press the Shift key and click the header button of the Postal Code field to select both the Country and Postal Code columns.

4. Click the Sort Ascending button of the toolbar or choose Records, Sort, Ascending.

The sorted table, shown in Figure 6.3, now makes much more sense. Applying a multi-field sort on a table (sometimes called a *composite sort*) is the equivalent of the following SQL statement:

```
SELECT * FROM Customers ORDER BY Country, [Postal Code]
```

| Customer ID | Company Name | Region | Country | Postal Code |
|---|---|---|---|---|
| RANCH | Rancho grande | | Argentina | 1010 |
| OCEAN | Océano Atlántico Ltda. | | Argentina | 1010 |
| CACTU | Cactus Comidas para llevar | | Argentina | 1010 |
| PICCO | Piccolo und mehr | | Austria | 5020 |
| ERNSH | Ernst Handel | | Austria | 8010 |
| MAISD | Maison Dewey | | Belgium | B-1180 |
| SUPRD | Suprêmes délices | | Belgium | B-6000 |
| QUEDE | Que Delícia | RJ | Brazil | 02389-673 |
| RICAR | Ricardo Adocicados | RJ | Brazil | 02389-890 |
| GOURL | Gourmet Lanchonetes | SP | Brazil | 04876-786 |
| COMMI | Comércio Mineiro | SP | Brazil | 05432-043 |
| FAMIA | Família Arquibaldo | SP | Brazil | 05442-030 |
| HANAR | Hanari Carnes | RJ | Brazil | 05454-876 |
| QUEEN | Queen Cozinha | SP | Brazil | 05487-020 |
| TRADH | Tradição Hipermercados | SP | Brazil | 05634-030 |

Record: 1 of 91

**FIG. 6.3**   The effect of a multiple-field sort on the Country and Postal Code fields of the Customers table.

## Removing a Table Sort Order and Thawing Columns

After you freeze columns and apply sort orders to a table, you might want to return the table to its original condition. To do so, Access offers you the following choices:

■  To return to Datasheet view of an Access table with a primary key to its original sort order, select the field(s) that comprise the primary key (in the order of the primary key fields).

- To return to the original order when the table has no primary key field, close the table, *don't* save the changes, and reopen the table.

- To thaw your frozen columns, choose Format, Unfreeze All Columns.

- To return the sequence of fields to its original state, either drag the fields you moved back to their prior position or close the table *without* saving your changes.

If you make substantial changes to the layout of the table and apply a sort order, it is usually quicker to close and reopen the table. (*Don't* save your changes to the table layout.)

Removing the sort order from a field is the equivalent of issuing the following SQL statement:

```
SELECT * FROM Customers
```

# Finding Matching Records in a Table

To search for and select records with field values that match (or partially match) a particular value, use Access's Find feature. To find Luleå—a relatively large city in northern Sweden close to the Arctic Circle—in the City field, follow these steps:

1. Select the field—City—you want to search. You can select the City field by either clicking the header button or placing the caret in the field.

2. Click the Find button of the toolbar or choose Edit, Find to display the Find in field dialog shown in Figure 6.4. You can also display the Find dialog by pressing Ctrl+F.

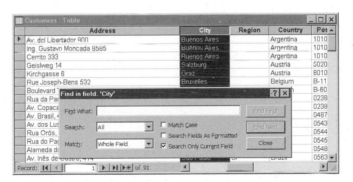

**FIG. 6.4** The opened Find in Field dialog with the City field selected.

3. Type the name of the city, **Lulea**, in the Find What text box (see Figure 6.5). When you make an entry in the Find What text box, the Find First and Find Next command buttons are enabled.

4. Select Whole Field from the Match drop-down list. (The other choices, Start of Field and Any Part of Field, are just as effective in this case.)

    The default value of the Search option button is satisfactory, and matching case or format is not important here.

5. Click the Find First button. If you do not have a Scandinavian keyboard, Access displays the "finished searching" message box shown in Figure 6.6.

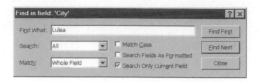

**FIG. 6.5**  Attempting to find Luleå in the City field.

**FIG. 6.6**  The message box that appears when Access cannot find a match to the content of the Find What text box.

The "finished searching" message indicates that the Find feature did not locate a match between the present position of the record pointer and the last record of the table. The reason Access missed your entry is that the Scandinavian diacritical ° is missing over the *a* in *Lulea*. In the ANSI character set, "a" has a value of 97, and "å" has a value of 229.

> **Note**
>
> You can enter international (extended) characters in the Find What text box by typing the English letters and then using Windows 95's or Windows NT 4.0's Character Map (Charmap.exe) applet to find and copy the extended character to the Clipboard. (Don't worry about choosing the correct font.) Paste the character into the Find What text box at the appropriate location.

If the letters preceding an extended character are sufficient to define your search parameter, follow this set of steps to find Luleå:

1. Type **Lule**, deleting the "a" from Lulea, in the Find What text box.

2. Select Start of Field from the Match drop-down list.

3. Click the Find First button. Access finds and highlights Luleå in the City field, as shown in Figure 6.7.

You also can find entries in any part of the field. If you type **ule** in the Find What text box and choose Any Part of Field from the Match drop-down list, you get a match on Luleå. However, you would also match Thule, the location of the Bluie West One Airfield (also known as Thule AFB) in Greenland. (There is no actual entry for Thule in the Customers table.)

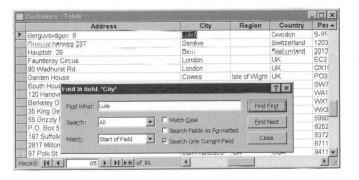

**FIG. 6.7**   Finding a record that contains a special character.

---

**Note**

Searching all fields for an entry is usually much slower than searching a single field, especially if you have an index on the field being searched. Unless you specify the Any Part of Field option, Access uses the index to speed the searching operation.

---

Following is a list of the options available in the Find in Field dialog:

- To specify a case-sensitive search, mark the Match Case check box.

- To search using the field's format, mark the Search Fields as Formatted check box. This enables you to enter a search term that matches the formatted appearance of the field rather than the native (unformatted) value if you applied a Format property value to the field. Using the Search Fields as Formatted option slows the search operation; indexes are not used.

- To find additional matches, if any, click the Find Next button. If the Search option is set to Down, then clicking the Find First button starts the search at the first record in the table, regardless of the current position of the record pointer. If the Search option is set to All, then clicking the Find First button starts the search at the current record pointer.

- To start the search at the last record of the table, select Up in the Search drop-down list.

SQL has no direct equivalent to a Find First or Find Next operation. SQL is a set-oriented language, so the following SQL statement

```
SELECT * FROM Customers WHERE City = "Luleå"
```

returns the set of all records that meet the criterion. The SQL CURSOR construct enables you to move between records of a set, but the CURSOR reserved word is not supported in Access SQL and its use is beyond the scope of the SQL discussion in this chapter.

# Replacing Matched Field Values Automatically

A variation on the Find in field dialog's theme—the Replace in field dialog—enables you to replace values selectively in fields that match the entry in the Find What text box. To display the Replace in Field dialog, choose Edit, Replace, or press Ctrl+H. (No button on the standard Table Datasheet toolbar exists for the search and replace feature.) The derivation of the shortcut key combination for Edit, Replace—Ctrl+H—is a mystery.

The entries to search for *Luleå* and replace with *Lulea* appear in Figure 6.8. To replace entries selectively, click the Find Next button, and then click the Replace button for those records in which you want to replace the value. You can do a bulk replace in all matching records by clicking the Replace All button.

**FIG. 6.8**    The Replace in Field dialog.

 ▶▶ See "Updating Values of Multiple Records in a Table," p. 383

In SQL, the statement to replace all occurrences of *Luleå* with *Lulea* is as follows:

```
UPDATE Customers SET City = 'Lulea' WHERE City = 'Luleå'
```

 ▶▶ See "Specifying Action Query Syntax," p. 860

# Filtering Table Data

Access enables you to apply a filter to specify the records that appear in Datasheet view of a table or a query result set. For example, if you wanted to view only those customers located in Germany, you would use a filter to limit the displayed records to only those whose Country field contains the text Germany. Access gives you three different ways to apply filters to the data in a table:

■ *Filter by Selection.* This is the fastest and simplest way to apply a filter. In a filter by selection, you establish the filter criteria by selecting all or part of the data in one of the table's fields; Access displays only records that match the selected sample. You can only filter records based on criteria in a single field of the table with a filter by selection.

- *Filter by Form.* This is the second-fastest way to apply a filter. In a filter by form, you enter the filter criteria into a blank datasheet form of the table; Access displays records that match the combined criteria in each field. Use a filter by form to quickly filter records based on criteria in more than one field.

- *Advanced Filter/Sort.* This is the the most powerful, and also the most difficult type of filter to use. With an advanced filter/sort you can make an Access filter do double-duty because you also can add a sort order on one or more fields.

Each of the three available types of filters is described in the next few sections.

### Filtering by Selection

Creating a filter by selection is as easy as selecting (highlighting) text in a field. When you apply the filter, Access uses the selected text to determine which records to display. Table 6.1 summarizes what records are displayed, depending on how you select text in the field. In all cases, Access applies the filter criteria only to the field in which you have selected text. Filter by selection only allows you to establish filter criteria for a single field at one time.

| **Table 6.1  How Selected Text Affects Filter by Selection** | |
| --- | --- |
| **Selected Text** | **Filter Effect** |
| Entire field | Displays only records whose fields contain exactly matching values. |
| Beginning of field | Displays records where the text at the beginning of the field matches the selected text. |
| End of field | Displays records where the text at the end of the field matches the selected text. |
| Characters anywhere in field, except beginning or end | Displays records where any part of the field matches anywhere in the selected text. |

To create a Filter by Selection on the Customers table (displaying only those customers located in Germany), follow these steps:

1. If necessary, open the Customers table in Datasheet view, and use the scroll bars to make the Country field column visible in the table window.

2. Click the First Record button to make the first record in the table the active record.

3. Select all of the text in the Country field of the first record in the Customers table. (This should be Germany.)

4. Click the Filter by Selection button on the toolbar, or choose <u>R</u>ecords, <u>F</u>ilter, Filter by <u>S</u>election. Access applies the filter, as shown in Figure 6.9.

   Notice that the Apply Filter button on the toolbar is now displayed in a "down" position, indicating that a filter is being applied to the table and the ScreenTip changes to `Remove Filter`. The legend (`Filtered`) is also added to the record selection and information bar at the bottom of the table window.

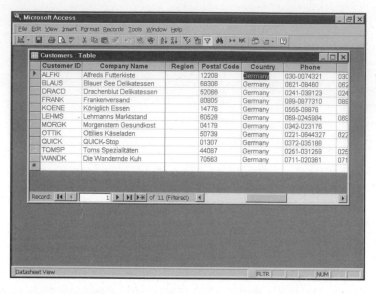

**FIG. 6.9**    A Filter by Selection applied to the Customers Table to display only those customers in Germany.

---

**Tip**

Use the Find dialog to quickly locate the first record of a group you're interested in filtering, and then apply a filter by selection.

---

As mentioned previously, you can also apply a filter by selection based on partially selected text in a field. Figure 6.10 shows the Customers table with a different filter by selection applied—this time, only the letters *er* in the Country field were selected.

**FIG. 6.10**    The Customers table, this time filtered by selecting the letters "er" in the Country field.

> **Tip**
>
> You can apply a filter by selection to more than one field at a time. For example, after applying a filter by selection to display only those customers located in Germany, you could then move to the City field and apply a second filter by selection for Berlin. The resulting table display will then include only those customers in both Germany and in Berlin. An easier way to apply filters based on more than one field value is to use a Filter by Form, described in the next section of this chapter.

Run

> **Note**
>
> To remove a filter, click the Remove Filter button on the toolbar. This is really the same as the Apply Filter button—the button is "down" whenever a filter is in effect, and "up" otherwise.

### Filtering by Form

Filtering by form is slightly more complex than filtering by selection, but allows you to filter records based on criteria in more than one field at a time. For example, you saw in the preceding section how to use a filter by selection to view only those customers located in Germany. To further limit the displayed records to those customers located in Berlin, Germany, use a Filter by Form.

▶▶ See "Understanding the Elements in Expressions," p. 288
▶▶ See "Creating Access Expressions," p. 309
▶▶ See "Expressions for Query Criteria," p. 310

In a Filter by Form, Access presents you with a blank form for the table (see Figure 6.11). This window is called a *form* to distinguish it from the Table Design grid and the table datasheet windows, although it is not the same as the data-entry forms discussed later in this book. You can use any query expression you want in the fields of the Filter by Form window. Query expressions are described Chapter 9, "Understanding Operators and Expressions in Access." You can combine criteria in a Filter by Form with either a logical **Or** condition or a logical **And** condition. For example, you can filter the Customers table to display only those customers in the United States or in Canada. As another example, you could filter the Customers table to display only those customers in the United States and in ZIP codes beginning with the digit 9 (such as 94609 or 90807).

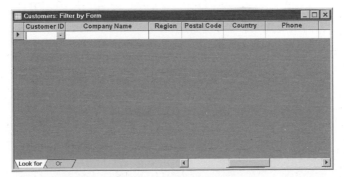

**FIG. 6.11**  An empty Filter by Form window for the Customers table.

To create a Filter by Form on the Customers table (displaying only those customers located in the United States or Canada), follow these steps:

1. If necessary, open the Customers table in Datasheet view, and use the scroll bars to make the Country field column visible in the table window.

2. Click the Filter by Form button on the toolbar, or choose Records, Filter, Filter by Form. Access displays the Filter by Form window (refer to Figure 6.11).

3. Use the scroll bars to make the Country field visible in the Filter by Form window, if necessary. (The Customer ID and Company Name columns in the figures have been frozen, as described previously in this chapter.)

4. Click inside the Country field to move the caret to that field, and then click the arrow to open the Country list box, or press F4. The drop-down list contains a list of all the unique values in the Country field (see Figure 6.12).

5. Select Canada in the list box, as shown in Figure 6.12. Access automatically adds the quotation marks around the value you select, and enters it into the Country field form box.

6. Click the Or tab at the bottom of the Filter by Form window. Access combines criteria that you enter on separate tabs in the Filter by Form window with a logical Or condition.

7. Click the arrow to open the Country list box, or press F4, and select USA from the drop-down list (see Figure 6.13).

8. Click the Apply Filter button, or choose Filter, Apply Filter/Sort. Access applies the new filter to the table, displaying the records shown in Figure 6.14.

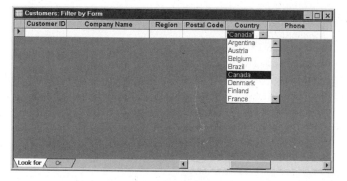

**FIG. 6.12**  Selecting the first country to filter for in the Customers table.

You can also combine filter criteria in a logical **And** condition by entering criteria in more than one field on the same tab of the form window. For example, say you wanted to filter the Orders table to find all orders handled by Nancy Davolio and shipped to France. You could easily use a Filter by Form to do so, as the following example shows:

1. Open the Orders table, if necessary, and freeze the Order ID, Customer, and Employee columns, then use the field scroll bars to position the Ship Country field so that it is visible in the window (see Figure 6.15). (Freezing the columns isn't an essential step, but it makes setting up the filter and viewing the filtered data easier.)

2. Click the Filter by Form button on the toolbar, or choose Records, Filter, Filter by Form. Access displays the Filter by Form window.

3. Click the Clear Grid button on the toolbar, or choose Edit, Clear Filter to clear any previous filter criteria from the Filter by Form grid.

4. Use the drop-down list in the Employee field to select Davolio, Nancy, and then use the drop-down list in the Ship Country field to select France (see Figure 6.16).

5. Click the Apply Filter button, or choose Filter, Apply Filter/Sort. Access applies the new filter to the table, displaying the records shown in Figure 6.17.

This filter only shows those records for orders that were both handled by Nancy Davolio and were shipped to France.

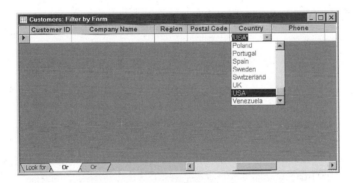

**FIG. 6.13**   Selecting the Or condition for the Filter by Form in the Customers table.

| Customer ID | Company Name | Region | Postal Code | Country | Phone |
|---|---|---|---|---|---|
| BOTTM | Bottom-Dollar Markets | BC | T2F 8M4 | Canada | (604) 555-4729 |
| GREAL | Great Lakes Food Market | OR | 97403 | USA | (503) 555-7555 |
| HUNGC | Hungry Coyote Import Store | OR | 97827 | USA | (503) 555-6874 |
| LAUGB | Laughing Bacchus Wine Ce | BC | V3F 2K1 | Canada | (604) 555-3392 |
| LAZYK | Lazy K Kountry Store | WA | 99362 | USA | (509) 555-7969 |
| LETSS | Let's Stop N Shop | CA | 94117 | USA | (415) 555-5938 |
| LONEP | Lonesome Pine Restaurant | OR | 97219 | USA | (503) 555-9573 |
| MEREP | Mère Paillarde | Québec | H1J 1C3 | Canada | (514) 555-8054 |
| OLDWO | Old World Delicatessen | AK | 99508 | USA | (907) 555-7584 |
| RATTC | Rattlesnake Canyon Grocer | NM | 87110 | USA | (505) 555-5939 |
| SAVEA | Save-a-lot Markets | ID | 83720 | USA | (208) 555-8097 |
| SPLIR | Split Rail Beer & Ale | WY | 82520 | USA | (307) 555-4680 |
| THEBI | The Big Cheese | OR | 97201 | USA | (503) 555-3612 |
| THECR | The Cracker Box | MT | 59801 | USA | (406) 555-5834 |
| TRAIH | Trail's Head Gourmet Provis | WA | 98034 | USA | (208) 555-8257 |

Record: 1 of 16 (Filtered)

**FIG. 6.14**   The result of the Filter by Form displays only those records for customers in Canada or the USA.

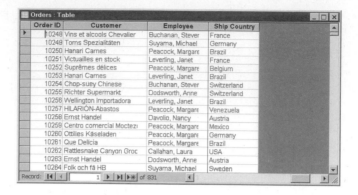

**FIG. 6.15**   The Orders table with the Order ID, Customer, and Employee columns frozen, and the Ship Country scrolled into visibility.

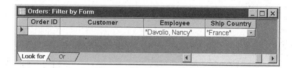

**FIG. 6.16**   Combining criteria in two fields in a logical And condition.

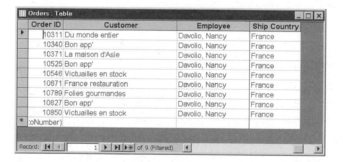

**FIG. 6.17**   The Orders table records displayed by the Filter by Form shown in Figure 6.16.

---

## Troubleshooting

*My Filter by Form filters don't produce the records I expect. I'm seeing either too few records, or records extraneous to the filter I've selected.*

Access keeps your last filter settings for a table until you close the table. If you've applied a different filter, whether through Filter by Selection or Filter by Form earlier in your current work session, Access may be applying additional filter criteria that you're not expecting. Use the Clear Grid button or choose Edit, Clear Filter in Filter by Form to clear all previous filter criteria and ensure that the new filter criteria you enter are the only ones in effect.

---

### Advanced Filters and Sorts

Filters in Access, as mentioned previously, are queries in disguise. Creating an Advanced Filter/Sort is very much like creating a query, with some basic differences. The basic differences between the Filter Design window and the Query design window are as follows:

- The Show Table dialog does not appear.

- The SQL button is missing from the toolbar, so you can't display the underlying SQL statement.

- The Show row is missing from the Filter Design grid.

Filters are limited to using one table or query that Access automatically specifies when you enter Filter Design mode. You can save a filter you create as a query, or load a filter from a query, but Access has no provision for saving a filter as a filter. The sections that follow describe how to add criteria to filter records and to add a sort order in the Filter Design window.

### Adding a Multi-Field Sort and Compound Filter Criteria

In its default configuration, the Datasheet toolbar doesn't have an Advanced Filter/Sort button. Instead, you start the Advanced Filter/Sort operation by choosing Records, Filter, Advanced Filter/Sort. To create a filter on the Orders table (which provides more records to filter than the Customers table), follow these steps:

**1.** Open the Orders table in Datasheet view.

**2.** Choose Records, Filter, Advanced Filter/Sort to display the Filter window. The Filter window appears as shown in Figure 6.18. The default filter name, Filter1, is concatenated with the table name to create the default name of the first filter, OrdersFilter1. The field list window for the Orders table appears in the upper pane of the Filter window.

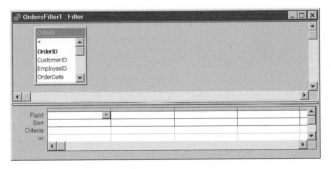

**FIG. 6.18**   The Filter Design window opened by choosing Records, Filter, Advanced Filter/Sort.

**3.** One of the fields that you might want to use to sort or limit displayed records is OrderID. Click the OrderID field in the Orders field list window in the upper pane and drag the field to the first column of the Fields row of the Filter Design grid in the lower pane and drop it. (When your mouse pointer reaches the lower pane, it turns into a field symbol.)

4. Repeat step 3 for other fields on which you want to sort or establish criteria. Candidates are CustomerID, ShipName, ShipCountry, ShipPostalCode, OrderDate, and ShippedDate fields.

5. Add an ascending sort to the ShipCountry and ShipPostalCode fields to check the sorting capabilities of your first advanced filter. Your Filter Design window appears as shown in Figure 6.19.

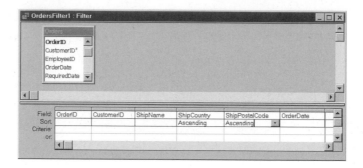

**FIG. 6.19**   Adding fields and sort orders to the Filter design window.

6. Click the Apply Filter button of the toolbar, or choose Filter, Apply Filter/Sort.

7. Use the horizontal scroll bar of the datasheet to reveal the ShipCountry and ShipPostalCode fields. Your sorted table appears as shown in Figure 6.20.

**FIG. 6.20**   The Orders table, ordered by the ShipCountry and ShipPostalCode fields.

8. Choose Records, Filter, Advanced Filter/Sort to display the Filter Design window so you can edit the filter criteria. Access displays the Filter Design window with all of the criteria from the preceding filter already entered.

9. Type **USA** in the Criteria row of the ShipCountry column to limit records to those orders shipped to an address in the United States. Access automatically adds double-quotes (") around "USA", indicating that the entry is text, not a number.

10. Click the Apply Filter button of the toolbar or choose Filter, Apply, Filter/Sort and scroll to display the sorted fields. Only records with destinations in the United States appear, as shown in Figure 6.21. (The first three columns of the table have been frozen, and the Ship Country and Ship Postal Code columns have been scrolled into visibility to achieve the table appearance in Figure 6.21.)

| Order ID | Customer | Employee | Ship Postal Code | Ship Country |
|---|---|---|---|---|
| 10624 | The Cracker Box | Peacock, Margaret | 59801 | USA |
| 10775 | The Cracker Box | King, Robert | 59801 | USA |
| 11003 | The Cracker Box | Leverling, Janet | 59801 | USA |
| 10271 | Split Rail Beer & Ale | Suyama, Michael | 82520 | USA |
| 10385 | Split Rail Beer & Ale | Davolio, Nancy | 82520 | USA |
| 10369 | Split Rail Beer & Ale | Callahan, Laura | 82520 | USA |
| 10349 | Split Rail Beer & Ale | King, Robert | 82520 | USA |
| 10821 | Split Rail Beer & Ale | Davolio, Nancy | 82520 | USA |
| 10432 | Split Rail Beer & Ale | Leverling, Janet | 82520 | USA |
| 10974 | Split Rail Beer & Ale | Leverling, Janet | 82520 | USA |
| 10329 | Split Rail Beer & Ale | Peacock, Margaret | 82520 | USA |
| 10758 | Split Rail Beer & Ale | Callahan, Laura | 82520 | USA |
| 10678 | Save-a-lot Markets | King, Robert | 83720 | USA |
| 10748 | Save-a-lot Markets | Leverling, Janet | 83720 | USA |
| 10757 | Save-a-lot Markets | Suyama, Michael | 83720 | USA |
| 10815 | Save-a-lot Markets | Fuller, Andrew | 83720 | USA |
| 10607 | Save-a-lot Markets | Buchanan, Steven | 83720 | USA |
| 10393 | Save-a-lot Markets | Davolio, Nancy | 83720 | USA |
| 10722 | Save-a-lot Markets | Callahan, Laura | 83720 | USA |

Record: 1 of 122 (Filtered)

**FIG. 6.21**   The result of applying a "USA" criterion to the Ship Country field.

### Tip

Although the Datasheet toolbar doesn't have an Advanced Filter/Sort command button in its default configuration, you can customize the Datasheet toolbar to add an Advanced Filter/Sort button to it.

### Using Composite Criteria

You can apply composite criteria to expand or further limit the records that Access displays. Composite criteria are applied to more than one field. To display all orders received on or after 1/1/95 with destinations in North America, try the following:

1. Choose Records, Filter, Advanced Filter/Sort to display the Filter Design window.

2. Type **Canada** in the second criteria line of the ShipCountry column and **Mexico** in the third line, and then move the caret to a different cell. When you add criteria under one another, the effect is to make the criteria alternative—that is, combined in a logical Or condition. (Adding criteria in successive rows is the equivalent of using the OR operator in SQL.)

3. Type **>=#1/1/95#** in the first criteria line of the OrderDate field. When you add criteria on the same line as another criterion, the criteria is additive (a logical And condition); that is, orders for the United States placed on or after 1/1/95. (Adding criteria in the same row is the equivalent of using the SQL AND operator.) The # symbols indicate to Access that the enclosed value is of the Date/Time data type.

4. Press F2 to select the entry of step 2, and then press Ctrl+C to copy the expression to the Clipboard. Position the caret in the second row of the Order Date column, and press Ctrl+V to add the same expression for Canada. Repeat this process to add the date criterion for Mexican orders. Your Filter Design grid now appears as shown in Figure 6.22. You need to repeat the date criterion for each country criterion because of a limitation in constructing SQL statements from QBE grids, which is discussed shortly.

5. Click the Apply Filter button to display your newly filtered datasheet (see Figure 6.23).

| Field: | OrderID | CustomerID | ShipName | ShipCountry | ShipPostalCode | OrderDate |
|---|---|---|---|---|---|---|
| Sort: | | | | Ascending | Ascending | |
| Criteria: | | | | "USA" | | >=#1/1/95# |
| or: | | | | "Canada" | | >=#1/1/95# |
| | | | | "Mexico" | | >=#1/1/95# |

**FIG. 6.22** The Filter grid with composite criteria added.

The SQL statement equivalent to this filter/sort combination is as follows:

```
SELECT * FROM Orders
   WHERE ([Ship Country] = 'USA' AND [Order Date] >= #1/1/95#)
      OR ([Ship Country] = 'Canada' AND [Order Date] >= #1/1/95#)
      OR ([Ship Country] = 'Mexico' AND [Order Date] >= #1/1/95#)
   ORDER BY [Ship Country], [Ship Postal Code]
```

The following is a more efficient SQL statement that accomplishes the same objective:

```
SELECT * FROM Orders
   WHERE ([Ship Country] = 'USA'
      OR [Ship Country] = 'Canada'
      OR [Ship Country] = 'Mexico')
      AND [Order Date] >= #1/1/95#
   ORDER BY [Ship Country], [Ship Postal Code]
```

| Order ID | Customer | Employee | Order Date | Ship Country | Requ |
|---|---|---|---|---|---|
| 10376 | Mère Paillarde | Davolio, Nancy | 09-Jan-95 | Canada | 06-Feb |
| 10424 | Mère Paillarde | King, Robert | 23-Feb-95 | Canada | 23-Mar |
| 10724 | Mère Paillarde | Callahan, Laura | 30-Nov-95 | Canada | 11-Jan |
| 10619 | Mère Paillarde | Leverling, Janet | 04-Sep-95 | Canada | 02-Oct |
| 10618 | Mère Paillarde | Davolio, Nancy | 01-Sep-95 | Canada | 13-Oct |
| 10605 | Mère Paillarde | Davolio, Nancy | 21-Aug-95 | Canada | 18-Sep |
| 10590 | Mère Paillarde | Peacock, Margaret | 07-Aug-95 | Canada | 04-Sep |
| 10570 | Mère Paillarde | Leverling, Janet | 18-Jul-95 | Canada | 15-Aug |
| 10565 | Mère Paillarde | Callahan, Laura | 12-Jul-95 | Canada | 09-Aug |
| 10505 | Mère Paillarde | Leverling, Janet | 15-May-95 | Canada | 12-Jun |
| 10439 | Mère Paillarde | Suyama, Michael | 10-Mar-95 | Canada | 07-Apr |
| 10411 | Bottom-Dollar Markets | Dodsworth, Anne | 10-Feb-95 | Canada | 10-Mar |
| 10975 | Bottom-Dollar Markets | Davolio, Nancy | 24-Apr-96 | Canada | 22-May |
| 10389 | Bottom-Dollar Markets | Peacock, Margaret | 20-Jan-95 | Canada | 17-Feb |
| 10949 | Bottom-Dollar Markets | Fuller, Andrew | 12-Apr-96 | Canada | 10-May |
| 10944 | Bottom-Dollar Markets | Suyama, Michael | 11-Apr-96 | Canada | 25-Apr |
| 10918 | Bottom-Dollar Markets | Leverling, Janet | 01-Apr-96 | Canada | 29-Apr |
| 10431 | Bottom-Dollar Markets | Peacock, Margaret | 02-Mar-95 | Canada | 16-Mar |
| 10410 | Bottom-Dollar Markets | Leverling, Janet | 10-Feb-95 | Canada | 10-Mar |

Record: 1 of 153 (Filtered)

**FIG. 6.23** The result of the filter of Figure 6.22 applied to the Orders datasheet.

A statement using the SQL IN predicate is even simpler:

```
SELECT * FROM Orders
    WHERE [Ship Country] IN('USA', 'Canada', 'Mexico')
        AND [Order Date] >= #1/1/94#
    ORDER BY [Ship Country], [Ship Postal Code]
```

You can't generate either of the more efficient forms of the SQL statement with QBE because Access has to take into consideration that you might want a different range of order dates for each country.

### Saving Your Filter as a Query and Loading a Filter

Access does not have a persistent Filter object. A *persistent* database object is an object you create that is stored as a component of your database's .mdb file. All persistent database objects appear as items in one of the list boxes of the Database window. A filter is the equivalent of a single-table query, so Access lets you save your filter as a QueryDef object. Access saves the names of the filters associated with each table in the system tables of your database when you save a filter as a query. This is the principle advantage of using a filter rather than a query when only a single table is involved.

To save your filter and remove the filter from the Orders table, follow these steps:

1. Choose Records, Filter, Advanced Filter/Sort to display the Filter design window, if it is not already displayed.

2. Choose File, Save As Query to display the Save As Query dialog, or click the Save As Query toolbar button.

3. Enter a descriptive name for your filter in the Query Name text box. Using the **flt** prefix distinguishes the filters you save from conventional queries (see Figure 6.24).

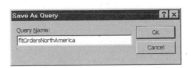

**FIG. 6.24**  Naming the QueryDef object that contains a filter.

4. Click OK to save the filter.

5. Click the Close Window button to close the Filter window.

6. Click the Remove Filter on the toolbar or choose Records, Remove Filter/Sort to remove the filter from the Orders datasheet.

7. A filter remains in memory while the table to which it applies is open. To close the filter, click the Close Window button to close the Orders table.

Re-creating a filter from the filter you saved as a query requires the following steps:

1. Reopen the Orders table in Datasheet view.

2. Choose Records, Filter, Advanced Filter/Sort to open the Filters window with an empty filter.

**I**

**Learning Fundamentals**

**3.** Click the Load from Query toolbar button, or choose <u>F</u>ile, Load from <u>Q</u>uery to display the Applicable Filter dialog, shown in Figure 6.25.

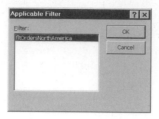

**FIG. 6.25**   A saved filter listed in the Applicable Filter dialog.

**4.** Double-click the fltOrdersNorthAmerica filter to load the saved query into the Filter window.

 **5.** Click the Apply Filter button on the toolbar to display the resulting filter set in the Orders datasheet.

You can save the preceding steps by simply executing the saved query. You execute a query the same way you open a table:

**1.** Close the Orders table.

 **2.** Click the Queries tab of the Database window to list the saved queries.

**3.** Double-click the fltOrdersNorthAmerica item. The datasheet of the fltOrdersNorthAmerica: Select Query window that appears is identical to the datasheet you created in step 5 of the preceding operation.

 **4.** Click the Design View button of the toolbar to display the query design, shown in Figure 6.26. Notice that the columns of your original filter, in which no selection criteria or sort order were entered, don't appear in the query's grid.

**5.** Choose <u>V</u>iew, <u>S</u>QL to display the SQL statement behind the query, illustrated by Figure 6.27.

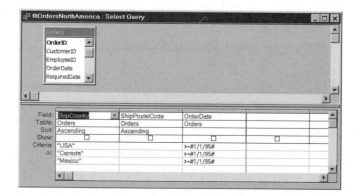

**FIG. 6.26**   The Query Design view of a saved filter.

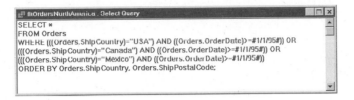

**FIG. 6.27**  The SQL statement for the filter saved as a query.

Access adds a multitude of parentheses, plus table name qualifiers, to the field names of the statements created from QBE grids. Most of the parentheses are superfluous. (They are present to help the Jet database engine's query parser execute more complex queries.) Table name qualifiers are not necessary in an SQL statement when only one table is included in the FROM clause.

# Customizing Datasheet View

You can customize the appearance of Datasheet view by hiding the fields you don't want to appear in your datasheet, changing the height of the record rows, eliminating the grid lines, and selecting a different font for your display. The following list describes each of the options for customizing Table and Query Datasheet view:

- To hide a field, select the field by clicking the field header or placing the caret in the column for the field and then choose Format, Hide Columns. Alternatively, you can use the Unhide Columns method described in the next option.

- To show a hidden field, choose Format, Unhide Columns to display the Unhide Columns dialog shown in Figure 6.28. Columns that appear in Datasheet view are indicated by a check mark next to the field name in the Column list. Click the box to the left of the field name to toggle between hiding and showing the column.

**FIG. 6.28**  The Unhide Columns dialog, which allows you to show and hide datasheet fields.

- To change the font used to display and print the datasheet, use the Font drop-down list on the Formatting toolbar (if it is displayed), or choose Format, Font to display the Font dialog, shown in Figure 6.29. (The Font dialog is one of the common dialogs of Windows 95 and Windows NT 4.0. Other common dialogs include the Open and Save dialogs.)

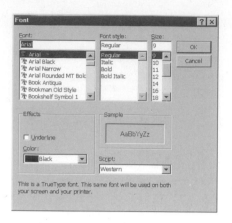

**FIG. 6.29**   Choosing a display and printing font for datasheets.

■ To remove gridlines from the display and printed versions of the datasheet, click the Gridlines Shown drop-down list button on the Formatting toolbar, or choose Format, Cells. If you choose the Gridlines Shown drop-down list, Access displays a palette of four gridline display choices: Both, Horizontal, Vertical, and None; click the button corresponding to the gridline display you want. If you choose Format, Cells, Access displays the Cells Effects dialog, which contains check boxes for the horizontal and vertical gridlines; select or clear the check boxes to obtain the desired gridline display.

■ To change the height of the rows as displayed and printed, position the mouse pointer at the bottom edge of one of the record selector buttons. The mouse pointer turns into a double-headed arrow, as shown in Figure 6.30. Drag the bottom edge of the button to adjust the height of all the rows. Alternatively, choose Format, Row Height and set the height in points in the Row Height dialog. (Multiply the size of your font by about 1.25 to obtain normal row spacing; printers call 10-point type with 12-point spacing 10 on 12.)

■ To change the width of the columns to accommodate a larger font, choose Format, Column Width and then click the Best Fit button to let Access determine the size of your columns. You might need to adjust individual column widths by dragging the right edge of the field header with the mouse.

Figure 6.30 shows the Orders datasheet with several columns hidden, gridlines off, 9-point Century Schoolbook TrueType font, and the height of the rows adjusted to accommodate the larger font.

---

### Tip

For the greatest printing speed, choose a typeface family native to your printer, such as Helvetica for PostScript or Swiss for LaserJet printers. (Native fonts are indicated by a printer and page symbol next to the typeface family name in the Font list.) Alternatively, choose a TrueType face, such as the default Arial, for both display and printing.

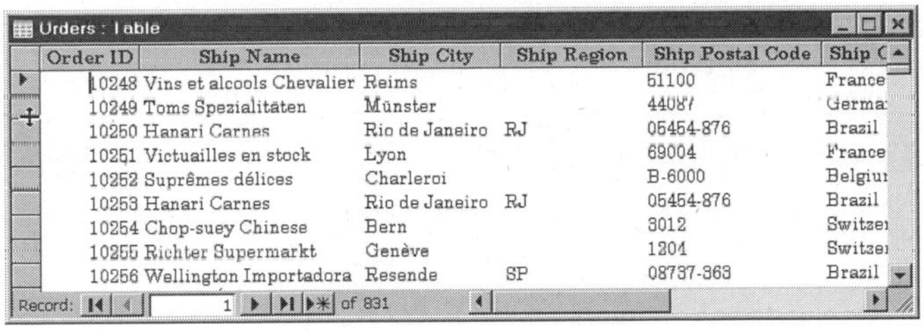

| Order ID | Ship Name | Ship City | Ship Region | Ship Postal Code | Ship C ▲ |
|---|---|---|---|---|---|
| 10248 | Vins et alcools Chevalier | Reims | | 51100 | France |
| 10249 | Toms Spezialitäten | Münster | | 44087 | Germa |
| 10250 | Hanari Carnes | Rio de Janeiro | RJ | 05454-876 | Brazil |
| 10251 | Victuailles en stock | Lyon | | 69004 | France |
| 10252 | Suprêmes délices | Charleroi | | B-6000 | Belgiu |
| 10253 | Hanari Carnes | Rio de Janeiro | RJ | 05454-876 | Brazil |
| 10254 | Chop-suey Chinese | Bern | | 3012 | Switzel |
| 10255 | Richter Supermarkt | Genève | | 1204 | Switzel |
| 10256 | Wellington Importadora | Resende | SP | 08737-363 | Brazil ▼ |

Record: ◄ ◄   1   ► ►► ►* of 831

**FIG. 6.30**   The Orders datasheet in a customized view.

# Copying, Exporting, and Mailing Sorted and Filtered Data

A primary use for filters and customized datasheets is so that you can export the filtered records to another application, such as Microsoft Excel or Word. A variety of methods for exporting filtered and custom-formatted records is available, each of which is described in the following list:

▶▶ See "Exporting Data from Access Tables," p. 253

- Copy the entire datasheet to the Clipboard, and then paste it into the other application. Hidden columns don't appear, but formatting (font, font attributes, and row height) is preserved.

- Use the Save As/Export feature to export the datasheet to an Excel worksheet (.xls) or a rich text format (.rtf) file for Word or other Windows word processing applications. (Choose File, Save As/Export, select To an external File or Database in the Save As dialog, and then select the file type you want in the Save As Type drop-down list of the Save Table In dialog.) Save As/Export preserves the attributes you use to customize the filtered and sorted data when you choose Excel format. Hidden columns, however, appear when you open the resulting file in any version of Excel.

- Choose Tools, Office Links, Analyze It with MS Excel to save the filtered or sorted data in an Excel worksheet, or choose Tools, Office Links, Publish It with MS Word to save the data as an .rtf document. Whether you choose to Analyze It or Publish It, Access starts Excel or Word (whichever is appropriate) with the exported document displayed.

- Choose Tools, Office Links, Merge It with MS Word to create form letters with Microsoft Word. Using Mail Merge with Microsoft Word is discussed in Chapter 22, "Using Access with Microsoft Word and Mail Merge."

- Send the file as an attachment to a Microsoft Mail or Exchange message. Hidden columns don't appear, but formatting is not preserved in Microsoft Mail messages. (The attached file is in Excel BIFF format.)

If you make the Database window the active window and choose File, Save As/Export, the entire content of the table is exported without regard to the filter you added.

**Troubleshooting**

*When attempting to use the Merge It With Word feature, a* Must save object first *or* Name not found in this collection *message box appears.*

You applied a filter or created a query for your Mail Merge operation that you did not save before clicking the Merge It button. The filter or query object (filters are saved as QueryDef objects) must be a member of the QueryDefs collection before the DDE conversation between Access and Word commences. Save the filter or the query, and then try clicking the Merge It button again. Chapter 29, "Understanding the Data Access Object Class," provides detailed information on database objects and object collections.

# Chapter 7

# Linking, Importing, and Exporting Tables

Undoubtedly, more than 90 percent of personal computer users have data that can be processed by database management techniques. Any data a computer can arrange in tabular form, even tables in word processing files, can be converted to database tables. The strength of a relational database management system (RDBMS) lies in its capability to handle large numbers of individual pieces of data stored in tables, and to relate the pieces of data in a meaningful way.

PC users acquire RDBMSs when the amount of data created exceeds the application's capability to manipulate the data effectively. A common example of this situation is a large mailing list created in a word processing application. As the number of names in the list increases, using the word processor to make selective mailings and maintain histories of responses to mailings becomes increasingly difficult. A PC RDBMS is the most effective type of application for manipulating large lists.

One Access strong point is its capability to transform existing database tables, spreadsheets, and text files created by other DOS and Windows applications into the Access .mdb format—a process known as *importing* a file. Access can *export* (create) table files in any format in which it can import the files. Most PC RDBMSs share this capability, but Access can import and export Borland Paradox files—many other systems cannot. Most client/server RDBMSs can import and export only text-type files.

Access can link a database table file created by Access or another RDBMS to your current Access database; Access then acts as a database front end. Because Access has a linking capability, it can use a file created by another RDBMS in its native form. This capability is far less common in other PC and client/server RDBMSs. When you link a database table from a different RDBMS, you can display and update the linked table as if it were an Access table contained in your .mdb file. If the file that contains the table is shared on a network, other users can employ the file with their applications, while it is linked to your database. This capability to link files is an important feature for two reasons: you can have only one Access database open at a time, and you can create new applications in Access that can coexist with applications created by other database managers.

This chapter deals primarily with what are known as *desktop database-development applications*—a term used to distinguish them from client/server RDBMSs, such as Microsoft and Sybase SQL Server, ORACLE, Informix, and Ingres databases. (Client/server RDBMSs are designed specifically for use with networked PCs and—except for Microsoft SQL Server for Windows NT—require you to set aside a PC for use as a database application and file server to run the RDBMS and store the database files.) Desktop RDBMSs, such as dBASE, FoxPro, and Paradox, are more widely used than client/server systems. The majority of desktop RDBMSs can share files on a network, but several publishers of desktop RDBMSs require that you purchase a special multiuser version of the RDBMS to do so. Multiuser desktop RDBMSs—while accommodating the workstation-server configuration required by conventional networks such as Novell NetWare, Windows NT Server, or IBM LAN Server—are especially well-suited to the peer-to-peer networks discussed in Chapter 25, "Securing Multiuser Network Applications," such as Windows 95 peer networking, NetWare Lite, and LANtastic. Chapter 25 explains how to use Access with shared database files in general, and Chapter 26, "Connecting to Client/Server Databases," deals with client/server databases in particular.

## Learning How Access Handles Tables in Other Database File Formats

Conventional desktop database development applications maintain each table in an individual file. Each file contains a header followed by the data. A *header* is a group of bytes that provides information on the structure of the file, such as the names and types of fields, number of records in the table, and length of the file. When you create a table file in dBASE, FoxPro, or Paradox, for example, the file contains only a header. As you add records to the file, the file grows by the number of bytes required for one record, and the header is updated to reflect the new file size and record count.

Desktop RDBMSs create a variety of supplemental files, which are shown in the following list—some of which are required to import, link, or export RDBMSs:

- Paradox stores information about the primary-key index file (.px) in the associated table (.db) file; the .px file for the .db file must be available for Access to open a Paradox .db file for updating. Access links the .px file automatically if it exists.

- dBASE and FoxPro store memo-type data in a separate .dbt file. If a dBASE table file contains a memo field, the .dbt file must be available. If the .dbt file is missing, you cannot import or link dBASE or FoxPro tables that contain a memo field.

- Use of .ndx (dBASE III), .mdx (dBASE IV), or .idx or .cdx (FoxPro) index files is optional. You always should use index files when you have them. If you don't link the index files when you link an indexed .dbf table file, modifications you make to the linked tables aren't reflected in the index, which causes errors to occur when you try to use the indexed tables with dBASE or FoxPro.

All supplemental files must be in the same folder as the related database file to be used by Access.

The header of an Access 97 .mdb file differs from conventional PC RDBMS files in that an .mdb header consists of a collection of system tables that contain information on all the tables, indexes, macros, and Access VBA functions and procedures stored in a single Access file. The Access system tables also contain information on the location and characteristics of other PC RDBMS files that you linked to your Access database. Access's system tables are similar to the tables used in client/server databases that maintain information on the content of database devices (files), plus the databases and tables contained in the devices.

---

**Note**

You can view the Access 97 system tables by choosing Tools, Options. Select the View tab, and in the Show group, select System Objects.

Never modify anything in these tables (most of them are read-only). Some database developers have used the data and values in these tables to aid in referencing items in the database. This is not a good practice, because the design of these tables is not guaranteed to remain consistent from version to version and could result in substantial rework to convert a database application to a new version of Access.

---

**Identifying PC Database File Formats**

Access can import, link, and export the following types of database table files used by the most common PC database managers:

- *dBASE .dbf table and .dbt memo files, and dBASE III .ndx and dBASE IV .mdx index files.* dBASE III and IV files and indexes are the standard language of the PC RDBMS industry. The majority of PC RDBMSs, and also all common spreadsheet applications, can import and export .dbf files. Most of these RDBMSs can update existing .ndx and .mdx index files, and some RDBMSs can create these index files.

  The .dbf file structure is native to other xBase clone applications such as FoxPro, but not all these RDBMSs create fully compatible dBASE file structures. Compilers like CA-Clipper have their own native index-file structures, but they can use .ndx indexes when necessary. The capability to use .mdx multiple-index files is less widespread.

  Access can link and create .ndx and .mdx files. Access updates both types of dBASE index files when you edit or add records to a linked .dbf file. The section "Setting Primary Keys and Using Index Files" later in this chapter, discusses index files in linked tables. When you export an Access table with a memo field, a .dbt memo file with the same name you assign to the dBASE file is created.

- *FoxPro 2+ .dbf table files.* You can import, export, and link FoxPro 2+ .dbf files and files created by earlier versions of FoxPro. The procedures for handling FoxPro 2+ .dbf files are the same as the procedures used for dBASE III and IV. Access maintains the currency of FoxPro 2+ .idx (single) and .cdx (multiple) index files.

- *Paradox 3.x, 4.x, and 5.0 .db table and .px primary key files.* You can link Paradox for DOS 3.x and 4.x table and index files, and those files created by Paradox for Windows 5.0. The following section presents the specific limitations applicable to Paradox files.

The majority of applications that use table and index files also use the standard file extensions presented in the preceding paragraphs. The dBASE memo file, for example, requires a standard extension—.dbt. Using the standard extensions for all types of files, however, is not a requirement. Some developers of xBase applications disguise their files by using arbitrary extensions. You may have to do some detective work to determine which files contain data and which are indexes.

> **Note**
>
> If you work in a multiuser environment, you must have exclusive access to the file you intend to import. No other user can have this file open when you initiate the importing process, and other users are denied access to the file until you close the Import dialog.

> **Caution**
>
> Make sure that you work on a backup, not on the original copy of the linked file, until you are certain that your updates to the data in the linked table are valid for the existing database application.

### Linking and Importing External Tables

To link or import an xBase or Paradox file as a table in an open Access database, such as Northwind.mdb, follow these steps:

> **Note**
>
> *Linking* an external file to an Access database was referred to as *attaching* a table in versions of Access prior to Access 95. Don't confuse linking an external file to an Access database with OLE links; when you link an external file, you just give Access information about the external file so it knows how to open, read, and modify the data in that file.

1. Click the Show Database Window button on the toolbar or choose <u>W</u>indow, <u>1</u> Database. Access doesn't require that all open tables are closed before you link or import a table.

2. If you have a test database that you can use for this procedure, click the Open Database button of the toolbar or choose <u>F</u>ile, <u>O</u>pen Database; then select the test database, open it, and skip to step 5.

3. If you don't have a test database, create a sample to use throughout this chapter. Click the New Database button of the toolbar or choose File, New Database to display the New dialog.

4. Double-click the Blank Database icon in the New dialog; Access displays the File New Database dialog. Type a name, such as **Mdb Test.mdb**, in the File Name text box and click Create. You must wait while Access creates and tests the new database.

5. In this example, you link an external table to the database. Choose File, Get External Data, Link Tables. The Link dialog appears (see Figure 7.1); the Link dialog is a variation of the common Windows 95 and Windows NT 4.0 Open dialog. If you choose File, Get External Data, Import, the Import dialog appears.

6. Use the Files of Type drop-down list to select the type of file you want to link. (If you have a suitable Paradox table to link, select Paradox. Otherwise, select dBASE III, dBASE IV, or another database type as appropriate to the format of your table file.)

7. Double-click the name of the table you want to link or import (or click the name to select it, and then click the Link button). Access supplies the standard extensions for dBASE, FoxPro, and Paradox table files.

If you're linking a .dbf file that has indexes, the Select Index Files dialog appears. The section "Setting Primary Keys and Using Index Files" later in this chapter explains how to use the Select Index Files dialog.

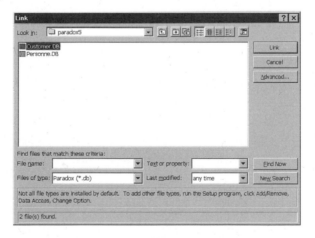

**FIG. 7.1**  The Link dialog used to select external files for linking to an Access database.

> **Note**
>
> You can link Access 1.x, Access 2.0, and Access 95 files to an Access 97 database. Linking Access 1.x, 2.0, and 95 files solves the problem of not being able to convert an Access 97 mdb file to any previous Access version .mdb format for backward compatibility, which is another reason to always use one .mdb file for tables and another .mdb file for your application database objects.

**8.** If the file you choose is encrypted (coded) and requires a password to decrypt it, the Password Required dialog appears. Type the password in the box and press Enter.

**9.** After you successfully link or import the file, a dialog appears, confirming this operation (see Figure 7.2). If you link more than one table with the same name, Access automatically appends a sequential digit to the table name.

The Link (or Import) dialog remains open; if you have additional external tables you want to link or import to this database—most Paradox and xBase databases consist of several separate table files—repeat steps 6–9 for all the files you want to link or import. If you are linking external Access tables, you may select at once all the tables you want to link by simply clicking each one.

**FIG. 7.2**    Access displays this message after successfully linking an external table to a database.

**10.** In the Link dialog, click Close. The table(s) you linked or imported now are listed in the Database window. If you linked a file, Access adds an icon that indicates the type of database table and an arrow that indicates that the table is linked (see Figure 7.3).

**11.** Select the table you linked, and then click the Open button to display the records in Table Datasheet view (see Figure 7.4). Alternatively, you can double-click the table name.

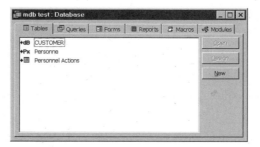

**FIG. 7.3**    The special icons displayed in the Database window indicating linked tables.

After you link an external file as a table, you can use it almost as if it were a table in your own database. The only general limitation is that you cannot change the structure of a linked table: field names, field data types, or the Field Size properties. In linked Paradox files, Access prevents you from changing a table's primary-key field that previously was defined because this property determines the contents of the associated .px index file.

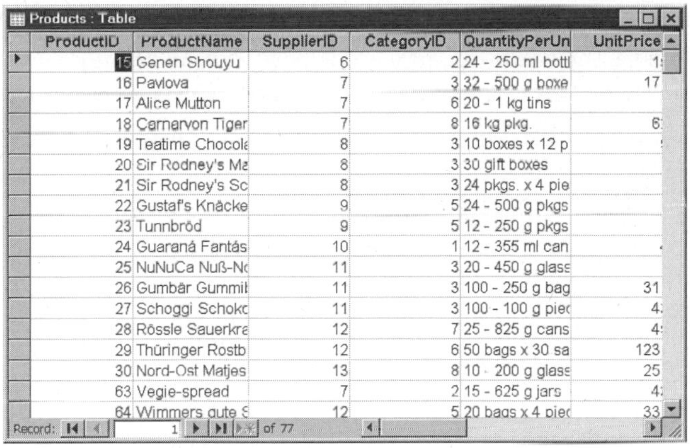

| Products : Table | | | | | | |
|---|---|---|---|---|---|---|
| ProductID | ProductName | SupplierID | CategoryID | QuantityPerUn | UnitPrice | |
| 15 | Genen Shouyu | 6 | 2 | 24 - 250 ml bottl | 1! | |
| 16 | Pavlova | 7 | 3 | 32 - 500 g boxe | 17 | |
| 17 | Alice Mutton | 7 | 6 | 20 - 1 kg tins | | |
| 18 | Carnarvon Tiger | 7 | 8 | 16 kg pkg. | 6: | |
| 19 | Teatime Chocola | 8 | 3 | 10 boxes x 12 p | | |
| 20 | Sir Rodney's Ma | 8 | 3 | 30 gift boxes | | |
| 21 | Sir Rodney's Sc | 8 | 3 | 24 pkgs. x 4 pie | | |
| 22 | Gustaf's Knäcke | 9 | 5 | 24 - 500 g pkgs | | |
| 23 | Tunnbröd | 9 | 5 | 12 - 250 g pkgs | | |
| 24 | Guaraná Fantás | 10 | 1 | 12 - 355 ml can | | |
| 25 | NuNuCa Nuß-Nc | 11 | 3 | 20 - 450 g glas: | | |
| 26 | Gumbär Gummit | 11 | 3 | 100 - 250 g bag | 31 | |
| 27 | Schoggi Schokc | 11 | 3 | 100 - 100 g piec | 4: | |
| 28 | Rössle Sauerkra | 12 | 7 | 25 - 825 g cans | 4: | |
| 29 | Thüringer Rostb | 12 | 6 | 50 bags x 30 sa | 123 | |
| 30 | Nord-Ost Matjes | 13 | 8 | 10 - 200 g glas: | 25 | |
| 63 | Vegie-spread | 7 | 2 | 15 - 625 g jars | 4: | |
| 64 | Wimmers aute S | 12 | 5 | 20 bags x 4 piec | 33 | |

Record: 14 ◄ | 1 ► ►I ►* of 77 | ◄

**FIG. 7.4**  The Datasheet view of a linked Paradox file.

> ### Note
>
> Although you cannot change field properties for linked tables, you can change the name of the
> attached table, *within this database only*. Choose Edit, Rename and type the new name for the
> table. The name for the table (called an *alias*) is changed only in the current Access database and
> not in the native database.

### Solving Problems with Importing or Linking Files

Access detects problems with linked or imported tables that may cause errors when you
try to use the tables with Access. The following sections describe these problems and how
to overcome most of them.

**The Incorrect Password Dialog.** If you enter a wrong password or just press Enter,
Access informs you that it cannot decrypt the file. You do, however, get another opportunity to enter the password or click Cancel to terminate the attempt (see Figure 7.5).

**FIG. 7.5**  The message indicating an incorrect password entry to a Paradox 5 table.

**The Null Value in Index Dialog.** Occasionally, older Paradox .px index files don't have
an index value for a record; when this situation occurs, you see a warning dialog with
the message, Can't have Null value in Index. Usually, you can disregard the message
and continue linking or importing the file. The offending record, however, may not
appear in the table; fixing the file in Paradox and starting over is better than ignoring the
message.

**The Missing Memo File Dialog.** Both dBASE and Paradox use additional memo files to store the data from memo fields in a particular table. dBASE memo files have the .dbt file type, and Paradox memo files have the .mb file type. Access correctly decides that it can't import or link an external table if it can't open the table's associated memo file—either because the memo file doesn't exist, isn't in the same folder as the table with which it is associated, or contains nontext data.

If the table you're trying to link or import is a dBASE table, Access displays the error dialog shown in Figure 7.6. If the table you're trying to link is a Paradox table, however, you receive the less informative error message shown in Figure 7.7. For assistance in solving the problem, click the Help button. To close the error dialog, click OK; Access then cancels the linking or importation.

**FIG. 7.6**   The error message when Access can't open a required dBASE memo file.

**FIG. 7.7**   The error message when Access can't open a required Paradox memo file.

**The Graphics Field Type Restriction.** If the successful-link dialog doesn't appear, your table or its accompanying dBASE or Paradox memo file probably contains a graphics field type. The following section discusses how to modify files with graphics content so that you can link or import them as Access tables.

### Dealing with Graphics in External Files

Most database managers designed for Windows include some form of graphics field data type. Superbase, Paradox 4.x, and Paradox for Windows provide a special field data type for graphics. Although dBASE IV lacks a field data type for graphics, third-party software firms publish applications that enable you to store graphic images in dBASE memo fields. A variety of add-on applications enables CA-Clipper programmers to display and edit graphic images. The images usually are in individual files but a few third-party applications place images in memo files. CA-dbFast, for example, can display—but not edit—images stored in Windows bitmap (.bmp) files. CA-dbFast doesn't add a graphics field type to store bitmapped data within tables.

When you try to import or link Paradox 4.x, Paradox for Windows files, or dBASE .dbt files that contain images or other binary data, you may receive an error message that the memo file is corrupted or a message that you cannot import the .db or .dbf file that contains the offending memo or graphics field. In rare cases—usually involving tiny images—you can import the .dbf and .dbt files, but you see random characters in the Access memo field. With Paradox tables, the graphic or binary fields simply disappear from the table.

If a dialog appears that reports a problem during importing or linking a file, the linking or importing process is canceled.

The following recommendations can help you deal with graphic images processed with other RDBMSs and add-on applications:

- Use add-on applications for xBase clones and compilers that operate with the original graphics files in their native format, such as .tif, .pcx, .gif, or .tga. In nearly all cases, the original graphics file is on your computer's fixed disk or on a file server. You can link or embed the graphics file in an Access OLE Object field by using the techniques described in Chapter 20, "Adding Graphics to Forms and Reports."

- Do not use add-on applications that incorporate graphics in .dbt files. If you are committed to this approach, use the method that follows to place the offending memo file in a new file.

- If you use Paradox 4.x or Paradox for Windows with application development in Access, maintain files with graphics fields (as well as any OLE fields in Paradox for Windows tables) separate from files containing conventional data types.

- Use an OLE server that can process the graphics file type of the original image. Windows Paint is limited to Windows bitmap files (.bmp and .dib) and can only read—not save—.pcx files. To display the image in a form or report, you can create a reduced-size, 16-color or 256-color, Windows bitmap file to be displayed as a bound object. Chapter 20 discusses methods of handling images in this way.

To link or import an xBase file that contains a memo field or a Paradox file that contains graphics fields, you must be familiar with file-restructuring methods for dBASE or Paradox. To restructure an xBase file with a memo file that contains graphic images, follow these steps:

1. Make a copy of the file and give it a new name.

2. Modify the structure of the original file by deleting all but the related fields and the memo or graphics field of the original file. Modifying the new file with Modify Structure creates a backup of the original file with a .bak extension.

3. Modify the structure of the new file by deleting the memo or graphics field.

4. Add a field for the path and file name of the original graphics file, if it isn't already included. Access then can use the location of the original graphics file to pass the file name to an OLE server. You must write some Access VBA code, however, to handle this process. See Chapter 28, "Writing Visual Basic for Applications Code," and Chapter 30, "Responding to Events with VBA 5.0," for examples of writing Access VBA code.

**5.** Modify the source code of your original application, establishing a one-to-one relationship between the new files.

### Converting Field Data Types to Access Data Types

When you import or link a file, Access reads the header of the file and converts the field data types to Access data types. Access usually is quite successful in this conversion; Access offers a greater variety of data types than most of the other widely used PC RDBMSs. Table 7.1 shows the correspondence of field data types between dBASE, Paradox, and Access files.

| Table 7.1   Field Data Type Conversion Between Access and Other RDBMSs | | |
|---|---|---|
| **dBASE III/IV/5** | **Paradox 3.x, 4.x, 5.0** | **Access** |
| Character | Alphanumeric | Text (Specify Size property) |
| Numeric, Float* | Number, Money, BCD* | Number (Double) Number (Single) Number (Byte) |
| | Short Number | Number (Integer) |
| | Long Number | Number (Long) |
| | AutoIncrement | AutoNumber |
| Logical | Logical | Yes/No |
| Date | Date, Time, Timestamp* | Date/Time |
| Memo | Memo, Formatted Memo, Binary* | Memo |
| | OLE | OLE |

*Sometimes two types of field data, separated by commas, are shown within a single column in Table 7.1. When Access exports a table that contains a data type that corresponds with one of the two field data types, the first of the two data types is assigned to the field in the exported table. The Float data type is available only in dBASE IV and 5.*

◀◀ See"Choosing Field Data Types, Sizes, and Formats," p. 119
◀◀ See"Adding Indexes to Tables," p. 154

If you are importing tables, you can change the field data type and the Field Size property to make them more suitable to the type of information contained in the field. When you change a data type or Field Size, however, follow the precautions noted in Chapter 4, "Working with Access Databases and Tables." Remember that you cannot change the field data type or Field Size property of linked tables. You can, however, use the Format property with imported or linked tables to display the data in any format compatible with the field data type of imported or linked files. You can change any remaining properties applicable to the field data type, such as validation rules and text. By using the Caption property, you can give the field a new and more descriptive name.

### Setting Primary Keys and Using Index Files

Methods of setting primary keys and creating indexes differ according to the type of file you use to link a table. Tables based on Paradox and client/server RDBMS files usually have predefined primary-key fields and are indexed on the key fields. Files based on dBASE structures, however, don't have fields specified as primary-key fields and use separate index files. The following two sections discuss the effects these differences have on the tables you create.

**Establishing Key Fields in Linked Paradox Tables.** When you link or import a Paradox or Btrieve table that has a primary-key index, Access establishes this primary key as the primary key for the new table. To verify that Access establishes a primary key for a linked Paradox table, click the Design View button on the toolbar. A message box states that you cannot modify some properties of the table and asks if you want to open the table anyway (see Figure 7.8). Click Yes.

**FIG. 7.8**   The message box that appears when you open a linked table in Design view.

The table appears in Design mode. The primary key of the linked table is shown with the key icon next to the field name, as with primary keys for Access tables you create yourself.

When you link a Paradox .db table file that has a primary key, Access uses the Paradox .px file to establish the primary key. If you modify the values in a key field, the .db and .px files simultaneously reflect this modification.

**Linking dBASE Index Files.** Key-field indexing is not automatic with dBASE files linked as tables; dBASE file headers do not include data about the indexes used by the application that has the .dbf file. The first time you link the .dbf file as an Access table, you must manually link the index files associated with a dBASE file. Then, when you open the Access database with the linked table again, Access links the indexes you specify.

---

**Note**

Access cannot open or update index files in proprietary formats of xBase clones and compilers. You cannot, for example, link CA-Clipper .ntx files. CA-Clipper (5+), however, can create and maintain .ndx files as an addition to, or a substitute for, their original index structures. Access cannot use secondary indexes of Paradox tables. If you create or commission custom database applications that use nonstandard or secondary indexes and you plan to use Access to update these files while they are linked, you must modify your applications so that they use only .ndx or .px indexes. You probably don't need to make a major revision of the source code, but you may find that your present applications run more slowly with .ndx indexes.

When you link a dBASE file as a table in your database and select the file name for the table, Access displays a Select Index Files dialog (see Figure 7.9). When you import a dBASE file, this dialog doesn't appear.

If you select a dBASE III source file, Access supplies the default .ndx file extension in the Select Index Files dialog. Your dBASE III file may have one or more .ndx index files associated with it. The five indexes that appear in Figure 7.9 are for the Customer.dbf table (a dBASE III file, created by exporting the Customers table from the Northwind.mdb sample database).

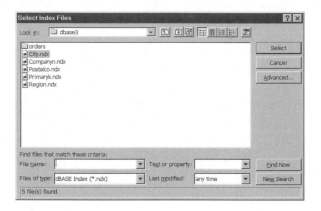

**FIG. 7.9**  Selecting dBASE II, III, IV, and 5 index files.

dBASE IV and 5 can create a multiple-index (.mdx) file that includes all the indexes associated with the .dbf file. The .mdx file usually has the same file name as the .dbf file. Access supplies both .mdx and .ndx as default index-file extensions when you select a dBASE IV or 5 file. The Select Index Files dialog appears whenever you select an xBase file type for linking or importing into an Access database, as described in the section "Linking and Importing External Tables," earlier in this chapter.

To link index files to tables created from dBASE files, follow these steps:

1.  From the file list in the Select Index Files dialog, select the index file name, and then click Select. Access adds the index and displays a message dialog, confirming that the index was added (see Figure 7.10).

> ### Caution
>
> Access does not test to determine whether the table's .ndx or .mdx index file matches the structure of its associated Access .dbf file. If the index file doesn't match the Access file, Access doesn't update the index file. Unfortunately, Access does not advise you that it is ignoring the nonconforming index. If you add records to the table in Access, and then attempt to use the table with an xBase application that uses the proper index, you receive the error message, Index does not match database. You then must re-index the .dbf file.

**FIG. 7.10**    Confirming the addition of a dBASE index to a linked table.

> ### Caution
>
> When you link a dBASE file that is used by another application, you must select all indexes associated with this file if your Access application modifies fields in the index expressions of each index file. If you do not update all the associated index files while updating the .dbf file with Access, the other application may display the error message, Index does not match file. Worse, the application may produce erroneous or unpredictable results. If the message or errors occur, you must re-index the file in the other application.

2. If more than one index file is associated with the dBASE .dbf file, you must repeat step 1 for each .ndx file until you add the names of all the indexes needed for your Access table, and then click Close in the Select Index Files dialog. Access displays the Select Unique Record Identifier dialog (see Figure 7.11).

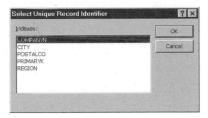

**FIG. 7.11**    The dialog for selecting a unique index for a linked dBASE file.

3. If you want Access to use one of the linked dBASE indexes to ensure that records have a unique value in the indexed field (that is, to use the dBASE index as a primary key in the table), double-click this index's name in the Indexes list of the Select Unique Record Identifier dialog.

4. Click the Close button in the Select File dialog.

5. Click the Design button in the Database window to display the structure of your linked dBASE table.

6. If the Indexes window is not visible, click the Indexes button on the toolbar or choose View, Indexes. The field names that are the basis for any linked single- or multiple-field indexes appear in the Index Name text boxes of the Indexes window (see Figure 7.12).

> **Caution**
>
> Access does not distinguish between dBASE indexes created with SET UNIQUE ON and SET UNIQUE OFF. If there are multiple identical entries in the field you select as the primary key, Access rejects your choice of that field in the Select Unique Record Identifier dialog. You must copy the dBASE file with SET UNIQUE ON to another file, re-index the file, and then repeat the attachment process.

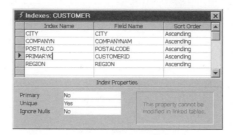

**FIG. 7.12**    The Indexes window of a linked dBASE table.

If you try to modify the primary-key field or change the data type or the Field Size property of a linked table, and then click the Datasheet button in Run mode, Access displays a dialog (see Figure 7.13). Click Yes. (Clicking No restores the original values.) Access doesn't change the properties in the linked file, nor do the Design and Datasheet windows display the changes.

**FIG. 7.13**    The message to remind you that design changes to linked tables are not permitted.

**Creating Access .inf Files for dBASE Indexes.** When you link one or more indexes to a table created from a dBASE file, Access creates a file with the same file name as the .dbf file but with an .inf extension. The *Filename*.inf file is a text file that contains the path and the file name of the index you linked, in the following format (the following .inf file is for the Customer dBASE III indexes shown in Figure 7.12, and shows UNC file names to a network location):

```
[dBase III]
NDX1=\\Zeus\zeusd\DOC\TESTDATA\dbase3\CITY.NDX
NDX2=\\Zeus\zeusd\DOC\TESTDATA\dbase3\COMPANYN.NDX
NDX3=\\Zeus\zeusd\DOC\TESTDATA\dbase3\POSTALCO.NDX
NDX4=\\Zeus\zeusd\DOC\TESTDATA\dbase3\PRIMARYK.NDX
NDX5=\\Zeus\zeusd\DOC\TESTDATA\dbase3\REGION.NDX

[UIDX1 PRIMARYK]
NDX5=\\Zeus\zeusd\DOC\TESTDATA\dbase3\REGION.NDX
```

The .inf file is located in the same folder as the .dbf file you are linking. If you create an invalid .inf file or if one or more of the indexes listed in the .inf file isn't found in the specified location, Access terminates the current link operation, and you must link the dBASE file again. Figure 7.14 shows the error message you see if Access can't find an index specified in the .inf file. When you relink the dBASE file to correct a prior error, a message box indicates that an .inf file already exists (see Figure 7.15). If the indexes changed or you moved the indexes, click Yes to create a new .inf file.

---

**Note**

If you try to find an .inf file by selecting the folder in which it should be located, the .inf extension may be missing. This is because .inf files are registered by their type, which is Setup Information.

---

**FIG. 7.14**   The warning that a linked index for a dBASE file wasn't found.

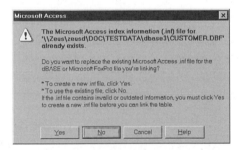

**FIG. 7.15**   The warning that an .inf file for a linked dBASE file already exists.

### Linking Tables from Other Access Databases

The procedure for linking a table from one Access database to another Access database is like the procedure for linking other tables. To link a table from Northwind.mdb to your test database, for example, follow these steps:

1. Choose File, Get External Data, Link tables, select Northwind.mdb in the Link dialog, and click the Link button. The Link Tables dialog appears (see Figure 7.16).

2. Select the name of the table to link from the Tables list that displays the names of tables in the other Access database. You can select more than one table in this list; just click each table in the list you want to link, or click Select All to link all the tables.

3. Click OK. Access adds the linked table(s) and closes all dialogs. The name(s) of your linked Access table(s) appears in the Database window.

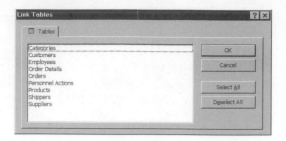

**FIG. 7.16** The Link Tables dialog displaying the tables in the external .mdb file.

Access maintains a record of the drive and folder containing the files responsible for your linked tables. If you rename or change the location of a file that you linked as a table, Access no longer can find the file and displays an error dialog (see Figure 7.17).

**FIG. 7.17** The dialog indicating that Access cannot find a linked file.

### Using the Linked Table Manager Add-In to Relink Tables

Before Access 2.0, if you moved a file that was linked to or contained objects linked to an Access database, you had to delete the linked tables, and then relink the tables from their new location. Access 97 provides an add-in assistant known as the *Linked Table Manager*, which simplifies relinking tables. (The Linked Table Manager was known as the Attachment Manager in Access 2.0.)

If you move an Access, dBASE, FoxPro, or Paradox file that provides a table linked to an Access 97 database, choose Tools, Add-Ins, Linked Table Manager. The Linked Table Manager's window lists all the linked tables (except linked ODBC tables). Access also displays the path to the database containing the linked table(s) at the time the link was created. (You also can view the path to the database containing a linked table by opening the linked table in Design view and opening the Table Properties window.) Click the check box of the file(s) whose location(s) changed (see Figure 7.18).

Click OK to display the Select New Location of the *TableName* dialog shown in Figure 7.19. Select the folder and file where the table is located, and then click Open to change the link reference and close the dialog. If Access successfully refreshes the table links, it displays a dialog saying so; click OK to close the success message dialog. Click the Close button of the Linked Table Manager to close the add-in.

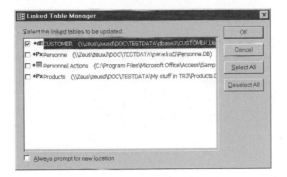

**FIG. 7.18**    The Linked Table Manager add-in, which enables you to update the path to linked tables.

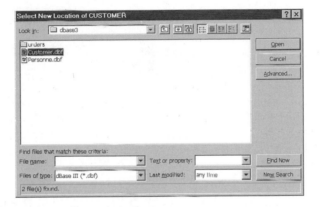

**FIG. 7.19**    Changing the location of a table with the Linked Table Manager add-in.

> **Note**
>
> The Linked Table Manager is capable of only refreshing links for tables that have been moved to another disk or folder—the table must have the same name. If the linked table's file was renamed, you must delete the table link from your Access database and relink the table under its new name.

### Importing versus Linking Database Files as Tables

The preceding examples demonstrate the differences between the behavior of Access with linked and imported database files. You should link tables contained in another database file if any of the following conditions exist:

- You share the file with other users who are allowed to update the file, or you make updates of the file available to other users.

- You use another RDBMS to modify the file in any way.

- The file is resident on another computer, such as a server, and its size is larger than fits comfortably on your fixed disk.

- You observe the recommended database application development practice of maintaining separate .mdb files for tables and your application's objects.

You should import a table when one of the following conditions exists:

- You are developing an application and want to use data types or Field Size properties different from those chosen for you by Access.

- You or the users of your application do not have online access to the required database files and cannot link them.

- You want to use a key field different from the field specified in a Paradox or client/server table. This situation can occur when the structure of one or more of the files you plan to use seriously violates one or more of the normalization rules described in Chapter 23, "Exploring Relational Database Design and Implementation."

- You need Access to allow duplicate values in your table when a primary-key field precludes duplicate values.

If you decide to use a temporarily imported table in an application that, when completed, also will use a linked table, make sure that you do not change any field names, field data types, or Field Size properties after you import the table. If you change Field Name properties, you may have to make many changes to forms, reports, macros, and Access VBA code when you change to a linked table. If your application involves Paradox and client/server database tables, do not change the primary-key fields of these tables. With dBASE tables, make sure that the indexes you create correspond to the indexes of the associated .ndx or .mdx files.

# Importing and Linking Spreadsheet Files

Access can import files created by spreadsheet and related applications, such as project management systems, in the following formats:

- Excel 2.x, 3.0, 4.0, 5.0, and 95 .xls files, and task and resource files created by Microsoft Project in .xls format.

- Lotus 1-2-3 .wks (Release 1 and Symphony), .wk1 (Release 2), and .wk3 (Release 3 and later) files. Most spreadsheet applications can export files to at least one of these Lotus formats.

You can use OLE to embed or link charts created by Microsoft Excel that are stored in files with an .xlc extension. Copy the contents of the file to the Windows Clipboard from Excel. Then choose Edit, Paste to embed or link (via OLE) the chart in fields of the OLE Object type, and display the chart on a form or print it on a report as an unbound object. Similarly, you can embed or link views displayed in Project for Windows 3.0 or 4.0, which also uses the Microsoft Chart applet, except task and resource forms and the Task PERT chart. Chapters 19–22 describe OLE linking and embedding techniques.

### Creating a Table by Importing an Excel Worksheet

Figure 7.20 illustrates the preferred format for exporting data from Excel and other spreadsheet applications to Access tables. Most spreadsheet applications refer to the format as a *database*. The names of the fields entered in the first row and the remainder of the database range consist of data. The type of data in each column must be consistent within the database range you select.

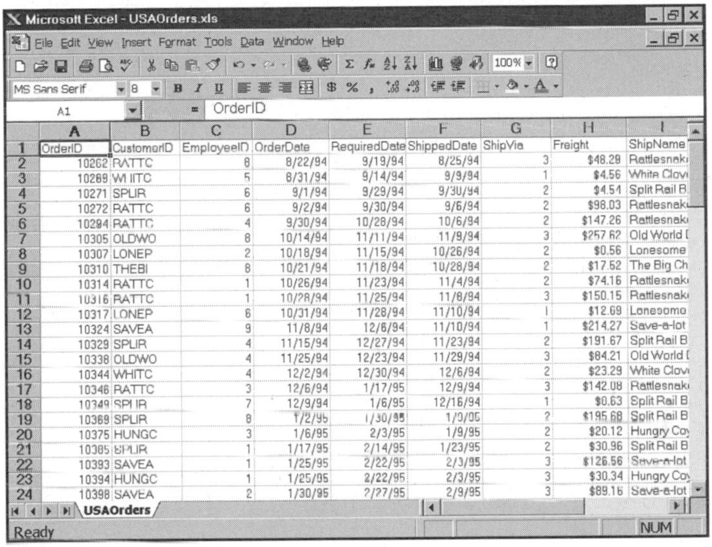


| | A | B | C | D | E | F | G | H | I |
|---|---|---|---|---|---|---|---|---|---|
| 1 | OrderID | CustomerID | EmployeeID | OrderDate | RequiredDate | ShippedDate | ShipVia | Freight | ShipName |
| 2 | 10262 | RATTC | 8 | 8/22/94 | 9/19/94 | 8/25/94 | 3 | $48.29 | Rattlesnak |
| 3 | 10269 | WHITC | 5 | 8/31/94 | 9/14/94 | 9/9/94 | 1 | $4.56 | White Clov |
| 4 | 10271 | SPLIR | 6 | 9/1/94 | 9/29/94 | 9/30/94 | 2 | $4.54 | Split Rail B |
| 5 | 10272 | RATTC | 6 | 9/2/94 | 9/30/94 | 9/6/94 | 2 | $98.03 | Rattlesnak |
| 6 | 10294 | RATTC | 4 | 9/30/94 | 10/28/94 | 10/6/94 | 2 | $147.26 | Rattlesnak |
| 7 | 10305 | OLDWO | 8 | 10/14/94 | 11/11/94 | 11/9/94 | 3 | $257.62 | Old World |
| 8 | 10307 | LONEP | 2 | 10/18/94 | 11/15/94 | 10/26/94 | 2 | $0.56 | Lonesome |
| 9 | 10310 | THEBI | 8 | 10/21/94 | 11/18/94 | 10/28/94 | 2 | $17.52 | The Big Ch |
| 10 | 10314 | RATTC | 1 | 10/26/94 | 11/23/94 | 11/4/94 | 2 | $74.16 | Rattlesnak |
| 11 | 10316 | RATTC | 1 | 10/28/94 | 11/25/94 | 11/8/94 | 3 | $150.15 | Rattlesnak |
| 12 | 10317 | LONEP | 6 | 10/31/94 | 11/28/94 | 11/10/94 | 1 | $12.69 | Lonesome |
| 13 | 10324 | SAVEA | 9 | 11/8/94 | 12/6/94 | 11/10/94 | 1 | $214.27 | Save-a-lot |
| 14 | 10329 | SPLIR | 4 | 11/15/94 | 12/27/94 | 11/23/94 | 2 | $191.67 | Split Rail B |
| 15 | 10338 | OLDWO | 4 | 11/25/94 | 12/23/94 | 11/29/94 | 3 | $84.21 | Old World |
| 16 | 10344 | WHITC | 4 | 12/2/94 | 12/30/94 | 12/6/94 | 2 | $23.29 | White Clov |
| 17 | 10346 | RATTC | 3 | 12/6/94 | 1/17/95 | 12/9/94 | 3 | $142.08 | Rattlesnak |
| 18 | 10349 | SPLIR | 7 | 12/9/94 | 1/6/95 | 12/16/94 | 1 | $8.63 | Split Rail B |
| 19 | 10369 | SPLIR | 8 | 1/2/95 | 1/30/95 | 1/9/95 | 2 | $195.68 | Split Rail B |
| 20 | 10375 | HUNGC | 3 | 1/6/95 | 2/3/95 | 1/9/95 | 2 | $20.12 | Hungry Co |
| 21 | 10385 | SPLIR | 1 | 1/17/95 | 2/14/95 | 1/23/95 | 2 | $30.96 | Split Rail B |
| 22 | 10393 | SAVEA | 1 | 1/25/95 | 2/22/95 | 2/3/95 | 3 | $126.56 | Save-a-lot |
| 23 | 10394 | HUNGC | 1 | 1/25/95 | 2/22/95 | 2/3/95 | 3 | $30.34 | Hungry Co |
| 24 | 10398 | SAVEA | 2 | 1/30/95 | 2/27/95 | 2/9/95 | 3 | $89.16 | Save-a-lot |

**FIG. 7.20** Data from the Orders table in a Microsoft Excel 97 worksheet.

#### Caution

All the cells that comprise the range of the worksheet to be imported into an Access table must have frozen values. *Frozen values* substitute numeric results for the Excel expressions used to create the values. When cells include formulas, Access imports the cells as blank data cells. Freezing values causes Access to overwrite the formulas in the spreadsheet with the frozen values. If the range to import includes formulas, save a copy of your .xls file with a new name. By using the worksheet window with the new file name, select the range to import and freeze the values by choosing Edit, Copy, or by pressing Ctrl+C. Choose Edit, Paste Special, select the Values option, and click OK. Save the new spreadsheet by its new name and use this file to import the data. The section "Using the Clipboard to Import Data" that follows in this chapter presents an alternative to this procedure.

#### Tip

You get an opportunity to assign field names to the columns in the worksheet during the importation process, although it's easier if you add field names as column headings first.

To prepare the data in an Excel spreadsheet for importation into an Access table, follow these steps:

1. Launch Excel, and then open the .xls file that contains the data you want to import.

2. Add field names above the first row of the data you plan to export (if you haven't done so). Field names cannot include periods (.), exclamation points (!), or square brackets ([ ]). You cannot have duplicate field names. If you include improper characters in field names or use duplicate field names, you see an error message when you attempt to import the worksheet.

3. If your worksheet contains cells with data you don't want to include in the imported table, select the range that contains the field names row and all the rows of data needed for the table. In Excel, choose Insert, Name, Define and name the range.

4. If the worksheet cells include expressions, freeze the values as described in the caution that precedes these steps.

5. Save the Excel file (using a different file name if you froze values), and exit Excel to conserve Windows resources for Access if your computer has less than 8M of memory.

Now you are ready to import worksheets from the Excel workbook file.

To import the prepared data from an Excel spreadsheet into an Access table, follow these steps:

1. Launch Access, if it's not running, and open the database to which you want to add the new table. The Database window must be active (with a dark title bar, usually blue) before you can import a file.

2. Choose File, Get External Data, Import in Access. The Import dialog appears (see Figure 7.21). The Files of Type drop-down list provides several more formats for importing tables than it provides for linking files.

3. Select Microsoft Excel (*.xls) in the Files of Type drop-down list, and then double-click the name of the Excel workbook that contains the spreadsheet you want to import (you also can click the file name to select it, and then click Import). Access now invokes the Import Spreadsheet Wizard, which displays the dialog shown in Figure 7.22.

4. If you're importing an entire worksheet, select the Show Worksheets option; if you're importing a named range, select the Show Named Ranges option. The Import Spreadsheet Wizard lists the worksheets or named data ranges, depending on the option you select in the list box in the upper-right corner of the wizard's opening dialog (refer to Figure 7.22).

5. Select the worksheet or the named data range that you want to import in the list box. The Import Spreadsheet Wizard shows a sample view of the data in the worksheet or named range in the scrollable area at the bottom of the dialog.

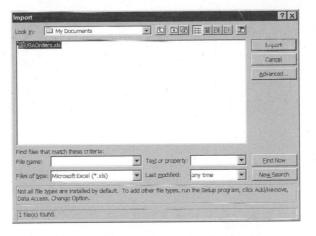

**FIG. 7.21**   The Import dialog is used to import Excel and Lotus 1-2-3 spreadsheets.

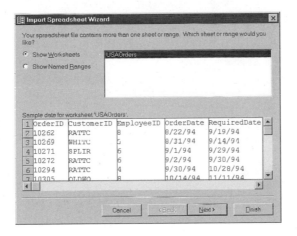

**FIG. 7.22**   The opening dialog of the Import Spreadsheet Wizard.

6. Click the Next button to move to the next step of the Spreadsheet Import Wizard. The wizard displays the dialog shown in Figure 7.23.

7. If the first row of your spreadsheet data contains the field names for the imported table, select the First Row Contains Column Headings check box. Click Next to continue with the third step; the Import Spreadsheet Wizard displays the dialog shown in Figure 7.24.

8. If you want to create a new table to hold the imported spreadsheet data, select the In a New Table option. To add the imported data to an existing table, select the In an Existing Table option and select the table you want to add the imported data to in the drop-down list. Click Next to continue with the fourth step; the Import Spreadsheet Wizard displays the dialog shown in Figure 7.25.

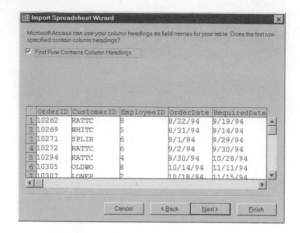

**FIG. 7.23**   Selecting whether the first row of imported data contains field names.

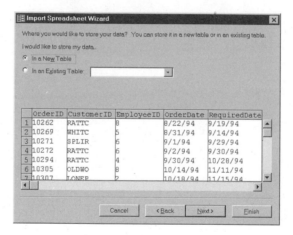

**FIG. 7.24**   Choosing whether to create a new table from the imported data, or to add it to an existing table.

> **Note**
>
> If you elect to add the imported data to an existing table, the Import Spreadsheet Wizard skips over all intervening steps, and goes immediately to its final dialog, described in step 16 of these instructions.

   **9.** If you want to exclude a column from the imported database, select the column by clicking it, and then select the Do Not Import Field (Skip) check box, and skip to step 12.

 **10.** The Import Spreadsheet Wizard enables you to edit or add the field names for the spreadsheet columns; click the column whose name you want to edit or add, and then type the name in the Field Name text box.

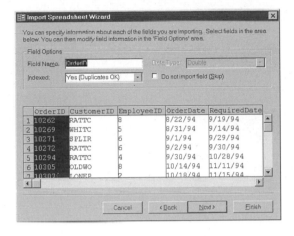

**FIG. 7.25**   Selecting field names, indexes, and the field's data type.

11. If you want Access to index this field, choose the appropriate index type in the Indexed list box; you may choose No index, Yes (Duplicates OK), or Yes (No Duplicates).

12. If the data in the spreadsheet column is unformatted or is formatted as text, Access enables you to select the data type for the field in the Data Type drop-down list. The Data Type control is disabled in Figure 7.25 because the cells in the selected column of the Excel worksheet have a Double number format; Access recognizes the Double format, and automatically selects a Double data type for this field.

13. Repeat steps 9–12 for each column in the worksheet or data range that you import. When you are satisfied with your options for each column, click Next to move to the next dialog in the Import Spreadsheet Wizard (see Figure 7.26).

> **Tip**
>
> Use an existing field column in the worksheet for a primary key field if the column contains unique values only. In Figure 7.26, the OrderID field is known to contain unique values.

14. Select the Let Access add Primary Key option to have Access add an AutoNumber field to the imported table; Access fills in a unique number for each existing row in the worksheet that you're importing. Select the Choose my own Primary Key option and select the primary key field in the drop-down list if you know there is a column in the worksheet or data range that you can use as a primary key for the imported table. If this imported table doesn't need a primary key, select the No Primary Key option.

▶▶ See "Using Access 97's Table Analyzer Wizard," p. 813

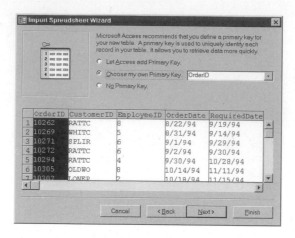

**FIG. 7.26** Selecting a primary key for the new table.

15. Click Next to move to the final dialog of the Import Spreadsheet Wizard (see Figure 7.27). Type the name of the new table in the Import to Table text box; Access uses the name of the worksheet or data range as the default table name. If you want to use the Table Analyzer Wizard to split the imported table into two or more related tables, select the check box labeled, I Would Like the Wizard to Analyze the Structure of My Table After it Finishes Importing the Data. (You can use the Table Analyzer Wizard at any time, on any table by choosing Tools, Analyze, Table.)

16. Click Finish to complete the importing process. Access closes the Import Spreadsheet Wizard and imports the data. When Access completes the import process without errors, it displays the dialog shown in Figure 7.28.

Access analyzes, approximately, the first 20 rows of the spreadsheet you are importing, and assigns data types to the imported fields based on this analysis. If every cell in a column has a numeric or date value, the columns convert to Number and Date/Time field data types, respectively. If a column contains mixed text and numbers, Access converts the column as a text field. If, however, a column contains numeric data in the first 20 rows (the rows that Access analyzes), and then has one or more text entries, Access does not convert these rows.

If Access encounters cell values that it cannot convert to the data type that it assigned to the imported field, Access creates an Import Errors table with one record for each error. You can review this table, select the records in which the errors are reported, and fix them. A better approach, however, is to correct the cells in the spreadsheet, resave the file, and import the corrected data.

> **Note**
>
> The Import Spreadsheet Wizard doesn't display an error message when it encounters inconsistent field data types; it just creates the Import Errors table. You must look in the Database window to

> see if the Import Errors table is present. After you resolve the import errors, make sure that you delete the Import Errors table so that you can more easily tell whether or not there are errors the next time you import a spreadsheet or other external file.

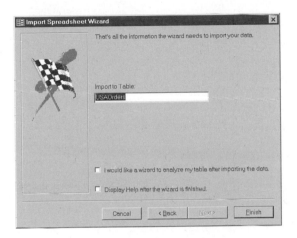

**FIG. 7.27**    Giving the new table a name in the Import Spreadsheet Wizard's final dialog.

**FIG. 7.28**    This is the message displayed by the Import Spreadsheet Wizard after successfully importing a spreadsheet.

The Database window now contains a new table with the name you entered in the final step of the Import Spreadsheet Wizard. If you import another file with the same name as your spreadsheet file name, Access adds the number 1 to the file name.

To verify that you obtained the desired result, double-click the name of the imported table in the Database window to display the new table in Datasheet view. Figure 7.29 illustrates a portion of the Access table created from the USA Orders worksheet in the USAOrders.xls spreadsheet file of Figure 7.20.

To display the .xls file data types that Access chose, click the Design View button on the toolbar. Figure 7.30 shows the structure of the new USA Orders table.

After you successfully import the table, you may want to change the properties of the fields. Unlike the procedure with linked files, Access places no restrictions on altering the field properties of imported files. The section, "Modifying Linked and Imported Tables," that follows in this chapter discusses how to change the default field data types of tables created by imported files.

| OrderID | CustomerID | EmployeeID | OrderDate | RequiredDate | ShippedI |
|---|---|---|---|---|---|
| 10262 | RATTC | 8 | 8/22/94 | 9/19/94 | 8/ |
| 10269 | WHITC | 5 | 8/31/94 | 9/14/94 | 9 |
| 10271 | SPLIR | 6 | 9/1/94 | 9/29/94 | 9/ |
| 10272 | RATTC | 6 | 9/2/94 | 9/30/94 | 9 |
| 10294 | RATTC | 4 | 9/30/94 | 10/28/94 | 10 |
| 10305 | OLDWO | 8 | 10/14/94 | 11/11/94 | 1 |
| 10307 | LONEP | 2 | 10/18/94 | 11/15/94 | 10/ |
| 10310 | THEBI | 8 | 10/21/94 | 11/18/94 | 10/ |
| 10314 | RATTC | 1 | 10/26/94 | 11/23/94 | 1 |
| 10316 | RATTC | 1 | 10/28/94 | 11/25/94 | 1 |
| 10317 | LONEP | 6 | 10/31/94 | 11/28/94 | 11/ |
| 10324 | SAVEA | 9 | 11/8/94 | 12/6/94 | 11/ |
| 10329 | SPLIR | 4 | 11/15/94 | 12/27/94 | 11/ |
| 10338 | OLDWO | 4 | 11/25/94 | 12/23/94 | 11/ |
| 10344 | WHITC | 4 | 12/2/94 | 12/30/94 | 12 |
| 10346 | RATTC | 3 | 12/6/94 | 1/17/95 | 12 |
| 10349 | SPLIR | 7 | 12/9/94 | 1/6/95 | 12/ |
| 10369 | SPLIR | 8 | 1/2/95 | 1/30/95 | |

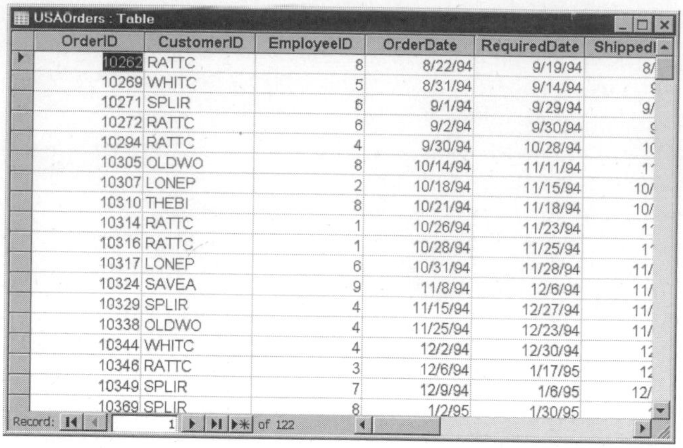

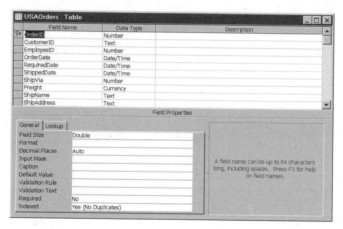

**FIG. 7.29** The imported Excel worksheet data in an Access table.

**FIG. 7.30** The structure of the imported USA Orders table based on Excel data types.

## Linking an Excel Worksheet by Using the ODBC API

Office 97 installs 32-bit Excel, FoxPro, Paradox, Access, dBASE, and Text file ODBC drivers, plus the SQL Server driver. ODBC and the ODBC drivers are installed if you choose a Complete Microsoft Office 97 or Access 97 setup, but you must explicitly specify installation of the SQL Server driver during the setup process. If you don't have the ODBC drivers on your system, you can rerun Setup to install them. Additional ODBC drivers are available from various third-party vendors.

You can use the ODBC drivers provided with Office 97 to link Excel worksheets to your Access databases. Linking an Excel worksheet has the advantage of providing up-to-date information if the data in the worksheet is subject to periodic updates. You can use the 32-bit ODBC Manager application supplied with Access 97 (and installed into the Windows 95 and Windows NT 4.0 Control Panel) to create an ODBC data source from your Excel worksheet. You also can link Excel worksheets directly to a database by using

ODBC directly from Access. *Data source* is a synonym for *database* when you use the ODBC API to link tables. (In Windows NT, the ODBC Manager is referred to as the *ODBC Administrator*.)

▶▶ See "Understanding ODBC Drivers," p. 918

> **Note**
>
> To link data in an Excel worksheet, you must create a named data range for the worksheet data you want to link. Usually, you should make sure that the worksheet you link via ODBC meets all the requirements for a worksheet that you intend to import, as described in the preceding section of this chapter. That is, make sure that the data in the worksheet is laid out in a tabular format. You don't, however, have to freeze values for an ODBC-linked worksheet.

Linking an Excel worksheet via ODBC is similar to the spreadsheet importing and linking you learned about previously in this chapter. Assuming that you installed the ODBC Manager and ODBC drivers, follow these steps to link an Excel worksheet to an Access database via ODBC:

1.  Launch Access and open a database, if necessary. Choose File, Get External Data, Link Table to display the Link dialog (refer to Figure 7.1).

2.  Select ODBC Databases in the Files of Type drop-down list. Access closes the Link dialog and displays the Select Data Source dialog (see Figure 7.31).

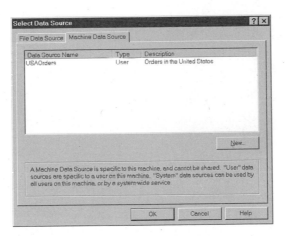

**FIG. 7.31**   Selecting an ODBC data source in the Select Data Source dialog.

3.  Click the Machine Data Source tab to select a previously defined ODBC data source, or to connect to another data source. (You use the File Data Source page to specify a data source file that you can share with other users.)

▶▶ See "Creating a File Data Source Within Access 97," p. 931

4. If you previously defined an ODBC data source for the worksheet you want to link, select its name in the Select Data Source list. Otherwise, click New to display the first dialog of the Create New Data Source Wizard (see Figure 7.32).

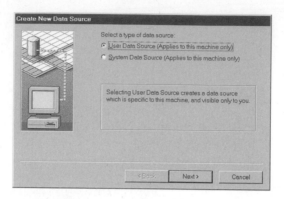

**FIG. 7.32**   The opening dialog of the Create New Data Source Wizard.

5. Select the User Data Source option if you want the new data source to be available only to you. If you want anyone who logs on to your computer to be able to use your new data source, select the System Data Source option. Click Next to continue with the second dialog of the Create New Data Source Wizard (see Figure 7.33).

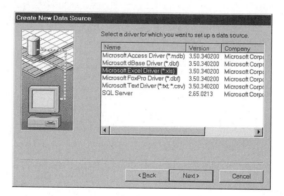

**FIG. 7.33**   Selecting a database driver for an Excel worksheet.

6. Select the database driver appropriate for the database you want to link. For an Excel worksheet, select Microsoft Excel Driver (*.xls)—refer to Figure 7.33. Click Next to display the Create New Data Source Wizard's third dialog.

7. The final dialog of the Create New Data Source Wizard displays summary information about the type of data source you have created (system or user) and the name of the database driver you selected (see Figure 7.34). Click Finish to complete the creation of your new data source.

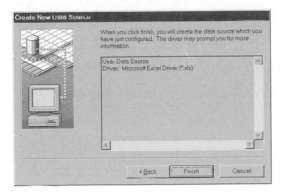

**FIG. 7.34**  The Create New Data Source Wizard's final dialog.

8. After creating a new data source, you must configure it. Access now displays the ODBC Microsoft Excel Setup dialog (see Figure 7.35). Enter a name for your data source in the Data Source Name text box, and enter a description of the data source in the Description text box.

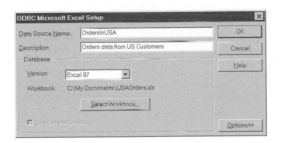

**FIG. 7.35**  Configuring a new Excel ODBC data source.

9. Click Select Workbook to display the Select Workbook dialog, shown in Figure 7.36. The Select Workbook dialog is a Windows 3.x-style file opening dialog. If needed, use the Drives and Directories lists to navigate to the correct folder in which your workbook is stored and select its name in the Database Name list. Click OK; Access closes the Select Workbook dialog and adds the new data source to the list in the Select Data Source dialog (refer to Figure 7.31).

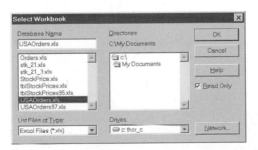

**FIG. 7.36**  Choosing the workbook for the new data source in the Select Workbook dialog.

Learning Fundamentals

10. Select your new data source in the Select Data Source dialog's list (refer to Figure 7.31) and then click OK. Access opens the Link Tables dialog (see Figure 7.37).

11. The Link Tables dialog lists the named data ranges and worksheets in the workbook. Click a worksheet or range name to select it. After you select all the worksheets or ranges that you want to link, click OK. Access closes the Link Tables dialog, and displays the Select Unique Record Identifier dialog (see Figure 7.38).

**FIG. 7.37**   Selecting the worksheet or named range to link to your database.

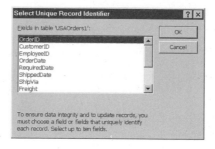

**FIG. 7.38**   Selecting a field in the linked table to create a primary key for the linked spreadsheet.

12. If you want to be able to update the data in the ODBC-linked worksheet, you must select a field (or combination of fields) that creates a unique record identification for each row in the worksheet—essentially, you create a primary key for the linked table. To select a field, click it with the mouse.

13. After you are satisfied with your key field selection, click OK. At this point, Access formulates the SQL query to establish indexes for the linked worksheet and analyzes the data in the worksheet. Depending on the outcome of this analysis, Access either immediately links the worksheet, or invokes the Link Spreadsheet Wizard.

    Using the Link Spreadsheet Wizard is the same as using the Import Spreadsheet Wizard described in the preceding section of this chapter, except that Access doesn't allow you to edit the field names it assigns to the linked data.

14. Your linked worksheet table appears in the Database window (with the ODBC globe turned to display Africa), as shown in Figure 7.39.

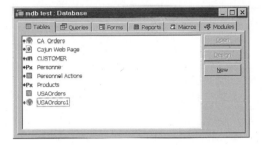

**FIG. 7.39**    Identifying tables linked with ODBC drivers by the globe icon.

Click the Open button of the Database window to display your linked worksheet. The look of the worksheet as a linked table is identical to a table imported from a worksheet with one major difference—you cannot update a linked worksheet. When you link a table to an Access database by using the ODBC API and the Microsoft ODBC drivers, you can update the table only if the table has a designated primary-key field. (The linked worksheet table is represented by a read-only `Recordset` object of the `Snapshot` type.)

> **Note**
>
> Some third-party ODBC drivers, such as the Intersolve ODBC drivers in the ODBC Driver Pack, have an option that enables you to edit Excel worksheet and text files that you link to Access tables. For more information, see Chapter 26, "Connecting to Client/Server Databases."

# Importing Text Files

If the data you want to import into an Access table was developed in a word processor, database, or other application that cannot export the data as a .dbf, .wk?, or .xls file, you need to create a text file in one of the text formats supported by Access. (A *text file* is a file with data consisting of characters that you can read with a text editor, such as Windows Notepad or the DOS Edit.com text editor.) Most DOS- and Windows-compatible data files created from data in mainframe computers and files converted from nine-track magnetic tapes are text files, and Access imports these files in various formats.

Access refers to the characters that separate fields as *delimiters* or *separators*. In this book, the term *delimiter* refers to characters that identify the end of a field; the term *text identifiers* refers to the single and double quotation marks that you can use to distinguish text from numeric data.

> **Note**
>
> EBCDIC (*Extended Binary-Coded-Decimal Interchange Code*) is a proprietary format used by IBM to encode data stored on nine-track tape and other data interchange media. EBCDIC is similar to the
>
> (continues)

(continued)

ANSI (American National Standards Institute) and ASCII (American Standard Code for Information Interchange) codes. You need to convert EBCDIC-encoded data to ANSI or ASCII code before you can import the data into an Access table. Nine-track tape drives designed for PC applications and service bureaus who provide tape-to-disk conversion services handle the EBCDIC-ASCII conversion. The printable (text) characters with values 32 through 127 are the same in ANSI and ASCII, so conversion from ASCII to ANSI, the character set used by Windows and Access, is seldom necessary.

Table 7.2 details the formats that Access supports.

| Table 7.2   Text File Formats Supported by Access 97 | |
| --- | --- |
| **Format** | **Description** |
| Comma-delimited text files (also called *CSV* [Comma-Separated Value] files) | Commas separate (delimit) fields. The newline pair, carriage return (ASCII character 13), and line feed (ASCII character 10) separate records. Some applications enclose all values within double quotation marks; this format often is called *mail-merge* format. Other applications enclose only text (strings) in quotation marks to differentiate between text and numeric values, the standard format for files created by the xBase command, COPY TO FILENAME DELIMITED. |
| Tab-delimited text files (also called ASCII files) | These files treat all values as text and separate fields with tabs. Records are separated by newline pairs. Most word-processing applications use this format to export tabular text. |
| Space-delimited files | Access can use spaces to separate fields in a line of text. The use of spaces as delimiter characters is uncommon because it can cause what should be single fields, such as names and addresses, to be divided inconsistently into different fields. |
| Fixed-width text files | Access separates (parses) the individual records into fields based on the position of the data items in a line of text. Newline pairs separate records; every record must have exactly the same length. Spaces pad the fields to a specified fixed width. Using spaces to specify field width is the most common format for data exported by mainframes and minicomputers on nine-track tape. |

## Using the Text Import Wizard

To import any of the text file types listed in Table 7.2, you follow a procedure similar to the procedure for importing any external data into Access. To import a text file, follow these steps:

1. Open the database into which you want to import the text file and make the Database window active, if necessary.

2. Choose File, Get External Data, Import. Access displays the Import dialog.

3. In the Import dialog, select Text Files (*.txt, *.csv, *.tab, *.asc) in the Files of Type drop-down list. Use the Look In drop-down list to select the folder that contains the text file you want to import, and double-click the text file's name. Access now starts the Text Import Wizard (see Figure 7.40).

**4.** Select the Delimited option to import a delimited text file, or select the Fixed Width option to import a fixed-width text file. The Text Import Wizard displays a sample of the text file's contents in the lower portion of the dialog to help you determine the correct file type. Figure 7.40 shows a comma-delimited text file being imported. Click Next to proceed to the next step in the Text Import Wizard. If you selected Delimited as the file type, the Text Import Wizard displays the dialog shown in Figure 7.41; if you selected the Fixed Width option, the wizard displays the dialog in Figure 7.42.

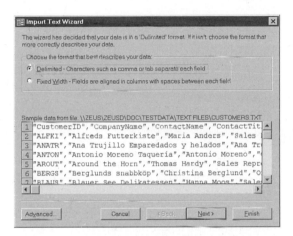

**FIG. 7.40**   Choosing whether the text file you're importing is delimited or fixed-width text.

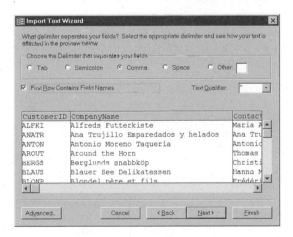

**FIG. 7.41**   The second step of the Text Import Wizard for delimited text files.

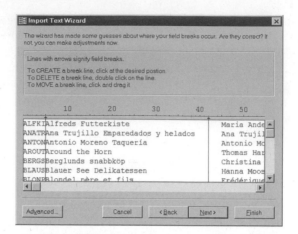

**FIG. 7.42**    The second step of the Text Import Wizard for fixed-width text files.

> **Note**
>
> In almost every case, you will select the Delimited option. Use the Delimited option for comma-delimited, tab-delimited, and all other types of delimited text files. Use fixed-width for space-delimited text files and also text files actually formatted as fixed-width.

5. If you're importing a fixed-width text file, skip to step 6. Otherwise, select the delimiter character that separates fields in the table (most delimited files use the default comma separator). If the text file you're importing uses a text qualifier other than the double quote, enter it in the Text Qualifier text box. If the first line in the text file contains field names (such as the column headings in a spreadsheet file), select the First Row Contains Field Names check box. Click Next to move to the next step of the Text Import Wizard.

6. If you're importing a delimited text file, skip to step 7. In a fixed-width text file, the Text Import Wizard analyzes the columns and makes an approximation about where the field breaks lie. Scan through the sample data at the bottom of the dialog; if the field breaks aren't in the right place, there are too many field breaks, or there aren't enough field breaks. You can add, delete, or move the field breaks that the Text Import Wizard suggests. To move a field break, drag it with the mouse. To remove a field break, double-click it. To add a field break, click at the location where you want the field break added. When you're satisfied with the field break arrangement, click Next to continue with the Text Import Wizard.

7. The Text Import Wizard now displays the dialog shown in Figure 7.43. Choose the In a New Table option to create a new Access table for the imported text file. Choose the In an Existing Table option to add the data in the text file to an existing database table, then select the table to which you want the data added in the accompanying drop-down list. Click Next to continue with the next step in the Text Import Wizard. (If you selected the In an Existing Table option, the Text Import Wizard skips directly to its final step, step 10 of this procedure.)

## Caution

Access matches fields from left to right when you import a text file into an existing table. You must make sure that the data types of the fields in the imported text file match those in the Access table; otherwise, the added data values aren't inserted into the correct fields. In most cases, you end up with many import errors in the Import Errors table. If you're not absolutely certain that the format of your input data matches the format of the desired table exactly, you can choose the In a New Table option, and then place your data in the existing table with an Append query, as discussed in Chapter 11, "Using Action Queries."

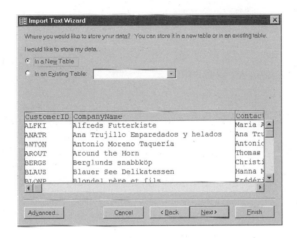

**FIG. 7.43**  Choosing whether to create a new table, or add the imported text data to an existing table.

8. The Text Import Wizard now displays the dialog shown in Figure 7.44. The Text Import Wizard enables you to edit field names, choose whether and what kind of index to use for each field, and to adjust each field's data type. To set the options for each field, click the field column at the bottom of the dialog to select it; you then may edit the field name, select an index method in the Indexed drop-down list, and select the data type for the field in the Data Type drop-down list. Select the Do Not Import Field (Skip) check box if you don't want to import the select field column. When you're satisfied with your field settings, click Next.

9. Now the Text Import Wizard displays the dialog in Figure 7.45. Choose the appropriate option for the primary keys you want—whether to allow Access to add a new field with an automatically generated primary key, select an existing field to use as a primary key, or import the table without a primary key. After selecting the primary key options, click Next.

10. The Text Import Wizard now displays its final dialog, shown in Figure 7.46. You now must enter the name for the new imported table. The Text Import Wizard displays this dialog even if you chose to import the text file into an existing table. Access enters either a default table name that is the same as the original name of

the text file or the table name you selected for importing the data into. Edit the table name, or type a different table name, if you want. Click Finish to import the text file.

The Text Import Wizard imports the text file, and displays a success message. As with other import operations, Access creates an Import Errors table to document any errors that occurred during the import process, and displays a message informing you that errors occurred.

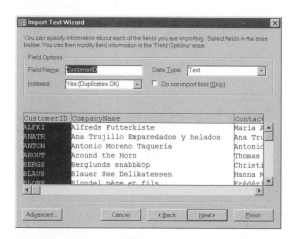

**FIG. 7.44**    Editing field names and selecting the index type and the data types for fields.

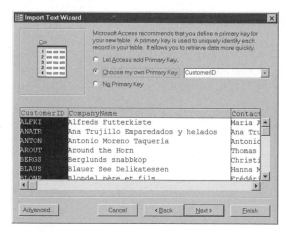

**FIG. 7.45**    Selecting a primary key for the imported text data.

The specific values you should select for field delimiters and text qualifiers are described in following sections, along with some tips on importing fixed-width text files.

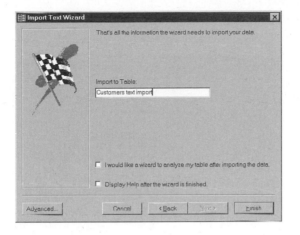

**FIG. 7.46**  Giving the new table a name in the Text Import Wizard's final dialog.

### The Text Import Wizard Advanced Options

Occasionally, you may find that you import text data from the same text file more than once, or that you have several text files that all have the same format. A typical situation in many corporations is that data from the company's mainframe computer system is provided to desktop computer users in the form of a text file report. Frequently, reports are delivered over the network to users in a text file, using the same name for the text file each time. You can use the Text Import Wizard's advanced options to configure Access to import a text file, and save these options so that you don't have to go through every step in the wizard every time you import the text file.

Every step of the Text Import Wizard has an Advanced button. Clicking this button displays a special dialog that shows all the Text Import Wizard settings in a single dialog and allows you to select a few options, such as date formatting, that don't appear in the regular Text Import Wizard dialogs. If you select the Delimited option, the Advanced dialog has the options and field grid shown in Figure 7.47. If you select the Fixed-Width option, the Advanced dialog has the options and field grid shown in Figure 7.48.

> **Tip**
>
> For text files you intend to import only once, it's much easier to import the file by going step-by-step through the Text Import Wizard.

The following list summarizes the options you can select in the Advanced dialog:

- *File Format.* Use these option buttons to choose which type of text file format you're importing: Delimited, or Fixed Width. Depending on the file format you select, the specific options available to you change.

- *Field Delimiter.* Use this drop-down list to select the symbol that delimits fields in the text file. This option is disabled for fixed-width text files.

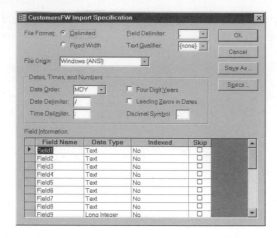

**FIG. 7.47** The Advanced options for delimited text files.

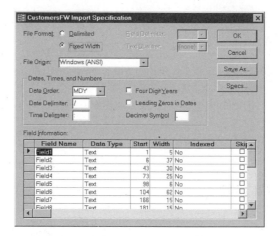

**FIG. 7.48** The Advanced options for fixed-width text files.

- *Text Qualifier.* Use this drop-down list to select the symbol that marks the beginning and end of text strings in the text file. This option is disabled for fixed-width text files.

- *File Origin.* Select the character set used for the text file in this drop-down list. If you're importing a text file that originated on a Macintosh computer, for example, select Macintosh in this list.

- *Date Order.* If the data in the text file uses a European or other date format that differs from the month-day-year format typical in the United States, select the appropriate date order in the Date Order drop-down list.

■ *Date Delimiter* and *Time Delimiter*. Type the symbol used to separate the month, day, and year in a date in the Date Delimiter text box, and type the symbol used to separate hours, minutes, and seconds in the Time Delimiter text box. For example, in the United States, the Date Delimiter is the slash (/) character, and the Time Delimiter is the colon (:).

■ *Four Digit Years*. Mark this check box if the dates in the text file use four digits for the year, such as 8/28/1997.

■ *Leading Zeroes in Dates*. Mark this check box if the dates in the text file have leading zeroes, such as 08/09/97.

■ *Decimal Symbol*. Type the symbol used for the decimal separator in numeric values in the text box. In the United States, the decimal symbol is the period (.), but many European nations use a comma (,).

■ *Field Information*. The appearance of this grid varies, depending on the file format that you select. For a delimited text file, the Field Information grid allows you to edit field names, select the field's data type and indexing, and specify whether to skip the field in importing (refer to Figure 7.47). For a fixed-width text file, the Field Information grid allows you to perform the same operations, but adds specifications for the starting column and width of each field (refer to Figure 7.48).

■ *Save As*. Click this button to display the Save Import/Export Specification dialog. By entering a name for the specification and clicking OK, you can save the file import settings for later use.

■ *Specs*. Click this button to display the Load Import/Export Specification dialog. Select a previously saved specification and click OK to use import settings that you defined previously.

The following sections on using delimited and fixed-width text files discuss the application of some of these Advanced options in greater detail.

### Using Delimited Text Files

Delimited files can accept a wide variety of field- and record-delimiting characters. The native format (used by files created within WordPerfect) of WordPerfect secondary merge files, for example, uses control characters to separate fields and records. Access provides commas, tabs, and spaces as standard field delimiters. You can type any printable character, such as an asterisk or a dollar sign, in the text box as a delimiter (refer to Figure 7.41). Because spaces and other special-character delimiting are seldom used, only comma-delimited (.csv) and tab-delimited files are presented in this chapter.

Word-processing applications use both commas and tabs as delimiters in the mail-merge files that they or other applications create for personalized documents. The newline pair is universally used to indicate the end of a record in mail-merge files; a record always consists of a single line of text.

**Comma-Delimited Text Files Without Text-Identifier Characters.** Comma-delimited files come in two styles: with or without quotation marks surrounding text fields. The quotation marks, usually the standard double quotation marks ("), identify the fields within them as having the Text data type. Fields without quotation marks are processed as numeric values if they contain numbers only. Not all applications offer this capability; .csv files, for example, exported by Excel don't enclose text within quotation marks. Figure 7.49 shows a typical Excel .csv file opened in the Windows Notepad applet.

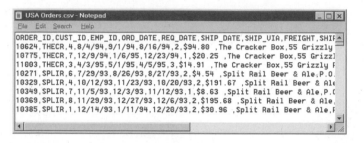

**FIG. 7.49**   A .csv text file exported by Excel, displayed in Windows Notepad.

> **Note**
>
> Using Notepad to view files that fit within its 60K file-size limitation is a quick way to determine the type of text file with which you are dealing. If the file is longer than 60K, you can use Windows WordPad to view the file. Make sure, however, that you do not save the file as a .doc file after you view or edit it. If you used WordPad to edit the file, choose File, Save As and specify a text (.txt) file.

> **Caution**
>
> If you export the Orders table from Northwind.mdb to Excel, and then use Excel to create an Orders.csv file and import the file into an Access table, you may receive an extraordinary number of errors. Most of these errors are due to a mixture of numeric values for United States ZIP codes and alphanumeric values used for Canadian, U.K., and European postal codes.
>
> The first data cell in the Postal Code column is a number, so the Access import procedure determines that the field should have the Number field data type. Therefore, mixed value fields (letters and numbers) cause import errors. A wise policy is to not import delimited text files without text-identification characters to Access tables.

**Comma-Delimited Text Files with Text-Identifier Characters.** The default delimited text file type of dBASE, named .sdf for Standard Data Format, created by the COPY TO FILENAME DELIMITED command, creates comma-delimited files with text fields surrounded by double quotation marks. (Date and Numeric field types do not have quotation marks.) This type of delimited file is standard in many other database systems, as well as project and personal information management applications. Figure 7.50 shows an example of a delimited text file that contains text qualifiers.

> **Note**
>
> When you create a DOS dBASE III+ file from an Access file, Access translates characters with ANSI values 128 through 255 to the PC-8 character set used by character-based DOS and OS/2 applications. Letters with diacriticals and special characters of Scandinavian and romanized Slavic languages do not have the same values in the PC-8. These letters and characters appear on-screen as black rectangles because the PC-8 values do not correspond to printable ANSI values. For text files that don't use the Windows ANSI character set, use the Text Import Wizard's advanced options to select the appropriate character set.

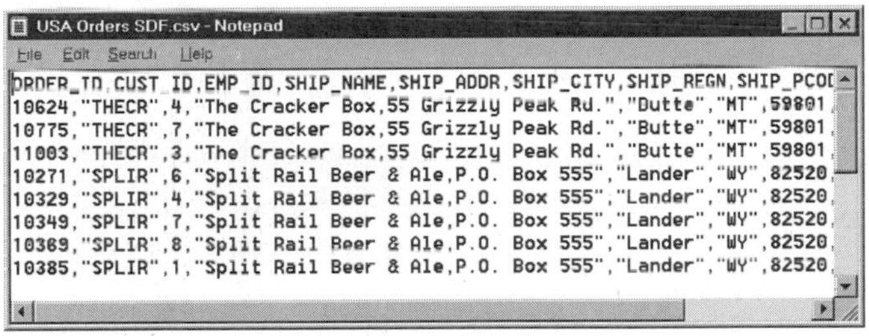

```
USA Orders SDF.csv - Notepad                    _ □ ×
File  Edit  Search  Help
ORDER_ID,CUST_ID,EMP_ID,SHIP_NAME,SHIP_ADDR,SHIP_CITY,SHIP_REGN,SHIP_PCO
10624,"THECR",4,"The Cracker Box,55 Grizzly Peak Rd.","Butte","MT",59801
10775,"THECR",7,"The Cracker Box,55 Grizzly Peak Rd.","Butte","MT",59801
11003,"THECR",3,"The Cracker Box,55 Grizzly Peak Rd.","Butte","MT",59801
10271,"SPLIR",6,"Split Rail Beer & Ale,P.O. Box 555","Lander","WY",82520
10329,"SPLIR",4,"Split Rail Beer & Ale,P.O. Box 555","Lander","WY",82520
10349,"SPLIR",7,"Split Rail Beer & Ale,P.O. Box 555","Lander","WY",82520
10369,"SPLIR",8,"Split Rail Beer & Ale,P.O. Box 555","Lander","WY",82520
10385,"SPLIR",1,"Split Rail Beer & Ale,P.O. Box 555","Lander","WY",82520
```

**FIG. 7.50**   A dBASE .sdf file displayed in Windows Notepad.

**Tab-Delimited Text Files.** Word-processing applications often use tab characters to separate fields in mail-merge files. These tab characters usually define the fields of tables when you convert conventional text to tabular format (and vice versa) in word processors such as Word 97. Tab-delimited text files rarely use text-qualifier characters. When exporting tab-delimited text files (described in a following section of this chapter), Access adds double quotation marks as text-identifier characters so that Word doesn't interpret embedded newline pairs (carriage return and line feed, or CR/LF) in text fields as the end of the record. (Allowing embedded newline pairs in text fields isn't a recommended database design practice.)

Many organizations acquire RDBMSs because the amount of their data is too large for their word-processing application to maintain mailing lists for direct-mail advertising and other promotional and fundraising purposes. RDBMSs also enable you to create specialized merge data files for specific types of customers, ranges of ZIP codes, and other parameters you select.

Fortunately, Access has a simple process for converting the merge data files used by most word processors to text files that can be imported and maintained by an Access database application. In Word 97, for example, you simply open the merge data file in whatever format you use (usually the native .doc) and save the document in Text Only (.txt) format under a different file name. WordPerfect 5+ (using CONVERT.EXE) and WordPerfect for Windows offer a variety of export formats for their secondary merge files. Unless you have a specific file type in mind, select the tab-delimited format for these files.

### Handling Fixed-Width Text Files

If you have a choice of text file formats for the data you plan to import into Access, avoid using fixed-width text files by choosing a delimited file format. If you are importing data created by a mainframe or minicomputer, however, the data probably is in fixed-width format. In a fixed-width text file, you must name the fields, rather than relying on the first line of the text file to provide names for you. Fixed-width text files seldom come with a field name header in the first line.

A fixed-width text file resembles the file in Figure 7.51. Fixed-width text files often contain more spaces than data characters. In a tab-delimited file, the spaces between fields aren't included in the file itself, but are added by the text editor when tab characters (ASCII or ANSI character 9) are encountered. In a fixed-width file, each space is represented by ASCII or ANSI character 32.

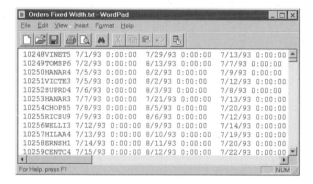

**FIG. 7.51**    Padding fixed-width records to the same length with spaces.

---

### Note

The fields of fixed-width text files often run together; the first four fields of the Orders Fixed Width.txt file shown in Figure 7.51 are Order ID (five digits), Customer ID (four letters), Employee ID (one digit), and Order Date (16 characters). The Order Date field is padded with spaces to a width of 16 characters. The appearance of the data in Figure 7.51 is typical of COBOL "text dumps" from mainframe and minicomputer tables. If you have the COBOL file description for the fixed-width table, it's far easier to complete the import specification.

---

### Troubleshooting

*When importing tables created from fixed-width text files, a large number of errors occur.*

You probably miscalculated one or more of the starting positions of a field. Locate the first field name with a problem; the names following it usually have problems, too. Close all open tables. From the Database window, select the table you imported and press the Delete key. If you have an Import Errors table, delete it, too. You cannot delete an open table. Perform the importation process again, and reposition the field breaks in the Text Import Wizard. Remember that Access only analyzes the first 20 lines of the text file, so its guesses about where to position the field breaks may be incorrect, and may not allow enough room for the actual width of a field.

### Appending Text Data to an Existing Table

If the data you import is provided on a floppy disk, you may need several disks to store the data. Fixed-width text files usually require more floppy disks because in most cases, they are derived from data on mini- and mainframe computers, and the fixed-width format is quite inefficient. If you ever imported multiple-disk data into dBASE files, for example, you probably learned that you must concatenate all the files on your hard disk into one large text file. You concatenate files by using the DOS `COPY file1+file2 file3` command or by appending each file to a separate dBASE file and then appending the remaining dBASE files to the file created from the first disk. This process is very tedious.

Access enables you to append data from text files to an existing table. Besides simplifying the process described in the preceding paragraph, you can update an imported file with new text data by appending it directly from the source text file—rather than by creating a new Access table—and then appending the new table to the existing one.

You can append a text file to an existing table by following these steps:

1. Make a backup copy of your table in the same database or another database, in case an error occurs during the importing operation.

2. Choose File, Get External Data, Import, and select a text file as though you are going to import it to a new table.

3. Make sure that you select the In an Existing Table option and specify a table name in step 3 of the Text Import Wizard (refer to Figure 7.43).

4. If you used the Advanced button to create and save an import specification, click Advanced to display the advanced options dialog, and then click Specs to load the previously saved import specification.

5. Proceed with the importation process as you would for any other text file.

At the end of the appending process, a message box appears. The Import Errors table displays any errors made.

> **Note**
>
> Maintaining a backup copy of the table to which you are appending files is important. If you have a problem with field delimiters or field lengths, or accidentally select the wrong import specification for the file, you can end up with one error for each appended record. Then, if you do not have a backup file, you must delete the appended records and start over. To use a backup table file, close and delete the damaged table. Then choose Edit, Rename to change the name of the backup table to the name of the damaged table.

# Using the Clipboard to Import Data

If another Windows application generates the data you want to import, you can use the Windows Clipboard to transfer the data without creating a file. This technique is useful for making corrections to a single record with many fields or for appending new records to a table. This process requires a table with the proper field structure so that you can paste the data copied to the Clipboard into the other application. Pasting rows from an Excel spreadsheet, for example, requires a table with fields containing data types that correspond to those of each column that you copy to the Clipboard. Other Windows applications that can copy tabular data to the Clipboard use similar techniques.

### Pasting New Records to a Table

To import data from the Clipboard, and then append the data to an existing table or table structure, use the following procedure:

1. Open the application you are using to copy the data to the Clipboard—in this case, Microsoft Excel. Then, open the file that contains the data.

2. Select the range to be appended to the table (see Figure 7.52). The Excel columns you select must start with the column that corresponds to the first field of your Access table. You do not, however, need to copy all the columns that correspond to fields in your table. Access supplies blank values in the columns of your appended records that are not included in your Excel range. Remember that if any of the columns you select contain formulas, the values must be frozen.

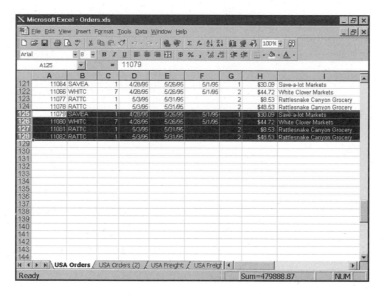

**FIG. 7.52** Selecting cells in Excel to be appended to an Access table by copying to the Clipboard.

3. To copy the selected cells to the Clipboard, press Ctrl+C or choose Edit, Copy.

4. Launch Access (if necessary), and open the table to which you are appending the records in Datasheet view.

5. Choose Edit, Paste Append in Access. If no errors occur during the pasting process, a message box reports how many new records you are about to add (see Figure

7.53). Click Yes. The records are appended to the bottom of your Access table (see Figure 7.54). Choose <u>R</u>ecords, <u>R</u>emove Filter/Sort to place the appended records in the correct order.

---

**Note**

The fields you add to a table by using Paste Append must correspond (in left to right order) to the fields in the table you are pasting the data into. You cannot, therefore, Paste Append records into a table that has an AutoNumber field, unless the records you are appending have already been assigned unique numeric values greater than the highest AutoNumber value currently existing in the table you are appending the records to. Otherwise, the fields of the pasted data don't match the left to right order of the fields in the table you're pasting into, and all of the pasted records will end up in the Paste Errors table.

---

**FIG. 7.53**  The message that appears when Access successfully appends records pasted from the Clipboard.

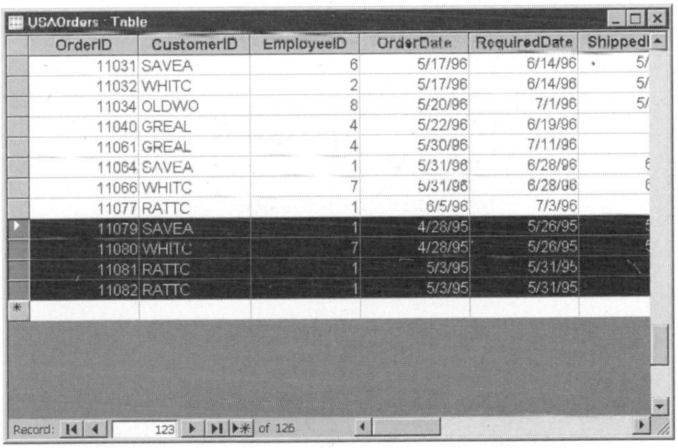

| OrderID | CustomerID | EmployeeID | OrderDate | RequiredDate | ShippedI |
|---------|-----------|-----------|-----------|-------------|----------|
| 11031 | SAVEA | 6 | 5/17/96 | 6/14/96 | 5/ |
| 11032 | WHITC | 2 | 5/17/96 | 6/14/96 | 5/ |
| 11034 | OLDWO | 8 | 5/20/96 | 7/1/96 | 5/ |
| 11040 | GREAL | 4 | 5/22/96 | 6/19/96 | |
| 11061 | GREAL | 4 | 5/30/96 | 7/11/96 | |
| 11064 | SAVEA | 1 | 5/31/96 | 6/28/96 | 6 |
| 11066 | WHITC | 7 | 5/31/96 | 6/28/96 | 6 |
| 11077 | RATTC | 1 | 6/5/96 | 7/3/96 | |
| 11079 | SAVEA | 1 | 4/28/95 | 5/26/95 | 5 |
| 11080 | WHITC | 7 | 4/28/95 | 5/26/95 | 6 |
| 11081 | RATTC | 1 | 5/3/95 | 5/31/95 | |
| 11082 | RATTC | 1 | 5/3/95 | 5/31/95 | |

Record: 123 of 126

**FIG. 7.54**  Records appended from the Clipboard to an Access table.

---

**Troubleshooting**

*Paste errors occur when pasting spreadsheet cells into a table.*

Errors usually occur during the Paste/Append process for one of two reasons—the data types in the Excel cells don't match those in the corresponding fields of your Access table, or you attempted to

*(continues)*

(continued)

paste records with data that duplicates information in key fields of the table. Both types of errors result in Access creating a Paste Errors table that contains information on the records with the errors. The Paste Errors table for field-type mismatches is similar in purpose and appearance to the Import Errors table described previously in this chapter.

Errors caused by duplicate primary-key violations result in the following series of cascading message boxes:

1. Figure 7.55 shows the first message you receive that indicates a primary-key violation. Access does not offer a Cancel option; therefore, you must click OK.

2. Next, a message box appears enabling you to suppress further error messages (see Figure 7.56). To cancel the append operation, click Cancel. Otherwise, click Yes to try to paste the remaining records without reporting further errors. If you want to see which errors occur as they are encountered, click No.

**FIG. 7.55**  The message informing you that a pasted record duplicates a primary key value.

**FIG. 7.56**  Choosing whether to view error messages for each pasted record.

3. Finally, a message box reports where the records that couldn't be pasted were placed (see Figure 7.57). Click OK.

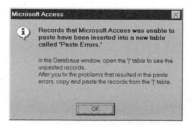

**FIG. 7.57**  The message reporting that some records could not be pasted.

Figure 7.58 illustrates the result of this Pandora's box of messages. The set of four records copied to the Clipboard from Excel had all been previously pasted into the Access table; all four records duplicated key-field values in the existing table. Access pasted records without problems into the table and inserted the four records with duplicate key values into a Paste Errors table.

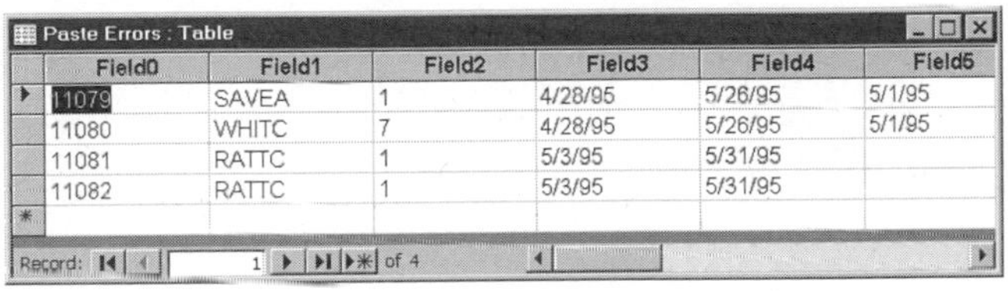

Paste Errors : Table

| Field0 | Field1 | Field2 | Field3 | Field4 | Field5 |
|---|---|---|---|---|---|
| 11079 | SAVEA | 1 | 4/28/95 | 5/26/95 | 5/1/95 |
| 11080 | WHITC | 7 | 4/28/95 | 5/26/95 | 5/1/95 |
| 11081 | RATTC | 1 | 5/3/95 | 5/31/95 | |
| 11082 | RATTC | 1 | 5/3/95 | 5/31/95 | |

Record: 1 of 4

**FIG. 7.58** The Paste Errors table showing records that Access couldn't paste from the Clipboard.

If you specified one or more primary-key fields for your table, records that duplicate key field values are not appended. Tables without primary-key fields do not preclude adding duplicate records. The capability to index a nonkey field with the condition, "no duplicates allowed," is useful when you make new entries into a spreadsheet or word-processing document and you want to append the new entries as records to a table. You preserve the uniqueness of the records by preventing the addition of records that duplicate records already in your table.

**Note**

When pasting or importing large numbers of records to a table, you must specify primary-key fields or a no-duplicates-allowed index for fields that later may become the primary key before you import any data. If you import the data before you create the primary-key fields index, you might find many duplicate records in the table. Then, when Access tries to create a no-duplicates index on the key fields, you see the message, `Can't have duplicate key`. You must manually review all the added records for duplicates because Access doesn't create an Errors table in this case.

If, however, the data you are importing contains redundant information that you ultimately will remove to one or more secondary tables, you must import every record. Do not assign key fields or no-duplicates indexes in this case. The section, "Deleting Redundant Fields in Imported Tables," that follows in this chapter, discusses the requirement to import every record when records contain one-to-many relations.

**Tip**

If you do encounter the `Can't have duplicate key` error message when trying to establish a primary key, there is a quick way to find the duplicates. Open a new query and select the Find Duplicates Query Wizard. This Wizard creates a query that you can use to quickly find exactly where the duplicates are, without having to search record-by-record through your data.

### Replacing Records by Pasting from the Clipboard

You can replace existing records in an Access table by pasting data in the Clipboard over the records. This process is useful when you are updating records with data from another

Windows application. The data you paste must have a one-to-one column-to-field corre-spondence and must begin with the first field of the table. You need not, however, paste new data in all the fields. If no data is pasted in a field that is not included in the copied data's range, that field retains its original values.

To use data in the Clipboard to replace existing records in a table, follow this procedure:

1. Select and copy the data from the other application that you want to paste to the Clipboard, using the method previously described for appending records from Clipboard data.

   If you choose more than one row of data in Excel, for example, the rows must have a one-to-one correspondence with the records to be replaced in the Access table. The one-to-one correspondence is likely to occur only if the table is indexed and the source data you are copying is sorted in the same order as the index. You can paste only contiguous rows from Excel.

2. Open your Access table. To select the records to be replaced by the Clipboard data, click the selection button for a single record or drag the mouse across the buttons for multiple records.

   If you are replacing multiple records, the number of records you select must be equal to or exceed the number of rows you copied to the Clipboard. If the number of records selected is less than the number of rows, the remaining rows are ignored.

   If you are replacing records in a table with key fields or a no-duplicates index, the columns of the replacement data corresponding to the key or indexed fields of the table must match exactly the key fields of the selected records. Otherwise, you see the key duplication error message sequence.

3. Choose Edit, Paste in Access. In this case, rather than appending the records, the contents of the existing records are overwritten, and you see a dialog that tells you how many records will be replaced.

When you use Paste for a replacement record rather than Paste Append for a new record with an identical key field value, Access suppresses the key violation error messages.

---

**Note**

If you do not select one or more records to be replaced by the Pasting operation, and the caret is located within a data cell of one of your records or a data cell is selected, Access attempts to paste all the data in the Clipboard to this one cell, rather than to the records. If the data doesn't create a mismatch type error or exceed 255 characters (if the caret is in a Text field), you do not receive a warning message. If you notice unexpected data values in the cell, Access pasted all the data to a single cell. Press Esc before selecting another record; Access restores the original value of the data cell.

---

# Modifying Linked and Imported Tables

Access provides a great deal of flexibility in the presentation of the Datasheet view of tables. You can rearrange the sequence of fields in Datasheet view without changing the underlying structure of the database. You also can alter the Caption property of the fields to change the names of the field name buttons. Although you cannot modify the field names, field data types, or Field Length properties of linked tables, you can use the Format property to display the data in linked or imported tables in various ways, as described in the sections that follow.

### Restructuring the Presentation of Tables

The basic structure of the tables you link or import is controlled by the structure of the files from which the table was created. The original structure, unfortunately, may not be in the sequence you want to use for data entry. Database design, for example, often displays the key fields in a left-to-right sequence, starting with the first field. This sequence may not be the best sequence for entering data. You can change the order of the fields displayed by dragging and dropping the field name buttons of linked or imported tables to new locations, using the method described in Chapter 4, "Working with Access Databases and Tables."

◄◄  See "Rearranging the Sequence of Fields in a Table," p. 155

### Adding Fields to Tables with Imported Data

You can add fields to tables that use imported data. During the development of your database application, you may need to repeatedly import data into your table. Therefore, you should append new fields to the end of the field list in Design view rather than insert them between existing fields. The imported data fills the fields in the sequence of the rows in the field list, and the added fields contain null values. You then can rearrange the display position of the new fields in Datasheet view, as described in the preceding section.

### Changing Field Data Types of Imported Files

Access converts all numeric data within imported files to the Double data type. The following list contains recommendations for field data type changes for data imported from any type of source file:

- Use *Integer* or *Long Integer* field data types for numeric fields that do not require decimal values. Your database files consume less disk space, and your applications run faster.

- Change the data type of values that represent money to the data type, *Currency*, to eliminate rounding errors.

- Assign Field Length property values to text-type fields. You should assign Field Length values no greater than the longest text entry you expect to make. If you assign a Field Length value less than the number of characters in the field, characters in positions beyond the Field Length value are lost irretrievably.

Because Paradox versions prior to Paradox 4.x do not provide a memo field data type, you often can find comments in large, fixed-width alphanumeric fields. If you import Paradox files that contain fields of comments, you should convert the fields to memo fields unless you plan to export the data back to a Paradox 3.x file. (You cannot export a table that contains a memo-type field to Paradox 3.x files, although you can export tables with memo fields to Paradox 4.x and Paradox for Windows 5.)

### Adding or Modifying Other Field Properties

The following table includes properties of both linked and imported tables that you can change:

| Property | Description |
| --- | --- |
| Caption | Use to change the caption of the field name buttons when using linked files. You can assign any `FieldName` property to imported tables. |
| Decimal Places | Use to specify the number of decimal places to be displayed for numeric values other than Byte, Integer, and Long Integer. |
| Default Value | Default values are substituted for data elements missing in the imported or linked file. The default values, however, do not replace zeroes and blank strings that represent "no entry" in the fields of most PC database files. |
| Format | Use to create custom formats to display the data in the most readable form. |
| Validation Rule | Validation rules do not affect importing data; they affect only editing the data or appending new records in Access. You cannot use a validation rule to filter imported records. *Filtering*, in this case, means importing only records that meet the validation rule. |
| Validation Text | Prompts created from validation text assist data entry operators when they begin using a new table. |

### Deleting Redundant Fields in Imported Tables

The purpose of a relational database is to eliminate redundant data in tables. If you design a database that doesn't use data imported or linked from existing databases, you can eliminate data redundancy by following the normalization rules of relational database design described in Chapter 23, "Exploring Relational Database Design and Implementation."

When you link files, however, you are at the mercy of the database designer who originally created the files. Any redundant data the linked file contains is likely to remain a permanent characteristic of the file. Existing database structures are substantially inert; developers of applications that work usually are reluctant to make changes. Changes may introduce new problems that can later return to haunt the developers.

If you import table data from a file or append records by pasting from the Clipboard, you can eliminate data redundancy by restructuring the resulting tables. An Invoice table, for example, may contain one record for each invoice. When a customer makes more than one purchase, the customer information is duplicated in the invoice file for each purchase. In this situation, you need to create separate tables for customers and invoices.

The Customer table should contain one record per customer, with name and address information. The Invoice table should contain one record per customer with date, amount, and other information specific to the transaction.

Removing redundancy from existing tables by dividing them into two or more related tables is not a simple task, even if you use the Table Analyzer Wizard (accessed by choosing Tools, Analyze, Table). You must either manually (or with the help of the Table Analyzer) create a query that establishes the relationship between two tables that contain one record for each invoice based on a new primary-key field. Then, you delete the duplicate records from the Customer table. Fortunately, the Import Errors table can do much of the work; import the data into a new table with primary-key fields or a no-duplicate index on the customer name and address.

Another type of redundancy is the presence of fields in tables that have values calculated from other fields, either within the table or in the fields of related tables. Any field with values derived from combinations of values within the table or accessible in any other related table within the database or linked to the database contains redundant data. In this case, just remove the redundant field and perform the calculation with a query. Do not remove redundant fields, however, until you verify that your calculated values match those in the redundant field to be replaced.

You need to learn about queries and joining tables—the subject of the next four chapters—to know how to eliminate redundancy in imported tables. The point of this discussion is to let you know that you can perform much of the restructuring by using specialized Access operations and to caution you not to try to remove duplicate data from imported tables prematurely.

# Exporting Data from Access Tables

You can export data contained in Access tables in any format you can use to import data. The most common export operation with PC RDBMSs is the creation of mail-merge files, used with word-processing applications and spreadsheet files, for data analysis. In most cases, you might want to export the result of a query, enabling you to select specific records to export rather than the entire contents of a file. Exporting tables created from action queries is discussed in Chapter 11, "Using Action Queries."

▶▶  See "Joining Tables to Create Multitable Queries," p. 322

### Exporting Data Through the Windows Clipboard

If a Windows application is to use your exported data, the simplest method to export data is to copy the records you want to export to the Windows Clipboard, and then paste the data into the other application. You can copy specific groups of contiguous records to the Clipboard by using the techniques described in Chapter 5, "Entering, Editing, and Validating Data in Tables."

To create a merge data file from the Customers table of the Northwind sample database for use with Word, follow these steps:

1. Open the Northwind.mdb database.

2. Open the Customers table from the table list.

3. Select the records to copy by selecting the upper-left corner of the block with the F2 key, and then holding down the Shift key and using the arrow keys to define the records you want to copy to the Clipboard. Alternatively, you can select the area to copy by placing the cursor at the upper left corner of the block you want to copy; the cursor turns into a big plus symbol. Hold down the left mouse button and drag to the lower-right corner of the block. Datasheet view should look like the window in Figure 7.59. (If you want to select all fields of all records in the table, choose Edit, Select All Records.)

4. Press Ctrl+C or choose Edit, Copy to copy the selected records to the Clipboard.

5. Open Word and choose File, New to create a new document for your merge data file.

6. Press Ctrl+V or choose Edit, Paste to paste the records from the Clipboard into your new document. Access 97 pastes the records as a fully formatted table in Word, as illustrated by Figure 7.60. The column widths you select in Access are used to define the column widths of the Word table.

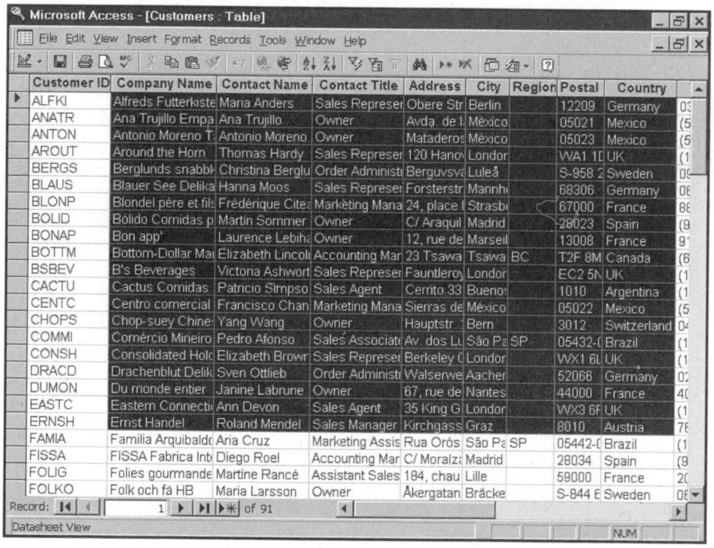

**FIG. 7.59** Selecting records in an Access table to copy to the Clipboard.

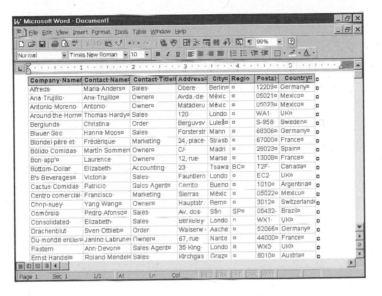

**FIG. 7.60**  Access data pasted into a Word document as a fully formatted table.

When you copy Access records to the Clipboard, the first line contains field names, no matter what group of records you select. If you append individual records or groups of records to those already pasted to a document in another application, you must manually remove the duplicated field names.

> **Note**
>
> The field names pasted into Word documents contain spaces. Spaces, however, are not allowed in the first (field names) row for merge data documents. Delete the spaces or replace them with underscores so that Word accepts the names. If you do not remove the spaces, you receive an error message when you try to use the document during the Merge operation.

### Exporting Data as a Text File

Exporting a table involves a sequence of operations similar to importing a file with the same format. To export a table as a comma-delimited file that you can use as a merge file with a wide variety of word processing applications, complete these steps:

1. Activate the Database window, display the Tables tab, and select the table you want to export.

2. Choose <u>F</u>ile, Save <u>A</u>s/Export. The Save As dialog appears (see Figure 7.61). Select the To an External File or Database option, and then click OK.

3. Access now displays the Save Table *Filename* In dialog (see Figure 7.62). Select Text Files in the Save As Type drop-down list (the title of the dialog changes to Save Table *Filename* As, as shown in Figure 7.62). Use the Save In drop-down list to select the drive and folder in which you want to store the exported file, enter a name for the exported file in the File Name text box, and then click Export.

**FIG. 7.61** Choosing whether to export a table to an external file.

4. Access starts the Text Export Wizard. Using the Text Export Wizard, including its advanced options, is the same as using the Text Import Wizard described previously, except that the end result is an external file instead of an Access table. (When exporting a text file, the Text Export Wizard doesn't have a step to edit field names, or select field data types; these options aren't relevant when exporting data.)

To finish exporting the text file, follow the procedures as if you were importing a text file. Figure 7.63 shows the exported Customers table from the Northwind.mdb database displayed by Windows Notepad.

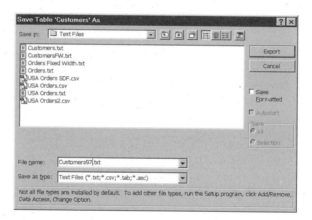

**FIG. 7.62** Starting the Text Export Wizard by saving a table as a text file.

> **Note**
>
> The two highlighted lines in Figure 7.63 are a single record from the Access table that was split into two text records during the export process. A newline pair is included in the Address field of the record for Consolidated Holdings. The purpose of the newline pair is to separate a single field into two lines—Berkeley Gardens and 12 Brewery. Use of newline pairs within fields causes many problems with exported files. As mentioned previously in this chapter, use of embedded newline pairs in text fields isn't good database design practice. Use two address fields if you need secondary address lines.

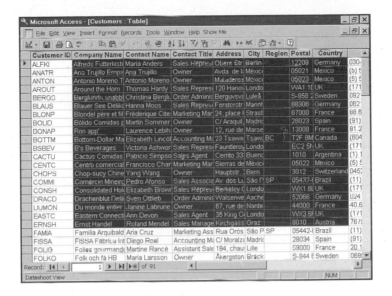

**FIG. 7.63**  A comma-delimited text file exported from the Customers table.

The records in files created by Access are exported in the order of the primary key. Any other order you may have created is ignored. If you do not assign primary-key fields, the records are exported in the sequence that you entered them into the table.

### Exporting Data in Other File Formats

In addition to text files, you can export data to any other file format that Access can import. Access supports export to the following file formats:

- Excel .xls files (versions 3.0 through 97)

- Lotus 1-2-3 and Symphony .WK?

- Rich-text format (.RTF) files for Microsoft Word and other Windows word processing applications

- Paradox for DOS 3.x, 4.x, and 5.0

- FoxPro 2.x and 3.0

- dBASE III/III+, IV, and 5

- Any format supported by an installed ODBC driver

> **Note**
>
> When you export a dBASE file in Access 97, Access creates .ndx files that correspond to the primary key and any additional indexes you may have created in Access. Exporting a Paradox .db file, however, does not create an associated .px file to accompany it. You must use Paradox to re-create any index files required for your application.

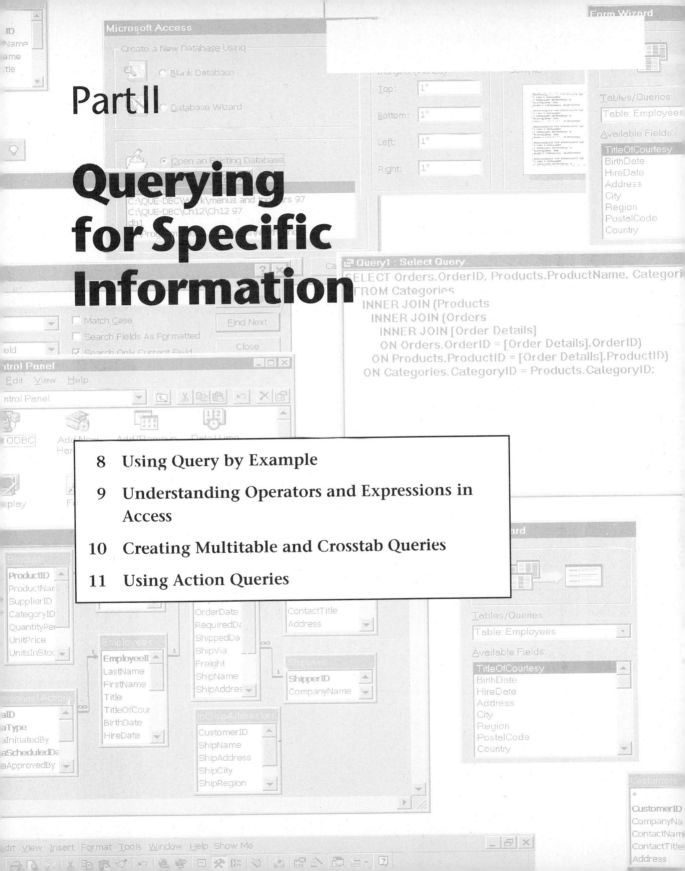

# Part II

# Querying for Specific Information

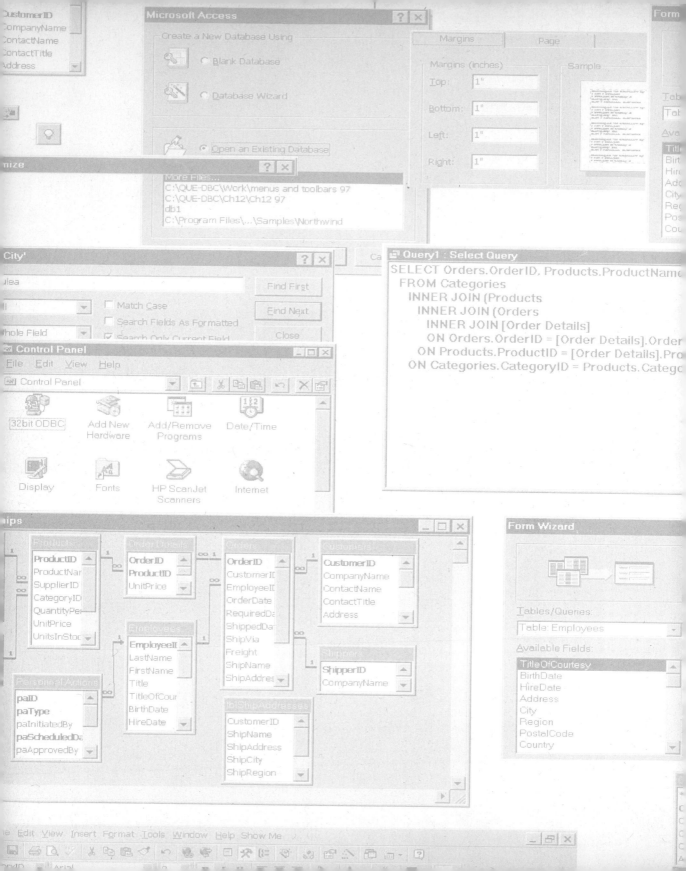

# Chapter 8

# Using Query by Example

Queries are essential tools in any database management system. You use queries to select records, update tables, and add new records to tables. Most often, you use queries to select specific groups of records that meet criteria you specify. You can also use queries to combine information from different tables, providing a unified view of related data items. In this chapter, you learn the basics of creating your own queries. You learn how to specify selection criteria in a query and use the results of your queries.

## Introducing Queries

Query by Example, usually abbreviated QBE, was originally developed to enable users of mainframe-computer database applications to find and display pieces of data (or collections of data) without having to know a computer language. Many database management systems eventually came to use QBE in one form or another. (In fact, dBASE, the first commercially successful PC database manager, used a variant of QBE for its dot-prompt commands.)

At a command prompt, for example, QBE users enter such statements as this:

```
LIST ALL lastnames LIKE Lin* WITH state IL IN us_hist
```

These are known as *give me an example of* statements. The QBE application program then searched the lastnames field of the us_hist table file for all names beginning with Lin. The program disregarded the remaining characters in the names and displayed only those records that met the lastname and state (IL) requirements.

As computer display terminals became more sophisticated, *graphical QBE* developed as the preferred method of creating queries. Graphical QBE displays the field names of one or more database tables as headers of a column. Users can type partial example statements, or *expressions*, in these columns to create a query. Because terminals capable of displaying actual graphics were a rarity when graphical QBE was developed, the standard 80-character by 25-line text mode was used. The term *graphical* is a misnomer, therefore, in today's world of truly graphical user environments like Windows. In the original version of graphical QBE, the preceding example statement might resemble the following display:

```
LASTNAME      FIRSTNAME      ADDRESS        CITY           STATE
Like LIN*                                                  IL
```

Fields corresponding to the columns in which no expressions are entered are not checked for compliance with the query.

After checking the designated fields and finding all matches within the searched file, the application displays those addresses containing matching values. The parts of each address appear in their respective columns, as in the following example:

```
LASTNAME      FIRSTNAME      ADDRESS        CITY           STATE
Lincoln       Abraham        123 Elm St.    Springfield    IL
Lincoln       Mary Todd      123 Elm St.    Springfield    IL
```

Learning to type query expressions in graphical QBE columns proved easier for most computer users than typing QBE expressions at a prompt. The user had to know the syntax of only a few expressions to create relatively complex queries. The use of graphical QBE was one feature that made Ansa Software's original Paradox RDBMS a success in the PC desktop RDBMS market, dominated at the time by dBASE II and dBASE III.

Microsoft Windows introduced a graphical user environment ideally suited to a truly graphical QBE database management system. Microsoft has taken full advantage of the wide range of graphical features incorporated in Windows 95 and Windows NT 4.0, as you see when you create your first true Access query.

# Creating Your First Real Query

Chapter 6, "Sorting, Finding, and Filtering Data in Tables," introduced the concepts of creating queries. You applied a sort order to tables and added record selection criteria to filters for data contained in tables. Access's Query Design window, however, gives you greater flexibility than the Filter window because it lets you choose the fields that appear in the query result set. You also can create more complex queries by joining primary and related tables.

This chapter explains the basics of QBE. You learn to create multitable queries in Chapter 10, "Creating Multitable and Crosstab Queries," after you learn the details of how to use operators and create expressions in Chapter 9, "Understanding Operators and Expressions in Access." Expressions often are used as criteria for more complex queries.

To devise a simple query that enables you to customize mailing lists for selected customers of Northwind Traders, for example, follow these steps:

1. Open the Northwind Traders database (filename Northwind.mdb in the \Program Files\Microsoft Office\Office\Samples folder). The Northwind Database window appears.

**2.** Click the arrow adjacent to the New Object button in the toolbar and choose New Query from the drop-down menu; alternatively, click the Query tab in the Database window and then click the New button. The New Query dialog appears (see Figure 8.1). This dialog enables you to select between creating a query yourself (Design view) or using one of the Query Wizards to design specialized queries. Select the Design View item and click OK to display the Query Design window.

The Show Table dialog is superimposed on the Query Design window, as shown in Figure 8.2. The tabbed lists in the Show Table dialog let you select from all existing tables, all queries, or a combination of all tables and queries. You can base a new query on one or more previously entered tables or queries. (The tables and queries listed in the Show Table list come with Access as samples for the Northwind Traders database.)

> **Note**
>
> If you select a table in the Tables page of the Database window, and then click the New Query toolbar button, Access 97 automatically places the selected table in the Query Design window, without displaying the Add Tables dialog described in step 2 of this procedure.

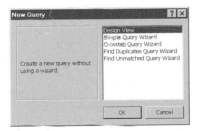

**FIG. 8.1**  The New Query dialog, in which you choose how you want to create a new query.

**FIG. 8.2**  Starting the design of a new query with the Show Table dialog.

**II**

**Querying for Information**

3. This example uses only tables in the query, so accept the default selection of Tables. Click (or use the down-arrow key to select) Customers in the Show Table list to select the Customers table, and then choose the Add button. Alternatively, double-click Customers to add a table to the query. You can use more than one table in a query by choosing another table name from the list and choosing Add again. This example, however, uses only one table. After selecting the tables that you want to use, choose Close. The Show Table dialog disappears.

The Field list for the Customers table appears at the left in the upper pane of the Query Design window, and a blank Query Design grid appears in the lower pane, as shown in Figure 8.3. The Field list displays all the names of the fields listed in the Customers table.

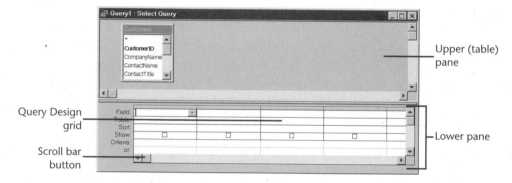

**FIG. 8.3**   The Field list box of the Customers table in a Query Design window.

By clicking the Query and New buttons in the Database window, you enter Access's Query Design view. By default, you create Select queries that return selected data from tables or the result set of other Select queries. Access assigns a default name, Query1, to the first query that you create (but have not yet saved) in this mode. You assign your own names to queries when you save them. If you create additional queries without saving the first query, Access assigns them the default names Query2, Query3, and so on, in sequence.

### Choosing Fields for Your Query

After you choose a table from the Show Table dialog, the next step is to decide which of the table's fields to include in your query. Because you plan to use this query to create a customer mailing list, you must include the fields that make up a personalized mailing address.

As this chapter's introduction explained, the first row of any graphical QBE query contains the names of each field involved in the query. (These field names also are called *field headers*.) The sample query that you are creating, therefore, must include in its first row the names of all the fields that constitute a mailing address.

To choose the fields that you want to include in the Query Design grid, follow these steps:

1. When you open the Query Design window, the caret is located in the Field row of the first column. Click the List Box button that appears in the right corner of the first column, or press F4, to open the Field Name list (see Figure 8.4).

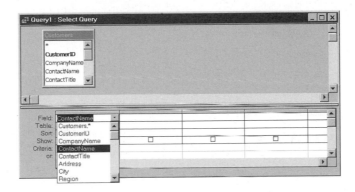

**FIG. 8.4**  Adding a field name to the Query Design grid.

2. Choose the ContactName field as the first field header of the query, or use the down-arrow key to highlight the name and press Enter. The Field list in the lower pane closes.

3. Move the caret to the second column by using the right arrow or Tab key. (Notice that the List Box button moves to the second column along with the caret.) Double- click CompanyName in the Customers Field list in the upper pane to add CompanyName as the second field of your query. Double-clicking entries in the upper pane's list is the second method that Access provides to add fields to a query.

   Access offers a third method of adding fields to your query: the drag-and-drop method. You can add the Address, City, and Region fields to columns 3–5, respectively, in one step by using the drag-and-drop method (see steps 4 and 5).

4. To use the drag-and-drop method of adding fields, you must first select the fields. In the Customers field list of the upper pane's Query Design window, click Address and hold the Shift or Ctrl key as you click City and Region. Alternatively, select Address with the down-arrow key, hold the Shift or Ctrl key, and press the down-arrow key twice more. You have selected the Address, City, and Region fields, as shown in Figure 8.5.

5. Position the mouse pointer over the selected fields and click the left mouse button. Your mouse pointer turns into a symbol representing the three selected field names. Drag the symbol for the three fields to the third column of your query's Field row, as shown in Figure 8.5, and release the left mouse button.

Access adds the three fields to your query, in sequence, starting with the column in which you drop the symbol. When the mouse pointer is in an area where you cannot drop the fields, it becomes the international Do Not Enter symbol shown in the upper pane of the Query Design window of Figure 8.5.

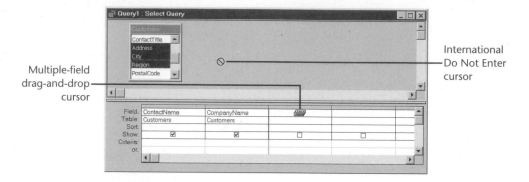

Multiple-field drag-and-drop cursor

International Do Not Enter cursor

**FIG. 8.5** Selecting multiple fields and using the drag-and-drop method to add fields to the Query Design grid.

6. The Query Design grid in the lower pane displays four columns (in the default width) in a normal Query Design window. This query uses seven fields, so you need to drag the edges of the Query Design window to increase the width of the grid's display to expose two additional empty fields. You can reduce the columns' width by dragging the divider of the grid's header bars to the left. Click the scroll-right button (on the horizontal scroll bar at the bottom of the window) twice to display two blank fields, or drag the scroll bar slider button to the right to expose empty fields as necessary.

7. Click the scroll-down button in the Customers field list to display the PostalCode and Country fields. Hold the Shift or Ctrl key and select PostalCode and Country. Drag the symbol for these two fields to the first empty field cell (column 6), and drop the two fields there. Your Query Design window appears similar to the one shown in Figure 8.6. (Notice that the check boxes in the Show row for the columns that contain a field name now are marked.)

> **Note**
>
> Most of the figures in this book are created with windows in *Normal* style, which occupies a portion of the display, rather than *Maximized* style, which occupies all the display. Normal style is used so that figures can be reproduced on a larger scale, which improves legibility.

8. Click the Query View button on the toolbar to enter Run mode. Expect a brief waiting period while Access processes your query on the Customers table. Alternatively, click the Run button on the toolbar to run your query against the Customers table.

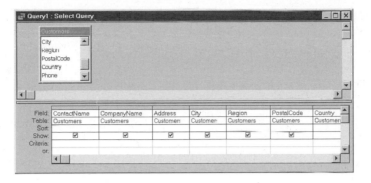

**FIG. 8.6**  The seven field names included in the new query.

Because you have not yet entered any selection criteria in the Criteria row of the Query Design grid, your query results in the Customers table displaying all records. These records appear in the order of the primary key index on the CustomerID field because you have not specified a sorting order in the Sort row of the Query Design grid. (The values in the CustomerID field are alphabetic codes derived from the Company Name field.) Figure 8.7 shows the result of your first query.

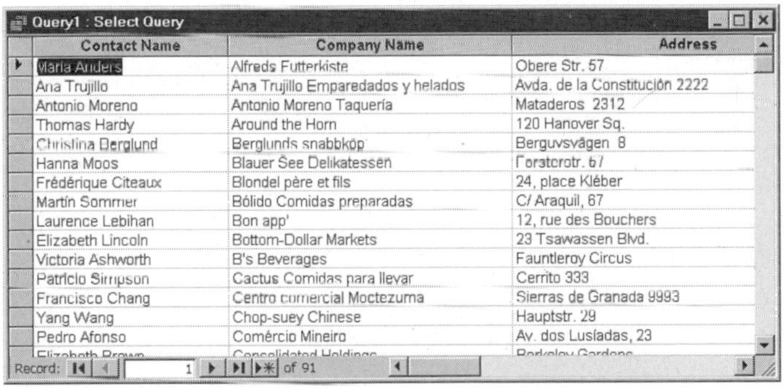

| Contact Name | Company Name | Address |
|---|---|---|
| Maria Anders | Alfreds Futterkiste | Obere Str. 57 |
| Ana Trujillo | Ana Trujillo Emparedados y helados | Avda. de la Constitución 2222 |
| Antonio Moreno | Antonio Moreno Taquería | Mataderos  2312 |
| Thomas Hardy | Around the Horn | 120 Hanover Sq. |
| Christina Berglund | Berglunds snabbköp | Berguvsvägen  8 |
| Hanna Moos | Blauer See Delikatessen | Forsterstr. 57 |
| Frédérique Citeaux | Blondel père et fils | 24, place Kléber |
| Martín Sommer | Bólido Comidas preparadas | C/ Araquil, 67 |
| Laurence Lebihan | Bon app' | 12, rue des Bouchers |
| Elizabeth Lincoln | Bottom-Dollar Markets | 23 Tsawassen Blvd. |
| Victoria Ashworth | B's Beverages | Fauntleroy Circus |
| Patricio Simpson | Cactus Comidas para llevar | Cerrito 333 |
| Francisco Chang | Centro comercial Moctezuma | Sierras de Granada 9993 |
| Yang Wang | Chop-suey Chinese | Hauptstr. 29 |
| Pedro Afonso | Comércio Mineiro | Av. dos Lusíadas, 23 |
| Elizabeth Brown | Consolidated Holdings | Berkeley Gardens |

Record: 1 of 91

**FIG. 8.7**  A list of all records contained in the Customers table.

> **Note**
>
> Many field names of tables in Access 2.0's NWIND.MDB sample database contained spaces. Most RDBMSs don't permit spaces in field names or table names. Starting with Access 95, field names in Northwind.mdb no longer include spaces. Access 97's Northwind.mdb uses the Caption property of table fields to alter (alias) the field headers of tables to add spaces where appropriate. For example, to alias the Customers table's CompanyName field, you set the Caption property's value to **Company Name**.

### Selecting Records by Criteria and Sorting the Display

The mailing for which you are creating a list with your sample query is to be sent to U.S. customers only, so you want to include in your query only those records that have USA in their Country fields. Selecting records based on the values of fields—that is, establishing the criteria for the records to be returned (displayed) by the query—is the very heart of the query process.

 ◀◀ See "Working with Relations, Key Fields, and Indexes," p. 146

Perform the following steps to establish criteria for selecting the records to comprise your mailing list:

1. Click the Design View button on the toolbar to return to Design mode. The partially filled Query Design grid replaces the mailing list on-screen.

2. To restrict the result of your query to firms in the United States, type the expression **USA** in the Criteria row of the Country column. Entering a criterion's value without preceding the value with an operator indicates that the value of the field must match the value of the expression USA. You do not need to add quotation marks to the expression; Access adds them for you (see the Country column in Figure 8.8).

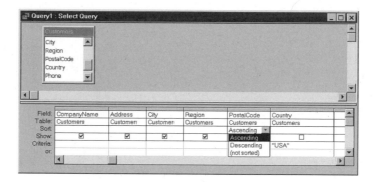

**FIG. 8.8** Adding the Ascending sort order to the PostalCode field.

3. Click the Show check box in the Country column to remove the check mark that appeared when you named the column. After you deactivate the Show check box, the Country field does not appear when you run your query. (You do not need to include the Country column in your mailing list address if you are mailing from within the United States to another location within the United States.) If you do not deactivate a Show check box, that field in the query appears in the query's result by default.

4. Move the caret to the PostalCode column's Sort row and press F4 to display the sorting options for that field: Ascending, Descending, and Not Sorted. Choose the Ascending option to sort the query by PostalCode from low codes to high.

At this point, the Query Design grid appears as shown in Figure 8.8.

**5.** Click the Query View or Run button on the toolbar to display the result of your criterion and sorting order. Use the horizontal scroll bar to display additional fields.

Figure 8.9 displays the query result table (also called a *query result set*) that Access refers to as an updatable `Recordset` (a `Recordset` object of the `Dynaset` type, to be more precise). A `Recordset` object is a temporary table stored in your computer's memory; it is not a permanent component of the database file. A `Recordset` object differs from the conventional view of an object created by the SQL `VIEW` reserved word because you can update the data in a `Recordset` object of the `Dynaset` type. After you save the query, the Northwind.mdb file saves only the design specifications of the query, not the values that the query contains. The query design specification is called a `QueryDef` object.

| Contact Name | Company Name | Address | City | Region | Postal Code |
|---|---|---|---|---|---|
| Liu Wong | The Cracker Box | 55 Grizzly Peak Rd. | Butte | MT | 59801 |
| Art Braunschweiger | Split Rail Beer & Ale | P.O. Box 555 | Lander | WY | 82520 |
| Jose Pavarotti | Save-a-lot Markets | 187 Suffolk Ln. | Boise | ID | 83720 |
| Paula Wilson | Rattlesnake Canyon Grocer | 2817 Milton Dr. | Albuquerque | NM | 87110 |
| Jaime Yorres | Let's Stop N Shop | 87 Polk St. | San Francisco | CA | 94117 |
| Liz Nixon | The Big Cheese | 89 Jefferson Way | Portland | OR | 97201 |
| Fran Wilson | Lonesome Pine Restaurant | 89 Chiaroscuro Rd. | Portland | OR | 97219 |
| Howard Snyder | Great Lakes Food Market | 2732 Baker Blvd. | Eugene | OR | 97403 |
| Yoshi Latimer | Hungry Coyote Import Store | City Center Plaza | Elgin | OR | 97827 |
| Helvetius Nagy | Trail's Head Gourmet Provis | 722 DaVinci Blvd. | Kirkland | WA | 98034 |
| Karl Jablonski | White Clover Markets | 305 - 14th Ave. S. | Seattle | WA | 98128 |
| John Steel | Lazy K Kountry Store | 12 Orchestra Terrace | Walla Walla | WA | 99362 |
| Rene Phillips | Old World Delicatessen | 2743 Bering St. | Anchorage | AK | 99508 |

Query1 : Select Query

Record: 1 of 13

**FIG. 8.9**  The query result, sorted in ascending order by PostalCode.

**Creating More Complex Queries**

To limit your mailing to customers in a particular state or group of states, you can add a Criteria expression to the Region or PostalCode field. To restrict the mailing to customers in California, Oregon, and Washington, for example, you can specify that the value of the PostalCode field must be equal to or greater than 90000. Alternatively, you can specify that Region values must be CA, OR, and WA.

Follow these steps to restrict your mailing to customers in California, Oregon, and Washington:

**1.** Click the Design View button on the toolbar to return to Design mode.

Design

**2.** Use the right-arrow or Tab key to move the caret to the Region column. If the Region column is not on-screen, click the scroll-right button until that column appears.

**3.** Type **CA** in the first criteria row of the Region column. Access adds the quotation marks around CA (as it did when you restricted your mailing to U.S. locations with the USA criterion).

**4.** Press the down-arrow key to move to the next criteria row in the Region column. Type **OR**, and then move to the third criteria row and type **WA**. Your query design now appears as shown in Figure 8.10. Access adds the required quotation marks to these criteria, also.

II

**Querying for Information**

5. Click the Datasheet View or Run button on the toolbar to return to Run mode. The query result set appears as shown in Figure 8.11.

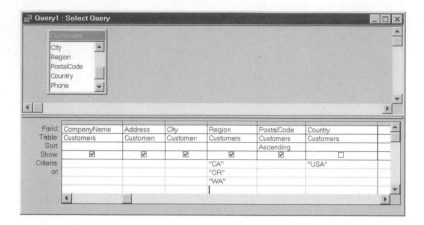

**FIG. 8.10** Adding criteria to the Region field of the Query Design grid.

| Contact Name | Company Name | Address | City | Region | Postal Code |
|---|---|---|---|---|---|
| Jaime Yorres | Let's Stop N Shop | 87 Polk St. | San Francisco | CA | 94117 |
| Liz Nixon | The Big Cheese | 89 Jefferson Way | Portland | OR | 97201 |
| Fran Wilson | Lonesome Pine Restaurant | 89 Chiaroscuro Rd. | Portland | OR | 97219 |
| Howard Snyder | Great Lakes Food Market | 2732 Baker Blvd. | Eugene | OR | 97403 |
| Yoshi Latimer | Hungry Coyote Import Store | City Center Plaza | Elgin | OR | 97827 |
| Helvetius Nagy | Trail's Head Gourmet Provis | 722 DaVinci Blvd. | Kirkland | WA | 98034 |
| Karl Jablonski | White Clover Markets | 305 - 14th Ave. S. | Seattle | WA | 98128 |
| John Steel | Lazy K Kountry Store | 12 Orchestra Terrace | Walla Walla | WA | 99362 |

Record: ◄ ◄ 1 ► ►► ►* of 8

**FIG. 8.11** The query result set for customers in California, Oregon, and Washington.

---

**Note**

After you type a criterion on the same line as a previously entered criterion in another field, only those records that meet both criteria are selected for display. In the preceding example, therefore, only those records with Region values equal to CA and Country values equal to USA are displayed.

To be displayed, records for Region values OR and WA need not have Country values equal to USA because the USA criterion is missing from the OR and WA rows. This omission does not really affect the selection of records in this case because all OR and WA records are also USA records. To eliminate possible ambiguity, however, USA should appear in each criterion row that contains a state code.

(Note that the remaining criteria rows in the different columns on the Query Design grid enable you to enter additional criteria to qualify further which records to display. In the current example, you need no additional criteria, so Access leaves these cells blank.)

---

### Editing Table Data in Query View

You can edit the data in any visible fields of the table in the query display. Any table that underlies the Recordset reflects the changes that you make to data cells in an updatable Recordset object of the Dynaset type. To edit an entry in a query and then verify the change to the corresponding record in the underlying table, perform these steps:

1. Use the right-arrow or Tab key to move the caret to the first row of the Company Name column (Let's Stop N Shop).

2. Press F2 to deselect the field and to enter Edit mode.

3. Use the arrow keys to position the cursor to immediately before the N and add an apostrophe to change the Company Name value to **Let's Stop 'N Shop**.

4. Press Enter or move the caret down another line to make the change to Let's Stop 'N Shop permanent. (Data in the underlying table does not change until you press Enter or move to a different record.)

> **Note**
>
> Changes made to sorted fields in Access do not actually move the edited records to their correct locations in the query tables until you press Shift+F9 to rerun the query.

5. Click the Database Window button of the toolbar, or choose <u>W</u>indow, <u>1</u> Database and then click the Tables tab of the Database window.

6. Double-click the Customers table to display the table in Datasheet view. Scroll down to verify that the underlying Customers table reflects your update to the query data (see Figure 8.12).

| Customer ID | Company Name | Contact Name | Co |
|---|---|---|---|
| LAMAI | La maison d'Asie | Annette Roulet | Sales Manage |
| LAUGB | Laughing Bacchus Wine Cellars | Yoshi Tannamuri | Marketing Ass |
| LAZYK | Lazy K Kountry Store | John Steel | Marketing Mar |
| LEHMS | Lehmanns Marktstand | Renate Messner | Sales Repres |
| LETSS | Let's Stop 'N Shop | Jaime Yorres | Owner |
| LILAS | LILA-Supermercado | Carlos González | Accounting M: |
| LINOD | LINO-Delicateses | Felipe Izquierdo | Owner |
| LONEP | Lonesome Pine Restaurant | Fran Wilson | Sales Manage |
| MAGAA | Magazzini Alimentari Riuniti | Giovanni Rovelli | Marketing Mar |
| MAISD | Maison Dewey | Catherine Dewey | Sales Agent |
| MEREP | Mère Paillarde | Jean Fresnière | Marketing Ass |
| MORGK | Morgenstern Gesundkost | Alexander Feuer | Marketing Ass |
| NORTS | North/South | Simon Crowther | Sales Associa |
| OCEAN | Océano Atlántico Ltda | Yvonne Moncada | Sales Agent |

Record: 45 of 91

**FIG. 8.12**  Viewing the original table data confirms the alteration made to a record in the query results window.

### Changing the Names of Query Column Headers

You can substitute a query's field header names with column header names of your choice—a process called *aliasing*—but only if the header name has not been changed by an entry in the field Caption property of the table. If you are a U.S. firm, for example, you might want to change Region to **State** and PostalCode to **ZIP**. (Canadian firms might want to change only Region to **Province**.)

As demonstrated in the following example, you cannot make the change to the PostalCode field for queries based on the Customers table because the PostalCode field previously has been changed (aliased) to Postal Code by the Caption property for the field. You can, however, make the change to the Region field because this field is not aliased at the table level.

**Tip**

If you already have a main document for the merge operation, substitute the main merge document's merge field names for the table's field header names in your query.

**Note**

The inability to alias field names in queries that have been altered by use of the Caption property in the source table is a good reason not to use the Caption property of table fields. If you want to display different field headers, use a query for this purpose. In a client/server RDBMS, such a query is called an SQL VIEW. Aliasing field names in tables, rather than queries, is not considered a generally accepted database design practice.

To attempt to change the query column header names, perform the following steps:

1. Switch to Design mode by clicking the toolbar's Design View button. Then use the right-arrow or Tab key to move the caret to the Field column containing the field header name that you want to change—in this case, the Region column.

2. Press F2 to deselect the field; then press Home to move the caret to the first character position.

3. Type the new name for the column and follow the name with a colon (with no spaces):

   **State:**

   The colon separates the new column name that you type from the existing table field name, which shifts to the right to make room for your addition. The result, in this example, is State:Region (see Figure 8.13).

4. Use the arrow key to move to the PostalCode field and repeat steps 2 and 3, typing **ZIP:** as that header's new name. The result, as shown in Figure 8.13, is ZIP:PostalCode.

5. Change the column header for the ContactName field to **Contact**; change the column header for the CompanyName field to **Company** (refer to steps 2, 3, and 4).

6. Delete the CA, OR, and WA criteria from the State:Region column so that all records for the U.S. appear.

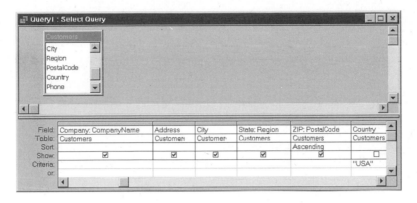

**FIG. 8.13** Changing the names of the Region and PostalCode column headers.

7. Click the toolbar's Query View or Run button to execute the query. Observe that only the Region column header is changed to State; the other columns are unaffected by the alias entry (see Figure 8.14).

| Contact Name | Company Name | Address | City | State | Postal Code |
|---|---|---|---|---|---|
| Liu Wong | The Cracker Box | 55 Grizzly Peak Rd. | Butte | MT | 59801 |
| Art Braunschweiger | Split Rail Beer & Ale | P.O. Box 555 | Lander | WY | 82520 |
| Jose Pavarotti | Save-a-lot Markets | 187 Suffolk Ln. | Boise | ID | 83720 |
| Paula Wilson | Rattlesnake Canyon Grocer | 2817 Milton Dr. | Albuquerque | NM | 87110 |
| Jaime Yorres | Let's Stop 'N Shop | 87 Polk St. | San Francisco | CA | 94117 |
| Liz Nixon | The Big Cheese | 89 Jefferson Way | Portland | OR | 97201 |
| Fran Wilson | Lonesome Pine Restaurant | 89 Chiaroscuro Rd. | Portland | OR | 97219 |
| Howard Snyder | Great Lakes Food Market | 2732 Baker Blvd. | Eugene | OR | 97403 |
| Yoshi Latimer | Hungry Coyote Import Store | City Center Plaza | Elgin | OR | 97827 |
| Helvetius Nagy | Trail's Head Gourmet Provis | 722 DaVinci Blvd. | Kirkland | WA | 98034 |
| Karl Jablonski | White Clover Markets | 305 - 14th Ave. S. | Seattle | WA | 98128 |
| John Steel | Lazy K Kountry Store | 12 Orchestra Terrace | Walla Walla | WA | 99362 |
| Rene Phillips | Old World Delicatessen | 2743 Bering St. | Anchorage | AK | 99508 |

Record: 1 of 13

**FIG. 8.14** The query result set, with only one new column header.

> **Note**
>
> To make field aliasing in queries operable, delete the entries in the Caption field for each of the aliased fields of the table. In the sections that follow, the entries in the Caption property of the ContactName, CompanyName, and PostalCode fields of the Customers table have been deleted. Deleting these entries makes the aliases you entered in the preceding example work as expected.

### Printing Your Query as a Report

Queries are often used to print quick, *ad hoc* reports. Access 97 lets you print your report to a Word for Windows .rtf (rich-text format) file, Excel worksheet .xls file, or a DOS .txt (text) file, or as an attachment to an Exchange message.

▶▶ See "Sending Reports by Microsoft Exchange and Outlook," p. 570

Previewing your query table's appearance to see how the table will appear when printed is usually a good idea. After you determine from the preview that everything in the table is correct, you can print the finished query result set in a variety of formats.

To preview a query result set before printing it, follow these steps:

 **1.** In Query view, click the Print Preview button on the toolbar. A miniature version of the query table appears in Report Preview mode.

 **2.** Position the Zoom mouse pointer (the magnifying glass cursor) at the upper-left corner of the miniature table and click the left mouse button or the Zoom button above the window to view the report at approximately the scale at which it will print.

**3.** Use the vertical and horizontal scroll bar buttons to position the preview in the window (see Figure 8.15).

| Contact | Company | Address | City | State | ZIP |
|---------|---------|---------|------|-------|-----|
| Liu Wong | The Cracker Box | 55 Grizzly Peak Rd. | Butte | MT | 59801 |
| Art Braunschweiger | Split Rail Beer & Ale | P.O. Box 555 | Lander | WY | 82520 |
| Jose Pavarotti | Save-a-lot Markets | 187 Suffolk Ln. | Boise | ID | 83720 |
| Paula Wilson | Rattlesnake Canyon Groce | 2817 Milton Dr. | Albuquerque | NM | 87110 |
| Jaime Yorres | Let's Stop 'N Shop | 87 Polk St. | San Francisco | CA | 94117 |
| Liz Nixon | The Big Cheese | 89 Jefferson Way | Portland | OR | 97201 |
| Fran Wilson | Lonesome Pine Restaurant | 89 Chiaroscuro Rd. | Portland | OR | 97219 |
| Howard Snyder | Great Lakes Food Market | 2732 Baker Blvd. | Eugene | OR | 97403 |
| Yoshi Latimer | Hungry Coyote Import Stor | City Center Plaza | Elgin | OR | 97827 |
| Helvetius Nagy | Trail's Head Gourmet Provi | 722 DaVinci Blvd. | Kirkland | WA | 98034 |
| Karl Jablonski | White Clover Markets | 305 - 14th Ave. S. | Seattle | WA | 98128 |
| John Steel | Lazy K Kountry Store | 12 Orchestra Terrace | Walla Walla | WA | 99362 |
| Rene Phillips | Old World Delicatessen | 2743 Bering St. | Anchorage | AK | 99508 |

**FIG. 8.15** Previewing the Mailing List query table at zoomed scale.

**Note**

Field width in the query table is based on the column width that you last established in Run mode. You might have to drag the right edge of the field header buttons to the right to increase the columns' width so that the printed report does not truncate the data. If the query data's width exceeds the available printing width (the paper width minus the width of the left and right margins), Access prints two or more sheets for each page of the report.

**4.** Click the Close button and then alter the width of the columns in Run mode so that all seven columns of the query fit on one sheet of paper when you print it. Return to Report Preview mode after you finish this process.

---

**Note**

Adjust the displayed width of query fields the same way that you adjusted table fields (as described in Chapters 4, "Working with Access Databases and Tables," and 6, "Sorting, Finding, and Filtering Data in Tables"). Access stores query column widths as properties of the query.

---

To print to the default printer a query table after previewing it and determining that all the data is correct, simply click the Print button of the toolbar. To change the default printing margins of one inch on all sides of the sheet (or any revised defaults that you might have set earlier by choosing Tools, Options and entering new values in the Print Options text boxes of the General page), or to print only data (but not field header names), follow these steps:

**1.** Choose File, Page Setup to open the Page Setup dialog shown in Figure 8.16. If necessary, click the Margins tab to display the Margins page.

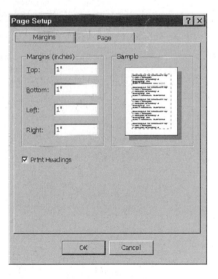

**FIG. 8.16**   The Margins page of the Page Setup dialog.

**2.** Enter any changes that you want to make to the margins; mark the Print Headings check box if you want to print the field header names. Click the Page tab to change the print orientation, paper size or source, or printer. Then click OK to return to Print Preview mode.

**3.** Click the Print button of the toolbar to print your query data.

### Using the Data from Your Query

Occasionally, you might want to use data from your query as part of a different Windows application without printing the data in a report. The simplest technique for transferring data in your query to another Windows application is to use the Clipboard. Clipboard operations for data in query tables are identical to those operations for tables described in Chapter 7, "Linking, Importing, and Exporting Tables."

◄◄ See "Using the Clipboard to Import Data," p. 245

Access 97 includes a Merge It choice when you click the arrow adjacent to the Office Links button on the toolbar. Merge It automatically creates a Word mail merge document. Performing automated operations manually, however, gives you insight into how Access 97 implements Office Links. To create manually a merge data file for Word directly from a query, for example, follow these steps:

**1.** In Query view, choose Edit, Select All Records.

> **Tip**
>
> For a partial mailing, such as to firms in California only, you can choose the individual records by dragging the mouse over the records' selection buttons.

**2.** Press Ctrl+C or choose Edit, Copy to copy the selected records to the Clipboard.

**3.** Run Word and, if necessary, choose File, New to open a new window.

**4.** Press Ctrl+V or choose Edit, Paste. Your Access mailing records are added as a table to the Word document (see Figure 8.17).

**5.** Convert the table to the tab-delimited format necessary for Word merge data files. Place the caret in one of the cells of the table and choose Table, Select Table to select all the rows and columns of the table.

**6.** Choose Table, Convert Table to Text to display the dialog that lets you choose the field-delimiter character. Accept the default Tab selection in the Convert Table to Text dialog and click OK. Your merge data file appears as shown in Figure 8.18.

> **Note**
>
> Some of the records of this query also contain *newline pairs* (paragraph marks) embedded in fields that result in premature ends of these records. An example of a spurious newline pair in the Address field is highlighted for the Let's Stop 'N Shop record in Figure 8.18. Replace the extra new line pairs with commas and spaces, and delete the quotation marks that enclose fields containing extra headline pairs before using the document in a merge operation.

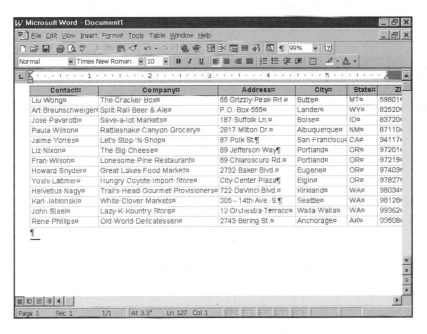

**FIG. 8.17**  The query result set copied to a Word for Windows document.

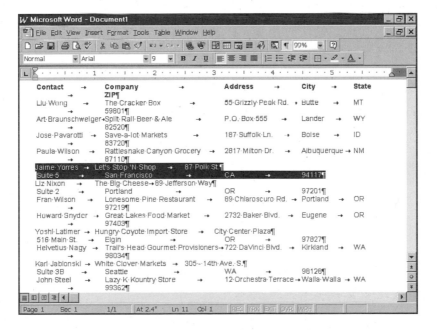

**FIG. 8.18**  A Microsoft Word merge data file with extra newline pairs embedded.

If you use a DOS word processor and want to import query data into a merge data file, save the query in the form of a table and export the table as a file in a format compatible with that of your word processor. This process requires that you create an action query to create a table. Then export the table's data in a compatible format, as described in Chapter 7, "Linking, Importing, and Exporting Tables." Action queries are discussed briefly in the section "Creating and Using a Simple Make-Table Action Query," later in this chapter, and in Chapter 11, "Using Action Queries."

### Saving and Naming Your Query

After completing your query, save it as an element of your database file, giving the query its own descriptive name.

Follow these steps to save and name your query:

1. Close your query by clicking the Close Window button. Access prompts you with a message box to save the new or modified query, as shown in Figure 8.19.

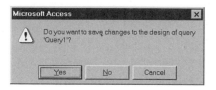

**FIG. 8.19**   The message reminding you to save a newly created or modified query.

2. Click the message box's Yes button to save your query. Because Access has already assigned a default name to your query, the Save As dialog appears (see Figure 8.20). If you click Cancel or press Esc, Access does not save your query.

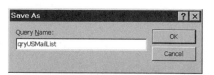

**FIG. 8.20**   The Save As dialog, in which you enter the name for your query.

3. Type in the Query Name text box a descriptive name for your query, in this case **qryUSMailList**, and then press Enter or click OK. Your query now is saved under the name that you assigned it rather than under the default name.

> **Note**
>
> Prefixes, called tags, are commonly used to identify types of Access objects you create. Tags are one of the subjects of Appendix B, "Naming Conventions for Access Objects and Variables."

Alternatively, you can save your query by choosing <u>F</u>ile, Save <u>A</u>s.

To rename a saved query, follow these steps:

**1.** Close the query by clicking the close window box. (You cannot rename an open query.)

**2.** In the Queries page of the Database window, select the query that you want to rename.

**3.** Choose <u>E</u>dit, Rena<u>me</u>. Alternatively, right-click the query you want to rename and choose Rename from the popup menu.

**4.** Type in the text box a new name to replace the caption adjacent to the query's icon.

**5.** Press Enter to accept the change. Access saves your query with the new name that you assigned.

# Creating Other Types of Queries

Access enables you to create the following four basic types of queries to achieve different objectives:

- *Select*. Select queries extract data from one or more tables and display the data in tabular form.

- *Crosstab*. Crosstab queries summarize data from one or more tables in the form of a spreadsheet. Such queries are useful for analyzing data and creating graphs or charts based on the sum of the numeric field values of many records.

- *Action*. Action queries create new database tables from query tables or make major alterations to a table. Such queries enable you to add or delete records from a table or to make changes to records based on expressions that you enter in a query design.

- *Parameter*.  Parameter queries repeatedly use a query and make only simple changes to its criteria. The mailing list query that you created earlier in this chapter is an excellent candidate for a parameter query because you can change the criterion of the Region field for mailings to different groups of customers. When you run a parameter query, Access displays a dialog to prompt you for the new criterion. Parameter queries are not actually a separate query type because you can add the parameter function to select, crosstab, and action queries.

Chapters 10, "Creating Multitable and Crosstab Queries," and 11, "Using Action Queries," explain how to create each of the four query types. Creating a table from the mailing list query to export to a mail merge file is an example of an action query. (In fact, this is the simplest example of an action query and also the safest because make-table queries do not modify data in existing tables.)

### Creating and Using a Simple Make-Table Action Query

To create a table from your mailing list query, you first must convert the query from a select to an action query. Follow these steps to make this change:

1. Open your mailing list query in Design mode by selecting the name that you gave the query in the Database window and clicking the Design button.

2. Choose Query, Ma<u>k</u>e-Table Query. (You can access the Query menu only in Query Design mode.) Alternatively, click the Query Type button on the toolbar and select Make Query Table. The Make Table dialog appears, as shown in Figure 8.21.

**FIG. 8.21**   The Make Table dialog, in which you enter a name for the table the query creates and specify the new table's location.

3. In the Table Name text box, type a descriptive table name for your query table, such as **tblUSMailList**.

    The Make Table dialog enables you to define your query table's properties further in several ways. You can add the table to the Northwind Traders database by choosing the Current Database option (the default). You also can choose the Another Database option to add the table to a different database that you specify in the File Name text box.

4. Click OK. Access converts your select query to the make-table type of action query.

5. Close your query by clicking the Close Window button. Access displays a message dialog asking if you want to save changes to your query; click Yes. Your query name in the Database window now is prefixed by an exclamation point, as shown in Figure 8.22. An exclamation point indicates that the query is an action query.

Now that you have converted your query from a select query to an action query, you can create a new U.S. mailing list table. To create the table, follow these steps:

1. Run the newly converted action query table to create your mailing list by double-clicking its name in the Queries page of the Database window (refer to Figure 8.22).

    When you open an action query table, it performs the desired action—in this case, creating the tblUSMailList table—instead of simply displaying a select query result set. Before Access carries out the action, however, a message appears (see Figure

8.23) and warns you that the query will modify the data in the tblUSMailList table (despite the fact that you haven't yet created the table).

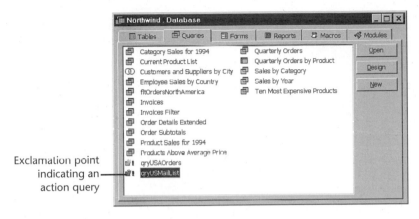

Exclamation point
indicating an
action query

**FIG. 8.22** A highlighted action query in the list of queries.

**FIG. 8.23** The message box that appears after you open an action query.

2. Click Yes to dismiss the message box and continue the operation. A second message, shown in Figure 8.24, appears to tell you what happens after you execute the action query.

**FIG. 8.24** A second message indicating the effects of running the action query.

3. Click Yes. Because you have not run this action query before, running it now creates the new tblUSMailList table.

4. Click the Table tab in the Database window. Access adds the new tblUSMailList table to the list of tables in the Northwind database, as shown in Figure 8.25.

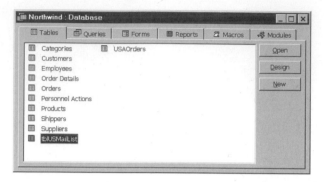

**FIG. 8.25**   The new table added to the Northwind Database's table list.

5. Double-click the tblUSMailList icon to open the table. Its contents, which are identical to the contents of the Datasheet view of the make-table query, appear as shown in Figure 8.26.

| Contact | Company | Address | City | State | ZIP |
|---|---|---|---|---|---|
| Liu Wong | The Cracker Box | 55 Grizzly Peak R | Butte | MT | 59801 |
| Art Braunschweig | Split Rail Beer & A | P.O. Box 555 | Lander | WY | 82520 |
| Jose Pavarotti | Save-a-lot Market: | 187 Suffolk Ln. | Boise | ID | 83720 |
| Paula Wilson | Rattlesnake Cany | 2817 Milton Dr. | Albuquerque | NM | 87110 |
| Jaime Yorres | Let's Stop 'N Shop | 87 Polk St. | San Francisco | CA | 94117 |
| Liz Nixon | The Big Cheese | 89 Jefferson Way | Portland | OR | 97201 |
| Fran Wilson | Lonesome Pine R | 89 Chiaroscuro R | Portland | OR | 97219 |
| Howard Snyder | Great Lakes Food | 2732 Baker Blvd. | Eugene | OR | 97403 |
| Yoshi Latimer | Hungry Coyote Im | City Center Plaza | Elgin | OR | 97827 |
| Helvetius Nagy | Trail's Head Gour | 722 DaVinci Blvd. | Kirkland | WA | 98034 |
| Karl Jablonski | White Clover Mark | 305 - 14th Ave. S. | Seattle | WA | 98128 |
| John Steel | Lazy K Kountry St | 12 Orchestra Terr | Walla Walla | WA | 99362 |
| Rene Phillips | Old World Delicat | 2743 Bering St. | Anchorage | AK | 99508 |

Record: 1 of 13

**FIG. 8.26**   The Datasheet view of the table created by the make-table query.

After you create the new table, you can export its data to any of the other file formats supported by Access. To do so, use the methods described in Chapter 7, "Linking, Importing, and Exporting Tables."

### Adding a Parameter to Your Make-Table Query

A simple modification to your mailing list query enables you to enter a selection criterion, called a *parameter*, from a prompt created by Access. Follow these steps:

 ◀◀ See "Setting Default Options," p. 81

1. Close the tblUSMailList table by clicking the Close Window button; then click the Queries tab in the Database window.

2. Choose the qryUSMailList query that you created earlier in the chapter, and then choose the Design button to display your make-table action query in Design mode.

3. Type **[Enter the state code:]** in the first criteria row of the State:Region column, as shown in Figure 8.27. The enclosing square brackets indicate that the entry is a prompt for a parameter when you run the action query.

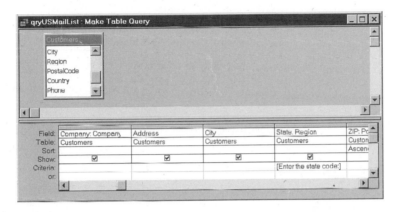

**FIG. 8.27** Entering a parameter prompt as a criterion in Query Design view.

4. Close and save changes to the action query, select the qryUSMailList query, and choose File, Edit, Rename.

5. Rename your query by typing **qryStateMailList** in the text box and pressing Enter.

6. Select the renamed qryStateMailList query from the list in the Database window, and then click the Open button. Alternatively, double-click the qryStateMailLis icon. You see the message indicating that data will be modified (refer to Figur 8.23)

7 Choose Yes. Another message appears, warning that you are about to overwrite th data in the table created by the last execution of your query (see Figure 8.28)

> **Note**
>
> Each time you execute a make-table query, it creates a new table with whatever name you have specified in the Make Table dialog. If a table with that name already exists, its contents are lost and replaced by the result set of the make-table query. If you want a make-table query to create a table with a different name, you must choose Query, MakeTtable Query,

Querying for Information

and enter a new name in the Make Table dialog.

**FIG. 8.28**  The message warning that you are about to overwrite data.

8. Choose Yes. Access displays the Enter Parameter Value dialog. This dialog contains a prompt for you to enter the state criterion, as shown in Figure 8.29.

**FIG. 8.29**  The text box for entering a parameter to be used as a select criterion.

9. Type **WA**, and press Enter or choose OK. (You do not need to type an equal sign before the state code because Access enters the equal sign for you.)

   Another message appears, similar to the one in Figure 8.24, indicating the number of records in the new version of the tblUSMailList table that have a value in the Regions field that matches your state parameter entry.

10. Choose Yes to close the message box and execute the make-table query.

11. Click the Tables tab in the Database window, and select tblUSMailList. Choose the Open button. Records only for customers in Washington appear in the table.

You can delete the new table from the Northwind Traders database by closing the table, selecting the tblUSMailList table in the Database window, and then pressing the Delete key. (Access requests that you confirm your deletion. Click OK, and Access removes the table from the database.)

# Translating Graphical QBE to Structured Query Language

*Structured Query Language*, or *SQL*, is a standard set of English words used to describe a query. Access translates the QBE expressions that you type in the Query Design grid into a series of statements in its own dialect of SQL, called *Jet SQL* in this book. Access then carries out these instructions on any tables that contain fields matching those specified in your query.

Access's use of SQL is important when you are dealing with client/server databases that process SQL statements on the server's computer. After processing the query, the server sends the data for the query result table to your Access client application for further processing.

To display the SQL statements created from your mailing list query, perform the following steps:

1. Open the mailing list query in Design mode by selecting the name you gave the query in the Database window and clicking the Design button.

2. Click the Query View button of the toolbar and choose SQL from the menu, or

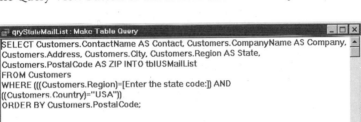

choose View, SQL View. The SQL window, which acts as a multiline text box, appears, as shown in Figure 8.30.

**FIG. 8.30**  Graphical QBE expressions translated by Access into Jet SQL.

SQL *reserved words* are displayed in uppercase letters. SQL reserved words are the instructions or the actions that the query is to perform. The names of the objects in your query appear in uppercase and lowercase letters. The following list explains the meanings of the reserved words used in your query:

- SELECT is usually the first reserved word in a SQL statement that returns records to a query result set. The expressions that follow specify the fields involved in the query. Fields are identified by the table's name followed by a period and the field's name.

- AS establishes the alias for the field name preceding the alias. ZIP, for example, is the alias for the PostalCode field. The alias is the caption that appears in the field header for the PostalCode field.

- INTO specifies the name of the table into which the results of the query are to be placed. INTO applies only to action queries.

- FROM is the name of the table in which the fields are located.

- WHERE identifies the expressions that follow as the query's selection criteria.

- AND is a logical operator that results in records that meet both the criterion that precedes the AND and the criterion that follows the AND.

■ ORDER BY specifies the field or fields by which the query result table is to be sorted.

When you finish viewing the SQL statements, close the SQL window.

This chapter and Chapter 6, "Sorting, Finding, and Filtering Data in Tables," provide only a brief glimpse of SQL, and this example uses only a small cross-section of SQL's reserved words. Chapter 24, "Working with Structured Query Language," explains in detail the syntax that you use to edit and create SQL statements.

     ▶▶ See "What Is Structured Query Language?" p. 836

# Chapter 9

# Understanding Operators and Expressions in Access

Chapter 5, "Entering, Editing, and Validating Data in Tables," briefly introduced you to operators and the expressions that use them when you added validation rules to table fields. Chapter 8, "Using Query by Example," touched on expressions again when you devised selection criteria for the query that you created. You must use expressions with the forms (Chapters 12 and 13), reports (Chapters 14 and 15), and queries (Chapters 8 and 10) that you combine when creating custom Access applications; furthermore, you use expressions extensively when programming with Access VBA (Chapters 28 through 31). To work effectively with Access, therefore, you must know how to create simple expressions that use Access's group of functions and operators.

If you use spreadsheet applications, such as Microsoft Excel or Lotus 1-2-3, you might be familiar with using operators to create expressions. In spreadsheet applications, expressions are called *formulas*. As discussed in Chapter 4, "Working with Access Databases and Tables," the syntax for expressions that create default values, such as **=Date** + 28, is similar to formula entries in Excel. Conditional expressions that use the **=IIF** function in Excel use the **IIf** function in Access.

Much of this chapter is devoted to describing the functions available in Access for manipulating data of the Numeric and Text field data type. Functions play important roles in every element of Access, from validation rules for tables and fields of tables, to the control of program flow in Access VBA. You use functions when creating queries, forms, reports, and when writing Access VBA code. To use Access effectively, you must know what functions are available to you.

# Understanding the Elements in Expressions

An *expression* is a statement of intent. If you want an action to occur after meeting a specific condition, your expression must specify that condition. To select records in a query that contains ZIP field values of 90000 or higher, for example, you type the expression

### ZIP>=90000

You can use expressions in arithmetic calculations also. If you need an Extended Amount field in a query, for example, you type

### [Extended Amount]: Quantity * [Unit Price]

as the expression to create calculated values in the data cells of the Extended Amount column.

---

**Note**

Square bracket pairs ([ ]) must surround object names, such as field names that contain spaces or punctuation other than the underscore character. You also use square bracket pairs to identify field names in expressions for validating data. The Northwind Traders sample database in prior versions of Access used field names that included spaces; in Access 97, the field names of tables in Northwind.mdb do not contain spaces, but table names include spaces. It is a Good Database Design Practice (GDBDP) never to use spaces in object names of any type. If you want to make object names more readable, separate words with the underscore character (_); for example, a field name of Postal_Code is preferable to the name Postal Code. In most cases, using upper- and lowercase object names provides adequate readability.

---

To qualify as an expression, a statement must have at least one operator and at least one literal, identifier, or function. The following list describes these elements:

- *Operators* include the familiar arithmetic symbols +, −, * (multiply), and / (divide), as well as many other symbols and abbreviations. Most other operators available in Access are equivalent to those operators found in traditional programming languages, such as BASIC, but some are specific to Access or SQL, such as the Between, In, Is, and Like operators.

- *Literals* consist of values that you type, such as **12345** or **ABCDE**. Literals are used most often to create default values and, in combination with field identifiers, to compare values in table fields.

- *Identifiers* are the names of objects in Access (such as fields in tables) that return distinct numeric or text values. The term *return*, when used with expressions, means that the present value of the identifier is substituted for its name in the expression. For example, the field name identifier [CompanyName] in an expression returns the value (a name) of the CompanyName field for the currently selected record. Access has five predefined named constants that also serve as identifiers: **True**, **False**, **Yes**, **No**, and **Null**. Named constants and variables that you create in Access VBA also are identifiers.

■ *Functions* return a value in place of the function name in the expression, such as the `Date` and `Format$` functions, which are used in the examples in Chapter 5, "Entering, Editing, and Validating Data in Tables." Unlike identifiers, most functions require that you supply with parentheses an identifier or value as an argument. Later in this chapter, the section "Functions" explains functions and their arguments.

When literals, identifiers, or functions are used with operators, these combinations are called *operands*. The following sections explain these four elements of expressions more thoroughly.

---

**Note**

Expressions in this book appear in monospace type to distinguish expressions from the explanatory text of the book. Operators, including symbolic operators, built-in functions, and other reserved words and symbols of VBA, are set in **monospace bold** type. (VBA reserved words appear in blue color in the code-editing window of modules.) SQL operators and names of Access objects are set in monospace type.

---

## Operators

Access provides six categories of operators that you can use to create expressions:

■ *Arithmetic* operators perform addition, subtraction, multiplication, and division.

■ *Assignment* and *comparison* operators set values and compare values.

■ *Logical* operators deal with values that can only be true or false.

■ *Concatenation* operators combine strings of characters.

■ *Identifier* operators create unambiguous names for database objects so that you can assign the same field name, for example, in several tables and queries.

■ Other operators, such as the `Like`, `Is`, and `Between` operators, simplify the creation of expressions for selecting records with queries.

Operators in the first four categories are available in almost all programming languages, including xBase and PAL (Paradox Application Language). Identifier operators are specific to Access; the other operators of the last category are provided only in relational database management systems (RDBMSs) that create queries using Query by Example (QBE) or Structured Query Language (SQL). The following sections explain how to use each of the operators in these categories.

**Arithmetic Operators.** Arithmetic operators operate only on numeric values and must have two numeric operands, with the following exceptions:

■ When the minus sign (-) changes the sign (negates the value) of an operand. In this case, the minus sign is called the *unary minus*.

■ When the equal sign (=) assigns a value to an Access object or an Access VBA variable identifier.

Table 9.1 lists the arithmetic operators that you can use in Access expressions.

| Table 9.1 | Arithmetic Operators | |
|---|---|---|
| **Operator** | **Description** | **Example** |
| + | Adds two operands | [Subtotal] + [Tax] |
| – | Subtracts two operands | **Date** – 30 |
| – (unary) | Changes the sign of an operand | – 12345 |
| * | Multiplies two operands | [Units] * [UnitPrice] |
| / | Divides one operand by another | [Quantity] / 12.55 |
| \ | Divides one integer operand by another | [Units] \ 2 |
| **Mod** | Returns the remainder of division by an integer | [Units] **Mod** 12 |
| ^ | Raises an operand to a power (exponent) | [Value] ^ [Exponent] |

Access operators are identical to operators used in Microsoft QuickBASIC, QBasic (supplied with DOS 5.0 and later), and Visual Basic. If you aren't familiar with BASIC programming, the following operators need further explanation:

\    The integer division symbol is the equivalent of "goes into," as used in the litany of elementary school arithmetic: *Three goes into 13 four times, with one left over.* When you use integer division, operators with decimal fractions are rounded to integers, but any decimal fraction in the result is truncated.

Mod    An abbreviation for *modulus*, this operator returns the *left over* value of integer division. Therefore, 13 **Mod** 4, for example, returns 1.

^    The exponentiation operator raises the first operand to the power of the second. For example, 2 ^ 4, or two to the fourth power, returns 16 (2*2*2*2).

These three operators seldom are used in business applications but often are used in Access VBA program code.

**Assignment and Comparison Operators.**  Table 9.1 omits the equal sign associated with arithmetic expressions because in Access you use it in two ways—neither of which falls under the arithmetic category. The most common use of the equal sign is as an assignment operator; = assigns the value of a single operand to an Access object or to a variable or constant. When you use the expression = "Q" to assign a default value to a field, the equal sign acts as an assignment value. Otherwise, = is a comparison operator that determines whether one of two operands is equal to the other.

*Comparison operators* compare the values of two operands and return logical values (**True** or **False**) depending on the relationship between the two operands and the operator. An exception is when one of the operands has the **Null** value. In this case, any comparison returns a value of **Null**. Because **Null** represents an unknown value, you cannot compare an unknown value with a known value and come to a valid **True** or **False** conclusion. The **Null** value is an important concept in database application, but few desktop RDBMSs support **Null** values.

Table 9.2 lists the comparison operators available in Access.

**Table 9.2 Comparison Operators**

| Operator | Description | Example | Result |
|----------|-------------|---------|--------|
| < | Less than | 123 < 1000 | True |
| <= | Less than or equal to | 15 <= 15 | True |
| = | Equal to | 2 = 4 | False |
| >= | Greater than or equal to | 1234 >= 456 | True |
| > | Greater than | 123 > 123 | False |
| <> | Not equal | 123 <> 456 | True |

The principal uses of comparison operators are to create validation rules, to establish criteria for selecting records in queries, to determine actions taken by macros, and to control program flow in Access VBA.

**Logical Operators.** *Logical operators* (also called *Boolean operators*) are used most often to combine the results of two or more comparison expressions into a single result. Logical operators can combine only expressions that return the logical values **True**, **False**, or **Null**. With the exception of **Not**, which is the logical equivalent of the unary minus, logical operators always require two operands.

Table 9.3 lists the Access logical operators.

**Table 9.3 Logical Operators**

| Operator | Description | Example 1<br>Example 2 | Result 1<br>Result 2 |
|----------|-------------|------------------------|----------------------|
| And | Logical and | True And True<br>True And False | True<br>False |
| Or | Inclusive or | True Or False<br>False Or False | True<br>False |
| Not | Logical not | Not True<br>Not False | False<br>True |
| Xor | Exclusive or | True Xor False<br>True Xor True | True<br>False |

The logical operators **And**, **Or**, and **Not** are used extensively in Access expressions. **Xor** is seldom used in Access. **Eqv** (equivalent) and **Imp** (implication) are rarely seen, even in programming code, so Table 9.3 omits these two operators.

**Concatenation Operators.** *Concatenation operators* combine two text values into a single string of characters. If you concatenate ABC with DEF, for example, the result is ABCDEF. The ampersand (**&**) is the preferred concatenation operator in Access because the character is SQL's standard concatenation symbol. Although you can use the + operator to link two strings of characters, using the + operator for concatenation can lead to ambiguities because the operator's primary purpose is to add two numeric operands.

**Identifier Operators.** The *identifier operators,* ! (the exclamation point, often called the *bang operator*) and . (the period, called the *dot operator* in Access), are separators and perform the following operations:

- Combine the names of object classes and object names to select a specific object or property of an object. For example, the following expression identifies the Personnel Actions form:

    ```
    Forms![Personnel Actions]
    ```

    This identification is necessary because you might also have a table called Personnel Actions.

- Distinguish object names from property names. Consider the following expression:

    ```
    TextBox1.FontSize = 8
    ```

    TextBox1 is a control object, and FontSize is a property.

- Identify specific fields in tables, as in the following expression, which specifies the Company Name field of the Customers table:

    ```
    Customers![Company Name]
    ```

You use the ! character to separate object references; the general syntax is *ObjectClass!ObjectName*. The . character separates objects and their properties or methods, as in *ObjectClass!Object.Property* or *ObjectClass!ObjectName.Method*.

**Other Operators.** The remaining Access operators are related to the comparison operators. These operators return **True** or **False**, depending on whether the value in a field meets the chosen operator's specification. A **True** value causes a record to be included in a query; a **False** value rejects the record. When you use these operators in validation rules, entries are accepted or rejected based on the logical value returned by the expression.

Table 9.4 lists the four other operators used in Access.

| Table 9.4 Other Operators | | |
| --- | --- | --- |
| **Operator** | **Description** | **Example** |
| Is | Used with **Null** to determine whether a value is **Null** or **Not Null**. | Is **Null**<br>Is **Not Null** |
| Like | Determines whether a string value begins with one or more characters (for Like to work properly, you must add a wild card, *, or one or more ?s). | Like "Jon*"<br>Like "FILE????" |
| In | Determines whether a string value is a member of a list of values. | In("CA", "OR", "WA") |
| Between | Determines whether a numeric value lies within a specified range of values. | Between 1 **And** 5 |

You use the wildcard characters * and ? with the Like operator the same way that you use them in DOS. The * (often called *star* or *splat*) takes the place of any number of characters. The ? takes the place of a single character. For example, Like "Jon*" returns **True** for values such as *Jones* or *Jonathan*. Like "*on*" returns **True** for any value that contains *on*. Like "FILE????" returns **True** for *FILENAME*, but not *FILE000* or *FILENUMBER*. Wildcard characters can precede the characters that you want to match, as in Like "*son" or Like "????NAME".

Except for Is, the operators in this other category are equivalent to the SQL reserved words LIKE, IN, and BETWEEN. Access includes these operators to promote compatibility with SQL. You can create each of these operators by combining other Access operators or functions. Like "Jon*" is the equivalent of Access VBA's **InStr**(**Left$**(*FieldName*, 3), "Jon"); In("CA", "OR", "WA") is similar to **InStr**("CAORWA", *FieldName*), except that no matches occur for the ambiguous AO and RW. Between 1 **And** 5 is the equivalent of >= 1 **And** <= 5.

## Literals

Access provides three types of literals that you can combine with operators to create expressions. The following list describes these types of literals:

- *Numeric* literals are typed as a series of digits, including the arithmetic sign and decimal point, if applicable. You don't have to prefix positive numbers with the plus sign; Access assumes positive values unless the minus sign is present. Numeric literals can include E or e and the sign of the exponent to indicate an exponent in scientific notation—for example, 1.23E 02.

- *Text* (or *string*) literals can include any printable character, plus unprintable characters returned by the **Chr$** function. The **Chr$** function returns the characters specified by a numeric value from the ANSI character table (similar to the ASCII character table) that Windows uses. For example, **Chr$**(9) returns the Tab character. Printable characters include the letters A–Z, numbers 1–0, punctuation symbols, and other special keyboard symbols such as the tilde (~). Access expressions require that you enclose string literals within double quotation marks (""). Combinations of printable and unprintable characters are concatenated with the ampersand. For example, the following expression separates two strings with a newline pair.

    "First line" **&** **Chr$**(13) **&** **Chr$**(10) **&** "Second line"

    **Chr$**(13) is the carriage return (CR), and **Chr$**(10) is the line-feed (LF) character; together they form the newline pair.

    When you enter string literals in the cells of tables and Query Design grids, Access adds the quotation marks for you. In other places, you must enter the quotation marks yourself.

- *Date/time* literals are enclosed within number or pound signs (#), as in the expressions #1-Jan-80# or #10:20:30#. Access adds the enclosing pound signs if the program detects that you are typing into a Design grid a date or time in one of the standard Access date/time formats.

## Identifiers

An *identifier* is usually the name of an object; databases, tables, fields, queries, forms, and reports are objects in Access. Each object has a name that uniquely identifies that object. Sometimes, to identify a subobject, an identifier name consists of a *family name* (object class) separated from a *given name* (object name) by a bang symbol or a period (an identifier operator). The family name of the identifier comes first, followed by the separator and then the given name. SQL uses the period as an object separator. An example of an identifier in an SQL statement is as follows:

```
Customers.Address
```

In this example, the identifier for the Address field object is contained in the Customers table object. *Customers* is the family name of the object (the table), and *Address* is the given name of the subobject (the field). In Access, however, you use the ! symbol to separate table names and field names. (The period separates objects and their properties.) If an identifier contains a space or other punctuation, enclose the identifier within square brackets, as in this example:

```
[Personnel Actions]![paID]
```

You cannot include periods or exclamation points within the names of identifiers; [PA!ID], for example, is not allowed.

In simple queries that use only one table, identifiers are usually the name of a field. You use identifiers to return the values of fields in form and report objects. Chapters 12 through 15 cover the specific method of identifying objects within forms and reports.

## Functions

*Functions* return values to their names; functions can take the place of identifiers in expressions. One of the most common functions used in Access expressions is **Now**, which returns to its name the date and time from your computer's internal clock. (The empty parentheses are optional for the **Now** function.) If you type **Now** as the `DefaultValue` property of a table's Date/Time field, for example, 5/15/97 9:00 appears in the field when you change to Datasheet view (at 9:00 A.M. on March 15, 1997).

 ▶▶ See "Modules, Functions, and Subprocedures," p. 981

Access and VBA define about 140 individual functions. The following list groups functions by purpose:

- *Date and time* functions manipulate date/time values in fields or date/time values that you enter as literals. You can extract parts of dates (such as the year or day of the month) and parts of times (such as hours and minutes) with date and time functions.

- *Text-manipulation* functions are used for working with strings of characters.

- *Data-type conversion* functions enable you to specify the data type of values in Numeric fields instead of depending on Access to pick the most appropriate data type.

■ *Mathematic and trigonometric* functions perform on numeric values operations that are beyond the capability of the standard Access arithmetic operators. You can use simple trigonometric functions, for example, to calculate the length of the sides of a right triangle (if you know the length of one side and the included angle).

■ *Financial* functions are similar to functions provided by Lotus 1-2-3 and Microsoft Excel. They calculate depreciation, values of annuities, and rates of return on investments. To determine the present value of a lottery prize paid out in 25 equal yearly installments, for example, you can use the PV function.

■ *General-purpose* functions don't fit any of the preceding classifications; you use these functions to create Access queries, forms, and reports.

■ Other functions include those that perform dynamic data exchange (DDE) with other Windows applications, domain aggregate functions, SQL aggregate functions, and functions used primarily in Access VBA programming.

The following sections describe these functions more fully.

You can create user-defined functions by defining them with Access VBA programming code. Chapter 28, "Writing Visual Basic for Applications Code," describes how to create user-defined functions.

**Using the Debug Window.** When you write Access VBA programming code in a module, the Debug window is available to assist you in debugging your code. You also can use the module's Debug window to demonstrate the use and syntax of functions.

To experiment with some of the functions described in the following sections, perform these steps:

1. Click the Modules tab in the Database window.

2. Choose the New button to create a temporary module. Access assigns the default name Module1 to the temporary module.

3. Click the Debug Window button of the toolbar or choose View, Debug Window. The Debug window appears, as shown in Figure 9.1. The entries shown in Figure 9.1 aren't visible at this point. You can create similar entries by using the functions for date and time discussed in the section "Functions for Date and Time" later in this chapter, and listed in Table 9.6.

4. Type **?Now** in the bottom portion of the Debug window (see Figure 9.1) and press Enter. The date and time from your computer's clock appear on the next line. The ? is shorthand for the VBA **Print** statement (which displays the value of a function or variable) and must be added to the **Now** function to display the function's value.

If you neglected to precede the function entry with ? or **Print**, an error message appears, indicating that Access expected you to type a statement or an equal sign. Click OK and type **?** before the function name in the Debug window. Press End to return the caret to the end of the line and then Enter to retry the test.

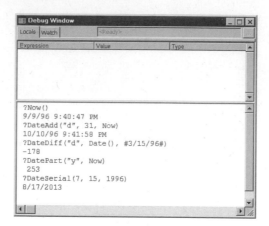

**FIG. 9.1** Using the Debug window of a temporary module to experiment with functions.

The following sections describe and provide the correct syntax for the various functions available to Access users. This information should help you get acquainted with using functions with queries, forms, and reports. These descriptions and syntax examples are brief compared to the information available from the Access online Help system and in the Microsoft Access Language Reference.

As you type in your functions in the Debug window, Access displays a popup help window, showing the function's name and its complete argument list. An *argument list* is the list of information that you specify for the function to work on—for example, if you use the **Sqr** function to compute the square root of a number, you must supply a number inside the function's parentheses for the function to work on. Figure 9.2 shows the popup help window for the **Sqr** function. You can turn this feature on and off by choosing Tools, Options, and selecting (on) or clearing (off) the Auto Quick Info option on the Module page.

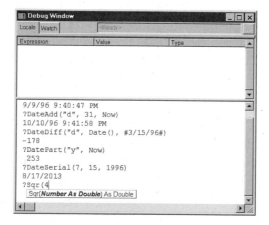

**FIG. 9.2** A popup help window appears as you type functions in the Debug window.

Another way to learn more about functions is to choose Help, Contents and Index, click the Index tab, and type in the Index dialog's text box the name of the function on which you want more information. For a faster method to learn more about a particular function, however, follow these steps:

1. In the Debug window, press Enter to move the caret to the beginning of a new line.

2. Type the name of the function; select the name by double-clicking it or by pressing Shift+left arrow several times (as shown for the Format function in Figure 9.3). Alternatively, you can press Home to place the cursor in front of the function name's first character.

3. Press F1. The Help window opens. If a function and a property or event share the same name, an intermediate Context Help On window appears that enables you to choose the function, the event, or the property.

4. Click the See Also hotspot. Related Help topics appear in a Topics Found dialog (see Figure 9.4). Select a related topic and choose Display to show the associated Help window, or click Cancel to close the dialog.

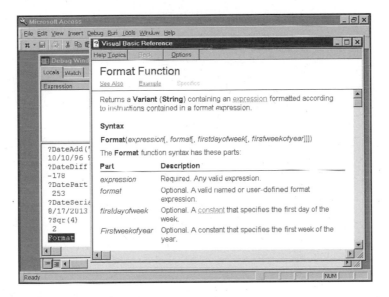

**FIG. 9.3** The Format function help window.

5. After reviewing the syntax and other information concerning the function, close the Help window by clicking its Close Window button.

Help windows for functions have a standard format, as shown in Figure 9.3. If you click the Example hotspot in any function Help window, another window displays an example of the function used in Access VBA code. These examples show the syntax of the functions and appropriate arguments.

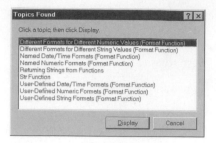

**FIG. 9.4** The Topics Found dialog displayed by clicking the See Also hotspot.

**The *Variant* Data Type in Access.** `Variant` is a special data type unique to Microsoft Visual Basic dialects. The `Variant` data type enables you to concatenate values that ordinarily have different data types, such as an integer and a character string. The capability to concatenate different data types is called *turning off data-type checking*. `Variant` values are related to the `As Any` data type that Access VBA uses to turn off data-type checking when declaring external functions contained in Windows Dynamic Link Libraries (DLLs).

The `Variant` data type enables you to concatenate field values of tables and queries that have dissimilar data types without using VBA's data-type conversion functions such as `Str$`. (`Str$` converts numeric values to the `String` data type.) The `Variant` data type also simplifies expressions that combine field values to create concatenated indexes. The `Variant` data type also enables you to use the `&` symbol to concatenate values of different data types. SQL requires you to use the ampersand for such concatenation.

 ▶▶ See "Access Intrinsic Constants," p. 996

Table 9.5 lists the 16 subtypes of the `Variant` data type of Access VBA, along with the names of the intrinsic Visual Basic constants, *vbConstant*, corresponding to the `Variant` subtype value. Access 2.0 defined only `Variant` subtypes 0–8. In addition to the Access intrinsic constants that Access 2.0 originally defined, VBA provides its own set of intrinsic constants, which are prefixed with vb. Access intrinsic constants are prefixed with ac. Intrinsic constants, which you use primarily when writing Access VBA code, are one of the subjects of Chapter 29, "Understanding the Data Access Object Class."

| Table 9.5 | Subtypes of the `Variant` Data Type | | |
|---|---|---|---|
| **Subtype** | **Constant** | **Corresponds To** | **Stored As** |
| 0 | (None) | **Empty** (uninitialized) | Not applicable |
| 1 | vbNull | **Null** (no valid data) | Not applicable |

| Subtype | Constant | Corresponds To | Stored As |
|---------|----------|----------------|-----------|
| 2 | vbInteger | **Integer** | 2-byte integer |
| 3 | vbLong | **Long** | 4-byte long integer |
| 4 | vbSingle | **Single** | 4-byte single-precision floating point |
| 5 | vbDouble | **Double** | 8-byte double-precision floating point |
| 6 | vbCurrency | **Currency** | 4-byte fixed point |
| 7 | vbDate | Date/Time | 8-byte double-precision floating point |
| 8 | vbString | **String** | Conventional string variable |
| 9 | vbObject | **Object** | Automation object |
| 10 | vbError | **Error** | **Error** data type (error number) |
| 11 | vbBoolean | **Boolean** | **True** or **False** values only |
| 12 | vbVariant | **Variant** | Used with **Variant** arrays |
| 13 | vbDataObject | Special | Non-Automation object |
| 17 | vbByte | **Byte** | Numeric value from 0–255 |
| 8192 | vbArray | **Array** | Used with **Variant** arrays |

You can concatenate **Variant** values with **Variant** subtypes 1–8 listed in Table 9.5. You can concatenate a subtype 8 **Variant** (**String**) with a subtype 5 **Variant** (**Double**), for example, without receiving from Access the Type Mismatch error message displayed when you attempt this concatenation with conventional **String** (text) and **Double** data types. Access returns a value with the **Variant** subtype corresponding to the highest subtype number of the concatenated values. This example, therefore, returns a subtype 8 (**String**) **Variant** because 8 is greater than 5, the subtype number for the **Double** value. If you concatenate a subtype 2 (**Integer**) value with a subtype 3 (**Long**) value, Access returns subtype 3 **Variant** data.

Distinguishing between the **Empty** and **Null Variant** subtypes is important. **Empty** indicates that a variable that you created with Access VBA code has a name but doesn't have an initial value. **Empty** applies only to Access VBA variables (see Chapter 28, "Writing Visual Basic for Applications Code"). **Null** indicates that a data cell doesn't contain an entry. You can assign the **Null** value to a variable, in which case the variable is initialized to the **Null** value, **Variant** subtype 1.

▶▶ See "Variables and Naming Conventions," p. 988

You can experiment with **Variant** subtypes in the Debug window to become more familiar with using the **Variant** data type. VBA provides a function, **VarType**, that returns the integer value of its argument's subtype. Figure 9.5 shows the data subtype values that **VarType** returns for four variables (A to D) and the result of the concatenation of these variables (E).

**FIG. 9.5**   The **Variant** subtype return values for four variables and the result of their concatenation.

    ◄◄ See "Choosing Field Data Types, Sizes, and Formats," p. 119
◄◄ See "Adding Indexes to Tables," p. 154

**Functions for Date and Time.**   Access offers a variety of functions for dealing with dates and times. If you have used Visual Basic, you probably recognize most of the functions applicable to the Date/Time field data types shown in Table 9.6. VBA has several Date/Time functions, such as **DateAdd** and **DateDiff**, to simplify the calculation of date values.

All Date/Time values are stored as double-precision values but are returned as **Variant** subtype 7 unless you use the function's **String** form. The **String** form is identified by the **String** data type identification character, **$**, appended to the end of the function name. Both **?** **VarType(Date$)** and **?** **VarType(Time$)** return a subtype 8 (**String**) **Variant**.

> **Note**
>
> The Debug window in Figure 9.1 shows a few of the entries used to test the syntax examples of Table 9.6.

| Table 9.6 | Access Functions for Date and Time | | |
|---|---|---|---|
| **Function** | **Description** | **Example** | **Returns** |
| Date, Date$ | Returns the current system date and time as a subtype 7 date **Variant** or a standard date **String** subtype 8. | Date | 7/15/97 07-15-97 |
| DateAdd | Returns a subtype 7 date with a specified number of days, weeks ("ww"), months ("m"), or years ("y") added to the date. | DateAdd ("d",31, #7/15/97#) | 8/15/97 |

| Function | Description | Example | Returns |
|---|---|---|---|
| DateDiff | Returns an **Integer** representing the difference between two dates using the d/w/m/y specification. | DateDiff ("d",Date, #4/15/95#) | -91 (assuming **Date** = 7/15/95) 7 (Saturday) |
| DatePart | Returns the specified part of a date such as day, month, year, day of week ("w"), and so on, as an **Integer**. | DatePart ("w", #7/15/95) | |
| DateSerial | Returns a subtype 7 **Variant** from year, month, and day arguments. | DateSerial (95,7,15) | 7/15/95 |
| DateValue | Returns a subtype 7 **Variant** that corresponds to a date argument in a character format. | DateValue ("15-Jul-95") | 7/15/95 |
| Day | Returns an **Integer** between 1 and 31 (inclusive) that represents a day of the month from a Date/Time value. | Day(Date) | 15 (assuming that the date is the 15th of the month) |
| Hour | Returns an **Integer** between 0 and 23 (inclusive) that represents the hour of the Date/Time value. | Hour (#2:30 PM#) | 14 |
| Minute | Returns an **Integer** between 0 and 59 (inclusive) that represents the minute of a Date/Time value. | Minute (#2:30 PM#) | 30 |
| Month | Returns an **Integer** between 1 and 12 (inclusive) that represents the month of a Date/Time value. | Month(#15-Jul-95#) | 7 |
| Now | Returns the date and time of a computer's system clock as a **Variant** of subtype 7. | Now | 7/15/95 11:57:28 AM |
| Second | Returns an **Integer** between 0 and 59 (inclusive) that represents the second of a Date/Time value. | Second (Now) | 28 |
| Time, Time$ | Returns the Time portion of a Date/Time value from the system clock. | Time (returns subtype 7) Time$ (returns String) | 11:57:20 AM |
| TimeSerial | Returns the time serial value of the time expressed in integer hours, minutes, and seconds. | TimeSerial (11,57,20) | 11:57:20 AM |
| TimeValue | Returns the time serial value of the time (entered as the **String** value) as a subtype 7 **Variant**. | TimeValue ("11:57") | 11:57 |
| Weekday | Returns day of the week (Sunday = 1) corresponding to the date as an **Integer**. | Weekday (#7/15/95#) | 7 |
| Year | Returns the year of a Date/Time value as an **Integer**. | Year (#7/15/95#) | 1994 |

II

Querying for Information

**Text-Manipulation Functions.** Table 9.7 lists the functions that deal with the Text field data type, corresponding to the **String** data type or **Variant** subtype 8. Most of these functions are modeled on BASIC string functions.

**Table 9.7 Functions for String and Subtype 8 Variant Data Types**

| Function | Description | Example | Returns |
|---|---|---|---|
| Asc | Returns ANSI numeric value of character as an **Integer**. | Asc("C") | 67 |
| Chr, Chr$ | Returns character corresponding to the numeric ANSI value as a **String**. | Chr(67) Chr$(10) | C (line feed) |
| Format, Format$ | Formats an expression in accordance with appropriate format strings. | Format (Date, "dd-mmm-yy") | 15-Jul-95 |
| InStr | Returns the position of one string within another. | InStr ("ABCD","C") | 3 |
| LCase, LCase$ | Returns the lowercase version of a string. | LCase ("ABCD") | abcd |
| Left, Left$ | Returns the leftmost characters of a string. | Left ("ABCDEF",3) | ABC |
| Len | Returns the number of characters in a string as a **Long**. | Len("ABCDE") | 5 |
| LTrim, LTrim$ | Removes leading spaces from string. | LTrim (" ABC") | ABC |
| Mid, Mid$ | Returns a portion of a string. | Mid ("ABCDE",2,3) | BCD |
| Right, Right$ | Returns the rightmost characters of a string. | Right ("ABCDEF",3) | DEF |
| RTrim, RTrim$ | Removes trailing spaces from a string. | RTrim ("ABC ") | ABC |
| Space, Space$ | Returns a string consisting of a specified number of spaces. | Space(5) | |
| Str, Str$ | Converts the numeric value of any data type to a string. | Str(123.45) | 123.45 |
| StrComp | Compares two strings for equivalence and returns the integer result of the comparison. | StrComp ("ABC", "abc") | 0 |
| String, String$ | Returns a string consisting of specified repeated characters. | String (5, "A") | AAAAA |
| Trim, Trim$ | Removes leading and trailing spaces from a string. | Trim (" ABC ") | ABC |
| UCase, UCase$ | Returns the uppercase version of a string. | UCase ("abc") | ABC |
| Val | Returns the numeric value of a string in a data type appropriate to the argument's format. | Val ("123.45") | 123.45 |

> **Note**
>
> There are two different types of **String** variables: variable-length and fixed-length. Access 97 table fields of the Text data type are variable-length (**Variant** subtype 8) and can range from 0–255 characters. In Access VBA, variable-length strings can contain up to about two billion (2 ^ 31) characters. (Access 2.0 Basic limited variable-length strings to about 64K characters.) Fixed-length strings, which you declare in VBA with the syntax **Dim** str*Variable* **As String** * lng*Length*, can range from 1 to about 64K (2 ^ 16) characters. Access 97 Memo fields remain limited to a maximum of 64K characters for data entered at the keyboard, but can contain up to approximately 2 billion characters when text is entered via Access VBA code.

Table 9.7 shows two versions of most of the functions: one with, and one without a string-identifier character (**$**). In these cases, the function without **$** returns a **Variant** subtype 8 (**String**); the function with **$** returns the Text field data type (**String** in VBA). Figure 9.6 shows tests of a few of the string functions in the Debug window.

**FIG. 9.6**    Testing the string-manipulation functions in the Debug window.

Access's **Format** and **Format$** functions are identical to the **Format** and **Format$** functions of Visual Basic 4.0 and VBA (see Chapter 4, "Working with Access Databases and Tables," for the arguments of these functions). Table 9.7 doesn't include the **Tab** and **Spc** functions because these functions are used primarily to format the printing of text strings, which Access's built-in report-generation feature handles.

 ◀◀ See "Custom Display Formats," p. 125

> **Note**
>
> Access 97 stores **String** and **Variant** subtype 8 values in 32-bit Windows' Unicode format, which requires 2 bytes to define a single character. Unicode has the advantage of providing 2-byte codes for both alphabetic characters and the pictographic characters used in Asian languages. Access 97's string-manipulation functions count characters, not bytes. The FieldSize property of fields of Access 97 Recordset objects, however, is measured in bytes. Thus, values returned by the FieldSize property of a Recordset are twice those returned by the **Len** function. The difference between characters and bytes is significant in VBA programming that uses the GetChunk and AppendChunk methods, but not in the ordinary use of Access 97.

**Numeric, Logical, Date/Time, and *String* Data-Type Conversion Functions.** You can assign a particular data type to a numeric value with any of the data-type conversion functions. After you *freeze* (or *coerce*) a data type with one of the numeric data-type conversion functions, you cannot concatenate that data type with the **String** data type or data **Variant** subtype 7.

Table 9.8 lists the 11 numeric data-type conversion functions of Access 97. Access 97 introduces VBA's **Boolean**, **Byte**, and **Error** data types. The *NumValue* argument in the Syntax column can be any numeric or **String** value. However, if you use a **String** value as the argument of a numeric-type conversion function, the first character of the argument's value must be a digit, a dollar sign, a plus symbol, or a minus symbol.

**Table 9.8   Data-Type Conversion Functions for Numeric, Time/Date, and String Values**

| Function | Description | Syntax |
|---|---|---|
| CBool | Converts a numeric value to a **Boolean** (**True** or **False**) data type. | **CBool**(*NumValue*) |
| Cbyte | Converts a numeric value to a **Byte** (0–255) data type. | **CByte**(*NumValue*) |
| CCur | Converts a numeric value to a **Currency** data type. | **CCur**(*NumValue*) |
| CDbl | Converts a numeric value to a **Double** data type. | **CDbl**(*NumValue*) |
| CInt | Converts a numeric value to an **Integer** data type. | **CInt**(*NumValue*) |
| CLng | Converts a numeric value to a **Long** integer data type. | **CLng**(*NumValue*) |
| CSng | Converts a numeric value to a **Single** data type. | **CSng**(*NumValue*) |
| CStr | Converts a numeric value to a **String** data type. | **CStr**(*NumValue*) |
| CVar | Converts a numeric value to a **Variant** data type. | **CVar**(*NumValue*) |
| CVDate | Converts a numeric value to a **Variant** subtype 7. | **CVDate**(*NumValue*) |
| CVErr | Converts a valid error number to create user-defined errors. | **CVErr**(*NumValue*) |

**Mathematic and Trigonometric Functions.** Access provides a sufficient number of mathematic and trigonometric functions to meet most scientific and engineering requirements. You can create additional trigonometric functions with more complex expressions. If you are interested in more obscure transcendental functions, such as cosecants or hyperbolic functions, choose <u>H</u>elp, <u>C</u>ontents and Index, click the Index tab, enter **math functions** in the text box, and then click Derived Math Functions in the Topics Found dialog. Table 9.9 lists the mathematic and trigonometric functions available directly in Access.

| Table 9.9    Mathematic and Trigonometric Functions | | | |
| --- | --- | --- | --- |
| **Function** | **Description** | **Example** | **Returns** |
| Abs | Returns the absolute value of a numeric value. | Abs(--1234.5) | 1234.5 |
| Atn | Returns the arctangent of a numeric value, in radians. | Atn(1) | .7853982 |
| Cos | Returns the cosine of the angle represented by a numeric value, in radians. | Cos(pi/4) | .707106719949 |
| Exp | Returns the exponential (antilog) of the numeric value. | Exp(2.302585) | 9.9999990700 (rounding errors) |
| Fix | Identical to **Int**, except for negative numbers. | Fix(--13.5) | 13 |
| Int | Returns a numeric value with the decimal fraction truncated; the data type isn't changed unless the argument is a string. | Int(13.5)<br>Int(--13.5) | 13<br>14 |
| Log | Returns natural (Napierian) logarithm of a numeric value. | Log(10) | 2.302585 |
| Rnd | Creates a random single-precision number between 0 and 1 when no argument is supplied. Must be initialized by first executing the **Randomize** statement. | Rnd (varies) | .533424 |
| Sgn | Returns the sign of a numeric value: 0 if positive, –1 if negative. | Sgn(--13.5) | --1 |
| Sin | Returns the sine of a numeric value, in radians. | Sin(pi/4) | .707106842423 |
| Sqr | Returns the square root of a numeric value. | Sqr(144) | 12 |
| Tan | Returns the tangent of a numeric value, in radians. | Tan(pi/4) | 1.0000001732 (fraction because of rounding) |

The angles returned by the trigonometric functions are expressed in radians, as is the argument of the arctangent (**Atn**) function shown in the table. To obtain the values shown in Table 9.9's examples, type the expression **Pi = 3.141593** in the Debug window before entering the syntax example expressions. The returned values of the trigonometric functions are for an angle of approximately 45 degrees, corresponding to /4 radians.

> **Note**
>
> Because a 360-degree circle contains 2 radians, you convert radians to degrees with the expression radians * 360/2 . Because Pi is a rounded value of  and the trigonometric functions round results, you usually obtain values with rounding errors. The cosine of 45 degrees, for example, is 0.7070707... but Access returns 0.7071067.... These rounding errors are not significant in most applications.

**Int** and **Fix** differ in the following way: **Fix** returns the first negative integer less than or equal to the argument; **Int** returns the first negative integer greater than or equal to the argument. **Int** and **Fix**, unlike other mathematic and trigonometric functions, return the integer value of a string variable but not the value of a literal string argument. Entering **?Int("13.5")**, for example, returns a data-type error message; however, if you type **A = 13.5** and then **? Int(A)**, Access returns 13.

**Financial Functions.** You might be interested in the financial functions of Access because you have used similar functions in Microsoft Excel or Lotus 1-2-3 spreadsheets. The financial functions of Access (supplied by VBA and listed in Table 9.10) are identical to their capitalized counterparts in Excel and employ the same arguments. If you have a table of fixed asset records, for example, you can use the depreciation functions to calculate monthly, quarterly, or yearly depreciation for each asset and then summarize the depreciation schedule in an Access report.

> **Note**
>
> A full description of the use and syntax of these functions is beyond the scope of this book. If you are interested in more details about these functions, choose <u>H</u>elp, <u>C</u>ontents and Index, click the Index tab, and enter the function name in the text box.

### Table 9.10  Financial Functions for Calculating Depreciation and Annuities

| Function | Description |
| --- | --- |
| DDB | Returns the depreciation of a fixed asset over a specified period by using the double-declining balance method. |
| FV | Returns the future value of an investment based on a series of constant periodic payments and a fixed rate of interest. |
| IPmt | Returns the amount of interest for an installment payment on a fixed-rate loan or annuity. |
| IRR | Returns the internal rate of return for an investment consisting of a series of periodic incomes and expenses. |
| MIRR | Returns the modified internal rate of return for an investment consisting of a series of periodic incomes and expenses. |
| NPer | Returns the number of payments of a given amount required to create an annuity or to retire a loan. |
| NPV | Returns the net present value of an annuity paid in equal periodic installments. |
| Pmt | Returns the amount of the periodic payment that must be made to create an annuity or to retire a loan. |
| PPmt | Returns the amount of principal in an installment payment on a fixed-rate loan or annuity. |
| PV | Returns the present value of an annuity paid in equal periodic installments. |
| Rate | Returns the interest rate of a loan or annuity based on a constant interest rate and equal periodic payments. |
| SLN | Returns the depreciation of a fixed asset over a specified period by using the straight-line method. |
| SYD | Returns the depreciation of a fixed asset over a specified period by the |

| Function | Description |
|----------|-------------|
|          | sum-of-the-years'-digits method. |

**Miscellaneous Functions.** Access provides several functions that don't fit in any of the preceding categories but that you can use for creating queries and validating data entries, or with forms, reports, and macros. Table 9.11 lists these general-purpose functions.

**Table 9.11  Miscellaneous Access Functions**

| Function | Description | Syntax |
|----------|-------------|--------|
| Choose | Returns a value from a list of values, based on the value's position in the list. | `Choose([Unit of Measure], "Each", "Dozen", "Gross")` |
| IIf | Returns one value if the result of an expression is **True**, another if the result is **False**. | `IIf([Order Quantity]Mod 12 = 0, "Dozen", "Each")` |
| IsArray | Returns **True** if the argument is an array; otherwise, returns **False**. | `IsArray(varName)` |
| IsDate | Returns **True** if the argument is the Date/Time field data type; otherwise, returns **False**. | `IsDate(FieldName)` |
| IsEmpty | Returns **True** if the argument is a noninitialized variable; otherwise, returns **False**. | `IsEmpty(varName)` |
| IsError | Returns **True** if the argument is an Error object; otherwise, returns **False**. | `IsError(varName)` |
| IsMissing | Returns **True** if an optional argument has not been passed to a procedure; otherwise, returns **False**. | `IsMissing(argOptional)` |
| IsNull | Returns **True** if the argument is **Null**; otherwise, returns **False**. | `IsNull(FieldName)` |
| IsNumeric | Returns **True** if the argument is one of the Number field data types; otherwise, returns **False**. | `IsNumeric(FieldName)` |
| IsObject | Returns **True** if the argument refers to a valid Automation object; otherwise, returns **False**. | `IsObject(objName)` |
| Partition | Returns a **String** value indicating the number of occurrences of a value within a range of values. | `Partition (Number, Start, Stop, Interval)` |
| Switch | Returns the value associated with the first of a series of expressions evaluating to **True**. | `Switch([Unit of Measure], "Each", 1, "Dozen", 12, "Gross", 144)` |
| TypeName | Returns the **String** value representing the name of the **Variant** data type; for instance, "Byte." | `TypeName(varName)` |

`Choose` creates a lookup table that returns a value corresponding to a position from a list of values that you create. `Choose` is related closely to the `Switch` function, which returns a value associated with the first of a series of expressions evaluating to **True**. In Table 9.11's `Choose` example, if the value of the Unit of Measure field is 1, the function returns Each; if the value is 2, `Choose` returns Dozen; and if the value is 3, the function returns Gross. Otherwise, the function returns **Null**.

The `Switch` example returns a divisor value for an order. If the value of the Unit of Measure field is Each, **Switch** returns 1. If Unit of Measure is Dozen, the function returns 12; if Unit of Measure is Gross, **Switch** returns 144. The function returns **Null** for no matching value. **Choose** and **Switch** have similarities to the **Select Case** statement in VBA and other BASIC dialects (**Null** is the **Case Else** value).

The **IIf** function is called *in-line If*, or *immediate If*, because it substitutes for the multiline If...Then...Else...End If structure of the VBA conditional expression. In the example shown in Table 9.11, the **IIf** function returns Dozen if the quantity ordered is evenly divisible by 12; otherwise, the function returns Each.

The **Partition** function creates histograms. A *histogram* is a series of values (usually displayed as a bar chart) representing the frequency of events that can be grouped within specific ranges. A familiar histogram is a distribution of school examination grades, indicating the number of students who received grades A, B, C, D, and F. The grades might be based on a range of test scores from 90 to 100, 80 to 89, 70 to 79, 60 to 69, and less than 60. You establish the upper and lower limits of the data and then add the partition value.

Effective use of the **Partition** function requires typing or editing a SQL statement; the result of the query is most useful if presented in graphical form. Adding a histogram chart to a form is much easier than using the **Partition** function.

The eight **IsDataType** functions, four of which were new in Access 95, determine the type or value of data. You can use **IsNull** in validation rules and query criteria of one field to determine whether another field—whose field name is used as the argument—contains a valid entry. Although *FieldName* is the argument in the example syntax in Table 9.11, you can substitute an Access VBA variable name.

**Other Functions.** The chapters that cover other aspects of Access 97 describe and provide the syntax for the following special-purpose functions:

- *SQL aggregate functions* are described in Chapter 10, "Creating Multitable and Crosstab Queries." You use these functions most often with multiple-table queries that provide the data source forms. SQL aggregate functions return statistical data on the records selected by a query. You cannot use these functions in macros or call them from Access VBA modules, except within quoted strings used to create SQL statements to populate Recordset objects.

- *Domain aggregate functions* perform the same functions as the SQL aggregate functions, but on calculated values rather than the values contained in query fields. Chapter 12, "Creating and Using Forms," covers these functions. One domain aggregate function, **DCount**, is useful in validating entries in tables; this function is explained later in this chapter in the section "Expressions for Validating Data."

- The two dynamic data exchange functions, **DDE** and **DDESend**, are used to transfer data from and to other applications, respectively. In most cases, you use DDE functions with applications that don't support ActiveX Automation (formerly known as OLE Automation), the preferred method of interapplication data exchange.

■ The remaining Access functions are used exclusively or almost exclusively in Access VBA modules, and are described in Part VII of this book, "Programming, Distributing, and Converting Access Applications."

### Intrinsic and Named Constants

As noted earlier in this chapter, VBA and Access have many predefined intrinsic constants. The names of these constants are considered *keywords* because you cannot use these names for any purpose other than returning the value represented by the names, such as −1 for **True** and Yes, 0 for **False** and No. (**True** and Yes are synonyms, as are **False** and No, so you can use these pairs of values interchangeably.) As mentioned earlier in the chapter, **Null** indicates a field with no valid entry. **True**, **False**, and **Null** are the most commonly used VBA intrinsic constants.

*Named constants*, which you define, return a single, predetermined value for the entire Access session. You can create named constants for use with forms and reports by defining them in the declarations section of an Access VBA module. Chapter 28, "Writing Visual Basic for Applications Code," describes how to create and use named constants such as Pi (used in the examples of trigonometric functions).

▶▶ See "Access Intrinsic Constants," p. 996

# Creating Access Expressions

Chapter 5, "Entering, Editing, and Validating Data in Tables," uses several functions to validate data entry for most fields in the Personnel Actions table. Chapter 8, "Using Query By Example," uses an expression to select the states to be included in a mailing list query. These examples provide the foundation on which to build more complex expressions that can define more precisely the validation rules and query criteria for real-life database applications.

◀◀ See "Validating Data Entry," p. 170
◀◀ See "Creating Your First Real Query," p. 262

The topics that follow provide a few examples of typical expressions for creating default values for fields, validating data entry, creating query criteria, and calculating field values. The examples demonstrate the similarity of syntax for expressions with different purposes. Part III of this book, "Creating Forms and Reports," provides additional examples of expressions designed for use in forms and reports; Part VII, "Programming, Distributing, and Converting Access Applications," explains the use of expressions with Access VBA code.

### Expressions for Creating Default Values

Expressions that create default field values can speed the entry of new records. Assigning values ordinarily requires you to use the assignment operator (=). When entering a default value in the Properties pane for a table in Design mode, however, you can enter a simple literal. An example is the Q default value assigned to the paType field in Chapter 4, "Working with Access Databases and Tables." In this case, Access infers the = assignment operator and the quotation marks surrounding the Q. To adhere to the rules of creating expressions, the default value entry must be = "Q". You often can use shorthand techniques when typing expressions because Access infers the missing characters. If you enter = "Q", you achieve the same result; Access doesn't infer the extra characters.

You can use complex expressions for default values if the result of the expression conforms to or can be converted by Access to the proper field data type. You can enter = 1 as the default value for the paType field, for example, although 1 is a Numeric field data type and paType is a Text type field.

### Expressions for Validating Data

The Personnel Actions table uses several expressions to validate data entry. The validation rule for the paID field is > 0; the rule for the paType field is "S" Or "Q" Or "Y" Or "B" Or "C"; the rule for the paApprovedBy field is > 0 Or Is Null. The validation rule for the paID field is equivalent to the following imaginary in-line IIf function:

```
IIf(DataEntry > 0, paID = DataEntry,
    MsgBox("Please enter a valid employee ID number."))
```

Access tests *DataEntry* in the validation rule expression. If the validation expression returns **True**, the value of *DataEntry* replaces the value in the current record's field. If the expression returns **False**, a message box displays the validation text that you typed. **MsgBox** is a function used in VBA programming to display a message box on-screen. You cannot type the imaginary validation rule just described; Access infers the equivalent of the imaginary **IIf** expression after you add the ValidationRule and ValidationText properties with entries in the two text boxes for the paID field.

You might change the expression "S" Or "Q" Or "Y" Or "B" Or "C", which you use to test the paType field, to a function. The **In** function provides a simpler expression that accomplishes the same objective:

```
In("S", "Q", "Y", "B", "C")
```

Alternatively, you can use the following table-level validation expression:

```
InStr("SQYBC",[paID]) > 0
```

Both expressions give the same result, but you can use **InStr** only for table-level validation because one of its arguments refers to a field name. Thus, the **In** function provides the better solution.

### Expressions for Query Criteria

When creating Chapter 8's qryUSMailingList query to select records from the states of California, Oregon, and Washington, you enter ="CA", ="OR", and ="WA" on separate lines. A better expression is **In**("CA", "OR", "WA"), entered on the same line as the ="USA" criterion for the Country field. This expression corrects the failure to test the Country field for a value equal to USA for the OR and WA entries.

◀◀ See "Creating More Complex Queries," p. 269

You can use a wide range of other functions to select specific records to be returned to a query table. Table 9.12 shows some typical functions used as query criteria applicable to the Northwind Traders tables.

| **Table 9.12** | **Typical Expressions Used as Query Criteria** | | |
|---|---|---|---|
| **Table** | **Field** | **Expression** | **Records Returned** |
| Customers | Country | **Not** "USA" **And** **Not** "Canada" | Firms other than those in the U.S. and Canada. |
| Customers | Country | **Not** ("USA" **Or** "Canada") | Firms other than those in the U.S. and Canada; the parentheses apply the condition to both literals. |
| Customers | CompanyName | Like "[N—Z]*" | Firms with names beginning with N through Z, outside the U.S. |
| Customers | CompanyName | Like S* **Or** Like V* | Firms with names beginning with S or V (Access adds Like and quotation marks). |
| Customers | CompanyName | Like "*shop*" | Firms with *shop*, *Shop*, *Shoppe*, or *SHOPPING* in the firm name. |
| Customers | PostalCode | >=90000 | Firms with postal codes greater than or equal to 90000. |
| Orders | OrderDate | **Year**([OrderDate]) = 1995 | Orders received to date, beginning with 1/1/1995. |
| Orders | OrderDate | Like "*/*/95" | Orders received to date, beginning with 1/1/1995; using wild cards simplifies expressions. |
| Orders | OrderDate | Like "1/*/95" | Orders received in the month of January 1995. |
| Orders | OrderDate | Like "1/?/95" | Orders received from the 1st to the 9th of January 1995. |
| Orders | OrderDate | **Year**([OrderDate] = 1995 **And** DatePart("q", [OrderDate]) = 1 | Orders received in the first quarter of 1995. |
| Orders | OrderDate | Between #1/1/95# **And** #3/31/95# | Orders received in the first quarter of 1995. |
| Orders | OrderDate | **Year**([OrderDate] = 1995 **And** DatePart("ww", [OrderDate]) = 10 | Orders received in the 10th week of 1995. |
| Orders | OrderDate | >= **DateValue** ("1/15/95") | Orders received on or after 1/15/95. |
| Orders | Shipped Date | **Is Null** | Orders not yet shipped. |
| Orders | Order Amount | >= 5000 | Orders with values greater than or equal to $5,000. |

*(continues)*

II

Querying for Information

| Table 9.12 | Continued | | |
| Table | Field | Expression | Records Returned |
| --- | --- | --- | --- |
| Orders | Order Amount | Between 5000 And 10000 | Orders with values greater than or equal to $5,000 and less than or equal to $10,000. |
| Orders | Order Amount | < 1000 | Orders less than $1,000. |

The wildcard characters used in Like expressions simplify the creation of criteria for selecting names and dates. As in DOS, the asterisk (*) substitutes for any legal number of characters, and the question mark (?) substitutes for a single character. When a wildcard character prefixes or appends a string, the matching process loses its default case-sensitivity. If you want to match a string without regard to case, use the following expression:

UCase$(*FieldName*) = "*MATCH STRING*"

> **Note**
>
> The Orders table of the Northwind Traders sample database supplied with Access 1.0 and 1.1 included an Order Amount field. The value in the Order Amount field was set equal to the sum of the products of the Quantity and Unit Price fields, less the Discount percentage, of the records in the Order Details table. Including the Order Amount field violates the rule of relational databases that requires that all data in the fields of primary tables (Orders is a primary table) be dependent on the primary key and independent of other fields, either in the table or in other tables. The Order Amount field's value depends on the entries in the Order Details table.

**Entering a Query Criterion.** To experiment with query criteria expressions, follow these steps:

1. Click the Queries tab of the Database window, click the New button to open a new query, then click OK when the New Query dialog appears.

2. Select the Customers table from the Tables list of the Show Table dialog, and click the Add button. Repeat this process for the Orders and Order Details table. (Alternatively, you can add a table from the Show Table dialog by double-clicking the table.) Click the Close button to close the Add Table dialog. The CustomerID fields of the Customers and Orders tables and the OrderID fields of the Orders and Order Details tables are joined; *joins* are indicated by a line between the fields of the two tables. (The next chapter covers joining multiple tables.)

3. Add the CompanyName, PostalCode, and Country fields of the Customers table to the query. You can add fields by selecting them from the Field drop-down list in the Query Design grid, by clicking a field in the Customers field list above the grid and dragging the field to the desired Field cell in the grid, or by double-clicking a field in the Customers field list above the grid.

**4.** Add to the query the OrderID, OrderDate, ShippedDate, and Freight fields of the Orders table. Use the horizontal scroll bar slider under the Query Design grid to expose additional field columns as necessary. Choose <u>V</u>iew, Table <u>N</u>ames to display the table names in the Tables row of the Query Design grid, if necessary. Place the caret in the Sort row of the OrderID field, press F4 to open the Sort list box, and select Ascending Sort.

**5.** Click the Totals button of the toolbar or choose <u>V</u>iew, <u>T</u>otals to add the Total row to the Query Design grid. The default value, Group By, is added to the Total cell for each field of your query.

**6.** Scroll the grid so that the Freight column appears. Click the selection bar above the Field row to select the Freight column and press the Insert key to add a new column.

**7.** Type **Amount: CCur([UnitPrice]\*[Quantity]\*(1—[Discount]))** in the new column's Field cell (see Figure 9.7). This expression calculates the net amount of each line item in the Order Details table and formats the column as if the field data type were Currency. The next section discusses how to use expressions to create calculated fields.

**8.** Move the caret to the Total row of the new column and press F4 to open the drop-down list. Choose **Sum** from the list (refer to Figure 9.7). The Sum option totals the net amount for all the line items of each order in the Orders table. In the next chapter, you learn the details of how to create queries that group data.

The Total row for all the other columns of the query shows Group By. Make sure that you mark the Show check box so that your new query column appears when you run the query. (Do not make an entry in the Table row of your new query column; if you do, you receive an error message when you run the query.)

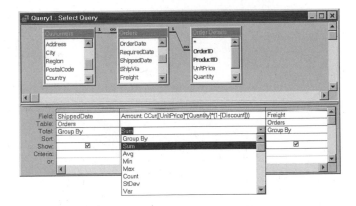

**FIG. 9.7** The query design for testing the use of expressions to select records with values that meet criteria.

9. Click the Run or Datasheet View button of the toolbar to run your new query. Your query appears as shown in Figure 9.8. The Amount column contains the total amount of the order and the net of discounts, if any.

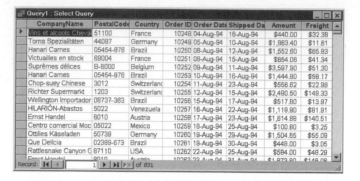

**FIG. 9.8** The query result set for the query design shown in Figure 9.7.

**Using the Expression Builder to Add Query Criteria.** After creating and testing your query, you can apply criteria to limit the number of records that the query returns. You can use Access's Expression Builder to simplify the process of adding record-selection criteria to your query. To test some of the expressions listed in Table 9.12, follow these steps:

1. Click the Design View button of the toolbar to change to Query Design mode.

2. Place the caret in the Criteria row of the field for which you want to establish a record-selection criterion.

3. Click the Build button of the toolbar to display the Expression Builder's window. Alternatively, you can right-click the Criteria row, then choose Build from the popup menu.

4. In the expression text box at the top of Expression Builder's window, type one of the expressions from Table 9.12. Figure 9.9 shows the sample expression Like "*shop*" that applies to the Criteria row of the Company Name column. You can use the Like button under the expression text box as a shortcut for entering Like.

5. Click OK to return to the Query Design grid. In the field where the caret is located, the Expression Builder places the expression that you built (see Figure 9.10).

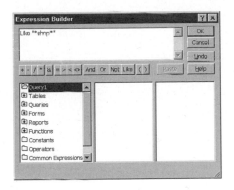

**FIG. 9.9** Entering a criterion in the Expression Builder to create a criterion to match *shop*.

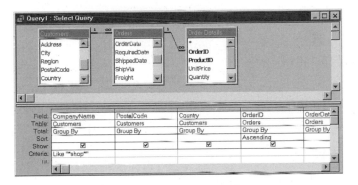

**FIG. 9.10** The Query Design grid with the expression that you created in the Expression Builder.

6. Click the Run button of the toolbar to test the expression. The query result for the example in Figure 9.10 appears as shown in Figure 9.11.

7. Return to Query Design mode, then select and delete the expression by pressing the Delete key.

8. Repeat steps 2–7 for each expression that you want to test. When you test expressions using Date/Time functions, sort the OrderDate field in ascending order. Similarly, sort on the Amount field when queries are based on amount criteria. You can alter the expressions and try combinations with the implied And condition by entering criteria for other fields in the same row. Access warns you with an error message if you make a mistake in an expression's syntax.

9. After you finish experimenting, save your query with a descriptive name, such as **qryOrderAmount**.

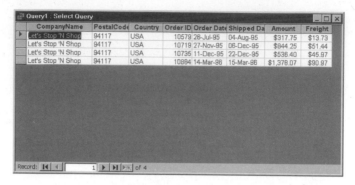

**FIG. 9.11**   The query result set resulting from adding the `Like  "*shop*"` criteria to the Company Name field.

## Expressions for Calculating Query Field Values

The preceding section demonstrated that you can use expressions to create new, calculated fields in query tables. Calculated fields display data computed based on the values of other fields in the same row of the query table. Table 9.13 shows some representative expressions that you can use to create calculated query fields.

| Table 9.13   Typical Expressions to Create Calculated Query Fields |||
| --- | --- | --- |
| **Column Name** | **Expression** | **Values Calculated** |
| TotalAmount | [Amount] + [Freight] | Sum of the OrderAmount and Freight fields. |
| FreightPercent | 100 * [Freight]/[Amount] | Freight charges as a percentage of the order amount. |
| FreightPct | Format([Freight]/[Amount], "Percent") | Freight charges as a percentage of the order amount, but with formatting applied. |
| SalesTax | Format([Amount] * 0.05, "$#,###.00") | Sales tax of 5 percent of the amount of the order added with a display similar to the Currency data type. |

To create a query containing calculated fields, follow these steps:

1. In Query Design view, move to the first blank column of the query that you created in the preceding section. Type the column name shown in Table 9.13, followed by a colon and then the expression. (Click the Build button of the toolbar to use the Expression Builder to enter the expression, as shown in Figure 9.12, or press Shift+F2 to use the Zoom box to enter the expression.) The expression for the example in Figure 9.12 is

```
FreightPct: Format([Freight]/[Amount],"Percent")
```

If you don't type the field name and colon, Access provides the default Expr1 as the calculated field name.

**FIG. 9.12**    Entering an expression in the Expression Builder to create a calculated field in a query.

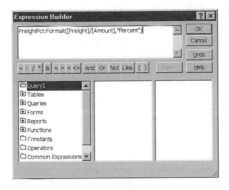

2. Place the caret in the Total cell of the calculated field and select Expression from the drop-down list, as shown in Figure 9.13. (If you don't select Expression, your query opens a Parameters dialog or returns an error message when you attempt to execute it.)

**FIG. 9.13**    The query design for two of the calculated fields of Table 9.13

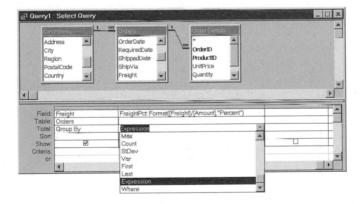

3. Run the query. The result set for the query with the calculated field appears as shown in Figure 9.14.

4. Repeat steps 1, 2, and 3 for each of the four examples in Table 9.13.

Query1 : Select Query

| CompanyName | PostalC | Country | Order ID | Order D | Shipped Da | Amount | Freight | FreightPct |
|---|---|---|---|---|---|---|---|---|
| Vins et alcools C | 51100 | France | 10248 | 04-Aug-9 | 16-Aug-94 | $440.00 | $32.38 | 7.36% |
| Toms Spezialitäte | 44087 | Germany | 10249 | 05-Aug-9 | 10-Aug-94 | $1,863.40 | $11.61 | 0.62% |
| Hanari Carnes | 05454-87 | Brazil | 10250 | 08-Aug-9 | 12-Aug-94 | $1,552.60 | $65.83 | 4.24% |
| Victuailles en stoc | 69004 | France | 10251 | 08-Aug-9 | 15-Aug-94 | $654.06 | $41.34 | 6.32% |
| Suprêmes délice: | B-6000 | Belgium | 10252 | 09-Aug-9 | 11-Aug-94 | $3,597.90 | $51.30 | 1.43% |
| Hanari Carnes | 05454-87 | Brazil | 10253 | 10-Aug-9 | 16-Aug-94 | $1,444.80 | $58.17 | 4.03% |
| Chop-suey Chine | 3012 | Switzerlai | 10254 | 11-Aug-9 | 23-Aug-94 | $556.62 | $22.98 | 4.13% |
| Richter Superma | 1203 | Switzerlai | 10255 | 12-Aug-9 | 15-Aug-94 | $2,490.50 | $148.33 | 5.96% |
| Wellington Import | 08737-36 | Brazil | 10256 | 15-Aug-9 | 17-Aug-94 | $517.80 | $13.97 | 2.70% |
| HILARIÓN-Abastc | 5022 | Venezuel: | 10257 | 16-Aug-9 | 22-Aug-94 | $1,119.90 | $81.91 | 7.31% |
| Ernst Handel | 8010 | Austria | 10258 | 17-Aug-9 | 23-Aug-94 | $1,614.88 | $140.51 | 8.70% |
| Centro comercial | 05022 | Mexico | 10259 | 18-Aug-9 | 25-Aug-94 | $100.80 | $3.25 | 3.22% |
| Ottilies Käseladei | 50739 | Germany | 10260 | 19-Aug-9 | 29-Aug-94 | $1,504.65 | $55.09 | 3.66% |
| Que Delícia | 02389-67 | Brazil | 10261 | 19-Aug-9 | 30-Aug-94 | $448.00 | $3.05 | 0.68% |
| Rattlesnake Cany | 87110 | USA | 10262 | 22-Aug-9 | 25-Aug-94 | $584.00 | $48.29 | 8.27% |

Record: 1 of 831

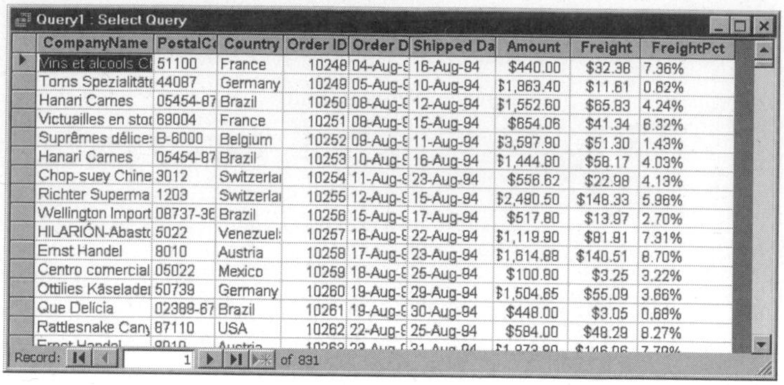

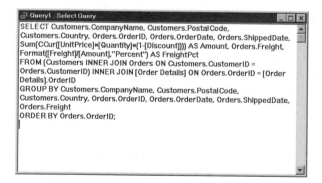

**FIG. 9.14** The query result set displaying the order total and freight charges as a percent of the order amount.

You use the **Format** function with your expression as its first argument to display the calculated values in a more readable form. When you add the percent symbol (`%`) to a format expression or specify `"Percent"` as the format, the value of the expression argument multiplies by 100, and the percent symbol preceded by a space appends to the displayed value. (Access 2.0 introduced `"Percent"` as a new format specifier equivalent to entering `"0.00%"`.)

Figure 9.15 shows the rather complex SQL statement that creates the query with two calculated fields in Access's SQL window. (Choose View, SQL or right-click a blank area of the upper pane and choose View SQL from the popup menu to display the SQL window.) Note that you cannot include periods to indicate abbreviations in field names. Periods and exclamation points are identifier operators, and you cannot include them within identifiers.

Query1 : Select Query

```
SELECT Customers.CompanyName, Customers.PostalCode,
Customers.Country, Orders.OrderID, Orders.OrderDate, Orders.ShippedDate,
Sum(CCur([UnitPrice]*[Quantity]*(1-[Discount]))) AS Amount, Orders.Freight,
Format([Freight]/[Amount],"Percent") AS FreightPct
FROM (Customers INNER JOIN Orders ON Customers.CustomerID =
Orders.CustomerID) INNER JOIN [Order Details] ON Orders.OrderID = [Order
Details].OrderID
GROUP BY Customers.CompanyName, Customers.PostalCode,
Customers.Country, Orders.OrderID, Orders.OrderDate, Orders.ShippedDate,
Orders.Freight
ORDER BY Orders.OrderID;
```

**FIG. 9.15** The SQL statement used to create a query with two calculated fields.

## Troubleshooting

*When attempting to execute a query that contains an expression, a* `Can't evaluate expression` *or* *Wrong data type message box appears.*

The Can't evaluate expression message usually indicates a typographic error in naming a function or an object. Depending on the use of the function, an Enter Parameter Value dialog might appear if the named object does not exist. The Wrong data type message is most likely to occur as a result of attempting to use mathematic or trigonometric operators with values of the Text or Date/Time field data types. If your expression refers to a control contained in a Form or Report object, the form or report must be open when you execute the function.

**Other Uses for Expressions**

You can use expressions with update queries, to calculate fields in forms and reports, as conditions for the execution of a VBA procedure, or as an argument for an action you program in VBA SQL SELECT statements use expressions as in the following fragment:

```
WHERE [Birth Date] >= #1/1/60#
```

See Chapter 24, "Working with Structured Query Language," for more information. Access VBA code also uses expressions extensively to control program flow and structure. The chapters focusing on SQL and Access VBA programming (Parts VI and VII) describe these uses for expressions.

II

Querying for Information

# Chapter 10

# Creating Multitable and Crosstab Queries

Your purpose in acquiring Access is undoubtedly to take advantage of this application's relational database management capabilities. To do so, you have to be able to link related tables based on key fields that have values in common—a process known as a *join* in database terms. Chapters 8, "Using Query by Example," and 9, "Understanding Operators and Expressions in Access," showed you how to create simple queries based on a single table. If you tried the examples in Chapter 9, you saw a glimpse of a multiple-table query when you joined the Order Details table to the Orders table, which you then joined to the Customers table to create the query for testing expressions. The first part of this chapter deals exclusively with queries created from multiple tables that are related through joins.

This chapter provides examples of queries that use each of the four basic types of joins that you can create in Access's Query Design View: *equi-joins*, *outer joins*, *self-joins*, and *theta joins*. Two of the three new query features introduced by Access 2.0, subqueries and UNION queries, cannot be used in the queries that you design in Access's graphic Query by Example (QBE) window. You can implement these two new query features only by writing SQL statements—the subject of Chapter 24, "Working with Structured Query Language." Some of the example queries in this chapter use the Personnel Actions table that you created in Chapter 4, "Working with Access Databases and Tables." If you didn't create the Personnel Actions table, refer to the "Creating the Personnel Actions Table" section of Chapter 4 or to Appendix C, "Data Dictionary for the Personnel Actions Table," for instructions on how to build this table.

Other example queries build on queries that you create in preceding sections. You will find, therefore, that reading this chapter and creating the example queries sequentially, as the queries appear in text, is more efficient than taking the random approach.

This chapter also includes descriptions and examples of four of the five categories of queries that you can create with Access: *select*, *summary*, *parameter*, and *crosstab* queries. Four types of action queries exist that you can use to create or modify data in tables: *Make-table*, *Append*, *Delete*, and *Update*. The next chapter, "Using Action Queries," presents typical applications for and examples of each type of action query.

# Joining Tables to Create Multitable Queries

Before you can create joins between tables, you must know the contents of the tables' fields and which fields are related by common values. As mentioned in Chapter 4, assigning identical names to primary- and foreign-key fields in different tables that contain related data is a common practice. This approach, used by Microsoft when creating the Northwind Traders sample database, makes determining relationships and creating joins among tables easier. The CustomerID field in the Customers table and the CustomerID field in the Orders table, for example, are used to join orders with customers.

Figure 10.1 shows the structure of the Northwind Traders database with a graphical display of the joins between the tables. Access query designs indicate joins with lines between field names of different tables. Bold type indicates primary-key fields. Each join usually involves at least one primary-key field.

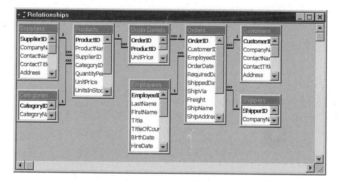

**FIG. 10.1** The joins between the tables of the Northwind Traders sample database.

You can display the structure of the joins between the tables in Access 97's Northwind Traders database by giving the Database window the focus (click the Database Window button of the toolbar) and then clicking the Relationship button of the toolbar or choosing Tools, Relationships. The 1 above the line that shows the join between two tables in Figure 10.1 indicates the "one" side of a one-to-many relationship; the infinity symbol ( ) indicates the "many" side.

> **Note**
>
> Access 97 lets you choose between displaying only the direct relationships for a single table (the Show Direct Relationships button on the toolbar) or all relationships for all tables in a database (the

Show All Relationships button). All tables of Northwind.mdb appear by default when you open the Relationships window of the Northwind sample database. In this case, clicking the Show Direct Relationships button has no effect.

To show relationships for only one table, click the toolbar's Clear Layout button, click the Show Table button to display the Show Table dialog, select the table to display in the Tables list, and then click Add and Close. Click the Show Direct Relationships button to display the relationships for the selected table. Clearing the layout of the Relationships windows does not affect the underlying relationships between the tables. The Show Direct Relationships feature is useful primarily with databases that contain many related tables.

Access supports four types of joins in the graphical QBE Design mode:

- *Equi-joins* (also called *inner joins*) are the most common join for creating select queries. Equi-joins display in one table all of the records with corresponding records in another table. The correspondence between records is determined by identical values (WHERE *field1* = *field2* in SQL) in the fields that join the tables. In most cases, joins are based on a unique primary-key field in one table and a foreign-key field in the other table in a one-to-many relationship. If none of the table's records that act as the *many* side of the relationship have a field value that corresponds to a record in the table of the *one* side, the corresponding records in the *one* side don't appear in the query result.

  Access automatically creates the joins between tables if the tables share a common field name that is a primary key of one of the tables. These joins are also automatically created if you previously specified the relationships between the tables in the Relationships window.

- *Outer joins* are used in database maintenance to remove orphan records and duplicate data from tables by creating new tables that contain records with unique values. Outer joins display records in one member of the join, regardless of whether corresponding records exist on the other side of the join.

- *Self-joins* relate data within a single table. You create a self-join in Access by adding to the query a duplicate of the table (Access provides an alias for the duplicate) and then creating joins between the fields of the copies.

- *Theta joins* relate data by using comparison operators other than =. Theta joins include *not-equal joins* (<>) used in queries designed to return records that lack a particular relationship. You implement theta joins by WHERE criteria rather than by the SQL JOIN reserved word. The Query Design window does not indicate theta joins by drawing lines between field names, nor do theta joins appear in the Relationships window.

### Creating Conventional Single-Column Equi-Joins

Joins based on one column in each table are known as *single-column equi-joins*. Most relational databases are designed to employ single-column equi-joins only in one-to-many relationships. The following list details the basic rules for creating a database that enables you to use simple single-column equi-joins for all queries:

 ◄◄ See "Establishing Relationships Between Tables," p. 146

■ Each table on the *one* side of the relationship must have a primary key with a No Duplicates index to maintain referential integrity. Access automatically creates a No Duplicates index on the primary-key field(s) of a table.

■ Many-to-many relationships, such as the relationship of Orders to Products, are implemented by an intermediary table (in this case, Order Details) having a one-to-many relationship (Orders to Order Details) with one table and a many-to-one relationship (Order Details to Products) with another.

■ Duplicated data in tables, where applicable, is extracted to a new table that has a primary-key, no-duplicates, one-to-many relationship with the table from which the duplicate data is extracted. Using a multicolumn primary key to identify extracted data uniquely often is necessary because individual key fields might contain duplicate data. The combination (also known as *concatenation*) of the values of the key fields, however, must be unique. Access 97's Table Analyzer Wizard locates and extracts most duplicate data automatically. Chapter 11 describes how to extract duplicate data manually from tables.

 ▶▶ See "Creating New Tables with Make-Table Queries," p. 371

All of the joins in the Northwind Traders database, shown by the lines that connect field names of adjacent tables in Figure 10.1, are single-column equi-joins between tables with one-to-many relationships. Access uses the ANSI SQL-92 reserved words INNER JOIN to identify conventional equi-joins, and LEFT JOIN or RIGHT JOIN to specify outer joins.

Among the most common uses for queries based on equi-joins is to match customer names and addresses with orders received. You might want to create a simple report, for example, that lists the customer name, order number, order date, and amount. To create a conventional one-to-many, single-column equi-join query that relates Northwind's customers to the orders that the customers place, sorted by company and order date, follow these steps:

1. If Northwind.mdb is open, close all windows except the Database window by double-clicking the windows' close box. Otherwise, choose File, 1 Northwind.mdb to open the Northwind Traders database.

New
2. Click the Queries tab of the Database window and then choose New to create a new query. The New Query dialog appears. With the Design View item selected, click OK. Access displays the Show Table dialog superimposed on an empty Query Design window.

3. Select the Customers table from the Show Table list and click the Add button. Alternatively, you can double-click the Customers table name to add the table to the query. Access adds to the Query Design window the Field Names list for Customers.

4. Double-click the Orders table in the Show Table list, and then click the Close button. Access adds to the window the Field Names list for Orders, plus a line that indicates a join between the CustomerID fields of the two tables, as shown in Figure 10.2. Access creates the join automatically because CustomerID is the key field of the Customers table, and Access found a field with the same field name (a foreign key) in the Orders table.

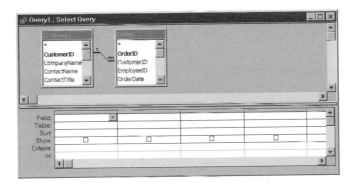

**FIG. 10.2**  A join between fields of two tables with a common field name, created automatically by Access.

5. To identify each order with the customer's name, select the CompanyName field of the Customers table and drag the field symbol to the Field row of the Query Design grid's first column.

6. Select the OrderID field of the Orders table and drag the field symbol to the second column's Field row. Drag the OrderDate field to the third column. Your query design appears as shown in Figure 10.3.

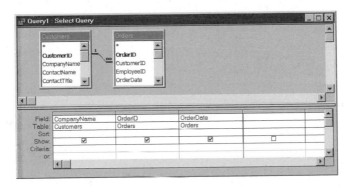

**FIG. 10.3**  A query to display orders placed by customers, sorted by company name and order date.

**7.** Click the Run or Query View button to display the result of the query, the Recordset shown in Figure 10.4. Notice that the field headers of the query result set show the captions for the table fields, which include spaces, rather than the actual field names, which don't have spaces.

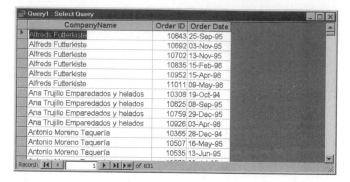

**FIG. 10.4** The result of the query design of Figure 10.3 that joins the Customers and Orders tables.

### Specifying a Sort Order for the Query Result Set

Access displays query result sets in the order of the index on the primary-key field. If more than one column represents a primary-key field, Access sorts the query result set in left-to-right key-field column precedence. Because Company Name is the primary-key field located farthest to the left, the query result set displays all orders for a single company in order-number sequence. You can override the primary-key display order by adding a sort order. For example, if you want to see the latest orders first, you can specify a descending sort by the order date. To add this sort sequence to your query, follow these steps:

◀◀ See "Adding Indexes to Tables," p. 154

**1.** Click the Design View button to return to Query Design mode.

**2.** Place the caret in the Sort row of the Order Date column of the Query Design grid and press F4 to open the drop-down list.

**3.** Select Descending from the drop-down list to specify a descending sort on date—latest orders first (see Figure 10.5).

**4.** Click the Run button or the Query View button to display the query result set with the new sort order (see Figure 10.6).

### Creating Queries from Tables with Indirect Relationships

You can create queries that return indirectly related records, such as the categories of products purchased by each customer. You must include in the queries each table that serves as a link in the chain of joins. If you are creating queries to display the categories of products purchased by each customer, for example, include each of the tables that link the chain of joins between the Customers and Categories tables. This chain includes the Customers, Orders, Order Details, Products, and Categories tables. You don't need to add any fields, however, from the intermediate tables to the Query Design grid; the CompanyName and the CategoryName fields suffice.

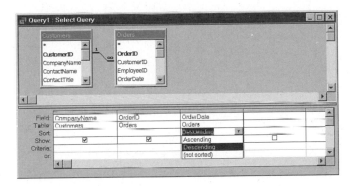

**FIG. 10.5**  Adding a special sort order to the query.

**FIG. 10.6**  The result of adding a descending sort on Order Date to the query.

To modify your customers and orders query so that you create a query that displays fields of indirectly related records, follow these steps:

1. In Query Design view, delete the OrderID column of the query by clicking the thin bar above the Field row to select (highlight) the entire column, then press Delete. Perform the same action for the OrderDate columns so that only the CompanyName column appears in the query.

2. Click the Show Table button of the toolbar or choose Query, Show Table and add the Order Details, Products, and Categories tables to the query, in sequence, then click the Close button of the Add Table dialog. The upper pane of Figure 10.7 shows the chain of joins that Access automatically creates between Customers and Categories based on the primary-key field of each intervening table and the identically named foreign-key field in the adjacent table.

As you add tables to the Query Design window, the table field lists might not appear in the upper pane. Use the upper pane's vertical scroll bar to display the "hidden" tables. You can drag the table field lists to the top of the upper pane and then rearrange the field lists to match the appearance of Figure 10.7.

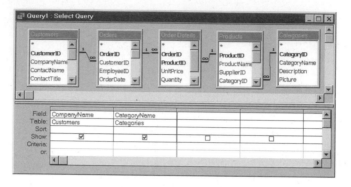

**FIG. 10.7**  The chain of joins required to create queries from tables that have an indirect relationship.

**3.** Drag the CategoryName from the Categories field list to the Field row of the grid's second column. Alternatively, you can double-click the field name to add it to the next empty column of the grid.

**4.** If you want to see the SQL statement that Access uses to create the query, choose View, SQL to display the SQL window, shown in Figure 10.8. The table's joins appear as INNER JOIN...ON... clauses. Cascaded joins use the INNER JOIN...ON...ON... syntax, which is explained in Chapter 24, "Working with Structured Query Language."

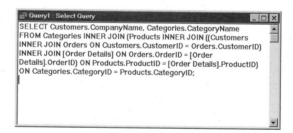

**FIG. 10.8**  The SQL statement that creates the query to determine which customers purchased specific categories of products.

**5.** Click the toolbar's Query Design View button to close the SQL window. Then click the Run button on the toolbar. The query result set shown in Figure 10.9 appears.

**6.** Close the query by clicking the window close box. This query is only an example, so you don't need to save it.

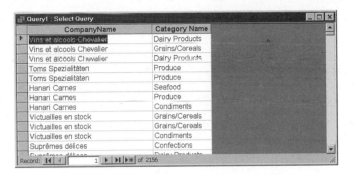

**FIG. 10.9**  The Customers-Categories `Recordset`, resulting from the query of Figure 10.7.

Queries made on indirectly related tables are common, especially when you want to analyze the data with SQL aggregate functions or Access's crosstab queries. For more information, see the sections "Using the SQL Aggregate Functions" and "Creating Crosstab Queries" later in this chapter.

### Creating Multicolumn Equi-Joins and Selecting Unique Values

You can have more than one join between a pair of tables. You might, for example, want to create a query that returns the names of customers for which the billing and shipping addresses are the same. The billing address is the Address field of the Customers table, and the shipping address is the ShipAddress field of the Orders table. Therefore, you need to match the Customer ID fields in the two tables and `Customers.Address` with `Orders.ShipAddress`. This task requires a *multicolumn equi-join*.

To create this example of an address-matching multicolumn equi-join, follow these steps:

1. Create a new query by giving the Database window the focus, clicking the Queries tab (if necessary), and then choosing the New button. With Design View selected in the New Query dialog, click OK.

2. Add the Customers and Orders tables to the query by selecting each table in the Show Table dialog and clicking the Add button. Click Close.

3. Click and drag the Address field of the Customers table's Field List box to the ShipAddress field of the Orders table's Field List box. This creates another join, indicated by the new line between Address and ShipAddress (see Figure 10.10). The new line in the graphical QBE window has dots at both ends, indicating that the join is between a pair of fields that do not have a specified relationship, the same field name, or a primary-key index.

4. Drag the Customers table's CompanyName and Address fields to the Field row of the first and second query columns, and drop the fields. Drag the Orders table's ShipAddress field to the query's third column, and drop the field in the Field row.

5. Add an ascending sort to the CompanyName column.

New

II

Querying for Information

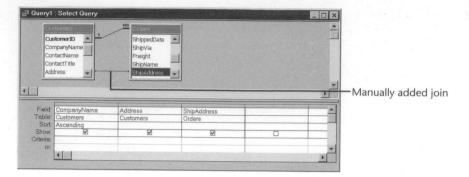

**FIG. 10.10** Creating a multicolumn equi-join by dragging one field name to a field in another table.

 **6.** Click the Run button on the toolbar. Figure 10.11 shows the query's result.

**FIG. 10.11** A query result set of orders for customers who have the same billing and shipping addresses.

**7.** To eliminate the duplicate rows, you must use the Unique Values option of Access's Query Properties window. To display the Query Properties window, which is shown in Figure 10.12, click the Design View button, and then click the toolbar's Properties button or double-click an empty area in the Query Design window's upper pane. If the title bar of the Properties window displays Field Properties or Field List, click an empty area in the Query Design window's upper pane so that the title bar displays Query Properties. Alternatively, right-click an empty region of the upper pane and select Properties from the popup menu.

**8.** By default, both the UniqueRecords query property and the UniqueValues property are set **False** (No). Place the caret in the Unique Values text box and press F4 to open the drop-down list. Select Yes and close the list. Setting the UniqueValues property True adds the ANSI SQL reserved word DISTINCT to the query. Click the Properties button again to close the Properties window.

**Tip**

You can also change the property settings for the `UniqueRecords` and `UniqueValues` properties by double-clicking their text boxes in the Properties window.

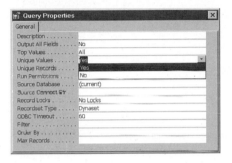

**FIG. 10.12** Using the Query Properties window to display only rows with unique values.

**9.** Click the Run button of the toolbar. The result set no longer contains duplicate rows, as shown in Figure 10.13.

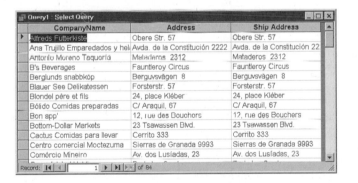

**FIG. 10.13** The query result set after you remove duplicate rows.

**10.** Choose <u>V</u>iew, S<u>Q</u>L to display the SQL statement (see Figure 10.14). The DISTINCT modifier of the SELECT statement causes the query to display only those records whose field values included in the query differ.

**11.** Click the Close Window button to close the query without saving it. You then avoid cluttering the Database window's Queries list with obsolete query examples.

Because most of the orders have the same billing and shipping addresses, a more useful query is to find the orders for which the customer's billing and shipping addresses differ. You cannot create this query with a multicolumn equi-join, however, because the INNER JOIN reserved word in Access SQL doesn't accept the <> operator. Adding a not-equal join uses a criterion rather than a multicolumn join, as explained in the section "Creating Not-Equal Theta Joins with Criteria" later in this chapter.

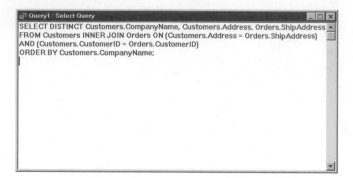

**FIG. 10.14** The SQL statement that results in the query result set of Figure 10.13.

**Troubleshooting**

*When I run my query, an Enter Parameter Value dialog appears that asks me to enter a value. I didn't specify a parameter for the query.*

The Enter Parameter Value dialog appears when the Jet engine's query parser cannot identify an object specified in the query or evaluate an expression. Usually, the Enter Parameter Value dialog appears because of a typographic error. Intentionally creating parameter queries is the subject of the section "Designing Parameter Queries" later in this chapter.

# Using Lookup Fields in Tables

Access 97's lookup feature for table fields lets you substitute combo (drop-down list) boxes or list boxes for conventional field text boxes. The lookup feature lets you provide a list of acceptable values for a particular field. When you select the value from the list, the value automatically is entered in the field of the current record. You can specify either of the following two types of lookup field:

- In a field that contains foreign-key values, a list of values from one or more fields of a related base table is provided. As an example, the Orders table of Northwind.mdb has two foreign key fields: CustomerID and EmployeeID. The lookup feature of the CustomerID field displays in a combo box the CompanyName field value from the Customers table. The EmployeeID field displays the LastName and FirstName fields of the Employees table, separated by a comma and space (see Figure 10.15). The foreign key lookup feature is implemented by a simple Access SQL select query, `SELECT DISTINCTROW [CustomerID],[CompanyName] FROM [Customers] ORDER BY [CompanyName];`, in the case of the CustomerID field.

- With any field except a single primary-key field, a list of fixed values from which to select is provided.

> **Note**
>
> Lookup is a feature of a field, not a field data type. The field data type is that of the content of the field, such as Number (Long Integer) for the EmployeeID field of the Orders table. The lookup feature is implemented by a special set of Access-specific properties that are stored with the common (Data Access Object, or DAO) field properties of the table. (Lookup properties are included in the `Properties` collection of the `Field` object of the `TableDef` object for the table. These objects are described in Chapter 29, "Understanding the Data Access Object Class.")

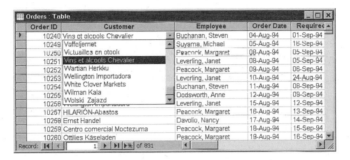

**FIG. 10.15**   A lookup field's combo box and value list.

You can add a new lookup field in either Design view or Table Datasheet view; however, you only can add the lookup feature to an existing field in Design view. In Datasheet view, only the combo box control is displayed, even if you specify a list box control. You can display a combo box or a list box on a form that is bound to a table with lookup fields. In practice, the drop-down list (a combo box with the Limit to List property set to Yes) is the most common type of lookup field control. The following sections describe how to add foreign key and fixed list lookup features to table fields.

### Adding a Foreign Key Drop-Down List with the Lookup Wizard

The Personnel Actions table you created in earlier chapters of this book is a candidate for a lookup field that uses a foreign-key drop-down list. Follow these steps to use the Lookup Wizard to change the paID field of the Personnel Actions table to a lookup field:

1. In the Database window, select the Personnel Actions table, and press Ctrl+C to copy the table to the Clipboard.

2. Press Ctrl+V to display the Paste Table As dialog. Enter a name for the copy, such as **tblLookup**, and click the OK button to create the copy.

3. Open the table copy in Design view and select the paInitiatedBy field. Click the Lookup tab to display the current lookup properties; a text box control has no lookup properties. Open the Data Type drop-down list and select Lookup Wizard (see Figure 10.16). The first dialog of the Lookup Wizard appears.

4. You want the field to look up values in another table (Employees), so accept the first (default) option (see Figure 10.17). Click the Next button to display the Lookup Wizard's second dialog.

5. With the View Tables option enabled, select the Employees base table to which the paInitiatedBy field is related (see Figure 10.18). Click the Next button to display the third dialog.

6. Click the > button three times to add the EmployeeID, LastName, and FirstName fields to your lookup list (see Figure 10.19). You must include the base table key field that is related to your foreign key field. Click the Next button for the fourth dialog.

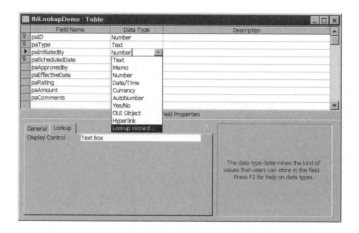

**FIG. 10.16**  Selecting the Lookup Wizard to add the lookup feature to a field.

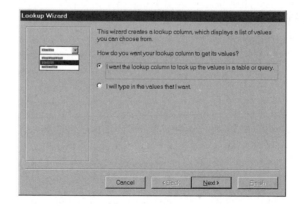

**FIG. 10.17**  Selecting between a foreign-key and fixed-list lookup in the first dialog of the Lookup Wizard.

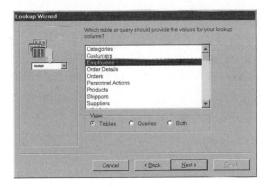

**FIG. 10.18** Choosing the base table or query of a foreign-key lookup field.

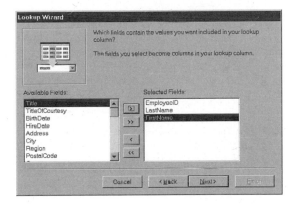

**FIG. 10.19** Selecting the fields to include in your lookup list.

**7.** Adjust the widths of the columns to display the first and last names without excessive trailing "white space." The wizard determines that EmployeeID is the key column and recommends hiding the key column (see Figure 10.20). Click Next to display the fifth and final dialog.

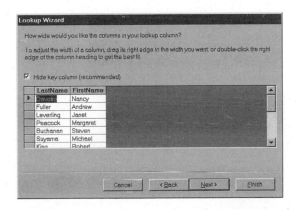

**FIG. 10.20** Adjusting column widths of the lookup list and hiding the key column.

8. Accept the default "label" for the lookup field in the text box (see Figure 10.21). (If you change the default value, you change the field name, not the caption.)

9. Click the Finish button to complete the wizard's work. Click OK when the wizard asks whether you'd like to save the table design. Your new lookup field properties appear as shown in Figure 10.22. The Access SQL statement created by the wizard is `SELECT DISTINCTROW [Employees].[EmployeeID], [Employees].[LastName], [Employees].[FirstName] FROM [Employees];`.

10. Click the Table View button to display the table datasheet. Only the first visible column of the list appears in the Initiated By column. Adjust the width of the Initiated By column to the width of the drop-down list, about 1.5 inches. With the caret in the Initiated By column, open the drop-down list to display the wizard's work (see Figure 10.23).

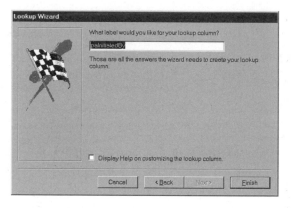

**FIG. 10.21** Specifying the caption for the lookup field.

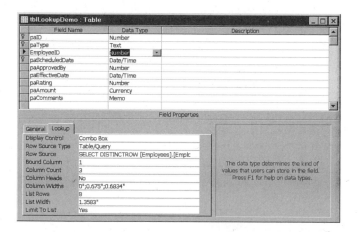

**FIG. 10.22** Lookup properties added to the paInitiatedBy field.

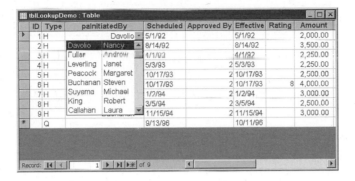

**FIG. 10.23**  The drop-down lookup list created by the Lookup Wizard.

**11.** Return to Design view, select the Row Source property of the paInitiatedBy field, and click the Build button to display the Row Source SQL statement in Query Design view (see Figure 10.24), then close the Query Design window.

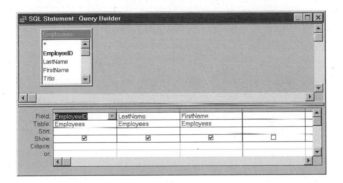

**FIG. 10.24**  The Query Design view of the SQL statement of the Row Source property in Query Design view.

> **Note**
>
> The properties of the combo box control created by the wizard are described in the "Using List Boxes and Combo Boxes" section of Chapter 13, "Designing Custom Multitable Forms." You can alter the lookup properties of a field to customize the basic work done for you by the wizard. The wizard's entries are quite adequate for most Access applications.

### Adding a Fixed Value Lookup List to a Table

You add the alternative lookup feature—a fixed list of values—using the Lookup Wizard in much the same way as you created the foreign-key lookup list in the preceding section. To add a fixed-list lookup feature to the paType field of your copy of the Personnel Actions table, follow these steps:

**1.** Select the paType field, open the Data Type list, and select Lookup Wizard to launch the wizard.

**2.** In the first Lookup Wizard dialog, select the I Will Type in the Values That I Want option, and click the Next button.

**3.** In the second Lookup Wizard dialog, type **2** in the Number of Columns text box, and press the Tab key to create the second list column.

**4.** Enter **H**, **Hired**; **Q**, **Quarterly Review**; **Y**, **Yearly Review**; and **S**, **Salary Adjustment** in the Col1 and Col2 columns of four rows. Adjust the width of the columns to suit the entries (see Figure 10.25). Click the Next button to display the wizard's third dialog.

**5.** The paType field uses single-character abbreviations for the type of personnel actions, so select Col1 as the "field that uniquely identifies the row," as shown in Figure 10.26. (The paType field does not uniquely identify the row; Col1 contains the single-character value that you want to insert into the field.) Click the Next button to display the fourth and final wizard dialog.

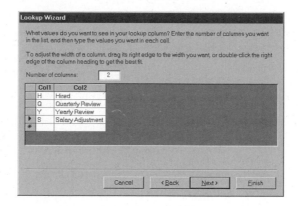

**FIG. 10.25** Adding the lookup list values in the Lookup Wizard's second dialog.

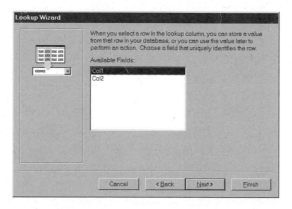

**FIG. 10.26** Selecting the column that contains the value to insert into the field.

6. Accept the default "label" for your column and click the Finish button. The lookup properties for the paType field appear as shown in Figure 10.27. The Row Source Type is Value List. The Row Source contains the following values: `"H"`;`"Hired"`; `"Q"`;`"Quarterly Review"`;`"Y"`;`"Yearly Review"`;`"S"`;`"Salary Adjustment"`.

7. Click the Table View button and save the changes to your table. Increase the width of the Type column to about 1.5 inches, place the caret in the Type column, and open the fixed value list to check the wizard's work (see Figure 10.28).

8. If you don't want the abbreviation to appear in the drop-down list, change the first entry of the Column Widths property value to **0**.

9. If you want to remove the lookup feature from a field, select the field, click the Lookup tab, and choose Text Box from the drop-down Display Control list.

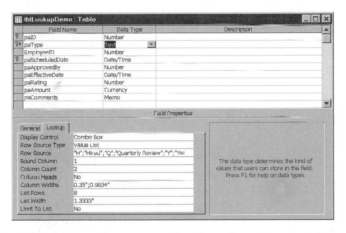

**FIG. 10.27**   Selecting the column that contains the value to insert into the field.

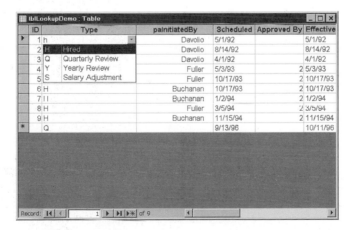

**FIG. 10.28**   The fixed value list created by the Lookup Wizard.

---

**Note**

The lookup feature has generated controversy among seasoned database developers. Relational database purists object to the principle of modifying the properties of tables with embedded queries. Another objection to the use of foreign-key, drop-down lists is that it is easy for uninitiated users to inadvertently change data in a table after opening the list. Access 97's lookup feature, however, is a useful tool, especially for new database users.

---

# Outer, Self, and Theta Joins

The preceding sections of this chapter described the equi-join or, in the parlance of SQL-92, an inner join. Inner joins are the most common type of join in database applications. Access also lets you create three other joins: outer, self, and theta. The following sections describe these three less-common types of joins.

### Creating Outer Joins

*Outer joins* allow you to display the fields of all records in a table participating in a query, regardless of whether corresponding records exist in the joined table. With Access, you can choose between left and right outer joins.

When diagramming database structures (a subject of Chapter 23, "Exploring Relational Database Design and Implementation"), you traditionally would draw the primary *one* table to the left of the secondary *many* table. A left outer join (LEFT JOIN or *= in SQL) query in Access, therefore, displays all of the records in the table with the unique primary key, regardless of whether matching records exist in the *many* table. Conversely, a right outer join (RIGHT JOIN or =*) query displays all of the records in the *many* table, regardless of a record's existence in the primary table. Records in the *many* table without corresponding records in the *one* table usually, but not necessarily, are orphan records; these kinds of records may have a many-to-one relationship to another table.

To practice creating a left outer join to detect whether records are missing for an employee in the Personnel Actions table, follow these steps:

New

1. Open a new query and add the Employees and Personnel Actions tables.

2. Drag the EmployeeID field symbol to the paID field of Personnel Actions to create an equi-join between these fields if Access didn't create the join. (Access automatically creates the join if you established a relationship between these two fields when you created the Personnel Actions table in Chapter 4, "Working with Access Databases and Tables.")

3. Select and drag the LastName and FirstName fields of the Employees table to columns 1 and 2 of the Query Design grid. Select and drag the paType and paScheduledDate fields of the Personnel Actions table to columns 3 and 4.

4. Click the line joining EmployeeID with paID to select it, as shown in Figure 10.29. The thickness of the center part of the line increases to indicate the selection. (In Figure 10.29, the two Field List boxes are separated so that the thin section of the join line is apparent.)

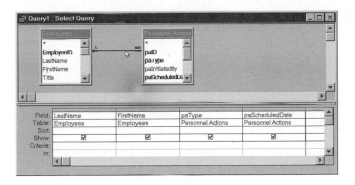

**FIG. 10.29**   Selecting a join to change its property from an inner to a left or right outer join.

**5.** Choose <u>V</u>iew, <u>J</u>oin Properties. (The Join Properties command is active only after you select an individual join with a mouse click.) You also can double-click the thin section of the join line. (Double-clicking either of the line's thick sections displays the Query Properties window.) The Join Properties dialog in Figure 10.30 appears. Type <u>1</u> is a conventional inner join, Type <u>2</u> is a left join, and Type <u>3</u> is a right join.

**FIG. 10.30**   The Join Properties dialog for choosing inner, left, or right joins.

**6.** Select a Type <u>2</u> join—a left join—by choosing <u>2</u>. Click OK to close the dialog.

Notice that Access adds an arrowhead to the line that joins EmployeeID and paID. The direction of the arrow, left to right, indicates that you have created a left join between the tables.

**7.** Click the Run button of the toolbar to display the result of the left join query. In Figure 10.31, three employees without a record in the Personnel Actions table appear in the result table's last rows. Your query result set may differ, depending on the number of entries that you made when creating the Personnel Actions table. (If all employees show a personnel action, open the Personnel Actions table, delete the entries for a few employees, and then rerun the query.)

**8.** Close, but don't save, the query.

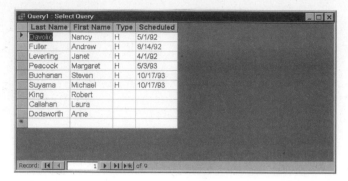

**FIG. 10.31**   The result of creating a left join between the ID fields of the Employees and Personnel Actions tables.

If you could add a personnel action for a nonexistent EmployeeID (the validation rule that you added in Chapter 9, "Understanding Operators and Expressions in Access," prevents you from doing so), a right join would show the invalid entry with blank employee name fields.

### Creating Self-Joins

*Self-joins* relate values in a single table. Creating a self-join requires that you add to the query a copy of the table and then add a join between the related fields. An example of self-join use is to determine whether supervisors have approved personnel actions that they initiated, which is prohibited by the imaginary personnel manual for Northwind Traders.

To create this kind of self-join for the Personnel Actions table, follow these steps:

1. Open a new query and add the Personnel Actions table.

2. Add to the query another copy of the Personnel Actions table by clicking the Add button again. Access names the copy Personnel Actions_1. Close the Show Tables dialog.

3. Drag the original table's paInitiatedBy field to the copied table's paApprovedBy field. The join appears as shown in the upper pane of Figure 10.32.

4. Drag the paID and paInitiatedBy fields of the original table, and the paApprovedBy and paType fields of the copy of the Personnel Actions table, to the Field row of columns 1–4, respectively, of the Query Design grid.

5. With self-joins, you must specify that only unique values are included. Click the Properties button on the toolbar or double-click an empty area in the Query Design window's upper pane, and set the value of the Query Properties window's UniqueValues property to Yes. Click the Properties button again to close the Query Properties window.

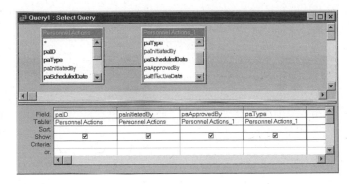

**FIG. 10.32**  Designing the query for a self-join on the Personnel Actions table.

6. Click the Run button of the toolbar to display the records in which the same employee initiated and approved a personnel action, as shown in Figure 10.33. In this case, EmployeeID 2 (Mr. Fuller) is a vice president and can override personnel policy. (Your results may differ, depending on the number of entries that you made in the Personnel Actions table.)

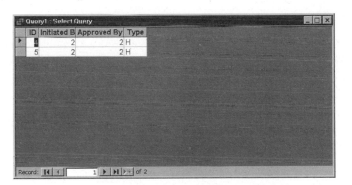

**FIG. 10.33**  The result of a self-join that tests for supervisors approving personnel actions that they initiated.

In this example, you can add the Employees table to the query in order to display the employee name. Adding the Employees table creates an additional join between the original paID field of the Personnel Actions table and the EmployeeID field of the Employees table. You then must drag the LastName field to the Query Design grid's fifth column. Because this join includes a primary-key field, EmployeeID, the default DISTINCT process yields unique values. To verify that the values are unique, click the Properties button of the toolbar, or double-click an empty area in the Query Design window's upper pane. Set the value of the UniqueValues property to Yes and then rerun the query.

▶▶ See "Maintaining Referential Integrity," p. 834

Full-fledged relational database applications seldom use self-joins because validation criteria and enforcement of referential integrity can (and should) eliminate the types of problems that self-joins can detect.

### Creating Not-Equal Theta Joins with Criteria

Most joins are based on fields with equal values, but sometimes you need to create a join on unequal fields. Joins that you create with graphical QBE in Access are restricted to conventional equi-joins and outer joins. You can create the equivalent of a not-equal theta join by applying a criterion to one of the two fields you want to test for not-equal values.

Finding customers that have different billing and shipping addresses, as mentioned previously, is an example in which a not-equal theta join is useful. To create the equivalent of this join, follow these steps:

1. Create a new query and add the Customers and Orders tables.

2. Select the Customers table's CompanyName and Address fields and the Orders table's ShipAddress field. Drag them to the Query Design grid's first three columns.

3. Type **<> Customers.Address** in the Criteria row of the ShipAddress column. (Access automatically adds square brackets surrounding table and field names, regardless of whether the names include spaces or other punctuation.) The Query Design window appears as shown in Figure 10.34. This criterion adds the WHERE Orders.ShipAddress <> [Customers].[Address] clause to the SQL SELECT statement shown in Figure 10.35.

   Typing **<> Orders.ShipAddress** in the Address column gives an equivalent result. This criterion adds a WHERE Customers.Address <> Orders.[ShipAddress] clause to the SQL SELECT statement.

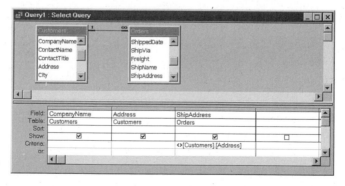

**FIG. 10.34**  Designing the query for a not-equal theta join.

4. Click the toolbar's Properties button or double-click an empty area in the Query Design window's upper pane to open the Query Properties window and set the value of the Unique Values property to Yes.

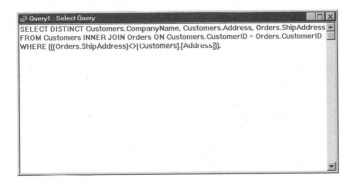

**FIG. 10.35**   The SQL statement for a not-equal theta join.

5. Run the query. Only the records for customers that placed orders with different billing and shipping addresses appear, as shown in Figure 10.36.

6. Click the Close Window button and save your query, if desired.

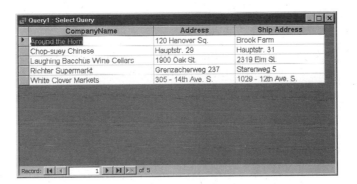

**FIG. 10.36**   The result of a not-equal theta join designed to identify different billing and shipping addresses.

# Updating Table Data with Queries

Many of the queries that you create with the Unique Records property set to Yes are updatable because you use Access SQL's DISTINCTROW modifier to create them. (Setting the Unique Records property to Yes causes Access to add the DISTINCTROW modifier to the query's SQL statement.) These queries create Recordset objects of the updatable Dynaset type. You cannot update a query unless you see the tentative (blank) append record (with the asterisk in the select button) at the end of the query result table. Queries that you create with the Unique Values property set to Yes create Recordset objects of the Snapshot type by substituting ANSI SQL's DISTINCT modifier. You cannot edit, add new records to, or otherwise update a Recordset object of the Snapshot type. The next few sections describe the conditions under which you can update a record of a table included in a query. The following sections also discuss how to use the Output Field Properties window to format a query data display and edits.

> **Note**
>
> You cannot set both the Unique Values and Unique Records properties to Yes—these choices are mutually exclusive. Setting Unique Values to Yes causes Access to include the `DISTINCT` modifier in the SQL statement for the query, resulting in a `Recordset` that cannot be updated. Setting the Unique Records property to Yes causes Access to include the `DISTINCTROW` modifier in the SQL statement, resulting in a Recordset that *can* be updated. In Access 97, the default setting of both the Unique Values and Unique Records properties is No.

> **Note**
>
> Dynaset and Snapshot are subtypes of Access 97's Recordset object. Microsoft states that the use of the reserved words Dynaset and Snapshot as object names is supported in Access 97 only for compatibility with Access 1.x. Although the distinctive terminology of Dynaset and Snapshot makes it unlikely that these two terms will disappear from common use among Access developers, future versions of Access might not support Dynaset and Snapshot objects and might instead require you to specify Recordset objects of different types in Access VBA.

### Characteristics That Determine Whether You Can Update a Query

Adding new records to tables or updating existing data in tables included in a query is a definite advantage in some circumstances. Correcting data errors that appear when you run the query is especially tempting. Unfortunately, you cannot append or update records in most of the queries that you create. The following properties of a query prevent you from appending and updating records:

- The Unique Values property is set to Yes in the Query Properties window.

- Self-joins are used in the query.

- SQL aggregate functions, such as `Sum()`, are employed in the query. Crosstab queries, for example, use SQL aggregate functions.

- No primary-key fields with a unique (No Duplicates) index exist for the *one* table in a one-to-many relationship.

When designing a query to use as the basis of a form for data entry or editing, make sure that none of the preceding properties apply to the query.

If none of the preceding properties apply to the query or all tables within the query, you can append records to and update fields of queries in the following:

- A single-table query

- Both tables in a one-to-one relationship

- The *many* table in a one-to-many relationship

- The *one* table in a one-to-many relationship if none of the fields of the *many* table appear in the query

Updating the *one* table in a one-to-many query is a special case in Access. To enable up-dates to this table, follow these steps:

1. Add to the query the primary-key field or fields of the *one* table and additional fields to update.

2. Add the field or fields of the *many* table that correspond to the key field or fields of the *one* table; this step is required to select the appropriate records for updating.

3. Add the criteria to select the records for updating to the fields chosen in step 2.

4. Click the Show box so that the *many* table field(s) does not appear in the query.

After following these steps, you can edit the non-key fields of the *one* table. You cannot, however, alter the values of key fields that have relationships with records in the *many* table. Such a modification violates referential integrity. You also cannot update a calculated column of a query; tables cannot include calculated values.

---

**Note**

By adding lookup fields to tables, you often can avoid writing one-to-many queries and precisely following the preceding rules to make such queries updatable. For example, the Orders table, which includes three lookup fields (CustomerID, EmployeeID, and ShipVia), is updatable. If you want to allow updates in Datasheet view (called *browse updating*), using lookup fields is a better approach than creating an updatable query. Most database developers consider simple browse updating to be a poor practice because of the potential for inadvertent data-entry errors.

---

### Formatting Data with the Output Field Properties Window

The display format of data in queries is inherited from the format of the data in the tables that underlie the query. You can override the table format by using the `Format(ColumnName, FormatString)` function described in Chapter 9, "Understanding Operators and Expressions in Access," to create a calculated field.

Access 97 provides an easier method: it adds a Field Properties window that you can use  to format the display of query data. You also can create an input mask to aid in updating the query data. To open the Field Properties window, place the caret in the Field cell of the query column that you want to format, and then click the Properties button of the toolbar or double-click an empty area in the upper pane of the Query Design window. Figure 10.37 shows the Field Properties window for the Order Date column of a simple one-to-many query that was created from the Customers and Orders tables.

- *Description.* Enables you to enter the text to appear in the status bar when the user selects the field in Datasheet view.

- *Format.* Enables you to control the appearance of the data in Datasheet view, such as Medium Date.

Query1 : Select Query
Customers
CustomerID
CompanyName
ContactName
ContactTitle
Orders
OrderID
CustomerID
EmployeeID
OrderDate
Field Properties
General
Lookup
Description
Format
Input Mask
Caption
Medium Date
General Date 6/19/94 5:34:23 PM
Long Date Sunday, June 19, 19
Medium Date 19-Jun-94
Short Date 6/19/94
Long Time 5:34:23 PM
Medium Time 5:34 PM
Short Time 17:34
Field: OrderDate
Table: Orders
Sort:
Show:
Criteria:
or:

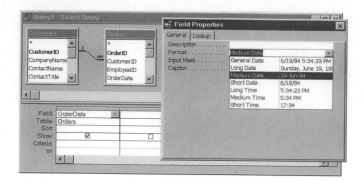

**FIG. 10.37** Changing the display format for a query column of the Date/Time field data type.

The Field Properties window displays the following subset of the properties that apply to a table's fields:

- *Input Mask*. Enables you to establish the format for entering data, such as `90/90/00`. (To create an input mask that is appropriate for the field data type, click the ellipsis button to open the Input Mask Wizard.)
- *Caption*. Enables you to change the query column heading, such as Received, for the Order Date column.

Each of the preceding query properties follows the rules described in Chapter 4, "Working with Access Databases and Tables," for setting table field properties. Adding a value (Received) for the Caption property is the equivalent of adding a column alias by typing **Received**: as a prefix in the Order Date column's Field cell. The value of the Input Mask property need not correspond to the value of the Format property. For example, the Received (OrderDate) field in Figure 10.38, which shows the effect of setting the property values shown in the preceding list, has a Medium Date display format and an input mask for updating in Short Date format.

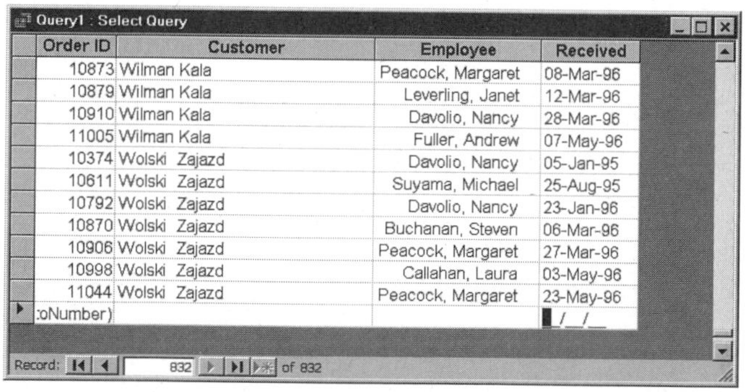

Query1 : Select Query
Order ID | Customer | Employee | Received
10873 | Wilman Kala | Peacock, Margaret | 08-Mar-96
10879 | Wilman Kala | Leverling, Janet | 12-Mar-96
10910 | Wilman Kala | Davolio, Nancy | 28-Mar-96
11005 | Wilman Kala | Fuller, Andrew | 07-May-96
10374 | Wolski Zajazd | Davolio, Nancy | 05-Jan-95
10611 | Wolski Zajazd | Suyama, Michael | 25-Aug-95
10792 | Wolski Zajazd | Davolio, Nancy | 23-Jan-96
10870 | Wolski Zajazd | Buchanan, Steven | 06-Mar-96
10906 | Wolski Zajazd | Peacock, Margaret | 27-Mar-96
10998 | Wolski Zajazd | Callahan, Laura | 03-May-96
11044 | Wolski Zajazd | Peacock, Margaret | 23-May-96
:oNumber) | | | _/_/_
Record: 832 of 832

**FIG. 10.38** Adding a new order record with an Order Date input mask.

### Troubleshooting

*I can't create an updatable one-to-many query with my attached dBASE tables, despite the fact that my query only displays fields from the many side of the relationship.*

You must specify (or create) primary-key indexes for each dBASE table that participates in the query. The field or fields that you choose must uniquely identify a record; the index doesn't allow duplicate values. Delete the attachment to the dBASE tables, and then reattach the table with the primary-key indexes. Make sure that you specify which index is the primary-key index in the Select Unique Record Identifier dialog that appears after you attach each table.

Also, make sure that you don't include the field of the *many*-side table on which the join is created in the query. If you add the joined field to the field list, your query is not updatable.

# Making All Fields of Tables Accessible

Most queries that you create include only the fields you specifically choose. To choose these fields, you either select them from or type them into the drop-down combo list in the Query Design grid's Field row, or you drag the field names from the field lists to the appropriate cells in the Field row. You can, however, include all fields of a table in a query. Access provides three methods, which are covered in the following sections.

### Using the Field List Title Bar to Add All Fields of a Table

One way to include all fields of a table in a query is to use the field list title bar or asterisk. To use this method in your query to include all fields, together with their field name headers, follow these steps:

1. Open a new query and add the tables required for your query.

2. Double-click the field list title bar of the table for which you want to include all fields. This selects all of the fields in the field list.

3. Click and drag a field name to the Query Design grid's Field cell, and drop the field name where you want the first field to appear. Figure 10.39 shows an example of the result of the preceding steps for the Customers table.

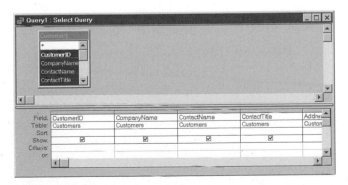

**FIG. 10.39** Adding all fields of the Customers table to a query by double-clicking the header of the Customers field list and dragging the fields to the Query Design grid.

II

Querying for Information

New

Adding all fields to the query by this method creates a SQL statement that is the equivalent of the following:

```
SELECT TableName.FirstField,
       TableName.SecondField, ... TableName.LastField
   FROM TableName
```

### Using the Asterisk to Add All Fields Without Field Names

To include in the query all fields of the table without displaying their field names, click and drag the asterisk to the first Field cell of the Query Design grid, and drop the asterisk where you want all of the fields to appear in the query result table. The asterisk column is equal to the Access SQL statement SELECT * FROM TableName.

You cannot sort on a column with an asterisk in its Field cell, nor can you establish criteria on such a column. If you choose the asterisk approach, you can sort or apply criteria to one or more fields in the table by following this technique:

1. After you add the asterisk to the Field cell, drag the name of the field that you want to sort or to which you want to apply a criterion. Drop that field name in the adjacent column's Field row.

2. Add the sort specification to the Sort cell or add the criterion to the Criteria cell.

3. Click the Show box, which removes the check mark, so that the field doesn't appear twice in the query. Figure 10.40 shows the resulting query design with the Customers table.

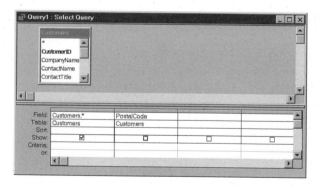

**FIG. 10.40** Adding all fields of the Customers table with the asterisk field and providing a hidden column for sorting by PostalCode.

You can use this method to add to the query as many columns from the asterisk table as you need. The field on which you sort the data is added to the SQL statement as an ORDER BY TableName.FieldName clause, and a criterion is added in a WHERE CriterionExpression clause.

### Selecting All Fields with the Output All Fields Property

Usually, only the fields whose names appear in the query are available for updating in forms or including in reports. All other fields are excluded from the result set. You can make all fields of every table used in the query available to the forms and reports that you create—even though the query design does not include the fields by name—by setting the Output All Fields property to Yes. To use the Output All Fields property to make all table fields available, follow these steps:

1. Open a new query and add the table(s) that participate(s) in the query.

2. Click the Properties button of the toolbar or double-click an empty area in the Query Design window's upper pane to display the Query Properties window.

3. In the Query Properties window, place the caret in the Output All Fields text box, press F4 to open the drop-down list, and change the default value—No—to Yes.

4. If the Unique Values Only text box displays Yes, you cannot update fields.

5. Click the Properties button to close the Query Properties window.

Turning on the Output All Fields option adds an all-fields asterisk to the list of specified fields in the SQL statement, as in the following example:

```
SELECT Customers.[CompanyName],
    Categories.[CategoryName], *
```

When you include all fields in your queries, you might find that running the query takes longer, especially with queries that create many rows in the result set.

# Making Calculations on Multiple Records

One of QBE's most powerful capabilities is that of obtaining summary information almost instantly from specified sets of records in tables. Summarized information from databases is the basis for virtually all management information systems (MIS). Such systems usually answer questions such as, "What are our sales to date for this month?" or "How did last month's sales compare with the same month last year?" To answer these questions, you must create queries that make calculations on field values from all or selected sets of records in a table. To make calculations on table values, you must create a query that uses the table and employs Access's SQL aggregate functions to perform the calculations.

### Using the SQL Aggregate Functions

Summary calculations on fields of tables included in query result tables use the SQL aggregate functions listed in Table 10.1. These are called *aggregate functions* because they apply to groups (aggregations) of data cells. The SQL aggregate functions satisfy the requirements of most queries needed for business applications. You can write special user-defined functions with Access VBA code to apply more sophisticated statistical, scientific, or engineering aggregate functions to your data.

| Table 10.1 | SQL Aggregate Functions | |
|---|---|---|
| **Function** | **Description** | **Field Types** |
| Avg() | Average of values in a field | All types except Text, Memo, and OLE Object |
| Count() | Number of Not Null values in a field | All field types |
| First() | Value of a field of the first record | All field types |
| Last() | Value of a field of the last record | All field types |
| Max() | Greatest value in a field | All types except Text, Memo, and OLE Object |
| Min() | Least value in a field | All types except Text, Memo, and OLE Object |
| StDev(), StDevP() | Statistical standard deviation of values in a field | All types except Text, Memo, and OLE Object |
| Sum() | Total of values in a field | All types except Text, Memo, and OLE Object |
| Var(), VarP() | Statistical variation of values in a field | All types except Text, Memo, and OLE Object |

StDev() and Var() evaluate population samples. You can choose these functions from the drop-down list in the Query Design grid's Total row. (The Total row appears when you click the Totals button of the toolbar or choose View, Totals.) StDevP() and VarP() evaluate populations and must be entered as expressions. If you're familiar with statistical principles, you recognize the difference in the calculation methods of standard deviation and variance for populations and samples of populations. The following section explains the method of choosing the SQL aggregate function for the column of a query.

> **Note**
>
> ANSI SQL and most SQL (client/server) databases support the equivalent of Access SQL's Avg(), Count(), First(), Last(), Max(), Min(), and Sum() aggregate functions as AVG(), COUNT(), FIRST(), LAST(), MAX(), MIN(), and SUM(), respectively. ANSI SQL and few, if any, SQL databases provide equivalents of the StdDev(), StdDevP(), Var(), and VarP() functions.

### Making Calculations Based on All Records of a Table

Managers, especially sales and marketing managers, are most often concerned with information about orders received and shipments made during specific periods of time. Financial managers are interested in calculated values, such as the total amount of unpaid invoices and the average number of days between the invoice and payment dates. Occasionally, you might want to make calculations on all records of a table, such as finding the historical average value of all invoices issued by a firm. Usually, however, you apply criteria to the query in order to select specific records that you want to total.

 Access considers all SQL aggregate functions to be members of the Totals class of functions. You create queries that return any or all SQL aggregate functions by clicking the Totals button (with the Greek sigma, Σ, which represents summation) on the toolbar.

The Orders table of Access 97's Northwind.mdb sample database does not include an OrderAmount field that represents the total amount of the order, less freight. (The "Entering a Query Criterion" section of Chapter 9 used a simplified version of this example to demonstrate the use of functions to calculate field values.) To create a sample query that uses the SQL aggregate functions to display the total number of orders, total sales, and the average, minimum, and maximum order values, you need a field that contains the total amount of each order. Follow these steps to create a new table that includes an additional field with a computed Order Amount:

1. Create a new query and add the Orders and Order Details tables to it.

2. Drag the OrderID field of the Orders table to the first column of the Query Design grid, and then drag the OrderDate field to the second column.

3. Type **Order Amount: Sum([Quantity]\*[UnitPrice]\*(1-[Discount]))** in the Field row of the third (empty) column. This expression sums the net amount of all line items for each order. With the caret in the Order Amount column, click the Properties button of the toolbar to open the Field Properties window. Type **Currency** in the text box for the Format property to format your new column.

4. Click the Totals button on the toolbar. A new row, Total, is added to the Query Design grid. Access adds Group By, the default action, to each cell in the Totals row. The following section discusses the use of Group By.

5. Move to the third column's Total row and press F4 to display the drop-down list of SQL aggregate functions. Select Expression from the list. Your Query Design grid appears as shown in Figure 10.41.

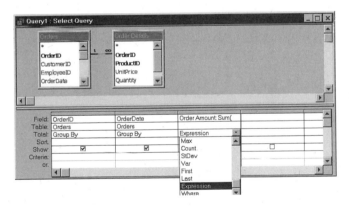

**FIG. 10.41** Creating a calculated field with the Sum() function.

6. Click the Run button of the toolbar to test your initial entries. Your query in Datasheet view appears as in Figure 10.42.

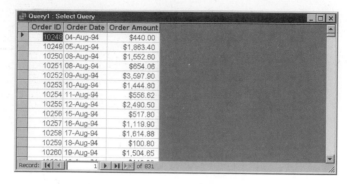

**FIG. 10.42** Running the query design shown in Figure 10.41.

**7.** Close and save your query with the name **Order Totals**.

> **Note**
>
> When you apply the Format property to the Order Amount column by selecting or typing **Currency** in the Field Properties window, successive queries that you create do not inherit the value of the Format property (instead, the default Format value, Double, is applied). If you type **Order Amount: CCur(Sum([Quantity]*[Unit Price]*(1-[Discount])))** in the Order Amount column's Field row, however, the Format property of successive queries containing the Order Amount field will be set to Currency. The **CCur**( ) function coerces the field's data type to Currency.

Follow these steps to apply the SQL aggregate functions to the Order Amounts field of the query result set of the Order Totals query:

**1.** Open a new query and add the Order Totals query. (To base a query on a prior-saved query, click the Queries tab of the Show Table dialog, and add the query as you would a table.)

**2.** Drag the OrderID field to the first column and then drag the Order Amount column four times to the adjacent column to create four Order Amount columns.)

**3.** Choose View, Totals to add the Totals row to your Query Design grid. Alternatively, right-click in the grid region and choose Totals from the popup menu.

**4.** Move to the Total row of the OrderID column and press F4 to display the drop-down list of SQL aggregate functions. Choose Count as the function for the Order ID, as shown in Figure 10.43.

**5.** Move to the first Order Amount column, open the list, and choose Sum from the Total drop-down list. Repeat the process, choosing Avg for the second Order Amount column, Min for the third, and Max for the fourth.

**6.** Place the caret in the Count field, and click the Properties button of the toolbar (or right-click in the Count field and then click Properties in the popup menu) to display the Field Properties window. Type **Count** as the value of the Caption property.

7. Repeat step 6 for the four Order Amount columns, typing **Currency** for the Format property and typing **Sum**, **Average**, **Minimum**, and **Maximum** as the values of the Caption property for the four columns, respectively. (You don't need to set the Format property if you used the CCur() function in the Order Totals query.)

8. Click the Run button of the toolbar to display the query's result. You haven't specified criteria for the fields, so the result shown in Figure 10.44 is for the whole table. (The values in the result may differ from the values in Figure 10.44 because of records that Microsoft might add to the sample database after this book is published.)

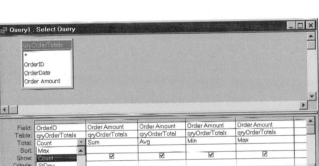

**FIG. 10.43**  Choosing the SQL aggregate function for calculations based on multiple records in a table.

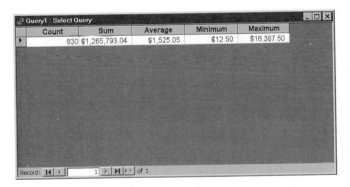

**FIG. 10.44**  The result of the all-records query shown in Figure 10.43.

9. Save your query with a descriptive name, such as **qrySQLAggregates**, because you use this query in the two sections that follow.

> **Note**
>
> When you run qrySQLAggregates, the Jet database engine determines that Order Totals is a query (QueryDef object) rather than a table (TableDef object). Thus Jet executes the Order Totals query before executing the qrySQLAggregates query. One of the most important features of Access is that you can execute queries against the query result sets (Recordset objects) of other queries—a process called *nesting* queries. In theory, at least, there is no limit to the depth to which you can nest Access queries. As you increase the number of queries in the chain, however, execution slows for the last query in the nested sequence.

## Making Calculations Based on Selected Records of a Table

The preceding example query performed calculations on all orders received by Northwind Traders that were entered in the Orders table. Usually, you are interested in a specific set of records—a range of dates, for example—from which to calculate aggregate values. To restrict the calculation to orders that Northwind Traders received in March 1995, follow these steps:

1. Click the Query View button on the toolbar to return to design mode so that you can add criteria to select a specific group of records based on the date of the order.

2. Drag the OrderDate field onto the OrderID column to add OrderDate as the first column of the query. You need the OrderDate field to restrict the data to a range of dates.

3. Open the Total drop-down list in the Order Date column, and choose Where to replace the default Group By. Access deselects the Show box of the OrderDate column. (If you attempt to show a column that provides the SQL WHERE restriction, you receive an error message when you run your query.)

4. In the Order Date column's Criteria row, type **Like "3/*/95"** to restrict the totals to orders received in the month of March 1995 (see Figure 10.45). When you use the Like criterion, Access adds the quotation marks if you forget to type them.

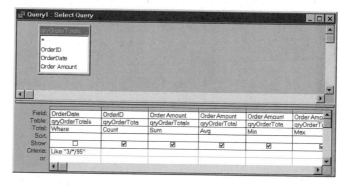

**FIG. 10.45**  Adding a Where criterion to restrict the totals to a range of records.

5.  Choose <u>V</u>iew, S<u>Q</u>L to display your query's SQL statement. The Where criterion in the Total row adds a WHERE clause to the SQL statement—in this case, WHERE (((([Order Totals.OrderDate Like "3/*/94")))—to restrict the totaled records to the records for the specified date range. (The Access query parser tends to add extra sets of parentheses to expressions.) If you don't add the Where instruction to the Total row, the query result consists of rows with the totals of orders for each day of March 1995, not for the entire month.

6.  Click the Run button on the toolbar to display the result: the count, total, and average value of orders received during the month of March 1995 (see Figure 10.46).

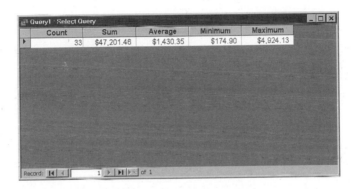

**FIG. 10.46**  The result of adding the Where criterion to the query.

You can create a more useful grouping of records by replacing the field name with an expression. For example, you can group aggregates by the year and month (or year and quarter) by grouping on the value of an expression created with the Format() function. The following steps produce a sales summary record for each month of 1995, the latest year for which 12 months of data are available in the Orders table:

1.  Click the Query View button of the toolbar, and then click the header bar of the query's OrderDate column to select the first column. Press the Insert key to add a new, empty column to the query.

2.  Type **Month: Format([OrderDate],"yy-mm")** in the first (empty) column's Field row. (You use the "yy-mm" format so that the records sort in date order. For a single year, you also can use "m" or "mm", but not "mmm" because "mmm" sorts in alphabetic sequence starting with Apr.)

3.  Change the Where criterion of the Order Date column to **Like "*/*/95"**. Your query design appears as shown in Figure 10.47.

4.  Click the toolbar's Run button to display the result of your query (see Figure 10.48). The query creates sales summary data for each month of 1995.

II

Querying for Information

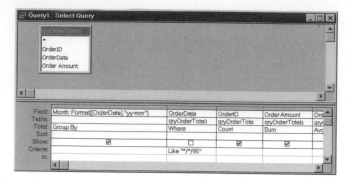

**FIG. 10.47**  Designing a query for a yearly sales summary by month.

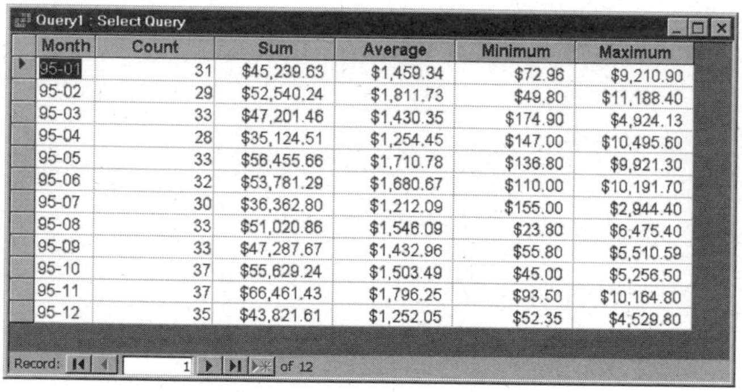

| Month | Count | Sum | Average | Minimum | Maximum |
|---|---|---|---|---|---|
| 95-01 | 31 | $45,239.63 | $1,459.34 | $72.96 | $9,210.90 |
| 95-02 | 29 | $52,540.24 | $1,811.73 | $49.80 | $11,188.40 |
| 95-03 | 33 | $47,201.46 | $1,430.35 | $174.90 | $4,924.13 |
| 95-04 | 28 | $35,124.51 | $1,254.45 | $147.00 | $10,495.60 |
| 95-05 | 33 | $56,455.66 | $1,710.78 | $136.80 | $9,921.30 |
| 95-06 | 32 | $53,781.29 | $1,680.67 | $110.00 | $10,191.70 |
| 95-07 | 30 | $36,362.80 | $1,212.09 | $155.00 | $2,944.40 |
| 95-08 | 33 | $51,020.86 | $1,546.09 | $23.80 | $6,475.40 |
| 95-09 | 33 | $47,287.67 | $1,432.96 | $55.80 | $5,510.59 |
| 95-10 | 37 | $55,629.24 | $1,503.49 | $45.00 | $5,256.50 |
| 95-11 | 37 | $66,461.43 | $1,796.25 | $93.50 | $10,164.80 |
| 95-12 | 35 | $43,821.61 | $1,252.05 | $52.35 | $4,529.80 |

Record: ◄◄ ◄ [ 1 ] ► ►◄ ►* of 12

**FIG. 10.48**  The result set of the query design shown in Figure 10.47.

5. Choose <u>V</u>iew, SQL to display the SQL statement that created the query result set. The SQL statement in the SQL window of Figure 10.49 has been reformatted for clarity. (Formatting a SQL statement with spaces and newline pairs does not affect the statement's execution.)

6. Choose <u>F</u>ile, Save <u>A</u>s and save the query under a different name, such as **qryMonthlySales**, because you modify the query in the next section.

# Designing Parameter Queries

If you expect to run a summary or another type of query repeatedly with changes to the criteria, you can convert the query to a *parameter query*. Parameter queries—which Chapter 8, "Using Query by Example," explained briefly—enable you to enter criteria with the Enter Parameter Value dialog. You are prompted for each parameter required. For the example qryMonthlySales query that you created previously in this chapter, the only parameter likely to change is the range of dates for which you want to generate the product sales data. The two sections that follow show you how to add a parameter to a query and specify the data type of the parameter.

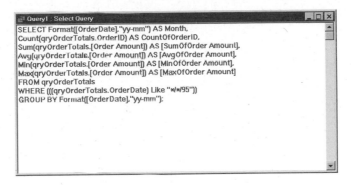

**FIG. 10.49** The SQL statement for a yearly sales summary by month.

### Adding a Parameter to the Monthly Sales Query

To convert the qryMonthlySales summary query to a parameter query, you first create prompts for the Enter Parameter Value dialog that appears when the query runs. You create parameter queries by substituting the text with which to prompt, enclosed within square brackets, for actual values. Follow these steps:

1. In Design mode, open the qryMonthlySales query that you created in the preceding section.

2. With the caret in the Month column's Field row, press F2 to select the expression in the Field cell. Then press Ctrl+C to copy the expression to the Clipboard.

3. Move the caret to the OrderDate column's Field row, and press F2 to select OrderDate. Then press Ctrl+V to replace OrderDate with the expression used for the first column.

4. Move to the OrderDate column's Criteria cell and replace Like "*/*/95" with **[Enter the year and month in YY-MM format:]** (see Figure 10.50).

5. Click the Run button of the toolbar. The Enter Parameter Value dialog appears with the label that you assigned as the value of the criterion in step 4.

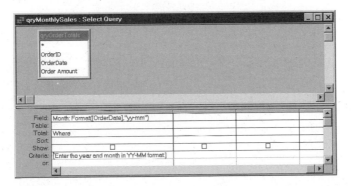

**FIG. 10.50** The expression to create the Enter Parameter Value dialog with boxes for the year and month.

6. Type **96-04** in the text box to display the data for April 1996, as shown in Figure 10.51.

**FIG. 10.51** The Enter Parameter Value dialog for entering the year and month.

7. Click OK to run the query. The result appears as shown in Figure 10.52.

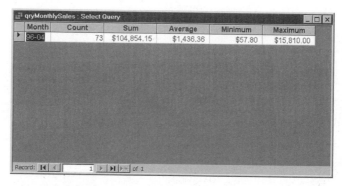

**FIG. 10.52** The query result for the 96-04 parameter.

### Specifying the Parameter's Data Type

The default field data type for parameters of Access queries is Text. If the parameter creates a criterion for a query column of the Date/Time or Number field data type, you must assign a data type to each entry that is made through an Enter Parameter Value dialog. Data types for values entered as parameters are established in the Query Parameters dialog. Follow these steps to add an optional data type specification to your parameter:

1. Use the mouse to select Enter the Year and Month in YY-MM Format: in the Month column's Criteria cell (omit the square brackets) and copy the text of the prompt to the Clipboard by pressing Ctrl+C.

2. Choose Query, Parameters to display the Query Parameters dialog.

3. To insert the prompt in the Parameter column of the dialog, place the caret in the column and press Ctrl+V. The prompt entry in the Parameter column must match the prompt entry in the Criteria field exactly; copying and pasting the prompt text ensures an exact match. Do not include the square brackets in the Parameter column.

4. Press Tab to move to the Data Type column, press F4 to open the Data Type drop-down list, and choose Date/Time (see Figure 10.53). Click OK to close the dialog.

> **Note**
>
> Complete your query design and testing before you convert any type of query to a parameter query. Using fixed criteria with the query maintains consistency during the testing process. Furthermore, you can make repeated changes between Design and Run mode more quickly if you don't have to enter one or more parameters in the process. After you finish testing the query, edit the criteria to add the Enter Parameter Value dialog.

**FIG. 10.53**  The Query Parameters dialog for assigning data types to user-entered parameters.

The parameter-conversion process described in this section applies to all types of queries that you create if one or more of the query columns includes a criterion expression. The advantage of the parameter query is that you or a user of the database can run a query for any range of values—in this case, dates—such as the current month to date, a particular fiscal quarter, or an entire fiscal year.

# Creating Crosstab Queries

*Crosstab queries* are summary queries that enable you to determine exactly how the summary data appears on-screen. Crosstab queries display summarized data in the traditional row-column form of spreadsheets. Crosstab queries use the Access SQL TRANSFORM keyword to indicate that the statements following the keyword are for a crosstab query. (TRANSFORM is not an ANSI SQL keyword.) With crosstab queries, you can perform the following processes:

- Specify the field that creates labels (headings) for rows by using the Group By instruction.

- Determine the field(s) that create(s) column headers and the criteria that determine the values appearing under the headers.

- Assign calculated data values to the cells of the resulting row-column grid.

The following list details the advantages of using crosstab queries:

- You can display a substantial amount of summary data in a compact format familiar to anyone who uses a spreadsheet application or columnar accounting form.

- The summary data is presented in a format that is ideally suited for creating graphs and charts automatically with the Access Chart Wizard.

■ Designing queries to create multiple levels of detail is quick and easy. Queries with identical columns but fewer rows can represent increasingly summarized data. Highly summarized queries are ideal to begin a drill-down procedure by instructing the user, for example, to click the Details button to display sales by product.

Using crosstab queries imposes only one restriction: You cannot sort your result table on calculated values in columns. You cannot, therefore, create a query that ranks products by sales volume. Columns are likely to have values that cause conflicts in the sorting order of the row. You can choose an ascending sort, a descending sort, or no sort on the row label values in the first column.

One of Access 97's Query Wizards is designed to help you create crosstab queries. However, the Crosstab Query Wizard is limited to creating crosstab queries for a single table or query. If your database follows the rules of relational database design, a usable crosstab query is far more likely to be based on at least two tables. Using the Crosstab Query Wizard requires that you create a query including the tables needed for the crosstab query. Thus, you create the examples of crosstab queries in the next two sections with help from this book instead of the Crosstab Query Wizard.

### Creating a Monthly Product Sales Crosstab Query

To create a typical crosstab query that displays products in rows and the monthly sales volume for each product in the corresponding columns, follow these steps:

1. Open a new query and add the Products, Order Details, and Orders tables to the query.

2. Drag the ProductID and ProductName fields from the Products table to the query's first two columns, and then drag the OrderDate field of the Orders table to the third column.

3. Choose Query, Crosstab Query. The title bar of the query changes from Query1: Select Query to Query1: Crosstab Query. Another row, Crosstab, is added to the Query Design grid.

4. Open the drop-down list of the ProductID column's Crosstab row and select Row Heading. Repeat this process for the ProductName column. These two columns provide the required row headings for your crosstab.

5. Open the Total drop-down list of the OrderDate column and select Where. Type **Like "*/*/95"** in this column's Criteria row to restrict the crosstab to orders received in 1995, the latest year for which 12 months of data are available.

6. Move to the next (empty) column's Field row and type the following:

    **Sales: Sum([Order Details].[Quantity]* [Order Details].[UnitPrice])**

    Move to the Total row, choose Expression from the drop-down list, and then choose Value from the Crosstab row. The expression calculates the gross amount of the orders received for each product that populates your crosstab query's data cells. (You need to specify the Orders Detail table name; if you don't, you receive an `Ambiguous field reference` error message.)

7. In the next (empty) column's Field row, type **Format([OrderDate], "mmm")**.
   Access adds a default field name, Expr1:. Accept the default because the Format()
   function that you added creates the column names, the three-letter abbreviation
   for the months of the year ("mmm" format), when you run the query. The months of
   the year (Jan through Dec) are your column headings, so move to the Crosstab row
   and choose Column Heading from the drop-down list. The design of your crosstab
   query appears as shown in Figure 10.54.

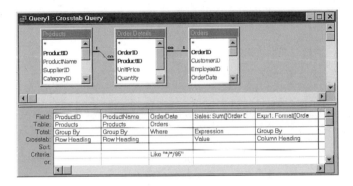

**FIG. 10.54**   The design of a crosstab query for monthly sales of products.

8. Click the Run button on the toolbar to execute the query. A period of disk activity
   occurs, followed by a display of the crosstab query's result, shown in Figure 10.55.

Notice that the crosstab query result contains a major defect: The columns are arranged
alphabetically by month name rather than in calendar order. You can solve this problem
by using fixed column headings, which you learn about in the following section, "Using
Fixed Column Headings with Crosstab Queries."

| Product ID | Product Name | April | August | Decem |
|---|---|---|---|---|
| 1 | Chai | $216.00 | $522.00 | $1,0 |
| 2 | Chang | $912.00 | $190.00 | $2 |
| 3 | Aniseed Syrup | $160.00 | $140.00 | $2 |
| 4 | Chef Anton's Cajun Seasoning | $281.80 | $440.00 | $5 |
| 5 | Chef Anton's Gumbo Mix | | | |
| 6 | Grandma's Boysenberry Spread | | | $7 |
| 7 | Uncle Bob's Organic Dried Pears | $720.00 | $1,650.00 | |
| 8 | Northwoods Cranberry Sauce | | | |
| 9 | Mishi Kobe Niku | | | |
| 10 | Ikura | $498.00 | $2,480.00 | |
| 11 | Queso Cabrales | $504.00 | $294.00 | $1 |
| 12 | Queso Manchego La Pastora | | | |
| 13 | Konbu | $4.80 | $408.00 | $ |
| 14 | Tofu | $223.20 | | $4 |
| 15 | Genen Shouyu | | $387.50 | $3 |

Record: 1 of 77

**FIG. 10.55**   The first result set from the crosstab query design shown in Figure 10.54.

## Using Fixed Column Headings with Crosstab Queries

Access uses an alphabetical or numerical sort on row and column headings to establish
the sequence of appearance in the crosstab query result table. For this reason, if you use

short or full names for months, the sequence is in alphabetic rather than calendar order. You can correct this problem by assigning fixed column headings to the crosstab query. Follow these steps to modify and rerun the query:

◄◄  See "Functions for Date and Time," p. 300

1. Return to query design mode and click the Properties button of the toolbar, or double-click an empty area in the Query Design window's upper pane. The Query Properties window contains an option that appears only for crosstab queries: Column Headings.

2. In the Column Headings text box, type the three-letter abbreviations of all 12 months of the year (see Figure 10.56). You must spell the abbreviations of the months correctly; data for months with spelling mistakes does not appear. You can separate entries with commas or semicolons, and you don't need to type quotation marks because Access adds them. Spaces are unnecessary and undesirable between the Column Headings values. After you complete all 12 entries, close the Query Properties window.

3. Click the Run button of the toolbar. Now the result table, shown in Figure 10.57, includes columns for all 12 months, although you can see only January through April in Figure 10.57. (Scroll to the right to see the remaining months.) If the crosstab appears differently, check whether you properly entered the fixed column headings in the Query Properties window. A misspelled month causes Access to omit the month from the query result set; if you specified "mmmm" instead of "mmm", most of your month columns will be blank.

4. Choose File, Save As and save the query with an appropriate name, such as **qry1995MonthlyProductSales**.

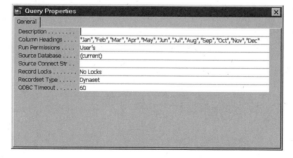

**FIG. 10.56**  Entering fixed column headings in the crosstab Query Properties window.

You can produce a printed report quickly from the query by clicking the Print Preview button on the toolbar and then clicking the Print button.

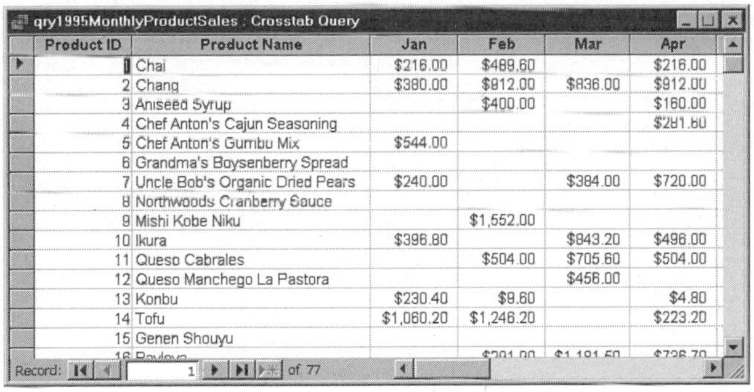


| Product ID | Product Name | Jan | Feb | Mar | Apr |
|---|---|---|---|---|---|
| 1 | Chai | $216.00 | $489.60 | | $216.00 |
| 2 | Chang | $380.00 | $812.00 | $836.00 | $912.00 |
| 3 | Aniseed Syrup | | $400.00 | | $160.00 |
| 4 | Chef Anton's Cajun Seasoning | | | | $281.60 |
| 5 | Chef Anton's Gumbu Mix | $544.00 | | | |
| 6 | Grandma's Boysenberry Spread | | | | |
| 7 | Uncle Bob's Organic Dried Pears | $240.00 | | $384.00 | $720.00 |
| 8 | Northwoods Cranberry Sauce | | | | |
| 9 | Mishi Kobe Niku | | $1,552.00 | | |
| 10 | Ikura | $396.80 | | $843.20 | $496.00 |
| 11 | Queso Cabrales | | $504.00 | $705.60 | $504.00 |
| 12 | Queso Manchego La Pastora | | | $456.00 | |
| 13 | Konbu | $230.40 | $9.60 | | $4.80 |
| 14 | Tofu | $1,060.20 | $1,246.20 | | $223.20 |
| 15 | Genen Shouyu | | | | |

**FIG. 10.57** The result table from the crosstab query design with fixed column headings and a date-limiting criterion.

**Note**

You might want to use fixed column headings if you use the Group By instruction with country names. Users in the United States will probably place USA first, and Canadian firms will undoubtedly choose Canada as the first entry. If you add a record with a new country, you must remember to update the list of fixed column headings with the new country value. Fixed column headings have another hidden benefit: they usually make crosstab queries operate more quickly.

### Decreasing the Level of Detail in Crosstab Queries

The result table created by the preceding example query has a row for every product for which Northwind Traders received an order in each month of 1995. Higher-level management usually wants information in the form of a graph or chart to analyze trends in the data. Therefore, you must reduce the number of rows and columns so that you can create a readable graph from the values in the query result table.

To create a summary query that reports quarterly gross sales of products by category (rather than by ProductID), follow these steps:

1. Choose File, Save As and save a copy of the query that you created in the preceding section with a descriptive name, such as **qry1995QuarterlyCategorySales**.

2. In Query Design view, click the Show Table button on the toolbar and add the Categories table to the query.

3. To make the relationships among the tables more clear, click the title bar of each of the field lists in the upper pane and drag the field lists to the positions shown in Figure 10.58.

4. Drag and drop the Categories table's CategoryID and CategoryName fields to the first column's Field cell, which contains ProductID. New CategoryID and CategoryName columns are added to the query. Move down to the Crosstab cell and choose Row Heading from the drop-down list for both new columns.

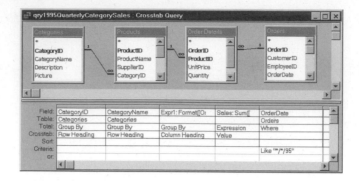

**FIG. 10.58** The design of a summary query for quarterly sales by product category.

5. Click the selection bar above the third column's ProductID cell, and then press Delete to delete this column. Repeat this process for the ProductName column. The Crosstab Query Design grid then appears as shown in Figure 10.58.

6. Edit Expr1:, which creates the column headings, so that the expression appears as **Format([OrderDate],""""Quarter ""q"""")**. This results in column headings of Quarter 1 through Quarter 4. (The multiple quotation marks are necessary to specify `Quarter` and a space as literals and `q` as a formatting character.)

7. Double-click an empty area in the Query Design window's upper pane to open the Query Properties window. Delete the Column Headings entries for the month abbreviations, then close the Query Properties window. If you don't delete the fixed column headings, your query can't return any rows. To make your query run more quickly, you can add the four Quarter number headings, separated by commas or semicolons, as the value of the Column Heading property in the Query Properties window.

8. Click the Run button on the toolbar. The query result set appears as shown in Figure 10.59.

qry1995QuarterlyCategorySales : Crosstab Query

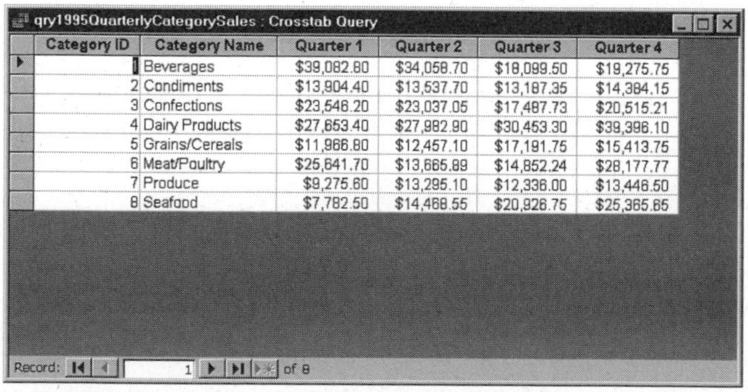

| Category ID | Category Name | Quarter 1 | Quarter 2 | Quarter 3 | Quarter 4 |
|---|---|---|---|---|---|
| 1 | Beverages | $39,082.80 | $34,058.70 | $18,099.50 | $19,275.75 |
| 2 | Condiments | $13,904.40 | $13,537.70 | $13,187.35 | $14,384.15 |
| 3 | Confections | $23,546.20 | $23,037.05 | $17,487.73 | $20,515.21 |
| 4 | Dairy Products | $27,653.40 | $27,982.90 | $30,453.30 | $39,396.10 |
| 5 | Grains/Cereals | $11,966.80 | $12,457.10 | $17,191.75 | $15,413.75 |
| 6 | Meat/Poultry | $25,641.70 | $13,665.89 | $14,852.24 | $28,177.77 |
| 7 | Produce | $9,275.60 | $13,295.10 | $12,336.00 | $13,446.50 |
| 8 | Seafood | $7,782.50 | $14,468.55 | $20,926.75 | $25,365.65 |

Record: 1 of 8

**FIG. 10.59** The result set of the query design for the quarterly sales by product category.

9. Choose <u>V</u>iew, SQL to view the SQL statement that creates the crosstab query (see Figure 10.60). The Access SQL TRANSFORM clause, which corresponds to the Values crosstab property, defines the values that appear in the data cells. The PIVOT statement defines the column headings. (The IN predicate following the PIVOT statement specifies the fixed column headings, if any.) TRANSFORM and PIVOT are not reserved words of ANSI SQL. Access crosstab queries and conventional SQL SELECT queries interpret the ANSI SQL IN predicate differently.

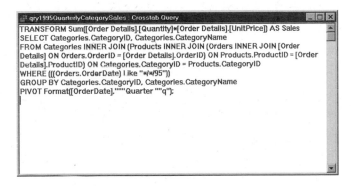

**FIG. 10.60**  The SQL statement that creates the quarterly sales-by-product query.

10. Choose <u>F</u>ile, <u>S</u>ave to save your query. The qry1995QuarterlyCategorySales query is used for many different purposes in later chapters of this book.

Crosstab queries that display time-series data, such as monthly and quarterly sales for products or categories of products, are often used as the basis for graphs. Chapter 20, "Adding Graphics to Forms and Reports," uses the qry1995QuarterlyCategorySales query to create two types of Access graphs.

# Creating Queries from Tables in Other Databases

Access's Query Properties window includes two properties that let you create a query based on tables contained in a database other than the current database. Access calls the database that you open after you launch Access the *current database*. Databases other than the current database commonly are called *external* databases. The use of these two properties is as follows:

- The value of the Source Database property for desktop databases is the path to the external database and, for Access databases, the name of the database file. To run a query against tables contained in the Solutions.mdb sample database, replace (current) in the Source Database text box with the following, as shown in Figure 10.61:

**C:\Program Files\Microsoft Office\Access\Samples\Solutions.mdb**

To run a query against a set of Paradox tables in the D:\Paradox folder, you type the path only (**d:\paradox**, where *d:* is the logical drive letter). If you're using the ODBC API to connect to a client/server database, you leave the Source Database text box empty.

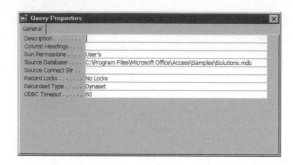

**FIG. 10.61**    Setting the Source Database property for a query against an external database.

■ The value of the Source Connect Str property also depends on the type of external database being used. If your external Access database is not secure, leave the Source Connect Str text box empty; otherwise, type **UID=UserID;PWD=Password** to specify the user ID and password needed to open the external database. For other desktop databases, type the product name, such as **Paradox 3.5** or **dBASE IV**. ODBC data sources require the complete ODBC connect string. Using ODBC databases is one of the subjects of Chapter 25, "Securing Multiuser Network Applications."

Running a query against an external database is related to running a query against linked tables. When you link tables, the data in the tables is available at any time that your application is running. When you run a query against an external database, the connection to the external database is open only while your query is open in Design or Run mode. A slight performance penalty exists for running queries against an external database—each time that you run the query, Access must make a connection to open the database. The connection is closed when you close the query.

Figure 10.62 shows a query design based on tables contained in the Solutions.mdb sample database that accompanies Access 97. In this case, Access 97's Northwind.mdb is the current database. Figure 10.63 shows the result of executing the query design of Figure 10.62 against the Example Objects, Examples, and Example Topics tables of Solutions.mdb.

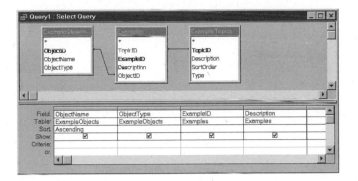

**FIG. 10.62**  A query design based on tables in an external Access database.

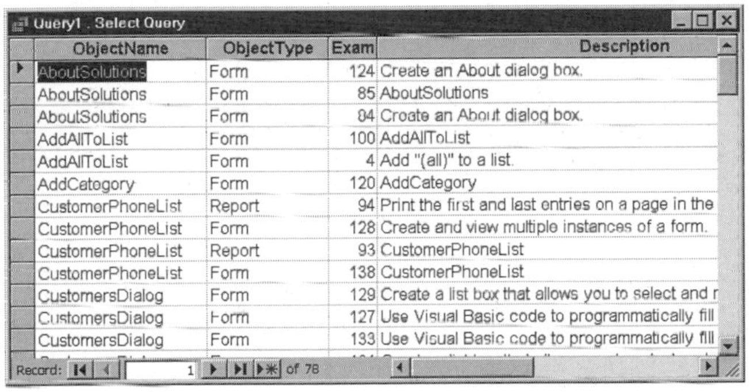

| ObjectName | ObjectType | Exam | Description |
|---|---|---|---|
| AboutSolutions | Form | 124 | Create an About dialog box. |
| AboutSolutions | Form | 85 | AboutSolutions |
| AboutSolutions | Form | 84 | Create an About dialog box. |
| AddAllToList | Form | 100 | AddAllToList |
| AddAllToList | Form | 4 | Add "(all)" to a list. |
| AddCategory | Form | 120 | AddCategory |
| CustomerPhoneList | Report | 94 | Print the first and last entries on a page in the |
| CustomerPhoneList | Form | 128 | Create and view multiple instances of a form. |
| CustomerPhoneList | Report | 93 | CustomerPhoneList |
| CustomerPhoneList | Form | 138 | CustomerPhoneList |
| CustomersDialog | Form | 129 | Create a list box that allows you to select and r |
| CustomersDialog | Form | 127 | Use Visual Basic code to programmatically fill |
| CustomersDialog | Form | 133 | Use Visual Basic code to programmatically fill |

Record: 1 of 78

**FIG. 10.63**  The query result set of the query design shown in Figure 10.62.

II

Querying for Information

# Chapter 11

# Using Action Queries

*Action queries* create new tables or modify the data in existing tables. Four types of action queries are available in Access:

- *Make-table* creates new tables from the data contained in query result sets. One of the most common applications for make-table queries is to create tables that you can export to other applications, or that summarize data from other tables. A make-table query provides a convenient way to copy a table to another database. In some cases, you can use make-table queries to speed the generation of multiple forms and reports based on a single, complex query.

- *Append* adds new records to tables from the query's Recordset.

- *Delete* deletes records from tables that correspond to the rows of the query result set.

- *Update* changes the values of existing fields of table records corresponding to rows of the query result set.

This chapter shows you how to create each of the four types of action queries and how to use Access's cascading deletions and cascading updates of related records. This chapter covers cascading deletions and cascading updates because these features are related to delete and update action queries, respectively.

## Creating New Tables with Make-Table Queries

In the following sections, you learn how to use a make-table query to create a new table, Shipping Address, for customers that have different shipping and billing addresses. This process enables the deletion of the shipping address data that, in most of the records in the Orders table, duplicates the address data in the Customers table. Removing duplicated data to new tables is an

Important step when you are converting data contained in a flat (non-relational) database to a relational database structure. You can use the Table Analyzer Wizard, described in Chapter 23, "Exploring Relational Database Design and Implementation," to perform an operation similar to that described in the following sections. Removing duplicated data manually, however, is one of the best methods of demonstrating how to design make-table queries.

> ### Caution
>
> Always make a backup copy of a table that you are going to modify with an action query. Changes made to table data with action queries are permanent; an error can render a table useless. Invalid changes made to a table with an action query containing a design error often are difficult to detect.

◄◄ See "Creating Not-Equal Theta Joins with Criteria," p. 344
►► See "Using Access 97's Table Analyzer Wizard," p. 813

The example that you create in the following sections extracts data from the Orders table based on data in the Customers table and creates a new table, tblShipAddresses. A modification of the query that you created in the "Creating Not-Equal Theta Joins with Criteria" section of Chapter 10 generates the data for the new table. Make-table queries are useful in converting flat-file tables that contain duplicated data, including tables created by spreadsheet applications, to relational form.

### Designing and Testing the Select Query

To create the new shipping addresses table from the data in the Orders table, you first must build a select query. To build a select query, follow these steps:

1.  Create a new query and add the Customers and Orders tables to it.

2.  Drag the CustomerID field from the Customers table and drop it in the query's first column. The CustomerID field links the Shipping Address table to the Orders table.

3.  Drag the ShipName, ShipAddress, ShipCity, ShipRegion, ShipPostalCode, and ShipCountry fields and drop them in columns 2–7, respectively. You use these fields, in addition to CustomerID, to create the new Shipping Address table.

    Next, you want to add criteria to select only those records of the Orders table for which the ShipName doesn't match the CompanyName or the ShipAddress doesn't match the Customers table's address.

4.  In the ShipName column's first Criteria row, type the following:

    **<>[*Customers*].[*CompanyName*]**

5.  In the next row of the ShipAddress column, type the following:

    **<>[*Customers*].[*Address*]**

This entry must be in a different Criteria row than the CompanyName criterion so that the **or** operator is applied to the two criteria. The Query Design grid appears as shown in Figure 11.1.

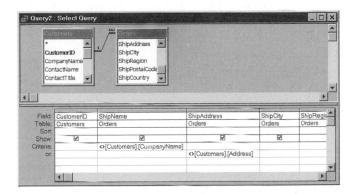

**FIG. 11.1** Creating the select query for the new Shipping Address table.

> **Note**
>
> A more precise approach is to add additional **Or** criteria to test for not-equal cities, regions, postal codes, and countries. A customer having exactly the same address in two different cities, however, is highly improbable.

6. Double-click an empty area in the Query Design window's upper pane to open the Query Properties window. Open the Unique Values drop-down list and select Yes.

7. Click the toolbar's Run button to run the select query. Data for customers that placed orders with different billing and shipping addresses appears, as shown in Figure 11.2. (Figure 11.2 contains the CustomerID LETSS, which appears only if you performed the exercises in Chapter 8.)

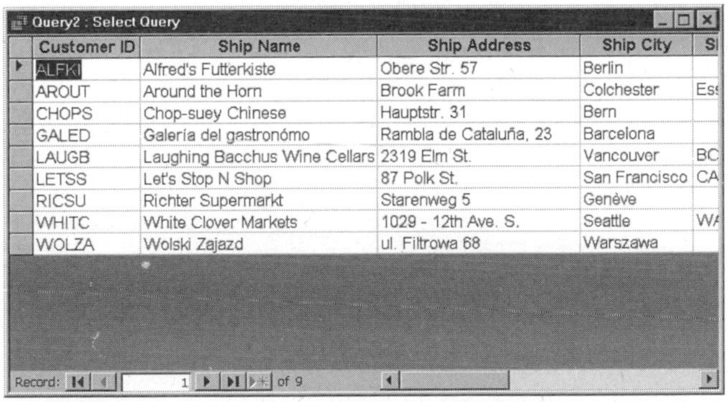

| Customer ID | Ship Name | Ship Address | Ship City | S |
|---|---|---|---|---|
| ALFKI | Alfred's Futterkiste | Obere Str. 57 | Berlin | |
| AROUT | Around the Horn | Brook Farm | Colchester | Ess |
| CHOPS | Chop-suey Chinese | Hauptstr. 31 | Bern | |
| GALED | Galería del gastrónomo | Rambla de Cataluña, 23 | Barcelona | |
| LAUGB | Laughing Bacchus Wine Cellars | 2319 Elm St. | Vancouver | BC |
| LETSS | Let's Stop N Shop | 87 Polk St. | San Francisco | CA |
| RICSU | Richter Supermarkt | Starenweg 5 | Genève | |
| WHITC | White Clover Markets | 1029 - 12th Ave. S. | Seattle | WA |
| WOLZA | Wolski Zajazd | ul. Filtrowa 68 | Warszawa | |

**FIG. 11.2** The data to be added to the new Shipping Address table.

II

Querying for Information

### Converting the Select Query to a Make-Table Query

Now that you have tested the select query to make sure that it creates the necessary data, you can create the table from the query. To create the table, follow these steps:

**1.** Choose Query, Ma**k**e-Table Query. The Make Table dialog appears. Type the name of the table, **tblShipAddresses**, in the Table Name text box (see Figure 11.3). Click OK.

**FIG. 11.3**  The Make Table dialog for make-table queries.

**2.** Click the Run button on the toolbar. A message confirms the number of records that you are adding to the new table (see Figure 11.4). Choose Yes to create the new tblShipAddresses table.

**FIG. 11.4**  The confirmation message box that precedes the creation of the new table.

**3.** Click the toolbar's Database Window button to activate the Database window, click the Table tab, and open the new tblShipAddresses table. The entries appear as shown in Figure 11.5.

| CustomerID | ShipName | ShipAddress | ShipCity | ShipRegion | ShipPostalC |
|---|---|---|---|---|---|
| ALFKI | Alfred's Futterki | Obere Str. 57 | Berlin | | 12209 |
| AROUT | Around the Horn | Brook Farm | Colchester | Essex | CO7 6JX |
| CHOPS | Chop-suey Chir | Hauptstr. 31 | Bern | | 3012 |
| GALED | Galería del gast | Rambla de Cata | Barcelona | | 8022 |
| LAUGB | Laughing Bacch | 2319 Elm St. | Vancouver | BC | V3F 2K1 |
| LETSS | Let's Stop N Sho | 87 Polk St. | San Francisco | CA | 94117 |
| RICSU | Richter Superm | Starenweg 5 | Genève | | 1204 |
| WHITC | White Clover Ma | 1029 - 12th Ave | Seattle | WA | 98124 |
| WOLZA | Wolski Zajazd | ul. Filtrowa 68 | Warszawa | | 01-012 |

Record: |◄ ◄|  1  ► ►| ►* of 9

**FIG. 11.5**  The tblShipAddresses table created by the make-table query.

Now complete the design of the new tblShipAddresses table by following these steps:

1. Click the Design View button of the toolbar. The table's basic design is inherited from the properties of the fields of the tables used to create the new table. The tblShipAddresses table does not, however, inherit the primary-key assignment from the Customers table's CustomerID field.

2. Click the toolbar's Properties button to display the Table Properties window. In the Table Properties window's Description text box, type **Shipping addresses different from billing addresses**, as shown in Figure 11.6. Click the Properties button to close the Properties window.

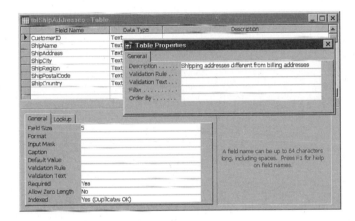

**FIG. 11.6**    The design of the newly created tblShipAddresses table.

3. The tblShipAddresses table presently has a partial one-to-one relationship with the Customers table because only one shipping address record exists for each customer that has different shipping and billing addresses. A customer might have many different shipping addresses, however, so the relationship of Customers to tblShipAddresses is one-to-many, and you must allow duplicate values in the CustomerID field of tblShipAddresses. You cannot, therefore, create a primary key for the tblShipAddresses table unless you include three fields—CustomerID, ShipName, and ShipAddress—to make multiple entries for one customer unique. This particular example doesn't use a primary key. Choose the CustomerID field, open the Indexed property drop-down list, and choose the Yes (Duplicates OK) value. Indexing improves the performance of queries when you have many different shipping addresses for customers.

4. The CustomerID, ShipName, ShipAddress, ShipCity, and ShipCountry fields are required, so set the value for each of these fields' Required property to **Yes**. (Many countries do not have values for the ShipRegion field, and a few countries do not use postal codes.)

## Establishing Relationships for the New Table

Now you need to complete the process of adding the new table to your database by establishing default relationships and enforcing referential integrity so that all records in the tblShipAddress table have a corresponding record in the Customers table. Access 97's graphical Relationships window makes this process simple and intuitive. To establish the relationship of tblShipAddress and the Customers table, follow these steps:

1. Close the tblShipAddress table. Answer Yes when asked whether you want to save changes to the table's design, and answer Yes again when asked whether you want to apply the new data integrity rules to the table. Click the toolbar's Database Window button to make the Database window active.

2. Click the Relationships button of the toolbar or choose Tools, Relationships to open the Relationships window that establishes the default relationships between tables. Click the toolbar's Show Table button and double-click the tblShipAddresses table to add the table to the Relationships window; then click the Close button. Move the field list to the position shown in Figure 11.7. (Drag up the bottom of the Orders field list to make room for the tblShipAddress field list.)

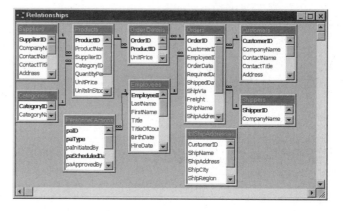

**FIG. 11.7** Adding the tblShipAddresses table to the Relationships window.

3. Click the Customers table's CustomerID field, drag the field symbol to the tblShipAddresses table's CustomerID field, and drop the symbol. This example emphasizes the table names, so the direction in which you drag the field is important. The Relationships dialog appears (see Figure 11.8). The field that you select to drag appears in the Table/Query list (the *one* side of the relationship), and the field on which you drop the dragged field appears in the Related Table/Query list (the *many* side of the relationship).

4. Select the Enforce Referential Integrity check box. Access sets the default relation type, One-To-Many, which is the correct choice for this relation. Access also establishes a conventional equi-join as the default join type, so in this case you don't

need to click the Join Type button to display the Join Properties window. Select the Cascade Update Related Fields and the Cascade Delete Related Records check boxes to maintain referential integrity automatically.

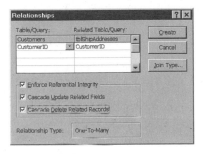

**FIG. 11.8** The Relationships dialog for the new shipping addresses table.

5. Choose the Create button of the Relationships dialog to close it. Your Relationships window appears as shown in Figure 11.9. (The tables in Figure 11.9 have been rearranged slightly, and the new join line has been selected to make it more visible.)

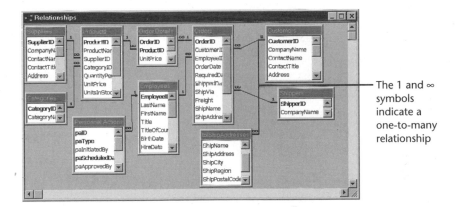

The 1 and ∞ symbols indicate a one-to-many relationship

**FIG. 11.9** The Relationships window showing a relationship established for the new table.

6. Close the Relationships window and click Yes to save your changes. Save your make-table query with an appropriate name, such as **qryMakeShipAddressesTable**.

### Using the New tblShipAddresses Table

After creating a new table from a make-table query, you must take care of several "housekeeping" chores before you can take advantage of your new table. The purpose of creating the new shipping addresses table is to eliminate the data in the Orders table that duplicates information in the Customers table. The additional steps that you must take to use the new table include the following:

- You need a new Number (Long Integer) field, ShipID, for the tblShipAddresses and Orders tables. In the Orders table's ShipID field, you can have a 0 value indicate that the shipping and billing addresses are the same. You then assign a sequential number to each shipping address for each customer. (In the present case, the value of the ShipID field is 1 for all records in tblShipAddresses.) By adding the ShipID field to the tblShipAddresses table, you can create a composite primary key on the CustomerID and ShipID fields. The no-duplicates index on the composite primary key prevents accidental duplication of a ShipID value for a customer.

- Do not delete fields that contain duplicate data extracted to a new table until you confirm that the extracted data is correct and modify all the queries, forms, and reports that use the table. You use the update query described later in this chapter to assign the correct ShipID field value for each record in the Orders table. After you verify that you have assigned the correct value of the ShipID field, you can delete the duplicate fields.

- Add the new table to any queries, forms, reports, macros, and modules that require the extracted information.

- Change references to fields in the original table in all database objects that refer to fields in the new table.

During this process, you have the opportunity to test the modification before deleting the duplicated fields from the original table. Making a backup copy of the table before you delete the fields also is a low-cost insurance policy.

## Creating Action Queries to Append Records to a Table

A make-table query creates the new table structure from the structure of the records that underlie the query. Only the fields of the records that appear in the query are added to the new table's structure. If you design and save a Shipping Address table before extracting the duplicated data from the Orders table, you can use an Append query to add the extracted data to the new table.

 Another situation in which append queries are useful is when removing duplicate data from a table currently in use. In this case, you use make-table queries to create the related tables and then change them to append queries. You change the type of query by opening the Query menu and choosing Select, Crosstab, Make Table, Append, or Delete, or by clicking the Query Type button of the toolbar while in Design mode and choosing the type of query from the menu.

An append query also differs from a make-table query because an append query can have fewer fields than the table to which the query is appending the data. Otherwise, the make-table and append processes are basically identical. To append records to the tblShipAddress table, for example, follow these steps:

1. Open the tblShipAddresses table in Datasheet view, choose Edit, Select All Records, and then press the Delete key to delete all the records from the table. Click Yes when asked to confirm the deletion, and then close the table.

2. Open your make-table query, qryMakeShipAddressTable, from the Database window in Design mode (or choose the query from the Window menu if it is open). If you double-click qryMakeShipAddressTable or open qryMakeShipAddressTable in Datasheet view, you run the make-table query.

3. Choose Query, Append Query. The Append dialog appears with tblShipAddresses as the default value in the Table Name drop-down list, as shown in Figure 11.10. Click the OK button to close the Append dialog.

**FIG. 11.10**  The Query Properties window for an append query.

> **Note**
>
> To append data to a table, the field names of the query and of the table to which you are appending the records must be identical, or you must specify the field of the table to which the append query column applies. Access does not append data to fields in which the field name differs by even a single space character. The Query Design grid for append queries has an additional row, Append To (shown in Figure 11.11), that Access attempts to match by comparing field names of the query and the table. Default values appear in the Append To row of columns for which a match occurs. If a match does not occur, open the Append To row's drop-down list and select the table's field.

4. Click the toolbar's Run button to execute the append query. A message box displays the number of records that the query will append to the table (see Figure 11.12). Choose Yes to append the records.

5. Open the tblShipAddresses table to verify that you have added the records.

Querying for Information

II

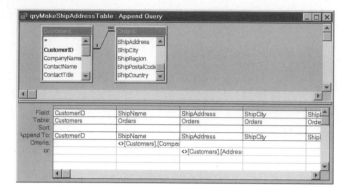

**FIG. 11.11** The Append Query Design grid with the added Append row.

**FIG. 11.12** The message box announcing an impending append.

---

**Troubleshooting**

*After appending records to an existing table, I can't create a primary key on the table.*

The Unique Values Only test that you specify in the Query Properties window applies only to the query, not to the table to which you are appending the records. If you want to preclude the possibility of appending duplicate records to the tblShipAddress table, you must first create the composite primary key, discussed in the preceding section, which creates a No Duplicates index on the primary key, and then append the records.

---

You cannot append records that contain values that duplicate those of the key fields in existing records. If you try to do so, you see a message box that indicates the number of records that cause key-field violations. Unlike the Paste Append operation described in previous chapters, however, Access does not create a Paste Errors table that contains the unappended records.

# Deleting Records from a Table with an Action Query

**Tip**

It's a good practice to run a select query to display the records that you are about to delete and then convert the select query to a deleted query.

Often, you might have to delete records from a table. For example, you might want to delete records for canceled orders, or records for customers that have made no purchases for several years. Deleting records from a table with a delete query is the reverse of the append process. You create a select query with all fields (using the * choice from the field list) and then add the individual fields to be used to specify the criteria for deleting specific records. If you don't specify any criteria, Access deletes all the table's records when you convert the select query into a delete query and run it against the table.

To give you some practice at deleting records—you stop short of actual deletion in this case, however—suppose that Northwind Traders' credit manager has advised you that Austrian authorities have declared Ernst Handel (CustomerID ERNSH) insolvent and that you are to cancel and delete any orders from Ernst Handel not yet shipped. To design the query that selects all of Ernst Handel's open orders, follow these steps:

1. Open a new query and add the Orders table to it.

2. Drag the * (all fields) item from the field list to the Field cell of the query's first column.

3. Drag the CustomerID field to the second column's Field cell. You need this field to select a specific customer's record. The fields that comprise the query must be exactly those of the Orders table, so click the Show box to prevent the CustomerID field from appearing in the query's result twice. This field is already included in the first column's * (all fields) indicator.

4. In the CustomerID field's Criteria cell, type **ERNSH** to represent Ernst Handel's ID.

5. A **Null** value in the ShippedDate field indicates orders that have not shipped. Drag the ShippedDate field from the field list to the third column's Field cell. Click the Show box to prevent the ShippedDate field from appearing in the query's result twice, because the first column also includes that field.

6. In the ShippedDate field's Criteria cell, type **Is Null**. To ensure that you delete only records for Ernst Handel *and* those that have not been shipped, you must place this criterion on the same line as that for the CustomerID field. The select query design for the delete query appears as shown in Figure 11.13.

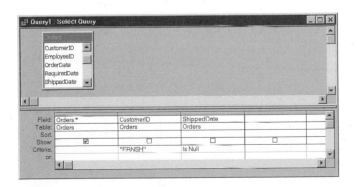

**FIG. 11.13**  The select query design for a delete query.

**7.** Run the select query to display the records to delete when the delete query runs. Figure 11.14 shows the query result set.

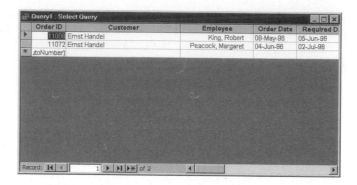

**FIG. 11.14** The unshipped orders for Ernst Handel to be deleted from the Orders table.

To proceed with the simulated deletion, follow these steps:

**1.** Click the toolbar's Database Window button to activate the Database window, then click the Tables button to display the table list. Create a copy of the Orders table by clicking the Orders table entry and pressing Ctrl+C to copy the table to the Clipboard. Press Ctrl+V. The Paste Table As dialog appears. Type **tblOrders** as the name of the new table copy and press Enter. Repeat this process for the Order Details table, naming it **tblOrderDetails**. These two tables are backup tables in case you actually delete the two records for Ernst Handel.

**2.** Activate your select query and click the toolbar's Design button to return to Design mode. Choose Query, Delete Query. Access then replaces the select query grid's Sort and Show rows with the Delete row, as shown in Figure 11.15. The From value in the Delete row's first column, Orders, indicates that Access will delete records that match the Field specification from the Orders table. The Where values in the remaining two cells indicate fields that specify the deletion criteria.

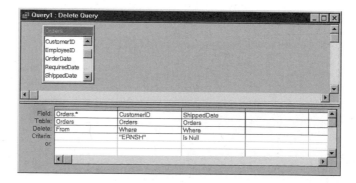

**FIG. 11.15** The delete query design created from the select query of Figure 11.13.

**3.** Click the Run button. The message box shown in Figure 11.16 appears, asking you to confirm the deletion of the rows. Click No to prevent the deletion.

**FIG. 11.16**   The deletion confirmation message box.

> **Note**
>
> Deleting records in a one table when records corresponding to the deleted records exist in a related many table violates the rules of referential integrity; the records in the many table would be made orphans. In this situation, referential integrity is enforced between the Order Details and Orders table, preventing the creation of orphan Order Details records for the two records of the Orders table that you want to delete.
>
> To delete the two records of the Orders table, you must use a process called cascading deletion. First, you delete the Order Details records, then you delete the Orders records. Northwind.mdb's one-to-many relationship between Orders and Order details includes cascading deletions. If you clear the Relationships dialog's Cascade Delete Related Records check box, attempting to delete the two open Orders records for Ernst Handel results in the message shown in Figure 11.17.

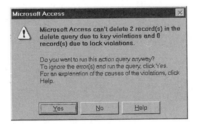

**FIG. 11.17**   The message box that indicates a violation of the rules of referential integrity.

If you accidentally delete records for Ernst Handel, reverse the process that you used to make the backup tables: Copy the backup tables—tblOrders and tblOrderDetails—to Orders and Order Details, respectively.

# Updating Values of Multiple Records in a Table

*Update queries* change the values of data in a table. Such queries are useful when you must update field values for many records with a common expression. For example, you might need to increase or decrease the unit prices of all products or products within a particular category by a fixed percentage.

To see how an update query works, you perform some of the housekeeping chores discussed earlier in the chapter that are associated with using the tblShipAddress table. To implement this example, you must have created the tblShipAddress table, as described in the "Creating New Tables with Make-Table Queries" section earlier in this chapter. You also must modify the tblOrders and tblShipAddresses tables to include a field for the ShipID code, by following these steps:

1. Click the Tables tab in the Database window and open the tblOrders table in Design mode. If you didn't create the tblOrders table as a backup table for the example of the preceding section, do so now.

2. Select the OrderDate field by clicking the selection button, and press Insert to add a new field between EmployeeID and OrderDate. (Access inserts fields in tables above the selected field.)

3. Type **ShipID** as the field name, select Number as the field data type, and select Long Integer as the field's Field Size. Set the `Required` property's value to **Yes**. The table design pane appears as in Figure 11.18 (which shows the new ShipID field selected).

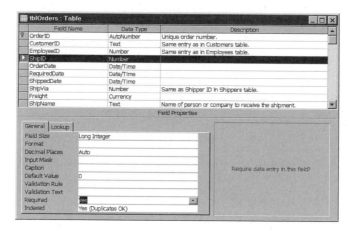

**FIG. 11.18**   Adding the ShipID field to the tblOrders table.

4. Close the tblOrders table and save the changes to your design. You changed the domain integrity rules when you added the `Required` property, so the message box in Figure 11.19 appears. Choose No to avoid the test, which would fail because no values have been added to the ShipID field.

5. Open the tblShipAddresses table in Datasheet view.

**FIG. 11.19**   Choosing whether to test changes to domain integrity rules.

6. Click the ShipName field header and choose Insert, Column to add a Field1 field between the CustomerID and the ShipName fields. The capability to add new columns (fields) in Table Datasheet view was a new feature of Access 95.

7. Type **1** in the Field1 cell for each record of the tblShipAddress table.

8. Change to Design mode, and change the name of Field1 to **ShipID**. Access 97 detects from your data entries that the field should be a Number field, and assigns Long Integer as the default Field Size property value. Change the value of the Required property to **Yes**.

9. Select both the CustomerID and the ShipID field by clicking and dragging the mouse.

10. Click the toolbar's Primary Key button to create a composite primary key on the CustomerID and ShipID fields, and then close the tblShipAddress table. This time, you test the changes that you made to the table.

Now, you need to set up a query to select the orders to which you want to add a value of 1 to the ShipID field to indicate the use of data from the tblShipAddresses table. This query is quite similar to that which you used to create the tblShipAddresses table earlier in this chapter. Follow these steps to design your update query:

1. Create a new query and add the Customers and tblOrders tables to it.

2. Drag the Customers table's CompanyName and Address fields to columns 1 and 2, and the tblOrders table's ShipName and ShipAddress fields to columns 3 and 4 of the Query Design grid.

3. Type **<>[Customers].[CompanyName]** in the first Criteria row of the ShipName column and **<>[Customers].[Address]** in the second Criteria row of the Ship Address column. Your query design appears as shown in Figure 11.20.

4. Run the query to verify that you have correctly selected the set of records to be updated. If you changed the name of Let's Stop N Shop to Let's Stop 'N Shop in the section "Editing Table Data in Query View" in Chapter 8, "Using Query by Example," the five records for orders placed by this firm appear when you run the query. Using the apostrophe in the entries for Alfred's Futterkiste is inconsistent in

the versions of the Customers and Orders tables that were used to write this book (see the highlighted records in Figure 11.21).

Checking for errors of this type is one reason for running the select query before you run the update query. If these records appear, however, you also have a tblShipAddress record for the firm. This is only an example, so you can proceed with the update or you can correct the errors in the query, because the query is updatable.

**FIG. 11.20**  The select query to test for orders that will require 1 as the value of ShipID.

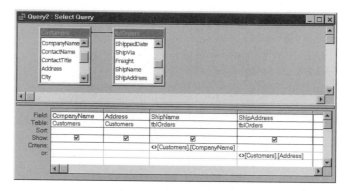

**FIG. 11.21**  The result of the select query used to test the records to be updated.

After ensuring that you have selected the appropriate records of the tblOrders table for updating, you are ready to convert the select query to an update query by following these steps:

1. Return to Design mode and drag the tblOrders table's ShipID field to the query's first column.

2. Choose Query, Update Query. A new Update To row replaces the Sort and Show rows of the Select Query Design grid.

3. In the ShipID column's Update To cell, type **1** to set ShipID's value to 1 for orders that require the use of a record from the tblShipAddresses table. The Update Query Design grid appears as shown in Figure 11.22. The Update To cells of the remaining fields are blank, indicating that Access is not to update values in these fields.

4. Run the update query. A message box such as that shown in Figure 11.23 indicates the number of records that you will update. (The query might return a different number of records because of changes made to the sample database since this book was written.)

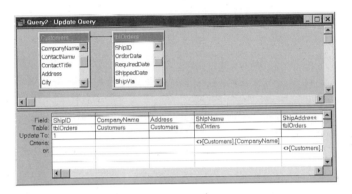

**FIG. 11.22**   The completed update query's Design grid.

**FIG. 11.23**   The message box that indicates the number of records to be updated.

5. Click the Database Window button and open the tblOrders table. Check a few records to see that you correctly added the ShipID value of 1.

6. You must add 0 values to the ShipID cells of records that have the same shipping and billing addresses. Close the update query, create a new query, and add only the tblOrders table.

7. Drag the ShipID field to the query's first column and choose Query, Update Query.

8. Type **0** in the Update To row, and **Is Null** in the Criteria row. Then click the Run Query button to replace **Null** values in the ShipID column with 0.

After you check the tblOrders table to verify the result of your second update query, you can change to Table Design mode and safely delete the ShipName, ShipAddress, ShipCity, ShipRegion, ShipPostalCode, and ShipCountry fields.

# Testing Cascading Deletion and Updating

Access 2.0 introduced two new features that were requested by Access 1.x users: cascading deletion and cascading updating of records having a many-to-one relationship. When you delete a record in a primary or base table on which records in a related table depend, *cascading deletion* automatically deletes the dependent records. Similarly, if you modify the value of a table's primary-key field and a related table has records related by the primary-key field's value, *cascading updating* changes the value of the related foreign-key field for the related records to the new primary-key field value.

Cascading deletions and cascading updates are special types of action queries that the Jet engine executes for you. The following three sections show you how to use Access's cascading deletion and cascading updating features with a set of test tables copied from the Orders and Order Details tables of Northwind.mdb.

### Creating the Test Tables and Establishing Relationships

When experimenting with database features, you should work with test tables rather than "live" data. As mentioned in the note at the beginning of this chapter, using copied test tables is particularly advisable when the tables are participants in action queries. The remaining sections of this chapter use the two test tables, tblOrders2 and tblOrderDetails, that you create in the following steps:

**1.** Click the Database window's Tables tab and then select the Orders table from the list.

**2.** Press Ctrl+C to copy the table to the Clipboard.

**3.** Press Ctrl+V to display the Paste Table As dialog.

**4.** In the Table Name text box, type **tblOrders2**, then click OK or press Enter to create the test tblOrders2 table.

**5.** Repeat steps 1–4 for the Order Details table, naming the copy **tblOrderDetails**.

**6.** Open the tblOrders2 table in Table Design view and change the field data type of the OrderID field from AutoNumber to **Number**, and make sure that the Field Size property is set to **Long Integer**. (This change is necessary to test cascading updates in the next section.)

Cascading deletions and updates require that you establish a default relationship between the primary and related tables, and enforce referential integrity. To add both cascading deletions and updates to the tblOrderDetails table, follow these steps:

**1.** Click the toolbar's Relationships button to display the Relationships window.

**2.** Click the Clear Layout button to clear the display of the Relationships window. A message box appears warning you that the Relationships window will be cleared. Click Yes to continue.

3. Click the toolbar's Show Table button to display the Add Table dialog. Alternatively, right-click the upper pane of the Query window and choose Show Table.

4. Double-click the tblOrders2 and tblOrderDetails items in the list, and then click the Close button to close the Show Table dialog.

5. Click the OrderID field of tblOrders2, then drag the field symbol to the tblOrderDetails table's OrderID field to establish a one-to-many join on the OrderID field. The Relationships window appears.

6. Select the Enforce Referential Integrity check box to enable the two cascade check boxes.

7. Select the Cascade Update Related Fields and Cascade Delete Related Records check boxes, as shown in Figure 11.24.

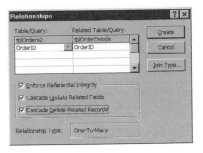

**FIG. 11.24**   Setting the cascading deletions and updates options.

8. Click the Relationships dialog's Create button to make your changes to the join effective, and then click the Close Window button to close the Relationships window. Click Yes when Access asks if you want to save your changes to the window's layout.

## Troubleshooting

*When I try to enforce referential integrity, I get a* `Can't create relationship to enforce referential integrity` *message.*

You dragged the field symbols in the wrong direction when you created the relationship. The related table is in the Table/Query list and the primary or base table is in the Related Table/Query list. Close the Relationships dialog, click the thin area of the join line to select the join, and then press the Delete key to delete the join. Make sure that you drag the field name that you want from the primary table to the related table.

### Testing Cascading Deletion

To try cascading deletion with the test tables, follow these steps:

 Tables

1. Open the tblOrders2 and tblOrderDetails tables in Datasheet view.

2. Click the surface of the tblOrders2 datasheet to make it the active window, and then click a record-selection button to pick an order in tblOrders2 to delete.

3. Press the Delete key to delete tentatively the selected records and the related order's line-item records in tblOrderDetails.

4. The message shown in Figure 11.25 appears requesting that you confirm the deletion. Choose Yes to delete the records.

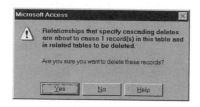

**FIG. 11.25**    Confirming the cascading deletion.

To verify that you have deleted the related records, you can scroll to the related record or records for the order that you deleted in the tblOrderDetails table. If you opened tblOrderDetails in step 1, the data cell values for the deleted related records are replaced with #Deleted.

### Testing Cascading Updates

Cascading updates to the foreign-key field of records that depend on a primary-key value that you want to change in a primary table is a valuable feature of Access. Performing updates of primary-key values while enforcing referential integrity is not a simple process; Chapter 4, "Working with Access Databases and Tables," briefly discusses the problems associated with performing such updates manually. To see how Access takes the complexity out of cascading updates, follow these steps:

1. With the tblOrders2 and tblOrderDetails windows open, size and position the two datasheets as shown in Figure 11.26. Then click the surface of the tblOrders2 datasheet to make it the active window. Positioning the two table datasheet windows as shown in Figure 11.26 enables you to see the cascading updates in the tblOrderDetails window as they occur.

2. Change the value of the OrderID cell of the first record to the order number that you deleted in the preceding section. Alternatively, change the value of the OrderID cell to a value, such as **20000**, that is outside the range of the values of the test table.

3. Move the caret to another record to cause the cascading update to occur. You see the changes in the OrderID foreign-key field of the related dependent records immediately (see Figure 11.26).

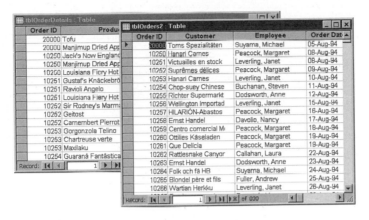

**FIG. 11.26**   An example of a cascading update.

No confirmation message appears when you execute a cascading update, because the effect of a cascading update is reversible. If you make an erroneous entry that causes an undesired cascading update, you can simply change the entry to its original value by choosing Edit, Undo Saved Record. Alternatively, you can simply reenter the original or the correct value manually.

# Part III

# Creating Forms
and Reports

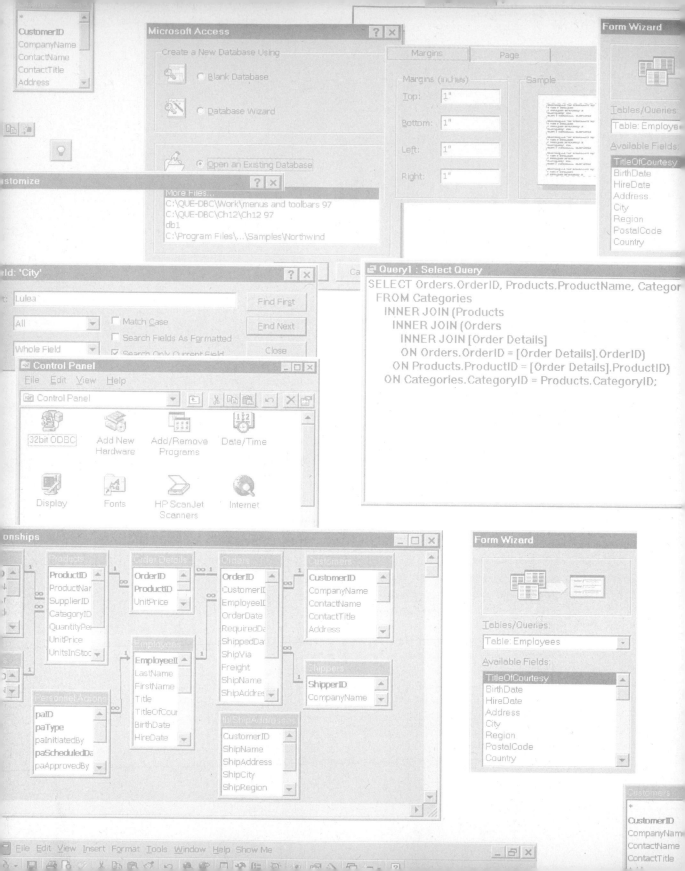

# Chapter 12

# Creating and Using Forms

Access *forms* create the user interface to your tables. Although you can use Table view and Query view to perform many of the same functions as forms, forms offer the advantage of presenting data in an organized and attractive manner. You can arrange the location of fields on a form so that data entry or editing operations for a single record follow a left-to-right, top-to-bottom sequence. Forms let you create multiple-choice selections for fields that use shorthand codes to represent a set of allowable values. A properly designed form speeds data entry and minimizes operator keying errors.

Forms are constructed from a collection of individual design elements called *controls* or *control objects*. Controls are the components you see in the windows and dialogs of Access and other Windows applications. You use *text boxes* to enter and edit data, *labels* to hold field names, and *object frames* to display graphics. A form consists of a window in which you place two types of controls: some that display the data in your tables, and others that display static data such as labels or logos.

This chapter concentrates on creating forms that consist only of text-based controls. Part V, "Integrating Access with Other Office 97 Applications," provides explanations of object linking and embedding (OLE), the method Access uses to incorporate graphs and other graphical elements in forms and reports.

Access forms are versatile; they let you complete tasks that you cannot complete in Table view or Query view. You can validate entries based on information contained in a table other than the one you are editing. You can create forms that incorporate other forms (a form within a form is called a *subform*). Forms can calculate values and display totals. This chapter shows you how to create a form using the Access Form Wizard and how to modify the form to speed up data entry. Chapter 13, "Designing Custom Multitable Forms," explains how to use the Form Toolbox to add controls to forms, as well as how to establish default values and validation rules with forms.

# Identifying Types of Forms

The content and appearance of your form depend on its use in your database application. Database applications fall into three basic categories:

- *Transaction processing* applications add new records to tables or edit existing records. Transaction-processing applications require write access to (permissions for) the tables that are linked to the form.

- *Decision support* applications supply information as graphs, tables, or individual data elements but don't allow the user to add or edit data. Decision-support applications require only read access to the tables that are linked to the form.

- *Database maintenance* applications perform administrative functions such as creating databases or database tables, controlling database access by users, providing security assurance via encryption, performing periodic database compaction, and providing backup operations. Database-maintenance applications require full permissions for all of the objects in the database.

Forms are key elements in transaction-processing and decision-support applications, which are described in the following sections. Common database maintenance operations don't require forms, but forms can be useful for maintaining records of maintenance activities.

## Forms for Transaction Processing

Forms for transaction processing usually operate directly on tables when only one table is involved. If a single form is used for adding or editing information in more than one table, you can create a query that includes all of the fields you need and then base the form on the query. Your primary form also can use a single table as its data source but use a subform that has a related table as its data source. An example of a transaction-processing form that uses the subform approach is the Orders form of the Northwind Traders sample database (see Figure 12.1). The datasheet subform that appears below the Order ID, Order Date, Required Date, and Shipped Date text boxes is used to display and add line items on an invoice.

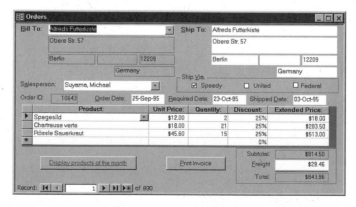

**FIG. 12.1** The Orders form of the Northwind Traders database is a typical form for transaction processing.

This chapter concentrates on forms used for transaction processing, but the techniques you learn are applicable to forms used for any other purpose.

### Forms for Decision Support

Forms designed only to present information fall into the category of decision support; these forms provide historical data that managers and supervisors use to determine a course of action. You can design decision-support forms for long-range planning or short-term decisions. Short-term decisions relate to a single action, such as granting a larger credit line to a customer or sending a sales representative to determine why the customer's purchases have declined. An example of a form to support a short-term decision is Northwind's Quarterly Orders form (see Figure 12.2).

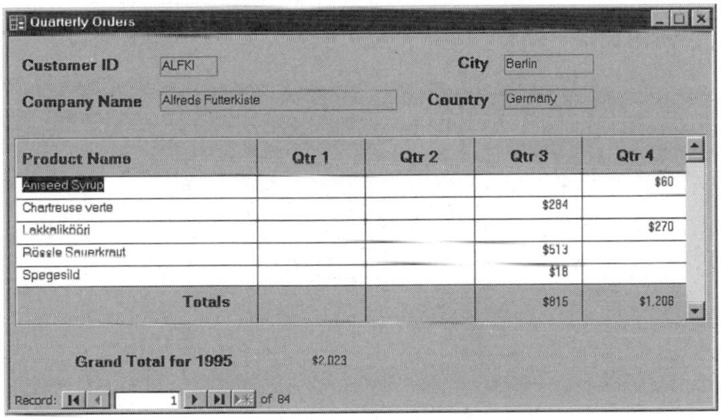

**FIG. 12.2**  Quarterly Orders is an example of a form used for decision support.

The Quarterly Orders form consists of a main form that displays the Customer ID, Company Name, City, and Country, and a subform that displays quarterly sales of products to the customer. The main form is based on the Customers table. The subform consists of a separate form based on the Quarterly Orders by Product crosstab query. Access enables you to include subforms within forms and even subforms within subforms. (Including a subform within a subform is called *nesting*). You can have up to three levels: main form, subform, and sub-subform.

Forms that support short-term decisions often are based on crosstab queries that summarize data in a time series, such as sales to a customer totaled by month, quarter, or year. A table used to support the decision to grant additional credit to a customer might list by quarters the number of invoices issued to the customer, total purchases, and average payment times in days.

# Creating a Transaction-Processing Form with the Form Wizard

The form that you create in this example is typical of the transaction-processing forms used to add new records to the *many* side of a one-to-many relationship. Adding line items to an invoice is an example of when a form of this kind—called a *one-to-many form*—is necessary. The object of the Personnel Actions form is to add new records to the Personnel Actions table or allow you to edit the existing records. If you didn't add the Personnel Actions table shown in Figure 12.3 to the Northwind Traders database in Chapter 4, "Working with Access Databases and Tables," or Chapter 5, "Entering, Editing, and Validating Data in Tables," do so before proceeding with this example. The structure of the Personnel Actions table is provided in Appendix C, "Data Dictionary for the Personnel Actions Table."

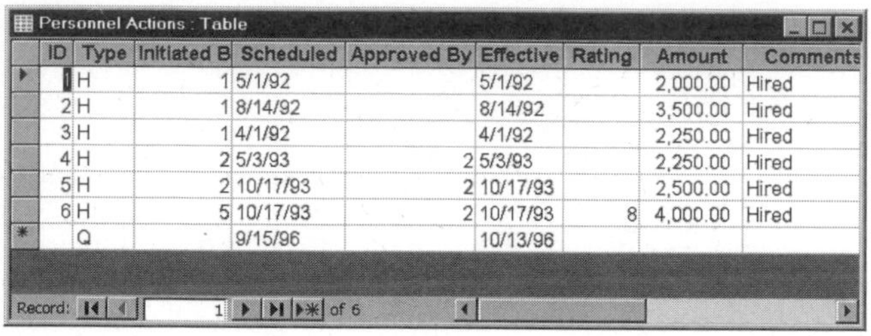


| ID | Type | Initiated B | Scheduled | Approved By | Effective | Rating | Amount | Comments |
|---|---|---|---|---|---|---|---|---|
| 1 | H | 1 | 5/1/92 | | 5/1/92 | | 2,000.00 | Hired |
| 2 | H | 1 | 8/14/92 | | 8/14/92 | | 3,500.00 | Hired |
| 3 | H | 1 | 4/1/92 | | 4/1/92 | | 2,250.00 | Hired |
| 4 | H | 2 | 5/3/93 | 2 | 5/3/93 | | 2,250.00 | Hired |
| 5 | H | 2 | 10/17/93 | 2 | 10/17/93 | | 2,500.00 | Hired |
| 6 | H | 5 | 10/17/93 | 2 | 10/17/93 | 8 | 4,000.00 | Hired |
| * | Q | | 9/15/96 | | 10/13/96 | | | |

**FIG. 12.3** The Personnel Actions table.

If you didn't add records to the Personnel Actions table when you created it in Chapter 4, you can add them with the Personnel Actions form you're going to create now with the assistance of Access's Form Wizard.

### Choosing the Form Type

The Personnel Actions form that you create in this exercise allows you to add new entries to the Personnel Actions table. The form also has a subform that displays all of the previous personnel actions for a given employee. The majority of forms found in common database applications are one-to-many forms, and most one-to-many forms require a subform to display data from the many side of the relationship.

The Personnel Actions form is intended as both a transaction-processing form and a decision-support form. You can take two approaches to designing a form that accomplishes the objectives of the Personnel Actions form:

- Use the Employees table as the source of the data for the main form, and use the subform to display, add, and edit records to the Personnel Actions table. This method allows you to add a new employee to the Employees table as well as to add a new Personnel Actions record.

- Use the Personnel Actions table as the source of data for both the main form and the subform. You cannot construct forms of this type with the Form Wizard. In this case, you could not add a new employee using this form because the Employees table has a one-to-many relationship with the Personnel Actions table being edited. This approach is demonstrated in Chapter 13, "Designing Custom Multitable Forms."

The first approach is by far the easiest and is the approach you'll use to create this version of the Personnel Actions form.

### Creating the Basic Form with the Form Wizard

The easiest way to create a form and subform is with the Access Form Wizard. The Form Wizard allows you to create forms (with or without subforms) that contain fields from one or more tables or queries. The Form Wizard creates the basic design of the form and adds text box controls to display and edit the values of data items.

To create the Personnel Actions form with the Form Wizard, follow these steps:

1. Click the Forms tab of the Database window, then click the New button. The New Form dialog appears, as shown in Figure 12.4.

**FIG. 12.4**  The New Form dialog.

2. Select Form Wizard from the list in the New Form dialog. Access 97's Form Wizard allows you to create either a simple form without a subform, or a data form that does contain a subform. The Design View choice opens a blank form in Design mode. The various AutoForm choices automatically create forms with the specified layouts: Columnar, Tabular, and Datasheet. The Chart Wizard choice invokes the ChartWizard to add a graph or chart to your form, while the PivotTable Wizard choice helps you create a form based on Excel pivot tables.

3. The drop-down list at the bottom of the New Form dialog lists all of the existing tables and queries that can serve as a source of data for a form. Click the arrow to open the drop-down list, then click to select the Employees table. Click OK, and Access displays the first dialog of the Form Wizard (see Figure 12.5).

4. Click to select the EmployeeID field in the Available Fields list, then click the > button to move the EmployeeID field from the Available Fields list to the Selected Fields list. Alternatively, you can double-click the field name to move it.

   Repeat this step for the LastName, FirstName, and Title fields of the Employees table. (Placing these fields on the form allows you to edit data from these fields in the Employees table.)

5. Open the Tables/Queries drop-down list and select the Personnel Actions table. The Available Fields list changes to show the available fields in the Personnel Actions table.

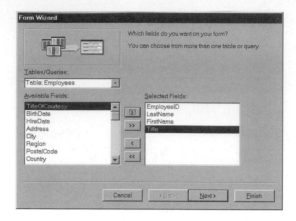

**FIG. 12.5**  Selecting the fields that you want on your form.

6. Click the >> button to copy all of the fields from the Available Fields list to the Selected Fields list. (You copy all fields from the table onto this form because you need to be able to edit every field in the Personnel Actions table; copying all fields from the table also allows you to edit the FirstName and LastName fields from the Employees table.)

7. Because the EmployeeID field from the Employees table is included in the Selected Fields list, you don't need to include the paID field from the Personnel Actions table on the form. Select the paID field in the list of Selected Fields, then click the < button to move this field out of the Selected Fields list and back to the Available Fields list. Finally, click the Next button to display the second step of the Form Wizard, shown in Figure 12.6.

> **Note**
>
> If you realize that you made an error—or if you change your mind about something—and you're on a later step of the Form Wizard, you can click the Back button to return to and modify your previous choices. You can also click Cancel at any time to abort the form creation and get back to the Database window.

8. Because the fields you have selected to appear on the form come from two different tables, the Form Wizard asks how you want to view the data. Because you want to view the data by employee, with the employee's personnel action data in a subform, click By Employees, and make sure that the Form With Subform(s) option is selected (see Figure 12.6). The picture in the upper-right area of the Form Wizard dialog changes to show the fields of the master form (from the Employees table), with a sunken area containing the fields of the subform (from the Personnel Actions table). Click Next to reach the third step of the Form Wizard.

**Note**

In one-to-many forms, the subform needs to be linked to the main form so that all records displayed in the subform are related to the current record displayed in the main form. The Access 97 Form Wizard obtains the information it needs to link the main form and subform from a join in the Relationships window (in this case, between the Employees table and the Personnel Actions table).

If you haven't established a relationship between the two tables in the Relationships window, the Form Wizard skips the step that asks you to choose how to view the data and lay out the subform (steps 8 and 9). The Form Wizard then goes directly to the dialog that asks which style you want for the form (step 10). For this procedure to work correctly, you must establish a relationship between the two tables, as described in Chapter 4, "Working with Access Databases and Tables."

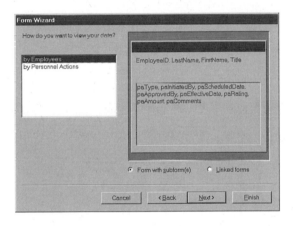

**FIG. 12.6**   Selecting the master table in the form-subform relationship.

9. The Form Wizard now displays the dialog shown in Figure 12.7, which asks you to select the layout style for the subform. Select the Tabular option. This option creates a subform that displays the data from the Personnel Actions table in a tabular format that is similar to Datasheet view but one in which you can change the formatting (colors, column headings, and so on). Click Next to reach the fourth step in the Form Wizard.

10. The Form Wizard displays the dialog shown in Figure 12.8, which asks you to select a style for the new form. The Access Form Wizard has several predefined styles. Because the sample form we're creating is for use by a data-entry operator—and doesn't require special effects to highlight or decorate any fields—you can click Standard. Click Next to reach the Form Wizard's final dialog, shown in Figure 12.9.

11. The Form Wizard asks you to type a name for the master form and any subforms. The Form Wizard also asks you to select what should happen with the form after the Form Wizard has finished creating it. Type **frmPersonnelActions**

in the Form text box and **sbfPersonnelActions** in the Subform text box. Select the Open the Form to View or Enter Information option, then click Finish to complete your form. (If you want Access to display help for working with your completed form, select the Display Help on Working with the Form check box before you click Finish.)

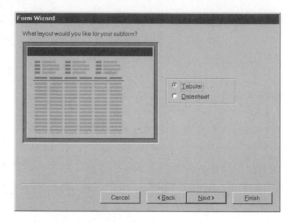

**FIG. 12.7**   Selecting a tabular layout for the Personnel Actions subform.

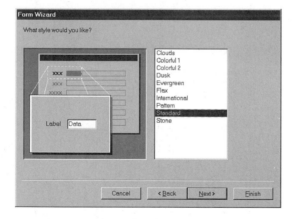

**FIG. 12.8**   Selecting a predefined form style in the Form Wizard.

> **Tip**
>
> Access suggests default names for the form and any subforms; make sure that you type in names that describe what the form really does. Also, make sure that you include the name of the main form (or an abbreviation) in the name of your subform so that the relationship between the form and subform is evident.

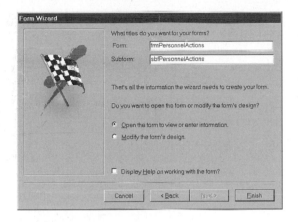

**FIG. 12.9**  Entering a name for the main form and its subform.

> **Note**
>
> In previous versions of Access, the title you entered for a form was inserted as a heading in the actual form. Instead of doing this, Access 95 and Access 97 use the form title you enter in the final step of the Form Wizard as the name of the form. The title is displayed in the Form window's title bar but not as part of the actual form.

The Form Wizard creates the form and any subforms, then automatically saves them. When the Form Wizard has finished creating the forms, it displays the main form (see Figure 12.10).

> **Caution**
>
> If you didn't select the Open the Form to View or Enter Information option in the final step, you'll be placed automatically into Design view to work with your new form.

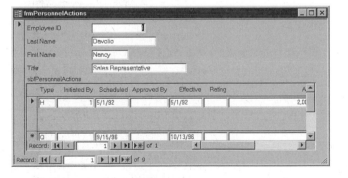

**FIG. 12.10**  The basic Personnel Action form created by the Form Wizard.

On the main form, the Form Wizard creates a single column of text boxes—each with an associated label—for entering or editing data values in each of the fields from the Employees table that you placed on this form. The subform contains all of the fields from the Personnel Actions table (except the paID field) arranged in a tabular layout. Access uses the field names as default text box labels and also as column headings for the tabular subform. Access uses the name that you entered for the subform as the label for the subform area.

In Figure 12.10, notice that the paAmount and paComments fields are partially or completely obscured, and scrollbars appear in the subform area. The subform is larger than the area created for it in the main form, so Access automatically adds scrollbars to let you access all data displayed in the subform.

The basic form as created by the Form Wizard is immediately usable, but could benefit from cosmetic adjustments to the layout of both the main form and subform. The remaining discussions and exercises in this chapter show you how to modify forms created with the Form Wizard; you can apply these form-editing skills when you create your own forms from scratch, as described in the next chapter.

No matter how expert you become at designing Access forms, using the Form Wizard to create the basic form design saves you time.

## Using the Form Design Window

 To modify the design of your new form, click the Design View button on the toolbar. The Form Design window appears (see Figure 12.11, where the Design window has been maximized). The floating window that appears in Form Design mode contains an undocked toolbar, called the *Toolbox*, that allows you to place new control elements on a form. Using the Toolbox to add new control elements to the form is covered in the next chapter. For this exercise, hide the Toolbox by clicking the Toolbox button on the Forms toolbar or by clicking the Close Window button in the upper-right corner of the Toolbox.

---

**Note**

 Access usually shows the Toolbox automatically whenever you enter Form Design mode. If you've manually closed the Toolbox, Access does not automatically display it the next time you open the Form Design window. To display the toolbox, click the Toolbox button on the Forms toolbar, or choose View, Toolbox.

---

The Personnel Action Entry (frmPersonnelActions) form lets you experiment with methods of modifying forms and their contents, which are described in the following sections.

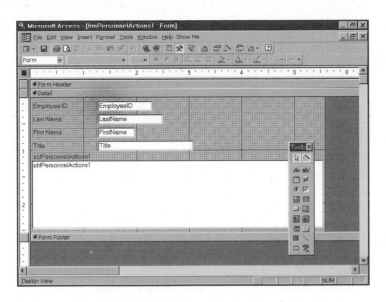

**FIG. 12.11** The basic frmPersonnelActions form in Design view.

---

**Caution**

Do not save the form with the changes you make when following the instructions in this section. These changes are for demonstration purposes only. Saving these changes would permanently modify the form you created in the preceding section. If you really want to experiment, you can make a copy of the frmPersonnelActions main form and sbfPersonnelActions subform, and then work with the form copies. (Make a backup copy of a form the same way you make a backup copy of a table: choose Edit, Copy to copy the selected form, and then choose Edit, Paste to paste a copy of the form.)

---

### Elements of the Form Design Window

Forms can be divided into three sections: Form Header, Detail, and Form Footer. Headers and footers are optional. The Form Design window includes the following basic elements:

- The Form Design toolbar contains buttons that are shortcuts for menu selections in Form Design mode. The functions of the buttons, and their equivalent menu choices, are listed in tables in the next section, "Form Design Toolbar Buttons and Menu Choices."

- The Formatting toolbar contains buttons that are shortcuts for color, text, border, and various other formatting options. The functions of the formatting buttons and their equivalent menu choices are listed in tables in the next section.

- Vertical and horizontal rulers help you determine the size and placement of objects on the form. The rulers are calibrated in inches for the United States version of Access and in centimeters for versions of Access that are supplied to countries where the metric system is used.

- A bold vertical line (shown to the right of the toolbox in Figure 12.11) indicates the position of the right margin of the form. You can move this margin indicator line by clicking and dragging it to the desired location.

- A bold horizontal line indicates the bottom margin of the form. You can click and drag this line to a new location. Margins are important when you are designing a subform to fit within a rectangle of a predetermined size on the main form.

- Vertical and horizontal scroll bars let you view portions of the form outside the boundaries of the form window.

- A Form Header bar defines the height of the form's header section. The form header bar applies only if you choose to add a header and footer to your form. The Form Header section contains static text, graphic images, and other controls that appear at the top of form. The header only appears on the first page of a multipage form.

- A Form Detail bar divides the Form Header from the rest of the form. Form controls that display data from your tables and queries, plus static data elements such as labels and logos, are on the Form Detail bar.

- A Form Footer bar defines the height of the form's footer section. The Form Footer section is similar in function to the Form Header section. If you print a multipage form, the Form Footer appears only at the bottom of the last page.

> **Note**
>
> Although the form shown in Figure 12.11 has both Form Header and Form Footer sections, neither section takes up any space on the form—that's why the Form Header bar touches the Detail bar, and the Form Footer bar touches the bottom margin of the form. Even though no text or other information is in the header and footer areas, the Form Wizard adds these elements to the form automatically. When you create a new, blank form without using the Form Wizard, header and footer sections are not added automatically.

You can add Form Header and Form Footer sections to a form—or delete these sections—by choosing View, Form Header/Footer. (If the form currently contains these sections, a check mark appears to the left of the Form Header/Footer menu choice.) Clear the check marks to delete the Header and Footer sections of the form.

> **Note**
>
> If a header or footer section contains any text or other form controls when you try to delete it, Access displays a dialog warning that you will lose the contents of the header and footer.

### Form Design Toolbar Buttons and Menu Choices

The Form Design toolbar of Access 97 contains several buttons that apply only to the design of forms. You select color and font options from the Format toolbar, which was a new feature in Access 95. Table 12.1 lists the function and equivalent menu choice for

---

each of the Form Design toolbar buttons. The buttons that relate to text and color formatting are described in the following section, "The Formatting Toolbar."

**Table 12.1 Standard Toolbar Buttons in Form Design Mode**

| Button | Function | Menu Choice |
|---|---|---|
| | Displays the form in Run mode (clicking the arrow at the right of this button displays a drop-down list that allows you to select Datasheet view). | View, Form View |
| | Saves the current form. | File, Save |
| | Prints all records in the table using the on-screen form to format the printed data and using the current printer settings. | n/a |
| | Selects Print Preview to display how your form appears if printed. You can print the form from the Print Preview window. | File, Print Preview |
| | Starts the spelling checker to check the spelling of the selected label control. | Tools, Spelling |
| | Cuts selected objects from the form and puts them on the Clipboard. | Edit, Cut |
| | Copies selected objects from the form onto the Clipboard. | Edit, Copy |
| | Pastes the contents of the Clipboard onto the form. | Edit, Paste |
| | Copies formatting from selected objects to another object of similar type. | n/a |
| | Undoes the last change you made to the form. | Edit, Undo |
| | Inserts a new Hyperlink control, or allows you to edit an existing Hyperlink control. | Insert, Hyperlink |
| | Toggles the display of the Web toolbar. | n/a |
| | Displays a list of the fields in the query or table that is the data source for the main form. | View, Field List |
| | Displays or closes the Toolbox. | View, Toolbox |
| | Applies your choice of several predefined form formats, including formatting for the background bitmap of a form, text fonts, and color settings. | Format, AutoFormat |

(continues)

III

Creating Forms and Reports

| Button | Function | Menu Choice |
|---|---|---|
| Table 12.1 Continued | | |
| | Opens the code editing window for Access VBA code contained in a module as an integral part of the form (the form's class module). | View, Code |
| | Displays the Properties window for one of the two sections of the form when you click the section bars, or displays the properties of a control when you select it. | View, Properties |
| | Displays the Build Wizard for the selected object or property in the form. This is enabled only if Access has a builder for the selected item. | n/a |
| | Displays the Database window. | Window, 1 Database |
| New Object: Table | Creates a new object. Click the arrow at the right of this button to see a drop-down list of the objects you can create. | n/a |
| | Displays the Microsoft Office Assistant that, in turn, displays help text related to the actions you are performing. | Help, Microsoft Access Help |

The appearance of the Form Design window after clicking the Properties button is shown in Figure 12.12.

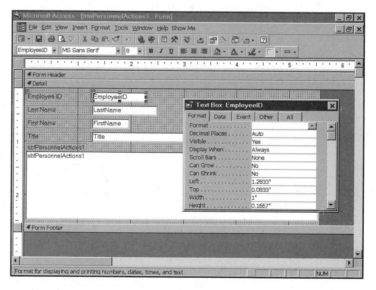

**FIG. 12.12** The Form Design window with the Properties window open.

You can close the Properties window by clicking the Close Window button or by clicking the Properties button on the toolbar.

### The Formatting Toolbar

Access 97 displays in Form and Report Design view shortcut buttons and drop-down lists for all of the text formatting, line, color, and cell effects options on a separate toolbar: the Formatting toolbar. When you select an object (such as a text box) on a form, Access enables the relevant Formatting toolbar buttons. Drop-down lists allow you to choose the desired typeface and type size for the text. Additional buttons on this toolbar, used to format the text, are similar to the buttons you find on the toolbar of Microsoft Word for Windows and other Windows word-processing applications.

Access 97 adds a new drop-down list to the toolbar, the Object list. The Object list displays the name of the currently selected object on the form and allows you to rapidly select another object on the form by selecting its name in the list. In Figure 12.12, the EmployeeID text box is the currently selected object.

The default typeface for forms is MS Sans Serif in an 8-point font. You can select any bitmapped or TrueType family that is installed on your computer from the drop-down list containing type families.

You can choose from a drop-down list of preset type sizes or type a size in points in the Size combo box. You apply attributes and formatting with the text buttons. Table 12.2 lists the function of each text-formatting button and its equivalent property setting.

| **Table 12.2   Toolbar Buttons for Text Controls in Form Design Mode** | | |
|---|---|---|
| **Button** | **Function** | **Property and Value** |
| **B** | Sets text style to bold (the default for titles and labels). | Font Weight = Bold |
| *I* | Sets italic text style. | Font Italic = Yes |
| U | Sets underline text style. | Font Underline = Yes |
| ≣ | Left-justifies text within border. | Text Align = Left |
| ≣ | Centers text horizontally within border. | Text Align = Center |
| ≣ | Right-justifies text within border. | Text Align = Right |
| ◈ ▾ | Displays a color palette from which you choose the background color for the selected object. | Back Color = number |
| A ▾ | Displays a color palette from which you choose the color of the text in the selected object. | Fore Color = number |

(continues)

| Table 12.2 Continued | | |
| --- | --- | --- |
| **Button** | **Function** | **Property and Value** |
| | Displays a color palette from which you choose the color for the border of the selected object. | Border Color = number |
| | Displays a drop-down list from which you choose the width of the selected object's borders. You may select a hairline width or widths ranging from 1 to 6 points. | Border Width = width |
| | Displays a drop-down list from which you choose a special effect for how the selected object is displayed. You may choose Flat, Raised, Sunken, Etched, Shadowed, or Chiseled. | Special Effect = name |

### Default Values for Forms

You can change some of the default values used in the creation of all forms by choosing Tools, Options and then selecting the Forms/Reports tab (see Figure 12.13). You can create a form to use as a template and replace the standard template, and you can determine how objects are displayed when chosen. The effects of these options are described in the sections that follow. The options that you or other Access users choose in the Options dialog are saved for each user ID in the MSysOptions table of the current System.mdw workgroup system file.

You can change the default values for the current form, section, or controls by choosing the object and then changing the default values displayed in the Properties window for that object. You can also use the AutoFormat feature to quickly apply a predefined format to all of the controls in the form. The next section describes using AutoFormat to change a form's appearance, and subsequent sections describe ways to change the format of text or controls manually on a form.

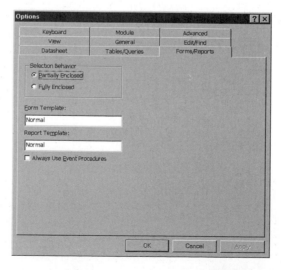

**FIG. 12.13** Displaying Forms/Reports options in the Options dialog.

## Using AutoFormat

The AutoFormat feature was new in Access 95. AutoFormat enables you to apply a pre-defined format to an entire form with only a few mouse clicks. Access 97 comes with several predefined formats, and you also can create your own formats for use with AutoFormat.

**Applying an AutoFormat.** To apply a format to a form with AutoFormat, follow these steps:

1. Click the AutoFormat button on the toolbar. Access displays the AutoFormat dialog, shown in Figure 12.14.

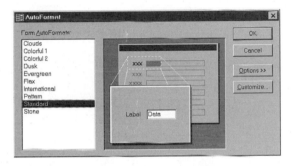

**FIG. 12.14**  Using AutoFormat to apply a predefined format to an entire form.

2. Click to select the format you want to use in the Form AutoFormats list; a preview of the format you select appears in the window in the center of the dialog.

3. Click OK to apply the format to the form. Figure 12.15 shows the frmPersonnelActions form after the International format has been applied.

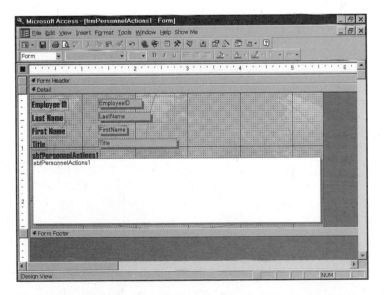

**FIG. 12.15**  The frmPersonnelActions form after applying the International format.

The AutoFormat dialog allows you to omit the application of font, color, or border style information to your form when you apply the AutoFormat. When the AutoFormat dialog is open, click the Options button; the AutoFormat dialog expands to display three additional check boxes (see Figure 12.16). Deselect the check box for the elements of the AutoFormat that you want omitted when you apply the AutoFormat to your form.

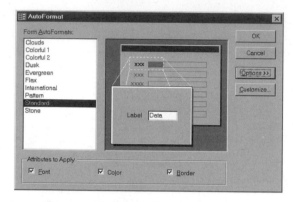

**FIG. 12.16** The expanded AutoFormat dialog.

**Creating, Customizing, and Deleting AutoFormats.** The predefined AutoFormat styles might not suit your tastes, or you might want to create AutoFormat styles specific to your company or application.

To create a new AutoFormat or customize an existing one, follow these steps:

1. Create a form and alter its appearance (using the techniques described in the next five sections of this chapter) so that the form has the font, border, background picture, and other options adjusted exactly the way you want them for your new or customized AutoFormat.

2. Click the AutoFormat button to display the AutoFormat dialog. If you want to modify an existing AutoFormat, select it in the Form AutoFormats list now.

3. Click the Customize button to display the Customize AutoFormat dialog shown in Figure 12.17.

**FIG. 12.17** The Customize AutoFormat dialog used to create, modify, or delete an AutoFormat.

4. Select the Create a new AutoFormat based on the Form *formname* option, or the Update *formatname* with values from the Form *formname* option to create or modify an AutoFormat, respectively. (Deleting AutoFormats is covered later in this section.)

5. Click OK. If you're creating a new AutoFormat, the New Style Name dialog appears (see Figure 12.18). Type an appropriate name for your new AutoFormat, and click OK. Access now creates or updates the AutoFormat and returns you to the AutoFormat dialog.

6. Click Close to close the AutoFormat dialog.

**FIG. 12.18**    Entering a name for a new AutoFormat.

If you have created your own AutoFormats, you may want to delete an AutoFormat that you no longer use. To delete an AutoFormat, follow these steps:

1. Open any form in Design view.

2. Click the AutoFormat button to display the AutoFormat dialog.

3. Click to select the AutoFormat you want to delete in the Form AutoFormats list, then click the Customize button. Access displays the Customize AutoFormat dialog.

4. Select the Delete *formname* option, and click OK. Access deletes that AutoFormat from the list.

> **Caution**
>
> Access does not ask for confirmation when you delete an AutoFormat; make sure to select the correct AutoFormat for deletion before you click OK.

5. Click Close to close the AutoFormat dialog.

Applying formatting to a form through an AutoFormat style is by far the easiest way to create standardized forms for your database application—especially because the Form Wizard uses the same format style list as the AutoFormat feature. In other words, any AutoFormats you create become available in the Form Wizard dialog, also.

The next few sections of this chapter describe how you can customize the appearance of various objects on a form.

### Changing an Object's Colors

You select object colors through the buttons on the Formatting toolbar, as well as through property settings that are accessible through the Properties window of the form and individual objects on the form. The following sections describe how to use the Formatting toolbar controls and the Property dialog to change background and foreground colors of form sections and control objects, as well as border properties of control objects.

**Background Colors.** The background color (Back Color property) of a form section (Header, Detail, or Footer) applies to all areas of that section except those occupied by control objects. The default background color of all sections of forms created by the Form Wizard depends on the specific form style you choose when you create the form; the Standard format scheme used to create the frmPersonnelActions form, for example, is light gray.

The default color choices on the palette displayed by the Fill/Back Color toolbar button are 16 of the standard system colors of Windows 95 and Windows NT 4.0. If you are creating a form that you intend to print, a gray or deeply textured background will not only be distracting but will also consume substantial amounts of printer toner. Data-entry operators often prefer a white background rather than a gray, colored, or textured background. Colored backgrounds hinder text visibility.

> **Note**
>
> If you have selected a picture as the background for a form—or used an AutoFormat style that includes a background picture, such as the International style pictured in Figure 12.15—then any changes you make in the background color of the form are hidden by the overlying picture.

To change the background color of a section of a form, follow these steps:

1. Click an empty area within the section of the form (Header, Detail, or Footer) whose background color you want to change. This selects the appropriate section.

2. Click the Fill/Back Color button on the toolbar to display the color palette.

3. Click the box that contains the color you want to use.

Because the background color of each form section is independent, you must repeat the process if you want to change the color for other sections of your form. The Transparent button of the Fill/Back Color palette is disabled when a form section is chosen, because a transparent background color isn't applicable to forms.

You choose the background color of a control object, such as a label, just as you do for forms. In most cases, the chosen background color of labels is the same as that of the form, so click the Transparent button to allow the background color to appear. The default value of the Back Color property of text boxes is white so that text boxes (and the data they contain) contrast with the form's background color.

**Changing the Background Bitmap.** You can use a bitmap picture as the background for a form. Unlike background colors, of which you can have several, you select a single bitmap picture for the entire form. Access 97 comes with a few bitmap pictures that it uses in the AutoFormat formats—International, for example, uses the Globe.wmf graphics file (stored in the Program Files\Microsoft Office\Access\Bitmaps\Styles folder) as the background for the form. You can use any .wmf, .bmp, .emf, or .dib graphics file as a background for a form.

> **Note**
>
> Forms with bitmap graphics as a background can look dramatic and, therefore, are best suited for public-access information terminals or decision-support forms. These forms, however, tend to be more visually complex, which might make it difficult for users to read text labels or identify specific fields on the form. For accurate, high-speed data-entry, you should keep your transaction-processing forms visually simple so that users can easily distinguish data fields on the form and easily read text labels.

You set or remove a form's background bitmap through the Properties window of the form; you can also specify several viewing and formatting properties for the background picture. Follow these steps to set the background picture properties of a form:

1. Open the form in Design view, if necessary.

2. Click the square at the upper-left corner of the Form Design window (where the horizontal and vertical rulers meet) to select the form as a whole. A black square appears when the form is selected (see Figure 12.19).

3. If the Properties window isn't already open, click the Properties button on the toolbar to display this window.

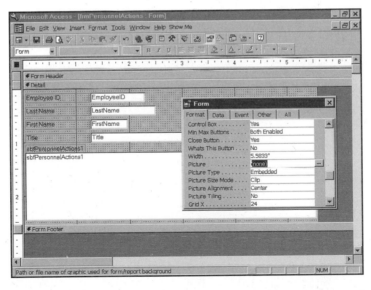

**FIG. 12.19**  Setting the file name and formatting properties for a form's background picture.

III

Creating Forms and Reports

4. Click the Format tab in the Properties window, and scroll down to the end of the Format properties list to view the various Picture properties: Picture, Picture Type, Picture Size Mode, Picture Alignment, and Picture Tiling. Each of these properties and their effects are described in the list following these numbered steps.

5. Set the various Picture properties until you are satisfied with the appearance of the form. As you change each property, results of the change become immediately visible on the form.

6. Click the Close window button in the Properties window to close this window.

The following list summarizes form properties related to the background picture, available choices for each property, and the effects of each choice.

■ The Picture property contains the folder path and file name of the graphics file that Access uses as the form's background. You may either type the folder path and file name directly in the Picture property text box, or you may use the builder to help you select the background graphics file. To use the builder, click the Picture property field to select that field, then click the Build button that appears next to the text box. Access displays the Insert Picture dialog shown in Figure 12.20. The Insert Picture dialog is a standard Windows 95 or Windows NT 4.0 dialog for opening files. Click the Preview button (second button from the right), if necessary, to display the background image. When you locate the graphics file you want, click to select its name, then click OK to have Access fill in the Picture property.

> **Tip**
>
> To remove a background picture, simply delete the entry in the Picture text box.

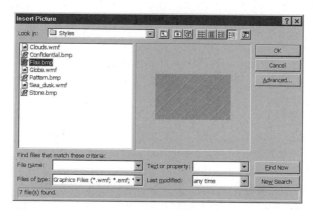

**FIG. 12.20**  The Insert Picture dialog used to select a picture as a form's background.

■ The Picture Type property specifies the OLE or ActiveX method that Access uses to attach the background picture to the form. You can select either Embedded or Linked as the picture type. You usually should use the Embedded picture type, especially if you intend to distribute your database application—the resulting form is self-contained and doesn't rely on the presence of external files that might be moved or deleted. If you have many forms that use the same background bitmap graphic, however, linking the background picture can save some disk space.

- The Picture Size Mode property controls how Access sizes the background picture. The available choices are Clip, Stretch, and Zoom. Clip causes Access to display the picture at its full size behind the form; if the picture is larger than the form, it is clipped to fit the form. If the picture is smaller than the form, the form's own background color shows in any part of the form background not covered by the picture. Stretch causes Access to stretch the picture vertically and horizontally to match the size of the form; the Stretch option permits distortions in the picture. Zoom causes Access to magnify the picture, without distortion, to fit the size of the form.

- The Picture Alignment property controls where Access positions the background picture. The available choices are Top-left (aligns the upper-left corner of the picture with the upper-left corner of the form window), Top-right (aligns the upper-right corner of the picture with the upper-right corner of the form window), Center (places the picture in the center of the form window), Bottom-left (aligns the lower-left corner of the picture with the lower-left corner of the form), Bottom-right (aligns the lower-right corner of the picture with the lower-right corner of the form), and Form Center (centers the picture on the form).

> **Tip**
>
> To ensure that a background picture is displayed relative to the form, rather than the form's window, select Form Center as the value for the Picture Alignment property.

- The Picture Tiling property has two permissible values: Yes or No. *Tiling* means that the picture is repeatedly displayed to fill the entire form or form window (if the Picture Alignment property is set to Form Center, the tiling fills just the form).

Now that you know how to adjust the background picture and colors of a form, the next section describes how to adjust the foreground colors and border properties of the form and objects on the form.

**Foreground Color, Border Color, and Border Style.** You may set the foreground color, border color, and border width through buttons on the Formatting toolbar or directly in the Properties window for a selected control. To set a border style (solid style or a variety of dashed-line styles), you must set the property directly in the Properties window.

Foreground color (the Fore Color property) is applicable only to control objects. (The Font/Fore Color button on the toolbar is disabled when you select a form section.) Foreground color specifies the color for the text in labels and text boxes. The default value of the Fore Color property is black. You choose border colors for control objects that have borders by using the Line/Border Color toolbar button.

**III**

**Creating Forms and Reports**

The Special Effects button of the Formatting toolbar allows you to simulate special effects for control objects, such as a raised or sunken appearance. The Line/Border Width button allows you to control the width of the border of controls. The Formatting toolbar buttons were listed earlier in this chapter in Table 12.2. Table 12.3 lists the property name for each border property and the specific values that each may have.

To set a control's foreground color, border width, or border color by using the Formatting toolbar buttons, first click the control whose properties you want to change, then click the arrow to the right of the toolbar button for the property you want to change. Click the color or line width you want for the control.

To set a control's foreground color, border width, border color, or border style in the Properties window, first select the control whose properties you want to change by clicking it. If necessary, open the Properties window by clicking the Properties button on the toolbar. Click the Format tab in the Properties window, then scroll to the text box for the property you want to change. Most of the border properties are selected from drop-down lists; color properties require you to type a number that represents the desired color in Windows 95 or Windows NT 4.0 color notation. (Windows 95/NT 4.0 color notation is too complex to explain here; the easiest way to enter color values is with the toolbar buttons or by using the color builder described in the following section of this chapter, "Creating Custom Colors with the Color Builder.")

**Table 12.3   Border Style Properties and Values**

| Property Name | Function | Values |
|---|---|---|
| Border Style | Determines the line style of the border. | Transparent, Solid, Dashes, Short Dashes, Dots, Sparse Dots, Dash Dot, Dash Dot Dot |
| Border Color | Sets the color of the border. | Depends on the color |
| Border Width | Determines the width of the border. | Hairline, or any whole point size from 1 to 6 |

**Creating Custom Colors with the Color Builder.** If you aren't satisfied with one of the 16 Windows system colors for your form sections or control objects, you can create your own custom colors by following these steps:

1. Place the caret in the Back Color, Fore Color, or Border Color text box of the Properties window for a control.

2. Click the ellipsis button to display the Color dialog. The basic form of this dialog enables you to choose from a set of 48 colors. If one of these colors suits your taste, click the color square and then click OK to assign that color as the value of the property, and close the dialog. If you want a custom color, proceed to step 3.

3. Click the Define Custom Colors button to expand the Color dialog to include the Hue/Saturation and Luminance windows, as shown in Figure 12.21.

4. Click and drag the cursor within the square Hue/Saturation area to choose the color you want.

5. Click and drag the arrow at the right of the rectangular luminance area while observing the Color block; release the mouse button when the Color block has the luminance (brightness) value you want.

6. Click Add to Custom Colors to add your new color to the first of the 16 custom color blocks.

7. Click the new custom color block to select it. Click OK to add this color value to the property, and close the Color dialog.

Many PCs used for data entry and editing applications run in 16-color VGA mode because this mode is slightly faster than the standard 256-color mode used by most of today's PCs. In 16-color VGA mode, any colors you choose or create, other than the standard Windows system colors, are simulated by a dithering process. *Dithering* alternates pixels of differing colors to create the usually imperfect illusion of a solid color. Thus, it is good programming practice to stick with the 16 system colors of Windows unless you have a very good reason to do otherwise.

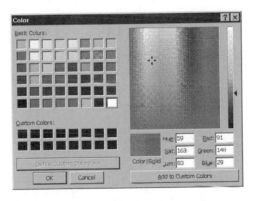

**FIG. 12.21**   Defining a custom color in the expanded Color dialog.

# Selecting, Editing, and Moving Form Elements and Controls

The properties that apply to the entire form, to the five sections of the form, and to each control object on the form are determined by the values shown in the Properties window. To view the Properties window for a control, select the control by clicking anywhere on its surface; then click the Properties button on the toolbar. The sections of an Access form are shown in Figure 12.22.

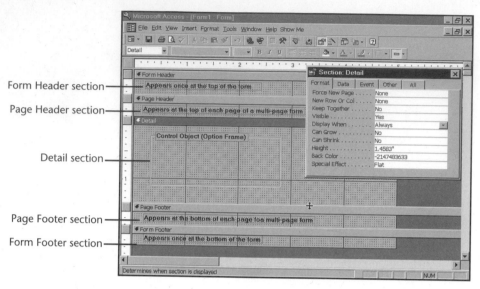

Form Header section ——

Page Header section ——

Detail section ——

Page Footer section ——

Form Footer section ——

**FIG. 12.22**    The five sections of an Access form with the Detail section selected.

The following list describes how to choose and display the properties of the entire form, its sections, and its control objects:

- *Form.* To select the Form object, click the area of the form to the right of the right-margin indicator line. Alternatively, click the square where the ruler lines meet or choose Edit, Select Form to select the Form object. (If the Properties window isn't open, you must double-click the square where the ruler lines meet.) Selecting the form allows you to set properties for the form as a whole by entering values for the properties listed in the Properties window.

- *Header section only.* To select the Form Header, click the Form Header or Page Header bar. The set of properties you work with applies only to the Form Header or Page Header section. A Form Header and Footer appear when you choose View, Form Header/Footer. A Page Header and Footer appear when you choose View, Page Header/Footer. Page Headers and Footers primarily are used in conjunction with printing forms. You delete headers and footers by choosing View, Form Header/Footer or View, Page Header/Footer a second time.

- *Detail section only.* To select the Detail section, click the Detail bar. You get a set of properties similar to those of the Form Header section, but all of these apply to the Detail section.

- *Footer section only.* To select the Footer section, click the Form Footer or Page Footer bar. A set of properties identical to the header properties is available for the footer sections. A Form Footer appears only if a Form Header has been added. The same applies to Page Headers and Footers.

- *Control object* (or both elements of a control with an associated label). Click the surface of the control to select the control. Each type of control has its own set of properties. Displaying the properties of multiple-control objects is the subject of the section "Selecting, Moving, and Sizing a Single Control" later in this chapter.

### Changing the Size of the Form Header and Form Footer

You can change the height of a form section by dragging the Form Header, Page Header, Detail, Page Footer, or Form Footer bar vertically with the mouse. When you position the mouse pointer at the top edge of a section divider bar, it turns into a line with two vertical arrows (refer to Figure 12.22). You drag the pointer with the mouse to adjust the size of the section above the mouse pointer.

The height of the Detail section is determined by the vertical dimension of the window in which the form is displayed, less the combined heights of all the header and footer sections that are fixed in position. When you adjust the vertical scroll bar, only the Detail section scrolls.

### Selecting, Moving, and Sizing a Single Control

When you select a control object by clicking its surface, the object is enclosed by a shadow line with an anchor rectangle at its upper-left corner and five smaller, rectangular sizing handles (see Figure 12.23).

---

**Note**

Text boxes, combo boxes, check boxes, and option buttons have associated (attached) labels. When you select one of these objects, the label and object are selected as a unit.

---

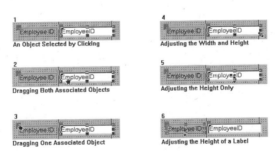

**FIG. 12.23** The appearance of a control object selected for relocation and resizing.

The following choices are available for moving or changing the size of a control object (the numbered choices correspond with the numbers in Figure 12.23):

1. *To select a control (and its associated label, if any)*, click anywhere on its surface.

2. *To move the control (and its associated label, if any) to a new position*, move the mouse pointer within the outline of the object at any point other than the small resizing handles or the confines of a text box (where the cursor can become an editing caret). The mouse pointer becomes a hand symbol when it's on an area that you can use to move the entire control. Press and hold down the left mouse button while dragging the hand symbol to the new location for the control. An outline of

the control indicates its position as you move the mouse. When the control is where you want it to be, release the mouse button to drop the control in its new position.

> **Tip**
>
> If the control doesn't have an associated label, you can drag the control's anchor handle at the upper-left corner to move the control.

3. *To separately move the elements of a control that has an associated label,* position the mouse pointer on the anchor handle in the upper-left corner of the control that you want to move. The mouse pointer becomes a hand with an extended finger. Click and drag the individual element to its new position, then release the mouse button.

4. *To simultaneously adjust the width and height of a control,* click the small sizing handle at any of the three corners of the outline of the control. The mouse pointer becomes a diagonal two-headed arrow. Click and drag this arrow to a new position, then release the mouse button.

5. *To adjust only the height of the control,* click the sizing handle on one of the horizontal surfaces of the outline. The mouse pointer becomes a vertical, two-headed arrow. Click and drag this arrow to a new position, then release the mouse button.

Selecting and deselecting controls is a *toggling* process. Toggling means repeating an action with the effect of alternating between On and Off conditions. The Properties, Field List, and Toolbox buttons on the toolbar—as well as their corresponding menu choices—are toggles. The Properties window, for example, appears and disappears if you repeatedly click the Properties button.

### Aligning Controls to the Grid

The Form Design window includes a grid that consists of one-pixel dots with a default spacing of 24 to the inch horizontally and 24 to the inch vertically. When the grid is visible, you can use the grid dots to assist in maintaining the horizontal and vertical alignment of rows and columns of controls. Even if the grid isn't visible, you can cause controls to "snap to the grid" by choosing Format, Snap to Grid. This menu command is a toggle, and when Snap to Grid is active, the menu choice is checked. Whenever you move a control while Snap to Grid is active, the upper-left corner of the object jumps to the closest grid dot.

You can cause the size of control objects to conform to grid spacing by choosing Format, Size, To Grid. You also can make the size of the control fit its content by choosing Format, Size, To Fit.

> **Tip**
>
> If Snap to Grid is on and you want to locate or size a control without reference to the grid, press and hold the Ctrl key while you move or resize the control.

Toggling the <u>V</u>iew, Grid menu command controls the visibility of the grid; by default, the grid is visible for all new forms. If the grid spacing is set to more than 24 per inch or 10 per centimeter, the dots aren't visible. To change the grid spacing for a form, follow these steps:

1.  Choose <u>E</u>dit, Select Fo<u>r</u>m.

2.  Click the Properties button on the toolbar to make the form properties appear.

3.  Click the Format tab in the Properties window to display the formatting properties, and scroll through the list until the Grid X and Grid Y properties are visible.

4.  Change the value of Grid X to 10 dots per inch (dpi) and Grid Y to 12 dpi, or change both values to 16 (if you want controls to align with inch ruler ticks). Users with metric rulers are likely to prefer a value of 10 for both Grid X and Grid Y.

> **Tip**
>
> The default values of grid spacing of Access 97 is 24 dpi. Better values are 10 for Grid X and 12 for Grid Y. This grid dot spacing is optimum for text controls that use the default 8-point MS Sans Serif font. The Form Wizards also use 24 dpi horizontally and vertically.

### Selecting and Moving a Group of Controls

You can select and move more than one object at a time by using one of the following methods:

■ *Enclose the objects with a rectangle.* Begin by clicking the surface of the form outside the outline of a control object. Press and hold down the mouse button while dragging the mouse pointer to create an enclosing rectangle that includes each of the objects you want to select (see Figure 12.24). Release the mouse button. You may now move the group of objects by clicking and dragging the anchor handle of any one of them.

■ *Click to select one object, then hold down the Shift key while you click to select the next object.* You can repeat this step as many times as necessary to select all of the objects you want.

■ *To remove a selected object from a group,* hold down the Shift key, and click the object with the mouse to deselect it. To deselect an entire group, click any inactive area of the form. An inactive area is an area outside the outline of a control.

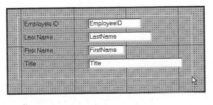

**FIG. 12.24**  Selecting a group of objects by dragging a selection rectangle.

If you select or deselect a control with an associated label, the label is selected or deselected along with the control.

---

**Note**

The selection rectangle selects a control if any part of the control is included within the rectangle. This behavior is unlike many drawing applications in which the entire object must be enclosed to be selected. You can change the behavior of Access's selection rectangle to require full enclosure of the object by choosing Tools, Options, selecting the Forms/Reports tab, and changing the value of the Selection Behavior option from Partially Enclosed to Fully Enclosed.

---

### Aligning a Group of Controls

You can align selected individual controls, or groups of controls, to the grid or each other by choosing Format, Align and completing the following actions:

- To align a selected control (or group of controls) to the grid, choose To Grid from the submenu.

- To adjust the positions of controls within a selected columnar group so that their left edges fall into vertical alignment with the far-left control, choose Left from the submenu.

- To adjust the positions of controls within a selected columnar group so that their right edges fall into vertical alignment with the right edge of the far-right control, choose Right from the submenu.

- To align rows of controls at their top edges, choose Top from the submenu.

- To align rows of controls at their bottom edges, choose Bottom from the submenu.

Your forms have a more professional appearance if you take the time to align groups of controls vertically and horizontally.

### Using the Windows Clipboard and Deleting Controls

All of the conventional Windows Clipboard commands apply to control objects. You can cut or copy a selected control or group of controls to the Clipboard. After that, you can paste the control or group to the form using Edit menu commands and then relocate the pasted control or group as desired. Access uses the Windows 95 and Windows NT 4.0 keyboard shortcut keys: Ctrl+X to cut, Ctrl+C to copy selected controls to the Clipboard, and Ctrl+V to paste the Clipboard contents. The traditional Shift+Delete, Ctrl+Insert, and Shift+Insert commands perform the same operations.

You can delete a control by selecting it and then pressing Delete. If you accidentally delete a label associated with a control, do the following: select another label, copy it to the Clipboard, select the control with which the label needs to be associated, and paste the label to the control.

### Changing the Color and Border Style of a Control

As mentioned earlier in this chapter, the default color for the text and borders of controls is black. Borders are one pixel wide (called *hairline* width). Some objects, such as text boxes, have default borders. Labels have a gray background color by default, but a better choice for the default label color would have been transparent. *Transparent* means that the background color of the object under the control (the form section, in this case) appears within the control except in areas of the control that are occupied by text or pictures.

You control the color and border widths of a control from the Line/Border Color and Line/Border Width buttons on the Formatting toolbar. You must select a border style directly in the Properties window.

To change the color or border width of a selected control or group of controls, follow these steps:

1. Select the control(s) whose color or border width you want to change.

2. Click the arrow of the Fill/Back Color toolbar button to open the color palette popup window. Click the color square you want, or click the Transparent button to make the background transparent.

3. Click the arrow of the Line/Border Color toolbar button to open the color palette popup window, where you change the border color for any selected control with borders.

4. Click the arrow of the Line/Border Width toolbar button to open the border width popup window, where you change the thickness of the border for any selected control whose borders are enabled.

5. Click the arrow of the Font/Fore Color toolbar button to open the color palette popup window, where you change the color of the text of selected controls.

> **Note**
>
> The general practice for Windows database entry forms is to indicate editable elements with borders and clear backgrounds. Still, some popular software (most notably, the DOS versions of dBASE and Paradox) uses reverse video as the default to indicate editable text. You can create the effect of reverse video by choosing black or another dark color for the fill of a text box control and a light color for its text. If you decide to implement reverse text, remember that reverse text is more difficult to read than normal text, and consider using a larger font and adding the bold attribute to ensure legibility.

To set the border style, you must select the Border Style property directly in the Properties window, as explained earlier in this chapter.

### Changing the Content of Text Controls

You can edit the content of text controls by using conventional Windows text-editing techniques. When you place the mouse pointer within the confines of a text control and click the mouse button, the mouse pointer becomes the Windows text-editing caret that you use to insert or delete text. You can select text by dragging the mouse over it or by holding down Shift and moving the caret with the arrow keys. All Windows Clipboard operations are applicable to text within controls. Keyboard text selection and editing techniques using the arrow keys in combination with Shift are available, also.

If you change the name of a field in a text box and make an error naming the field, you receive a #Name? error message in the offending text box when you select Run mode. Following is a better method of changing a text box with an associated label:

1. Delete the existing field control by clicking to select it and then pressing Delete.

2. Click the Field List button in the Properties bar to display the Field List dialog.

3. Scroll through the entries in the list until you find the field name you want.

4. Click the field name to select it, then drag the field name to the location of the deleted control. Release the mouse button to drop the new name.

5. Close the Field List dialog when you are finished.

You can relocate and resize the new field caption and text box (or edit the caption) as necessary.

### Using the Format Painter

The Format Painter allows you to quickly copy the format of any control on the form to any other control on the form. The Format Painter copies only those formatting properties that are relevant to the control on which you apply the Format Painter. To use the Format Painter, follow these steps:

1. Select the control with the formatting you want to copy.

2. Click or double-click the Format Painter button on the toolbar; the mouse cursor changes to a pointing arrow with a paintbrush icon attached to it. (Double-clicking "locks" the Format Painter on. Double-click the Format Painter button only if you want to copy the formatting to more than one control.)

3. Click any control that you want to copy the formatting to; the Format Painter copies all relevant formatting properties to this control. If you didn't double-click the Format Painter button, the Format Painter turns itself off after copying the formatting properties to one control.

4. If you locked the Format Painter on by double-clicking its button, you can repeat step 3 as many times as you want. Click the Format Painter button again to turn the Format Painter off.

Typically, you use the Format Painter to quickly set the formatting properties for field text labels, or in any situation where selecting several controls by dragging a selection rectangle seems undesirable. By locking the Format Painter on, it's easy to format several controls one after another.

## Rearranging the Personnel Actions Form

The objective of the following set of instructions is to rearrange the controls on the frmPersonnelActions form so that all of the elements on the form (and its subform) are completely visible in the form window. The objective of these instructions is also to optimize the position of the fields for data entry. After you complete the following steps, your main form appears as shown in Figure 12.25, and your subform appears as shown in Figure 12.26.

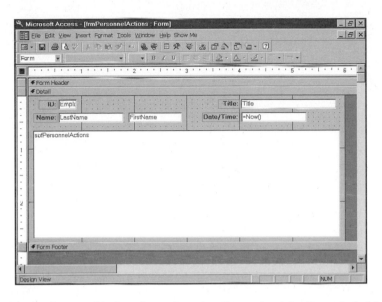

**FIG. 12.25**    The frmPersonnelActions form after relocating and resizing its control objects.

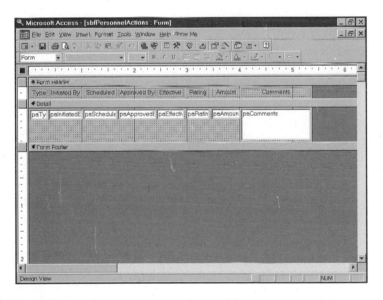

**FIG. 12.26**    The sbfPersonnelActions subform after modifying its appearance.

### Setting Properties of the Main Form

To change the color of form objects and rearrange the controls of the frmPersonnelActions form to correspond with the positions shown in Figure 12.25, follow these steps:

1.  Close the frmPersonnelActions form by clicking the Close Window button. Do not save any changes you made in the preceding section.

2.  Choose frmPersonnelActions from the Forms list in the Database window, and click the Design button.

3.  Click the Maximize window button to maximize the Form Design window if it isn't already maximized.

4.  Choose <u>E</u>dit, Select Fo<u>r</u>m, and then click the Properties button on the toolbar.

5.  Click the Format tab of the Properties window, and then scroll through the properties list until you see Grid X and Grid Y. Change the Grid X property to 10 and the Grid Y property value to 12. (Metric users may prefer a 5-by-5 grid, providing 2 mm resolution.)

6.  Close the Properties window by clicking the Properties button on the toolbar again.

7.  Drag the right margin of the form from its present position (5.5 inches) to 6 inches.

8.  Click the Title field text box to select the text box and its label.

9.  Move the mouse pointer onto the selected Title field until the pointer changes to the shape of a hand. Click and drag the Title field to the right of the EmployeeID text box.

10. Delete the FirstName label (click the label, then press Delete). Next, use the technique described in steps 8 and 9 to select the FirstName field and drag it to a position to the right of the LastName field (refer to Figure 12.25).

11. Edit the LastName label to read **Name:**, the EmployeeID label to read **ID:,** and the Title label to read **Title:.**

12. Delete the sbfPersonnelActions field label (the size and content of the subform is sufficient to identify it), and drag the subform control to a position below the FirstName and LastName fields (refer to Figure 12.25).

13. Click and drag the Form Footer bar to approximately 2.75 inches. (Alternatively, you can type the detail section's height directly in the Height property on the Format sheet of the Properties window.) At present, the dimensions of your form are 6×2.7 inches.

14. Resize the sbfPersonnelActions subform control on the form so that its left, right, and bottom edges are one grid mark inside the edges of the form (this makes the sbfPersonnelActions subform control about 5.8×1 7/8 inches).

15. Click the text label of the EmployeeID field to select it, and then click the Bold and Align Right buttons on the Formatting toolbar to make the text label bold and right justified.

16. Double-click the Format Painter button on the toolbar (remember that this locks the Format Painter).

**17.** In turn, click the text labels for all of the remaining controls on the form to apply the formatting with the Format Painter.

**18.** Click the Format Painter button on the toolbar again to turn off the Format Painter.

**19.** Adjust the widths of the labels and text boxes to suit their content (refer to Figure 12.25).

**20.** Click the Save button on the toolbar (or choose File, Save) to save your changes to the frmPersonnelActions form.

You may need to adjust the sizes of some controls individually to make their appearance consistent with other controls. When you complete your rearrangement, click the Form View button. Your form appears as shown in Figure 12.27.

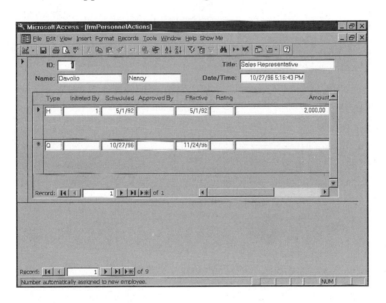

**FIG. 12.27**   The revised frmPersonnelActions form in Run mode.

### Setting the Properties of a Subform

You can learn about modifying the properties of a subform by working with the subform used to create the history of prior Personnel Actions for an employee. In this example, editing or deleting entries using the subform is not allowed, but you can add new entries. The subform needs to be modified so that all of its columns are readable without horizontal scrolling. To change the properties of the Personnel Actions subform, follow these steps:

**1.** Close the frmPersonnelActions form.

**2.** Open the sbfPersonnelActions subform from the Database window in Design view.

3. Select the form and use the Properties window to make sure that the Grid X and Grid Y properties are both set to 24. Close the Properties window.

4. Using the same techniques you used when working with the main form, resize the label boxes in the Form Header section of the form so that they match what you saw in Figure 12.26. Use the Format Painter to center the text in every text label in the Form Header section.

5. Adjust the field text boxes in the Detail section of the form, if necessary, to line up with the headings in the Form Header section (refer to Figure 12.26).

6. Drag the right edge of the form to the left until the form is 5 3/8 inches in width, and then drag the Form Footer upward so that the Detail section is about 5/8 inches high.

7. Choose Edit, Select Form to select the form, then click the Properties button on the toolbar to display the Properties window for the subform.

8. Click the Data tab in the Properties window so that the Allow Edits, Allow Deletions, and Allow Additions properties are visible.

9. Set the Allow Edits property to **No**; this prevents the user from editing records displayed in this subform.

10. Set the Allow Deletions property to **No**; this prevents the user from deleting records displayed in this subform.

11. Set the Allow Additions property to **Yes**; this enables the user to add new records in this subform.

12. Close the sbfPersonnelActions subform and save your changes.

    To see how the new form and subform look, open the frmPersonnelActions form; the adjusted form and subform should appear similar to Figure 12.28. Notice that there's no horizontal scroll bar, and that the appearance and visibility of fields and column headings in the subform has improved. By changing the size of the subform control in the main form and resizing the subform to fit completely within the subform control (allowing room for the vertical scrollbar), the subform now fits completely in the main form. Notice also the tentative append record that is visible as the second record in the subform.

> **Note**
>
> You can set the Data Entry property to Yes to achieve a result that is similar to setting the Allow Edits and Allow Deletions property to No and the Allow Additions property to Yes. When you set the Data Entry property to Yes, however, only the tentative new record appears—no prior entries appear in the subform.

You can change the default view of the subform to a continuous form that you can modify to display the data in another format. When displaying historical data, Datasheet view (a tabular view) is usually the best choice because it is the easiest to implement.

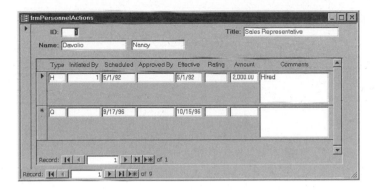

**FIG. 12.28**  The completed frmPersonnelActions and sbfPersonnelActions forms in Form view displayed in normal window mode.

# Using Transaction-Processing Forms

As noted near the beginning of this chapter, the purpose of transaction-processing forms is to add new records to, delete records from, or edit data in one or more tables that underlie the form. This section describes how to add new records to the Personnel Actions table with the frmPersonnelActions form.

### Toolbar Buttons in Form View

When you display your form in Run mode (Form view), the toolbar contains the command buttons listed in Table 12.4. This table lists all of the buttons that appear on the toolbar, along with each button's function and the equivalent menu choice.

| Table 12.4 | Standard Toolbar Buttons in Form Run Mode | |
|---|---|---|
| **Button** | **Function** | **Menu Choice** |
| | Selects Form Design mode. | View, Design View |
| | Saves the form layout. | File, Save |
| | Prints the form. | File, Print |
| | Selects Print Preview to display how your form will appear if printed. You can print the form directly from the Print Preview window. | File, Print Preview |
| | Starts the spelling checker to check the spelling of the current selection or field. | Tools, Spelling |
| | Cuts the current selection and places it on the Windows Clipboard. | Edit, Cut |

(continues)

| **Table 12.4** | **Continued** | |
|---|---|---|
| **Button** | **Function** | **Menu Choice** |
| | Copies the current selection to the Windows Clipboard. | Edit, Copy |
| | Pastes the current contents of the Windows Clipboard onto the form. | Edit, Paste |
| | Format Painter. This button is always disabled in Form view. | n/a |
| | Undoes the most recent change to a record. | Edit, Undo |
| | Inserts a new Hyperlink or allows you to edit an existing Hyperlink. | Insert, Hyperlink |
| | Toggles the display of the Web Toolbar. | n/a |
| | Sorts records in ascending order based on the current field. | Records, Sort, Ascending |
| | Sorts records in descending order based on the current field. | Records, Sort, Descending |
| | Filters records based on selected text in a field. | Records, Filter, Filter by Selection |
| | Filters records based on criteria you enter in a form's fields. | Records, Filter, Filter by Form |
| | Applies a filter. Click this button a second time to show all records. | Records, Apply Filter/Sort or Records, Remove Filter/Sort |
| | Searches for a value in the selected field or in all fields. Displays the Find dialog. | Edit, Find |
| | Goes to the tentative append record. | Edit, Go To, New |
| | Deletes the current record. | Edit, Delete Record |
| | Gives the Database window the focus. | Window 1 Database |

| Button | Function | Menu Choice |
|---|---|---|
| [icon] | Displays a drop-down list of new database objects. | n/a |
| [icon] | Displays the Microsoft Office Assistant which, in turn, displays help text related to the actions you are performing. | Help, Microsoft Access Help |

The Find button serves the same purpose for forms in Run mode as it does for tables and queries. You type characters in the Find dialog using wild cards, if needed. When you execute the search, Access displays the first record that matches your entry.

The Sort Ascending, Sort Descending, Filter by Selection, and Filter by Form buttons work the same way in Form view as they do in Datasheet view. Using these filter buttons was described in Chapter 6, "Sorting, Finding, and Filtering Data in Tables." Sorting specified in the form overrides the sort criteria of the primary query used as the source of the data (if your form is based on a query, rather than directly on one or more tables). The filter or sort criteria you specify do not take effect until you click the Apply Filter/ Sort button or make the equivalent Records, Apply Filter/Sort menu choice.

### Using the Personnel Actions Form

Forms you create with the Form Wizard use the standard record-selection buttons located at the bottom of the form. The record-selection buttons perform the same functions with forms as they do with tables and queries. You can select the first or last records in the table or query that is the source of data for your main form, or you can select the next or previous record. Subforms always include their own set of record-selection buttons that operate independently of the set for the main form.

Navigation between the text boxes used for entering or editing data in the form is similar to navigation in queries and tables in Datasheet view, except that the up-arrow and down-arrow keys cause the caret to move between fields rather than between records. Accept the values you've entered by pressing Enter or Tab.

To edit records in a table in Form view, the Allow Editing property must be set to Yes (which is the default). To append new records to a table in Form view, the Allow Additions property must be set to Yes (which is also the default). You can only change these properties by using the Properties window for the form in Form Design view (as you did earlier in this chapter for the subform).

### Appending New Records to the Personnel Actions Table

In Datasheet view of a table or query, the last record in the datasheet is provided as a *tentative append record* (indicated by an asterisk on the record-selection button). If you enter data in this record, the data automatically is appended to the table, and Access starts a new tentative append record. Forms also provide a tentative append record, unless you have set the Allow Additions property for the form to No.

To append a new record to the Personnel Actions table and enter the required data, follow these steps:

1. Open the frmPersonnelActions form if it is not already open, or click the Form View button if you are in Design view. Data for the first record of the Employees table—with the matching data from the corresponding record(s) in the Personnel Actions table—appears in the text-box controls of your form.

   Because data from the Employees table is included in the main form, the ID number, name, and title of the employee appear in the text boxes on the main form. Access lets you edit the LastName, FirstName, and Title data, although these fields are incorporated in the table (Employees) on the one side of a one-to-many relationship. The editing capability of a form is the same as that for the underlying table or query that serves as its source, unless you change the form's editing capabilities by setting the form's Allow Editing property and other related properties.

   If you added an entry for the chosen employee ID when you created the Personnel Actions table in Chapter 4, "Working with Access Databases and Tables," the entry appears in the subform's fields. The subform's data display is linked to the data in the main form through the one-to-many relationship between the Employees table and the Personnel Actions table. The subform only displays records from the Personnel Actions table whose paID fields match the value of the EmployeeID field of the record currently displayed by the main form.

2. Access places the caret in the first text box of the main form, the ID text box. The first example uses Steven Buchanan, whose employee ID is 5, so you should do the following: click the Find button on the toolbar to open the Find dialog, type **5** in the Find What text box, make sure that the Search Only Current Field option is selected, and click Find First. Access displays the Employees table data for Steven Buchanan in the main form and his Personnel Actions records in the subform. Click Close to close the Find dialog.

3. Click in the Type field of the tentative append record in the subform. If the tentative append record in the subform isn't visible, click in any field in the subform, then click the New Record button on the toolbar to move to the tentative append record at the end of the existing Personnel Actions table entries for Steven Buchanan.

4. The controls of the tentative append record in the subform become empty, except for those fields with default values assigned to them.

5. Access places the caret in the first text box of the subform, the Type (paType field) text box. Type a valid Personnel Action type (H, S, Q, Y, B, or C, because of the field's validation rule) in the Type text box. In this example, you bring Steven Buchanan's Personnel Actions records up to date by adding quarterly performance review information, so you can stick with the default value, **Q**. Press Tab or Enter to accept the Type and move the caret to the next data-entry text box, Initiated By.

6. Mr. Buchanan reports to the Vice President of Sales, Andrew Fuller, whose employee ID is 2. Type **2** in the Initiated By text box and press Enter.

   The pencil symbol, which indicates that you are editing a record, replaces the triangle at the top of the Record Selector bar to the left of the record that you are entering. The Description property you entered for the field in the table underlying this query appears in the status bar and changes as you move the caret to the next field. (To change a previous entry, press Shift+Tab, or use the up- and down-arrow keys to maneuver to whichever text box contains a value you want to change.)

7. Mr. Buchanan was hired on 10/17/93, so his first quarterly performance review should be dated about three months after that. Therefore, use a date near **1/2/94** for the Scheduled text box. Today's date is the default for the paScheduled date. Edit the date, or press F2 to select the default date, and then replace the default value with a new date.

8. Because Mr. Fuller is a vice president, he has the authority to approve salary increases. Type Mr. Fuller's employee ID, **2**, in the Approved By text box, and press Enter to move the caret to the next field.

9. The effective date for salary adjustments for Northwind Traders is the first or 15th day of the month in which the performance review is scheduled. Type the appropriate date in the Effective text box.

10. You can type any number from **0** (terminated) to **9** (excellent) in the Rating text box, which reflects the employee's performance.

11. You can be as generous as you want with the salary increase that you enter in the New Amount text box. The value of the New Amount is a new monthly salary (or a new commission percentage), not an incremental value.

12. In the Comments multiline text box to the right of the New Amount field, add any comments you care to make concerning how generous or stingy you were with this salary increase. The multiline text box includes a scroll bar that appears when the caret is within the text box.

13. When you complete your entries, Access stores them in a memory buffer but does not add the new record to the Personnel Actions table. You can add the record to the table by doing any of the following: pressing Shift+Enter; choosing Records, Save Record; clicking the New Record button; or changing the position of the record pointer with the Prior or Next record selector button. If you want to cancel the addition of a record, press Esc.

14. Repeat steps 3 through 13 to add a few additional records.

**Tip**

If you ever click the New Record button on the toolbar (or the Next record selector button) and decide that you don't want to add any more data, simply click the Prior button to make sure this new record is not added to the table.

After you add several records, your form appears like the one shown in Figure 12.29. Each record for an employee appears in the subform datasheet in the order of the primary key fields of the Personnel Actions table.

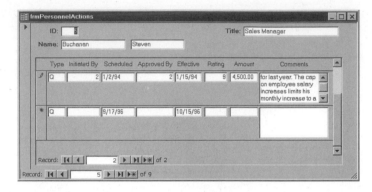

**FIG. 12.29**   The Personnel Actions form after appending subform records for a single employee.

The key fields of the Personnel Actions table are paID, paType, and paScheduledDate; duplicate values of the combination of the three fields aren't allowed. If you try to enter a duplicate of another record, the message box shown in Figure 12.30 appears. If you still want to add the new record, you must change the Type or Scheduled Date entry to be different from the existing record.

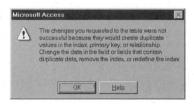

**FIG. 12.30**   The message box that results when you try to complete a duplicate entry.

### Editing Existing Data

You can edit existing records the same way you add new records. Use the Next button to find the record you want to edit, and then make your changes. You can use the toolbar's Find button to locate records by employee ID, by one of the dates in the record, or by a word or phrase contained in the paComments field. If you prefer that the records be ordered by paEffective date to find all records for which an effective date hasn't been entered, use the Filter by Form button and specify an Ascending Sort on the paEffective field. Click the Apply Filter button to apply the sort to the records.

### Committing and Rolling Back Changes to Tables

As with tentative append records, Access does not apply record edits to the underlying table until you move the record pointer with the record-selection buttons (or choose Records, Save Record). Either action is the equivalent of the CommitTrans instruction in transaction-processing terminology.

Rollback reverses a CommitTrans instruction. You can do the equivalent of rolling back a single transaction by clicking the Undo button on the toolbar immediately after you save the record to the table (or by choosing Edit, Undo Saved Record if that choice is available).

### Deleting a Record in Form View

To delete the current record underlying the form (either the main form or a subform), click the Delete Record button on the toolbar (or choose Edit, Delete Record). Access displays the message box, shown in Figure 12.31, and asks you to confirm the permanent removal of the record you selected. Click Yes to delete the record.

Access also allows you to delete records by clicking the vertical record selection bar to the left of the Detail section of the form. The vertical record selection bar becomes a darker shade of gray, and the triangle that is used to identify a selected record appears at the top of the bar. Press Delete, and the confirmation message appears. Click Yes to delete the record, or click No if you've changed your mind.

**FIG. 12.31**    The message box that asks you to confirm or cancel the deletion of a record.

---

**Note**

You can't use the sbfPersonnelActions form to delete records from the Personnel Actions table because you set the Allow Deletions property to No when you modified the subform earlier in this chapter. The main form won't permit you to delete records from the Employees table, either, because the Employees table has dependent records in other tables.

Furthermore, the Enforce Referential integrity option for the join between the Employees and Personnel Actions tables is enabled without cascading deletes also being enabled. Access therefore prevents the deletion of records in the Employees table if it would create orphan records in another table. If you want to experiment with deleting records from the Personnel Actions table in the subform, open the sbfPersonnelActions form in Design mode, and change the Allow Deletions property (on the Data tab of the Properties window for the form) to Yes.

---

# Modifying the Properties of a Form or Control After Testing

The entries you added and edited gave you an opportunity to test your form. Testing a form to ensure that it accomplishes the objectives you have in mind usually takes much longer than creating the form and the query that underlies it. During the testing process, you might notice that the order of the fields isn't what you want, or that records in the subform aren't displayed in an appropriate sequence. The following two sections deal with modifying the properties of the form and subform control.

### Changing the Order of Fields for Data Entry

The order in which the editing caret moves from one field to the next is determined by the Tab Order property of each control. The Form Wizard established the tab order of the controls when you first created the form. The default Tab Order property of each field is assigned, beginning with the value 0, in the sequence in which you add the fields. Because the Form Wizard created a single-column form, the order of the controls in Personnel Actions is top to bottom. The tab order originally assigned doesn't change when you relocate a control.

To change the sequence of entries—for example, to match the pattern of entries on a paper form—follow these steps:

**1.** Click the Design View button on the toolbar.

**2.** Choose <u>V</u>iew, Ta<u>b</u> Order to display the Tab Order dialog shown in Figure 12.32. The order of entry is shown by the sequence of field names in the Custom Order list. (In this example, changing the sequence of the entries is unnecessary because the sequence is logical, even after moving the controls to their present locations on the Personnel Actions form.)

**3.** Click the Auto Order button if you want to reorder the entry sequence going left to right across each row of fields, then top to bottom.

**4.** Drag any control to a new location by clicking the button at the left of its name and dropping it wherever you want it to be in the sequence.

**5.** Click OK to implement the changes you made; click Cancel to retain the original entry sequence.

> **Note**
>
> Using the Auto Order button to change the tab order of fields on a form also changes the left-to-right order of the table fields in Datasheet view to correspond to the Auto Order field sequence.

**FIG. 12.32**  Changing the sequence of data-entry fields in the Tab Order dialog.

### Removing Fields from the Tab Order

Access 97 allows you to set the value of the Tab Stop property to No in order to prevent controls from receiving the focus in the tab order. To remove a control from the tab order, select the control; open the Properties window; select Other Properties; and change the value of Tab Stop to **No** (see Figure 12.33). You cannot edit the EmployeeID field, so set the Tab Stop property to No for this control.

---

**Note**

Setting the Tab Stop property's value to No does not disable a given control, but it removes the control from the tab sequence. This means that the control can't be selected by pressing the Tab key, but can still be selected by clicking it with the mouse.

---

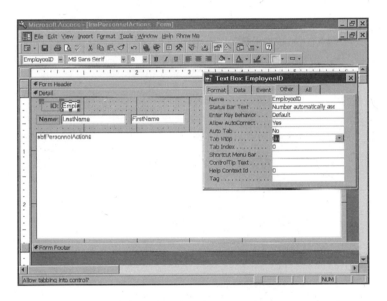

**FIG. 12.33**  Removing a field from the tab order.

### Changing the Source of Data for the Subform and Sorting the Subform Data

The Personnel Actions table is indexed by paType and paScheduledDate, but the sequence of the records appears in the order of the primary key: paID, paType, and paScheduledDate. Because only paID is used to link the records, records for a particular employee appear in the order of the remaining key fields, paType and paScheduledDate. Eventually, the number of records for an employee can become quite large, so having the records appear in type and date order is convenient. Because only a few records can be displayed in the subform datasheet, the latest entries should appear by default. This requires a descending sort on the Personnel Actions table. You can establish a descending sort only by substituting a sorted query that contains all records of the Personnel Actions table, as described in the following two procedures.

To create a new sorted query, follow these steps:

1. Close the Personnel Action entry form, and make the Database window active.

2. Click the Queries tab of the Database window, and then click the New button to create a new query. With Design view selected in the New Query dialog, click OK.

3. In the Show Table dialog, select Personnel Actions as the table on which to base the query; click Add and then click Close.

4. Drag the * field to the Query grid, and drop it in the first column.

5. Drag the paScheduledDate field to the Query grid, and drop it in the second column.

6. Click to remove the check mark from the Show box in the new paScheduledDate column so that you don't duplicate a field name in the query. Add a descending sort to the paScheduledDate column (see Figure 12.34).

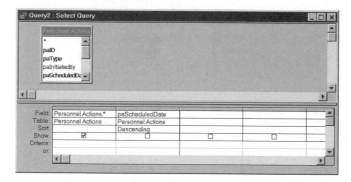

**FIG. 12.34**    The query design for the subform with all of the personnel actions sorted in descending date sequence.

7. Click the Run Query button to check to see that the records are sorted in reverse chronological order.

8. Close your query and name it **qryPersonnelActionsSubform**.

To change the data source for the subform to the new sorted query, complete the following steps:

1. Click the Forms tab in the Database window, and open the sbfPersonnelActions subform in Design mode.

2. Click the Properties button to display the Properties window, then click the Data tab.

3. Click the Record Source box, open the list, and select qryPersonnelActionsSubform as the new data source for the subform (see Figure 12.35).

4. If you want to review the design of the table or query you select as the value of the Record Source property, click the ellipsis button to display the source object in Design mode.

5. Close the Properties window, and click the Form View button on the toolbar to verify that the datasheet display is correct.

6. Close the sbfPersonnelActions subform, and save your changes.

7. Reopen the Personnel Actions form. Use Find in the main part of the form to locate the employee for whom you added additional records in the Personnel Actions table. The history in the subform is now sorted with the most recent dates first.

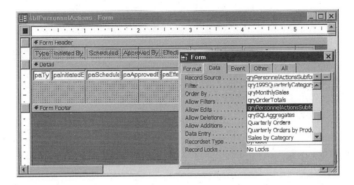

**FIG. 12.35**  Changing the Record Source property of the subform to change the underlying data source.

8. To verify that the sort stays active when you add new entries, add a new record with today's date, and then click the Prior button to save the new entry. Click Next to display the new entry so that you can be sure the sorting is functional.

You can use the same method described in the preceding steps to change the data source of a main form. For example, you could create a query for the main form so that the records in the form are displayed alphabetically by last name instead of in numerical order by EmployeeID.

---

### Troubleshooting

*I receive an error message in the Scheduled column of the subform datasheet every time I try to run the query.*

You didn't click the Show box in step 6 of the set of instructions given earlier for creating the new query. When a field is duplicated in a query, Access doesn't know which of the two fields to use if the Show check box is marked for both fields.

> **Note**
>
> Pressing Shift+Enter (or choosing <u>R</u>ecords, Save Rec<u>o</u>rd) to save a record does not update the subform, and the new entry is not displayed in the subform. You must choose <u>R</u>ecords, Refres<u>h</u> to update the subform's display. The Refres<u>h</u> command doesn't requery the database but does cause any updates that have occurred since the last automatic refreshing operation to appear. The best approach, therefore, is to use the record position buttons to commit the new or edited record. The Refresh command is discussed in Chapter 25, "Securing Multiuser Network Applications."

# Chapter 13

# Designing Custom Multitable Forms

The controls that the Form Wizard adds to the forms it creates are only a sampling of the 20 native control objects offered by Access 97. Until now, you used the Form Wizard to create the labels, text boxes, and subform controls for displaying and editing data in the Personnel Actions table. These three kinds of controls are sufficient for creating a conventional transaction processing form.

The remaining 17 controls described in this chapter allow you to take full advantage of the Windows graphical user environment. You add controls to the form by using the Access Toolbox. List and combo boxes increase data entry productivity and accuracy by allowing you to choose from a list of predefined values rather than requiring you to type the value. Option buttons, toggle buttons, and check boxes supply values to Yes/No fields. If you place option buttons, toggle buttons, and check boxes in an option frame, these controls can supply the numeric values you specify. The Image control (which was a new feature of Access 95) supplements the Bound and Unbound Object Frame controls for adding pictures to your forms. Page breaks control how forms print. Access 97's new Tab control allows you to create tabbed forms to display related data on forms and subforms in a space-saving and more clearly organized fashion. Command buttons allow you to execute Access VBA procedures. ActiveX controls, which greatly expand the versatility of Access forms, are one of the subjects of Chapter 19, "Using 32-Bit OLE Components."

## Understanding the Access Toolbox

The Access 97 Toolbox is based on the Toolbox created for Microsoft Visual Basic. Essentially, the Access Toolbox is a variation of toolbar. You choose one of the 20 buttons that appear in the Toolbox to add a control, represented by that tool's symbol, to the form. When you create a report, the Toolbox serves the same purpose—although tools that require user input, such as combo boxes, are seldom used in reports.

### Control Categories

Three control object categories exist in Access forms and reports:

■ *Bound controls* are associated with a field in the data source for the form or subform. The data source can be a table or query. Bound controls display and update values of the data cell in the associated field of the currently selected record. Text boxes are the most common bound control. You can display the content of graphic objects or play a waveform audio file with a bound OLE object. You can bind toggles, check boxes, and option buttons to Yes/No fields. All bound controls have associated labels that display the Caption property of the field; you can edit or delete these labels without affecting the bound control.

■ *Unbound controls* display data you provide that is independent of the data source of the form or subform. You use the unbound OLE object to add a drawing or bitmapped image to a form. You can use lines and rectangles to divide a form into logical groups, or simulate boxes used on the paper form. Unbound text boxes are used to enter data that is not intended to update a field in the data source but is intended for other purposes, such as establishing a value used in an expression. Some unbound controls, such as unbound text boxes, include labels; others, such as unbound OLE objects, don't include labels.

■ *Calculated controls* use expressions as their source of data. Usually, the expression includes the value of a field, but you also can use values created by unbound text boxes in calculated control expressions.

### The Toolbox

 You use the Access Toolbox to add control objects to forms and reports. The Toolbox appears only in Design mode for forms and reports, and it appears only if you click the Toolbox button on the toolbar or toggle the View, Toolbox menu command. When the Toolbox is visible, the Toolbox menu choice is checked; the Toolbox is shown in Figure 13.1. You can choose from the 20 controls and one wizard button, whose names and functions are listed in Table 13.1.

**FIG. 13.1** The Access 97 Toolbox in its floating window.

### Table 13.1  Control Objects of the Access Toolbox

| Tool | Name | Function |
|------|------|----------|
| ▷ | Select Objects | Changes mouse pointer to object selection tool. Deselects a previously selected tool and returns the mouse pointer to normal selection function. Select Objects is the default tool when you display the Toolbox. |
| ✸ | Control Wizards | Turns the Control Wizards on and off. Control Wizards aid you in designing complex controls, such as option groups, list boxes, and combo boxes. |
| Aa | Label | Creates a box that contains fixed descriptive or instructional text. |
| ab | Text Box | Creates a box to display and allow editing of text data. |
| [xyz] | Option Group | Creates a frame of adjustable size in which you can place toggle buttons, option buttons, or check boxes. Only one of the objects within an object group frame may be selected. When you select an object within an option group, the previously selected object is deselected. |
| ⊟ | Toggle Button | Creates a button that changes from On to Off when clicked. The On state corresponds to Yes (–1), and the Off state corresponds to No (0). When used within an option group, toggling one button On toggles a previously selected button Off. You can use toggle buttons to let the user select one value from a set of values. |
| ◉ | Option Button | Creates a round button (originally called a *radio button*) that behaves identically to a toggle button. Option buttons are most commonly used within option groups to select between values in a set where the choices are mutually exclusive. |
| ☑ | Check Box | Creates a check box that toggles On and Off. Multiple check boxes should be used outside of option groups so that you can select more than one check box at a time. |
| ▤ | Combo Box | Creates a combo box with an editable text box where you can enter a value, as well as a list, from which you can select a value from a set of choices. |
| ▤ | List Box | Creates a drop-down list box from which you can select a value. A list box is simply the list portion of a combo box. |
| ▭ | Command Button | Creates a command button that, when clicked, triggers an event that can execute an Access VBA event-handling procedure. |
| ▨ | Image | Displays a static graphic on a form or report. This is not an OLE-type picture, so you can't edit it after placing it on the form. |

(continues)

**III**

**Creating Forms and Reports**

| Tool | Name | Function |
|---|---|---|
| | Unbound Object | Adds an OLE object created by an OLE server application, such as Microsoft Graph or Microsoft Draw, to a form or report. The ActiveX Control object is a special version of the Unbound Object that contains ActiveX Controls. |
| | Bound Object | Displays the content of an OLE field of a record if the field contains a graphic object. If the field contains no graphic object, the icon that represents the object appears, such as the Sound Recorder's icon for a linked or embedded .wav file. Data-bound ActiveX Controls are stored in a special version of the Bound Object. |
| | Page Break | Causes the printer to start a new page at the location of the page break on the form or report. Page breaks don't appear in form or report Run mode. |
| | Tab Control | Inserts a tab control to create tabbed forms. (The tab control looks like the tabbed pages you've seen in the various Properties windows throughout this book.) Pages of a tab control can contain other bound or unbound controls, including subform/subreport controls. |
| | Subform | Adds a subform or subreport to a main form or report, respectively. The subform or subreport you intend to add must exist before you use this control. |
| | Line | Creates a straight line that you can size and relocate. The color and width of the line can be changed by using the Formatting toolbar buttons or the Properties window. |
| | Rectangle | Creates a rectangle that you can size and relocate. The border color, width, and fill color of the rectangle are determined by selections from the palette. |
| | More Controls | Clicking this tool opens a scrolling list of additional ActiveX controls that you can use in your forms and reports. The ActiveX controls available through the More Controls list aren't part of Access; ActiveX controls are supplied as .ocx code libraries with Office 97, Visual Basic, and various third-party tool libraries. |

**Table 13.1 Continued**

Using controls in the design of reports is discussed in the following two chapters, which are devoted entirely to the subject of Access reports. The use of bound and unbound OLE objects is described in Chapter 20, "Adding Graphics to Forms and Reports." Using command buttons to execute Access VBA code is covered in Part VII of this book, which deals with Access VBA programming. You learn how to use the remaining 16 controls on your forms in the following sections.

### Access's Control Wizards, Builders, and Toolbars

Access provides a number of features to aid you in designing and using more complex forms. Three of these features—Control Wizards, Builders, and customizable toolbars—are described in the three sections that follow.

**Access Control Wizards.** Much of the success of Access is attributable to the Form Wizard, Report Wizard, and Chart Wizard that simplify the process of creating database objects. The first wizard appeared in Microsoft Publisher, and most of Microsoft's productivity applications now include a variety of wizards. Chapter 12, "Creating and Using Forms," introduced the Form Wizard; the Report Wizard is discussed in Chapter 14, "Printing Basic Reports and Mailing Labels"; and the Chart Wizard is described in Chapters 19, "Using 32-Bit OLE Components," and 20, "Adding Graphics to Forms and Reports." Developers can create custom wizards to perform a variety of duties. You can expect a wide range of wizards to become available from independent software vendors (ISVs) as Access continues to gain adherents.

Access's repertoire of wizards includes Control Wizards that lead you step-by-step through the design of more complex control objects, such as option groups, list boxes, and combo boxes. Designing and populating list and combo boxes requires several steps. In this chapter, you are introduced to a Control Wizard each time you add a control for which a wizard is available.

**Access Builders.** Builders are another feature that makes Access easy to use. You use the Expression Builder, introduced in Chapter 4, "Working with Access Databases and Tables," to create expressions that supply values to calculated controls on a form or report. The Query Builder creates the SQL statements you need when you create list boxes or combo boxes whose Row Source property is a SQL statement that executes a select query. Using the Query Builder to insert SQL statements created by graphical QBE is much simpler than the method originally used with Access 1.x: You had to create a query, open the SQL window, copy the SQL statement to the Clipboard, and then paste the SQL statement to the Row Source property's text box. Using the Query Builder is described in the section "Using the Query Builder to Populate a Combo Box" near the end of this chapter.

**Customizable Toolbars.** The preceding chapters demonstrated that the toolbars of Access include many shortcut buttons to expedite the design and use of Access database objects. Access 97, like most other contemporary Microsoft applications, lets you customize the toolbars to your own set of preferences. Access 1.x stored toolbars as forms in UTILITY.MDA. Access 2.0 used the 16-bit common toolbar Dynamic Link Library, COMMTB.DLL, to manipulate toolbars. Access 95 used the 32-bit version of the common toolbar dynamic link library, Commtb32.dll, and (like Access 2.0) stored definitions of your customized versions of standard toolbars in the MSysToolbars table of System.mdw. (The significance of storing your preferences in System.mdw is discussed in Chapter 25, "Securing Multiuser Network Applications.") Access 97 also uses the Commtb32.dll to manipulate toolbars, and it stores customized toolbars in System.mdw. Toolbars that you create yourself are stored in a hidden system table—MSysCmdbars—in each database.

You can convert conventional floating design tools, such as the Toolbox, to conventional toolbars by the drag-and-drop method. To anchor the Toolbox as a toolbar, also called *docking the toolbar*, follow these steps:

1. Press and hold down the mouse button while the mouse pointer is on the title bar of the Toolbox, and then drag the Toolbox toward the top of Access's parent window.

   When the Toolbox reaches the toolbar area, the dotted outline changes from a rectangle that is approximately the size of the Toolbox into a wider rectangle with only as much height as a toolbar.

2. Release the mouse button to change the Toolbox to an anchored toolbar positioned below the standard Form Design toolbar.

> **Note**
>
> You can anchor or dock a toolbar to any edge of Access's parent window. Press and hold down the mouse button on an empty area of the toolbar (not covered by a button), and then drag the toolbar until its outline appears along the left, right, or bottom edge of the window. If you drop the toolbar within the confines of Access's main window, it becomes a floating toolbar.

You can add or delete buttons from toolbars with the Customize Toolbars dialog. If you are using the conventional VGA display format (640×480 pixels), there is very little room to add new buttons to the Form Design toolbar, and no room exists for adding buttons to the Formatting toolbar. However, the Toolbox toolbar has room to add seven or eight additional buttons when Access's main window is maximized. To add form design utility buttons to the Toolbox toolbar (whether it's docked or floating), do the following:

1. Choose View, Toolbars, Customize to display the Customize dialog.

2. Click the Toolbars tab to display the list of built-in and custom toolbars, and then select Toolbox in the list of toolbars to both display the Toolbox (if it isn't already visible) and select the Toolbox toolbar for customization.

> **Tip**
>
> You can also open the Customize dialog by right-clicking any part of a toolbar and then choosing Customize on the resulting popup menu.

3. Click the Commands tab, and then select Form/Report Design from the Categories list. The optional buttons applicable to form design operations appear in the Commands list, as shown in Figure 13.2.

4. The most useful optional buttons for form design are control alignment and sizing buttons. Press and hold down the mouse button on the Align to Grid command, and then drag this button to the Toolbox toolbar and drop it to the right of the Rectangle button. The right margin of the Toolbox toolbar expands to accommodate the new button (if you customize the Toolbox while it's floating, the window expands to accommodate the new button). You can drag the Snap to Grid button slightly to the right to create a gap between the new button and the Rectangle button.

**5.** Repeat step 4 for the Size to Fit, Size to Grid, and Align Left commands, dropping each button to the right of the preceding button. You now have four new buttons available in your Toolbox.

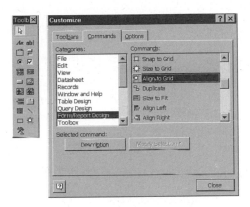

**FIG. 13.2**  The Toolbox with the Align to Grid command added and the open Customize dialog used to add commands.

The Customize dialog for toolbars provides the following additional capabilities:

■ To remove buttons from the toolbar, open the Customize dialog; click and drag the buttons you don't want, and drop them anywhere off the toolbar.

■ To reset the toolbar to its default design, open the Customize dialog. In the Toolbars list, select the toolbar you want to reset, then click the Reset button. A message box asks you to confirm that you want to abandon any changes you made to the toolbar.

■ To create a button that opens or runs a database object, open the Customize dialog, display the Commands page, and scroll the Categories list to display the All *Objects* items. When, for example, you select All Tables, the tables of the current database appear in the Commands list. Select a table name, such as Employees, and drag the selected item to an empty spot on a toolbar. The ScreenTip for the new button displays `Open Table 'Employees'`. (If you select All Macros and drag a macro object to the toolbar, the button you add runs the macro when clicked.)

■ To substitute text or a different image for the picture on the buttons you add to a toolbar, open the Customize dialog. Then click the button you want to change with the right mouse button to display the button shortcut menu. Click Choose Button Face to display the Choose Button Face dialog. Click one of the images offered, or click the Text check box and type the text you want to display in the text box. To edit the image of the button, click Edit Button Image.

■ To create a new empty toolbar that you can customize with any set of the supplied buttons you want, open the Customize dialog and select Utility 1 or Utility 2 on the Toolbars page. If space exists to the right of an existing toolbar, the empty toolbar appears in this space. Otherwise, Access creates a new toolbar row for the empty toolbar. The Utility 1 and Utility 2 toolbars are available in any Access database; changes you make to these toolbars will be universally available.

■ To create a custom toolbar that becomes part of your database, open the Customize dialog and click New on the Toolbars page of the dialog. The New Toolbar dialog appears, requesting a name for the new toolbar (Custom 1 is the default). Access creates a new floating tool window to which you add buttons from the Commands page of the Customize dialog. You can anchor the custom tool window to the toolbar if you want.

■ To delete a custom toolbar, open the Customize dialog, select the custom toolbar on the Toolbars page, and click the Delete button. You are requested to confirm the deletion. The Delete button is disabled when you select one of Access's standard toolbars in the list.

Custom toolbars to which you assign names become part of your database application and are stored in the current database file; they are available only when the database in which they are stored is open. Built-in Access toolbars that you customize are stored in System.mdw and are available in any Access work session.

### The Appearance of Controls in Design and Run Modes

The appearance in Form Design mode of the 17 different controls you can create with the Toolbox is shown in Figure 13.3. Labels were added to the page break, image, unbound object, line, and rectangle controls to identify them in the illustration. The labels aren't actually components of the controls.

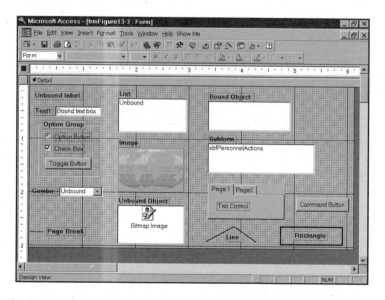

**FIG. 13.3** The 17 controls you can create by using the Toolbox, shown in Design mode (with four custom buttons added to the Toolbox toolbar).

When you click the Form View button, the controls appear as shown in Figure 13.4. The text box displays a #Name? error message because no value is assigned to the content of the text box. The list and combo boxes show some test values, which are provided only to show how the control appears in Form view. The image field displays a bitmap copied from the Globe.wmf graphic with the Size Mode property set to Zoom; the contents of the image field aren't editable. The unbound object field contains the Stone.bmp graphics file. This file is an embedded OLE object displayed as an icon. The bound object field is empty because no value for its content is assigned to it. The subform field displays a portion of the sbfPersonnelActions subform (the field is too small to display a significant portion of the subform). You can't create a subform control unless you enter the name of an existing form as the value. No fields have been placed on the tab control, which shows the default number of tab pages (2). An unbound label was added to the first page to help identify the control.

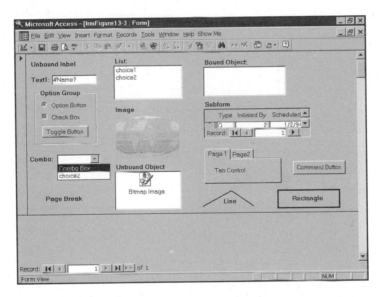

**FIG. 13.4**  The 17 controls you can create by using the Toolbox, shown in Form view. Notice that the list in the combo box has been dropped down.

# Using the Toolbox to Add Controls

Experimenting is the best way of learning how to use a new computer application. No matter how well the product's documentation—or a book such as this—describes a process, no substitute exists for trying the methods. This axiom holds true whether you are designing a form or writing program code. The Microsoft programmers who created Access cleverly designed the user interface for creating custom forms so that the interface is intuitive and flexible. After you complete the examples in this chapter, you probably will agree that this statement is true.

III

Creating Forms and Reports

The examples in this chapter use the Personnel Actions table that you created in Chapter 4, "Working with Access Databases and Tables," and two queries: qryPersonnelActions (which you create in the next section of this chapter, "Creating the Query on Which to Base the Main Form") and qryPersonnelActionsSubform (which you created in Chapter 12, "Creating and Using Forms"). The data dictionary needed to create the Personnel Actions table appears in Appendix C.

◄◄ See "Creating the Personnel Actions Table," p. 141

◄◄ See "Changing the Source of Data for the Subform and Sorting the Subform Data," p. 439

### Creating the Query on Which to Base the Main Form

The Personnel Actions table identifies employees only by their ID numbers, located in the paID field. As before, you need to display the employee's name and title on the form to avoid entering records for the wrong person. To obtain the employee's name and title data for the form, you need to create a one-to-many query that joins the Employees table, which has only one entry per employee, with the Personnel Actions table, which can have many entries for one employee.

> **Note**
>
> In the form you created in Chapter 12, you used the Form Wizard to specify the tables from which you wanted to display data on the form. When you create a multitable form from scratch, you need to create a query as a data source for the form. The query joins the data from the tables into a unified source for use by the form.

To create the Personnel Actions query that serves as the data source for your main form, follow these steps:

1. Close any open forms, click the arrow to the right of the New Object button on the toolbar to open the drop-down menu, and click Query. Next, select Design View in the list of the New Query dialog and click OK. Double-click the Personnel Actions table in the list of tables of the Show Table dialog to add the Personnel Actions table to your query.

   New Object: Query

   Alternatively, you can bypass the Show Table dialog step by clicking the Table button of the Database window and then selecting Personnel Actions in the table list. When you click the New Query button with a table selected, the table is added automatically to the new query.

2. Double-click the Employees table in the table list, and then click Close. The field list windows for the Personnel Actions and Employees tables appear in the upper pane of the Query Design window.

   If you used the alternative method to add the Personnel Actions table to the query described in step 1, you need to click the Show Table button on the toolbar to open the Show Table dialog to add the Employees table to your query.

3. Choose <u>V</u>iew, Table <u>N</u>ames to add the Tables row to your Query Design grid. (If the Table Names command already has a check mark next to it, you don't need to choose it.)

4. If you defined relationships for the Personnel Action table as described in Chapter 4, "Working with Access Databases and Tables," the upper pane of the query window appears as shown in Figure 13.5. The line connecting the two tables indicates that a many-to-one relationship exists between the paID field in the Personnel Action table and the EmployeeID field of the Employees table.

**FIG. 13.5**   The upper pane of the Query Design window for the Personnel Actions query.

If you didn't define any relationships, the join line won't appear. In this case, you need to drag the paID field from the Personnel Actions field list to the EmployeeID field of the Employees field list to create a join between these two fields.

5. Click the * field of the Personnel Actions table, drag it to the first column of the Query Design grid, and drop it in the Personnel Actions column. This adds all of the fields to the Personnel Actions table to your query.

6. Click the LastName field of the Employees table, drag it to the Query grid, and drop it in the second column.

7. From the Employees table, click and drag the FirstName, Title, HireDate, Extension, Notes, ReportsTo, and Photo fields. Drop them in columns 3, 4, 5, 6, 7, 8, and 9 of the Query grid, respectively, as shown in Figure 13.6.

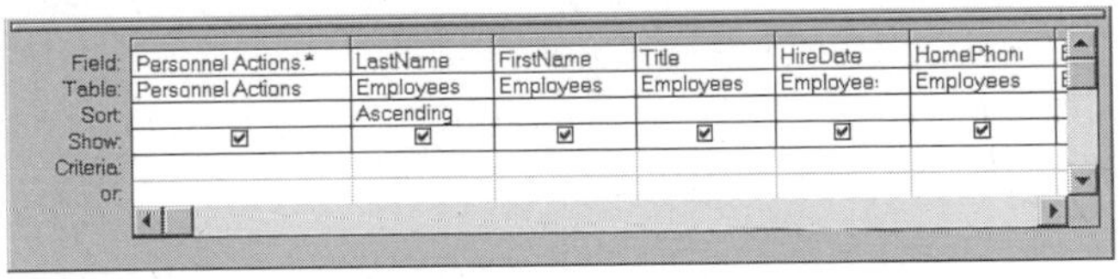

**FIG. 13.6**   The Query grid for the Personnel Actions query.

8. To simplify finding an employee, click the Sort row of the LastName column and select an Ascending sort.

9. Close the new query. Click Yes when the message box asks if you want to save the query.

10. In the Save As dialog, name the query **qryPersonnelActions** and click OK (see Figure 13.7).

**FIG. 13.7** The Save As dialog for the Personnel Actions query.

Now that you've created the query that will provide a unified record source for the main form, you're ready to begin creating your custom multitable form.

### Creating a Blank Form with a Header and Footer

When you create a form without using the Form Wizard, Access provides a default blank form to which you add controls that you choose from the Toolbox. To create a blank form with which to experiment with Access controls, perform the following steps:

1. With the Database window active, click the Forms tab in the Database window, and then click the New button. Access displays the New Form dialog.

2. Even an experimental form requires a data source, so choose qryPersonnelActions from the drop-down list, choose Design View from the list in the upper-right corner of the New Form dialog, and click OK.

3. Access creates a new blank form with the default title Form1. Click the Maximize button to expand the form to fill the document window.

4. If the Toolbox isn't visible, click the Toolbox button on the toolbar (or choose View, Toolbox) to display the Toolbox. Drag the Toolbox to the top or bottom of the form to anchor it there as a toolbar (do this if the Toolbox isn't already in a docked position—docking the toolbar usually makes working on a form easier because the floating Toolbox window obscures the form underneath it).

5. Choose View, Form Header/Footer. The blank form appears as shown in Figure 13.8. If the grid doesn't appear on the form, choose View, Grid.

   The default width of blank forms is 5 inches. The default height of the Form Header and Footer sections is 0.25 inch, and the height of the Detail section is 2 inches.

6. To adjust the height of the Detail section of the form, place the mouse pointer on the top line of the Form Footer bar. The mouse pointer becomes a double-headed arrow with a line between the heads. Hold down the left mouse button and drag the bar to create a height of about 3.5 inches, measured by the left vertical ruler. The active surface of the form, which is gray with the default 24×24 grid dots, expands vertically as you move the Form Footer bar, as shown in Figure 13.9.

7. Minimize the Form Footer section by dragging the bottom margin of the form to the bottom of the Form Footer bar.

8. Drag the right margin of the form to 6 inches as measured by the horizontal ruler at the top of the form.

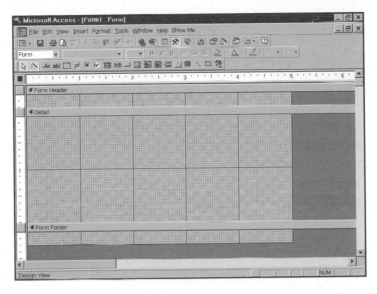

**FIG. 13.8**  Access's default blank form with Form Header and Form Footer sections added.

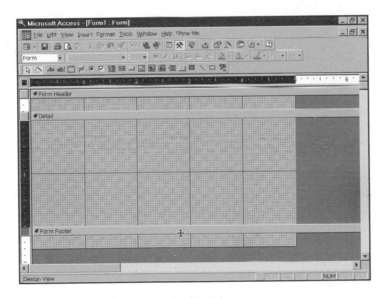

**FIG. 13.9**  Expanding the Detail section of the blank form.

You are using the blank form to create a form similar to the frmPersonnelActions form that you created in Chapter 12, "Creating and Using Forms."

### Adding a Label to the Form Header

The label is the simplest control in the Toolbox to use. Labels are unbound and static, and they display only the text you enter. *Static* means that the label retains the value you originally assigned as long as the form is displayed. To add a label to the Form Header section, complete the following steps:

1. Click the Label button in the Toolbox. When you move the mouse pointer to the active area of the form, the pointer becomes the symbol for the Label button, combined with a crosshair—the center point of the crosshair defines the position of the upper-left corner of the control.

2. Locate the crosshair at the upper-left of the Form Header section. Press and hold down the left mouse button while you drag the crosshair to the position for the lower-right corner of the label (see Figure 13.10).

   As you drag the crosshair, the outline of the container for the label follows your movement. The number of lines and characters that the text box can display in the currently selected font is shown in the status bar.

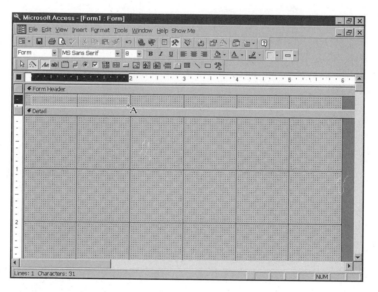

**FIG. 13.10**   Adding a label control to the Form Header.

3. If you move the crosshair beyond the bottom of the Form Header section, the Form Header bar expands to accommodate the size of the label after you release the left mouse button. When the label is the size you want, release the mouse button.

4. The mouse pointer becomes the text editing caret inside the outline of the label. Enter **Personnel Action Entry** as the text for the label, and then click anywhere outside the label to finish its creation. If you don't type at least one text character in a label after creating it, the box disappears the next time you click the mouse.

◄◄ See "Selecting, Moving, and Sizing a Single Control," p. 421

You use the basic process described in the preceding steps to add most of the other types of controls to a form. (Some Toolbox buttons, such as the graph and command buttons, launch a Control Wizard to help you create the control if the Control Wizards button is activated.) After you add the control, you use the anchor and sizing handles described in Chapter 12, "Creating and Using Forms," to move the control to the desired position and to size the control to accommodate the content. The location of the anchor handle determines the Left (horizontal) and Top (vertical) properties of the control. The sizing handles establish the control's Width and Height properties.

### Formatting Text and Adjusting Text Control Sizes

When a control is selected that accepts text as the value, the typeface and font size combo boxes appear on the toolbar. To format the text that appears in a label or text box, complete the following steps:

1. Click the Personnel Action Entry label you created in the preceding section to select the label.

2. Double-click the label (or click the Properties button on the toolbar) to display the Properties window. (You don't actually need to use the Properties window to make these formatting changes. You open the Properties window to learn about how the changes you make to a control with toolbar buttons and menu commands affect the control's properties.)

3. Open the Font list on the Formatting toolbar and select the typeface family you want. MS Sans Serif, the default, is recommended because all users of Windows 95 and Windows NT 4.0 have this bitmapped font. (MS Sans Serif is quite similar to Linotype Company's Helvetica typeface or the Arial TrueType typeface also supplied with Windows.) Sans serif faces are easier to read on forms than faces with serifs, such as MS Serif or Times New Roman. (Serif faces are easier to read when a large amount of text is involved, such as in newspapers or the body text of this book.)

4. Open the Font Size list and select 14 points.

5. Click the Bold attribute button on the toolbar.

6. The size of the label you created isn't large enough to display the larger font. To adjust the size of the label to accommodate the content of the label, click the Size to Fit button—if you added it to the Toolbox—or choose Format, Size, To Fit. Access resizes the label's text box to display the entire label; if necessary, Access also increases the size of the Form Header section.

---

**Note**

The two sizing commands (Size, To Grid and Size, To Fit) work slightly differently, depending on whether one or more controls are selected. If one or more controls are selected when you execute

(continues)

---

**Creating Forms and Reports**

(continued)

one of the sizing commands, the command is applied to the selected control(s). If no controls are selected, the chosen sizing command applies as the default to all objects you subsequently create, move, or resize.

When you change the properties of a control, the new values are reflected in the Properties window for the control, as shown in Figure 13.11. If you move or resize the label, you see the label's Left, Top, Width, and Height values change in the Properties window. You usually use the Properties window to actually change the characteristics of a control only if a toolbar button or menu choice isn't available.

You can choose different fonts and the bold, italic, and underline attributes (or a combination) for any label or caption for a control. You can assign the text content of list boxes and combo boxes to a typeface or size other than the default, but this practice is uncommon in Windows applications.

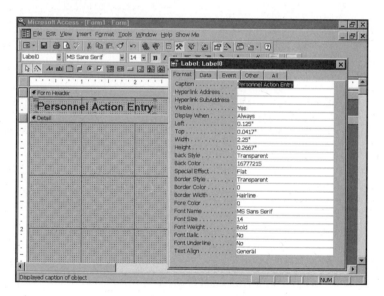

**FIG. 13.11**  The form title label and its Properties window.

### Creating Bound, Multiline, and Calculated Text Boxes

Access uses the following four basic kinds of text boxes:

- *Single-line text boxes* usually are bound to controls on the form or to fields in a table or query.

- *Multiline text boxes* usually are bound to Memo field types and include a vertical scroll bar to allow access to text that doesn't fit within the dimensions of the box.

■ *Calculated text boxes* obtain values from expressions that begin with = (equal sign) and are usually a single line. If you include a field value, such as [paScheduledDate], in the expression for a calculated text box, the text box is bound to that field. Otherwise, calculated text boxes are unbound. You cannot edit the value of a calculated text box.

■ *Unbound text boxes* can be used to supply values—such as limiting dates—to Access VBA procedures. An unbound text box that doesn't contain a calculation expression can be edited.

The following sections show you how to create the first three types of text boxes.

**Adding a Text Box Bound to a Field.** The most common text box used in Access forms is the single-line bound text box that comprises the majority of the controls of the frmPersonnelActions form you created in Chapter 12. To add a text box that is bound to a field of the form's data source with the field list window, complete the following steps:

1. Click the Field List button on the toolbar. The field list window appears.

2. Click the paID field in the field list window. Hold down the mouse button and drag the field to the upper-left corner of the form's Detail section. When you move the mouse pointer to the active area of the form, the pointer becomes a field symbol, but no crosshair appears. The position of the field symbol indicates the upper-left corner of the text box, not the label, so drop the symbol in the approximate position of the text box anchor handle, as shown in Figure 13.12.

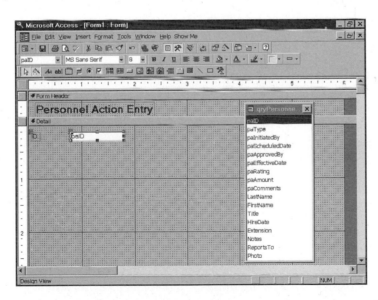

**FIG. 13.12**  Adding a text box control that is bound to the paID field.

III

Creating Forms and Reports

3. Drag the text box by the anchor handle closer to the ID label, and decrease the box's width.

4. Small type sizes outside of a field text box are more readable when you turn the bold attribute on. Choose the ID label and click the Bold button.

5. Choose File, Save, and then type the name **frmPersonnelActionsEntry** in the Form Name text box of the Save As dialog. Click OK.

---

**Note**

When Access creates a text label that is associated with a form control, it uses the bound object's name as the value for the text label. If the form control is bound to a table object, such as a field, that has a Caption property (and the Caption property isn't blank), then Access uses the value of the Caption property as the default value for the text label of the bound form control. When you created the Personnel Actions table in Chapter 4, "Working with Access Databases and Tables," you set the Caption property for each field name. The paID field has a Caption property set to ID, so the label for the text box bound to the paID field is also ID.

---

Steps 3 and 4 in the preceding example are included to show how to make minor design adjustments to controls that improve the appearance of forms. Step 5 was included because you've already put some effort into this sample form (which you'll continue to experiment with and eventually complete in the following sections of this chapter). Furthermore, it's good working practice to save your documents frequently.

**Adding a Multiline Text Box with Scroll Bars.** Although you can use a conventional text box to display comments or other text fields with lengthy content, you must then scroll the caret through the text box to read the content. Multiline text boxes allow you to display long strings of text as a series of lines whose width is determined by the width of the multiline text box. To create a multiline text box, perform the following steps:

1. Click and drag paComments from the field list window to about the middle of the Detail section and drop it there.

2. Delete the Comments label, and size the text box as shown in Figure 13.13.

3. Click the Properties button on the toolbar, and click the Format tab in the Properties window. Scroll the Format Properties list for the text box until the Scroll Bars property appears.

4. Open the drop-down list for the Scroll Bars property, and choose Vertical to add a vertical scroll bar to the Comments text box.

5. If you plan to print the form, change the Can Grow and Can Shrink properties from No to Yes (for the height of the printed version of the form to vary with the number of lines of text in the box). The Can Grow and Can Shrink properties don't affect the appearance of the form in Run mode.

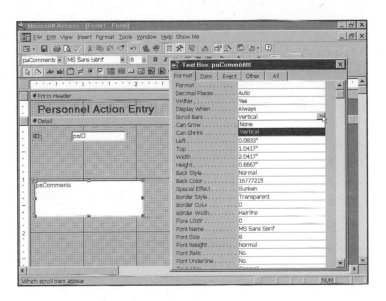

**FIG. 13.13**  Adding the multiline paComments text box.

---

**Note**

The vertical scroll bar of a multiline text box is visible only in the form's Run mode, and then only when the multiline text box has the focus (when the caret is within the text box).

---

**Creating a Calculated Text Box.** You can display the result of all valid Access expressions in a calculated text box. An expression must begin with = and may use Access functions to return values. As mentioned in the introduction to this section, you can use calculated text boxes to display calculations based on the values of fields. To create a calculated text box that displays the current date and time, complete the following steps:

1. Close the field list and Properties windows. Click the Text Box tool in the Toolbox to add an unbound text box at the right of the Form Header section of the form.

2. Edit the label of the new text box to read Date/Time:, and relocate the label so that it is adjacent to the text box.

3. Type **=Now()** in the text box to display the current date and time from your computer's clock. (In Design view, the form displays the calculation formula; it displays the actual date and time only in Form view.)

4. Adjust the length of the text box to accommodate the number of characters—20—in the default DD/MM/YY HH:MM:SS PM format used for dates and times. The entry appears as shown in the Date/Time text box of Figure 13.14. You add the other two text boxes in the following section.

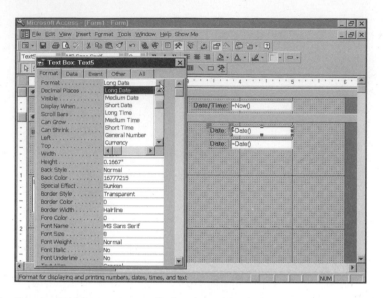

**FIG. 13.14**    Creating and formatting a calculated text box to display the date and time.

**Formatting Values.** You can use the Format property you learned about in Chapter 4 to determine how dates, times, and numbers are displayed in a text box on a form. To format a date entry, perform the following steps:

1. Using the Text Box tool, add a second unbound text box in the Detail section of the form under the first text box in the Form Header section. Adjust the new box's dimensions to correspond to the other text box.

2. Edit the label to read Date: and enter **=Date()** in the text box.

3. Select the text box, then display the Properties window in one of two ways: click the right mouse button to display a popup menu, and choose Properties; or click the Properties button on the toolbar. Click the Format tab in the Properties window.

4. Click the Format property and open the drop-down list. Select Long Date from the list.

A Format property applied to a bound text box on a form or report overrides the format assigned to the field in the table design that supplies the value to the text box.

---

**Note**

When you display a form in Run mode, the value displayed in the Date/Time text box is the time that you open the form. To update the time, choose Records, Refresh. The refreshing process that occurs at an interval determined by the Refresh Interval property of the Multiuser Options (the default value is 15 seconds) doesn't update unbound text boxes.

---

**Using the Clipboard with Controls.** You can use the Windows Clipboard to easily make copies of controls and their properties. As an example, create a copy of one of the Date/Time controls using the Clipboard by performing the following steps:

1. Select the unbound control and its label by clicking the field text box of the second date text box you added in the preceding section. Both the label and the text box are selected, as indicated by the selection handles on both controls.

2. To copy the selected control to the Clipboard, do one of the following: press Ctrl+C, click the Copy button on the toolbar, or choose Edit, Copy.

3. To paste the copy of the control below the original version, do one of the following: press Ctrl+V, click the Paste button on the toolbar, or choose Edit, Paste.

4. Click the Format property in the Properties window for the copied control, and select Short Date from the drop-down list.

5. To display the controls you've created, click the Form View button on the toolbar, and then return to Design view.

6. Delete the two Date text boxes and labels. To do so, enclose both with a selection boundary created by dragging the mouse pointer across the text boxes from the upper-left to the lower-right corner. Then press Delete. (You only need the Date/Time text box in the Form Header section for this form.)

7. Click the Form View button to view the form (see Figure 13.15).

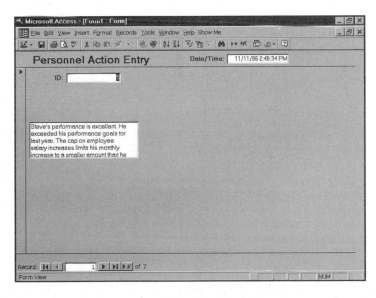

**FIG. 13.15** The form title and text boxes displayed in Form view.

Text boxes (and their associated labels) are the most commonly used control objects on Access forms.

### Changing the Default View and Obtaining Help for Properties

A form that fills Access's Design window might not necessarily fill the window in Run mode. Run mode may allow the beginning of a second copy of the form to appear. The second copy is created because the Default View property has a value of Continuous Forms. (In Access 2.0, the default property value for Default view was Continuous Forms; in Access 95 and 97, the default value of Default view is Single Form—your test form won't show the second form at the bottom of the screen.) Forms have the following three Default View property values from which you can choose:

■ *Single Form* displays one record at a time in one form.

■ *Continuous Forms* displays multiple records, each record having a copy of the Detail section of the form. You can use the vertical scroll bar or the record selection buttons to select which record to display. Continuous Forms view is the default value for subforms created by the Form Wizard.

■ *Datasheet* displays the form fields arranged in rows and columns.

To change the Default View property of the form, complete the following steps:

**1.** Click the Design View button on the toolbar.

**2.** Choose Edit, Select Form.

**3.** Click the Properties button on the toolbar if the Properties window isn't visible. Click the Format tab in the Properties window.

**4.** Click the Default View property to open the list.

**5.** Select the value you want for this property for the current form. For this exercise, select Single Form (the default) from the list.

**6.** While Default view is selected, press F1. The Help window for the Default View property appears. This Help window also explains how the Default view and Views Allowed properties relate to each other.

The vertical scroll bar disappears from the form in Run mode if a single form fits within its MDI child window.

You can verify your changes to the Default View property by clicking the Form View button to review the form's appearance.

### Adding Option Groups, Binding Controls, and Locking Tools

Option buttons, toggle buttons, and check boxes can return only Yes/No (—1/0 or True/False) values when used by themselves on a form. Here, their use as bound controls is limited to providing values to Yes/No fields in a table. When you place any of these controls within an option group, the buttons or check boxes can return a number you specify for the Option Value property of the control.

The capability of assigning numbers to the Option Value property allows you to use one of the preceding three controls inside an option group frame for assigning values to the paRating field of the Personnel Actions table. Option buttons are most commonly employed in Windows applications to select one value from a limited number of values.

---

**Caution**

Placing check boxes within option groups violates the Windows user interface design guidelines. According to the guidelines, a group of check boxes provides multiple additive choices. Thus, if you have more than one check box in a group, any or all of the check boxes can be marked. Use the shape control to create a frame around check boxes. Only option buttons and toggle buttons should be used in option groups.

---

By default, all controls you add with the Toolbox are unbound controls. You can bind a control to a field by choosing the control you want to use and then clicking the field name in the Field List window to which you want the control bound. Another way of binding a control is to create an unbound control with a tool and then type the name of a field in the Control Source property text box (reach the Control Source text box by clicking the Data tab in the Properties window for the control).

Access 97 offers two means of creating an option group: using the Option Group Wizard or manually adding option buttons or toggle buttons to the option group. The following two sections describe these methods.

**Using the Option Group Wizard.** The Option Group Wizard is one of three Control Wizards that take you step by step through the creation of complex controls. To create an option group for the paRating field of the Personnel Actions table with the Option Group Wizard, follow these steps:

1. Click the Control Wizards tool to turn on the wizards if the toggle button is not On (the default value). Toggle buttons indicate the On (True) state with a sunken appearance.

2. Click the Option Group tool, position the pointer where you want the upper-left corner of the option group, and then click the mouse button to display the first dialog of the Option Group Wizard, shown in Figure 13.16.

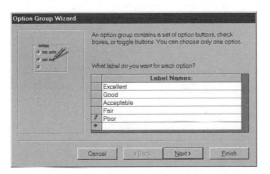

**FIG. 13.16** The opening dialog of the Option Group Wizard.

3. Type five of the nine ratings in the Label Names datasheet: **Excellent**, **Good**, **Acceptable**, **Fair**, and **Poor** (see Figure 13.16). Click the Next button to display the second dialog of the Option Group Wizard, shown in Figure 13.17.

> **Tip**
>
> You can create accelerator keys in the captions of your option buttons by placing an ampersand (**&**) before the letter to be used as an accelerator key. Thereafter, pressing Alt in combination with that letter key selects the option when your form is in Run mode.

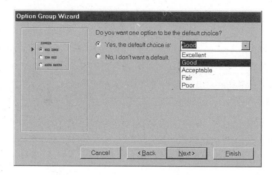

**FIG. 13.17**   Choosing a default value for the options group.

4. The second dialog lets you set an optional default value for the option group. Select the option named Yes, the Default Choice Is, and then open the drop-down list. Select Good, as shown in Figure 13.17, and then click Next. If you need to, you can always return to the prior step by clicking Back.

5. The third dialog of the Option Group Wizard provides for the assignment of option values to each option button of the group. Type **9**, **7**, **5**, **3**, and **1** in the five text boxes, as illustrated by Figure 13.18, and then click the Next button.

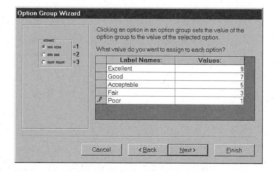

**FIG. 13.18**   Assigning the numeric OptionValue property to the option buttons.

The domain integrity rule for the paRating field provides for nine different ratings. Nine option buttons, however, occupy too much space on a form. Thus, only five of the nine ratings are provided here. In the section "Creating an Option Group Manually" later in this chapter, you add to this form a drop-down combo list with all nine ratings.

**6.** The fourth Option Group Wizard dialog enables you to bind the option frame to a field of a table or a column of a query that acts as the Record Source of the bound form. Select the paRating column of the qryPersonnelActions query to which your form is bound (see Figure 13.19). Click Next to continue with the next stage of the wizard.

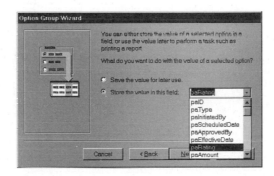

**FIG. 13.19**  Binding the option group to a column of the form's Record Source.

**7.** The fifth dialog lets you determine the style of the option group, as well as the type of controls (option buttons, check boxes, or toggle buttons) to add to the option group. You can preview the appearance of your option group and button style choices in the Sample pane. For this example, accept the defaults, Option Buttons and Etched (see Figure 13.20).

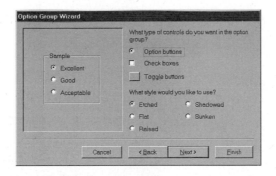

**FIG. 13.20**  Selecting a style for the option group and determining the type of button to add.

The sunken and raised styles of option groups, option buttons, and check boxes are applicable only to control objects on forms with a Back Color property other than white. Light gray is used to aid in the three-dimensional simulation, and neither option buttons nor check boxes have a Back Color property. Thus, option buttons and check boxes with special effects are best suited for light gray backgrounds (Back Color = 12632256).

8. The last dialog provides a text box for entering the value of the Caption property of the label for the option group. Type **Rating**, as shown in Figure 13.21, and then click Finish to let the wizard complete its work. Your completed Rating option group appears as shown in Figure 13.22.

**FIG. 13.21**  Assigning the value of the Caption property for the option group's label.

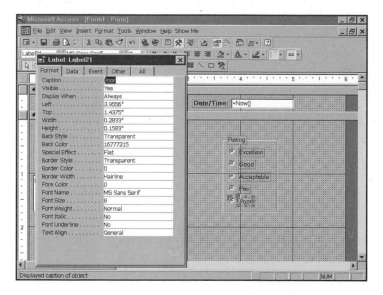

**FIG. 13.22**  The option group created by the Option Group Wizard.

To test your new bound option group, add a text box that is bound to the paRating column of the query underlying the form. Figure 13.23 shows the option group in Form view with the space between the buttons closed up, the bold attribute applied to the option group label, and the Rating text box added. Click the option buttons to display the rating value in the text box.

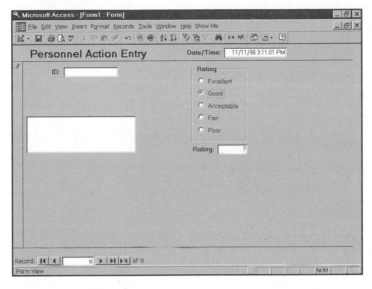

**FIG. 13.23** The new option group in Form view with a text box for the Rating field added to show the effect of selecting different options.

**Creating an Option Group Manually.** Although the Option Group Wizard does a good job of creating option groups, it's useful to know how to create a bound option group on your own. To bind an option group frame to the paRating field of the Personnel Actions query without taking advantage of the Control Wizard, complete the following steps:

1. Deactivate the Control Wizard's toggle button in the Toolbox (make sure the button has a raised appearance), so you won't get any help from a wizard, and then click the Option Group tool in the Toolbox.

2. Click the Field List button on the toolbar to display the Field List window and choose the paRating column of your query.

3. Hold down the mouse button and drag the field pointer to a position to the right of the Rating option group you created in the preceding section. Then release the mouse button to create an option group of the default size.

   When you create a bound option group by dragging a field from the Field List window, the option group name is automatically assigned to the Caption property of the associated label.

**4.** Resize the option group frame so that it is the same size as the other Rating option group. Apply the bold attribute to the option group's label.

Option buttons, toggle buttons, and check boxes within bound frames inherit many of their properties, such as Control Source, from the frame. The option frame provides the binding of these tools when they are inside of a frame. Therefore, you don't use the field list with these controls. Adding multiple copies of a control is easier if you double-click the tool's button in the Toolbox to lock the tool on. (Click the tool at any time to unlock it.) To add five option buttons to assign values to the paRating field, perform the following steps:

**1.** Double-click the Option Button tool.

**2.** Using the crosshair as a reference to the upper-left corner of an imaginary rectangle that surrounds the option button, drop the option button at the appropriate location in the option group frame. When the option button symbol enters the option group frame, the button, frame, and contents appear in reverse video as shown in Figure 13.24.

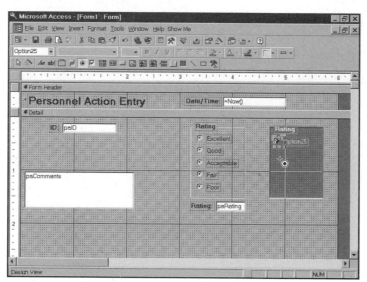

**FIG. 13.24** Manually adding a second option button to an option frame.

**3.** Repeat step 2 four times to include a total of five Rating option buttons inside of the Rating option group frame. The labels of the buttons are assigned numbers in the sequence in which they were added.

**4.** Click the Option Button tool in the Toolbox again to unlock this tool; Access automatically changes back to the pointer tool.

**5.** Edit the labels to read the following from top to bottom: **Excellent**, **Good**, **Acceptable**, **Fair**, and **Poor**, corresponding to the option values of 9, 7, 5, 3, and 1, respectively.

6. Double-click the option button at the top to display its Properties window. Click the Data tab, and then replace 1 with **9** as the Option Value in the Data Properties list. A default Option Value is assigned in sequence from 1 to the number of buttons in the frame.

7. Repeat step 6 for the four remaining buttons, replacing the default values 2, 3, 4, and 5 with **7**, **5**, **3**, and **1**, respectively. No two buttons in an option frame can have the same value.

8. To test the entries, click the Form View button on the toolbar. The form appears as shown in Figure 13.25.

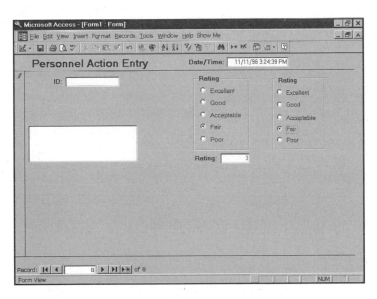

**FIG. 13.25**  The option group frame and option buttons displayed in Form view.

9. Using the record selection buttons, choose a record to edit. If you previously assigned ratings with odd-numbered values, the option button that corresponds to the value is selected.

10. Click the option buttons in sequence to verify that the proper numeric values appear in the Rating text box.

11. Click the Design View toolbar button to return to Design view.

12. You won't need either of the Rating option group boxes currently on the form, so delete both.

The drop-down lists and combo boxes you learn about in the following sections of this chapter are a better control type to use than an option group for the relatively large number of choices available in the ratings field. Option groups are best for choosing one of only three or four choices.

If you have a Yes/No field in the table, you can use a single option button bound to a field (not inside an option frame) to create the Yes/No values for the user.

---

**Note**

If you add a button or a check box within a frame with the Field List drag-and-drop method, the button is independently bound to the selected field rather than to the field through the option frame. In this case, the button's Properties window doesn't include the Option Value property, and the button assigns Yes/No values to the field.

An independently bound button inside an option frame doesn't follow the rules of the option frame; you can choose this button and another button simultaneously.

Adding independently bound buttons within option frames results in the assignment of inconsistent values to fields.

---

### Using the Clipboard to Copy Controls to Another Form

Access's capability of copying controls and their properties to the Windows Clipboard allows you to create controls on one form and copy them to another. If you use a standard header style, you can copy the controls in the header of a previously designed form to a new form and edit the content as necessary. The form that contains the controls to be copied need not be in the same database as the destination form in which the copy is pasted. You can create a library of standard controls in a dedicated form that is used only for holding standard controls.

The Time/Date calculated text box is a candidate to add to the frmPersonnelActions form you created in Chapter 12, "Creating and Using Forms." You may want to add a Time/Date text box to the Form Header or Detail section of all your transaction forms. To add the Time/Date control to the frmPersonnelActions form, perform the following steps:

1.  Click the Design View button, and select the Time/Date control and its label by clicking the field text box.

2.  To copy the selected control(s) to the Clipboard, do one of the following: press Ctrl+C; click the Copy button on the toolbar; or choose Edit, Copy.

3.  Click the Show Database Window button on the toolbar. Then open the frmPersonnelActions form from the Database window in Design mode.

4.  Click the Detail section selection bar, and then do one of the following: press Ctrl+V; click the Paste button on the toolbar; or choose Edit, Paste. A copy of the control appears at the upper-left corner of the Detail section.

    Controls are pasted to the section of the form that is presently selected. You cannot drag controls between sections of a form.

5.  Position the mouse pointer over the copied option group so that the pointer becomes a hand symbol.

**6.** Hold down the mouse button and drag the option group to the position shown in Figure 13.26, and then release the mouse button.

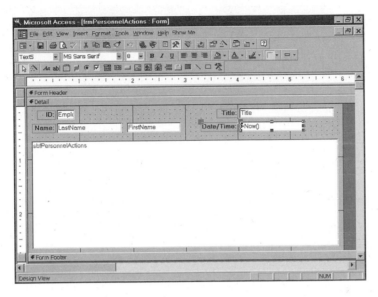

**FIG. 13.26**  Copying the Date/Time calculated field to the frmPersonnelActions form by using the Clipboard.

**7.** Click the Form View button on the toolbar. The Personnel Action Entry form appears as shown in Figure 13.27.

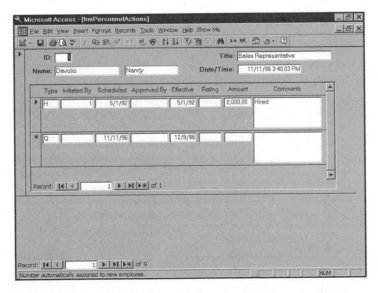

**FIG. 13.27**  The Date/Time text box displayed in Form view.

8. Return to Design mode, click the Save button to save your changes, and then click the Close window button to close the frmPersonnelActions form.

---

### Troubleshooting

*I've copied a control to another form, but when I attempt to use the form, I get an error message whenever that control gets the focus.*

When you copy a control to a form that uses a data source that is different from the one used to create the original control, you need to change the Control Source property to correspond with the field to which the new control is to be bound. Changing the Control Source property doesn't change the Status Bar Text, Validation Rule, or Validation Text properties for the new control source. You must enter the appropriate values manually.

---

### Using List Boxes and Combo Boxes

List boxes and combo boxes both serve the same basic purpose by enabling you to pick a value from a list, rather than type the value in a text box. These two kinds of list boxes are especially useful when you need to enter a code that represents the name of a person, firm, or product. You don't need to refer to a paper list of the codes and names to make the entry. The differences between list boxes and combo boxes are shown in the following list:

- *List boxes* don't need to be opened to display their content; the portion of the list that fits within the size of the list box you assign is visible at all times. Your choice is limited to values included in the list.

- *Drop-down combo boxes and drop-down lists* consume less space than list boxes in the form, but you must open these controls to select a value. Combo boxes in Access are drop-down lists plus a text box, not traditional combo boxes that display the list at all times. You can allow the user to enter a value in the text box element of the drop-down combo list or limit the selection to just the members in the drop-down list. If you limit the choice to members of the drop-down list (sometimes called a *pick list*), the user can still use the edit box to type the beginning of the list value—Access searches for a matching entry. This feature reduces the time needed to locate a choice in a long list.

Drop-down lists and combo boxes are two of the most powerful controls that Microsoft programmers developed for Access. The data source for these controls may be a table, a query, a list of values you supply, or the names of Access VBA functions. The boxes may have as many columns as you need to display the data for making the correct choice.

**Adding a Combo Box with a Table or Query as the Data Source.** In the majority of cases, you bind the drop-down list or combo box to a field so that the choice updates the value of this field. Two-column controls are most commonly used. The first column contains the code that updates the value of the field to which the control is bound, and the second column contains the name associated with the code. An example of where a limit-to-list, multiple-column, drop-down list is most useful is the assignment of supervisor and manager employee ID numbers to the paInitiatedBy and paApprovedBy fields in the frmPersonnelActionsEntry form. The Combo Box Wizard is used to add the paInitiatedBy drop-down list, and then you employ manual methods to add the paApprovedBy drop-down list in the two sections that follow.

**Using the Combo Box Wizard.** Designing combo boxes is a more complex process than creating an option group, so you're likely to use the Combo Box Wizard for most of the combo boxes you add to forms. Follow these steps to use the Combo Box Wizard to create the paInitiatedBy drop-down list that lets you select from a list of Northwind Traders' employees:

1. Open the frmPersonnelActionsEntry form (that you created and saved earlier in this chapter) from the Database window in Design mode if it is not presently open.

2. Click the Control Wizards button, if necessary, so that the wizards are turned on.

3. Click the Combo Box tool in the Toolbox. The mouse pointer turns into a combo box symbol while on the active surface of the form.

4. Click the Field List button to display the Field List window.

5. Drag the paInitiatedBy field to a position at the top and extreme right-hand edge of the Detail section of the form, opposite the paID field (look ahead to Figure 13.34). The first Combo Box Wizard dialog appears.

6. You want the combo box to look up values in the Employees table, so accept the default option button and then click Next (see Figure 13.28). Your selection specifies Table/Query as the value of the Record Source property of the combo box. The second Combo Box Wizard dialog appears.

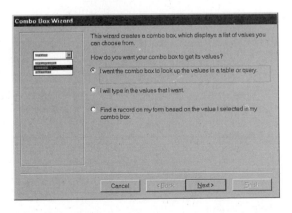

**FIG. 13.28** Selecting the source of list values in the opening dialog of the Combo Box Wizard.

7. Select Employees from the list of tables in the list (see Figure 13.29). Click Next to reach the third dialog.

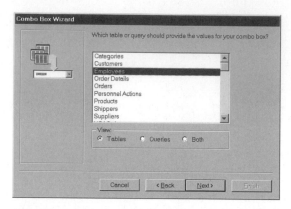

**FIG. 13.29** Selecting the Record Source property of the combo box.

8. You need the EmployeeID and LastName fields of the Employees table for your combo box. EmployeeID serves as the bound field, and your combo box displays the LastName field. EmployeeID is selected in the Available Fields list by default, so click the > button to move EmployeeID to the Selected Fields list. LastName is selected automatically, so click the > button again to move LastName to the Selected Fields list. Your Combo Box Wizard dialog appears as shown in Figure 13.30. This selection specifies the SQL SELECT query that serves as the value of the Row Source property and populates the combo box's list. Click Next to reach the fourth dialog.

9. The fourth dialog (see Figure 13.31) displays the value list for the combo box. Access has successfully determined that the EmployeeID field is the key field of the Employees table and has assumed (correctly) that the EmployeeID field is the bound field for the combo box. The Hide key column check box is selected by default; this option causes Access to hide the bound column of the combo box. The result is that, although you've selected two columns for the combo box, only one column (the LastName field) is displayed in the combo box's list. The EmployeeID column is hidden and used only to supply the data value for the paInitiatedBy field. Resize the LastName column by dragging the right edge of the column leftward—you want the column wide enough to display everyone's last name but not any wider than absolutely necessary. Click Next to continue to the fifth Combo Box Wizard dialog.

10. Your combo box supplies the EmployeeID value corresponding to the name you select to the paInitiatedBy field. You previously specified that the Control Source property is paInitiatedBy when you dragged the field symbol to the form in step 5. The Combo Box Wizard uses your prior selection as the default value of the Control Source property (see Figure 13.32), so accept the default value by clicking the Next button to display the sixth and final dialog.

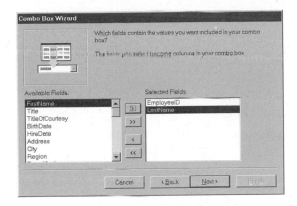

**FIG. 13.30**  Selecting the fields of the table with which to populate the combo box.

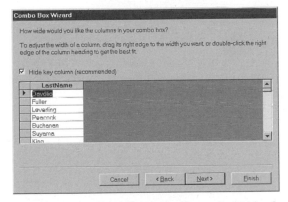

**FIG. 13.31**  Selecting the column width for the combo box and a hidden key field column.

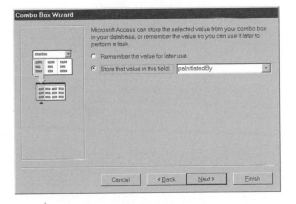

**FIG. 13.32**  Assigning the Control Source property value.

**11.** The last dialog lets you edit the label associated with the combo box (see Figure 13.33). Type **Initiated By:** and click Finish to add the combo box to your form. Your combo box in Design mode appears as shown in Figure 13.34.

**FIG. 13.33** The final Combo Box Wizard dialog allows you to edit the control's label.

**12.** Click the Form View button on the toolbar to test your combo box (see Figure 13.35). Change the Initiated By value to another person, such as Mr. Fuller, the Vice President of Sales, and then move the record pointer to make the change permanent. Return to the original record, and open the combo box to verify that the combo box is bound to the paInitiatedBy field.

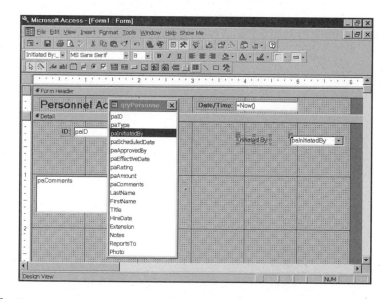

**FIG. 13.34** The new combo box in Design mode.

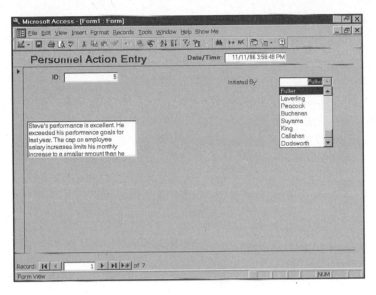

**FIG. 13.35**  The Initiated By combo box in Run mode.

**Adding a Combo Box Manually.** As mentioned previously in this chapter, it is good practice to create control objects manually so that you learn the properties associated with each control. To substitute a two-column combo box that you create yourself for the paApprovedBy text box in the frmPersonnelActionsEntry form, complete the following steps:

1. Open the frmPersonnelActionsEntry form from the Database window in Design mode if it is not presently open.

2. If necessary, click the Control Wizards button in the Toolbox to disable the wizards (make sure the button is raised).

3. Click the Field List button on the toolbar to open the Field List window if it isn't already open.

4. Click the Combo Box tool in the Toolbox. Then click paApprovedBy in the Field List window, and drag and drop the field symbol underneath the Initiated By combo box you created previously. Size the combo box and its label to match the Initiated By combo box above it.

5. Double-click the combo box to display the Properties window, and then click the Data tab.

6. The source of the data for the combo box is the Employees table, so the default value of the Row Source Type property, Table/Query, is correct. Place the caret in the Row Source property box, open the list, and select Employees as the value of the Row Source property.

7. When you choose the name of a table or query as the Row Source property, all fields of the table or columns of the query are included automatically as combo box columns. The first two columns of the Employees table provide EmployeeID to be assigned as the value of the paApprovedBy field and LastName to identify the supervisor. Click the Format tab in the Properties window, and type **2** as the Column count to create a two-column combo box.

8. The default width of each column of the combo box is 1 inch. The EmployeeID column can be less than 1 inch wide because it consists of only one digit. In the Column Width box, type **0.2** as the width of the first column followed by a semicolon (or comma) separator, and type **0.8** as the width of the second column. Access adds inch units (") for you.

9. Click the Data tab to return to the data properties. The first column of the Employees table—EmployeeID—contains the value to assign to the paApprovedBy field, so the default value of the Bound Column property—column 1—is correct. You can choose any column by its number (in left-to-right sequence) as the value to be assigned to the field to which the combo box is bound.

10. Only an employee included in the Employees table can initiate or approve a Personnel Action, so open the Limit to List drop-down list and select Yes. (If you want to allow the user to add a value not included in the list, accept the default No value. Adding a user-defined value is not applicable in this case.) The Personnel Actions form appears as shown in Figure 13.36.

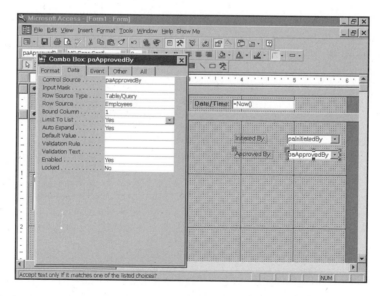

**FIG. 13.36** Setting the values of the data properties of the combo box.

11. Click the Form View button on the toolbar to test the combo boxes. When you open the Approved By combo box, the display appears as shown in Figure 13.37.

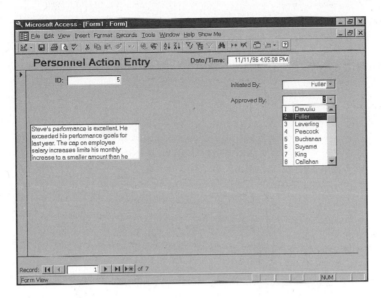

**FIG. 13.37**  The Approved By multiple-column combo box in Form view.

Notice that the EmployeeID field value appears in the text element of the combo box rather than the LastName field value, as in the Initiated By combo box. If the bound column appears in the list element, the value of the bound column appears in the text element.

**12.** To display only the name of the supervisor or manager in the list and text boxes, return to Design mode and change the value of the Column Widths property (on the Format tab of the Properties window) of the first column to 0 from 0.2 inches. This action causes only the second column to appear in the text box and list elements of the combo box, making the two combo boxes of your form consistent.

As an example, if the fourth column of the table or query is the column you want to display in the combo box, type three zero-width columns preceding the width you want for the column that you want to display (0,0,0, and 1).

List and combo boxes are a boon to developers because Access does all of the work. Users who, in early versions of Clipper or later versions of dBASE, wrote the code necessary to create a popup window that contains a drop-down list, will appreciate the ease of creating a combo box in Access.

**Using the Query Builder to Populate a Combo Box.** If the Row Source Type property for a combo box is Table/Query, you can substitute a SQL statement for a named table or query as the value of the Row Source property. In the case of queries, the advantage of the substitution is that this process prevents the list of queries in the Database window from becoming cluttered with named queries used to create a multitude of combo boxes. For either tables or queries, you can choose only the fields or columns you want for the text box, eliminating the need to hide columns. In addition, you can specify a sort order for the list element of your combo box.

To invoke Access 97's Query Builder to create a SQL statement for populating the Approved By combo box, follow these steps:

1. Return to or open frmPersonnelActions in Design mode, and double-click the paApprovedBy combo box to open the Properties window. Click the Data tab of the Properties window, if necessary.

2. Select the Row Source property, and click the Build button (...) to launch the Query Builder. You previously selected the Employees table as the value of the Row Source property, so the message box shown in Figure 13.38 appears. Click Yes to confirm the replacement and open the Query Builder window.

**FIG. 13.38** Confirming you want to build a Row Source query based on the Employees table.

3. The Query Builder's window is identical in most respects to the Query Design window, but its title and behavior differ. The Employees table automatically appears in the upper pane. Drag the EmployeeID and LastName fields to columns 1 and 2 of the Query Design grid.

4. You want an ascending sort on the LastName field, so select Ascending in the Sort list box. Your query design appears as shown in Figure 13.39.

   When you use the Query Builder, you can test the results of your query by clicking the Run button on the toolbar. Access executes the query and displays a Datasheet view of the query's results.

5. Click the Close window button to close the Query Builder. The message box shown in Figure 13.40 appears for confirmation of your change to the Row Source property value, instead of asking if you want to save your query. Click Yes and the SQL statement derived from the graphical QBE design appears as the value of the Row Source property.

6. SQL statements, especially those created by Access, have a tendency to be lengthy. With the caret in the Row Source property text box, press Shift+F2 to display the SQL statement in the Zoom box, as shown in Figure 13.41.

   In this case, the field name prefix is applied in each field reference, although it is really only necessary in the FROM clause because just one table is involved in the query.

Switch to Form view to test the effect of adding the sort (the ORDER BY clause) to the query. Writing your own SQL statements to fill combo boxes with values is discussed in Chapter 24, "Working with Structured Query Language."

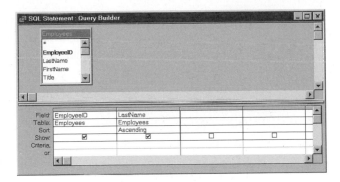

**FIG. 13.39**   The design of the query to create the SQL statement for the Approved By combo box.

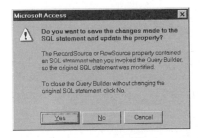

**FIG. 13.40**   Confirming your change to the Row Source property value.

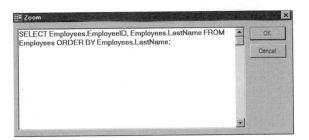

**FIG. 13.41**   The new SQL statement for the Approved By combo box's Row Source property displayed in the Zoom box.

**Creating a Combo Box with a List of Static Values.** Another application for list boxes and combo boxes is picking values from a static list of options that you create. A drop-down list to choose a Rating value saves space in a form compared with the equivalent control created with option buttons within an option frame. As you design more complex forms, you find that display "real estate" becomes increasingly valuable.

The option frame you added to the frmPersonnelActionsEntry form provides a choice of only five of the possible 10 ratings. To add a drop-down list with the Combo Box Wizard to allow entry of all possible values, perform the following steps:

1. Click the Design View button on the toolbar (if the form isn't already in Design view). Click the Control Wizards button in the Toolbox, if necessary, to enable the Combo Box Wizard (the button should have a sunken appearance).

2. Open the Field List window, then click the Combo Box tool in the Toolbox. Drag the paRating field symbol to a position underneath the Approved By combo box you added previously. The first Combo Box Wizard dialog appears.

3. Select the I Will Type in the Values That I Want option, and then click Next to reach the second dialog.

4. The Rating combo box requires two columns: the first column contains the allowable values of paRating, 0–9, and the second column contains the corresponding description of each rating code. Enter **2** as the number of columns.

5. Access assigns Row Source property values in column-row sequence; you enter each of the values for the columns in the first row, and then do the same for the remaining rows. Type **9 Excellent**, **8 Very Good**, **7 Good**, **6 Average**, **5 Acceptable**, **4 Marginal**, **3 Fair**, **2 Sub-par**, **1 Poor**, **0 Terminated**, as shown in Figure 13.42 (don't type the commas). Click Next to reach the third dialog.

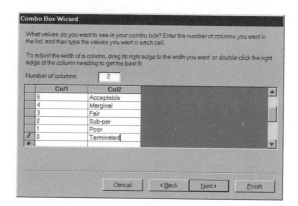

**FIG. 13.42** Entering Static values in the Combo Box Wizard's datasheet.

6. Set the widths of the columns you want by dragging the edge of each column header button to the left, as shown in Figure 13.43. If you don't want the rating number to appear, drag the left edge of column 1 fully to the left to reduce its width to 0. When you've adjusted the column widths, click Next to reach the fourth dialog.

7. Select Col1, the rating number code, as the bound column for your value list—that is, the column containing the value you want to store or use later (see Figure 13.44); this column must contain unique values. Click Next to reach the fifth dialog.

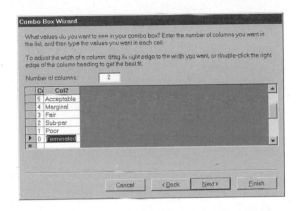

**FIG. 13.43**  Setting the column widths of the combo box.

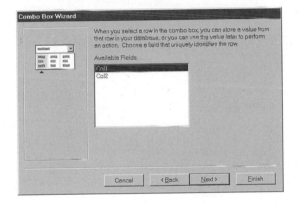

**FIG. 13.44**  Choosing a column to bind to a field of a table or a column of a query.

8. Accept the default value (the paRating field) in this dialog by clicking Next to go to the final dialog of the Combo Box Wizard.

9. Type **Rating:** as the label for the new combo box control, and click Finish to complete the combo box specification and return to Design mode.

10. Open the Properties window for the combo box, then click the Data tab in the Properties window. Set Limit to List to Yes to convert the drop-down combo to a drop-down list. The frmPersonnelActionsEntry form's Data properties appear as shown in Figure 13.45. Notice that Access has added commas after the numbers, semicolons between the row entries, and quotation marks to surround the text values in the Row Source property. You use this format when you enter list values manually.

11. Click the Form View button on the toolbar to display the form. The open Rating static-value combo box appears as shown in Figure 13.46.

Another opportunity to use a static-value combo box is as a substitute for the Type text box. Several kinds of performance reviews exist: Quarterly, Yearly, Bonus, Salary, Commission, and so on, each represented by an initial letter code.

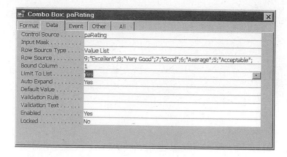

**FIG. 13.45** The data properties for the value list combo box.

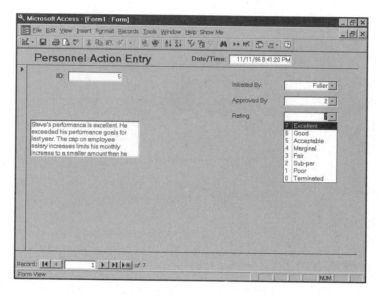

**FIG. 13.46** The Rating static-value combo box opened in Form view.

> **Note**
>
> You can improve the appearance of columns of labels and associated text, list, and combo boxes by right-aligning the text of the labels and left-aligning the text of the boxes. Select all of the labels in a column with the mouse, and click the Align Right button on the toolbar. Then select all of the boxes and click the Align Left button.

### Creating a Combo Box to Find Specific Records

The Combo Box Wizard in Access 97 includes a third type of combo list box that you can create—a combo list that locates a record on the form based on a value you select from the list. You can use this type of combo box, for example, to create a Find Last Name box on the frmPersonnelActionsEntry form that contains a drop-down list of all last names from the Employees table. Thus, you can quickly find Personnel Actions records for those employees.

To create a combo box that finds records on the form based on a value you select in the combo box, follow these steps:

1. Click the Design View button on the toolbar (if the form isn't already in Design view). Click the Control Wizards button in the Toolbox, if necessary, to enable the Combo Box Wizard (the button should have a sunken appearance).

2. Click the Combo Box tool in the Toolbox, and then click and drag on the surface of the form's Detail section to create the new combo box in a position underneath the Rating drop-down box you created previously. Release the mouse, and the first Combo Box Wizard dialog appears.

3. Click the Find a Record on My Form Based On the Value I Selected in My Combo Box option. Click Next to reach the second dialog.

4. Scroll the Available Fields list until the LastName field is visible. Click to select this field, and then click the > button to move it to the Selected Fields list. Click Next to reach the third dialog.

> **Note**
>
> When creating a combo box to find records, select only one field. The combo box won't work for finding records if you select more than one field for the combo box's lists.

5. The Combo Box Wizard now displays a list of the field values from the column you just selected. Double-click the right edge of the LastName column to get the best column-width fit for the data values in the column, and then click Next to go to the fourth and final step of the wizard.

6. Type **Zoom to:** as the label for the new combo box, and then click Finish to complete the new combo box control. Your form should appear as shown in Figure 13.47.

7. Click the Form View button on the toolbar to display the form. The open Zoom To combo box appears as shown in Figure 13.48.

When you create this type of combo box, the Combo Box Wizard automatically creates an Access VBA event procedure for the After Update property of the combo box (refer to the Property window in Figure 13.47). An event procedure is a VBA procedure that Access executes automatically whenever a particular event occurs—in this case, updating the combo box. Chapter 28, "Writing Visual Basic for Applications Code," describes how to write Access VBA code and Chapter 30, "Responding to Events with VBA 5.0" describes how to write event-handling procedures.

To view the event procedure code that the wizard created for your new combo box, open the Properties window for the Zoom to: combo box, click the Events tab in the window, select the After Update property text box, and then click …. Access opens the Code Builder window shown in Figure 13.49. After you've looked at the code, click the Close window button to close the Code Builder window and return to Design mode.

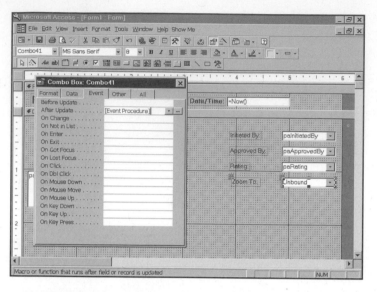

**FIG. 13.47**    The new combo box that will find a record on the form based on a value selected in the combo box.

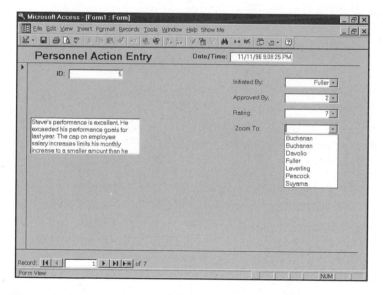

**FIG. 13.48**    The combo box for finding a record on the form in Form view.

To use a combo box of this type, select a value from the list. As soon as you select the new value, Access updates the combo box's text box, which then invokes the Access VBA code for the After Update event procedure. The VBA code in the After Update procedure finds the first record in the form's record set with a matching value and displays it. You can only use this type of combo box to find the first matching record in a record set.

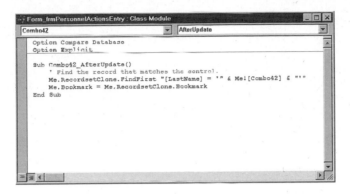

**FIG. 13.49** The Module window for the After Update event property of the locating combo box.

Because the field on the form is based on the LastName column of the form's underlying query, you'll see an entry in the list for each and every last name entry in the record set produced by the qryPersonnelActions query. If, let's say, more than one Personnel Action record exists for Steve Buchanan, then Buchanan appears in the combo list as many times as there are records for him. To display a unique list of last names to be located on the form, change the Row Source property to obtain the LastName field values for the combo box list through a SQL statement based on a query from the Employees table.

To change the Row Source property, follow the procedure you learned in the "Using the Query Builder to Populate a Combo Box" section, earlier in this chapter: open the Properties window of the Zoom To combo box, click the Data tab, select the Row Source text box, and then open the Query Builder. Change the query so that it uses the Employees table, as shown in Figure 13.50. You should also change the Limit to List property value to Yes.

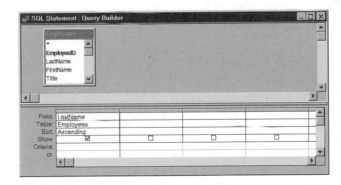

**FIG. 13.50** The Query Builder window for the new combo box, showing the Employees table selected as the new Row Source property value for the combo box.

### Creating a Tab Control

The Tab control is an important addition to Access 97's Toolbox. With the Tab control, you can easily create multipage forms in a tabbed dialog, similar to the tabbed pages you've seen in the Properties window, in the Options dialog, and elsewhere in Access.

The Tab control is a relatively easy and very efficient alternative to creating multipage forms with the Page Break control. You can use the Tab control to conserve space on-screen, and to show information from one or more tables. This section shows you how to add a Tab control to a form. You also learn to set the important properties of the Tab control as a whole, as well as the properties of individual pages of the Tab control.

To add a Tab control to the frmPersonnelActionsEntry form, follow these steps:

1. Click the Design View button on the toolbar if the frmPersonnelActionsEntry form isn't already in Design view. No wizard for the Tab control exists, so the status of the Control Wizards button doesn't matter.

2. Click the Tab Control tool in the Toolbox; the mouse cursor changes to the Tab Control icon while it is over the active surface of the form.

3. Click and drag on the surface of the Detail section of the form to create the new tab control near the bottom center of the form (see Figure 13.51).

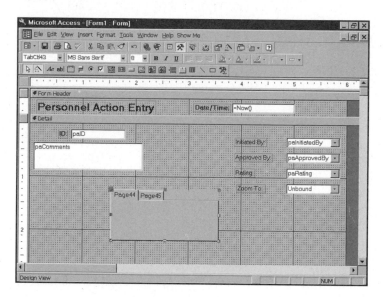

**FIG. 13.51** A new Tab control showing the default two pages and default page captions.

Access creates the new Tab control when you release the mouse button, as shown in Figure 13.51. By default, Access creates a Tab control with two pages. Each page's tab displays the name of the page combined with a sequential number corresponding to the number of controls you placed on your form in this work session. The next few sections describe how to change the page tab's caption, add or delete pages in the Tab control, add controls to the pages, and set the page and Tab control properties.

**Adding Tab Control Pages.** Depending on the data you want to display and how you want to organize that data, you may want to include more than two pages in your Tab control. To add a page to a tab control, follow these steps:

**1.** Click the tab of the page you want the new page inserted in front of. Access brings the page you select to the front of the Tab control.

**2.** Using the right mouse button, click the edge of the Tab control (the blank space along the top of the tab rows is easiest). Access displays the popup menu shown in Figure 13.52.

**3.** Choose Insert Page; Access inserts a new page in the Tab control in front of which-ever existing page is currently selected.

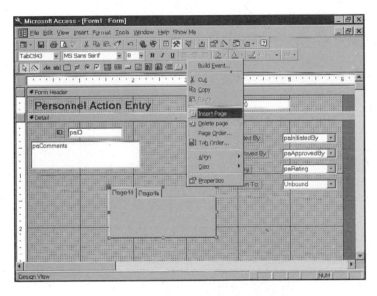

**FIG. 13.52**  The popup menu for adding, deleting, or changing the order of pages in a Tab control.

**Changing the Page Order.** Because Access adds new pages to a Tab control in front of the currently selected page, it isn't possible to add a new page at the end of the existing tab pages. As a result, if you want the new Tab control page to appear as the last page in the Tab control, you'll need to change the order of pages in the Tab control. You may also want to change the order of Tab control pages as you work with and test your forms—in general, you should place the most frequently used (or most important) page at the front of the Tab control. To change the order of pages in a Tab control, follow these steps:

**1.** Using the right mouse button, click the edge of the Tab control. Access displays the Tab control's popup menu (see Figure 13.52).

2. Choose Page Order; Access displays the Page Order dialog shown in Figure 13.53.

3. In the Page Order list, select the page whose position you want to change.

4. Click the Move Up or Move Down buttons, as appropriate, until the page is in the position you want.

5. Repeat steps 3 and 4 until you have arranged the Tab control pages in the order you want, and then click OK to close the Page Order dialog and apply the new page order to the Tab control.

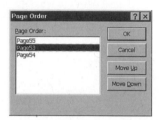

**FIG. 13.53**   Changing the page order of the tab control in the Page Order dialog.

**Deleting a Tab Control Page.** At some point, you may decide that you don't want or need a page in a Tab control. The frmPersonnelActionsEntry form only needs two pages in its Tab control. If you added a page to the Tab control by following the steps at the beginning of this section, you can delete a page from the Tab control by following this procedure:

1. Click the page tab of the page you want to delete; Access brings that page to the front of the Tab control.

2. Right-click the edge of the Tab control; Access displays the Tab control's popup menu (refer to Figure 13.52).

3. Choose Delete Page; Access deletes the currently selected Tab control page.

**Setting the Tab Control's Properties.** Two sets of properties govern the appearance and behavior of a tab control. A set of properties exists for the entire Tab control, and a separate set of properties exists for each page in the Tab control. The following list summarizes the important properties of the Tab control and its pages; the remaining property settings for the Tab control and its pages are similar to those you've seen for other controls (height, width, color, and so on):

- *Caption*. This text property controls the text that appears on the page's tab and applies to individual Tab control pages only. If this property is blank (the default), then the page's Name property is displayed on the page's tab.

- *MultiRow*. This Yes/No property applies to the Tab control as a whole and controls whether the Tab control can display more than one row of tabs. (The Options dialog, reached by choosing <u>T</u>ools, <u>O</u>ptions, is an example of a multirow tabbed dialog.) The default setting is No; in this case, if there are more tabs than fit in the width of the Tab control, Access displays a scroll button in the Tab control. If you change this property to Yes and there are more page tabs than will fit in the width of the Tab control, Access displays multiple rows of tabs.

■ *Picture*. You can display an icon in any or all of the page tabs in a Tab control using this property, which applies to pages only. You can use any of Access's built-in icons or insert any bitmapped (.bmp) graphic file as the page's tab icon.

■ *Style*. The Style property applies to the Tab control as a whole and controls the style in which the Tab control's page tabs are displayed. The default setting, Tabs, produces the standard page tabs you're accustomed to seeing in the Properties window and in various dialogs in Access and Windows. Two other settings are available: Buttons and None. The Buttons setting causes the page tabs to display as command buttons in a row across the top of the Tab control. The None setting causes the Tab control to omit the page tabs altogether. Use the None setting if you want to control which page of the Tab control has the focus with command buttons or option buttons located outside of the Tab control. However, using command buttons external to the Tab control to change pages requires writing Access VBA program code. You should use the default Tabs setting unless you have a very specific reason for doing otherwise—using the Tabs setting ensures that the appearance of your Tab controls is consistent with other portions of the Access user-interface. Using this setting also saves you the effort of writing VBA program code.

■ *TabFixedHeight* and *TabFixedWidth*. These two properties, which apply to the Tab control as a whole, govern the height and width of the page tabs in the control, respectively. The default setting for these properties is 0. When these properties are set to 0, the Tab control sizes the page tabs to accommodate the size of the Caption for the page. If you want all of the page tabs to have the same height or width, enter a value (in inches or centimeters, depending on your specific version of Access) in the corresponding property text box.

To display the Properties window for the entire Tab control, right-click the edge of the Tab control, and select <u>P</u>roperties from the resulting popup menu (see Figure 13.52). Alternatively, click the edge of the Tab control to select it (clicking the blank area to the right of the page tabs is easiest), and then click the Properties button on the toolbar to display the Properties window.

To display the Properties window for an individual page in the Tab control, click the page's tab to select it, and then click the Properties button on the toolbar to display the page's Properties window.

The Tab control in the frmPersonnelActionsEntry form uses one page to display company information about an employee: the employee's job title, supervisor, company telephone extension, hire date, and photo. The second Tab control page displays a history of that employee's personnel actions. Follow these steps to set the Caption property for the frmPersonnelActionsEntry form's Tab control:

1. Click the Design View button on the toolbar if the frmPersonnelActionsEntry form isn't already in Design view.

2. Click the first page of the Tab control to select it, and then click the Properties button on the toolbar to display that page's Properties window (see Figure 13.54).

3. Click the Format tab, if necessary, to display the Format properties for the Tab control page.

4. Type **Company Info** in the Caption property's text box.

5. Click the second page of the Tab control to select it; the contents of the Property dialog change to show the properties of the second Tab control page.

6. Type **History** in the Caption property text box for the second page of the Tab control, and close the Properties window.

Figure 13.54 shows the Tab control with both page captions set and the first page of the Tab control selected. Notice that the sizing handles visible in the Tab control are *inside* of the control—this position indicates that the page, not the entire control, is currently selected. When the entire Tab control is selected, the sizing handles appear at the edge of the Tab control.

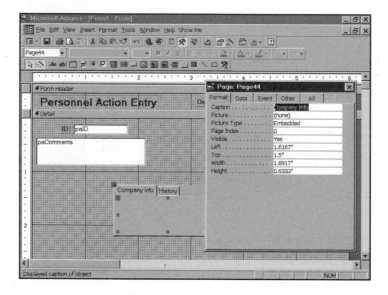

**FIG. 13.54** Setting the Caption property of a page in the Tab control.

**Placing Other Controls on Tab Pages.** You can place any of Access's 16 other types of controls on the pages of a Tab control—labels, text boxes, list boxes, even subforms. To add a control of any type to a Tab control's page, follow this procedure:

1. In Design view, click the page tab you want to add the control to; Access selects the page and brings it to the front of the Tab control.

2. Add the desired control to the Tab control's page using the techniques presented earlier in this chapter for creating controls on the Detail or Header/Footer sections of a form.

   Alternatively, you can copy controls from the same or another form and paste them into the Tab control's pages by using the same techniques you learned for copying and pasting controls on a form's Detail and Header/Footer sections. You cannot drag controls from the form's Detail or Header/Footer sections onto the Tab control's page.

As you proceed with the examples in this chapter and complete the frmPersonnelActionsEntry form, you'll place various bound and unbound controls on the pages of the Tab control.

### Changing One Control Type to Another

If you made a mistake in selecting the type of control in earlier versions of Access, you would have to delete the control and start over. Access 97 allows you to "morph" a control of one type to become a control of a compatible type. You can change an option button to a check box, for example, or you can change a toggle button to an option button. You can't, however, change a text box to an object frame or other control with a different field data type. To change a control to a different type, follow these steps:

1. In the form's Design view, select the control whose type you want to change.

2. Choose F<u>o</u>rmat, <u>C</u>hange To to see a submenu of form control types. Only the submenu choices for control types that are compatible with the selected control are enabled.

3. Select the control type you want from the submenu. Access changes the control type.

## Completing the Main Personnel Actions Entry Form

In the following sections of this chapter, you learn how to use the Control Wizards to help you add a subform to a form. Before you add the subform, however, you should complete the main frmPersonnelActionsEntry form. Like the form that you created with the Form Wizard in Chapter 12, the purpose of this form is to display records from the Personnel Actions table so that a user can view the history of an employee's personnel actions. The form also conveniently provides a means of adding new personnel action records.

In the form you created in Chapter 12, you viewed the history of personnel records and also added new records in a tabular subform, while information from the Employees table was displayed only on the main form. In this custom form, you place fields from the Personnel Actions table on the main form to make adding new records to the Personnel Actions table easier, and the Tab control is used to contain the subform as well as additional information from the Employees table. The subform on the second page of the Tab control displays only historic personnel action records. The frmPersonnelActionsEntry form has fields from the Personnel Actions table on both the main form and the subform, and it uses the qryPersonnelActions form you created at the beginning of this chapter as the form's data source. If you were creating a full-scale human resources database application, you might choose the Employees table as the data source for the form and design a subform for editing the Personnel Actions table. You might then put this subform on a third Tab control page or display the history in a subform of the subform.

---

**Note**

Creating a form and subform that are both based on the same underlying table—in this example, the Personnel Actions table—is a somewhat unconventional but totally acceptable database application design method. Most forms that employ subforms employ a base table (such as Employees) or a query whose data source is a base table as the record source of the main form. A related table or query based on a related table serves as the record source of the subform. Many of the forms of Northwind.mdb demonstrate the conventional form-subform design. Our form example, frmPersonnelActionsEntry, uses a common underlying table for both the form and subform to illustrate some of the unique characteristics of this approach to one-to-many form design.

---

To complete the main form, follow these steps (refer to Figure 13.55 for field placement):

1. Click the Design View button on the toolbar (if the frmPersonnelActionsEntry form isn't already in Design view).

2. If necessary, click the Toolbox button to enable the Control Wizards (make sure the button has a sunken appearance), and then click the Field List button on the toolbar to open the Field List dialog if it isn't already open.

3. Drag the LastName field from the Field List to a position to the right of the ID field text box; when you release the mouse, Access creates a text box for the field. Edit the field's label to read **Name:**.

4. Drag the FirstName field from the Field List to a position to the right of the LastName field; delete the FirstName field's label.

5. Drag the paType field from the Field List to a position at the right of the FirstName field.

6. Repeat step 5 for the paScheduledDate, paEffectiveDate, and paAmount fields (refer to Figure 13.55 for field positioning and sizing). You'll need to move the Approved By, Rating, and Zoom To fields that you placed on the form earlier in this chapter.

**7.** Resize the paComments field so that it is underneath the paID and name fields (see Figure 13.55). Next, resize the Tab control so that it fills the width of the form and extends from an area below the paComments field to the bottom of the form. The Tab control needs to be as large as possible in order to display the most data in the subform that you'll later add to its second page.

**8.** Click the first tab of the Tab control to bring it to the front, and then drag the Title field from the Field List to a position near the top left corner of the Company Info page.

**9.** Repeat step 8 for the ReportsTo, Extension, and HireDate fields (refer to Figure 13.55 for field placement).

**10.** Drag the Photo field onto the right side of the Tab control's first page and delete its label (the fact that this field displays a photo of the employee is enough to identify the field). Size and position the Photo field at the right edge of the Tab control's page; you may need to resize the Tab control and the form after inserting the Photo field.

**11.** Double-click the Photo field to display its Properties window, click the Format tab, and select the Size Mode property's text box (see Figure 13.56). Select Zoom from the drop-down list to have the employee photo scaled down to fit the photo field's size.

> **Tip**
>
> Use the Format Painter to format the text labels of the fields. Using the Format Painter is described in Chapter 12, "Creating and Using Forms."

**12.** Drag the Notes field onto the bottom left side of the Tab control's first page and delete its label. Refer to Figure 13.55 for placement and sizing.

**13.** Use the techniques you learned in Chapter 12 to move, rearrange, and change the label formats to match the appearance of Figure 13.55. (All labels are bold and right-aligned.)

**14.** Test your new fields by clicking the Form View button on the toolbar. Your form appears as shown in Figure 13.57.

> **Note**
>
> In Figure 13.55, all of the toolbars and the Form Design window's rulers have been turned off so that you can see the entire form in Design view.

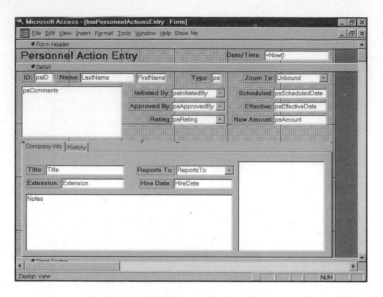

**FIG. 13.55** The frmPersonnelActionsEntry form in Design view, showing the final placement and formatting of the main form fields and the first page of the tab control.

**FIG. 13.56** Setting the Photo field's Size Mode property so that photos are scaled to fit the size of the field on the form.

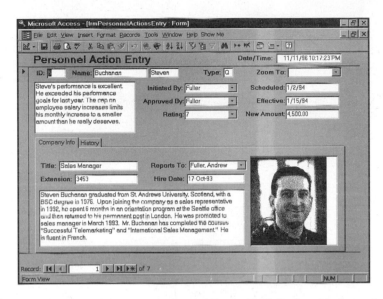

**FIG. 13.57**   The frmPersonnelActionsEntry form of Figure 13.55 displayed in Form view.

# Creating a Subform Using the Subform/Subreport Wizard

The frmPersonnelActionsEntry form needs a subform in which to view the history of personnel actions for the employee displayed in the main part of the form. Access 97's new Subform/Subreport Wizard makes it possible for you to create a new subform at the same time that you add the subform field to the main form or, as in this example, a page in a Tab control. To do so, follow these steps:

1. Click the Design View button on the toolbar if the frmPersonnelActionsEntry form isn't already in Design view.

2. Click the Control Wizards button to enable the Control Wizards if the button isn't already down.

3. Click the second tab of the Tab control to bring its second page to the front. Click the Subform button in the Toolbox, and then click at the top-left corner of the second tab control page. Access displays the first dialog of the Subform/Subreport Wizard.

4. You can use this wizard either to create a new subform based on a table or query or to insert an existing subform (see Figure 13.58). (You learn how to insert an existing form as a subform in the section "Creating and Using Continuous Forms" later in this chapter.) For this exercise, select the Table/Query option, and click Next to reach the second dialog.

5. The Subform/Subreport Wizard asks you to indicate which table or query the new subform is based on and which fields appear in the subform (see Figure 13.59).

Select Query: qryPersonnelActionsSubform in the Tables and Queries drop-down list. To expedite field selection, click the >> button to copy all of the fields to the Selected Fields list. Select the paComments field in the Selected Fields list, and click the < button to remove this field from the list. Click Next to reach the third dialog.

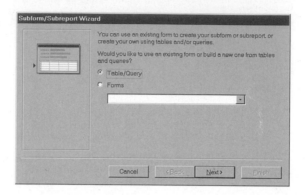

**FIG. 13.58**   Choosing whether to use an existing form as the subform or to use a table or query to create a new subform.

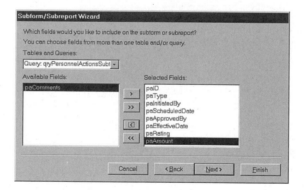

**FIG. 13.59**   Selecting the data source and fields for the new subform.

6. The wizard now asks you to specify the link between the main form and the subform. You may select from a list of possible relationships that Access has determined, or define your own link. Click the Define my own option, and the Wizard dialog changes to show four drop-down list text boxes (see Figure 13.60).

7. In the upper Form/Report Fields list, select paID as the linking field; in the upper Subform/Subreport Fields list, also select paID as the linking field. Click Next to go to the fourth and final dialog of the wizard.

8. Type **sbfTest** as the name of this new subform, and click Finish to complete the subform's specifications (see Figure 13.61). Access creates and saves the new form; it inserts the completed subform into the subform field on the main form and sizes

the subform field to accommodate the new subform (see Figure 13.62). The text you entered for the subform's name is assigned to the label for the subform. The subform itself is saved under the same name.

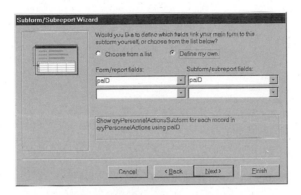

**FIG. 13.60**   Defining the link between the main form and the subform.

**FIG. 13.61**   Entering a name for your new subform.

9. Click the Form View button on the toolbar to check the appearance of the new subform. Your form appears as shown in Figure 13.63.

As you can see from Figure 13.63, the Subform/Subreport Wizard always creates new subforms with Datasheet view. In many cases, this is acceptable—or even desirable. For the frmPersonnelActionsEntry form, however, a better view of the data can be achieved with a tabular continuous form view of the data. The following sections of this chapter explain the advantages of a tabular continuous form and guide you through the steps necessary to create such a form and insert it as a subform into the main form.

**10.** Close the frmPersonnelActionsEntry form by clicking the Close window button. Click No when Access asks if you want to save changes to the form's design.

You'll create a much more useful form in the next section.

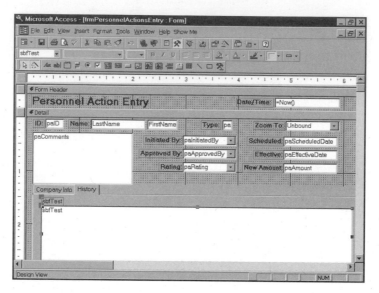

**FIG. 13.62**  The completed subform field in Design view.

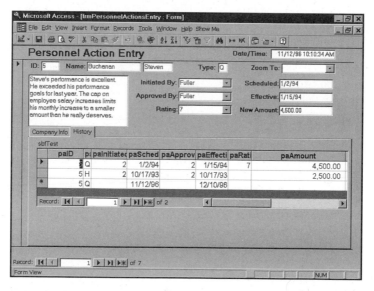

**FIG. 13.63**  The new subform in Form view.

# Creating and Using Continuous Forms

Continuous forms are useful for displaying data contained in multiple records of a table or query in a format other than Datasheet view. The sbfPersonnelActions subform you created in Chapter 12, for example, is designed only to display the most recent Personnel Action records for an employee. Editing isn't allowed in the subform, so you don't need the field headers, record selection buttons, and scroll bars associated with Datasheet view. These graphic elements focus more attention on the subform than is deserved. You need a plain vanilla display of the history for the employee; this basic display requires a continuous form.

The Form Wizard offers the choice of creating a tabular continuous form, so using the Form Wizard is the quickest method of creating a plain, vanilla subform. To create a tabular continuous form with the Form Wizard, perform the following steps:

1. Click the Forms tab, then click New in the Database window to create a new form. Access displays the New Form dialog.

2. Select qryPersonnelActionsSubform as the source of data for the new form.

3. Select Autoform: Tabular from the list at the top of the New Form dialog, then click OK. Access immediately creates a tabular form based on the fields in the query qryPersonnelActionsSubform and then displays the form in Form view (see Figure 13.64).

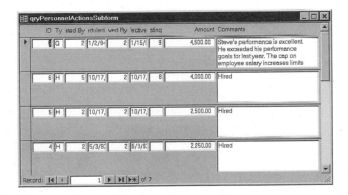

**FIG. 13.64**  The tabular form produced by the Form Wizard from qryPersonnelActionsSubform.

4. Click the Save button on the toolbar; Access displays the Save As dialog.

5. Type **sbfTest1** as the name of the form, and click OK.

The Form Wizard created the tabular form using the qryPersonnelActionsSubform query as the data source. To customize the form to make the size and appearance compatible with the frmPersonnelActionsEntry form, follow these steps:

1. Click the Design View button to switch the sbfTest1 form to Design view, and then maximize the form window.

2. Delete the paID and paComments fields from the Detail section of the form. Delete the paID and paComments labels from the Form Header section of the form.

3. Click the Form Header bar, and use the Fill/Back Color button on the Formatting toolbar to change the background color (Back Color property) to white. Change the background color of the Detail section to white, also.

4. Drag a selection box around all of the labels in the Form Header section. Click the Bold button on the Formatting toolbar, and then click the Center button.

5. Choose Format, Size, to Fit; then choose Format, Size, To Grid. This sequence of commands makes the label text boxes large enough to display their entire contents and then sizes them to the nearest regular grid mark. This sizing makes it easier to position the labels into columns with the fields in the Detail section of the form.

6. Choose Format, Horizontal Spacing, Make Equal to spread the field labels apart evenly so that they are touching each other without overlapping.

7. Drag the Type label to the upper-left corner of the Form Header section; position the remaining labels along the top edge of the same section, one grid mark apart from each other (see Figure 13.65). Then drag the Detail section header bar to the bottom of the labels.

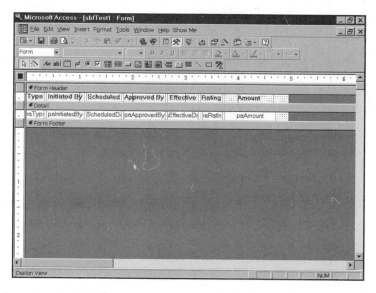

**FIG. 13.65** The modified tabular form in Design view.

8. Drag the paType field to the upper-left corner of the Detail section, and resize it to match the Type label in the Form Header section. Position each of the remaining fields from left to right under the corresponding label in the Form Header section, sizing each field to match its label. Drag the Form Footer section header bar to the bottom of the text boxes.

9. Drag a selection box around all of the fields in the Detail section of the form, and then click the Center button on the formatting toolbar to center the data in each field. Click the Line/Border Color button, and then click Transparent to make all of the fields' borders transparent.

10. Choose Edit, Select Form, and then click the Properties button on the toolbar.

11. Click the Data tab, and set the value of the Allow Edits property to No, the Allow Deletions property to No, and the Allow Additions property to No. These changes prevent records displayed by this form from being edited, added to, or deleted.

12. Click the Format tab, set the value of the Scroll Bars property to Neither, and then set the Record Selectors and Navigation Buttons properties to No. The default GridX and GridY property values of 24 correspond to the grid spacing of the frmPersonnelActionsEntry form.

13. Close the Properties window, and drag the right edge of the form leftward until the form is just under 5 inches wide. Your form should look like the one you saw in Figure 13.65.

14. Click the Form View button on the toolbar. The continuous form displays all records in the Personnel Actions subquery, as shown in Figure 13.66.

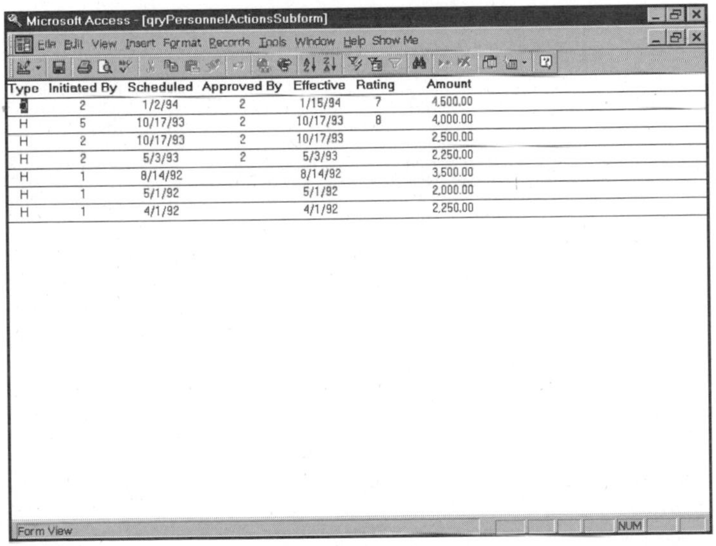

| Type | Initiated By | Scheduled | Approved By | Effective | Rating | Amount |
|------|-------------|-----------|-------------|-----------|--------|--------|
| S | 2 | 1/2/94 | 2 | 1/15/94 | 7 | 4,500.00 |
| H | 5 | 10/17/93 | 2 | 10/17/93 | 8 | 4,000.00 |
| H | 2 | 10/17/93 | 2 | 10/17/93 | | 2,500.00 |
| H | 2 | 5/3/93 | 2 | 5/3/93 | | 2,250.00 |
| H | 1 | 8/14/92 | | 8/14/92 | | 3,500.00 |
| H | 1 | 5/1/92 | | 5/1/92 | | 2,000.00 |
| H | 1 | 4/1/92 | | 4/1/92 | | 2,250.00 |

**FIG. 13.66** The appearance of the continuous form of Figure 13.65 in Form view.

Creating Forms and Reports

**15.** Choose <u>F</u>ile, Save <u>A</u>s/Export. Select Within the Current Database As, and type **sbfPersonnelActionsTab** in the New Name text box. Click OK to save the form under its new name. Click the Close window button to close the form.

Now, you need to add the tabular form you just created as a subform in the Tab control of the frmPersonnelActionsEntry form. You'll use the Subform/Subreport Wizard to insert this form into the Tab control on your main form. (Whether you add the subform directly on a form or onto a page of a Tab control, the procedure is the same.) To complete this procedure, perform the following steps:

**1.** Open the frmPersonnelActionsEntry form, and click the Design View button on the toolbar.

**2.** If necessary, click the Control Wizards button on the toolbar to enable the Control Wizards (the button position should be down).

**3.** On the Tab control, click the tab of the second page to bring it to the front. (This is the History tab you created earlier in this chapter.)

**4.** Click the Subform button on the Toolbox, and then click at the upper-left corner of the Tab control's second page. Access displays the first dialog of the Subform/Subreport Wizard.

**5.** To insert an existing form, select the Forms option, and then select sbfPersonnelActionsTab in the drop-down list (see Figure 13.67). Click Next to reach the second dialog.

**FIG. 13.67**   Using the Subform/Subreport Wizard to insert an existing form as a subform.

**6.** The wizard asks you to specify the link between the main form and the subform. You may select from a list of possible relationships that Access has determined or define your own link. Click the Define my own option. Select paID in the upper Form/Report Fields list, and select paID in the upper Subform/Subreport Fields list. Click Next to go to the third dialog.

**7.** Accept the default label name for the new subform field, and click Finish to complete the new subform field. Access now inserts the form you specified as a subform on the second page of the Tab control and sizes the subform field to accommodate the new subform, as shown in Figure 13.68.

**8.** Delete the label from the subform field, and resize the field so that it fills the width of the main form. Scroll the Form Design window downward, and resize the subform field so that it fills the Tab control page (see Figure 13.69). At this point, your form should be approximately 3.5 inches high, and the Tab control should be about 2 inches high.

**9.** Click the Form View button on the toolbar to check the appearance of the new  subform. Your form appears as shown in Figure 13.70 after clicking the History tab to display the second page of the Tab control. (Refer to Figure 13.57 for a view of the completed form showing the Company Info page of the Tab control.) If the subform displays scroll bars or a record selector, close the Personnel Action Entry form and reopen it from the Database window to remove these features (called *adornments*).

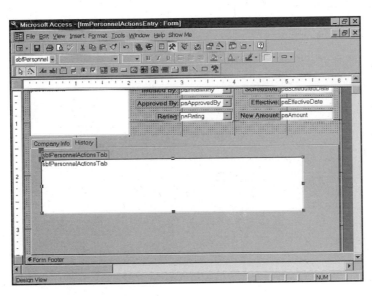

**FIG. 13.68** The new subform field for the sbfPersonnelActionsTab form, inserted by the Subform/Subreport Wizard.

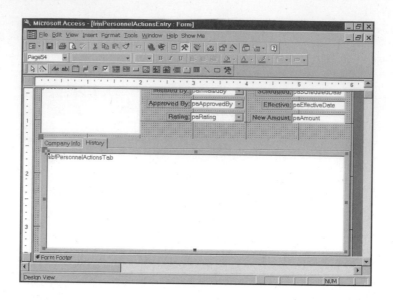

**FIG. 13.69** The modified sbfPersonnelActionsTab form in Design view.

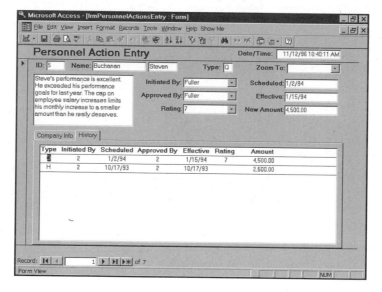

**FIG. 13.70** The completed subform and main form in Form view.

> **Note**
>
> Delete the vertical scroll bar when all control objects of the noncontinuous form fit in a maximized form window. The horizontal scroll bar need not be present when record selectors are used. Unnecessary graphic elements are distracting and have a negative influence on the overall appearance of a form.

**10.** Choose File, Save, and then click the Close window button to close the frmPersonnelActionsEntry form.

The frmPersonnelActionsEntry form's fields and field formatting are essentially complete. In a real-world application, you would now adjust the tab order of the form and test the form by entering and editing records—you learned to do these steps in Chapter 12, "Creating and Using Forms."

# Overriding the Field Properties of Tables

Access uses the table's property values assigned to the fields as defaults. The form or subform inherits these properties from the table or query on which the form is based. You can override the inherited properties, except for the Validation Rule property, by assigning a different set of values in the Properties window for the control. Properties of controls bound to fields of tables, or queries that are inherited from the table's field properties are shown in the following list:

- Format
- Decimal Places
- Status Bar Text
- Validation Rule
- Validation Text
- Default Value
- Typeface characteristics (such as Font Name, Font Size, Font Bold, Font Italic, and Font Underline)

Values of field properties that you override with properties in a form apply only when the data is displayed and edited with the form. You can establish validation rules for controls bound to fields that differ from properties of the field established by the table, but you can only narrow the rule. The table-level validation rule for the content of the paType field, for example, limits entries to the letters H, S, Q, Y, B, and C. The validation rule you establish in a form cannot broaden the allowable entries; if you add T as a valid choice by editing the validation rule for the paType field to InStr("HSQYBCT",[PA Type])>0, you receive an error when you type **T**.

However, you can narrow the range of allowable entries by substituting `InStr("SQYB",[PA Type])>0`. Notice that you can use expressions that refer to the field name in validation rule expressions in forms; such expressions are not permitted in table validation rule expressions in Access 97.

# Adding Page Headers and Footers for Printing Forms

Access allows you to add a separate pair of sections, Page Header and Page Footer, that appear only when the form prints. You add both of these sections to the form at once by choosing View, Page Header/Footer. The following list shows the purposes of Page Headers and Footers:

- *Page Header* sections enable you to use a different title for the printed version. The depth of the Page Header can be adjusted to control the location where the Detail section of the form is printed on the page.

- *Page Footer* sections enable you to add dates and page numbers to the printed form.

Page Header and Page Footer sections appear only in the printed form, not when you display the form on-screen in Form view. The frmPersonnelActionsEntry form in Design mode with Page Header and Page Footer sections added is shown in Figure 13.71. The Tab control has been deleted so that both the Form Footer and Page Footer sections appear in the window. Usually, you need to use the vertical scroll bar to display these sections in Design mode.

With the Display When (Format) property of the Properties window for the Form Header and Form Footer sections, you can control whether these sections appear in the printed form. In Figure 13.71, the Form Header duplicates the information in the Page Header (except for the Date/Time label and text box), so you don't want to print both. To control when a section of the form prints or is displayed, perform the following steps:

1. Double-click the title bar of whichever section of the form you want to change; this opens the related Properties window. (The Page Header and Page Footer sections don't have a Display When property; these sections only appear when printing.)

2. Click the Format tab if the formatting properties aren't already showing. Click to drop down the Display When list.

3. To display but not print this section in Form view, select Screen Only.

4. To print but not display this section, select Print Only.

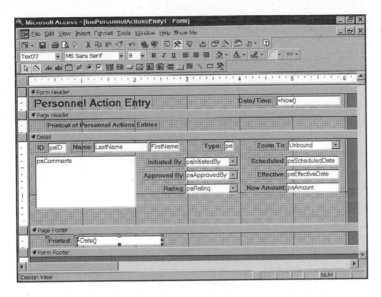

**FIG. 13.71**  The frmPersonnelActionsEntry form with Page Header and Page Footer sections added.

# Chapter 14

# Printing Basic Reports and Mailing Labels

The final product of most database applications is a report. In Access, a report is a special kind of continuous form that is designed specifically for printing. Access combines data in tables, queries, and even forms to produce a report that you can print and distribute to people who need or request it. A printed version of a form can serve as a report, which often is the case for reports designed for decision support, one of the topics of Chapter 20, "Adding Graphics to Forms and Reports." By printing a continuous form, you can create a report that displays some or all of the values of fields in a table or query.

This chapter describes how you create relatively simple reports, including multicolumn mailing labels, using the Report Wizards. The chapter also tells how you modify the design of the wizard's reports to suit your particular needs. The next chapter describes how you design a report from scratch without using the Report Wizards.

## Differences and Similarities Between Forms and Reports

Most methods of creating transaction-processing forms, which you learned about in Chapter 11, "Using Action Queries," and Chapter 12, "Creating and Using Forms," also apply to reports. The following list details the principal differences between reports and forms:

- Reports are intended for printing only and, unlike forms, aren't designed for display in a window. When you view an 8 1/2×11-inch report in Print Preview, its content is not legible. In the zoomed (full-page) view, only a portion of the report is visible in the Print Preview window.

- You cannot change the value of the underlying data for a report with a control object from the toolbox as you can with forms. With reports, Access disregards user input from option buttons, check boxes, and the like. You can use these controls, however, to indicate the status of Yes/No option buttons, check boxes, and fields with values derived from multiple-choice lists.

■ Reports do not provide a Datasheet view. Only Print Preview and Report Design views are available.

■ You can create an unbound report that isn't linked to a source of data. Unbound reports are used as "containers" for individual subreports that use unrelated data sources.

■ The Printer Setup dialog controls the minimum left, right, top, and bottom printing margins of reports. If a report is less than the printable page width, the report's design determines the right margin. You can increase the left margin over the default setting by positioning the print fields to the right of the display's left margin.

■ In multicolumn reports, the number of columns, the column width, and the column spacing are controlled by settings in the Printer Setup dialog, not by controls that you add or properties that you set in Design mode.

Access reports share many characteristics of forms, including the following:

■ *Report Wizards* can create the three basic kinds of reports: single-column, groups/ totals, and mailing labels. You can modify as necessary the reports that the Report Wizard creates. The function of the Report Wizard is similar to that of the Form Wizard discussed in Chapter 12, "Creating and Using Forms," and Chapter 13, "Designing Custom Multitable Forms."

■ *Sections* include report headers and footers that appear once at the beginning and at the end of the report, and page headers and footers that print at the top and bottom of each page. The report footer often is used to print grand totals. Report sections correspond to similarly named form sections.

■ *Group sections* of reports, as a whole, comprise the equivalent of the Detail section of forms. Groups often are referred to as *bands*, and the process of grouping records is known as *banding*. You can add Group Headers that include a title for each group, and Group Footers to print group subtotals. You can place static (unbound) graphics in header and footer sections and bound graphics within group sections.

■ *Controls* are added to reports from the Access toolbox and then moved and sized with their handles.

■ *Subreports* can be incorporated into reports the same way you add subform controls within main forms.

# Types of Access Reports

Reports created by Access fall into six basic types, also called *layouts*, that are detailed in the following list:

■ *Single-column reports* list in one long column of text boxes the values of each field in each record of a table or query. A label indicates the name of a field, and a text box to the right of the label provides the values. Access 97's AutoReport feature creates a single-column report with a single click of the toolbar's AutoReport button. Single-column reports are seldom used because the format wastes paper.

■ *Tabular reports* provide a column for each field of the table or query and print the value of each field of the records in rows under the column header. If you have more columns than can fit on one page, additional pages print in sequence until all of the columns are printed; then the next group of records is printed. Figure 14.1 shows in Report Preview mode a tabular report that is based on Northwind.mdb's Customers table.

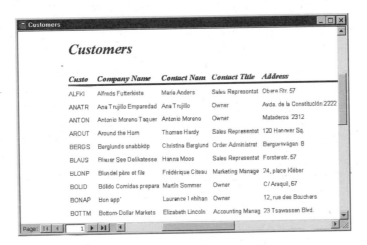

**FIG. 14.1**   A preview of a tabular report created from Northwind.mdb's Customers table.

■ *Multicolumn reports* are created from single-column reports by using the "newspaper" or "snaking" column approach of desktop publishing and word processing applications. Information that doesn't fit in the first column flows to the top of the second column, and so on. The format of multicolumn tables wastes less paper but the uses are limited because the column alignment is unlikely to correspond with what you want.

■ *Groups/totals reports* are the most common kind of report. Access groups/totals reports summarize data for groups of records and then adds grand totals at the end of the report.

■ *Mailing labels* are a special kind of multicolumn report designed to print names and addresses (or other multifield data) in groups. Each group of fields constitutes a cell in a grid. The design of the stock adhesive label on which you are printing determines how many rows and columns are on a page.

■ *Unbound reports* contain subreports based on unrelated data sources, such as tables or queries.

The first four types of reports use a table or query as the data source, as do forms. These kinds of reports are said to be *bound* to the data source. The main report of an unbound report is not linked to a table or query as a data source. The subreports contained by an unbound report, however, must be bound to a data source. *Unbound reports* allow you to incorporate subreports that are bound to independent tables or queries.

III

**Creating Forms and Reports**

# Creating a Grouping Report with the Report Wizard

This section shows you how to use the Report Wizard to create a grouping report based on data in the Products and Suppliers tables of the Northwind Traders sample database. (Like the Form Wizard, the Report Wizard allows you to create reports that contain data from more than one table without first creating a query.) This report displays the quantity of each specialty food product in inventory, grouped by product category.

To create an inventory report, you modify the basic report created by the Report Wizard. The process of creating a basic report with the Report Wizard is similar to the process that you used to create a form in Chapter 12, "Creating and Using Forms." An advantage of using the Report Wizard to introduce the topic of designing Access reports is that the steps for this process are parallel to the steps you take when you start with a default blank report. Chapter 15, "Preparing Advanced Reports," explains how to start with a blank report and create more complex reports.

To create a Products on Hand by Category report, follow these steps:

1. Click the Reports tab in the Database window, and then click the New button. Access displays the New Report dialog (see Figure 14.2).

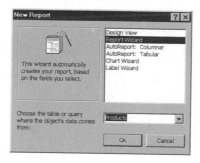

**FIG. 14.2** The New Report dialog, in which you select the report's type and data source.

2. Like forms, reports require a data source, which can be a table or query. Select the Products table from the choices offered in the New Report dialog's drop-down list (refer to Figure 14.2). Select Report Wizard in the list in the dialog's upper-right corner and click OK. The Report Wizard displays its opening dialog.

3. The fields that you choose to display represent rows of the report. You want the report to print the product name and supplier so that users do not have to refer to another report to associate codes with names. The fields from the Products table that you need for this report are CategoryID, ProductID, ProductName, SupplierID, and UnitsInStock. With the > button, select these fields in sequence from the Available Fields list (see Figure 14.3). As you add fields to the Selected Fields list, Access removes the field names from the Available Fields list. Alternatively, you can double-click the field name in the Available Fields list to move the field name to

the Selected Fields list. The fields appear from left to right in the report based on the top-to-bottom sequence in which the fields appear in the Selected Fields list.

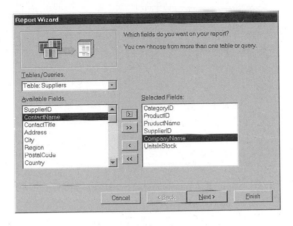

**FIG. 14.3**   Selecting the fields of a report from one or more tables or queries in the Report Wizard's opening dialog.

4. To avoid having to look up Supplier ID numbers in a separate report, you need to add to this report the CompanyName field from the Suppliers table. Open the Tables/Queries drop-down list and select Table: Suppliers (refer to Figure 14.3).

5. Instead of presenting the supplier name as the report's last field, you want the report's CompanyName column to follow the SupplierID report column. Select the SupplierID field in the Selected Fields list. Now select the CompanyName field from the Available Fields list and click the > button. Access moves the CompanyName field from the Available Fields list and inserts the field into the Selected Fields list, after the SupplierID field and before the UnitsInStock field (refer to Figure 14.3). Choose Next to continue with the second Wizard dialog, shown in Figure 14.4.

> **Note**
>
> If you want to change the field order shown in the right pane of Figure 14.4, use the < button to move the field back to the Available Fields list. You can retrace your steps to correct an error by clicking the Back button whenever it is activated. The Finish button accepts all defaults and jumps to the end of the wizard, so you shouldn't use this button until you're familiar with the Report Wizard's default selections.

6. The Report Wizard asks you to choose how you want to view the data in the report. Notice the Show Me More Information button near the left center of the wizard dialog. Click this button to display the first of a series of hint dialogs for the Report Wizard (see Figure 14.5). If you click the Show Me Examples option, Access displays additional hint screens. These screens use examples from the Sales Reps, Customers, and Orders tables to show you the different groupings that the Report Wizard can automatically add to the report. Click the Close button repeatedly until you return to the Report Wizard dialog shown in Figure 14.4.

III

**Creating Forms and Reports**

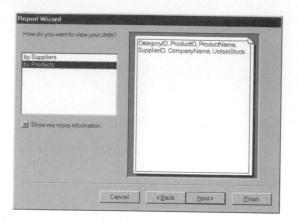

**FIG. 14.4**  Choosing how you want to view your data in the second Report Wizard dialog.

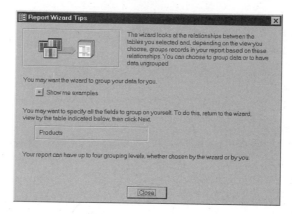

**FIG. 14.5**  The first of the Report Wizard's hint screens.

7.  For this report, you select your own groupings. Select By Products in the list, and choose Next to continue with the third Report Wizard dialog.

8.  The Report Wizard asks whether you want to add any grouping levels to the report. Select the CategoryID field in the list, and click the > button to establish the grouping By Products category. The Report Wizard dialog now appears as shown in Figure 14.6.

9.  Click the Grouping Options button. The Report Wizard displays the Grouping Intervals dialog shown in Figure 14.7. By changing the grouping interval, you can affect how Access groups data in the report. For numeric fields, you can group items by 10s, 50s, 100s, and so on. For text fields, you can group items based on the first letter, the first three letters, and so on.

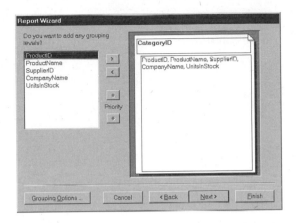

**FIG. 14.6**   Selecting grouping levels for your report.

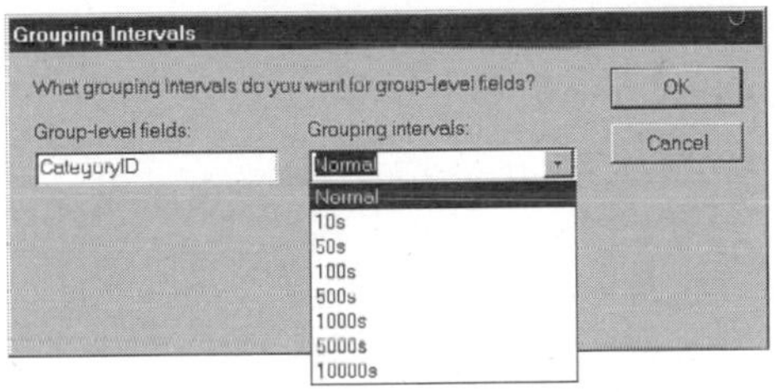

**FIG. 14.7**   Selecting grouping intervals for your report.

---

**Note**

If your application uses a text-coding scheme, such as BEVA for alcoholic beverages and BEVN for nonalcoholic beverages, you can combine all beverages in a single group by selecting 1st 3 Characters from the Grouping Intervals list. Access 97 provides this option for numeric fields and for fields of the Text data type.

---

**10.** This report doesn't require any special grouping interval, so select Normal in the Grouping Intervals list, and click OK to return to the Report Wizard's third dialog (refer to Figure 14.6). Choose Next to continue with the fourth wizard dialog.

**11.** You can sort the records within groups by any field that you choose (see Figure 14.8), with up to four different sorted fields. The dialog does not offer CategoryID as a choice because the records are grouped in this field, and the field on which the grouping is based is therefore automatically sorted. Select ProductID in the first drop-down list. By default, the sort order is ascending; if you want a descending sort order, click the button to the right of the drop-down list. (This button is a toggle control; click it again to return to an ascending sort.)

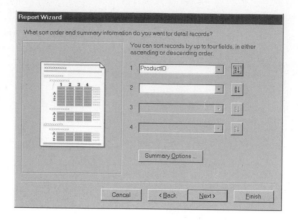

**FIG. 14.8**   Selecting a sort order for fields within groups.

12. Choose the Summary Options button to display the Summary Options dialog (see Figure 14.9). If you want to add summary information to a report column, set the options for that column in this dialog. The Report Wizard lists all of the numeric fields on the report that aren't AutoNumber fields and offers you check boxes to select a Sum, Average, Minimum, and Maximum for that report column. Depending on the check boxes that you select, the Report Wizard adds those summary fields to the end of the report.

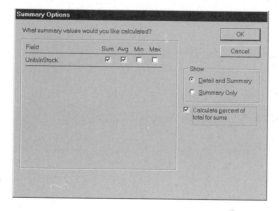

**FIG. 14.9**   Choosing the summary data you want included in your report in the Summary Options dialog of the Report Wizard.

The Show option group allows you to select whether the report shows the summary fields only or the full report with the summary fields added at the end of each group and at the end of the report. For this report, select the Sum and Avg check boxes, the Detail and Summary option, and the Calculate Percent of Total for Sums check box. (The Calculate Percent of Total for Sums check box displays the group's total as a percentage of the grand total for all groups.) Click OK to return to the Report Wizard dialog.

13. Choose Next to continue with the fifth Wizard dialog, shown in Figure 14.10. The Report Wizard asks you to select one of six layout styles for your report. The window in the left side of the wizard dialog shows a preview of the layout style that you select. For this report, choose Stepped in the Layout option group.

14. By default, the Report Wizard selects the Adjust the Field Width So All Fields Fit on a Page check box. As a rule, you should select this option to save paper and make your report more legible. In the Orientation option group, you select the report's printing orientation. Make sure that you select the Portrait option. Choose Next to continue with the sixth Report Wizard dialog.

15. Select one of the predefined report styles for your report. The window on the left shows a preview of the selected style (see Figure 14.11). (You can customize or create your own styles for the Report Wizard to use. This activity is described in the "Using AutoFormat and Customizing Report Styles" section later in this chapter.) Select the Compact style, and then choose Next to continue with the seventh and final Report Wizard dialog.

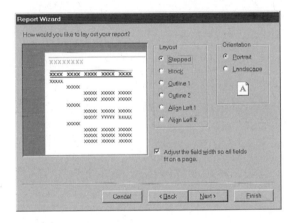

**FIG. 14.10**   Choosing a layout format for a report.

16. Type **Products On Hand by Category** as the title for the new report; the Report Wizard also uses this title as the name of the saved report it creates (see Figure 14.12). Select the Preview the Report option and click Finish to complete your report specification. The Report Wizard creates the report and displays it in print preview mode. (To get Help with the report, click the Display Help on Working with the Report? check box.)

Figure 14.13 shows the basic report that the Report Wizard creates. Use the vertical and horizontal scroll bars to position the preview as shown. (Leave the report in Print Preview mode for now because you use this report as the basis for examples in subsequent sections of this chapter.)

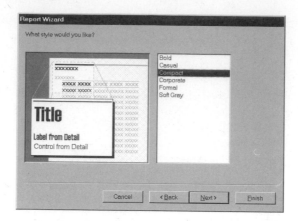

**FIG. 14.11**   Selecting a style for your report.

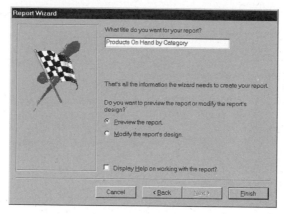

**FIG. 14.12**   Giving your report a name and title, and choosing how you want to view the completed report.

◀◀ See "Using Lookup Fields in Tables," p. 332

In Figure 14.13, notice that the report appears to have duplicate columns—a Supplier column, which lists the name of the product's supplier, and the Company Name column, which also lists the name of the product's supplier. The reason for this duplication is twofold:

- A Caption property is set for the SupplierID field of the Products table. This property establishes an alias for the field. The Report Wizard substitutes the text in the Caption property for the field name in field labels on the report.

- The SupplierID field of the Products table is defined as a lookup field. Therefore, Access automatically looks up the value that corresponds to the SupplierID code in the Suppliers table and displays that value, rather than the actual code number stored in the field.

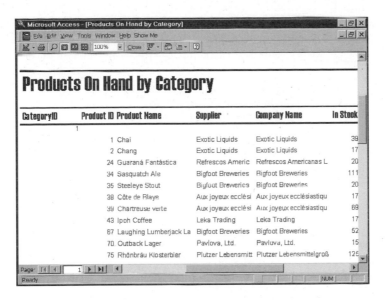

**FIG. 14.13**  The basic report created by the Report Wizard, shown in a maximized window.

When you view the lookup field in Design view, a nonfunctional drop-down list button (see Figure 14.14 in the next section, "Using Access's Report Windows") designates lookup fields. This report doesn't need to include the CompanyName field of the Suppliers table because the SupplierID field is a lookup field.

With a few simple modifications, you can obtain a finished report with the information necessary to analyze Northwind's current inventory. (See "Modifying a Basic Report Wizard Report" later in this chapter.)

# Using Access's Report Windows

The windows that you use to design and run Access reports are easier to use than those windows that you use for other basic Access functions. To open an existing Access report, click the Report tab in the Database window and then select a report name from the Database window. If you click the Design button or the New button to create a new report, the Design Mode toolbar appears with the buttons listed in Table 14.1.

| Table 14.1 | Standard Toolbar Buttons in Report Design Mode | |
| --- | --- | --- |
| **Button** | **Function** | **Menu Choice** |
| | Selects Print Preview to display how your report appears when printed. You can print the form from the Print Preview window. (Same as the Print Preview button.) | File, Print Preview |
| | Saves the current report. | File, Save |

(continues)

**Table 14.1 Continued**

| Button | Function | Menu Choice |
|---|---|---|
| | Prints the report without displaying the Print dialog. Access prints the report using the current printer settings. | Not applicable |
| | Selects Print Preview to display how your report appears when printed. You can print the form from the Print Preview window. | File, Print Preview |
| | Starts the spelling checker to check the selected label control's spelling. | Tools, Spelling |
| | Cuts the selected object(s) from the report and puts it on the Clipboard. | Edit, Cut |
| | Copies the selected object(s) from the report onto the Clipboard. | Edit, Copy |
| | Pastes the Clipboard's contents onto the report. | Edit, Paste |
| | Copies formatting from the selected object to another object of a similar type. | Not applicable |
| | Undoes the last change that you made to the report. | Edit, Undo |
| | Inserts a new Hyperlink control or allows you to edit an existing Hyperlink control. | Insert, Hyperlink |
| | Toggles the display of the Web toolbar. | not applicable |
| | Displays a list of fields in the query or table that is the main report's data source. | View, Field List |
| | Displays or closes the toolbox. | View, Toolbox |
| | Displays the Sorting and Grouping dialog in which you can establish the structure of reports and the order in which the report presents the data. | View, Sorting and Grouping |
| | Applies your choice of several predefined report formats, including formatting for the text fonts and color settings. | Format, AutoFormat |
| | Opens the window in which you can edit event-handling code. | View, Code |
| | Displays the Properties dialog for the entire report, the sections of the report when you click the section divider bars, or the properties of a control when a control is selected. | View, Properties |
| | Displays a Build Wizard for the selected object or property in the report. This button is enabled only if Access has a builder for the selected item. | Not applicable |
| | Displays the Database window. | Window, 1 Database |

| Button | Function | Menu Choice |
|---|---|---|
| | Creates a new object. Click the arrow to the right of this button to see a drop-down list of objects that you can create. | Not applicable |
| | Displays the Microsoft Office Assistant that, in turn, displays help text related to the actions you are performing. | Help, Microsoft Access Help |

Many of the buttons listed in Table 14.1 serve the same purposes for both forms and reports. As is the case for Form Design mode, the Formatting toolbar's buttons for formatting text are enabled only when a control object that can contain text is selected. The Formatting toolbar for reports is identical to the Formatting toolbar for forms. The Formatting toolbar was described in Chapter 12, "Creating and Using Forms."

If you double-click the name of an existing report, or click the Preview button in the Database window, the report displays in Print Preview mode, which is the Run mode for reports. Table 14.2 lists the toolbar's buttons in Print Preview mode.

| **Table 14.2** | **Standard Toolbar Buttons in Report Print Preview Mode** | |
|---|---|---|
| **Button** | **Function** | **Menu Choice** |
| | Prints the report without displaying the Print dialog. The report is printed using the current printer settings. | Not applicable |
| | Toggles between full-page and full-size views of the report. Clicking the mouse when its pointer appears as the magnifying glass symbol produces the same effect. | View, Zoom |
| | Displays one full page. | View, Pages, 1 |
| | Displays two full pages. | View, Pages, 2 |
| | Displays a palette from which you can select several multiple-page views of the report. | |
| 100% | Changes the size of the view from 200 percent to 10 percent or fits the report to the window. | View, Zoom |
| Close | Closes Print Preview and returns to Report Design view or to the Database window. | File, Print Preview |
| | Displays a drop-down list of shortcut commands for Microsoft Office Links: Merge It, Publish It with MS Word, and Analyze It with MS Excel. | Tools, OfficeLinks |
| | Opens the Database window. | Window, 1 Database |
| | Creates a new object. Click the arrow at the right of this button to display a drop-down list of objects that you can create. | Not applicable |
| | Displays the Microsoft Office Assistant that, in turn, displays help text related to the actions you are performing. | Help, Microsoft Access Help |

Chapter 22, "Using Access with Microsoft Word and Mail Merge," discusses using the Office Links button to print reports as files in rich-text format. Chapter 21, "Using Access with Microsoft Excel," discusses printing files in Excel BIFF format. Chapter 15, "Preparing Advanced Reports," describes linking files created from reports to Microsoft Mail messages.

# Using AutoFormat and Customizing Report Styles

The AutoFormat toolbar button works the same way for reports as for forms. Chapter 12, "Creating and Using Forms," contains a detailed, step-by-step explanation of how to use Access 97's AutoFormat button and customize the predefined AutoFormat styles or create your own AutoFormat styles. Follow the instructions in the "Using AutoFormat" section of Chapter 12 to apply an AutoFormat style to a report or define or customize a report AutoFormat style. Access stores styles for reports and forms separately, so you'll need to create separate AutoFormat styles for your reports.

 ◀◀ See "Using AutoFormat," p. 411

As with forms, to create an AutoFormat style for customized reports, you must first create a report that contains controls that are formatted the way you want for your new style. You click the AutoFormat button on the toolbar and then click the Customize button in the AutoFormat dialog to customize the format.

# Modifying a Basic Report Wizard Report

The Report Wizard tries to create the optimum final report in the first pass. Usually, the wizard comes close enough to a finished product that you spend far less time modifying a wizard-created basic report than creating a report from the default blank template.

In the following sections, you use Access's report design features to make the report more attractive and easier to read.

### Deleting, Relocating, and Editing Existing Controls

The first step in modifying the wizard's report is to modify the existing controls on the report. You don't need to align the labels and text boxes precisely during the initial modification; the section "Aligning Controls Horizontally and Vertically" later in this chapter covers control alignment. To modify the wizard's report in order to create space for adding additional controls, follow these steps:

1. Click the Close button of the Print Preview toolbar to enter Report Design mode; click the Maximize Window button to maximize the design window, if necessary. The Products on Hand by Category report, as created by the Report Wizard, appears as shown in Figure 14.14.

**2.** The SupplierID and CompanyName fields are redundant in this report because the SupplierID field is a lookup field. Select the Company Name label in the Page Header section, then hold down the Shift key, and click the CompanyName field in the Detail section. Press Delete to remove the field and label from the report. (Don't worry about aligning the fields and labels yet.)

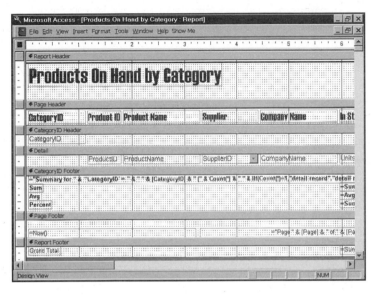

**FIG. 14.14**   The basic report in Design mode (all toolbars have been hidden to make the entire report visible).

**3.** This report is more useful if you include the dollar value of both the inventory and number of units on hand. To accommodate one or two additional columns, you must compress the fields' widths. CategoryID occupies a column, but you can display this column's content in the CategoryID footer (or header) without using the extra column space. Select and delete the CategoryID label from the Page Header section, and select and delete the CategoryID text box from the CategoryID Header section. For this report, you'll put the CategoryID name in the footer section of the group, so drag the Detail section bar upward to eliminate the space occupied by the CategoryID Header. Your report appears as shown in Figure 14.15.

**4.** All of the Page Header labels, Detail text boxes, and Totals text boxes in the CategoryID Footer and Report Footer sections must move to the left as a group. Click the Product ID label to select it, and then press and hold down Shift. Click the remaining Page Header labels, each of the Detail text boxes, the three summary field text boxes in the CategoryID Footer section, and the Grand Total text box in the Report Footer section. Then release Shift. (To select all of the labels and text boxes, you'll need to scroll the report to the right and left and up and down.)

5. Position the mouse pointer over the Product ID label at a location where the pointer turns into the graphic of a palm of a hand. Hold down the left mouse button and drag the selected fields to the left margin. Your report appears as shown in Figure 14.16.

6. You can more easily edit and position the labels if you left-justify them. Click a blank area of the report to deselect the group, select all of the Page Header labels, and click the Align Left button on the toolbar. Do the same for the Grand Total label in the Report Footer section.

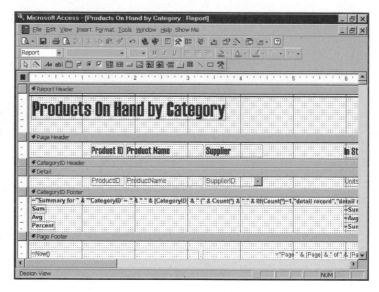

**FIG. 14.15** The basic report after deleting the CategoryID label and text box and closing the space for the CategoryID Header.

7. Edit the Product ID label to read **Product**, and edit the Units In Stock label to read only **Units**. Select all of the labels in the Page Header and choose Format, Size, To Fit. Resize the widths of the ProductID, SupplierID, and UnitsInStock text boxes in the Detail section to match the width of the labels in the Page Header. Relocate the labels to provide more space on the right side of the report, as shown in Figure 14.17.

8. By default, the Report Wizard adds to the CategoryID Footer a calculated field (visible in Figure 14.17) that displays the group's field name (CategoryID) and value to help identify the group footer's summary fields. For example, for CategoryID 1, the calculated field displays the following:

```
"Summary for 'CategoryID' = 1 (12 detail records)."
```

For this report, you want a more explicit description of the product category—more than just the CategoryID number. Delete this calculated field; you'll replace it in the next step.

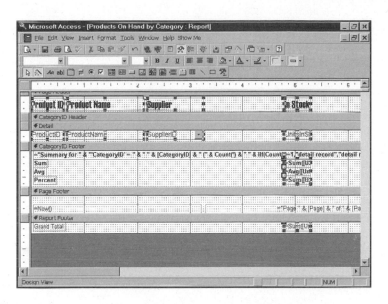

**FIG. 14.16**   Moving selected labels and text boxes to the report's left margin.

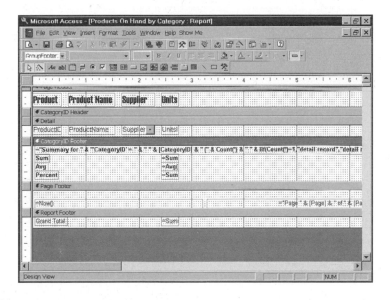

**FIG. 14.17**   The Products on Hand by Category report after you edit, resize, and relocate existing controls.

9. You now need to add a bound text box to identify the subtotal in the CategoryID Footer section. Click the Field List button on the toolbar. Select CategoryID from the list in the Field List window.

10. Click and drag the field symbol mouse pointer to the left margin of the CategoryID Footer. Because the CategoryID field is a lookup field, it displays with a drop-down list button for the field box. When printed or displayed in Print Preview, this field shows the CategoryID name rather than the numeric code. Click the Field List button on the toolbar to close the Field List window.

11. Select the label of the CategoryID field that you just placed, and use the Font and Size drop-down lists on the Formatting toolbar to set the label's font to Arial and the label's size to 8 points. Next, select the CategoryID text box, click the Bold button on the toolbar to add the bold attribute to the CategoryID text box, and also select the Arial font at a size of 8 points. Figure 14.18 shows the new bound CategoryID field in place of the calculated field that you deleted in step 8. (In the figure, the report has been scrolled upward in the window to make the Report Footer and Page Footer sections visible.)

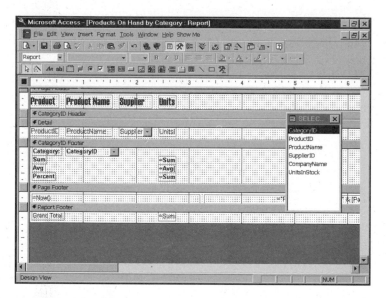

**FIG. 14.18** The Products On Hand by Category report, after adding the CategoryID field to the CategoryID Footer section.

12. Drag the two calculated fields in the Page Footer section until they are one grid mark away from the top of the Page Footer section. Drag the Report Footer bar upward to reduce the Page Footer's height, as shown in Figure 14.18.

13. For this report, the Average field is unnecessary; delete it and its label, and then rearrange the remaining fields and labels. Click and drag the =Sum([UnitsInStock])/ [UnitsInStock Grand Total Sum] text box from its present location below the =Sum([UnitsInStock]) text box to a position at the top of the CategoryID Footer, near the page's right edge. Drag the =Sum([UnitsInStock]) field to a position at the

top of the CategoryID text box and near the center of the page. Finally, move up the Page Footer divider bar to reduce the footer's depth (see Figure 14.19).

**14.** Click the toolbar's Save button to save your report.

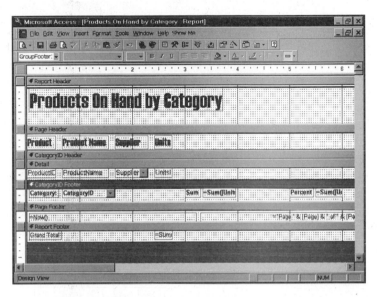

**FIG. 14.19**  The completely modified Products On Hand by Category report in Design mode.

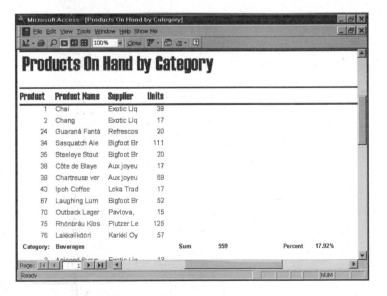

**FIG. 14.20**  Previewing the Products on Hand by Category report.

> ### Troubleshooting
>
> *When I preview or print my report, Access displays or prints a blank page after each page with data.*
>
> If a report's width becomes greater than the net printable width (the paper width minus the sum of the left and right margins), the number of report pages doubles. Columns of fields that do not fit a page's width print on a second page, similar to the printing method used by spreadsheet applications. If you set your right margin beyond the right printing margin, or if the right edge of any control on the report extends past the right printing margin, the added pages often are blank. Change the printing margins or reduce the width of your report so that it conforms to the printable page width. (See the section "Adjusting Margins and Printing Conventional Reports" later in this chapter.)

 To check the progress of your work, periodically click the toolbar's Print Preview button to display the report prior to printing. At this point, your Products On Hand by Category report appears in Print Preview mode, as shown in Figure 14.20.

### Using the DLookUp() Domain Aggregate Function to Print Product Category Names

As you saw in the preceding section of this chapter, lookup fields in a table are placed on a report as a limited-function combo box. You can't use the combo box to select values, but it causes a value looked up from another table to be displayed instead of the actual field value. For example, if you place the CategoryID field on the report (as you did in the preceding section), Access displays the category name in the report rather than the actual CategoryID number, because the CategoryID field in the Products table has lookup field properties assigned to it. When you place the CategoryID field on the report, Access automatically creates a combo box control with the properties needed to look up the CategoryName field from the Categories table.

Not every table that you use in your reports will have lookup fields, however, nor is it necessarily desirable to create lookup fields for all numeric code fields (such as CategoryID and SupplierID). If you want to display a looked-up value for a field that isn't defined as a lookup field, you use Access's domain aggregate function, DLookUp(), to find values from another table that correspond to a value in one of the report's fields. For example, if you want to display both the actual CategoryID number and the CategoryName in the Group Footer of the Products On Hand by Category report, you can use the DLookUp() function to display the text of the CategoryName field from the Categories table, and a bound text field to display the CategoryID number from the Products table.

To change the CategoryID combo box control to a standard text box and add a new Category Name field that uses the DLookUp() function to the CategoryID Footer section of the Products On Hand by Category report, follow these steps:

1. In Report Design mode, select the CategoryID combo box, and then choose Format, Change To, Text Box to convert the combo box to a regular text box field. This field will no longer display the looked-up CategoryName field but will display the actual number stored in the CategoryID field.

**2.** Edit the CategoryID field label to read ID:, then resize the CategoryID text box so that it is approximately 3/8 of an inch wide. Move both the text and field boxes closer together, near the left edge of the report's CategoryID Footer section (see Figure 14.21).

**3.** Click the Toolbox button to display the toolbox if it is not already displayed.

**4.** Click the Text Box tool and add a new unbound text box to the right of the CategoryID text box with the approximate dimensions shown in Figure 14.21.

**5.** Delete the field label for the new text box control, and give the text box itself the bold text attribute.

**6.** Click the new text box, and type the following as the text box's value:

> **=DLookUp("[CategoryName]","Categories","[CategoryID] = Report!CategoryID") & " Category"**

[CategoryName] is the value that you want to return to the text box. Categories is the table that contains the CategoryName field. [CategoryID] = Report!CategoryID is the criterion that selects the record in the Categories table with a CategoryID value that is equal to the value in your report's CategoryID text box. The Report prefix is necessary to distinguish between the CategoryID field of the Categories table and a control object of the same name. (Report is necessary in this example because Access has automatically named the report's CategoryID text box control as CategoryID.)

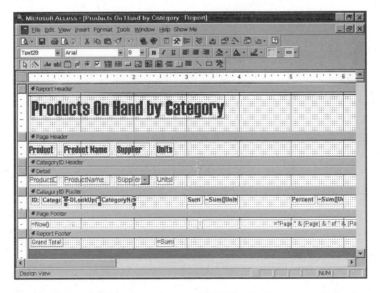

**FIG. 14.21** The transformed and resized CategoryID field with the new, unbound text box containing the DLookUp() function.

7. Select the CategoryID text box and verify that the name CategoryID appears in the Object Name text box (at the left side of the Formatting toolbar). If not, click the Properties button of the toolbar, select the Other tab in the Properties window, and type **CategoryID** as the value of the control's Name property (see Figure 14.22).

8. Click the Report View button of the toolbar. Your Products On Hand by Category report appears as shown in Figure 14.23.

---

### Troubleshooting

*When I preview or print my report, the text box that contains the* DLookUp( ) *function displays* #error *or just the word* Category.

Your DLookUp expression contains a typographical error, or one of the objects that you specified does not exist. Make sure that you have typed the entry in the CategoryName text box exactly as shown in the preceding step 6. If the field name in the table or query for which you are searching is the same as the control name, make sure that you add the Report! prefix to the control name. For example, you must add **Report**! if you assign Category Name as the name of the new control that you added in the preceding example.

---

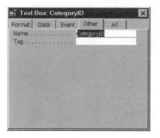

**FIG. 14.22**   Verifying the name of the CategoryID text box.

### Adding Other Calculated Controls to the Report

Calculated controls, such as the DLookUp( ) control that you added in the preceding section, are quite useful in reports. You use calculated controls to determine extended values, such as quantity times unit price or quantity times cost. Now you have enough space at the right of the report to add a column for the UnitPrice field and a column for the extended inventory value, which is UnitPrice multiplied by UnitsInStock. To add these controls, follow the steps described in the following subsections.

**Changing the Report's Record Source.**   You created the Products On Hand by Category report by selecting fields directly from the Products and Suppliers table in the Report Wizard. As a result, the Record Source property for the report, as a whole, is a SQL statement that selects only those fields that you chose initially in the Report Wizard. Although it's possible to add fields to the report by creating unbound text box controls and using the Expression Builder to create an expression to retrieve the desired value, it's much easier to create a query to select the fields desired for the report and substitute the new query as the report's data source.

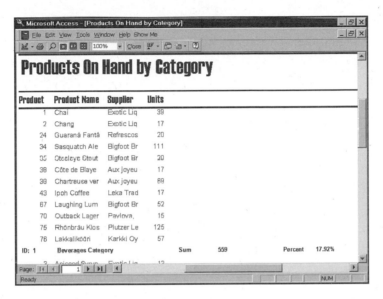

**FIG. 14.23**   The Products On Hand by Category report with the DLookUp() field added.

To create a query for use with the Products on Hand by Category report, follow these steps:

1. Click the toolbar's Database Window button to display the Database window. Click the Queries tab and then click New to create a new query.

2. In the New Query dialog, select Design View and then click OK.

3. Double-click the Products table in the Show Table dialog to add the table to the query. Then click Close to dismiss the Show Table dialog.

4. Drag the * field to the first column of the query grid to add to the query all of the Products table's fields.

5. Drag the Discontinued field to the query grid's second column.

6. Clear the Show check box for the Discontinued field, and then type **=False** in the Discontinued field's first Criteria row (see Figure 14.24).

7. Click the Close Window button to close the Query window. A prompt asks whether you want to save changes to the query design. Click Yes.

8. In the Save As dialog's Query Name text box, type **qryProductOnHand**. Then click OK to save the query.

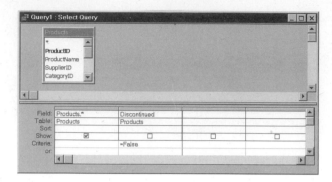

**FIG. 14.24**    The qryProductOnHand query that contains all fields from the Products table and excludes discontinued products.

The query that you have just created contains all of the fields from the Products table and excludes discontinued products from the record set. (In other words, the query includes only those records whose Discontinued field contains the **False** or **No** value.)

To change the report's Record Source property, follow these steps:

1. Open the Products on Hand by Category report in Design mode.

2. Choose Edit, Select Report.

3. Click the toolbar's Properties button to open the report's Properties window. Then click the Data tab to display the report's various data properties.

4. Click the Record Source text box, and then use the drop-down list to select the qryProductOnHand query as the report's new Record Source property.

5. Click the toolbar's Save button to save the changes to the report.

**Adding the Calculated Fields.** Now that you've changed the report's record source, you have easy access to the UnitPrice field that you need for adding the additional calculated fields to the report. To add the UnitPrice field and the Value calculated field to the report, follow these steps:

1. Display the Products on Hand by Category report in Design mode, if necessary. Then click the toolbar's Toolbox button to display the Access toolbox if it isn't already displayed.

2. Click the Label tool in the toolbox and place the label to the right of the Units label in the Page Header section. Type **Price** as the label.

3. Add another label to the right of Price and type **Value**.

4. Click the toolbar's Field List button to display the Field List window. Select UnitPrice and drag the field symbol to a position under the Price label in the Detail section. Drop the text box, and then delete the UnitPrice field's label in the report's Detail section.

**5.** To create the calculated Value text box, click the Text Box button in the toolbox and add the text box to the right of the Unit Price text box.

> **Tip**
>
> Entering expressions is easier if you display the Properties window and enter the expression as the Control Source property. Press Shift+F2 to open the Zoom box so you can see the entire expression as you enter it.

**6.** Type **=[UnitsInStock]\*[UnitPrice]** as the expression for the Value text box. Delete the field label for this text box in the report's Detail section.

**7.** Drag the Page Footer section bar downward to increase the height of the report's CategoryID Footer section, and rearrange the text labels and fields as shown in Figure 14.25. Edit the Sum label to read **Total:** and the Percentage label to read **Percentage:**.

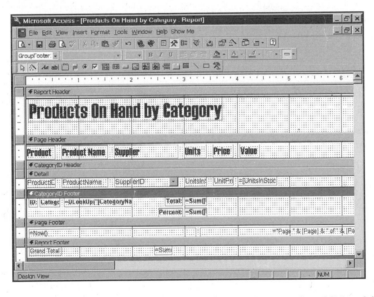

**FIG. 14.25** Rearranging the CategoryID Footer section to make room for additional fields.

**8.** Repeat steps 5 and 6 to create the Value Subtotal text box in the CategoryID Footer section, but type **=Sum([UnitsInStock]\*[UnitPrice])** as the subtotal expression. Click the toolbar's Bold button to set the Font Weight property to Bold. In the Properties window, click the Other tab and then set this text box's Name property as **txtTotalValue**.

9. Repeat step 8 to create the Value grand total box in the Report Footer section. In the Other page of the Properties window, set this text box's Name property as **txtGrandTotalValue**.

10. Add another unbound text box underneath the txtTotalValue text box. Type **=[txtTotalValue]/[txtGrandTotalValue]** as the value of the Control Source property and set the Format property's value to Percent. The report design appears as shown in Figure 14.26.

> **Tip**
>
> If the Parameter dialog appears, you misspelled one or more field names in the expressions. Click Cancel and check the properties that you added in steps 6 through 10.

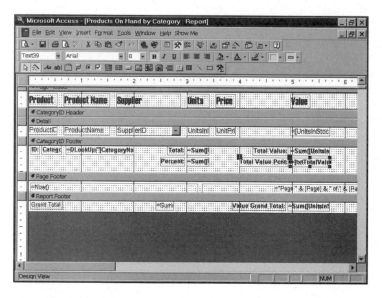

**FIG. 14.26** Adding the Price, Value, Total Value, Total Value Pcnt, and Grand Total Value fields to the report.

11. Click the toolbar's Report View button to check the result of your additions. The report appears as in Figure 14.27. Use the vertical scroll bar, if necessary, to display the category subtotal. The next section describes how you can correct any misaligned values and the spacing of the Detail section's rows.

12. Click the Bottom of Report page selector button to display the grand totals for the report (see Figure 14.28). The record selector buttons become page selector buttons when you display reports in Run mode.

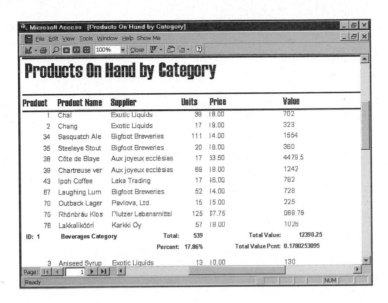

**FIG. 14.27** Page 1 of the report, with calculated product values and value subtotals.

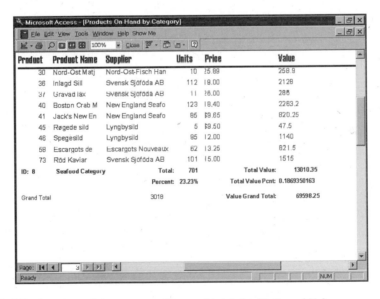

**FIG. 14.28** The last page of the report, with grand totals for Units and Value.

### Aligning and Formatting Controls, and Adjusting Line Spacing

On reports, the exact alignment of label and text box controls is more important than alignment on forms because in the printed report, any misalignment is obvious. Formatting the controls further improves the report's appearance and readability.

III

**Creating Forms and Reports**

The spacing of the report's rows in the Detail section is controlled by the section's depth. Likewise, you can control the white space above and below the headers and footers by adjusting the depth of their sections and the vertical position of the controls within the sections. To create a professional-looking report, you must adjust the controls' alignment and formatting as well as the sections' line spacing.

**Aligning Controls Horizontally and Vertically.** You align controls by first selecting the rows to align and then aligning the columns. Access provides several control-sizing and alignment options to make the process easier. To size and align the controls that you created, follow these steps:

1. Click the Report View toolbar's Close button to return to Design mode.

2. You can simultaneously adjust the height of all text boxes to fit the font used for their contents. Choose Edit, Select All to select all of the controls in the report.

3. Choose Format, Size, To Fit to adjust the height of the selected controls. Access adjusts all of the controls to the proper height. To deselect all of the controls, click a blank area of the report.

4. Select all labels in the Page Header sections. Choose Format, Align, Top. This process aligns the tops of each selected label with the uppermost selected label. Click a blank area of the report to deselect the labels.

5. Select all text boxes in the Detail section, and repeat step 4 for the text boxes.

6. Select the labels and text boxes in the CategoryID Footer and Report Footer sections and repeat step 4.

7. Select all controls in the Units column. Choose Format, Align, Right so that Access aligns the column to the right edge of the text farthest to the right of the column. Next, click the toolbar's Align Right button to right-align the contents of the labels and text boxes. (The first part of this step aligns the controls themselves to the right-most control, and the second part right-aligns the text or data displayed by the selected controls.)

8. Select all controls in the Price column and repeat step 7.

9. Select all controls in the Values column (except the Page Footer text box) and repeat step 7.

10. Click the toolbar's Report View button to display the report with the improved alignment of rows and columns.

**Formatting Controls.** As you can see in Figure 14.27, you must revise the formatting of several controls. Although ProductID values are right-aligned, centering or left-justification is more appropriate for values used as codes rather than numbers to total. The repeated dollar signs in the Unit Price field detract from the report's readability, and the Value column's left-justification is inappropriate.

To change the Format property of these fields, follow these steps:

1. Click the toolbar's Close button to return to Design mode.

2. Select the ProductID text box in the Detail section and click the toolbar's Center button.

3. Select and then center the CategoryID text box in the CategoryID Footer section.

4. Double-click the Unit Price text box to open its Properties window, then click the Format tab of the Properties window.

5. In the Format text box, type **#,#00.00**. This procedure eliminates the dollar sign but preserves the monetary formatting.

6. Repeat steps 4 and 5 for the Values text box. The Detail section doesn't require dollar signs.

> ### Tip
>
> If you select Currency formatting instead of typing **$#,#00.00** to add a dollar sign to the value, your totals do not align. Currency formatting offsets the number to the left to provide space for the parentheses that accountants use to specify negative monetary values.

7. Select the Values subtotal in the CategoryID Footer. Click the Properties window's Format tab and type **$#,#00.00** in the Format field. Accountants use dollar signs to identify subtotals and totals in ledgers.

8. Select the Values grand total in the Report Footer and type **$#,#00.00** as the Format property of the Values grand total.

9. Select the Total Value Percent text box in the CategoryID Footer. Choose Percent from the Format property's drop-down list to display the text box's contents as a percentage.

10. The Values grand total in the Report Footer is the report's most important element, so click the toolbar's Line/Border Color button and then click the black box to give this field a black border. Next, click the Line/Border Width button and then the 2-point border button. This procedure increases the thickness of the border around the grand total.

11. Click the toolbar's Report View button to check your formatting modifications. Click the Bottom of Report page selector button to display the last page of the report (see Figure 14.29).

**Adjusting Line Spacing.** In the Page Header section, shown in Figure 14.27, the controls are placed further apart than is necessary, and the depth of the controls in the Report Header section is out of proportion with the size of the text. The line spacing of the remainder of the report's sections is satisfactory, but you can also change this spacing. Minimizing line spacing allows you to print a report on fewer sheets of paper.

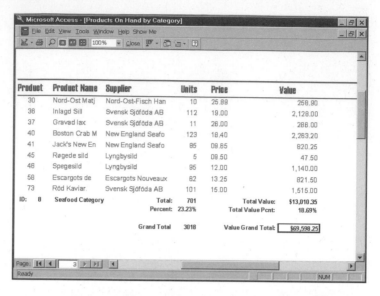

**FIG. 14.29** The last page of the report, with the correct Format property assigned to the values.

> **Tip**
>
> You might have to return to Design mode and adjust the width or position of the Subtotals and Grand Totals text boxes to align these values with those for the individual products.

To change the spacing of the report's Page Header and Detail sections, follow these steps:

> **Tip**
>
> You can adjust the size of controls and the line spacing more precisely if you choose Format, Snap to Grid. This command toggles the Snap to Grid feature on and off.

1. Click the toolbar's Close button to return to Design mode.

2. Select all of the labels in the Page Header and move the group as close to the top of the section as possible.

3. Click the bottom line of the Page Header and move the line as close to the bottom of the text boxes as possible. (To select the line, you may have to move the CategoryID Header section downward temporarily.)

4. Click a blank area of the report and then move the CategoryID Header section to the bottom of the labels. You cannot reduce a section's depth to less than the Height property of the label that has the maximum height in the section.

5. Select all of the text boxes in the Detail section, and move those boxes as a group to the top of the section. Move the CategoryID footer up to the bottom of the text boxes.

6. Move the line and label in the Report Header section upward to minimize the amount of white space in the Report Header.

7. Click the toolbar's Report View button to check the Page Header depth and line spacing of the Detail section. The spacing shown in Figure 14.30 is close to the minimum that you can achieve. You cannot reduce a section's line spacing to less than that required by the tallest text box or label by reducing the section's Height property in the Properties box because Access rejects the entry and substitutes the prior value.

8. Click the toolbar's Zoom button to display the report in full-page view. Clicking the mouse when the pointer is the magnifying glass symbol has the same effect as clicking the Zoom button. Alternate clicks toggle between full-size and full-page views.

9. Choose File, Save to save your changes.

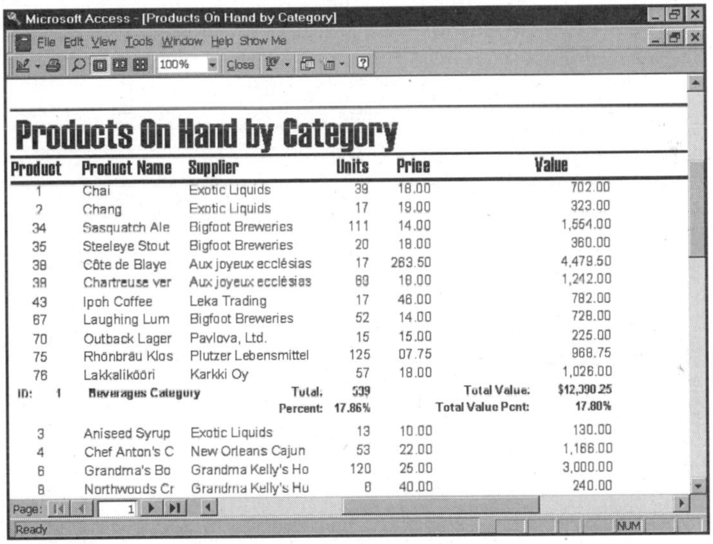

**FIG. 14.30**   The report in Report view after you adjust the depth of the Report Header, Page Header, and Detail sections.

# Adjusting Margins and Printing Conventional Reports

The full-page Report View of the report shows the report as it would print using Access's default printing margins of one inch on the top, bottom, and sides of the report (see Figure 14.31). In the Print Setup dialog, you can adjust the printed version of the report. The procedure for printing a report also applies to printing the data contained in tables and queries as well as single-record or continuous forms.

To change the printing margins for a report, follow these steps:

1. Choose File, Page Setup to open the Page Setup dialog (see Figure 14.32).

2. The Page Setup dialog is similar to the Print and Page Setup dialogs of other Windows applications, with a section for printing margins included. To increase the amount of information on a page, decrease the top and bottom margins. By selecting the Print Data Only check box, you can print only the data in the report; the Report and Page Headers and Footers do not print.

3. In the Left text box, type **2.0** to specify a two-inch left margin. In the Right, Top, and Bottom text boxes, type **0.75** inches. Click OK. The full-page view of the report with the revised margins appears (see Figure 14.33).

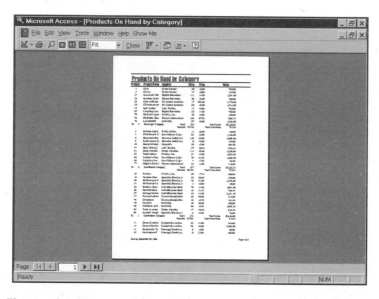

**FIG. 14.31** The completed report in full-page view.

> **Tip**
>
> The printing margins that you establish for a report in the Page Setup dialog apply to the active report only; each report has a unique set of margins. When you save the report, Access saves the margin settings.

4. To print the report, click the toolbar's Print button. Access immediately prints the report using the current printer options. If you want to change the selected printer, page orientation, graphics quality, or other printer options, choose File, Print. The standard Print dialog appears for the printer specified in Windows as the default printer. Figure 14.34 shows, for example, the Print dialog for an IBM Laser Printer shared on a network.

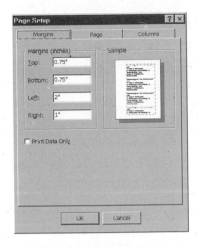

**FIG. 14.32**    The Page Setup dialog for printing data sheets, forms, and reports.

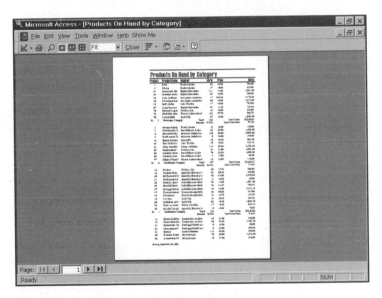

**FIG. 14.33**    The full-page preview of the report with new printing margins applied.

5. You can choose to print all or part of a report, to print the report to a file for later printing, and select the number of copies to print. By choosing the Properties button, you can change the parameters that apply to the printer you are using. Click OK to print the report.

The Page Setup dialog includes a Page tab that allows you to select the paper size and orientation. The dialog also includes a Columns tab that allows you to establish specifications for printing mailing labels and other multiple-column reports. The next section describes these specifications and how you set them.

III

Creating Forms and Reports

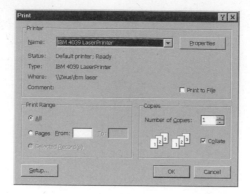

**FIG. 14.34** The Print dialog controls printing of datasheets, forms, and reports.

# Preventing Widowed Records with the Group Keep Together Property

Access includes a Keep Together property for groups that prevents widowed records from appearing at the bottom of the page. Depending on your report section depths, you might find that only a few records of the next group (called *widowed records*) appear at the bottom of the page. You can force a page break when an entire group does not fit on one page by following these steps:

1. With the report in Design view, click the toolbar's Sorting and Grouping button to open the Sorting and Grouping dialog.

2. Select the field with the group symbol in the selection button that corresponds to the group that you want to keep together. In this example, select CategoryID.

3. Open the Keep Together drop-down list and select Whole Group, as shown in Figure 14.35.

**FIG. 14.35** Setting the report group's Keep Together property.

4. Close the Sorting and Grouping dialog, and click the Report View button to see the result of applying the group Keep Together property.

> **Tip**
>
> If you want to delete or add a Group Header or Footer singly (rather than in pairs), select Yes or No in the appropriate property field of the Sorting and Grouping dialog.

The Report Wizard makes the other entries in the Sorting and Grouping dialog for you. The next chapter describes how to use the Sorting and Grouping dialog to design reports without the aid of the wizard.

# Printing Multicolumn Reports as Mailing Labels

Access allows you to print multicolumn reports. You can create a single-column report with the Report Wizard, for example, and then arrange the report to print values from the Detail section in a specified number of columns across the page. The most common application of multicolumn reports is the creation of mailing labels.

You can create mailing lists with the Report Wizard, or you can start with a blank form. The Report Wizard's advantage is that it includes the dimensions of virtually every kind of adhesive label for dot-matrix or laser printers made by the Avery Commercial Products division. You select the product number of the label that you plan to use, and Access determines the number of columns, rows per page, and margins for the report's Detail section. You can also customize the Mailing Label Wizard for labels with unusual sizes or that other manufacturers produce.

The Northwind Traders database includes a Customer Labels report that you can modify to suit the design of any mailing label. Figure 14.36 shows the Detail section of the Customer Labels report with the font changed to Courier New in a 10-point font and the size of the label adjusted to 2.5×0.833 inches.

You specify the number of columns in a row and the number of rows on a page by selecting settings in the Columns tab in the Page Setup dialog, as shown in Figure 14.37. This dialog appears when you choose File, Page Setup in either Print Preview or Report Design mode.

The dialog's text boxes, check boxes, and option buttons allow you to perform the following procedures:

- The Items Across property sets the number of labels across the page. In this example, this property is set to 3, so the labels will print three across.

> **Note**
>
> The Left and Top margin settings (which you set on the Margins tab of the Page Setup dialog) specify the position at which Access prints the upper-left corner of the first label on the page. For most laser and inkjet printers, these values cannot be less than about 0.25 inches. Labels designed for laser and inkjet printers are die-cut so that the marginal areas remain on the backing sheet when you remove the individual labels.

- The Width property in the Item Size group overrides the left margin, and the Height property overrides the bottom margin that you establish in Report Design view only if you don't select Same as Detail to use the margins you set in the Detail section.

- Column Spacing specifies the position of the left edge of columns to the right of the first column.

- Row Spacing and the Height property determine the number of labels that fit vertically on a page and the vertical distance between successive labels. If you set Row Spacing to zero, the depth of your Detail section determines the vertical spacing of the labels.

- The Across, Then Down option causes the labels to print in columns from left to right and then in rows from the top to the bottom of the page. This setting is preferred for mailing labels because it wastes less label stock for continuous-feed printers.

- The Down, Then Across option causes the labels to print in *snaking* column style. The first column is filled from top to bottom, then the second column is filled from top to bottom, and so on.

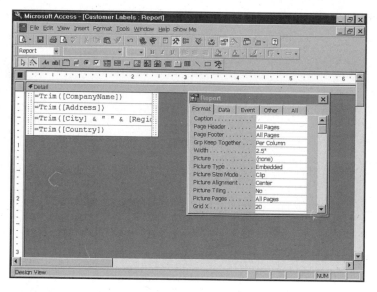

**FIG. 14.36** The modified Customer Labels report in Design mode.

You set these properties' values for three columns of 12 labels per page. You can access the settings for all of these columns and pages in the Page Setup dialog's Layout page.

After you set the dimensions of the mailing labels and click OK, the full-size view of the labels appears in Print Preview mode, as shown in Figure 14.38.

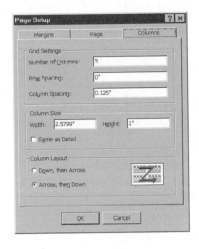

**FIG. 14.37**   The Columns tab of the Page Setup dialog.

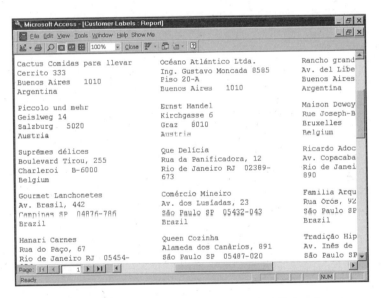

**FIG. 14.38**   Three-across mailing labels shown in Report View's full-size view.

Click the toolbar's Zoom button to display the full-page layout. To test the label layout properties that you set, print only the label's first page on standard paper or a xerographic duplicate of the label template supplied with labels designed for laser printing.

You might have to make minor alignment adjustments because the upper-left corner of the printer's image and the upper-left corner of the paper might not correspond exactly.

If you select the Down, then Across option, the technique for printing successive Detail rows is identical to that which word processing and page layout applications such as

Aldus PageMaker use to create newspaper (snaking) columns. When the first column fills to the page's height, Detail rows fill the next column to the right.

---

**Note**

Newspaper columns are suitable for mailing labels but are difficult to format correctly when you convert other kinds of single-column reports to multiple columns. For newspaper columns to operate at all, you must set the Keep Together property of the report's Detail section to No, and then set the Detail section's height so that the field data for a single record appears in a single set of rows. If the Detail data includes Memo fields with variable amounts of text in a text box with the Can Grow property set to Yes, formatting newspaper columns properly becomes almost impossible. Instead of having Access attempt to create newspaper columns, an easier approach is to lay out the Detail section with multiple columns in Design mode.

---

# Chapter 15

# Preparing Advanced Reports

Access 97's Report Wizard can create reports that you can use "as is" or modify to suit most of your database reporting requirements. In some cases, however, you might have to create reports that are more complex than or differ from those offered by the Report Wizard. For example, you might have to apply special grouping and sorting methods to your reports. Including subreports within your reports requires that you start from a blank report form instead of using the Report Wizard.

To understand fully the process of designing advanced Access reports, you must be familiar with Access functions, which is one of the subjects of Chapter 9, "Understanding Operators and Expressions in Access." You also must understand the methods that you use to create and design forms, which are covered in Chapters 12 and 13. Reports extensively use Access functions such as Sum() and expressions like ="Subtotal of" & [Field Name] & ":". The toolbox that you use to add controls to forms also adds controls when you create or modify reports. You assign properties of controls, such as labels and text boxes, with the methods that you use with forms. If you skipped Chapters 9, 12, or 13, you might want to refer to the appropriate sections of those chapters whenever you encounter unfamiliar subjects or terminology in this chapter.

## Grouping and Sorting Report Data

Most reports you create require that you organize their data into groups and subgroups in a style similar to the outline of a book. The Report Wizard lets you establish the initial grouping and sorting properties for your data, but you might want to rearrange your report's data after reviewing the Report Wizard's first draft.

The Sorting and Grouping dialog (see Figure 15.1) allows you to modify these report properties in Design mode. This section uses the Products On Hand by Category report that you created in the preceding chapter. The sorting and grouping methods described here, however, apply to any report that you create. To display the dialog, open the report in Design view and click the toolbar's Sorting and Grouping button.

**FIG. 15.1** The Sorting and Grouping dialog lets you create or alter report groups and the sort order within groups.

The Sorting and Grouping dialog allows you to determine the fields or expressions on which Access is to group the products, up to a maximum of three levels. You can sort the grouped data in ascending or descending order, but you must select one or the other; "unsorted" is not an option. The Sorting and Grouping symbol in the selection button at the left of the window indicates that Access uses the field or expression in the adjacent column to group the records.

### Grouping Data

The method that you use to group data depends on the data in the field by which you group. You can group by categories, in which case a unique value must represent each category. You can group data by a range of values, which usually are numeric but also can be alphabetic. You can use the data in a field to group the data, or you can substitute an expression as the basis for the grouping.

**Grouping by Category.** When you told the Report Wizard to use CategoryID as the field by which to group, you elected to group by category. You can alter the grouping sequence easily by using the Sorting and Grouping dialog. To group by SupplierID, for example, select SupplierID as the first group field. (When you change the group field, Access automatically renames the Group Header and Footer sections.) In the SupplierID Footer section, change the ID text box's Control Source property to the SupplierID field, and rename the text box to **txtSupplierID**. Next, change the title label in the Report Header to Products on Hand by Supplier, and use the DLookUp function to change the text box's expression to the following:

```
="Supplier: " & DLookUp("[CompanyName]","Suppliers",
"[txtSupplierID]=Report!SupplierID")
```

Increase the DLookUp text box's width so that more of the supplier's name is visible in the report. The report appears as shown in Figure 15.2. Choose File, Save As, and save the report under the new name **Products On Hand by Supplier**.

Microsoft Access - [Products On Hand by Category]

File  Edit  View  Tools  Window  Help  Show Me

100%  ▾  Close

# Products On Hand by Supplier

| Product | Product Name | Supplier | Units | Price | | Value |
|---|---|---|---|---|---|---|
| 1 | Chai | Exotic Liquids | 39 | 18.00 | | 702.00 |
| 2 | Chang | Exotic Liquids | 17 | 19.00 | | 323.00 |
| 3 | Aniseed Syrup | Exotic Liquids | 13 | 10.00 | | 130.00 |
| ID:  1 | **Supplier: Exotic Liquids** | Total: | 69 | | Total Value: | $1,155.00 |
| | | Percent: | 2.29% | | Total Value Pcnt: | 1.66% |
| 4 | Chef Anton's C | New Orleans Cajun | 53 | 22.00 | | 1,166.00 |
| 65 | Louisiana Fier | New Orleans Cajun | 76 | 21.05 | | 1,599.80 |
| 66 | Louisiana Hot | New Orleans Cajun | 4 | 17.00 | | 68.00 |
| ID:  2 | **Supplier: New Orleans Cajun** | Total: | 133 | | Total Value: | $2,833.80 |
| | | Percent: | 4.41% | | Total Value Pcnt: | 4.07% |
| 6 | Grandma's Bo | Grandma Kelly's Ho | 120 | 25.00 | | 3,000.00 |
| 7 | Uncle Bob's Or | Grandma Kelly's Ho | 15 | 30.00 | | 450.00 |
| 8 | Northwoods Cr | Grandma Kelly's Ho | 6 | 40.00 | | 240.00 |
| ID:  3 | **Supplier: Grandma Kelly's H** | Total: | 141 | | Total Value: | $3,690.00 |
| | | Percent: | 4.67% | | Total Value Pcnt: | 5.30% |
| 10 | Ikura | Tokyo Traders | 31 | 31.00 | | 961.00 |
| 74 | Longlife Tofu | Tokyo Traders | 4 | 10.00 | | 40.00 |
| ID:  4 | **Supplier: Tokyo Traders** | Total: | 35 | | Total Value: | $1,001.00 |

Page:  1

Ready    NUM

**FIG. 15.2**    The effect of changing the report grouping so that it displays records by SupplierID.

---

### Note

You cannot let a report's properties or controls limit the number of rows of detail data that a report presents, unless you write a TopN or TopNPercent query using Access SQL. (Search the online Help for the TopValues property to learn more about TopN and TopNPercent queries.) All rows of a table or query appear somewhere in the report's Detail section if the report includes a Detail section with at least one control. To include only a selected range of dates in a report, for example, you must base the report on a query with the criteria necessary to select the Detail records. If the user is to choose the range of records to include in the report, use a parameter query as the report's data source.

---

◀◀  See "Text-Manipulation Functions," p. 302

If you use a systematic code for grouping, you can group by the first five or fewer characters of the code. With an expression, you can group by any set of characters within a field. To group by the second and third digits of a code, for example, use the following expression:

=**Mid**([*FieldName*],2,2).

If your table or query contains appropriate data, you can group reports by more than one level by creating subgroups. The Employee Sales by Country report (one of the Northwind Traders sample reports), for example, uses groups (Country) and subgroups (the employee's name—the actual group is an Access expression that combines the FirstName and LastName fields) to organize orders received within a range of dates. Open the Employee Sales by Country report in Design mode to view the additional section created by a subgroup.

**Grouping by Range.** You often must sort reports by ranges of values. (If you opened the Employee Sales by Country report, close this report and reopen the Products On Hand by Category report in Design mode.) If you want to divide the Products on Hand by Category report into a maximum of six sections—each beginning with a five-letter group of the alphabet (A through E, F through J, and so on) based on the ProductName field—the entries in the Sorting and Grouping dialog should look like the entries in Figure 15.3.

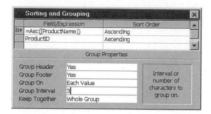

**FIG. 15.3** Sorting and Grouping criteria to group records in alphabetical intervals.

Access VBA's **=Asc**([*ProductName*]) function returns the ASCII (numeric) value of the first character of its string argument, the ProductName field. You set the Group On specification to Interval and then set the Group Interval to 3. This setup groups the data into names beginning with A through C, D through F, and so on (see Figure 15.4). You delete all text boxes in the Group Footer because subtotals by alphabetic groups are not significant. Although of limited value in this report, an alphabetic grouping often is useful for grouping long, alphabetized lists to assist readers in finding a particular record.

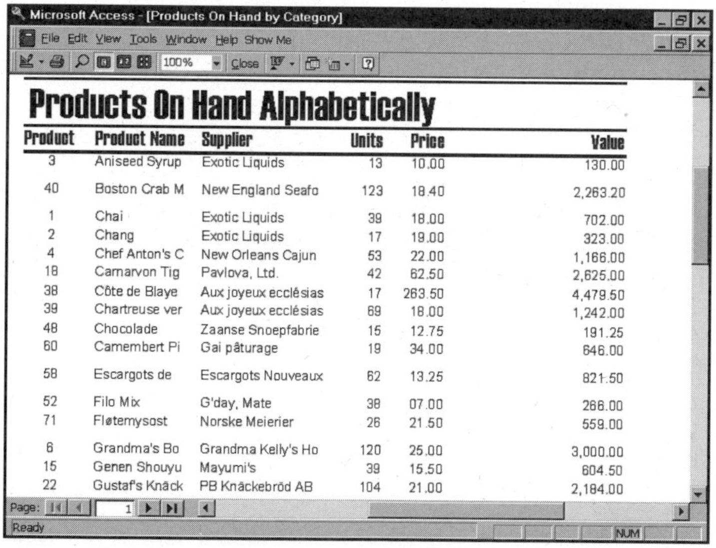

| Product | Product Name | Supplier | Units | Price | Value |
|---|---|---|---|---|---|
| 3 | Aniseed Syrup | Exotic Liquids | 13 | 10.00 | 130.00 |
| 40 | Boston Crab M | New England Seafo | 123 | 18.40 | 2,263.20 |
| 1 | Chai | Exotic Liquids | 39 | 18.00 | 702.00 |
| 2 | Chang | Exotic Liquids | 17 | 19.00 | 323.00 |
| 4 | Chef Anton's C | New Orleans Cajun | 53 | 22.00 | 1,166.00 |
| 18 | Carnarvon Tig | Pavlova, Ltd. | 42 | 62.50 | 2,625.00 |
| 38 | Côte de Blaye | Aux joyeux ecclésias | 17 | 263.50 | 4,479.50 |
| 39 | Chartreuse ver | Aux joyeux ecclésias | 69 | 18.00 | 1,242.00 |
| 48 | Chocolade | Zaanse Snoepfabrie | 15 | 12.75 | 191.25 |
| 60 | Camembert Pi | Gai pâturage | 19 | 34.00 | 646.00 |
| 58 | Escargots de | Escargots Nouveaux | 62 | 13.25 | 821.50 |
| 52 | Filo Mix | G'day, Mate | 38 | 07.00 | 266.00 |
| 71 | Fløtemysost | Norske Meierier | 26 | 21.50 | 559.00 |
| 6 | Grandma's Bo | Grandma Kelly's Ho | 120 | 25.00 | 3,000.00 |
| 15 | Genen Shouyu | Mayumi's | 39 | 15.50 | 604.50 |
| 22 | Gustaf's Knäck | PB Knäckebröd AB | 104 | 21.00 | 2,184.00 |

**FIG. 15.4** A report that categorizes products by three-letter alphabetic intervals.

◄◄  See "Functions," p. 294

If you group data on a field with a Date/Time data type, Access allows you to set the Sorting and Grouping dialog's Group On property to Year, Qtr (quarter), Month, Week, Day, Hour, or Minute. To group records so that values of the same quarter for several years print in sequence, type the following in the Field/Expression column of the Sorting and Grouping dialog:

```
=DatePart("q",[FieldName])
```

### Sorting Data Groups

Although most data sorting within groups is based on the values contained in a field, you also can sort by expressions. When compiling an inventory valuation list, the products with the highest inventory value are the most important. The report's users might want these products listed first in a group. This decision requires a record sorting within groups on the expression =[UnitsInStock]*[UnitPrice], the same expression that Access uses to calculate the report's Value column. Figure 15.5 shows the required entries in the Sorting and Grouping dialog.

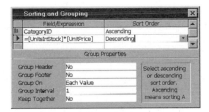

**FIG. 15.5**   Sorting data by each record on an expression.

The descending sort on the inventory value expression results in the report shown in Figure 15.6. As expected, the products with the highest inventory value appear first in each category.

# Working from a Blank Report

Usually, the fastest way to set up a report is to use the Report Wizard to create a basic report and then modify the basic report as described in Chapter 14, "Printing Basic Reports and Mailing Labels," and previous sections of this chapter. If you are creating a simple report, however, it could take you longer to modify a standard report style created by the Report Wizard than it would take to create a report by using the default blank report that Access provides.

### The Basis for a Subreport

To create a report to use as the Monthly Sales by Category subreport (rptMonthlyCategorySales) in the following section of this chapter, "Adding and Deleting Sections of Your Report," follow these steps:

◄◄ See "Creating a Monthly Product Sales Crosstab Query," p. 362

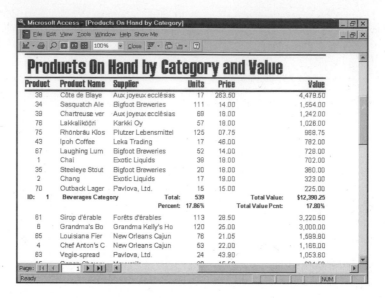

**FIG. 15.6** The Products On Hand by Category and Value report, showing records sorted by inventory value within groups.

1. Close the Products On Hand by Category report, and click the Query tab in the Database window.

2. Select the qry1995MonthlyProductSales query that you created in Chapter 10, "Creating Multitable and Crosstab Queries." Click the Design button. A slightly modified version of this crosstab query serves as the data source for the report of the same name.

3. Change the first column's field name from ProductID to CategoryID by opening the Field list and clicking the CategoryID field name. You need the CategoryID field to link with the CategoryID field in the qryProductOnHand query that the Products On Hand by Category report uses as its data source.

4. Delete the ProductName column. The modified query appears as shown in Figure 15.7.

5. Choose File, Save As and name the modified query **qry1995MonthlyCategorySales**. Your query result set appears as shown in Figure 15.8.

6. Open the New Object drop-down list on the toolbar, and select New Report from the list. The New Report dialog appears.

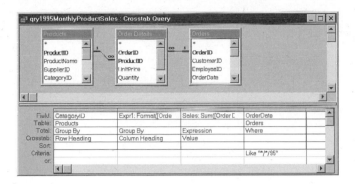

**FIG. 15.7**  The modified crosstab query for the Monthly Sales by Category subreport.

**FIG. 15.8**  The result set returned by the crosstab query of Figure 15.7.

7. Access automatically selects qry1995MonthlyCategorySales as the query on which to base the report. Select Design view from the list and click OK. Access creates the default blank report shown in Figure 15.9.

### Adding and Deleting Sections of Your Report

When you create a report from a blank template or modify a report created by the Report Wizard, you might want to add a new section to the report by using the following guidelines:

- To add Report Headers and Footers as a pair, choose View, Report Header/Footer.

- To add Page Headers and Footers as a pair, choose View, Page Header/Footer.

- To add a Group Header or Footer, click the toolbar's Sorting and Grouping button  and set the Group Header or Group Footer property value to Yes.

Figure 15.10 shows a blank report, with the headers and footers for each section that you can include in a report. (Although Figure 15.10 shows only one group, you may add as many group levels as you want to your report.)

III

**Creating Forms and Reports**

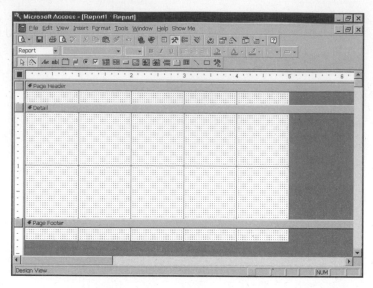

**FIG. 15.9** The default report presented by Access after you select Design view in the New dialog.

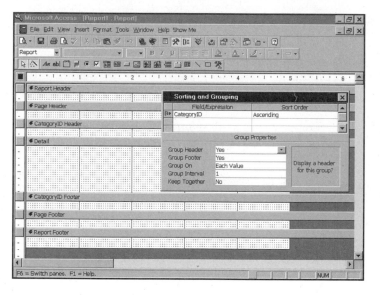

**FIG. 15.10** A blank report with all sections added.

If you group the data in more than one level (group, subgroup, sub-subgroup), you can add a Group Header and Footer for each level of grouping. This action adds to your report another pair of sections for each subgroup level.

You delete sections from reports by using methods similar to those that you use to create the sections. To delete unwanted sections, use the following guidelines:

- To delete the Detail section or an individual Report Header, Report Footer, Page Header, or Page Footer section, delete all controls from the section, and then drag up the divider bar below so that the section has no depth. To delete a report footer, drag the report's bottom margin to the Report Footer border. These actions do not actually delete the sections, but sections with no depth do not print or affect the report's layout.

- To delete Report Headers and Footers as a pair, choose <u>V</u>iew, Report <u>H</u>eader/Footer. If the Report Header or Footer includes a control, a message box warns you that you will lose the controls in the deleted sections.

- To delete Page Headers and Footers as a pair, choose <u>V</u>iew, P<u>a</u>ge Header/Footer. A warning message box appears if either section contains controls.

- To delete a Group Header or Footer, click the toolbar's Sorting and Grouping button and set the Group Header or Group Footer property's value to No.

> **Note**
>
> Page and Report Headers and Footers that incorporate thin lines at the header or footer's upper border can be difficult to delete individually. To make these lines visible, choose <u>E</u>dit, Select <u>A</u>ll to add sizing anchors to the lines. Hold down the Shift key and click the controls that you want to save in order to deselect these controls. Then press the Delete key to delete the remaining selected lines.

### Controlling Page Breaks and the Printing of Page Headers and Footers

The Force New Page and Keep Together properties of the report's Group Header, Detail, and Group Footer sections control manual page breaks. To set these properties, double-click the group's section border to display the section's Properties window. Force New Page causes an unconditional page break immediately before printing the section. If you set the Keep Together property to Yes, and insufficient room is available on the current page to print the entire section, a page break occurs and the section prints on the next page.

To control whether Page Headers or Footers print on the first or last page of a report, choose <u>E</u>dit, Select <u>R</u>eport and then click the toolbar's Properties button. You then select the Page Headers and Page Footers printing option in the Format page of the Properties window (see Figure 15.11).

### Creating the Monthly Sales by Category Report

Earlier in this chapter, you started creating the Monthly Sales by Category report, which is a good example of a report that you might want to create by starting with a blank report. The report includes information about total monthly sales of products by category. Comparing the monthly sales to the inventory level of a category allows the report's user to estimate inventory turnover rates. This report serves two purposes: as a report and as a subreport within another report. You add the Monthly Sales by Category report as a subreport in the "Incorporating Subreports" section later in this chapter.

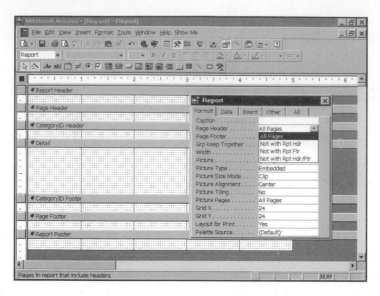

**FIG. 15.11** The Properties window for a report, displaying page-section printing options.

The crosstab query that acts as the report's data source is closely related to a report, but the crosstab query doesn't include detail records (see Chapter 10, "Creating Multitable and Crosstab Queries"). Each row of the query consists of subtotals of sales for a category for each month of the year. One row appears below the inventory value subtotal when you link the subreport to the main report, so the report needs only a Detail section. Each detail row, however, requires a header label to print the month. The CategoryID field is included so that you can verify that the data is linked correctly.

To create the Monthly Sales by Category report (and subreport), follow these steps:

1. Delete all sections of your blank report except the Detail section. By default, blank reports have 24×24 grid dots, and Snap to Grid is selected.

2. Drag down the bottom margin of the Detail section so that the section has an inch or two of depth. You need maneuvering room to relocate the text boxes and associated labels that you add in the following steps. Drag the right margin of the Detail section to the right so that the report is 6.5 inches wide.

3. Click the toolbar's Sorting and Grouping button to display the dialog, and select CategoryID as the field to use to sort the data with a standard ascending sort. Close the Sorting and Grouping dialog.

4. Click the toolbar's Field List button, select CategoryID, and drag the field symbol to the Detail section.

5. Click the CategoryID label, and relocate the label to the Detail section's upper left so that the CategoryID combo box is directly underneath it. (CategoryID appears as a dummy combo box, not a text box, in Report Design view because CategoryID is a lookup field.) Adjust the depth of the label and text box to 0.2 inches (four grid dots) and the width to 1 inch. Edit the label's text to **ID**.

6. Click and drag the field list's Jan field to the right of the CategoryID field. Move the label to the top of the section, adjacent to the right border of the field to its left. Move the text box under the label. Adjust the label and text box depth to four dots and the width to 16 dots. Edit the label's text to delete the colon.

7. Repeat step 6 for the month fields of Feb through Jun. The report design now appears as shown in Figure 15.12.

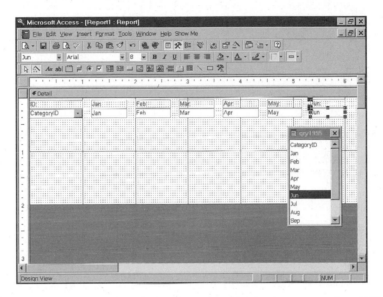

**FIG. 15.12** The report with labels and text boxes added for the first six months of 1995.

8. Click each label while holding down the Shift key so that you select all labels (but only the labels).

9. Click the toolbar's Bold button to add the bold attribute to the labels. Then click the Center button to center the labels above the text boxes.

10. Select the CategoryID text box, and click the toolbar's Bold button.

11. Choose Edit, Select All, and drag the labels and text boxes so that the tops of the labels are two dots down from the top of the Detail section. Click a blank area of the report to deselect the controls.

12. If the toolbox is invisible, click the Toolbox button of the toolbar. Click the Line tool and add a line at the top edge of the labels. Drag the line's right-end handle to the right edge of the Jun text box.

13. Click the drop-down list of the Line/Border Width button on the toolbar, and click the 2-point line-thickness button.

14. Repeat steps 12 and 13 for another identical line, but add the new line under the labels (and above the text boxes).

15. Drag the Detail section's margins to within two dots of the bottom and right edge of the controls. The report's design appears as shown in Figure 15.13.

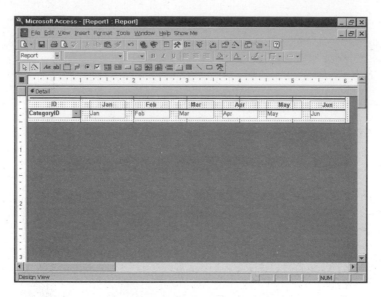

**FIG. 15.13** The layout of the new report's Detail section.

 16. Click the toolbar's Report View button to verify the design. The full-size view of the report appears (see Figure 15.14).

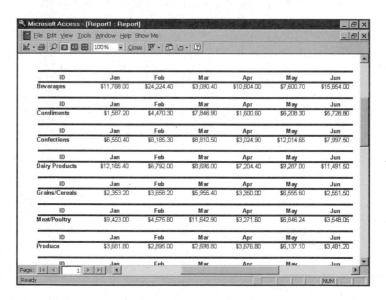

**FIG. 15.14** The monthly category sales report in Print Preview mode.

17. Choose File, Save As and type **rptMonthlyCategorySales** as the report's name.

To add to your report the remaining months of the year, follow these steps:

1. To accommodate another row of labels and text boxes, increase the depth of the Detail section by dragging the bottom margin down (about 1 inch).

2. Choose Edit, Select All.

3. Click the Copy button on the toolbar, or press Ctrl+C to copy the labels and text boxes to the Clipboard.

4. Click the Paste button on the toolbar, or press Ctrl+V to paste a copy of the labels and text boxes to the Detail section.

5. Move this copy under the original labels and text boxes. Space the copy two grid dots below the originals, as shown in Figure 15.15.

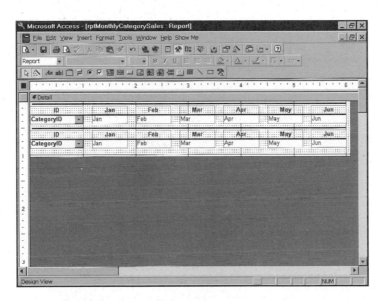

**FIG. 15.15**  The rptMonthlyCategorySales report after adding a copy of all text boxes and labels.

6. Click a blank area of the report to deselect the controls, and then select the new CategoryID text box. Delete the CategoryID text box. When you delete this text box, you also delete the associated label.

7. Edit both the labels and text boxes to display Jul through Dec. (Access automatically resizes the labels to fit the new text value and automatically sets the text boxes' Control Source property to match the field name you type into the text box.)

8. Delete the ID label in the first row, and drag the CategoryID text box to the position that its label formerly occupied.

III

Creating Forms and Reports

9. Drag up the bottom margin to within two dots of the bottom of the text boxes in the second row. The final design appears in Figure 15.16.

10. Click the toolbar's Print Preview button to display the double-row report (see Figure 15.17).

11. Close the rptMonthlyCategorySales report and save the changes.

The technique of copying controls to the Clipboard, pasting copies to reports, and then editing the copies is often faster than creating duplicate controls that differ from one another only in the text of labels and text boxes.

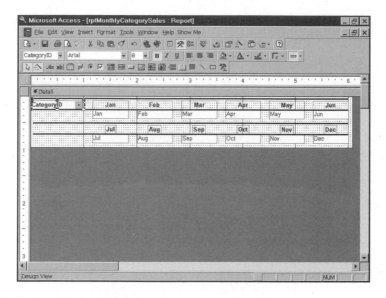

**FIG. 15.16**   The final design of the rptMonthlyCategorySales report.

# Incorporating Subreports

Reports, like forms, can include subreports. Unlike the Form Wizard, however, the Report Wizard offers no option of automatically creating reports that include subreports. You can add subreports to reports that you create with the Report Wizard, or you can create subreports from blank reports, as shown in the preceding section, "Working from a Blank Report."

### Adding a Linked Subreport to a Bound Report

If a main report is bound to a table or query as a data source, and the subreport's data source can be related to the main report's data source, you can link the subreport's data to the main report's data.

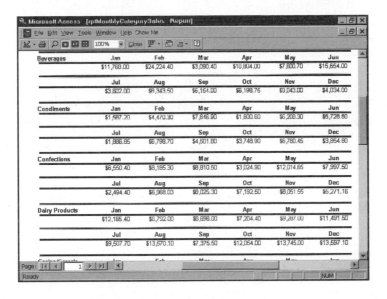

**FIG. 15.17**    The rptMonthlyCategorySales report in Print Preview.

To add and link the rptMonthlyCategorySales report as a subreport to the Products On Hand by Category report, for example, follow these steps:

1. Open the Products On Hand by Category report in Design mode.

2. Drag down the top of the Page Footer border to make room for the subreport in the CategoryID Footer section (about 0.5 inches).

3. Click the toolbar's Database Window button. If the Database window is maximized, click the Restore button.

4. Click and drag the small Report icon from the left of the rptMonthlyCategorySales report to a location inside the CategoryID Footer section. Drop the icon below the CategoryID text box. You must be able to see the location where you want to drop the new subreport in the Report Design window, as shown in Figure 15.18.

5. At the point where you drop the icon, Access creates a subreport box that is similar to a text box. This subreport box has an associated label (see Figure 15.18). Delete the label.

6. Click the Maximize button to restore the Report Design window.

7. Adjust the CategoryID Footer's depth to provide about 0.1-inch margins above and below the section's controls. The report appears in Design view as shown in Figure 15.19.

8. You need to link the data in the subreport to the data of the main report so that only the sales data corresponding to a specific group's CategoryID value appears on screen. Select the subreport box and click the Properties button to display the

III

Creating Forms and Reports

subreport's Properties window. Click the Data tab, type **CategoryID** as the value of the Link Master Fields property, and type **CategoryID** as the value of the Link Child Fields property.

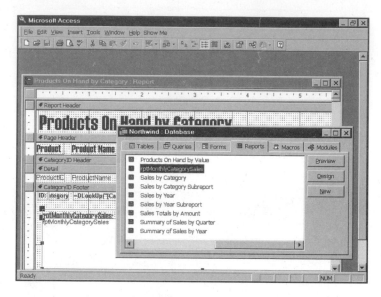

**FIG. 15.18** Dragging and dropping a report as a subreport within another report.

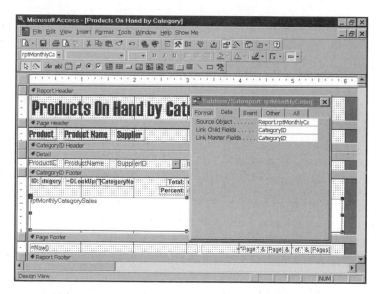

**FIG. 15.19** Setting the properties to link the subreport to the main report.

Access attempts to create the link. If the main report and subreports are based on tables and a relationship is set between the tables, Access creates the link to the related fields. If the main report is grouped to a key field and the subreport's table or query contains a field of the same name and data type, Access creates the link.

9. Click the toolbar's Print Preview button to display the report in the full-size view. The subreport appears as shown at the bottom of Figure 15.20. Click the page selector buttons to view other parts of the subreport to confirm that the linkage is correct.

10. Choose File, Save to save the changes.

You can add and link several subreports to the main report if each subreport has a field in common with the main report's data source.

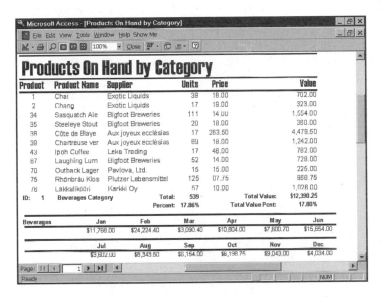

**FIG. 15.20** The rptMonthlyCategorySales subreport linked to the Products On Hand by Category report.

---

**Note**

You can use calculated values to link main reports and subreports. Calculated values often are based on time—months, quarters, or years. To link main reports and subreports by calculated values, you must create queries for both the main report and subreport that include the calculated value in a field, such as Month or Year. You create the calculated field in each query by using the corresponding Access date function, Month or Year. To group by quarters, select Interval for the Group On property and set the value of the Group Interval property to 3. You cannot use Qtr as the Group On property because the calculated value lacks the Date/Time field data type.

---

> **Troubleshooting**
>
> *When I try to create a link between the main report and subreport, I get a* `Can't evaluate expres-`
> `sion` *error message.*
>
> The most likely cause is that you are trying to create a master-child (or, more properly, parent-
> child) link with an incompatible data type. Parent-child linkages are similar to joins of queries that
> use the `WHERE` *SubreportName*.*FieldName* = *ReportName*.*FieldName* criterion. As with joins, the
> data types of the linked fields of tables or columns of queries must be identical. You cannot, for
> example, link a field of the Text data type with a field of the Integer data type, even if your text
> field contains only numbers. If you use an expression to create the link, the data type that the
> expression returns must match the field value. You can use the data type conversion functions
> described in Chapter 9, "Understanding Operators and Expressions in Access," to change the data
> type that the expression returns to that of the linked field. For example, you can link a text field
> that contains numbers to a field of the Long Integer data type by entering **=CLng**(*TextField*) as
> the linking value.

### Using Unlinked Subreports and Unbound Reports

Most reports that you create use subreports that are linked to the main report's data
source. You can, however, insert independent subreports within main reports. In this
case, you don't enter values for the Link Child Fields and Link Master Fields properties—
in fact, if Access adds values, you delete them. The subreport's data source can be related
to or completely independent of the main report's data source. Figure 15.21 shows the
affect of including an unlinked subreport. Figure 15.21 shows a portion of page 2 of the
rptMonthlyCategorySales subreport within the Products on Hand by Category report
after deleting the CategoryID values of the Link Child Fields and Link Master Fields properties. Notice that, without the link, the subreport displays all records instead of just
those records related to the particular category in which subreport appears.

You can add multiple subreports to an unbound report if all of the subreports fit on one
page of the report or all subreports fit across the page. In the latter case, you can use
landscape printing orientation to increase the available page width. To create an unbound report with multiple subreports, follow these steps:

1. Click the Report tab in the Database window, and then click the New button to
   display the New Report dialog.

2. Keep the text box for the New Report dialog's data source blank, select Design view
   in the list, and then click OK. This action creates an unbound report.

3. Click the toolbar's Database Window button to display the Database window, and
   drag the Report icon for the first subreport to the blank form's Detail section.

4. Drag the Report icon for the second subreport to the blank form's Detail section. If
   the two subreports fit vertically on one page, place the second subreport below the
   first subreport. If either of the two subreports requires more than a page, place the
   second subreport to the right of the first. In this case, you must add column labels
   for the subreports in the main report's Page Header section so that each page identifies the columns.

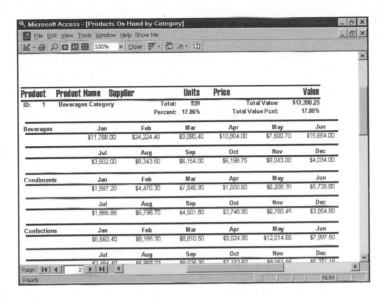

**FIG. 15.21**  The appearance of the rptMonthlyCategorySales subreport for the beverages category when the linking properties have been deleted.

> **Note**
>
> You can also add subreports to a report by using the Toolbox's subform/subreport tool. Use the same procedures for adding subforms that you learned in Chapter 13, "Designing Custom Multitable Forms."

## Adding Other Controls to Reports

Access places no limit on the toolbox controls that you add to reports. So far, the controls that you have modified or added have been limited to labels, text boxes, lines, and the combo boxes that Access places automatically for fields configured as lookup fields. These four kinds of controls are likely to comprise more than 90 percent of the controls used in the reports you create. Controls that require user interaction, such as lists and combo boxes, can be used in a nonprinting section of the report, but practical use of these controls in reports is limited. The following list describes other controls that you might want to add to reports:

■ *Bound object frames* print the contents of the OLE Object field data type. An OLE  object can be a still or animated graphic, a video clip, a waveform or CD audio, or even MIDI music. Reports are designed only for printing, so animated graphics, video, and sound are inappropriate for reports.

■ *Unbound object frames* display OLE objects created by server applications, such as  Microsoft Graph 97 (included with Access), Windows Paint, Excel, or the Microsoft WordArt or Equation Editor OLE applets included with Microsoft Word. Usually, you place unbound objects in the report's Form Header or Form Footer section, but you can add a logo to the top of each page by placing the image object in the Page Header section. A graph or chart created by the Chart Wizard is a special kind of unbound OLE object.

 ■ *Lines* and *rectangles* (also called *shapes*) create decorative elements on reports. Lines of varying widths can separate the sections of the report or emphasize a particular section.

 ■ *Check boxes* and *option buttons* can be used to indicate the values of Yes/No fields or within group frames to indicate multiple-choice selections. Group frames, option buttons, and check boxes used in reports indicate only the value of data cells and do not change the values. Reports seldom use toggle buttons.

 ■ *Command buttons* execute Access VBA procedures.

Bound and unbound object frames are the subject of Chapter 20, "Adding Graphics to Forms and Reports." Access VBA programming is the topic of Part VII, "Programming, Distributing, and Converting Access Applications."

# Sending Reports by Microsoft Exchange and Outlook

If you have installed the Microsoft Exchange client (Inbox) along with the Microsoft Outlook messaging application, you can send a report to others as an attachment to a Microsoft Mail or other Microsoft Exchange message. Exchange lets you send the report output as a fax, through CompuServe mail, Internet Mail, Microsoft Network mail, or through any other messaging system that you have configured to work with Microsoft Exchange. To send a report by Microsoft Exchange, follow these steps:

> **Note**
>
> A full discussion of Microsoft Exchange is beyond the scope of this book. Search the Windows online Help for more information about Microsoft Exchange.

> **Note**
>
>  You can also publish your reports as HTML pages to make them available to Internet users or your company's intranet users. Part IV of this book describes using HTML in Access.

Reports

1. In Print Preview mode, open the report that you want to send. (You do not need to have Microsoft Mail or other Exchange client software running when you create the message, although it must be installed and correctly configured.) You can also select the report that you want to send in the Reports tab of the Database window.

2. Choose File, Send to display the Send dialog (see Figure 15.22).

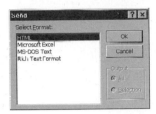

**FIG. 15.22**   Choosing the format for the Microsoft Exchange attachment.

3. In the Select Format list box (refer to Figure 15.22), select the format in which you want to send the report file. This example sends the Products on Hand by Category report in Microsoft Excel 97 (.xls) format.

4. Click OK to create the message. A progress-reporting dialog appears while Access creates the Excel worksheet (.xls) file. When the process is complete, Microsoft Exchange's Choose Profile dialog appears (see Figure 15.23).

**FIG. 15.23**   Choosing the Microsoft Outlook profile for sending a report as a mail attachment.

5. In the Profile Name drop-down list box, select the profile name that you want to use for this message, and then click OK. (Refer to Exchange's online Help for information about Exchange's profiles.) The Microsoft Exchange's New Message window now appears (see Figure 15.24).

6. Enter the recipients' names, a subject, and an optional transmittal message, as shown in Figure 15.24. Click the Send button (the left-most button of the upper toolbar) to send the message with the attached report file.

> **Note**
>
> Depending on your report's formatting, some of the field values might not appear in an Excel worksheet file. For example, the subtotals for the Values fields (as well as both percentage fields) are missing. However, you can easily reconstruct these fields in Excel. Access cannot incorporate subreports that are contained in reports printed to files of any of the three available formats. You must provide individual columns for subtotals and other section footers to ensure that the values appear in an .xls file.

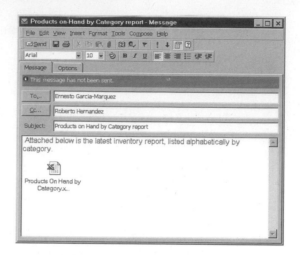

**FIG. 15.24** Completing the Microsoft Outlook message.

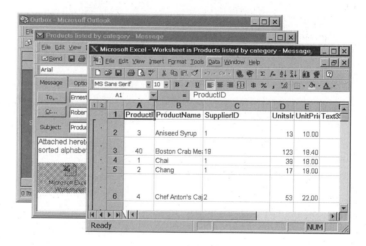

**FIG. 15.25** The appearance of the report attachment in Microsoft Excel 97.

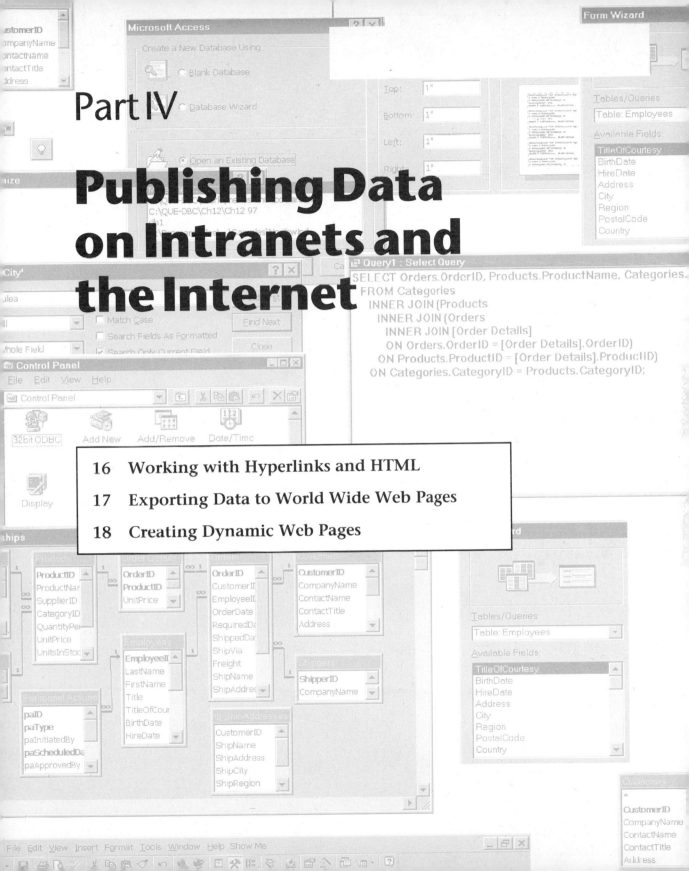

# Part IV

# Publishing Data on Intranets and the Internet

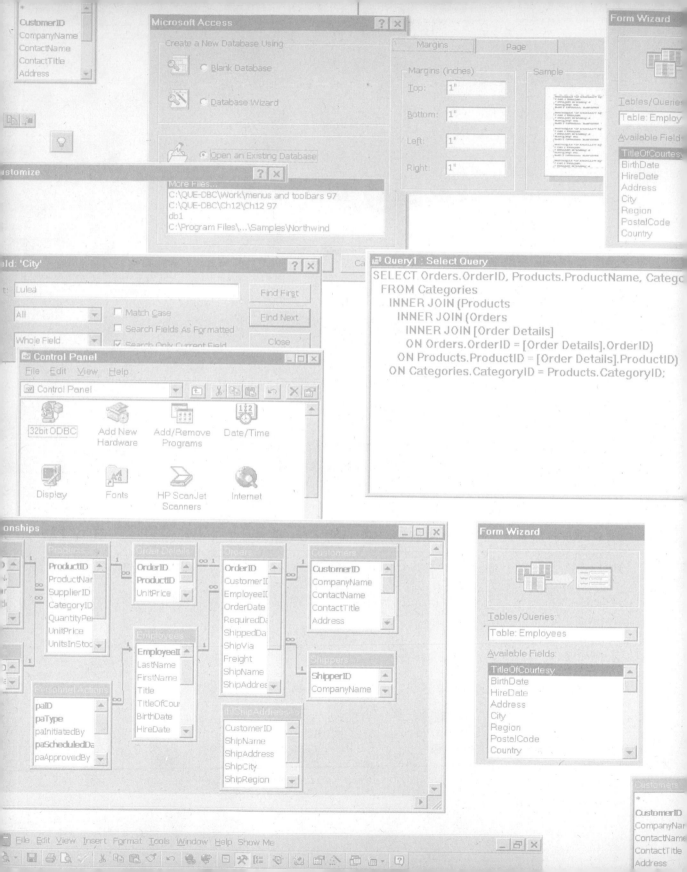

# Chapter 16

# Working with Hyperlinks and HTML

The Internet has made the most profound change in the direction of the computer software industry since the introduction of Windows 3.0. Virtually every new software product published in 1996 had some connection with the Internet, even if tenuous, and there currently is no indication of a slackening in this trend. All of the members of Microsoft Office 97 are "Internet-enabled" to a varying degree. Word 97 lets you convert conventional .doc files to .htm Web pages. PowerPoint 97 encourages you to create presentations for delivery via the World Wide Web. Excel 97 lets you export worksheets to HTML tables. Each of these enhancements rely on *hyperlinks* that lead from one document to another related document and *HyperText Markup Language (HTML)*, a variant of the *Standard Generalized Markup Language (SGML)* designed for text document formatting.

Databases currently play an important role in Internet publishing and are destined to become the backbone of commercial transactions conducted on the Internet (called *electronic commerce* or *e-commerce*). Private intranets, which quickly deliver up-to-date information within an organization, have even greater potential for exploiting relational database technology. Microsoft has equipped Access 97 with a variety of enhancements for distributing data via private intranets and the public Internet. Access 97 also includes features that enable your Access applications to interact directly with documents located on the World Wide Web. This chapter, plus the two chapters that follow, shows you how to take best advantage of these new Access 97 features.

## Putting Microsoft's Internet Program in Perspective

The astounding growth in the use of the Internet that occurred in 1994 and early 1995 appeared to have gone unnoticed by Microsoft. The World Wide Web, with its hyperlinked documents and easy-to-use browsers, had extended the reach of the Internet to ordinary computer users. Sales of Internet server software and hardware mushroomed. Commercial versions of Web browsers, based on the original NCSA Mosaic browser design, gained a major market presence. Ultimately, Netscape Communications, Inc. gained the lion's share of the rapidly expanding Internet server and Web browser software market. The consensus of the computer trade press by late 1995 was that Microsoft had "missed the Internet boat."

Bill Gates announced on December 7, 1995, that Microsoft Corporation would, hence-forth, "embrace and extend the Internet." To achieve his goal, Gates initiated a major reorganization that gave Internet-related development programs top priority at Microsoft. The result of diverting a large part of Microsoft's considerable technical and economic resources to the Internet was a 1996 flood of new products and technology incentives, plus Internet upgrades to existing products. Just keeping up with Microsoft's product announcements bordered on a full-time occupation. What's more, Microsoft distributed most of its new Internet-related products, often in the beta (or pre-beta) testing stage, to users at no charge.

### An Overview of Microsoft's Internet Products

Virtually all of Microsoft's newly-released Internet-related products incorporate or em-ploy database technology. Following is a list of the most important new Internet-related products introduced by Microsoft as of late 1996:

- *Internet Explorer 3.0 (IE)* is Microsoft's entry in the Web browser sweepstakes at the time this book was written. Unlike Netscape Navigator 3.0, which has a retail list price of $49.95, IE 3.0 is free. Office 97 includes IE 3.0, and IE 3.0 is required to take full advantage of the Office 97 Internet feature set, but Office 97 applications also support Netscape Navigator 3.0 as your preferred browser. Figure 16.1 shows Internet Explorer 3.0 displaying the home page of the Volcano Coffee Company example application included with Internet Information Server 2.0.

  Microsoft has succeeded in convincing all of the major online services and many large Internet Service Providers (ISPs) to make IE 3.0 their preferred browser. The next version of IE will be incorporated directly within the Windows 95 and Windows NT operating system. Ultimately, all PC operating systems will have built-in browser capability.

On the Web

  Download the latest Internet Explorer from:

  **http://www.microsoft.com/ie/**

- *NetMeeting 2.0* is an extension to IE 3.0 for collaborative computing. NetMeeting currently includes Internet telephony for voice communication, multiuser data conferencing for application sharing, an electronic whiteboard for diagramming, chat, and binary file transfer. Future versions of NetMeeting are expected to include videoconferencing capability over ISDN and faster connections. NetMeeting uses a database to maintain a list of locations of other NetMeeting users.

On the Web

  You can download your own copy of NetMeeting from:

  **http://www.microsoft.com/netmeeting/**

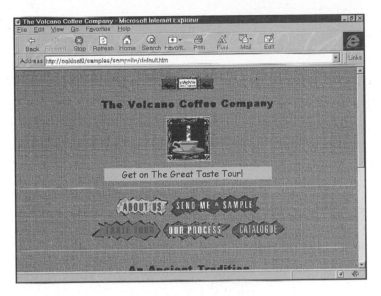

**FIG. 16.1**    Internet Explorer 3.0 displaying the home page for the Volcano Coffee Company example included with Internet Information Server 2.0.

- *NetShow* delivers live and on-demand multimedia content over the Internet and intranets with IE 3.0. NetShow currently enables multicasting of live audio and data, plus storing and streaming of graphics (*illustrated audio*). Future versions of NetShow will include streaming video content for high-bandwidth connections. Databases store locations of NetShow sites and program guides for upcoming live NetShow performances.

  More information on NetShow is available from:

  **http://www.microsoft.com/netshow/**

On the Web

- *Internet Information Server 2.0 (IIS)* is included with Windows NT Server 4.0, a high-performance Internet/intranet delivery system that's closely integrated with Windows NT 4.0's security features. IIS 2.0 includes the Internet Database Connector (IDC), which is the subject of Chapter 18, "Creating Dynamic Web Pages." Figure 16.2 shows a Web page created from a simple IDC query against SQL Server 6.5's Pubs database.

  Get the latest information about Internet Information Server at:

  **http://www.microsoft.com/ntserver/iis/**

On the Web

- *Proxy Server*, originally code-named *Catapult*, provides secure access to the Internet via internal local-area networks (LANs). Proxy Server, which now is a member of Microsoft BackOffice 2.5, improves performance for networked users by *caching* (holding local copies of) commonly accessed Internet content. You can download a free 60-day evaluation copy of Proxy Server from Microsoft's Web site. (Windows NT 4.0 Service Pack 1 is required to run Proxy Server.)

On the Web

The details on Proxy Server are found at:

**http://www.microsoft.com/proxy/**

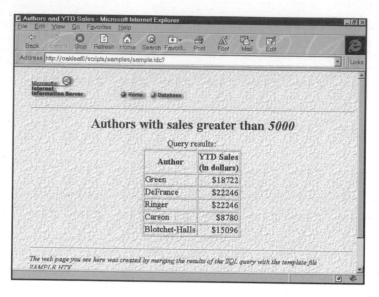

**FIG. 16.2**    Internet Explorer 3.0 displaying a Web page created from a query processed by the Internet Database Connector.

■ *Index Server 1.1* performs full-text searches and retrieves information from any Web browser. Index Server is a free, downloadable service for Windows NT Server 4.0 and Internet Information Server 1+. Index Server 1.1 supports HTML, text, and Microsoft Office document formats, so you need not convert documents to HTML for indexing. Index Server 1.1 uses a special database structure for locating documents stored on one or more Windows NT servers. The Search feature of the Microsoft Web site uses Index Server 1.1.

On the Web

You can download your own copy of Index Server 1.1 from:

**http://www.microsoft.com/ntserver/search/step111dl.htm**

■ *Merchant Server* contains a set of Windows NT services designed for conducting secure electronic commerce on the Internet. Merchant Server lets retailers first build "electronic storefronts" and accept credit-card payment via Secure Electronic Transaction (SET) technology. Microsoft acquired the storefront technology from eShop, an early Internet shopping mall. Merchant Server uses SQL Server 6.5 as its database back-end. Microsoft is expected to charge for licensing Merchant Server.

On the Web

A variety of information on Merchant Server is located at:

**http://www.microsoft.com/merchant/**

- *Media Server*, code-named *Cougar* when this book was written, is an Internet/ intranet server designed expressly for delivering streaming MPEG-1 video content using the ActiveMovie Streaming Format (ASF). Media Server is a downsized version of Microsoft's Tiger server designed to support full-scale interactive video-on-demand (IVOD) using MPEG-2 compression, the standard compression system for DVD, plus digital direct broadcast satellite (DBS) and Advanced TV (ATV, also known as HDTV) transmission. Bandwidth limitations dictate that users connect to Media Server over a LAN or a high-speed WAN.

- *Commercial Internet System* (code-named *Normandy*) *for Windows NT 4.0* provides the following components: Internet Chat Server, Internet News Server, Internet White Pages and Locator Server, Information Retrieval Server, Content Replication System, and Personalization System. Normandy is intended primarily for use by commercial ISPs and large corporations that host their own Web sites. In mid-1996, CompuServe Information Services, Inc. announced that it would use the Normandy platform to implement its new Internet-based online service. Normandy uses SQL Server 6.5 for many of its services. Some of the components of Normandy, such as the Chat Server, are available for free downloading from the Microsoft Web site.

  You can download a few components of Normandy from:

  **http://www.microsoft.com/internet/normandy/**

On the Web

- *dbWeb 1.1a* is a free, downloadable application that creates fully-formatted Web pages from data stored in databases that offer ODBC (Open Database Connectivity) drivers, such as Access and SQL Server. dbWeb consists of a ISAPI (Internet Server API) service, which runs on Internet Information Server 1+, and a stand-alone dbWeb Administrator component for creating schemas that define the data-related content of Web pages.

  You can download dbWeb 1.1a from:

  **http://www.microsoft.com/intdev/dbweb/**

On the Web

▶▶ See "Defining Open Database Connectivity," p. 917

- *FrontPage 97* is an easy-to-use Web page authoring and Web site management system that supports ActiveX technologies and Java components. FrontPage 97 includes a Database Connectivity Wizard that simplifies the design of Web pages that offer user-defined queries. Figure 16.3 shows the FrontPage Explorer's map of the Volcano Coffee Company sample Web site. Although FrontPage 97 is a member of Office 97, Microsoft sells it as a separate retail product. When this book was written, the beta version of FrontPage 97 was available for downloading from the Microsoft Web site.

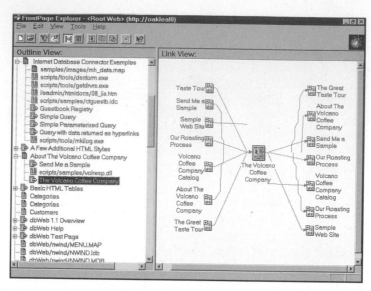

**FIG. 16.3**    The Volcano Coffee Company Web site displayed in the FrontPage Explorer application.

**On the Web**

Get the latest information on FrontPage 97 from:

**http://www.microsoft.com/frontpage/**

The preceding list of Internet-related products introduced in 1996 demonstrates that Microsoft is, to use Bill Gates' expression, "hard-core about the Internet." By mid-1996, the computer press simultaneously praised Microsoft for its "amazing Internet turn-around" and condemned the firm for its aggressive Internet-related marketing practices. Regardless of the outcome of complaints by its competitors to federal regulators, you can expect a continuing stream of new and upgraded Microsoft products for the Internet and intranets in 1997 and beyond.

### Microsoft Technologies Supporting Internet-Related Products

Behind the new products listed in the preceding section are Microsoft technologies that make the products possible. The following list, current as of the fall of 1996, describes both the mature and the new specifications that provide the foundation for current and future Microsoft Internet products:

- *Common Object Model (COM)* is the foundation for OLE (Object Linking and Embedding) and OLE's lightweight successor for the Internet, ActiveX. COM is a specification for creating interactive software components, called *objects*, that become the building blocks of larger applications. In the fall of 1996, Microsoft appointed the Open Group, a computer software industry association, to manage the COM specification. Microsoft's objective in making COM an "open specification" is to gain support for COM as an industry-wide standard for defining programming objects.

IV

Publishing Data

▶▶ See "Introducing Object Building Blocks, p. 670

You can read the 15 chapters of the COM specification at:

**http://www.microsoft.com/oledev/olecom/title.htm**

On the Web

■ *Distributed COM (DCOM)* implements COM over local- and wide-area networks, including the Internet. Microsoft first implemented the final version of DCOM (formerly *NetworkOLE*) in Windows NT 4.0. A beta version of DCOM for Windows 95 was available for downloading from Microsoft's Web site when this book was written. DCOM technology is critical to the implementation of Internet electronic commerce.

The working draft of the DCOM specification is at:

**http://www.microsoft.com/oledev/olecom/dcomspec.txt**

On the Web

■ *ActiveX* contains a collection of COM technologies intended by Microsoft to "activate the Internet" by enabling authors and graphics designers to create dynamic Web pages. The most important ActiveX components for Access 97 users are ActiveX Controls, a replacement for the OLE Controls of earlier versions of Access. IE 3.0 basically is a container for Microsoft's ActiveX Internet Control, which you can insert into an Access 97 form. OLE Documents, which first appeared in the Office 95 Binder, now are called *ActiveX Documents*.

The following URL leads you to a wide range of information on ActiveX technologies:

**http://www.microsoft.com/ActiveX/**

On the Web

▶▶ See "Introducing Microsoft's ActiveX Technology," p. 1096
▶▶ See "Adding ActiveX Controls to Your Application," p. 1122

■ *ActiveMovie* is the replacement for Microsoft's aging Video for Windows (VfW 1.1e for Windows 95 and Windows NT) that enables real-time playback of motion video (.avi files) under Windows. ActiveMovie 1.0 includes the ability to play MPEG-1 movies on a fast Pentium PC without the need for special hardware and eliminates the 2G .avi file size limit, but otherwise is uninspiring. Future versions of ActiveMovie are expected to support full-motion video capture and other features offered by VfW 1.1e.

Current information on ActiveMovie is at:

**http://www.microsoft.com/imedia/activemovie/activem.htm**

On the Web

■ *Visual Basic, Scripting Edition (VBScript, VBS)* is a simplified subset of Visual Basic, Applications Edition (VBA) 5.0, which is included as an application programming (macro) language with all of the members of Office 97, plus Visual Basic 5.0. You can incorporate VBS code in Web pages to program ActiveX controls. VBS also is used for server-side scripting in the ActiveX Server Framework. Once you learn VBA, it's relatively easy to write VBS code embedded in Web pages.

The following URL provides links to pages that describe VBScript:

**On the Web**

**http://www.microsoft.com/vbscript/**

■ *Internet Services API (ISAPI)* contains a set of extensions to Internet Information Server 1+ that lets developers write Windows DLLs to replace slower-performing CGI (Common Gateway Interface) scripts. The most useful ISAPI extension for Access users is the Internet Database Connector (IDC), discussed in the preceding section.

■ *Active Server Pages (ASP)*. Formerly *ActiveX Server Framework* and code-named *Denali* when this book was written; an extension to IIS 2.0 that lets you include VBS on the server to automate the creation of custom Web pages based on input from Web browsers. ASP is included in the forthcoming Internet Information Server 3.0.

■ *OLE DB* contains an SDK (Software Development Kit) and specification for simplifying access to tabular data stored in a variety of formats, such as ODBC-enabled databases (Access and SQL Server, for example), worksheets, e-mail, and text files. OLE DB enables the creation of *ActiveX Data Objects* (ADOs) which provide simplified data connectivity with VBS for Web pages distributed with the ASF. In its FAQs (Frequently Asked Questions) for OLE DB, Microsoft says, "We intend for ADO to be an evolution of our earlier object models. Over time, all our products will standardize on ADO and OLE DB."

You can download version 1.0 of the OLE DB SDK and a preview edition of ADO from:

**On the Web**

**http://www.microsoft.com/oledb/**

■ *OLE Transactions* has a specification for handling updates to databases that involve more than one table. SQL Server 6.5's *Distributed Transaction Controller* (DTC) uses OLE Transactions to handle database updates across multiple databases, including databases residing on remote servers. Both OLE Transactions and DTC play an important role in Microsoft's newly-announced *Transaction Server* (MTx, code-named *Viper* when this book was written.)

■ *DirectX* contains a series of hardware-related Windows 95 and Windows NT technologies for improving video (DirectDraw and Direct3D), audio (DirectSound, Direct3DSound, and DirectMusic), joystick (DirectInput) performance, and game playing over the Internet (DirectPlay).

The details on DirectX are at:

**On the Web**

**http://www.microsoft.com/mediadev/**

- *PC97*, a specification (*PC97 Hardware Design Guide 1.0*), defines three types of Windows-based personal computers: Basic, Workstation, and Entertainment PC. As of July 1, 1997, PCs must meet the requirements of one of the three PC97 types to qualify for use of Microsoft's "Designed for Windows 95" logo. The Entertainment PC includes basic specifications for large-screen PCs designed for family rooms, sometimes called *PCTVs* or *TVPCs*.

The PC97 specification is available from:

**http://www.microsoft.com/hwdev/desguid/pc97des.htm**

**On the Web**

> **Note**
>
> The DirectX and PC97 items of the preceding list are included because they represent the hardware-enabling technology to make high-bandwidth multimedia Internet content, such as ActiveMovie/Media Server MPEG-1 video, practical for users with T-1 or faster connections to the Internet. Individual consumers of Internet multimedia must wait for cable, satellite, or xDSL (high-speed telephone line) access to view real-time, full-motion Internet video broadcasts.

# Navigating with Hyperlinks

The key to the rapid adoption of the Internet's World Wide Web is the ability to jump quickly from one document to a related document or a particular page of a related document with *hyperlinks*. Apple Computer was one of the first firms to commercialize hyperlinks with its original HyperCard development environment, which used HyperTalk as a scripting language. Windows help files also use hyperlinks to display help topics, as do many CD-ROM titles created with CD-ROM authoring applications, such as Microsoft's MediaView and Macromedia's Authorware.

HyperCard, Windows help files, and CD-ROM authoring software allow the linked document files to be located on your PC's fixed disk drive or on a CD-ROM, or be accessible via a conventional LAN or WAN. The public Internet expanded the geographic scope of the hyperlinking process to the entire world. If you're reading a North American Web page on consumer electronics products, it's likely that many of the hyperlinks will point to the Web sites of Japanese manufacturers of TV sets, VCRs, and camcorders, such as **http://www.sony.co.jp**, which usually provide both English and Japanese versions of their text content.

> **Note**
>
> On the Web, *document* and *page* are synonyms; a Web page basically is a file, usually with an .htm or .html extension, stored in a folder on a Web server. *ActiveX documents* (formerly called *document objects* or *DocObjects*) created by Office 97 applications or Visual Basic 5.0 can be embedded within a Web page, which also may include other text and graphic elements.

Another feature of hyperlinking is the ability to return quickly to prior documents, then move on to another related document via a hyperlink. It's this forward-backward navigation system that led to the terms Web *browsing* and *browser*. To provide improved performance, Web browsers store .htm or .html files, together with required graphics files (usually as .gif or .jpg files) on your local disk drive, a process called *caching*. The browser checks to see if a local copy of the file is present before requesting a download from the Web server.

### Hyperlinks and File Paths

Hyperlinks can point to the default home page of a Web site, such as **http://www. microsoft.com**, or to the default page of an intranet server, as in **http://oakleaf0**, the IIS 2.0 intranet server used to write the Internet-related chapters of this book. (OAKLEAF0 is the name of the server on which IIS 2.0 is installed.) You don't need to specify the default page, which usually is Default.htm or Index.htm, as in **http:// oakleaf0/default.htm**. You can jump directly to the default page for a specific topic by extending the address entry, for example **http://www.microsoft.com/msaccess** or **http://oakleaf0/samples/sampsite/default.htm** (refer to Figure 16.1).

Hyperlinks to Web pages use *relative paths* to specify the folders that store HTML pages, graphic images, or scripts that control the customization of pages. As an example, the default folder for the content OAKLEAF0 server is C:\InetPub\wwwroot; the Volcano Coffee Company home page is at C:\InetPub\wwwroot\samples\sampsite. The server name (**oakleaf0**) you include in the Uniform Resource Locator (URL) for the Volcano home page specifies the first part of the path (C:\InetPub\wwwroot) for an intranet server. Extended paths in the URL (**...\samples\sampsite**) are relative (added) to the default Web server path. Understanding the difference between fully-qualified paths (starting with a logical drive letter or \\*SERVERNAME*) and relative paths is very important to your use of hyperlinks with Access 97.

---

> **Note**
>
> The Internet was developed with and, until recently, dominated by UNIX hosts (servers). The UNIX operating system uses the virgule (forward slash, / ) instead of the backslash as the separator in path statements. Another UNIX tradition is the use of lowercase letters for virtually everything, ranging from program names (grep and ftp) to Internet URLs (**http://www.microsoft.com**). UNIX ordinarily is case-sensitive, which would make InetPub a different folder from inetpub, but URLs and path extensions for Web sites are not case-sensitive.

---

### Hyperlinks and Intranets

The combination of hyperlinks and browsing capability makes Web browsers effective competitors to custom database front-ends created with conventional database development platforms, such as Access and Visual Basic. All Web browsers share a relatively standard, simple interface with button-based navigation. Training costs are minimized because most users already are familiar with browsing the Web. Another advantage of browsers compared with custom database front-end applications is the promise of platform independence. Netscape Navigator runs under 16-bit and 32-bit Windows, the Macintosh operating system, and the more popular flavors of UNIX. Microsoft promises that updated versions of Internet Explorer for the Macintosh and UNIX will be available in 1997.

It remains to be seen if Web browsers will take over the role of forms-based database applications, such as Access 97 or Visual Basic 5.0, for delivering data via private networks. The primary incentive for establishing intranets is quick and easy deployment of new and updated Web pages that take the place of Access forms. As an example, you can duplicate the function of the Main Switchboard form of Northwind.mdb with a home page that replaces the form's command buttons with hyperlinks leading to Web pages that imitate the Categories, Products, Suppliers, and Orders forms. If you want to change the Categories page, you need only copy the page from the Web server, edit and test the page, then replace the page on the server. To add a new page, you need only place another hyperlink on the Main Switchboard page. The updating process is considerably easier than altering Northwind.mdb and delivering the new version to every user.

# Understanding Access 97's Hyperlink Field Data Type

Access 97 adds a new member, *Hyperlink*, to its repertoire of field data types. Hyperlink is not a Jet 3.5 data type, because Jet 3.5 stores Access Hyperlink values in Memo fields. Access 97's Hyperlink data type simply interprets the value of the Memo field as a hyperlink and formats the display accordingly.

A Hyperlink field value may consist of the following three components:

- *Display text,* an optional descriptive name for the hyperlink that appears as emphasized text, usually underlined and having a distinctive color.

- *Address,* a required reference to the location of a related document. The reference can be an Internet URL for World Wide Web and FTP (File Transfer Protocol) sites, a relative or fully-qualified path and file name, or a file on a network server specified by UNC (Uniform Naming Convention).

- *Subaddress,* an optional reference to a named location in a related document, such as a bookmark in a Word or HTML document, or a named range in an Excel worksheet.

Individual components of Hyperlink values are separated by the pound sign, the same delimiter used for Jet date values. Following are examples of typical Hyperlink values:

- `Microsoft Web Site#http://www.microsoft.com` displays Microsoft Web site and jumps to the home page of **www.microsoft.com**.

- `Yen Conversion#c:\currency\1996dec.xls#Yen` displays Yen Conversion and points to the c:\currency\1996dec.xls file's Yen named range.

- `#\\Server1\Documents\Reports\1996sales.doc#Drugs` displays and points to the Drugs bookmark in the 1996sales.doc Word document in the shared \Documents \Reports folder of Server1. If you don't include a display text value, the address and subaddress values are displayed.

- `##frmProducts` points to the frmProducts form in the currently-open database.

### Testing Hyperlinks in the Northwind Orders Table

Northwind.mdb's Suppliers table, shown in Figure 16.4, includes a Home Page Hyperlink field that includes links to Web pages located in your \Program Files\Microsoft Office\Office\Samples folder and to placeholder pages at **http://www.microsoft. com/accessdev/sampleapps**. Hyperlinks stored in tables are useful for creating searchable databases for storing links to your favorite Web sites. Hyperlinks in tables also offer automatic navigation assistance within large corporate intranets. As an example, you can create a table with document names, keywords, and other identifying information, then use a query to locate and display only those documents meeting criteria you establish.

The CAJUN.HTM and FORMAGGI.HTM hyperlinks point to individual Cajun.htm and Formaggi.htm files, respectively, using relative paths. Clicking either of these two hyperlinks opens Internet Explorer 3.0 (or another browser you've specified as your default browser) to display the file. Figure 16.5 shows Cajun.htm open in Internet Explorer 3.0. If you click one of the links with (on the World Wide Web) in the display text, your browser connects to the Web site and opens the specified page.

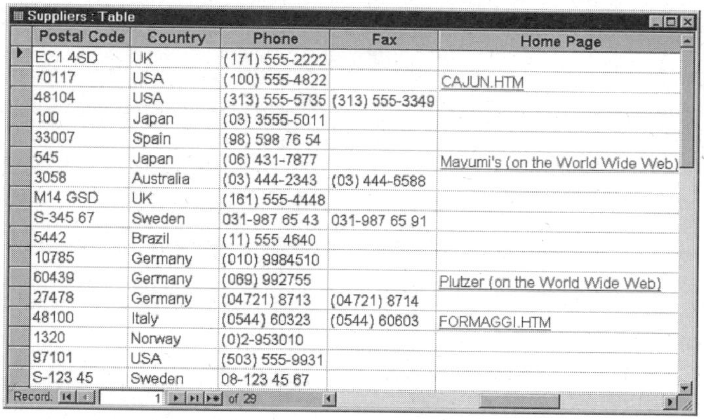


| Postal Code | Country | Phone | Fax | Home Page |
|---|---|---|---|---|
| EC1 4SD | UK | (171) 555-2222 | | |
| 70117 | USA | (100) 555-4822 | | CAJUN.HTM |
| 48104 | USA | (313) 555-5735 | (313) 555-3349 | |
| 100 | Japan | (03) 3555-5011 | | |
| 33007 | Spain | (98) 598 76 54 | | |
| 545 | Japan | (06) 431-7877 | | Mayumi's (on the World Wide Web) |
| 3058 | Australia | (03) 444-2343 | (03) 444-6588 | |
| M14 GSD | UK | (161) 555-4448 | | |
| S-345 67 | Sweden | 031-987 65 43 | 031-987 65 91 | |
| 5442 | Brazil | (11) 555 4640 | | |
| 10785 | Germany | (010) 9984510 | | |
| 60439 | Germany | (069) 992755 | | Plutzer (on the World Wide Web) |
| 27478 | Germany | (04721) 8713 | (04721) 8714 | |
| 48100 | Italy | (0544) 60323 | (0544) 60603 | FORMAGGI.HTM |
| 1320 | Norway | (0)2-953010 | | |
| 97101 | USA | (503) 555-9931 | | |
| S-123 45 | Sweden | 08-123 45 67 | | |

**FIG. 16.4** The Home Page Hyperlink field of Northwind.mdb's Suppliers table.

> **Note**
>
> When you open IE 3.0 from an Access 97 hyperlink, Access automatically minimizes. Each hyperlink you click opens another independent instance of IE 3.0 to display the page.

### Editing and Inserting Conventional Hyperlinks

To edit an existing hyperlink value or to add a new hyperlink to a table, right-click a cell in a Hyperlink field to open the popup menu, then choose Hyperlink, Edit Hyperlink (see Figure 16.6) to open the Edit Hyperlink dialog. Figure 16.7 shows the URL entry for the Plutzer home page located on the Microsoft Web site. If you're creating a new hyperlink, type the Internet URL of the page in the Link to File or URL drop-down combo box. Alternatively, you can open the drop-down list and select from prior URLs that you've opened in IE 3.0. To link to a file, click the Browse button to open the Link to File dialog and select the file for the link.

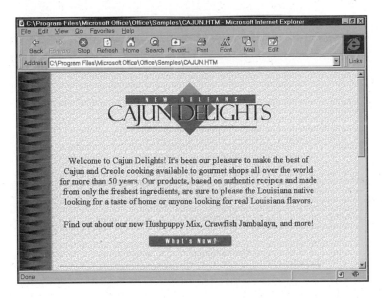

**FIG. 16.5**  The home page for the Cajun Delights (Cajun.htm) hyperlink of the Suppliers table opened in Internet Explorer 3.0.

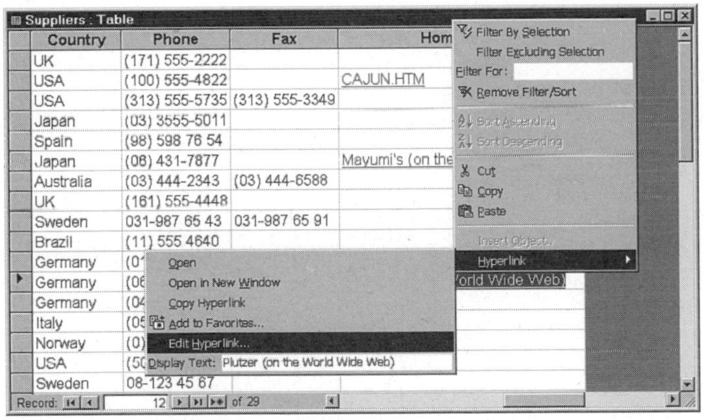

**FIG. 16.6**  The popup menu and submenu for editing or creating a hyperlink value.

| **Note** |
| --- |
| You can edit the display text element of the hyperlink value in the text box of the popup submenu that opens when you choose Hyperlink from the first popup menu (refer to Figure 16.6). |

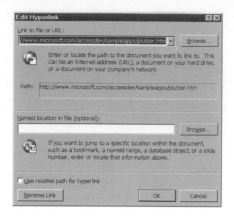

**FIG. 16.7**    The Edit Hyperlink dialog with an entry for a hyperlink to a page on the World Wide Web.

### Linking to Bookmarks in a Word Document

To create a link to an existing Word document having one or more bookmarks that uses a hyperlink subaddress to locate a specific bookmark in the document, follow these steps:

1. Create a new table with at least one Text field to identify the subject matter and a Hyperlink field to contain the links to the bookmarks. Open the new table in Datasheet view.

2. Type the description in the text field and move to the Hyperlink field, but don't enter display text.

> **Note**
>
> If you enter display text in the Hyperlink field, an **http://** URL prefix is added to the display text to create a default URL in the Edit Hyperlink dialog's Link to URL or File combo box. This is not helpful when you want to link to a file.

3. Right-click the empty cell in the Hyperlink field, then choose Hyperlink, Edit Hyperlink to open the Edit Hyperlink dialog.

4. Click the Browse button to the right of the Link to URL or File combo box to open the Link to File dialog (see Figure 16.8). Select the .doc file to link and click the OK button to close the dialog. The fully-qualified path to the selected file appears in the Link to URL or File combo box (see Figure 16.9).

5. Type the name of the bookmark in the Named Location in File text box. If you want to use the relative path to the file, mark the Use Relative Path for Hyperlink check box (see Figure 16.10). A relative path is most useful when your document is in the same folder as the Access .mdb file; in this case only the file name appears in the Path label. Click OK to close the Edit Hyperlink dialog.

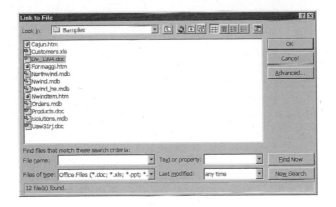

**FIG. 16.8** Specifying the file for a hyperlink in the File to Link dialog.

**FIG. 16.9** The full path to the file displayed in the URL or File to Link combo box.

**FIG. 16.10** Specifying a bookmark for the hyperlink in the Word .doc file and the use of a relative path for the link to the file.

> **Note**
>
> You can't use the Browse button to the right of Named Location in File text box to display a list of bookmarks in Word .doc files or named ranges in Excel worksheets. The Browse button only displays objects in the currently open Jet database.

**6.** The file name (address element of the hyperlink value) appears in the Hyperlink cell of the table (see Figure 16.11). If you want display text to appear in the cell, rather than the file name, right-click the cell, choose Hyperlink, and type the entry in the Display Text text box of the popup submenu (refer to Figure 16.6).

> **Note**
>
> If you type over the file name in the current cell of the Hyperlink field that displays the file name, you replace the address element. Thus you must make the change in the popup submenu's Display Text text box.

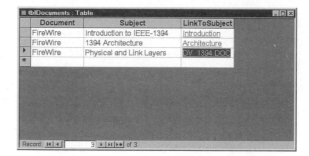

**FIG. 16.11**    A hyperlink entry without display text showing the address of the file (Dv_1394.doc).

**7.** When you click the new hyperlink entry, Word 97 opens the specified .doc file and positions the caret to the bookmark name you entered in step 5 (see Figure 16.12).

 **8.** Click the Back button of Word's Web toolbar to return to Access.

 **9.** Click the Forward button of Access's Web toolbar to return to Word and the open document.

**10.** Close Word when you're finished experimenting.

The preceding procedure also applies to Excel worksheets and PowerPoint presentations. Specify the name of an Excel 97 range or the number of a PowerPoint slide in the Named Location in File text.

### Specifying Hyperlinks to Pages on an Intranet Server

You can establish links to pages on an intranet server using the following generalized URL format:

**http://*servername*/*folder*[/*pagename*.htm]**

As an example, to specify a link to the default page of the FireWire subfolder of the \InetPub\wwwroot folder for Internet Information Server 2.0 running on a server named OAKLEAF0, type **http://oakleaf0/firewire** in the Link to URL or File text box. Alternatively, you can specify a particular page in the folder, such as **.../1394wirc.htm** (see Figure 16.13). To define a jump to an *anchor* (the term for the HTML equivalent of a bookmark) in the Web page, type the anchor name in the Named Location in File (subaddress) text box. Figure 16.17 shows IE 3.0 displaying the 1394wire.htm file, which was created by using Word 97 to save the Dv_1394.doc file in HTML format.

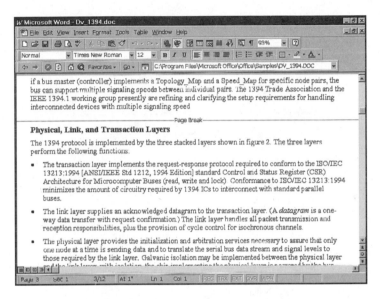

**FIG. 16.12**   The hyperlinked document opened in Word 97 with the caret positioned at the specified bookmark.

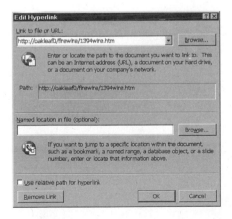

**FIG. 16.13**   Specifying a hyperlink jump to a page on an intranet server.

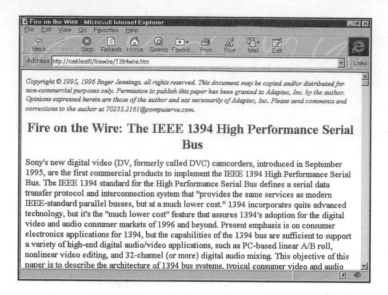

**FIG. 16.14** A Web page displayed by making the jump to a document stored on an intranet server.

### Using Hyperlinks to Open an Access Object

In addition to using hyperlinks to open documents in IE 3.0, Word 97, Excel 97, or PowerPoint 97, you can specify an object to open in an Access 97 database file. As an example, you can open a designated form in the Solutions.mdb database by following these steps:

1. Open the Suppliers table of Northwind.mdb and move to an empty cell in the Home Page field.

2. Right-click the empty Hyperlink cell and choose Hyperlink, Edit Hyperlink to open the Edit Hyperlink dialog.

3. Click the upper Browse button, select Solutions.mdb, and click OK to specify the Solutions database as the address of the hyperlink (see Figure 16.15).

4. Click the lower Browse button to open the Select Location dialog, a modal version of the Database window that displays the objects in the selected .mdb file.

5. Click the Forms tab and select one of the forms in Solutions.mdb, such as the SolutionsHyperForm (see Figure 16.16). Click OK to close the Select Location dialog.

6. The type of object, Form in this case, followed by a space and the name of the object appears in the Named Location in File text box (see Figure 16.17). Click OK to close the Edit Hyperlink dialog.

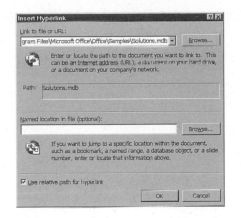

**FIG. 16.15**    An Access .mdb file specified as the address of a hyperlink.

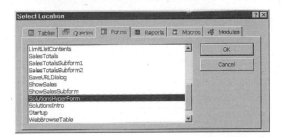

**FIG. 16.16**    Selecting the Access object to open in a hyperlinked .mdb file.

**FIG. 16.17**    Selecting the Access object to open in a hyperlinked .mdb file.

7. Click the new hyperlink. A second instance of Access launches, opens Solutions. mdb, and then opens the SolutionsHyperForm form (see Figure 16.18). You might need to close the Solutions splash screen to make the form visible.

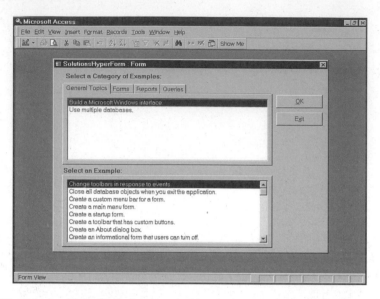

**FIG. 16.18**    The SolutionsHyperForm form opened by the hyperlink of Figure 16.17.

8. Click the Exit button to close Solutions.mdb, close the second instance of Access, and clear the test hyperlink value you created.

> **Note**
>
> Access 97 uses Windows dynamic data exchange (DDE) to process Hyperlinks to applications that reside on your PC. If you're familiar with DDE, following is the correspondence of hyperlink value components with DDE command arguments.
>
> The address component of the hyperlink value corresponds to DDE's TopicName argument of the DDEInitiate command; the ServiceName argument is derived from the file extension. The subaddress component corresponds to the ItemName argument of the DDERequest command. If you're not familiar with DDE, disregard this note.

# Specifying Internet Uniform Resource Locators

Internet Uniform Resource Locators consist of an abbreviation for a protocol that defines the type of object (usually a document) and the location (address) of the desired object on the Internet or an intranet. In most cases, the protocol and the address are separated by two virgules (forward slashes) and a colon, as in **http://www.microsoft.com** or **ftp://ftp.microsoft.com**. Access 97 hyperlinks support the http (HyperText Transport Protocol) and FTP URL prefixes with IE 3.0 and other Web browsers. Access 97's Hyperlink fields recognize the URL prefixes listed in Table 16.1. You need the appropriate software installed and registered on your PC to use prefixes other than http and ftp.

**Table 16.1   Uniform Resource Locator (URL) Prefixes Recognized by Access 97 Hyperlink Fields**

| URL Prefix | Protocol Name | Description of Protocol |
|---|---|---|
| cid | CompuServe Information Dialer (CID) | Attempt to create a connection using Point-to-Point Protocol (PPP) to the Internet using the CompuServe dialer. |
| file | File | Opens a file specified by a fully-qualified path and file name. |
| ftp | File Transfer | Transfers files stored on an FTP server. |
| gopher | Gopher | Obtains information from a Gopher server. |
| http | Hypertext Transfer | Opens a Web page. |
| https | Hypertext Transfer with Security | Attempts to open a connection to a Web page with Secure Sockets Layer (SSL) encryption. |
| mailto | Electronic mail | Sends a message using your preferred e-mail program using the mailto:mailbox@domainname URL format. |
| mid | Musical Instrument Digital Interface (MIDI) | Uses your audio adapter card to play MID files. |
| mms | Microsoft Media Server (MMS) | Plays streaming media files (such as ASF files). |
| msn | Microsoft Network | Jumps to a location on The Microsoft Network. |
| news | News protocol | Starts your news reader program for the specified news group using the news: newsgroupname URL format. |
| nntp | Network News Transfer | Same as news, but uses the conventional nntp://newsgroupname URL format. |
| pnm | RealAudio protocol | Uses your audio adapter card to play Progressive Networks' RealAudio files. |
| prospero | Prospero | Accesses the Prospero distributed file system for UNIX hosts. |
| rlogin | Terminal login | Tries to start a Rlogin terminal emulation program on a UNIX host. |
| telnet | Terminal emulation | Tries to start a telnet terminal emulation program with a UNIX host. |
| tn3270 | IBM 3270 terminal emulation | Tries to start an IBM 3270 terminal emulation program. |
| wais | Wide Area Information Servers | Connects to a WAIS search services database. |

# Using Hyperlinks with Access Controls

You can use hyperlinks with Access controls, such as command buttons, combo boxes, and labels, to jump to another document or open an object within the current or another Access database. To create a form with a command button to open Northwind. mdb's Orders form with a hyperlink, follow these steps:

1. Create a new form in Design view.

2. Disable the Control Wizards and add a command button to the form.

3. With the command button selected, click the Properties button of the toolbar to open the Properties window and click the Format tab.

4. In the Caption property text box, type **Open Orders Form** to create the display text component of the hyperlink.

5. Leave the Hyperlink Address property text box empty, specifying that the object you want to open is in the current database.

6. Select the Hyperlink Subaddress property text box and click the Builder button to open the Select Location dialog.

7. Click the Forms tab, select the Orders form, then click OK to close the dialog. Form Orders appears in the Hyperlink Subaddress property text box, and the command button's caption appears in blue type with an underscore (see Figure 16.19).

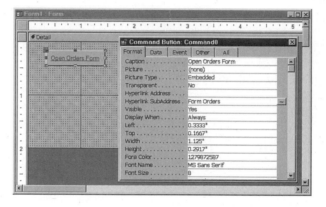

**FIG. 16.19**  A command button that uses a hyperlink to open a form in the current database.

8. Change to Form view and click the command button to open the Orders form.

9. Close, but don't save, your test form.

---

**Note**

Using command buttons with hyperlinks to open forms lets you take advantage of Access 97's *lightweight forms* (forms without VBA code in class modules). You can open, but not close, a form with a hyperlink. As a result, users of your application may be confronted a large number of simultaneously-open forms. Having more than two open forms at a time is likely to confuse users new to Access applications.

---

# Chapter 17

# Exporting Data to World Wide Web Pages

The easiest approach to creating Web pages is to export existing content from applications with which you're familiar. Each member of Office 97, except Outlook, is capable of exporting its documents to formatted HTML files with a File menu choice or a wizard. Access 97 gives you several options for creating static and dynamic Web pages from data contained in Jet tables. This chapter covers methods for generating static Web pages, which you must replace when the underlying data changes. Chapter 18, "Creating Dynamic Web Pages," describes how to create Web pages that automatically display the most current information.

You don't need to be an HTML (HyperText Markup Language) expert to export data from Access 97 objects to static Web pages. In fact, you don't need to have any knowledge of HTML and its formatting tags to perform the examples in this chapter. An elementary understanding of use of basic HTML tags, however, lets you alter the predetermined format of exported data to improve the appearance or utility of your Web pages. Thus, the HTML source for some of the examples in this chapter is included in the form of code listings or examples in the text.

## Exporting Table and Query Datasheets to HTML

Northwind.mdb's Suppliers table is a good choice for exporting to a Web page because it contains relatively few fields and records. The Suppliers table also includes four hyperlinks, two of which link to sample home pages in your ...\Office\Samples folder. To create a formatted Web page from the Suppliers table, follow these steps:

1. Open the Suppliers table of Northwind.mdb in Datasheet view.

2. Choose File, Save As/Export to open the Save As dialog. With the To an External File or Database option selected, click the OK button to close the dialog and open the Save Table 'Suppliers' In dialog.

3. In the Files of Type drop-down list, select HTML Documents (*.html, *.htm), as shown in Figure 17.1. The .html extension is used most often by UNIX servers, while .htm is most common for Windows NT 4.0 servers. Internet Explorer (IE) 3.0 handles .html (the default) and .htm extensions equally well.

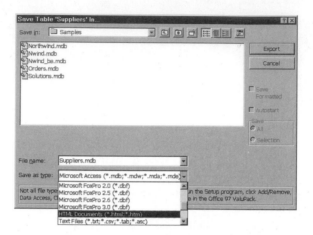

**FIG. 17.1** Choosing HTML Documents as the format for exporting the content of an Access 97 table.

4. Selecting HTML Documents enables the Save Formatted check box, which you must mark to include Access 97's automatic HTML formatting. When you mark the Save Formatted check box, the Autostart check box is enabled. Mark the Autostart check box to have IE 3.0 or another default browser display the page when exporting completes (see Figure 17.2).

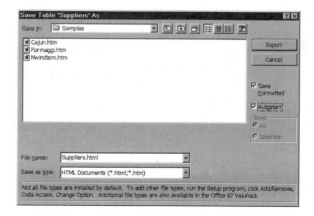

**FIG. 17.2** Specifying HTML formatting with the Save Formatted option and opening the exported .html file in your default browser with the Autostart option.

5. Click the Export button to close the Save Table 'Suppliers' In dialog and begin the export process. Click OK to close the HTML Output Options dialog, leaving the

HTML Template text box empty (see Figure 17.3). The section "Using HTML Templates" later in the chapter describes how to base the design of your Web page on an HTML template.

**FIG. 17.3** Bypassing use of an existing HTML template file by leaving the text box of the HTML Output Options dialog empty.

6. When the formatted Suppliers.html Web page automatically appears in your browser (see Figure 17.4), scroll to the right to display the Home Page table column (see Figure 17.5). Click one of the local hyperlinks (CAJUN.HTM or FORMAGGI.HTM) to test the links to the sample Web pages in your …\Office\Samples folder. HTML formats hyperlinks with `<A HREF=location>` tags that include the location of the linked document.

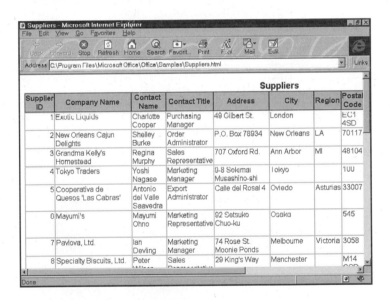

**FIG. 17.4** The formatted Web page created from the Suppliers table.

> **Note**
>
> HTML uses *tags* to identify the beginning and end of HTML documents (`<HTML>` and `</HTML>`), titles (`<TITLE>` and `</TITLE>`), and other elements of the page. HTML 3.2, the current version of HTML when Microsoft released Access 97, has hundreds of tags for formatting, creating control objects on pages, and other uses.

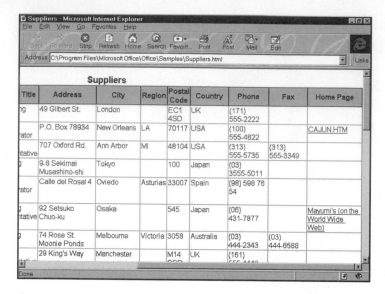

**FIG. 17.5**  Hyperlinks to local (CAJUN.HTM) and Internet (Mayumi's) Web pages in the Suppliers.html file.

**On the Web**

The World Wide Web Consortium (W3C) is responsible for maintaining the standards for HTML. You can obtain the latest information on HTML 3.2 and its successors from

**http://www.w3.org/pub/WWW/MarkUp/Wilbur/**

7. Choose <u>V</u>iew, Sour<u>c</u>e from IE 3.0's menu to display the HTML source for the Suppliers.html file in Windows Notepad (see Figure 17.6). If the size of the file is larger than about 50K, you receive a message that the file is too large for Notepad and are given the option to open the file in WordPad.

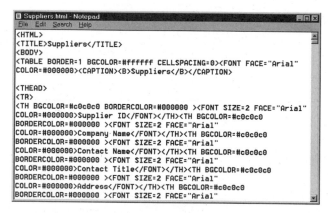

**FIG. 17.6**  The first few lines of the HTML source for the Suppliers.html file.

8. Close Notepad and your browser, then return to Access.

### Creating an Unformatted Web Page

The vast majority of the content of the Suppliers.html file is HTML formatting instructions for colors and text fonts. The color and font formatting instructions obscure the HTML text that creates the tabular structure of the Web page. Much of the formatting content is duplicated throughout the source code; duplicate formatting is typical when you use tools that automatically create Web pages for you.

To create a Web page with a simple HTML table that doesn't include extra formatting instructions, modify the process described in the preceding example as follows:

1. Repeat steps 2 and 3 of the preceding example. In step 3, change the name of the file to **Suppliers (Unformatted).html**.

2. With the Save Formatted check box cleared, click the Export button to create the unformatted Web page. In this case, the HTML Output Options dialog doesn't appear.

3. Open Explorer, navigate to your …\Office\Sample folder, and double-click the Suppliers (Unformatted).html item to launch your browser and display the unformatted Web page (see Figure 17.7). To improve the readability of Web pages in the figures of this book, the background color of IE 3.0 is set to white.

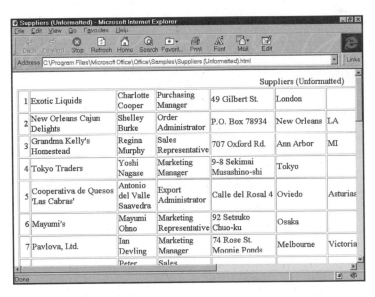

**FIG. 17.7**  The Suppliers (Unformatted).html file displayed in Internet Explorer 3.0.

4. Choose View, Source from IE 3.0's menu to display in Notepad the simplified HTML source for the page (see Figure 17.8). All of the font and color formatting is removed, along with the source only the most basic HTML tags use to create a title for the browser's title bar, caption, and the table containing the data. The unformatted table doesn't include a header for field names and uses the default HTML table borders.

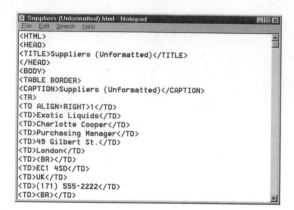

**FIG. 17.8** Simplified HTML source for the unformatted version of the Page created from the Suppliers table.

**5.** After you've reviewed the HTML source code, close Notepad and your browser to return to Access.

Listing 17.1 shows the HTML source for the unformatted page, with only the first two and the last rows of data. (An ellipsis (...) replaces missing table data rows.) <TR>... </TR> tags define the beginning and end of a table row. Individual data cells of the table are defined by <TD>...</TD> pairs. Unless the ALIGN=RIGHT attribute for numeric values is applied to a cell, the default left alignment for text prevails.

**Listing 17.1   HTML Source for the Suppliers (Unformatted).html File with Source Only for the First Two and Last Records**

```
<HTML>
<HEAD>
<TITLE>Suppliers (Unformatted)</TITLE>
</HEAD>
<BODY>
<TABLE BORDER>
<CAPTION>Suppliers (Unformatted)</CAPTION>
<TR>
<TD ALIGN=RIGHT>1</TD>
<TD>Exotic Liquids</TD>
<TD>Charlotte Cooper</TD>
<TD>Purchasing Manager</TD>
<TD>49 Gilbert St.</TD>
<TD>London</TD>
<TD><BR></TD>
<TD>EC1 4SD</TD>
<TD>UK</TD>
<TD>(171) 555-2222</TD>
<TD><BR></TD>
<TD><BR></TD>
</TR>
<TR>
<TD ALIGN=RIGHT>2</TD>
<TD>New Orleans Cajun Delights</TD>
```

```
          <TD>Shelley Burke</TD>
          <TD>Order Administrator</TD>
          <TD>P.O. Box 78934</TD>
          <TD>New Orleans</TD>
          <TD>LA</TD>
          <TD>70117</TD>
          <TD>USA</TD>
          <TD>(100) 555-4822</TD>
          <TD><BR></TD>
          <TD><A HREF="CAJUN.HTM">CAJUN.HTM</A></TD>
          </TR>
          ...
          <TR>
          <TD ALIGN=RIGHT>29</TD>
          <TD>For&ecirc;ts d'&eacute;rables</TD>
          <TD>Chantal Goulet</TD>
          <TD>Accounting Manager</TD>
          <TD>148 rue Chasseur</TD>
          <TD>Ste-Hyacinthe</TD>
          <TD>Qu&eacute;bec</TD>
          <TD>J2S 7S8</TD>
          <TD>Canada</TD>
          <TD>(514) 555-2955</TD>
          <TD>(514) 555-2921</TD>
          <TD><BR></TD>
          </TR>
          </TABLE>
          </BODY>
          </HTML>
```

HTML uses the &*charname*; format to specify special characters. As an example, &ecirc; inserts the letter "e" with a circumflex (ê) for Forêts, and &eacute inserts the letter "e" with an acute (é) in both d'érables and Québec in the last row of the table in Listing 17.1. </TABLE>, </BODY>, and </HTML> denote the end of the table, body part, and document.

> **Note**
>
> Files containing conventional (unformatted) HTML tables are much smaller than Access 97's formatted files. As an example, Suppliers.html (33K) is almost four times the size of Suppliers (Unformatted).html (9K). It's uncommon to export tables with large numbers of records to single Web pages because they are slow to load in the user's browser and make finding the desired row a chore. If you must create a static Web page from a table or query with a large number of rows, choose the unformatted version to reduce file size and speed display in the browser.

### Creating a Web Page from a Query

Tables in Web pages exported from entire Access tables often contain much more than users want to know. Thus, most static Web pages include only a subset of the records and columns of large tables. The objective of reducing the number of columns is to eliminate the need for horizontal scrolling to review the information presented. Queries let you specify the columns that appear in the page. Multiple queries with different criteria let you create a series of Web pages opened by hyperlinks on a home page.

> **Note**
>
> If you use a parameterized query, you are prompted to enter the parameter value before Access creates the HTML file. If you use parameterized queries to create multiple pages, remember to save the resulting file with an appropriate file name to prevent overwriting files created with other parameter values. All of the Web pages you create from a single parameterized query have the same title and caption, which limits the utility of parameterized queries for creating static Web pages.

The following example uses a query to display only the North American customers of Northwind Traders in a format that doesn't require horizontal scrolling. The resulting Web page almost fills the width of the display area of a browser on PCs using either 640×480 or 800×600 video resolution. Although 800×600 is the most common resolution for today's desktop PCs with 15-inch and larger monitors, you also should make sure your Web page design is suitable for the 640×480 resolution used by the majority of the installed base of laptop computers.

Follow these steps to create the sample query and Web page:

 Queries

1. Create a new query and add only the Customers table.

2. Add the CustomerID, CompanyName, City, Region, PostalCode, Phone, and Country fields to the query design grid.

3. Add **USA**, **Canada**, and **Mexico** in the Criteria cells of the Country field and save your query with the name **North American Customers** (see Figure 17.9).

> **Note**
>
> The export process uses the query object name for the title and caption of the Web page. Thus, using the qry prefix for query names isn't recommended when you design queries for export to Web pages.

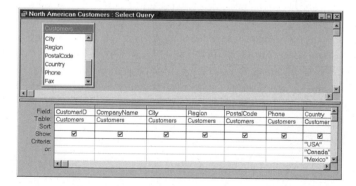

**FIG. 17.9** The design of a query to display selected records in a Web page without a horizontal scroll bar.

4. Run your query to change to Datasheet view and test the design (see Figure 17.10).

**FIG. 17.10**   The query result set of the query design of Figure 17.9.

5. Choose File, Save As/Export, select the To an External File or Database option, and click OK to open the Save Query 'North American Customers' In dialog. Select HTML Files (*.html, *.htm) in the Files of Type drop-down list and mark the Save Formatted and Autostart check boxes. Change the name of the file from North American Customers.html in the File Name combo box, if you want to use a shorter file name.

6. Click Export, then click OK when the HTML Options dialog appears. After a few seconds, your query result set appears in your default Web browser. Figure 17.11 shows the formatted page in IE 3.0 at 800×600 resolution with large fonts specified. The appearance of the page is identical in 640×480 resolution.

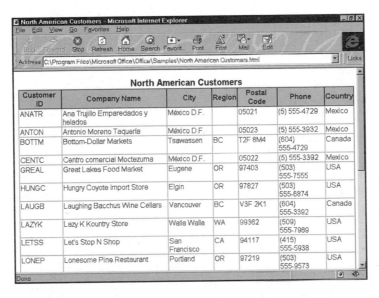

**FIG. 17.11**   The Web page created from the query datasheet of Figure 17.10.

> **Note**
>
> The Web browser is responsible for determining much of the formatting of table display. The browser attempts to display tables within the width of the display area when possible, making a best guess on the relative width of columns. There are a variety of HTML tags that you can add to the HTML source created by Access 97's export feature to format the tables. Refer to the HTML 2.0 and 3.2 specifications or Que's *Special Edition Using HTML* for further information on custom formatting of tables.

# Using HTML Templates

Most commercial Web sites use HTML templates to provide a consistent corporate or organizational image and to add visual interest to Web pages without writing a lot of HTML source for each page. The majority of Web page authoring applications, such as Microsoft FrontPage, include a variety of templates from which you quickly can create Web pages with a standardized appearance.

### Using the Access HTML Templates Included with Office 97

Microsoft includes a variety of HTML templates (.htm files) in your \Program Files\ Microsoft Office\Templates\Access folder. These templates each include a "Created with Microsoft Access" logo and a different background color and pattern. Figure 17.12 shows the 100.htm template displayed in IE 3.0. Other templates in the ...\Templates\Access folder include:

- Default.htm
- Mc.htm
- Stones.htm

- Gray.htm
- Mcst.htm
- Tiles.htm

- Grayst.htm
- Sky.htm
- Zigzag.htm

Background patterns are provided by .jpg graphics files with the same file name as the template. Background pattern files usually are small graphics files that the browser tiles to create a pattern over the entire page display region. The "Created with Microsoft Access" logo is provided by Msaccess.jpg.

When you choose <u>V</u>iew, Sou<u>r</u>ce from IE 3.0's menu to display the HTML source of an Access HTML template file, the content appears similar to that shown for 100.htm in Figure 17.13. The `<! Text >` tag normally is used to add invisible comments to a Web page. The Access 97 export feature interprets comment text in the format `<!--AccessTemplate_Element-->` to mean replace this line with the specified `Element`. Microsoft calls these comment lines *Access HTML Template Tags*. Table 17.1 lists the Access HTML Template Tags recognized by Access 97. The `...Page` anchor tags listed in Table 17.1 are used with multiple-page exports from Access reports, the subject of the section "Exporting Reports to HTML" later in the chapter.

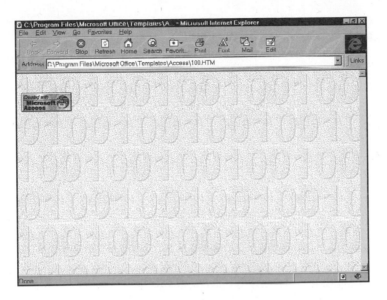

**FIG. 17.12**　The 100.htm template file displayed in Internet Explorer 3.0.

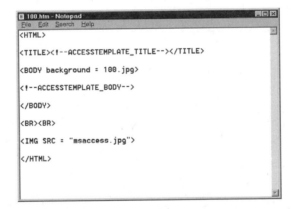

**FIG. 17.13**　The HTML source for the 100.htm template file.

| Table 17.1    Replaceable Access HTML Template Tags Recognized by Access 97 | |
|---|---|
| **Access HTML Template Tag** | **Purpose** |
| `<!--AccessTemplate_Title-->` | The object name that appears in the browser's title bar. |
| `<!--AccessTemplate_Body-->` | The table created from the object's output. |
| `<!--AccessTemplate_FirstPage-->` | Anchors tag to first page. |
| `<!--AccessTemplate_PreviousPage-->` | Anchors tag to previous page. |

(continues)

| Table 17.1 Continued | |
|---|---|
| **Access HTML Template Tag** | **Purpose** |
| `<!--AccessTemplate_NextPage-->` | Anchors tag to next page. |
| `<!--AccessTemplate_LastPage-->` | Anchors tag to last page. |
| `<!--AccessTemplate_PageNumber-->` | Displays the current page number. |

### Exporting a Query Datasheet with a Template

To add a template to a Web page created from a query datasheet, follow these steps:

1. Create the query design, save the query with an appropriate name for the title and caption, and execute the query to open it in Datasheet view. This example uses a modified version (US Customers) of the North American Customers query that displays only customers in the U.S.

2. Copy the graphics files required by the template to the folder in which you intend to save your exported Web page. For the 100.htm template, copy the 100.jpg and Msaccess.jpg files to …\Office\Samples, assuming you are using this folder to store your .html files.

3. Choose File, Save As/Export, select the To an External File or Database option, and click OK to open the Save Query '*Query Name*' In dialog. Select HTML Files (*.html, *.htm) in the Files of Type drop-down list and mark the Save Formatted and Autostart check boxes. Change the name of the file in the File Name combo box, if you want to use a non-default file name. Click Export to continue.

4. When the HTML Options dialog appears, click the Browse button to select your template in the HTML Template To Use dialog—…\Templates\Access\100.htm for this example (see Figure 17.14).

**FIG. 17.14** Specifying the Access HTML template for an exported Web page.

> **Note**
>
> When you specify a template in the HTML Options dialog, the template becomes the default template for the succeeding Web pages you export. The location and name of the template file appears in the HTML Template text box of the Hyperlinks/HTML page of the Options dialog. Choose Tools, Options, and click the Hyperlinks/HTML tab to display the HTML Template text box.

5. Click OK to export the query datasheet and open the Web page in your browser. Scroll to the bottom of the page to see the background and the "Created with

Microsoft Access" logo (see Figure 17.15). The background of the table and its caption is opaque, so the background texture of 100.jpg doesn't appear behind the table region.

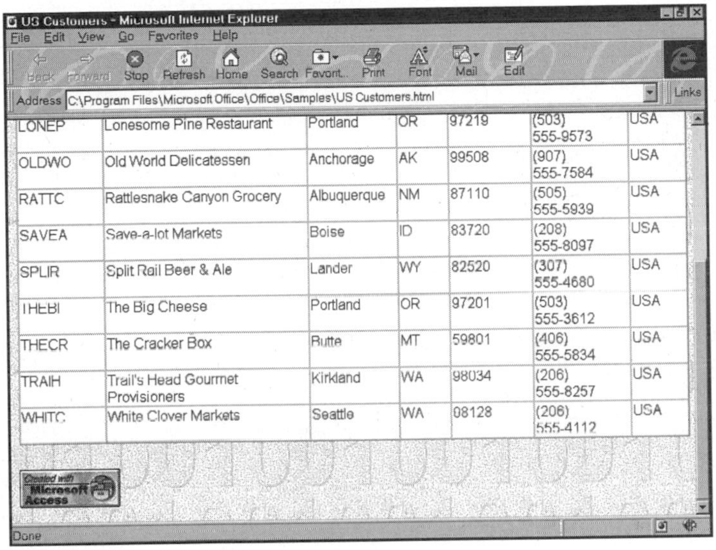

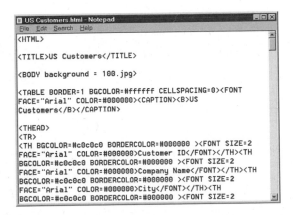

**FIG. 17.15**    The bottom of the Web page created with the 100.htm template that adds a background and the "Created with Microsoft Access" logo.

6. Choose <u>V</u>iew, Sour<u>c</u>e from IE 3.0's menu to view in Notepad the HTML lines added by the 100.htm template. Figure 17.16 shows the <BODY background = 100.jpg> line added from the template. Scrolling to the end of the file displays the <IMG SRC = "msaccess.jpg"> tag for the logo.

```
US Customers.html - Notepad
File  Edit  Search  Help
<HTML>

<TITLE>US Customers</TITLE>

<BODY background = 100.jpg>

<TABLE BORDER=1 BGCOLOR=#ffffff CELLSPACING=0><FONT
FACE="Arial" COLOR=#000000><CAPTION><B>US
Customers</B></CAPTION>

<THEAD>
<TR>
<TH BGCOLOR=#c0c0c0 BORDERCOLOR=#000000 ><FONT SIZE=2
FACE="Arial" COLOR=#000000>Customer ID</FONT></TH><TH
BGCOLOR=#c0c0c0 BORDERCOLOR=#000000 ><FONT SIZE=2
FACE="Arial" COLOR=#000000>Company Name</FONT></TH><TH
BGCOLOR=#c0c0c0 BORDERCOLOR=#000000 ><FONT SIZE=2
FACE="Arial" COLOR=#000000>City</FONT></TH><TH
BGCOLOR=#c0c0c0 BORDERCOLOR=#000000 ><FONT SIZE=2
```

**FIG. 17.16**    The first few lines of the HTML source for a Web page created with the 100.htm template.

> **Note**
>
> If you want the background to show through the table, you can export the datasheet without marking the Save Formatted check box. Open the .html file in Notepad and replace the <BODY> tag with <BODY background = 100.jpg> and add the <IMG SRC = "msaccess.jpg"> tag immediately above the <\HTML> tag. Standard HTML tables with no background color specified are transparent, so the background appears under the table region.

# Exporting Reports to HTML

You can export an Access report to HTML in a manner similar to that for table or query datasheets. Unlike static datasheets, exporting a multipage report creates multiple Web pages, one for each page of the report. Office 97 includes a special template, Nwindtem.htm in the ...\Office\Samples folder, specifically designed for reports. Nwindtem.htm, shown in Figure 17.17, includes hyperlinks to provide paging through of multipage reports.

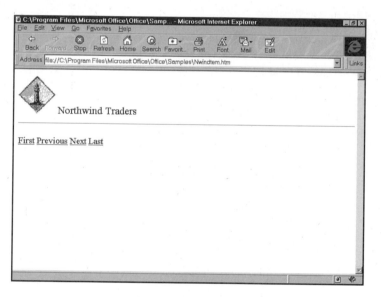

**FIG. 17.17** The Nwindtem.htm template for exported Access reports.

Figure 17.18 shows the HTML source for Nwindtem.htm in Notepad. <META ...> tags provide HTML metadata to indicate the type of content of the page and other information to aid the browser in formatting the document. The <A HREF=...>*Position*</A> anchor tags provide First, Previous, Next, and Last navigation hyperlinks at the bottom of each report page.

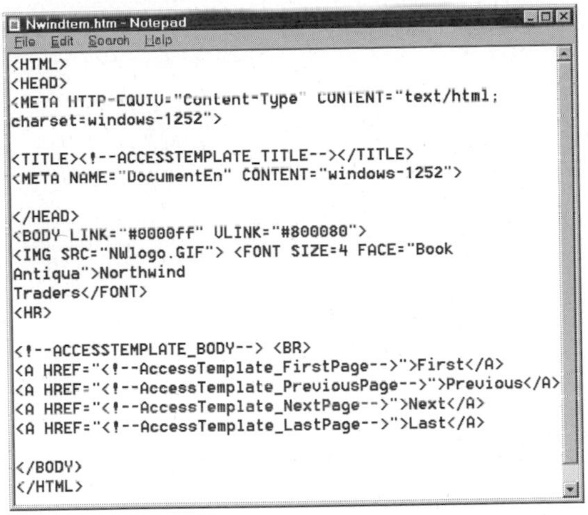


```
<HTML>
<HEAD>
<META HTTP-EQUIV="Content-Type" CONTENT="text/html;
charset=windows-1252">

<TITLE><!--ACCESSTEMPLATE_TITLE--></TITLE>
<META NAME="DocumentEn" CONTENT="windows-1252">

</HEAD>
<BODY LINK="#0000ff" VLINK="#800080">
<IMG SRC="NWlogo.GIF"> <FONT SIZE=4 FACE="Book
Antiqua">Northwind
Traders</FONT>
<HR>

<!--ACCESSTEMPLATE_BODY--> <BR>
<A HREF="<!--AccessTemplate_FirstPage-->">First</A>
<A HREF="<!--AccessTemplate_PreviousPage-->">Previous</A>
<A HREF="<!--AccessTemplate_NextPage-->">Next</A>
<A HREF="<!--AccessTemplate_LastPage-->">Last</A>

</BODY>
</HTML>
```

**FIG. 17.18** The HTML source for the Nwindtem.htm report template with navigation hyperlinks.

> **Note**
>
> You can only export Access Reports to static Web pages. This limitation is logical because a Web page is the equivalent of a printed report, which must be physically replaced when updated. Unlike Word 97's File, Export to HTML menu choice, the exporting process for Access 97 reports doesn't process graphic images. If you want to add graphics to a report beyond the image(s) added by the template, you must create a .gif, .jpg, or .png file from each graphic image of the report, then manually add a `<IMG SRC="`*`filename.ext`*`">` tag in the appropriate location of each report page. The graphics files must be located in the same folder as the associated .html file, unless you add a well-formed path to the *`filename.ext`* element of the tag.

To export the Catalog report of Northwind.mdb to a series of Web pages using Nwindtem.htm to add a logo and navigation features, follow these steps:

1. Open the Catalog report in Preview mode.

   > **Note**
   >
   > If you haven't copied the graphics files required for your template file to the folder in which you intend to store the .html files of the Catalog report, do so at this point. Step 2 in the preceding section describes how to copy the required graphics files.

2. Choose File, Save As, select the To an External File or Database option, and click OK to open the Save Report 'Catalog' In dialog. Select HTML Files (*.html, *.htm) in the Files of Type drop-down list and mark the Autostart check box. (The Save Formatted check box is marked and disabled; you can't export an unformatted report.) Click Export to continue.

3. When the HTML Options dialog appears, click the Browse button and select the Nwindtem.htm template in the HTML Template to Use dialog.

4. Click OK to complete the export process and open the first page of the Catalog report in your browser (see Figure 17.19). As expected, the large Northwind Traders graphic is missing from the first page, Catalog.html.

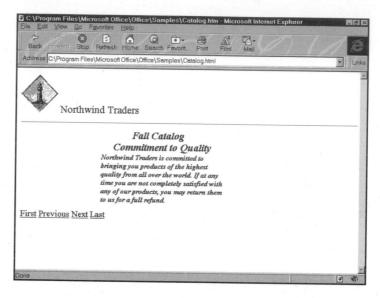

**FIG. 17.19** The first Web page (Catalog.html) of the exported Catalog report.

5. Click the Next hyperlink to proceed to the second page of the Catalog, then scroll to the bottom of the page and click the Next button to display the third page (see Figure 17.20). When you export a report, the Access export feature appends `Page#` to the file name of the report for pages 2 and higher.

6. Choose View, Source from IE 3.0 to display the HTML source for CatalogPage3.html in Notepad, then scroll to the bottom of the file (see Figure 17.21). Each page of a report has a different set of HTML Previous and Next anchor lines for navigation. For page 3 of the catalog, the Previous and Next anchor lines are `<A HREF="CatalogPage2.html">Previous</A>` and `<A HREF="CatalogPage4.html">Next</A>`, respectively. The First (`<A HREF="Catalog.html">First</A>`) and Last (`<A HREF="CatalogPage9.html">Last</A>`) anchors are the same for all pages of the report.

Reports are formatted as HTML tables without borders (`<TABLE BORDER=0>`), which emulates on a Web page the appearance of Access 97's reports in Preview mode and when printed. As a general rule, Access reports are the best choice for exporting large amounts of data to Web pages. You have much more control over the appearance of the Web page with exported reports than when you export a datasheet with the same content. To optimize the appearance of Web pages created from reports, you must design the report specifically for export to HTML.

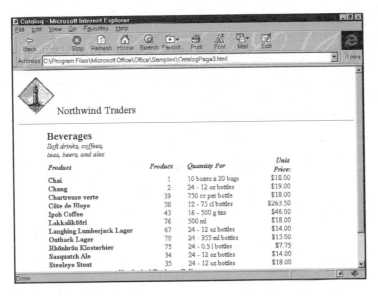

**FIG. 17.20**  The third Web page (CatalogPage3.html) of the Catalog report.

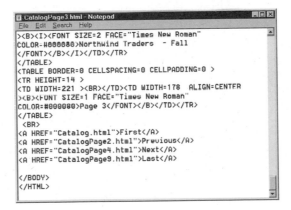

**FIG. 17.21**  The anchor tags of the third page (CatalogPage3.html) of the Catalog report.

---

**Note**

Report formatting fails for complex reports that contain a combination of graphic elements and text. As an example, compare the last Web page (CatalogPage9.html) of the Catalog series with the last page of the Catalog report in Access' Report Preview mode. All of the graphic elements in the order form are missing from the last Web page.

# Using the Web Publishing Wizard to Create a Static Web Site

If you have a Web server, such as Internet Information Server 2+ or you've installed the Microsoft Personal Web Server from the Office Value Pack, you can create a complete Web site, including a rather drab home page, with the Web Publishing Wizard. The Web Publishing Wizard is an alternative to creating individual pages or sets of pages from Access objects. The wizard provides an additional level of automation that can speed the creation of larger Web sites that distribute data from Access or ODBC data sources.

To try the Web Publishing Wizard with Northwind.mdb and the Nwindtem.htm template, create a folder on your Web server, such as \InetPubs\wwwroot\Nwind, for the Web page files and follow these steps:

1. With Northwind.mdb open in Access, choose File, Save As HTML to open the first Web Publishing Wizard dialog (see Figure 17.22). When you first use the wizard, you haven't created any publication profiles, so the I Want to Use a Web Publishing Profile I Already Created with This Wizard check box is disabled. Click Next to continue.

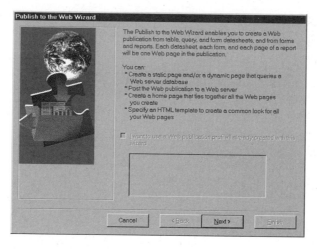

**FIG. 17.22**  The Web Publishing Wizard's opening dialog.

2. In the second wizard dialog, select the objects you want to export by clicking the object type tab, then marking the check boxes of each object you want to include (see Figure 17.23). You can select any combination of tables, queries, and reports for a static Web site. Forms are restricted to dynamic Web sites that use Active Server Page (.asp) files. Dynamic Web sites are the subject of the next chapter. Click Next.

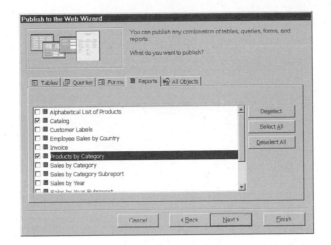

**FIG. 17.23** Selecting table, query, and report objects for export to static Web pages.

3. Type the well-formed path and file name of the template you want to use for your Web pages, in this case **Nwindtem.htm** (see Figure 17.24). Alternatively, click the Browse button and locate the template file in the HTML Template to Use dialog. If you mark the I Want to Select Different Templates for Some of the Selected Objects check box, you are prompted to choose a template file for each object. Click Next.

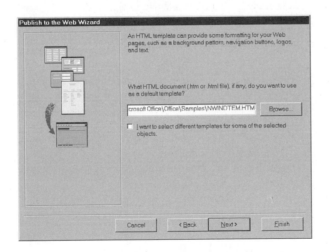

**FIG. 17.24** Specifying a single template for all exported Web pages.

4. Select the Static HTML option to create static HTML pages from your selected objects (see Figure 17.25). The next chapter shows you how to use the Dynamic HTX/IDC and Dynamic ASP options. Click Next.

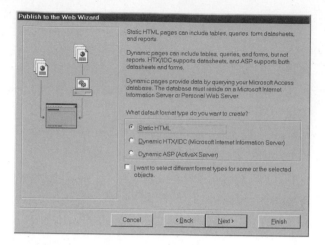

**FIG. 17.25** Selecting the Static HTML option for the exported Web pages.

5. Type the well-formed path to the folder for your Web pages in the text box (see Figure 17.26); use UNC if you're connected to the server via a network. Select the No, I Want to Publish Objects Locally option if you are creating the Web pages on a PC that's running or is connected via a network to the Web server. Click Next.

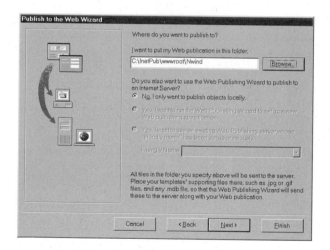

**FIG. 17.26** Specifying the path to the Web server's folder for the exported pages.

6. To create a Spartan home page, consisting of a switchboard table with hyperlinks to Web pages created from your Access object, mark the Yes, I Want to Create a Home Page check box. Accept Default in the text box to use Default.htm for the home page file (see Figure 17.27). Click Next.

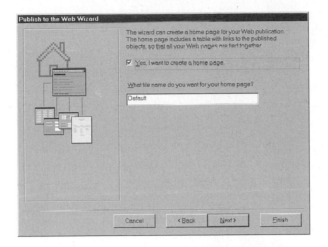

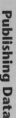

**FIG. 17.27**  Instructing the wizard to create a home page "switchboard."

7. To save a Web Publication Profile, mark the Yes, I Want to Save Wizard Answers to a Web Publication Profile check box. Type a name for the Profile in the Profile Name text box (see Figure 17.28). Saving a Profile lets you skip the specification process when you update your Web pages. Click Finish to create the Web site by exporting the Access objects.

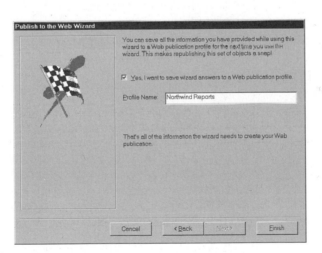

**FIG. 17.28**  Saving your export specification as a Web Publication Profile.

8. Copy the graphics file(s) for your template (Nwlogo.gif for Nwindtem.htm) to the Web server folder you specified in step 5.

9. Launch your browser and type the **http://*servername*/Nwind** URL in the Address text box to open the Northwind Traders home page you just created (see Figure 17.29). Click the hyperlinks in the Object column of the Switchboard table to open the individual Web pages.

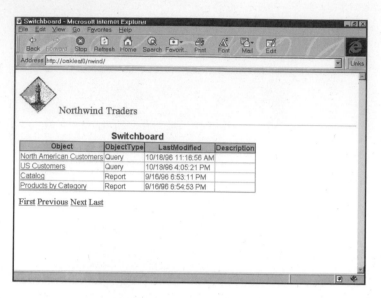

**FIG. 17.29** The home page's Switchboard table with jumps to each of the exported pages.

---

**Note**

The hyperlinks for the anchors of the Nwindtem.htm template aren't appropriate for the Switchboard page or single Web pages created from datasheets. If you include reports in your Web site, create one template for pages based on datasheets and another template for pages created from reports. Mark the I Want to Select Different Templates for Some of the Selected Objects check box in the third wizard form (in the preceding step 3) and specify the template to use with each selected object when prompted.

---

# Importing Data from HTML Tables

Access 97 includes the capability to import or link data from an HTML table to a Jet 3.5 table. This feature appears to have been included in Access 97 for HTML symmetry; the theory apparently is that if one can export to HTML, one also should be able to import from HTML. Few Access users are likely to employ this feature because relatively little useful tabular data is available on the Internet. For completeness, however, following is an example of importing data from an HTML page created in the section "Exporting Table and Query Datasheets to HTML" earlier in this chapter:

1. Choose File, Get External Data, Import to open the Import dialog. Select HTML Documents (*.html, *.htm) in the Files of Type drop-down list (see Figure 17.30).

2. Select the Suppliers.html file you created in the "Exporting Table and Query Datasheets to HTML" section at the beginning of this chapter and click the Import button to close the Import dialog and open the first Import HTML Wizard dialog.

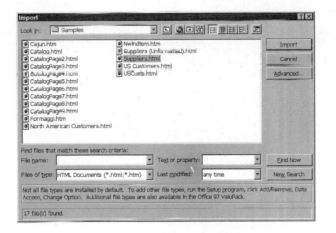

**FIG. 17.30** Displaying .html and .htm files in the Import dialog.

3. The wizard imports the table header data, if present, together with the table data. The formatted version of Suppliers.html includes headers, so check the First Row Contains Column Headings check box (see Figure 17.31).

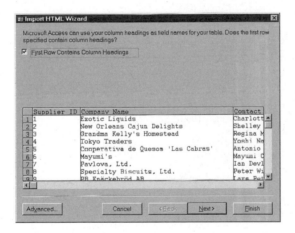

**FIG. 17.31** Specifying column headers in the Import HTML Wizard's first dialog.

4. Click the Advanced button to open the Suppliers Import Specification dialog. This dialog lets you customize import operations on date and time fields and choose the decimal symbol. You can change the field names, data types, and indexing for each of the fields, as well as skip the import of specific fields. Change the data type of the Supplier ID field to Long Integer, and specify a No Duplicates index on the field (see Figure 17.32). Data types and indexes for the remaining fields are satisfactory.

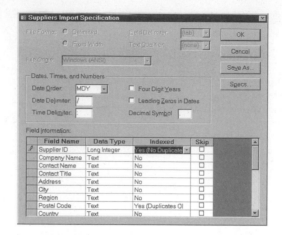

**FIG. 17.32**   Specifying field data types and indexes in the Suppliers Import Specification dialog.

> **Note**
>
> Alternatively, you can specify field data types and indexing in the third wizard dialog. The wizard proposes to add Duplicates OK indexes on any field that contains ID or Code in the column name.

**5.** Click the Save As button to save the Import Specification. Edit or type a new name for the specification in the Specification Name of the Save Import/Export Specification dialog (see Figure 17.33). Click OK to close the dialog, then click OK to close the Suppliers Import Specification dialog.

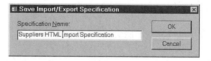

**FIG. 17.33**   Editing the default name for the saved Suppliers Import Specification.

**6.** Click Next to display the second Import HTML Wizard dialog. Select the In a New Table option to store the data in a new table whose name you specify at the end of the import process (see Figure 17.34). Click Next.

**7.** You can make last-minute changes to field names, data types, and indexes in the third wizard dialog (see Figure 17.35). If you made the required changes to the Suppliers Import Specification dialog in preceding step 4, click Next.

**8.** By default, the wizard proposes to add a numeric primary key field to the table. The Supplier ID field qualifies as a primary key, so select the Choose My Own Primary Key option and pick the Supplier ID field in the drop-down list (see Figure 17.36). Click Next.

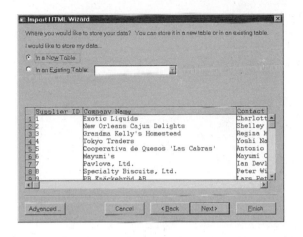

**FIG. 17.34**  Specifying import of the tabular HTML data to a new table.

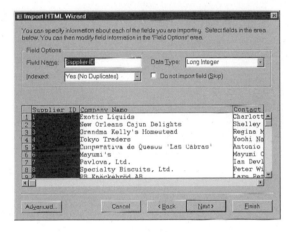

**FIG. 17.35**  A second chance to change field names, data types, and indexes offered by the third wizard dialog.

9. There is a Suppliers table in Northwind.mdb, so edit the proposed table name to tblSuppliers (see Figure 17.37). You don't need to analyze the Suppliers table, so don't mark the I Would Like a Wizard to Analyze check box. Click Finish to export the HTML table to tblSuppliers and terminate the wizard.

10. Open the tblSuppliers table to verify the import wizardry. The table is essentially identical to the original Suppliers table from which the Web page was created (see Figure 17.38). The most significant differences are the field data type of the Supplier ID column (Long Integer, not AutoNumber) and the field names (derived from the Caption property of the original table).

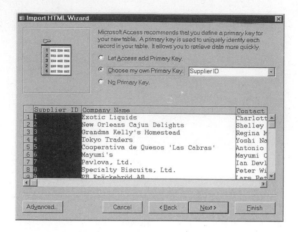

**FIG. 17.36** Selecting the Supplier ID field as the primary key for the imported table.

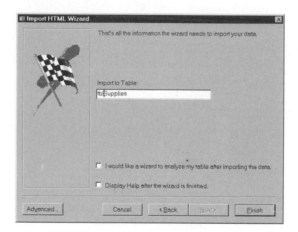

**FIG. 17.37** Editing the name of the new table in the final wizard dialog.

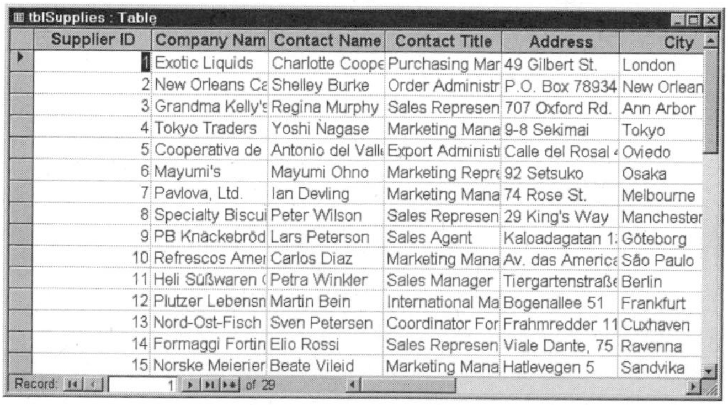

| Supplier ID | Company Nam | Contact Name | Contact Title | Address | City |
|---|---|---|---|---|---|
| 1 | Exotic Liquids | Charlotte Coope | Purchasing Mar | 49 Gilbert St. | London |
| 2 | New Orleans Ca | Shelley Burke | Order Administr | P.O. Box 78934 | New Orlean |
| 3 | Grandma Kelly's | Regina Murphy | Sales Represen | 707 Oxford Rd. | Ann Arbor |
| 4 | Tokyo Traders | Yoshi Nagase | Marketing Mana | 9-8 Sekimai | Tokyo |
| 5 | Cooperativa de | Antonio del Vall | Export Administi | Calle del Rosal | Oviedo |
| 6 | Mayumi's | Mayumi Ohno | Marketing Repr | 92 Setsuko | Osaka |
| 7 | Pavlova, Ltd. | Ian Devling | Marketing Mana | 74 Rose St. | Melbourne |
| 8 | Specialty Biscui | Peter Wilson | Sales Represen | 29 King's Way | Manchester |
| 9 | PB Knäckebröd | Lars Peterson | Sales Agent | Kaloadagatan 1 | Göteborg |
| 10 | Refrescos Amer | Carlos Diaz | Marketing Mana | Av. das America | São Paulo |
| 11 | Heli Süßwaren ( | Petra Winkler | Sales Manager | Tiergartenstraße | Berlin |
| 12 | Plutzer Lebensn | Martin Bein | International Ma | Bogenallee 51 | Frankfurt |
| 13 | Nord-Ost-Fisch | Sven Petersen | Coordinator For | Frahmredder 11 | Cuxhaven |
| 14 | Formaggi Fortin | Elio Rossi | Sales Represen | Viale Dante, 75 | Ravenna |
| 15 | Norske Meierier | Beate Vileid | Marketing Mana | Hatlevegen 5 | Sandvika |

**FIG. 17.38** The exported tblSuppliers table in Datasheet view.

**Note**

Most of the information available on the Internet is subject to copyright, either explicitly (by a copyright notice on the Web site's home page) or implicitly (by statute). Importing and using copyrighted content from the Internet for most purposes is prohibited by federal copyright statutes, unless you have express permission of the copyright owner to use the content. If you intend to import and use information created by others and published on the Internet, consult an attorney before using the information.

# Chapter 18

# Creating Dynamic Web Pages

Microsoft's rallying cry, "Activate the Internet," and the firm's use of the "Active" prefix for the majority of its new Internet-related technologies are intended to do away with the static Web pages described in the preceding chapter. Static pages constitute by far the majority of the content available on today's Internet. Microsoft wants you to use Internet Information Server (IIS) 3.0, ActiveX controls, and Visual Basic Script (VBS) to create interactive Web pages. Flashy graphics, hot audio riffs, and even some digital video content now greet members of the newly revamped and highly activated Microsoft Network. Of course, users need Internet Explorer (IE) 3+ to take full advantage of what Microsoft calls "exciting, compelling, and rich" content. By advancing the technology to create interactive Web pages, Microsoft also gains market share in the browser war.

Giving intranet and Internet users the ability to define their own Web-based view of data isn't as exciting as delivering "rich multimedia content" (one of Microsoft's favorite clichés) from your Web site. Corporate intranets and the Internet offer the opportunity for users to interact with databases, displaying custom views of information and updating entries from Web browsers. Electronic commerce on the Internet depends almost entirely on consumer- and business-related interaction with databases.

This chapter introduces you to the use of new Microsoft technologies, the *Internet Database Connector* (IDC) and the *Active Server Pages* (ASP, formerly *ActiveX Server Framework*), that let you create dynamic Web pages for displaying and updating data. The IDC examples of this chapter require you to have IIS 2+ or the Microsoft Personal Web Server installed and operating. The ASP examples require IIS 3.0 (or IIS 2.0 and the ASP extensions, code-named *Denali*), which was in the beta-testing stage when this book was written. You also can use the ASP extensions with the Personal Web Server running under Windows 95.

> **Note**
>
> The term *users* to define consumers of information implies to many that information providers should be referred to as *pushers*.

# Understanding Microsoft's View of Databases and the Web

Giving away Web browsers, including Web servers with Windows NT Server 4.0, and distributing free Internet enhancements for browsers and servers isn't a business model that's likely to add much to Microsoft's bottom line. To earn a return on its Internet investment, Microsoft ultimately must sell, not give away, products. The initial objective of Microsoft's Internet program is to increase sales of Windows NT Server 4.0 as an Internet/intranet server and to make SQL Server 6.5 the client/server database of choice for conducting Internet commerce and distributing information from corporate databases over private intranets. Data marts, data malls, and distributed transactions are the keys to Microsoft's success in the back-end of the Internet/intranet business.

### Rolling Up Data to Marts and Malls

Most large organizations have established or plan to establish intranets that let networked users of Web browsers query data that is stored in databases running on mainframes or minicomputers. Letting users run queries directly against these business-critical transaction databases is an anathema to the vast majority of information services managers. *Data warehouses* make organization-wide information available without disturbing day-to-day database operations.

Periodically, data from the transaction databases is downloaded, often in summarized form (called *rollups*), to a client/server data warehouse. Smaller *data marts*, which hold up to about 250G of data, serve individual divisions or departments. Data malls consist of groups of data marts against which users can execute *distributed queries*. A distributed query can create joins between databases running on separate data mart servers. Data marts and malls are ideal applications for SQL Server 6.5 running under Windows NT Server 4.0. Microsoft doesn't give Windows NT Server or SQL Server away; you must pay for these products and, in addition, pay a license fee for each client PC that connects to them.

> **Note**
>
> The demand for data warehouses, marts, and malls became so great in mid-1996 that the large, fast fixed-disk drives (4G and up) that are needed for database servers were difficult to find. 20G and larger Wide, Fast SCSI-2 and SCSI-3 drives are expected to be available from several suppliers beginning in early 1997. If the remarkable increase in the demand for large disk drives continues its 1996 growth rate, these new drives also are likely to be scarce.

Although you're not likely to see Jet 3.5 databases used for data marts and malls, Access 97 is a candidate for designing, testing, and maintaining such client/server databases.

Access 97 makes it easy to link Jet 3.5 tables to SQL Server 6.5 databases by using the SQL Server ODBC driver included with Office 97. This chapter uses the Access ODBC driver for Jet 3.5 databases to create dynamic Web pages for displaying and updating data. The experience you gain in this chapter is directly applicable when you move to the client/server RDBMS model.

◄◄ See "Linking an Excel Worksheet by Using the ODBC API," p. 228
►► See "Understanding ODBC Drivers," p. 918

### Managing Distributed Transactions

One of the primary requirements of electronic commerce on the Internet is the ability to update multiple databases, regardless of their location. As an example, a Web-based credit-card purchase requires verifying the purchaser's account, testing for available inventory of the ordered items, placing a hold amount against the purchaser's available credit limit, and entering the order. Such a transaction might involve three or more databases residing on mainframes, minicomputers, or PCs. A transaction requires that all updates involved in a purchase succeed; if any update fails, the transaction must be rolled back. Rolling back a transaction restores the state of the participating database tables to the state that existed immediately prior to the start of the transaction. A *distributed transaction* is a transaction that takes place on tables residing in more than one database. In the case of a credit-card purchase, the databases are likely to be owned by different firms and connected over a wide-area network (WAN), such as (but not necessarily) the Internet.

A discourse on distributed transaction technology is beyond the scope of this book, but the subject is of vital importance to the future of Internet-based commerce. SQL Server 6.5 now includes a Distributed Transaction Controller (DTC) to coordinate the execution of transactions on multiple servers running SQL Server 6.5. DTC and the new *Microsoft Transaction Server* (MTx) technology, code-named *Viper* when this book was written, extends DTC to the full range of database servers, including IBM mainframes connected via Microsoft SNA Server. If MTx is successful, Microsoft will gain a greater share of the market for Internet commerce back-ends, which are typified by the firm's fledgling Microsoft Merchant Server and Commercial Internet Services.

# Using the IDC for Delivering Information

The IDC is an *Internet Services API* (ISAPI) application that simplifies the creation of active Web pages. These Web pages automatically deliver updated information and let users process queries against any database for which a 32-bit ODBC driver is available. ISAPI applications use Windows *dynamic link libraries* (DLLs) as a substitute for the *Common Gateway Interface* (CGI) applications (scripts) originally developed for UNIX Web servers. ISAPI runs only on Microsoft's Internet Information Server and Personal Web Server. The advantage of ISAPI DLLs is that they run in the Web server's process space, which makes ISAPI DLLs run faster than executable CGI applications. IDC is implemented by Httpodbc.dll, a 32-bit ISAPI DLL.

An IDC application requires the following two types of files:

- *Internet Data Connector (.idc) files* specify the ODBC data source and the query that supplies the data for the Web page in a simple text format. The .idc file also can contain optional information, such as a user name and password for access to the data source.

- *HTML Extension (.htx) files*, commonly called template files, provide the HTML source to format the data for viewing. The data generated by the .idc file is merged with the .htx file to create a Web page. The .idc and .htx files are paired for a particular Web page, although it's possible to use a single .idc file with multiple .htx files. Templates can contain HTML forms with common Windows control objects, such as text boxes and drop-down lists to create Web pages with customized data content.

The process of generating a dynamic Web page with .idc and .htx files follows this sequence:

1. The browser sends a URL in the format `pagename.idc?` to IIS 2.0, usually from a hyperlink on another page.

2. The IDC DLL, Httpodbc.dll, reads *Pagename*.idc to obtain the information that is necessary to connect to the database and execute the query.

3. Httpodbc.dll connects to the data source and sends the query statement, which must be in the dialect of SQL for the RDBMS specified by the data source.

4. Httpodbc.dll receives the rows from the data source and merges the rows with the *Pagename*.htx file.

5. Httpodbc.dll sends the merged document, *Pagename*.htm, to IIS 2.0, which delivers the page to the requesting browser.

Fortunately, IDC does all this work for you. You need to create only an .idc text file and a relatively simple .htx file.

### The IDC Demonstration Applications Included with IIS 2.0

Internet Information Server 2.0, included with Windows NT Server 4.0, offers a simple demonstration of the use of .idc and .htx files with the pubs sample database of SQL Server 6.5. To use the IDC samples included with IIS 2.0, you must have access to SQL Server 6.x from the server on which you run IIS 2.0 or a copy of the pubs database in Jet 3.0 (Access 95) or Jet 3.5 (Access 97) format. If you don't have these capabilities, the section "A Dynamic Web-Based Access Application" later in this chapter directs you to an Internet site that offers a more complex demonstration of dynamic Web-page generation with the IDC.

> **Note**
>
> Microsoft's dbWeb 1.1a, described in the "An Overview of Microsoft's Internet Products" section of Chapter 16, "Working with Hyperlinks and HTML," includes Pubs.mdb, a Jet version of the pubs sample database. If you've installed dbWeb 1.1 or 1.1a, you can use the Microsoft Access ODBC driver to connect to Pubs.mdb.

Before you can run the IIS 2.0 database example applications, you must create an ODBC data source named Web SQL. This procedure assumes that you are working at the server PC on which IIS 2.0 is running because you must create a system data source for IIS 2.0. To create the data source and run a simple IDC query, follow these steps:

1. Launch IE 3.0 or the default browser and type **http://*servername*/samples/ dbsamp/dbsamp.htm** in the Address text box to open the Internet Database Connector Examples page.

2. Scroll to the line that includes <u>click here to create it</u> and click the <u>hear</u> hyperlink to display the Create ODBC Datasource on the Microsoft Internet Information Server page.

   If you have and want to use Pubs.mdb, instead of SQL Server's pubs database, click the ODBC data source tools hyperlink, and then click the Microsoft Access Driver (*.mdb) hyperlink.

3. In the Datasource Name to Create text box, type **Web SQL** (with a space between **Web** and **SQL**). In the Server Name text box, type the name of the server on which SQL Server 6.x is installed.

4. In the Attribute String text box, type **DATABASE=pubs** (see Figure 18.1).

   If you're using Pubs.mdb, type **d:\\*path*\pubs.mdb**, where **d:\\*path*** is the location of Pubs.mdb, in the Database Name text box.

5. Click the Create Datasource button to create the data source. A new page displays a message indicating that the data source was created successfully.

> **Note**
>
> The IDC samples assume that you are using integrated security for SQL Server. Integrated security authenticates SQL Server users based on their Windows NT logon ID and password. If you are not using integrated security, the samples assume that you can connect to SQL Server 6.x with the default system administrator account, sa, with no password.
>
> To use another account and/or a password, you must edit the Sample.idc file, as described in the following section, before you attempt to run the query in the following steps. Unfortunately, the password you specify is accessible to others in the clear text of the .idc file, which is a breach of SQL Server security.

6. Use the Back button to return to the dbsamp1.htm page and scroll to the Other Database Examples section at the bottom of the page (see Figure 18.2). Click the Simple database query hyperlink to open the Internet Database Connector Example 1: Simple Query page.

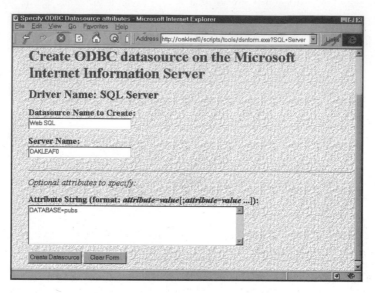

**FIG. 18.1** Specifying the parameters for the Web SQL ODBC data source for SQL Server.

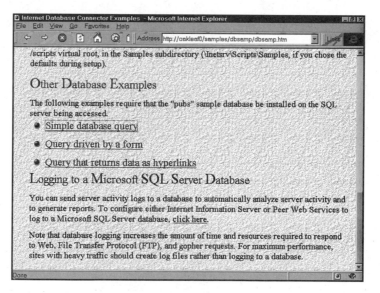

**FIG. 18.2** Hyperlinks to the sample database applications that are included with IIS 2.0.

**7.** Click the single hyperlink below the caption line to run the query. The query displays the names of authors whose books have generated more than $5,000 in year-to-date sales (see Figure 18.3).

**8.** If you choose View, Source, Notepad displays the HTML source for Sample.htm—the name of the Web page created by the Sample.htx template file and the Sample.idc IDC file (see Figure 18.4). By default, the .htx, .idc, and .htm files have the same file name.

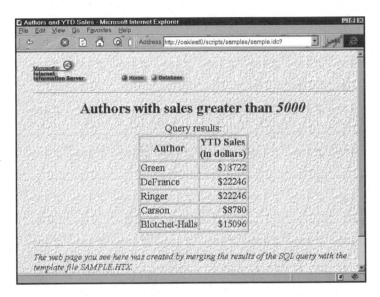

**FIG. 18.3**  The Sample.htm page created by Sample.htx and a static query.

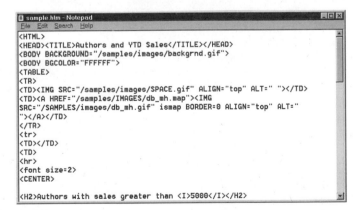

**FIG. 18.4**  Part of the HTML source for the Sample.htm Web page.

**The Sample.idc and Sample2.idc File.** The Sample.idc file, located in the \InetPub\Scripts\Samples folder, specifies the name of the ODBC data source, the user name for SQL Server, a password (if needed), the name of the template file, and the SQL statement required to execute the query. For Jet data sources, you can copy and paste the SQL statement for an Access query to create the `SQLStatement:` parameter. Listing 18.1 shows the content of Sample.idc.

**Listing 18.1    The Data Source Parameters and SQL Query Statement of Sample.idc**

```
Datasource: Web SQL
Username: sa
Template: sample.htx
SQLStatement:
+ SELECT au_lname, ytd_sales
+ FROM pubs.dbo.titleview
+ WHERE ytd_sales>5000
```

The plus (+) symbols preceding the lines of the SQL statement are continuation characters, indicating that the text is a continuation of the line above. Minor formatting changes have been made to the text of Listing 18.1 to improve readability.

> **Note**
>
> If you need a password to log in to SQL Server, add `Password:` *password* after the `Username: userid` line. When using integrated security, IDC ignores the `Username:` and `Password:` entries.

The Internet Database Connector Examples page provides a link to a parameterized query that lets you enter the year-to-date sales criteria in an HTML form. Click the Query driven by a form hyperlink to display the Dbsamp2.htm form, shown in Figure 18.5. You enter the criterion value in the text box, and then click the Run Query button to execute Sample2.idc.

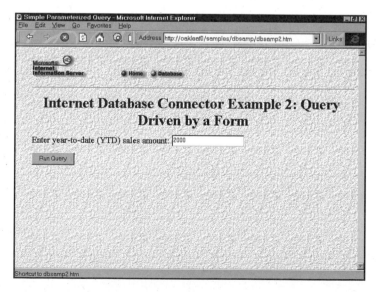

**FIG. 18.5**  The Dbsamp2.htm form for executing a parameterized query.

**Listing 18.2    The HTML Source for the Form Page**

```
<HTML>
<HEAD><TITLE>Simple Parameterized Query</TITLE></HEAD>
<BODY BACKGROUND="/samples/images/backgrnd.gif">
<BODY BGCOLOR="FFFFFF">
<TABLE>
<TR>
<TD><IMG SRC="/samples/images/SPACE.gif" ALIGN="top" ALT=" "></TD>
<TD><A HREF="/samples/IMAGES/db_mh.map">
<IMG SRC="/SAMPLES/images/db_mh.gif" ismap BORDER=0 ALIGN="top" ALT=" ">
➥</A></TD>
</TR>
<TR>
<TD></TD>
<TD>
<HR>
<FONT SIZE=2>
<CENTER>
<H2>Internet Database Connector Example 2: Query Driven by a Form</H2>
</CENTER>
<FORM METHOD="POST" ACTION="/scripts/samples/sample2.idc">
<P>
Enter year-to-date (YTD) sales amount: <INPUT NAME="sales" VALUE="5000">
<P>
<INPUT TYPE="SUBMIT" VALUE="Run Query">
</FORM>
</FONT>
</TD>
</TR>
</TABLE>
</BODY>
</HTML>
```

The `<FORM METHOD="POST" ACTION="/scripts/samples/sample2.idc">` tag defines an HTML form that executes Sample2.idc. Paths within Web pages stored on the server are relative to the Web server root folder, \InetPub, not the default \InetPub\Wwwroot folder. The sales text box created by the `<INPUT NAME="sales" VALUE="5000">` tag has a default value of 5000. When you click the Run Query button created by the `<INPUT TYPE="SUBMIT" VALUE="Run Query">` tag, the sales value is passed to Sample2.idc's replaceable parameter, `%sales%`. Listing 18.3 shows the text of Sample2.idc with `%sales%` as the criterion for the ytd_sales field of `titleview`.

**Listing 18.3    The Parameterized Query of Sample2.idc**

```
Datasource: Web SQL
Username: sa
Template: sample.htx
SQLStatement:
+ SELECT au_lname, ytd_sales
+ FROM pubs.dbo.titleview
+ WHERE ytd_sales > %sales%
```

---

**Note**

Only the `Datasource`, `Template`, and `SQLStatment` fields are required for .idc files. You can add many optional values to .idc files for fine-tuning query execution, supplying default parameter values, and setting the maximum number of records to return. For a full explanation of these optional fields, read the 08_iis.htm page of the IIS 2.0 documentation in the \Winnt\System32\ Inetsrv\lisadmin\Htmldocs folder.

---

**The Sample.htx File.** Listing 18.4 shows the content of the Sample.htx file, also located in the \InetPub\Scripts\Samples folder. Sample.htx supplies the template for the simple Sample.idc query and for the parameterized query, Sample2.idc. All IDC-specific tags in the HTML source for .htx files use the format `<%...%>`. IDC supports conditional display using the `<% if expression %>...<%else%>...<%endif%>` structure, similar to VBA's **If** *expression* **Then...Else...End If** statements. Sample.htx displays the `<H2>Authors with sales greater than <I><%idc.sales%></I></H2>`. The `<%idc.sales%>` tag is replaced by the value from the sales text box of the Dbsamp2.htm form. If the value is missing, as is the case when you use Sample.idc, the `<H2>Authors with sales greater than <I>5000</I></H2>` line appears in the generated page.

**Listing 18.4    The HTML Source and IDC-Specific Tags of the Sample.htx File**

```
<HTML>
<HEAD><TITLE>Authors and YTD Sales</TITLE></HEAD>
<BODY BACKGROUND="/samples/images/backgrnd.gif">
<BODY BGCOLOR="FFFFFF">
<TABLE>
<TR>
<TD><IMG SRC="/samples/images/SPACE.gif" ALIGN="top" ALT=" "></TD>
<TD><A HREF="/samples/IMAGES/db_mh.map">
<IMG SRC="/SAMPLES/images/db_mh.gif" ismap BORDER=0 ALIGN="top" ALT=" ">
➥</A></TD>
</TR>
<tr>
<TD></TD>
<TD>
<hr>
<font size=2>
<CENTER>
<%if idc.sales eq ""%>
<H2>Authors with sales greater than <I>5000</I></H2>
<%else%>
<H2>Authors with sales greater than <I><%idc.sales%></I></H2>
<%endif%>
<P>
<TABLE BORDER>
<%begindetail%>
<%if CurrentRecord EQ 0 %>
<caption>Query results:</caption>
<TR>
<TH><B>Author</B></TH><TH><B>YTD Sales<BR>(in dollars)</B></TH>
</TR>
```

```
<%endif%>
<TR><TD><%au_lname%></TD><TD align="right">$<%ytd_sales%></TD></TR>
<%enddetail%>
<P>
</TABLE>
</center>
<P>
<%if CurrentRecord EQ 0 %>
<I><B>Sorry, no authors had YTD sales greater than </I><%idc.sales%>.</B>
<P>
<%else%>
<HR>
<I>
The web page you see here was created by merging the results
of the SQL query with the template file SAMPLE.HTX.
<P>
The merge was done by the Microsoft Internet Database Connector and
the results were returned to this web browser by the Microsoft Internet
Information Server.
</I>
<%endif%>
</FONT>
</TD>
</TR>
</TABLE>
</BODY>
</HTML>
```

Merged data from execution of the .idc file appears between <%begindetail%> and <%enddetail%> tags. <%*columnname*%> tags, such as <%au_lname%> and <%ytd_sales%>, are replaced by the value of the query columns for the current row of the table. If no records are returned by the query, the <%if CurrentRecord EQ 0 %> expression evaluates true, and the Sorry... message appears.

### A Dynamic Web-Based Access Application

Microsoft's Access JobForum application is an example of more complex dynamic Web page generation with .idc and .htx files. The JobForum site, which is similar to newspaper classified advertising, lists job openings for Access developers and also lets developers place jobs wanted listings. Microsoft created this application in January 1996 as a demonstration of the use of IDC with Jet databases. Subsequently, the site became quite active, with many "help wanted" entries added every month.

You can view a good example of a complex, dynamic Web page at:

**http://www.microsoft.com/access/internet/jobforum/**

**On the Web**

From the JobForum home page, you can choose to view, enter, or update a listing in Job Available or Job Wanted. When you choose view, you can display all listings, all listings on or after a specified date, or a specific listing by number. Figure 18.6 shows a few of the Job Available listings on and after October 1, 1996. Clicking a listing hyperlink opens a Job Available page (see Figure 18.7) derived from data stored in the JobAvailable table of the .mdb file.

The JobForum white paper provides a complete description of the JobForum application with detailed explanations of the .idc and .htx files used to create the JobForum pages. You can download the white paper in Word 6 .doc format or read the paper at the following URL:

**http://www.microsoft.com/AccessDev/accwhite/JobForPa.htm**

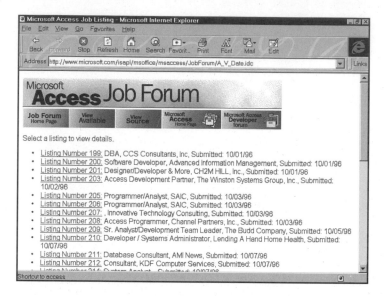

**FIG. 18.6** A few of the Job Available listings as of October 1996 that are displayed by the Access JobForum application.

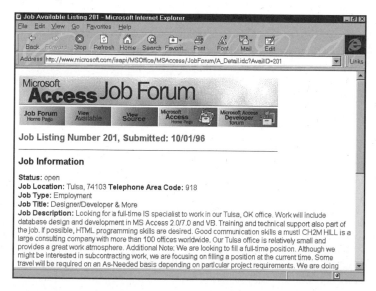

**FIG. 18.7** A Job Information page created from data stored in a Jet database.

Clicking the View Source button at any point in the JobForum application displays a Web page with the HTML source for the .idc and .htx files used to create the page, together with an explanation of the source in the form of comments (<!--explanation-->tags). Figure 18.8 shows part of the commented HTML source for the Job Information page shown in Figure 18.7. The commented source pages with the JobForum white paper are very useful when learning to write .idc and .htx files.

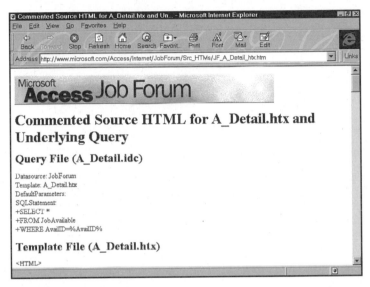

**FIG. 18.8**  The first part of the commented HTML source Web page for the Job Information page of Figure 18.7.

# Exporting Datasheets to Dynamic Web Pages

Access 97's File, Save As/Export and File, Save As HTML menu choices let you save table or query datasheets to dynamic Web pages. The advantage of a dynamic Web page compared with the static Web pages described in the preceding chapter, "Exporting Data to World Wide Web Pages," is that a dynamic Web page displays up-to-date information. Using a dynamic Web page eliminates the need to periodically re-create Web pages.

> **Note**
>
> You can't create dynamic Web pages from Access reports. Like printed reports, you must re-create the Web page when the content of a report changes.

### Creating a System ODBC Data Source by Using Access 97

Before you can use the .idc and .htx files, you must create a system ODBC data source on the Web server for the database that supplies the information for the table of the generated Web page. To create a system ODBC data source for Northwind.mdb, follow these steps:

1. On the PC running IIS 2+, open Northwind.mdb (or any other .mdb file) in Access 97. Select any table in the database.

---

**Note**

You can only export table and query objects to an ODBC database.

---

2. Choose File, Save As/Export. Select the To Another File or Database in the Save As dialog, and click OK to open the Save Table '*Tablename*' dialog.

3. Select ODBC Databases( ) in the Save as Type drop-down list (see Figure 18.9). When you make the selection, the Export dialog appears.

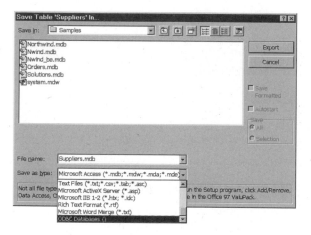

**FIG. 18.9** Selecting an ODBC data source to start the ODBC data source creation process in Access.

4. Accept the default table name in the Export dialog (see Figure 18.10), and click OK to open the Select Data Source dialog.

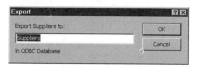

**FIG. 18.10** Specifying a temporary table name for the export process.

5. Click the Machine Data Source tab to display the user and system ODBC data sources presently installed on your computer (see Figure 18.11). The number of

data sources that appear depends on the software you've installed. All of the User data sources are installed by Office 97.

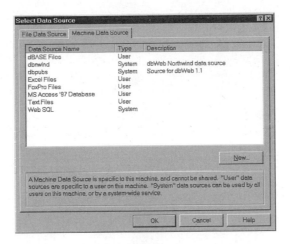

**FIG. 18.11** Displaying existing system and user ODBC data sources.

6. Click the New button to display the first dialog of the Create New Data Source (Wizard). Microsoft doesn't include "Wizard" in the dialog's caption, but the dialog resembles that of other Access wizards. The New Data Source (Wizard) automates a multistep process. Select the System Data Source option (see Figure 18.12). Click Next to continue.

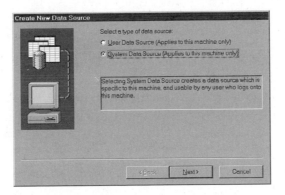

**FIG. 18.12** Selecting the System Data Source option in the second Create New Data Source dialog.

7. Select the Microsoft Access Driver (*.mdb) in the list box (see Figure 18.13). Click Next.

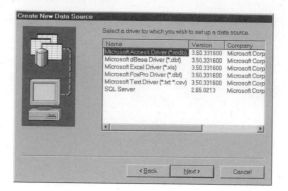

**FIG. 18.13** Selecting the Microsoft Access Driver for the data source in the third Create New Data Source dialog.

8. The final (wizard) dialog confirms your prior choices (see Figure 18.14). Click Finish to open the ODBC Microsoft Access Setup dialog of the 32-bit ODBC Administrator application.

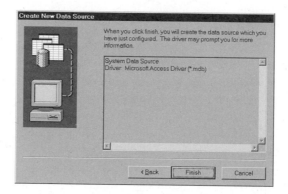

**FIG. 18.14** Confirming your data source selections in the final Create New Data Source dialog.

9. Type a name, such as **Nwind Web**, in the Data Source Name text box, and add an optional description in the Description text box (see Figure 18.15). Click the Select button to open the Select Database dialog.

10. Navigate to the …\Office\Samples folder, if necessary, and select Northwind.mdb as the Database Name (see Figure 18.16). Click OK to return to the ODBC Microsoft Access Setup dialog.

---

**Note**

If you want to use tables in a secure Jet database for the Web pages, select the Database option in the System Database frame, and click the System Database button. Select the workgroup file in the Select System Database dialog and click OK.

---

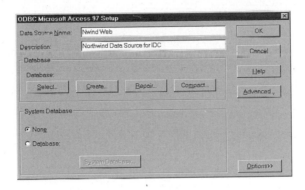

**FIG. 18.15**   Specifying a data source name and adding a description in the ODBC Microsoft Access Setup dialog.

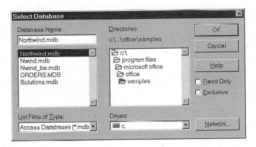

**FIG. 18.16**   Selecting the Jet 3.5 database for the ODBC data source.

**11.** Click OK to create the ODBC data source entry in the Registry. Your new data source appears as a System Data Source in the list of Machine Data Sources for the Web server (see Figure 18.17).

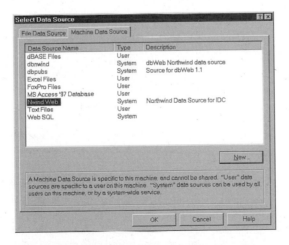

**FIG. 18.17**   The new data source added to the list of Machine Data Sources.

**12.** Click Cancel to stop the export process, because you only want to create the data source and don't want to export the table.

> **Note**
>
> It's important to specify a system ODBC data source, rather than a file or user data source, for ODBC data sources used with the IDC. System data sources are accessible to Httpodbc.dll immediately after the server boots up, without the need for a user to be logged on to the server. You must log on as the user who created the data source to make a user data source available to Httpodbc.dll.

### Specifying a Default ODBC Data Source

The Hyperlink/HTML page of the Options dialog lets you set a default ODBC data source for the .idc files you create with Access export operations. To make the Nwind Web data source the default, follow these steps:

**1.** Choose Tools, Options to open the Options dialog and click the Hyperlink/HTML tab.

**2.** Type the name of your data source—**Nwind Web,** in this case—in the Data Source Name text box.

**3.** Type **Admin** (the default user name) or a valid user name for a secure Jet database in the User to Connect As text box.

**4.** If your Jet database is secure, type the password to use with the user name in the Password for User text box (see Figure 18.18). For the default Admin user, leave the Password for User text box empty.

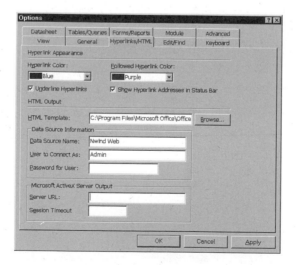

**FIG. 18.18** Specifying the data source name, user name, and password (if required) for the default ODBC data source of the .idc files you export.

**5.** Click OK to save the default database information and close the Options dialog.

## Using HTML Export to Create the Web Pages

You can use the File, Save As/Export command to create the .idc and .htx files for your dynamic Web page, but you need a home page (Default.htm) to execute the .idc file. Using the File, Save As HTML menu choice to activate the Publish to the World Wide Web Wizard (described in the preceding chapter) offers you the option of automatically creating a Switchboard form to execute the .idc file. The example that follows uses the North American Customers query (described in the preceding chapter) and Publish to the World Wide Web Wizard with Internet Information Server 2.0 running under Windows NT 4.0. You also can use the Microsoft Personal Web Server, included on the CD-ROM version of Office 97, for this example. If you use the Personal Web Server, only the paths to the folders in which you store the files differ.

◄◄ See "Creating a Web Page from a Query," p. 603
◄◄ See "Using the Web Publishing Wizard to Create a Static Web Site," p. 614

To create a dynamic Web page from the North American Customers query, follow these steps:

**1.** Create a new folder, \InetPub\wwwroot\NwindWeb, in which to create your Default.htm, .idc, and .htx files.

**2.** Create a second new folder, \InetPub\scripts\NwindWeb, to which you move the .idc and .htx files after the Publish to the World Wide Web Wizard creates the files in \InetPub\wwwroot\NwindWeb.

> **Note**
>
> All .idc and .htx files must be located in subfolders of the \InetPub\scripts folder. You cannot execute .idc files (or any other executable file) from subfolders of the \InetPub\wwwroot folder.

**3.** If you want to use a template for your Default.htm home page, copy the template files, including the required .gif or .jpg graphics files, to the \InetPub\wwwroot\ NwindWeb folder. This example uses the 100.htm template, which requires 100.jpg and Msaccess.jpg. If you want to use the same or another template with the .htx file, copy the graphics files to \InetPub\scripts\NwindWeb.

**4.** Open Northwind.mdb in Access 97 and choose File, Save As HTML to start the Publish to the Web Wizard (see Figure 18.19). You create a new publication profile in this example, so leave the I Want to Use a Web Publication Profile check box unmarked. Click Next to display the second Wizard dialog.

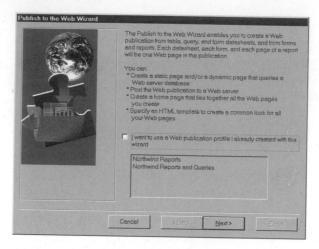

**FIG. 18.19** The first dialog of the Publish to the Web Wizard.

5. Click the Queries tab and select the North American Customers query (see Figure 18.20). You can create .idc and .htx files for more than one query or combine tables and queries, but you can't create .idc and .htx files for Access reports. Click Next to display the third wizard dialog (see Figure 18.21).

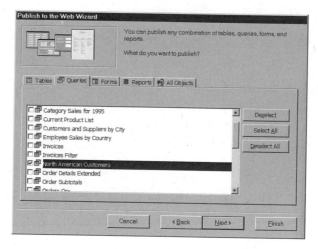

**FIG. 18.20** Selecting the query for the Web page in the second wizard dialog.

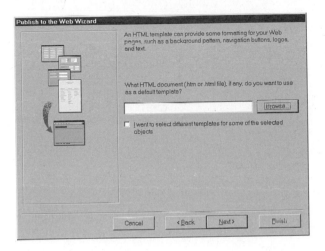

**FIG. 18.21** The third wizard dialog that lets you specify an HTML template for your Default.htm home page.

6. Click the Browse button to open the Select a HTML Template dialog, navigate to the \InetPub\Wwwroot\NwindWeb folder, and select the template—100.htm for this example (see Figure 18.22). Click Next to display the fifth wizard dialog.

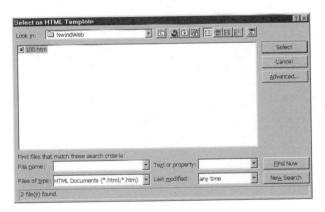

**FIG. 18.22** Selecting a template for the Default.htm page.

7. Select the Dynamic HTX/IDC (Microsoft Internet Information Server) option to create .htx and .idc files (see Figure 18.23). Click Next to display the sixth wizard dialog.

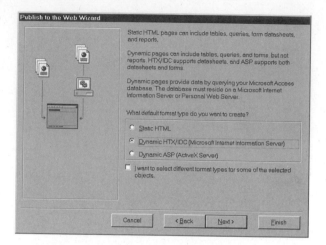

**FIG. 18.23** Specifying a dynamic Web page created with the Internet Database Connector.

8. The default ODBC data source name you specified in the preceding section appears in the text boxes of the Data Source Information frame (see Figure 18.24). The Data Source Name value is required; User Name and Password entries are required only for secure Access databases for which you specify a workgroup file. Click Next.

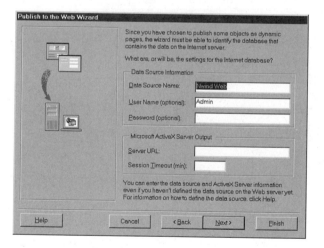

**FIG. 18.24** Accepting the default ODBC data source entries from the data source specified in the Hyperlink/HTML page of the Access 97 Options dialog.

9. Type **\InetPub\wwwroot\NwindWeb** as the folder to store the files that the wizard creates (see Figure 18.25). Alternatively, click the Browse button to navigate to the correct folder. The .idc and .htx files move to the \InetPub\scripts\

NwindWeb folder later in this example. Accept the default No, I Only Want to Publish Objects Locally, assuming that you are creating the files on the PC that's running IIS 2+. Click Next.

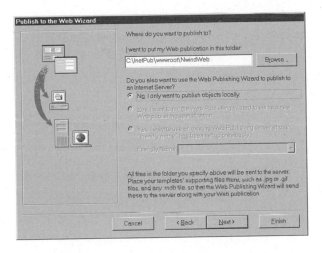

**FIG. 18.25**   Specifying the folder in which to store the files you create.

10. You need a home page to execute the .idc file, so mark the Yes, I Want to Create a Home Page check box and accept Default(.htm) as the name of the home page file (see Figure 18.26). Click Next.

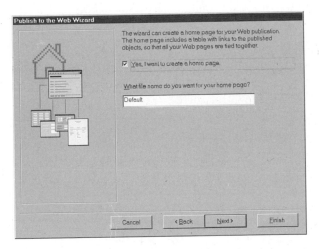

**FIG. 18.26**   Specifying a Switchboard home page to execute the .idc file.

11. In the final wizard page, mark the Yes, I Want to Save Wizard Answers to a Web Publication Profile check box, and type **NwindWeb Specification** in the Profile Name text box (see Figure 18.27). Click Finish to create the Web page files and terminate the wizard.

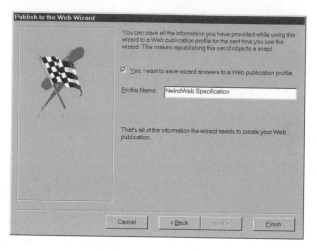

**FIG. 18.27** Specifying a Web publication profile in the last wizard dialog.

After the wizard creates the files, you must take the following steps to test the dynamic Web page you designed:

1. Move the North American Customers_1.htx and North American Customers_1.idc files from \InetPub\Wwwroot\NwindWeb to \InetPub\scripts\NwindWeb.

2. Open in Notepad the Default.htm file in \InetPub\Wwwroot\NwindWeb. Find the `<A HREF="North American Customers_1.idc?">` tag, and change the link to `<A HREF="/scripts/nwindweb/North American Customers_1.idc?">` (see Figure 18.28). Close Notepad and save the changes to the file.

> **Note**
>
> The paths you specify for hyperlinks to other files on the Web server are relative to the main publishing directory, \InetPub for IIS 2.0.

3. Open IE 3.0 or your default browser and type the **http://servername/ nwindweb** URL in the Address text box. The Default.htm Switchboard page appears (see Figure 18.29).

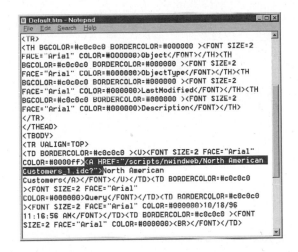

**FIG. 18.28** Changing the hyperlink to the North American Customers_1.idc file in Default.htm.

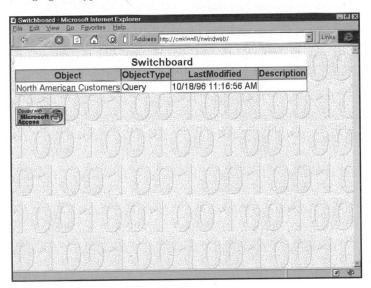

**FIG. 18.29** The Switchboard page created by Default.htm with the 100.htm template.

4. Click the North American Customers hyperlink to cause North American Customers_1.idc to execute a SQL query against Northwind.mdb, to return the query result set to North American Customers_1.htx, and to display the dynamic Web page (see Figure 18.30).

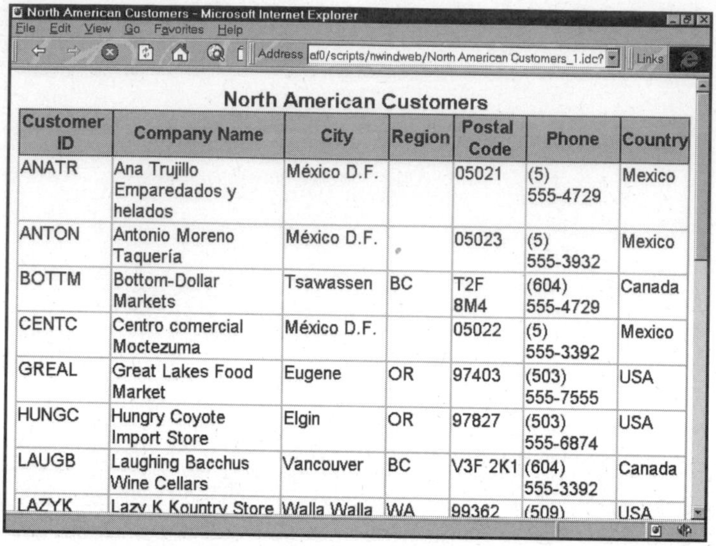

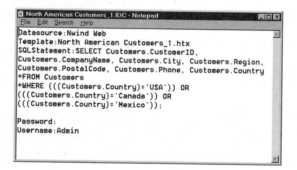

**FIG. 18.30** Internet Explorer 3.0 displaying the North American Customers dynamic Web page.

5. Open North American Customers_1.idc in Notepad to view the first half of the Publish to the Web Wizard's work (see Figure 18.31). The Wizard creates the `SQL Query` element of the file from the Jet SQL statement used to create the North American Customers query. (The field names of the query are a single line in the .idc file but appear on multiple lines in Figure 18.31 because of line wrapping.)

```
Datasource:Nwind Web
Template:North American Customers_1.htx
SQLStatement:SELECT Customers.CustomerID,
Customers.CompanyName, Customers.City, Customers.Region,
Customers.PostalCode, Customers.Phone, Customers.Country
+FROM Customers
+WHERE (((Customers.Country)='USA')) OR
(((Customers.Country)='Canada')) OR
(((Customers.Country)='Mexico'));

Password:
Username:Admin
```

**FIG. 18.31** Notepad displaying the content of the North American Customers_1.idc file.

Listing 18.5 shows the HTML source of the North American Customers_1.htx file called by the `Template:` element of North American Customers_1.idc.

**Listing 18.5    The HTML Source of the North American Customers_1.htx Template File**

```
<HTML>
<TITLE>North American Customers</TITLE>


TABLE BORDER=1 BGCOLOR=#ffffff CELLSPACING=0><FONT FACE="Arial"
OLOR=#000000><CAPTION><B>North American Customers</B></CAPTION>

THEAD>
T R >
TH BGCOLOR=#c0c0c0 BORDERCOLOR=#000000 >
FONT SIZE=2 FACE="Arial" COLOR-#000000>Customer ID</FONT></TH>
TH BGCOLOR-#c0c0c0 BORDERCOLOR=#000000 >
FONT SIZE=2 FACE="Arial" COLOR=#000000>Company Name</FONT></TH>
TH BGCOLOR=#c0c0c0 BORDERCOLOR=#000000 >
FONT SIZE=2 FACE="Arial" COLOR=#000000>City</FONT></TH>
TH BGCOLOR=#c0c0c0 BORDERCOLOR=#000000 >
FONT SIZE=2 FACE="Arial" COLOR=#000000>Region</FONT></TH>
TH BGCOLOR=#c0c0c0 BORDERCOLOR=#000000 >
FONT SIZE=2 FACE="Arial" COLOR=#000000>Postal Code</FONT></TH>
TH BGCOLOR=#c0c0c0 BORDERCOLOR=#000000 >
FONT SIZE=2 FACE="Arial" COLOR=#000000>Phone</FONT></TH>
TH BGCOLOR=#c0c0c0 BORDERCOLOR=#000000 >
FONT SIZE=2 FACE="Arial" COLOR=#000000>Country</FONT></TH>
/ T R >
/THEAD>

TBODY>
%BeginDetail%>
TR   VALIGN=TOP>
TD BORDERCOLOR=#c0c0c0 ><FONT SIZE=2 FACE="Arial"
OLOR=#000000><%CustomerID%><BR></FONT></TD>
TD BORDERCOLOR=#c0c0c0 ><FONT SIZE=2 FACE="Arial" COLOR=#000000>
%CompanyName%><BR></FONT></TD>
TD BORDERCOLOR=#c0c0c0 ><FONT SIZE=2 FACE="Arial" COLOR=#000000>
%City%><BR></FONT></TD>
TD BORDERCOLOR=#c0c0c0 ><FONT SIZE=2 FACE="Arial" COLOR=#000000>
%Region%><BR></FONT></TD>
TD BORDERCOLOR=#c0c0c0 ><FONT SIZE=2 FACE="Arial" COLOR=#000000>
%PostalCode%><BR></FONT></TD>
TD BORDERCOLOR=#c0c0c0 ><FONT SIZE=2 FACE="Arial" COLOR=#000000>
%Phone%><BR></FONT></TD>
TD BORDERCOLOR=#c0c0c0 ><FONT SIZE=2 FACE="Arial" COLOR=#000000>
%Country%><BR></FONT></TD>
/ T R >
%EndDetail%>
/TBODY>
TFOOT></TFOOT>
/TABLE>
/BODY>
BR><BR>

/HTML>
```

# Exporting Tables, Queries, and Forms to Active Server Pages

Active Server Pages (ASPs) play the primary role in Microsoft's strategy to gain for IE and IIS the predominate position in the Internet browser and server markets. ASP uses server-side scripting and *ActiveX Data Objects* (ADOs) to generate HTML files from desktop and client/server databases. ADO is an Automation wrapper (interface) for Microsoft's new OLE DB API, which first appeared in late 1996. OLE DB's objective is to provide a simpler mechanism than SQL-oriented ODBC for accessing data stored in any type of row/column format. ADO defines an Automation object, similar in concept to Access's ODBCDirect and Visual Basic's Remote Data Object (RDO). ADO supplies a Recordset object created from a table or query that you can manipulate with *Visual Basic Script* (*VBScript* or *VBS*) contained in .asp files stored on the Internet server. VBS is a simplified subset of VBA 5.0. Jet and ODBCDirect Recordset, and RDO's rdoResultset objects require the full version of VBA 5.0.

▶▶ See "Using ODBCDirect and the Remote Data Object," p. 1044

When this book was written, the only OLE DB data provider was Microsoft's "OLE DB Over ODBC," formerly code-named *Kagera*. You can expect Microsoft and third parties to deliver a variety of OLE DB data providers in 1997 and beyond. Until an OLE DB data provider is available for Jet 3.5 .mdb files, you must use an ODBC data source with OLE DB. The Nwind Web data source, described in the section "Creating a System ODBC Data Source Using Access 97" earlier in this chapter, is used for the ASP examples that follow.

### Creating \InetPub Subfolders for ASP Files

When an Internet client requests an .asp file from the server, the code in the .asp file executes to create an .htm(l) file that that the browser can display. Thus, the folders that contain .asp files require Execute permission. By default, subfolders of the \InetPub\Wwwroot folder do not have Execute permission. To create an IIS 3.0 \InetPub subfolder in which to store the .asp files you create in the following sections, perform these steps:

1. Use Windows Explorer to create a subfolder of \InetPub, \InetPub\NwindASP, for the examples that follow. If you are using IIS 3.0 and NTFS, make sure that the anonymous IUSER_*SERVERNAME* user has at least Read, Write, and Execute permissions for the folder.

2. Choose Start, Programs, Microsoft Internet Server, Internet Service Manager to launch Internet Service Manager.

3. Double-click the Computer entry for the WWW Service to open the WWW Service Properties for *Servername* properties sheet.

**4.** Click the Directories tab and click the Add button to open the Directory Properties dialog. Click the Browse button to open the Select Directory dialog and navigate to the \InetPub\NwindASP folder (see Figure 18.32). Click OK to enter the folder name in the Directory text box.

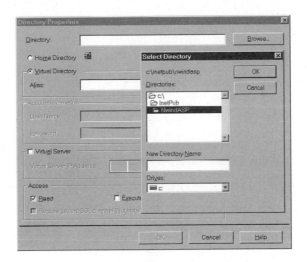

**FIG. 18.32**   Making the \InetPub\NwindASP folder accessible to Internet or intranet users.

**5.** Select the Virtual Directory option and type a name for the folder, **Northwind** for the following examples, in the Alias text box. The URL for the folder is **http:// servername/northwind**; OAKLEAF3 is the name of the server used to create the following figures.

▶▶ See "Defining the Client/Server Environment," p. 915

**6.** Mark the Execute check box to give users permission to execute files contained in this folder (see Figure 18.33). Click OK to add your new folder to IIS 3.0 and close the Directory Properties dialog.

> **Caution**
>
> If you don't enable Execute permissions, .asp files fail to deliver .htm(l) files to the browser. Depending on the browser you use and your location on the network, you might see the source code for the .asp file or an empty browser window.

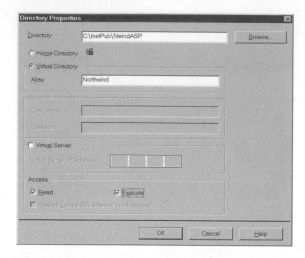

**FIG. 18.33** Specifying a virtual directory alias and enabling execution of .asp files in the folder.

7. Select the C:\InetPub\NwindASP Directory item, mark the Enable Default Document check box, and modify the default entry to Default.html (see Figure 18.34). The Switchboard page created by the Publish to the Web Wizard uses the .html file extension.

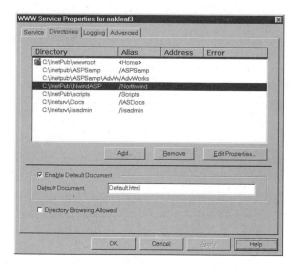

**FIG. 18.34** Specifying a default document for the \InetPub\NwindASP folder.

8. Click the OK button to close the WWW Service Properties for *Servername* properties sheet, and then close the Internet Service Manager window.

9. If you want to use a template with your .asp files, copy the template files to the \InetPub\NwindASP folder. The examples that follow use the 100.htm, 100.jpg, and Msaccess.jpg files for the template.

**IV**

**Publishing Data**

◀◀ See "Using HTML Templates," p. 606

### Exporting a Query to an ASP File

Creating a single .asp file is considerably simpler than using .idc/.htx files to create dynamic Web pages that display tabular data. You can export complete tables or a query result set to a single .asp file, which generates the .htm file from the database specified in the ODBC data source. The following example uses the File, Save As/Export method to create the ASP version of the IDC example described in the section "Using HTML Export to Create the Web Pages" earlier in this chapter.

◀◀ See "Creating a Web Page from a Query," p. 603

To create the North American Customers.asp file, follow these steps:

1. Open Northwind.mdb, if necessary, and select the North American Customers query that you created in the preceding chapter, "Exporting Data to World Wide Web Pages."

2. Choose File, Save As/Export to open the Save As dialog. Select the To an External File or Database option and click OK to open the Save Query 'North American Customers' In dialog.

3. Navigate to the \InetPub\NwindASP folder, and then select Microsoft ActiveX Server (*.asp) from the Save as Type list (see Figure 18.35). Click Export to open the Microsoft ActiveX Server Pages Output Options dialog.

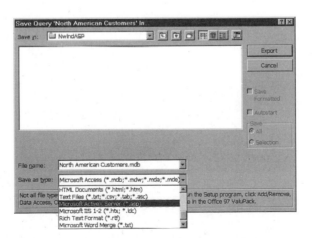

**FIG. 18.35**  Saving the North American Customers query in ASP format.

4. If you added a template file to your \InetPub\NwindASP folder in the last step of the preceding section, type the file name of the template in the HTML Template text box. Type **Nwind Web** in the Data Source Name text box and **http://servername/northwind** in the Server URL text box (see Figure 18.36).

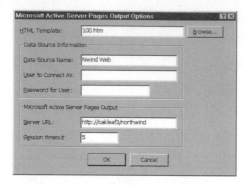

**FIG. 18.36** Specifying the template file, ODBC data source, and URL for the North American Customers.asp file.

5. Click OK to export the file to North American Customers.asp and close the dialog.

6. Launch IE 3+ and type **http://servername/North American Customers.asp** in the Address text box to execute the .asp file. The resulting HTML page appears as shown in Figure 18.37.

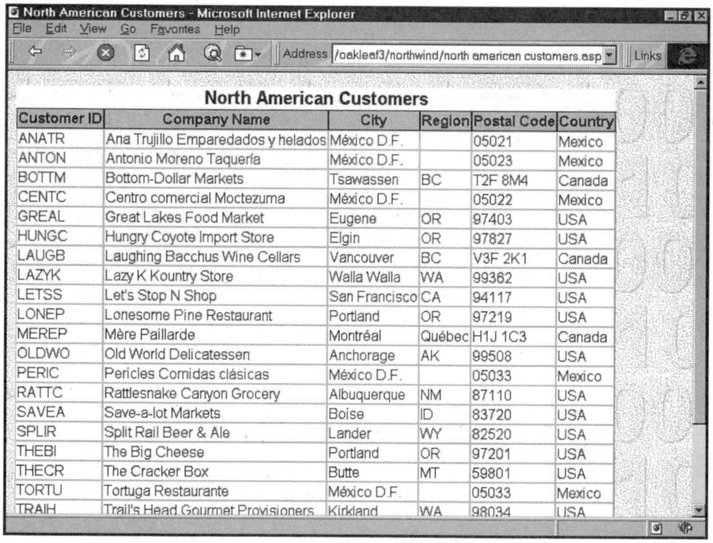

| Customer ID | Company Name | City | Region | Postal Code | Country |
|---|---|---|---|---|---|
| ANATR | Ana Trujillo Emparedados y helados | México D.F. | | 05021 | Mexico |
| ANTON | Antonio Moreno Taquería | México D.F. | | 05023 | Mexico |
| BOTTM | Bottom-Dollar Markets | Tsawassen | BC | T2F 8M4 | Canada |
| CENTC | Centro comercial Moctezuma | México D.F. | | 05022 | Mexico |
| GREAL | Great Lakes Food Market | Eugene | OR | 97403 | USA |
| HUNGC | Hungry Coyote Import Store | Elgin | OR | 97827 | USA |
| LAUGB | Laughing Bacchus Wine Cellars | Vancouver | BC | V3F 2K1 | Canada |
| LAZYK | Lazy K Kountry Store | Walla Walla | WA | 99362 | USA |
| LETSS | Let's Stop N Shop | San Francisco | CA | 94117 | USA |
| LONEP | Lonesome Pine Restaurant | Portland | OR | 97219 | USA |
| MEREP | Mère Paillarde | Montréal | Québec | H1J 1C3 | Canada |
| OLDWO | Old World Delicatessen | Anchorage | AK | 99508 | USA |
| PERIC | Pericles Comidas clásicas | México D.F. | | 05033 | Mexico |
| RATTC | Rattlesnake Canyon Grocery | Albuquerque | NM | 87110 | USA |
| SAVEA | Save-a-lot Markets | Boise | ID | 83720 | USA |
| SPLIR | Split Rail Beer & Ale | Lander | WY | 82520 | USA |
| THEBI | The Big Cheese | Portland | OR | 97201 | USA |
| THECR | The Cracker Box | Butte | MT | 59801 | USA |
| TORTU | Tortuga Restaurante | México D.F. | | 05033 | Mexico |
| TRAIH | Trail's Head Gourmet Provisioners | Kirkland | WA | 98034 | USA |

**FIG. 18.37** The Web page generated by North American Customers.asp.

Internet Explorer 3.01 is the browser used to test the .asp pages created in these examples. IE 3.01 provides a number of minor improvements to the original IE 3.0 version. You can download the current version of IE from:

**http://www.microsoft.com/ie/**

7. Choose View, Source to display in Notepad the HTML source generated by the .asp file (see Figure 18.38). The HTML source is essentially identical to that created by the .idc/.htx files you created earlier in the chapter.

Spaces ordinarily aren't allowed in URLs, so ASP replaces spaces in generated HTML file names with %20.

```
north%20american%20customers.htm - Notepad
File  Edit  Search  Help
<HTML>

<TITLE>North American Customers</TITLE>

<BODY background = 100.jpg>


<TABLE BORDER=1 BGCOLOR=#ffffff CELLSPACING=0><FONT FACE=

<THEAD>
<TR>
<TH BGCOLOR=#c0c0c0 BORDERCOLOR=#000000 ><FONT SIZE=2 FAC
<TH BGCOLOR=#c0c0c0 BORDERCOLOR=#000000 ><FONT SIZE=2 FAC
<TH BGCOLOR=#c0c0c0 BORDERCOLOR=#000000 ><FONT SIZE=2 FAC
<TH BGCOLOR=#c0c0c0 BORDERCOLOR=#000000 ><FONT SIZE=2 FAC
<TH BGCOLOR=#c0c0c0 BORDERCOLOR=#000000 ><FONT SIZE=2 FAC
<TH BGCOLOR=#c0c0c0 BORDERCOLOR=#000000 ><FONT SIZE=2 FAC
```

**FIG. 18.38**  Part of the HTML source for the Web page generated by North American Customers.asp.

8. Use Notepad to open the North American Customers.asp file to display the VBS source code used to create the .htm file (see Figure 18.39).

```
North American Customers.asp - Notepad
File  Edit  Search  Help
<HTML>

<TITLE>North American Customers</TITLE>

<BODY background = 100.jpg>

<%
Param = Request.QueryString("Param")
Data = Request.QueryString("Data")
%>
<%
Session.timeout = 5
If IsObject(Session("Nwind Web_conn")) Then
    Set conn = Session("Nwind Web_conn")
Else
    Set conn = Server.CreateObject("ADODB.Connection")
    conn.open "Nwind Web","",""
    Set Session("Nwind Web_conn") = conn
End If
%>
```

**FIG. 18.39**  Part of the VBS source code contained in North American Customers.asp.

> **Note**
>
> The reason for using a fully descriptive query name is to create an appropriate title for the query result set table. You can rename the North American Customers.asp file to NACusts.asp or the like to minimize the length of the URL and avoid including spaces.

Listing 18.6 contains the complete source, including VBS code, of North American Customers.asp. Server-side VBS code is enclosed within `<%...%>` tags. The following three VBS statements establish a connection to Northwind.mdb using the ActiveX Data Object (ADODB) and the Nwind Web data source:

```
Set conn = Server.CreateObject("ADODB.Connection")
conn.open "Nwind Web","",""
Set Session("Nwind Web_conn") = conn
```

The SQL statement in the `sql = ...` lines is the Jet SQL statement of the North American Customers query that opens an ADO `Recordset` object with the `rs.Open sql, conn, 3, 3` VBS statement. The VBA code between the `Do While Not rs.EOF` and `Loop` statements populates the cells of the table.

**Listing 18.6  The HTML Source and VBS Code of the North American Customers.asp File**

```
<HTML>
<TITLE>North American Customers</TITLE>
<BODY background = 100.jpg>


%
aram = Request.QueryString("Param")
ata = Request.QueryString("Data")
>
%
ession.timeout = 5
f IsObject(Session("Nwind Web_conn")) Then
  Set conn = Session("Nwind Web_conn")
lse
  Set conn = Server.CreateObject("ADODB.Connection")
  conn.Open "Nwind Web","",""
  Set Session("Nwind Web_conn") = conn
End If
%>
<%
    sql = "SELECT Customers.CustomerID, Customers.CompanyName,
Customers.City, Customers.Region, Customers.PostalCode,
Customers.Country FROM Customers WHERE (((Customers.Country)='USA'))
OR (((Customers.Country)='Canada')) OR
(((Customers.Country)='Mexico'))"
    If cstr(Param) <> "" And cstr(Data) <> "" Then
        sql = sql & " And " & cstr(Param) & " = " & cstr(Data)
    End If
    Set rs = Server.CreateObject("ADODB.Recordset")
    rs.Open sql, conn, 3, 3
%>
```

```
<TABLE BORDER=1 BGCOLOR=#ffffff CELLSPACING=0><FONT FACE="Arial"
COLOR=#000000><CAPTION><B>North American Customers</B></CAPTION>


THEAD>
TR>
TH BGCOLOR=#c0c0c0 BORDERCOLOR=#000000 ><FONT SIZE=2
FACE="Arial"  COLOR=#000000>Customer ID</FONT></TH>
TH BGCOLOR=#c0c0c0 BORDERCOLOR=#000000 ><FONT SIZE=2
FACE="Arial"  COLOR=#000000>Company Name</FONT></TH>
TH BGCOLOR=#c0c0c0 BORDERCOLOR=#000000 ><FONT SIZE=2
FACE="Arial"  COLOR=#000000>City</FONT></TH>
TH BGCOLOR=#c0c0c0 BORDERCOLOR=#000000 ><FONT SIZE=2
FACE="Arial"  COLOR=#000000>Region</FONT></TH>
TH BGCOLOR=#c0c0c0 BORDERCOLOR=#000000 ><FONT SIZE=2
FACE="Arial"  COLOR=#000000>Postal Code</FONT></TH>
TH BGCOLOR=#c0c0c0 BORDERCOLOR=#000000 ><FONT SIZE=2
FACE="Arial"  COLOR=#000000>Country</FONT></TH>

/TR>
/THEAD>
TBODY>

%
n Error Resume Next
s.MoveFirst
o While Not rs.EOF
% >

TR  VALIGN=TOP>
TD BORDERCOLOR=#c0c0c0 ><FONT SIZE=2 FACE="Arial"
OLOR=#000000><%=Server.HTMLEncode(rs.Fields("CustomerID").Value)%>
BR></FONT></TD>
TD BORDERCOLOR=#c0c0c0 ><FONT SIZE=2 FACE="Arial"
OLOR=#000000><%=Server.HTMLEncode(rs.Fields("CompanyName").Value)%>
BR></FONT></TD>
TD BORDERCOLOR=#c0c0c0 ><FONT SIZE=2 FACE="Arial"
OLOR=#000000><%=Server.HTMLEncode(rs.Fields("City").Value)%>
BR></FONT></TD>
TD BORDERCOLOR=#c0c0c0 ><FONT SIZE=2 FACE="Arial"
OLOR=#000000><%=Server.HTMLEncode(rs.Fields("Region").Value)%>
BR></FONT></TD>
TD BORDERCOLOR=#c0c0c0 ><FONT SIZE=2 FACE="Arial"
OLOR=#000000><%=Server.HTMLEncode(rs.Fields("PostalCode").Value)%>
BR></FONT></TD>
TD BORDERCOLOR=#c0c0c0 ><FONT SIZE=2 FACE="Arial"
OLOR=#000000><%=Server.HTMLEncode(rs.Fields("Country").Value)%>
BR></FONT></TD>
/TR>

<%
rs.MoveNext
Loop
%>
```

(continues)

---

**Listing 18.6    Continued**

```
</TBODY>
<TFOOT></TFOOT>
</TABLE>
</BODY>
<BR><BR>
<IMG SRC = "msaccess.jpg">
</HTML>
```

---

If you're familiar with VBA, the similarities between server-side VBS and VBA code in the preceding listing are quite evident. Using .asp files to create dynamic Web pages from tables and queries saves a substantial amount of server disk space compared with exporting a corresponding static Web page.

### Exporting Access Forms to ASP Files

Access 97 lets you export existing forms to .asp files. The form export process creates the necessary HTML text boxes and navigation buttons to emulate simple Access forms, including forms with subforms. IE 3+ uses the ActiveX HTML Layout Control to create the page design in a *Formname*alx.asp file; subforms are implemented by an embedded Web browser control. Both *Formname*.asp and *Formname*alx.asp files are required to emulate Access forms.

To create Customers.asp and Customersalx.asp and test the Web-based form, follow these steps:

1. Select the Customers form and choose File, Save As/Export to open the Save As dialog. Make sure that the To an External File or Database option is selected and click OK to open the Save Form 'Customers' In dialog.

2. Navigate to the \InetPub\NwindASP folder, and then select Microsoft ActiveX Server (*.asp) from the Save as Type list (refer to Figure 18.35). Click Export to open the Microsoft ActiveX Server Pages Output Options dialog.

3. The default background color of the exported form is gray, the same as the default background color of most browsers, so don't specify a template file. If necessary, type **Nwind Web** in the Data Source Name Text box and type **http://** *servername*/**northwind** in the Server URL text box (refer to Figure 18.36).

   If you complete this example immediately after completing the example of the prior section, the text boxes of the Microsoft ActiveX Server Pages output Options dialog retain their prior settings.

4. Click OK to export the file to Customers.asp and Customersalx.asp and close the dialog.

5. Launch IE 3+ and type **http://***servername*/**Customers.asp** in the Address text box to execute the two .asp files. The resulting HTML page appears as shown in Figure 18.40.

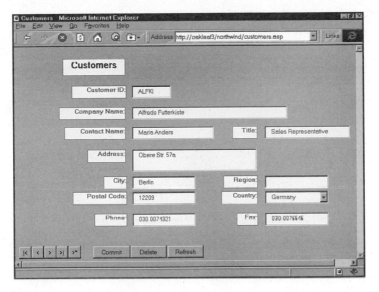

**FIG. 18.40** The Web page generated by Customers.asp and Customersalx.asp.

**6.** Choose View, Source to display in Notepad the HTML source generated by the Customers.asp file (see Figure 18.41). Very little source is required in the Customers(1).htm file because all the action takes place in the ActiveX HTML Layout Control of the Customersalx.asp file identified by the OBJECT ID= and PARAM NAME= tags.

**FIG. 18.41** The Web page generated by Customers.asp and Customersalx.asp.

You can edit any of the entries that appear in text boxes and select a country from the drop-down list. Clicking the Commit button sends changes you make to the server, which performs an UPDATE operation on the affected table(s)—only Customers, in this case. Each time you move the record pointer with the navigation buttons, commit changes, or delete or refresh a record, the server resends the modified page to the client. Thus, browsing a table with a Web form is a relatively slow process, even if you're connected to the server via a local-area network (LAN). The ActiveX Database Connector (ADC), which wasn't released by Microsoft when this book was written, lets you store "disconnected" ADO Recordset objects on the client, browse and make multiple updates to the Recordset, and then return the changes to the server. ADC eliminates the need for a round-trip to the server each time you update, delete, or add a new record.

> **Note**
>
> Changing the value of the primary key field of a table on which other records rely violates referential integrity rules. If referential integrity is enforced by Access relationships, changes you make to primary key values (such as to the CustomerID field of the Customers table) are ignored. You don't receive an error message, because the VBS code in Customersalx.asp includes an On Error Resume Next statement.

 ▶▶ See "Handling Run-Time Errors," p. 1005

# Part V

# Integrating Access with Other Office 97 Applications

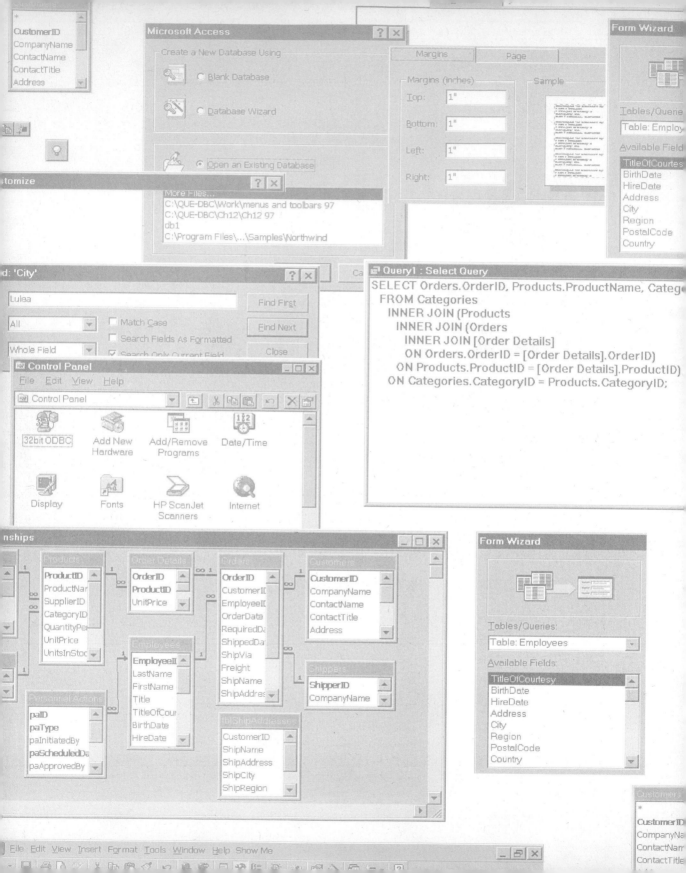

Chapter 19

# Using 32-Bit OLE Components

Windows 95 and Windows NT 3.51 introduced 32-bit *Object Linking and Embedding* (OLE, pronounced as the Spanish *¡olé!*) 2.1 to the PC. The new version 8.0 members of the Microsoft Office 97 suite—Access 97 (in the Professional Edition only), Excel 97, Word 97, and PowerPoint 97—provide a variety of new capabilities with OLE 2.1. OLE is a method of transferring information in the form of *objects* between different Windows applications. This method is similar in concept to, although more sophisticated than, copying text or graphics to the Clipboard and pasting the copied text or graphic to other applications.

OLE 2.+ is based on Microsoft's *Component Object Model* (COM), which is the industry standard for object-oriented application programming in the Windows environment. This chapter introduces you to the principles of OLE and how your Access 97 applications can take advantage of the features offered by 32-bit OLE 2.1. The new ActiveX components included in Office 97 are also a form of OLE objects; ActiveX components are described in Chapter 31, "Exchanging Data with Automation and ActiveX Controls."

## Understanding the Importance of OLE

Understanding OLE principles is important because OLE is the sole method by which you can add graphic images to your Access forms and reports, as well as add or edit data in OLE Object fields of Access. The benefits of using OLE for applying and storing nontext information (instead of using built-in graphics processing offered by some RDBMSs) include the following:

■ You can use any image-processing application that functions as an OLE server to create and edit bitmapped graphics: from the simple Windows 95/NT 4.0 Paint application to photographic-quality editors, such as Adobe Photoshop and Corel PhotoPAINT.

■ You can embed or link vector-based images from template-based OLE servers, such as Visio 4.0, or from professional illustration packages, such as CorelDRAW! 6.0—both 32-bit OLE 2.1 servers that are designed for Windows 95. Access 97 also supports 16-bit OLE 2.0 servers. Microsoft Graph 97, called MSGraph8 in this book, is included with Access 97; MSGraph8 is a 32-bit implementation of the 16-bit OLE 2.0 server applet included with Access 2.0 and Access 95.

■ The added overhead that is associated with bitmap editors incorporated in the application is eliminated. Self-contained bitmap editors and drawing functions are seldom as capable as stand-alone, shrink-wrapped OLE server applications.

■ You don't need to install a collection of import and export filters for different kinds of files. OLE server applications provide file import from, and export to, a variety of file types.

■ You can export objects stored in OLE Object fields in Access tables or within bound or unbound object frames to other applications via the Clipboard. Bound object frames display the presentation of OLE objects stored in OLE Object fields of Access tables. Unbound object frames display the presentation of static OLE objects, such as company logos used to embellish forms and reports.

■ You can store a variety of OLE objects in one OLE Object field. You can link or embed in one OLE Object field waveform audio (.wav), MIDI music (.mid), animation (.fli and .mmm), and audio/video interleaved (.avi) files. You need a large-capacity fixed disk to embed .avi and long-duration .wav files, however.

■ You can choose between embedding the data within a table, form, or report and linking the OLE object to a file that contains the data. The behavior of an OLE 2.1 object differs, depending on whether you link or embed an object.

The most common kinds of OLE objects used in Access applications are 16-color and 256-color embedded bitmap graphic images. Figure 19.1 shows a portion of a page from the Northwind Traders Catalog report that includes an embedded bitmap image. The image is a Windows 95 Paint bitmap that is embedded by OLE in the Picture field of the Categories table.

# Defining OLE

OLE is a member of a class of computer operations known as *interprocess communication* (*IPC*). IPC operations enable different applications to send data to and receive data from other applications by an agreed-on procedure. The Clipboard is the primary IPC path for Windows; most present-day communication of data between running applications (other than by reading or writing to disk files) involves using the Windows Clipboard.

Windows defines a set of standard data types that you can copy to, or paste from, the Clipboard. OLE uses these standard Windows data types: bitmapped and vector-based graphic images, plain and formatted text, digital audio sound, and so on. You may have used (or tried to use) dynamic data exchange (DDE) as an IPC method to transfer data between Windows applications. OLE is a major improvement over DDE because OLE is easier to implement than DDE. OLE 2.1+ ultimately is expected to replace DDE.

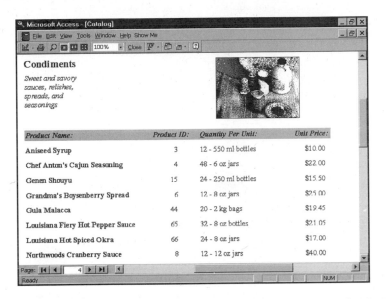

**FIG. 19.1**   A part of one page of the Northwind Traders Catalog report in Print Preview mode.

OLE operations differ from conventional Windows copy-and-paste operations—performed with Ctrl+C and Ctrl+V or by way of DDE—because OLE includes a substantial amount of information about the source of the data along with the actual data. An OLE object copied to the Clipboard by Excel 97, for example, includes the following information:

- The name of the application from which the data originated (in this case, Excel).

- The type of data, such as worksheet, module, or chart (Excel worksheet).

- The full path to the file, beginning with the drive letter and the file name, if the data is derived from or was saved to a file.

- A name assigned to the sheet or chart that contains the data if the data isn't derived from or saved to a file. The name usually is a long combination of numbers and letters.

- The name or coordinates of the range of the data if only a portion of an object is included.

- The presentation of the object in Windows Metafile Format (.wmf). If the object is not an image, the icon of the application that created the object is the object's presentation.

- For file-based OLE 2.1 objects, a set of property values obtained from entries in the property pages of the Properties window for the file (see Figure 19.2).

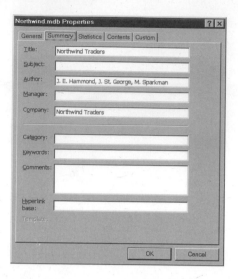

**FIG. 19.2** The Summary page of the Properties window for Northwind.mdb.

---

**Note**

All file-based OLE 2.1-compliant server applications that qualify for the "Designed for Windows 95" logo have a File, Properties menu command that opens a standard Properties page for the file. You can edit the property values of the Summary and Custom pages; values in the General, Statistics, and Contents pages are read-only. Only documents created by OLE 2.1 servers appear as choices of the Start, Documents menu.

---

When you paste data copied to the Clipboard from an Excel worksheet and then double-click the cell's surface, Excel pops up to allow you to edit the data, and it disappears when you finish. With OLE, you paste complete objects, rather than just data, into an element of the application.

# Classifying OLE 2.1-Compliant Applications

32-bit OLE 2.1-compliant applications fall into the following six categories:

- *Container applications*. These applications, such as Access 97, are stand-alone products that are capable of linking or embedding objects created by other 16-bit and 32-bit OLE 2+-compliant applications. Container applications, however, cannot create OLE objects for linking to, or embedding in, other OLE 2.1 applications. OLE container applications also are called *OLE client applications*.

- *Server-only applications*. These stand-alone applications create OLE objects for embedding in and linking to other applications, but you cannot embed an OLE object in or link an OLE object to them.

- *Mini-server applications.* Mini-servers (also called *OLE applets*) are similar to server-only applications, but mini-servers are not stand-alone products. You can execute an OLE mini-server only from within an OLE container application. MSGraph8 is an OLE 2.1 mini-server. Mini-servers also are called *components* or *ActiveX components*.

- *Full-server applications.* OLE full-servers are stand-alone applications that are capable of creating OLE objects for use by other applications. Full-server applications can embed or link objects created by other OLE servers. Excel 97, Word 97, and Project 97 are OLE 2.1 full-servers.

- *Automation-compliant applications.* Automation (formerly known as *OLE Automation*) lets an OLE 2+ container application manipulate an embedded or linked object by sending programming instructions to the OLE 2+ server that created it. Automation server applications are said to create *programmable objects*. Access 97 is an Automation server but not a conventional OLE 2.1 server, because you cannot embed Access 97 objects in 32-bit container applications. Microsoft Outlook also is an Automation server. Excel 97, Word 97, and Project 97 are all Automation-compliant container and server applications. Automation client applications, such as Access 97, use their programming language to send instructions to programmable objects. Using Automation is the subject of Chapter 31, "Exchanging Data with Automation and ActiveX Controls."

▶▶  See "Adding ActiveX Controls to Your Application," p. 1122

- *ActiveX Controls.* One of the advantages of Visual Basic as a Windows programming environment has been its extensibility through custom controls, originally called VBXs (Visual Basic eXtensions). Microsoft and third-party software publishers supply a variety of specialized custom control objects for Visual Basic 3.0 and earlier, including mini-spreadsheets, image editors, and report writers. In 1995, Microsoft created an OLE-based replacement for VBXs, called *OLE Controls*. Access 2.0 was the first product to offer extensibility through 16-bit OLE Controls. The 16-bit version of Visual Basic 4.0 accommodates both 16-bit OLE Controls and VBXs. Access 95 and 32-bit Visual Basic 4.0 use 32-bit OLE Controls.

The file size of OLE Controls was much larger than their VBX counterparts because of the overhead needed to support the OLE 2.x specifications. To make OLE Controls practical for use in Internet applications, Microsoft developed 32-bit ActiveX Controls based directly on COM. ActiveX Controls are a lightweight version of the 32-bit OLE Controls they replace. Office 97 components (except Outlook) and Visual Basic 5.0 can embed ActiveX Controls in forms. The original OLE Control design is obsolete, but Access 97 is backwardly compatible with most of the 32-bit OLE Controls supplied with the Access 95 Developer's Toolkit and Visual Basic 4.0.

> **Note**
>
> Server-only, mini-server, and full-server OLE applications collectively are called *local servers*, because these OLE servers must reside on the same PC as the OLE client application. The Professional Edition of Visual Basic 4+ lets you create *Remote Automation Objects* (RAOs), a special type of OLE server that can reside on a network server and communicate with OLE client applications on networked workstations using *Distributed COM* (*DCOM*). RAOs let you build three-tier client/server applications with Access 97. You also can create *in-process* OLE servers by using Visual Basic 4+. These special types of OLE servers are discussed briefly in Chapter 31.

# Introducing Object Building Blocks

When the term *object* is used in conjunction with a computer application or programming language, the term doesn't refer to a tangible object, such as a rock, saxophone, or book. Objects in computer programming and applications are intangible representations (called *abstractions*) of real-world objects.

A computer object combines *properties*—such as the properties you assign to an Access control object in a form or report—and *methods* that define the behavior of the object. Text box properties (such as the text the box contains, the size, the typeface, the font the text uses, and the colors and borders employed) vary widely. The ways text box controls behave when you type new text or edit existing text are the methods associated with text box objects of forms and reports. All text boxes in Windows applications use similar, but not identical, methods.

### Properties and Methods Encapsulated in Objects

A musical instrument, such as a saxophone, can serve as an example of a tangible object with an intangible representation: sound. Some properties of a saxophone are size (soprano, alto, tenor, bass, and baritone), type of fingering, materials of construction, and the name of the instrument's manufacturer.

The methods that are applicable to saxophones are the techniques used to play these instruments: blowing into the mouthpiece, biting the reed, and fingering the keys that determine the note that you play.

If you create a programming object that simulates all of the properties and methods of a particular kind of saxophone, and if you have the proper audio hardware for a computer, you can create an object that imitates the sound of Charlie Parker's, Art Pepper's, or Stan Getz's style. Stanford University's new WaveGuide acoustic synthesis computer programs create objects that are capable of this kind of imitation. The properties of a particular saxophone and the methods of the artist playing it are said to be *encapsulated* in a particular kind of saxophone object. The object acts as a container for the properties and methods that constitute the object.

One more item is found in the container of an OLE object: *presentation*. Presentation is how the user perceives the object—how the object looks or sounds. The presentation of a WaveGuide saxophone is a musical sound. If the saxophone object is used in a Windows

95 application, the sound probably is reproduced through digital audio techniques by an audio adapter card. The presentation of a large graphic image may be a miniature copy, called a *thumbnail*.

At first glance, presentation may appear to be a property. Presentation isn't a property in the true sense, however, because the presentation of an object is dependent on factors outside the object, such as the kind of hardware available, the computer operating system used, and the application in which the object is employed. The presentation of a 256-color bitmap on a 16-color VGA display, for example, is quite different from its presentation on a 256-color display driver.

### Object-Enabled Applications

Applications and programming languages—which are also applications—that programmers used to create these applications are *object-enabled* if the applications can encapsulate properties and methods within an object container. Before object-enabled programming was developed, programmers considered properties and methods as two separate entities. Programmers wrote code that defined the methods of an application. Separate data files contained the properties that the programmer's application manipulated. A classic example of this separation is xBase: a set of .dbf files contains properties (data), and a separate collection of .prg files contains the methods (programs) that apply to the set of .dbf files.

In contrast to the conventional programming technique, Access takes an object-enabled approach to database management. Access combines the data (tables) and methods (queries, forms, reports, and Access VBA code) in a single, often massive, .mdb container—known as the `Database` object. `Form` and `Report` objects act as containers for `Control` objects. `QueryDef` objects consist of Structured Query Language (SQL) methods applied to `Table` or other `QueryDef` objects. Although lacking some characteristics of a truly object-oriented programming language (OOPL), Access VBA comes close enough to the mark that you can consider Access VBA an object-enabled application programming language.

### The Advantages of Objects

Combining properties and methods into an object and then adding a standard presentation provides the following advantages to users of applications and the programmers who create them:

- Objects combine data (properties) and the program code that deals with the data (methods) into one object you can treat as a "black box." You need not understand the internal elements of the box to use a box in an application. This characteristic of objects aids in the programming of large-scale applications in which many programmers participate. You can modify an object without affecting how the object is used by other programmers.

- Objects can be reused when needed. You can create and use a library of objects in many programs or applications. If you create a library of vector-based images created by CorelDRAW! in an Access table, for example, you can edit these images from within Access and then save a copy of the edited drawing in a separate file.

■ Objects can be used with any Windows application that supports OLE 2+. You can use the same graphic or sound object with Access, Excel, or Word. If you copy a drawing embedded in an Excel spreadsheet to the Clipboard, you can paste the drawing as an unbound object in an Access form or report, or into an OLE Object field.

■ Objects are easy to create with OLE. If you copy all or a portion of the data you create in an OLE-compliant application, you create a temporary OLE object in the Clipboard.

### Object Classes, Types, Hierarchies, and Inheritance

Programming objects, like real-world objects, are organized in hierarchies of classes and subclasses, as well as in types without subclasses. The class hierarchy of musical instrument synthesis objects is shown in Figure 19.3 (the subclasses are shown for woodwinds only). At the top of the hierarchical structure you see the master class, Simulated Musical Instruments, that defines the presentation of all the subclasses as digital audio sound.

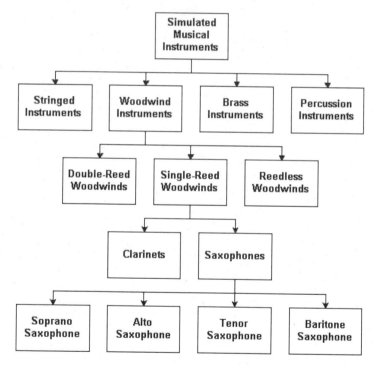

**FIG. 19.3**  A hierarchy diagram of objects representing the sound of simulated musical instruments.

Musical instruments are classified by the method used to create their sounds. Saxophones are members of the general woodwind class, which you can further subclass as single-reed woodwinds (refer to Figure 19.3). Single-reed woodwinds include clarinets and saxophones, which share many playing methods. Saxophones can be subclassed further by size and the musical key in which these instruments play. At the bottom of the hierarchy are types that have no further subclasses.

A B flat (tenor) saxophone has a unique set of property values (data), but the kinds of properties are common to all saxophones. Similarly, the tenor saxophone's playing methods are common to all saxophones. The tenor saxophone type inherits both the methods and the list of properties from the saxophone subclass, which in turn inherits properties from the single-reed woodwind class. Parent classes are a level above child classes in the genealogy of classes, and siblings are members of the same class or type. Access uses the term *master* to indicate a parent class object and *child* to indicate a descendent of the parent class, as in the Link Master Fields and Link Child Fields properties of subform and subreport controls.

▶▶ See "Understanding Objects and Object Collections," p. 1023

Figure 19.4 illustrates the hierarchy of objects within Access that are described up to this point in the book. Table, Form, and Report objects have distinctive properties and methods. Form and Report objects share the same group of Control objects, but some Control objects behave differently when contained in Form or Report objects.

Queries (called QueryDef objects) aren't true objects; QueryDef objects comprise a set of methods applied to Table objects. Control objects can be classified further into bound and unbound Control objects. Only object frames can incorporate OLE objects, and only a bound object frame can display or provide access to editing capability for OLE data in tables or queries without resorting to Access VBA code.

The Control objects in Access inherit some methods from the object that contains the control objects. Subform and subreport controls inherit all related methods and many properties from Form and Report objects, respectively. OLE child objects inherit a large number of their properties and methods from the parent OLE class that defines how OLE objects behave (or should behave). Each OLE child, however, has a complement of properties and methods that apply only to that child. OLE object subclasses at the bottom of Figure 19.4 aren't types because each subclass may have different OLE object types. The Bitmapped Graphic Class, for example, may include Paintbrush Picture, CorelPhotoPAINT Picture, and PicturePublisher Picture OLE object types.

# Containing Objects in Other Objects

OLE is designed to allow a single *container document* to be built with contributions, known as *source documents*, from foreign applications. (Container documents were *destination documents* in OLE 1.0 terminology.) The container document may be created by most applications that are OLE compliant. Access forms and reports, proposals created in Word for Windows, Excel worksheets, and PowerPoint presentation visuals are common container documents.

When more than one application contributes to the content of a document, the document is referred to as a *compound document*. The application that creates the compound document is the OLE container application (formerly the OLE client), and the foreign applications that contribute source documents to the compound document are OLE servers. Access 97 is an OLE 2.1 client and creates the compound container documents; Access forms, reports, and tables that incorporate OLE objects are compound documents.

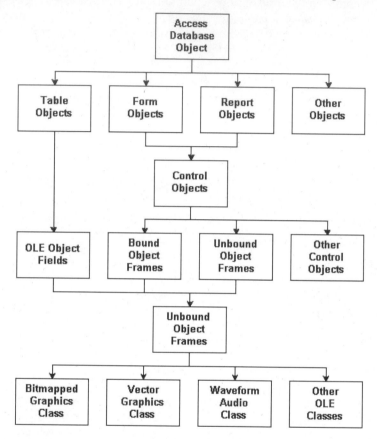

**FIG. 19.4**    A simplified hierarchy of database objects in Access.

Each source document created with OLE servers and contributed to a container document is an individual, identifiable object that possesses its own properties, possesses its own methods, and has its own presentation. You can choose to *embed* the source document within an Access container document that acts as a container for one or more source document objects. Embedding includes the object's data in the source document. You also can *link* the source document; in this case, the data resides in a separate file. The difference between embedding and linking objects is the subject of the next section, "Understanding Differences Between OLE and DDE."

**Note**

With OLE 1.0, you could activate an embedded or linked object within the container document, but you could not activate any objects contained within the first embedded or linked object. (To *activate* an OLE object means to open the object for editing in the source application.) OLE 2+ eliminates this restriction. Thus, if you embed a Word 97 document containing an embedded Excel 97 worksheet in the OLE object field of an Access table, you can activate the Word document in Word 97 and then activate the worksheet object in Excel 97. There is no limit to how deeply you can nest embedded or linked OLE 2+ objects.

Whether you embed or link the source document, the code to perform the server's methods isn't incorporated in the compound document. Consider the size of an Access table that contains several copies of Excel.exe. Instead, the server's methods are incorporated by a reference to the application's name, known as the *OLE type*, in the source document. You need a local copy of the server application that created the source document to edit an embedded source document or display most linked source documents. Information about OLE server applications is incorporated in your Windows 95 or Windows NT Registry, which takes the place of Windows 3.1's registration database file—REG.DAT. The importance of the Registry to OLE 2+ is explained in the section "The Windows Registry" at the end of this chapter.

### Understanding Differences Between OLE and DDE

If you previously used dynamic data exchange (DDE) between Windows applications, OLE gives you the opportunity to add a new dimension to DDE operations. The differences between OLE and DDE techniques for transferring data are illustrated by Figure 19.5. DDE transfers data (properties) from the server to Access text boxes, labels, or other controls that can accommodate text and numbers; OLE transfers data and methods from the server only to unbound or bound object frames.

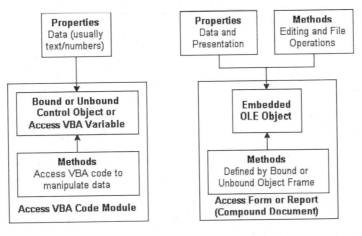

**FIG. 19.5**  A diagram showing the differences between DDE and OLE data transfer in Access.

Using DDE always requires a substantial amount of programming. Writing code to make full use of DDE with Access, or with any other Windows application, is and always was a difficult process. DDE data exchanges are also notoriously unreliable. Using the basic features of OLE, however, requires no programming. OLE data exchanges are also much more reliable than DDE. Simple OLE operations in Access use the Paste Special or Insert Object choices of the Edit menu. You can copy OLE objects in Access to the Clipboard from the Edit menu so that other OLE client applications can use the objects. There are relatively few Access VBA reserved words that apply exclusively to OLE objects; Microsoft deliberately designed OLE for use by nonprogrammers.

OLE 2.+ and ActiveX introduce a new programming methodology for OLE objects that is called *Automation*. The advantage of Automation is that you can alter the values of an object's properties and apply methods to the object by using conventional Access VBA syntax. Automation is the foundation upon which ActiveX Controls and other OLE server objects are built. Automation with OLE servers is discussed briefly in the section "Taking Advantage of Automation with OLE Objects" later in this chapter. Chapter 31, "Exchanging Data with Automation and ActiveX Controls," shows you how to write Access VBA code to manipulate Automation objects.

### Embedding versus Linking Source Documents

When you embed a source document, Windows creates a copy of the source document data and embeds the copy permanently in the container document. The source document retains no connection to the embedded data. Subsequent editing or deletion of the file or data from which the source document was created has no effect on the embedded copy in the table or displayed on the forms and reports.

Embedding is the only option if you do not or cannot save the source document as a file. The Microsoft Graph 8.0 and Visio Express OLE 2.0 mini-servers allow you only to embed a file. These applets have no Save or Save As choices in their File menus. When you choose Exit from an applet File menu, a dialog appears that asks whether you want to update the destination document with the edited source document.

The Windows 95 Paint application is the OLE 2.1 source application for all graphics displayed in bound or unbound objects of the Northwind Traders sample database. Paint allows you to import and save images in monochrome, 16-bit, or 24-bit .bmp files. Thus, you can use Paint to embed or link all bitmapped graphics you possess or create in either of these file formats. (Paint can open but not save PC Paintbrush .pcx files.)

Open the Categories form and then double-click the picture. Paint appears so that you can edit the image, as shown in Figure 19.6. All bitmaps in the Northwind Traders sample database are Bitmap Image objects that are embedded in OLE Object fields of tables and unbound object frames on forms and reports. Notice in Figure 19.6 that the menubar changes when you activate the embedded image for editing. Activating Paint grafts the Image and Options choices of Paint's menu to Access's menubar.

If you link an object, you create a reference to the data of the source document: the name of a file. When you or others change the data in a file linked to the object, the data in the source document permanently changes. The next time you display the data, if you set the value of the Update Options property of the bound object frame to Automatic, the presentation of the object incorporates all changes made to the data in the file. The ability to automatically update everyone's linked objects at once is useful in a networked Access application that displays data, which periodically is updated by others who share these files on the network.

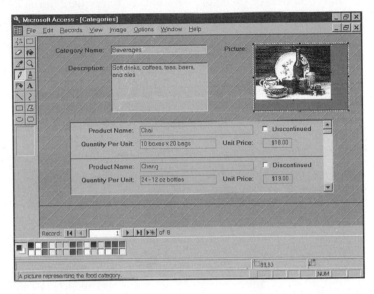

**FIG. 19.6**  The Windows Paint application editing an embedded bitmap that is displayed in a bound object frame.

| **Caution** |
| --- |
| If you want to try the following process for linking a range of an Excel worksheet to a record of Northwind.mdb's Categories table, make a copy of Northwind.mdb and open the copy in Access. You can't undo an embedding or linking update to an Access table. |

| **Note** |
| --- |
| The following steps use a dummy record in the Categories table of Northwind.mdb in which to embed data. The Categories table is displayed by using the Categories form included with Northwind.mdb. To duplicate on your own computer the figures shown in this section, open the copy of the Northwind.mdb sample database, then open the Categories form. Click the Tentative Append Record button on the toolbar to create a new record in which you can experiment with embedded or linked data. |

To link rather than embed an object created by an OLE server, perform the following steps:

1. Open the OLE server—Excel 97 in this example.

2. Load the workbook or other file that contains the data you want to link.

3. Select the range of data (or part of an image) to copy to the Clipboard. Most OLE 2+ server applications let you select all or part of the open document.

4. Press Ctrl+C to copy the data to the Clipboard.

5. Activate the container—in this case, an Access 97 form—and select a bound or unbound object frame. For this example, use the Picture field of the Categories form.

6. Choose Edit, Paste Special in the container application. If the application supports OLE 2+, the Paste Special dialog shown in Figure 19.7 appears.

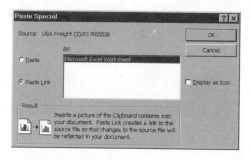

**FIG. 19.7**    The standard OLE 2+ Paste Special dialog.

7. Click the Paste Link option button, and then click OK to paste the image into the container document. In this example, the container is the Picture field of a dummy test record that is added to the Categories table of Northwind.mdb, and displayed by the Categories form.

> **Note**
>
> Before creating an OLE link in the destination application, you must open the source application and load the file because opening a file in most OLE servers breaks the existing OLE connection.

When you double-click to edit a linked object, the application opens its window and the title bar of the server's window displays the name of the file that created the image, as shown in Figure 19.8. This method is one quick way to determine whether an OLE object is linked, rather than embedded, in most OLE client applications (including Access).

Another advantage of linking some objects whose data resides in files is that you don't waste disk space with duplicate copies of the files in the database. Access creates a copy of the source document's presentation in the table, so you don't save disk space when you link graphic images, spreadsheets, or other source documents whose presentation consists of the data. The presentation of animation, waveform audio, and digital video files is either an icon or the first image of a sequence, so the presentation is small in size. Here, the disk space saved by linking rather than embedding is substantial.

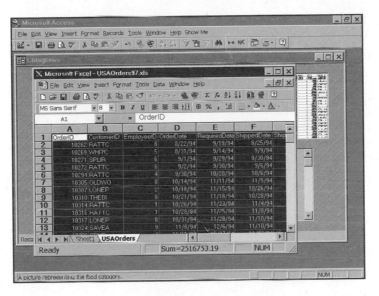

**FIG. 19.8**   Excel 97 editing a worksheet file with a range of cells linked to a bound object frame.

> **Note**
>
> Linking a bitmapped image doesn't save disk space; the presentation stored in .bmp format is the same size in bytes as the original image. (The size of the presentation is likely to be much larger if your image file was stored in a compressed format, such as .pcx, .gif, or .jpg.) If your OLE image server application lets you substitute a thumbnail image, the amount of file space saved is often substantial. A *thumbnail image* is a smaller version of the original image that often has less depth of color (8-bit instead of 24-bit color data, for instance).

The disadvantage of linking is that the linked files must be available to all users of the application. The files must reside in the same directory for their lifetime unless you edit the linkage to reflect a new location. A fully specified path, including the drive designator or UNC server address, is included with the file name in the linking information. If your application can't open the linked file, the presentation of the source document appears in the form or report, but when you double-click the bound object frame to edit the linked object, you see an error message that the linked file is not found.

> **Note**
>
> OLE 2+ has a limited capability to update the links to files that have moved. However, it is not a wise practice to depend on the present version, OLE 2.1, to maintain links to relocated files. If the object is contained in an unbound object frame, you can change the value of the SourceDoc property to point to the file in its new location. If the object is contained in a bound object frame, you need to open the file, copy its data to the Clipboard, and then re-create the link by using Paste Special to create a new link to the file.

## Activating OLE 2+ Objects in Place

One of the advantages of embedding, rather than linking, objects is that you can activate OLE 2+ objects in place. In-place activation (also called *in-situ editing* or *in-place editing*) causes the source application for the embedded object to "take over" the container application.

You activate an OLE object for editing by double-clicking the surface of the object frame that displays a simplified presentation of the worksheet. Figure 19.6 illustrates in-place activation of a Paintbrush Picture object. Figure 19.9 shows an Excel worksheet embedded in an unbound object frame of a form. The worksheet has been activated in place for editing. When an object is activated in place for editing, the object is surrounded by a frame that consists of alternating gray and black, diagonal hash marks. Eight sizing handles (black squares at each corner and at the midpoints of the frame) let you adjust the size of the editing frame.

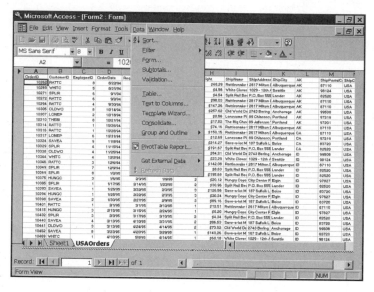

**FIG. 19.9**  An Excel 97 document activated for editing in an Access 97 form.

When you activate an embedded OLE 2+ object, the menubars of the application with which you created the object replace Access's menus with the same name. This process is called *grafting a menu*. If the source application has additional menus, they are added to Access's menubar.

In Figure 19.9, the Edit, View, Insert, Format, Tools, and Help menus are replaced by Excel's menus of the same name. Excel adds its own Insert, Tools, and Data menus to the menubar. Excel's anchored toolbars can become floating toolbars that you can reposition or hide. Depending on the specific object you have activated for in-place editing, various screen adornments will appear. *Adornments* are the rulers, column and row headers, sheet tabs, and scroll bars that are part of the object's presentation while being edited by its

OLE server. You have full control over the embedded object, and you can perform almost any operation on the object that is possible if you had opened a file containing the object directly in its server application.

> **Note**
>
> In-place activation is available only for embedded, not linked, OLE 2+ objects. When you double-click the presentation of a linked OLE 2+ object, the source application's window appears. In this respect, linked OLE 2+ objects behave identically to linked or embedded OLE 1.0 objects.

# Taking Advantage of Automation with OLE Objects

OLE 2+ server and mini-server applications that support Automation *expose* programmable objects. As an example, Excel 97 is an Automation server application that creates programmable Excel objects. Thus, when you activate an Excel worksheet object embedded in, or linked to, an Access 97 object frame, you can gain access to the worksheet through the Object property of the object frame control. The Object property is available only with Access VBA code; the Object property does not appear in the Properties window for object frames. The Object property provides access to all of the objects, and the properties and methods of the objects, exposed by the application that created the embedded or linked object.

▶▶ See "Manipulating an Excel 97 Workbook Object," p. 1102

Using Automation requires that you learn to program in Access VBA and that you understand the hierarchy of the collections of objects that you intend to program. Collections of objects are groups of objects of the same class that are contained within another object. As an example, the collection of Excel Worksheet objects are contained in Workbook objects. Collections of Automation objects follow the same general structure as Access 97's data access objects (DAOs) described in Chapter 29, "Understanding the Data Access Object Class." Excel 97, for example, has more than 100 different types of objects and several hundred properties and methods that apply to its objects.

Access 97's DBEngine object is at the top of the Access DAO pyramid; the Application object of Excel 97 (and most other Automation servers) is the equivalent of the DBEngine object. All other Excel objects are subclasses of the Application object. Access 97 exposes its Application object to OLE client applications, qualifying the object for Automation Server status.

Automation lets you construct applications by using the building block approach. If you need a worksheet in your Access application, insert an Excel Worksheet object in an unbound object frame. You then set the values for properties of, and apply methods to, the Worksheet object with Access VBA code. If you want word processing features, insert a

Word 97 Document object into an unbound object frame. You add command buttons or other controls to the form to execute the procedures or functions that contain the required Automation commands.

ActiveX Controls are a special class of OLE 2+ mini-servers that use Automation to provide access to their properties, methods, and events. (Conventional OLE and Automation objects don't expose events when activated.) When you embed an ActiveX Control in an unbound object frame, the Control object's events are not added to the Property window's list of events for unbound object frames. However, you can write Access VBA event-handling code for the events exposed by the ActiveX Control as subprocedures in code contained in forms.

The preceding brief discussion of Automation may appear out of context at this point in the book because writing Access VBA code is the subject of Part VII, "Programming, Distributing, and Converting Access Applications." However, future Windows operating systems and applications will extensively use Automation. A general description of OLE 2.1 without including Automation would be incomplete, at best.

As mentioned at the beginning of this section, taking advantage of Automation and ActiveX Controls requires that you write Access VBA code. Mastering Automation programming requires a very retentive memory and much experimentation. If you need interprocess communication in your Access 97 applications, use OLE 2.1 and Automation—not DDE—whenever you can. Your investment astride the OLE 2.1 learning curve will return substantial dividends as more and better Automation applications and, especially, 32-bit ActiveX Controls become available.

# The Windows Registry

In Windows 95 and Windows NT, the Registry takes the place of Windows 3.1+'s REG.DAT, plus WIN.INI, SYSTEM.INI, and application-specific INI files. (If you install Windows 95 over Windows 3.1+, Setup migrates all REG.DAT and many WIN.INI and SYSTEM.INI entries to the Registry.)

The Registry consists of two hidden system files: System.dat and User.dat. User.dat can be on your local fixed disk drive or stored on a network server. System.dat contains information on your PC, including the hardware and software installed. User.dat contains your user profile information. If your User.dat file is stored on a server, you can move to another networked computer, log on with your user name and password, and have your desktop configuration appear at the computer you're using.

System policy information, contained in .pol files, overrides entries in System.dat and User.dat. System policy files, such as Config.pol, are primarily of interest to PC administrators for maintaining control over the extent to which users can modify their Windows 95 or Windows NT Workstation 4.0 installation.

The registration process for early OLE 1.0 servers was relatively simple. Only a few entries in REG.DAT were required, primarily to create an association between individual file extensions and the OLE server for the type of file. The registration process for OLE 2+ servers is not so simple; much more information is required to register OLE 2+ servers, and even more entries are added for applications that support Automation through OLE or ActiveX technology.

ActiveX and OLE Controls also register themselves in the Registry. Although the setup program registers each OLE server and control automatically, you must understand the use of the Registry and the Registry Editor application in case you encounter a problem when you attempt to insert an OLE 2+ or ActiveX object in an Access 97 object frame. The following two sections are devoted to the Registry and concentrate on the OLE 2.1 aspects of server registration.

### The Registry Editor

The Registry Editor, RegEdit.exe, is included with Windows 95 and Windows NT so that users can display and edit the Registry, formerly the registration database of Windows 3.1+. The Registry Editor has a help file that explains how to use RegEdit, and the *Windows 95 Resource Kit* includes an explanation of the Registry's contents and also describes how to use RegEdit. None of this information provides even a hint about the new Registry data structures required by OLE 2.1. If you plan to use the OLE Object field data type, to use MSGraph8 to create graphs, or add sophisticated graphic images to your forms and reports, you need to know more about the Registry and RegEdit than appears in the Windows and Access 97 documentation.

Although the RegEdit program files are installed, the Windows Setup program doesn't install a program icon on the Start menu for RegEdit. To run RegEdit, choose Start, Run and type **regedit.exe** in the Command Line text box. Click OK to launch RegEdit. RegEdit's opening window appears, as shown in Figure 19.10.

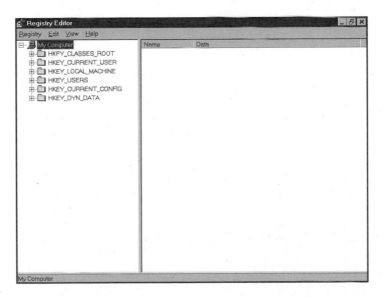

**FIG. 19.10**   RegEdit's opening window for viewing or editing the Registry files.

Information contained in the Registry is stored in the six subtrees, each beginning with HKEY, as shown in Figure 19.10. The type of information stored in each subtree is as follows:

- *HKEY_CLASSES_ROOT* contains association mappings between applications and file types identified by the file extension. HKEY_CLASSES_ROOT also contains information to support drag-and-drop operations, and contains data on the user interface. This subtree includes information similar to that stored in the REG.DAT file of Windows 3.1+ and Windows NT 3.1+.

- *HKEY_CURRENT_USER* stores a pointer to the *hive* (sub-subtree) of the HKEY_USERS subtree for the user currently logged on to Windows 95.

- *HKEY_LOCAL_MACHINE* contains information on the hardware and software installed on your PC. This subtree is employed by all users who log on to your PC.

- *HKEY_USERS* stores information on all users of your PC if Windows security is implemented. If only you use your PC, HKEY_USERS stores the data for HKEY_CURRENT_USER.

- *HKEY_CURRENT_CONFIGURATION* stores a pointer to a hive in HKEY_LOCAL_MACHINE that contains details about the current hardware setup of your PC.

- *HKEY_DYN_DATA* contains dynamic status information for Plug and Play devices, such as PC Cards (PCMCIA devices) that you "hot swap" while your PC is powered.

The primary subtrees used by OLE 2+ are HKEY_CLASSES_ROOT and the SOFTWARE hive of HKEY_LOCAL_MACHINE. To display hives below subtrees, double-click the folder symbol for the subtree, then double-click folders with a + symbol to expand the hierarchical list. HKEY_CLASSES_ROOT identifies a file extension with a particular class of object, such as .doc files with the Word.Document.8 object class—called the *programmatic ID* or *ProgID* (see Figure 19.11).

When you double-click a .doc file in My Computer or Explorer, the association launches the application's executable file specified by the ...\shell\open value that appears in the Data column of RegEdit's right pane. If you don't have Word 97 on your computer, Windows 95 launches WordPad to create a Wordpad.Document.1 object from .doc files. Similar entries associate .mdb files with the Access.Application.8 object class.

---

**Note**

You can see a list of registered file types by launching Explorer, choosing <u>V</u>iew, <u>O</u>ptions, and clicking the File Types tab. You can change the association between a file extension and an application by clicking the Edit button of the File Types tab. Editing associations in the File Types page is similar to the process used with the Modify File Type editing feature of Windows 3.1+'s REGEDIT.EXE. The most common change to file associations is changing the editing application for bitmapped graphics files.

---

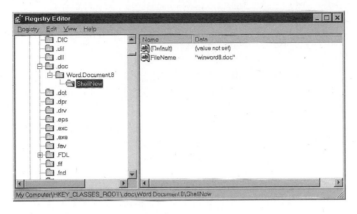

**FIG. 19.11** Entries in RegEdit's HKEY_CLASSES_ROOT subtree that associate .doc files with applications.

Following the list of file extension associations in HKEY_CLASSES_ROOT is an alphabetized list of ProgIDs for registered objects. Figure 19.12 shows the HKEY_CLASSES_ROOT\ Word.Document.8\shell\New\command entry that launches Word 97 with the /n parameter to specify a new (empty) document. If you move a registered application from one folder to another, you must change every Registry entry for the application that contains the pointer to its executable file.

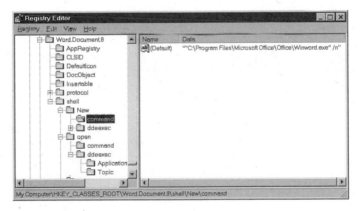

**FIG. 19.12** The Registry entry that enables Windows to create a new Word 97 document without first starting Word.

Windows' RegEdit includes a flexible Find feature that allows searching for entries' keys, values, and/or data (see Figure 19.13). Figure 19.14 shows the Edit String dialog that appears when you double-click the "ab" icon that indicates the entry is a string of characters. Unfortunately, RegEdit doesn't include a find and replace feature, so you must make multiple Registry entries manually.

**FIG. 19.13** Searching for the Registry entries that contain the Word.Document.8 programmatic ID.

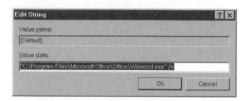

**FIG. 19.14** The Edit String dialog for changing a Registry value.

 ▶▶ See "Registry Entries for Automation Servers," p. 1108

Applications that support OLE 2+ add a variety of other entries to the Registry; an explanation of the purpose of each of these entries is beyond the scope of this chapter. What is important, however, is your ability to recover from problems that result from improper entries for OLE 2+ servers in the Registry.

---

### Troubleshooting

*When I try to insert an object into an unbound object frame, I get a message that Windows can't find the OLE server or one of its components.*

The Registry contains an entry that points to the wrong location of the OLE server, the server executable has been erased (or is corrupted), or one of its DLLs or other supporting components is missing. Although you can manually change the Registry entries for relocated OLE servers, reinstalling the server from its distribution diskettes or CD-ROM is a far more foolproof process. You're likely to have a better chance of satisfactorily correcting the Registry entries for the server if you launch the Add/Remove Programs feature of Control Panel, remove the server, and then reinstall the server. Many older OLE server applications, however, don't display entries in the Install/Uninstall page of the Add/Remove Programs dialog.

---

### How Access and Other OLE Applications Use the Registry

The primary Registry entries for each OLE server appear in the Object Type list box of the Insert Object dialog that appears when you choose Insert, Object in Form Design view. Figure 19.15 shows the Insert Object dialog that is standard for all OLE 2-compliant applications with the Microsoft Graph 97 entry (MSGraph.Chart.8 ProgID) selected.

If you have installed prior versions of current OLE 2.0 servers, such as Excel 5.0 and Word 6.0, entries may appear for these servers even if you have deleted the applications from your fixed disk. If you use the Uninstall option of the Maintenance Setup applications to remove applications, the Registry entries for these applications are deleted. Unfortunately, many older OLE 2.0 servers don't provide an uninstaller. All applications that display the "Designed for Windows 95" logo must include an uninstall feature that clears registry entries during the application removal process.

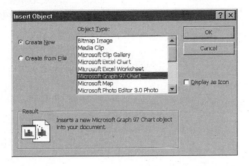

**FIG. 19.15**   The OLE 2+ Insert Object dialog that allows you to select an available object type based on the Registry entries.

Each Object Type in the Object Type list box is a specific type of the OLE object. The entries in the list box are derived from the Registry's value of each registered OLE server. The Microsoft Graph 97 type, for example, is entered from the `MSGraph.Chart.8 = Microsoft Graph 97 Chart` in `\HKEY_CLASSES_ROOT`. If you double-click the Microsoft Graph 97 Chart entry (or select the entry and click OK), Access creates an unbound object frame, and Graph8.exe opens with the example graph shown in Figure 19.16.

You can enter data in the datasheet at the upper left of Microsoft Graph's window to alter the height of the bars of the chart, or you can import an Excel .xlc chart file, but that's about all you can do without having a working knowledge of how graphs obtain data from Access 97. Creating graphs from Access data is one of the subjects of Chapter 20, "Adding Graphics to Forms and Reports."

### Replacing the Registry Files with Backups

When you start Windows, a backup copy of System.dat and User.dat (System.da0 and User.da0, respectively) is created automatically. If either of these files becomes corrupted, you may not be able to start Windows. If the `HKEY_CLASSES_ROOT` or `HKEY_LOCAL_MACHINE\ SOFTWARE` entries for an OLE server in System.dat are incorrect or missing, the server won't appear in the Object Type list of the Insert Object dialog, or you receive an error message when attempting to insert an object. Corruption of System.dat isn't a common occurrence, but it occasionally happens during the installation of a new application. You can replace the corrupted System.dat file with the backup System.da0 version by following these steps:

**V**

**Integrating Access**

1. If your corrupted System.dat file prevents Windows from starting, launch Windows and immediately press the F8 key for a fail-safe boot. Then choose Safe Mode Command Prompt Only. Skip the next two steps.

2. If you can run Windows, open Explorer and choose <u>V</u>iew, <u>O</u>ptions. In the View page of the Options dialog, click the Show All Files option, and then click OK to close the dialog.

3. Locate System.dat and System.da0 with Explorer. The location of these two files depends on how you installed Windows, but they are located most commonly in your \Windows folder.

4. If you are working from the MS-DOS command prompt, skip to step 7. In Explorer, right-click System.dat and choose Properties from the resulting popup menu. Clear the Read-Only and Hidden check boxes on the file's properties page. Repeat this step for the System.da0 file.

5. Click the System.da0 file to select it, choose <u>E</u>dit, <u>C</u>opy, then choose <u>E</u>dit, <u>P</u>aste; Windows creates a copy of System.da0 that is named Copy of System.da0.

6. Delete System.dat, and then rename Copy of System.da0 to **System.dat**. Skip to step 9 to finish this procedure.

7. If you're working from an MS-DOS prompt, change to the directory containing System.dat. System.dat and System.da0 are hidden, read-only system files, so entries for these files do not appear when you execute a `dir` command.

8. At the MS-DOS command prompt, type the following three instructions:

   **attrib -h -r -s system.dat**

   **attrib -h -r -s system.da0**

   **copy system.da0 system.dat**

9. Reboot your computer. (It is not necessary to reset the attributes of System.dat.)

To replace User.dat with User.da0, follow the preceding steps and substitute **user** for **system** in steps 5, 6, and 8.

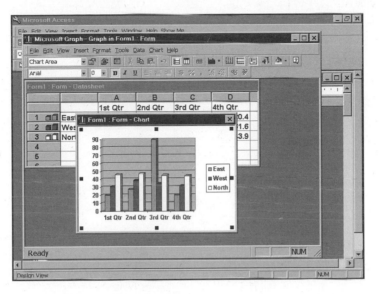

**FIG. 19.16**  An example graph created by inserting a new `MSGraph.Chart.8` object in Form Design view.

# Chapter 20

# Adding Graphics to Forms and Reports

One of the principal incentives for using a Windows desktop database manager is the ability to display graphic images contained in (or linked to) database tables. Early Windows RDBMSs could display images stored in individual bitmapped graphic files with common formats such as .bmp, .pcx, and .tif, but they could not store the bitmap data within the database file.

A few publishers enhanced some of these early desktop database products with Binary Large OBject (BLOB) field data types. A BLOB field is of variable length and can hold any type of data, regardless of its format. Other Windows desktop RDBMSs use auxiliary files (similar to dBASE's .dbt memo files) to store graphic images and other types of non-text data. When an auxiliary file is used, a field in a database table provides a reference (called a *pointer*) to the location of the data in the auxiliary file.

Many Windows graphic images are stored as combinations of lines, shapes, and patterns, rather than as copies of the pixel pattern of an image on your video display unit. Images of this type are called *vector-based graphics*. Windows illustration applications (such as Corel Systems' CorelDRAW! and Visio Corporation's Visio) create vector-based graphics. Microsoft Graph 97 (MSGraph8) uses vector-based graphics to create graphs from data in Access tables. Although each of these products has a proprietary file format, the illustration applications communicate with other applications through the Clipboard in standard Windows Metafile Format (.wmf).

This chapter describes how to use both bitmapped and vector-based graphics in conjunction with Access forms and reports. It also describes how you use MSGraph8 to create graphs and charts from Access 97 data.

## Adding a Bound Object Control to a Form or Report

Graphic images and other OLE objects stored in OLE Object fields of Access tables use a bound object frame control to display their presentation. The *bound object frame control* is an OLE container within which a bitmapped or vector-based image can be displayed. Other OLE objects that rely on data stored in OLE Object fields, such as Sound Recorder and Media Player objects, plus data-bound OLE Controls use the bound object frame.

In the case of still graphic images, the presentation within the bound object frame is a copy of the object's data property. Animated images and video objects usually display the first image in the animation sequence or video clip. Sound objects substitute the icon of the OLE server with which their file type is associated in the Registry. Double-clicking the bound object frame launches the OLE server that was used to add the object to a data cell in an OLE Object field of your table.

In Chapter 13, "Designing Custom Multitable Forms," you were introduced to adding a bound object frame to an Access form. Here, you learn the details of displaying and editing a photograph in the Personnel Actions Entry form you have built in the preceding chapters. You also learn how to scale the photograph within the bound object frame so that you get exactly the look you want.

### Including Photos in the Personnel Actions Query

The majority of Access applications use the OLE Object field data type to store only graphic images. The Northwind Traders Employees table includes a photograph for each employee as one such graphic image. You use the OLE Object field data type to add the photograph to your Personnel Actions form. The bound object frame is linked to the Photo field of the qryPersonnelActions query (see Figure 20.1).

 ◄◄ See "Creating the Query on Which to Base the Main Form," p. 452

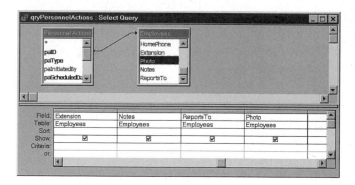

**FIG. 20.1**   The Photo field of the qryPersonnelActions query in Design view.

To run the qryPersonnelActions query so you can view one of the photographs in the Windows 95 Paint window, follow these steps:

1. From the Database window, open the qryPersonnelActions query.

2. Drag the horizontal scroll bar button to the right to display the Photo field in the resulting table.

3. Double-click one of the Bitmap Image data cells to display the image in Windows 95 Paint. The chosen image appears in the Paint window (see Figure 20.2).

**FIG. 20.2**   Editing the Photo field of the qryPersonnelActions query.

4. Choose Exit & Return to qryPersonnelActions:Select Query from Paintbrush's File menu to close the editing window.

5. Choose Close from Access's File menu to close the query.

◀◀ See "The Registry Editor," p. 683

### Troubleshooting

*An Insufficient memory or Application not properly registered message appears after double-clicking a data cell in the OLE Object field.*

Either of the two messages can occur under low-memory conditions. First, try closing all other running applications and then double-clicking the data cell again. If you continue to receive registration error messages, exit and restart Windows. If this procedure doesn't solve the problem, open the Registry Editor (RegEdit), choose Edit, Find, and search for the **Bitmap Image** value. Expand the CLSID entry for Bitmap Image and select the LocalServer32 item. Verify that the value for LocalServer32 is C:\PROGRA~1\ACCESS~1\MSPAINT.EXE—or the location of Mspaint.exe on your PC. (The LocalServer32 entry contains the DOS name of the folder in which Paint is installed: C:\Program Files\Accessories, by default.) If you need to change the entry, double-click the "ab" icon in the right pane to open the Edit String dialog and correct the entry as necessary.

The behavior of Windows Paint is similar to that of other OLE 2+ local server applications used to add or edit the values (contents) of data cells in OLE Object fields.

### Displaying the Employee's Picture in the Personnel Actions Form

You can edit OLE objects in Access tables and queries only through the window of the OLE server you used (Paint, in this example) to add the objects to the table. The presentation of OLE objects is, however, stored in the OLE field and displayed automatically in a bound or unbound object frame. You double-click within the object frame to edit the object.

You added a bound object frame to the Personnel Actions Entry form in Chapter 13, "Designing Custom Multitable Forms." For this exercise, you'll create a temporary form for the purpose of experimenting with bound object frames. To add a bound object frame to your experimental form so you can display the Photo field of your qryPersonnelActions query, follow these steps:

1. Click the Forms tab of the Database window, and then click New to display the New Form dialog.

2. Select qryPersonnelActions as the data source for the new form, select Design View in the list, and then click OK to display the new form in Design view.

3. Click the Field List button, and select Photo from the Field List window.

4. Select the Photo field and drag the Field symbol to the approximate position of the upper-left corner of the new form. Access creates a bound object frame rather than a text box when you create a control directly from a field of the OLE Object type in the Field List dialog.

5. Position and size the new bound object frame, as shown in Figure 20.3.

6. Click the Form View button to display your form with the photograph. The form appears as in Figure 20.4. Notice that the photo doesn't fill the entire frame. You may still need (or want) to scale the image, which is the subject of the next section.

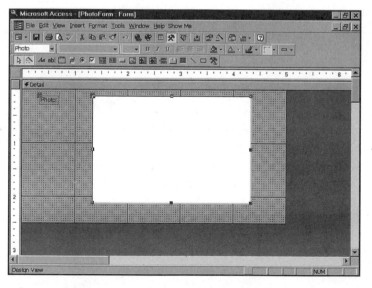

**FIG. 20.3** Adding a bound object frame to a form.

**FIG. 20.4**  Viewing the form with the added Photo bound object frame.

---

### Troubleshooting

*The employee's photo does not appear in Form view.*

If you add the Photo field to your query and follow the procedure for adding a bound object frame while the form is open, your frame is likely to be empty when you display the form in Run mode. In this case, the Photo field is added to the Datasheet view of your form, but the field's cells have Null values. Pressing Shift+F9 (Requery) does not replace the Null values with Bitmap Images. If this problem occurs, you must close the form and then reopen it from the Database window. Access runs the modified query when you open the form, and the picture appears.

---

An alternative method for creating a bound object frame is to click the bound object frame tool of the toolbox, click the Photo field, and drag the Field symbol to the form. The extra step involved in this process serves no purpose because Access chooses a bound object frame for you when you choose a field in the Field list that is of the OLE Object data type.

When you use either the bound object frame tool or the toolbox, the value of the Enabled property is set to Yes and the Locked property is set to No. (Access 2.0 set the Enabled property to No and the Locked property to Yes when using the toolbox to create a bound object frame.) The effect of these two properties is as follows:

- When an object frame is disabled (the Enabled property is set to No), you can't double-click the object to launch the OLE server that created the object's content. The setting of the Locked property has no effect in this case.

- When an object is enabled and locked (the Locked property is set to Yes), you can launch the OLE server, but any edits you make to the content of the object are discarded when you close the server application.

> **Note**
>
> In Form view with the default values of the Enabled and Locked properties—Yes and No, respectively—double-click the Photo object frame to launch Windows Paint, which assumes the role of the active application through in-place activation. Paint is an OLE 2.1 server, so Paint grafts its menu choices to the Access menubar, a process also called *menu negotiation*. Paint's View, Image, and Options menu choices replace several of Access's menu choices (see Figure 20.5). You can edit the bitmap in Paint and then save the changes to the OLE data in the Employees table when you close Paint. You click the form outside the Photo image to close (deactivate) Paint.

**FIG. 20.5**    Windows Paint activated in place to edit a Bitmap Image object.

### Scaling Graphic Objects

Access provides three methods for scaling graphic objects within the confines of a bound object frame. You select one of these methods by choosing the value of the Size Mode property in the Bound Object Frame Properties window, displayed in Figure 20.6.

**FIG. 20.6**    Setting the Size Mode property of an object frame.

The three options offered for the value of the Size Mode property display the image in the following ways:

- *Clip*, the default, displays the image in its original aspect ratio. The aspect ratio is the ratio of the width to the height of an image, measured in pixels or inches. A *pixel* is the smallest element of a bitmap that your computer can display—a single dot. The aspect ratio of the standard VGA display, for example, is 640×480 pixels, which is 1.33:1. If the entire image does not fit within the frame, the bottom or right of the image is cropped. *Cropping* is a graphic arts term that means cutting off the portions of an image outside of a window of a specified size, as shown in the top picture of Figure 20.7.

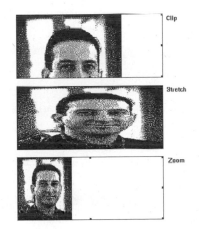

**FIG. 20.7**   Comparing the Clip, Stretch, and Zoom values of the Size Mode property.

- *Stretch* independently enlarges or shrinks the horizontal and vertical dimensions of the image to fill the frame. If the aspect ratio of the frame is not identical to that of the image, the image is distorted, as illustrated by the center image of Figure 20.7.

- *Zoom* enlarges or shrinks the horizontal or vertical dimension of the image so that it fits within the frame, and the original aspect ratio is maintained. If your frame has an aspect ratio different from that of the image, a portion of the frame is empty, as shown in the bottom image of Figure 20.7.

The bound object frames in Figure 20.7 have been shortened vertically and expanded horizontally to accent the effects of the Stretch and Zoom property values.

> **Note**
>
> The figures in this book were created using a screen resolution of 800×600 pixels. If you're working on a computer system using the standard VGA resolution of 640×480 pixels, the effects of the default Clip property on your image are likely to be much more noticeable than in the figures shown here.

Access cannot specify a particular area of the image to be clipped, so zooming to maintain the original aspect ratio is the best choice in this case. When you scale or zoom a bitmapped image, the apparent contrast is likely to increase, as shown in the center and bottom images of Figure 20.7. This increase results from deleting a sufficient number of pixels in the image to make it fit the frame, which increases the graininess. The increase in graininess and contrast is less evident in 256-color (8 bits per pixel) bitmaps; the photos of employees are 16-color (4 bits per pixel) bitmaps.

To apply the Zoom property to your bound object frame in Design mode, follow these steps:

1. Select the Photo bound object frame.

2. Click the Properties button on the toolbar to open the bound object frame Properties window. Click the Format tab.

3. Click the Size Mode text box, and open its list box.

4. Select Zoom.

To display the form so that you can view the photograph with its new property, follow these steps:

1. Click the Form View button of the toolbar to display your form, which now appears as shown in Figure 20.8.

**FIG. 20.8**  The bound object frame with Zoom Size Mode applied.

2. If your frame includes an empty area, as illustrated in Figure 20.8, return to design mode, adjust the size of the frame, and rerun the form to verify that the frame has the correct dimensions.

3. Choose File, Close, and save your changes to the form; you might save this experimental form as **frmPhotoForm**.

The technique described in this section allows you to add a bound object frame containing a vector image created with a drawing application, to add a sound clip from a .wav or .mid file, or to add any other OLE object type that you can select from the Insert Object dialog.

To add a bound object frame to the Detail section of a report, you also use the same method outlined here. The quality of the printed image depends on the type of image and the laser or inkjet printer you use. Vector-based images (such as drawings created in CorelDRAW! 6.0 or Visio 4.0) result in more attractive printed reports than do bitmapped images, especially when the bitmap is scaled. The contrast problem discussed previously may be aggravated when color images are printed in black and white.

### Examining Bitmap Image File Formats

Graphics files are identified by generally accepted file extensions; these serve to define most (or all) of the format's basic characteristics. The following file extensions identify bitmap image files that have achieved the status of "industry standards" for the PC. Most commercial bitmap image editing applications support these formats, though some do not import .gif files. The "standard" extensions follow:

- *.bmp* is for Windows bitmap files in 1-, 2-, 4-, 8-, and 24-bit color depths. .bmp files contain a bitmap information header that defines the size of the image, the number of color planes, the type of compression used (if any), and information on the palette used. A *header* is a block of data in the file that precedes the image data.

- *.dib* is for device-independent bitmap files. The .dib file format is a variant of the .bmp format; to define the RGB values of the colors used, it includes a color table in the header.

- *.pcx* is for files that are compatible with ZSoft Paintbrush applications. The .pcx file format is the common denominator for most bitmap file format conversions; almost every graphics application created in the past five years can handle .pcx files, but Windows Paint cannot save files in .pcx format. (Paint refers to .pcx files as PC Paintbrush format.) .pcx files are compressed by a method called *run-length encoding* (*RLE*), which can decrease the size of bitmap files by a factor of 3 or more, depending on their contents.

- *.tif* (an abbreviated form of TIFF) is for tagged image format files. The TIFF format was originally developed by Aldus Corporation and now is managed by Microsoft Corporation. Originally, TIFF files were used primarily for storing scanned images, but now they are used by a substantial number of applications (including those for Windows) as the preferred bitmap format.

  A special version of TIFF that uses file compression is used for fax transmission. TIFF files for conventional bitmaps are found in both uncompressed and compressed formats. A tag in the header of the file defines information similar to that found in the information header of .bmp files.

- *.jpg* is for files created by applications that offer compression and decompression options for Joint Photographic Experts Group (JPEG) graphics. JPEG has developed a standard methodology to compress and decompress still-color images. Special JPEG adapter cards are available to speed the compression and decompression processes.

  JPEG compression often is used for video images, especially for digital video editing, but Moving Pictures Experts Group (MPEG) compression is expected to predominate in the video field; it provides better compression ratios for video images than the JPEG method. MPEG compression is used by the Hughes Direct Broadcast System (DBS) satellites that beam DirecTV and USSB programming to 18-inch microwave dishes connected to RCA or Sony set-top boxes. MPEG compression requires special PC adapter cards to display live-motion video images at the standard 30 frames-per-second rate, but Pentium PCs can use software decoding at a somewhat lower frame rate.

- *.pcd* (an abbreviation for *Photo CD*, a Kodak trademark) is for photographic images that are digitized and stored on CD-ROMs by photofinishers. Photo CD files use a special compression system devised by the Eastman Kodak Company; you need Kodak's Photo CD Access application for Windows or an image editor, such as Adobe Photoshop or Corel PhotoPAINT, to display the images and save them to .pcd files.

- *.gif* is for the graphics interchange file format used to archive bitmapped images on CompuServe and other online services. Shareware and freeware .gif file conversion applications for all popular types of personal computers are available for downloading from CompuServe's Graphic Support forum (**GO GRAPHSUP**). The .gif format has been the standard bitmap format for background images of the Internet's World Wide Web pages, partially supplanted by the use of JPEG compression.

- *.png* is for Portable Network Graphics files. PNG is a new standard proposed by the World Wide Web Consortium (W3C), a group dedicated to "realizing the full potential of the Web." Graphics stored in PNG format load faster, and can be displayed on more hardware platforms (PC, Mac, and others) without alteration of the image's qualities. (Other graphics file formats display with brighter or darker colors, or shifts in the specific color tints depending on the specific system on which you display the image.) The PNG format was developed in late 1994, and was finalized in early 1995. PNG is now the native graphic image format for Microsoft Office 97 applications.

- *.tga* is for files in the TARGA file format developed by Truevision for its TARGA product line of graphics adapter cards. TARGA cards were the first to offer relatively high-resolution, wide-spectrum color images with PCs by employing a separate video monitor.

If you don't have a Windows image-editing application with OLE file server capability, you need to convert bitmap files in .tif, .gif, .pcd, or .tga format to .bmp or .pcx format. You can use Microsoft Word's bitmap file-conversion capability to insert a .tif file in a new document and then copy the image to the Clipboard as a picture. You cannot edit the Word picture that you paste into an Access table with Paste Special, however, because the image is not an OLE object; it is a bitmap picture created from a DDE link to Word.

> **Note**
>
> If you have an OLE server application that supports the .pcx format, store individual bitmap images in .pcx and not the .bmp files used by Windows Paint. Using .pcx files saves disk space compared with the .bmp format, because .pcx uses RLE file compression. Line-art tiles (black on a white background) compress the most; 24-bit, full-color photographic images compress the least. The JPEG compression offered by most current Windows image editing applications provides greater compression than .pcx for color images, especially images with more than 256 colors (16-bit or 24-bit color).
>
> If your use of images is intended primarily for printing (as in desktop publishing) and you do not have a color printer, use shades of gray for vector-based images. The 256-grayscale palette is preferred for printing bitmapped images; change color images to grayscale if your image-editing application supports this conversion.

# Adding an Unbound Object Frame to a Form or Report

Instead of using OLE Object fields, images in unbound object frames store their properties as data in the area of your .mdb file that is devoted to forms or reports. Like the methods you use with bound object frames, the methods that create (or edit) unbound objects are contributed temporarily by the OLE server. After you embed or link the unbound object, the Access application supplies the methods used to display the images.

◀◀ See "Adding a Linked Subreport to a Bound Report," p. 564

The use of unbound object frames differs from that of bound object frames in the following ways:

- You set the Enabled property of most unbound object frames to No so that the OLE server that supplied those unbound objects does not appear if you double-click the object in Run (Form view) mode. The Enabled property does not affect your ability to edit the object in Design mode. A bound object's Enabled property is usually set to Yes (the default value when the bound object frame is created).

- Unbound object frames have properties (such as Row Source, Link Child Fields, Link Master Fields, and Column Count) that are not applicable to bound object frames. Graphs and other unbound objects use these properties to obtain or present data in an unbound object field.

- You can create a master-child linkage between the content of an unbound object frame and the value of a field in the underlying table or query (or the value entered in a text box on your form).

V

Integrating Access

■ Multimedia objects, such as sound, video, or animated graphics, are often contained in unbound object frames.

The following sections provide examples that use the important additional properties that are available when using unbound object frames.

### Creating a New Logo for Your Personnel Actions Form

Logotypes and symbols that identify an organization are among the most common graphic objects on forms and in reports. The bitmap example in this section uses the image of a lighthouse from the Northwind Traders database, but you can substitute your organization's logo if you have a bitmap file or a scanner to create an image of suitable dimensions. Creating a logo from a bitmap file is the subject of the "Using the Image Control" section of this chapter.

The easiest way of adding an image to a new form is to copy to the Clipboard an existing unbound object frame of a form or report that contains the image. Then duplicate the image by pasting it into another form. This process is similar to the process for copying OLE objects that are to be used by other applications. You can edit the image as necessary with Windows Paint or another OLE-compliant image editor.

Northwind Traders' Forms Switchboard form contains an image that can easily be adjusted to fit on your Personnel Actions Entry form. However, the bitmap is contained in an image control, so the process is a bit more complicated than simply copying an unbound object frame from one form to another. Before adding the graphic image to the Personnel Actions Entry form, you should make a backup copy of the form by following these steps:

1. Click the Forms tab of the Database window and then click the Copy button on the toolbar.

2. Click the Paste toolbar button; Access displays the Paste As dialog.

3. Type a name for the copy of the form, such as **frmPersonnelActionsEntryCopy**, and then click OK. Access creates a copy of the form.

Follow these steps to copy the Northwind Traders logo from the Forms Switchboard to your Personnel Actions Entry form:

1. Click the Forms tab of the Database window, and open the frmPersonnelActionsEntry form. Rearrange the fields at the top of the form to make room for the logo; refer to Figure 20.9 for the sizing and placement of fields.

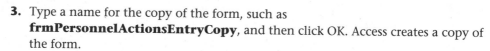

◀◀ See "Selecting, Editing, and Moving Form Elements and Controls," p. 419

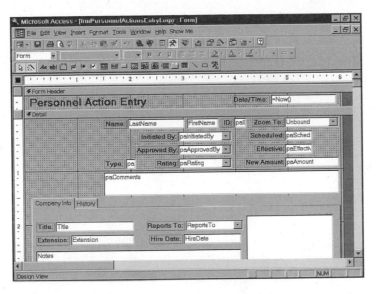

**FIG. 20.9**    The Personnel Actions Entry form with the main form controls rearranged to make room for the new logo.

2. Switch to the Database window, click the Forms tab, and choose the Main Switchboard form from the list; click the Design button to open the form in Design view.

3. Select the Northwind logo by clicking the lighthouse in the logo. The logo is an image control, which was new to Access 95. Image controls are the subject of the section "Using the Image Control," which follows shortly.

4. Press Ctrl+C or choose Edit, Copy to copy the logo's bitmap to the Clipboard. Close the Forms Switchboard form.

5. Click the Detail header bar of the Personnel Actions Entry form to select the Detail section of the form.

6. Choose Insert, Object to display the Insert Object dialog. Select Bitmap Image from the Object Type list, making sure that the Create New option button is selected (see Figure 20.10).

7. Click OK to open Paint with an empty image, and then press Ctrl+V or choose Edit, Paste to paste the image into Paint's window (see Figure 20.11). Click outside of the image to expose the bitmap sizing handles.

8. Click and drag the middle-bottom sizing handle to eliminate the white (empty) region below the image. Repeat the process with the middle-right sizing handle to eliminate the empty region to the right of the image (see Figure 20.12).

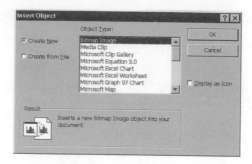

**FIG. 20.10**    The Insert Object dialog settings for opening an instance of Paint.

**FIG. 20.11**    Copying the bitmap from the Northwind logo into the open instance of Paint.

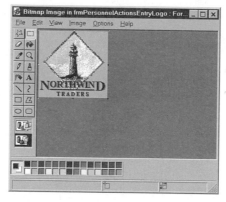

**FIG. 20.12**    The logo bitmap with white (empty) regions removed.

9. Choose File, Save Copy As and save a copy of the bitmap as **Nwind.bmp** in your working folder (usually C:\My Documents). You'll use this bitmap file later with the image control.

10. Choose File, Exit & Return to frmPersonnelActions:Form to close Paint and place the unbound object frame in your form. The default position of the frame is at the upper left of the selected section of your form (see Figure 20.13).

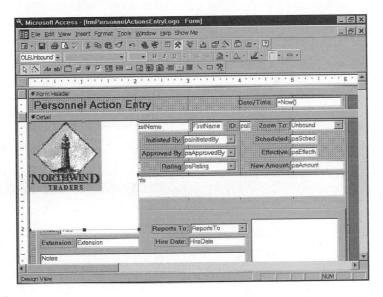

**FIG. 20.13**   The unbound object frame for the logo added to the Detail section of the Personnel Actions Entry form.

Access applies the Size Mode property to the presentation of the image; Size Mode does not modify the image itself. The copied image covers several controls. This problem is corrected when you manipulate the image in the next section.

### Sizing and Setting the Properties of the Unbound Object Frame

Sizing and setting the properties of unbound object frames is similar to the process for bound object frames. To finish adding the logo to your form, follow these steps:

1. Click and drag the unbound frame so that the top-left corner is about two grid marks from both the top and left edges of the Detail section of the form.

2. Use the bottom-middle and right-middle sizing handles to adjust the size of the frame to fit the available space (see Figure 20.14).

3. Open the Properties window and set the Size Mode property to Zoom for scaling the bitmap to the available space while retaining the original aspect ratio.

4. You don't need a border around the logo, so set the Special Effect property to Flat, the Border Style property to Transparent, and the Back Color property to light gray (12632256), as shown in Figure 20.15.

5. Click the Form View button to display the logo added to the Personnel Actions Entry form (see Figure 20.16).

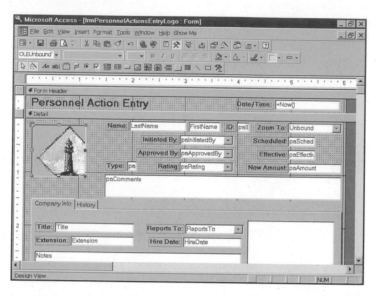

**FIG. 20.14** Sizing the clipped bitmap image in the unbound object frame to the available space.

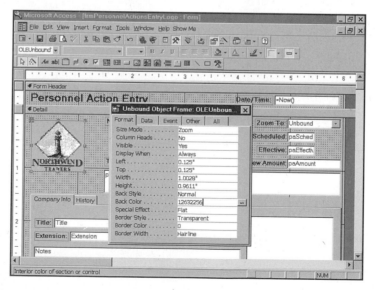

**FIG. 20.15** Setting the properties for the Northwind Traders logo.

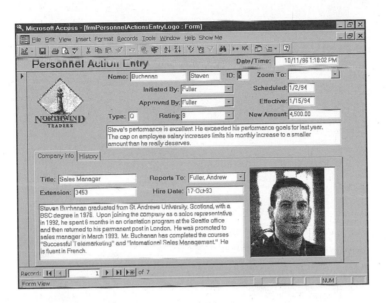

**FIG. 20.16**  The Northwind Traders logo in Form view.

# Using the Image Control

Versions of Access prior to Access 95 required use of object frames to contain bitmapped images. Access 95 and 97 add the image control—similar to the image control of Visual Basic 4.0 —to display bitmap (.bmp), device-independent bitmap (.dib), and Windows Metafile Format (.wmf) or enhanced metafile (.emf) vector images in forms and reports. To substitute the image control for the unbound object frame of your Personnel Actions Entry form, follow these steps:

1.  Open frmPersonnelActions in Design view and select the logo. Press Delete to delete the unbound object frame from the form.

2.  Click the Image button of the toolbox and draw the image control to the same dimensions as the deleted unbound object frame. The Insert Picture dialog appears.

3.  Maneuver to the folder in which you stored the Nwind.bmp file you created with Paint in the section "Creating a New Logo for Your Personnel Actions Form" earlier in this chapter (see Figure 20.17). If you like another image better, you can substitute its .bmp file in this example.

4.  Double-click Nwind.bmp or select Nwind.bmp and click OK. Your image control appears, as shown in Figure 20.18. Unlike object frames, image controls by default center clipped images in their frame. Image frames have a Picture Alignment property that lets you choose how the image is aligned.

5.  Image controls have default Special Effect, Border Style, and Back Color properties that are suitable for adding logos to forms. Thus, you need only change the Size Mode property of the image control to Zoom. Figure 20.19 shows the result of the preceding steps in Form view.

**FIG. 20.17**  Selecting the Nwind.bmp file created earlier in the chapter for the image control.

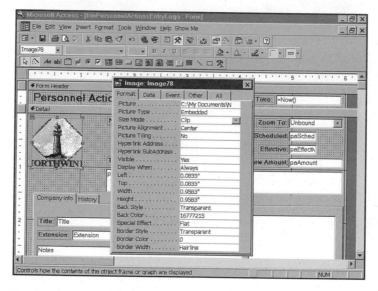

**FIG. 20.18**  The clipped Northwind logo in an image frame.

If you don't need to edit a static image from within your Access application, image controls are preferred over unbound object frames for display images of the file types supported by the image control. Image controls respond faster and use fewer Windows resources than unbound object frames.

Image controls also have a variety of additional properties that you can use to customize the presentation of the image. One of the most useful of these new properties is the Palette property that you can set to a Windows palette file (.pal) or a variety of other image file types to provide a custom set of 240 colors that enhance the appearance of 256-color bitmaps. Like its predecessors, Access 97 is limited to displaying 256-color bitmaps. Third-party, 32-bit ActiveX controls designed for image presentation and editing let you use high-color (16-bit color depth) and full-color (24-bit color depth) bitmaps.

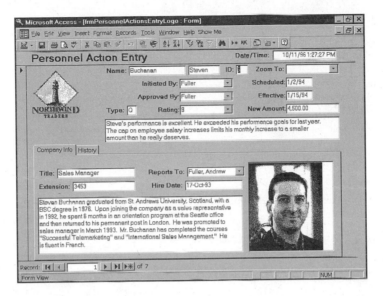

**FIG. 20.19**  The Northwind logo zoomed in an image frame.

# Creating Graphs and Charts with Microsoft Graph 97

Microsoft Graph 97 (called in this book by its Registry programmatic ID, MSGraph8) is a 32-bit OLE 2.1 miniserver application. MSGraph8 is the 32-bit replacement to MSGraph5; MSGraph8 is an OLE mini-server that provides graphing capabilities to all Microsoft productivity applications. The sections that follow describe how to use the Graph Wizard to add MSGraph8 graphs and charts to Access 97 forms and reports.

### Creating the Query on which to Base the Graph

Most graphs required by management are the time-series type; these track the history of financial performance data, such as orders received, product sales, gross margin, and the like. In smaller firms, this data comes from tables that store entries from the original documents (such as sales orders and invoices) that underlie the summary information.

This type of data often is called a *line-item source*. Because a multibillion-dollar firm can accumulate several million line-item records in a single year, larger firms usually store summaries of the line-item source data in tables; this technique improves the performance of queries. Summary data is referred to as *rolled-up* data or, simply, *rollups*. Rollups of data on mainframe computers often are stored in client/server RDBMSs running under UNIX or Windows NT to create *data warehouses*. Although rolling up data from relational tables violates one of the guiding principles of relational theory—don't duplicate data in tables and don't store derived data in tables—databases of rolled-up data are very common.

---

**Note**

The Chart Wizard of Access 95 and Access 97 differs substantially from the Graph Wizard of Access 2.0 and its predecessors. The Chart Wizard creates a crosstab query for you; the older Graph Wizard required you to create your own crosstab query. This section describes how to use the Chart Wizard in the manner Microsoft intended: from a table or SELECT query. The section "Creating a Graph from a Crosstab Query" later in this chapter shows you how to change the Row Source property of a graph object to use an existing crosstab query as the source of the data.

---

Northwind Traders is a relatively small firm, so it isn't necessary to roll up line-item data to obtain acceptable query performance on an Intel 80486-based or faster computer. To create a query designed specifically for the Chart Wizard, follow these steps:

1. In the Database window, open a new query and add the Categories, Products, Order Details, and Orders tables to the query. Joins are created for you between the primary-key and foreign-key fields of each table.

2. Drag the CategoryName field of the Categories table to the first column.

3. Drag the UnitPrice field of the Order Details table to the second column. Edit the Field row of the column to read **Amount: [Order Details].[UnitPrice]\* [Order Details].[Quantity]**.

4. Drag the ShippedDate field of the Orders table to the third column. Add an ascending sort on this column.

5. Add the criterion **Like "\*/\*/95"** to the ShippedDate column so as to only include 1995 orders. The year 1995 is used instead of 1996 in this example because data is available for all 12 months of 1995. Your query design appears, as shown in Figure 20.20.

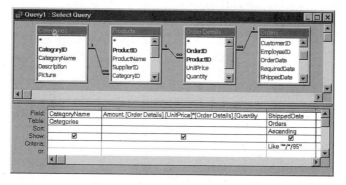

**FIG. 20.20**   A query design for creating a graph with Access 97's Chart Wizard.

6. Click the Run button to test your query (see Figure 20.21.) Close the query and save it with the name **qryChartWizard**.

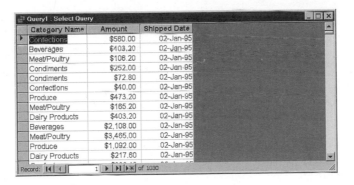

**FIG. 20.21**   The query result set of the query in Figure 20.20.

## Using the Chart Wizard to Create an Unlinked Graph

Although it's possible to create a graph or chart by using the Insert Object method and selecting the Microsoft Graph 97 object type, the Graph Wizard makes this process much simpler. You can use the Graph Wizard to create two different classes of graphs and charts:

- *Unlinked* (also called *non-linked*) line graphs display a line for each of the rows of your query. You can also create unlinked stacked-column charts and multiple-area charts.

- A *linked* graph or chart is bound to the current record of the form on which it is located and displays only a single set of values from one row of your table or query at a time.

This section shows you how to create an unlinked line graph based on a query. The next section describes how to use MSGraph8 to display alternative presentations of your data in the form of bar and area charts. In the last section of this chapter, you create a graph that is linked to a specific record of a query result set.

To create an unlinked graph that displays the data from the qryChartWizard query, follow these steps:

1. Open a new form, select Chart Wizard in the list box, and select qryChartWizard in the drop-down list (see Figure 20.22). Click OK to launch the first dialog of the Chart Wizard.

2. Click the >> button to add all three fields to your graph (see Figure 20.23). Click the Next button to display the Chart Wizard's second dialog.

3. Click the Line Chart button (the third from the left in the third row of the buttons that display the available graph styles), as shown in Figure 20.24. Click the Next button to display the third Chart Wizard dialog.

4. The Chart Wizard attempts to design a crosstab query based on the data types of the query result set. In this case, the Chart Wizard makes a mistake by assuming you want months in the legend box and product categories along the graph's horizontal x-axis (see Figure 20.25).

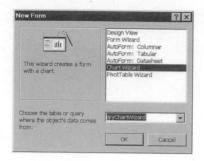

**FIG. 20.22**    Selecting the Chart Wizard and the query on which to base the graph.

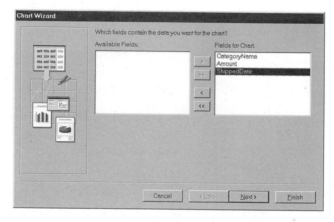

**FIG. 20.23**    Selecting the fields to include in the graph.

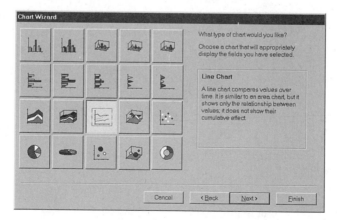

**FIG. 20.24**    Selecting the type of graph or chart.

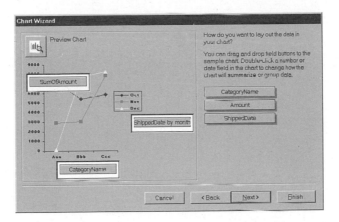

**FIG. 20.25**  The Chart Wizard's first try at guessing the type of crosstab query to create.

5. You want the categories in the legend and the months of 1995 across the x-axis. Drag the CategoryName button from the right side of the dialog to the drop box under the legend, and drag the ShippedDate button to the drop box under the x-axis. The button title, partly obscured, is ShippedDate by month (see Figure 20.26). You can double-click the ShippedDate by month button and select from a variety of GROUP BY date criteria, ranging from Year to Minute. Click the Next button to go to the fourth and final Chart Wizard Dialog.

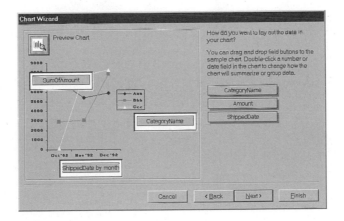

**FIG. 20.26**  Correcting the Chart Wizard's crosstab query guesswork.

6. Type **1995 Monthly Sales by Category** in the text box to add a title to your graph. Click the Yes, Display a Legend option button, if necessary, to display the Category Name legend (see Figure 20.27). Accept the remainder of the defaults.

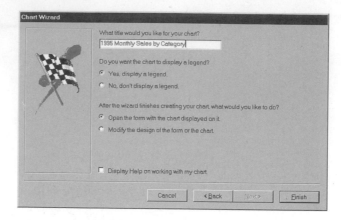

**FIG. 20.27** Adding a title and legend to your graph.

7. Click the Finish button to display your graph in Form view. In the miniature version illustrated by Figure 20.28, some month labels are missing and the legend crowds the graph and label. You fix these problems in the next section of this chapter, "Modifying the Design Features of Your Graph."

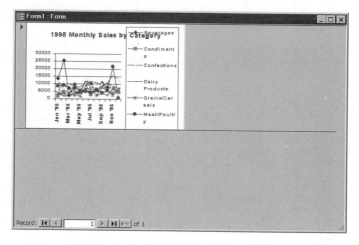

**FIG. 20.28** The unbound graph in Form view, as completed by the Chart Wizard.

8. Click the Design View button of the toolbar and increase the size of your graph to at least 5.5 inches wide by 2.5 inches high (see Figure 20.29). The graph that appears in Design View at this point is an example graph included with MSGraph8.

9. Set the Enabled property of the unbound object frame to Yes and the Locked Property to No.

10. The chart is in an unbound object frame, so you don't need form adornments for record manipulation. Select the form and set the Scroll Bars property of the form to Neither, the Record Selectors to No, and the Navigation Buttons to No.

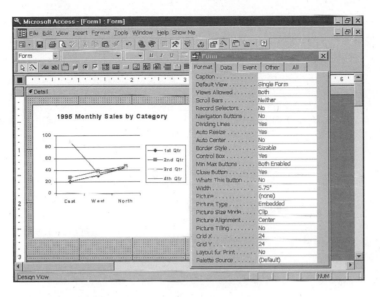

**FIG. 20.29**  The expanded object frame in Form Design view.

11. Use the sizing handles of the unbound object frame to create a 1/8-inch form border around the frame. Leaving a small form area around the object makes the activation process more evident.

12. Save your form with a descriptive name, such as **frmChartWizard**. Return to Form view in preparation for changing the size and type of your graph.

### Tip

When you complete your design, set the value of the Enabled property to No so that users of your application can't activate the graph and alter its design.

### Modifying the Design Features of Your Graph

MSGraph8 is an OLE 2.1 mini-server; you can activate MSGraph8 in place and modify the design of your graph. MSGraph8 also supports Automation, so you can use Access VBA code to automate design changes. This section shows you how to use MSGraph8 to edit the design of the graph manually, as well as how to change the line graph to an area or column chart.

▶▶ See "Understanding Automation," p. 1097

To activate your graph and change its design with MSGraph8, follow these steps:

1. Display the form in Form view, then double-click the graph to activate MSGraph8 in place. A diagonally hashed border surrounds the graph; MSGraph8's menus replace and supplement those of Access 97. (The activation border is missing from

the left and top of the object frame if you didn't create some space on the form around the object frame in step 11 of the preceding section.)

2. Drag the middle-right sizing handle to the right border of your enlarged unbound object frame. Drag the middle-bottom sizing handle to the bottom border of the object frame.

3. Choose <u>V</u>iew, <u>D</u>atasheet to inspect the data series that Access has transmitted to MSGraph8 (see Figure 20.30).

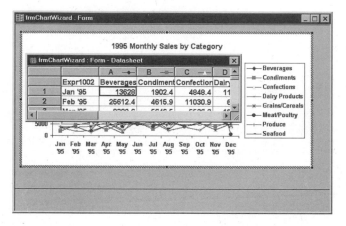

**FIG. 20.30**    The expanded version of the chart displaying part of the datasheet for the graph.

4. You can change the type family and font size of your chart's labels and legend. Select the graph title, and then choose F<u>o</u>rmat, S<u>e</u>lected Chart Title to open the Format Chart Title dialog. Select the Font tab, and set the size of the chart title to 12 points (see Figure 20.31), and then click OK to close the dialog. Select the legend, and then open the Format Legend dialog and set the size of the legend font to 7 points.

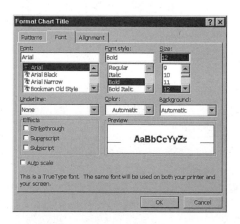

**FIG. 20.31**    Changing the font size of the graph's title.

**5.** The y-axis labels should be formatted as currency, so click one of the labels to select the y-axis. Then choose F̲ormat, S̲elected Axis to display the Format Axis dialog.

**6.** Click the Number tab, select Currency formats in the Category list, and enter **0** in the Decimal Places text box (see Figure 20.32). Click OK to close the dialog and apply the new format. Your line graph appears as shown in Figure 20.33.

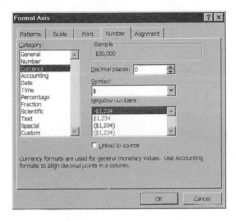

**FIG. 20.32**  Formatting the numeric values of the y-axis.

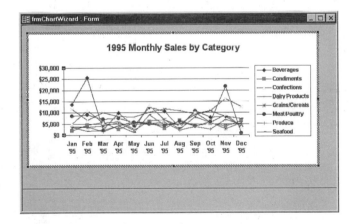

**FIG. 20.33**  The line graph with reformatted y-axis labels and a larger graph title.

You might want to change the line graph to some other type of chart (such as area or stacked column) for a specific purpose. Area charts, for example, are especially effective as a way to display the contribution of individual product categories to total sales. To change the line graph to another type of chart, follow these steps:

**1.** Choose C̲hart, Chart T̲ype to open the Chart Type dialog.

**2.** Click the Standard Types tab to display the standard chart selections, and select Area in the Chart Type list (see Figure 20.34).

**3.** Select Stacked Area chart in the Chart Sub-Type list (the second chart in the first row—see Figure 20.34). Click OK to change your line graph into an area chart, as shown in Figure 20.35. The contribution of each category appears as an individually colored area, and the uppermost line segment represents total sales.

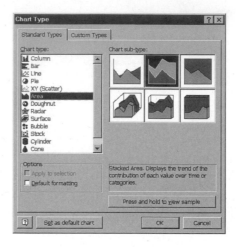

**FIG. 20.34**  Changing the line graph to a stacked area chart.

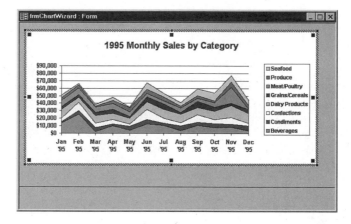

**FIG. 20.35**  The stacked area chart in Form view.

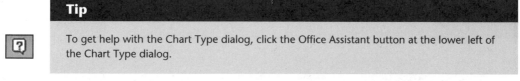

**Tip**

To get help with the Chart Type dialog, click the Office Assistant button at the lower left of the Chart Type dialog.

**4.** To convert the area chart into a stacked column chart, choose Chart, Chart Type, display the Standard Types page of the Chart Type dialog, select Column in the

Chart Type list, and then select Stacked Column (the second button in the first row) of the Chart Sub-Type list (see Figure 20.36).

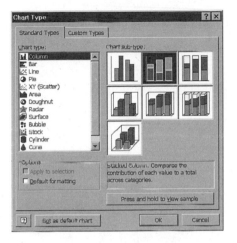

**FIG. 20.36**  Selecting a stacked column chart type.

5. Click OK to close the Chart Type dialog. Your stacked column chart appears, as shown in Figure 20.37.

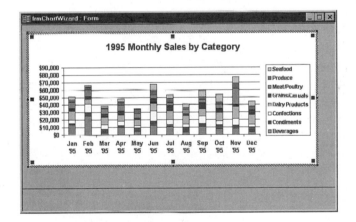

**FIG. 20.37**  The stacked column chart in Form view.

6. Another subtype of the area chart and stacked column chart is the *percentage distribution* chart. To create the distribution of the sales graph shown in Figure 20.38, repeat steps 4 through 5, but select the 100% Percent Column picture with equal column heights in the Chart Sub-type list of the Chart Type dialog.

7. Because you set the format of the y-axis previously to eliminate the decimals, you need to change the format of the y-axis manually to Percentage. Select the y-axis, choose Format, Selected Axis, select Percentage in the Category list, make sure that

Decimal Places is set to **0**, and then click OK to apply the format. Your chart appears as shown in Figure 20.38.

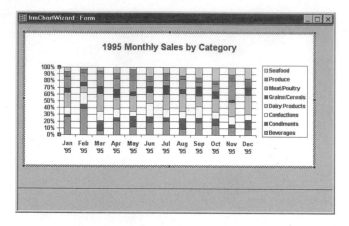

**FIG. 20.38**  The percentage distribution column chart.

**8.** Change the Chart Type back to a line graph in preparation for the linked graph example of the next section, "Creating a Graph from a Crosstab Query." Click inside the form border but outside the object frame to deactivate the graph, and save your form. Of the four types of charts demonstrated, most users find the area chart best for displaying time-series data for multiple values that have meaningful total values.

---

**Note**

The process of adding an unbound graph to an Access report is identical to that for forms. Unless you have a color printer, you need to select a line graph subtype that identifies data points with a different symbol for each category. For area and stacked column charts, select a series of hatched patterns to differentiate the product categories.

---

Creating graphs with MSGraph8 is not a speedy process. Each time you change from Design view to Form view, Access runs the query, launches MSGraph8 in the background, and passes the query data to MSGraph8. This process, using the qryChartWizard query, takes about 13 to 15 seconds on an 80486DX4/100 computer with a PCI bus video accelerator and a fast fixed-disk drive. The 32-bit graph OLEControl of Visual Basic 4.0 is much faster in operation than MSGraph8, but you must master programming Automation code in Access VBA to use Graph32.ocx.

Another problem with MSGraph8 is that you cannot easily transfer data to MSGraph8's datasheet with Access VBA code. (The Cells and Range properties of MSGraph8's DataSheet object are read-only, so you can't use Automation to set data series values directly.) You can expect third-party suppliers to provide faster-operating graphing applications in the form of OLE 2.x miniservers and ActiveX controls. You need to write Access VBA code, however, to send the data series to these applications.

### Creating a Graph from a Crosstab Query

Access 97's Chart Wizard is quite parochial: It insists on creating a crosstab query for you. Once you've created a chart with the Chart Wizard, however, you can change the Row Source property value to specify a previously created crosstab query of your own design. Thus, you can take one of the queries you created in Chapter 10, qry1995QuarterlyCategorySales, and modify this query to create the qry1995MonthlyCategorySalesChart query that provides the same result as the crosstab query created by the wizard. You need to specify a table or query as the Record Source for the chart to create the linked chart described in the next section, "Linking the Graph to a Single Record of a Table or Query."

◄◄ See "Creating a Monthly Product Sales Crosstab Query," p. 362
◄◄ See "Decreasing the Level of Detail in Crosstab Queries," p. 365

> **Note**
>
> You must create the qry1995MonthlyCategorySalesChart query and use the query as the Row Source of the unbound object frame to complete the linked graph example in the following section. The linked graph example does not work with the crosstab query created by the Chart Wizard in the preceding steps.

To create the qry1995MonthlyCategorySalesChart query, follow these steps:

1. Open the qry1995MonthlyCategorySales query in Design mode.

2. Click the Show Table button of the toolbar and add the Categories table to the query. A join is created between the CategoryID fields of the Categories and Products tables.

3. Delete the CategoryID column that provided the Row Heading.

4. Drag the CategoryName field from the Categories table to the first column of the query, and select RowHeading in the Crosstab row.

5. Alias the CategoryName field by typing **Categories:** at the beginning of the field text box.

6. Change the Expr1 statement in the Fields row to **Expr1:Format([OrderDate], "mmm")** to use three-letter month abbreviations. Your query appears as shown in Figure 20.39.

7. Double-click an empty region of the upper pane to open the Query Properties window's General page. Delete the current entry in the Column Headings text box of the General page. Enter the 12 month abbreviations, **Jan** through **Dec**, separating the month abbreviations with commas. Access adds the double quotation marks for you, as shown in Figure 20.40.

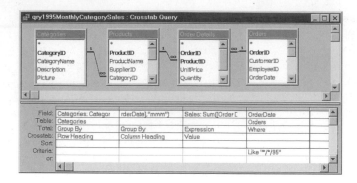

**FIG. 20.39**  The design of a query that displays monthly sales by product category.

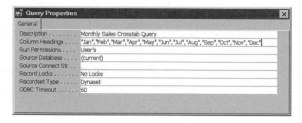

**FIG. 20.40**  Adding fixed column headings for 12 months.

  8. Choose <u>F</u>ile, Save <u>A</u>s, and save your query as
     **qry1995MonthlyCategorySalesGraph**.

  9. Click the Run button of the toolbar to check your query result set (see Figure
     20.41).

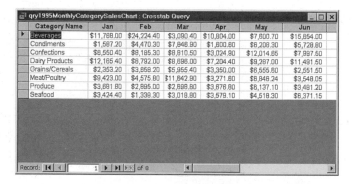

**FIG. 20.41**  Part of the result set of the qry1995MonthlyCategorySalesChartquery.

 10. Open frmChartWizard in Design view, if necessary, select the unbound object
     frame, and open the Properties window.

11. Click the Data tab, open the Row Source list box, and select qry1995MonthlyCategorySalesChart as the value of the Row Source property.

12. Change to Form view and verify that your line graph appears the same as that created by the Chart Wizard.

---

### Troubleshooting

*After changing the Row Source property of my chart to the qry1995MonthlySalesCategoryChart query, the product categories appear in the chart as the x-axis labels, and the total month sales are plotted on the chart.*

MSGraph8 might determine that the column headings of the Row Source query are the series to be plotted, resulting in the Category Name appearing as the x-axis legends. To obtain the correct data plotting, display the chart in Form view, and double-click it to activate in-place editing with MSGraph8. Next, choose Data, Series in Rows to change the series markers from the column headings to the rows; this causes the dollar amounts to be plotted on the chart, and the months of the year appear as the x-axis legend.

---

### Linking the Graph to a Single Record of a Table or Query

You create a linked graph or chart by setting the values of the MSGraph8 object's Link Child Fields and Link Master Fields properties. The link is similar to that between a form and subform. A linked graph displays the data series from the current row of the table or query that serves as the Record Source of the form. As you move the record pointer, the graph is redrawn to reflect the data values in the selected row.

To change the frmChartWizard form to accommodate a linked graph, follow these steps:

1. Open frmChartWizard in Design view; then click the Properties button of the toolbar to open the Properties window for the form.

2. Click the Data tab, open the Record Source list box, and select qry1995MonthlyCategorySalesChart as the value of the Record Source property of the form, which binds the form to the query.

3. Your form needs record-navigation buttons for a linked query, so click the Format tab and set the value of the Navigation Buttons property to Yes.

4. Select the unbound object frame, and then click the Data tab. Type **Categories** as the value of the Link Child Fields and Link Master Fields properties (see Figure 20.42). Using this technique, you create the link between the current record of the form and the row of the query that serves as the Row Source property of the graph (through the Categories field of the query).

5. To test your linked graph, click the Form View button of the toolbar. If (in the preceding section) you saved the line graph version of the form, your graph appears as shown in Figure 20.43.

V

Integrating Access

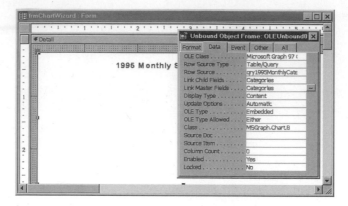

**FIG. 20.42** Linking the graph's Row Source property to the current record of the form.

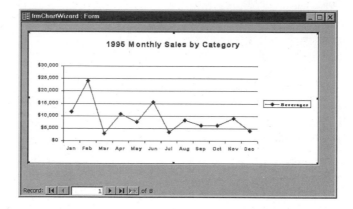

**FIG. 20.43** The linked version of the 1995 Monthly Sales by Category graph.

6. The single line appears a bit anemic for a graph of this size, so double-click the graph to activate it in place. Double-click anywhere on the line to display the Format Data Series dialog. Click the Patterns tab to bring that page to the front of the dialog. Open the Weight drop-down list, and choose the thickest line it offers. To change the data-point marker, open the Style drop-down list and select the square shape. Use the drop-down lists to set the Foreground and Background colors of the marker to a contrasting hue, such as red (see Figure 20.44). Click OK to close the dialog and implement your design changes.

7. Double-click the legend box to open the Format Legend dialog. On the Patterns page, click the None option button in the Border frame to remove the border from the legend (see Figure 20.45). Click the Font tab, set the Bold attribute on, and change the font size to 11 points. Click OK to close the dialog and apply your modification to the legend.

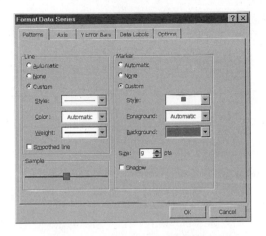

**FIG. 20.44**  Increasing the thickness of and changing the markers for the data series line.

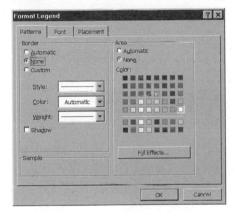

**FIG. 20.45**  Removing the border from the legend.

8. To use your enhanced legend as a subtitle for the chart, click and drag the legend to a location under the chart title, as shown in Figure 20.46. Click over the plot area to display the chart's sizing handles; drag the middle sizing handle to the right to increase the size of the plot area (see Figure 20.46).

9. Click anywhere on the form outside of the chart to close MSGraph8 and return to Access. Click the record selection buttons to display a graph of the sales for each of the eight categories.

10. You can smooth the data series line by activating the graph and double-clicking the line. Mark the Smoothed Line check box in the Line frame of the Patterns page, and then click OK. Your graph now appears as shown in Figure 20.47.

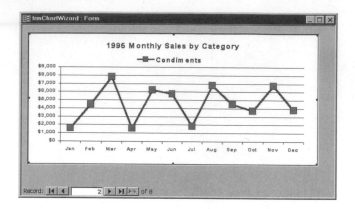

**FIG. 20.46**   The Form view of the graph with added design features.

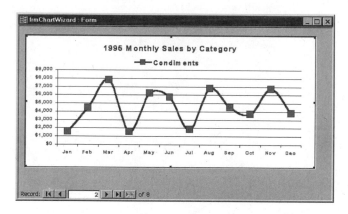

**FIG. 20.47**   Smoothing applied to the data series line, using best-fit curves.

11. MSGraph8 offers a variety of three-dimensional chart formats. Figure 20.48 illustrates a 3-D column chart. You can change the perspective of the graph by activating the chart and selecting the Corners part of the chart. Click one of the Corners' selection squares, and drag the square to change the perspective.

---

**Tip**

Use the Chart Objects list (at the top left of the MSGraph8 toolbar) to select objects in the chart, such as the corners, walls, series, and other elements of a bar chart.

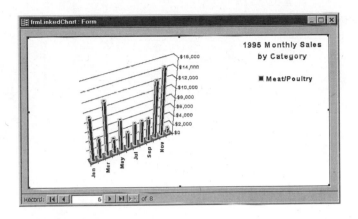

**FIG. 20.48**  The line graph converted to a 3-D column chart.

**12.** Deactivate the graph by clicking the form outside the bound object frame. Choose
File, Save <u>A</u>s, and save your bound form with a new name, such as
**frmLinkedChart**.

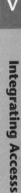

# Chapter 21

# Using Access with Microsoft Excel

Spreadsheet and word-processing applications dominate the Windows productivity application software market. According to industry reports, more than 70 percent of all Windows installations in the business environment include a spreadsheet application. Microsoft Office 97, which includes 32-bit Excel 97 and Word 97, is likely to take over the dominant position of 16-bit Microsoft Office 4+ as Windows 95 and Windows NT 4.0 Workstation gain popularity. Spreadsheets include the capability to emulate some features of database managers, such as sorting ranges of cells that are defined as a worksheet "database."

One of the principal uses of Access 97 is the conversion of data in large worksheets to tables in a relational database structure. Some of the primary justifications for converting from the familiar worksheet model to an Access 97 database include the following:

- Access queries provide much greater flexibility in selecting and sorting data than is offered by the limited sort and selection criteria of spreadsheet applications.

- You can create Access forms to simulate common business forms, which is difficult or impossible to do with present-day Windows spreadsheet applications. Excel 97 forms (dialog sheets in Excel 95), for example, offer the choice of only a few simple unbound control objects. Data-entry validation is much easier in Access than in worksheets.

- Access offers many more options for printing formatted reports from your data than are available with worksheets.

- Access VBA allows you to write programs in a full-featured language and does not restrict you to using a set of predetermined worksheet functions. (Spreadsheet applications that use VBA or other BASIC-like macro languages, however, don't suffer from this restriction.)

■ Properly designed Access relational databases minimize the duplication of information, speed data entry, and reduce disk file-storage requirements for large aggregations of data.

In many situations, however, changing a worksheet to a database is impractical. You may need to be able to view, import, or edit data that is contained in a worksheet within an Access application. In this case, linking the spreadsheet as an OLE object is the best method. You also can attach worksheet files in Excel 5+ formats to Access 97 tables with the Excel ODBC driver that is supplied with Microsoft Office.

The limited utility of attached worksheet files is demonstrated in the first sections of this chapter by the conversion process necessary to restructure the data to relational form. The second major topic of this chapter, "Using Excel as an OLE Server," describes how to link or embed worksheet data as OLE objects in bound or unbound object frames.

> **Note**
>
> Microsoft Excel 97 is used in the following examples, but you can use any Windows spreadsheet application that has OLE server capability. The first series of examples that show you how to reorganize spreadsheet data into Access tables doesn't require a spreadsheet application. You only need a suitable file in Excel .xls or Lotus .wk? format to import.

# Importing and Reorganizing Worksheet Data

Worksheets created by Excel and other spreadsheet applications often contain data that is suitable for processing with relational database techniques. The worksheet usually is organized for viewing the data quickly; however, this organization seldom is appropriate for data manipulation by an RDBMS.

STK_21_1 (described in the next section) is an example of a worksheet that is formatted for viewing data. Four rows of 22 columns each contain the equivalent of a database record—all available data for a single stock. This type of structure, where a group of individual rows constitute a database record, is common in worksheet design. This structure differs from the design of a proper worksheet database, in which all of the data for a single entity (in this case, a stock) is contained in a single row. The examples that follow in this section illustrate how to import a spreadsheet of multiple-row-per-record type and convert the data it contains to related Access tables. Make-table and update queries assist in the reorganization of the data into relational form.

> **Note**
>
> The example presented in the following sections is based on a specific worksheet format that contains New York Stock Exchange trading data for common stocks. The format of the data in the worksheet is similar to that used by online sources of financial information, many of whose sources

> organize their transmitted data for automatic or manual importing into worksheets. You're likely to find other time-series statistical data to have been created as worksheets. The following sections are specific to a single data format, but the process of converting almost all column-row, time-series data to database format is similar to that presented throughout this chapter.

## Obtaining the Example Worksheet

The file used to create many of the examples in this chapter, Stk_21.xls (Excel 97 format), contains the high price, low price, and trading volume of more than 300 individual stocks for a 21-day period beginning on April 10, 1992. This file was originally created as a Lotus 1-2-3 worksheet file (STK_21.WK1) by Ideas Unlimited.

The Stk_21.xls file is included in the example files for this book, available from the Macmillan Publishing USA Information SuperLibrary Web site. Follow the links from this URL to the *Special Edition Using Access 97* page for downloading instructions:

On the Web

## http://www.mcp.com/que/msoffice/

The examples files are archived in ZIP format. You can download an evaluation copy of the latest 32-bit version of WinZip, which expands the ZIP files, from:

On the Web

## http://www.winzip.com/

Figure 21.1 shows the Stk_21.xls workbook opened in Excel 97. Stk_21.xls contains three worksheets. The worksheet named STK_21_1 contains the entire set of sample data—more than 300 stocks in more than 1,200 rows. The worksheet named STK_21_2 contains 201 rows and 50 stocks, while STK_21_3 contains 17 rows and 4 stocks. The two smaller worksheets, STK_21_2 and STK_21_3, demonstrate the effect of worksheet size on Access's performance in sections related to OLE later in this chapter. The first row of each worksheet is used to provide field names for the table. The first column of the first row contains the entry "Day," and the remaining columns of the first row are numbered sequentially from 1 to 21.

| | A | B | C | D | E | F | G |
|---|---|---|---|---|---|---|---|
| 1 | Day | 1 | 2 | 3 | 4 | 5 | |
| 2 | AAL-S | 18.500 | 18.250 | 18.750 | 19.125 | 19.000 | 19. |
| 3 | High | 19.250 | 18.500 | 18.875 | 19.250 | 19.125 | 19. |
| 4 | Low | 18.500 | 18.125 | 18.500 | 18.875 | 18.875 | 18. |
| 5 | Volume | 59200.000 | 52800.000 | 84000.000 | 63400.000 | 16700.000 | 16700. |
| 6 | AAQ-S | 55.500 | 56.500 | 58.750 | 60.500 | 59.000 | 59. |
| 7 | High | 57.500 | 56.750 | 59.250 | 60.875 | 60.750 | 60. |
| 8 | Low | 55.000 | 55.250 | 57.250 | 57.500 | 58.500 | 58. |
| 9 | Volume | 2447000.000 | 1078200.000 | 1289300.000 | 1940700.000 | 2309700.000 | 2309700. |
| 10 | AA-S | 68.000 | 73.750 | 71.750 | 74.500 | 76.625 | 76. |
| 11 | High | 68.750 | 73.875 | 73.750 | 74.875 | 76.750 | 76. |
| 12 | Low | 68.000 | 67.000 | 71.250 | 72.000 | 74.375 | 74. |
| 13 | Volume | 381900.000 | 270800.000 | 1162900.000 | 723900.000 | 1079600.000 | 1079600. |
| 14 | ABT-S | 65.250 | 65.625 | 67.250 | 66.375 | 64.875 | 64. |
| 15 | High | 66.125 | 65.750 | 67.875 | 67.750 | 66.000 | 66. |
| 16 | Low | 64.625 | 64.875 | 65.625 | 65.625 | 64.375 | 64. |
| 17 | Volume | 1328400.000 | 561800.000 | 739900.000 | 898900.000 | 894700.000 | 894700. |
| 18 | ABY-S | 12.375 | 12.375 | 12.500 | 12.125 | 12.250 | 12. |

STK_21_3 / STK_21_2 \ STK_21_1 /

**FIG. 21.1**  The Stk_21.xls sample workbook opened in Excel 97.

V

Integrating Access

The organization of these worksheets is especially well-suited to the first example in the next section, "Importing the Example Worksheet," which shows you how to reorganize a worksheet to create a properly designed table. Alternatively, you can use for the examples any Excel or .wk? file that contains multiple series of numbers.

### Importing the Example Worksheet

The first step in the importing process is to create a new database in which to import the worksheet data. Follow these steps:

◄◄ See "Creating a New Database," p. 112

◄◄ See "Creating a Table by Importing an Excel Worksheet," p. 221

1.  Launch Access if it is not open, select Blank Database in the opening dialog, and click OK. Alternatively, if Access is already open, choose File, New Database, and double-click the Blank Database icon. The New Database dialog appears.

2.  In the New Database dialog, enter **Stocks.mdb** as the name of your new database, and then click Create.

3.  Choose File, Get External Data, Import. The Import dialog opens (see Figure 21.2).

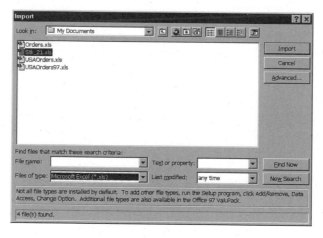

**FIG. 21.2**   Access 97's Import dialog.

4.  Select Microsoft Excel (.xls) from the Files of Type drop-down list. (Support for importing all Excel file versions with a single file-type selection was new with Access 95.)

5.  Select Stk_21.xls in the list, and click the Import button to display the first dialog of the Import Spreadsheet Wizard dialog (see Figure 21.3).

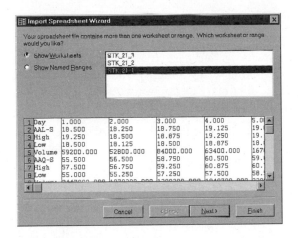

**FIG. 21.3**    Access 97's Import Spreadsheet Wizard's first dialog for importing worksheet files.

6. Select STK_21_1 from the worksheet name list. (Select one of the smaller sheets if you want to save disk space.) Click Next to display the second wizard dialog.

7. Mark the First Row Contains Column Headings check box (see Figure 21.4). Access displays a message informing you that the first row contains data that can't be used for valid Access field names and that the wizard will assign valid field names for you. (Access field names must begin with an alphabetic character, so the column headings 1–21 can't be converted directly to field names.) Click OK to dismiss the information dialog, and then click Next to display the third wizard dialog (selecting a destination for the imported data).

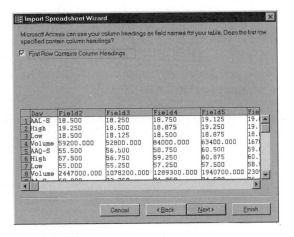

**FIG. 21.4**    The Import Spreadsheet Wizard's second dialog.

**V**

**Integrating Access**

8. Select the In a New Table option, and click Next to display the fourth wizard dialog (field options).

9. You don't need to specify field data types in this case, so click Next to display the fifth wizard dialog (primary key options). You don't need a primary key at this point, so click the No Primary Key option button, and click Next to display the final Wizard dialog.

10. Because you specified a new table for the imported data, Access now asks you for a name for the new table. The default name for the new table, STK_21_1, is correct, so click Finish to import the spreadsheet.

11. When the Wizard's message box announces that the import process has completed, click OK.

12. With the STK_21_1 table, click the Open button to display the table in Table view.

13. Select all 22 fields by clicking the Day column header button, holding down the mouse button, and dragging the mouse to the right. Choose Format, Column Width to display the Column Width dialog (see Figure 21.5).

14. Click the Best Fit button to reduce the column widths to suit the entries in the table.

**FIG. 21.5** Setting the column width of the STK_21_1 table.

Access has interpreted the field type of the Excel 97 numeric data as double-precision, which is not required for any of the values in the table. Single-precision numbers can accommodate all of the numeric values in the table. Using single-precision, rather than double-precision, values saves about 33 percent of the disk space.

To change the Field Size property of the numeric fields of the STK_21_1 table, follow these steps:

1. Click the Design View button.

2. Select the first Number field—the field named Field2. Change the Field Size value from Double to Single.

3. Repeat step 2 for the remaining 20 Number fields (Field3–Field23).

4. Click the Datasheet button to return to Table view. Click Yes when asked whether you want to save your changes and when notified that some data may be lost. Access converts the field sizes in the STK_21_1 table from Double to Single at this point, and no data is lost. Your table appears as shown in Figure 21.6.

| Day | Field2 | Field3 | Field4 | Field5 | Field6 | Field7 | Field8 | Field9 | Fie |
|---|---|---|---|---|---|---|---|---|---|
| AAL-S | 18.5 | 18.25 | 18.75 | 19.125 | 19 | 19 | 18.75 | 19.125 | |
| High | 10.25 | 18.5 | 18.875 | 19.25 | 19.125 | 19.125 | 19 | 19.125 | 1 |
| Low | 18.5 | 18.125 | 18.5 | 18.875 | 18.875 | 18.875 | 10.625 | 18.75 | |
| Volume | 59200 | 52800 | 84000 | 63400 | 16700 | 16700 | 21200 | 73400 | |
| AAQ-S | 55.5 | 56.5 | 58.75 | 60.5 | 59 | 59 | 56.75 | 56.25 | 5 |
| High | 57.5 | 56.75 | 59.25 | 60.875 | 60.75 | 60.75 | 59 | 57.25 | |
| Low | 55 | 55.25 | 57.25 | 57.5 | 58.5 | 58.5 | 56 | 56 | |
| Volume | 2447000 | 1078200 | 1289300 | 1940700 | 2309700 | 2309700 | 1839700 | 1610400 | 15: |
| AA-S | 68 | 73.75 | 71.75 | 74.5 | 76.625 | 76.625 | 77.75 | 76.25 | |
| High | 68.75 | 73.875 | 73.75 | 74.875 | 76.75 | 76.75 | 78.25 | 77.375 | 7 |
| Low | 68 | 67 | 71.25 | 72 | 74.375 | 74.375 | 75.625 | 75.5 | |
| Volume | 381900 | 270800 | 1162900 | 723900 | 1079600 | 1079600 | 531000 | 297500 | 2 |
| ABT-S | 65.25 | 65.625 | 67.25 | 66.375 | 64.875 | 64.875 | 63.25 | 62.875 | 6 |
| High | 66.125 | 65.75 | 67.875 | 67.75 | 66 | 66 | 64.5 | 64 | 6 |
| Low | 64.625 | 64.875 | 65.625 | 65.625 | 64.375 | 64.375 | 63 | 62 | |
| Volume | 1328400 | 561800 | 739900 | 898900 | 894700 | 894700 | 738300 | 907600 | 5: |
| ABY-S | 12.375 | 12.375 | 12.5 | 12.125 | 12.25 | 12.25 | 12.375 | 23.125 | 1 |
| High | 12.5 | 12.375 | 12.5 | 12.375 | 12.25 | 12.25 | 12.375 | 23.125 | 1 |

Record: 1 of 1221

**FIG. 21.6**  The revised version of the STK_21_1 table.

## Developing a Conversion Strategy

The second step in the conversion process is to define the tables to be created as a result of normalizing the data in the imported spreadsheet (*normalizing* the data means converting it to a form that follows the rules of relational database design). Very few worksheets can be converted to a single table that meets relational database standards. Designing the tables to contain the data and establishing the relationships of these tables to one another are the most important elements of the conversion process. Following are the two objectives of your design strategy:

▶▶ See "Normalizing Data to the Relational Model," p. 802

- *A design optimized for data display, entry, and editing.* This objective is primary if you plan to use Access for data entry. In the stock prices example, data entry and editing aren't a consideration because the data is supplied in worksheet format by Ideas Unlimited and other purveyors of stock price data.

- *A design allowing you to extract imported data with the fewest steps.* If you obtain periodic updates to your stock price data in worksheet format, for example, ease of importing the data is the principal consideration.

The initial design usually is a compromise between these two objectives. The stock price example does not involve a compromise because data entry and editing are unnecessary.

When planning the initial design of the tables to contain the stock price and volume data, consider these points:

V

Integrating Access

▶▶ See "Fifth Normal Form and Combined Entities," p. 807

- *The data for each element of the group—Close, High, Low, and Volume—is incorporated in an individual table.* A table with the 84 fields required to hold all data for a stock is unwieldy at best. Reconstructing a worksheet from a table with such a design results in a cumbersome worksheet. One of the principles of relational database design is that you should be able to reconstruct your original database from the relational data.

- *The key field of each table, Symbol, is the ticker symbol of the stock.* (The ticker symbol is the abbreviation for the name of the stock assigned by the New York Stock Exchange.) This key field allows the tables to be linked in a one-to-one relationship based on the unique values of the ticker symbols. One-to-one relationships are uncommon in relational databases, but in this example a one-to-one relationship is quite useful.

- *Queries organize the data in the tables as required for Access forms and reports.* Because each field in the query is prefaced by the table name, the names of the tables should be short to save keystrokes.

- *When multiple tables are combined in a query, the records in each table must be identified by type.* The second field, Type, is a single-letter abbreviation of the type of data: C(lose), H(igh), L(ow), and V(olume).

Now you need to develop the tactics to create the required tables in accordance with your strategy. The conversion plan involves these elements:

- The records to be included in the individual tables are extracted from the STK_21_1 table by make-table queries with criteria based on the values in the Day field.

- The Symbol field from the Close table must be added to the High, Low, and Volume tables.

- In the query used to create the final table, adding the Symbol field to a table requires a unique key to link the Close table and the tables without symbol values. An AutoNumber field added to the Close, High, Low, and Volume tables can serve as a temporary key field.

- Creating the new tables is a two-step process. First, the data is extracted to a temporary set of tables (Hi, Lo, and Vol). The second step combines these three tables with the Symbol field of another temporary table—Close—to create the final High, Low, and Volume tables. You need temporary tables in this case because make-table queries should never alter tables on which they are based.

■ Because the Close table lacks a type identifier field, a Type field must be added to this table. The remaining tables have a type identifier word that can be replaced by the corresponding code letter.

Now that you have a conversion strategy and have decided the tactics for carrying it out, you are ready to test the merits of both, as described in the next section.

### Extracting Data

Make-table queries are designed specifically for creating new tables from data in existing tables that meet a specified set of criteria. For STK_21_1, you use make-table queries to create one final table (Close) and three temporary tables (Hi, Low, and Vol). To create these four tables with make-table queries, follow these steps:

◄◄ See "Creating Action Queries to Append Records to a Table," p. 378

1.  With the STK_21_1 table open, click the arrow of the New Object button of the toolbar and select New Query from the list to create a new query based on STK_21_1.

2.  With Design View selected in the New Query dialog's list, click OK. Access creates a new query and automatically adds the STK_21_1 table to the query.

3.  Click the Day field, and drag the field symbol to the first column of the query.

4.  Click the asterisk (*, all fields), and drag the field symbol to the second column of the query.

5.  Click the Show check box in the Day field to clear the box. (Day is included in the fields in the second column of the query. You cannot include two fields of the same name in a make-table query.)

6.  In the Criteria row of the Day field, enter **High** to include only records for the high price of the stock in the temporary Hi table. Your query appears, as shown in Figure 21.7.

7.  Choose Query, Ma_k_e Table Query to display the Make Table dialog.

8.  Enter **Hi** in the Table Name text box and then click OK (see Figure 21.8). The default values for the remaining elements in the Make Table dialog are satisfactory.

9.  Click the Run button of the toolbar to create the temporary Hi table. Access displays a message box that indicates the number of records to be added to the new table (see Figure 21.9). Click Yes to complete the make-table query.

**V**

**Integrating Access**

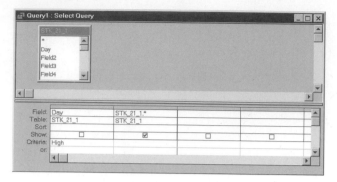

**FIG. 21.7**    Creating the temporary Hi table with a make-table query.

**FIG. 21.8**    Entering the temporary table name in the Make Table dialog.

**FIG. 21.9**    The message box that confirms the number of rows added to the new table.

**10.** Open the Database window, click the Tables tab, and double-click the Hi entry in the list to view the table (see Figure 21.10).

**11.** Change the Criteria value of your make-table query to **Low** and repeat steps 6–10, substituting **Lo** for the table name in steps 6 and 10.

**12.** Change the Criteria value to **Volume** and repeat steps 6–10, using **Vol** for the table name.

**13.** The closing prices are in the row with the ticker symbol. Each of the symbols has a hyphen followed by a character that identifies the type of security; -S represents a common stock. Change the Criteria value to **Like** "*-*" to select these rows and repeat steps 6 through 10, using **Close** for the table name. The expression *-* selects all records containing a hyphen. You don't need to create a temporary table in this case because the Close table includes the ticker symbols, as illustrated by Figure 21.11.

**Hi : Table**

| Day | Field2 | Field3 | Field4 | Field5 | Field6 | Field7 | Field8 | Field9 | Field10 | Fiel |
|-----|--------|--------|--------|--------|--------|--------|--------|--------|---------|------|
| High | 19.25 | 18.5 | 18.875 | 19.25 | 19.125 | 19.125 | 19 | 19.125 | 19.125 | 19. |
| High | 57.5 | 56.75 | 59.25 | 60.875 | 60.75 | 60.75 | 59 | 57.25 | 58 | 58 |
| High | 68.75 | 73.875 | 73.75 | 74.875 | 76.75 | 76.75 | 78.25 | 77.375 | 76.375 | 76. |
| High | 66.125 | 65.75 | 67.875 | 67.75 | 66 | 66 | 64.5 | 64 | 63.375 | 63. |
| High | 12.5 | 12.375 | 12.5 | 12.375 | 12.25 | 12.25 | 12.375 | 23.125 | 12.125 | 12. |
| High | 62.625 | 62.75 | 64.375 | 64.75 | 64.75 | 64.75 | 62.375 | 61.75 | 61.625 | 61. |
| High | 25.125 | 25.5 | 26 | 25.875 | 24.5 | 24.5 | 24.125 | 23.5 | 24.375 | 24 |
| High | 31.375 | 31.25 | 31.875 | 32 | 32.25 | 32.25 | 32.25 | 32.25 | 32.125 | 31. |
| High | 43.75 | 44.5 | 44.25 | 43.75 | 43.25 | 43.25 | 43.25 | 43.75 | 44.125 | 43. |
| High | 42 | 42 | 42.25 | 42.375 | 42.625 | 42.625 | 42.375 | 42.5 | 43.25 | |
| High | 40.5 | 40.125 | 41.5 | 42.375 | 42.625 | 42.625 | 42.375 | 41.875 | 41.375 | 39. |
| High | 16.625 | 16.625 | 16.75 | 16.875 | 17 | 17 | 16.875 | 17 | 17.375 | 1: |
| High | 77.75 | 77.75 | 82 | 81.875 | 80 | 80 | 77.875 | 77.25 | 76.875 | |
| High | 86 | 85.625 | 87.75 | 87.5 | 87.5 | 87.5 | 86.375 | 86.375 | 85.125 | 85. |
| High | 58.875 | 59.375 | 59.5 | 59.625 | 60.75 | 60.75 | 61.125 | 61.5 | 62.75 | 63. |

Record: |◄ ◄ | 1 | ► |►| |►* | of 305

**FIG. 21.10**    The temporary Hi table created by the make-table query.

**Close : Table**

| Day | Field2 | Field3 | Field4 | Field5 | Field6 | Field7 | Field8 | Field9 | Field10 | Field |
|-----|--------|--------|--------|--------|--------|--------|--------|--------|---------|-------|
| AAL-S | 18.5 | 18.25 | 18.75 | 19.125 | 19 | 19 | 18.75 | 19.125 | 19 | 18.8 |
| AAQ-S | 55.5 | 56.5 | 58.75 | 60.5 | 59 | 59 | 56.75 | 56.25 | 57.625 | |
| AA-S | 68 | 73.75 | 71.75 | 74.5 | 76.625 | 76.625 | 77.75 | 76.25 | 75 | 7! |
| ABT-S | 65.25 | 65.625 | 67.25 | 66.375 | 64.875 | 64.875 | 63.25 | 62.875 | 63.375 | 62.6 |
| ABY-S | 12.375 | 12.375 | 12.5 | 12.125 | 12.25 | 12.25 | 12.375 | 23.125 | 12.125 | 12.1 |
| ACY-S | 61.875 | 62.375 | 64.375 | 64.5 | 62.625 | 62.625 | 60.25 | 61.5 | 61 | 61.1 |
| ADM-S | 25 | 25.375 | 25.625 | 24.375 | 23.875 | 23.875 | 23.375 | 23.375 | 24.125 | 23.8 |
| AEP-S | 31.25 | 31.125 | 31.625 | 32 | 32.25 | 32.25 | 32.25 | 32.25 | 31.875 | 31. |
| AET-S | 43.5 | 44 | 43.625 | 43.125 | 43.25 | 43.25 | 43.125 | 43.75 | 43.875 | 43.8 |
| AGC-S | 41.875 | 41.375 | 42.125 | 42.375 | 42.625 | 42.625 | 42.25 | 42.5 | 43 | |
| AHC-S | 39.375 | 40 | 41.375 | 42.375 | 42.375 | 42.375 | 41.875 | 41.5 | 40 | 39.8 |
| AHM-S | 16.375 | 16.625 | 16.625 | 16.625 | 16.75 | 16.75 | 16.75 | 16.875 | 17.125 | 17. |
| AHP-S | 76.875 | 77.75 | 81.625 | 80 | 78.25 | 78.25 | 76.125 | 77.125 | 76.125 | |
| AIG-S | 85.375 | 85.5 | 86.75 | 87.25 | 86.75 | 86.75 | 80 | 85.25 | 84.875 | 85.1 |
| AIT-S | 58.75 | 58.875 | 59.375 | 59.625 | 60.75 | 60.75 | 61.125 | 61.125 | 62.625 | 63.6 |
| ALD-S | 53.75 | 53.75 | 54.625 | 55.5 | 57 | 57 | 56.5 | 56.75 | 56.25 | |

Record: |◄ ◄ | 1 | ► |►| |►* | of 305

**FIG. 21.11**    The Close table with the ticker symbol of the stocks.

### Modifying the Table Structure

Each table you created in the preceding section requires additional fields so that you can design an append query to create a properly structured table. An AutoNumber field is used as a temporary key field for each of the four tables. The Close table needs a Type field added, and the Day field of each temporary table needs the name changed to Type. Follow these steps to make the changes:

> **Tip**
>
> AutoNumber fields are the fastest way of adding a primary-key field to a table that does not contain unique values on which to base a primary key.

**1.** Click the Tables tab in the Database window, select the Hi table, and click the Design button.

Tables

Design

Integrating Access

V

**2.** Change the name of the first field from Day to **Type** and set the Field Size property to **1**, as shown in Figure 21.12. This action truncates the Type field value, High, to the required single-letter code H when you save your design changes.

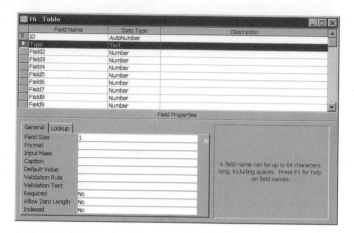

**FIG. 21.12**  Modifications to the design of the temporary Hi table.

**3.** Click the field selector button of the Type field, and press Insert to add a field at the beginning of the table. Type **ID** in the Field Name column, and select AutoNumber in the Data Type column. Click the Primary Key button of the toolbar to make the ID field the primary-key field.

**4.** Click the Table View button on the toolbar. Save the changes to the table. A message box advises you that some data may be lost as a result of truncating the Type field length (see Figure 21.13). Click Yes to approve the change. The table appears as shown in Figure 21.14.

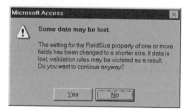

**FIG. 21.13**  The warning that some data may be lost as a result of truncating the Type field.

**5.** Repeat steps 1 through 4 for the Lo and Vol tables.

**6.** Open the Close table in Design mode. Change the Day field name to **Symbol**, and change its Field Size property to **10** to accommodate longer ticker symbols.

**7.** Click the Selection button for the Symbol field, and press Insert to add an **ID** AutoNumber field. Click the Primary Key button of the toolbar to create the primary-key index.

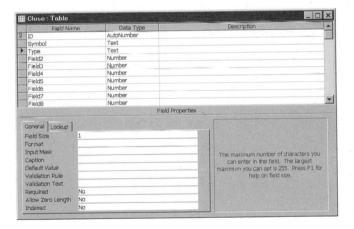

| ID | Type | Field2 | Field3 | Field4 | Field5 | Field6 | Field7 | Field8 | Field9 | Field10 | Field |
|---|---|---|---|---|---|---|---|---|---|---|---|
| 1 | H | 19.25 | 10.5 | 18.875 | 19.25 | 19.125 | 19.125 | 19 | 19.125 | 19.125 | 19. |
| 2 | H | 57.5 | 56.75 | 59.25 | 60.875 | 60.75 | 60.75 | 59 | 57.25 | 58 | 58 |
| 3 | H | 68.75 | 73.875 | 73.75 | 74.875 | 78.75 | 76.75 | 78.25 | 77.375 | 76.375 | 75 |
| 4 | H | 66.125 | 65.75 | 67.875 | 67.75 | 66 | 66 | 64.5 | 64 | 63.375 | 63. |
| 5 | H | 12.5 | 12.375 | 12.5 | 12.375 | 12.25 | 12.25 | 12.375 | 23.125 | 12.125 | 12. |
| 6 | H | 62.625 | 62.75 | 64.375 | 64.75 | 64.75 | 64.75 | 62.375 | 61.75 | 61.625 | 61. |
| 7 | H | 25.125 | 25.5 | 26 | 25.875 | 24.5 | 24.5 | 24.125 | 23.5 | 24.375 | 24 |
| 8 | H | 31.375 | 31.25 | 31.875 | 32 | 32.25 | 32.25 | 32.25 | 32.25 | 32.125 | 31. |
| 9 | H | 43.75 | 44.5 | 44.25 | 43.75 | 43.25 | 43.25 | 43.25 | 43.75 | 44.125 | 43. |
| 10 | H | 42 | 42 | 42.25 | 42.375 | 42.625 | 42.625 | 42.375 | 42.5 | 43.25 | |
| 11 | H | 40.5 | 40.125 | 41.5 | 42.375 | 42.625 | 42.625 | 42.375 | 41.875 | 41.375 | 39. |
| 12 | H | 16.625 | 16.625 | 16.75 | 16.875 | 17 | 17 | 16.875 | 17 | 17.375 | 17 |
| 13 | H | 77.75 | 77.75 | 82 | 81.875 | 80 | 80 | 77.875 | 77.25 | 76.875 | 7 |
| 14 | H | 86 | 85.625 | 87.75 | 87.5 | 87.5 | 87.5 | 86.375 | 86.375 | 85.125 | 85. |
| 15 | H | 58.875 | 59.375 | 59.5 | 59.625 | 60.75 | 60.75 | 61.125 | 61.5 | 62.75 | 63 |
| 16 | H | 54.125 | 54.375 | 55.75 | 55.5 | 57.125 | 57.125 | | 56.5 | 57.125 | 56.75 | |
| 17 | H | 18.125 | 18 | 17.75 | 17.875 | 18.25 | 18.25 | 18.25 | 18 | 18 | 18. |
| 18 | H | 19.625 | 20.625 | 20.375 | 20.25 | 21.125 | 21.125 | 21.375 | 21 | 21.125 | 21 |

Record: |◄ ◄   1  ► ►| ►* of 305   ◄

**FIG. 21.14**  The temporary Hi table with the ID key field added.

8. Select the Field2 field (the first of the Number fields), and then press Insert to add a new field. Enter **Type** as the Field Name of the new field (added fields default to the Text data type), and set its Field Size property to **1**. Figure 21.15 shows the design of the Close table.

| Field Name | Data Type | Description |
|---|---|---|
| ID | AutoNumber | |
| Symbol | Text | |
| Type | Text | |
| Field2 | Number | |
| Field3 | Number | |
| Field4 | Number | |
| Field5 | Number | |
| Field6 | Number | |
| Field7 | Number | |
| Field8 | Number | |

Field Properties

General | Lookup

| | |
|---|---|
| Field Size | 1 |
| Format | |
| Input Mask | |
| Caption | |
| Default Value | |
| Validation Rule | |
| Validation Text | |
| Required | No |
| Allow Zero Length | No |
| Indexed | No |

The maximum number of characters you can enter in the field. The largest maximum you can set is 255. Press F1 for help on field size.

**FIG. 21.15**  Modifications made to the design of the Close table.

9. Click the Table View button of the toolbar, save your changes, and accept the truncated field. Figure 21.16 shows the resulting Close table.

The extraction of data from STK_21_1 to the required tables is a relatively simple process because the labels used to identify the data are consistent throughout the worksheet. You may need to write a worksheet macro that creates consistent labels for rows to be included in a specific table if the labels don't exist or aren't consistent in the original version of the worksheet.

V

Integrating Access

| ID | Symbol | Type | Field2 | Field3 | Field4 | Field5 | Field6 | Field7 | Field8 | Field9 | F |
|---|---|---|---|---|---|---|---|---|---|---|---|
| 1 | AAL-S | | 18.5 | 18.25 | 18.75 | 19.125 | 19 | 19 | 18.75 | 19.125 | |
| 2 | AAQ-S | | 55.5 | 56.5 | 58.75 | 60.5 | 59 | 59 | 56.75 | 56.25 | |
| 3 | AA-S | | 68 | 73.75 | 71.75 | 74.5 | 76.625 | 76.625 | 77.75 | 76.25 | |
| 4 | ABT-S | | 65.25 | 65.625 | 67.25 | 66.375 | 64.875 | 64.875 | 63.25 | 62.875 | |
| 5 | ABY-S | | 12.375 | 12.375 | 12.5 | 12.125 | 12.25 | 12.25 | 12.375 | 23.125 | |
| 6 | ACY-S | | 61.875 | 62.375 | 64.375 | 64.5 | 62.625 | 62.625 | 60.25 | 61.5 | |
| 7 | ADM-S | | 25 | 25.375 | 25.625 | 24.375 | 23.875 | 23.875 | 23.375 | 23.375 | |
| 8 | AEP-S | | 31.25 | 31.125 | 31.625 | 32 | 32.25 | 32.25 | 32.25 | 32.25 | |
| 9 | AET-S | | 43.5 | 44 | 43.625 | 43.125 | 43.25 | 43.25 | 43.125 | 43.75 | |
| 10 | AGC-S | | 41.875 | 41.375 | 42.125 | 42.375 | 42.625 | 42.625 | 42.25 | 42.5 | |
| 11 | AHC-S | | 39.375 | 40 | 41.375 | 42.375 | 42.375 | 42.375 | 41.875 | 41.5 | |
| 12 | AHM-S | | 16.375 | 16.625 | 16.625 | 16.625 | 16.75 | 16.75 | 16.75 | 16.875 | |
| 13 | AHP-S | | 76.875 | 77.75 | 81.625 | 80 | 78.25 | 78.25 | 76.125 | 77.125 | |
| 14 | AIG-S | | 85.375 | 85.5 | 86.75 | 87.25 | 86.75 | 86.75 | 86 | 85.25 | |
| 15 | AIT-S | | 58.75 | 58.875 | 59.375 | 59.625 | 60.75 | 60.75 | 61.125 | 61.125 | |
| 16 | ALD-S | | 53.75 | 53.75 | 54.625 | 55.5 | 57 | 57 | 56.5 | 56.75 | |
| 17 | ALK-S | | 18.125 | 17.75 | 17.5 | 17.875 | 18.125 | 18.125 | 18 | 17.875 | |
| 18 | AL-S | | 19.625 | 20.625 | 20.125 | 20.25 | 20.875 | 20.875 | 21.125 | 20.875 | |

Record: ◄◄ ◄ 1 ► ►► ►* of 305

**FIG. 21.16** The Close table with the ID and Type fields added.

### Adding the Type Value to the Close Table

When you need to replace data in a field containing text values, the Replace command on the Edit menu is usually a faster process than creating an UPDATE query. Because the Replace What text box in the Replace in Field dialog doesn't accept a Null value, however, you cannot use the Replace command on the Edit menu to add the C code (for "Close") to the Type field of the Close table. Instead, you must use an update query to change the Type field value. Follow these steps:

◄◄ See "Updating Values of Multiple Records in a Table," p. 383

New Object: Query

1. Make the Close table active. Click the arrow of the New Object button of the toolbar, and choose New Query from the menu list.

2. Select Design View in the New Query dialog's list, and then click OK to create a new query with the Close table added.

3. Choose _Query, Update Query to change the query type from select to update.

4. Select the Type field and drag the field symbol to the first column of the query.

5. Type **C** in the Update To row. This action changes the Type field value in all records from the default Null to the single letter C. Figure 21.17 shows the Update Query design at this point.

6. Click the Run button on the toolbar to update the Type field of the Close table. When the message box shown in Figure 21.18 appears, click Yes.

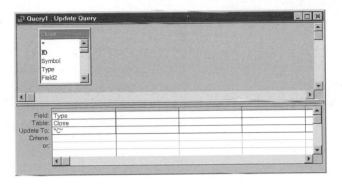

**FIG. 21.17**  The Update Query used to add C to the Type field of each record in the Close table.

**FIG. 21.18**  The message box that indicates the number of records to be updated.

### Creating the Final Tables

Now, you need to combine the Symbol field of the Close table with the data in the Hi, Lo, and Vol tables to create the final High, Low, and Volume tables. In this example, you use the same query each time, changing the temporary table name to create the three final tables.

> **Tip**
>
> If you are creating an application that uses Access VBA code to automate the conversion process, save each query with a unique name so that the query can be run by a VBA procedure.

To create your final High, Low, and Volume tables with make-table queries, follow these steps:

1. With the Close table active, click the arrow of the New Object button of the toolbar `New Object: Query` and select Design View. Then, click the OK button of the New Query dialog to create a new query based on the Close table.

2. Choose Query, Make Table Query to open the Make Table dialog. Enter **High** in the Table Name text box as the name of the final table to create, and click OK.

3. Select the Symbol field of the Close table, and drag it to the first column of the make-table query.

4. Click the Show Table button of the toolbar or choose Query, Show Table to open the Show Table dialog. Select Hi from the Tables list and click Add. Then choose the Close button. Access automatically creates the join between the ID fields of the Close and Hi tables for you.

> **Caution**
>
> This step is very important. If Access fails to establish this relationship and you don't add the relationship, you create a *Cartesian product* instead of the result you want. A Cartesian product is all possible combinations of all field values contained in the two tables. In this case, the Cartesian product contains about 95,000 (305 * 305) rows.

5. Click the asterisk (*, all fields) of the Hi table, and drag the field symbol to the second column of the query. The make-table query appears as shown in Figure 21.19.

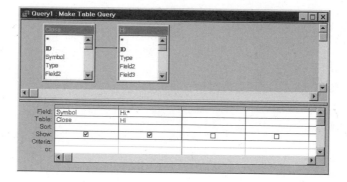

**FIG. 21.19** The make-table query that creates the final High table.

6. Click the Run button of the toolbar to create the final High table. Click OK in the message box that appears to confirm creating the new table.

7. In the query, select the Hi table field list, and press Delete to remove the field list from the query. Repeat steps 4 through 6 for the Lo table, substituting **Low** as the name for the new final table in the Make Table dialog.

8. Repeat step 7 for the Vol table, entering **Volume** as the name of the final table in the Make Table dialog.

9. Close the query, and don't save the changes.

You must remove the temporary key field, ID, from the Close table so that you can make Symbol the key field. Follow these steps:

1. Open the Database window, click the Tables tab, and select the Close table. Click the Design button.

2. Click the field selection button of the ID field, and then press Delete. When Access displays message boxes asking you to confirm deletion of the field and key field, click OK.

3. Select the Symbol field; then click the Primary Key button of the toolbar to make the Symbol field the primary-key field. Figure 21.20 shows the Design view of the Close table.

4. Click the Table View button on the toolbar to display the contents of the table. Click OK when asked to confirm your changes.

5. Select all columns of the table by dragging the mouse pointer over the column's field name buttons.

6. Choose Format, Column Width to open the Column Width dialog, and then click Best Fit to change the column sizes and close the Column Width dialog. Figure 21.21 shows the resulting Close table.

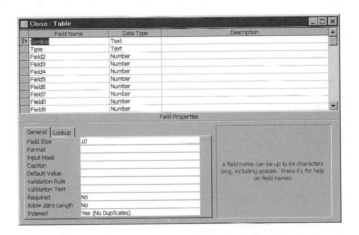

**FIG. 21.20**   The Close table with Symbol as the primary-key field.

| Symbol | Type | Field2 | Field3 | Field4 | Field5 | Field6 | Field7 | Field8 | Field9 | Field10 | F |
|--------|------|--------|--------|--------|--------|--------|--------|--------|--------|---------|---|
| AA-S | C | 68 | 73.75 | 71.75 | 74.5 | 76.625 | 76.625 | 77.75 | 76.25 | 75 | |
| AAL-S | C | 18.5 | 18.25 | 18.75 | 19.125 | 19 | 19 | 18.75 | 19.125 | 19 | |
| AAQ-S | C | 55.5 | 56.5 | 58.75 | 60.5 | 59 | 59 | 56.75 | 56.25 | 57.625 | |
| ABT-S | C | 65.25 | 65.625 | 67.25 | 66.375 | 64.875 | 64.875 | 63.25 | 62.875 | 63.375 | |
| ABY-S | C | 12.375 | 12.375 | 12.5 | 12.125 | 12.25 | 12.25 | 12.375 | 23.125 | 12.125 | |
| ACY-S | C | 61.875 | 62.375 | 64.375 | 64.5 | 62.625 | 62.625 | 60.25 | 61.5 | 61 | |
| ADM-S | C | 25 | 25.375 | 25.625 | 24.375 | 23.875 | 23.875 | 23.375 | 23.375 | 24.125 | |
| AEP-S | C | 31.25 | 31.125 | 31.625 | 32 | 32.25 | 32.25 | 32.25 | 32.25 | 31.875 | |
| AET-S | C | 43.5 | 44 | 43.625 | 43.125 | 43.25 | 43.25 | 43.125 | 43.75 | 43.875 | |
| AGC-S | C | 41.875 | 41.375 | 42.125 | 42.375 | 42.625 | 42.625 | 42.25 | 42.5 | 43 | |
| AHC-S | C | 39.375 | 40 | 41.375 | 42.375 | 42.375 | 42.375 | 41.875 | 41.5 | 40 | |
| AHM-S | C | 16.375 | 16.625 | 16.625 | 16.625 | 16.75 | 16.75 | 16.75 | 16.875 | 17.125 | |
| AHP-S | C | 76.875 | 77.75 | 81.625 | 80 | 78.25 | 78.25 | 76.125 | 77.125 | 76.125 | |
| AIG-S | C | 85.375 | 85.5 | 86.75 | 87.25 | 86.75 | 86.75 | 86 | 85.25 | 84.875 | |
| AIT-S | C | 58.75 | 58.875 | 59.375 | 59.625 | 60.75 | 60.75 | 61.125 | 61.125 | 62.625 | |
| AL-S | C | 19.625 | 20.625 | 20.125 | 20.25 | 20.875 | 20.875 | 21.125 | 20.875 | 21 | |
| ALD-S | C | 53.75 | 53.75 | 54.625 | 55.5 | 57 | 57 | 56.5 | 56.75 | 56.25 | |
| ALK-S | C | 18.125 | 17.75 | 17.5 | 17.875 | 18.125 | 18.125 | 18 | 17.875 | 17.875 | |

Record: 14 ◀ | 1 ▶ ▶I ▶* of 305

**FIG. 21.21**   The final version of the Close table.

**7.** Choose <u>F</u>ile, <u>S</u>ave to save the column width change.

At this point, you can delete the Hi, Lo, and Vol tables. Deleting temporary tables conserves disk space, but only after you compact the database.

### Verifying the Tables by Re-Creating the Worksheet

An important step when creating tables from external data sources is to verify that the tables contain the correct information. In most cases, the best method of testing is to use the tables to re-create the data in its original format—or as close to the original format as possible. This strategy allows you to make a direct comparison of the source data and the data contained in the tables.

◀◀ See "Copying and Pasting Tables," p. 159

To create a replica of the original STK_21_1 worksheet, follow these steps:

 **1.** Make the Database window active, click the Tables tab, and select the Close table.

**2.** Press Ctrl+C to copy the table to the Clipboard, and then press Ctrl+V to create a copy of the table. The Paste Table As dialog appears.

**3.** Type **tblStockPrices** as the name of the new table in the Paste Table As dialog (see Figure 21.22). Make sure that the default Structure and Data options button is selected, and then click OK. Access creates a new tblStockPrices table.

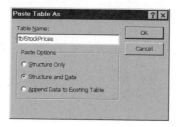

**FIG. 21.22**    Entering the table name in the Paste Table As dialog.

 **4.** Select the tblStockPrices table in the Tables list of the Database window, and then click the Design button.

 **5.** Click the Indexes button of the toolbar to display the Indexes dialog.

 **6.** Select both the Symbol and Type fields by holding down the Shift key and clicking the two field selection buttons. Then click the Primary Key button of the toolbar.

**7.** Select the Symbol field and click the Indexed text box in the Field Properties section of the Design window. Choose Yes (Duplicates OK) from the Indexed drop-down list. If you choose No (No Duplicates), you cannot append records. Indexing the Symbol field can speed up queries based on a specific symbol or set of symbols. Figure 21.23 shows the design for the tblStockPrices table.

8. Click the Table View button of the toolbar, and click OK when asked whether you want to save your changes. Review the data in the table, and then close the tblStockPrices window.

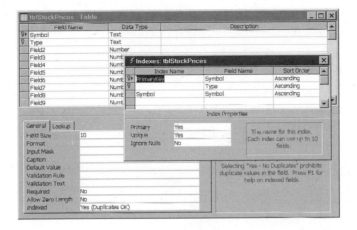

**FIG. 21.23** Modifying the key field and indexing properties of the tblStockPrices table.

In preparation for appending the data in the other tables to the tblStockPrices table, you need to remove the primary key (ID) field. In prior versions of Access, you could append data from tables without an identical set of fields. Access 97 issues an INSERT INTO statement contains unknown field name 'FieldName' message if the field names don't match in the source and destination tables. Open the High, Low, and Volume tables in Design view, and delete the ID field of each of these three tables.

> **Note**
>
> An alternative to deleting the ID fields is to add all fields, except the ID field, of the High, Low, and Volume fields to the queries you create in the following series of steps. If you do delete the ID fields from the tables, you should make backup copies of the High, Low, and Volume tables, because you'll use these tables again in the next section of this chapter, "Using the Tables You Created."

To add the data in the High, Low, and Volume tables to the Stock Data table, follow these steps:

1. Select the High table in the Database window; then click the New Object button of the toolbar, and select New Query from the menu list to display the New Query dialog.

2. With Design View selected, click OK to open a new query based on the High table.

3. Choose _Query, A_ppend to display the Append dialog. Open the Table Name dropdown list and select tblStockPrices (see Figure 21.24). The tblStockPrices table is the table to which you want to append the records. Click OK.

V

Integrating Access

**FIG. 21.24** Entering the name of the table to append records to in the Append dialog.

4. Select the asterisk (*) field of the High table field list and drag the field list symbol to the first column of the query. Figure 21.25 shows the append query design.

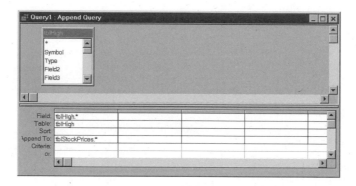

**FIG. 21.25** The append query design for adding records to tblStockPrices from the High table.

 5. Click the Run button on the toolbar to append the High records to Stock Data. The message box shown in Figure 21.26 indicates the number of records to be appended. Click Yes.

**FIG. 21.26** The message box confirming the append operation.

6. Delete the High table's field list from the query, and then click the Show Table button of the toolbar. Repeat steps 4 and 5 to append the Low and Volume table data to tblStockPrices.

 7. After you have appended the data from the High, Low, and Volume tables to tblStockPrices, open the tblStockPrices table from the Database window. The table appears as shown in Figure 21.27. The data for Close, High, Low, and trading Volume appears in the same sequence as in the worksheet because the table is indexed on the combination of the Symbol and the Type fields, the primary key. Access creates a no-duplicates index on the key field(s).

8. Drag the tblStockPrices table to the lower right of your display. Open the STK_21_1 table; then click the exposed surface of the tblStockPrices window to compare it with the original version (see Figure 21.28).

9. Indexing tblStockPrices has changed the order of some of the entries. Confirm that the data for a few stocks in both tables are the same.

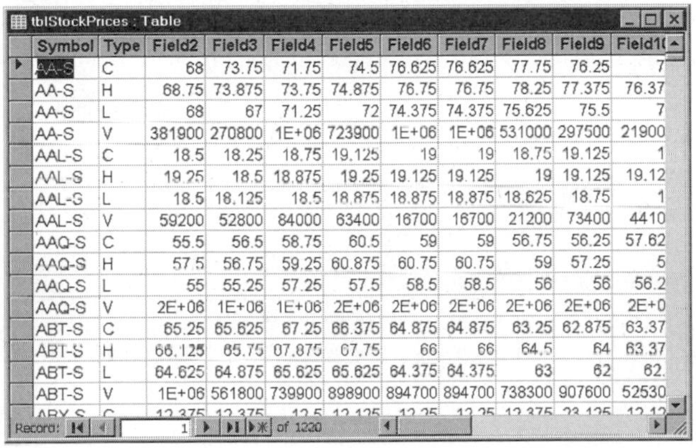

tblStockPrices : Table

| Symbol | Type | Field2 | Field3 | Field4 | Field5 | Field6 | Field7 | Field8 | Field9 | Field1( |
|---|---|---|---|---|---|---|---|---|---|---|
| AA-S | C | 68 | 73.75 | 71.75 | 74.5 | 76.625 | 76.625 | 77.75 | 76.25 | 7 |
| AA-S | H | 68.75 | 73.875 | 73.75 | 74.875 | 76.75 | 76.75 | 78.25 | 77.375 | 76.37 |
| AA-S | L | 68 | 67 | 71.25 | 72 | 74.375 | 74.375 | 75.625 | 75.5 | 7 |
| AA-S | V | 381900 | 270800 | 1E+06 | 723900 | 1E+06 | 1E+06 | 531000 | 297500 | 21900 |
| AAL-S | C | 18.5 | 18.25 | 18.75 | 19.125 | 19 | 19 | 18.75 | 19.125 | 1 |
| AAL-S | H | 19.25 | 18.5 | 18.875 | 19.25 | 19.125 | 19.125 | 19 | 19.125 | 19.12 |
| AAL-S | L | 18.5 | 18.125 | 18.5 | 18.875 | 18.875 | 18.875 | 18.625 | 18.75 | 1 |
| AAL-S | V | 59200 | 52800 | 84000 | 63400 | 16700 | 16700 | 21200 | 73400 | 4410 |
| AAQ-S | C | 55.5 | 56.5 | 58.75 | 60.5 | 59 | 59 | 56.75 | 56.25 | 57.62 |
| AAQ-S | H | 57.5 | 56.75 | 59.25 | 60.875 | 60.75 | 60.75 | 59 | 57.25 | 5 |
| AAQ-S | L | 55 | 55.25 | 57.25 | 57.5 | 58.5 | 58.5 | 56 | 56 | 56.2 |
| AAQ-S | V | 2E+06 | 1E+06 | 1E+06 | 2E+06 | 2E+06 | 2E+06 | 2E+06 | 2E+06 | 2E+0 |
| ABT-S | C | 65.25 | 65.625 | 67.25 | 66.375 | 64.875 | 64.875 | 63.25 | 62.875 | 63.37 |
| ABT-S | H | 66.125 | 65.75 | 67.875 | 67.75 | 66 | 66 | 64.5 | 64 | 63.37 |
| ABT-S | L | 64.625 | 64.875 | 65.625 | 65.625 | 64.375 | 64.375 | 63 | 62 | 62. |
| ABT-S | V | 1E+06 | 561800 | 739900 | 898900 | 894700 | 894700 | 738300 | 907600 | 52530 |

Record: 1 of 1220

**FIG. 21.27** The final version of the tblStockPrices table with all records appended.

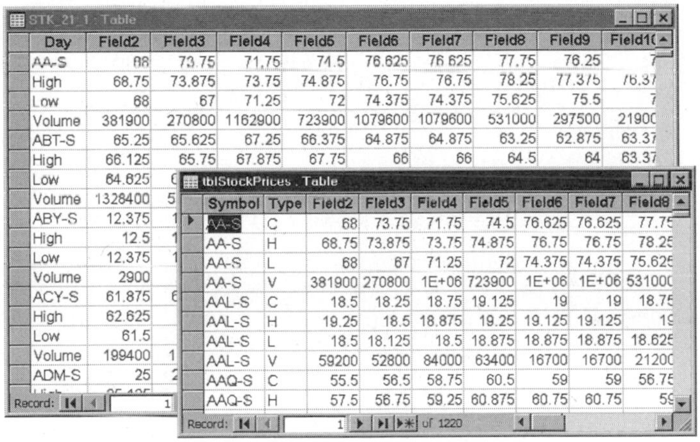

STK_21_1 : Table

| Day | Field2 | Field3 | Field4 | Field5 | Field6 | Field7 | Field8 | Field9 | Field1( |
|---|---|---|---|---|---|---|---|---|---|
| AA-S | 68 | 73.75 | 71.75 | 74.5 | 76.625 | 76.625 | 77.75 | 76.25 | 7 |
| High | 68.75 | 73.875 | 73.75 | 74.875 | 76.75 | 76.75 | 78.25 | 77.375 | 76.37 |
| Low | 68 | 67 | 71.25 | 72 | 74.375 | 74.375 | 75.625 | 75.5 | 7 |
| Volume | 381900 | 270800 | 1162900 | 723900 | 1079600 | 1079600 | 531000 | 297500 | 2190C |
| ABT-S | 65.25 | 65.625 | 67.25 | 66.375 | 64.875 | 64.875 | 63.25 | 62.875 | 63.37 |
| High | 66.125 | 65.75 | 67.875 | 67.75 | 66 | 66 | 64.5 | 64 | 63.37 |
| Low | 64.625 | 6 | | | | | | | |
| Volume | 1328400 | 5 | | | | | | | |
| ABY-S | 12.375 | 1 | | | | | | | |
| High | 12.5 | 1 | | | | | | | |
| Low | 12.375 | 1 | | | | | | | |
| Volume | 2900 | | | | | | | | |
| ACY-S | 61.875 | 6 | | | | | | | |
| High | 62.625 | | | | | | | | |
| Low | 61.5 | | | | | | | | |
| Volume | 199400 | 1 | | | | | | | |
| ADM-S | 25 | 2 | | | | | | | |

Record: 1

tblStockPrices : Table

| Symbol | Type | Field2 | Field3 | Field4 | Field5 | Field6 | Field7 | Field8 |
|---|---|---|---|---|---|---|---|---|
| AA-S | C | 68 | 73.75 | 71.75 | 74.5 | 76.625 | 76.625 | 77.75 |
| AA-S | H | 68.75 | 73.875 | 73.75 | 74.875 | 76.75 | 76.75 | 78.25 |
| AA-S | L | 68 | 67 | 71.25 | 72 | 74.375 | 74.375 | 75.625 |
| AA-S | V | 381900 | 270800 | 1E+06 | 723900 | 1E+06 | 1E+06 | 53100C |
| AAL-S | C | 18.5 | 18.25 | 18.75 | 19.125 | 19 | 19 | 18.75 |
| AAL-S | H | 19.25 | 18.5 | 18.875 | 19.25 | 19.125 | 19.125 | 19 |
| AAL-S | L | 18.5 | 18.125 | 18.5 | 18.875 | 18.875 | 18.875 | 18.625 |
| AAL-S | V | 59200 | 52800 | 84000 | 63400 | 16700 | 16700 | 2120C |
| AAQ-S | C | 55.5 | 56.5 | 58.75 | 60.5 | 59 | 59 | 56.75 |
| AAQ-S | H | 57.5 | 56.75 | 59.25 | 60.875 | 60.75 | 60.75 | 59 |

Record: 1 of 1220

**FIG. 21.28** Comparing the tblStockPrices table with the original version.

You can add stock price data for later dates by consecutively numbering the fields in successive Excel tables. As an example, the next 21 days of prices and trading volumes would use field names 23–44 for the numeric values. You could name the tables you create Close2, High2, Low2, and Volume2, and then add these tables to your queries to extend the range of dates to be included. Alternatively, you could create tables that have the high, low, close, and volume data for a given stock on a specific date. Making this type of transformation, however, requires that you write Access VBA code to restructure the tables.

> **Note**
>
> The structure of the tblStockPrices table does not conform to the rules of relational databases, although its structure is an improvement over the original Excel worksheet. Using individual fields for dates constitutes *repeating groups*, a violation of first normal form for relational tables. A fully normalized table would consist of a single record for the high, low, close, and volume data for a single stock on a single date. The composite primary key of such a table would be the stock ticker symbol and the date. Creating a fully normalized table from STK_21.xls requires the use of Automation and a substantial amount of Access VBA code.

### Using the Tables You Created

In this section, queries combine the data in the tables to create forms and reports that display the data in tabular or graph form. The relationships between the tables should be established automatically for the queries you create. In addition, you need to maintain referential integrity; that is, you shouldn't be able to delete a closing price for a stock for which you have high, low, and volume data. This obligation requires that you include relationships as properties of the tables.

◄◄ See "Establishing Relationships Between Tables," p. 146
◄◄ See "Enforcing Referential Integrity," p. 157

To establish the relationships between the tables, follow these steps:

1. Open the High table in Design view, select the Symbol field, and click the Primary Key button of the toolbar to make the Symbol field the primary key field. Repeat the process for the Low and Volume tables.

   Access 95 and 97 require a primary key to determine whether the relationship between tables is one-to-one or one-to-many. (Access 2.0 lets you specify the type of relationship.)

2. Make the Database window active, and then click the Relationships button of the toolbar or choose <u>T</u>ools, <u>R</u>elationships. The empty Relationships window opens with the Show Table dialog active.

3. Select the High table in the Tables list box, and click the Add button.

4. Repeat step 2 for the Low, Close, and Volume tables, and then click the Close button. Your Relationships window appears as shown in Figure 21.29.

5. Drag the Symbol field from the High table field list to the Symbol field of the Low table field list to create a join. Access opens the Relationships dialog.

6. Mark the Enforce Referential Integrity check box to enable cascading updates and deletions. Access automatically determines the relationship between each table as one-to-one by testing the joined fields.

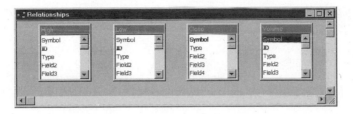

**FIG. 21.29** The Relationships window with the four tables added.

7. Mark the Cascade Update Related Fields check box. This action lets you change the Symbol value for a stock if its NYSE ticker symbol should change, an unlikely (but conceivable) event. If you change one Symbol value, the Symbol values for all of the related tables change in unison.

8. Mark the Cascade Delete Related Records check box. This action lets you remove all of the records for a stock that is delisted from the NYSE, a more likely event. Your Relationships dialog appears as shown in Figure 21.30.

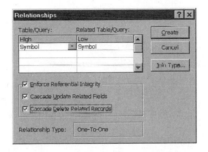

**FIG. 21.30** Setting referential integrity enforcement rules in the Relationships dialog.

9. Click the Create button to create the join and close the Relationships dialog.

10. Repeat steps 4 through 8 for the join between the Low and Close tables and the join between the Close and Volume tables. The Relationships window now appears as shown in Figure 21.31.

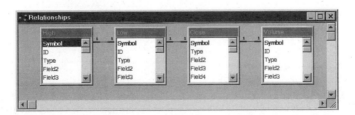

**FIG. 21.31** The Relationships window with one-to-one relationships between each table.

11. Close the Relationships window and save your changes.

> **Note**
>
> Always establish default relationships between the tables of your database so that these relation-ships are added automatically to the queries you create. If you don't establish default relationships and then Access doesn't create or you forget to add relationships to your query, you may obtain the Cartesian product (described earlier in this section) instead of the result you want. The Carte-sian product of large tables can be large and take several minutes to create. Pressing Ctrl+Break may not halt the process, and Windows may exhaust its resources in creating the Cartesian prod-uct, creating an out-of-memory error.

To create a test query that includes all of the data in your tables, follow these steps:

1. Select the High table in the Database window, click the arrow of the New Object button of the toolbar, and select New Query from the button menu to display the New Query dialog.

2. With Design View selected in the list, click OK to create a query with the High table added.

3. Click the Show Table button of the toolbar to add the Low, Close, and Volume tables. The joins between the tables are established automatically (by the relation-ships you established in the preceding series of steps) as you add each table, as shown by the lines connecting the Symbols fields in Figure 21.32. Click the Close button to close the Show Table dialog.

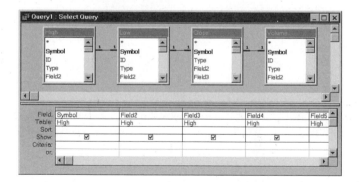

**FIG. 21.32**   Part of the query design for the 21-day stock prices query.

4. Double-click the header of the High table's field list to select all of the fields, and drag the multiple field column to the first column of the query.

5. Select and delete the Type and ID columns. Then use the horizontal scroll bar slider to display the first empty column after the 22 columns devoted to the High fields.

6. Repeat steps 4 and 5 for the Low, Close, and Volume tables, but also delete the Symbol field for these three tables.

**7.** Click the Run button of the toolbar to display the query. You can drag the columns of the query to reorder the columns in a logical sequence, as shown in Figure 21.33.

**8.** Choose View, S QL to display the SQL statement for the query (see Figure 21.34).

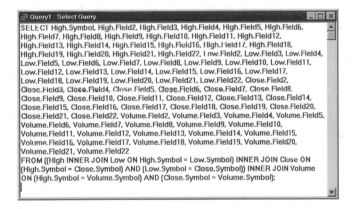

| Symbol | High.Field2 | Low.Field2 | Close.Field2 | Volume.Field2 | High.Field3 |
|--------|-------------|------------|--------------|---------------|-------------|
| AAL-S | 19.25 | 18.5 | 18.5 | 59200 | 18.5 |
| AAQ-S | 57.5 | 55 | 55.5 | 2447000 | 56.75 |
| AA-S | 68.75 | 68 | 68 | 381900 | 73.875 |
| ABT-S | 66.125 | 64.625 | 65.25 | 1328400 | 65.75 |
| ABY-S | 12.5 | 12.375 | 12.375 | 2900 | 12.375 |
| ACY-S | 62.625 | 61.5 | 61.875 | 199400 | 62.75 |
| ADM-S | 25.125 | 24.5 | 25 | 1819500 | 25.5 |
| AEP-S | 31.375 | 31 | 31.25 | 214300 | 31.25 |
| AET-S | 43.75 | 42.5 | 43.5 | 160700 | 44.5 |
| AGC-S | 42 | 41.75 | 41.875 | 66400 | 42 |
| AHC-S | 40.5 | 39.25 | 39.375 | 213300 | 40.125 |
| AHM-S | 16.625 | 16.125 | 16.375 | 266000 | 16.625 |
| AHP-S | 77.75 | 76.75 | 76.875 | 561800 | 77.75 |

**FIG. 21.33**  The query result set with the columns reordered.

```
SELECT High.Symbol, High.Field2, High.Field3, High.Field4, High.Field5, High.Field6,
High.Field7, High.Field8, High.Field9, High.Field10, High.Field11, High.Field12,
High.Field13, High.Field14, High.Field15, High.Field16, High.Field17, High.Field18,
High.Field19, High.Field20, High.Field21, High.Field22, Low.Field2, Low.Field3, Low.Field4,
Low.Field5, Low.Field6, Low.Field7, Low.Field8, Low.Field9, Low.Field10, Low.Field11,
Low.Field12, Low.Field13, Low.Field14, Low.Field15, Low.Field16, Low.Field17,
Low.Field18, Low.Field19, Low.Field20, Low.Field21, Low.Field22, Close.Field2,
Close.Field3, Close.Field4, Close.Field5, Close.Field6, Close.Field7, Close.Field8,
Close.Field9, Close.Field10, Close.Field11, Close.Field12, Close.Field13, Close.Field14,
Close.Field15, Close.Field16, Close.Field17, Close.Field18, Close.Field19, Close.Field20,
Close.Field21, Close.Field22, Volume.Field2, Volume.Field3, Volume.Field4, Volume.Field5,
Volume.Field6, Volume.Field7, Volume.Field8, Volume.Field9, Volume.Field10,
Volume.Field11, Volume.Field12, Volume.Field13, Volume.Field14, Volume.Field15,
Volume.Field16, Volume.Field17, Volume.Field18, Volume.Field19, Volume.Field20,
Volume.Field21, Volume.Field22
FROM ((High INNER JOIN Low ON High.Symbol = Low.Symbol) INNER JOIN Close ON
(High.Symbol = Close.Symbol) AND (Low.Symbol = Close.Symbol)) INNER JOIN Volume
ON (High.Symbol = Volume.Symbol) AND (Close.Symbol = Volume.Symbol);
```

**FIG. 21.34**  The SQL statement for the queries of Figures 21.32 and 21.33.

You can use queries of the preceding type to display or edit any data in the four tables by using a form, or these queries can be used to print part or all of the stock data with an Access report. You might design other queries that display only stocks which meet a specific criterion, such as minimum trading volume or a range of stock closing prices. The ability to rearrange data in almost any desired row and column sequence quickly, using simple queries, demonstrates that Access query datasheets are at least as flexible as worksheets.

V

Integrating Access

### Exporting Stock Data as a Worksheet

When you are collecting data on the same set of common stocks, you can simplify the conversion process by modifying the design of the Excel worksheet to correspond with the design of the tables. You can avoid making a large number of changes to the worksheet in Excel by exporting the Access tblStockPrices table back to Excel in Excel 97 format.

To export the Stock Data table to an .XLS workbook file, follow these steps:

1. Activate the Database window, and select the tblStockPrices table.

2. Click the arrow of the Office Links button of the toolbar, and choose Analyze It with Excel to export the table data and launch Excel with the tblStockPrices.xls worksheet active (see Figure 21.35).

| | A | B | C | D | E | F | G | H | I | J | K | L |
|---|---|---|---|---|---|---|---|---|---|---|---|---|
| 1 | Symbol | Type | Field2 | Field3 | Field4 | Field5 | Field6 | Field7 | Field8 | Field9 | Field10 | Field |
| 2 | AA-S | C | 68 | 73.75 | 71.75 | 74.5 | 76.625 | 76.625 | 77.75 | 76.25 | 75 | 7 |
| 3 | AA-S | H | 68.75 | 73.875 | 73.75 | 74.875 | 76.75 | 76.75 | 78.25 | 77.375 | 76.375 | 75.6 |
| 4 | AA-S | L | 68 | 67 | 71.25 | 72 | 74.375 | 74.375 | 75.625 | 75.5 | 75 | |
| 5 | AA-S | V | 381900 | 270800 | 1E+06 | 723900 | 1E+06 | 1E+06 | 531000 | 297500 | 219000 | 3973 |
| 6 | AAL-S | C | 18.5 | 18.25 | 18.75 | 19.125 | 19 | 19 | 18.75 | 19.125 | 19 | 18.8 |
| 7 | AAL-S | H | 19.25 | 18.5 | 18.875 | 19.25 | 19.125 | 19.125 | 19 | 19.125 | 19.125 | 19.1 |
| 8 | AAL-S | L | 18.5 | 18.125 | 18.5 | 18.875 | 18.875 | 18.875 | 18.625 | 18.75 | 19 | 18.8 |
| 9 | AAL-S | V | 59200 | 52800 | 84000 | 63400 | 16700 | 16700 | 21200 | 73400 | 44100 | 194 |
| 10 | AAQ-S | C | 55.5 | 56.5 | 58.75 | 60.5 | 59 | 59 | 56.75 | 56.25 | 57.625 | |
| 11 | AAQ-S | H | 57.5 | 56.75 | 59.25 | 60.875 | 60.75 | 60.75 | 59 | 57.25 | 58 | 58 |
| 12 | AAQ-S | L | 55 | 55.25 | 57.25 | 57.5 | 58.5 | 58.5 | 56 | 56.25 | | |
| 13 | AAQ-S | V | 2E+06 | 1E+06 | 1E+06 | 2E+06 | 2E+06 | 2E+06 | 2E+06 | 2E+06 | 2E+06 | 2E+ |
| 14 | ABT-S | C | 65.25 | 65.625 | 67.25 | 66.375 | 64.875 | 64.875 | 63.25 | 62.875 | 63.375 | 62.6 |
| 15 | ABT-S | H | 66.125 | 65.75 | 67.875 | 67.75 | 66 | 66 | 64.5 | 64 | 63.375 | 63.8 |
| 16 | ABT-S | L | 64.625 | 64.875 | 65.625 | 65.625 | 64.375 | 64.375 | 63 | 62 | 62.5 | 61.3 |
| 17 | ABT-S | V | 1E+06 | 561800 | 739900 | 898900 | 894700 | 894700 | 738300 | 907600 | 525300 | 9077 |
| 18 | ABY-S | C | 12.375 | 12.375 | 12.5 | 12.125 | 12.25 | 12.25 | 12.375 | 23.125 | 12.125 | 12. |

**FIG. 21.35**  The stock price data appears in the order of the table's primary-key fields.

3. Choose File, Save to save the sorted worksheet and then choose File, Exit to close Excel.

You can use the new worksheet as a template for the entry or import of stock price and trading volume data for other ranges of dates. Using the new format eliminates the necessity of creating temporary tables during the conversion process.

# Using Excel as an OLE Server

This section describes methods of creating links between data cells in OLE Object fields and worksheets created with Excel 97. You can duplicate some examples with Excel 3.0 and 4.0, but version 5 and later versions—with their OLE 2+ compatibility—have several added features that simplify the process. The step-by-step examples in this section are based on the assumption that you are familiar with the use of Excel 5+.

You can embed or link an Excel worksheet or graph as a bound or unbound OLE object. You can copy data from the OLE worksheet object to the Clipboard and then paste the data into a bound or unbound text box. The following sections provide examples of these techniques.

### Embedding an Excel Worksheet in a Form

You can embed an entire Excel worksheet in an unbound object frame using the simple process that follows. In this case, the presentation of an Excel worksheet (or what you can display of the worksheet in a bound object frame) is the entire content of the worksheet. Large embedded worksheets occupy considerable disk space and may require a substantial period of time to display their presentation; you may want to use a small worksheet (a file size of 5K or less, such as a workbook file created from the STK_21_3 worksheet) if you are short on disk space.

To embed an Excel worksheet in an unbound object frame of a new form, follow these steps:

1. Open the Stocks.mdb database, if necessary, and create a new blank form. Initially,  size the form to about 3.33 inches high by 6 inches wide.

2. Click the Toolbox button of the toolbar and select the unbound object frame tool. Create a frame with the left corner at about .5 inch from the form's left edge and about 0.3 inch from the top. (The dimensions of these margins are important; see the troubleshooting note at the end of this section.) The Insert Object dialog appears.

3. Click the Create from File option button, then click the Browse button to open the Browse Dialog and locate the folder containing the tblStockPrices.xls file. Select tblStockPrices.xls (or the name of any other Excel 5+ workbook file you want to embed) in the file list, and then click Open to close the Browse dialog. Then click OK to close the Insert Object dialog (see Figure 21.36).

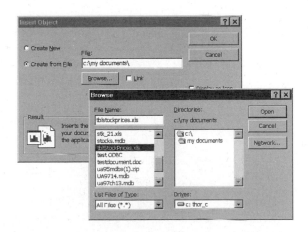

**FIG. 21.36**  Inserting an unbound object from an Excel 97 file.

---

**Troubleshooting**

A message box appears, indicating that the Excel worksheet is corrupted, that Excel is not properly registered, or that not enough available memory exists to open Excel.

Close other open applications and try again. If the procedure continues to display error messages, exit Windows and start over. (An application has failed to release its global memory blocks when closing.) If you continue to receive error messages that refer to the Registry, you need to verify that the Registry entries for Excel are correct. See Chapter 19, "Using 32-Bit OLE Components," for detailed instructions on the Registry entries required for local servers.

---

4. Select the unbound object frame and drag the right border to about 5.8 inches. Drag the bottom border to about 3.1 inches.

5. Click the Properties button of the toolbar. Click the Data tab and set the value of the Enabled property to Yes and the Locked property to No. If you don't enable and unlock the object frame, you can't activate the object (see Figure 21.37).

**FIG. 21.37**   Setting the Enabled and Locked properties of the object to allow in-place activation.

6. Click the Form View button of the toolbar to display the presentation of your worksheet (see Figure 21.38). If only part of a column displays, return to Design view and adjust the width of your object frame so that a full column is displayed with a 0.25-inch border at the right. You also may need to adjust the height of the form to provide a 0.25-inch border at the bottom. (The borders inside the object frame are necessary; see the following troubleshooting note.)

7. Double-click the object frame to activate the worksheet in place. If you have set the left and top positions of your object frame and provided the proper internal borders, your activated worksheet appears as shown in Figure 21.39. Excel 97's Edit and View menus replace Access's Edit and View menus, and Excel's Insert, Format, Tools, and Data menus are added to Access's menu. The toolbars that normally appear when you open Excel are added to Access 97's toolbars. Activated mode is indicated by a hashed border around the object frame.

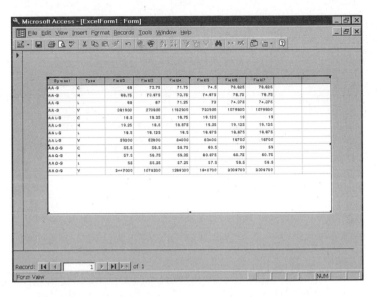

**FIG. 21.38**  The presentation of a worksheet in an unbound object frame.

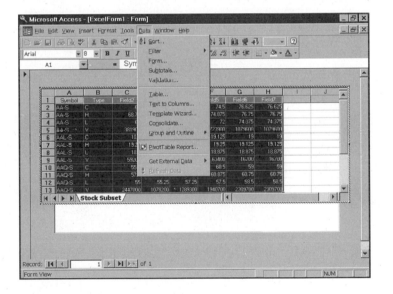

**FIG. 21.39**  The worksheet activated in place.

You can perform any operation that is possible in Excel 97 when the object is activated, except operations that require use of Excel's File menu—such as saving the workbook to a file or printing the worksheet.

8. Click outside the bound object frame to deactivate the object, and return to presentation mode so that Access's menubar is active.

9. Choose Edit, Worksheet Object, Open to open Excel 97's window with the embedded data as the source of Excel's current workbook (see Figure 21.40). When you open Excel, you can print the worksheet or save the embedded workbook to a file.

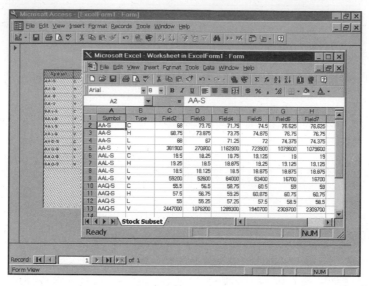

**FIG. 21.40**   Opening Excel 97 in its own window (from Presentation mode).

10. Choose File, Exit to close the instance of Excel and return to presentation mode.

11. Close your form and save the changes.

---

### Troubleshooting

Excel's column selection buttons, row selection buttons, worksheet tabs, horizontal scroll bar, or the vertical scroll bar don't appear when the object is activated.

Two sets of critical factors determine the visibility of *adornments*, as the preceding objects are called, when you activate an object in place. The top position of the object frame must provide room for the column selector buttons in the form area (0.25 inch), and the left position of the frame must provide space for the row selector buttons (0.5 inch). The visibility of the horizontal and vertical scroll bars is determined by the internal margin of the object, the space between the edge of the worksheet presentation, and the bottom and right edge of the object frame (0.25 inch each).

If, after setting these values, all of the adornments shown in Figure 21.39 do not appear, position the mouse pointer on the upper-left corner of the activation border and drag the corner diagonally downward to reduce the size of the activation frame. You may need to make repeated adjustments to the size of the object frame and the activation frame to ensure that all adornments appear.

Finally, you may need to set the Size Mode property of the unbound object frame to Zoom. If the embedded spreadsheet is very large, the default Clip property may cause the adornments at the right and bottom edges of the activated workbook object to be clipped off.

---

### Extracting Values from an OLE Object

You can copy individual numeric or text values from a linked or embedded Excel OLE object and place the values in a text box. To add the close, high, and low values of the AAL-S stock to a multiline text box added to the form you created in the preceding section, follow these steps:

1. In Design view, reduce the size of your unbound object frame containing the Excel worksheet object, and move the frame down to make room for a multiline text box at the top of the form.

2. Add a text box to the form, and set the value of the Scrollbars property to Vertical.

3. In Form view, double-click the unbound object frame to activate the workbook object.

> **Note**
>
> You must copy and paste the selected values while the form is in Form view; otherwise, the pasted text becomes the text box's Control Source property, resulting in the display of the #Name? error when you display the form in Form view.

4. Select the cell or range of cells you want to import to a text control object. In this case, select A2:H5 to return seven days of price data for the AA-S stock.

5. Choose Edit, Copy, or press Ctrl+C to copy the A2:H5 range to the Clipboard.

6. Select the text box, which deactivates the object frame, and then choose Edit, Paste Special to display the Paste Special dialog. When you paste data items from an embedded object into a text box, you only have the option of pasting them as text (see Figure 21.41). Click OK to paste the text into the text box.

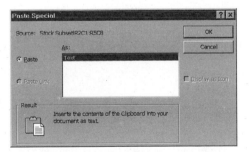

**FIG. 21.41** Pasting a selection from an embedded Excel worksheet as text.

7. The pasted data items appear as shown in Figure 21.42. The vertical bars between the values in the text box represent the tab characters that Excel uses to separate data columns in a row.

If you create one or more bound text boxes with a numeric data type, you can paste a number from a selected single cell to each text box and then use the values to update the fields of the table to which the text box is bound. A more efficient method, however, is to use Automation to update values in tables with data from another application.

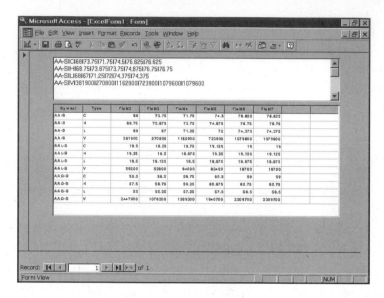

**FIG. 21.42** A selection from an embedded Excel worksheet pasted into an unbound text box.

### Linking to a Range of Cells in an Excel Worksheet

Embedding Excel objects is useful if you want to use Automation to transfer data from a Recordset object to embedded worksheet cells. In most cases, however, creating an OLE link to all or a range of cells in a worksheet is a more common practice. Linking allows you to display or edit the most recent version of the worksheet's data from its source file. Any changes you make in Access are reflected when you close Excel if you save the changes.

▶▶ See "Manipulating an Excel 97 Workbook Object," p. 1102

The conventional process of linking a file in Excel is similar to that for using OLE 1.0 to link graphics files; in-place activation is not available with linked objects. To create a link with a range of cells in an Excel file, perform the following steps:

1. Open a new, blank Access form.

2. Launch Excel independently of Access.

**3.** Choose File, Open, and in Excel's Open dialog select the file you want to link. This example uses tblStockPrices.xls.

**4.** Select the cells of the worksheet to be included in your Access table, and then copy the selected cells to the Clipboard with Ctrl+C. Cell range A1:E17 of the tblStockPrices.xls worksheet is used in this example.

**5.** In Access, choose Edit, Paste Special to display the Paste Special dialog. Click the Paste Link option button. Your only choices for a linked object are the object or text contained in the selected data items. The data source, tblStockPrices!R1C1:R17C5, appears in the Source label (see Figure 21.43).

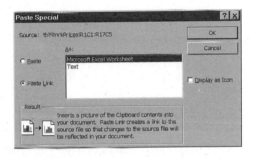

**FIG. 21.43**  The Paste Special dialog for a linked range of cells in an Excel worksheet.

**6.** Click OK to create the unbound object frame containing the presentation of the selected cells. You don't need to provide for margins in the design because in-place activation is not available with linked objects.

**7.** Open the Properties window and set the value of the Enabled property of the object frame to Yes and the Locked property of the frame to No.

**8.** Click the Form View button of the toolbar. The presentation of your linked object appears, as shown in Figure 21.44.

**9.** Double-click the presentation of the worksheet to launch Excel in its own window with the linked cells selected (see Figure 21.45). As noted earlier in this section, in-place activation does not apply to linked objects.

**10.** In Excel, choose File, Exit to return the focus to Access. If you have made changes to the data, you can elect to save the changes at this point.

V

Integrating Access

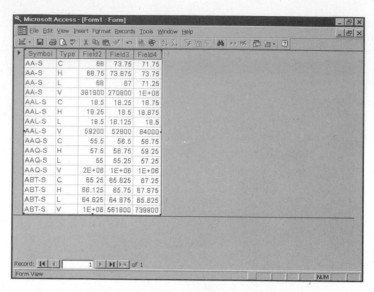

**FIG. 21.44**    The presentation of a linked range of worksheet cells.

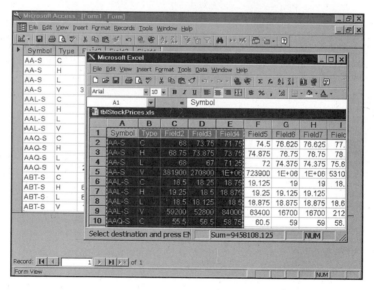

**FIG. 21.45**    The instance of Excel launched by double-clicking the linked cells' presentation.

# Chapter 22

# Using Access with Microsoft Word and Mail Merge

Members of the Microsoft Office 97 software suite are specifically designed to make constructing cooperative applications easy. *Cooperative applications* use two or more Windows productivity applications to perform a specified task. One of the principle uses for database applications is creating mailing lists for use in conjunction with form letters. Thus, Access 97—a member of the Professional Edition of Microsoft Office 97—includes a Mail Merge Wizard that not only automates the process of creating Word 97 Merge data files but also helps you create new form letters.

You also can use the reverse process and create form letters using Word 97's new mail merge process. Creating form letters from Word 97 accommodates users who do not have retail Access 97 on their computers. Word 97 uses 32-bit Microsoft Query (Msqry32.exe) and the new 32-bit Open Database Connectivity (ODBC) application programming interface (API) version 2.5 to connect to Access 97 and earlier .mdb files, as well as to a variety of other desktop database types.

As with Excel worksheets, you can embed or link Word documents in bound or unbound object frames and add a complete word-processing system to your Access application. If you embed the Word document in the object frame, you can take advantage of OLE 2.1's in-place activation to make the operating environment of Access almost identical to that of Word. Word's menu supplements the Access menu, and Word's toolbars appear as docked or floating toolbars on your display. Word's document editing window, in Page view, appears within the confines of your object frame.

## Using the Access Mail Merge Wizard

Access 97's Mail Merge Wizard can help you create a new main merge document or employ an existing main merge document from which to create form letters. The Mail Merge Wizard uses a table or a query as the data source for the merge data file. The sections that follow describe the following two methods of creating a form letter:

■ Using the Mail Merge Wizard to create a new main merge document whose merge data source is an Access table

■ Using an existing main merge document with a merge data source from an Access select query

### Creating and Previewing a New Form Letter

When you first try a new wizard, it's customary to create a new object rather than use the wizard to modify an existing object, such as a main merge document. The following steps use the Mail Merge Wizard to create a new main merge document from records in the Customers table of Northwind.mdb.

> **Note**
>
> Using the Mail Merge Wizard consumes an extraordinary amount of Windows resources because Word and two instances of Access run simultaneously. If you have less than 16M of RAM, close all running applications except Word and Access before starting the following process.

**1.** Open Northwind.mdb, if necessary, and select the Customers table in the Database window.

**2.** Click the arrow of the Office Links button of the toolbar, and select Merge-It from the drop-down menu to launch the Microsoft Mail Merge Wizard. The wizard's first and only dialog appears as shown in Figure 22.1.

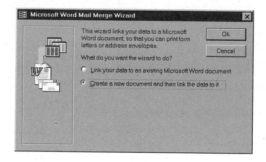

**FIG. 22.1**  The sole dialog of the Microsoft Word Mail Merge Wizard.

**3.** Select the Create a New Document and Then Link the Data To It option to create a new main merge document using fields from the Customers table.

**4.** Click OK to launch Word 97 if it is not running, and open a new mail merge main document. The Mail Merge Wizard uses dynamic data exchange (DDE) to communicate with Word and opens a new instance of Access 97.

**5.** Click the Insert Merge Field button to verify the fields from the Customers table in the drop-down list, as shown in Figure 22.2.

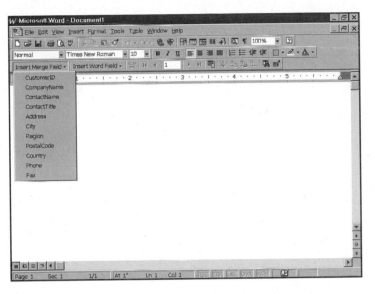

**FIG. 22.2**  Displaying the available merge fields in Word 97's Mail Merge window.

**6.** With the caret at the top of the document, choose <u>I</u>nsert, Date and <u>T</u>ime to display the Date and Time dialog; choose any date format you want, and then click OK to add a date field to the main document.

> ### Tip
>
> In Word 97, click the Show/Hide button on Word's toolbar to display end-of-paragraph marks, space characters, tab characters, and other document symbols that are usually hidden. All of the figures of Word 97 in this chapter were taken with the Show/Hide button in its down position.

**7.** Add a blank line, click the Insert Merge Field button to display the drop-down list, and insert the fields from the Customers table to create the address section of the main document (see Figure 22.3).

> ### Note
>
> Spaces and other punctuation in merge data field names are not permitted by Word. The Mail Merge Wizard substitutes underscores (_) for spaces and other illegal characters in Access field names, when present.

**8.** Click the View Merged Data button of the Mail Merge toolbar to preview the appearance of your form letter.

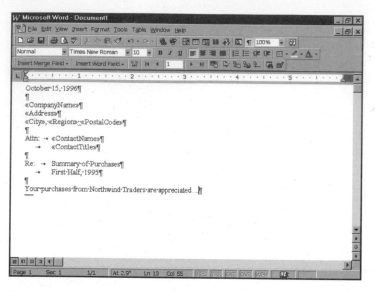

**FIG. 22.3**  Adding the merge fields to the main merge document.

9. The form letters go only to customers in the United States, so repeatedly click the Next Record button of the Mail Merge toolbar to find the first U.S. record. Alternatively, type **32** in the text box of the toolbar. The preview of the form letter for Great Lakes Food Market appears as shown in Figure 22.4.

10. You want to send letters to U.S. customers, so you need to create a query that returns only records whose Country column has the value "USA." Close Word, and save your main merge document with an appropriate file name, such as **PurchaseSummary1995H1.doc**. This file is used in the next section, as well as later in the chapter when you open the Access data source from Word.

**Note**

The Mail Merge Wizard uses DDE to communicate with Word, so you cannot use Word 97's query features to select and sort the merge data. If you attempt to do so, you break the DDE link between Word and Access. Thus, you need to base your final mail merge document on an Access query if you want to select or sort your records.

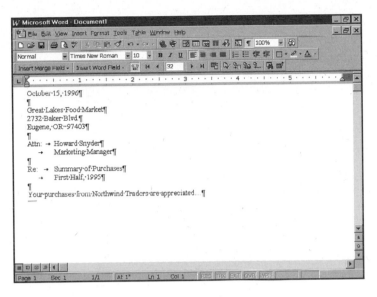

**FIG. 22.4**  Displaying a preview of a form letter to a U.S. customer.

### Using an Existing Main Merge Document with a New Data Source

Once you've created a standard main merge document, the most common practice is to use differing data sources to create form letters by addressee category. Take the following steps to use the main mail merge document you created in the preceding section, PurchaseSummary1995H1.doc, with a new data source based on a simple Access query:

1. Open a new query, and add the Customers table.

2. Add the CompanyName, ContactName, ContactTitle, Address, City, Region, PostalCode, and Country fields to the query.

3. Enter **USA** as the criterion for the Country field, and clear the Show check box to prevent Country from appearing in the query. Add an ascending sort to the PostalCode field. Your query design appears as shown in Figure 22.5.

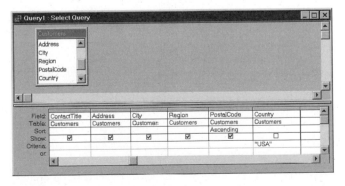

**FIG. 22.5**  The query design for the U.S. customers mailing list.

**4.** Click the Run button of the toolbar to verify the query result set (see Figure 22.6). Choose File, Save or Save As, and save the query with an appropriate name, such as **qryPurchaseSummaryUSA**.

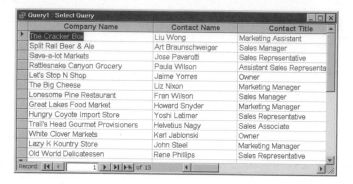

| Company Name | Contact Name | Contact Title |
|---|---|---|
| The Cracker Box | Liu Wong | Marketing Assistant |
| Split Rail Beer & Ale | Art Braunschweiger | Sales Manager |
| Save-a-lot Markets | Jose Pavarotti | Sales Representative |
| Rattlesnake Canyon Grocery | Paula Wilson | Assistant Sales Representa |
| Let's Stop N Shop | Jaime Yorres | Owner |
| The Big Cheese | Liz Nixon | Marketing Manager |
| Lonesome Pine Restaurant | Fran Wilson | Sales Manager |
| Great Lakes Food Market | Howard Snyder | Marketing Manager |
| Hungry Coyote Import Store | Yoshi Latimer | Sales Representative |
| Trail's Head Gourmet Provisioners | Helvetius Nagy | Sales Associate |
| White Clover Markets | Karl Jablonski | Owner |
| Lazy K Kountry Store | John Steel | Marketing Manager |
| Old World Delicatessen | Rene Phillips | Sales Representative |

**FIG. 22.6**  The query result set for U.S.-based customers.

**5.** With the query open, choose Tools, Office Links, Merge It with MS Word to launch the Mail Merge Wizard. With the Link Your Data to an Existing Microsoft Word Document option button marked (the default), click OK to display the Select Microsoft Word Document dialog (see Figure 22.7).

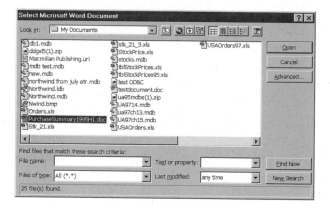

**FIG. 22.7**  Selecting the main merge document.

**6.** Select your main merge document in the file list and click Open. A message box, shown in Figure 22.8, appears when you change the data source for a merge document. Click Yes to change to the new data source.

**7.** Confirm that your query is the new merge data source by clicking the Insert Merge Field button and checking the field list. (The Country field shouldn't appear.)

Alternatively, you can click the Edit Data Source button of Word's Mail Merge toolbar to display the query in Access, as shown in Figure 22.9. (Click the Minimize button of Access's Query window, and then click the Word document to return the focus to Word.)

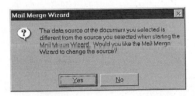

**FIG. 22.8**   The message box that appears when you change the merge data source.

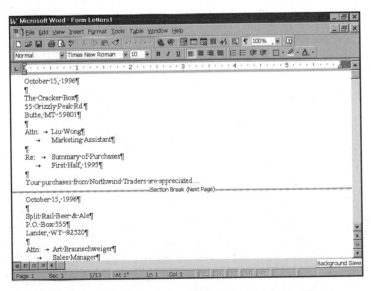

**FIG. 22.9**   Displaying the query result set from Word.

8. You can merge the main document and data source directly to the printer or create a series of form letters in a new document. The latter choice lets you inspect the letters before you print them. Click the Merge To New Document button to create the new form letter. The top of the first form letter appears—in ZIP code sequence—as shown in Figure 22.10.

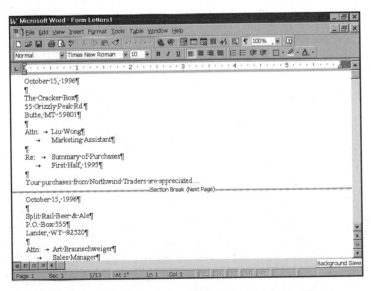

**FIG. 22.10**   The final version of the form letter addressed to U.S. customers.

If you close Word at this point, make sure you save your changes to
PurchaseSummary1995H1.doc. This file is used as the main merge document
in the sections that follow.

# Using Word 97's Mail Merge Feature with Access Databases

In many cases, Access 97 isn't available to Word users who need to create form letters
from data contained in Access .mdb files. Office 97 includes Microsoft Query and the
necessary 32-bit ODBC drivers to connect to Access .mdb files (all versions) and
Microsoft SQL Server databases, plus dBASE, FoxPro, and Paradox 3+ table files. (ODBC
drivers for Excel worksheets and text files also are included.) Microsoft Query is modeled
on Access's query design window, but Microsoft Query displays the query result set automatically in a separate pane below the design pane as you construct the query. Office 97
applications launch and control Microsoft Query with DDE.

 ▶▶ See "Understanding ODBC Drivers," p. 918

> **Note**
>
> You need Microsoft Office 97 installed on your PC to create the examples in this section. Access 97
> and Jet 3.5 require the 32-bit ODBC 3.0 drivers. Office 97 includes the 32-bit ODBC driver for
> Access 97 databases. The prior 16-bit Access drivers do not support 32-bit Access 97 .mdb files.

Word 97 includes the Mail Merge Helper, which is similar in concept to an Access wizard. The following three sections use the Mail Merge Helper to create a new Microsoft
Query (MSQuery) data source and to use an existing MSQuery data source.

### Creating a New Mail Merge Data Source with Microsoft Query and an ODBC Data Source

To use Microsoft Query (MSQuery) to create a merge data source from a Microsoft Access
database, follow these steps:

1. Launch Word 97, if necessary, and open the PurchaseSummary1995H1.doc main
   merge document you created earlier in this chapter in the section "Creating and
   Previewing a New Form Letter."

> **Note**
>
> ODBC and Microsoft Query must be installed on your computer system before you can use
> the procedures described in this and the following sections of this chapter. If ODBC and
> MSQuery are not installed on your computer, rerun the Microsoft Office 97 Setup program
> and add these items to your system configuration.

2. Click the Mail Merge Helper button of the mail merge toolbar to open the Mail Merge Helper dialog (see Figure 22.11). The entry in the Data label of the Data Source section is Northwind.mdb!Query qryPurchaseSummaryUSA. This syntax is used for specifying the topic of a DDE conversation when you use Access as a DDE server.

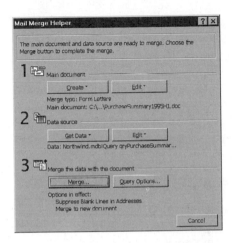

**FIG. 22.11** The Mail Merge Helper dialog with an Access DDE merge data source specified.

3. Click the Get Data button, and select Create Data Source from the drop-down list to open the Create Data Source dialog. Word includes a set of default field names you can use to create merge data files (see Figure 22.12).

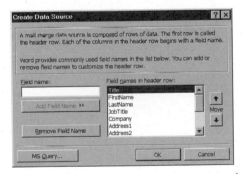

**FIG. 22.12** Word 97's Create Data Source dialog.

4. This example uses MSQuery to create the data source, so click the MS Query button to launch MSQuery. MSQuery opens with the Choose Data Source dialog active (see Figure 22.13).

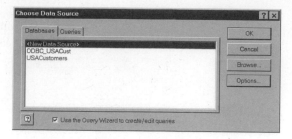

**FIG. 22.13** MSQuery's Choose Data Source dialog.

5. Click the Databases tab to bring the Databases list to the front of the dialog (if necessary); select <New Data Source> in the Databases list, and then click OK. MSQuery displays the Create New Data Source dialog (see Figure 22.14).

The Create New Data Source dialog contains four numbered controls: a text box, a drop-down list, a command button, and another drop-down list. When MSQuery first displays the Create New Data Source dialog, only the first text box is enabled. Each successive control is enabled as you complete each item. Figure 22.14 shows the Create New Data Source dialog after filling in all options for this data source. Each numbered control corresponds to an item of information that you must supply for MSQuery to create the data source: the data source's name, the driver for the data source, connection information for connecting to the data source, and an optional default table for the data source.

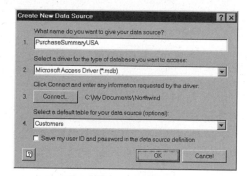

**FIG. 22.14** MSQuery's Create New Data Source dialog.

6. In the first text box, type **PurchaseSummaryUSA** as the name of the new data source. As you enter the data source name, MSQuery enables the drop-down list below it.

7. In the drop-down list (item 2 in the Create New Data Source dialog), select Microsoft Access Driver (*.mdb) as the driver for this data source.

8. Click the Connect command button to display the ODBC Microsoft Access 97 Setup dialog (see Figure 22.15). Click the Select button in the Database frame to display the Select Database dialog.

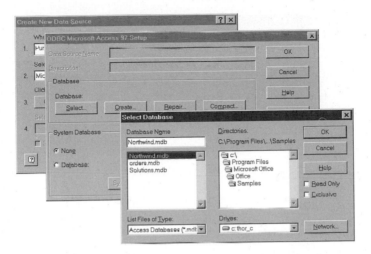

**FIG. 22.15**  Choosing the Connection for a new MSQuery data source.

9.  Maneuver to the folder containing Northwind.mdb (usually C:\Program Files\
    Microsoft Office\Office\Samples) and select Northwind.mdb in the Database
    Name list (see Figure 22.15). Click OK to close the Select Database dialog.

10. If you have secured Access or Northwind.mdb, click the Database option button in
    the System Database frame, and then click the System Database button to open the
    System Database dialog. Select the System Database you're using, and then click OK
    to close the dialog. Click the Advanced button to open the Advanced dialog, and
    enter your login name and password in the text boxes. Then click OK to close the
    Advanced dialog.

11. Click OK to close the ODBC Microsoft Access 97 Setup dialog. The Create New Data
    Source dialog now displays the connected database's folder path and file name (or
    as much of it as will fit) next to the Connect button.

12. Optionally, you can select a table or query from the connected database as the
    default table for queries created from this data source. In the final drop-down list
    (numbered 4 in the Create New Data Source dialog), select Customers (refer to
    Figure 22.14).

13. Click OK to close the Create New Data Source dialog. MSQuery adds the newly
    created data source to the Databases list in the Choose Data Source dialog.

14. Select PurchaseSummaryUSA in the Databases list of the Choose Data Source dialog
    and click OK. MSQuery automatically starts its Query Wizard; the first dialog of the
    Query Wizard is shown in Figure 22.16.

    The Choose Columns dialog of the Query Wizard displays an expandable tree list
    of all tables and queries in the connected database, with the default table or query's
    branch selected and expanded for you as shown in Figure 22.16.

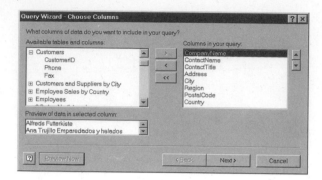

**FIG. 22.16**   MSQuery's Query Wizard dialog, in which you select the columns for the new query.

**15.** Select the CompanyName field in the Available Tables and Columns list, and then click the > button to copy the CompanyName field to the Columns in your query list. If you want, you may preview the data in any field by selecting that field in either list and clicking the Preview Now button.

**16.** Repeat step 15 to add the ContactName, ContactTitle, Address, City, Region, PostalCode, and Country fields to the Columns in your query list (see Figure 22.16). The specific order of the columns is unimportant. Click Next to continue with the second Query Wizard dialog.

**17.** In the second step of the Query Wizard, you enter criteria to restrict the data retrieved by MSQuery. Select the Country field in the Column To Filter list, then select **equals** in the first drop-down list in the Only Include Rows Where frame, and select **USA** in the second drop-down list (see Figure 22.17). Click Next to continue with the third Query Wizard dialog.

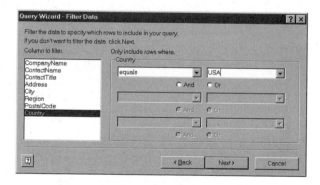

**FIG. 22.17**   The Filter Data dialog of MSQuery's Query Wizard.

**18.** In the Query Wizard's Sort Order dialog, you select how you want the retrieved data to be sorted. Select **PostalCode** in the first drop-down list; MSQuery automatically selects the Ascending option button (see Figure 22.18). Click Next to display the final Query Wizard dialog.

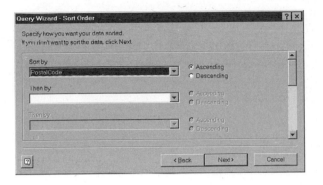

**FIG. 22.18**   The Sort Order dialog of MSQuery's Query Wizard.

**19.** Select the View Data or Edit Query in Microsoft Query option, and then click Finish to complete the query (see Figure 22.19). Although you can immediately return data to Word or click the Save Query button to save your query, you should usually take a look at the finished query to make sure that it produces the results you desire.

The completed query is shown in Figure 22.20; notice that the MSQuery query design grid is highly similar to the query design grid in Access, except that the query's results are shown in a table underneath the criteria rows. Use the scroll bars to view the data returned by the query. You can add or edit criteria in MSQuery much the same way you add or edit selection criteria in an Access query. MSQuery, however, uses single quotation marks (') for literal strings (as shown in Figure 22.20) instead of the double quotation marks (") used by Access. Also, MSQuery handles sorting differently than Access—there is no Sort row in the query design grid. Instead, you sort rows by selecting a column in the query's result and then clicking one of the sort order buttons on the toolbar. Essentially, the process is the same as sorting a table's view in Access.

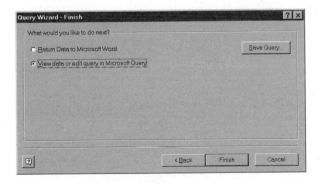

**FIG. 22.19**   The final dialog of the MSQuery Query Wizard.

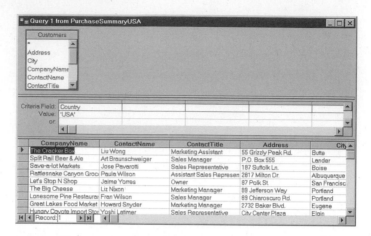

**FIG. 22.20**  The completed query in MSQuery.

20. Choose File, Save to open the Save dialog. Assign your query a name, such as **PurchaseSummary.dqy**, and click Save. By default, queries are saved in the \Program Files\Microsoft Office\Queries folder. You use the saved query in the section that follows, "Creating Form Letters from an Existing Query."

21. Choose File, Return Data to Microsoft Word to close MSQuery and return to the Mail Merge Helper. The entry in the Data label of the Data Source section is now C:\Program Files\Microsoft Office\Office\Samples\Northwind.mdb. Click the Merge button of Mail Merge Helper to open the Merge dialog.

22. Accept the default New Document selection in the Merge To drop-down list. Click the Check Errors button of the Merge dialog to display the Checking and Reporting Errors dialog. Click the Complete the Merge, Pausing to Report Each Error As It Occurs option button (see Figure 22.21).

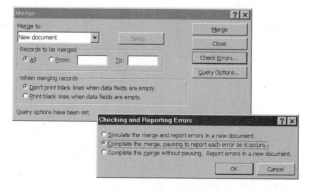

**FIG. 22.21**  The Merge dialog and the Checking and Reporting Errors dialog.

**23.** Click OK to close the Checking and Reporting Errors dialog, and click Merge to perform the merge. Word finishes merging the documents and displays the final form letter. After reviewing the form letters, close the form letter document; you don't need to save changes.

### Creating Form Letters from an Existing Query

Once you've created and saved a query with MSQuery, you can use the saved query to create another set of form letters. MSQuery's saved queries are similar to Access queries saved as QueryDef objects in .mdb files. To use an existing .dqy file as the data source for a merge document, follow these steps:

---

**Note**

Versions of MSQuery prior to Office 97 saved queries in files with the .qry file extension. MSQuery in Office 97 uses the .dqy file extension, instead.

---

**1.** In Word 97, click the Mail Merge Helper button to display the dialog.

**2.** Click the Get Data button, and select Open Data Source from the drop-down list to display the Open Data Source dialog.

**3.** Choose the MS Query Files (*.dqy) item in the Files of Type drop-down list.

**4.** Select the PurchaseSummary.dqy file you saved in the preceding section, and click Open (see Figure 22.22). The message box shown in Figure 22.23 appears.

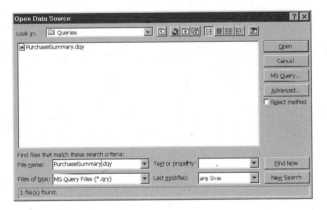

**FIG. 22.22**  Choosing an existing MSQuery .dqy file in the Open Data Source dialog.

**5.** To make PurchaseSummary.dqy the permanent source of data for the PurchaseSummary1995H1.doc main merge document, click the Yes button of the message box to return to the Mail Merge Helper dialog. The path to and the name of your query file appear in the Data label of the Data Source section.

**FIG. 22.23**  Making the .dqy file the permanent source of data for the main merge document.

# Embedding or Linking Word Documents in Access Tables

Many word-processing documents are a collection of individual paragraphs, each of which can change depending on the purpose of the document. If the document is a contract, many of the paragraphs are likely to be *boilerplate*: standard paragraphs that are added based on the jurisdiction and purpose of the contract and relationship between the parties. Similarly, books are collections of chapters; when an author is writing a book, each chapter may go through several editing stages. Keeping track of boilerplate files and maintaining collections of book chapter files in various editing stages can be a daunting project. Even if you establish a workable DOS filenaming convention, you can easily lose track of the relationship between the file name and the content of the file.

Applications that track documents and maintain revision records for documents fall into the category of *document management systems*. Document management systems differ from image management systems; the latter systems handle static bitmapped images (usually created by scanners) rather than dynamic document content (editable data). With its OLE 2.1 capability, Access 97 is a logical candidate for the creation of document management applications.

You can create a simple document management system by designing a table with one or more fields of the OLE Object data type to contain embedded documents or links to individual document files. You need a minimum of two other fields: one to identify the source file name of the document and the other to provide a document description. Additional fields can be added to indicate document ownership, track document status, hold key terms, and control who can modify the document. Figure 22.24 shows the design of a simple table that is devised to store the manuscript of this edition in the form of individual chapters in an OLE Object field.

After you define the fields for your document table, you need to determine whether you want to embed the document's data in the table or link the documents to their source files. Make your choice based on the following criteria:

- Embedding the document lets you use in-place activation to review the document within Access. In-place activation is a less-intrusive process.

- Activating a linked document launches Word 97 in its own window.

- Embedding the document provides an independent copy of the document that can serve as an archive. You can set the value of the Locked property of the object to Yes to allow the object to be activated but not altered.

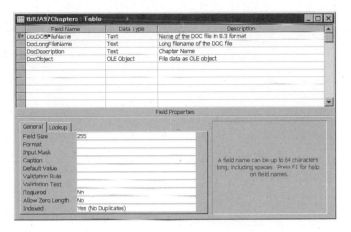

**FIG. 22.24**  The design of the table for a simple document management system.

- Linking the document allows you to view changes to the document as they occur.

- Linking requires that the document remain in the same location. In most cases, moving the document to another drive or directory breaks the link.

- You cannot save an embedded Word 97 or Excel 97 document to a file or print the embedded document using File menu choices in the in-place activated mode. The File menus of these applications do not replace the File menu of Access 97 when the embedded objects are activated. However, you can open Word's window to make the Word File menu accessible.

---

**Note**

You can use Automation instructions in Access VBA modules to save an embedded Word 97 document to a file or to print the document. The Object property of the object frame lets you manipulate embedded or linked objects with Access VBA code. Chapter 31, "Exchanging Data with Automation and ActiveX Controls," describes how to apply Automation methods to Word documents.

---

### Embedding or Linking a Word 97 Document in a Table

To embed or link a Word 97 document in an OLE Object field of a table with a design similar to that shown in Figure 22.24, follow these steps:

**1.** Place the caret in the OLE Object field, and choose Insert, Object to display the Insert Object dialog (see Figure 22.25).

**2.** You can create an empty Word document by accepting the default, Create New, and then clicking OK. To link or embed an existing document, click the Create from File option; the Object Type list changes to the File text box. (You don't need to select Microsoft Word Document when you insert an object from a file.)

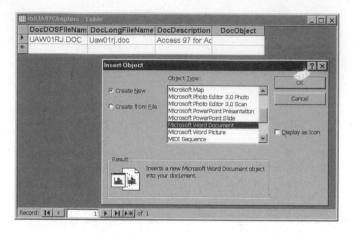

**FIG. 22.25**    The Insert Object dialog.

3. You can type the path and file name in the File text box or click the Browse button to display the Browse dialog (see Figure 22.26). Select the file you want to use in the File Name list, and then click Open to close the Browse dialog and return to the Insert Object dialog.

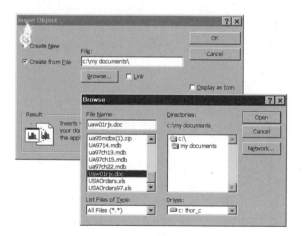

**FIG. 22.26**    Selecting a source document file in the Browse dialog.

4. The file you selected in the preceding step appears in the File text box. At this point, you can choose between linking and embedding the file. The example that follows uses embedded objects to demonstrate in-place activation (see Figure 22.27). If you want to link the file, mark the Link text box. Click OK.

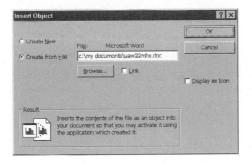

**FIG. 22.27**   Embedding a Word 97 document object from a file.

5. Position the record selector of the table to a different record to save the embedded object or the link to the object's file in your table, together with its OLE presentation.

Repeat the preceding steps for each document you want to add to the table. You can activate the document object in Word 97's window by double-clicking the OLE Object cell. Viewing the documents you insert in the file lets you verify that their contents correspond to their description.

## Troubleshooting

*The Microsoft Word 97 Document entry does not appear in the Insert Object dialog's Object Type list, or attempting to insert a Word 97 document results in a message box stating that the registration database entry is invalid or corrupted.*

The Registry entries for Word 97 are missing or invalid. If the Word 97 entry is missing, Word's Setup program probably did not complete its operation. (The last step of Setup adds entries to the Registry.) If the "corrupted" message appears, it is likely that you moved the Word files from the original directory in which Setup installed the files into a different directory. In either case, you need to use the Registry Editor (RegEdit.exe) to correct the problem. See the instructions for using the Registry editor in Chapter 19, "Using 32-Bit OLE Components."

### Creating a Form to Display the Document
If your table contains only a few fields, you can use the AutoForm feature to create a simple form to display and edit your linked or embedded object. To create the document display form, follow these steps:

1. With the table containing your Word objects, open with the focus in Datasheet view, click the arrow of the New Object button of the toolbar and select AutoForm from the drop-down menu. The Form Wizard automatically creates a standard form.

New Object: AutoForm

V

Integrating Access

**2.** Click the Design View button of the toolbar, and then relocate and resize the controls as necessary. Your bound object frame should occupy most of the display area. To view the entire document in its original format, set the Height property of the object frame to 11 inches and the Width property to 8.5 inches.

**3.** Return to Form view to display the presentation of the document. Figure 22.28 shows the presentation of the initial version of the manuscript for this chapter of the book. The size of the bound object frame of Figure 22.28 is about 8.5×11 inches.

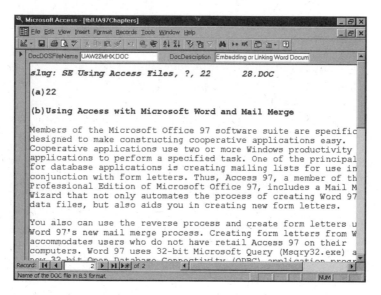

**FIG. 22.28**  The presentation of a Word 97 document in a bound object frame.

**4.** Double-click the surface of the object frame to activate the object. Activating the object launches Word 97 if it is not running. If you embedded the document, activation adds Word's toolbars to the display as docked toolbars. Word's menu choices take over Access's Edit and View menus, and Word adds its Insert, Format, Tools, and Table menus to the menubar (see Figure 22.29).

You can move through the document with the Page Up and Page Down keys. All editing features of Word 97 are available when the document object is activated, but you can only view the document in Page Layout view. You may use the scroll bar of the Access form to view parts of the page that are not visible on your display. (Using 800×600-pixel or higher resolution solves the partial display problem.)

**5.** Click the surface of the form, outside of the bound object frame area, to deactivate the object and return to Presentation view of the document.

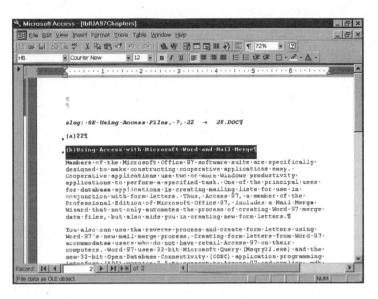

**FIG. 22.29**  An embedded Word 97 document activated in a bound object frame.

> **Tip**
>
> You can also click the record selection bar at the left edge of the form to deactivate the object and return to Presentation view.

6. To save the document to a file, to alter the page layout, or to print an embedded document, choose Edit, Document Object, and select Open. Microsoft Word opens a separate window in which to edit the embedded document, and you can access the File menu of Word to save changes, as shown in Figure 22.30.

7. Choose File, Close and Return to *FormName* to close Word's window and return to Access.

> **Note**
>
> The only available view of a Word document when the object is embedded is Page Layout view. You can change the layout of the embedded document by opening the document in Word (see the preceding step 8), choosing File, Page Setup, and then making the required adjustments.

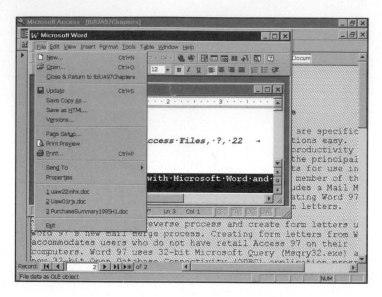

**FIG. 22.30**   Opening the embedded document in Word 97's window.

You also can insert additional document objects directly into the form. To embed or link an object in Form view, position the record pointer on the blank (tentative append) record. An empty presentation appears in the bound object frame. Choose Insert, Object, and follow steps 2 through 5 of the preceding section to embed or link additional document objects.

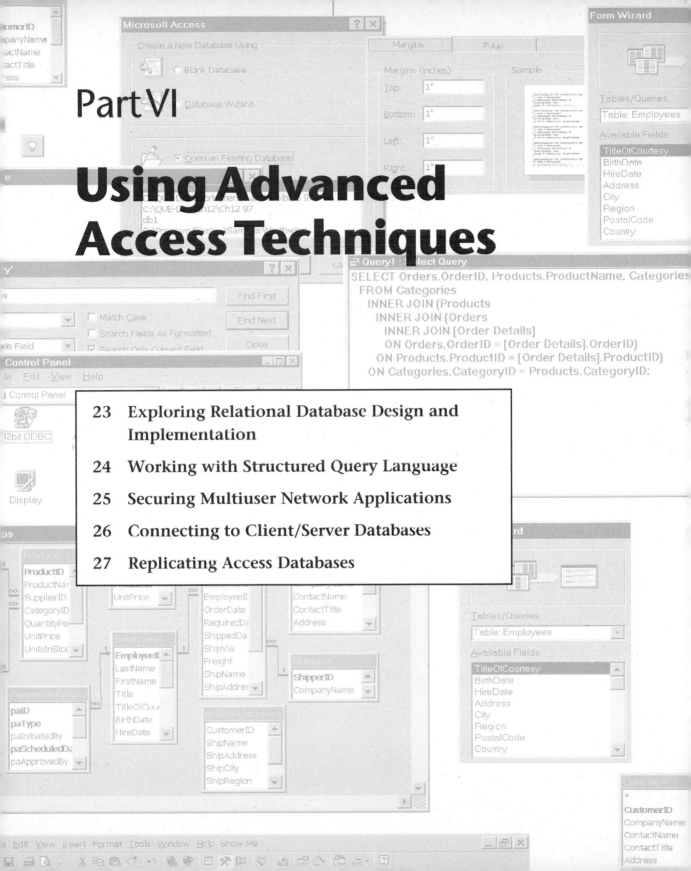

# Part VI

# Using Advanced Access Techniques

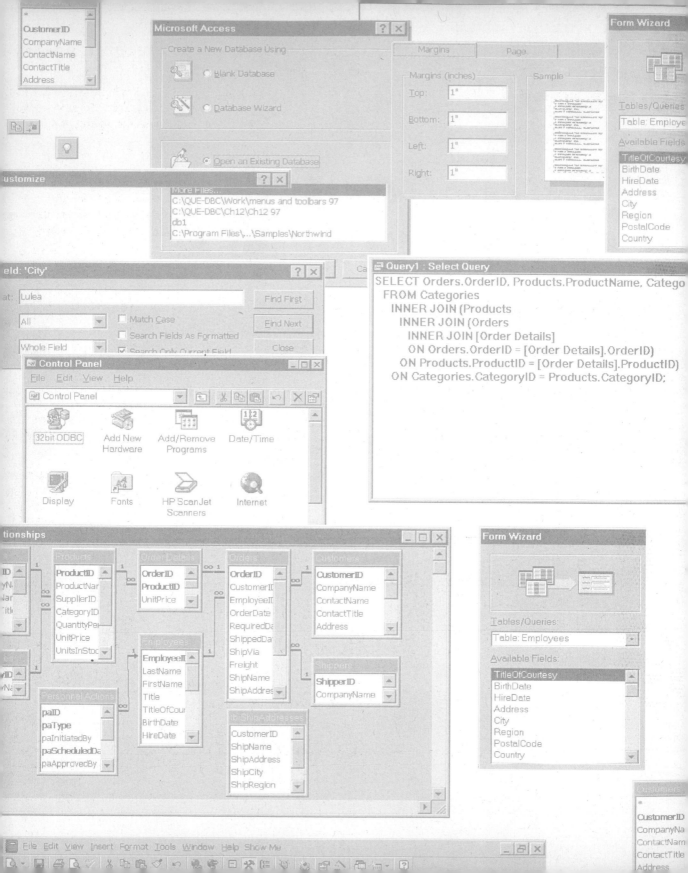

# Chapter 23

# Exploring Relational Database Design and Implementation

You were introduced to a few of the elements of relational database design when you created the Personnel Actions table and joined it with the Employees table of the Northwind Traders database in Chapter 10, "Creating Multitable and Crosstab Queries." Chapter 21, "Using Access with Microsoft Excel," gave you a bit more insight into how to create a relational database from information contained in a worksheet. However, when you're presented with the challenge of designing a database from ground zero—especially a complex or potentially complex database—you need to understand the theory of relational database design and its terminology.

## Integrating Objects and Relational Databases

This chapter takes a step back and starts with the definition of data objects and how you identify them. Because Access is an object-enabled database development tool, the concepts of database design presented in this chapter have an object-oriented bent. The reason for this approach is twofold:

- Access's relational tables incorporate many of the features of client/ server databases. Properties, such as validation rules and indexes, and methods, that include preventing duplicate primary key entries, are combined in the table object. Details of relationships between tables and methods of enforcing referential integrity are stored in the database object.

- Access VBA treats the database itself and each of Access's database elements—tables, queries, forms, and reports—as programming objects.

After you've identified the data objects that are to be included in the tables of your database, you need to design the tables to contain the data objects. You use a process called data *normalization* to create tables that conform to the relational database model. Normalization is the process of eliminating duplicate information in tables by extracting the duplicate data to new tables that contain records with unique data values. You then join the new tables by fields with common data values to create a relational database structure. Normalizing data is the subject of the "Normalizing Data to the Relational Model" section later in this chapter.

The role of indexes in maintaining unique values in primary-key fields and organizing data tables was described briefly in preceding chapters. This chapter provides an explanation of how indexes are constructed and maintained by Access 97 and the Jet 3.5 database engine. Properly designed indexes improve the performance of your applications without consuming excessive amounts of disk space or slowing the appending of new records to a crawl.

This chapter also deals with the rules that establish and maintain referential integrity—one of the most important considerations in designing a database. Referential integrity enforces uniqueness in primary keys and prevents the occurrence of orphaned records, such as records of invoices whose customer data records have been deleted.

# Understanding Database Systems

Prior to this chapter, you've used the Northwind Traders demonstration database, created a few simple databases, and perhaps imported your own data in another database format into an Access 97 table. No formal theories were presented to aid or hinder your understanding of the underlying design of the database examples. Now that you've gained some experience using Access, the more theoretical concepts of database design should be easier to understand.

This section takes a systems approach to database design, starting with a generalized set of objectives, outlining the steps necessary to accomplish the objectives, and then explaining the theory and practice behind each step.

### The Objectives of Database Design

The strategy of database design is to accomplish the following objectives:

- Fulfill your needs or the needs of the organization for information in a timely, consistent, and economical manner.

- Eliminate or minimize the duplication of database content across the organization. In a large organization, eliminating duplication may require a distributed database. Distributed databases use multiple servers to store individual databases. The individual databases are linked to one another (to use Access terminology) through a local-area network (LAN) or wide-area network (WAN) so that they appear as a single database to the user.

- Provide rapid access to the specific elements of information in the database required by each user category. Operating speed is a function of the relational database management system (RDBMS) itself, the design of the applications you create, the capabilities of the server and client computers, and network characteristics.

- Accommodate database expansion to adapt to the needs of a growing organization, such as the addition of new products and processes, complying with governmental reporting requirements, and incorporating new transaction-processing and decision-support applications.

- Maintain the integrity of the database so that it contains only validated, auditable information. Some client/server databases, such as Microsoft SQL Server, provide built-in triggers to maintain database integrity. Triggers are sets of rules that are included in the database. If you violate a rule, the trigger sends an error message instead of performing the transaction. The Enforce Referential Integrity check box in Access's Relationships dialog creates the equivalent of a trigger.

- Prevent access to the database by unauthorized persons. Access provides a security system that requires users to enter a password in order to use a particular database.

- Permit access only to those elements of the database information that individual users or categories of users need in the course of their work. You can permit or deny users the right to view the data in specific tables of the database.

- Allow only authorized persons to add or edit information in the database. Permissions in Access are multilevel; you can selectively allow users to edit tables or alter their structure, as well as edit or create their own applications.

- Ease the creation of data entry, editing, display, and reporting applications that efficiently serve the needs of the users of the database. The design of the RDBMS's front-end features determines the ease with which new applications are created or existing ones can be modified. You have seen in the preceding chapters that Access is especially adept as a front-end application generator.

The first two objectives are independent of the database manager you choose. The RDBMS influences or determines the other objectives. Operating speed, data validation, data security, and application creation are limited by the capabilities built into the RDBMS and the computer environment under which it operates. If your database is shared on a network, you need to consider the security features of the network operating system and the client/server database system (if one is used) in the security strategy.

> **Note**
>
> Database replication presents an exception to the objective of minimizing data duplication. Replication of entire databases or specific tables of databases often is used to improve performance of queries against remote databases that are accessed over a WAN. A local copy of the remote database is maintained on a LAN server. Updates to the tables of the remote database are periodically propagated over the WAN to the local replicate databases. If users don't need current information, replication is scheduled in the middle of the night when WAN traffic is minimal.
>
> Access 97 incorporates a small-scale replication system that is designed primarily to accommodate mobile computer users who maintain a copy of a database on their laptop PCs. Chapter 27, "Replicating Access Databases," describes Access 97's replication capabilities that take advantage of Windows 95's Briefcase feature.

### The Process of Database Design

The process of designing a relational database system consists of 10 basic steps:

1. Identify the objects (data sources) that the database system is to represent.

2. Discover associations between the objects (when you have more than one object).

3. Determine the significant properties and behaviors of the objects.

4. Ascertain how the properties of the objects relate to one another.

5. Create a preliminary data dictionary to define the tables that comprise the database.

6. Designate the relationships between database tables based on the associations between data objects contained in the tables, and incorporating this information in the data dictionary.

7. Establish the types of updates and transactions that create and modify the data in the tables, including any necessary data-integrity requirements.

8. Determine how to use indexes to speed up query operations without excessively slowing down the addition of data to tables or consuming excessive amounts of disk space.

9. Decide who can access and modify data in each table (data security), and alter the structure of the tables if necessary to assure data security.

10. Document the design of the database as a whole; complete data dictionaries for the database as a whole and each table it contains; and write procedures for database maintenance, including file backup and restoration.

Each step in the design process depends on preceding steps. The sections in this chapter follow steps 1–8 in sequence. Database security is the subject of Chapter 25, "Securing Multiuser Network Applications." A full discussion of database documentation is beyond the scope of this book, but this chapter explains how to use Access 97's improved Documentor feature to create a data dictionary.

### The Object-Oriented Approach to Database Design

Databases contain information about objects that exist in the real world. These objects may be people, books in a library, paper invoices or sales orders, maps, money in bank accounts, or printed circuit boards. Such objects are *tangible*. Whatever the object, it must have a physical representation, even if only an image on a computer display that never finds its way to the printer, as in the mythical "paperless office." References to objects in this book, if not preceded by a word describing the type of object—such as "table object" or "OLE object"—indicate real-world, tangible objects.

Tangible objects possess *properties* and *behavior*, just as the OLE objects discussed in Chapter 19, "Using 32-Bit OLE Components," have properties and methods. At first, this combination might appear to be applicable only to databases of persons, not books or bank balances. However, all database objects other than those in archival databases have both properties and behavior. (*Archival databases* store information that never changes—new data is simply added to such databases and the indexes to the data, if any, are updated. An example of an archival database is one containing the text of previously published newspapers.)

◀◀  See "Properties and Methods Encapsulated in Objects," p. 670

**Considering Static and Dynamic Properties of Objects.** An object's properties determine the content of a database or table that contains object representations of the same type. Books are assigned subject codes, which are derived from the Dewey decimal system. Modern books have an identifying ISBN code, and most now have a Library of Congress catalog number. These numbers are properties of a book, as are the title, author, number of pages, and binding type. Such properties are *static*: they are the same whether the book is in the stacks of a library or checked out by a cardholder. Customer information for a bank account, such as the account number, name, and address, also is considered static, even though customers occasionally change addresses. Book circulation status and bank account balances are *dynamic* properties: they change from day to day or hour to hour.

**Describing Data Entities and Their Attributes.** A single object, including all of its static properties, is called a *data entity*. Each individual data entity must be unique so that you can distinguish it from others. A bank's checking account customer is a data entity, for example, but money in the customer's account is not, because the money is fungible and cannot (and doesn't need to be) uniquely identified. A customer may have more than one account, so a Social Security number or federal employer identification number doesn't suffice as a unique identifier. An account number must be assigned to ensure the uniqueness of each customer data entity.

Deposit slips and checks are objects that are represented in the database as other data entities that *relate* to the customer entity. Check numbers aren't unique enough to distinguish them as entities; many different customers might use a check numbered 1553. Combining the customer and check number doesn't suffice as a unique identifier because different banking firms might use the same customer number to identify different people. A bank identification number, customer number, and check number together can uniquely identify a debit entity. Each check contains this information printed in magnetic ink. The amount property of each debit (check) or credit (deposit) entity is used to adjust the balance in the customer's account by simple subtraction and addition, a process called a *transaction*.

You don't want to wait while an ATM (originally Automated Transaction Machine, now commonly called an Automatic Teller Machine) calculates your balance by processing every transaction since you opened your account. Therefore, a derived static property, the last statement balance, can be included in the customer data entity and updated once per month. Only last-statement-to-date transactions need to be processed to determine the current balance—a dynamic, *calculated* property. In Figure 23.1, lines connect static properties of bank account objects to the data entities derived from them.

Properties of objects included in data entities, such as account number and customer name, are called *attributes*.

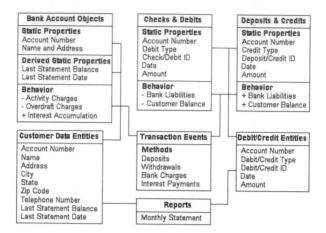

**FIG. 23.1**    Relationships between objects, entities, events, and methods in a banking database.

**Accounting for the Behavior of Objects with Methods.** The behaviors of related database objects determine the characteristics of transactions in which their data entities participate. Books in a library may be acquired, checked out, returned, and lost. Bank account behavior is very easy to describe: a customer opens the account; deposit transactions and interest accumulations (credits) increase the account balance; and checks, cash withdrawn from an ATM, and bank charges incurred (debits) reduce the balance. Crediting or debiting a bank account is an example of a transaction. Transactions occur in response to events, such as making a deposit or withdrawal at an ATM. Access implements transactions by using methods in response to events initiated by the user, such as opening a form or clicking a command button.

In conventional relational databases, you can represent tangible objects and object properties as data entities but not an object's real-world behavior. The OLE Object field data type, described in Chapter 20, "Adding Graphics to Forms and Reports," is an exception to this rule. The behavior of an OLE data object is determined by the methods available in the OLE server used to create the object or add the object to the OLE Object field. With conventional data entities, you emulate the behavior of tangible objects by applying the methods that you incorporate into your applications.

◀◀  See "Adding a Bound Object Control to a Form or Report," p. 691

Programs that you write using the RDBMS's native programming language(s) implement database methods. In the case of Access 97, VBA functions and procedures implement the methods. Most users of earlier versions of Access wrote Access macros to implement methods, because they deemed writing macros to be simpler than writing Access 1.x, Access Basic, or Access 2.0 VBA code.

Access is unique among today's mainstream PC database managers because, by default, Access saves application objects (the queries, forms, reports, macros, and VBA code that you create for the database) within the database file itself, not in separate SC, PRG, or .exe files as do other PC RDBMSs. Access data objects (tables) have self-contained properties and methods; most other PC RDBMSs require separate programs to validate data, display status text, and create indexes. Therefore, Access database files and the tables they contain conform to the object *paradigm*—a synonym for the word *model* that has become an object-oriented cliché.

---

**Note**

As observed in Chapter 25, "Securing Multiuser Network Applications," it has become a generally accepted database design practice (GADDP) to use separate .mdb files to contain application objects and data objects. Keeping your data object (tables) in a *Tables*.mdb file and linking the tables to your *AppObjs*.mdb file lets you update the application objects without affecting the existing data in the table objects.

A separate *Tables*.mdb file in Access 2.0 format is necessary if you must continue to support users running 16-bit Windows 3.1+. (You must also maintain a duplicate of your *AppObjs*.mdb file in Access 2.0 format, which is a major issue among Access developers.) Issues relating to 16-bit and 32-bit Access application versioning are covered in Chapter 33, "Migrating Access 2.0 and Access 95 Applications to Access 97."

---

▶▶ See "Splitting Databases for File Sharing," p. 873

**Combining Different Entities in a Single Table.** You can include representations of different types of objects in a single table as long as you can represent their properties and behavior in the same manner and yet distinguish between the different object types. For example, checks and debits are shown as a single data-object type in preceding Figure 23.1, although one originates from a paper check and the other from an Electronic Funds Transfer debit. A Debit Type field can indicate the different sources. You can combine cash deposits and transfers from a savings account into a single data-entity type in a Credits table. You might want to combine both debits and credits in a single table, which you can do by using different codes for Debit Types and Credit Types.

To identify a debit or credit uniquely, you need to include fields for bank ID, customer number, debit/credit type, and transaction number. Although a check number can serve as the transaction number, the system must assign transaction numbers to other types of transactions, such as those conducted at ATMs. Access 97 can use an AutoNumber field, called a Counter field in Access 2.0 and earlier, to add a unique transaction number (either incremented or random) to each data entity, including checks. The check number becomes a separate attribute.

### Database Terminology

The terms used to describe formally a database and the elements that comprise it derive from four different sources. The data-description language, of which entity and attribute are members, derives from the terminology of statistics. Another set of terms, which describe the same set of elements, is based on computer terminology and relates to how the elements are stored within disk files. Query by example introduced new terms—for example, *row*, *column*, and *cell*—to the language of databases. Structured Query Language adopted these terms.

Table 23.1 compares words that are used for data description, in QBE and SQL, and for describing data-storage methodologies employed by Access, xBase, and Paradox. The Access VBA language takes an object-oriented approach to programming, so Table 23.1 also includes terms that are applicable to object-oriented programming (OOP).

**Table 23.1   A Comparison of Data-Description and Data-Storage Terminology**

| Data Description | QBE and SQL | Object-Oriented | Access Storage | xBase/ Paradox |
|---|---|---|---|---|
| Heterogeneous Universe | Database Directory | Base Object Class | File | |
| Universe (homogeneous) | Table | Object Class | Table (Sub-File) | Data File |
| Entity (object, instance) | Row | Data Object | Record | Record |
| Attribute | Cell | Object Property | Field | Field |
| Attribute Data Type | Datatype | Data Type | Field Data Type | Field Type |
| Attribute Domain | Validation Rule Statement | Enumeration | Validation Rule | Valid |
| Attribute Value | Cell Value | Property Value | Field Value | Field Value |
| Identifier | Primary Key | Property Value | Key, Index | Index File |

The real-world object is the basic source of information that is represented in a database as an entity. In explaining the terms included in Table 23.1, therefore, the following definition list begins with an entity, breaks it down into its component parts, and then establishes its position in the hierarchy of databases and tables:

■ *Entity.* A unique representation of a single real-world object that is created by using the values of its attributes in computer-readable form. To ensure uniqueness, one or more of an entity's attributes must have values unlike the corresponding values of any other entity of the same class. An entity corresponds to a row in QBE and SQL or a record in data-storage terminology. Entities are also called data entities, data objects, data instances, or instances.

■ *Attribute.* A significant property of a real-world object. Every attribute carries a value that assists in identifying the entity of which it is a part and in distinguishing the entity from other members of the same entity class. Attributes are contained in fields (data-storage terminology) or columns (QBE and SQL). An attribute also is called a *cell* or *data cell*, terms that describe the intersection of a row and a column (or a field and a record).

■ *Attribute data type.* Basic attribute data types consist of all numeric (integer, floating-point, and so forth) and string (text or alphanumeric) data types without embedded spaces or separating punctuation. The string data type can contain letters, numbers, and special characters (such as those used in languages other than English). An attribute with a basic attribute data type is indivisible and called an *atomic type.*

Text data types with spaces or other separating punctuation characters are called *composite attribute data types.* You can divide most composite types into basic data types by parsing. Parsing means to separate a composite attribute into basic attributes. For example, you can parse "Smith, Dr. John D., Jr." to Last Name (Smith), Title (Dr.), First Name (John), Middle Initial (D.), and Suffix (Jr.) basic attribute types. Special field types, such as Memo and OLE, are composite attribute data types that cannot be parsed to basic data types by conventional methods. You cannot, therefore, create Access indexes that include Memo or OLE Object attribute data types; only attributes with basic attribute data types can be indexed.

■ *Attribute domain.* The allowable range of values for an attribute of a given attribute data type. The attribute data type determines the domain unless the domain is limited by a process that is external to the data in the table. As an example of attribute domain limitation, the domain of an employee age attribute that has an integer data type might be limited by a data validation method to any integer greater than 13 and less than 90. In object-oriented terms, the domain consists of an enumeration of acceptable values. A days-of-the-week enumeration (the domain of days) consists of a list of its members: Monday, Tuesday, and so on. Access validation rules, stored in tables, maintain domain integrity, limiting data entry to limits set by the data validation expression.

■ *Attribute value.* The smallest indivisible unit of data in an entity. Attribute values are limited to those within the attribute domain. Cell value and data value are synonyms for attribute value.

■ *Identifier.* An attribute or combination of attributes required to identify a specific entity (and no others) uniquely. Identifiers are called *primary-key fields* in Access and are used to create the primary index of the entities. When an entity's attribute values are duplicated in other entities' corresponding attributes, you need to combine various attributes to ensure a unique identifier for the entity. When more than one attribute is used as an identifier, the key fields are called a *composite* or *compound primary key.*

■ *Homogeneous universe.* The collection (set) of all data entities of a single data entity type. The data entities must have an identical set of attributes, attribute data types, and attribute domains. This set corresponds to an Access or Paradox table or a data file in xBase. The set also is called an *entity class* or *entity type,* and its members are sometimes called *entity instances,* or just *instances.*

■ *Heterogeneous universe.* The collection (set) of related entity classes comprising related homogeneous universes—the database. A database is stored as a single file in

Access and most client/server databases. Paradox and xBase store databases as collections of related files, usually in a single directory. Access databases include a special table that catalogs the objects the databases contain. You can reveal the content of the catalog by using the techniques described in the section "Access's Integrated Data Dictionary System" later in this chapter.

Much of the formal terminology used to describe data objects in relational databases is quite technical and rather abstract. You need to understand the meaning of these terms, however, when you create the data models that form the basis of the design of your database.

## Types of Tables and Keys in Relational Databases

Specific to relational databases are certain types of tables and keys that enable relationships between tables. Understanding these tables and keys is essential to comprehending relational databases and the rules of data normalization, which are discussed in the section "Normalizing Data to the Relational Model" later in this chapter. The following list defines the various relational keys and tables:

- *Base table.* In a relational database, a base table is the table that incorporates one or more columns of an object's properties and contains the primary key that uniquely identifies that object as a data entity. A base table must have a primary key. Base tables are often called *primary tables* because of the requirement for a primary key.

> **Note**
>
> Microsoft often uses the term *base table* to refer to a table in the native Jet MDB database structure. This book uses the term *base table* in accordance with the preceding definition.

- *Relation table.* A table that is used to provide linkages between other tables and isn't a base table (because it doesn't incorporate properties of an object or have a primary key field) is called a *relation table*. Key fields in relation tables each must be foreign keys related to a primary key in a base table.

  Technically, a true relation table is comprised wholly of foreign keys and contains no independent data entities. The Order Details table of the Northwind Traders database is an example of a relation table that contains data values that aren't foreign keys (the UnitPrice and Quantity fields, for example). Its OrderID field is related to the field of the same name in the Orders table. Likewise, the ProductID field is related to the ProductID field of the Products table. Although the Order Details table has a composite key, it isn't a true primary key; its purpose is to prevent duplication of a product entry in a specific order.

- *Primary key.* A primary key consists of a set of values that uniquely specifies a row of a base table, which in Access is the primary table. For any primary-key value, one and only one row in the table matches this value. You can base the primary key on a single field if each data cell's value is unique at all times.

- *Candidate keys.* Any column or group of columns that meets the requirements for a primary key is a candidate to become the primary key for the table. Name and

Social Security number are candidate keys for identifying a person in the United States; however, the Social Security number is the more appropriate choice because two people can have the same name but not the same valid Social Security number.

- *Composite keys.* If you need data from more than one column of the table to meet the uniqueness requirement of a primary key, the key is said to be a composite or concatenated key.

- *Foreign keys.* A foreign key is a column whose values correspond to those contained in a primary key, or the far-left portion of a composite key, in another related table. A foreign key can consist of one column or group of columns (a composite foreign key). If the length of a foreign key is less than the corresponding primary key, the key is called a *partial* or *truncated foreign key*.

Examples of the preceding keys and tables occur in the discussions of normal forms in the section "Normalizing Data to the Relational Model" later in this chapter. First, the following sections examine the process of data modeling.

### Data Modeling

The first step in designing a database is to determine which objects to represent within the database and which of the objects' properties to include. This process is called *data modeling*. The purpose of a data model is to create a logical representation of the data structure that is used to create a database. Data modeling can encompass an entire organization, a division or department, or a single type of object. Models that deal with objects, rather than the tables that you later create from the objects, are called *conceptual data models*.

Figure 23.2 illustrates two different approaches (conceptual data models) to database design: the bottom-up approach to create an application database, and the top-down method to develop subject databases. These two approaches, discussed in the following sections, result in databases with quite different structures.

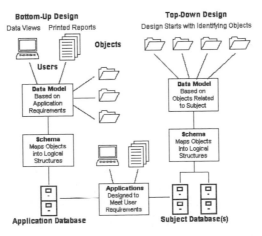

**FIG. 23.2** A comparison of bottom-up and top-down database designs.

VI

Using Advanced Techniques

**Application Databases.** You can base data models on specific needs for data presented in a particular manner. For such a needs-based model, you can use the bottom-up approach and start with a view of the data on a display, a printed report, or both, as shown in the left side of Figure 23.2. This approach results in an application database.

If you're creating a simple database for your own use or dealing with a single type of data object, the bottom-up approach might suffice because the presentation requirements and properties of the objects involved are usually well-defined. The problem with the bottom-up approach is that it often leads to multiple individual databases that may duplicate one another's information. Several persons or groups within an organization might have a requirement for an application database that includes, for example, a customer's table. When a new customer is added—or data for an existing customer is changed—in one application database, you need to update each of the other application databases. The updating process is time-consuming and subject to error.

Conceptual data models, such as those shown in Figure 23.2, are independent of the database manager you use and the type of database files it accesses. Therefore, the same data model accommodates databases in Access's native format as well as others with which Access is compatible. Data models aren't connected with any programming language or tools used to create applications. The applications box in Figure 23.2 isn't a component of conventional data models but is added to show where application design fits into the overall picture.

**Subject Databases.** A better approach is to base the design of the database on groups of objects that are related by subject matter. For a manufacturing firm, tables are usually grouped into databases devoted to a single department or function. The following lists some database examples:

- Sales database consisting of customer, sales order, sales quota, product discount, and invoice tables.

- Production database including product, price, parts, vendor, and cost accounting tables.

- Personnel database with employee, payroll, and benefits tables (large firms may include tables relating to health care providers and employment applicants).

- Accounting database incorporating general ledger and various journal tables.

Databases that consist of tables relating to a single class of subjects or functions are called *subject databases*. Even if you are creating the first database application for a small organization, starting with an overall plan for the organization's total information requirements in subject databases pays long-term dividends. If you decide or are assigned to create an invoicing application, for instance, you can establish sales, production, and personnel databases from the beginning, rather than split up a single invoice database at a later time and rewrite all of your applications to access tables within multiple databases.

Subject databases require top-down design, depicted in the right-hand diagram of Figure 23.2. In this case, the properties of the data objects, not the applications used with them, determine the design. Designing subject databases involves creating a diagram of the relevant objects and the associations between them and then creating models for each database involved. You distribute the model diagrams to users and then interview the users to determine their information needs based on the content of the model databases.

**Diagrammatic Data Models.** Large, complex data models resemble the work-flow and paper-flow diagrams commonly used in analyzing organizations' administrative procedures. If you have such diagrams or descriptions, they make the data-modeling process much easier. Generating an organization-wide data model may involve a substantial amount of research to determine the needs of the organization as a whole and of individuals using specialized applications. In many cases, users and potential users aren't able to define what information they need or how they want to see it presented.

Many methods exist of creating diagrams to represent data models. One of the more useful methods is the Entity-Relationship (E-R) diagram, developed by Peter Chen in 1976 and expanded on by David R. McClanahan in a series of articles entitled "Database Foundations: Conceptual Designs" in *DBMS* magazine (see Figure 23.3). You can use E-R diagrams to represent relationships between objects and to depict their behavior.

**FIG. 23.3**  An Entity-Relationship diagram of two data entities from Figure 23.1.

Data entities are enclosed within rectangles, data attributes within ovals, and relationships between entities within diamonds. Relationships between database objects, at the conceptual stage, can be defined by their behavior; therefore, E-R diagrams include at least one verb whose object, unless otherwise indicated, is to the right of the diamond relationship symbol. You add symbols to the diagram as the model's detail increases. One of the advantages of the E-R diagram is that you can use it to represent the conceptual design of very large systems with multiple databases in a relatively small amount of space.

**Database Schema.** A graphic description of the layout of tables in the form of bars that contain their field names and show a simplified version of relationships between them can be employed to aid users to grasp the concept of the database. A diagram that shows the logical representation of data is called a *schema*. A schema, such as the one shown in Figure 23.4 for an ocean shipping line, is independent of the RDBMS used to implement the database.

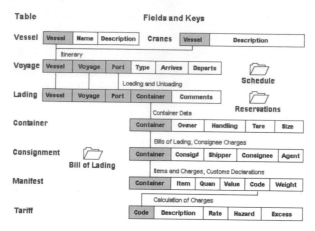

**FIG. 23.4** The schema for the operations database of a shipping line.

In Figure 23.4, the primary keys are shaded, and the relationships between the table keys are indicated by lines that connect the keys. Foreign keys are unshaded, except when they correspond to a component of a composite primary key. The descriptions shown between the bars are optional; they are useful in describing the relationships to users. You can expand a schema of this type to include the source documents involved, the reports to be generated, and the applications that pertain to all (or a portion) of the tables.

**External Determinants of Database Design.** Finding the data objects that provide the information to meet all of an organization's requirements may require extensive detective work. Many objects might not be available within the organization itself. For instance, if you're developing a database application that involves geographic positioning (called *geocoding*), you might need map tables such as the U.S. Census Bureau's TIGER/Line files, or tables derived from those files by others.

Images to be incorporated as OLE objects might not be available in file formats that are compatible with your OLE server applications; they would require file-type conversion. If the accounting department is using packaged accounting software, you must incorporate representations of the structure of its database into your model. In this case, you also must plan how to exchange information with the accounting data, but you need not include the access methodology in your conceptual data model.

# Using Data Modeling Tools to Create Access Databases

Data modeling tools are available from several publishers for designing and then automatically creating the structure of client/server relational databases, such as SQL Server, ORACLE, and SQLBase. Data modeling tools that run under Windows let you use graphic techniques, such as E-R diagrams, to design the structure of the tables and establish relationships between the tables. Database CASE tools save much time and prevent many errors when you implement a large and complex relational database.

> **Note**
>
> Data modeling tools often are called *Computer-Aided Software Engineering* (CASE) tools. CASE tools designed for enterprise-wide software design usually include data modeling as one of their features. Today's high-end CASE tools, some of which carry license fees of $100,000 or more, offer many additional capabilities. This book positions data modeling tools as a subset of CASE tools.

Most data modeling tools contain a *repository* that stores information about table design, primary and foreign key fields, constraints (validation rules) for fields, and types of relationships between the tables. The repository is a database maintained by the data modeling application itself. You can print database schema and generate data dictionaries from records in the repository. When your database design appears satisfactory, the data modeling tool translates the data in the repository to a SQL Data Definition Language (DDL) statement. You send the DDL statement to the client/server RDBMS on the server. This RDBMS can be used to create the entire database or just to add tables to the database. SQL's DDL commands are one of the subjects of the next chapter.

InfoModeler, published by Asymetrix Corporation of Bellevue, Washington, is the most popular data modeling tool for Access databases. InfoModeler uses a new approach to designing databases called *Object Role Modeling* (ORM), developed by Professor Terry Halpin of the University of Queensland, Australia. ORM lets you express the design of a database in simple, English terms through a structured language called *Formal Object Role Modeling Language* (FORML). InfoModeler translates FORML statements into a graphic schema, related to but more flexible than E-R diagrams. Figure 23.5 shows a portion of the ORM database diagram for a tutorial application of InfoModeler 2.0 derived from the pubs sample database included with Microsoft SQL Server 6.x.

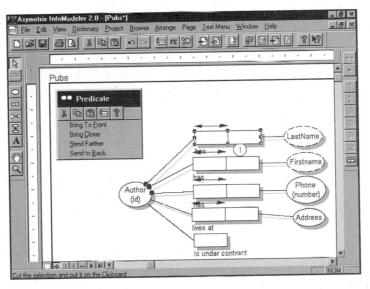

**FIG. 23.5** An Object Role Modeling diagram for an Access database.

InfoModeler lets you print the ORM graphic schema and creates a data dictionary for the database. This reduces the time required to describe the structure of the database to others, as well as much of the drudgery of creating a comprehensive data dictionary. 32-bit InfoModeler 2.0 for Windows 95 and Windows NT 4.0 offers a number of other useful features, such as reverse-engineering your Access database (creating an ORM schema from an .mdb file or client/server database), database structure version tracking, and automatic restructuring of databases and tables.

# Normalizing Data to the Relational Model

Up to this point, most of the subject matter in this chapter has been applicable to any type of database—hierarchical, relational, or even the new class of object database systems. However, because Access is a RDBMS, the balance of the chapter is devoted to relational databases. Access fully implements the relational model in its native database structure and you can link tables from other RDBMSs—including client/server tables—to Access databases. Thus, the discussion that follows is general in nature and applies to any database system with which Access is compatible or for which you have the appropriate 32-bit Open Database Connectivity (ODBC) driver. (Access 97 requires the use of 32-bit ODBC drivers.)

The theory of relational database design is founded in a branch of mathematics called *set theory*, with a great deal of combinatorial analysis and some statistical methodology added. The set of rules and symbols by which relational databases are defined is called *relational algebra*. This chapter doesn't delve into the symbolic representation of relational algebra, nor does it require you to comprehend advanced mathematics. The chapter does, however, introduce you to many of the terms used in relational algebra for the sake of consistency with advanced texts, which you may want to consult on the subject of database design.

### Normalization Rules

*Normalization* is a formalized procedure by which data attributes are grouped into tables and tables are grouped into databases. The purposes of normalization include the following:

- Eliminating duplicate information in tables.

- Accommodating future changes in the structure of tables.

- Minimizing the impact of database structural change on user applications that access the data.

Normalization is performed in steps; the first three and most common steps were described by Dr. E. F. Codd in his 1972 paper, "Further Normalization of the Data Base Relational Model." These steps are depicted in Figure 23.6. The following sections describe each of the five steps that comprise the entire normalizing process.

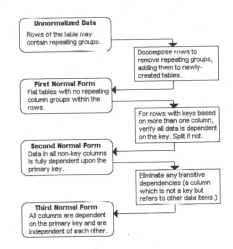

**FIG. 23.6** A graphic representation of relational database normalization to the third normal form.

**First Normal Form.** *First normal form* requires that tables be flat and contain no repeating groups. A flat table has only two dimensions—length (number of records or rows) and width (number of fields or columns)—and cannot contain data cells with more than one value. For a single cell to contain more than one data value, the representation of the cell's contents requires a third dimension, depth, to display the multiple data values. Flat tables and the flat-file databases referred to in Chapter 7, "Linking, Importing, and Exporting Tables," are similar in that both have two dimensions. Flat-file databases, however, consist of only one table and have no restrictions on the content of the data cells within the table.

> **Note**
>
> Access 97's Table Analyzer Wizard does a good job of detecting duplicate information in tables created from flat files, but the files must be in first normal form (no repeating groups) for the analysis to succeed. The "Using Access 97's Table Analyzer Wizard" section later in this chapter describes how to use the Table Analyzer Wizard to check for duplicate data and create a set of related tables to minimize or eliminate the duplication.

An example of unnormalized data for a shipping line appears in Figure 23.7. This presentation often is seen in the schedules published by transportation firms where the stops are displayed across the page. This example is representative of a schedule created by importing the worksheet file that was used to create the printed version of the schedule. In the various examples of tables that follow, missing borders are the equivalent of an ellipsis; that is, a missing right border indicates that additional columns (fields) exist beyond the far-right column. A missing bottom border means that more rows (records) follow. (Those readers who are seasoned mariners will recognize the example as a mythical schedule for vessels of the former Pacific Far East Lines.)

| Vessel | Name | Voyage | Embarks | From | Arrives | Port | Departs | Arrives | Port | Departs |
|--------|------|--------|---------|------|---------|------|---------|---------|------|---------|
| 528 | Japan Bear | 9203W | 5/31/92 | SFO | 6/6/92 | HNL | 6/8/92 | 7/15/92 | OSA | 7/18/92 |
| 603 | Korea Bear | 9203W | 6/05/92 | OAK | 6/19/92 | OSA | 6/21/92 | 6/25/92 | INC | 6/28/92 |
| 531 | China Bear | 9204W | 6/20/92 | LAX | 7/10/92 | PAP | 7/11/92 | 8/28/92 | SYD | 9/2/92 |
| 528 | Japan Bear | 9204W | 8/20/92 | SFO | 8/27/92 | HNL | 8/29/92 | 9/30/92 | OSA | 10/2/92 |

**FIG. 23.7**  A partial schedule of voyages for a shipping line.

Because the vessels stop at a number of ports, the Arrives, Port, and Departs columns are duplicated for each stop in the voyage. This type of data structure is allowed in COBOL, where the repeating group (Arrives, Port, and Departs) OCCURS any number of TIMES, but not in relational databases. The data in the preceding schedule isn't in first normal form because it contains repeating groups. The table must be decomposed (divided) into two tables, therefore, with the repeating groups (shown in shaded type in Figure 23.7) removed from the Schedule table and placed in two new tables, Ports and Vessel Voyages, as shown in Figure 23.8.

| Vessel | Name | Voyage | Embarks | From |
|--------|------|--------|---------|------|
| 528 | Japan Bear | 9203W | 5/31/92 | SFO |
| 603 | Korea Bear | 9203W | 6/5/92 | OAK |
| 531 | China Bear | 9204W | 6/20/92 | LAX |
| 528 | Japan Bear | 9204W | 8/20/92 | SFO |

| Arrives | Port | Departs |
|---------|------|---------|
| 6/6/92 | HNL | 6/8/92 |
| 6/19/92 | OSA | 6/21/92 |
| 7/10/92 | PAP | 7/11/92 |
| 8/27/92 | HNL | 8/29/92 |
| 7/15/92 | OSA | 7/18/92 |
| 6/25/92 | INC | 6/28/92 |
| 8/28/92 | SYD | 9/2/92 |
| 9/30/92 | OSA | 10/2/92 |

**FIG. 23.8**  The Ports and Vessel Voyages tables created from the Schedule table.

Now you need to provide for a link between the Ports and Vessel Voyages tables to retain the relationship between the data. This shipping line numbers voyages for each vessel with the year and which voyage this is for the year, as well as the general direction of travel (9204W is the fourth voyage of 1992, westbound). Thus, both Vessel and Voyage need to be used to relate the two tables. Neither Vessel nor Voyage is sufficient in itself because a vessel has multiple voyages during the year and the voyage numbers used here recur for other vessels. Because you must create a new Ports table to meet the requirements of the first normal form, you have the chance to order the columns in the order of their significance. Columns used to establish relationships are usually listed first, in the sequence in which they appear in the composite primary key, when more than one column is included in the key (see Figure 23.9).

| Vessel | Voyage | Port | Arrives | Departs |
|--------|--------|------|---------|---------|
| 528 | 9203W | HNL | 6/6/92 | 6/8/92 |
| 603 | 9203W | OSA | 6/19/92 | 6/21/92 |
| 531 | 9204W | PAP | 7/10/92 | 7/11/92 |
| 528 | 9204W | HNL | 8/27/92 | 8/29/92 |
| 528 | 9203W | OSA | 7/15/92 | 7/18/92 |
| 603 | 9203W | INC | 6/25/92 | 6/28/92 |
| 531 | 9204W | SYD | 8/28/92 | 9/2/92 |
| 528 | 9204W | OSA | 9/30/92 | 10/2/92 |

**FIG. 23.9**  Linking fields are added to the Ports relation table.

Next, you establish the key fields for the Ports table that uniquely identify a record in the table. You need a primary key for the Ports table because other tables may be dependent on this table. Clearly, Vessel and Voyage must be included because these columns constitute the relationship to the Vessel Voyages table. You need to add the Port field to create a unique key (Vessel + Voyage can have duplicate values). Vessel + Voyage + Port creates a unique composite primary key because the combination takes into account stopping at a port twice—when returning eastbound, the voyage carries an "E" suffix.

> **Note**
>
> A spreadsheet application, such as Microsoft Excel 97, can speed up the process of normalizing existing data, especially when the data contains repeating groups. Import the data into a worksheet, then cut and paste the data in the repeating groups into a new worksheet. When the data for both of the tables is normalized, save the worksheets and then import the files to Access tables. This process is usually faster than creating make-table queries to generate normalized tables.

**Second Normal Form.** *Second normal form* requires that data in all non-key columns be fully dependent on the primary key and each element (column) of the primary key when it is a composite primary key. *Fully dependent* means that the data value in each non-key column of a record is determined uniquely by the value of the primary key. If a composite primary key is required to establish the uniqueness of a record, the same rule applies to each value of the fields that comprise the composite key of the record. Your table must be in first normal form before examining it for conformity to second normal form. Second normal form removes much of the data redundancy that is likely to occur in a first normal table.

Returning to the Vessel Voyages table, you can see that it requires a composite key, Vessel + Voyage, to create a unique key because the vessel number and vessel name recur. When you create such a key, however, you observe that Vessel and Name aren't dependent on the entire primary key because neither is determined by Voyage. You also find that the vessel name occurs for each of a vessel's voyages; for example, the Japan Bear appears twice. This lack of dependency violates the rules of the second normal form and requires Vessel Voyages to be split into two tables, Vessels and Voyages. One row is required in the Vessels table for each ship, and one row is required in the Voyages table for each voyage made by each ship (eastbound and westbound directions are considered separate voyages for database purposes). As was the case for Ports, a unique key is required to relate voyages to the vessel, so the vessel number column is added to the Voyages table, as shown in Figure 23.10.

| Vessel | Vessel Name |
|--------|-------------|
| 528 | Japan Bear |
| 603 | Korea Bear |
| 531 | China Bear |

| Vessel | Voyage | Embarks | From |
|--------|--------|---------|------|
| 528 | 9203W | 5/31/92 | SFO |
| 603 | 9203W | 6/5/92 | OAK |
| 531 | 9204W | 6/20/92 | LAX |
| 528 | 9204W | 8/20/92 | SFO |

**FIG. 23.10**  The Vessels and Voyages tables created from the Vessel Voyages table.

**Third Normal Form.** *Third normal form* requires that all non-key columns of a table be dependent on the table's primary key and independent of one another. Tables must conform to both first and second normal forms to qualify for third normal status.

Your Vessels and Voyages tables are now in third normal form because there are no repeating groups of columns, and the data in non-key columns is dependent on the primary key field. The non-key columns of Ports, Arrives, and Departs are dependent on the composite key (Vessel + Voyage + Port) and independent of one another. Ports, therefore, meets the requirements of first, second, and third normal forms. The departure date is independent of the arrival date because the difference between the two dates is based on the vessel's lading into and out of the port, the availability of berths and container cranes, and the weather.

To demonstrate normalization to the third normal form, suppose that you want to identify the officers of the vessel—master, chief engineer, and so on—in the database. Your first impulse might be to add their employee numbers, the primary key of an Employee table, to the Vessels table (see Figure 23.11).

| Vessel | Vessel Name | Master | Chief | 1st Mate |
|---|---|---|---|---|
| 528 | Japan Bear | 01023 | 01155 | 01367 |
| 603 | Korea Bear | 00955 | 01203 | 00823 |
| 531 | China Bear | 00721 | 00912 | 01251 |

**FIG. 23.11** A table with a transitive dependency between vessels and crew members.

This table violates the third normal rule because none of the officers assigned to a vessel is dependent on the vessel itself. This type of dependency is called *transitive*. The master's, chief's, and first mate's maritime licenses allow them to act in their respective capacities on any vessel for which the license is valid. Any officer may be assigned to other vessels, as the need arises, or remain on board for only a portion of the voyage.

One method of removing the transitive dependency might be to add the employee numbers column to the Voyages table. This method doesn't provide a satisfactory solution, however, because the vessel may arrive at a port with one group of crew members and depart with another group. In addition, you need to specify the crew members who remain with the vessel while it is in port. A relation table, such as that shown for the Japan Bear in Figure 23.12, solves the problem. Duplicate values in the Port (departure port) and To (destination port) fields designate records for crew members responsible for the vessel while in port. The Crew table of Figure 23.12 qualifies as a relation table because all of its fields correspond to primary keys or parts of primary keys in the base tables—Vessels, Voyages, Ports, and Employees.

| Vessel | Voyage | Port | To | Master | Chief | 1st Mate |
|---|---|---|---|---|---|---|
| 528 | 9203W | SFO | HNL | 01023 | 01156 | 01367 |
| 528 | 9203W | HNL | HNL | 01023 | 01156 | 01367 |
| 528 | 9203W | HNL | OSA | 01023 | 01156 | 01367 |
| 528 | 9203W | OSA | OSA | 01023 | 01156 | 01367 |
| 528 | 9203W | OSA | INC | 01023 | 01156 | 01367 |

**FIG. 23.12** Removing transitive dependency with a relation table.

All of your tables are now flat, contain no duplicate information other than that in the columns used for keys, and conform to the first through third normal forms.

**Fourth Normal Form.** *Fourth normal form* requires that independent data entities not be stored in the same table when many-to-many relationships exist between these entities. The table of Figure 23.12 violates fourth normal form because many-to-many relationships exist between the Vessel and the fields that identify crew members. The fourth normal form is discussed in the "Many-to-Many Relationships and Fourth Normal Form" section later in this chapter, because it is the only normalization rule that is dependent on a specific type of relationship.

---

**Note**

Many database designers disregard the fourth and fifth normal forms; those designers consider these forms too esoteric or applicable only in specialized cases. Disregarding fourth normal form often results in poorly designed databases, but not necessarily malfunctioning ones.

---

**Fifth Normal Form and Combined Entities.** *Fifth normal form* requires that you be able to reconstruct exactly the original table from those tables into which it was decomposed. Re-creating the Excel spreadsheet from the tables in the example in Chapter 21, "Using Access with Microsoft Excel," demonstrates compliance with fifth normal form. Fifth normal form requires that the tables comply with the rules for third normal form and, when many-to-many relationships are present, with the rule for fourth normal form.

◀◀  See "Verifying the Tables by Re-Creating the Worksheet," p. 746

The Voyages table appears to be quite similar to that of Ports. The From column is equivalent to Port, and Embarks is the same as Departure. Therefore, you can move the data in the Voyages table to the Ports table and delete the Voyages table. Figure 23.13 shows the new Ports table. The rows from the Voyages table don't have values in the Arrives column because they represent points of departure.

| Vessel | Voyage | Port | Arrives | Departs |
|--------|--------|------|---------|---------|
| 528 | 9203W | HNL | 6/6/92 | 6/8/92 |
| 603 | 9203W | OSA | 6/19/92 | 6/21/92 |
| 531 | 9204W | PAP | 7/10/92 | 7/11/92 |
| 520 | 9204W | HNL | 8/27/92 | 8/29/92 |
| 528 | 9203W | OSA | 7/15/92 | 7/18/92 |
| 603 | 9203W | INC | 6/25/92 | 6/28/92 |
| 531 | 9204W | SYD | 8/28/92 | 9/2/92 |
| 528 | 9204W | OSA | 8/30/92 | 10/2/92 |
| 528 | 9203W | SFO | | 5/31/92 |
| 603 | 9203W | OAK | | 6/5/92 |
| 531 | 9204W | LAX | | 6/20/92 |
| 528 | 9204W | SFO | | 8/20/92 |

**FIG. 23.13**    Records from the Voyages table appended to the Ports table.

However, you cannot explicitly reconstruct the original table from the combined Voyages and Ports tables in all cases, because you cannot distinguish an embarkation row from the other rows by a value in the table. A Null value in the Arrives field is a candidate to distinguish an embarkation, but most PC RDBMSs don't support Null values. You eliminate any ambiguity that using a Null value might cause—and bring the table into fifth normal form—by adding a single-character field, Type, with single-letter codes to define the type of call. In Figure 23.14, the codes E and S represent Embarkation and Scheduled call, respectively. Other codes might include M for Maintenance stop and R for Return voyage.

**VI**

**Using Advanced Techniques**

| Vessel | Voyage | Port | Type | Arrives | Departs |
|---|---|---|---|---|---|
| 528 | 9203W | HNL | S | 6/6/92 | 6/8/92 |
| 603 | 9203W | OSA | S | 6/19/92 | 6/21/92 |
| 531 | 9204W | PAP | S | 7/10/92 | 7/11/92 |
| 528 | 9204W | HNL | S | 8/27/92 | 8/29/92 |
| 528 | 9203W | OSA | S | 7/15/92 | 7/18/92 |
| 603 | 9203W | INC | S | 6/25/92 | 6/28/92 |
| 531 | 9204W | SYD | S | 8/28/92 | 9/2/92 |
| 528 | 9204W | OSA | S | 9/30/92 | 10/2/92 |
| 528 | 9203W | SFO | E | | 5/31/92 |
| 603 | 9203W | OAK | E | | 6/5/92 |
| 531 | 9204W | LAX | E | | 6/20/92 |
| 528 | 9204W | SFO | E | | 8/20/92 |

**FIG. 23.14** The Type field has been added to comply with fifth normal form.

Figure 23.15 demonstrates that you can reconstruct the content of the original Schedule table from the Vessels and Ports tables. Query1 creates the first five columns of the Schedule table by adding the criterion E for the Type field, which isn't shown. You can re-create the remaining columns of the Schedule table from Query2, which uses the criterion S for the Type field.

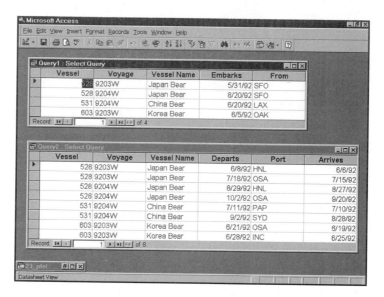

**FIG. 23.15** The datasheets of the two queries required to reconstruct the Schedule table.

On the Web The database used to create Figure 23.15—23_pfel.mdb—is included in the example files for this book, available from the Macmillan Publishing USA Information SuperLibrary Web site. Follow the links from this URL to the *Special Edition Using Access 97* page for downloading instructions:

**http://www.mcp.com/que/msoffice/**

The example files are archived in ZIP format. You can download an evaluation copy of the latest 32-bit version of WinZip, which expands the ZIP files, from

**http://www.winzip.com/**

### Types of Relationships

The subject of relationships between entities usually precedes discussions of normalization. Relationships come second in this book, however, because you can only create valid relationships between tables that have been structured in accordance with at least the first three normalization rules described in the preceding sections. This section describes the four basic types of relationships between tables and employs E-R diagrams to depict the relationships graphically.

**One-to-One Relationships.** The simplest relationship between tables is a one-to-one relationship. In such a relationship, the tables have exact one-to-one row correspondence; no row in one table has more than one corresponding row in the other table. You can combine one-to-one-related tables into a single table consisting of all the tables' columns.

One-to-one relationships are often used to divide very wide base tables into narrower ones. You might want to divide a wide table to reduce the time needed to view fields containing specific sets of data, such as the stock prices table in the example of Chapter 15, "Preparing Advanced Reports." Often you need to control access to the parts of tables that contain sensitive or confidential data. An example is an employee file: everyone might have read-only access to the employees' names, but only members of the personnel department are authorized to view salary and other payroll information (see Figure 23.16).

| Employee | Position | Last | First | MI |
|----------|----------|------|-------|-----|
| 00668 | Master | Johansson | Lars | F. |
| 00721 | Master | Karlsson | Bo | B. |
| 00885 | Chief | MacGregor | Paul | C. |
| 00912 | Chief | McDemott | John | R. |
| 00955 | Master | Olafson | Karl | T. |
| 01023 | Master | Kekkonen | Eino | K. |
| 01156 | Chief | McDougal | William | U. |
| 01203 | Chief | Kashihara | Matsuo | |

| Employee | Salary |
|----------|--------|
| 00668 | 6500.00 |
| 00721 | 6250.00 |
| 00885 | 5100.00 |
| 00912 | 5000.00 |
| 00955 | 6100.00 |
| 01023 | 6050.00 |
| 01156 | 4900.00 |
| 01203 | 4850.00 |

**FIG. 23.16**  Two tables with a one-to-one relationship.

Figure 23.17 shows the E-R diagram for the Employees and Salaries tables. The number 1 added to each side of the relationship diamond indicates a one-to-one relationship. The participation of entities in relationships can be mandatory or optional. Optional relationships are symbolized by a circle drawn on the line connecting the optional entity with the relationship diamond. In the figure, the Paid-Salaries relationship is optional because some employees can be paid on an hourly basis and linked to a Wages table. Tables with mandatory one-to-one relationships are base tables. A table with an optional one-to-one relationship to a base table is a related table. Multiple tables with one-to-one relationships where the corresponding records in the other tables are optional can reduce the database's disk space requirement.

Another example of a one-to-one relationship is between an xBase memo field and a corresponding entry in a memo .dbt file. Access treats free text as the content of a data cell in the table, so no relationship is involved.

**FIG. 23.17**   An E-R diagram for an optional one-to-one relationship.

**One-to-Many Relationships.** One-to-many relationships link a single row in one table with two or more rows in another table through a relationship between the primary key of the base table and the corresponding foreign key in the related table. Although the foreign key in the table containing the many relationships may be a component of a composite primary key in its own table, it is a foreign key for the purposes of the relationship. One-to-many relationships are the most common relationships.

The one-to-many relationship shown in Figure 23.18 links all records in the Ports table to one record in the Vessels table. The one-to-many relationship allows you to display all records in the Ports table for scheduled ports of call of the Japan Bear.

| Vessel | Vessel Name | | Vessel | Voyage | Port | Type | Arrives | Departs |
|--------|-------------|---|--------|--------|------|------|---------|---------|
| 528 | Japan Bear | | 528 | 9203W | HNL | S | 6/6/92 | 6/8/92 |
| | | | 528 | 9204W | HNL | S | 8/27/92 | 8/29/92 |
| | | | 528 | 9203W | OSA | S | 7/15/92 | 7/18/92 |
| | | | 528 | 9204W | OSA | S | 9/30/92 | 10/2/92 |
| | | | 528 | 9203W | SFO | E | | 5/31/92 |
| | | | 528 | 9204W | SFO | E | | 8/20/92 |

**FIG. 23.18**   A one-to-many relationship between the Vessels and Ports tables.

The E-R diagram of Figure 23.19 expresses this relationship, where the degree of the Vessel entity relationships between the two tables is indicated by the "1" and "m" adjacent to their entities.

**FIG. 23.19**   The E-R diagram for the one-to-many relationship of Figure 23.17.

**Many-to-One Relationships.** Many-to-one relationships are the converse of the one-to-many type. The many-to-one relationship allows you to display the vessel name for any record in the Ports table. If the roles of the participating entities are simply reversed to create the many-to-one relationship, the relationship is said to be *reflexive*; that is, the many-to-one relationship is the reflection of its one-to-many counterpart (see Figure 23.20). All many-to-one relationships in Access are reflexive; you can specify only a one-to-one or one-to-many relationship between the primary table and the related table by using the two option buttons in Access's Relationship dialog.

| Vessel | Voyage | Port | Type | Arrives | Departs |
|---|---|---|---|---|---|
| 528 | 9203W | HNL | O | 6/6/92 | 6/9/92 |
| 528 | 9204W | HNL | S | 8/27/92 | 8/29/92 |
| 528 | 9203W | OSA | S | 7/15/92 | 7/18/92 |
| 528 | 9204W | OSA | S | 9/30/92 | 10/2/92 |
| 528 | 9203W | SFO | E | | 5/31/92 |
| 528 | 9204W | SFO | E | | 8/20/92 |

| Vessel | Vessel Name |
|---|---|
| 528 | Japan Bear |

**FIG. 23.20**   The Ports and Vessels tables in a reflexive many-to-one relationship.

If you select a record on the many side of the relationship, you can display the record corresponding to its foreign key on the one side. E-R diagrams for reflexive relationships are often drawn like the diagram in Figure 23.21. Reflexive relationships are indicated by the appropriate form of the verb placed outside the diamond that defines the relationship.

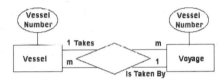

**FIG. 23.21**   The E-R diagram for a reflexive many-to-one relationship.

**Many-to-Many Relationships and Fourth Normal Form.** Many-to-many relationships cannot be expressed as simple relationships between two participating entities. You create many-to-many relationships by making a table that has many-to-one relationships with two base tables.

The Crews relation table, created in the "Third Normal Form" section of this chapter, for assigning crew members to legs of the voyage is shown again in Figure 23.22. The Crews table creates a many-to-many relationship between the Vessels table (based on the Vessel entity) and the Employees table (based on the employee number entities in the Master, Chief, and 1stMate fields).

| Vessel | Voyage | Port | To | Master | Chief | 1st Mate |
|---|---|---|---|---|---|---|
| 528 | 9203W | SFO | HNL | 01023 | 01156 | 01367 |
| 528 | 9203W | HNL | HNL | 01023 | 01156 | 01367 |
| 528 | 9203W | HNL | OSA | 01023 | 01156 | 01367 |
| 528 | 9203W | OSA | OSA | 01023 | 01156 | 01367 |
| 528 | 9203W | OSA | INC | 01023 | 01156 | 01367 |

**FIG. 23.22**   The first version of the Crews relation table.

The table in Figure 23.22 has a many-to-one relationship with the Vessels table and a many-to-one relationship with the Employees table. This version of the Crews table creates a many-to-many relationship between the Vessels and Employees tables. The employees who crew the vessel are independent of one another; any qualified employee can, in theory, be assigned to fill a crew position on any leg of a voyage. The table in Figure 23.22 violates the fourth normal form, therefore, because it contains independent entities.

**VI**

**Using Advanced Techniques**

Figure 23.23 shows the restructured Crews relation table that is needed to assign employees to legs of voyages. The table has one record for each employee for each leg of the voyage.

| Employee | Vessel | Voyage | Port | To |
|---|---|---|---|---|
| 01023 | 528 | 9203W | SFO | HNL |
| 01156 | 528 | 9203W | SFO | HNL |
| 01367 | 528 | 9203W | SFO | HNL |
| 01023 | 528 | 9203W | HNL | HNL |
| 01156 | 528 | 9203W | HNL | HNL |
| 01367 | 528 | 9203W | HNL | HNL |
| 01023 | 528 | 9203W | HNL | OSA |
| 01156 | 528 | 9203W | HNL | OSA |
| 01367 | 528 | 9203W | HNL | OSA |
| 01023 | 528 | 9203W | OSA | OSA |
| 01156 | 528 | 9203W | OSA | OSA |
| 01367 | 528 | 9203W | OSA | OSA |
| 01023 | 528 | 9203W | OSA | INC |
| 01156 | 528 | 9203W | OSA | INC |
| 01367 | 528 | 9203W | OSA | INC |

**FIG. 23.23** The Crews table restructured to fourth normal form.

You can add new entities to this table, provided that the entities are wholly dependent on all of the foreign key fields. An example of a dependent entity is payroll data that might include data attributes such as regular hours worked, overtime hours, and chargeable expenses incurred by each employee on each leg of a voyage. Such entities are called *weak* or *associative entities* because they rely on other base tables for their relevance. The Crews table is no longer considered strictly a relation table when you add associative entities because it no longer consists wholly of fields that constitute foreign keys.

The E-R diagram for the many-to-many relation table relating employees and the legs of a voyage to which the employees are assigned is shown in Figure 23.24. The encircled Date connected to the Assigned Crew relationship expresses cardinality: one employee can be assigned to only one voyage on a given date. The cardinality of the relationship, therefore, is based on the departure and arrival dates for the leg. Automatically enforcing the condition that employees not be in more than one place at one time can be accomplished by creating a no-duplicates index consisting of all fields of the Crews table. Associative entities are shown in E-R diagrams as a relationship diamond within an entity rectangle. If you add payroll data to the Crews table, an associative entity is created. Assignment of an employee to a voyage is optional, as indicated by the circled lines; employees may have shore leave, be indisposed, or be assigned to shoreside duties.

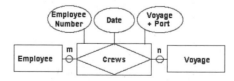

**FIG. 23.24** An E-R diagram for a many-to-many relationship with an associative entity.

Using graphic schema and E-R diagrams when you design an Access database helps ensure that the database meets your initial objectives. Schema also are useful in explaining the structure of your database to its users. E-R diagrams can uncover design errors, such as the failure to normalize tables at least to fourth normal form. Few experiences are more frustrating than having to restructure a large table because you realize its design wasn't fully normalized. Forethought, planning, and diagramming are the watchwords of success in database design.

# Using Access 97's Table Analyzer Wizard

Access 97's Table Analyzer Wizard detects cells containing repeated data in table columns and proposes to create two new related tables to eliminate the repetition. This wizard uses Access 97's Lookup Wizard, described in Chapter 10, "Creating Multitable and Crosstab Queries," to create the relationship between the two new tables. After the wizard creates the new related tables, tbl*NewName* and tlkp*Lookup*, your original table is renamed to *TableName*_OLD, and the wizard creates a one-to-many INNER JOIN query named *TableName* to return a result set that duplicates Datasheet view of the original table. Thus, you need not change the references to *TableName* in your Access application objects.

◄◄ See "Using Lookup Fields in Tables," p. 332

The tlkp*Lookup* table must have a valid primary key field to provide unambiguous association of a single record in the tlkp*Lookup* table with a foreign key field in the tbl*NewName* table. One of the problems associated with repetitious data is data entry errors, such as occasional misspelling of a company name or an address element in tlkp*Lookup*. The Table Analyzer Wizard detects and displays instances of minor mismatch in repeated cell values, such as a missing apostrophe, for correction. If such errors are not corrected, the tlkp*Lookup* table includes spurious, almost-duplicate entries that violate the rules of table normalization.

To demonstrate use of the TableAnalyzer Wizard to eliminate duplicate shipping address information in the Orders table of Northwind.mdb, follow these steps:

1. Open Northwind.mdb, if necessary, and launch the TableAnalyzer Wizard by choosing <u>T</u>ools, Analyze, <u>T</u>able.

2. Skip the two introductory dialogs by clicking the Next button twice to reach the Table Selection dialog shown in Figure 23.25.

3. Select the table with the duplicated data in the Tables list box (for this example, you select the Orders table). Next, clear the Show Introductory Pages check box to skip the two introductory dialogs whenever you use the Table Analyzer Wizard again. Click the Next button to continue.

4. If you let the wizard decide, you can't change the primary key field of tlkp*Lookup*, so select the No, I Want To Decide option (see Figure 23.26). Click Next.

VI

Using Advanced Techniques

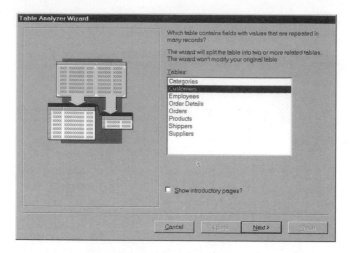

**FIG. 23.25** Selecting the table to analyze in the third TableAnalyzer Wizard dialog.

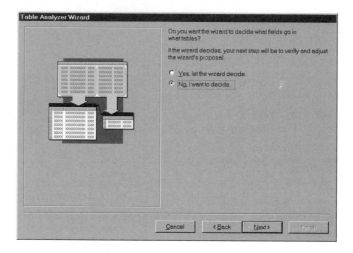

**FIG. 23.26** Analyzing the Orders table by deciding yourself which table fields contain duplicate data.

5. The wizard displays a list of fields of the Orders table renamed to Table1. Click to select the first of the fields with duplicated information, ShipName, then press Shift and click the last of the fields to move, ShipCountry (see Figure 23.27).

6. Holding the left mouse button down, drag the selected fields from the field list to an empty area to the right of the Table1 list. When you release the mouse button, the wizard creates a new field list for proposed Table2 with a many-to-one relationship between Table1 and Table2. The relationship is based on a lookup field in Table1 and a Generated Unique ID (AutoNumber) field in Table2. An input box opens to rename the table; type **tlkpShipAddress** in the Table Name text box (see Figure 23.28). Click OK to close the input box.

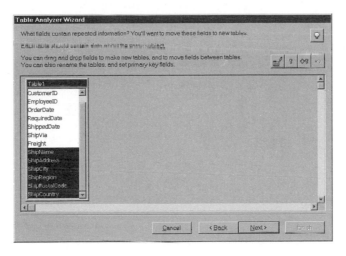

**FIG. 23.27**  Selecting the fields with duplicate data to move to a new table.

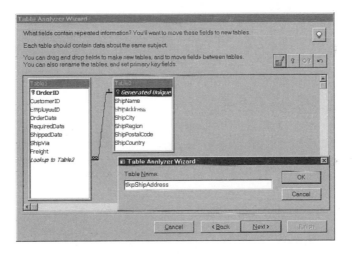

**FIG 23.28**  Naming the proposed tlkpShipAddress lookup table.

7.  CustomerID is a better choice than an AutoNumber field for the primary key
    field for tlkpShipAddress, because there is only one ShipAddress per customer
    in the Orders table. Click and drag the CustomerID field from the Table1 field
    list to the tlkpShipAddress field list. With the CustomerID field selected in the
    tlkpShipAddress field list, click the Set Unique Key button (with the key icon only).
    The Generated Unique ID field disappears and the CustomerID field becomes the
    primary key for the proposed tlkpShipAddress table (see Figure 23.29).

8.  Select Table1 and click the Rename Table button (the leftmost button in the group
    of three buttons near the top of the dialog) to display the Table Name input box.
    Give the table a new name—in this case, tblSalesOrders—and click OK to close the
    input box. Click Next to continue.

VI

Using Advanced Techniques

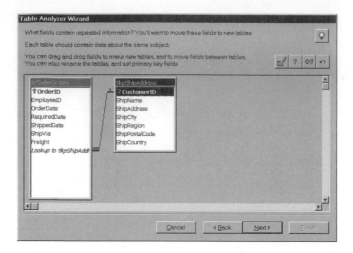

**FIG. 23.29** Specifying CustomerID as the primary key field for the tlkpShipAddress table.

9. If the wizard detects a misspelling of an entry in the lookup table, the dialog shown in Figure 23.30 appears. The wizard bases the marked check box in the Correct Record column on the frequency of exact duplication of records ("Alfred's Futter-kiste" appears several times, and "Alfreds Futterkiste" appears only once in the ShipName column). Verify which record is correct, and mark the Correct Record check box for the correct record(s), if necessary. The wizard automatically corrects the misspelled entries. Click Next to continue.

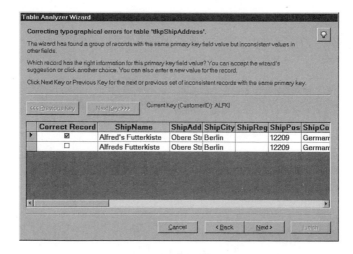

**FIG. 23.30** Correcting a misspelled entry in the ShipName field.

10. The wizard proposes to create a query, in this case named Orders, that substitutes for the original Orders table. Accept the Yes, Create the Query option. Clear the

Show Me Help check box to prevent two Lookup Wizard Help screens from appearing when you complete the operation (see Figure 23.31).

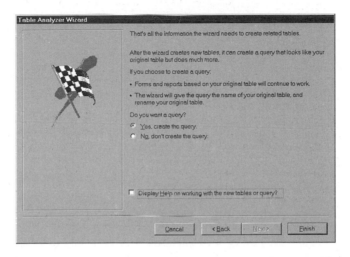

**FIG. 23.31**    Creating an Orders query as a substitute for the original Orders table.

11. Click Finish to create the Orders query and display the temporary Orders query  datasheet as shown in Figure 23.32. Click OK in the message box to create the final Orders query.

**FIG. 23.32**    The temporary Orders query displaying the Lookup to tlkpShipAddress column.

12. Verify that the Datasheet view of the final Orders query result set, which does not include the Lookup to Ship Addresses column, duplicates the original orders table. Figure 23.32 shows the Orders query in Query Design view.

13. The wizard has renamed the original Orders table to Orders_OLD. To return Northwind.mdb to its original state, open the Database window and delete the Orders query plus the tblSalesOrders and tlkpShipAddress tables, then rename the Orders_OLD table to Orders.

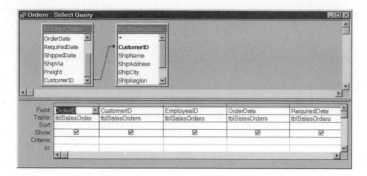

**FIG. 23.33** The final Orders query in Query Design view.

---

**Caution**

Extracting the duplicate shipping address information from the Orders table to a new tlkpShipAddress table is useful to demonstrate use of the Table Analyzer Wizard. But this extraction is not practical in the real world, where individual customers may have several shipping addresses. To make the tlkpShipAddress table useful, you must add a field, such as ShipToID, to identify multiple shipping addresses for a single customer. Assign a value of 0 for the ShipToID field for the default shipping information created by the wizard. Additional shipping addresses for a particular CustomerID are numbered 1, 2, 3, .... You need to redesign forms that specify shipping addresses to allow adding new tlkpShipAddress records for customers. You must change the primary key to a composite primary key consisting of CustomerID + ShipToID, and you must use Access VBA code to create successive ShipToID values automatically for a particular CustomerID.

---

# Working with Data Dictionaries

After you've determined the individual data entities that comprise the tables of your database and established the relationships between them, the next step is to prepare a preliminary written description of the database, called a *data dictionary*. Data dictionaries are indispensable to database systems; an undocumented database system is almost impossible to administer and maintain properly. Errors and omissions in database design often are uncovered when you prepare the preliminary data dictionary.

When you've completed and tested your database design, you prepare the final detailed version of the data dictionary. As you add new forms and reports to applications or modify existing forms and reports, you update the data dictionary to keep it current. Even if you're making a database for your personal use, a simplified version of a data dictionary pays many dividends on your time investment.

### Conventional Data Dictionaries

Data dictionaries contain a text description of the database as a whole, each table the database contains, the fields that comprise the table, primary and foreign keys, and values that may be assigned to fields when they contain coded or enumerated information.

The purpose and description of each application that uses the database is included. Data dictionaries shouldn't be dependent on the particular RDBMS used to create and manipulate the database. Because data dictionaries are hierarchical in nature, they lend themselves to the use of traditional outline formats that are implemented in Windows word processing applications. The following illustrates the structure of a conventional data dictionary using legal-style outline headings:

**1.** DATABASE—Proper name and file name

A text description of the purpose and general content of the database and who may use it. A list of applications that operate on the database is useful, along with references to any other databases that use the information that the database contains. If any graphic schema of the database have been prepared, they appear in this section.

1.1. DATA AREA—Name of the group of which tables are a member

When tables are classified by group, such as the Payroll group within the Human Resources database, include a description of the group.

1.1.1. TABLE—Individual tables that comprise the data area

1.1.1.1. PERMISSIONS—User domains with access to the table

1.1.1.2. RECORD—General definition of the data entities

1.1.1.2.1. PRIMARY KEY—Field(s) in the primary key

1.1.1.2.1.1. INDEX—Primary key index specification

1.1.1.2.2. FOREIGN KEY(S)—Other key fields

1.1.1.2.2.1 INDEX—Indexes on foreign keys

1.1.1.2.3. FIELDS—Non-key fields

1.1.1.2.3.1 ENUMERATIONS—Valid codes for fields

Text follows each heading and describes the purpose of the database element to which the heading refers. Subsequent headings include descriptions of the applications that use the database tables, with subheadings for queries, forms, and reports. Captured images of displays and copies of reports add to the usefulness of the data dictionary. Printouts of programming code usually are contained in appendixes. Complete data dictionaries are essential for database maintenance. An alternative format consists of content descriptions of each table in tabular form.

### Access's Integrated Data Dictionary System

Access 97's Database Documentor Add-In was introduced in Access 2.0. The Documentor creates a report that details the objects and values of the properties of the objects in the current database.

> **Note**
>
> The Access 2.0 version of Documentor printed reports, but couldn't export its data to tables or files. Access 97's Publish It with MS Word feature of the Office Links toolbar button allows you to save the report as an .rtf file (doc_rptObjects.rtf) for importing into Microsoft Word or any other word processor (such as WordPad) that handles rich-text files. Alternatively, you can export the report in BIFF format to an Excel doc_rptObjects.xls file by choosing the Analyze It with MS Excel option.

In many cases, Documentor tells you more than you want to know about your database; the full report for all objects in Northwind.mdb, for example, requires about 400 printed pages. Most often, you only want to document your tables and, perhaps, your queries to create a complete data dictionary. The following steps show you how to create a data dictionary with Database Documentor:

1. Open the database you want to document, and then choose Tools, Analyze, Documentor. Documentor's Select Objects opening tabbed dialog appears with Tables selected, as shown in Figure 23.34 for Nwind.mdb.

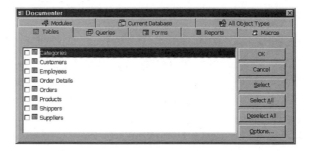

**FIG. 23.34** Database Documentor's opening tabbed dialog.

2. Click the tab for the type of object you want to document to display the list of objects. The All Object Types tab adds every object in the database to the list when you click Select All.

3. With the Tables list selected, click Options to display the Print Table Definition dialog. The most detailed set of information for tables and indexes is the default. If your Access database is not secure, you can clear the Permissions by User and Group check box to eliminate reporting permissions data (see Figure 23.35). Click OK to return to the Documenter dialog.

4. Select the table(s) you want to document in the Tables list, and then click Select. This marks the table's check box, as shown in Figure 23.36. (Clicking the check box for an item has the same effect.) Alternatively, if you want to document all tables of your database, click Select All. For this example, only the Orders and Order Details tables are documented.

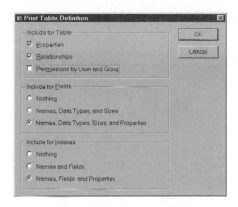

**FIG. 23.35**  Setting options for documenting tables.

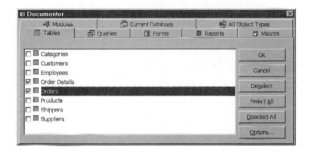

**FIG. 23.36**  Two tables selected for documenting.

**5.** Click the Queries tab to display the QueryDef objects in your database. Click the Options button to display the Print Query Definition dialog. Clear the Permissions by User and Group check box to eliminate security data from the report, and select the other options shown in Figure 23.37 to minimize duplication of table field data. Click OK to continue.

**6.** Click the Order Details Extended check box to add this query to the documentation, and then click OK to create the report, which is 13 pages long.

**7.** After a short period, the Object Definition print preview window appears (see Figure 23.38) with the Order Details table at the beginning of the list. Click the Last Page button to view the documentation for the Order Information query.

**8.** Click the Print button on the toolbar to print the report, or click the OfficeLinks button to create a doc_rptObjects.rtf or doc_rptObjects.xls file. Figure 23.39 shows part of a doc_rptObjects.xls file pertaining to the Order Details table.

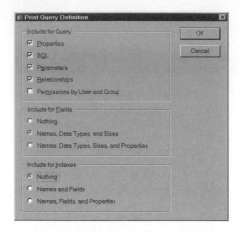

**FIG. 23.37** Selecting the options for printing query definitions.

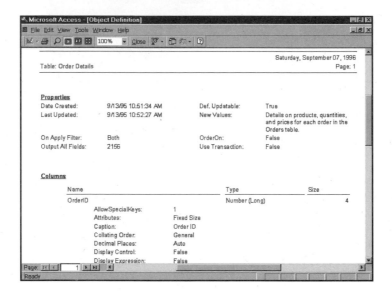

**FIG. 23.38** The first page of Database Documentor's report.

   **9.** Click the Close button on the toolbar, or double-click the Document Control-menu box to close the print preview window.

Documenting other objects in your database follows the same method outlined in the preceding steps. You can print data for the database itself by clicking the Current Database tab, or you can print data for selected forms, reports, macros, and modules.

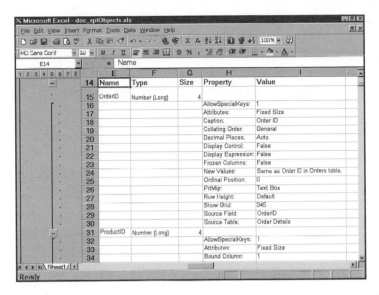

**FIG. 23.39**  Part of the doc_rptObjects.xls displayed in Microsoft Excel 97.

# Using Access Indexes

Database managers use indexes to relate the values of key fields to the location of the data entity on the disk. The basic purpose of an index is to speed up access to specific rows or groups of rows within a database table. You also use indexes to enforce the uniqueness of primary keys and establish upper and lower limits for queries. Using an index eliminates the necessity of re-sorting the table each time you need to create a se-quenced list based on a foreign key.

Different PC database managers create and use indexes in a variety of ways. Paradox uses a mandatory primary index (.px) to speed up queries and ensure nonduplicate keys. Secondary indexes on nonprimary-key fields are permitted by Paradox (.x## and .y##) and created either by the QuerySpeedUp menu choice or the PAL INDEX instruction. dBASE and some of its xBase dialects allow any number of indexes to be created in the form of individual .ndx files, for a single file or table. The number of xBase indexes that you can have open at once, so as to keep them current, is determined by the xBase RDBMS you choose. In xBase and FoxPro, you select the index you want to use with the SET ORDER TO *IndexFileName* instruction. Several xBase languages have their own index structures, such as Clipper's .ntx and FoxPro's .idx. dBASE IV+ and FoxPro go one step beyond with their multiple index structures (.mdx and .cdx, respectively) that combine several indexes in a single file. You specify a TAG name to identify which index is to be used to find the records you want.

### Indexed Sequential Access Method

*Indexed Sequential Access Method* (ISAM) describes a file structure in which the records are logically located (sorted) in their primary key's sequence of values, with an index used to provide random access to individual records. The term logically is applied to record location because the records' physical location on the disk may not be sequential; their physical location is determined by the disk's file allocation table (FAT, for Windows 95) and the degree of file fragmentation on the drive. ISAM is often used to describe any database structure that uses indexes for searching. This book adheres to the original definition, in which the records must be in the order of their primary key.

Classic mainframe ISAM databases have file structures that use *overflow sectors*, space reserved on the disk to handle insertion of new records. The database administrator periodically sorts the file to insert the data from the overflow sectors into the body of the table structure at appropriate locations. The periodic sorting clears the overflow sectors for future additions. The process is called *file maintenance*. Improved insertion techniques have been applied to databases created by PC and client/server RDBMSs. These methods are described in the sections that follow.

DOS RDBMSs duplicate ISAM structures by using an insertion technique. For instance, many xBase dialects allow you to INSERT a record in the middle of a file (the ISAM method), rather than APPEND a BLANK to the end of a file (the heap technique). When you INSERT a record near the top of a large, indexed xBase file, you can catch up on your sleep while the RDBMS moves all of the following records to make room for the new one, adjusting all index entries to refer to new locations. Figure 23.40 shows the difference between a record INSERT and APPEND. Paradox's native mode is ISAM, which explains why some of its operations, such as canceling an edit on a large table, take so long to complete.

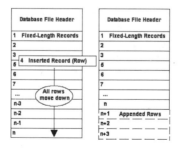

**FIG. 23.40**   Inserting versus appending new records in an xBase file.

Certain types of files created by DOS RDBMSs inherently fit the ISAM mold—sales order. Invoice records with a numeric key incremented by one for each addition are the best examples. Access's AutoNumber field data type performs the numbering function automatically. Other types of tables, such as lists of customers, are often sorted alphabetically. You have to INSERT each record in the proper location or re-sort the file each time you add a new customer to maintain a true ISAM structure. The faster method with xBase is to APPEND BLANKs and REPLACE the blanks WITH data; this procedure adds the new records in a heap at the bottom of the file. Periodically, DOS adds another cluster to the file to accommodate the newly added data. Some xBase dialects, such as Clipper, don't include the INSERT command.

The header of an xBase .dbf file, such as the one in Figure 23.40, includes the name of each field, its field data type, its length in bytes, and some additional data. All data records in the file are the same length, representing the sum of the field lengths plus one byte, to indicate whether the record is marked for deletion. xBase files are called the *fixed-length record type*. Values that don't fill the length of a field are padded with spaces; character fields are padded with spaces to the right of the text, and numbers are right-justified by padding to the left. xBase files often incorporate much more padding than data.

The record numbers shown in Figure 23.40 aren't present in the data but are deduced by calculating the offset (the intervening number of bytes) of the record from the beginning of the file. If the header is 300 bytes long, record 1 begins at offset 300, corresponding to the 301st byte (the offset of the first byte is 0). Assuming the fields total 80 bytes in width, record 2 begins at offset 380, record 3 begins at offset 460, and so forth. The location of a data item's value is determined by calculating the offset of the desired record, then adding the offset to the beginning of the column (field) containing the data.

### Access Data Pages and Variable Length Records

Access, like Microsoft SQL Server and many other SQL databases, divides the data stored in its table structures into 2K data pages, corresponding to the size of a conventional DOS fixed-disk file cluster. A header, similar to the one in Figure 23.41, is added to each page to create the foundation for a linked list of data pages. The header contains a reference, called a *pointer*, to the page that precedes it. The header contains another pointer to the page that follows. Linked lists use pointers to link the data pages to one another in order to organize the data table. If no indexes are in use, new data is added to the last page of the table until the page is full, and then another page is added at the end. The process is much like the heap method used by xBase or the manner in which DOS creates entries that link fixed-disk data clusters in its file allocation table.

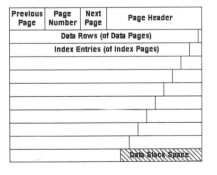

**FIG. 23.41**   The structure of a data page in an Access table.

VI

Using Advanced Techniques

Data pages contain only integral numbers of rows. The space that remains after the last row that fits in the page is called slack. You may be familiar with the concept of slack from the characteristic of current DOS versions that allocate fixed-disk file space in 2K clusters or larger. A small batch file, for example, may be displayed as having a file size of 120 bytes, but the file actually occupies a minimum of 2,048 bytes of disk space; the unused space is slack. Access uses variable-length records for its data rows instead of the fixed-length record structure of xBase. Variable-length records don't require padding for data that is shorter than the designated field size.

Data rows longer than 2K are contained in multiple pages. Avoid long rows if possible, as they can reduce storage efficiency by increasing the percentage of slack space in data pages. Access .mdb files with relatively short rows store data, especially character-based data, more efficiently than xBase or Paradox. Special fields containing text and images are stored in separate data structures linked to the data item in the data page. The storage concept is similar to that for xBase memo files, but the implementation differs in Access.

The advantage of data pages with their own headers (over the single-header, record-based xBase structure shown earlier in Figure 23.40) is that you can keep a table's data pages in ISAM order by altering only the pointers in the page header and not the structure of the file itself. This process, which uses a nonclustered index (discussed later in this chapter in the section "Nonclustered and Clustered Indexes"), is much faster than the INSERT method for xBase files and usually matches the speed of the APPEND technique.

### Balanced Binary Trees, Roots, and Leaves

Most database managers use an indexing method called a *binary tree*, or *B-tree*. In describing an index structure, the tree is inverted, with its root and trunk at the top, progressing downward to branches and leaves—the direction taken by the searching process. A binary tree is defined as a tree in which the trunk divides into two branches, with each branch dividing into two sub-branches and then into further twofold divisions until you reach the leaves, which are indivisible. The points of the two-way divisions are called *nodes*. B-trees for computer-based searching were first proposed in 1946 by John Mauchly, one of the pioneers of electronic computers.

When you make many insertions and deletions in a database, conventional B-tree structures can become very lopsided, with many sub-branches and leaves stemming from one branch and few from another. The reason for this pattern is explained by mathematical theory that is beyond the scope of this book. Lopsided B-trees slow the searching process for records that are in an especially active area of the database. This situation causes undesirable effects in, for example, an airline reservation system where passenger reservations are being added to or deleted from a flight at a rapid rate immediately prior to its scheduled departure.

To solve the lopsided B-tree problem, two Russian mathematicians, G. M. Adelson-Velski and E. M. Landis, proposed a balanced B-tree structure in 1963. In a balanced B-tree structure, the length of the search path to any leaf is never more than 45 percent longer than the optimum. Each time a new row is added to the index, a new node is inserted and the tree is rebalanced if necessary. A small, balanced B-tree structure appears in Figure 23.42. Its nodes are labeled + (plus) or − (minus), called the balance factor, according to whether the right subtree height minus the left subtree height is +1 or −1. If the subtrees are the same height, the node is empty. Balance factors are used to determine where a new node is added to maintain the tree in balance.

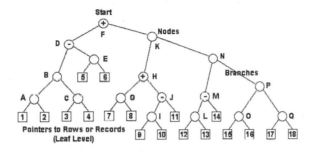

**FIG. 23.42**   A diagram of a simple balanced B-tree index.

Access and most other modern RDBMSs use the balanced B-tree structure to create indexes. Balanced B-trees improve search speed at the expense of increasing the time necessary to add new records, especially when the table is indexed on several keys. In a multitasking or client/server environment, however, the server conducts the addition process independently. The user can then perform other client operations, such as entering the key to search for another record, while the server's insertion and index rebalancing operations are going on.

### Nonclustered and Clustered Indexes

Most RDBMSs, including Access, use nonclustered indexes to locate records with specific key values. Nonclustered means that the RDBMS adds data by the heap or APPEND method. Furthermore, nonclustered means that the rows of the table aren't in the sequence of their primary key—that is, the table isn't structured as an ISAM table. Figure 23.43 shows the structure, compressed and truncated, of a nonclustered Access index. xBase indexes have a similar structure, substituting records for data pages.

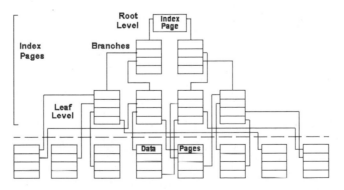

**FIG. 23.43**   A diagram of a conventional nonclustered index.

Notice the more-or-less random association of the data pages to the location of the pointers at the leaf level of the index. This lack of order is typical for indexes on foreign keys in all types of databases and for indexes on primary keys in non-ISAM files. If organized into an ISAM structure with the index created on the primary key, the file would have the more organized appearance of the diagram in Figure 23.44.

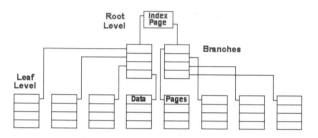

**FIG. 23.44**   A diagram of a clustered index.

Many client/server databases, such as Microsoft SQL Server, can use a clustered index to create ISAM order out of heap-induced chaos. When you use a clustered index, its table converts from heap-based row-insertion structure to the balanced B-tree structure you saw in Figure 23.42. In this case, the leaf level of the index consists of the data pages themselves. This organization is accomplished by rewriting the pointers in each data page's header in the order of the key on which the clustered index is based. Because the header can have only one set of pointers, fore and aft, you can have only one clustered index per table. In almost all cases, you create the clustered index from the primary key, but a clustered index need not be unique.

To retain the balanced B-tree organization of data pages, an RDBMS needs a balancing technique for insertions. Instead of using overflow sectors, the RDBMS adds a new page, readjusts the header pointers to include the new page in the linked list, and then moves the last half of the rows in the original page to the new page. The RDBMS then updates the index to reflect the changes. This process speeds up data access but slows updating; therefore, the process is practical only for an RDBMS running on a high-speed server computer under an advanced operating system, such as Windows NT 4.0, and that contains a lot of RAM.

### Query Speed versus Update Performance

Access automatically creates an index on the primary key field. Adding other indexes to Access tables is a doubled-edged sword. You speed up the performance of queries because the index assists the sort sequence; you don't need to sort the query's Recordset object on a primary key index. Furthermore, sorts in the order of other indexes you specify are faster. On the other hand, when you append a new record, Access must take the time to update all of the table's indexes. When you edit a field of a record that is included in one or more indexes, Access has to update each of the indexes affected by the edit.

Beginning with version 2.0, Access incorporates FoxPro's Rushmore technology that optimizes query operations on indexed tables with large numbers of records. Many decision-support queries can be speeded by a factor of 10 to 25 or more by adding the appropriate indexes, in addition to the index on the primary key field that is created for you. You can improve the performance of Access applications, especially when tables with large numbers of records or queries that join several tables are involved, by observing these guidelines:

- Minimize the number of indexes used with transaction-based tables, especially in networked multiuser applications that share tables. Access locks pages so that they aren't editable by other users while you are editing records and during the time it takes Access to update the indexes when you are finished.

- Minimize the number of indexes in tables that are used regularly with INSERT and DELETE queries. The time required to update indexes is especially evident when making changes to the data in bulk.

- Add indexes judiciously to tables that have large numbers of records and are used primarily in decision-support applications.

- Add indexes to foreign key fields of tables that participate in joins with primary tables. However, when specifying a selection criterion on the key field, always use the key field of the primary table rather than the foreign key field of the related table.

- Add indexes to fields on which you set criteria. If transaction-processing performance is more important than the speed of decision-support applications, add indexes only to those fields that occur most often in the criteria of your select queries.

Indexing becomes more important as the number of records in your tables increases. You might need to experiment to determine whether an index is effective in significantly increasing the speed of a query. If you find the index is warranted by improved query performance, check the speed of transaction processes with the new index before committing to its use.

> **Note**
>
> If you are using a shared database on a peer-to-peer network, such as Windows 95 networking, and the database is located on your computer, use another workgroup member's computer to test the effectiveness of indexes. Network characteristics may significantly affect the performance of indexes. Try to make the test during periods of maximum network traffic, not during off hours, when no one is contributing to network congestion.

# Enforcing Database Integrity

The integrity of a database is comprised of two elements: entity and referential integrity. Entity integrity requires that all primary keys must be unique within a table, and referential integrity dictates that all foreign keys must have corresponding values within a base table's primary key. Although the normalization process creates entity and referential integrity, either the RDBMS itself or your application must maintain that integrity during the data-entry process. Failure to maintain database integrity can result in erroneous data values and, ultimately, widespread corruption of the entire database.

### Ensuring Entity Integrity and Auditability

Database managers differ widely in their capabilities to maintain entity integrity through unique primary key values. Paradox, for instance, enforces unique primary keys within the RDBMS by flagging as a key violation any attempt to insert a row with an identical primary key. Paradox then places the offending record in the KeyViol table. Access uses a similar technique when you specify a no-duplicates index. If you paste or append records that have duplicate primary keys, Access appends those records to a Paste Errors or Append Errors table.

> **Note**
>
> In xBase, you can add as many records with duplicate index keys as you want. If you use SET UNIQUE ON, a SEEK finds only the first record with the same key. However, any duplicate keys remain in the file and, for example, appear in an indexed LIST operation. Indexed DELETEs affect only the first undeleted record found for the SEEK parameter; you must perform a DELETE for each duplicate. You need to write xBase code, therefore, to test for data duplicates before you APPEND the record that adds the data to the file.

Enforcing entity integrity within the table itself, the process used by Access, is more reliable than using application programming code to prevent the duplication of primary key values. Access provides two methods of ensuring entity integrity that are independent of the applications employing the tables:

- A key field that uses the AutoNumber data type that creates unique values based on an automatically incremented long integer. Using incremental AutoNumber fields is the most common method for creating primary key fields. You cannot create a duplicate primary key in this case because you cannot edit the values in fields of the AutoNumber data type. Random AutoNumber fields are not suitable for creating primary key values, because there is no assurance that a randomly-assigned number is not duplicated in tables with very large numbers of records.

- An index on the primary key field with the No Duplicates property. If you attempt to enter a duplicate value in the key field, Access displays an error message.

Either of these methods ensures unique key fields, but an AutoNumber field is helpful so that documents such as sales orders, invoices, and checks are sequentially numbered. Sequential numbering is necessary for internal control and auditing purposes. Auto-Number (Incremental) fields normally begin with 1 as the first record in a table, but rarely does a real-world cash disbursement or invoice table need 1 as its starting number. You cannot create a table with a Long Integer Number field, enter the beginning number, and then change the field data type to AutoNumber. Access issues a warning message if you attempt this procedure. You can use an append query, however, to establish a specific beginning AutoNumber value.

> **Note**
>
> Access increments the value of the AutoNumber field even if Access prevents you from adding a record to a table with an AutoNumber field. Such a situation can occur if domain or referential integrity rules are violated when the addition of a record is attempted. For this reason, an Access AutoNumber field is not likely to be satisfactory for applications where sequential documents must be accounted for.

To create a starting AutoNumber field value of 123456 in the Invoice field of the tblInvoices table's first record, perform the following steps:

1. Open the Database window, select the Orders table, and press Ctrl+C to copy the table to the Clipboard.

2. Press Ctrl+V and type **tblInvoices** as the name of the table to create. Then select the Structure Only option button to create the new tblInvoices table with no records.

3. Open the tblInvoices table in Design mode, click the select button of the Order ID field, and change the field data type from AutoNumber to Number (Long Integer).

4. Click the Datasheet View button on the toolbar, and click OK to save your changes. Alternatively, choose File, Save. (Access 97 does not allow two or more operations on AutoNumber fields in a single design operation.)

5. If you changed to Datasheet view, Reopen the table in Design mode, select the OrderID field, and press Insert to add a new field.

6. Enter InvoiceID as the Field Name, and choose AutoNumber (Increment) as the Data Type.

7. Click the Indexes button on the toolbar. Delete the Primary Key index on OrderID, which enables you to append a record that doesn't have a value for the key field (Null values aren't allowed in key fields). The tblInvoices table design appears as shown in Figure 23.45. Close the Indexes window.

   You also need to set the value of the Required property of the CustomerID field to No and the Allow Zero Length property to Yes. Otherwise, the append query that follows will not execute.

8. Close the tblInvoices table and save your changes. Don't create a primary key field at this point.

9. Create a new temporary table named tblFirstInvoice with one field, named InvoiceID.

10. Set the InvoiceID field's Data Type property to Number and the Field Size property to Long Integer.

11. Change to Datasheet view; don't create a primary key field when asked; and enter a value in InvoiceID that is one less than the starting number you want (for this example, type **123455**).

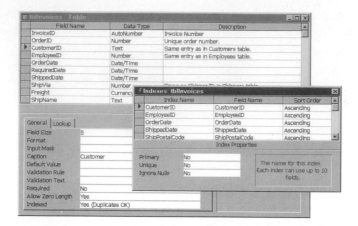

**FIG. 23.45** A table designed for adding an AutoNumber field with an arbitrary starting number.

**12.** Close the tblFirstInvoice table and save your changes.

**13.** Create a new query and add the tblFirstInvoice table. Click and drag the InvoiceID field symbol to the first column of the Query Design grid.

**14.** Choose Query, Append and type **tblInvoices** as the table to which to append the record. Click OK. Invoice automatically appears as the Append To field (see Figure 23.46). Click the Run button on the toolbar to add the single record in tblFirstInvoice to the tblInvoices table.

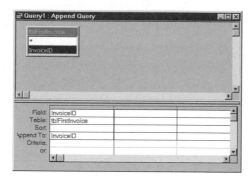

**FIG. 23.46** The append query to set the first value of an AutoNumber field.

**15.** Close Query1 without saving your changes.

The next record you append to tblInvoices is assigned the value 123456 in the InvoiceID (AutoNumber) field. To verify that this technique works properly for appended records, perform the following steps:

**1.** Create a new query, and add the Orders table. Click and drag the * symbol to the first column of the Query Design grid.

**2.** Choose Query, Append and enter tblInvoiceData as the table to which to append the records from the Orders table (see Figure 23.47). Click the Run Query button on the toolbar to add the records from the Orders table.

**3.** Close Query1 and don't save the changes.

**4.** Open the tblInvoices table.

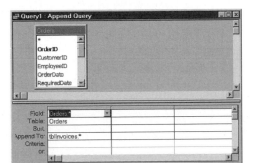

**FIG. 23.47**  The append query to add records from the Orders table to the tblInvoices table.

Access has added numbers beginning with 123456 to the new Invoice field, corresponding to OrderID values of 10000 and higher, as shown in Figure 23.48.

If you were adding an AutoNumber field to real-world data, you would delete the first blank record and then make the InvoiceID field the primary key field. Access creates a no-duplicates index when you assign an AutoNumber field as a primary key field.

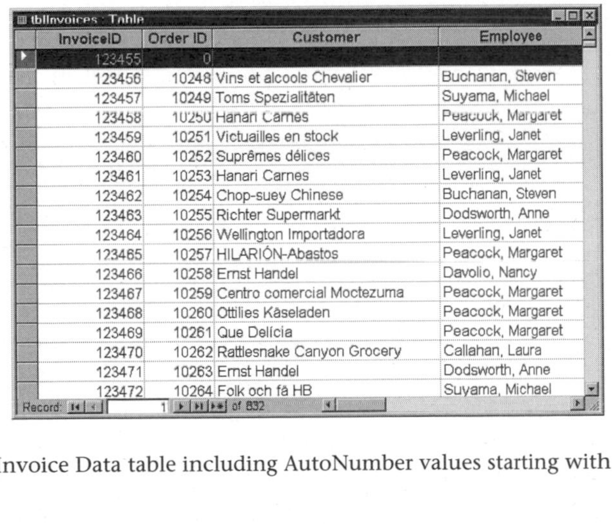

| InvoiceID | Order ID | Customer | Employee |
|---|---|---|---|
| 123455 | 0 | | |
| 123456 | 10248 | Vins et alcools Chevalier | Buchanan, Steven |
| 123457 | 10249 | Toms Spezialitäten | Suyama, Michael |
| 123458 | 10250 | Hanari Carnes | Peacock, Margaret |
| 123459 | 10251 | Victuailles en stock | Leverling, Janet |
| 123460 | 10252 | Suprêmes délices | Peacock, Margaret |
| 123461 | 10253 | Hanari Carnes | Leverling, Janet |
| 123462 | 10254 | Chop-suey Chinese | Buchanan, Steven |
| 123463 | 10255 | Richter Supermarkt | Dodsworth, Anne |
| 123464 | 10256 | Wellington Importadora | Leverling, Janet |
| 123465 | 10257 | HILARIÓN-Abastos | Peacock, Margaret |
| 123466 | 10258 | Ernst Handel | Davolio, Nancy |
| 123467 | 10259 | Centro comercial Moctezuma | Peacock, Margaret |
| 123468 | 10260 | Ottilies Käseladen | Peacock, Margaret |
| 123469 | 10261 | Que Delícia | Peacock, Margaret |
| 123470 | 10262 | Rattlesnake Canyon Grocery | Callahan, Laura |
| 123471 | 10263 | Ernst Handel | Dodsworth, Anne |
| 123472 | 10264 | Folk och fä HB | Suyama, Michael |

Record: 1 of 832

**FIG. 23.48**  The Invoice Data table including AutoNumber values starting with 123456.

> **Troubleshooting**
>
> *When I try to execute the append query that provides the starting value minus 1 to my table structure, I get an error message.*
>
> You have constraints on the fields of your destination table that do not allow Null values or empty strings in fields. Open your destination table in Design mode, and make sure that the Required property of each field is set to No and that the Allow Zero Length property of each field of the Text data type is set to Yes. Also, make sure that your destination table does not specify a primary key field.

## Maintaining Referential Integrity

Prior chapters have discussed the use of Access's database-level referential integrity enforcement capabilities, which were introduced in Access 2.0. Maintaining referential integrity requires strict adherence to a single rule: *Each foreign key field in a related table must correspond to a primary key field in a base or primary table.* This rule requires that the following types of transactions be prevented:

- Adding a record on the many side of a one-to-many relationship without the existence of a corresponding record on the one side of the relationship.

- Deleting a record on the one side of a one-to-many relationship without first deleting all corresponding records on the many side of the relationship.

- Deleting or adding a record to a table in a one-to-one relationship with another table without deleting or adding a corresponding record in the related table.

- Changing the value of a primary key field of a base table on which records in a relation table depend.

- Changing the value of a foreign key field in a relation table to a value that doesn't exist in the primary key field of a base table.

A record in a relation table that has a foreign key with a value that doesn't correspond to the value of a primary key in a relation table is called an *orphan record*.

Whenever possible, use Access's built-in INNER JOIN, cascading updates, and cascading deletions features to maintain referential integrity at the database level. Don't rely on applications to test for referential integrity violations when adding records to relation tables or deleting records from base tables. Access gives you the opportunity to enforce referential integrity automatically between tables in a database by marking the Enforce Referential Integrity check box in the Relationships dialog. As noted in Chapter 11, "Using Action Queries," you can specify cascade updates and deletes when you use Access's referential integrity enforcement capabilities. Access 97 also enforces referential integrity in linked Access tables.

> **Note**
>
> Most xBase RDBMSs don't have the capability to enforce referential integrity automatically. You need to write xBase code that tests for the required records with SEEK commands on indexed files.

# Chapter 24

# Working with Structured Query Language

This chapter describes Structured Query Language (SQL), the structure and syntax of the language, and how Access translates queries you design with Access's graphical query-by-example (QBE) technique into SQL statements. An SQL background helps you understand the query process and design more efficient queries. A knowledge of SQL syntax is necessary to use the new subquery and UNION query capabilities introduced by Access 2.0 and for many of the applications you write in Access VBA. Examples of SQL have been presented in other chapters in this book. These examples—usually figures that illustrate an SQL statement created by Access—demonstrate what occurs behind the scenes when you create a query or a graph.

In this chapter, you learn more about:

- SQL Reserved Words

- SQL Query Syntax

- Basic SQL SELECT Queries

- SQL INNER JOINs, OUTER JOINs, and UNION Queries

- SQL INSERT, UPDATE, and DELETE Queries

> **Note**
>
> There are no significant differences between the Access 2.0, Access 95, and Access 97 versions of SQL, previously known as *Access SQL*. The new name for Access SQL is *Microsoft Jet Database Engine SQL*, called *Jet SQL* in this book for brevity. The primary additions to Access SQL occurred during the upgrade from Access 1.1 to Access 2.0. The new Jet SQL terminology is more appropriate than Access SQL, because all members of Microsoft Office, Visual Basic, and any other application that supports VBA can use the Jet database engine.

## Using Access to Learn SQL

Access is a useful learning tool for gaining fluency in SQL. This chapter shows you how to create Access QBE queries from SQL statements entered in the SQL dialog. If you use SQL with another RDBMS, such as Microsoft SQL Server, this chapter can help you make the transition from ANSI/Access/Jet SQL to Transact-SQL, the extended version of SQL used by Microsoft SQL Server. A knowledge of SQL also is necessary for Visual Basic programmers because Visual Basic doesn't include a graphical QBE feature.

Many users of Access decision-support applications want to be able to define their own queries. When you open an Access 97 database with the run-time version of Access, the Query Design window is hidden. Thus, you must design forms that include control objects that users can manipulate to construct a Jet SQL statement that returns the desired query result set. You write Access VBA code to translate users' choices on the form into a Jet SQL statement; then create a QueryDef object (a persistent query definition whose name appears in the Database window) in the current database.

> **Note**
>
> This book uses the term *Access VBA* to mean the Access "flavor" of VBA that includes preestablished references to Microsoft Access 97 object collections, such as Forms and Reports, and elements of the Jet 3.5 Data Access Object (DAO), as well as VBA itself. The "flavor" of other VBA-enabled applications—such as Excel VBA, Word VBA, or Project VBA—is determined by the application's object collections that are referenced by default.

# What Is Structured Query Language?

Structured Query Language, abbreviated SQL (usually pronounced "sequel" or "seekel," but more properly "ess-cue-ell"), is the common language of client/server database management. The principal advantage of SQL is that it's standardized—you can use a common set of SQL statements with all SQL-compliant database management systems. The first U.S. SQL standard was established in 1986 as ANSI X3.135-1986. The current version is ANSI X3.135-1992, usually known as SQL-92.

> **Note**
>
> *ANSI*, an acronym for the *American National Standards Institute,* is an organization devoted to establishing and maintaining scientific and engineering standards. ANSI-standard SQL was first adopted as a worldwide standard in 1987 by the International Standards Organization (ISO), a branch of the United Nations. Microsoft states that Jet SQL "generally is ANSI SQL-89 Level 1-compliant."

SQL is an application language for relational databases, not a system or programming language. SQL is a set-oriented language; thus, ANSI SQL includes neither a provision for program flow control (branching and looping), nor keywords to create data entry forms and print reports. Programming functions usually are implemented in a system language such as xBase, C, C++, or COBOL. Some implementations of SQL, such as Transact-SQL used by Microsoft SQL Server, add flow control statements (IF...ELSE and WHILE) to the language. Publishers of ANSI SQL-compliant RDBMSes are free to extend the language if the basic ANSI commands are supported. The ANSI/ISO implementation of SQL is independent of any system language with which it might be used.

ANSI SQL includes a set of standard commands (keyword verbs) that are broadly grouped into six categories:

- Data definition
- Data query
- Data manipulation
- Cursor control
- Transaction processing
- Administration or control

Provisions for SQL keywords that maintain data integrity were added in a 1989 revision of the original standard as ANSI X3.135-1989, *Database Language—SQL with Integrity Enhancement*. Jet 3.5's implementation of SQL includes the data integrity keywords.

SQL has three different methods of implementation:

- *Direct Invocation*. Sends a series of SQL statements to the RDBMS. The RDBMS responds to the query by creating a table that contains the result and displays the table. Entering SQL commands at the dBASE IV SQL prompt is an example of Direct Invocation.

- *Module Language*. Lets you write a text file of SQL statements that later are executed by an application; you begin the SQL statement with the MODULE keyword and specify the programming LANGUAGE.

- *Embedded SQL*. The most common implementation; the SQL statements are generated by the application or included as strings of text in a command of an application language. Access queries, whether created by graphical QBE, by an SQL property in Access VBA, or by the Row Source property of a graph, use Embedded SQL.

# Looking at the Development of SQL

SQL was created because, early in the 1970s, IBM wanted a method with which nonprogrammers could extract and display the information they wanted from a database. Languages that nonprogrammers can use are called *fourth generation*, or *4GL*, and sometimes are referred to as *structured English*. The first commercial result of this effort was Query By Example (QBE), developed at IBM's laboratories in Yorktown Heights, New York. QBE was used, beginning in the late 1970s, on terminals connected to IBM System 370 mainframes. A user could obtain a result with less than an 80-character line of QBE code that required 100 or more lines to implement in COBOL or the other 3GL languages of the day. Access, dBASE IV and 5, and Paradox use QBE to display selected data from tables.

At the other end of the country, programmers at IBM's San Jose, California facility were developing System R, the progenitor of SQL/DS and IBM's DB2 relational database. In the mid-1970s, IBM scientist Dr. E.F. Codd proposed SQL (then known as SEQUEL for *S*tructured *E*nglish *Q*uery *L*anguage) as a means of accessing information from the relational database model he had developed in 1970. Relational databases based on the Codd model that use the SQL language to retrieve and update data within them have become, like QBE, computer-industry standards.

SQL has achieved the status of being the exclusive language of relational client/server databases. A *database server application* (the back end) holds the data. *Client applications* (front ends) add to or edit the data. The client application generates SQL statements. If you deal regularly with databases of any type, the odds are great that you ultimately will need to learn SQL. You need to learn Jet SQL *now* if you plan to create applications with user-defined queries that work with the run-time version of Access. You also need to learn SQL if you want to take full advantage of the Internet Database Connector (IDC/ HTX files) described in Chapter 18, "Creating Dynamic Web Pages."

## Comparing ANSI and Jet SQL

Jet SQL doesn't include many of the approximately 100 keywords incorporated in the ANSI standard for SQL. Few, if any, commercial SQL-compliant RDBMSes for the PC implement much more than half of the standard SQL keywords. The majority of the common SQL keywords missing from Jet's implementation are provided by the expressions you create with operators, built-in functions, or user-defined functions you write in Access VBA. The effect of many unsupported ANSI SQL keywords related to tables is achieved by making selections from Access's Database window or from menus.

When you learn a new language, it's helpful to categorize the vocabulary of the language by usage and then into the familiar parts of speech. SQL commands, therefore, first are divided into six usage categories:

- *Data Query Language (DQL)*. Sometimes referred to as *data retrieval commands*, obtain data from tables and determine how the results of the retrieval are presented. The SELECT command is the principal instruction in this category. DQL commands often are considered members of the Data Manipulation Language category.

- *Data Manipulation Language (DML)*. Provide INSERT and DELETE commands, which add or delete entire rows, and the UPDATE command, which can change the values of data in specified columns within rows.

- *Transaction Processing Language (TPL)*. Include BEGIN TRANS[ACTION], COMMIT [WORK], and ROLLBACK [WORK], which group multiple DML operations. If one DML operation of a transaction fails, the preceding DML operations are canceled (rolled back). Jet SQL doesn't support TPL; instead, you use the Access VBA BeginTrans, CommitTrans, and Rollback methods to support transaction processing.

- *Data Definition Language (DDL)*. Include CREATE TABLE and CREATE VIEW instructions that define the structure of tables and views. DDL commands are used also to modify tables and to create and delete indexes. The keywords that implement data integrity are used in conjunction with DDL statements. Jet SQL supports the CREATE TABLE and CREATE INDEX instructions.

■ *Cursor Control Language (CCL)*. Can select a single row of a query result set for processing. Cursor control constructs, such as UPDATE WHERE CURRENT, are implemented by the Jet database engine, so these commands are not discussed in this chapter.

■ *Data Control Language (DCL)*. Perform administrative functions that grant and revoke privileges to use the database, such as GRANT and REVOKE, a set of tables within the database, or specific SQL commands. Jet SQL does not include DCL; instead, you use Access's security objects for implementing security.

Keywords that comprise the vocabulary of SQL are identified further in the following categories:

■ *Commands*, such as SELECT, are verbs that cause an action to be performed.

■ *Qualifiers*, such as WHERE, limit the range of values of the entities that comprise the query.

■ *Clauses*, such as ORDER BY, modify the action of an instruction.

■ *Operators*, such as =, <, or >, compare values and are used to create joins when JOIN syntax is not used. Jet SQL uses JOIN syntax by default, but lets you use operators to create joins.

■ *Group aggregate functions*, such as MIN(), return a single result for a set of values.

■ Other keywords modify the action of a clause or manipulate cursors that are used to select specific rows of queries.

> **Note**
>
> SQL keywords usually are capitalized, but the keywords aren't case-sensitive. The uppercase convention is used in this book, and SQL keywords are set in the monospace type. You use *parameters*, such as *column_list*, to define or modify the action specified by keywords. Names of replaceable parameters are printed in lowercase italicized monospace type.

### SQL Reserved Words in Access

Access doesn't support all the ANSI SQL keywords with identical reserved words in the Jet SQL language. In this chapter, *keywords* are defined as the commands and functions that comprise the ANSI SQL language. Jet SQL commands and functions, however, are referred to here as *reserved words* to distinguish them from ANSI SQL.

The tables in the following section are intended to acquaint readers who are familiar with ANSI or similar implementations of SQL in other DBMs or database front-end applications with the Access implementation of SQL. If you haven't used SQL, the tables demonstrate that SQL is a relatively sparse language, having far fewer keywords than programming languages like VBA, and that Jet SQL is even more sparse. Jet SQL has few reserved words to learn. You learned in Chapter 9, "Understanding Operators and Expressions in Access," to use the Access operators and functions in expressions that Access substitutes for ANSI SQL keywords.

## Jet SQL Reserved Words Corresponding to ANSI SQL Keywords

Access supports the ANSI SQL keywords listed in Table 24.1 as identical reserved words in Jet SQL. Don't use these Jet SQL reserved words as the names of tables, fields, or variables. The reserved words in Table 24.1 appear in all capital letters in the Jet SQL statements Access creates for you when you design a query or when you add a graph to a form or report. Reserved words in are marked with an asterisk were introduced by Access 95:

| | | | | |
|---|---|---|---|---|
| ADD* | CONSTRAINT* | HAVING | MAX | REFERENCES* |
| ALL | COUNT | IN | MIN | RIGHT |
| ALTER* | CREATE* | INDEX* | NOT | SELECT |
| ANY* | DELETE | INNER | NULL | SET |
| AS | DESC | INSERT | ON | SOME* |
| ALIAS | DISALLOW* | INTO | OR | UNION* |
| ASC | DISTINCT | IS | ORDER | UNIQUE* |
| AVG | DROP* | JOINR | OUTE | UPDATE |
| BETWEEN | EXISTS* | KEY* | PARAMETERS | VALUE* |
| BY | FOREIGN* | LEFT | PRIMARY* | VALUES* |
| COLUMN* | FROM | LIKE | PROCEDURE | WHERE |

The keywords that relate to data types, CHAR[ACTER], FLOAT, INT[EGER], and REAL, aren't included in Table 24.1 because Jet SQL uses a different reserved word to specify these SQL data types. The comparison operators (=, <, <=, >, and =>) are common to both ANSI SQL and Jet SQL. Access substitutes the <> operator for ANSI SQL's not-equal (!=) operator.

As in ANSI SQL, the IN reserved word in Jet SQL can be used as an operator to specify a list of values to match in a WHERE clause or a list created by a subquery. (Beginning with Access 2.0, Jet SQL supports subqueries.) You also can use IN to identify a table in another database; this use is discussed near the end of this chapter in the section "Adding IN to Use Tables in Another Database."

## Access Functions and Operators Used in Place of ANSI SQL Keywords

Table 24.1 shows reserved words in Jet SQL that correspond to ANSI SQL keywords but are operators or functions used in Jet SQL expressions. Jet doesn't use ANSI SQL syntax for its aggregate functions; you cannot use the SUM(DISTINCT *field_name*) syntax of ANSI SQL, for instance. Jet, therefore, distinguishes between its use of the Sum() aggregate function and the SQL implementation, SUM(). Expressions that use operators such as And and Or are enclosed in parentheses in Jet SQL statements; Jet SQL uses uppercase AND and OR (refer to the previous section) when criteria are added to more than one column.

**Table 24.1  Jet SQL Reserved Words that Substitute for ANSI SQL Keywords**

| Jet SQL | ANSI SQL | Jet SQL | ANSI SQL |
|---|---|---|---|
| And | AND | Max() | MAX() |
| Avg() | AVG() | Min() | MIN() |
| Between | BETWEEN | Not | NOT |
| Count() | COUNT() | Null | NULL |
| Is | IS | Or | OR |
| Like | LIKE | Sum() | SUM() |

The Jet IsNull() function that returns True (-1) or False (0), depending on whether IsNull()'s argument has a Null value, has no equivalent in ANSI SQL, and isn't a substitute for IS NULL or IS NOT NULL qualifiers in WHERE clauses. Jet SQL does not support distinct aggregate function references, such as AVG(DISTINCT *field_name*); the default DISTINCTROW qualifier added to the SELECT statement by Jet serves this purpose.

### Jet SQL Reserved Words, Operators, and Functions Not in ANSI SQL

Jet SQL contains a number of reserved words that aren't ANSI SQL keywords (see Table 24.2). Most of these reserved words define Jet data types; some reserved words have equivalents in ANSI SQL, and others don't. You use Jet DDL reserved words to modify the properties of tables. Access VBA's SQL property DISTINCTROW is described in the following section. PIVOT and TRANSFORM are used in creating crosstab queries that are unique to Jet databases. (SQL Server 6.5's Transact-SQL adds the ROLLUP and CUBE functions that provide aggregation capabilities similar to PIVOT and TRANSFORM.)

**Table 24.2  Jet SQL Reserved Words Not in ANSI SQL**

| Jet SQL | ANSI SQL | Category | Purpose |
|---|---|---|---|
| BINARY | No equivalent | DDL | Not an official Jet field data type. |
| BOOLEAN | No equivalent | DDL | Jet Yes/No field data type. |
| BYTE | No equivalent | DDL | Byte field data type, 1 byte integer. |
| CURRENCY | No equivalent | DDL | Jet Currency field data type. |
| DATETIME | No equivalent | DDL | Jet Date/Time field data type. |
| DISTINCTROW | No equivalent | DQL | Updatable Jet Recordset objects. |
| DOUBLE | REAL | DDL | High-precision decimal numbers. |
| LONG | INT[EGER] | DDL | Long Integer field data type. |
| LONGBINARY | No equivalent | DDL | OLE Object field data type. |
| LONGTEXT | VARCHAR | DDL | Memo field data type. |
| OWNERACCESS | No equivalent | DQL | Run with owner's privileges parameters. |
| PIVOT | No equivalent | DQL | Used in crosstab queries. |
| SHORT | SMALLINT | DDL | Integer field data type, 2 bytes. |
| SINGLE | No equivalent | DDL | Single-precision real number. |

(continues)

**Table 24.2.** **Continued**

| TEXT | CHAR[ACTER] | DDL | Text field data type. |
|---|---|---|---|
| TRANSFORM | No equivalent | DQL | Creates crosstab query. |
| ? (LIKE wildcard) with LIKE. | _(wild card) | DQL | Single character. |
| * (LIKE wild card) | % (wild card) | DQL | Zero or more characters. |
| # (LIKE wild card) | No equivalent | DQL | Single digit, 0–9. |
| # (date specifier) | No equivalent | DQL | Encloses date/time values. |
| <> (not equal) | != | DQL | Jet uses ! as a separator. |

Jet provides four statistical aggregate functions that aren't incorporated in ANSI SQL. These functions are listed in Table 24.3.

**Table 24.3** **Aggregate SQL Functions Added in Jet SQL**

| Jet Function | Category | Purpose |
|---|---|---|
| StdDev() | DQL | Standard deviation of a population sample. |
| StdDevP() | DQL | Standard deviation of a population. |
| Var() | DQL | Statistical variation of a population sample. |
| VarP() | DQL | Statistical variation of a population. |

### Jet's *DISTINCTROW* and SQL's *DISTINCT* Keywords

The DISTINCTROW reserved word that follows the SQL SELECT keywords causes Jet to eliminate duplicated rows from the query's result. The effect of DISTINCTROW is especially dramatic in queries used to display records in tables that have indirect relationships. To create an example of a query that you can use to demonstrate the effect of Jet's DISTINCTROW SQL reserved word, follow these steps:

New

1. Open a new query in Nwind.mdb by clicking the Query tab in the Database window and then clicking the New button. Select Design View in the list box of the New Query window, and then click OK to bypass the Query wizards.

2. In the Show Table dialog, add the Customers, Orders, Order Details, Products, and Categories tables to the query, in sequence. Access automatically creates the required joins. Click Close to close the Show Table dialog.

3. Drag the CompanyName field from the Customers field list to the Field row of the first column of the Query Design grid. Select the Sort cell, open the drop-down list with F4, and choose Ascending Sort Order.

**4.** Drag the CategoryName field from the Categories field list to the Field row of the second column of the grid. Add an ascending sort to this field (see Figure 24.1).

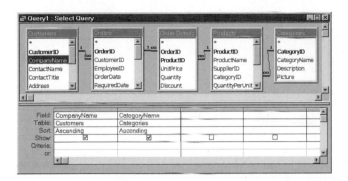

**FIG. 24.1** The QBE design of a query to determine customers purchasing categories of products.

**5.** Choose <u>V</u>iew, SQL View. The SQL statement that creates the query is shown in the SQL window in Figure 24.2.

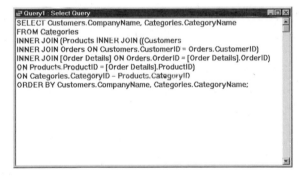

**FIG. 24.2** The SQL statement corresponding to the query design of Figure 24.1.

**6.** Click the Run Query button on the toolbar to execute the query. The number of rows (records) returned by the query—2,156 at the time of this writing—appears to the right of the navigation buttons at the bottom of the Query Datasheet window (see Figure 24.3). There are many duplicate rows in the query result set.

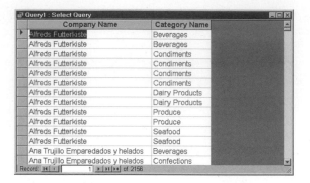

**FIG. 24.3** The query result set for the SQL statement of Figure 24.2.

To demonstrate the effect of adding the DISTINCTROW reserved word to the SQL statement and to verify, in this case, that the effect of ANSI SQL's DISTINCT keyword and Jet SQL's DISTINCTROW reserved word is the same, follow these steps:

1. Choose <u>V</u>iew, <u>S</u>QL to edit the SQL statement.

2. Add the DISTINCTROW keyword to the SQL statement after the SELECT command.

3. Click the Run Query button. The new query result set has 598 rows with no duplicated rows (see Figure 24.4).

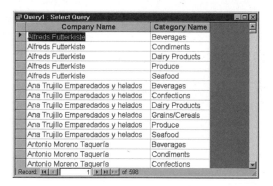

**FIG. 24.4** Eliminating duplicate rows with the Jet SQL DISTINCTROW modifier.

4. Choose <u>V</u>iew, <u>S</u>QL to edit the SQL statement again. Replace DISTINCTROW with DISTINCT.

5. Click the Run Query button again. You get the same result of 598 records that you obtain when you use the DISTINCTROW keyword.

6. Close, but do not save, the query.

> **Note**
>
> As an alternative to choosing <u>V</u>iew, SQL View from the Query menu, you can click the arrow adjacent to the View button of the toolbar, and then select SQL View from the drop-down menu. The number of mouse clicks is the same in either case.
>
> A second option is to right-click the mouse button on a blank area of the upper pane of the Query Design window and choose SQL View from the pop-up menu.

DISTINCTROW is a special Jet SQL reserved word and is unavailable in standard (ANSI) SQL; DISTINCTROW is related to, but not the same as, the DISTINCT keyword in ANSI SQL. Both words eliminate duplicate rows of data in query result tables, but they differ in execution. DISTINCT in ANSI SQL eliminates duplicate rows based only on the values of the data contained in the rows of the query, from left to right. You cannot update values from multiple-table queries that include the keyword DISTINCT.

DISTINCTROW, available only in Access, eliminates duplicate rows based on the content of the underlying table, regardless of whether additional field(s) that distinguish records in the table are included. DISTINCTROW allows values in special kinds of multiple-table Recordset objects to be updated.

To distinguish between these two keywords, assume that you have a table with a Last_Name field and a First_Name field and only 10 records, each with the Last_Name value, Smith. Each record has a different First_Name value. You create a query that includes the Last_Name field but not the First_Name field. DISTINCTROW returns all 10 Smith records because the First Name values differ in the table. DISTINCT returns one record because the First_Name field that distinguishes the records in the table is absent in the query result table.

Earlier versions of Access included the default reserved word DISTINCTROW, unless you purposely replaced it with the DISTINCT keyword by using the Query Properties dialog's Unique Values Only option. Access 97's Query Properties dialog sets the value of the Unique Values (DISTINCT) and Unique Rows (DISTINCTROW) properties to No (see Figure 24.5). Set either of these query property values to Yes to automatically add the modifier to SELECT queries.

**FIG. 24.5**  Access 97's Query Properties dialog with default query property values.

**VI**

**Using Advanced Techniques**

### Creating Tables with Jet DDL

You can create new tables in your current database with Jet 3.5's Data Definition Language reserved words. Using SQL to create new tables is of primary interest to developers, not users, of Access applications, because it is much easier to create new tables with the Access user interface. For the sake of completeness, however, a brief description of Access 95 SQL DDL statements follows:

- CREATE TABLE *table_name* (*field_name data_type* [*field_size*][, *field_name data_type*...]). Creates a new table with the fields specified by a comma-separated list. Properties of fields are space-delimited, so you need to enclose entries for *field names* with spaces in square brackets ([]). The *data_type* can be any valid Jet SQL field data type, such as TEXT or INTEGER. The *field_size* entry is optional for TEXT fields only. (The default value is 50 characters.)

- CONSTRAINT *index_name* {PRIMARYKEY¦UNIQUE¦REFERENCES *foreign_table* [(*foreign_field*)]}. Creates an index on the field name that precedes the expression. You can specify the index as the PRIMARYKEY or as an UNIQUE index. You also can establish a relationship between the field and the field of a foreign table with the REFERENCES *foreign_table* [*foreign_field*] entry. (The [*foreign_field*] item is required if the *foreign_field* is not a primary-key field.)

- CREATE [UNIQUE] INDEX *index_name* ON *table_name* (*field_name* [ASC¦DESC][, *field_name* [ASC¦DESC], ...]) [WITH {PRIMARY¦DISALLOW NULL¦IGNORE NULL}]. Creates an index on one or more fields of a table. If you specify the WITH PRIMARY modifier, UNIQUE is assumed (and not required). DISALLOW NULL prevents addition of records with NULL values in the indexed field; IGNORE NULL doesn't index records with NULL field_name values.

- ALTER TABLE. Allows you to add new fields (ADD COLUMN *field_name*...) or delete existing fields (DROP COLUMN field_name...).

- DROP INDEX *index_name* ON *table_name*. Deletes the index from a table specified by *table_name*.

- DROP TABLE *table_name*. Deletes a table from the database.

### Common ANSI SQL Keywords and Features
### Not Supported by Jet SQL Reserved Words

The majority of the ANSI SQL keywords that aren't supported by Jet 3.5 are elements of SQL's Data Control Language. Transactions, which are implemented automatically for most operations by the Jet 3.5 database engine, can be explicitly declared only in Access VBA code. The record position buttons of Access queries and forms substitute for most Cursor Control Language statements in ANSI SQL that choose a particular row in a query. Table 24.4 lists these substitutes.

**Table 24.4   Common ANSI SQL Reserved Words Not Supported in Jet SQL**

| Reserved Word | Category | Substitute |
|---|---|---|
| AUTHORIZATION | DCL | Privileges dialog |
| BEGIN | TPL | Access VBA BeginTrans method |
| CHECK | DQL | Table Validation Rule property |
| CLOSE | CCL | Document Control menu of query |
| COMMIT | TPL | Access VBA CommitTrans method |
| CREATE VIEW | DDL | Query Design mode and filters |
| CURRENT | CCL | Query Run mode, record position buttons |
| CURSOR | CCL | Query Run mode |
| DECLARE | CCL | Query Run mode (cursors are automatic) |
| DROP VIEW | DDL | Query Design mode |
| FETCH | DQL | Text boxes on a form or report |
| GRANT | DCL | Privileges dialog |
| PRIVILEGES | DCL | Privileges dialog |
| REVOKE | DCL | Privileges dialog |
| ROLLBACK | TPL | Access VBA Rollback method |
| TRANSACTION | TPL | Access VBA transaction methods |
| VALUES | DML | Data values entered in tables or forms |
| WORK | TPL | Access VBA BeginTrans method |
| : (variable) | DQL | Access VBA **Dim** statement prefix |
| != (not equal) | DQL | Access <> not-equal operator |

The Jet 3.5 database engine uses transaction processing for all Jet DML commands executed by action queries. You implement transaction processing (SQL's COMMIT and ROLLBACK [WORK]) on Recordset objects you create with code by writing Access VBA functions or procedures that contain the BeginTrans, CommitTrans, and Rollback reserved words. Many other less commonly used SQL keywords, such as COBOL and PASCAL, don't have Jet SQL reserved word equivalents.

# Writing Select Queries in SQL

When you create a SELECT query in Query Design mode, Access translates the QBE query design into a Jet SQL SELECT statement. You can view the Jet SQL equivalent of your design at any point by choosing View, SQL View. Displaying and analyzing the SQL statements that correspond to queries you design or queries in the Northwind Traders sample database is useful when you are learning SQL.

The heart of SQL is the SELECT statement used to create a select query. Every select query begins with the SELECT statement. The following lines of syntax are used for a SQL SELECT statement that returns a query table (called a *result set*, usually a Recordset object of the Dynaset type) of all or selected columns (fields) from all or qualifying rows (records) of a source table:

```
SELECT [ALL¦DISTINCT¦DISTINCTROW] [TOP n [PERCENT]] select_list
  FROM table_names
  [WHERE search_criteria]
  [ORDER BY column_criteria [ASC¦DESC]]
```

The following list shows the purpose of the elements in this basic select query statement:

- SELECT. The basic command that specifies a query. The *select_list* parameter determines the fields (columns) that are included in the result table of the query. When you design an Access QBE query, the *select_list* parameter is determined by the fields you add to the Fields row in the Query grid. Only those fields with the Show check box marked are included in *select_list*. Multiple field names are separated by commas.

  The optional ALL, DISTINCT, and DISTINCTROW qualifiers determine how rows are handled. ALL specifies that all rows are to be included, subject to subsequent limitation. DISTINCT eliminates rows with duplicate data. As discussed in the section "Jet's DISTINCTROW and SQL's DISTINCT Keywords" earlier in the chapter, DISTINCTROW is a Jet SQL keyword, similar to DISTINCT, that eliminates duplicate rows but also enables you to modify the query result set.

  The optional TOP *n* [PERCENT] modifier limits the query result set to returning the first *n* rows or *n* percent of the result set prior to the limitation. TOP and PERCENT are Jet SQL, not ANSI SQL, keywords. You use the TOP modifier to speed display when you only want to display the most significant rows of a query result set.

- FROM *table_name*. Specifies the name or names of the table or tables that form the basis for the query. The *table_names* parameter is created in Access QBE by the entries you make in the Add Table dialog. If fields from more than one table are included in the *select_list*, each table must be specified in the *table_names* parameter. Commas are used to separate the names of multiple tables.

- WHERE *search_criteria*. Determines which records from the select list are displayed. The search_criteria parameter is an expression with a text (string) operator, such as LIKE, for text fields or a numeric operator, such as >=, for fields with numeric values. The WHERE clause is optional; if you don't add a WHERE clause, all the rows that meet the SELECT criteria are returned.

- ORDER BY *column_criteria*. Specifies the sorting order of a Recordset object of the Dynaset or Snapshot type created by the query. A Recordset object of the Snapshot type is a query result set that is not updatable. Like the WHERE clause, ORDER BY is optional. You can specify an ascending or descending sort by the optional ASC or DESC keywords. If you don't specify a sort direction, ascending is the default.

The following lines show an example of a simple Jet SQL query statement:

```
SELECT CompanyName, CustomerID, PostalCode
   FROM Customers
   WHERE PostalCode LIKE '9*'
   ORDER BY CompanyName;
```

You must terminate a Jet SQL statement by adding a semicolon immediately after the last character on the last line.

---

**Note**

Examples of SQL statements in this book are formatted to make the examples more readable. Access doesn't format the SQL statements. When you enter or edit SQL statements in the Jet SQL window, formatting these statements so that commands appear on individual lines makes the SQL statements more intelligible. Use Ctrl+Enter to insert newline pairs (the return and newline characters) before SQL keywords. Jet ignores spaces and newline pairs when it processes the SQL statement.

---

The preceding query results in a Jet `Recordset` object of three columns and as many rows as the number of records in the Customers table for companies located in ZIP codes with values that begin with the character 9, sorted alphabetically by the company name. You don't have to specify the table name with the field name in the `select_list` because only one table is used in this query. When Access creates a SQL statement, the table name always precedes the field name. Usually, Access processes queries you write in either ANSI SQL or Jet SQL syntax. This example differs from ANSI SQL only in the substitution of the Jet SQL * (asterisk) for ANSI SQL's % wild card.

### Using SQL Punctuation and Symbols

In addition to the comparison operators used for expressions, SQL uses commas, periods, semicolons, and colons as punctuation. The following list of symbols and punctuation is used in ANSI SQL and the Jet SQL dialect; differences between the two forms of SQL are noted where appropriate:

- Commas are used to separate members of lists of parameters, such as multiple field names, as in `Name, Address, City, ZIP`.

- Square brackets surrounding field names are required only when the field name includes spaces or other symbols—including punctuation—not allowed by SQL, as in `[Company Name]`.

- If fields of more than one table are involved in the query, a period is used to separate the table name from the field name, as in `Customers.[Company Name]`.

- ANSI SQL uses the single quote symbol (') to enclose literal string values. You can use the double quote (") or the single quote symbol to enclose literal values in Jet SQL statements. Using the single quote makes writing SQL statements in Access VBA easier.

**VI**

**Using Advanced Techniques**

- ANSI SQL uses % and _ (underscore) symbols as the wild cards for the LIKE statement, rather than the * (asterisk) and ? used by Jet SQL to specify zero or more characters and a single character, respectively. The Jet wild cards correspond to the wild cards used in specifying DOS group file names.

- Jet provides the # wild card for the LIKE statement to represent any single digit. VBA also uses the # symbol to enclose date/time values in expressions. This symbol isn't available in ANSI SQL.

- The end of an Jet SQL statement is indicated by a optional semicolon (;).

- In Jet SQL, you cannot use colons as prefixes to indicate user-declared variables you create in ANSI SQL. You cannot create variables with Jet SQL; user-declared variables in Access are limited to the Access VBA functions and procedures you write. You can, however, pass variable values as parameters to stored procedures of client/server RDBMSes. Using stored procedures requires employing Access's SQL pass-through option.

- ANSI SQL uses the ! (bang symbol or exclamation mark) as a not in operator for character lists used with LIKE. ANSI SQL uses != for not equal; Jet SQL uses <>.

 ▶▶ See "Using Access 97's SQL Pass-Through Queries," p. 940

As the preceding list demonstrates, relatively minor differences exist in the availability and use of punctuation and symbols between ANSI and Jet SQL.

---

**Note**

Indentation often is used in writing multiple-line SQL statements. Indented lines indicate continuation of a preceding line or a clause that is dependent on a keyword in a preceding line.

---

### Using SQL Statements to Create Access Queries

You can enter SQL statements in Query Design mode to create simple Access queries that are reflected in changes to the design of the Query grid. This method is another useful way to learn the syntax of SQL. If your entries contain errors in spelling or punctuation, Access displays a message box that describes the error and its approximate location in the statement. When you choose OK in the SQL dialog, Access translates your SQL statement into a QBE design.

To create an Access QBE select query with the SQL statement, follow these steps:

1. Open the Northwind Traders database, if necessary, and then open a new query in Design view.

2. Close the Show Table dialog without adding a table name.

3. Choose View, SQL View to open the SQL window.

4. Delete any text, such as SELECT;, that may appear in the SQL window.

5. Enter the following SQL statement in the SQL window. Use Ctrl+Enter to create new lines. Your SQL statement appears as shown in Figure 24.6.

```
SELECT CompanyName, CustomerID, PostalCode
    FROM Customers
    WHERE PostalCode LIKE '9*'
    ORDER BY CompanyName;
```

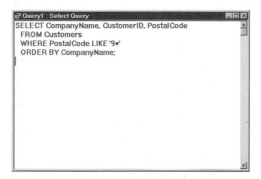

**FIG. 24.6**  An SQL statement for a simple select query.

> **Note**
>
> Access uses double quotes (") to identify string (text) values in SQL statements. As noted earlier in the chapter, the preferred SQL string identifier is the single quote (').

6. Choose <u>V</u>iew, <u>D</u>esign View. Access creates the equivalent of your SQL statement in graphical QBE (see Figure 24.7).

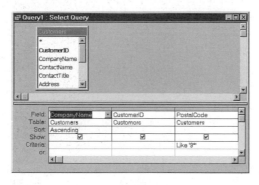

**FIG. 24.7**  The QBE design created by Access from the query in Figure 24.6.

7. Click the Run Query button on the toolbar. The result of your query in Datasheet view appears as shown in Figure 24.8.

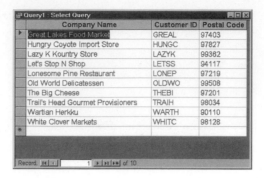

**FIG. 24.8** The query in Figure 24.7 in Datasheet view.

To change the order by which the query result is sorted, follow these steps:

1.  Choose View, S_QL View to open the SQL window.

2.  Change ORDER BY CompanyName to ORDER BY PostalCode, and choose View, Design View to open the Query Design window.

    The Query grid in Design mode displays Ascending in the PostalCode column rather than in the CompanyName column, indicating that the query result set is sorted by ZIP code.

3.  Click the Run button of the toolbar to display the result set sorted in ZIP code sequence (see Figure 24.9).

4.  Close, but do not save, the query.

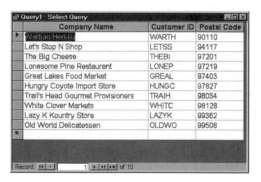

**FIG. 24.9** The query of Figure 24.7 in ZIP code order.

### Using the SQL Aggregate Functions

If you want to use the aggregate functions to determine totals, averages, or statistical data for groups of records with a common attribute value, you add a GROUP BY clause to your SQL statement. You can further limit the result of the GROUP BY clause with the optional HAVING qualifier:

```
SELECT [ALL|DISTINCT|DISTINCTROW]
    aggregate_function(field_name) AS alias_name
  [, select_list]
 FROM table_names
[WHERE search_criteria]
 GROUP BY group_criteria
   [HAVING aggregate_criteria]
[ORDER BY column_criteria]
```

The *select_list* includes the *aggregate_function* with a field_name as its argument. The field used as the argument of an aggregate function must have a numeric data type. The additional SQL keywords and parameters required to create a GROUP BY query are described in the following list:

- AS *alias_name*. Assigns a caption to the column. The caption is created in an Access QBE query by the *alias*:*aggregate_function*(*field name*) entry in the Field row of the Query grid.

- GROUP BY *group_criteria*. Establishes the column on which the grouping is based. In this column, GROUP BY appears in the Totals row of the Query grid.

- HAVING *aggregate_criteria*. One or more criteria applied to the column that contains the *aggregate_function*. The *aggregate_criteria* of HAVING is applied after the grouping is completed.

- WHERE *search_criteria*. Operates before the grouping occurs; at this point, no aggregate values exist to test against *aggregate_criteria*. Access substitutes HAVING for WHERE when you add criteria to a column with the *aggregate_function*.

> **Note**
>
> Not all client/server RDBMSes use the ANSI SQL AS *alias_name* construct. Microsoft SQL Server, Sybase System 10+, and IBM DB2, as examples, substitute a space for the AS keyword, as in SELECT *field_name alias_name*, .... The ODBC driver for these databases uses special codes (called *escape syntax*) to change from Access/ANSI use of AS to the space separator. If you use Access's SQL pass-through feature with Access VBA, you must use the space separator, not the AS keyword, for most client/server RDBMSes.

▶▶ See "Using Access 97's SQL Pass-Through Queries," p. 940

The following GROUP BY query is written in ANSI SQL, except for the # symbols that enclose date and time values:

```
SELECT ShipRegion, SUM(Freight) AS [Total Freight]
   FROM Orders
   WHERE ShipCountry="USA"
      AND OrderDate BETWEEN #01/1/94# AND #12/31/96#
   GROUP BY ShipRegion
   HAVING SUM(Freight)  > 50
   ORDER BY SUM(Freight) DESC;
```

**VI**

**Using Advanced Techniques**

The query returns a result set that consists of two columns: Ship Region (states) and the totals of Freight for each Ship Region in the United States, for the years 1994 through 1996. The result set is sorted in descending order.

To create an SQL GROUP BY query in Access, follow these steps:

1. Open a new query in Design view, close the Show Table dialog, and choose <u>V</u>iew, S<u>Q</u>L View. Type the preceding GROUP BY example code in the SQL window (see Figure 24.10).

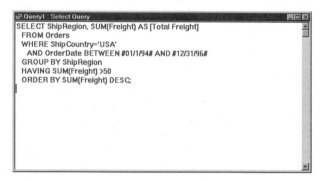

**FIG. 24.10**  An SQL statement that uses the SUM() aggregate function.

2. Choose <u>V</u>iew, <u>D</u>esign View. Your QBE GROUP BY query design appears as shown in Figure 24.11.

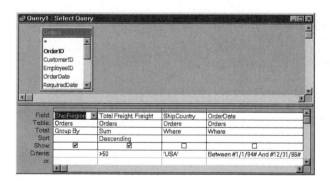

**FIG. 24.11**  Access's QBE design for the query shown in Figure 24.10.

3. Click the Run Query button on the toolbar. The states with orders having freight charges equal to $50 or more during the period 1/1/94 through 12/31/96 are shown ranked by total freight costs and are displayed in Datasheet view (see Figure 24.12).

4. Close, but do not save, your query.

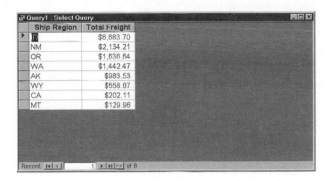

**FIG. 24.12** The aggregate query design in Figure 24.7 in Datasheet view.

### Creating Joins with SQL

Joining two or more tables with Access QBE uses the JOIN_ON structure that specifies the table to be joined and the relationship between the fields on which the JOIN is based:

```
SELECT [ALL¦DISTINCT¦DISTINCTROW]select_list
  FROM
  table_name {INNER¦LEFT¦RIGHT} JOIN join_table
    ON join_criteria
  [table_name {INNER¦LEFT¦RIGHT} JOIN join_table
    ON join_criteria]
  [WHERE search_criteria]
  [ORDER BY column_criteria]
```

The elements of the JOIN statement are shown in the following list:

- *table_name* {INNER¦LEFT¦RIGHT} JOIN *join_table*. Specifies the name of the table that is joined with other tables listed in *table_name*s. Each of the tables participating in a join must be included before the JOIN clause. When you specify a self-join by including two copies of the field list for a single table, the second table is distinguished from the first by adding an underscore and a digit to the table name.

  One of the three types of joins, INNER, LEFT, or RIGHT must precede the JOIN statement. INNER specifies an equi-join; LEFT specifies a left outer join; RIGHT specifies a right outer join. The type of join is determined in Access QBE by double-clicking the line connecting the joined fields in the table and clicking option button 1, 2, or 3 in the Join Properties dialog.

- ON *join_criteria*. Specifies the two fields to be joined and the relationship between the joined fields. One field is in join_table and the other is in a table in table_names. The *join_criteria* expression contains an equal sign (=) comparison operator and returns a True or False value. If the value of the expression is True, the record in the joined table is included in the query.

The number of JOIN statements you can add to a query usually is the total number of tables participating in the query minus one. You can create more than one JOIN between a pair of tables, but the result often is difficult to predict.

**VI**

**Using Advanced Techniques**

Access QBE creates nested JOIN statements for multiple JOINs. As an example, Figure 24.13 illustrates a query design with successive JOINs between the Orders, Order Details, Products, and Categories tables of Nwind.mdb. The SQL syntax for the three nested JOINs appears in Figure 24.14. The SQL statement has been formatted so that the ON clause for each JOIN statement is aligned vertically. The JOIN reserved word in Jet SQL creates the lines that connect the joined fields in Query Design view.

```
Query1 : Select Query
SELECT Orders.OrderID, Products.ProductName, Categories.CategoryName
  FROM Categories
    INNER JOIN (Products
      INNER JOIN (Orders
        INNER JOIN [Order Details]
        ON Orders.OrderID = [Order Details].OrderID)
      ON Products.ProductID = [Order Details].ProductID)
    ON Categories.CategoryID = Products.CategoryID;
```

**FIG. 24.13**   The Jet SQL implementation of three nested equi-joins.

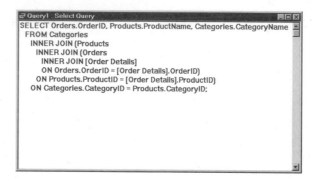

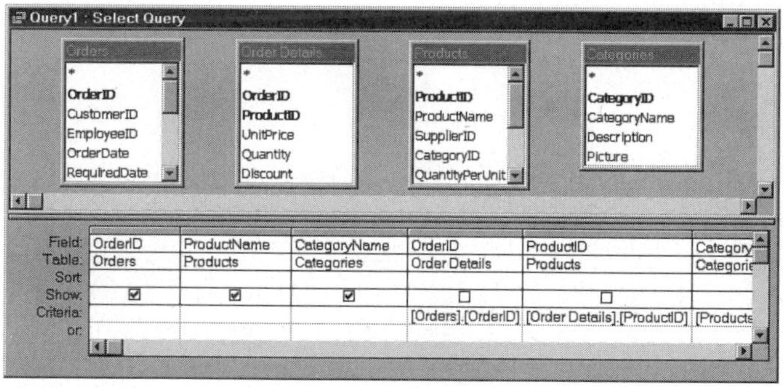

**FIG. 24.14**   The equi-join of Figure 24.13 created by a WHERE clause.

You create equi-joins in ANSI SQL with the WHERE clause, using the same expression to join the fields as that of the ON clause in the JOIN command. It's much simpler to write SQL statements using WHERE clauses for joins than employing the JOIN syntax. The WHERE clause also is more flexible than the JOIN\_... ON structure because you can use other operators such as BETWEEN\_AND, LIKE, >, and <. These operators result in error messages when they are substituted for the equal sign (=) in the ON clause of the JOIN statement.

The following ANSI SQL-89 statement gives the same result as the Jet SQL statement in Figure 24.13:

```
SELECT Orders.OrderID, Products.ProductName,
       Categories.CategoryName
  FROM Orders, [Order Details], Products, Categories
  WHERE [Order Details].OrderID = Orders.OrderID
```

```
    AND Products.ProductID = [Order Details].ProductID
    AND Categories.CategoryID = Products.CategoryID;
```

You create multiple joins with WHERE clauses by separating each join expression with an AND operator. Figure 24.14 shows the Query Design view of the preceding SQL statement. JOIN syntax isn't used, so no join lines appear between the field lists in the upper pane. In this case, the Criteria row of the QBE grid displays only the left element of the argument of each WHERE statement.

### Using *UNION* Queries

UNION queries let you combine the result set of two or more SELECT queries into a single result set. Nwind.mdb includes an example of a UNION query, which has the special symbol of two overlapping circles, in the Database window. You can create UNION queries only with SQL statements; if you add the UNION keyword to a query, the Query Design Mode button on the toolbar and the Query Design choice on the View menu are disabled. The general syntax of UNION queries is as follows:

```
SELECT select_statement
  UNION SELECT select_statement
    [GROUP BY group_criteria]
    [HAVING aggregate criteria]
  [UNION SELECT select_statement
    [GROUP BY group_criteria]
    [HAVING aggregate criteria]]
  [UNION. . .]
  [ORDER BY column_criteria]
```

The restrictions on statements that create UNION queries are the following:

■ The number of fields in the field_list of each SELECT and UNION SELECT query must be the same. You receive an error message if the number of fields is not the same.

■ The sequence of the field names in each field_list must correspond to similar entities. You don't receive an error message for dissimilar entities, but the result set is likely to be unfathomable. The field data types in a single column need not correspond; however, if the column of the result set contains both numeric and Text data types, the data type of the column is set to Text.

■ Only one ORDER BY clause is allowed, and it must follow the last UNION SELECT statement. You can add GROUP BY and HAVING clauses to each SELECT and UNION SELECT statement, if needed.

Figure 24.15 shows the SQL statement to create a UNION query derived from the Union Query included in Nwind.mdb. The syntax of the SQL statement illustrates the ability of UNION queries to include values from two different field data types, Text (CustomerID) and Long Integer (SupplierID), in the single, aliased ID column. The query result set appears in Figure 24.16 with the single record included from the Suppliers table selected.

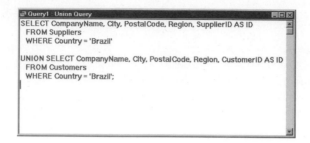

**FIG. 24.15**  Creating a multiple-column UNION query with a SQL statement.

| CompanyName | City | PostalCode | Region | ID |
|---|---|---|---|---|
| Comércio Minei | São Paulo | 05432-043 | SP | COMMI |
| Família Arquiba | São Paulo | 05442-030 | SP | FAMIA |
| Gourmet Lanch | Campinas | 04876-786 | SP | GOURL |
| Hanari Carnes | Rio de Janeiro | 05454-876 | RJ | HANAR |
| Que Delícia | Rio de Janeiro | 02389-673 | RJ | QUEDE |
| Queen Cozinha | São Paulo | 05487-020 | SP | QUEEN |
| Refrescos Ame | São Paulo | 5442 | | 10 |
| Ricardo Adocic | Rio de Janeiro | 02389-890 | RJ | RICAR |
| Tradição Hipern | São Paulo | 05634-030 | SP | TRADH |
| Wellington Impc | Resende | 08737-363 | SP | WELLI |

Record: 14 ◄ | 7 | ►| ►►| of 10

**FIG. 24.16**  The result of the UNION query of Figure 24.15.

### Implementing Subqueries

Versions of Access prior to 2.0 used nested queries to emulate the subquery capability of ANSI SQL. (A *nested query* is a query executed against the result set of another query.) Access 97 lets you write a SELECT query that uses another SELECT query to supply the criteria for the WHERE clause. Depending on the complexity of your query, using a subquery instead of nested queries often improves performance. The general syntax of subqueries is as follows:

```
SELECT field_list
  FROM table_list
  WHERE [table_name.]field_name
    IN (SELECT select_statement
[GROUP BY group_criteria]
  [HAVING aggregate_criteria]
[ORDER BY sort_criteria]);
```

Figure 24.17 shows the SQL statement for an example subquery that returns names and addresses of Northwind Traders customers who placed orders between January 1, 1996 and June 30, 1996. The SELECT subquery that begins after the IN predicate returns the CustomerID values from the Orders table against which the CustomerID values of the Customers table are compared.

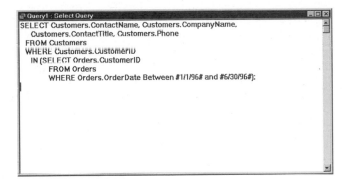

**FIG. 24.17** The SQL statement for a simple subquery.

Unlike UNION queries, you can create a subquery in Query Design mode. You type IN, followed by the SELECT statement as the criterion of the appropriate column, enclosing the SELECT statement within the parenthesis required by the IN predicate. Figure 24.18 shows the query design with part of the IN (SELECT statement in the Criteria row of the Customer ID column. Figure 24.19 shows the result set returned by the SQL statement of Figure 24.17.

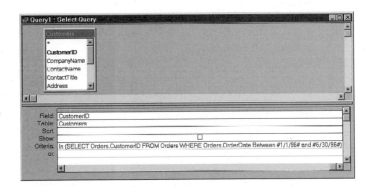

**FIG. 24.18** Entering the SQL statement for a subquery in the Criteria row.

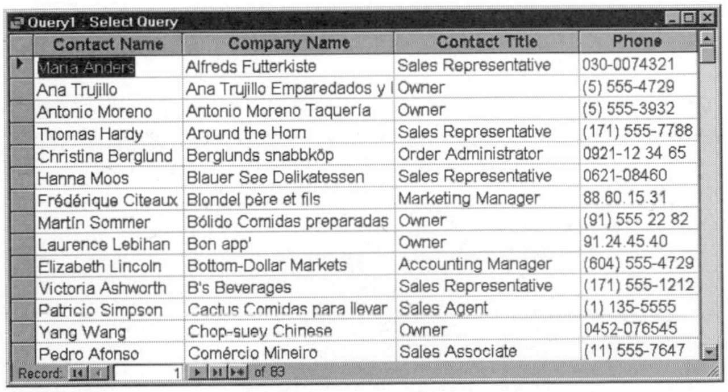

| Contact Name | Company Name | Contact Title | Phone |
|---|---|---|---|
| Maria Anders | Alfreds Futterkiste | Sales Representative | 030-0074321 |
| Ana Trujillo | Ana Trujillo Emparedados y l | Owner | (5) 555-4729 |
| Antonio Moreno | Antonio Moreno Taquería | Owner | (5) 555-3932 |
| Thomas Hardy | Around the Horn | Sales Representative | (171) 555-7788 |
| Christina Berglund | Berglunds snabbköp | Order Administrator | 0921-12 34 65 |
| Hanna Moos | Blauer See Delikatessen | Sales Representative | 0621-08460 |
| Frédérique Citeaux | Blondel père et fils | Marketing Manager | 88.60.15.31 |
| Martín Sommer | Bólido Comidas preparadas | Owner | (91) 555 22 82 |
| Laurence Lebihan | Bon app' | Owner | 91.24.45.40 |
| Elizabeth Lincoln | Bottom-Dollar Markets | Accounting Manager | (604) 555-4729 |
| Victoria Ashworth | B's Beverages | Sales Representative | (171) 555-1212 |
| Patricio Simpson | Cactus Comidas para llevar | Sales Agent | (1) 135-5555 |
| Yang Wang | Chop-suey Chinese | Owner | 0452-076545 |
| Pedro Afonso | Comércio Mineiro | Sales Associate | (11) 555-7647 |

**FIG. 24.19** The query result set from the subquery of Figures 24.17 and 24.18.

VI

Using Advanced Techniques

### Specifying Action Query Syntax

Data Manipulation Language (DML) commands are implemented by Access's action queries: append, delete, make-table, and update. Jet SQL reserved words that create crosstab queries—TRANSFORM and PIVOT—are included in this section because crosstab queries are related to DML queries. This sections shows the syntax for each type of Access action query.

Append queries use the following syntax:

```
INSERT INTO dest_table
   SELECT [ALL¦DISTINCT¦DISTINCTROW] select_list
   FROM source_table
   [WHERE append_criteria]
```

If you omit the WHERE clause, all the records of source_table are appended to dest_table.

Delete queries take the following form:

```
DELETE FROM table_name
   [WHERE delete_criteria]
```

If you omit the optional WHERE clause in a delete query, you delete all data in table_name.

Make-table queries use the following syntax:

```
SELECT [ALL¦DISTINCT¦DISTINCTROW] select_list
   INTO new_table
   FROM source_table
   [WHERE append_criteria]
```

To copy the original table, substitute an asterisk (*) for select_list and omit the optional WHERE clause.

Update queries use the SET command to assign values to individual columns:

```
UPDATE table_name
   SET column_name = value [, column_name = value[, ...]]
   [WHERE update_criteria]
```

Separate multiple column_name entries and corresponding values by commas if you want to update the data in more than one field. Jet SQL supports the ANSI SQL VALUES keyword for adding records to tables the hard way (specifying the VALUE of each column of each record).

Crosstab queries use the Jet SQL keywords TRANSFORM and PIVOT to create various types of summary queries using the SQL aggregate functions. The following syntax applies to time-series crosstab queries:

```
TRANSFORM aggregate_function(field_name) [AS alias]
SELECT [ALL¦DISTINCT¦DISTINCTROW] select_list
   FROM table_name
   PIVOT Format(field_name),"format_type")
   [IN (column_list)]
```

TRANSFORM defines a crosstab query, and PIVOT specifies the GROUP BY characteristics plus the fixed column names specified by the optional IN predicate. Crosstab queries, like queries with multiple or nested JOINs, are better left to Access QBE to create the query. You can edit the query as necessary after Access has written the initial SQL statement.

▶▶ See "Creating Crosstab Queries" p. 361

---

### Troubleshooting

*When I try to execute a query from my SQL statement, an Enter Parameter dialog appears.*

You misspelled one of the table names in your table_list, one of the field names in your field_list, or both. If the Jet engine's query parser can't match a table name or a field name with those specified in the FROM clause, Jet assumes that the entry is a parameter and requests its value. Check the spelling of the database objects in your SQL statement. (If you misspell a SQL keyword, you usually receive a syntax error message box.)

---

# Adding *IN* to Use Tables in Another Database

Access enables you to open only one database at a time, unless you write code to open another table with an Access VBA function or subprocedure. However, you can use Jet SQL's IN clause with a make-table, append, update, or delete query to create or modify tables in another database. Access provides the capability to make a table or append records to a table in another Access database through graphical QBE only. You click the Another Database option in the Query Properties dialog for the make-table or append query and type the file name of the other database.

You have to write an SQL query or edit a query created by Access to update data or delete records in tables contained in another database of any type, or to perform any operation on a dBASE, Paradox, or Btrieve file that isn't attached to your database. The SQL query uses the IN clause to specify the external database or table file. The advantage of using the IN clause is simplicity—you don't have to attach the table before using it. The disadvantage of using the IN clause is that indexes associated with dBASE and Paradox tables aren't updated when the content of the table is modified.

### Working with Another Access Database

You can create a table in another Access database, delete all the records, and then append the records back to the table from which the records were deleted, using the IN clause to specify the name of the other database that contains the table. To try using the IN clause, open a new query or an existing query and follow these steps:

1. Choose <u>V</u>iew, SQL View to open the SQL window.

2. Delete any existing text if you have a query open, and type the following line in the SQL window:

**SELECT * INTO Customers IN "OLE Objects.mdb" FROM Customers;**

SELECT_INTO creates a make-table query. If you haven't created OLE Objects.mdb, choose File, New Database and create a new blank database named OLE **Objects.mdb** or whatever you like in your ...\Office\Samples folder. If the new database is in a different location, you need to add the path to the IN string. Reopen Nwind.mdb.

**3.** Click the Run Query button of the toolbar to make the new Customers table in your OLE Objects database. Click OK when the message box advises you of the number of records that are copied to the new Customers table created in OLE Objects. You can open OLE Objects.mdb to verify the existence of the new table.

**4.** Choose View, SQL View again, delete the existing text, and type the following line:

**DELETE * FROM Customers IN "OLE Objects.mdb"**

DELETE...FROM creates a delete query.

**5.** Click the Run Query button on the toolbar to delete the records in the OLE_Objects Customers table. Click OK to confirm the deletion of the records.

> ### Tip
>
> You cannot use the IN identifier with Access DDL statements, such as DROP TABLE or CREATE TABLE.

To append the records you deleted back into the Customers table of the OLE Objects database, follow thesdßÀteps:

**1.** Choose File, Open Database and select your OLE Objects database, which contains the Customers table with no records.

**2.** Click the Query tab of the Database window, and then click the New button. Close the Show Table dialog without adding a table.

**3.** Choose View, S_QL View and type the following line in the SQL text box:

**INSERT INTO Customers SELECT * FROM Customers IN "Northwind.mdb"**

INSERT INTO creates an append query. If your OLE Objects database is located elsewhere, add the path to Northwind.mdb to the preceding statement.

**4.** Click the Run Query button on the toolbar to add the records from Northwind's Customers table. Confirm the append by clicking OK in the message box.

Although you accomplish the same objectives by attaching a table from another database or copying tables to the Clipboard and pasting the table into another database, using a SQL query for this purpose is a more straightforward process.

### Using the *IN* Clause with Other Types of Databases

You can create or modify xBase and Paradox tables by specifying in an IN statement the path to the file and the file type using the following special Jet SQL syntax reserved for foreign database file types:

```
IN "[drive:\]path" "database_type"
```

The path to the file is required, even if the database is located in your \Access folder; you receive an error if you omit the path entry. You can use an empty string, "", to identify the current folder.

The database_type expression must be enclosed in quotation marks. It consists of one of the seven foreign file types supported by ISAM DLLs supplied with Access 97, followed by a semicolon:

- dBASE III;
- dBASE IV;
- dBASE 5;
- FoxPro; (DBF)
- FoxPro 3.0; (DBC)
- Paradox; (DB)

The semicolon after the file type name is required, but the database file type names are not case-sensitive—dbase iii; is acceptable to Access.

You can create a dBASE IV table from a query by using the following statement:

```
SELECT *
    INTO supplier
        IN "c:\dbase\samples" "dBASE IV;"
    FROM Suppliers;
```

You can append records to a dBASE IV file with the following statement:

```
INSERT INTO supplier
        IN "c:\dbase\samples" "dBASE IV;"
    SELECT *
        FROM Suppliers;
```

When deleting and updating records in foreign tables, use the syntax shown in the "Specifying Action Query Syntax" section, with the IN clause added.

# Using SQL Statements in Forms, Reports, and Macros

If you create a large number of forms and reports based on queries or that use queries, or if you use macros to run Select and Action queries, the query list in your Database window can become cluttered. You can use SQL queries you write or copy from the SQL dialog in place of the names of query objects and then delete the query from your database. You can use SQL statements for the following purposes:

- *Record Source property of forms and reports.* Substitute the SQL query text for the name of the query in the Record Source text box.

■ *Row Source property in lists and drop-down combo lists on a form.* Using an SQL statement rather than a query object gives you greater control over the sequence of the columns in your list.

■ *Value of the* SQL *property of a* QueryDef *object or the* strSource *argument of the* OpenRecordset *method in Access VBA code.* You use SQL statements extensively as property and argument values when programming applications with Access VBA, especially for SQL pass-through queries.

■ *Argument of the* RunSQL() *macro action.* Only SQL statements that create action queries can be used with the RunSQL() macro action. Using macros is discouraged in Access 97.

▶▶ See "Using Access 97's SQL Pass-Through Queries," p. 940

You can create and test your Jet SQL statement in Query Design mode and then copy the statement to the Clipboard. Paste the text into the text box for the property or into your Access VBA module. Then close the test query design without saving it.

# Chapter 25

# Securing Multiuser Network Applications

Personal computer networking continues to be one of the fastest-growing areas in the PC marketplace. Many large organizations are downsizing database applications to personal computer networks. *Downsizing* means moving a database system that runs on a costly, large-scale computer, such as a mainframe, to smaller, lower-priced computers—usually server PCs running network operating systems, such as Windows NT Server 4.0. These networks use a dedicated server PC; PCs connected by the network to the server are called *clients* or *workstations*.

Small- to moderate-size organizations have discovered that installing a simple PC network can increase productivity and reduce the required investment in computing hardware. An organization need purchase only a single laser printer if all users cán share it on a network. The cost of purchasing large-fixed-disk drives is reduced when users share large files rather than keep multiple independent copies on local disk drives. Even families with more than one home PC are installing low-cost networks in order to share peripherals and files among family members.

Reducing capital expenditures and operating costs are the principal incentives for installing PC networks. In many cases, savings in the amount spent on peripheral equipment is the sole consideration in the decision to use a network. When you use a database application, however, productivity plays the most important role in the network decision-making process. The capability to share up-to-date information contained in a database file among many users is a strong incentive to install a PC network because it increases productivity. Increasing productivity with a networked database system can, in turn, reduce operating costs by many times the savings offered by the reduction of the investment when you share computer peripheral equipment.

## Networking Access Applications

Access 97 is likely to be the first networked Windows application many readers of this book will use. Windows 95's simple installation of low-cost and easy-to-administer Windows Networking should appeal to first-time network users. If you don't have a network now and you plan to create Access applications for other users to share, Windows 95's built-in network operating system is a logical choice as a peer-to-peer "starter" network. A *peer-to-peer network* is a network in which any PC connected to the network is capable of sharing files in all—or designated—folders with any other PC connected to the network. PCs connected by peer-to-peer networks often are called *members of a workgroup*. Access applications that share .mdb files on a network are termed *multiuser applications*.

Microsoft Corporation designed Access specifically for multiuser operation in a networked, workgroup environment. For example, Microsoft added a very sophisticated security system to Access designed for multiuser applications. If your network is already set up, you can choose to install Access on the network or install only the .mdb files you intend to share. (Sharing only .mdb files is the most practical approach.)

If you don't have a network when you begin using Access, the process is simple to change your database files from single-user to shared status when you do install a network. This chapter explains how to set up and use Access in a variety of network environments, share database files, establish database security, and administer a multiuser database system.

> **Caution**
>
> Access 2.0 users should be aware that Access 97 has a new .mdb file structure and uses entries in the Windows 95 or Windows NT Registry, not MSACC??0.INI, to hold the locations and names of workgroup system files.
>
> If you're upgrading to Access 97 from a prior version and plan to share existing .mdb and workgroup system (.mda) files, don't convert the .mdb or .mda files to Access 97 format unless all members of the workgroup have installed and are running Access 97. Access 2.0 and earlier versions cannot open Access 95 or Access 97 .mdb or .mdw files. However, Access 97 can link files created by earlier versions.
>
> Access 97 also can open Access 95 .mdb files, but you cannot change design features of an Access 95 .mdb file unless you convert the file to the Access 97 format.

 ▶▶ See "Using Access 1.x and 2.0 Data .MDB Files with Access 97," p. 1154

# Installing Access in a Networked Environment

If you're using a network operating system with application server capabilities, such as Windows NT Server 3.x/4.0 or Novell NetWare 3.x/4.x, you can use either of the following methods to install Access in a network environment:

■ Install Access 97 on the network server. All workstations run the server's copy of Access 97 and don't require a copy of Access on their local disk drives. This approach saves disk space on the workstations but results in much slower operation of Access. If workstations also run Windows 95 from the server, operation can slow down even more. The degree to which the operating speed is affected depends on your network's performance and the number of users accessing the network simultaneously.

■ Install a copy of Windows 95 and Access 95 on each workstation. In this case, users share only Access .mdb files. Access requires between 30M and 80M of disk space, depending on the features you include in the workstation installation and whether you previously have installed OLE 2+ server applications such as Microsoft Word 97 and/or Excel 97, or are installing Access 97 as a component of Microsoft Office 97 Professional Edition. Use this installation method for computers connected in a peer-to-peer network.

## Tip

If many users need to install or upgrade to Access 97, it is usually faster to use the administrator's installation on a network server and then install Access 97 on the workstations from the administrator's installation, rather than from the distribution disks. (See Acread80.wri and other .wri files on the CD-ROM.)

You need an individual copy of the Access software for each workstation that uses Access or a license for each workstation that runs an Access application with the retail version of Access 95. For additional details, refer to the license information that Microsoft supplies with Access.

The Office Developer Edition (ODE) lets you distribute a run-time version of Access 97. Run-time Access 97 enables users to run applications you create, but not to create or modify applications. Run-time Access enables multiple workstations to run Access applications without an individual license for each workstation.

Unlike Access 1.1 and 2.0, which used a separate run-time executable file (MSARN??0. EXE), Access 97 run-time uses the retail executable (Msaccess.exe) with a setting in the user's Registry that turns off the user's ability to use Msaccess.exe in Design mode. You can install run-time Access on the server or local workstations; installation of run-time Access on each workstation is recommended because you gain operating speed. A run-time Access installation consumes less disk space than the retail version of Access because run-time Access does not include (and cannot be used with) the Access help file and the Access wizards and builders.

## Note

Do not attempt to share the retail or run-time version of Access on a peer-to-peer network. Peer-to-peer networks are designed for sharing printers and data files, not the executable (.exe) and help (.hlp) files of large applications such as Access. The computer and network resources required to run Access from a peer server slow applications running on the server to a crawl and greatly increase network traffic.

**VI**

**Using Advanced Techniques**

# Sharing Your Access Database Files with Other Users

While you're learning how to use Access and designing your first Access applications, you use Access in single-user mode and maintain exclusive use of the database files you create. If your application is designed for use in a networked environment, however, you need to set up a workgroup for the users who will share the database you created. The sections that follow describe how to create a directory for sharing files, modify Access applications for a multiuser environment, and set up a workgroup to provide security for shared .mdb files.

 ▶▶ See "Examining the Content of the Office Developer's Kit," p. 1135

> **Tip**
>
> If you intend to share your Access applications, make a backup copy of System.mdw, preferably on disk. Use the backup copy to make a new System.mdw file in case your original System.mdw file becomes corrupted.

### Creating a Folder and System File for File Sharing

Sharing a database application requires that each user of the database share a common system file, derived from Access' System.mdw workgroup file, that contains information on the members of the workgroup, such as their logon names, passwords, and the groups of which they are members. Permissions for individual users to open and to modify objects are stored in the .mdb file. Permissions are discussed in the section "Maintaining Database Security" later in this chapter.

When you develop an application intended for shared use, it's a common practice to create a new local folder to hold the application's .mdb file(s). You then use the Workgroup Administrator application (Wrkgadm.exe) to create a new system file specifically for the application and develop the application in its own folder. Access 97's default extension for workgroup system files is .mdw. When the application is completed, you can copy the .mdb and .mdw files in this folder to the workgroup folder of the network or peer-to-peer server that is used to share them.

The location and name of the system file that Access 97 uses when it is launched is specified by the SystemDB entry of the `HKEY_LOCAL_MACHINE\SOFTWARE\Microsoft\Office\8.0\Access\Jet\3.5\Engines` hive of the Registry. For Windows 95, the default Registry entry (key) for SystemDB is your \*Windows*\System folder, as shown in Figure 25.1. For Windows NT, the default location is the \*WinNT*\System 32 folder.

**Caution**

Unless you're familiar with editing Windows 95's or Windows NT's Registry with the Registry Editor application (RegEdit.exe), don't edit Registry entries manually. An incorrect entry can cause Access or Windows to behave unexpectedly.

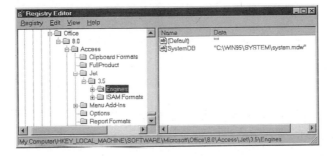

**FIG. 25.1**  The Windows 95 Registry Editor displaying the Registry value for the SystemDB key that specifies the name and location of your Access 97 system file.

To establish a folder and a workgroup system file for the development of an example shared database application, complete the following steps:

1. Launch Explorer and add a new folder, called \Shared in this example, to the root folder of a local drive on your PC.

2. Open the \Shared folder and create a new subfolder, \Shared\Nwind.

3. Create a copy of Northwind.mdb in \Shared\Nwind, rename the file to **Nwind.mdb**, and then close Explorer. Alternatively, you can use Access's Compact feature to create a compacted copy of Northwind.mdb to Nwind.mdb in the \Shared\Nwind folder.

◄◄ See "Compacting Databases," p. 102

4. Launch Workgroup Administrator (Wrkgadm.exe). Setup does not install Workgroup Administrator in your Start menu hierarchy. Wrkgadm.exe is located in Windows 95's \\*Windows*\System folder or in Windows NT's \\*WinNT*\System32 folder. Create a Desktop shortcut to Wrkgadm.exe to make the Workgroup Administrator easily accessible. The opening dialog of Workgroup Administrator displays the name and location of the default system file, System.mdw (see Figure 25.2).

**VI**

**Using Advanced Techniques**

**FIG. 25.2** Workgroup Administrator's opening dialog when running under Windows 95.

> **Note**
>
> Previous versions of Access used the ...\Access directory or folder as the default location for the workgroup file (System.mda or System.mdw), as well as Wrkgadm.exe.

5. Click the Create button to open the Workgroup Owner Information dialog in which you specify the Name, Organization, and optional Workgroup ID for the new workgroup system file (see Figure 25.3). The Name and Organization entries default to entries you made when installing Office 97 or Access 97. Write down the Name, Organization, and Workgroup ID entries, which are case-sensitive, and keep them in a safe place. If you need to re-create the workgroup system file in the future, your entries must exactly match the original entries.

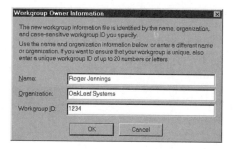

**FIG. 25.3** Specifying the Name, Organization, and optional Workgroup ID for a new workgroup system file.

6. Click the OK button to display the Workgroup Information File dialog. Type the path and name of your workgroup folder, **\SHARED\NWIND\SYSTEM.mdw** in this case, in the Database text box (see Figure 25.4).

**FIG. 25.4** Entering the location and name of the shared workgroup file in the Workgroup Information File dialog.

7. Click the OK button to display the Confirm Workgroup Information dialog (see Figure 25.5). If the workgroup information is correct, click the OK button. A message appears to confirm that the new workgroup system file has been created (see Figure 25.6). Click OK to close the message box and return to the initial Workgroup Administrator dialog (see Figure 25.7).

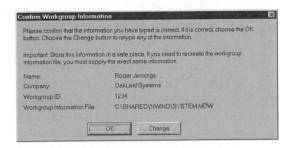

**FIG. 25.5** Confirming the owner information for the new workgroup system file.

**FIG. 25.6** Access confirming that the new System.mdw workgroup system file is created.

**FIG. 25.7** The Workgroup Administrator dialog, displaying the name and location of the new workgroup system file.

8. Click Exit to close Workgroup Administrator. Access doesn't use the new workgroup system file until you close and relaunch Access.

9. Launch Explorer to verify that the copy of Northwind.mdb and System.mdw appear in \Shared\Nwind, as shown in Figure 25.8.

10. Close Access, if it is open. Launch Access and open the \Shared\Nwind\ Northwind.mdb database file with the new System.mdw system file active.

The dedicated System.mdw file contains information pertaining only to the database applications that you open when System.mdw is your active system file. You can develop an application using Access' default operating options and System.mdw and then change the options and create a new workgroup system file to provide for file sharing when you complete the application.

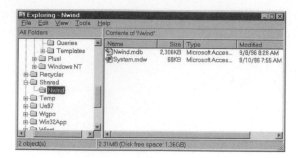

**FIG. 25.8**  Windows Explorer displaying the files in the \Shared\Nwind folder.

You can change with the Workgroup Administrator the system database file that Access uses when launched. The procedure is described in the section "Choosing Workgroups with the Workgroup Administrator" later in this chapter.

> **Note**
>
> Minimize the number of database objects you create when you develop applications to be shared. You must specifically grant or revoke permissions to groups or individual users for each object you create. Use SQL statements to replace query objects when possible (see Chapter 24, "Working with Structured Query Language"). Minimizing the number of objects also reduces the number of entries you need to make when you establish database security restrictions (permissions) for your application.

### Preparing to Share Your Database Files

To set up Access to share database files, you should verify the settings in the Advanced page of the Options properties sheet. You can open the Advanced page by choosing Tools, Options and then clicking the Advanced tab (see Figure 25.9). The changes you make to Access options (called preferences) are stored for your account (Admin, the default) in the system database and apply to all databases you open thereafter using that system database.

Following is a list of the Advanced options that affect multiuser applications:

- *Default Open Mode* set to Shared by default. Changing this setting to Exclusive so that only one user can open files improves performance. If you've changed the file open mode to Exclusive, you must return to the default Shared mode so that more than one user can open the file.

- *Default Record Locking* has three options designed to prevent more than one user from making simultaneous changes to the same record. No Locks, the default, only causes a lock when the edit occurs (*optimistic locking*). All Records locks the entire table when a user opens it for editing (*table locking*). Edited Records locks only the record(s) during the editing process (*pessimistic locking*).

■ *Number of Update Retries* specifies the number of times Access attempts to update a locked record, at a rate determined by the value in the Update Retry Interval text box, before issuing a message box that the record is locked and cannot be updated.

■ *Refresh Interval* determines how often the data displayed in a datasheet or form is rewritten automatically to reflect changes made by other members of the workgroup. *ODBC Refresh Interval* applies only to tables attached using the ODBC driver for tables linked from a foreign database, usually a client/server database.

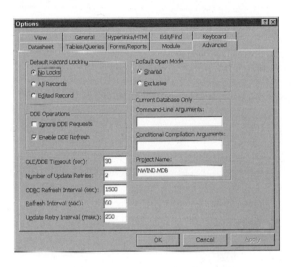

**FIG. 25.9**   The Advanced page of the Options properties sheet.

Access 97's default values are suitable for most multiuser applications. Unless you have a specific reason for making changes, accept the default values.

---

**Note**

Record locking is a misnomer in Access. An Edited Record lock is applied to a 2K page that may contain many records if the fields of the records have small Size property values. Using No Locks, the default, speeds operation of Access in a multiuser environment because the time required to lock and unlock table pages is saved. No Locks is called optimistic locking, because No Locks assumes that the probability is low that two or more users might attempt to alter the same record simultaneously.

If you attempt to update a record in a table with No Locks that is being updated simultaneously by another user, Access displays a message box that lets you choose to accept or overwrite the other user's changes. The conservative approach is to use Edited Record locking, but doing so may impair performance when many users simultaneously update data in a single table.

---

### Splitting Databases for File Sharing

All Access developers agree that Access applications should be divided into two .mdb files: one containing only Access tables (also called *data objects*) and the other containing all other objects (called *application objects*). Splitting Access applications lets you link (attach) tables from the shared .mdb to your application objects in a local .mdb file. Keeping the application objects on the user's computer minimizes network traffic and improves performance, especially on peer-to-peer networks. The major benefit of splitting Access applications, however, is the ability to easily update a user's application .mdb file without affecting current data stored in Jet tables.

Microsoft recognized that most production database applications created with Access use the split design, so Access 97 has an add-in to automate the process. Follow these steps to separate the tables from the application objects of the Northwind.mdb file using the Database Splitter Add-In:

1. Open Nwind.mdb in your \Shared\Nwind folder with \Shared\Nwind\ System.mdw as your system database. (Do not use your original copy of Northwind.mdb in …\Office\Samples for this example.)

2. With the Database window active, choose <u>T</u>ools, Add-<u>I</u>ns, <u>D</u>atabase Splitter to open the Database Splitter Add-Ins dialog, as shown in Figure 25.10.

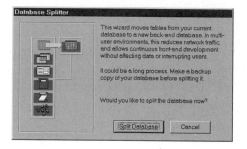

**FIG. 25.10**    The Database Splitter Add-Ins opening dialog.

3. Verify that you have the copy of Nwind.mdb open, and then click the Split Database button to display the Database Splitter's Save As dialog. The default file name is Nwind_be.mdb; "be" is an abbreviation for *back-end*.

4. Move to the \Shared\Nwind folder and type **NwindData.mdb** as the name of your back-end database file containing tables to link to application objects in Nwind.mdb (see Figure 25.11).

5. Click the Split button to create the back-end database. After a few seconds (depending on your computer's speed) of disk activity, you receive the message shown in Figure 25.12.

6. Click OK to close the Database Splitter Add-In. The tables page of your Database window appears as shown in Figure 25.13. Arrows to the left of the table icons indicate linked files.

7. To verify that the links to the tables are correct, choose <u>T</u>ools, Add-<u>I</u>ns, <u>L</u>inked Table Manager to display the Linked Table Manager's dialog, as shown in Figure 25.14.

**FIG. 25.11**   Selecting the directory and naming the back-end database file to contain the table objects.

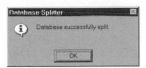

**FIG. 25.12**   The message informing you that the tables are split from your source .mdb file and links to the tables are created.

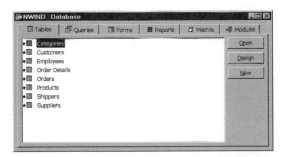

**FIG. 25.13**   Newly created links to the tables moved to the back-end database.

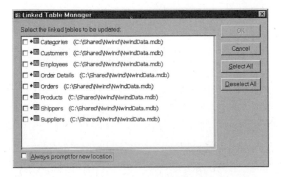

**FIG. 25.14**   The Linked Table Manager Add-In, confirming the location and name of the back-end .mdb file containing the linked tables.

### Choosing Workgroups with the Workgroup Administrator

If you have several workgroups that have overlapping user membership, you might want to place all of the workgroup system databases in a single directory, such as \Shared, to make it easy for users to choose a particular workgroup. (The workgroup system database does not have to be in the same directory as the shared .mdb file(s).) To use the Workgroup Administrator to change workgroups, follow these steps:

1. Launch Workgroup Administrator. Your current workgroup is identified by the .mdw file that appears in Workgroup Administrator's opening dialog.

2. Click the Join button to open the Workgroup Information File dialog. Your current workgroup system file appears in the Database text box (see Figure 25.15).

**FIG. 25.15**   Your current workgroup displayed in the Workgroup Information File dialog.

3. Type the well-formed path and name of the workgroup database file for the workgroup you want to join in the Database text box, or click the Browse button to display the Select Workgroup Information File dialog shown in Figure 25.16. In this case, choose the System.mdw in your \Program Files\Microsoft Office\Office folder to return to the normal Access configuration.

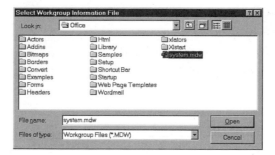

**FIG. 25.16**   Selecting the workgroup database file for the new workgroup.

4. Select the drive and directory in which the System.mdw file for the new workgroup is located, and click Open to close the Select Workgroup Information File dialog. Your selection appears in the Select Workgroup Information File dialog shown in Figure 25.17.

5. Click OK to confirm your new workgroup selection; click OK when the message box confirms that you have joined the workgroup, and then click the Exit button

of the Microsoft Workgroup Administrator's dialog (see Figure 25.18) to complete the process.

**6.** If Access is running, close it. Restart Access to use the new workgroup system file.

**FIG. 25.17**    Confirming the workgroup system file for the new workgroup.

**FIG. 25.18**    The Workgroup Administrator dialog after changing to a new workgroup.

# Using Command-Line Options to Open a Shared Database

Access provides a number of options that you can employ to customize how Access starts for each user. All users in a workgroup may share a common database, but you may want individual users to start Access with a different form. You can open a workgroup database automatically, execute a macro that opens a specific form, and supply a user name or password when you start Access by entering options on the command line that you use to start Access for each workgroup member, as in the following example:

```
d:\msa_path\msaccess.exe [n:\mdb_path\mdb_name.mdb]
  [/User user_name ][/Pwd pass_word ][/X macro_name]
  [/Ro ][/Excl ] [{/Profile user_profile¦/Ini profile.ini}]
  [/Repair] [/Nostartup]
  [/Compact [target.mdb]] [/Convert target.mdb] [/Run-time]
  [/Wrkgrp w:\mdw_path\system.mdw] [/Cmd cmd_value]
```

Spaces separate each of the optional command-line parameters. Table 25.1 describes the elements of the Access startup command-line options.

| Table 25.1    Command-Line Options for Launching Access | |
| --- | --- |
| **Command-Line Element** | **Function** |
| d:\*msa_path*\msaccess.exe | Command to launch Access. |
| n:\*mdb_path*\*mdb_name*.mdb | Path and name of startup database file. |

(continues)

### Table 25.1 Continued

| Command-Line Element | Function |
|---|---|
| /User user_name | Start with user_name as user name. |
| /Pwd pass_word | Start with pass_word as password. |
| /X macro_name | Run macro_name on startup. |
| /Ro | Open mdb_name for read-only use. |
| /Excl | Open mdb_name for exclusive use. |
| /Profile user_profile | Specify a user profile stored in the Registry named user_profile. |
| /Ini profile.ini | Open \Windows\profile.ini instead of using Registry entries. |
| /Repair | Repair the database, and then close Access. |
| /NoStartup | Don't display the Access startup dialog. |
| /Compact target.mdb | Compact into target.mdb or into the startup database if you omit target.mdb. |
| /Convert target.mdb | Converts a prior version .mdb file to an Access 97 .mdb file with the name specified by target.mdb, which is required and cannot be the same name as mdb_name. |
| /Run-time | Starts Msaccess.exe in Run-time mode for testing or to restrict users from entering Design mode. |
| /Wrkgrp system.mdw | Specifies a workgroup system file, system.mdw, on startup. |
| /Cmd cmd_value | Specifies a value to be returned by the VBA **Command** function. |

### Tip

Opening the local application .mdb with the /Excl parameter speeds operation of the application. The /Excl option applies to the local database, not the attached tables of the shared data .mdb file. Do not use the /Excl option if you want other users to be able to share the database. When you omit the /Excl option, shared or exclusive use of databases is determined by the Default Open Mode for Databases choice of the Multiuser Options, discussed in the previous section "Preparing to Share Your Database Files."

### Caution

Do not use the /Ro option if you want some members of the workgroup to be able to modify the tables or other objects of the database. If you specify the /Ro option for one workstation, all workstations in the workgroup are restricted to read-only use of the database. Use the permissions features of Access, described in the "Maintaining Database Security" section of this chapter, to designate the users who can update the data in tables and those who cannot.

The sequence in which you enter the command-line options doesn't affect the options' operation; however, a convention is that the name of the file to open always immediately follows the command that launches the application. The /Cmd cmd_value entry must be the last command-line option.

The /Profile parameter replaces the /Ini option of the run-time version of Access 2.0, but requires a substantial amount of editing of your Registry to use. The /Profile parameter is of limited usefulness, unless you're a full-fledged Access developer with experience editing the Registry. In Access 97, you still can use the argument of Access 2.0's /Ini parameter to point to a private profile (.ini) file, such as Nwind.ini, in your \Windows folder. (You can locate the .ini file in another folder by prefixing the well-formed path to the .ini file.) This feature is an alternative to the /Wrkgrp option, which is new to Access 97, letting you specify a particular workgroup system file in the [Options] section of the .ini file. To create and use a profile with the /Profile option, follow these steps:

1. Launch Notepad and type **[Options]** as the first line.

2. Type **SystemDB=** and the well-formed path and name of your workgroup system database as the second line.

3. Choose File, Save and save your text file in your \Windows or \Winnt directory as **Nwind.ini** (see Figure 25.19), and then close Notepad.

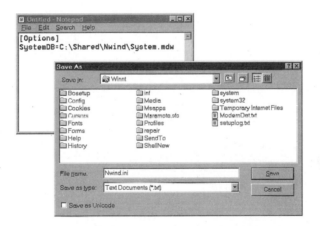

**FIG. 25.19**  Specifying a workgroup database file in a profile (.ini) file.

4. Create a desktop shortcut to Msaccess.exe, and then left-click the shortcut and choose Rename from the pop-up menu. Give the shortcut an appropriate name, in this case **Northwind.**

5. Right-click the shortcut and choose Properties from the pop-up menu. Click the Shortcut tab to display the Shortcut properties page.

6. After …\**Msaccess.exe**, add the path and name of your .mdb file, **/Ini** and the name of your .ini file, and then add **/Nostartup**. For this example, the full command line for the Windows 95 shortcut is **C:\Program Files\Microsoft Office\Office\Msaccess.exe C:\Shared\Nwind\Nwind.mdb /Ini Nwind.ini /Nostartup** (see Figure 25.20).

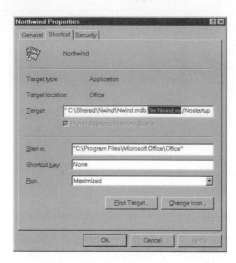

**FIG. 25.20**    Entering command-line parameters for an Access shortcut in Windows NT 4.0.

> **Note**
>
> If you are using Windows NT 4.0, the name of the executable file must be enclosed within double quotes ("....exe"). The full command line for the Windows NT 4.0 shortcut is **"C:\Program Files\Microsoft Office\Office\Msaccess.exe" C:\Shared\Nwind\ Nwind.mdb /Ini Nwind.ini /Nostartup**.

**7.** If you want to change the icon for your shortcut, click the Change Icon button to display a collection of icons in Shell32.dll from which to choose (see Figure 25.21). Select the icon you want, then click OK to close the Change Icon dialog.

**FIG. 25.21**    Changing the icon for an Access shortcut.

When you double-click the new shortcut, Access launches, uses the workgroup system database specified by the /Profile command-line parameter, and automatically opens the file specified on the command line parameter. When you distribute your Access application .mdb to other users, include a copy of the shortcut and the *Profile*.ini file.

> **Caution**
>
> Adding a user's password as an option to the startup command line violates one of the basic rules of database security: do not disclose your password to any other person. The preceding example that uses a password as a command-line option does so only for the purpose of completely defining the options available. You should not use the /Pwd command-line option under any circumstances.

# Maintaining Database Security

Database security prevents unauthorized persons from accidentally or intentionally viewing, modifying, deleting, or destroying information contained in a database. Database security is of primary concern in a multiuser environment, although you may want to use Access' security features to prevent others from viewing or modifying databases stored on your single-user computer. This section describes the multi-layered security features of networked Access databases and how you use these features to ensure a secure database system.

### Specifying the Principles of Database Security on a LAN

Ten basic principles of database security exist for databases installed on a LAN. Five of these principles are associated with the network operating system:

- Each user of a network must be positively identified before the user can gain access to the network. Identification requires a unique user name and secret password for each user. Users must not share their passwords with one another, and all passwords used should be changed every 60 to 90 days.

- Each identified user of the network must be authorized to have access to specific elements of the network, such as server directories, printers, and other shared resources. Each user has a network account that incorporates the user's identification data and authorizations. The network file that contains this information is always encrypted and is accessible only by the network administrator(s).

- Actions of network users should be monitored to determine whether users are attempting to access elements of the network for which they don't have authorization. Users who repeatedly attempt to breach network security should be locked out of the network until appropriate administrative action can be taken.

- The network should be tamper-proof. Tamper-proofing includes installing security systems immune to hacking by ingenious programmers and testing routinely for the presence of viruses.

- Data stored on network servers must be protected against hardware failure and catastrophic destruction (fires, earthquakes, hurricanes, and so on) by adequate and timely backup. Backup systems enable you to reconstruct the data to its state at the time the last backup occurred.

The measures required to establish the first five principles are the responsibility of the network administrator for a server-based system. In a peer-to-peer network, network security measures are the responsibility of each person who shares his or her resources with others. The remaining five principles of database security are determined by the security capabilities of the database management system and the applications you create with it:

■ The contents of tables in a database should be encrypted to prevent viewing the data with a file-reading or other snooping utility.

■ Users must be further identified before they are allowed to open a database file. A secret password, different from a user's network access password, should be used. The database file that contains user identification and password data (database user accounts) must be encrypted. The encryption technique used should be sophisticated enough to prevent hackers from deciphering it. Only the database administrator(s) has access to this file.

■ Users must be assigned specific permission to use the database and the tables it contains. If users are to be restricted from viewing specific columns of a table, access to the table should be in the form of a query that includes only the fields that the user is authorized to view. The RDBMS must provide for revoking specific permissions as the need arises.

■ The data in tables should be auditable. Lack of auditability is an incentive to computer-based embezzling. Updates made by users to tables that contain financial data should be maintained in a log—preferably in another database—that identifies the user who made the entry and the date and time the update was made. Logs are useful in reconstructing database entries that occurred between the time the database was last backed up and the time data was restored from the backup copy.

■ Operations that update records in more than one table should be accomplished by transaction techniques that can be reversed (or *rolled back*) if updates to all the tables involved cannot be completed immediately.

Most network operating systems in use on PCs provide for the first five database security principles, but enforcement of password secrecy, monitoring of user transgressions, and virus surveillance often are ignored, especially in peer-to-peer networks. Access provides all five of the database security principles, but you must take specific actions to invoke and maintain these principles.

> **Note**
>
> One of the most frequent breaches of database security occurs when a temporary worker is hired to stand in for a user who is ill or on vacation. Instead of establishing a new network account, including a user name, password, and new user (or guest) account for the database, the employee's user names and passwords are divulged to the temporary worker for the sake of expediency. A temporary worker should be assigned his or her own identification for the network and database; the temporary worker's authorizations should be removed when the regular employee returns to the job.

### Password-Protecting a Single Database

Access 97 adds password protection for individual database files. Setting a database password is the easiest way to partially secure a database while allowing others who don't know the password to use the copy of Access on your PC with other databases. To activate the database password for a specific .mdb file, complete the following steps:

1. You cannot set a database password in shared access mode, so close the open database, and then choose File, Open Database to display the Open dialog. Select your .mdb file, mark the Exclusive check box, and click Open to open the database in exclusive access mode.

2. Choose Tools, Security, Set Database Password to display the Set Database Password dialog.

3. Type a password in the Password text box. Your entry is shown as a series of asterisks to prevent disclosing your password to others as you enter it. Passwords are case-sensitive, so Uxmal is a different password from uxmal.

4. Type the password in the Verify text box to test your entry (see Figure 25.22). The verification test is not case-sensitive. Click OK.

**FIG. 25.22**   The Set Database Password dialog, establishing a password required to open a specific database.

5. Close the database, and then reopen it. The Password Required dialog shown in Figure 25.23 appears.

**FIG. 25.23**   Attempting to open a password-protected database.

6. Enter the password exactly as you typed it in step 3. Press Enter or click OK. If you enter the password correctly, Access continues the startup procedure. If you type an incorrect password, Access displays an error message and won't open the database.

To remove a password protection from a database, open the database for exclusive access, and then choose Tools, Security, Unset Database Password. Type the password in the Password text box of the Unset Database Password dialog, and then click OK.

VI

Using Advanced Techniques

> **Caution**
>
> Don't use database password protection for databases that you intend to replicate using Access 97's Briefcase Replication, described in Chapter 27, "Replicating Access Databases." Database password protection causes the replication process to fail.

## Managing Groups and Users

Most client/server databases establish the following three groups of database users:

- *Administrators* (Admins) have the authority to view and update existing tables and add or delete tables and other database objects from the database. Members of the Admins group usually have permission to modify the applications contained in databases.

- *Regular members of workgroups* (Users) are assigned permission to open the database and are granted permission to view and modify databases on a selective basis. Users ordinarily aren't granted permission to modify Access applications. In Access, Admins also are members of the Users group.

- *Occasional users of databases* (Guests) are granted limited rights to use a database and the objects it contains but aren't assigned a user account. Guest privileges often are assigned to persons being trained in the use of a database application. Access 97 does not define a Guests group.

When you install Access 97, you are automatically made a member of the Admins and Users groups with the name Admin and have all permissions granted. You have an empty password and Personal ID Number (PIN), which means that you don't need to enter a password to log onto the database(s) associated with the System.mdw database installed in the …\Office folder. When you are learning Access, you have little reason to establish database security. After you begin to create a useful database application, especially if it contains confidential information, you should implement basic security provisions on your own computer.

**Establishing Your Own Admins Name, Password, and PIN.** Access has two levels of security: application level and file level. The *application-level security system* requires each user of Access to enter a user name and a password to start Access.

*File level security* is established by the network operating system, such as Windows NT 4.0 Server, and grants users permissions for access to shared folders and/or individual files. Establishing single-user application-level security and preparing for multiuser security requires that you perform the following sequence of tasks:

1. Activate the logon procedure for Access. This action requires that you add a password for the Admin user. To remain Admin, you need not complete the remaining steps, but your only security is your password.

2. Create a new account for yourself as a member of the Admins group.

3. Log onto Access using your new Admins user account.

**4.** Remove the default Admin user account from the Admins group. The Admins group should include entries for active database administrators only. You cannot remove the Admin user from the Users group.

Before you begin the following procedure, make a disk backup copy of the System. mdw file in use and any database files that you created or modified while using this System.mdw. If you forget the user name or password you assigned to yourself after deleting the Admin user, you cannot log onto Access. In this case, you must restore the original version of the System.mdw file. Then you may not be able to open the database files with which the original version of the System.mdw file is associated unless you restore the backed-up versions. It is recommended that you modify the System.mdw file you created in the \Shared\Nwind folder as your system database for all of the examples that follow in this chapter.

---

### Caution

Do not use the Northwind.mdb database in your ...\Office\Samples folder for the examples that follow. You should preserve Northwind.mdb and the System.mdw file of your ...\Office\Access folder in the original state. Use the Nwind.mdb file created earlier in this chapter with the Database Splitter and use the System.mdw workgroup file located in the \Shared\Nwind directory.

---

### Tip

You don't need to open a database to add or modify user accounts. All user account information is stored in System.mdw, which Access automatically opens when launched.

---

To activate the logon procedure for Access, complete the following steps:

**1.** A temporary password to the Admin user is necessary to activate Access's logon procedure. Choose Tools, Security, User and Group Accounts to open the User and Group Accounts properties sheet (see Figure 25.24). You are logged on as Admin, a member of the Admins and Users group, by default.

**FIG. 25.24**  The default opening page, Users, of the User and Group Accounts properties sheet.

**2.** Click the Change Logon Password tab to display the Change Logon Password page.

> **Note**
>
> If you don't change the Admin user's password, you automatically are logged on as Admin with a blank password each time you start Access.

**3.** Press the Tab key to bypass the Old Password text box (this enters the equivalent of an empty password), and enter a difficult-to-guess password, such as **Xy8zW3ab**, in the New Password text box. Your entry is shown as a series of asterisks to prevent disclosing your password to others as you enter it. Passwords are case-sensitive, so Xy8zW3ab is a different password from xy8zw3ab.

**4.** Type the password in the Verify text box to test your entry, as shown in Figure 25.25. The verification test is not case-sensitive. Click OK to close the properties sheet.

**FIG. 25.25**    The Change Logon Password page used to establish your new Admin password.

**5.** Exit Access and launch it again. The Admin account is password-protected, so the Logon dialog appears.

**6.** Type **admin** in the Name text box, press Tab, and type the password exactly as you typed it in step 3 (see Figure 25.26). Press Enter or click OK. If you enter the password correctly, Access continues the startup procedure.

**FIG. 25.26**    The Logon dialog that appears when you protect the Admin account with a password.

To add your new user account in the Admins group, perform the following steps:

1. Choose Tools, Security, User and Group Accounts to display the User and Group Accounts properties sheet (refer to Figure 25.24). All members of the Admins group automatically are included (and must be included) in the Users group. Both Admins and Users appear in the Member Of list.

2. Click the New button to add your new account. The New User/Group dialog appears.

3. Type the name you want to use to identify yourself to Access in the Name text box and enter a four-digit PIN in the Personal ID text box (see Figure 25.27). The PIN, with the Name entry, uniquely identifies your account. This precaution is necessary because two people may use the same logon name; the Name and PIN values are combined to create a no-duplicates index on the Users table in your current system database file. Click OK to close the New User/Group dialog and return to the User and Group Accounts page.

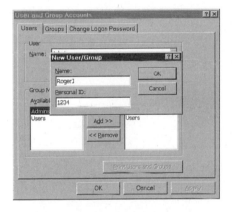

**FIG. 25.27** Adding a new account for the Admins group with the New User/Group dialog.

4. This is a critical step. Select Admins in the Available Groups list and click the Add button to add the Admins group to your new user name (see Figure 25.28). If you fail to do this, you cannot remove the Admin account from the Admins group. (Access requires that there be at least one member of the Admins group in each system database file.)

> **Note**
>
> When you log on with your new user name, you can't see the names of the last four databases you opened as Admin when you choose File, Open. Prior database selections are specific to each user.

**FIG. 25.28**    Adding the Admins group to your new user account.

5. You don't enter a password for the new user at this time because you still are logged onto Access as Admin. Click the OK button to close the User and Group Accounts properties sheet and then exit Access.

6. Launch Access, type your new user name in the Logon dialog, and press Enter or click OK. Do not enter a password because you have an empty password at this point. User names aren't case-sensitive; Access considers NewAdmin and newadmin to be the same user.

7. Choose Tools, Security, User and Group Accounts, select your new user name from the Name drop-down list, and click the Change Logon Password tab. Press Tab to bypass the Old Password text box and type the password you plan to use until it is time to change your password (to maintain system security). Passwords can be up to 14 characters long and can contain any character, except ASCII character 0, the Null character. Verify your password, and then press Enter or click OK to close the Password sheet.

8. Close and reopen Access and log on with your new user name and password. This step verifies that your new Admins user name and password are valid.

9. Choose Tools, Security, User and Group Accounts. Open the Users list of the User and Group Accounts page and select your new user name from the list. Verify that you are a member of the Admins and Users group.

10. Open the Users list again and select the Admin user. Select Admins in the Member Of list; then click Remove. Admin remains a member of the Users group, as shown in Figure 25.29. Click OK to close the properties sheet.

You use the same procedure to add other users as members of the default Admins, Users, or Guests group or of new workgroups you create. You have not fully secured the open database because the Admin user still has full permissions for the objects in the database. Revoking the Admin user's permissions is discussed in the section "Changing the Ownership of Database Objects" later in the chapter.

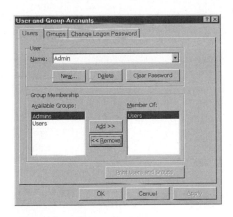

**FIG. 25.29**   Removing the Admin user from the Admins group.

---

**Note**

Write down and save your PIN and the PIN of every user you add to the workgroup for future reference. User names and PINs aren't secure elements, so you can safely keep a list without compromising system security. This list should be accessible only to database administrators. You need a user's PIN so that the user can be recognized as a member of another workgroup when the need arises. (See the section "Granting Permissions for a Database in Another Workgroup" near the end of this chapter.)

---

**Establishing Members of Access Groups.**   Groups within Access's security system are not the same as workgroups. As discussed previously, a workgroup shares the same system database file that is located in a designated directory. The entries you made in the preceding steps were saved in the workgroup or system database file that was active when you launched Access. This section describes how to add new users to a group, a process similar to the one you used to add your new Admins account.

To add a new user to a group, you must be logged onto Access as a member of the Admins group and complete the following steps:

1. Choose Tools, Security, User and Group Accounts to open the User and Group Accounts dialog.

2. With the Users page active, click New. The New User/Group dialog appears. Type the new user's name and PIN. Click OK to create the account and close the dialog. The Users dialog reappears. Make a note of the PIN you used to add the new user. You need to know the user's PIN so that you can duplicate an entry for the new user in other workgroups.

3. The default group for all new users is Users. To add the user to the Admins group, select Admins in the Available Groups list and click the Add button to add Admins to the Member Of list (refer to Figure 25.24). All Access users must be members of the Users group. Click OK to return to Access's main window when your selections are complete.

4. Request the new user log onto Access with the user name and change his or her password from the default empty value to a legitimate password.

   You can improve the level of security by typing the new user's password yourself, so that users cannot bypass the password step by leaving their password blank. To enter a password for a new user, close Access, log on as the new user, and enter the user's chosen password in the Change Logon Password page.

Before you add a significant number of users, decide whether you need additional groups and determine the permissions that should be assigned to each group other than Admins. These aspects of database security are discussed in the following sections.

> **Tip**
>
> When requesting new users enter their first password, emphasize the advantage of the use of longer passwords that combine upper- and lowercase characters and numbers because they improve system security. Users should not use their initials, names of spouses or children, birth dates, or nicknames; these are the entries that unauthorized users try first to gain access to the system.

**Adding a New Group.** In most cases, Admins and Users are the only groups necessary for each workgroup you create. Members of a group usually share the same permissions to use database objects (which is the subject of the next section). Adding a new Access group is not necessary, therefore, unless you have a category of users who are to have a different set of permissions than members of the Users group. Such a category may distinguish Users (who may be limited to viewing data) from members of a Data Entry group who have permission to update the data in tables.

To add a new group, perform the following steps:

1. Choose Tools, Security, User and Group Accounts. Then click the Groups tab. Currently defined groups appear in the Name drop-down list, as shown in Figure 25.30.

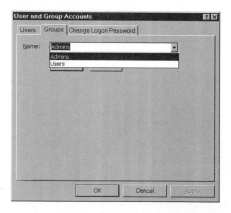

**FIG. 25.30**    The Groups page for adding a new user group to a database.

2. Click the New button to open the New User/Group dialog.

3. Type the name of the group in the Name dialog and a four-digit Personal ID Number, as shown in Figure 25.31. Group names can be up to 20 characters long and can contain spaces, but punctuation symbols aren't allowed. You don't need to make a note of the PIN in the case of groups because the PIN is used only for indexing purposes.

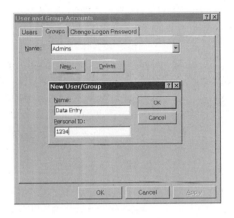

**FIG. 25.31**   Adding a new Data Entry group to the workgroup.

4. Press Enter or click OK. The Groups dialog reappears.

5. Click OK from the Groups dialog. You can delete the newly added group by clicking the Delete button.

After you add a new group, you need to assign the default permissions that apply to all members of the group by the procedure outlined in the "Granting and Revoking Permissions for Database Objects" section that follows.

**Deleting Users and Groups.** Members of the Admins group have the authority to delete users from any group and to delete any group except Admins, Users, and Guests. To delete a user or group, choose Tools, Security, User and Group Accounts, select the user or group to delete from the list box, and click Delete. You are asked to confirm the deletion. Admins and Users groups must each contain one user account; you cannot delete all users for either of these groups.

**Clearing Forgotten Passwords.** If a user forgets his or her password and you are logged into Access as a member of the Admins group, you can delete the user's password, so that you or the user can enter a new password.

To clear a user's password, complete the following steps:

1. Choose Tools, Security, User and Group Accounts. Make sure the Users tab is active.

2. Open the Name list and select the user whose password you want to clear.

3. Click the Clear Password button (refer to Figure 25.29).

4. Make sure that the user whose password you cleared enters a new password, or log onto Access as the new user and enter a new password for the user.

As mentioned previously, entering the user's password as the database administrator is the only means of ensuring that the database security is enforced. There is no other means of ensuring that users assign themselves passwords. (Of course, perverse users can change their passwords to empty strings or "password" if they choose to do so.)

# Understanding Database Object Ownership

The user who creates an object becomes the owner of the object. (Access calls the owner of an object the object's *creator*.) Object owners have special status within the Access security system. The following two sections briefly describe owners' permissions and how to change the ownership of database objects. A more detailed description of object ownership is contained in the file SECURE.ZIP, written for Access 2.0, that you can download from the **MSACCESS** forum on CompuServe.

### Owner Permissions for Objects

The owner of an object has full (Administer) permissions for the object. No other user, including members of the Admins group, can alter the object owner's permissions for the object directly. For example, the Admin user is the owner of all the database objects in Northwind.mdb. Thus, anyone who uses the Admin user account has full permissions for all objects in Northwind.mdb. This is one of the reasons for assigning a password for the Admin account.

When a user other than the object's creator adds a new object to the database or to one of the existing objects in the database, this user becomes the owner of the object. For example, if user Margaret adds a control object to a form created by Larry, Margaret is the owner of the control object, not Larry. Mixed ownership of objects can lead to bizarre situations, such as the inability of the owner of a query to execute the query because the owner of the underlying tables has changed. (You can overcome this problem, however, by adding the WITH OWNERACCESS OPTION to the Jet SQL statement for the query.)

When you create new database objects using the default Admin user ID, anyone else who has a retail copy of Access 97 and uses the default Admin user ID also has full permissions for these objects. Thus, when you begin development of an application that you intend to share with others or that you want to prevent others from using or modifying, create a new account in the Admins group as described earlier in the chapter. Use your new Admins account when you create new applications.

### Changing the Ownership of Database Objects

Following are the three methods of changing the ownership of existing Access database objects:

■ Create a new database file, and then choose File, Get External Data, Import. Open the .mdb file containing the objects, and import all of the objects into the new

.mdb file. The user who creates the new .mdb file becomes the owner of the imported objects.

- Use the Change Owner page of the User and Group Permissions dialog.

- Use the Security Wizard to create a new secure database file, import the objects, and then encrypt the new database.

The following two sections describe the second and third methods for changing database object ownership.

**Using Access 97's Change Owner Feature.** To use the Change Owner feature that originated in Access 95, you must be a member of the Admins group for the database, and must follow these steps:

1. Open the database containing the objects whose ownership you want to change.

2. Choose Tools, Security, User and Group Permissions to open the User and Group Permissions dialog, and then click the Change Owner tab.

3. Choose the class of object you want to change in the Object Type drop-down list.

4. If you want to change the ownership of all of the objects of the selected class, select the first item in the Object list, move to the bottom of the list, press the Shift key, and click the last item of the list.

5. Select the new owner's name from the New Owner drop-down list.

6. Click the Change Owner button to change the ownership of the selected items, from Admin to **RogerJ** in this example (see Figure 25.32).

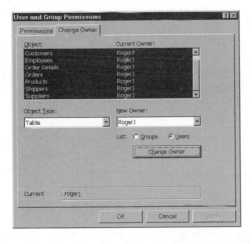

**FIG. 25.32**  Changing the ownership of all Table objects from Admin to a new owner.

7. Repeat steps 3–6 for each class of objects whose ownership you want to change.

The preceding process is the fastest way to remove permissions of the Admin user accrued from ownership of the original objects.

**Using the Security Wizard.** You can change the ownership of all the objects in a database for which you have Administer permissions by importing all the database objects into a new database you create with a user ID other than Admin. Access 2.0 made it easy to import all the database objects from one .mdb file into another .mdb file with its Import Database Add-In. Access 97's Security Wizard goes the Import Database Add-In one better by letting you choose the database objects to secure and encrypting the new secure copy of the database in a single (long) step. The Security Wizard automatically imports every object in the source database into the new encrypted destination database.

> **Caution**
>
> Do not use the Security Wizard with the Northwind.mdb database in your ...\Office\Samples directory. Use the NwindData.mdb file created earlier in this chapter with the Database Splitter, and use the System.mdw file in your \Shared\Nwind directory. The Security Wizard can take a long time to perform its operations with a slow processor, so using the smaller NwindData.mdb file is recommended.

To test the Security Wizard, follow these steps:

1. If you aren't logged onto Access, launch Access and log on with your new user ID that includes Admins group membership and open the database to secure, NwindData.mdb in this case.

2. Choose Tools, Security, User-Level Security Wizard to display the Security Wizard's opening dialog.

3. Clear the check box that corresponds to the class of database objects that you don't want to make secure (see Figure 25.33). If you want to secure all database objects, accept the wizard's default.

**FIG. 25.33**    Setting the types of objects to secure in the new database.

4. Click the OK button to open the Destination Database dialog. Select the folder in which to store the new secure database file and give the file a new name. The default is Secure *database*.mdb (see Figure 25.34).

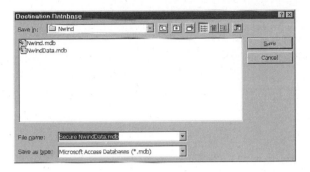

**FIG. 25.34**  Specifying the path and file name for the new secure database file.

5. Click the Save button to put the Security Wizard to work. After a few seconds, the message shown in Figure 25.35 appears, indicating successful creation of the new secure database. Click OK to close the dialog.

**FIG. 25.35**  The message indicating successful completion of the Security Wizard's task.

The owner of all the objects in the new database is the user ID you used when you opened the source database. Only members of the Admins group have access of any kind to the newly secured database.

> **Note**
>
> This chapter uses the term *user ID* to identify users of Access. Internally, Access uses a *system ID* (*SID*) to identify users. The SID is a value that Access computes from the user ID, password, and PIN. The SID is stored in the MSysUsers table of System.mda as an encrypted binary value in a field of the Binary (varbinary) data type.

# Granting and Revoking Permissions for Database Objects

The second layer of Access security is at the *database level*. Access lets the database administrator grant or revoke permissions to use specific database objects to all members of a group or to specific members of a group. Permissions grant authority for users to view or alter specific database objects. The permissions granted to the group are inherited by each member as he or she is added to the group. Thus, it is important that you establish the group permissions you want before adding users to a group.

Users who are members of more than one group, such as Admins and Users, inherit database object permissions from each group. You can grant additional permissions to individual members of a group, but you cannot revoke permissions that individual members inherit from the group. Permissions are stored within the database file as properties of individual database objects. Only members of the Admins group or users who have Administer permission can grant or revoke permissions for database objects.

> **Caution**
>
> If you use the split-database design, you do not need to add groups and users to the data .mdb. Permissions for use of the linked data .mdb file are managed by the permissions for links to the tables in your application .mdb file. However, it is important that you change the ownership of Table objects in the data .mdb file from the Admin account to your secure account in Admins. If you do not change ownership, any user of retail Access who uses the default Admin account can open the data .mdb file and make changes at will to the file.

Table 25.2 lists the permissions offered by Access for database objects, ranked in descending level of authority. Full Permissions allow the user to use all the features of Access, including design functions. The description of the specific action allowed by a permission is listed in the Explicit Permissions column. Permissions at an authority level below Full Permissions require other permissions to operate; these required permissions are called implicit permissions.

**Table 25.2  Permissions to Use Access Database Objects**

| Permission | Database Objects | Explicit Permissions | Implicit Permissions |
|---|---|---|---|
| Open/Run | Forms, reports, macros | Use or run objects | Read Data |
| Read Design | All | View objects | Execute for macros only |
| Modify Design | All | Alter, replace, or delete objects | Update Data and Execute |
| Administer | All database objects | All permissions | Not applicable |
| Read Data | Tables, queries, forms | View data in objects | Read Design |
| Update Data | Tables, queries, forms | Edit table data | Read Data |
| Insert Data | Tables, queries, forms | Append data in tables | Read Data |
| Delete Data | Tables, queries, forms | Delete data in tables | Read Data |

If, for example, you allow a user to modify design, this user also must be able to modify data and execute objects. Therefore, Update Data and Open/Run permissions are implied by the Modify Design permission. This user, and any other users allowed to modify data, must be able to read data. All users having permission to read data must be able to read designs. When you establish permissions for a database object, Access adds the implicit permissions automatically.

The Admins and Users groups have full permissions for any new database objects you create. If you intend to share the database with other users, you probably don't want all members of the Users group to have permission to update database tables, and certainly you don't want members of the Users Group to be able to modify the design of your database objects. A more conservative set of permissions for the two groups follows:

- The Admins group has full permissions for all objects. Admins privileges should be assigned to as few individuals as possible. Make sure you have enough backup database administrators with Admins privileges to cover for the absence of the primary administrator. Members of the Admins group are also members of the Users group.

- The Users group has Open/Run and Read Data permissions. Update, Insert, and Delete Data permissions are granted for specific forms and reports. Users are never granted Modify Design permission in databases.

You can add new groups with specific group permissions, such as Data Entry or Developers, to make assigning individual user permissions for database objects simpler.

> **Note**
>
> You can use the Run with Owner's Permissions check box or add the WITH OWNERACCESS option to Jet SQL statements to enable users without the required permissions to execute a query.

### Altering Group Permissions

After you design your hierarchy of permissions and add any new user groups you need, you are ready to assign group permissions for each of the objects in your database. Only members of the Admins group can alter permissions for Groups or Users. The Permissions check boxes that are enabled depend on the type of object you choose. Open/Run, for example, is enabled only for database, form, report, and macro objects.

> **Note**
>
> When you first select the Admins group, none of the Admins group's permission check boxes are marked. Members of the Admins group inherit full object permissions from membership in the Users group. (By default, Users have full permissions for all objects.) If you revoke object permissions for the Users group, you add Administer permissions for the Admins group.

To change the permissions for a group, complete the following steps:

1. Open the database for which group permissions are to be granted or revoked with the appropriate workgroup system database active.

2. Choose Tools, Security, User and Group Permissions to open the User and Group Permissions dialog.

3. Click the Groups option button to display the permissions for groups of users; then select Users in the User/Group Name list.

4. Open the Object Type drop-down list and select the type of database object whose permissions you want to change.

5. Select the specific object to which the new permissions will apply in the Object Name list. To select all objects, click the first item in the list, press the Shift key, and then click the last item in the list. Do not include <New ObjectType> in your multiple selection.

6. In the User/Group Names list, select the Group whose permissions you want to revise, Users for this example. Figure 25.36 shows the full permissions for Table objects that Access assigns by default to the Users group.

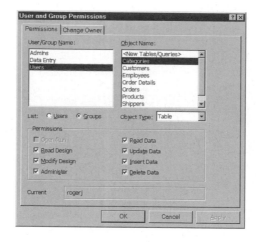

**FIG. 25.36**   The default permissions for the Users group.

7. Permissions currently granted to the group are shown by a check mark in the Permissions check boxes. Click the Modify Design, Update Data, Insert Data, and Delete Data check boxes to allow the users groups only to display forms and read table data. If you have made multiple selections, you may need to click the check box twice to make a selection effective. When you remove a permission, Access automatically removes the Administer permission. Your Permissions dialog appears as shown in Figure 25.37.

8. Click the Apply button to make the new permissions effective for the selected database object(s).

9. With the object(s) selected in step 5, select the Admins group, mark the Administer check box, and click the Apply button. This step assures that the Admin users continue to have full permissions for the objects (see Figure 25.38).

10. Repeat steps 4–9 for each database object and object type whose User group permissions you want to change.

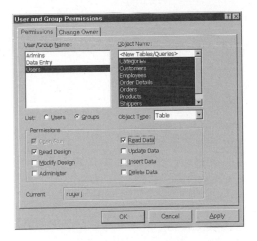

**FIG. 25.37**  Revising permissions for all Table objects for the Users group.

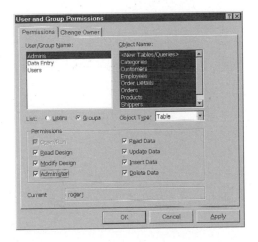

**FIG. 25.38**  Granting Administer permissions for all Table objects to the Admins group.

---

**Note**

If you create macro objects that contain several individually named macros (to minimize the number of objects in the database), make sure that each macro object contains named macros that correspond to a specific category of permissions. Named macros, for example, that invoke action queries to modify tables or add new records should be grouped in one macro object, and named macros that only display the contents of database objects should be located in a different macro object.

When you assign permissions to execute macro objects, you need to assign Modify Data permission to those users who can execute macro objects that run action queries. Microsoft discourages the use of macros with Access 97, and macros may not be supported in future versions of Access.

### Granting Additional Permissions to Specific Users

The process of granting additional permissions to a specific user is similar to the process used to alter group permissions. Permissions inherited by the user from the group to which the user is assigned are not shown in the Permissions dialog. To grant additional permissions to a specific user, complete the following steps:

1. Choose <u>T</u>ools, Security, User and Group <u>P</u>ermissions. The Users option is the default for the User and Group Permissions dialog.

2. Select the user to whom additional permissions are to be granted in the User/Group Name list (see Figure 25.39).

   TestUser is a member of the Users group whose account was added after the changes to User group permissions were made in the preceding section. As mentioned in the introduction to this section, the Read Design and Read Data permissions that were inherited by TestUser from the modified permissions of the Users group aren't shown in the Permissions check boxes.

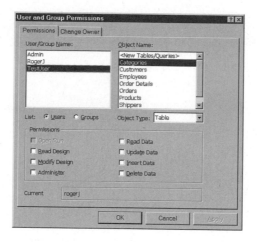

**FIG. 25.39**    The Permissions dialog for a new user with inherited permissions.

3. To assign permissions to a specific user so that the user can update data for an object, select the object using the Object Type and Object Name lists, and then click the Update Data, Insert Data, and Delete Data check boxes. Access automatically marks the implicit permissions, Read Design and Read Data, associated with the explicit permission, Update Data (see Figure 25.40). Click the Apply button after selecting each object whose permissions you want to change.

   Implicit permissions for individual users are displayed in the Permissions check boxes regardless of whether the implicit permissions also were inherited from group membership.

4. Repeat step 3 for each user who requires permissions for an object that aren't inherited from the user's group permissions. Click the OK button when you complete the permission changes for all users who require such changes.

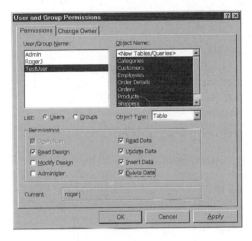

**FIG. 25.40**  The Permissions dialog for a new user with the new data permissions added.

> **Note**
>
> You can use the /Ro command-line option, described in the preceding section, "Using Command-Line Options to Open a Shared Database," to revoke Update Data, Insert Data, and Delete Data permissions for the database on specific workstations. This method isn't secure because the user can edit the command-line option, remove the /Ro entry, and log on again with read-write privileges. If you use this method, Access displays a message box indicating that the database is being opened in read-only mode and that the user cannot modify data.

### Granting Permissions for a Database in Another Workgroup

If your application requires that you attach a table in a secure database used by a different workgroup, the user needs to be a member of a group in the other workgroup and needs to be assigned appropriate permissions for the attached table. At this point, you need the list of PINs for users, mentioned in the section "Establishing Your Own Admins Name, Password, and PIN" earlier in this chapter.

To grant permission for a user to modify data in a table attached from another workgroup's database, perform the following steps:

1. Close Access; you need to relaunch Access when you select another workgroup.

2. Launch the Workgroup Administrator application and specify the path to the workgroup database file of the workgroup that uses the database that contains the table to be attached.

3. Launch Access and open the database that contains the table to be attached.

4. Add an account for the user to the Users group with exactly the same user name and PIN as was used to add the user account to his or her workgroup.

5. If you don't want this user to join the other workgroup, enter a password and don't disclose the password to the user.

6. Open the Permissions properties sheet, select the table object to be attached, and assign the appropriate data permission for the table to the user.

You need to use the same PIN for the user in both workgroups because the account for the user is created from the user name and PIN, and the accounts must be identical in both databases. You also must use the same PIN number to reinstate the user's account if the workgroup system file becomes corrupted; you don't have a current backup, and Access cannot repair it.

# Sharing Databases on the Network

Once you've set up your user groups and modified the database object permissions for the groups as necessary, you can safely share the workgroup system database and your data .mdb file, and then distribute copies of your application .mdb file to the users. Before sharing the files, make sure to create a backup copy of each of the shared files and store the copies in a safe location. The following sections describe how to share files.

### Sharing Database Files on a Windows 95 Network

With a peer-to-peer Windows 95 network, you need only set up a network share of the folder in which you developed the application, \Shared\Nwind for the example of this chapter. The most common method of sharing folders with Windows 95 networking is to use share-level security. To share a folder on your computer with share-level security, follow these steps:

1. Launch Control Panel and double-click the Network tool to open the Network properties sheet.

2. Click the Access Control tab and select the Share-Level Access Control option (see Figure 25.41). Click OK to close the Network properties sheet, then close Control Panel.

> **Note**
>
> If you previously have specified the User-Level Access Control option and change to Share-Level Access Control, all of your current shares will be removed, and you must reboot Windows 95 for the new access control option to take effect.

3. Launch Explorer and select the folder to be shared, \Shared\Nwind for this example.

4. Choose File, Properties or right-click the folder icon and choose Sharing to open the *FileName* Properties sheet. Click the tab of the Sharing properties page.

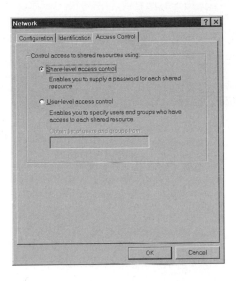

**FIG. 25.41**   Setting share-level access control in Control Panel's Network properties sheet.

5. Click the Shared As option button. The name of the folder appears as the default share name, NWIND in this example. Share names are limited to 12 characters and must not contain names, punctuation, or other special characters. Add an optional brief description of the share in the Comment text box.

6. To update data, users must have read-write access to the shared folder (often simply called a share). Other users only need read access to the folder. Click the Depends on Password option button in the Access Type frame.

7. Type the Read-Only Password and the Full Access Password in the two text boxes, as shown in Figure 25.41, and then click OK to create the share.

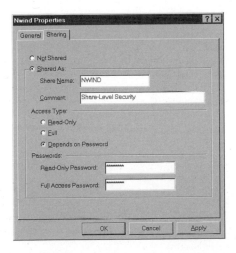

**FIG. 25.42**   Creating a shared subfolder with share-level access for a peer-to-peer Windows 95 network server.

In the examples presented in this chapter, both Nwind.mdb (the application database) and NWData.mdb (the data .mdb file) are shared for read-write access, allowing users to launch Nwind.mdb from the server if they choose. Users should copy Nwind.mdb from the server share to their local computer and run the local copy to minimize network traffic. When connecting to the server share, users must enter the appropriate password for full or read-only access.

### Sharing Files with User-Level Security

Specifying individual users with access to shares is a more secure alternative to simple share-based access control. You can specify users that are members of the Windows 95 workgroup to which you log on. If you're connected to a Windows NT network, you can grant share access to designated Windows NT groups or individual users. To set up user-level security, follow these steps:

1. Launch Control Panel and double-click the Network tool to open the Network properties sheet.

2. Click the Access Control tab and select the User-Level Access Control option (refer to Figure 25.41). Type your workgroup name or the Windows NT domain name in the Obtain List of Users and Groups From text box. Click OK to close the Network properties sheet, then close Control Panel.

> **Note**
>
> As noted in the preceding section, if you previously have specified the Share-Level Access Control option and change to User-Level Access Control, all of your current shares will be removed and you must reboot Windows 95 for the new Access Control option to take effect.

3. Launch Explorer and select the folder to be shared, \Shared\Nwind for this example.

4. Choose File, Properties or right-click the folder icon and choose Sharing to open the *ShareName* Properties sheet. Click the tab of the Sharing properties page. The Sharing page contains an empty list of names and access rights.

5. Click the Shared As option button. Add an optional brief description of the share in the Comment text box (see Figure 25.43).

6. To specify groups or users having access to the share, click the Add button to open the Add Users dialog. Members of your workgroup appear in the left-hand list if you're using Windows 95 networking. If you're connected to a Windows NT Server domain, which is the case for this example, all of the Windows NT groups and users appear in the list.

7. Select a group or user, then click the Read Only, Full Access, or Custom button, as appropriate for your selection. Ordinarily, only you and Domain Admins should be granted Full Access to the share (see Figure 25.44).

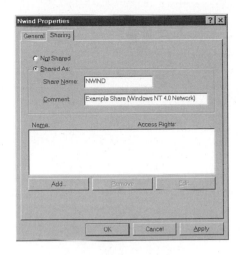

**FIG. 25.43** The Sharing properties page for user-level access control.

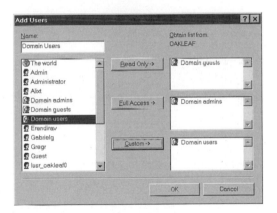

**FIG. 25.44** Adding Windows NT Server groups for Read Only, Full, and Custom access to the share.

8. When you add a user or group with Custom access to the share, the Change Access Rights dialog appears. Mark the check boxes for the specific rights you want to grant, as shown for Domain Users in Figure 25.45, then click OK to close the dialog.

9. When you finish adding groups or users, click OK to close the Add Users dialog. The groups (and users, if any) you added for the share appear in the Sharing page, as shown in Figure 25.46. Click OK to close the *ShareName* Properties sheet.

**VI**

**Using Advanced Techniques**

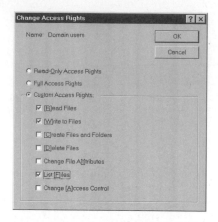

**FIG. 25.45** Specifying custom share access rights for a user or group.

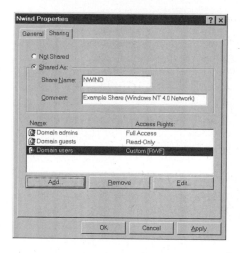

**FIG. 25.46** Three Windows NT groups with varying rights to a Windows 95 share.

The advantage to user-level access is that users don't need to enter a password when connecting to the share; the user ID and password used to log onto the network grants access to the share.

> **Note**
>
> It is a relatively uncommon practice to share files from a Windows 95 peer-to-peer server when workgroup members are connected to a Windows NT server. Sharing the files from a Windows NT server that uses the Windows NT File System (NTFS), the subject of the next section, offers improved security.

## Sharing Database Files from a Network Server

The specific method of creating a server share on a dedicated network server depends on the network operating system (NOS) in use. Ordinarily, the network administrator will create the server share for you, and you need only move the files to be shared from your local folder to the shared server directory. If your NOS supports permissions for individual files, request full access rights to your workgroup database and data .mdb files. Windows NT Server supports permissions for individual files, if the files are located on an NTFS partition.

If you want users to be able to run the application .mdb from the server, grant read and execute access; otherwise, grant copy-only access so users can copy the application .mdb file to their local computer. Make sure, however, that you (the share owner) have full network permissions for all of the shared files. Do not grant users more permissions for the shared files than they need.

## Accessing the Shared Files

Users access the server share by mapping the server share to a drive letter or by using Uniform Naming Convention (UNC). Using UNC eliminates the problem with users assigning different logical drive letters to server shares when mapping the share to their computer. Unlike Access 2.0, Access 97 supports UNC, as well as long file names (LFNs).

The network share you create, whether from your computer or from a network server, appears in the Network Neighborhood window for the selected server. In this example, Oakleaf0 is a Windows NT 4.0 Server (Primary Domain Controller) and Oakleaf1 is the workstation used to write this edition. Oakleaf3 is another Windows NT 4.0 Server that acts as a Backup Domain Controller. The \Shared\Nwind directory of Oakleaf0 is shared as NWIND, but appears as NWIND in the list of shares available from Oakleaf0 (see Figure 25.47). Double-clicking the nwind share displays icons for the shared files. (Use of the term *directory*, rather than *folder*, is more common when referring to file servers.)

**FIG. 25.47**   The \Shared\Nwind directory shared as NWIND on the Oakleaf0 server appears in Network Neighborhood as NWIND.

**Attaching the Shared Workgroup System File.** Users of your application ordinarily use Workgroup Administrator to join the workgroup using the shared workgroup database file. You copy the shared data .mdb file and the System.mdw file to the server's shared directory. To access files using UNC, type **\\ServerName\ShareName\ FileName.ext**. If you're sharing files from your computer, *ServerName* is the name you assigned to your computer when you installed Windows 95 or Windows NT. Figure 25.48 shows how to specify a workgroup database file using UNC.

> ### Caution
>
> Do not use a logical drive letter mapped from a share to specify the location of System.mdw. Users are likely to map shares to different logical drive letters.

**FIG. 25.48**  Specifying the workgroup to join using UNC.

> ### Troubleshooting
>
> *After changing the location of the workgroup database file, Access opens with a 'd:\path\ filename.mdw' isn't a valid path message, and then Access closes.*
>
> Either the drive letter, path, or file name entry isn't valid, or you cannot connect to the server share specified by the UNC name, or, if mapped to a drive letter *n*:[\*path*]. Use Explorer or Network Neighborhood to verify that your entry is correct and that your network connection to the server is working. In Explorer, choose <u>V</u>iew, <u>R</u>efresh to verify that the server connection currently is valid.

**Refreshing the Links to the Shared Data File.** Prior to distributing your application .mdb file, you must change the links to point to the shared data .mdb file. This step is especially important if you have revoked the design mode permissions for the Users group because the revocation prevents members of the Users group from refreshing the links. To refresh the links to point to the shared data .mdb file, follow these steps:

**1.** As a member of the Admins group, open the application .mdb file and choose <u>T</u>ools, Add-<u>I</u>ns, <u>L</u>inked Table Manager.

> ### Note
>
> If you share the files from your computer with the Windows 95 network, you must perform this step on another networked computer because your share does not appear in Network Neighborhood and you do not have access to files on your computer through UNC file names. In this case, open the shared application .mdb to refresh the links.

2. Click the Select All button, and then mark the Always Prompt for New Location check box. (If you don't mark this check box and the existing links are valid, you won't be able to refresh the links.) The Linked Table Manager's dialog appears as shown in Figure 25.49, assuming you performed the database splitting example earlier in this chapter.

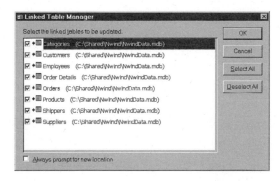

**FIG. 25.49**   Preparing to move table links to a shared data .mdb file with the Linked Table Manager.

3. Click the OK button to open the Select New Location of Categories dialog.

---

**Note**

If a local copy of the linked file specified in the opening dialog of Linked File Manager exists and you don't mark the Always Prompt for New Location check box, the links are simply refreshed and the Select New Location of *TableName* dialog doesn't appear.

---

4. Open the Look In list and select Network Neighborhood, and then select the server and share to display the files in the share (see Figure 25.50). Select the data .mdb file and click the Open button.

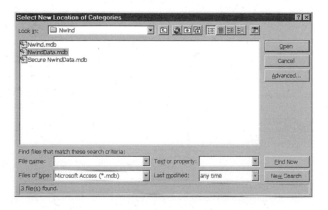

**FIG. 25.50**   Selecting the shared data .mdb file in the \Network Neighborhood\\*ServerName*\ *ShareName* folder.

5. The Linked File Manager automatically refreshes links for all of the linked tables it finds in the selected data .mdb file. On completion of the refresh process, a message confirms that all linkages were refreshed and the Linked File Manager's dialog appears as shown in Figure 25.51. Click the OK button to close both the message box and the dialog.

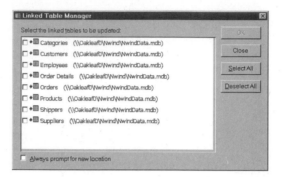

**FIG. 25.51**    The Linked Table Manager confirms the links to the data .mdb on the file server.

Once you refresh the links with the UNC location of the shared data .mdb file, you can distribute the application .mdb file to users.

# Administering Databases and Applications

Administering a multiuser database involves a number of duties besides adding and maintaining user accounts. The most important function of the database administrator is to ensure that periodic valid backup copies are made of database and system files. The database administrator's other responsibilities consist of routine database maintenance, periodic compacting of database files, and repairing databases.

### Backing Up and Restoring Databases

The following maxims relate to maintaining backup copies of database files:

- The time interval between successive backups of databases is equal to the amount of data you are willing and able to reenter in the event of a fixed disk failure. Except in unusual circumstances, such as little or no update activity, daily backup is the rule.

- Rotate backup copies. Make successive backups on different tapes or disk sets. One of the tapes or disks may have defects that could prevent you from restoring the backup. The backup device, such as a tape drive, can fail without warning you that the recorded data isn't valid.

- Test backup copies of databases periodically. You should test one different copy in the backup rotation sequence for restorability. If you rotate five daily backup tapes, for example, you should randomly choose one of the tapes, restore the database file from the tape, and open it with Access to ensure its validity every fifth day. Access tests each database object for integrity when you open the database file.

■ Maintain off-site backups that you can use to restore data in case of a disaster, such as a fire or flood. The copy of the backup tape or disk that you test for restorability is a good candidate for an off-site backup copy.

You can back up database files on a network server by copying them to a workstation that has a fixed disk, but this technique doesn't provide backup security. The user of the workstation can erase or damage the backup copy if you don't create the off-site copy required for security against disasters.

Backing up data on network and peer-to-peer servers usually is accomplished with a tape drive device. These devices usually include an application that backs up all data on a network server or selected files on peer-to-peer servers at intervals and times you select. The simpler the backup operation, the more likely you are to have current backups. Regardless of how automated the backup procedure is, however, you need to manually restore the test copy.

### Compacting and Repairing Database Files

Compacting and repairing database files was discussed in Chapter 3, "Navigating Within Access." You should compact database files in which applications add and delete data to recover the disk space occupied by the deleted data. The procedure for compacting a database is similar to that described for encrypting and decrypting databases, the subject of the next section, except that you choose <u>T</u>ools, Database <u>U</u>tilities, <u>C</u>ompact Database rather than <u>T</u>ools, Securi<u>t</u>y, <u>E</u>ncrypt/Decrypt Database.

◀◀ See "Compacting Databases," p. 102
◀◀ See "Repairing Databases," p. 104

> **Note**
>
> You can improve the operating speed of Access if you periodically defragment database files. Windows 95's Disk Defragmenter utility tells you whether a disk drive has sufficient fragmentation to justify running the utility.

If you receive a message that a database is corrupted or if the database behaves in an irregular manner, one or more of the objects it contains may be corrupt as the result of a hardware error. Databases can become corrupt as the result of a power failure when the computer is writing to the database file. The Repair Database choice of Access's File menu attempts to repair the damage. If Access cannot repair the corruption, you must restore the latest backup copy. Test the backup copy with the existing System.mda or Workgroup.mdw file; in some cases, you may need to restore the prior .mda or .mdw file that contains the user account data for the database.

### Encrypting and Decrypting Database Files

File-level security isn't complete until you encrypt the database. Encrypting the database prevents others from reading its contents with a text editing or disk utility application, such as is included with Symantec's Norton Utilities. Encryption of databases causes

Access' operations on tables to slow perceptibly because of the time required to decrypt the data. Only members of the Admins group can encrypt or decrypt a database.

> **Note**
>
> If you are using a fixed disk data-compression utility, you will find that encrypting your database files reduces the percentage of compression to zero or a very small number. Encrypting files eliminates the groups of repeating characters that form the basis of most data-compression algorithms.

To encrypt or decrypt an Access database file, complete the following steps:

1. Make sure that the disk drive of the computer on which the database is stored has sufficient free space to create a copy of the database you intend to encrypt or decrypt. Access makes a new copy of the file during the process.

2. All other workstations, including your own, need to close the database file to be encrypted. You cannot encrypt or decrypt a database file that is in use on any workstation.

3. Choose Tools, Security, Encrypt/Decrypt Database. The Encrypt/Decrypt Database dialog appears.

4. Select the name of the database file to be encrypted and click OK.

5. If the file already is encrypted, it is decrypted, and vice-versa. The title bar of the dialog that opens indicates whether the file will be encrypted or decrypted in this operation. If you are interested only in whether the file has been encrypted, you can click Cancel now.

6. Type the name of the encrypted or decrypted file to create in the Encrypt FileName As dialog, and click OK. Normally, you type the same name as the original file; Access does not replace the original copy of the file if the process does not succeed.

Databases are compacted by Access when they are encrypted or decrypted.

> **Note**
>
> You don't need to encrypt files while you're developing applications using files that aren't shared with others unless the files contain sensitive information. After the files are made shareable, a good security practice is to encrypt them, even if they don't contain confidential data.

# Chapter 26

# Connecting to Client/Server Databases

One of the computer buzzwords of the mid-1990s, *downsizing*, was mentioned in the context of local area networks (LANs) in the preceding chapter. Downsizing has another element: moving database management systems from mainframe computers to client/server RDBMSs that run on PCs and reduced instruction set computing (RISC) workstation-servers.

Another newly minted term, *rightsizing*, means choosing the best combination of computer platforms to ensure maximum availability of corporate data to those who need it. Rightsizing often involves retaining mainframe computers as giant database servers but moving the applications that access and manipulate the data from the mainframe to PCs.

The final member of the sizing trio is upsizing. *Upsizing* means moving tables from a desktop database, such as Access 97, to a client/server RDBMS. You can continue to use the application components of your desktop database if the desktop database can link to the tables of the client/server RDBMS. This chapter introduces you to Access front-ends for client/server databases and shows you how to use the Access Upsizing Wizard to move Access databases to Microsoft SQL Server 6.5.

## Creating Scalable Access Applications

Regardless of the linguistic legitimacy of terms such as rightsizing, these words have become ingrained in today's computerese. Each of these expressions relates to the *scalability* of applications. Scalable applications can run on a variety of platforms, communicate by industry-standard LAN and wide area networking (WAN) protocols, and access data stored in a variety of different types of databases. 32-bit Access 97 runs under Windows 95 or Windows NT 3.51+, so Access itself is moderately scalable. Access 97 is a threaded application and Jet 3.5 is multithreaded; thus, Access can take advantage of the symmetrical multiprocessing (SMP) capabilities of Windows NT running on workstations with multiple processors. Windows NT runs on Intel-based PCs and RISC systems, such as DEC Alpha servers and IBM PowerPC platforms, but you need a version of Access 97 that's compiled for the specific RISC processor in use. It remains to be seen whether Microsoft intends to release versions of Office 97 for use with Windows NT running on RISC machines.

On the networking front, Windows 95 and Windows NT support the three most common networking protocols: NetBEUI, IPX/SPX, and TCP/IP. Following is a brief description of each of these protocols:

- *NetBEUI (NetBIOS Extended User Interface)* is the foundation of Windows Networking and the simplest LAN protocol to implement. NetBEUI isn't a routable protocol, so it isn't suitable for large-scale networks. NetBEUI, however, is quite efficient and useful for setting up LANs in small- to medium-sized organizations.

- *IPX/SPX (Internetwork Packet Exchange/Sequenced Packet Exchange)* is the primary protocol for Novell NetWare LANs. IPX/SPX is the default network protocol for Windows 95 because of the large installed base of NetWare 3.x/4.x LANs.

- *TCP/IP (Tranmission Control Protocol/Internet Protocol)* is the protocol of the Internet and UNIX systems. TCP/IP is a routable protocol that enables the creation of very large LANs and WANs. The remarkable growth of the Internet in the mid-1990s has established TCP/IP as the standard protocol for scalable networking.

Fortunately, Windows 95 and Windows NT 3.5+ let you run all three of these protocols simultaneously. Unless you're connected to a NetWare LAN, it's more efficient to use only NetBEUI and TCP/IP. As an example, you might connect to SQL Server 6.5 running under Windows NT Server 4.0 with NetBEUI and to Sybase System 11 or Oracle7 running on a UNIX server with TCP/IP.

The third element of scalability, the capability to access data that resides in a variety of SQL-compliant databases, is provided by Microsoft's Open Database Connectivity (ODBC) products. Office 97 includes the new 32-bit ODBC 3.0 Administrator application and a 32-bit ODBC driver for Microsoft SQL Server. There are about 150 third-party suppliers of ODBC drivers. ODBC provides Access with the capability to connect virtually to any popular mainframe-, minicomputer-, RISC-, and PC-resident SQL-compliant database through Microsoft and third-party 32-bit ODBC drivers. This chapter describes how ODBC works and how you can connect to client/server databases with ODBC drivers.

---

**Note**

Access 97 requires 32-bit ODBC drivers to connect to client/server RDBMSs. Existing 16-bit ODBC 2.0 drivers used with Access 2.0 and its predecessors do not work with Access 97. If you are upgrading from Access 2.0 (or an earlier version), and are using 16-bit ODBC drivers for RDBMSs other than Microsoft SQL Server, you must obtain 32-bit versions of ODBC drivers from the RDBMS vendor or a third-party publisher.

---

# Defining the Client/Server Environment

Client/server databases are designed specifically for use on application server-based networks. An *application server* uses a network operating system, such as Windows NT Server, that is optimized specifically for running applications rather than sharing files or peripheral devices. Client/server databases have many advantages over conventional database systems, including increased database security, the incorporation of all components of the database. In a single file, and faster access to networked data. The clients of a client/server database are workstations, often called *front-ends*, that are connected to the server, called the *back-end*. In these respects, the "split" Access databases, described in the preceding chapter, and client/server databases are similar. The principal difference between Access and a typical client/server database manager, such as Microsoft SQL Server, is that the client/server RDBMS performs many operations on the server that traditionally are carried out by database applications running on the client workstation.

Client/server database managers accept SQL statements from client applications. The client/server RDBMS interprets the SQL statement and executes the actions specified in the statement. If you send a SELECT query SQL statement to the server, the server returns only the result set to the client; processing of the query occurs on the server computer. This action speeds query generation two ways: The amount of information traveling over the network is reduced, and server computers often have much more powerful and faster microprocessors than the workstation clients.

> **Note**
>
> SQL Server isn't limited to traditional client/server architecture in which clients connect to the server via a network. You can use Access front-ends on the same Windows NT server that runs SQL Server. Microsoft also offers a developer's version of SQL Server that runs as a service on Windows NT Workstation. Microsoft announced in the fall of 1996 its intention to port SQL Server to Windows 95, making SQL Server a direct competitor to the Jet database engine.

To understand many of the examples in this chapter, you need to know how the computers that create the examples are set up. The following list describes the computers and network used to create this chapter's examples of employing ODBC for connecting to client/server databases:

- The primary server (OAKLEAF0) is a 133-MHz Pentium clone with 64M of RAM and a 4.3G Seagate Barracuda Fast, Wide SCSI-2 fixed-disk drive that is connected to an Adaptec AHA-2940UW fixed-disk controller on the PCI bus. Windows NT Server 4.0 is installed as a Primary Domain Controller (PDC) on the 2G C: drive formatted with NTFS (Windows NT's New Technology File System). The 2.3G D: partition is used for file sharing. The E drive is a Toshiba double-speed SCSI CD-ROM drive. A 1G Tandberg tape backup drive also connects to the SCSI bus.

- A second server (OAKLEAF3) is a 166-MHz Pentium PC with a PCI bus, 32M of RAM, and two 4.3G Seagate Barracuda Wide, Fast SCSI-2 drives that are connected to an Adaptec AHA-2940UW. \\OAKLEAF3, which dual-boots Windows 95 and Windows NT Server 4.0 (as a Backup Domain Controller or BDC), is used primarily for digital video capture with an Interactive Images Plum card and non-linear digital video editing by using Adobe Premiere 4.2. OAKLEAF3 has a 4x SCSI-2 CD-ROM and a Hewlett-Packard ScanJet IIcx scanner that are connected to the narrow SCSI port of the AHA-2940UW.

■ Microsoft SQL Server 6.5 runs as a service under Windows NT Server 6.5 (NTS) on the OAKLEAF0 and OAKLEAF3 servers. (A Windows NT service is an application that starts automatically when you boot Windows NT, before the user logs on.) Exchange Server 4.0, Internet Information Server 3.0 (beta version), and Microsoft Media Server 1.0 also run as services on OAKLEAF0. SQL Enterprise manager, the administrative application for SQL Server 6.5, is installed on all computers except OAKLEAF2.

■ The client used to write this edition (OAKLEAF1) is an 80486DX4-100 PCI-bus clone with 16M of RAM, and 300M, 600M, and 1.2G IDE fixed disks, plus a 2X SCSI CD-ROM drive connected to the SCSI port of a Sound Blaster 16 audio adapter. OAKLEAF1 dual-boots Windows NT Workstation 4.0 and Windows 95. OAKLEAF1 is scheduled for retirement at the end of 1996.

■ Another client (OAKLEAF2) is an 80486DX2-66 ISA clone with 8M of RAM and a 300M IDE disk drive that runs Windows 95. OAKLEAF2 is used primarily for composing and sequencing music. It is equipped with a variety of legacy (pre-Plug and Play) sound cards and several MIDI synthesizer modules. The 80486 client is used for testing the performance of custom applications (except Access 97 applications) on yesterday's average client workstation configuration. 16-bit MIDI sequencing applications run fine under Windows 95 on OAKLEAF2, but trying to run Access 97 applications on 80486DX-33 PCs with 8M of RAM definitely is not recommended.

■ All servers and clients are equipped with Intel EtherExpress 16 Pro network interface cards (NICs) that are connected via thin Ethernet coaxial cabling. The LAN uses both NetBEUI and TCP/IP protocols. OAKLEAF0 and OAKLEAF3 also have Intel 100BaseT Fast Ethernet adapters for transferring compressed digital video data at rates up to about 42 Mbps. Remote Access Services (RAS), which allow dial-up (modem and ISDN) connections to the OAKLEAF0 server, are also implemented. Figure 26.1 shows the configuration of the network used for the examples discussed in this chapter.

If the preceding description appears to be written in Greek, don't despair; knowing the computer setup is necessary only to explain the entries in the text boxes of the dialogs that are illustrated in this chapter. Network systems of the complexity of the above configuration are common where a variety of operating systems, sometimes in both retail and beta versions, are used.

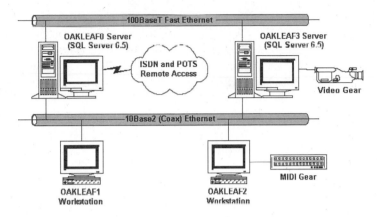

**FIG. 26.1**  The network topology of the computers used to write this book.

# Defining Open Database Connectivity

Access uses the Microsoft Open Data Base Connectivity (ODBC) application programming interface (API) to provide access to any database system for which ODBC drivers
are available. An API is a standardized method by which an application communicates
with elements of the computer's operating system or environment. For example, applications use the Windows 95 (Win32) API in GDI32.EXE, a mostly 32-bit Windows 95 dynamic link library (DLL), to perform all display operations. The ODBC API enables a
standard set of SQL statements in any application to be translated to commands that are
recognized by the server database. The role of ODBC drivers is explained in the following
section, "Understanding ODBC Drivers."

The ODBC API was the first element of Microsoft's Windows Open Services Architecture
(WOSA) used to create a variety of classes of commercial Windows applications. (32-bit
ODBC 3.0 is the fourth iteration of the ODBC API, and ODBC 3.5 is expected to be avail-
able by mid-1997). Messaging API (MAPI) and Telephony API (TAPI) also are members of
WOSA, which includes industry-specific APIs such as WOSA/XRT for handling real-time
stock market data.

Today, WOSA includes a group of APIs that enable Windows applications to manipulate
data that resides in virtually any format on any type of computer, anywhere in the
world. Enterprise-wide data sharing through LANs and WANs employs large mainframe
computers as centralized database servers that feed data to or through client/server
RDBMSs. A recent trend in enterprise-scale computing is for PC clients to connect to
large client/server RDBMSs that are configured as data warehouses or data marts, rather
than to connect directly to databases stored on mainframe computers.

One of today's trends in enterprise-wide computing is the use of distributed database
systems. Distributed database systems enable elements of a large database to be stored
on servers in different locations that act as if they were a single, large server. SQL Server
6.5 includes replication services and a Distributed Transaction Controller (DTC) to

implement the first phase of Microsoft's distributed database architecture. As advanced Windows operating systems—such as the next version of Windows NT (presently called Cairo)—are developed, and as additional members of WOSA become a commercial reality, PCs using Intel $80 \times 86$ architecture and RISC processors will capture a larger share of the server market. Access is designed to play an important role in enterprise-wide, distributed database systems: to create the applications that users need to view and update the myriad of databases to which they can connect. The advantage of Access as a client/server front-end is the ease with which you can create relatively simple decision-support and transaction-processing applications.

# Understanding ODBC Drivers

The ODBC API consists of a driver manager and one or more ODBC drivers, as illustrated by the shaded boxes in Figure 26.2. Windows uses drivers to adapt its standard API to specific combinations of hardware such as displays, keyboards, and printers. Likewise, the ODBC API uses drivers to translate instructions passed from the application through the driver manager to instructions that are compatible with various RDBMSs. When the ODBC driver manager receives instructions from Access that are intended for a data source, such as a SQL Server database, the driver manager opens the appropriate ODBC driver for the database. The relationship of the ODBC driver manager and ODBC drivers parallels the relationship of Access 97's built-in, 32-bit Jet 3.5 database engine and the 32-bit ISAM drivers that are used to connect to Access, dBASE, FoxPro, and Paradox files.

ODBC drivers are classified as one of the following two types:

- *Single-tier drivers* translate SQL statements into low-level instructions that operate directly on files. Single-tier drivers are required for RDBMSs that don't process SQL statements directly. The widely used PC RDBMSs fall into this category. The 32-bit ISAM drivers included with Access for connecting to dBASE, FoxPro, and Paradox databases are single-tier drivers (but they aren't ODBC drivers). The Access, dBASE, FoxPro, Paradox, Excel, and Text ODBC drivers included with Microsoft Office 97 are 32-bit ODBC drivers.

- *Multiple-tier drivers* process ODBC instructions but pass SQL statements directly to the data source using SQL syntax that is acceptable to the back-end RDBMS. All popular client/server RDBMSs that can run on PCs—and most mini- and main-frame RDBMSs—process SQL statements directly. The SQL Server ODBC driver is a multiple-tier driver because SQL Server processes SQL statements directly.

One 32-bit ODBC driver is required for each type of client/server database whose tables you want to attach to an Access 97 database, but a single driver can be used to connect to several databases of the same type. Each connection to a database is called an *instance* of a driver. In addition to the ODBC driver, you may need additional files (usually license and/or communication files supplied by the RDBMS publisher) to connect to the back-end RDBMS. As an example, Microsoft supplies the required named pipes DLLs— 16-bit Dbnmp3.dll and 32-bit Dbnmpntw.dll—to connect to Microsoft SQL Server. Named Pipes is the protocol through which you make connections to SQL Server. To connect to an Oracle database, for example, you need a local copy of Oracle's SQLNet.dll.

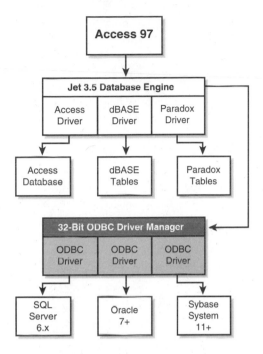

**FIG. 26.2**  A comparison of the ODBC 3.0 and Jet 3.5 driver systems used with Access.

The ODBC API is based on a standard called the *X/Open SQL Call Level Interface (CLI)*, which was developed by the SQL Access Group (an organization comprised of hardware manufacturers, software suppliers, and users of SQL databases). Microsoft published the standards for creating ODBC drivers, so any RDBMS supplier can make its database product compatible with Access by writing the appropriate driver. Microsoft provides a 32-bit ODBC driver with Office 97 that is compatible with Microsoft SQL Server 4.21a and later.

Most publishers of major client/server database management systems provide ODBC drivers for their database products. Oracle Corporation (Redwood Shores, CA) provides and supports ODBC drivers for its Oracle Server RDBMSs. Intersolv, Inc. (Rockville, MD) offers its DataDirect ODBC drivers for a variety of client/server RDBMSs, desktop databases, and file types.

You can obtain up-to-date information on Oracle and Intersolve ODBC drivers at the following URLs:

**On the Web**

**http://www.oracle.com/products/oracle7/odbc/overview.html**
**http://www.intersolv.com/solution/dw_odbc.htm**

Each workstation that needs to attach SQL Server tables to Access databases must be connected to the SQL Server through the network: Microsoft Windows Network, TCP/IP, Microsoft LAN Manager, IBM LAN Server, Banyan VINES, or Novell NetWare. In most cases, you set up your network adapter card and established the network protocol(s) in

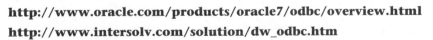

**VI**

**Using Advanced Techniques**

use when you installed Windows 95 or Windows NT. You can modify your network configuration, if necessary, with Control Panel's Network option.

# Installing the Microsoft ODBC Driver for SQL Server

 The members of Office 97, except Access 97, depend on 32-bit ODBC drivers for interoperability with Jet, dBASE, FoxPro, Paradox, and SQL Server databases, plus Excel and text files. Microsoft Query also uses ODBC to connect to the preceding data sources. Thus, Office 97 automatically installs the 32-bit ODBC 3.0 administrator application, called the ODBC Data Source Administrator, as a Control Panel tool when you choose the Typical or Custom Setup option. Figure 26.3 shows the 32-bit ODBC tool installed in Windows 95's Control Panel. In Windows NT 4.0's Control Panel, the 32-bit ODBC icon does not have the 32-bit caption prefix.

**FIG. 26.3** Windows 95's Control Panel with the 32-bit ODBC 3.0 Administrator tool installed.

> **Note**
>
> If you installed Microsoft Access 2.0, Word 6.0, or Excel 5.0 under Windows 95, and if you have elected to install the ODBC driver for Access or the Desktop Database Drivers for Word or Excel, you see an ODBC icon in Control Panel. This is the icon for the 16-bit ODBC Administrator and drivers, which do not work with Access 97. You must install the 32-bit ODBC Administrator and drivers for use with Access 97, Word 97, or Excel 97.

To install the SQL Server ODBC driver on a Windows 95 or Windows NT 4.0 workstation on which Office 97 is installed, perform the following steps:

1. Close all open Windows applications and launch Control Panel's Add/Remove Programs tool. When you install Office 97, the Setup program creates an entry in the list of installed programs. Click to select the Microsoft Office 97 Professional entry (see Figure 26.4).

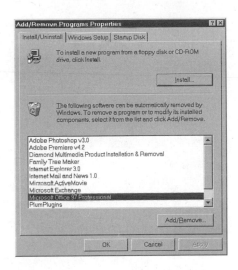

**FIG. 26.4**  The Add/Remove Programs feature of Control Panel lists previously installed 32-bit applications.

  **2.** With the Microsoft Office 97 Professional item selected, click the Add/Remove button to launch the Office 97 Setup maintenance program.

  **3.** Insert the Office 97 CD-ROM when prompted and click OK. The first dialog of the Setup maintenance program appears, as shown in Figure 26.5.

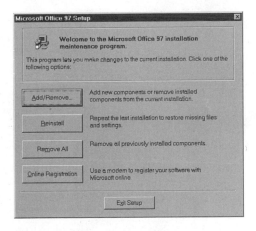

**FIG. 26.5**  The first dialog of the Access 95 Setup maintenance program.

  **4.** Click the Add/Remove button to display the Microsoft Office 97—Maintenance dialog. Select the Data Access item in the Options list, as shown in Figure 26.6. The appearance of other items in the Options list varies, depending on how you originally installed Office 97.

**VI**

**Using Advanced Techniques**

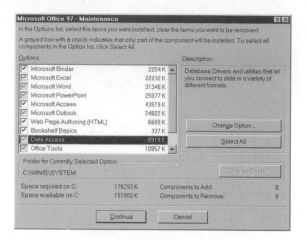

**FIG. 26.6**    The Microsoft Office 97—Maintenance dialog.

   **5.** With the Data Access entry in the Options list selected, click the Change Option button to display the Microsoft Office 97—Data Access dialog. Select the Database Drivers item in the Options list (see Figure 26.7) and click the Change Option button.

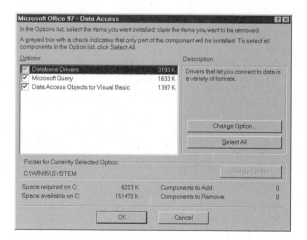

**FIG. 26.7**    The Microsoft Office 97—Data Access dialog.

   **6.** Double-click the Microsoft SQL Server Driver item in the Options list to mark the check box for installation (see Figure 26.8).

   **7.** Click OK to close the Database Drivers and Data Access dialogs, and click Continue to install the SQL Server driver from the Office 97 CD-ROM. Click OK to close the Setup maintenance application when you receive the message that installation is complete.

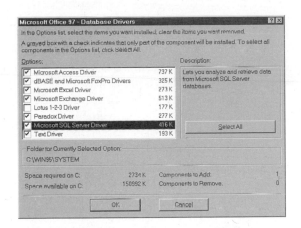

**FIG. 26.8**  Selecting the SQL Server driver for installation in the Microsoft Office 97—Database Drivers dialog.

**8.** Click the OK button of the Add/Remove Programs tool to close it, then close Control Panel.

When Setup installs the SQL Server ODBC driver, it creates the required entries for SQLsrv32.dll in the Registry in the HKEY_LOCAL_MACHINE\SOFTWARE\ODBC hive (see Figure 26.9).

---

**Note**

Previous 16-bit versions of ODBC stored data in ODBCINST.INI (which lists the installed ODBC drivers) and ODBC.INI files (which list installed ODBC data sources) in your \WINDOWS directory. The Registry entries include similar information in the \ODBC\ODBCINST.INI and ODBC\ODBC.INI groups.

---

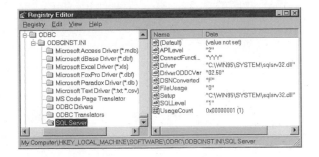

**FIG. 26.9**  The Registry Editor (Regedit.exe) displaying the Registry entry for the 32-bit SQL Server driver.

# Adding and Removing SQL Server Data Sources

An ODBC data source for a client/server RDBMS is a definition of a database—including the name of the server on which the RDBMS and database is located, the name of the ODBC driver required to connect to the database, and, optionally, the name of the database. You need at least one SQL Server data source to enable Access to attach, export, or import SQL Server tables. You can use Control Panel's ODBC Administrator tool or Access's built-in ODBC data source feature to create SQL Server data sources.

Following are the three different types of ODBC data sources supported by Access 97:

- *User data sources* are specific to each user of the workstation. The definitions of these data sources are stored in the \HKEY_CURRENT_USER\Software\ODBC\ODBC.INI section of the Registry. You can create conventional data sources using the ODBC Administrator tool or from within Access.

- *System data sources (System DSNs)* are stored in the HKEY_LOCAL_MACHINE\SOFTWARE \ODBC\ODBC.INI section of the Registry. All users of the workstation can choose from available System DSNs. Like user data sources, you can create system data sources using the ODBC Administrator tool or from within Access. Windows NT Server 4.0 requires System DSNs for operations that run as Windows NT services, such as logging usage of an Internet Information Server 2.0 Web site.

- *File data sources* are individual text files that define the ODBC data source, which you can share with other Access 97 users. File data sources are a standard feature of ODBC 3.0; Access is unique in its ability to create file data sources for ODBC 2.5. File data sources don't appear in the Registry.

The following sections describe how to use ODBC Administrator and Access 97 to create SQL Server data sources for the pubs example database of Microsoft SQL Server 6.x.

> **Note**
>
> It's a tradition in SQL Server to use all lowercase names for databases and most other database objects. Early versions of SQL Server used case-sensitive object names by default; the default for SQL Server 6.5's installation is case-insensitive object names.

### Using the ODBC Data Source Administrator to Create a SQL Server Data Source

The traditional approach is to use Control Panel's ODBC Administrator tool to add or remove SQL Server data sources. To add a SQL Server data source with ODBC Administrator, follow these steps:

1. Double-click the 32-bit ODBC icon in Control Panel to launch the ODBC Data Source Administrator and display the default User DSN page (see Figure 26.10).

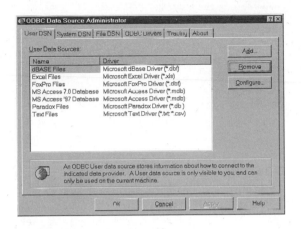

**FIG. 26.10**  The Data Sources dialog of the ODBC Administrator with default data sources installed.

Figure 26.10 shows the user ODBC data sources created during the installation of Office 97 ODBC drivers. Microsoft Office 97 installs the ODBC drivers for dBASE, Excel, FoxPro, and Access 97, plus optional drivers for Paradox and Text files. The list in Figure 26.10 reflects the ODBC driver choices made in Figure 26.8. There is no default data source for the SQL Server driver.

2. Click the Add button to add a new user ODBC data source with the Create New Data Source dialog. Alternatively, click the System DSN tab, then click Add to add a system data source. (Default system data sources aren't added when you install Office 97.) Select the SQL Server item in the Installed ODBC Drivers list of the Add Data Source dialog, as shown in Figure 26.11.

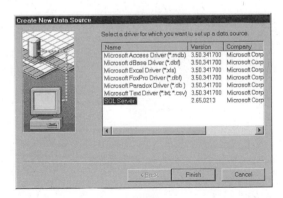

**FIG. 26.11**  Selecting the SQL Server ODBC driver in the Create New Data Source dialog.

3. Click Finish to display the ODBC SQL Server Setup dialog. Enter a short descriptive name of the SQL Server database in the Data Source Name text box. Unless you have a particular database that contains the tables you want to attach to Access,

type **pubs** to specify the pubs sample database supplied with SQL Server. Type a description of the database, such as **SQL Server Sample Database**, in the Description text box.

4. Select the name of the server from the Server combo list that holds the SQL Server database you want to use. If no entries appear in the combo list, type the name of the server (without the preceding \\) in the text box. If you are creating the data source on the Windows NT server running SQL Server, select (local) from the drop-down list. Unless you are using a special network library (netlib) for the data source, accept the (Default) entries for the Network Address and Network Library text boxes (see Figure 26.12). (The default 32-bit network library for SQL Server is Dbnmpntw.dll.) Mark the Use Trusted Connection check box if SQL Server is set up with Windows NT integrated security and you want the user to log on with his or her network user ID and password instead of a SQL Server user ID and password.

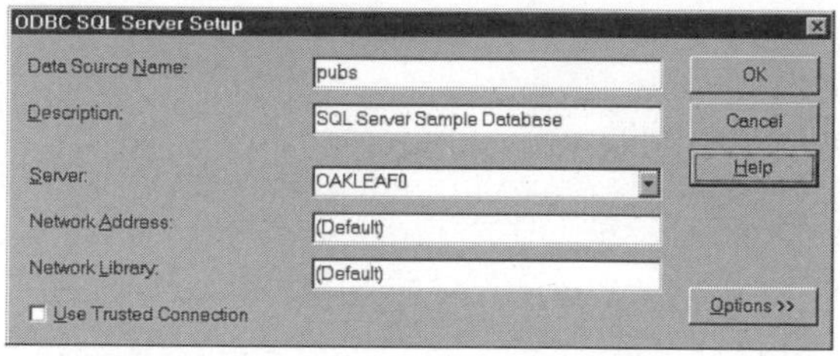

**FIG. 26.12**  Beginning the definition of a new ODBC data source.

5. Click the Options button to expand the dialog to specify a default database. Type **pubs** in the Database Name text box, as shown in Figure 26.13.

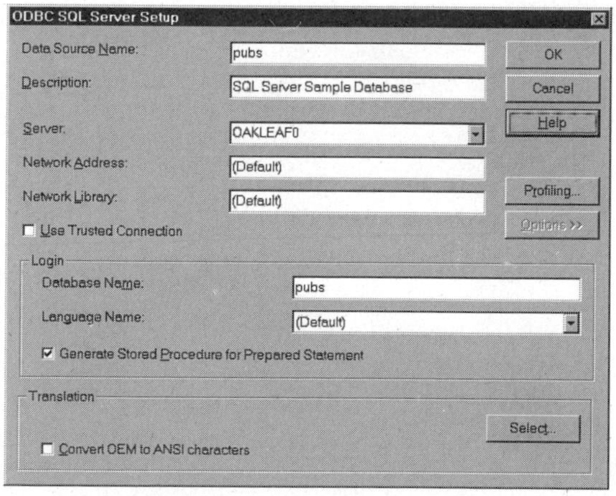

**FIG. 26.13**  Completing the definition of the ODBC data source.

The Generate Stored Procedure for Prepared Statement check box, when marked (the default), creates a temporary SQL Server stored procedure (a precompiled query) from prepared statements written in Transact-SQL, the SQL dialect of SQL Server. Access 97's new ODBCDirect feature, which you can implement only with Access VBA, is capable of creating multiple prepared statements that exist until you close the connection with SQL Server.

The Language Name drop-down list displays the national languages that the database supports. (The national language of the database is not necessarily the same as the Locale of Windows 95.) Accept the (Default) entry.

The Convert OEM to ANSI characters check box changes special characters in SQL Server database tables to their Windows (ANSI) equivalents when an ANSI equivalent is available. If you or the database administrator installed SQL Server with the default code page and you're using Windows 95 or Windows NT clients, you don't need to be concerned with OEM-to-ANSI conversion. Clear the check box if it is marked.

6. Click OK to add the new data source and close the Data Source dialog. Your new data source is added to the User Data Sources (Driver) list of the Data Sources dialog, as shown in Figure 26.14.

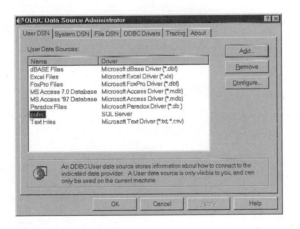

**FIG. 26.14** The new pubs SQL Server data source added to the ODBC User Data Sources List.

7. Click OK to close the ODBC Data Source Administrator tool, and then close Control Panel.

You can add additional SQL Server data sources for a workstation by repeating steps 1 through 6 before exiting the ODBC Administrator application. The entries you make for each new conventional data source are added to the HKEY_CURRENT_USER\ Software\ODBC\ODBC.INI section of the Registry, as shown in Figure 26.15. The ODBC data source entries are located under the HKEY_CURRENT_USER key, because other users of your PC may have different sets of ODBC data sources.

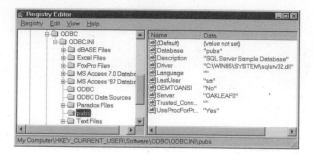

**FIG. 26.15**    The Registry entry for the pubs data source on the OAKLEAF0 server.

> **Note**
>
> Examples of entries in the Windows 95 Registry are provided in this chapter so that you can com-
> pare Registry entries for your computer in the event that you have problems making a connection
> to a client/server database. Each ODBC driver for a particular client/server RDBMS has its own set
> of properties, but the entries for the driver and data source should resemble Figures 26.9 and
> 26.15, respectively. If you have problems while connecting to a client/server database that you
> can't solve yourself, it's likely that the vendor's technical support person will ask for the values of
> your Registry entries for the ODBC driver and/or data source.

If you have problems connecting to your ODBC data source, you can turn ODBC tracing
on by clicking the Tracing tab of the ODBC Create Data Source Administrator's dialog to
display the Tracing page. Select either the All the Time or One-time Only options to
create an ODBC log in the default Sql.log file (see Figure 26.16). You can choose a different file name and location by clicking the Browse button. Entries in the log file can pin-
point the source of a problem if the ODBC error messages you receive aren't sufficiently
explicit.

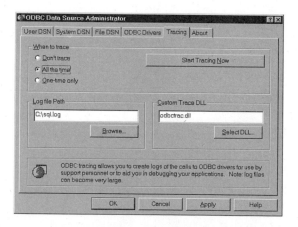

**FIG. 26.16**    Turning on the trace feature of the SQL Server ODBC driver.

> **Caution**
>
> Only turn on ODBC tracing when you are debugging a problem. The Sql.log file can become very large, and adding entries to the log reduces front-end performance dramatically.

The File Data Source page lets you create a sharable ODBC data source in the form of a .dsn file. The section "Creating a File Data Source Within Access 97," later in this chapter, describes how to create and use a file data source. The ODBC Drivers page provides details about the current set of 32-bit ODBC drivers installed on your PC. The About page displays the version numbers of the ODBC 3.0 files that are common to all ODBC drivers. The Windows 95 or Windows NT 4.0 Registry provides the information that appears in the ODBC Drivers and About pages.

### Creating a User or System SQL Server Data Source Within Access 97

Access 97's File, Get External Data, Import and Link Tables choices let you create ODBC data sources without opening Control Panel and launching the ODBC Administrator tool. To create the data source within Access 97, follow these steps:

1. Create a new database named pubs.mdb, and then choose File, Get External Data, Link Tables to open the Link dialog. Select ODBC Databases () from the Files of Type drop-down list (see Figure 26.17) to open the Select Data Source dialog.

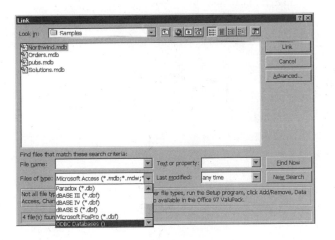

**FIG. 26.17**  Selecting ODBC Databases in the Link dialog.

2. Click the Machine Data Source tab. The default data sources for the ODBC drivers previously installed, and the pubs data source you created in the preceding section, appear as shown in Figure 26.18. The Machine Data Source page displays both user and system data sources.

3. Click the New button to open the Create New Data Source dialog, and accept the default User Data Source option (see Figure 26.19). Click Next to open the dialog in which you select the ODBC driver.

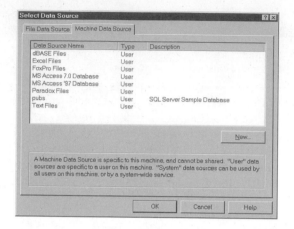

**FIG. 26.18**    The default data sources added with installation of the Office 97 desktop ODBC database drivers and the pubs data source.

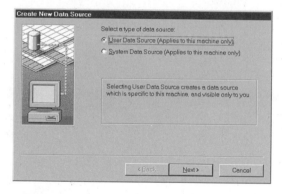

**FIG. 26.19**    Specifying the creation of a new user data source.

**4.** Select the SQL Server driver in the ODBC drivers list (see Figure 26.20), and click Next to continue.

**5.** The last Create New Data Source dialog lets you confirm the choice you made in the preceding dialogs (see Figure 26.21). Click Finish to open the ODBC SQL Server Setup dialog.

**6.** Click the Options button to expand the ODBC SQL Server Setup dialog and complete the entries as described in steps 3, 4, and 5 of the preceding section (refer to Figure 26.13).

**7.** Click OK to create the pubs data source and close the ODBC SQL Server Setup dialog. If you created the pubs data source in the preceding section, a message box appears asking whether you want to overwrite the existing data source. The data source is added as a User data source to the Machine Data Source list or replaces the existing entry (refer to Figure 26.18).

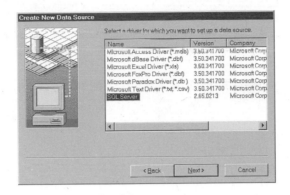

**FIG. 26.20**  Selecting the SQL Server driver in the third Create New Data Source dialog.

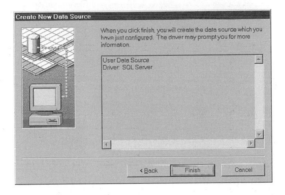

**FIG. 26.21**  Confirming creation of a user datasource with the SQL Server ODBC driver.

   **8.** Click cancel to return to Access. The section "Using Databases Connected by ODBC" later in this chapter describes how to import tables from or link tables to SQL Server databases.

### Creating a File Data Source Within Access 97

Access 97 supports 32-bit ODBC 3.0 file data sources. A *file data source* contains the Registry information for the data source but in conventional text format. File data sources are roughly equivalent to a single set of entries for a 16-bit ODBC data source stored in Windows 3.x's ODBC.INI. The advantage of a file data source is that it isn't machine- or user-dependent; you can share a *Filename*.dsn file with other users across the network. (The .dsn extension is the default for file data sources.)

To create a file data source for SQL Server's pubs database in a shared folder on a server, follow these steps:

   **1.** Create a new pubs.mdb database, if you didn't create this database in preceding section.

2. Choose File, Get External Data, Link Tables. Select ODBC Databases () in the Files of Type drop-down list of the Link dialog to open the Select Data Source dialog with the default File Data Sources page open (see Figure 26.22).

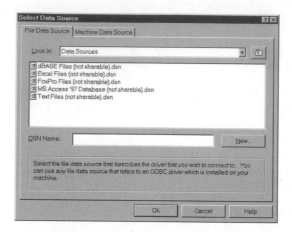

**FIG. 26.22**  The File Data Sources page of Access 97's Select Data Source dialog.

The file data sources installed by Office 97 appears with each data source described as not sharable. These data source files are located in your \Program Files\ Common Files\ODBC\Data sources folder.

3. Click the New button to open the first Create New Data Source dialog, and select the SQL Server item in the list (refer to Figure 26.20).

4. Click the Advanced button to open the Advanced File DSN Creating Settings dialog.

5. In the Enter Driver-Specific Keywords and Values text box, type the additional lines **SERVER=*ServerName*** and **DATABASE=pubs** (see Figure 26.23). The Driver={SQL Server} line is added automatically from the selection you made in step 3. Make sure the Verify This Connection check box is marked (the default). Click OK to close the dialog, then click Next in the Create New Data Source dialog to continue.

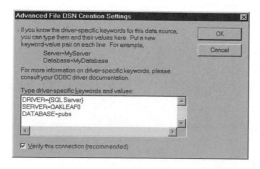

**FIG. 26.23**  Specifying the server and database names for an ODBC file data source.

**6.** Type the UNC path to the shared folder and the file name in the text box
(`\\OAKLEAF0\Shared\Nwind\pubs.dsn` for this example). Alternatively, click the
Browse button to open the Save As dialog, type **pubs** in the File Name text box,
and then select the server share from Network Neighborhood in the Save In navigation list. Access automatically adds the .dsn extension for you. Alternatively,
specify a server share mapped to a local drive letter (see Figure 26.24). Click Save to
close the Save As dialog and return to the Create New Data Source dialog.

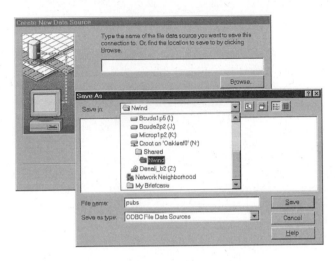

**FIG. 26.24**   Specifying the file name and share location for the pubs.dsn file data source.

The path and file name you specified appears in the Create New Data Source dialog
(see Figure 26.25).

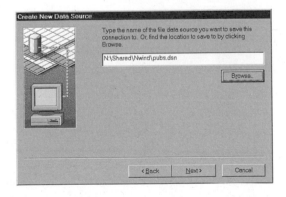

**FIG. 26.25**   The share path and file name used to test the new shared file data source.

7. Click Next to confirm your entries (see Figure 26.26). Click Finish to save and test the pubs.dsn file.

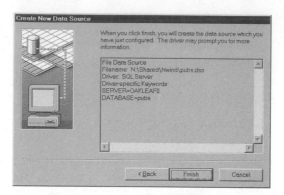

**FIG. 26.26** Confirming the entries and location of the pubs.dsn file data source.

8. In the SQL Server Login dialog, verify that the server name you specified appears in the Server combo list, type your SQL Server login ID and password, and click the Options button to expand the dialog. Verify that the database you specified appears in the Database text box. The Application Name and Workstation ID values are added automatically (see Figure 26.27). Click OK to close the SQL Server Login dialog and test the connection. You receive an error message if the connection fails.

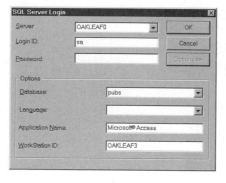

**FIG. 26.27** Testing SQL Server login with the new file data source.

Figure 26.28 shows Notepad displaying the content of the pubs.dsn file data source. The workstation ID (WSID) entry specifies the computer name on which the file data source was created, but any computer can share the pubs.dsn file.

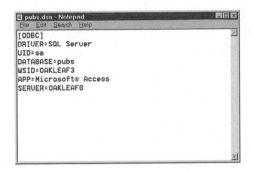

**FIG. 26.28**  The pubs.dsn file data source displayed in Windows Notepad.

# Using Databases Connected by ODBC

After you add the SQL Server database as a user, system, or file data source, you can link, import, or export tables in the SQL Server database to your Access database, depending on the permissions granted by SQL Server to your SQL Server account. If you have full permissions for the database, you can use tables attached from the client/server database in the same manner that you use attached Access, dBASE, FoxPro, or Paradox tables. You don't specify primary key indexes to be used with client/server tables because primary key indexes are opened automatically when you open the table for which indexes have been created, just as with Access tables.

◀◀ See "Linking and Importing External Tables," p. 206

Pubs is a demonstration database that contains tables for a fictional book distributor. Pubs' tables include information on imaginary book publishers, titles, and authors. To attach the tables in the pubs SQL Server database to a new Access database (pubs.mdb in this example), follow these steps:

1. Launch Access and create a new database named pubs.mdb if you didn't create pubs.mdb earlier in this chapter. Choose File, Get External Data, Link Tables to display the Link dialog.

2. Open the Files of Type drop-down list. Select the ODBC Databases() entry in the list, as shown in preceding Figure 26.17, to open the Select Data Source dialog.

3. Click the Machine Data Sources tab to display a list of user and system data sources. Select the data source name—in this case, pubs—in the list (see Figure 26.29). Alternatively, click the File Data Source tab and type in or browse to the file data source you created in the preceding section. Click OK to open the SQL Server Login dialog.

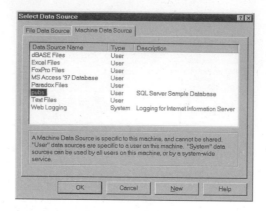

**FIG. 26.29** Selecting the SQL Server pubs user data source.

4. Type your login identification and password in the Login ID and Password text boxes, respectively. The default login ID, sa (system administrator) with no password is used in this example (see Figure 26.30).

**FIG. 26.30** Logging into the pubs SQL Server sample database as the system administrator with no password.

5. Click OK to log into SQL Server. After you connect to the pubs database with the ODBC API, the Link Tables dialog appears, as shown in Figure 26.31. The names of tables are prefixed with dbo, a SQL Server abbreviation for database owner.

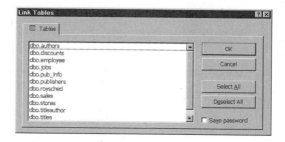

**FIG. 26.31** The list of tables in the pubs database of SQL Server 6.5 available for linking to an Access database.

**6.** Click the Select All button and mark the Save Password check box. Click OK to attach all of the tables to pubs.mdb.

Selecting the Save Password check box eliminates the need to reenter your login ID and password each time you attach another table. If the database administrator adds additional security provisions to a database (by adding a special MSysConf table to the SQL Server database), this check box is disabled.

**7.** To make the tables updatable by Access, a unique index is required on one or more fields to identify each record uniquely in the table. If the SQL Server table does not have a primary-key index, Access 97 opens the Select Unique Record Identifier dialog and offers to create a local "pseudo-index" on the table. As an example, the discounttype and stor_id fields of the dbo.discounts table create a composite primary key (see Figure. 26.32). Select the field(s) for the primary key and click OK (or click Cancel to omit the pseudo-index). Do not add a pseudo-index for the dbo.royaltysched or dbo.titleview tables. Add a pseudo-index on the stor_id, ord_num, and title_id fields of the dbo.sales table.

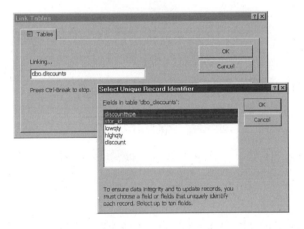

**FIG. 26.32**  Creating a pseud-oindex in the Select Unique Record Identifier dialog.

**8.** When the linking process is complete, the linked tables appear in the Tables page of the Database window (see Figure 26.33). The globe to the left of the table name indicates that the table is attached by ODBC. An underscore substitutes for the period between dbo and the table name because periods are not allowed within Access table names. (Periods are separators between objects and properties or methods in Access 97.)

Double-click the dbo_*tablename* item you want to examine. To verify that you can update or append dbo_sales records, for which you created an Access pseudo-index, click the Last Record button to check for a tentative append record at the bottom of the table (see Figure 26.34).

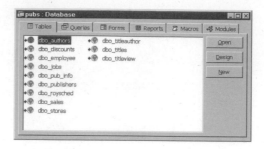

**FIG. 26.33** The 11 tables and one view attached from the pubs database.

| stor_id | ord_num | ord_date | qty | payterms | title_id |
|---------|---------|----------|-----|----------|----------|
| 7067 | D4482 | 9/14/94 | 10 | Net 60 | PS2091 |
| 7067 | P2121 | 6/15/92 | 40 | Net 30 | TC3218 |
| 7067 | P2121 | 6/15/92 | 20 | Net 30 | TC4203 |
| 7067 | P2121 | 6/15/92 | 20 | Net 30 | TC7777 |
| 7131 | N914008 | 9/14/94 | 20 | Net 30 | PS2091 |
| 7131 | N914014 | 9/14/94 | 25 | Net 30 | MC3021 |
| 7131 | P3087a | 5/29/93 | 20 | Net 60 | PS1372 |
| 7131 | P3087a | 5/29/93 | 25 | Net 60 | PS2106 |
| 7131 | P3087a | 5/29/93 | 15 | Net 60 | PS3333 |
| 7131 | P3087a | 5/29/93 | 25 | Net 60 | PS7777 |
| 7896 | QQ2299 | 10/28/93 | 15 | Net 60 | BU7832 |
| 7896 | TQ456 | 12/12/93 | 10 | Net 60 | MC2222 |
| 7896 | X999 | 2/21/93 | 35 | ON invoice | BU2075 |
| 8042 | 423LL922 | 9/14/94 | 15 | ON invoice | MC3021 |
| 8042 | 423LL930 | 9/14/94 | 10 | ON invoice | BU1032 |
| 8042 | P723 | 3/11/93 | 25 | Net 30 | BU1111 |
| 8042 | QA879.1 | 5/22/93 | 30 | Net 30 | PC1035 |

Record: 22 of 22

**FIG. 26.34** The dbo_sales table displaying the tentative append record enabled by specifying a local Access pseudo-index for the table.

To create a query that joins the tables and displays the author name, book title, and book publisher, follow these steps:

1. Create a new query in Design view and add the dbo_authors, dbo_titleauthor, dbo_titles, and dbo_publishers tables to your query. Click the Close button of the Add Tables dialog.

   Key fields of SQL Server tables are indicated in bold type, the same way Access emphasizes key fields of its tables. Access creates and joins automatically based on the key fields and identically named foreign-key fields of the SQL Server tables.

2. Click and drag the au_lname field from the dbo_authors table to the field row of the first column of the query.

3. Repeat step 2 for the title field of the dbo_titles table and the pub_name field of the dbo_publishers table. Your Query Design window looks like the one shown in Figure 26.35.

Query1 : Select Query
*
au_id
au_lname
au_fname
phone
address
*
au_id
title_id
au_ord
royaltyper
*
title_id
title
type
pub_id
price
*
pub_id
pub_name
city
state
country
Field: au_lname title pub_name
Table: dbo_authors dbo_titles dbo_publishers
Sort:
Show:
Criteria:
or:

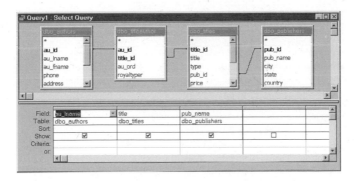

**FIG. 26.35** The Query Design window for the example based on tables attached from the pubs database.

4. Click the Run button on the toolbar to display your query result set, as shown in Figure 26.36.

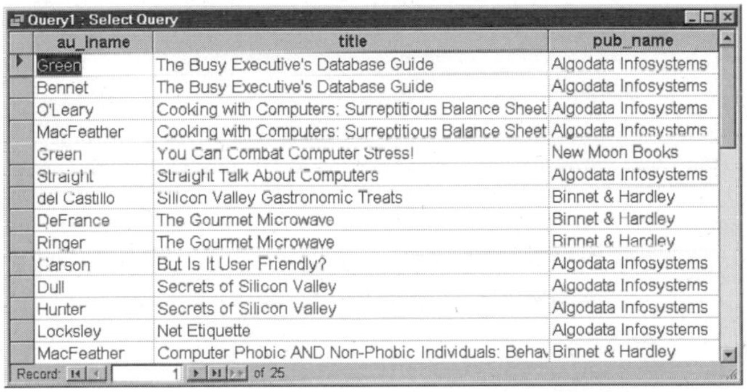

Query1 : Select Query
au_lname | title | pub_name
Green | The Busy Executive's Database Guide | Algodata Infosystems
Bennet | The Busy Executive's Database Guide | Algodata Infosystems
O'Leary | Cooking with Computers: Surreptitious Balance Sheet | Algodata Infosystems
MacFeather | Cooking with Computers: Surreptitious Balance Sheet | Algodata Infosystems
Green | You Can Combat Computer Stress! | New Moon Books
Straight | Straight Talk About Computers | Algodata Infosystems
del Castillo | Silicon Valley Gastronomic Treats | Binnet & Hardley
DeFrance | The Gourmet Microwave | Binnet & Hardley
Ringer | The Gourmet Microwave | Binnet & Hardley
Carson | But Is It User Friendly? | Algodata Infosystems
Dull | Secrets of Silicon Valley | Algodata Infosystems
Hunter | Secrets of Silicon Valley | Algodata Infosystems
Locksley | Net Etiquette | Algodata Infosystems
MacFeather | Computer Phobic AND Non-Phobic Individuals: Behav | Binnet & Hardley
Record: 1 of 25

**FIG. 26.36** The query result set from the query design shown in Figure 26.35.

5. Close and save your query for use in the next section.

To remove a linked table from the Northwind Traders database, click the Tables tab in the Database Window, and select the name of the linked table to delete—in this case, dbo_tableview. Press Delete. A message box appears, asking you to confirm that you want to delete the link to the table (see Figure 26.37). Click Yes because the SQL Server view is not needed in the sections that follow.

Microsoft Access
Do you want to remove the link to the table 'dbo_titleview'?
If you delete the link, you delete only the information Microsoft Access uses to open the table, not the table itself.
Yes
No

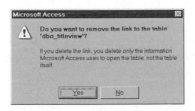

**FIG. 26.37** The message box that confirms the deletion of a link to a table.

> **Note**
>
> You can eliminate the need to add the dbo_ prefix to a table name by renaming the attachments to the table name without the dbo_ prefix. Close any open attached tables, select the table, and then choose <u>E</u>dit, Rena<u>m</u>e to enter the new name. Alternatively, right-click the table name, then choose Rename from the popup menu.

The preceding example, using the pubs database, is typical of the procedure that you use to attach tables from any client/server database for which an ODBC driver is available.

> **Troubleshooting**
>
> *A* `Cannot connect to server` *or similar error message occurs when I attempt to attach to SQL Server.*
>
> There are a variety of problems that can lead to your inability to connect to SQL Server. The most common cause is the lack of (or an outdated version of) the Dbnmpntw.dll library on your computer. Dbnmpntw.dll is the 32-bit named pipes library that is required to connect to SQL server. Choose Start, <u>F</u>ind, <u>F</u>iles or Folders, and verify that Dbnmpntw.dll is installed in your \Windows \System folder. (The size of the version of Dbnmpntw.dll that was current when this edition was written is 22K. The date should correspond to the dates of other files installed by Access or other applications that install Dbnmpntw.dll.) If you have additional copies of Dbnmpntw.dll with earlier dates in folders other than \Windows\System, delete these unneeded copies.

# Using Access 97's SQL Pass-Through Queries

SQL pass-through queries allow you to write queries in the dialect of SQL used by the server RDBMS. SQL Server, as an example, lets you write stored procedures that you can execute by name, instead of by sending individual SQL statements to the server. Executing a stored procedure query is faster than executing the query through the Jet database engine because of reduced network traffic and faster execution of the query by the server. (Stored procedure queries are precompiled by SQL Server.) You also need to use SQL pass-through if you want to take advantage of special Transact-SQL reserved words not included in Jet SQL. In many cases, SQL pass-through queries execute faster than queries that use Jet's built-in query optimizer.

### Executing a Simple Pass-Through Query

Access 1.x required that you use Access Basic to declare the functions of MSASP110.DLL, a SQL pass-through library supplied by Microsoft. Beginning with version 2.0, Access provides built-in SQL pass-through capability, similar to that offered by Visual Basic 3.0 and later. You can convert the query you created in the preceding section to a SQL pass-through query by following these steps:

  **1.** Open the saved query you created in the previous section in Design view; then choose Query, SQL-Specific, Pass-through.

2. The SQL window opens with the SQL statement behind your query. The Query Design button is disabled when you convert a conventional Access query to the SQL pass-through type.

3. Table names with the dbo_ prefix aren't acceptable to SQL Server, so replace all of the underscores (_) with periods (.), as shown in Figure 26.38. Alternatively, you can delete the dbo_ prefix from each table name.

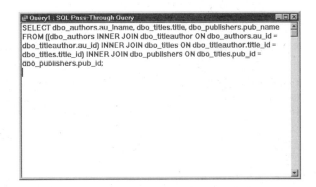

```
Query1 : SQL Pass-Through Query
SELECT dbo_authors.au_lname, dbo_titles.title, dbo_publishers.pub_name
FROM ((dbo_authors INNER JOIN dbo_titleauthor ON dbo_authors.au_id =
dbo_titleauthor.au_id) INNER JOIN dbo_titles ON dbo_titleauthor.title_id =
dbo_titles.title_id) INNER JOIN dbo_publishers ON dbo_titles.pub_id =
dbo_publishers.pub_id;
```

**FIG. 26.38** The SQL window for a SQL pass-through query with the dbo. prefix for SQL Server table names.

4. Choose File, Save to save your pass-through query. (If you don't save the query, it may attempt to execute against the attached tables.)

5. Click the Run button on the toolbar to execute your pass-through query. When the Select Data Source dialog appears, click the appropriate tab to specify your machine or file data source. When you click OK, you must enter your SQL Server login ID and password, then click OK again. You receive the same query result set as that from the conventional query executed through the Jet database engine against the linked tables.

> **Note**
>
> Query result sets returned by SQL pass-through queries are Recordset objects of the Snapshot type, which are not updatable. Other query result sets against databases linked by ODBC are Recordset objects of the Dynaset type but may or may not be updatable, depending on the query design and whether you set a local pseudo-index on the table.

When you save a SQL pass-through query, the ODBC symbol appears next to the name of the pass-through query in the Queries list of the Database window (see Figure 26.39). SQL pass-through queries are especially useful for creating high-performance client/ server front-ends with Access VBA.

**VI**

**Using Advanced Techniques**

**FIG. 26.39**    The Queries page of the Database window with a saved SQL pass-through query.

### Setting the Connect String Property for SQL Pass-Through Queries

You can use the ODBC Connect Str(ing) property of the SQL pass-through QueryDef object to avoid the need to respond to the Select Data Source dialog and, if desired, by-pass the SQL Server Login dialog. When you create a SQL pass-through query, Access automatically sets the value of the ODBC Connect Str property to "ODBC;". To specify the machine data source, the SQL Server login ID, and password in the ODBC Connect Str property value, follow these steps:

1. Right-click the title bar of the SQL window and choose Properties from the popup menu to open the Query Properties sheet with default values for all properties (see Figure 26.40).

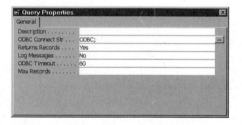

**FIG. 26.40**    The Query Properties sheet with default values for SQL pass-through queries.

2. Position the caret in the ODBC Connect Str text box and click the builder button to open the Select Data Source dialog. Click the Machine Data Source tab and select the data source for the query (see Figure 26.41).

3. Click OK to open the SQL Server Login dialog. Type your Login ID and Password (see Figure 26.42), then click OK. If you want to include your password in the ODBC connect string, click Yes when the Connection String Builder message box appears (see Figure 26.43).

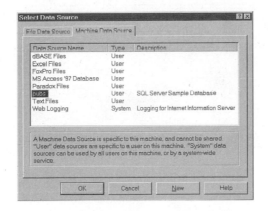

**FIG. 26.41** Using the Select Data Source dialog to add the data source (DSN=) and database (DATABASE=) entries to the ODBC Connect Str property.

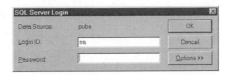

**FIG. 26.42** Using the SQL Server Login dialog to add the Login ID (UID=) and Password (PWD=) entries to the ODBC Connect Str property value.

**FIG. 26.43** Confirming inclusion of your password in the ODBC Connect Str property value.

> ### Caution
>
> Including your password, which appears in plain text, in the ODBC Connect Str property value is a breach of security. Any user with the retail version of Access and Read Design permission for the database can open the query and read your SQL Server password. The security breach is less serious with the runtime version of Access because users can't open objects in Design mode.

4. The final ODBC Connect Str value appears as shown in Figure 26.44. Close the Query Properties sheet, and choose File, Save to save your query. Then click the Run button to execute your SQL pass-through query.

VI

**Using Advanced Techniques**

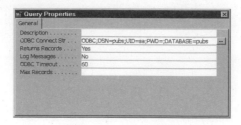

**FIG. 26.44** The Query Properties sheet with the final ODBC Connect Str value, including an empty password for the system administrator (sa) account.

### Logging ODBC Queries

You can trace the execution of ODBC operations by selecting the appropriate option on the Tracing page of the ODBC Data Source Administrator, as shown in Figure 26.16 in the earlier section "Using the ODBC Administrator to Create a SQL Server Data Source." The ODBC API function call for SQL pass-through queries is SQLExecDirect(). Figure 26.45 shows WordPad displaying the SQLExecDirect() function call in the Sql.log file created by the preceding SQL pass-through query.

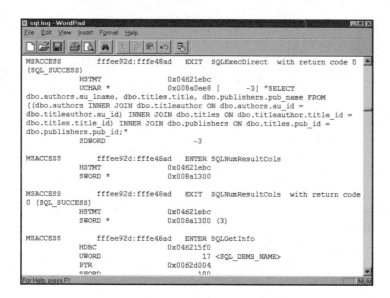

**FIG. 26.45** A few of the ODBC API function calls that result from executing a SQL pass-through query.

> **Note**
>
> SQL pass-through queries bypass the query parser of the Jet database engine, but Access SQL and ANSI SQL-92 INNER JOIN statements are not accepted by version 4.x of SQL Server. (SQL Server 4.x uses WHERE clauses to create joins.) The Microsoft ODBC driver for SQL Server 4.x traps the INNER JOIN statement and converts (or *escapes*, in ODBC terminology) the Access/ANSI SQL statements to an equivalent SQL WHERE clause. SQL Server 6.5 accepts INNER JOIN syntax. As an example, you can copy the SQL pass-through statement from the Query window (without the trailing semicolon), paste the query into ISQL/w, SQL Server 6.5's query tool, and then execute the query directly against SQL Server 6.5.

# Exporting Access Tables to a Client/Server Database

Creating the definition of tables in a client/server database can be a very lengthy process, especially if you need to write SQL DDL statements in ISQL/w to create the tables. SQL Server's SQL Enterprise Manager simplifies the process of creating new client/server tables. It's even easier, however, to export your existing Access tables to a database in SQL Server. When you export Access tables to SQL Server, you ensure that the SQL Server table's field data types correspond to the data types of your Access table.

### Using Access's Built-In Export Feature

To export a table from Northwind.mdb to the pubs database, follow these steps:

1. Open Northwind.mdb. In the Tables page of the Database window, select the table you want to export to the SQL data source.

2. Choose File, Save As/Export, then click OK when the Save As dialog with the To an External File or Database option selected appears to display the Export dialog. Select ODBC Databases( ) in the Save As Type drop-down list. The Export dialog appears to confirm your selection (see Figure 26.46). You can change the SQL Server table name, if you want, but you don't need to add the dbo. prefix for SQL Server tables. Click OK to display the Select Data Source dialog.

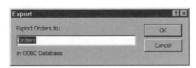

**FIG. 26.46** Confirming the export of a table to SQL Server.

**VI**

**Using Advanced Techniques**

**3.** Double-click the data source for the database to which you want to export the table—pubs, in this case—to display the SQL Server Login dialog.

**4.** Enter your user ID and password, then click OK to export the table to the server database.

The status bar shows the progress of exporting the table to the server. Exporting an Access table with a large number of records is not as fast as importing the content of the table to SQL Server from an ASCII text file with a bulk copy program (BCP). However, exporting the table is much faster when the table contains fewer than about 10,000 records.

Figure 26.47 shows SQL Server 6.5's SQL Enterprise Manager displaying the structure of the Orders table of Northwind.mdb exported to the pubs database. When you export a table containing an Access AutoNumber field, the field data type is converted to SQL Server's int data type, which is equivalent to the Access Long Integer field data type. The export process does not add SQL Server's identity attribute, the equivalent of Access's AutoNumber, Increment attribute, to the field.

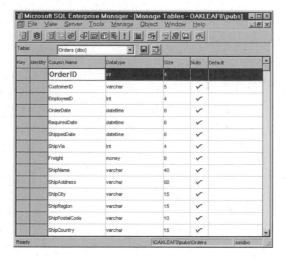

**FIG. 26.47**   SQL Enterprise Manager displaying the structure of the exported Orders table.

> **Note**
>
> When you export an Access table to SQL Server, the indexes, validation rules, default values, and other properties of the table are not exported. You need to use SQL Object Manager or a similar tool to add indexes and other properties to the new server table. Alternatively, you can use SQL Enterprise Manager's Manage Tables feature to add the indexes and other properties. The Access 97 Upsizing Wizard, the subject of the next section, automatically adds Access indexes, validation rules, and other properties to the SQL Server database.

### Using the Access 97 Upsizing Wizard

The Access 97 Upsizing Wizard, which is almost identical to the Access 95 Upsizing Wizard, makes it quick and easy to upsize an entire Access application to the use of tables attached from SQL Server 6.5. You can download the Access 97 Upsizing Wizard at no charge from **http://www.microsoft.com/msaccess/**. Once you install the Wizard library (Wzcs97.mde) with the Access Add-In Manager, you can upsize an Access 97 database to SQL Server 4.21, 6.0, or 6.5.

---

**Note**

The Access 97 Upsizing Wizard includes the Upsize to SQL Server and SQL Server Browser add-ins. These add-ins work only with Microsoft SQL Server because they rely on Transact-SQL syntax for many operations and specify SQL Server-specific field data types. You cannot use the Upsizing Wizard or the SQL Server Browser with other client/server RDBMSs, such as Oracle or Informix. The SQL Server Browser add-in is the subject of the section that follows.

---

To test the Access 97 Upsizing Wizard with a copy of the Northwind Traders sample database, follow these steps:

1. Create a SQL Server 6.x database, nwind for this example, with 5M of available space. If the SQL Server DBA creates the database for you, make sure you have full permissions (database owner) for the database. Make sure to set the database's Truncate Log on Checkpoint option to avoid creating a large log file.

2. Create a user or system data source, Nwind, specifying the newly created database (nwind). Make sure that the Convert OEM to ANSI Characters check box is cleared. Also verify that the Don't Trace options is selected in the Tracing Page of the ODBC Data Source Administrator.

---

**Caution**

If you specify the All the Time or One Time Only tracing options, operation of the Upsizing Wizard slows dramatically because tracing writes a very large number of entries to Sql.log. If you experience an extraordinary amount of disk activity during the wizard's operation, it's likely that you have specified one of these two tracing options. Tracing the operation of the Upsizing Wizard is likely to result in a Sql.log file of 30M or greater.

---

3. Launch Access, if necessary, and compact Northwind.mdb to a new database, Nwind.mdb. Upsizing modifies the database, so don't use the original version of Northwind.mdb for this example.

4. Choose Tools, Add-Ins, Upsize To SQL Server to launch the Upsizing Wizard.

5. In the first wizard dialog, select the Use Existing Database option (see Figure 26.48). Click Next to open the Select Data Source dialog.

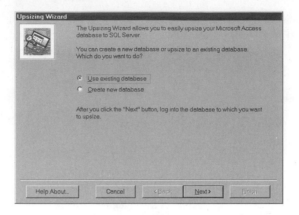

**FIG. 26.48**   Specifying an existing SQL Server database for the upsizing process.

   **6.** Select your new data source (Nwind) in the Machine Data Sources page of the
      Select Data Source dialog (see Figure 26.49). Click OK to log into SQL Server.

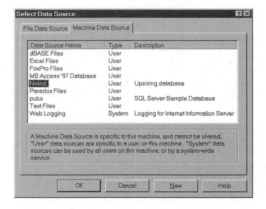

**FIG. 26.49**   Selecting the user data source for the upsizing operation.

   **7.** After you log into the nwind database, the wizard displays an Available Tables list
      of the database. Click the >> button to move all of the entries to the Export to SQL
      Server list (see Figure 26.50). Click Next to continue.

   **8.** Accept the default values offered by the wizard for table attributes and data op-
      tions. Mark the Attach Newly Created SQL Server Tables and Save Password and
      User ID with Linked Table check boxes (see Figure 26.51). Click Next to open the
      last Upsizing Wizard dialog.

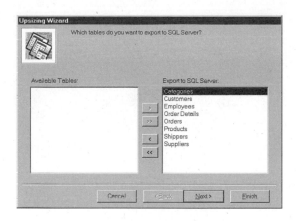

**FIG. 26.50** Specifying all tables to be upsized to the SQL Server database.

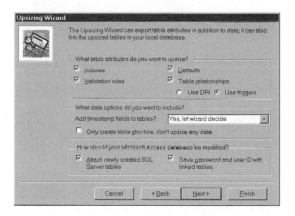

**FIG. 26.51** Setting options for the upsizing the tables and modifying the existing database.

**9.** If you want to create an Access report to document the upsizing process, mark the Create Upsizing Report check box (see Figure 26.52). Click Finish to begin the upsizing operation.

**10.** The Upsizing Wizard displays a progress bar with messages describing the status of the upsizing process (see Figure 26.53). Click OK when the message box advises that upsizing is complete. If you specified an Upsizing report in step 9, the report opens in Preview mode.

**VI**

**Using Advanced Techniques**

**FIG. 26.52** The final dialog of the Upsizing Wizard.

**FIG. 26.53** The dialog that displays the progress of the upsizing operation.

The Upsizing Wizard renames the existing tables of your database to *TableName*_local, then renames the table links from *TableName*_remote to *TableName*, taking the place of the original tables. Figure 26.54 shows the appearance of the Database window after upsizing is complete. Once you verify that there are no problems with your application, you can delete the *TableName*_local tables and compact the database to save disk space.

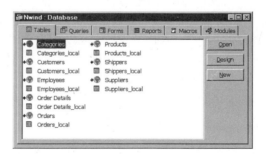

**FIG. 26.54** The Database window with the new linked tables and the original tables renamed to *TableName*_local.

The Upsizing Wizard adds SQL Server timestamp fields to tables with OLE Object or Memo fields (Categories and Employees), as well as to tables with composite primary keys (Order Details). Figure 26.55 shows the Categories table in Design view with an added upsize_ts timestamp (Binary) field. Timestamp data is used by SQL Server to resolve multiple, simultaneous edits to a single record. Unlike the table export operation, described in the preceding section, the Upsizing Wizard adds the SQL Server 6.5 primary key and identity attributes to primary key table fields of the Access AutoNumber field data type. These attributes appear as a primary key icon and check mark in the SQL Enterprise Manager's Manage Tables window's Key and Identity columns (see Figure 26.56).

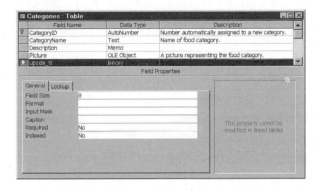

**FIG. 26.55**  The link to the exported Categories table in Design view.

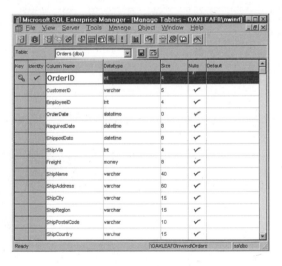

**FIG. 26.56**  The exported Orders table with SQL Server primary key and identity attributes set on the OrderID column.

### Using the SQL Server Browser Add-In

Access 97's Upsizing Wizard library includes the new SQL Server Browser utility that you can use to view, add, and/or modify the properties of SQL Server tables, views, default values, rules, and stored procedures. To give the SQL Server Browser a test drive with the nwind database, follow these steps:

VI

**Using Advanced Techniques**

1. Choose Tools, Add-Ins, SQL Server Browser to open the Select ODBC Data Source dialog.

2. Select the Nwind data source and click OK. Log on to SQL Server to display the main Browser window for the nwind database (see Figure 26.57).

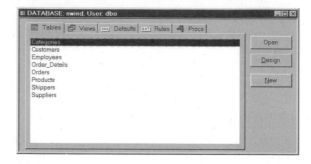

**FIG. 26.57** The main window of the SQL Server Browser add-in displaying the tables in the nwind database.

3. To display the records of a table in a datasheet view, double-click the table item in the list, or select the table and click the Open button.

4. Select the Orders table and click the Design button to display the field and table properties (see Figure 26.58). SQL Server field data types, such as int, datetime, and varchar appear in the Data Type column. Name of SQL Server triggers that the Upsizing Wizard creates to enforce referential integrity appear in the Table Properties pane.

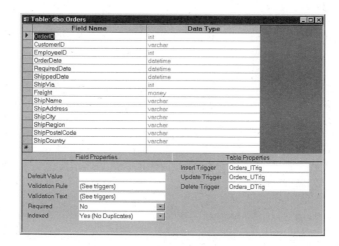

**FIG. 26.58** The SQL Server Orders table in the SQL Server Browser's Table Design window.

> **Note**
>
> Triggers are the most common method of enforcing referential integrity of SQL Server
> databases. *Triggers* are a set of stored procedures (similar to an Access `QueryDef` object)
> that execute immediately prior to performing an INSERT, UPDATE, or DELETE operation.
> SQL Server 6.x lets you replace triggers with SQL-92's declarative referential integrity (DRI)
> syntax. If you specified the DRI option in step 8 of the preceding section, the Upsizing
> Wizard doesn't create triggers.

**5.** Select one of the triggers in the Table Properties pane to activate the builder button. Click the Builder button to open the Triggers window (see Figure 26.59).

If you're experienced with writing SQL Server triggers, you can edit the trigger code and click Save to update the trigger in the nwind database. You also can delete the trigger by clicking the Drop Trigger button.

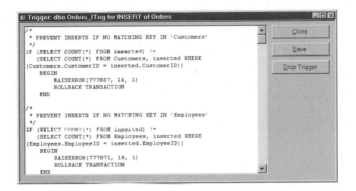

**FIG. 26.59**   The SQL Server Browser's Triggers window displaying the *INSERT* trigger for the Order table.

**6.** Click Close to return to the Orders table design window, then close the table design window to return to SQL Server Browser's main window.

> **Note**
>
> The nwind table created by the Upsizing Wizard doesn't include SQL Server views or stored proce-
> dures. If you created the pubs data source in the section "Using the ODBC Data Source Adminis-
> trator to Create a SQL Server Data Source" earlier in this chapter, you can display the view
> (titleview) and several stored procedures included in the pubs sample database. To open another
> SQL Server database, close SQL Server Browser's main window and restart the Browser Add-In.

**VI**

**Using Advanced Techniques**

# Chapter 27

# Replicating Access Databases

Laptop and notebook computers now comprise a substantial percentage of PCs running Windows, and the market share of portable PCs is expected to increase during the late 1990s. Microsoft designed Windows 95 specifically to accommodate the needs of mobile computing by adding features such as hot-swapping of PC Card (formerly PCMCIA) adapters and hot-docking to connect portable PCs to stationary keyboards and displays (called *docking stations*). The growing number of home PCs that are used part-time for business purposes also fits the mobile computing pattern. A large percentage of portable and home PC users connect to office networks by modem using Windows 95's Dial-Up Networking client and Windows NT Server's Remote Access Services (RAS) or the Windows 95 Dial-Up Networking Server included with Microsoft Plus!. Using RAS or Dial-Up Networking lets mobile computer users update the current versions of files on the server or their office PC.

 If you don't have a RAS or Dial-Up Networking connection to a server or your office PC, Windows 95 provides a Briefcase feature to synchronize the contents of multiple copies of a file. This chapter explains the principles of Briefcase synchronization and how Access 97 synchronizes updates to table data using database replicas stored in Windows 95 Briefcases. Briefcase synchronization was new in Access 95, and enabled users to replicate entire databases. Access 97's new features extend Briefcase replication to include the ability to replicate selected portions of a database. Access 97's Briefcase replication lets you create database replicas on a local disk drive, on a disk drive connected to your computer through a local-area network, or to FTP locations reached through the Internet or an intranet.

> **Note**
>
> The My Briefcase icon appears on the Windows 95 or Windows NT 4.0 desktop only if you installed Windows by using the Portable option, or if you installed Windows using the Custom option and then specified that Briefcase be included. Microsoft Office 97 Professional Edition
>
> (continues)

(continued)

also includes Briefcase replication. To install Briefcase replication with Microsoft Office, you must choose a Custom installation and specifically include Briefcase replication as part of your installation. If you didn't install Briefcase and want to try this chapter's examples of Briefcase synchronization, launch Control Panel's Add/Remove Programs feature and add the Briefcase files from your Microsoft Office 97 CD-ROM.

# Understanding the Principles of Briefcase Replication

To synchronize updates to Access 97 databases, you must create a *replica set*. An Access 97 replica set consists of one *design-master* replica, to which you can make design changes, and one or more replicas that do not support Design mode. One (and only one) design-master and all other replicas comprise an Access *replica set*. The design-master replica is the .mdb file from which all Briefcase replicas are created. In most cases, the .mdb file designated the design-master replica is the original application or, more often, the original data .mdb file stored on your local fixed disk or shared from a file server. You can designate one of the Briefcase replicas as the design-master, if desired.

OLE (Object Linking and Embedding) 2+ provides a set of functions, called *OLE interfaces*, that support operations such as embedding or linking objects within container documents. The chapters in Part V, "Integrating Access with Other Office 97 Applications," describe the basic features of OLE 2.1 as they apply to Access 97. Windows 95's implementation of OLE 2.1 includes an additional OLE 2.1 interface, not discussed in Part V, that adds the following Briefcase functions:

■ *Binding a reconciliation handler to an application.* A *reconciliation handler* is a set of methods, specific to the type of document created by the application, to reconcile accumulated changes to replicas of a particular document file made at different times by multiple users. *Binding* is a Windows programming term that means attaching a process to an application when the application needs to use the process.

 ◀◀ See "The Registry Editor," p. 683

■ *Tracking the contents of the Briefcase.* Access replica sets are identified by a unique number, called a *Globally Unique ID* (*GUID*, also called a *Universally Unique ID*, or *UUID*), created by Windows 95. Each member of a replica set uses the same GUID. GUIDs are automatically generated, 128-bit hexadecimal numbers that have an almost infinitesimal probability of duplication. (Access 97 provides the GUID data type for creating and manipulating GUIDs.) If you have explored the Windows 95 Registry with the Registry Editor (RegEdit.exe), you probably have seen a large number of entries with 32-character GUIDs. (The OLE Class ID, CLSID, entries in the Registry are GUIDs assigned to each OLE object class and interface by the author of the object.) Only classes of documents that are supported by an OLE 2.1 application with a reconciliation handler are candidates for Briefcase synchronization.

■ *Reconciling the contents of the Briefcase*. Reconciling Briefcase documents updates the original design-master file with the content of the replica file(s) in Briefcase(s) with accumulated changes. The updating process is relatively simple for a conventional OLE document, such as a Microsoft Word 97 or Excel 97 file that has built-in revision handling features, but it is a much more involved procedure for Access .mdb files, which may include a wide variety of different objects.

All participants in the Briefcase replication process must use Windows 95 or Windows NT 4.0. Prior versions of Windows NT Workstation and Server (version 3.55 and earlier) do not support Briefcase replication.

# Creating and Updating a Briefcase Replica

To create a design-master and Briefcase replica of a document, follow these basic steps:

1. Drag the database's icon from Windows 95's Explorer (or any folder window) into Briefcase's window or onto its icon. (Access 97 also offers the Tools, Replication, Create Replica command to create a design-master replica.)

2. Create additional Briefcases containing replicas by copying and pasting My Briefcase to the desktop, and then renaming the copy. Other database users update the Briefcase replica(s).

3. Open My Briefcase, and choose Briefcase, Update All. All replicas of the same replica set in all Briefcases on the desktop update the design-master replica.

Figure 27.1 illustrates the steps involved in Briefcase replication of Access 97 databases.

Once the replica is in the Briefcase of the host computer, mobile users can update the Briefcase replica on the host or on the guest (mobile) computer by the following four methods:

■ *Network connection*. If you can connect your guest computer to the host computer's Briefcase, you can update the Briefcase replica directly. If the replica is opened in shared mode (the default), multiple users can update the Briefcase replica simultaneously. Unless there is a particular reason to use the Briefcase replica, networked users should connect directly to and update the design-master (original) .mdb file.

■ *Direct cable connection*. You can use a serial cable (called a *null-modem cable*) between the serial (COM) ports of host and guest computers to make the host Briefcase accessible to the guest computer. If you have an ECP-enabled parallel port, you can use an ECP (Extended Communication Protocol) cable to connect the parallel (LPT) ports of the host and guest PCs. A parallel ECP connection is much faster than a serial connection. You can use a Universal Cable Module (UCM) cable to connect different types of PC parallel ports.

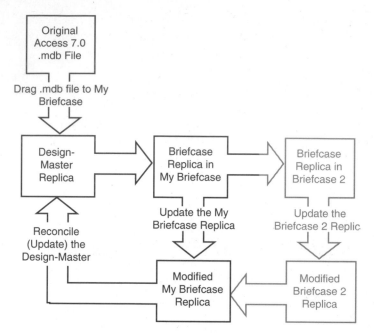

**FIG. 27.1** Creating an Access replica set and updating the design-master replica with updates made to Briefcase replicas.

- *Dial-up modem connection.* If you've installed on the host computer the Dial-Up Networking Server component included on the Microsoft Windows 95 Plus! Pack, your guest computer can connect to the Briefcase on the host computer and update the Briefcase replica.

- *Disk.* You can move the Briefcase replica on the host computer to a disk, and then move the Briefcase replica from the disk to a Briefcase on the desktop of the guest PC. After you make changes on the guest PC, you reverse the process and move the updated files from the disk to the host PC's Briefcase. Most Briefcase users are likely to employ the disk method, so the example in this chapter uses disks for synchronizing changes to Access tables.

> **Note**
>
> To use the network, direct cable, or dial-up modem connection method, you need to have the File and Printer Sharing services for either the Microsoft or Novell networks installed.

### Creating the Contact Management Application for Replication

Contact management is one of the most common applications for Briefcase replication. Salespersons take their laptops on sales calls and record important information relating to sales contacts. To use the Database Wizard to create a new Contact Management database, ContactManager.mdb, follow these steps:

1. Launch Access and select Database Wizard from the opening window or, if Access is open, choose File, New Database to open the New dialog (see Figure 27.2); then click the Database tab.

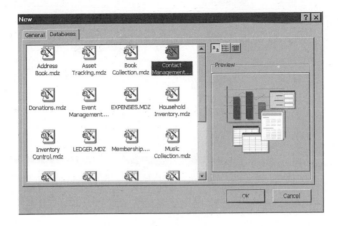

**FIG. 27.2**    The New dialog displaying icons for databases you can create with the Database Wizard.

2. Double-click the Contact Management icon in the Database list to create a new database based on the Contact Management template. The File New Database dialog opens.

3. Navigate to the directory for the new database and give the file a name, such as **ContactManager.mdb** (ContactManagement1.mdb is the default file name), as shown in Figure 27.3. The location of the file is not important; in this example, the new database is located in C:\My Documents. Click Create to have the Database Wizard generate the new database.

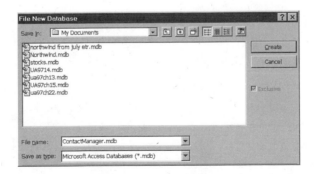

**FIG. 27.3**    Specifying a name and location for the new Contact Management database.

**4.** When the first Database Wizard screen appears, click the Next button to display the tables and fields dialog. Mark the Yes, Include Sample Data check box to add the sample data to the tables (see Figure 27.4). Accept the remainder of the dialog's defaults and click the Next button.

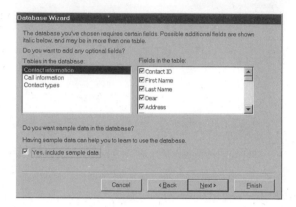

**FIG. 27.4**  Specifying addition of sample data to the Contact Management database.

**5.** In the first style selection dialog, select the style you like for forms and click the Next button. This example uses the International style.

**6.** In the second style selection dialog, select the report style you want and click the Finish button to accept the remainder of the Database Wizard's defaults. This example uses the Corporate style.

Access 97 displays a progress dialog as it creates the new database; after a few minutes of intense disk activity, the Database Wizard completes the task of building the ContactManager.mdb database, and the Contact Management Switchboard appears (see Figure 27.5).

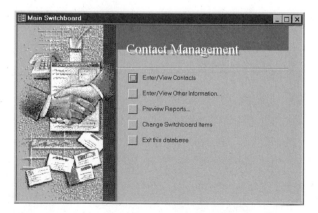

**FIG. 27.5**  The Switchboard form of the Contact Manager database.

Replicating only the tables of the database is more efficient than replicating the entire database, so follow these steps to split the tables of ContactManager.mdb into ContactData.mdb and create the links to the tables:

1. With ContactManager.mdb open and the Main Switchboard form closed, choose Tools, Add-Ins, Database Splitter to open the Database Splitter dialog.

2. Click the Split Database button to open the Database Splitter's Save As dialog. Maneuver to the same folder that contains ContactManager.mdb, if necessary, and type **ContactData.mdb** in the File Name text box (see Figure 27.6).

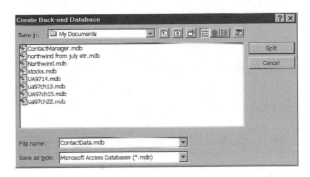

**FIG. 27.6.**  Naming the "back-end" database to contain the Contact Manager tables.

3. Click the Split button to complete the splitting and linking process. The Tables page of the Database window appears as shown in Figure 27.7.

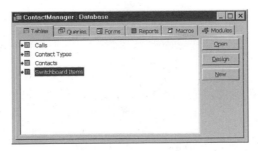

**FIG. 27.7**  The tables linked from ContactData.mdb to ContactManager.mdb.

4. Choose Tools, Add-Ins, Linked Table Manager to display the links from ContactManager.mdb's application objects to the tables of ContactData.mdb (see Figure 27.8). Close the Linked Table Manager.

---

**Caution**

Do not password-protect Access .mdb files that you intend to use with Briefcase replication. Providing a password requires opening Access. All reconciliation operations operate behind the scenes (using the Jet 3.5 database engine directly) and do not launch Access. You receive an error message if you attempt to reconcile updates to a password-protected replica.

---

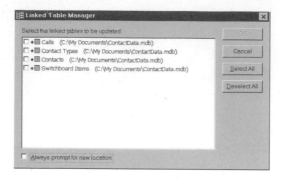

**FIG. 27.8** Verifying the links between the application and data .mdb file for the Contact Management application.

### Creating a Replica Set

To create a design-master and a Briefcase replica (a replica set) from ContactData.mdb, follow these steps:

1. Close Access and launch Explorer. Open the Explorer folder that contains ContactData.mdb.

2. Move Explorer's window, if necessary, to expose the My Briefcase desktop icon. Drag ContactData.mdb's icon to the desktop and drop the icon on the My Briefcase icon. (If My Briefcase is open, you can drop the icon in My Briefcase's window.) My Briefcase begins to create a replica set of ContactData.mdb.

3. After a brief period of disk activity, the message shown in Figure 27.9 appears. Click Yes to continue.

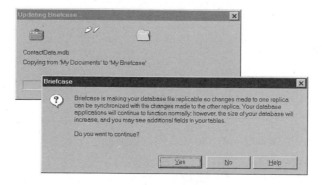

**FIG. 27.9** The message requesting confirmation for creating the Access replica set.

4. A second message appears offering you the option to make a backup copy of your replicated database (see Figure 27.10). Click No to continue because you don't need a backup copy of this example database. (Ordinarily, you create a backup copy of your database at this point.)

5. A third message appears that lets you select whether to make the Original Copy or the Briefcase Copy the design-master set (see Figure 27.11). Unless you plan to do off-site development work on your database, select the default (Original Copy) option. Ordinarily, you don't want users making changes to the design of your tables, especially if the tables are attached to an Access application. Click OK to complete the replication process.

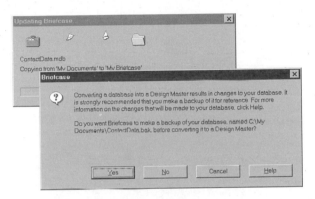

**FIG. 27.10**    The message offering to create a backup copy of your design-master replica database.

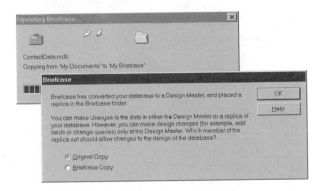

**FIG. 27.11**    The dialog to select whether the original or the Briefcase copy is the design-master replica.

6. Launch My Briefcase, if necessary. Your replica copy appears in My Briefcase's file list, as shown in Figure 27.12.

7. Right-click ContactData.mdb's icon and choose Properties from the popup menu to open the Properties window. Click the Update Status tab to display the synchronization status. The original and replica of ContactData.mdb are Unmodified and the status is Up-to-Date because you haven't yet made changes to either replica (see Figure 25.13). Click Close to return to Briefcase.

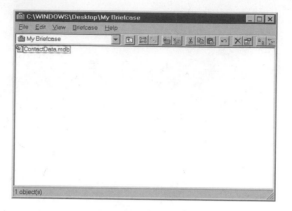

**FIG. 27.12** The Briefcase copy of ContactData.mdb in My Briefcase's file list.

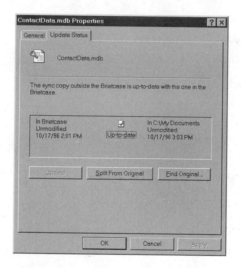

**FIG. 27.13** The Update Status properties page of the of ContactData.mdb Briefcase replica.

8. To view the tables of the replica, double-click ContactData.mdb's Briefcase icon. Access launches with the replica copy of ContactData.mdb active. `Replica` appears in the title bar of the Database window, indicating you're working with a replica of the original database; replicated tables in the database are indicated with a special icon (see Figure 27.14).

9. Choose Tools, Options and click the View tab. Mark the Hidden Objects and System Objects check boxes of the Show frame and click OK to close the Options sheet. Note that many new hidden tables for replication management, such as MSysExchangeLog, MSysReplicas, and MSysTombstones, have been added to ContactData.mdb (see Figure 27.14).

10. Choose <u>T</u>ools, <u>O</u>ptions again, and clear the Hidden Objects and System Objects check boxes. Then click OK to close the Options sheet. Close the Briefcase copy of ContactData.mdb.

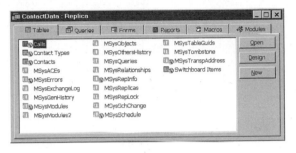

**FIG. 27.14**  The Tables page of the Database window displaying hidden and system tables, including hidden and system tables for replication management.

### Synchronizing the Design-Master and Briefcase Replicas

Modifying data or options in either the Briefcase replica or the design-master sets the status of the file to Modified. If either of the replicas has been modified since the last reconciliation, either the Briefcase or the design-master replica is a candidate for updating. Follow these steps to verify the preceding statements:

1. Open Briefcase, if necessary. Right-click ContactData.mdb's icon, and select Properties from the popup menu. Click the Update Status tab of the Properties window. The status of the Briefcase copy is Modified, as shown in Figure 27.15, although you didn't change any data in the preceding steps. Changing the View options in preceding steps 9 and 10 set the "Dirty" flag for the Briefcase copy, which determines if the copy's status is set to Modified.

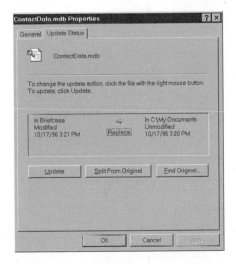

**FIG. 27.15**  The Update Status properties page of the modified Briefcase replica.

2. Click Update to update the design-master replica.

3. Open the original (design-master) copy of ContactData.mdb. The title bar of the Database window displays Design Master, and the replicated tables are marked with a special icon, as shown in Figure 27.16.

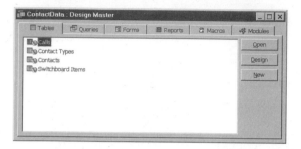

**FIG. 27.16** The Tables page of the Database window for the design-master replica of ContactData.mdb.

4. Open the Calls table of ContactData.mdb and modify an entry, such as changing the date in the Call Date field of a record.

5. Open Briefcase, if necessary, and check the Update status using the procedure described in step 1. The original version now shows modified status and the Update button is enabled (see Figure 27.17). Click Update to propagate the change from the original (design-master replica) file to the Briefcase replica.

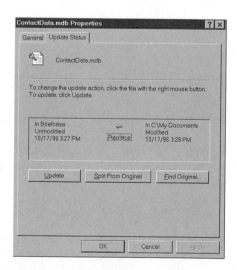

**FIG. 27.17** Updating the Briefcase replica with changes made to the design-master replica.

# Emulating Replica Set Reconciliation with Disks

As noted earlier in this chapter, most Access 97 users will use disks to replicate Briefcases and reconcile replica sets. You can emulate floppy disk Briefcase update operations on a single computer by following these steps:

1. Create a copy of your application .mdb file. For example, copy ContactManager. mdb and name the copy **ContactRemote.mdb**.

2. Right-click the My Briefcase icon and choose Copy from the popup menu. Right-click the desktop and choose Paste to add a copy of My Briefcase icon to the desktop. (The copy of My Briefcase is a backup.)

3. Insert a blank formatted disk in your A: drive. Open Explorer and drag the My Briefcase icon to Explorer and drop the icon on the A: drive icon. This step *moves* My Briefcase from the desktop to the A: drive.

> **Note**
>
> *Moving* the Briefcase is an important step in understanding the concept of a Windows Briefcase. You keep replicas of all the office files you want to update while on the road in My Briefcase. You take My Briefcase with you when you leave; a real briefcase cannot be two places at once, and neither can a briefcase's abstraction as a Windows desktop object. When you return, you move My Briefcase from the disk to the desktop, as described later in this procedure. If you share your Briefcase on a network, the real-world object corresponding to the Briefcase is an in-basket.

4. Now you need to change the links to ContactData.mdb to the copy of ContactData.mdb in the \My Briefcase folder on the disk to emulate disk operations with your guest computer. Open ContactRemote.mdb, and then choose Tools, Add-Ins, Linked Table Manager to open the Linked Table Manager's dialog.

5. Click the Select All button and mark the Always Prompt for New Location check box (see Figure 27.18). Click the OK button to open the Select New Location of Calls dialog.

VI

Using Advanced Techniques

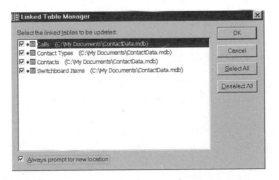

**FIG. 27.18**   Selecting all links for refreshing by the Linked Table Manager Add-In.

6. Open the Look In drop-down list and select the A:\My Briefcase folder, which contains the replica of ContactData.mdb, as shown in Figure 27.19.

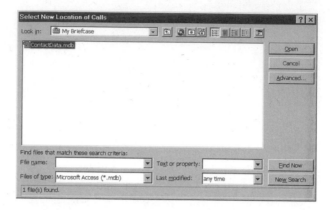

**FIG. 27.19**   Selecting A:\My Briefcase as the location of the ContactData.mdb file for linking.

7. Select ContactData.mdb and click the Open button to close the dialog and refresh the table links. The Linked Table Manager displays a message dialog indicating the successful refreshing of table links. Click OK to clear the message dialog; the Linked Table Manager's dialog appears as shown in Figure 27.20. Click Close to close the dialog.

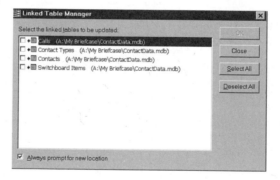

**FIG. 27.20**   Tables in ContactRemote.mdb linked to the My Briefcase replica of ContactData.mdb on the disk.

8. Open the Contacts form and change an entry, such as giving Nancy Davolio a promotion from Sales Representative to **Sales Director** (see Figure 27.21), and then close ContactRemote.mdb.

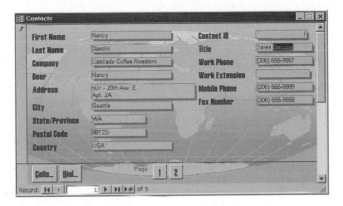

**FIG. 27.21**   Changing an entry in the Contacts form of the ContactRemote.mdb copy of the Contact Management application.

Operations using .mdb files stored on floppy disk are very slow; you need patience to perform steps 7 and 8. In real-world applications, you move the Briefcase from the disk to the desktop of your guest PC and attach the files from My Briefcase (or whatever you've named your Briefcase) to the desktop. When returning to the office, you move the Briefcase back to the disk.

**9.** Open Explorer and select the A: drive, as shown in Figure 27.22. Briefcase folders in Explorer are indicated by a small Briefcase icon. Drag the small My Briefcase icon in Explorer's window back to your desktop.

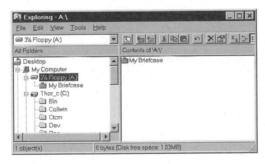

**FIG. 27.22**   Explorer displaying the My Briefcase folder on the floppy disk.

**10.** Open My Briefcase from the desktop and choose View, Details to display the location of the design-master copy to synchronize, the status of the replica set, and other file details, as illustrated in Figure 27.23.

VI

**Using Advanced Techniques**

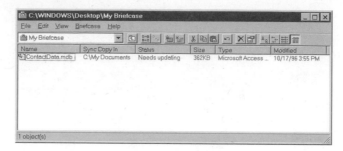

**FIG. 27.23** My Briefcase's windows displaying details of the modified Briefcase replica.

11. Choose <u>B</u>riefcase, Update <u>A</u>ll to update the design-master .mdb. The Update My Briefcase dialog appears, as shown in Figure 27.24. Click Update to make the changes to the design-master copy of ContactData.mdb.

The Update <u>A</u>ll menu choice updates the design-master .mdb from all Briefcases on the desktop that are synchronized with the .mdb, not just the open Briefcase.

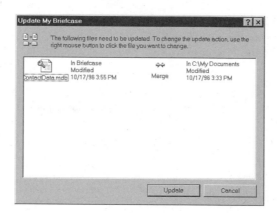

**FIG. 27.24** The Update My Briefcase dialog that confirms reconciliation of the design-master replica with the updated Briefcase replica.

12. Reopen My Briefcase to check the status of your Briefcase replica, which now is Up-to-Date (see Figure 27.25).

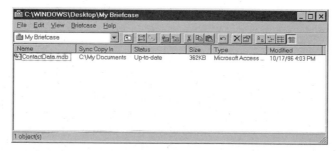

**FIG. 27.25** My Briefcase's window displaying the status of an up-to-date replica set.

**13.** Close My Briefcase and delete the copy of My Briefcase on the desktop.

> **Tip**
>
> If you create multiple Briefcases to accommodate several mobile users who update Briefcase replicas using disks, try to organize the process so that you obtain the disks from all users at the same time. This allows you to use a single Update <u>A</u>ll operation to reconcile all changes for a given period simultaneously.

# Replicating Part of a Database

Frequently, you might want to replicate only a portion of the data contained in a database, instead of replicating the entire contents of a database. For this reason, Microsoft has created the Partial Replication Wizard. By using the Partial Replication Wizard, you can create replica databases that have the same tables and structure as other databases in the replica set, but contain only a specific subset of the information stored in the database.

Partial database replicas provide three basic advantages:

- *Data restriction.* A partial replica enables you to restrict the data included in a particular replica database to only those records relevant to the particular use for which you prepare the replica. Using the Contact Management database you created in the preceding sections of this chapter as an example, there may be no reason or need for a salesperson to be able to view any other salesperson's contact information. In some cases, it might even be undesirable to have salespeople able to access the contact information of other salespersons. You could therefore use the Partial Replication Wizard to create replica databases for each salesperson, including only the contact information that belongs to that specific salesperson's contacts. Each salesperson would then use a partial replica containing only their own contact information, which could be synchronized to a full database for perusal by authorized managers.

- *Smaller size.* Because the partial replica contains less data (although it has the same structure), partial replicas tend to be smaller than the full database. Depending on how you choose the data included in the partial replica, a partial replica may be substantially smaller than the full database. This increases the likelihood that your partial replica will fit on a floppy disk, or on the typically smaller hard disks of laptop and notebook computers. The smaller size of a partial replica also means that you won't waste disk space storing data that isn't needed by a particular user, and that copying the Briefcase folder containing the partial replica will be faster.

- *Faster synchronization.* Because the partial replica contains fewer records than the full database, fewer data items have to be compared or exchanged in order to reconcile the two versions of the database. As a result, Briefcase updating operations with partial replicas tend to be faster than updating two full copies of the database.

**VI**

**Using Advanced Techniques**

### Obtaining and Installing the Partial Replica Wizard

The Partial Replica Wizard isn't included in Microsoft Office 97 Professional Edition, nor is it included with the Access 97 stand-alone product. Instead, you must obtain the Partial Replica Wizard directly from Microsoft, by downloading it from its Web site.

**On the Web**

The following URL is the home page for Access 97 that provides links to pages from which you can download Microsoft add-ins for Access 97:

**http://www.microsoft.com/msaccess**

After downloading Partial.exe, follow these steps:

1. At a DOS prompt, type **Partial** and then press Enter; alternatively, display the Partial.exe file in the Windows Explorer and double-click it. Partial.exe is a self-extracting archive file, and will unpack itself into a Readme.txt file and a file named Wzprtl80.mde.

2. Copy Wzprtl80.mde into the folder in which Access 97 is installed, usually C:\Program Files\Microsoft Office\Office.

3. Start Access and open any database file. Choose Tools, Add-Ins, Add-In Manager. Access opens the Add-In Manager dialog.

4. Select the Partial Replica Wizard in the Available Add-Ins list, and then click Install. An X appears at the left of the Partial Replica Wizard entry to indicate that it is installed (see Figure 27.26).

5. Click Close to close the Add-In Manager dialog.

**FIG. 27.26**    Installing the Partial Replica Wizard using the Add-In Manager.

### Using the Partial Replica Wizard

To use the Partial Replica Wizard, follow these steps:

1. Open any full replica of the database. It need not be the Design Master, but it must be a replica that contains the full data set.

**2.** Select <u>T</u>ools, Add-<u>I</u>ns, <u>P</u>artial Replica Wizard. Access starts the Partial Replica Wizard. Follow the on-screen instructions to complete the partial replica.

---

**Note**

The Partial Replica Wizard was not available at the time this book was in preparation. A working version is promised for the release of retail Access 97. Make sure to check the Readme.txt file that comes with the Partial Replica Wizard for last-minute installation and operating instructions.

---

VI

Using Advanced Techniques

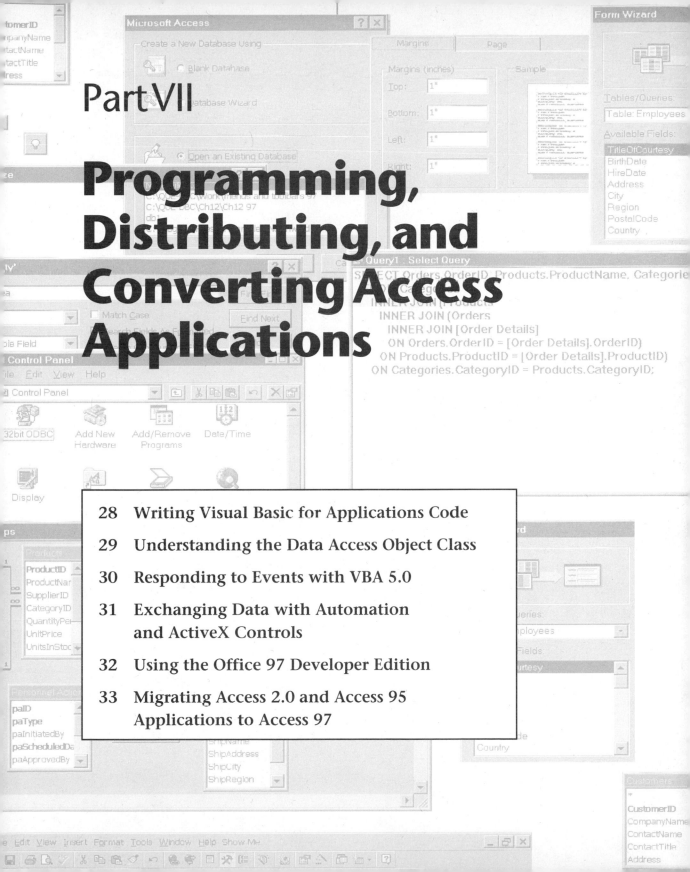

# Part VII

# Programming, Distributing, and Converting Access Applications

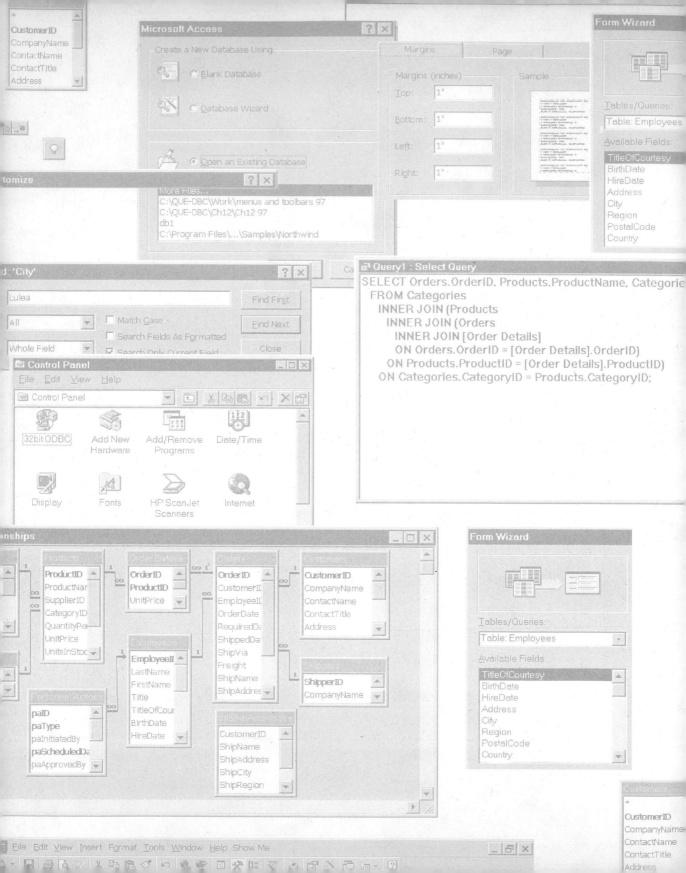

# Chapter 28

# Writing Visual Basic for Applications Code

Most Access applications you create require you to write little or no Access Visual Basic for Applications (VBA) code. A few commercial Access applications rely primarily on macros rather than Access VBA code for automating applications. Starting with Access 95, however, Microsoft recommended that Access developers use VBA code instead of macros, with the clear implication that macros may not be supported in future versions of Access. (Access 97 does support macro operations, but the Microsoft documentation states that it does so primarily for backward compatibility.) Short VBA procedures using the DoCmd object usually are sufficient to provide the methods needed by simple applications to run queries, display forms, and print reports. The built-in functions of Access allow you to perform complex calculations in queries. You may want or need to use Access VBA code for any of the following reasons:

- To create user-defined functions (UDFs) that substitute for complex expressions you use repeatedly to validate data, compute values for text boxes, and perform other duties. Creating a UDF that you refer to by a short name minimizes potential typing errors and allows you to document the way your expression works.

- To write expressions that include more complex decision structures than allowed by the standard IIf() function (in an **If...Then...Else...End If** structure, for example), or to write expressions that need loops for repetitive operations.

- To perform transaction processing actions with the Access VBA equivalents of SQL COMMIT and ROLLBACK statements.

- To manipulate other applications' objects with Automation code. Using Automation is the primary subject of Chapter 31, "Exchanging Data with Automation and ActiveX Controls."

- To open more than one database in an application where attaching a table or using the SQL IN statement is not sufficient for your application.

- To provide hard-copy documentation for your application. If you include actions in Access VBA code, you can print the Access VBA code to improve the documentation for your application.

- To provide graceful error-handling if something goes wrong in your application. With Access VBA code, you can closely control how your application responds to errors such as missing forms, missing data, incorrect values entered by a user, and other problems.

This chapter describes Access VBA, introduces you to Access VBA modules and procedures, shows you how to use the Module window to enter and test Access VBA code, and helps you start writing user-defined functions. The chapter also includes examples of Access VBA programs.

# Introducing Access VBA

Several years ago, Bill Gates, the founder and chairman of Microsoft Corporation, stated that all Microsoft applications using macros would share a common macro language built on BASIC. BASIC is the acronym for Beginner's All-Purpose Symbolic Instruction Code, originally developed at Dartmouth College. Gates' choice of BASIC is not surprising when you consider that Microsoft was built on the foundation of his BASIC interpreter that ran in 8K on the early predecessors of the PC. Gates reiterated his desire for a common macro language in an article that appeared in *One-to-One with Microsoft* in late 1991.

Before Access 1.0 was released, the results of Gates' edict were observed in only one Microsoft product, Word for Windows. If you have created Microsoft Word macros or just made minor changes to macros you have recorded, you will find that Access VBA is similar to WordBasic. With the arrival of Excel 5.0, Visual Basic, Applications Edition (more commonly known as Visual Basic for Applications, or VBA), became the *lingua franca* for programming Microsoft's productivity applications.

Access 95 joined Excel 5+, Project 4+, and Visual Basic 4.0 in implementing VBA as Microsoft's "common macro language." With the advent of Microsoft Office 97, Microsoft Word and Excel now share a common VBA programming environment, and even PowerPoint uses VBA to program presentations. Access 97 does not yet contain the same VBA programming environment used by Excel 97 and Word 97, but otherwise Access 97 fully supports VBA.

---

**Note**

Each application that uses VBA automatically adds references for its built-in application objects to the language. Thus, each application has its own "flavor" of VBA. As an example, the Access DoCmd object used to execute actions in code is specific to the Access "flavor" of VBA. For this reason, this book uses the term *Access VBA* to describe VBA with the standard set of Access object references added to the root language.

---

VBA is a real programming language, not a "macro language;" Access has its own macro language. You can expect Access VBA to replace Access macros gradually—Microsoft recommends that you develop applications in Access by using Access VBA instead of macros. You create the preferred equivalent of macros with Access VBA functions and subprocedures. Although you can execute Access VBA subprocedures directly from an open code module, you more typically execute Access VBA subprocedures by specifying the name of the subprocedure as the value of a specific event. (Chapter 30, "Responding to Events with VBA 5.0," explains how to use VBA subprocedures as event-handlers.) You typically execute Access VBA functions by using them in calculated controls in forms and reports, in the Validation Rule property of a field or table, or by calling the function from within a VBA subprocedure.

### Access VBA Compared with xBase, PAL, and Visual VBA

Programmers experienced with dBASE or other DOS xBase dialects, such as Clipper and FoxBase, will find that Access VBA uses many of the same xBase keywords or minor variations of familiar xBase keywords. Borland's PAL is related to xBase, so PAL and ObjectPAL programmers will also find the translation of PAL to Access VBA keywords straightforward. A large number of DOS-based RDBMS applications running on PCs remain, many of which are likely to be converted to 32-bit Access applications running under Windows 95 or Windows NT. Therefore, a comparison of Access VBA and DOS database applications continues to be warranted.

User-defined functions are almost identical in structure in Access VBA and the DOS versions of xBase and PAL. This similarity in code structure ends, however, with user-defined functions. Writing code for Windows applications in general and for Access in particular requires an entirely different code structure. Applications for DOS RDBMSs use top-down programming techniques, which means that a main program calls (executes) other subprograms or procedures that perform specific actions. The user of the application makes choices from a menu that determine which subprograms or procedures are invoked. Menus that let the application remain idle are enclosed within DO WHILE...ENDDO loops while the user decides what menu command to choose next. Your code is responsible for all actions that occur while the application is running.

The situation with Windows and Access differs from that of top-down programming. Access itself is the main program, and Windows is responsible for many functions that you must code in DOS RDBMS languages. This fact is a blessing for new programmers because Windows and Access simplify the development of complex applications. However, contributions from Access and Windows are a curse for top-down DOS programmers, because Access and Windows require an entirely new approach to writing RDBMS code.

The guiding principles for DOS RDBMS developers who write Access VBA applications are the following:

■ Don't try to write a great deal of Access VBA code during the development stage of your first applications. Create all forms, reports, and queries for your application first, and then write the minimum VBA code required to carry out the pre-programmed actions. Most applications do not need any code other than an occasional user-defined function and a few event-handling procedures.

■ Use command buttons and associated event actions to substitute for the traditional menu commands of DOS RDBMSs. In many applications, you create a menu that gives the user only the File, Exit command. All other user-initiated choices in the application are handled by control objects on forms.

■ Concentrate on using event procedures to respond to user- and application-initiated events, such as opening forms. Study the event-oriented properties of form and control objects and the DoCmd actions that are available for responding to the event properties. Learn the full capabilities of each DoCmd action that is native to Access before you write your own actions in Access VBA. Event properties combined with the appropriate DoCmd actions usually can substitute for about 95 percent of the code you write for DOS RDBMSs.

■ After your application is up and running, consider writing Access VBA code to add the nuances that distinguish professionally written database applications.

### Where You Use Access VBA Code

You probably will first use Access VBA to create functions that make complex calculations. Creating an Access VBA function to substitute for calculations with many sets of parentheses is relatively simple and a good introduction to writing Access VBA code. Writing expressions as Access VBA functions allows you to add comments to the code that make the purpose and construction of the code clear to others. Also, comments aid your memory when you decide to revise an application after using it for a few months.

Your next step is to create Access VBA event-handling subprocedures in form or report modules. You use event-handling subprocedures to perform operations in response to events such as clicking a command button on a form, updating a value in a field, or when a field gains or loses the focus. Access 97 gives you the choice of calling a function contained in an Access module or executing an event-handling subprocedure contained in a form or report module. Microsoft called Access VBA contained in forms or reports Code Behind Forms (CBF) in Access 2.0 and 95; event-handling code in Access 97 is contained in class modules. (Chapter 30, "Responding to Events with VBA 5.0," describes class module programming in more detail.)

### Typographic and Naming Conventions Used for Access VBA

This book uses a special set of typographic conventions for references to Access VBA keywords and object variable names in Access VBA examples:

■ Monospace type is used for all Access VBA code in the examples, as in `lngItemCounter`.

■ Bold monospace type is used for all VBA reserved words and type-declaration symbols, as in **Dim** and **%**. Standard function names in Access VBA, as described in Chapter 9, "Understanding Operators and Expressions in Access," also are set in bold type so that reserved words, standard function names, and reserved symbols stand out from variable and function names and values you assign to variables. Keywords incorporated by reference in Access, such as `DoCmd`, are not set in bold.

■ Italic monospace type indicates a replaceable item, as in `Dim `*`DataItem`*` As String`. *`DataItem`* is replaced by a name that you supply.

■ Bold-italic monospace type indicates a replaceable reserved word, such as a data type, as in `Dim `*`DataItem`*` As `***`DataType`***; ***`DataType`*** is replaced by a VBA-reserved word corresponding to the desired VBA data type.

■ Names of variables that refer to Access objects, such as forms or reports, use a three-letter prefix derived from the object name, as in `frm`*`FormName`* and `rpt`*`ReportName`*. The prefixes for object variables are listed in Appendix B, "Naming Conventions for Access Objects and Variables."

■ Names of other variables are preceded by a one-letter or three-letter data type identifier, such as `var`*`VariantVariable`* and `int`*`IntegerVariable`*. Boolean variables (flags) that return only **True** or **False** values use the f prefix, as in `fIsLoaded`.

■ Optional elements are included within square brackets, as in `[`*`OptionItem`*`]`. Square brackets also enclose object names that contain spaces or special punctuation symbols.

■ An ellipsis (...) substitutes for code that is not shown in syntax and code examples, as in `If...Then...Else...End If`.

### Modules, Functions, and Subprocedures

A *module* is a container for Access VBA code, just as a form is a container for control objects. Access 97 provides the following three types of modules:

■ *Access Modules*. You create an Access module to contain your Access VBA code the same way that you create any other new database object: click the Module tab in the Database window and then click the New button. Alternatively, you can click the New Object button on the toolbar and choose New Module from the drop-down menu. Figure 28.1 shows the `IsLoaded()` function of the Utility Functions module of Northwind.mdb. Access modules are also called *standard modules*.

> **Tip**
>
> Using Access modules to contain all of your Access VBA code speeds the opening of forms and reports but slows the initial opening of your application.

■ *Form Modules*. Form modules contain code in class modules to respond to events triggered by forms or controls on forms. Essentially, when you add code to a form object, you create a new class of object in the database. The event-handling procedures you create for the form are its new methods, hence the term *class module* for the code module associated with a particular form. You open a form module by clicking the Code button of the toolbar in Form Design view. Alternatively, choose

View, Code. Either of these methods opens a module that Access automatically names Form_*FormName*, where *FormName* is the name of the selected form. (Access 2.0 named the modules Form.*FormName*.) Prior to Access 97, forms automatically included a module as part of the form. Forms in Access 97, however, have a new property—Has Module. If this property is set to Yes, then the form has an attached module; otherwise, it does not. Leave the Has Module property set to No unless you really do need to add code to the form.

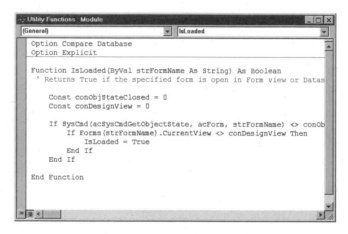

**FIG. 28.1**    The Access module window for the IsLoaded() function.

Another method of opening a form module is to click the ellipsis button for one of the event properties for a form or a control object on a form. Selecting Code Builder from the Choose Builder dialog displays the Form_*FormName* module with a procedure stub, **Private Sub** *ObjectName_EventName*()...**End Sub**, written for you. Access 97 adds the VBA **Private** prefix by default. Figure 28.2 shows the Access VBA code for the CustomerID_AfterUpdate procedure of Northwind.mdb's Orders form.

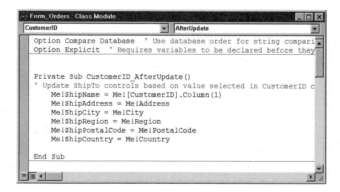

**FIG. 28.2**    A typical event-handling procedure in a class module.

■ *Report Modules*. Report modules contain code for responding to events triggered by reports, sections of reports, or group headers and footers. (Control objects on reports do not trigger events.) You open a report's class module the same way you open a form's class module. Report modules are named Report_*ReportName* automatically. Like forms, whether an Access 97 report has a class module depends on the setting of the Has Module property.

A module consists of a *Declarations section* and usually one or more *procedures* or *functions*. As the name suggests, the Declarations section of a module is used to declare items (usually variables and constants, the subjects of following sections) used by the procedures and functions contained in the module. You can use a module without functions or procedures to declare **Public** variables and constants that can be used by any function or procedure in any module. Similarly, you use the **Public** prefix for functions and subprocedures to allow their use by code in any module. (**Public** replaces Access 2.0's **Global** keyword, but **Global** continues to work in Access 97.)

> **Note**
>
> The Module windows of Figures 28.1 and 28.2 show the Declarations section and a function or procedure separated by a horizontal line. The ability to display the Declarations sections and all procedures in a single scrollable window, called Full Module view, is a feature shared by the Module windows of all flavors of VBA. If you see only the Declarations section when you open a module, click the Full Module View button at the bottom left of the module window (shown in its "down" position in both Figures 28.1 and 28.2). Alternatively, choose Tools, Options to display the Options dialog. Click the Module tab and mark the Full Module View and Procedure Separator check boxes.

*Procedures* are typically defined as subprograms referred to by name in another program. Referring to a procedure by name *calls* or *invokes* the procedure; the code in the procedure executes, and then the sequence of execution returns to the program that called the procedure. Another name for a procedure is *subroutine*. Procedures can call other procedures, in which case the called procedures are called *subprocedures*. Procedures are defined by beginning (**Sub**) and end (**End Sub**) reserved words with a **Public**, **Private**, or **Static** prefix, as in the following example:

```
Private Sub ProcName
    [Start of procedure code]
    ...
    [End of procedure code]
End Sub
```

> **Note**
>
> You can refer to the procedure name to invoke the procedure, but Access VBA provides a keyword, **Call**, that explicitly invokes a procedure. Prefixing the procedure name with **Call** is a good programming practice because this keyword identifies the name that follows as the name of a procedure rather than a variable.

*Functions* are a class of procedures that return values to their names, as explained in Chapter 9, "Understanding Operators and Expressions in Access." C programmers would argue that procedures are a class of functions, called *void functions*, that do not return values. Regardless of how you view the difference between functions and subprocedures, keep the following points in mind:

■ Access macros require that you write Access VBA functions (not subprocedures) to act in place of macro actions when using the `RunCode` macro action.

■ The only way you can call a subprocedure in an Access VBA module is from an Access VBA function or another procedure. You cannot directly execute a procedure in an Access module from any Access database object.

■ Unlike Access modules, form and report class modules use subprocedures (not functions) to respond to events. Using form- and report-level subprocedures for event-handling code mimics Visual VBA's approach for events triggered by forms and controls on forms.

■ Function names in Access modules are global in scope with respect to Access modules unless they are declared **Private**. Thus, you cannot have duplicate **Public** function names in any Access module in your application. However, form and report class modules can have a function with the same name as a **Public** function in a standard module because form and report function and procedure names have form- or report-level scope. A function in a form module with the same name as a function in an Access module takes priority over the Access module version. Therefore, if you include the `IsLoaded()` function in a form module and call the `IsLoaded()` function from a procedure in the form module, the `IsLoaded()` function in the form module executes.

■ To execute an Access VBA function in Access VBA code, you must use the function in an expression, such as

```
intReturnValue = nilFunctionName([Arguments])
```

even when the function returns no value.

Functions are created within a structure similar to procedures, as in the following example:

```
Private Function FuncName([Arguments])
    [Start of function code]
    ...
    [End of function code]
End Function
```

You cannot use **Call** to execute a function; you must refer to the function by name. Function calls are identified by the parentheses that follow the function name—even if the function requires no arguments.

You can add as many individual procedures and functions to a module as you want. If you write a substantial amount of Access VBA code, you should take one of the following two approaches:

■ Use form and report modules to contain the code that responds to the events on forms. Adding a class module to a form or report creates a new class of object within your database. Other forms and reports created from the originals will inherit the class module of the form or report and the VBA code that it contains. Procedures common to several forms, however, should be incorporated in Access modules. As mentioned in the tip earlier in this chapter, adding substantial amounts of code to form modules slows the opening of the form.

■ Create separate Access modules for code that is associated with a particular class of object, such as forms. A form that requires an appreciable amount of code usually deserves its own module. When you take the Access module approach, your application opens more slowly, but forms open more rapidly. Users are likely to favor applications that respond more quickly after they are launched.

Access VBA introduces another class of procedure called property procedures that use the `{Property Let ¦ Property Get ¦ Property Set}...End Property` structure to create custom properties for Access objects, such as forms or controls. Property procedures are used by VBA developers primarily for creating custom wizards. A discussion of property procedures is beyond the scope of this book.

### References to VBA and Access Modules

Access 97 uses references to make objects available for use in modules. Access 97's default references are Visual Basic for Applications, Microsoft Access 97, Microsoft DAO 3.5 Object Library, and the currently open database. To view the default references, open a module, then choose <u>T</u>ools, <u>R</u>eferences to open the References dialog (see Figure 28.3). Current references, except to the open database, are indicated by a mark in the adjacent check box.

Access 97 implements VBA by establishing references to collections of objects exposed by VBA's object library, Vbaen32.olb. Vbaen32.olb is the English (en) version of VBA, 32-bit version (32). Similarly, Access exposes its application objects through an object library, Msacc8.olb, and the Jet database engine exposes data access objects (DAOs) through Dao2535.olb (the Jet 3.5 engine is compatible with DAO 2.5 and 3.5, hence the 2535 in the object library's name). Each application that supports VBA has a similar, but not identical, set of default references.

Referenced objects appear in the Project/Library drop-down list of the Object Browser. To view the Object Browser, open a module and click the Object Browser button on the toolbar (or choose <u>V</u>iew, Object Browser). <All Libraries> is the default selection in the Project/Library list. Figure 28.4 shows a few of the references to `Report` objects in Northwind.mdb and the Utility Functions module in the Classes list. Only objects that can act as VBA containers appear in the Classes list.

When you select a function or subprocedure name in a module, the function or subprocedure name and arguments, if any, appear in the window at the bottom of the Object Browser dialog. You can obtain help on Access, VBA, and other objects by clicking the help (?) button, which is disabled for user-defined functions and the event-handling subprocedures you write. Chapter 29, "Understanding the Data Access Object Class," describes object classes and the use of the Object Browser in detail.

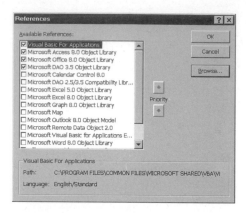

**FIG. 28.3**    The four default object references for Access 97.

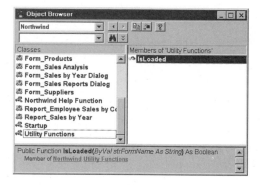

**FIG. 28.4**    The Object Browser displaying the calling syntax for the IsLoaded() function.

### Data Types and Database Objects in Access VBA

When you create Access VBA tables, all data types that you use to assign field data types and sizes (except for OLE and Memo field data types) have data type counterparts in Access VBA. With the exception of the **Variant** and **Currency** data types, Access VBA data types are represented in most other dialects of BASIC, such as Microsoft QuickBASIC and the QBasic interpreter supplied with MS-DOS 5 and later.

Traditional BASIC dialects use a punctuation symbol called the *type-declaration character*, such as **$** for the **String** data type, to designate the data type. The Access VBA data types, the type-declaration characters, the corresponding field data types, and the ranges of values are shown in the VBA Type, Symbol, Field Type, Minimum Value, and Maximum Value columns, respectively, of Table 28.1. The Field Types **Byte**, **Integer**, **Long Integer**, **Single**, and **Double** correspond to the Field Size property of the Number data type in tables, queries, forms, and reports. Access VBA adds the **Byte** and **Boolean** data types to support the 8-bit Byte and 16-bit Yes/No field data types.

**Table 28.1    Access VBA and Corresponding Field Data Types**

| VBA Type | Symbol | Field Type | Minimum Value | Maximum Value |
|---|---|---|---|---|
| **Byte** | None | Byte | 0 | 255 |
| **Integer** | % | Integer | –32,768 | 32,767 |
| **Boolean** | None | Yes/No | **True** | **False** |
| **Long** | & | Long Integer, AutoNumber | –2,147,483,648 | 2,147,483,647 |
| **Single** | ! | Single | –3.402823E38 1.401298E–45 | –1.401298E–5 3.402823E38 |
| **Double** | # | Double | –1.79769313486232E308 4.94065645841247E–324 | 4.9406564841247E–324 1.79769313486232E308 |
| **Currency** | @ | Currency | –922,337,203,685, 477.5808 | 922,337,203,685, 477.5807 |
| **String** | $ | Text or Memo | 0 characters | Approximately 2 billion characters |
| **Date** | None | Date/Time | January 1, 100 | December 31, 9999 |
| **Variant** | None | Any | January 1, 100 (date) | December 31, 9999 (date) |
| | | | Same as **Double** (numbers) | Same as **Double** (numbers) |
| | | | Same as **String** (text) | Same as **String** (text) |

**Tip**

All data returned from fields of tables or queries is of the **Variant** data type by default. If you assign the field value to a conventional data type, such as **Integer**, the data type is said to be *coerced*.

You can dispense with the type-declaration character if you explicitly declare your variables with the **Dim...As** *DataType* statement, discussed later in this section. If you do not explicitly declare the variables' data type or use a symbol to define an implicit data type, Access VBA variables default to the **Variant** data type.

The # sign is also used to enclose values specified as dates, as in varNewYears = #1/1/97#. In this case, bold type is not used for the enclosing # signs because these symbols are not intended for the purpose of the # reserved symbol that indicates the **Double** data type.

Database objects—such as databases, tables, and queries—and application objects (forms and reports), all of which you used in prior chapters, also have corresponding object data types in Access VBA. Here, Access VBA departs from other BASIC languages with the exception of Visual Basic. The most commonly used object data types of Access VBA and the object library that includes the objects are listed in Table 28.2.

**Table 28.2    The Most Common Database Object Data Types Supported by Access**

| VBAObject Data | Library | Corresponding Database Object Type |
|---|---|---|
| Database | DAO 3.5 | Databases opened by the Jet database engine |
| Form | Access 97 | Forms, including subforms |
| Report | Access 97 | Reports, including subreports |
| Control | Access 97 | Controls on forms and reports |
| QueryDef | DAO 3.5 | Query definitions (SQL statement equivalents) |
| TableDef | DAO 3.5 | Table definitions (structure, indexes, and other table properties) |
| Recordset | DAO 3.5 | A virtual representation of a table or the result set of a query |

**Note**

The Table, Dynaset, and Snapshot object data types of Access 1.x have been replaced by the all-encompassing Recordset data type of Access 2+. You distinguish the type of Recordset object (Table, Dynaset, or Snapshot) by the Recordset object's Type property. The Table, Dynaset, and Snapshot object types are supported by Access 97 for backward compatibility with Access 1.x code. However, it is a good practice to use the new Recordset data type because no guarantee exists that the obsolete Access 1.x object data types will be supported in future Access versions. DAO data types and object collections are discussed in Chapter 29, "Understanding the Data Access Object Class."

## Variables and Naming Conventions

*Variables* are named placeholders for values of a specified data type that change when your Access VBA code is executed. You give variables names, as you name fields, but the names of variables cannot include spaces or any other punctuation except the under-score character (_). The other restriction is that a variable cannot use an Access VBA key-word by itself as a name; keywords are called *reserved words* for this reason. The same rules apply to giving names to functions and procedures. Variable names in Access VBA typically employ a combination of upper- and lowercase letters to make them more readable.

**Implicit Variables.** You can create variables by assigning a value to a variable name, as in the following example:

```
NewVar = 1234
```

A statement of this type *declares* a variable, which means to create a new variable with a name you choose. The statement in the example creates a new implicit variable, NewVar, of the **Variant** data type with a value of 1234. (Thus, NewVar would be more appropriately named varNewVar.) When you do not specify a data type for an implicit variable by ap-pending one of the type-declaration characters to the variable name, the **Variant** data type is assigned by default. The following statement creates a variable of the Integer data type:

```
NewVar% = 1234
```

Declaring variables of the **Integer** or **Long** (integer) type when decimal fractions are not required speeds the operation of your code. Access takes longer to compute values for **Variant**, **Double**, and **Single** variables.

**Explicit Variables.** It is a better programming practice to declare your variables and assign those variables a data type before you give variables a value. Programming languages such as Pascal, C, C++, and Delphi require you to declare variables before you use them. The most common method of declaring variables is by using the **Dim...As** *Datatype* structure where **As** specifies the data type. This method declares explicit variables. An example follows:

```
Dim intNewVar As Integer
```

If you do not add the **As Integer** keywords, intNewVar is assigned the **Variant** data type by default.

You can require that all variables be explicitly declared prior to their use by adding the statement **Option Explicit** in the Declarations section of a module. The advantage of using **Option Explicit** is that Access detects misspelled variable names and displays an error message when misspellings are encountered. If you do not use **Option Explicit** and you misspell a variable name, Access creates a new implicit variable with the misspelled name. The resulting errors in your code's operation can be difficult to diagnose. Access automatically adds an Option Explicit statement to the Declarations section of each module if you set the Require Variable Declaration option on in the Module sheet of the Options dialog (see Figure 28.5).

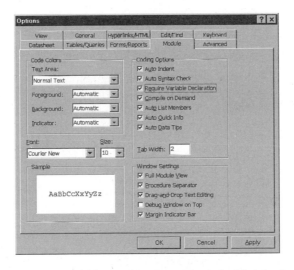

**FIG. 28.5**    Setting the Require Variable Declaration option in the Module sheet of the Options dialog.

**Scope and Duration of Variables.** Variables have a property called *scope*, which determines when the variables appear and disappear in your Access VBA code. Variables appear the first time you declare them and then disappear and reappear on the basis of the scope you assign to them. When a variable appears, it is said to be *visible*—meaning that you can assign the variable a value, change its value, and use it in expressions. Otherwise, the variable is *invisible*; if you use a variable's name while it is invisible, you instead create a new variable with the same name.

The following lists the four scope levels in Access VBA:

- *Local (procedure-level) scope.* The variable is visible only during the time when the procedure in which the variable is declared is executed. Variables that you declare, with or without using `Dim...As Datatype` in a procedure or function, are local in scope.

- *Form-level and report-level scope.* The variable is visible only when the form or report in which it is declared is open. You declare form-level and report-level variables in the Declarations section of form and report modules with `Private...As Datatype`. (`Dim...As Datatype` also works.)

- *Module-level scope.* The variable is visible to all procedures and functions contained in the module in which the variable was declared. (Modules open when you open the database.) You declare variables with module scope in the Declarations section of the module with the same syntax as form- and report-level variables.

- *Global or public scope.* The variable is visible to all procedures and functions within all modules. You declare variables with global scope in the Declarations section of a module using `Public...As Datatype`.

The scope and visibility of variables declared in two different Access modules of the same database, both with two procedures, are illustrated by the diagram in Figure 28.6. In each procedure, variables declared with different scopes are used to assign values to variables declared within the procedure. Invalid assignment statements are shown crossed out in the figure. These assignment statements are invalid because the variable used to assign the value to the variable declared in the procedure is not visible in the procedure.

Variables also have a property called *duration*, or *lifetime*. The duration of a variable is your code's execution time between the first appearance of the variable (its declaration) and its disappearance. Each time a procedure or function is called, local variables declared with the `Dim...As Datatype` statement are set to default values with 0 for numeric data types and the empty string ("") for string variables. The duration of these local variables is usually equal to the lifetime of the function or procedure—from the time the function or procedure is called until the `End Function` or `End Sub` statement is executed.

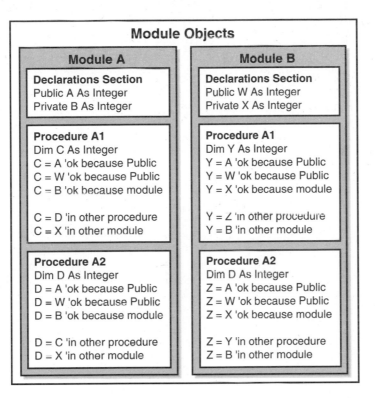

**FIG. 28.6** Valid and invalid assignment statements for variables of different scopes.

To preserve the values of local variables between occurrences (called *instances*) of a procedure or function, you substitute the reserved word **Static** for **Dim**. Static variables have a duration of your Access application, but their scope is determined by where you declare them. Static variables are useful when you want to count the number of occurrences of an event. You can make all variables in a function or procedure static variables by preceding **Function** or **Sub** with the **Static** keyword.

> **Note**
>
> Minimize the number of local variables that you declare **Static**. Local variables do not consume memory when they are not visible. This characteristic of local variables is especially important in the case of arrays, discussed in the "Access VBA Arrays" section that follows shortly, because arrays are often very large.

**User-Defined Data Types.** You can create your own data type that consists of one or more Access data types. User-defined data types are discussed in this section pertaining to variables because you need to know what a variable is before you can declare a user-defined data type. You declare a user-defined data type between the **Type...End Type** keywords, as in the following example:

```
Type DupRec
    Field1 As Long
    Field2 As String * 20
    Field3 As Single
    Field4 As Double
End Type
```

User-defined data types are particularly useful when you create a variable to hold the values of one or more records of a table that uses fields of different data types. The **String** * 20 statement defines Field2 of the user-defined data type as a fixed-length string of 20 characters, usually corresponding to the Size property of the Text field data type. String variables in user-defined data types are always specified with a fixed length. You must declare your user-defined data type (called a *record* or *structure* in other programming languages) in the Declarations section of a module.

You must explicitly declare variables to be of the user-defined type with the **Dim**, **Private**, **Public**, or **Static** keywords because no reserved symbol exists to declare a user-defined data type, as in **Dim** usrCurrentRec **As** tagDupRec. To assign a value to a field of a variable with a user-defined data type, you specify the name of the variable and the field name, separating the names with a period, as in usrCurrentRec.lngField1 = 2048.

**Access VBA Arrays.** Arrays are variables that consist of a collection of values, called *elements* of the array, of a single data type in a regularly ordered structure. Implicitly declared arrays are not allowed in Access VBA (or in Visual VBA). You declare an array with the **Dim** statement, adding the number of elements in parentheses to the variable name for the array, as in the following example:

```
Dim astrNewArray(20) As String
```

This statement creates an array of 21 elements, each of which is a conventional, variable-length string variable. You create 21 elements because the first element of an array is the 0 (zero) element unless you specify otherwise by adding the **To** modifier, as in the following example:

```
Dim astrNewArray(1 To 20) As String
```

The preceding statement creates an array with 20 elements.

You can create multidimensional arrays by adding more values separated by commas. The statement

```
Dim alngNewArray(9, 9, 9) As Long
```

creates a three-dimensional array of 10 elements per dimension. This array, when visible, occupies 4,000 bytes of memory (10×10×10×4 bytes/long integer).

You can create a *dynamic array* by declaring the array using **Dim** without specifying the number of elements and then using the **ReDim** reserved word to determine the number of elements the array contains. You can **ReDim** an array as many times as you want. Each time you do so, the values stored in the array are reinitialized to their default values, determined by the data type, unless you follow **ReDim** with the reserved word, **Preserve**. The following sample statements create a dynamic array:

```
Dim alngNewArray() As Long          'In Declarations sections
ReDim Preserve alngNewArray(9, 9, 9) 'In procedure, preserves prior values
ReDim alngNewArray(9, 9, 9)          'In procedure, reinitializes all
```

Dynamic arrays are useful when you don't know how many elements an array requires when you declare it. You can **ReDim** a dynamic array to zero elements when you no longer need the values it contains; this tactic allows you to recover the memory that the array consumes while it is visible. Alternatively, you can use the **Erase** reserved word followed by a dynamic array's name to remove all of the array's elements from memory. (**Erase** used on an array with fixed dimensions merely reinitializes the array to its condition before you assigned any values to it.) Arrays declared with **Dim** may have up to 60 dimensions. You can use the **ReDim** statement only to alter the size of the last dimension in a multidimensional array.

Scope, duration rules, and keywords apply to arrays in the same way in which they apply to conventional variables. You can declare dynamic arrays with global and module-level scope by adding the **Public** or **Private** statement to the Declarations section of a module and then using the **ReDim** statement by itself in a procedure. If you declare an array with **Static**, rather than **Dim**, the array retains its values between instances of a procedure.

> **Note**
>
> Do not use the **Option Base** keywords to change the default initial element of arrays from 0 to 1. **Option Base** is included in Access VBA for compatibility with other BASIC dialects. Many arrays you create from Access VBA objects must begin with element 0. If you are concerned about the memory occupied by an unused zeroth element of an array, use the **Dim** *ArrayName*(1 **To** N) **As** *DataType* declaration. In most cases, you can disregard the zeroth element.

**Named Database Objects as Variables in Access VBA Code.** Properties of database objects you create with Access can be treated as variables and assigned values within Access VBA code. For example, you can assign a new value to the text box that contains the address information for a customer by name. Use the following statement:

```
Forms!Customers!Address = "123 Elm St."
```

The collection name Forms defines the type of object. The exclamation point (called the *bang* symbol by programmers) separates the name of the form and the name of the control object. The ! symbol is analogous to the \ path separator that you use when you are dealing with folder and file names. If the name of the form or the control object contains a space or other punctuation, you need to enclose the name within square brackets, as in the following statement:

```
Forms!Customers![Contact Name] = "Joe Hill"
```

Alternatively, you can use the **Set** keyword to create your own named variable for the control object. This procedure is convenient when you need to refer to the control object several times. It is more convenient to type txtContact rather than the full "path" to the control object—in this case, a text box:

```
Dim txtContact As Control
```

```
Set txtContact = Forms!Customers![Contact Name]
txtContact = "Joe Hill"
```

You can assign any database object to a variable name by declaring the variable as the object type and using the **Set** statement to assign the object to the variable. You do not create a copy of the object in memory when you assign it a variable name; the variable refers to the object in memory. Referring to an object in memory is often called *pointing* to an object; many languages have a pointer data type that holds the address of the location in memory where the variable is stored. Access VBA does not support pointers. Chapter 29, "Understanding the Data Access Object Class," deals with creating variables that point to the Access 97 database objects supplied by the Jet 3.5 DAO.

**Object Properties and the *With...End With* Structure.** Access VBA introduces the **With...End With** structure that offers a shorthand method of setting the values of object properties, such as the dimensions and other characteristics of a form. The **With...End With** structure also lets you set the values of fields of a user-defined data type without repeating the variable name in each instance. To use the **With...End With** structure to set object property values, you must first declare and set an object variable, as in the following example:

```
Dim frmFormName As Form
Set frmFormName = Forms!FormName
With frmFormName
    .Top = 1000
    .Left = 1000
    .Width = 5000
    .Height = 4000
End With
```

When using the **With...End With** structure with user-defined data types, you don't use the **Set** statement. Names of properties or fields within the structure are preceded by periods.

**Variable Naming Conventions.** In the event that you need to write large amounts of Access VBA code, you probably will employ a large number of variable names and data types. On forms and reports, many different types of named control objects can be used, each of which you can assign to a variable name with the **Set** keyword in your Access VBA code. As your code grows in size, remembering the data types of all variables becomes difficult.

Stan Leszynski, a Seattle database consultant, has created a set of variable-naming conventions for Access VBA. The *Leszynski Naming Conventions for Microsoft Access* employs *Hungarian notation*, which is used primarily in the C and C++ languages. "Hungarian" refers to the nationality of the method's inventor, Charles Simonyi (who was involved in the development of Access), and the fact that only Hungarians are likely to be able to pronounce some of the abbreviations correctly, such as "lpsz." Leszynski adapted Hungarian notation for use in the Access VBA environment.

Hungarian notation uses a set of codes for the data type. You prefix the variable name with the code in lowercase letters. For example, the prefix code for a text box is txt, so the variable name for the text box in the preceding example is `txtContact`. Strings in C code are identified by the prefix `lpsz`, an abbreviation for long pointer to a string that is zero-terminated (with `Chr$(0)` or ASCII `Null`). Access VBA does not support the pointer data type (but it does use pointers for the location of string variables), and it does not use zero-terminated strings. Therefore, `str` is a more appropriate prefix for Access VBA strings.

The data type identifier of a user-defined data type is called a *created tag*. In Hungarian notation, created tags are capitalized as in the following:

```
Type REC
    lngField1 As Long
    strField2 As String
    sngField3 As Single
    dblField4 As Double
End Type
```

A variable of type `REC` is declared with the lowercase `rec` prefix, such as in the following:

```
Dim recCurRecord As REC
```

Created tags should be short but should not duplicate one of the standard data-type prefix codes.

Using standard data type prefixes makes your code easier to read and understand. Many of the code examples in this book use the new proposed naming conventions. The complete list of the Leszynski notation for Access VBA objects and variables appears in Appendix B, "Naming Conventions for Access Objects and Variables."

### Symbolic Constants

*Symbolic constants* are named placeholders for values of a specified data type that do not change when your Access VBA code is executed. You precede the name of a symbolic constant with the keyword, `Const`, as in `Const sngPI As Single = 3.1416`. You declare symbolic constants in the Declarations section of a module or within a function or procedure. Precede `Const` with the `Public` keyword if you want to create a global constant that is visible to all modules, as in `Public Const gsngPI = 3.1416`. Public constants can be declared only in the Declarations section of an Access VBA module.

Typically, symbolic constants take names in all capital letters to distinguish them from variables. Underscores often are used to make the names of symbolic constants more readable, as in `sngVALUE_OF_PI`. This naming convention no longer applies to system-defined constants in Access 97 or Access 95. System-defined intrinsic constants are the subject of the next section, "Access System-Defined Constants."

You do not need to specify a data type for constants because Access VBA chooses the data type that stores the data most efficiently. Access VBA can make this choice because it knows the value of the data when it "compiles" your code. It is a good programming practice, however, to add `As Datatype` when declaring constants.

> **Note**
>
> Access is an interpreted language, so the term *compile* in an Access VBA context is a misnomer. When you "compile" the Access VBA source that you write in code-editing windows, Access creates a tokenized version of the code (called *pseudo-code*, or *p-code*). This subject is discussed in the section "The Access VBA Compiler" later in the chapter.

**Access System-Defined Constants.** Access VBA includes seven system-defined constants—**True**, **False**, Yes, No, On, Off, and **Null**—that are created by the VBA and Access type libraries when launched. Of these seven, you can use **True**, **False**, and **Null**, which are declared by the VBA library, in Access VBA code. The remaining four are declared by the Access type library and are valid for use with all database objects except modules. When the system-defined constants **True**, **False**, and **Null** are used in Access VBA code examples in this book, they appear in bold, monospace type.

**Access Intrinsic Constants.** Access VBA provides a number of predeclared, intrinsic, symbolic constants that are primarily for use as arguments of DoCmd.*Action* statements. These statements let you execute standard database actions in Access VBA (such as opening forms, printing reports, applying sorts or filters, and so on). Access 97 intrinsic constants carry the prefix ac, as in acExportMerge. You can display the list of Access intrinsic constants in the Object Browser by selecting Access in the Project/Library list and then selecting Constants in the Classes list.

When you select a constant in the Members of list, its numeric value appears at the bottom of the Object Browser window (see Figure 28.7). A good programming practice is to use constants rather than their numeric values when applicable. You may not use any of these intrinsic constants' names as names for constants or variables that you define.

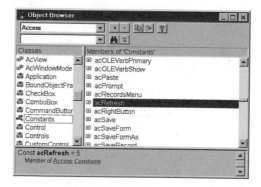

**FIG. 28.7** Displaying Access 97 intrinsic constants in the Object Browser.

> **Note**
>
> In Access 2.0 and earlier versions, intrinsic constants were classified as action constants (pre-fixed with A_), database constants (prefixed with DB_), and the Variant data type constants (prefixed with V_). In Access 97, each object library contributes its own set of intrinsic constants, prefixed with db for Jet 3.5 DAO constants and with vb for VBA constants. If you convert an Access 2.0 or earlier application to Access 97, the prior constant names are valid. These prior constants appear when you select OldConstants in the Classes list.

### Access VBA Named and Optional Arguments

Procedures often have one or more arguments that pass values from the calling state-ment to the called procedure. Traditionally, you must pass all of the values required by the procedure in your calling statement. As an example, if a procedure accepts four argu-ments, *Arg1...Arg4*, your calling statement must provide values for Arg1...Arg4, as in the following example:

```
Sub CallingProc()
    ...
    Call CalledProc(100000, 200000, 300000, 400000)
    ...
End Sub

Sub CalledProc(Arg1 As Long, Arg2 As Long, Arg3 As Long, _
               Arg4 As Long)
    [Subprocedure code]
End Sub
```

Access 97 lets you declare the arguments of the subprocedure to be **Optional**, eliminating the need to pass every parameter to the procedure. You use *named arguments* to pass val-ues to specific arguments, as in the following example:

```
Sub CallingProc()
    ...
    Call CalledProc(Arg2:=200000, Arg3:=300000)
    ...
End Sub

Sub CalledProc(Optional Arg1, Optional Arg2, Optional Arg3, _
               Optional Arg4)
    [Subprocedure code]
End Sub
```

The **:=** operator specifies that the preceding element is the name of an argument; named arguments need not be entered in the order that the arguments appear in the called pro-cedure. However, if you want to omit an argument or arguments, the corresponding argument name(s) of the called procedure must be preceded by the keyword **Optional**. Optional arguments must be of the **Variant** data type, and missing arguments return **Null** values to subprocedure code. If you omit the **As** *Datatype* modifier of an argument in the called procedure, the argument assumes the default **Variant** data type.

# Controlling Program Flow

Useful procedures must be able to make decisions based on the values of variables and then take specified actions based on those decisions. Blocks of code, for example, may need to be repeated until a specified condition occurs. Statements used to make decisions and repeat blocks of code are the fundamental elements that control program flow in Access VBA and all other programming languages.

All programming languages require methods of executing different algorithms based on the results of one or more comparison operations. You can control the flow of any program in any programming language with just three types of statements: conditional execution (**If...Then...End If**), repetition (**Do While...Loop** and related structures), and termination (**End...**). The additional flow control statements in Access VBA and other programming languages make writing code more straightforward.

The code examples used in the following sections do not include **Dim** statements, so Hungarian notation is not used here. Data type identification symbols are used for brevity to indicate the data types of variables.

### Branching and Labels

If you have written DOS batch files or WordPerfect macros, you are probably acquainted with branching and labels. Both the DOS batch language and the WordPerfect macro language include the **GoTo** *Label* command. DOS defines any word that begins a line with a colon as a label; WordPerfect requires the use of the keyword LABEL and then the label name.

When BASIC was first developed, the only method of controlling program flow was through its GOTO *LineNumber* and GOSUB *LineNumber* statements. Every line in the program required a number that could be used as a substitute for a label. GOTO *LineNumber* caused the interpreter to skip to the designated line and continue executing the program from that point. GOSUB *LineNumber* caused the program to follow that same branch, but when the BASIC interpreter that executed the code encountered a RETURN statement, program execution jumped back to the line following the GOSUB statement and continued executing at that point.

◄◄  See "Assignment and Comparison Operators," p. 290

**Skipping Blocks of Code with *GoTo*.** Procedural BASIC introduced named labels that replaced the line numbers for GOTO and GOSUB statements. Access VBA's **GoTo** *Label* statement causes your code to branch to the location named *Label:* and continue from that point. Note the colon following *Label:*, which identifies the single word you assigned as a label. However, the colon is not required after the label name following the **GoTo**. In fact, if you add the colon, you get a Label not found error message.

A label name must begin in the far-left column (1) of your code. This positioning often interferes with the orderly indenting of your code (explained in the next section), which is just one more reason, in addition to those following, for not using GoTo.

**Avoiding Spaghetti Code by Not Using *GoTo*.** The sequence of statements in code that uses multiple **GoTo** statements is very difficult to follow. It is almost impossible to understand the flow of a large program written in line-numbered BASIC because of the jumps here and there in the code. Programs with multiple **GoTo** statements are derisively said to contain "spaghetti code."

The **GoTo** statement is required for only one purpose in Access VBA: to handle errors with the **On Error GoTo** *Label* statement. Although Access VBA supports BASIC's **ON...GOTO** and **ON...GOSUB** statements, using those statements is not considered good programming practice. You can eliminate all **GoTo** statements in form and report modules by using Access's **Error** event and DAO 3.5's new **Errors** collection. The **Error** event is described in the "Handling Run-time Errors" section later in this chapter, and the **Errors** collection is explained in Chapter 29, "Understanding the Data Access Object Class."

### Conditional Statements

A *conditional statement* executes the statements between its occurrence and the terminating statement if the result of the relational operator is true. Statements that consist of or require more than one statement for completion are called *structured statements*, *control structures*, or just *structures*.

**The *If...Then...End If* Structure.** The syntax of the primary conditional statement of procedural BASIC is as follows:

```
If Condition1% [= True] Then
    Statements to be executed if Condition1 is true
[Else[If Condition2%[ = True] Then]]
    Optional statements to be executed if Condition1%
    is false [and Condition2% is true]
End If
```

The **= True** elements of the preceding conditional statement are optional and typically not included when you write actual code. **If** *Condition1%* **Then** and **If** *Condition1%* **= True Then** produce the same result when *Condition1%* is **True**.

You can add a second condition with the **ElseIf** statement. The **ElseIf** condition must be true to execute the statements that are executed if *Condition1%* is false. Note that no space is used between **Else** and **If**. An **If...End If** structure that incorporates the **ElseIf** statement is the simplified equivalent of the following:

```
If Condition1% Then
    Statements to be executed if Expression1 is true
Else
    If Condition2% Then
        Statements to be executed if Condition1% is
        false and Condition2% is true]
    End If
End If
```

A statement is executed based on the evaluation of the immediately preceding expression. Expressions that include **If...End If** or other flow-control structures within other **If...End If** structures are said to be *nested*, as in the preceding example. The number, or depth, of `If...End If` structures that can be nested within one another is unlimited.

Note that the code between the individual keywords that make up the flow-control structure is indented. Indentation makes code within structures easier to read. You usually use the Tab key to create indentation.

To evaluate whether a character is a letter and to determine its case, you can use the following code:

```
If Asc(Char$) > 63 And Asc(Char$) < 91 Then
    CharType$ = "Uppercase Letter"
ElseIf Asc(Char$) > 96 And Asc(Char$) < 123 Then
    CharType$ = "Lowercase Letter"
End If
```

> **Note**
>
> You have seen a single-line version of the `If...End If` statement, `IIf()`, in the "Assignment and Comparison Operators" section of Chapter 9, "Understanding Operators and Expressions in Access." The single-line (also called *inline*) version in Access VBA, `If Condition% Then ...`, does not require the terminating `End If` statement. Although acceptable for simple statements, the use of the single-line version is questionable (not necessarily poor) programming practice, so this book avoids it.

You use the `If...End If` structure more often than any other flow control statement.

**The *Select Case...End Select* Construct.** When you must choose among many alternatives, `If...End If` structures can become very complex and deeply nested. The `Select Case...End Select` construct was added to procedural BASIC to overcome this complexity. In addition to testing whether an expression evaluates to true or false, `Select Case` can evaluate variables to determine whether those variables fall within specified ranges. The generalized syntax is in the following example:

```
Select Case VarName
    Case Expression1[, Expressions, ...]
        (Statements executed if the value of VarName
         = Expression1 or Expressions)
    [Case Expression2 To Expression3
        (Statements executed if the value of VarName
         is in the range of Expression2 to Expression3)]
    [Case Is RelationalExpression
        (Statements executed if the value of
         VarName = RelationalExpression)]
    [Case Else
        (Statements executed if none of the
         above cases is met)]
End Select
```

`Select Case` evaluates *VarName*, which can be a string, a numeric variable, or an expression. It then tests each `Case` expression in sequence. `Case` expressions can take one of the following four forms:

- A single value or list of values to which to compare the value of *VarName*. Successive members of the list are separated from their predecessors by commas.

- A range of values separated by the keyword **To**. The value of the first member of the range limits must be less than the value of the second. Each string is compared by the ASCII value of its first character.

- The keyword **Is** followed by a relational operator, such as <>, <, <=, =, >=, or >, and a variable or literal value.

- The keyword **Else**. Expressions following **Case Else** are executed if no prior **Case** condition is satisfied.

The **Case** statements are tested in sequence, and the code associated with the first matching **Case** condition is executed. If no match is found and the **Case Else** statement is present, the code following the statement is executed. Program execution then continues at the line of code following the **End Select** terminating statement.

If *VarName* is a numeric type, all expressions with which it is to be compared by **Case** are forced to the same data type.

The following example is of **Select Case** using a numeric variable, Sales#:

```
Select Case Sales#
    Case 10000 To 49999.99
        Class% = 1
    Case 50000 To 100000
        Class% = 2
    Case Is < 10000
        Class% = 0
    Case Else
        Class% = 3
End Select
```

Note that because Sales# is a double-precision real number, all of the comparison literals also are treated as double-precision (not the default, single-precision) real numbers for the purpose of comparison.

A more complex example that evaluates a single character follows:

```
Select Case Char$
    Case "A" To "Z"
        CharType$ = "Upper Case"
    Case "a" To "z"
        CharType$ = "Lower Case"
    Case "0" To "9"
        CharType$ = "Number"
    Case "!", "?", ".", ",", ";"
        CharType$ = "Punctuation"
    Case ""
        CharType$ = "Empty String"
    Case < 32
        CharType$ = "Special Character"
    Case Else
        CharType$ = "Unknown Character"
End Select
```

This example demonstrates that **Select Case**, when used with strings, evaluates the ASCII value of the first character of the string—either as the variable being tested or the expressions following **Case** statements. Thus, **Case < 32** is a valid test, although Char$ is a string variable.

### Repetitive Operations: Looping

In many instances, you must repeat an operation until a given condition is satisfied, whereupon the repetitions terminate. You may want to examine each character in a word, sentence, or document, or you may want to assign values to an array with many elements. Loops are used for these and many other purposes.

**Using the *For...Next* Statement.** Access VBA's **For...Next** statement allows you to repeat a block of code for a specified number of times, as shown in the following example:

```
For Counter% = StartValue% To EndValue% [Step Increment%]
    Statements to be executed
    [Conditional statement
    Exit For
    End of conditional statement]
Next [Counter%]
```

The block of statements between the **For** and **Next** keywords is executed (*EndValue%* - *StartValue%* + 1) / *Increment%* times. As an example, if *StartValue%* = 5, *EndValue%* = 10, and *Increment%* = 1, the execution of the statement block is repeated six times. You need not add the keyword **Step** in this case—the default increment is 1. Although **Integer** data types are shown, **Long** (integers) may be used. The use of real numbers (**Single** or **Double** data types) as values for counters and increments is possible but uncommon.

The dividend of the previous expression must always be a positive number if the execution of the internal statement block is to occur. If *EndValue%* is less than *StartValue%*, *Increment%* must be negative; otherwise, the **For...Next** statement is ignored by Access VBA.

The optional **Exit For** statement is provided so that you can prematurely terminate the loop using a surrounding **If...Then...End If** conditional statement. Changing the value of the counter variable within the loop itself to terminate its operation is discouraged as a dangerous programming practice. You might make a change that would cause an infinite loop.

---

**Note**

If you use a numeric variable for *Increment%* in a **For...Next** loop and the value of the variable becomes 0, the loop repeats indefinitely and locks up your computer, requiring you to reboot the application. (You can also sometimes halt an infinite loop by pressing the Esc key to interrupt code execution.) Make sure that your code traps any condition that could result in *Increment%* becoming 0.

---

The repetition of *Counter%* following the **Next** statement is optional but considered good programming practice—especially if you are using nested **For...Next** loops. Adding *Counter%* keeps you informed of which loop you are counting. If you try to use the same variable name for a counter of a nested **For...Next** loop, you receive an error message.

When the value of *Counter%* exceeds *EndValue%* or the **Exit For** statement is executed, execution proceeds to the line of code following **Next**.

**Using *For...Next* Loops to Assign Values to Array Elements.** One of the most common applications of the **For...Next** loop is to assign successive values to the elements of an array. If you have declared a 26-element array named Alphabet$( ), the following example assigns the capital letters *A* through *Z* to its elements:

```
For Letter% = 1 To 26
    Alphabet$(Letter%) = Chr$(Letter% + 63)
Next Letter%
```

The preceding example assigns 26 of the array's 27 elements if you used **Dim** Alphabet$(26) rather than **Dim** Alphabet$(1 To 26). 63 is added to Letter% because the ASCII value of the letter *A* is 64, and the initial value of Letter% is 1.

**Understanding the *Do While...Loop* and *Do Until...Loop*.** A more general form of the loop structure is **Do While...Loop**, which uses the following syntax:

```
Do While Condition% [= True]
    Statements to be executed
    [Conditional statement
    Exit Do
    End of conditional statement]
Loop
```

This loop structure executes the intervening statements only if *Condition%* equals **True** (**Not False**, a value other than 0) and continues to do so until *Condition%* becomes **False** (0) or the optional **Exit Do** statement is executed.

From the preceding syntax, the previous **For...Next** array assignment example can be duplicated by the following structure:

```
Letter% = 1
Do While Letter% <= 27
    Alphabet$(Letter%) = Chr$(Letter% + 63)
    Letter% = Letter% + 1
Loop
```

Another example of a **Do** loop is the **Do Until...Loop** structure, which loops as long as the condition is not satisfied, as in the following example:

```
Do Until Condition% <> True
    Statements to be executed
    [Conditional statement
    Exit Do
    End of conditional statement]
Loop
```

Access VBA also supports the `While...Wend` loop, which is identical to the `Do While...Loop` structure, but you cannot use the `Exit Do` statement within it. The `While...Wend` structure is provided for compatibility with earlier versions of BASIC and should be abandoned in favor of `Do {While|Until}...Loop` in Access VBA.

**Making Sure Statements in a Loop Occur at Least Once.** You may have observed that the statements within a `Do While...Loop` structure are never executed if `Condition%` is `Not True` when the structure is encountered in your application. You also can use a structure in which the conditional statement that causes loop termination is associated with the `Loop` statement. The syntax of this format is in the following example:

```
Do
     Statements to be executed
     [Conditional statement then
     Exit Do
     End of conditional statement]
Loop While Condition%[ = True]
```

A similar structure is available for `Do Until...Loop`:

```
Do
     Statements to be executed
     [Conditional statement
     Exit Do
     End of conditional statement]
Loop Until Condition%[ = False]
```

These structures ensure that the loop executes at least once *before* the condition is tested.

**Avoiding Infinite Loops.** You have already received warnings about infinite loops in the descriptions of each of the loop structures. If you create a *tight loop* (one with few statements between `Do` and `Loop`) that never terminates, executing the code causes Access VBA to appear to freeze. You cannot terminate operation; and you must use Ctrl+Alt+Delete to reboot, then relaunch Access VBA and correct the code.

These apparent infinite loops are often created intentionally with code such as the following:

```
Temp% = True
ExitLoop% = False
Do While Temp% [= True]
    Call TestProc(ExitLoop%)
    If ExitLoop%[ = True] Then
        Exit Do
    End If
Loop
```

The preceding example repeatedly calls the procedure TestProc, whose statements are executed, until ExitLoop% is set **True** by code in TestProc. You must make sure one way or another that ExitLoop% eventually becomes **True**, no matter what happens when the code in TestProc is executed.

**Note**

To avoid locking up Access VBA with tight infinite loops, include the **DoEvents** command in loops during the testing stage, as in the following example:

```
Do While Temp%[ = True]
    Call TestProc(ExitLoop%)
    If ExitLoop% Then
        Exit Do
    End If
    DoEvents
Loop
```

**DoEvents** tests the Windows environment to determine whether any other event messages, such as a mouse click, are pending. If so, **DoEvents** allows the messages to be processed and then continues at the next line of code. You can then remove **DoEvents** to speed up the loop after your testing verifies that infinite looping cannot occur. The **DoEvents** statement should not be required in production 32-bit VBA code because threaded applications, such as Access 97, take advantage of preemptive multitasking in Windows 95 and Windows NT. However, not all 32-bit Windows applications are threaded, so **DoEvents** is likely to remain in use for some time.

# Handling Run-Time Errors

No matter how thoroughly you test and debug your code, run-time errors appear eventually. Run-time errors are errors that occur when Access executes your code. Use the **On Error GoTo** instruction to control what happens in your application when a run-time error occurs. **On Error** is not a very sophisticated instruction, but it is your only choice for error processing in Access modules. You can branch to a label or ignore the error. The general syntax of **On Error...** follows:

```
On Error GoTo LabelName
On Error Resume Next
On Error GoTo 0
```

**On Error GoTo** *LabelName* branches to the portion of your code with the label *LabelName*:. *LabelName* must be a label; it cannot be the name of a procedure. The code following *LabelName*, however, can (and often does) include a procedure call to an error-handling procedure, such as ErrorProc, as in the following:

```
On Error GoTo ErrHandler
...
 [RepeatCode:
(Code using ErrProc to handle errors)]
...
GoTo SkipHandler
ErrHandler:
Call ErrorProc
[GoTo RepeatCode]
SkipHandler:
...
(Additional code)
```

In this example, the `On Error GoTo` instruction causes program flow to branch to the `ErrHandler` label that executes the error-handling procedure `ErrorProc`. Ordinarily, the error-handler code is located at the end of the procedure. If you have more than one error handler or if the error handler is in the middle of a group of instructions, you need to bypass it if the preceding code is error-free. Use the `GoTo` `SkipHandler` statement that bypasses `ErrHandler:` instructions. To repeat the code that generated the error after `ErrorProc` has completed its job, add a label such as `RepeatCode:` at the beginning of the repeated code, and then branch to the code in the `ErrHandler:` code. Alternatively, you can add the keyword **Resume** at the end of your code to resume processing at the line that created the error.

`On Error Resume Next` disregards the error and continues processing the succeeding instructions.

After an `On Error GoTo` statement executes, it remains in effect for all succeeding errors until another `On Error GoTo` instruction is encountered or error processing is explicitly turned off with the `On Error GoTo 0` form of the statement.

If you do not trap errors with an `On Error GoTo` statement or if you have turned error trapping off with `On Error GoTo 0`, a dialog with the appropriate error message appears when a run-time error is encountered.

If you do not provide at least one error-handling routine in your Access VBA code for run-time applications, your application quits abruptly when the error occurs.

### Detecting the Type of Error with the *Err* Function

The **Err** function (no arguments) returns an integer representing the code of the last error or returns 0 if no error occurs. This function is ordinarily used within a **Select Case** structure to determine the action to take in the error handler based on the type of error incurred. Use the **Error$()** function to return the text name of the error number specified as its argument, as in the following example:

```
ErrorName$ = Error$(Err)
Select Case Err
    Case 58 To 76
        Call FileError 'procedure for handling file errors
    Case 281 To 297
        Call DDEError 'procedure for handling DDE errors
    Case 340 To 344
        Call ArrayError 'procedure for control array errors
End Select
Err = 0
```

Some of the error codes returned by the **Err** function are listed in the Error Codes topic of the Access help file. Choose Help, Contents and Index to display the Help Topics dialog. Then type **Error Codes** in the text box of the Index page, and press Enter. Double-click Error Codes in the Topics Found dialog to display a help window with an abbreviated list of code numbers and their descriptions. Click the underlined description text to display a window that describes each error code in detail.

You can substitute the actual error-processing code for the **Call** instructions shown in the preceding example, but using individual procedures for error handling is the recommended approach. The **Err** *statement* is used to set the error code to a specific integer. This statement should be used to reset the error code to 0 after your error handler has completed its operation, as shown in the preceding example.

The **Error** statement is used to simulate an error so that you can test any error handlers you write. You can specify any of the valid integer error codes or create a user-defined error code by selecting an integer that is not included in the list. A user-defined error code returns User-defined error to **Error$()**.

### Using the *Error* Event in Form and Report Modules

Access includes an event, Error, that is triggered when an error occurs on a form or report. You can use an event-handling procedure in a form or report to process the error, or you can assign a generic error-handling function in an Access module to the Error event with an =ErrorHandler() entry in order to call the ErrorHandler() function.

When you invoke an error-handling function from the Error event, you need to use the **Err** function to detect the error that occurred and take corrective action, as described in the preceding section.

# Exploring the Module Window

You write Access VBA functions and procedures in the Module window. To display a Module window, click the Module tab of the Database window, and then double-click the name of the module you want to display. To open a new Access VBA module, click the New button. A Module code-editing window appears, as shown in Figure 28.8. This figure shows part of the IsItAReplica() function of the Startup module that is included in Access 97's Northwind.mdb example database. You choose the function or procedure to display from the procedures drop-down list at the upper-right portion of the Module window. The Module window incorporates a text editor, similar to Windows Notepad, in which you type your Access VBA code. Access VBA color-codes keywords and comments.

The Access VBA code in Figure 28.8 demonstrates two principles of writing code in any language: adding comments that explain the purpose of the statements and using indentation to make your code more readable. Comments in Access VBA are preceded with an apostrophe ('); alternatively, use the prefix **Rem** (for "remark" in earlier versions of BASIC) to indicate that the text on the line is a comment. **Rem** must be the first statement on a line (unless preceded by a colon that separates statements), but the apostrophe prefix can be used anywhere in your code.

Comments that precede the code identify the procedure, explain its purpose, and indicate the function or procedure that calls the code. If the function returns a value, a description of the returned value and its data type are included.

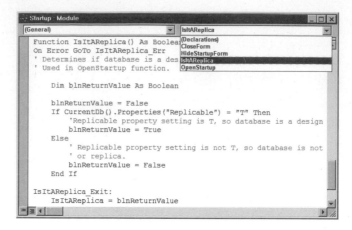

```
Startup : Module                                        _ □ ×
(General)                      ▼   IsItAReplica                    ▼
Function IsItAReplica() As Boolea  (Declarations)
On Error GoTo IsItAReplica_Err     CloseForm
' Determines if database is a des  HideStartupForm
' Used in OpenStartup function.    IsItAReplica
                                   OpenStartup
    Dim blnReturnValue As Boolean

    blnReturnValue = False
    If CurrentDb().Properties("Replicable") = "T" Then
        'Replicable property setting is T, so database is a design
        blnReturnValue = True
    Else
        ' Replicable property setting is not T, so database is not
        ' or replica.
        blnReturnValue = False
    End If

IsItAReplica_Exit:
    IsItAReplica = blnReturnValue
```

**FIG. 28.8**   Opening an Access VBA function in the Module window.

### The Toolbar of the Module Window

Table 28.3 lists the purpose of each item in the toolbar of the Module window and the menu commands and key combinations that you can substitute for toolbar components. Buttons marked with an asterisk (*) in the Items column are new with Access 97 or 95. Buttons whose design or name has changed but perform the same function in Access 97 as in Access 2.0 are not marked with an asterisk.

### Table 28.3   Elements of the Module Window's Toolbar

| Button | Item | Alternate Method | Purpose |
|--------|------|------------------|---------|
| Module | Insert Module* | Insert, Module | Creates a new, empty module. Click the down arrow next to this button to create a new class module or to insert a new procedure or function. |
| 💾 | Save | File, Save | Saves changes to the current module. |
| 🖨 | Print* | File, Print | Prints the content of the module as text. |
| ✂ | Cut | Edit, Cut | Cuts selected text from the module and places it on the Windows Clipboard. |
| 📋 | Copy | Edit, Copy | Copies selected text from the module and places it on the Windows Clipboard. |
| 📋 | Paste | Edit, Paste | Pastes the contents of the Window Clipboard into the module at the current position of the caret. |
| 🔍 | Find* | Edit, Find | Similar to the Find feature used in Table or Form view; allows you to search for a specific word or phrase in a module. |

| Button | Item | Alternate Method | Purpose |
|---|---|---|---|
| | Undo | Edit, Undo | Rescinds the last keyboard or mouse operation performed, if possible. |
| | Redo* | Edit, Redo | Rescinds the last undo operation, if possible. |
| | Go/Continue* | Run, Go/Continue or press F5 | Starts the execution of the current procedure, or continues executing a procedure after the execution of a procedure has been halted by a break condition or after use of the Single Step or Procedure Step button. |
| | End* | Run, End | Terminates execution of a procedure. |
| | Reset | Run, Reset or press Shift+F5 | Terminates execution of an Access VBA procedure and reinitializes all variables to their default values. |
| | Debug Window* | View, Debug Window | Opens the Debug Window. |
| | Object Browser | View, Object Browser | Opens the Object Browser dialog. |
| | Quick Watch* | Tools, Instant Watch or Shift+F9 | Adds a watch expression to the Debug window that causes a break in execution when the expression returns **True**. |
| | Call Stack | View, Call Stack | Displays the Calls dialog that lists all procedures called prior to reaching a breakpoint in your code. |
| | Compile Loaded Modules | Debug, Compile Loaded Modules | Creates pseudo-code (p-code) from the text version of all Access modules and all form and report modules currently open. |
| | Toggle Breakpoint | Debug, Toggle Breakpoint or press F9 | Toggles a breakpoint at the line of code in which the caret is located. Breakpoints are used to halt execution at a specific line. If a breakpoint is set, the Breakpoint button turns it off. |
| | Step Into | Debug, Step Into or press F8 | Moves through an Access VBA procedure one statement (line) at a time. |
| | Step Over | Debug, Step Over or press Shift+F8 | Moves through an Access VBA procedure one subprocedure at a time. |
| | Step Out* | Debug, Step Out or Ctrl+Shift+F8 | Executes the remaining statements in a VBA procedure or function at full speed, returning to single-step mode at the point after the current procedure or function was called. |
| | Database Window | Window, 1 | Opens the Database window. |

(continues)

| Button | Item | Alternate Method | Purpose |
|---|---|---|---|
| **Table 28.3 Continued** | | | |
| [?] | Office Assistant | Help, Microsoft Access Help | Starts the Office Assistant for help. |
| N/A | Object List* | None | Displays a list of objects in form or report modules. Only (General) appears for Access modules. |
| N/A | Procedure List | None | Displays a function or procedure in a module. Select the procedure or event name from the drop-down list. Procedures are listed in alphabetical order by name. |

### Module Shortcut Keys

Additional shortcut keys and key combinations listed in Table 28.4 can help you as you write and edit Access VBA code. Only the most commonly used shortcut keys are listed in Table 28.4.

| Key Combination | Purpose |
|---|---|
| **Table 28.4 Primary Key Combinations for Entering and Editing Access VBA Code** | |
| F3 | Finds next occurrence of a search string. |
| Shift+F3 | Finds previous occurrence of a search string. |
| F9 | Sets or clears a breakpoint on the current line. |
| Ctrl+Shift+F9 | Clears all breakpoints. |
| Tab | Indents a single line of code by four (default value) characters. |
| Tab with selected text | Indents multiple lines of selected code by four (default) characters. |
| Shift+Tab | Outdents a single line of code by four characters. |
| Shift+Tab with selected text | Outdents multiple lines of selected code by four characters. |
| Ctrl+Y | Deletes the line on which the caret is located. |

You can change the default indentation of four characters per tab stop by choosing Tools, Options. Click the Module tab and then enter the desired number of characters in the Tab Width text box.

### Menu Commands in the Module Window

Menu commands to perform operations not included in Table 28.3 are listed in Table 28.5. Menu commands that are common to other database objects, such as File, Save, are not included in the table.

**Table 28.5    Module Window Menu Commands**

| Menu | Commands | Purpose |
|------|----------|---------|
| File | Save As Text | Displays the Save Text dialog to save the module's code to a text file in ASCII format. |
|      | Replace | Replaces all or selected occurrences of the text entered in the Find text box with the text in the Replace text box. |
| View | Procedure Definition | If the caret is on a line that contains a procedure call, it finds and displays the called procedure. |
| Insert | File | Opens the Insert File dialog to allow insertion of code contained in a text file. |
| Debug | Run to Cursor | Continues execution until reaching the line above the position of the caret. |
|       | Set Next Statement | Sets the next statement to be executed, by passing other code. |
|       | Show Next Statement | Displays the next statement to be executed. |
|       | Clear All Breakpoints | Clears all breakpoints set in the module. Active only when breakpoint(s) are set. (See "Adding a Breakpoint to the IsLoaded() Function" in this chapter.) |
|       | Compile All Modules | Compiles all modules in the database. |
|       | Add Watch | Opens the Add Watch dialog to add a watchpoint. |
|       | Edit Watch | Opens the Edit Watch dialog to modify or delete a watchpoint. |
| Tools | ActiveX Controls | Opens the ActiveX Controls dialog to display a list of registered ActiveX Controls, and provides for the registration of new ActiveX Controls. |
|       | References | Opens the References dialog for adding or deleting references to objects exposed by libraries. |

### The Access VBA Help System

Microsoft provides an extensive, multilevel Help system to help you learn and use Access VBA. The majority of the help topics for Access VBA are supplied by a generic VBA help file that's applicable to all flavors of VBA. If you place the caret on a keyword or select a keyword and then press the F1 key, for example, a help window for the keyword appears. If you click the "Example" hotspot under the name of the keyword and an example that is specific to Access VBA is available, the Topics Found dialog appears to let you choose between the generic VBA and Access VBA example (see Figure 28.9). Double-clicking the topic with the (Microsoft Access) suffix displays the example that is specific to Access VBA (see Figure 28.10).

If you press F1 when the caret is not located on a keyword, the Help system displays an Ambiguous selection topic. Choosing Help, Contents and Index and then clicking the Contents tab displays a list of "books" that comprise the entire Access 97 Help system. To obtain additional information on VBA programming, double-click the Microsoft Access and Visual Basic for Applications Reference book. Then double-click the topic you want, such as Keywords by Task. Expanding the Keywords by Task item displays a list of chapters (represented by a "?" icon) that are devoted to specific programming subjects (see Figure 28.11). When you double-click the chapter icon, a keyword summary for the topic appears (see Figure 28.12). Clicking an underlined keyword hotspot displays the corresponding help topic.

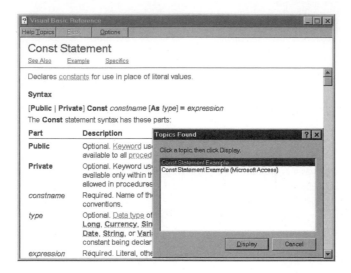

**FIG. 28.9**    A help window for the **Const** keyword with generic VBA and Access VBA examples available.

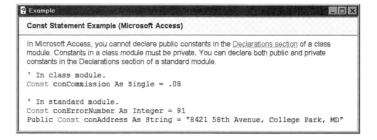

**FIG. 28.10**    The example that is specific to Access VBA for the **Const** keyword.

### The Access VBA Compiler

Programming languages, such as Pascal and C, use compilers. *Compilers* are applications that convert the code statements—*source code*—you write into instructions that the computer can understand—*object code*. These languages use punctuation symbols to identify where statements begin and end; Pascal, for example, uses a semicolon to tell the compiler that a statement is complete. Separating code into individual statements and determining which words in a statement are keywords is called *parsing the code*.

**FIG. 28.11** Help topics for VBA tasks beginning with the letters A through E.

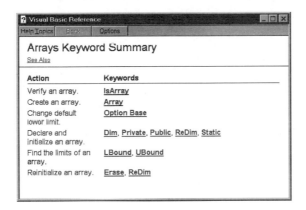

**FIG. 28.12** The Keyword Summary help topic for tasks related to arrays.

After you compile Pascal or C code, you link the code with *libraries* to create an *executable file*. *Libraries* are additional object code that perform standard operations, such as mathematical calculations. Access libraries, such as Utility.mda, have a similar purpose. An executable file for a Windows application has the extension .exe; you run executable files as independent applications. Compiling and linking an application, especially a Windows application, can be a complex process. Microsoft Visual C++, Professional Edition, for example, requires more than 60M for a typical installation. (A minimum installation consumes about 10M.)

Traditional BASIC languages, such as QBasic as well as the native dBASE and Paradox programming languages, employ interpreters to execute code. An *interpreter* is an application that reads each line of code, translates the code into instructions for your computer, and then tells the computer to execute these instructions. The interpreter parses code line by line, beginning with the first non-blank character on a line and ending with the newline pair, carriage return (CR, `Chr$(13)`), and line feed (LF, `Chr$(10)`). A newline pair is created by pressing the Enter key. Compilers for the dBASE language, such as the Borland dBASE compiler and CA-Clipper, also use the newline pair to indicate the end of a statement.

You must execute interpreted code within the application in which the code was created. You run QBasic code, for example, from QBasic—not as a stand-alone application. An interpreter's advantage is that it can test the statements you enter for proper syntax as you write them. Compiled languages don't issue error messages until you compile the source code to object code. Another advantage of interpreters is that you don't need to go through the process of compiling and linking the source code every time you make a change in the code. Unfortunately, interpreters usually execute code more slowly than the computer executes a compiled (.exe) application.

Access VBA combines the features of both a compiler and an interpreter. VBA interprets the code you write when you terminate a line with the Enter key. If possible, the VBA interpreter corrects your syntax; otherwise, you receive a syntax error message that usually is accompanied by a suggestion for correcting the mistake. Each line of code, therefore, usually contains a syntactically correct statement. (In some cases, you must run the "compiler" to interpret the source code.) Most languages, such as xBase and Paradox, allow you to continue a statement on another line; xBase, including Clipper, uses the semicolon for this purpose. Access VBA offers a statement continuation character: a space followed by an underscore.

After you write the source code, the VBA interpreter converts this code into a cross between interpreted and object code known as pseudo-code, or p-code. Pseudo-code runs faster than conventional interpreted code. Access compiles to p-code the code you write or modify the first time that the code is used in an application. Access discovers most errors not caught during entry as the code compiles. You can choose Run, Compile All Modules to force the VBA interpreter to compile all of the code in Access modules and in form/report modules. Forcing compilation before running the code—especially if the form or macro that executes the code takes a long time to load—can save substantial time during development.

# Examining the Utility Functions Module

One recommended way to learn a new programming language is to examine simple examples of code and analyze the statements used in the example.

The sections that follow show how to open a module, display a function in the Module window, add a breakpoint to the code, and then use the Debug window to execute the function.

### Adding a Breakpoint to the *IsLoaded()* Function

When you examine the execution of Access VBA code written by others, and when you debug your own application, breakpoints are very useful. This section explains how to add a breakpoint to the IsLoaded() function so that the Suppliers form stops executing when the Suppliers macro calls the IsLoaded() function and Access displays the code in the Module window.

To add a breakpoint to the IsLoaded() function, follow these steps:

1. Display the Database window, click the Modules tab, select the Utility Functions module, and then click Design to make the Module window active.

2. Place the caret on the line that begins with If SysCmd(acSysCmdGetObjectState,...).

3. Click the Breakpoint button of the toolbar, choose Run, Toggle Breakpoint, or press F9. The breakpoint you create is indicated by changing the display of the line to reverse red and by the placement of a red dot in the margin indicator at the left of the window (see Figure 28.13).

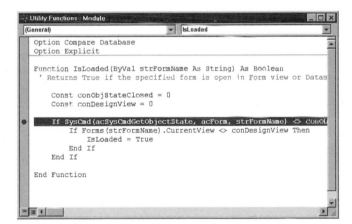

**FIG. 28.13**   The IsLoaded() function with a breakpoint set.

4. Close the Utility Functions module and open the Suppliers form to execute the Form_Open procedure attached to the On Open event of the form. When the Suppliers form's Form_Open procedure calls the IsLoaded() function, the execution of IsLoaded() begins with the Const conObjStateClosed = 0 line and halts at the line with the breakpoint. When execution encounters a breakpoint, the module containing the breakpoint opens automatically. The line with the breakpoint is enclosed in a highlighted rectangle (see Figure 28.14).

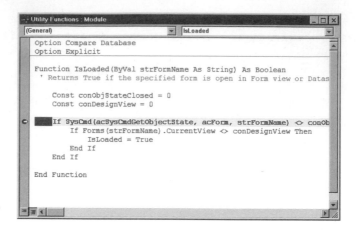

```
Utility Functions : Module
(General)                                    IsLoaded
Option Compare Database
Option Explicit

Function IsLoaded(ByVal strFormName As String) As Boolean
    ' Returns True if the specified form is open in Form view or Datas

    Const conObjStateClosed = 0
    Const conDesignView = 0

    If SysCmd(acSysCmdGetObjectState, acForm, strFormName) <> conOb
        If Forms(strFormName).CurrentView <> conDesignView Then
            IsLoaded = True
        End If
    End If

End Function
```

**FIG. 28.14**   The `IsLoaded()` function when the breakpoint is reached and the Utility Functions module opens.

5.  Click the Go/Continue button to resume execution of the VBA code. Access displays the Suppliers form.

6.  Close the Suppliers form to execute the `Form_Close` procedure that is attached to the form's `On Close` event. When the Suppliers form's `Form_Close` procedure calls the `IsLoaded()` function, execution occurs as described in step 4, and the `IsLoaded()` function again halts at the line with the breakpoint.

The element of the Forms collection to be tested is specified by `strFormName`. Access's `SysCmd()` function tests the `Forms` collection for the value of `strFormName` with the `SysCmd(acSysCmdGetObjectState, acForm, strFormName)` statement. If the specified form is open in either Form or Design view, `SysCmd()` returns **True**. The second test checks the value of the `CurrentView` property of the form to see whether the form is open in Form view. If the result of the `CurrentView` comparison is **True**, the `IsLoaded = True` line executes and the `IsLoaded()` function returns **True** to the calling procedure, in this case the Suppliers form's `Form_Open` procedure. (When `IsLoaded()` is called as the form is opened, it actually returns **False**, because the form isn't yet loaded.) The `IsLoaded()` function is called again by the Suppliers form's `Form_Close` procedure, which is attached to the `On Close` event. At this time, because the Suppliers form is loaded, the `IsLoaded()` function does return **True**.

### Using the Debug Window

In the "Using the Debug Window" section of Chapter 9, "Understanding Operators and Expressions in Access," you learned to use the Debug window to display the results of computations and values returned by functions. The Debug window also is useful when you want to display the value of variables when the breakpoint is encountered. To display the value of local (procedure-level) variables, the execution of your code must be halted at a breakpoint beyond the point at which the variables are assigned their values.

To open the Debug window and display the value of a variable while execution is halted at the breakpoint shown in Figure 28.14, and after completing step 6 of the preceding instructions, follow these steps:

1. Click the Debug Window button of the toolbar or choose <u>V</u>iew, Debug Window.

2. Click the Locals tab of the Debug window to display a split window. The upper portion of the Locals window displays the value of all constants and variables declared locally in the current function or procedure (see Figure 28.15).

3. Type **? strFormName** in the bottom window of the Locals page and then press Enter to display the value of the strFormName variable (see Figure 28.15). The ? symbol is shorthand for the reserved word Print. Using the ? symbol to print specific variable values or the results of test expressions in the Debug window can be a useful technique as you develop your code.

4. Click the Step Into button of the toolbar; choose <u>R</u>un, Single Step; or press F8 to continue the execution of the function, one line at a time. The **End If** statement is encountered. Press F8 again and execution moves to the **End Function** line. Press F8 again and execution proceeds to the **Sub** Form_Close procedure of the Suppliers form.

5. Press F5 twice to continue the execution of the code, closing the Suppliers form.

6. Choose <u>R</u>un, Clear <u>A</u>ll Breakpoints, or press Ctrl+Shift+F9 to toggle the breakpoint off.

When you write your own code, the Debug window is very handy for debugging purposes.

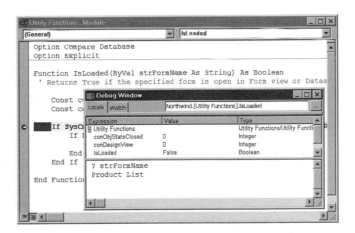

**FIG. 28.15**   Displaying a variable's value in the Debug window.

### Printing to the Debug Window with the *Debug* Object

When you need to view the values of several variables, you can use the **Debug** object to automate printing to the Debug window. If you add the **Debug** object to a function that tests the names of each open form, you can create a list in the Debug window of all the forms that are open.

To create a `WhatsLoaded()` function to list all open forms, follow these steps:

1. Load three or more forms by repeatedly opening the Database window, clicking the Form tab, and double-clicking a form icon. The Customers, Categories, Employees, and Main Switchboard forms are good choices because these forms load quickly.

2. Choose Module: Utility Functions from the Window menu and type **Sub WhatsLoaded()** below the End Function line of the `IsLoaded()` function. The Access VBA interpreter adds the **End Sub** statement for you automatically.

3. Type the following code between the **Sub...** and **End Sub** lines:

```
Dim intCtr As Integer
For intCtr = 0 To Forms.Count - 1
    Debug.Print Forms(intCtr).FormName
Next intCtr
```

The **For...Next** loop iterates the Forms collection. The **Debug.Print** statement prints the name of each open form in the Debug window.

> **Note**
>
> Access 97 contains a powerful new feature to help you write VBA code. The interpreter monitors each line of code as you type it in. When you type variable declarations, use built-in Access and VBA functions, or use object methods and properties in your code, the interpreter displays a popup window to help you select appropriate values. Figure 28.16 shows the popup list window that appears after you type the **As** keyword in the first **Dim** statement of the code you enter in step 3. For procedures, functions, and methods, the popup help window lists all of the arguments for the procedure, function, or method, so you don't have to remember all of the possible arguments. You can turn this feature on and off by choosing Tools, Options and then selecting or clearing the Auto Quick Info check box on the Module tab of the Options dialog.

4. Click the Debug Window button to open the Debug window. Type **WhatsLoaded** and press Enter. The name of each form is added to the Debug window by the `Debug.Print` statement (see Figure 28.17).

5. Close and don't save changes to the Utility Functions module. Then close the other forms that you opened for this example.

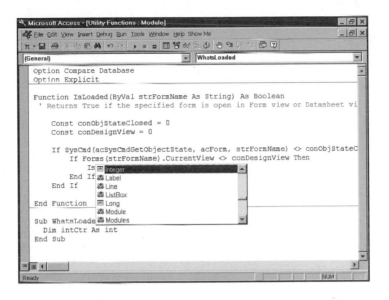

**FIG. 28.16**    The popup list of data types displayed as you enter the **Dim** statement.

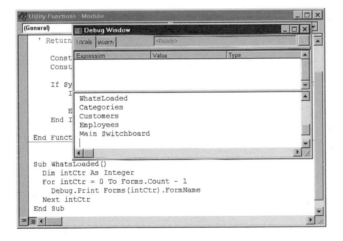

**FIG. 28.17**    The Debug object used to print values of variables to the Debug window.

The **Debug.Print** statement is particularly useful for displaying the values of variables that change when you execute a loop. When you have completed the testing of your procedure, you delete the **Debug** statements.

### Using Text Comparison Options

Tests of text data in fields of tables, query result sets, and Recordset objects against **String** or **Variant** text data in modules depends on the value of the **Option** Compare... statement, which appears in the Declarations section of the Utility Functions module.

To determine how text comparisons are made in the module, you can use any of the following statements:

- **Option** Compare Binary comparisons are case-sensitive. Lowercase letters are not equivalent to uppercase letters. To determine the sort order of characters, Access uses the character value assigned by the Windows ANSI character set.

- **Option** Compare Text comparisons are not case-sensitive. Lowercase letters are treated as the equivalent of uppercase letters. For most North American users, the sort order is the same as **Option** Compare Binary, ANSI. Unless you have a reason to specify a different comparison method, use **Option** Compare Text.

- **Option** Compare Database comparisons are case-sensitive, and the sort order is that specified for the database.

**Option** Compare Binary is the default if you do not include an **Option** Compare... statement in the Declarations section of the module. However, Access adds **Option** Compare Database to the Declarations section when you create a new module, overriding the default. Binary and Database are keywords in Access VBA, but these words do not have the same meaning when used in the **Option** Compare... statement. For compatibility with changes in possible future releases of Access, you should not use Compare or Text as names of variables.

# Writing Your Own Functions and Procedures

You do not need to be an Access VBA expert to write a user-defined function. The information you learned about operators and expressions in Chapter 9, "Understanding Operators and Expressions in Access," as well as the introduction to Access VBA statements presented in this chapter, allow you to create UDFs that supplement Access VBA's repertoire of standard functions.

After you master user-defined functions, you can try your hand at writing procedures to be executed as the result of an event. Access VBA procedures offer flexibility in manipulating database and control objects but require more knowledge of programming techniques than is needed to create UDFs. This section describes how you write a simple user-defined function.

User-defined functions are required when you need a conditional statement that is more complex than that accommodated by the IIf() function. An example is a fixed set of quantity discounts that apply to all or a group of products. You can create a table of quantity discounts; however, a user-defined function that returns the discount is easier to implement and faster to execute.

For this example, the discounts are 50 percent for 1,000 or more of an item; 40 percent for 500 to 999; 30 percent for 100 to 499; 20 percent for 50 to 99; 10 percent for 10 to 49; and no discount for purchases of fewer than 10 items. Discount structures of this type lend themselves well to **Select Case...End Select** structures.

To create the user-defined function `sngDiscount()` that returns a fractional percentage discount based on the value of the argument, `intQuantity`, follow these steps:

1. Click the Modules button of the Database window, and double-click the Utility Functions module.

   [Modules]

2. Position the cursor on the line following the last `End Function` statement, and type **Function sngDiscount(intQuantity As Integer) As Single**. After you press Enter, Access adds the `End Function` statement. This process is quicker than choosing Insert, Procedure.

   The `sng` prefix of the function name indicates to users of the function that it will return a value of the **Single** data type. The **As Integer** modifier for the `intQuantity` argument specifies that the function treats `intQuantity` as an **Integer** data type. If you do not specify the data type, your function assigns the default **Variant** data type to `intQuantity`. The **As Single** keywords at the end of the line tell Access VBA that the function's result should be returned as a **Single** data type. Whereas the `sng` prefix gives users of the function a clue as to the data type returned by the function, the function will return a **Variant** data type unless you specify a data type.

   > **Tip**
   >
   > You don't need to enter the `Is` keyword because Access checks the syntax of each statement you write when you press Enter. If you omit the `Is` keyword, Access adds it for you.

3. Position the caret at the beginning of the blank line and press Tab. To establish the discount schedule, enter the following lines of code:

```
Select Case intQuantity
    Case Is >= 1000
        sngDiscount = 0.5
    Case Is >= 500
        sngDiscount = 0.4
    Case Is >= 100
        sngDiscount = 0.3
    Case Is >= 50
        sngDiscount = 0.2
    Case Is >= 10
        sngDiscount = 0.1
    Case Else
        sngDiscount = 0
End Select
```

   Use the Tab key to duplicate the indentation illustrated in the preceding example. **Case** statements are executed from the first statement to the last, so quantities are entered in descending sequence. If sngQuantity = 552, the criterion is not met for **Case Is >= 1000**, so the next **Case** statement is tested. **Case Is >= 500** is satisfied, so sngDiscount receives the value 0.4 and execution proceeds directly to the **End Select** statement.

**4.** To make sure that the function is acceptable to Access VBA's compiler, click the Compile Loaded Modules button of the toolbar or choose <u>R</u>un, Compile Loa<u>d</u>ed Modules. Access converts the entries to a form that it can process. When you compile the code, Access indicates any errors that are not caught by line-by-line syntax checking.

**5.** You do not need to create a table or macro to test the function; the Debug window performs this task adequately for sample code. If the Debug window is not open, click the Debug Window button of the toolbar or choose <u>V</u>iew, <u>D</u>ebug Window.

**6.** Test the `sngDiscount()` function by entering **? sngDiscount(*Quantity*)** in the Debug window, and then press Enter. Substitute numeric values for *Quantity* (see Figure 28.18).

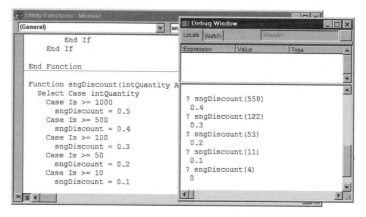

**FIG. 28.18**   Testing the `sngDiscount()` user-defined function.

**7.** To save the UDF, click the Save button of the toolbar or choose <u>F</u>ile, <u>S</u>ave.

You can employ user-defined functions in expressions to compute values for calculated fields, to validate data entry, to construct queries, and to fulfill other purposes where an expression can be used.

---

### Troubleshooting

*An `Expected Shared or identifier` message box appears when entering a `Dim VariableName As DataType` statement.*

You attempted to name a variable with a reserved word. For example, you receive the preceding error message if you attempt to create a **`Dim`** `Option` **`As Integer`** statement. **`Option`** is a VBA-reserved word. Change the name of the object, preferably using the data type tag prefix, as in `intOption`.

---

# Chapter 29

# Understanding the Data Access Object Class

Access VBA lets you create and manipulate databases, tables, and queries using the Jet 3.5 database engine. Access 97 also offers a new alternative to the full-feature Jet 3.5 engine: ODBCDirect which uses the Remote Data Object (RDO) version 2.0 for connecting to client/server databases. This chapter introduces you to the many data access object (DAO) classes of Jet 3.5 and explains how you can manipulate the DAOs with Access VBA code. The chapter also describes how to use ODBCDirect, which is accessible only with VBA code.

No *Data Access Object* exists, per se; the term refers to all collections of Access 95 objects. The structure of the hierarchy of DAO classes was, to a major extent, designed to conform to the requirements and recommendations of the Object Linking and Embedding (OLE) 2.1 specification. Jet 3.5 is a very large in-process (OLE) Automation server; thus, much of this chapter uses OLE 2.1 terminology. Microsoft has adopted ActiveX as the name for its family of lightweight OLE components, primarily directed to Internet applications. Jet 3.5, to say the least, is a heavyweight; according to Microsoft, the size and resource consumption of Jet 3.5 is similar to that of SQL Server 6.5.

> **Note**
>
> Microsoft announced in the fall of 1996 that it plans to introduce a version of SQL Server that runs under Windows 95. The announcement caused several PC trade publications to run stories predicting the demise of Access when SQL Server becomes easily accessible to desktop (and even laptop) database users. The future Windows 95 version of SQL Server is intended as a high-performance substitute for the Jet database engine, not as a replacement for Access.

## Understanding Objects and Object Collections

Access 97, like other members of the Office 97 productivity software suite, organizes programmable objects into a hierarchical structure of classes of objects. Two members of Access object classes that you have used extensively are Forms and Reports. You use these class names as identifiers, such as Forms!*FormName*. *PropertyName* and Reports!*ReportName*!*ControlName*.*PropertyName*, in expressions. In these expressions, Forms or Reports is the class name, and *FormName* or *ReportName* is the literal name of the member object of the class.

Groups of objects from the same class are called *object collections*. Forms is the collection of open Form objects, and Reports is the collection of open Report objects. Unopened objects do not appear in these collections. Collections are similar to arrays, except that collections consist of references (called *pointers*) to member objects. On the other hand, Access VBA arrays consist of elements with assigned values. Unlike arrays, collection members may appear or disappear without your intervention. As an example, the members of the Forms collection change as you open and close the Form objects of your application. Access 97 is also capable of creating user-defined collections with the **Dim** col*UserDefined* **As New** Collection statement. You then add user-defined objects to the collection by invoking the AddItem method of Collection objects.

### Naming Standards for Object Collections

To conform to OLE 2.x standards for creating programmable objects, collections are named by the English-language plural of the class name of objects contained in the collection. As an example, Microsoft Graph 7 (MSGraph7) has Axis objects; the collection of these objects is called the Axes collection. Collections have relatively few properties; the most common is Count, the current number of members in the collection. You use the Count property in the **For** intCtr = 0 **To** Forms.Count — 1...**Next** intCtr statement to iterate (enumerate) the Forms collection. To *enumerate* a collection usually means to test all (or a particular set of) collection members for values of a specified property.

Figure 29.1 shows the hierarchy of the data access objects in Access 97. The uppermost member of the hierarchy is the DBEngine object, representing the Jet database engine, which contains the Workspaces and Errors collections. The Workspaces collection contains Databases, Users, and Groups collections, plus the new Connections collection. Exposing a collection makes the members of the collection accessible to Access VBA code. As an example, the Errors collection contains one or more Error objects when an error is encountered by Jet 3.5. Notice that the Forms and Reports collections do not appear in Figure 29.1. The Forms and Reports collections, like the Scripts (macros) and Modules collections, are not DAOs. The Forms and Reports collections are defined by Access, not by Jet, and have two distinct identities:

- Forms and Reports collections, which contain only members of the Forms and Reports Containers collection that are currently open in your application.

- Documents collections, which consist of all saved forms and reports, together with modules and macros are members of the Containers collection. The primary use for Document objects is to set security permissions with Access VBA. Forms and Reports collections have a much larger repertoire of properties than their corresponding Document objects. (The DAO defines the Databases, Tables, and Relations documents that refer to saved databases, tables and queries, and relations, respectively.)

VII

Developing Access

In the case of Containers and Documents, Access departs from the OLE 2.x rules for naming collections. Documents are collections that are members of the Containers collection; no "Container" objects are in the collection. The list in the Database window enumerates the Name property of members of the class in the Documents collection that you select by clicking a tab. When you refer to Form and Report objects in expressions, you use the Forms and Reports collections, not the member of the Containers collection with the same name.

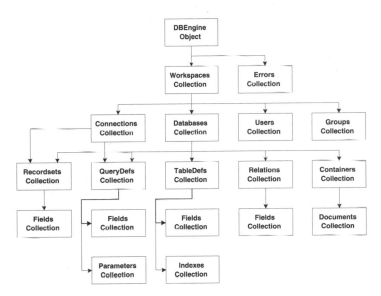

**FIG. 29.1** The hierarchy of Access 97's data access objects.

The Connections collection, which is new to Access 97, contains the set of open ODBCDirect Connection objects. A Connection object is a single ODBC connection to a client/server RDBMS, such as SQL Server, and occupies a position in the DAO hierarchy that is equivalent to the position of the Databases collection. A Connection object is similar to the RDO's rdoConnection object, so both ODBCDirect and the RDO are discussed in the section "Using ODBCDirect and the RDO" near the end of this chapter.

### Creating a Reference to the Data Access Object

VBA requires references to OLE objects that are exposed by components of OLE container applications. All flavors of VBA, including the Access, Excel, Project, and Visual Basic 5.0 versions, include references to application objects and to a common version of VBA. When you install Access 95, references are created automatically to the following four object libraries stored in various folders:

- Visual Basic for Applications (Vba332.dll, 32-bit VBA Version 5.0), which contains references to all of the commands and constants of VBA. The type library of this DLL is common to all members of Office 97 that support VBA. Vba332.dll is stored in the \Program Files\Common Files\Microsoft Shared\VBA folder.

- Microsoft Access 97 Object Library (Msacc8.olb), which contains references to all Access-specific objects, Access-only VBA commands (for example, `DoCmd`), and constants. Msacc8.olb is stored in the \Program Files\Microsoft Office\Office folder.

- Microsoft DAO 3.5 Object Library (Dao350.dll), which contains references to all of the objects exposed by the Jet 3.5 database engine. Dao350.dll is stored in the \Program Files\Common Files\Microsoft Shared\DAO folder.

- Microsoft Office 8.0 Object Library (Mso97.dll), which contains references to objects and constants that Access shares with other members of Office 97, primarily `CommandBar` objects and constants. Like Msacc8.olb, Mso97.dll is stored in the \Program Files\Microsoft Office\Office folder.

References to object libraries (.olb), object type libraries (.tlb), and OLE dynamic link libraries (.dll) appear in the References dialog shown in Figure 29.2. To open the References dialog, open the Utility Functions module of Northwind.mdb in Design view, and choose _T_ools, _R_eferences. The items that appear in the Available References list depend on the OLE-compliant applications and ActiveX controls installed on your computer. You cannot remove the references to or change the priority of Visual Basic for Applications or the Microsoft Access 8.0 Object Library. You can, however, click the check box for the Microsoft DAO 3.5 Object Library to remove references to the Jet 3.5 DAO. Removing the reference to Jet's DAO 3.5 doesn't unload the Jet database engine; most of Jet is required for Access 97 to run.

If you remove the DAO 3.5 reference, you cannot use data access objects in your VBA code. The references you establish with the References dialog apply only to VBA code, not to operations involving the Access user interface. You establish references to objects of other Automation servers and ActiveX controls to manipulate their Automation objects with VBA code, the subject of Chapter 31, "Exchanging Data with Automation and ActiveX Controls." All Automation client applications that use VBA as their application programming language have a References dialog similar to that of Access 97.

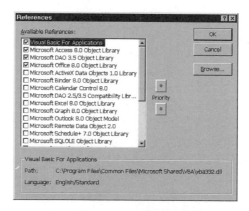

**FIG. 29.2**  Access 97's default VBA object references displayed by the References dialog.

> **Note**
>
> The Available References list of the References dialog also includes a reference for the 32-bit version of the Microsoft DAO 2.5/3.5 Compatibility Library (Dao2535.tlb). You can substitute Dao2535.tlb for Dao350.dll to preserve compatibility with Access Basic DAO code in Access 1.x and 2.0 applications that you convert to Access 95. You cannot add references to both Dao350.dll and Dao2535.dll; you receive an error message if you attempt to do so. To assure compatibility of your VBA code with future versions of Access, it is advisable to use the Dao350.dll reference and change your VBA code to comply with Access 97 VBA syntax for data access objects.

## Using the Object Browser

Access 97's upgraded Object Browser displays the objects exposed by OLE Automation servers to which references have been created, plus the properties and methods of the objects. To open Access 97's Object Browser dialog, press F2 and click the Object Browser button in the toolbar, or choose View, Object Browser. To choose the class of objects to view, open the upper drop-down list. You can select from the object classes supplied by the three references described in the preceding section, any additional references you have added, and objects in the current database (Northwind.mdb in this example). This chapter is devoted to data access objects, so select DAO.

The Object Browser is very useful for becoming acquainted with the names of objects exposed by the Jet 3.5 DAO and the properties and methods of data access objects. When you select an object or collection in the Classes list and a member function of the object or collection in the Members of '*ClassName*' list, the syntax for the method or property appears in a pane below the lists. Figure 29.3 shows the Object Browser displaying the syntax for the `OpenRecordset` method of the `Database` object. All members of Office 97 use the same Object Browser.

**FIG. 29.3**  Object Browser displaying the syntax for the `OpenRecordset` method of the `Database` object.

Clicking the ? button of the toolbar displays the help topic for the method or property—in this case for the OpenRecordset method (see Figure 29.4). You can type a word for which to search in the lower combo list of the Object Browser, and then click the Search and Search List buttons to display a list of objects, methods, and properties where the word appears. Figure 29.5 shows part of the result for a search on "Recordset."

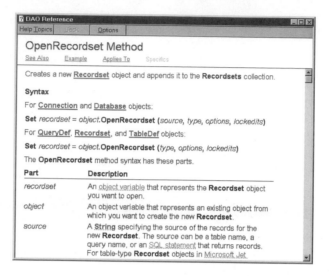

**FIG. 29.4**    The help topic for the OpenRecordset method opened by clicking the ? button of the Object Browser.

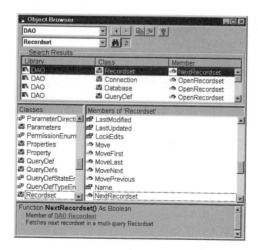

**FIG. 29.5**    Object Browser displaying part of the search result for "Recordset."

### Referring to Data Access Objects in VBA

Knowing the hierarchy of data access objects is critical to their manipulation by your Access VBA code. As an example, if you want to refer directly to a property value of the currently open database, you specify the full "path" through the hierarchy to your object and its properties or methods with an expression similar to the following:

```
strQDFName = DBEngine.Workspaces(0).Databases(0).QueryDefs(0).Name
```

The zeroth member of the Workspaces collection is the current Workspace object, also called the *current session* or *instance* of the Jet database engine. The current session comes into existence when you first launch Access. Similarly, Databases(0) specifies the database you open after launching Access, called the *current database*. QueryDefs(0) specifies the first QueryDef object of the QueryDefs collection. Name is a property of the QueryDef object. You can open additional Workspace objects and add one Database object or more to the newly created Workspace object with Access VBA code. Adding new members to DAO collections is described in the sections that follow.

---

**Note**

The currently open Database object, specified by DBEngine.Workspaces(0).Databases(0), is the same object identified by the CurrentDB() function in all versions of Access. Access 2.0 introduced Container(*i*) syntax, as in

**Set** dbCurrent = DBEngine.Workspaces(0).Databases(0)

The preferred statement in Access 97 to refer to the database opened in Access is

**Set** dbCurrent = CurrentDB()

that points to the instance of the current database. Using the CurrentDB() function is advisable to assure compatibility with future versions of Access. (See the "Creating Object Variables" section further in this chapter.) The CurrentDB() function (method) is a member function of the Access Application object, not the DAO. Thus, CurrentDB() is not applicable when using Visual Basic 5.0, Excel VBA, Word VBA, or Project VBA.

---

A Database object can contain TableDef, QueryDef, Recordset, and Relation objects, as well as Documents collections in the Containers collection. A brief description of each of these objects, except the Containers collection, follows:

- TableDef objects represent the definition of saved tables. TableDef objects contain Fields and Indexes collections, which contain one member for each field and index of the table represented by the TableDef object. TableDef objects have several properties, such as Name, RecordCount, and ValidationRule, that apply to the table as a whole. The Field and Index objects have their own sets of properties.

- QueryDef objects represent the definition of saved queries and contain Fields (which might better have been named Columns) and Parameters collections. QueryDef objects have properties, such as Name, SQL, and Updatable.

- Recordset objects, which have been mentioned throughout this book, represent virtual tables (images) that are stored in RAM. Recordset objects are said to be "created over" a table or a query result set. Recordset objects, which mimic the behavior of the underlying object, can be of the Table, Dynaset, or Snapshot type. As mentioned in earlier chapters of this book, the Table, Dynaset, and Snapshot object types appear in Access 97 for compatibility with Access 1.x code, but you must specify a reference to the Microsoft DAO 2.5/3.5 Compatibility Library to use these object types in VBA code. You should use Access 97's Recordset objects and the DAO 3.5 Object Library to assure compatibility with future versions of Access.

- Relation objects represent default relationships between fields of tables that, in most cases, you create in the Relationships window. Relation objects contain a Fields collection.

> **Note**
>
> If the size of a Recordset object exceeds the available RAM, the remainder of the object is placed in a temporary "spill file" in the \Windows\Temp folder.

Following are the three different methods of creating a reference to a member of a collection:

- The index method uses conventional array subscripts to specify a particular member of a collection by its position in the collection: CollectionName(i), where i ranges from 0 to CollectionName.Count − 1. Using the index to the object is the fastest method of referring to members of collections. The problem with the index method is that the index of a particular member object is likely to change as you open (add) and close (remove) objects in the collection.

- The argument method uses a literal identifier, either a quoted string or a variable holding the value of a literal identifier: CollectionName("ObjectName") or CollectionName(strObjectName). This method is preferred when you know the name of the member object.

- The literal method uses the bang operator to separate the literal name of the object from the collection name: CollectionName!ObjectName. If the literal name contains spaces or punctuation other than the underscore, enclose the literal in square brackets, as in CollectionName![Object Name]. This method is used primarily with Form and Report objects but is applicable to members of any collection. In this case, you can't use a variable in place of the member object's name. The literal method is the least flexible of the three.

### Properties of and Methods Applicable to DAOs

Most objects have a Properties collection that you can use to enumerate the properties of the object. You can read (get) the value of properties and set the value of most properties of an object in Run mode. The Debug window is a handy tool to experiment with getting and setting the values of properties as well as invoking methods. The example statements in this section use the Debug window syntax to print the value of properties.

The `? DBEngine.Workspaces(0).Properties.Count` statement returns 3, the number of `Workspace` object properties. You can obtain the name of a property with the `CollectionName(i).Properties(j).Name` statement, where `j = 0` to `CollectionName(i).Properties.Count — 1`. As an example, `? DBEngine.Workspaces(0).Properties(0)` returns the value of the `Name` property. `Name` is the zeroth (default) property of almost all DAOs. `? DBEngine.Workspaces(0).Properties(0)` returns `#DefaultWorkspace#`; `_Properties(1)` returns the value of `UserName`, admin for unsecure databases; and `_Properties(2)` returns the value of the `IsolateODBCTrans` property, 0 (False), as shown in Figure 29.6.

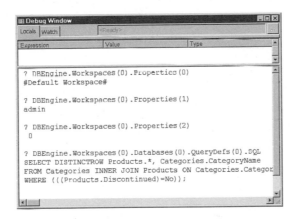

**FIG. 29.6** Using the Debug window to print the values of properties of data access objects.

---

**Note**

In Access 2.0, the `Workspaces` object had four properties. `DBEngine.Workspaces(0).Properties(2)` held the `Password` property of the user. This property was write-only; you could set this value but not read it. The `Password` property has been removed from the `Workspaces` object of Access 97.

---

To read or set property values of objects lower than `Workspaces` in the hierarchy, you should declare an object variable and then assign the object variable the object you want to manipulate from its collection. Creating object variables is the subject of the next section, "Creating Object Variables." Declaring an object variable for objects deep in the hierarchy improves the performance of your application by eliminating the need of VBA to parse the upper object layers.

You can apply methods to members of collections, such as applying `Append` to add a new member to a collection. The `Properties` collection is interesting in this respect: Access 2.0 and later versions allow you to append user-defined properties to the Properties collection. Some properties of objects are called *Access-defined properties*; you must append the Access-defined property to the collection in order for Access to assign the property a value.

> **Note**
>
> Publishing limitations preclude listing the properties and methods for each DAO. Use the Object Browser's ? button to display the online help topic for the object class (items only in the Classes/Modules list), as shown in Figure 29.7. You also can open the help topic for a specific member function (items in both the Classes/Modules and Methods/Properties lists), as illustrated by the preceding Figure 29.4. Using the Object Browser to open a help topic for a DAO is a much easier process than choosing Help, Microsoft Access Help Topics, selecting the Microsoft DAO book, and then attempting to find what you want in the book's table of contents.

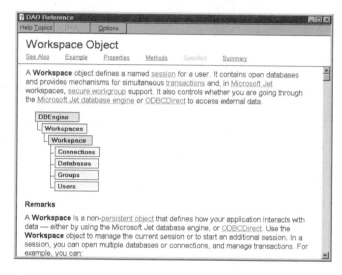

**FIG. 29.7**   The help topic for the Workspace object class.

## Creating Object Variables

It's a good programming practice to declare object variables to represent a specified object lower than Workspace objects in the DAO hierarchy. All object variables must be declared explicitly. Object variables are declared with **Private** *objName* **As** *ObjectType* statements in the Declarations section of a module to create an object variable with module-level scope or in a procedure to create a local object variable. Use the **Public** reserved word to create a variable with global scope in a VBA code module. **Private** and **Public** replace the **Dim** and **Global** reserved words of Access Basic, although you can continue to use **Dim** and **Global**. The following code creates an object variable, dbCurrent, that refers to the current database:

```
Private dbCurrent As Database
Set dbCurrent = CurrentDB()
```

The **Set** reserved word is used to assign values to variables of object data types. The value of the variable is a reference (pointer) to a block of memory in which the object is located. Thus, dbCurrent is said to point to the current database.

Once you've declared a Database variable, such as dbCurrent, you can use dbCurrent as a shorthand method of assigning pointers to the database objects. To refer to the TableDefs collection of the current database, which is a subclass of the Database object, use the following statements:

```
Private tdfCurrent As TableDef
Set tdfCurrent = dbCurrent.TableDefs("Categories")
```

As a general practice, you create a module-level variable of the Database type to point to the current database. If more than one module contains DAO manipulation code, substitute **Public** dbCurrent **As** Database for **Private** dbCurrent **As** Database. The subclass scope of your dbCurrent object depends on your use of the object subclasses in your code.

### Using Object Variables in the Debug Window

You cannot declare variables explicitly in the Debug window; thus, you need to declare object variables in the Declarations section of a module and then enter **Set** statements in the Debug window to assign object pointers to the variables. Figure 29.8 provides examples of declaring object variables at the module level and of assigning pointer values to the variables in the Debug window. Database objects contain one TableDef object for each table listed in the Database window, and each TableDef object contains one Field object for each field of the table.

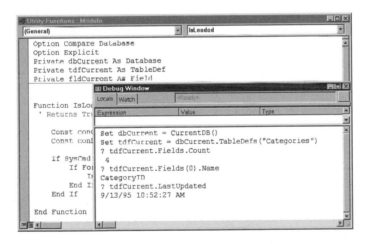

**FIG. 29.8**   Declaring and assigning values to object variables.

# Creating New Data Access Objects

As mentioned in the section "Creating Object Variables" earlier in this chapter, Access 97 lets you create new DAOs with Access VBA code. The most common DAOs you create with Access VBA are Recordset and QueryDef objects. QueryDef objects, like TableDef objects, are called *persistent objects* because QueryDef and TableDef objects also are Document objects: Query and Table objects, respectively. QueryDef and TableDef objects are stored as elements of your .mdb file and appear in the Queries and Tables lists, respectively, of the Database window. Recordset objects are impersistent objects; they exist in memory only from the time you open them until they are closed. You can close a Recordset object by applying the Close method; Recordset objects are closed automatically when the variable that points to them goes out of scope. When you close a Recordset object, the memory that the object consumes is released to your application.

> **Note**
>
> Using Access VBA to create new Workspace, Database, User, Group, TableDef, and Relation objects is beyond the scope of this book. You can create these objects, with the exception of the Workspace object, much easier with Access's user interface. You also can create new TableDef objects with make-table queries or by using Jet SQL Data Definition Language statements.

### Opening a New *Recordset* Object

You create a new Recordset object with the OpenRecordset method of Database, TableDef, and QueryDef objects. The general syntax of the OpenRecordset method has two forms:

```
Set rsdName = dbName.OpenRecordset(strSource[, intType[,_
    intOptions[, intLockEdits]]])
Set rsoName = objName.OpenRecordset([intType[, intOptions[, intLockEdits]]])
```

The first form, which is applicable only to Recordset objects created over Database objects, requires a value for the strSource argument. The value of the strSource argument can be the name of a TableDef object, or QueryDef object, or a Jet SQL statement. You also can use VBA's named arguments feature in the following statements:

```
Set rsdName = OpenRecordset(Name:=strSource[, Type:=intType[,_
    Options:=intOptions[, LockEdits:=intLockEdits]]])
Set rsoName = objName.OpenRecordset([Type:=intType[,_
    Options:=intOptions[, LockEdits:=intLockEdits]]])
```

Tables 29.1, 29.2, and 29.3 list values allowed for the intType, intOptions, and intLockEdits arguments for both of the preceding syntax examples. The values shown in the three tables are the names of predefined (intrinsic) global constants that are defined by the Jet 3.5 DAO. In earlier versions of Access, Access intrinsic global database constant names were uppercase and included underscore separators for readability, as in DB_OPEN_TABLE. Database intrinsic constants now are supplied by enumerations of the Jet 3.5 DAO and use the lowercase prefix db with intermediate capitalization to improve readability. A MethodArgumentEnum selection in the Class list of the Object Browser displays the names and values of applicable constants in the Members list (see Figure 29.9). In the case of the intOptions values listed in Table 29.2, you can combine the options you want with the VBA **Or** operator, as in dbDenyWrite **Or** dbDenyRead.

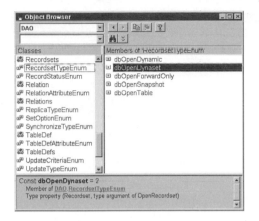

**FIG. 29.9** Some of the predefined (intrinsic) constants supplied by the Jet 3.5 DAO.

**Table 29.1   Values for the *intType* Argument of the *OpenRecordset* Method Comparing DAO 3.5 and Access 2.0 Intrinsic Constants**

| DAO 3.5 | Access 2.0 | Description of Type |
|---|---|---|
| dbOpenTable | DB_OPEN_TABLE | Table (default value for local TableDef source) |
| dbOpenDynaset | DB_OPEN_DYNASET | Dynaset (default value for Database, QueryDef, Recordset, or an attached TableDef) |
| dbOpenSnapshot | DB_OPEN_SNAPSHOT | Snapshot (not updatable) |
| dbOpenForwardOnly | Not defined | Similar to a Snapshot, but you can move only forward through the Recordset (default for ODBCDirect Recordset objects). |
| dbOpenDynamic | Not defined | Dynamic cursor (ODBCDirect Recordset objects only) |

**Table 29.2   Values for the *intOptions* Argument of the *OpenRecordset* Method Using DAO 3.5 and Access 2.0 Intrinsic Constants**

| DAO 3.5 | Access 2.0 | Purpose of Option |
|---|---|---|
| dbDenyWrite | DB_DENYWRITE | Prevents others from making changes to any records in the underlying table(s) while the Recordset is open. |
| dbDenyRead | DB_DENYREAD | Prevents others from reading any records in the underlying table while the Recordset is open. This option, which applies to Table-type Recordset objects only, should be used for administrative purposes only in a multiuser environment. |

(continues)

**Table 29.2   Continued**

| DAO 3.5 | Access 2.0 | Purpose of Option |
|---------|-----------|-------------------|
| dbReadOnly | DB_READONLY | Does not allow updates to records in the table. Read-only access increases the speed of some operations. |
| dbAppendOnly | DB_APPENDONLY | Allows appending only new records. (Applies to Dynaset-type Recordset objects only.) |
| dbInconsistent | DB_INCONSISTENT | You can update the one side of a one-to-many relationship. (Applies to Dynaset-type Recordset objects only.) |
| dbConsistent | DB_CONSISTENT | You cannot update the one side of a one-to-many relationship, the default. (Applies to Dynaset-type Recordset objects only.) |
| dbForwardOnly | DB_FORWARDSCROLL | Creates a Recordset object of the forward-scrolling-only Snapshot type. |
| dbSQLPassThrough | Not defined | Specifies a SQL pass-through query against an ODBC database using Jet; returns a Snapshot-type Recordset. |
| dbSeeChanges | Not defined | Generates a runtime error when the user attempts to change data that another user is currently editing (Dynaset-type Recordset only). |
| dbRunAsync | Not defined | Executes the query asynchronously, allowing the query to be canceled during execution (ODBCDirect only). |
| dbExecDirect | Not defined | Runs a query with no parameters directly, instead of creating a prepared statement (ODBCDirect only). |

**Table 29.3   Values for the *intLockEdits* Argument of the *OpenRecordset* Method of DAO 3.5**

| DAO 3.5 | Purpose of Option |
|---------|-------------------|
| dbReadOnly | Does not allow updates to the Recordset. |
| dbPessimistic | Uses pessimistic locking (locks the edited page during editing). |
| dbOptimistic | Uses optimistic locking (locks the edited page only when applying the edits). |
| dbOptimisticValue | Uses optimistic locking based on row values (ODBCDirect only). |
| dbOptimisticBatch | Uses optimistic locking for batch updates (ODBCDirect only). |

**Note**

There are many limitations on the use of constant values for the int*Options* and int*LockEdits* arguments of the OpenRecordset method. For instance, you receive an error if you use the dbReadOnly constant in both of these arguments. The "Remarks" section of the help topic for the OpenRecordset method explains the conflicts in detail.

The following two sections show how to create two different types of `Recordset` objects.

**A *Recordset* Object that Represents the Image of a Table.** You can create the following two types of `Recordset` objects over a table, both of which create a virtual table in memory:

- A `Recordset` object of the `Dynaset` type created from the current `Database` object. To open a `Dynaset`-type `Recordset` object over the Orders table, add the **Private** `rstCurrent` **As** `Recordset` variable declaration statement to the Declarations section of the module. Then use the following statement to assign the pointer, assuming that you have previously executed the **Set** `dbCurrent = CurrentDB()` statement:

    ```
    Set rsdCurrent = dbCurrent.OpenRecordset("Orders", dbOpenDynaset)
    ```

- A `Recordset` object of the `Table` type created from a `TableDef` object. To open a `Table Recordset` object over the Orders table, add the **Private** `tdfCurrent` **As** `TableDef` variable declaration statement to the Declarations section of the module. Then use the following statements to assign the pointers:

    ```
    Set tdfCurrent = dbCurrent.TableDefs("Orders")
    Set rstCurrent = tdfCurrent.OpenRecordset(dbOpenTable)
    ```

Figure 29.10 illustrates the creation of both of the preceding types of `Recordset` objects in the Debug window.

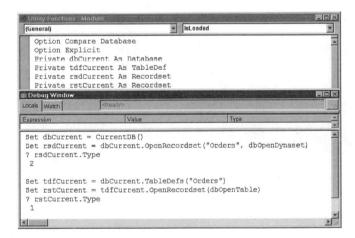

**FIG. 29.10**   Creating `Recordset` objects of the `Dynaset` and `Table` type in the Debug window.

**Moving to a Specific Record in a *Recordset* Object.** Opening a `Recordset` of the `Table` type lets you quickly find a record in a table with the `Seek` method. This method is applicable only to `Table`-type `Recordset` objects whose underlying table contains an index on the field in which the value you want to find is located. To apply the `Seek` method, you first must specify the index name. The following example sets the record pointer to the record in the Orders table of Northwind.mdb with a value of 10833 in the OrderID field, the primary key of the table:

```
Set dbCurrent = CurrentDB()
Set tdfCurrent = dbCurrent.TableDefs("Orders")
Set rstCurrent = tdfCurrent.OpenRecordset()
rstCurrent.Index = "PrimaryKey"
rstCurrent.Seek "=", 10833
If rstCurrent.NoMatch Then
    'Record not found, display message box
Else
    'Record found, add code to process the record here
End If
```

> **Note**
>
> You can't enter conditional statements in the Debug window, but you can test the preceding code by typing the entries up to and including the Seek line and then executing **?** **rstCurrent.NoMatch** to determine whether the Seek method was successful in finding a matching record. The NoMatch property uses the **Boolean** data type. If False is returned, the record pointer rests on the matching record.

If the field in which you are Seeking the value is not the primary key field, you specify the field's name. The NoMatch property returns False if the value specified by the Seek expression is found; it returns True if a matching record is not found. Figure 29.11 shows typical entries to test the Seek method in the Debug window. Test the Indexes collection of the TableDef object to verify that the index you specify exists. The Seek method allows the use of a variety of other operators, such as < or >=, in place of the = operator.

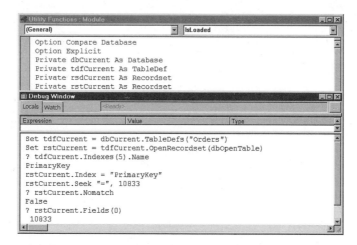

**FIG. 29.11**   Applying the Seek method to Recordset objects of the Table type.

> **Tip**
>
> You cannot apply the Find... methods to a forward-scrolling-only Recordset object of the Snapshot type. The only method applicable to such objects is MoveNext.

You use the Find... methods to locate a specific record in Recordset objects of the Dynaset and Snapshot type. There are four Find... methods: FindFirst, FindNext, FindLast, and FindPrevious. Not surprisingly, each method does what its name indicates. The general syntax of the Find... methods is

```
rsdName.Find{First|Next|Last|Previous} strCriteria
```

The single strCriteria argument of the Find... methods must be a valid SQL WHERE clause without the WHERE reserved word. As with the Seek method, the NoMatch property returns False if a match occurs. Figure 29.12 shows examples of the use of the four Find... methods.

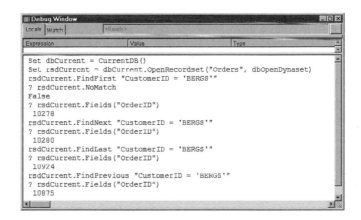

**FIG. 29.12** Applying the Find methods to Recordset objects of the Dynaset or Snapshot type.

**A *Recordset* that Emulates a *QueryDef* Object.** You can substitute a valid Jet SQL statement for a table or query name as the value of the strSource property to create a Recordset object of the Dynaset or Snapshot type. You only can create such a Recordset over the Database object because more than one TableDef object may participate in the query. Such a Recordset is the equivalent of an "impersistent QueryDef" object (a QueryDef object that is not a Document object). Figure 29.13 shows you how to create a Recordset object using a SQL statement in the Debug window. You must add a **Private** strSQL **As String** statement to the Declarations section of the module if the **Option** Explicit statement has been executed. The entire strSQL = _ statement is

```
strSQL = "SELECT * FROM Orders, [Order Details]
WHERE [Order Details].OrderID = Orders.OrderID
AND Orders.CustomerID = 'BERGS'"
```

If you need to manipulate a Recordset's records only temporarily, creating the "impersistent QueryDef" Recordset is faster than creating a legitimate, persistent QueryDef object.

**FIG. 29.13**    Creating a `Recordset` object with a Jet SQL statement.

### Defining a New *QueryDef* Object

You use the `CreateQueryDef` method to create a new, persistent `QueryDef` object and add it to the `QueryDefs` collection. One of the advantages of creating a `QueryDef` is that you can use the name you give the `QueryDef` in place of a table name in a Jet SQL statement. The name of the `QueryDef` must not duplicate the name of an existing `QueryDef` or `TableDef` object. The syntax for creating a new `QueryDef` object is

```
Set qdfName = dbName.CreateQueryDef(strName, strSQL)
```

> **Tip**
>
> You need to apply the `MoveLast` method before testing the value of the `RecordCount` property. If you omit the `MoveLast` method, you usually receive an erroneous `RecordCount` value (1). However, you can test whether any recorders were returned by testing with an **If** `rstName`. `RecordCount` **Then ... End If** structure.

`QueryDef` objects are what their object class name implies: the definition of a query. If `strSQL`'s SQL statement represents an action query, you apply the `Execute` method to the `QueryDef` object to execute the query. You must create a `Recordset` over `QueryDef` objects that define select queries in order to read values in the query result set. Figure 29.14 illustrates how you create a new `QueryDef` object and open a `Recordset` object based on the `QueryDef`. You need to add **Private** `qdfCurrent` **As** `QueryDef` to the Declarations section of your code before you can execute the code shown in the Debug window of Figure 29.14. When you execute a statement that includes the `CreateQueryDef()` method, the new `QueryDef` appears in the Queries page of the Database window. You can open a `QueryDef` created by Access VBA, as shown in Figure 29.15.

```
Set dbCurrent = CurrentDB()
strSQL = "SELECT * FROM Orders, [Order Details] WHERE [Order Details].
Set qdfCurrent = dbCurrent.CreateQueryDef("qryCurrent", strSQL)
Set rsdCurrent = dbCurrent.OpenRecordset("qryCurrent", dbOpenDynaset)
rsdCurrent.MoveLast
? rsdCurrent.RecordCount
 52
? rsdCurrent.Fields(1).Name
CustomerID
rsdCurrent.FindFirst "Orders.CustomerID = 'BERGS'"
? rsdCurrent.NoMatch
False
? rsdCurrent.Fields("Orders.OrderID")
 10280
? rsdCurrent.Fields(8)
Berglunds snabbköp
? rsdCurrent.Fields(9)
Berguvsvägen  8
```

**FIG. 29.14**  Creating a new `QueryDef` object and opening a `Recordset` over the `QueryDef`.

**FIG. 29.15**  Opening a new `QueryDef` object created with Access VBA code.

# Writing a Function that Uses Database Objects

All database objects that you can create and manipulate with Access's graphical develop-ment environment also can be created and manipulated with Access VBA code. You can use Access VBA to create a new table, to add records to the table, to define a query to select records from the table, to create a form to display the data, and then to print a report. In other words, you can use Access VBA to create an application exactly the same way you use the dBASE language or PAL. The purpose of Access's graphical development environment, however, is to minimize the need for code in applications.

The `nilTestQuery` function you write in the following example uses the `QueryDef` and `Database` object data types to create a query with a SQL statement and then displays that query in Datasheet view.

The `nilTestQuery` function contains a number of Access VBA reserved words that have been explained in the preceding sections of this chapter, but an example of one reserved word (`DoCmd`) has not yet been provided. Describing every Access VBA reserved word requires a book in itself, as you can see by the length of the Access VBA Language Reference if you have the Office Developer Edition. As you enter the keywords in this example, place the caret inside the keyword and press the F1 key to obtain a detailed explanation of the keyword and its use from Access VBA's Help system.

To create the `nilTestQuery` function, follow these steps:

**1.** Close any open module; then make the Database window active, click the Modules tab, and click the New button to create a new module.

**2.** You can accept the default `Option Compare Database` statement that Access adds to the Declarations section of a new module, or you can change the compare modifier to `Text` so that comparisons will not be case-sensitive. Add the `Option Explicit` statement to force explicit declaration of variables if you haven't specified Require Variable Declaration in the options for modules.

**3.** You need to declare and assign data types to the variables that the procedure uses. Below the **Option** `Explicit` statement, type the following statements to create object variables with module-level scope:

```
Private dbNWind As Database
Private qdfTest As QueryDef
```

**4.** To create the new procedure, type **Function nilTestQuery** below the preceding two statements. It's equally effective to create a subprocedure by typing **Sub TestQuery**.

**5.** You need to specify the database, in this case Northwind.mdb, that contains the table for the query. Type the following statement:

```
Set dbNWind = CurrentDB()
```

**6.** You cannot have two `QueryDef` objects of the same name, so you need to delete the `QueryDef` created by multiple executions of the procedure with the `Collection`.Delete method. Enter the following statements:

```
On Error Resume Next
dbNWind.QueryDefs.Delete "qryTest"
On Error GoTo 0
```

An error is generated if the `QueryDef` you attempt to delete doesn't exist; qryTest doesn't exist the first time you run the function, so an error occurs. The **On Error Resume Next** statement causes Access to disregard errors that occur in code below the statement. **On Error GoTo 0** resumes run-time error checking.

**7.** You need a variable to hold (point to) the definition of the query. Type the following:

```
Set qdfTest = dbNWind.CreateQueryDef("qryTest")
```

**8.** Now enter the SQL statement that you use to create and run the query. You can add the SQL statement as the optional second argument of the `CreateQueryDef` method instead of setting the value of its SQL property. Type the following:

```
qdfTest.SQL = "SELECT * FROM Suppliers WHERE SupplierID < 11;"
```

**9.** Execute the query and display the `Recordset` object created over the `QueryDef` in a datasheet. The Access action, `OpenQuery`, creates a `Recordset` and displays the rows of the `Recordset` in Datasheet view. You use the `DoCmd` object (a reserved word in Access) to execute actions in Access VBA. Enter the following statement:

```
DoCmd.OpenQuery "qryTest"
```

Your Module window appears, as shown in Figure 29.16.

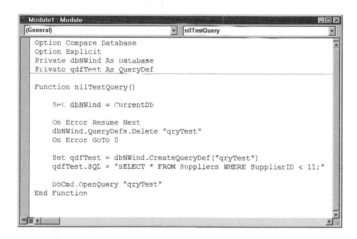

**FIG. 29.16**  Code for the `nilTestQuery` function.

**10.** Click the Compile Loaded Modules button of the toolbar or choose <u>D</u>ebug, Compile All <u>M</u>odules to verify the syntax of the Access VBA statements you entered.

**11.** Click the Save button of the toolbar, or choose <u>F</u>ile, <u>S</u>ave, and give the new module a name, such as `modTestQuery`.

**12.** Open the Debug window and delete any existing entries. Type **? nilTestQuery()**, press Enter, and then close the Debug window. Your query result set appears in the datasheet (see Figure 29.17).

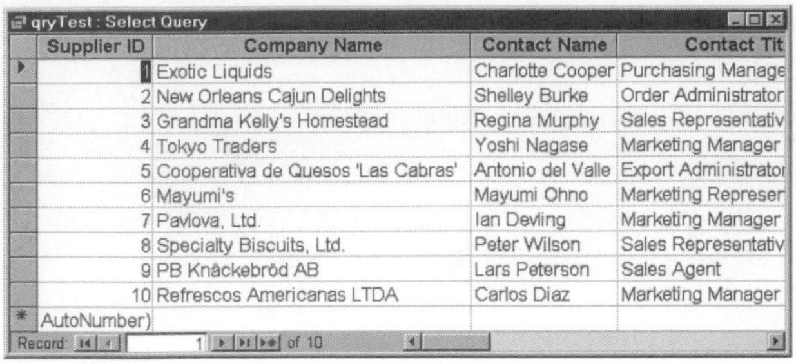

| Supplier ID | Company Name | Contact Name | Contact Tit |
|---|---|---|---|
| 1 | Exotic Liquids | Charlotte Cooper | Purchasing Manage |
| 2 | New Orleans Cajun Delights | Shelley Burke | Order Administrator |
| 3 | Grandma Kelly's Homestead | Regina Murphy | Sales Representativ |
| 4 | Tokyo Traders | Yoshi Nagase | Marketing Manager |
| 5 | Cooperativa de Quesos 'Las Cabras' | Antonio del Valle | Export Administrator |
| 6 | Mayumi's | Mayumi Ohno | Marketing Represen |
| 7 | Pavlova, Ltd. | Ian Devling | Marketing Manager |
| 8 | Specialty Biscuits, Ltd. | Peter Wilson | Sales Representativ |
| 9 | PB Knäckebröd AB | Lars Peterson | Sales Agent |
| 10 | Refrescos Americanas LTDA | Carlos Diaz | Marketing Manager |

**FIG. 29.17**   The Datasheet view of the query result set created by the `nilTestQuery` function.

# Using ODBCDirect and the Remote Data Object

ODBCDirect is a simplified interface to the RDO. Version 1.0 of the 32-bit (only) RDO was introduced with Visual Basic 4.0 and was included only in the Enterprise Edition. The objective of RDO was to provide a means of using ODBC to connect to client/server RDBMSs without incurring the overhead of the Jet database engine. RDO provides faster processing of SQL pass-through queries, especially for INSERT and UPDATE operations that involve many records.

In addition, the RDO provides flexible handling of cursors in RDBMSs that implement cursors in their ODBC driver. A *cursor* is a pointer to a row in a query result set, similar to Jet's record pointer. If the RDBMS supports server-side cursors, RDO lets VBA code in your Access 97 front-end manipulate the remote cursor. In situations that involve operations on large query result sets, server-side cursors improve performance and minimize network traffic. Figure 29.18 illustrates the collection hierarchy of the RDO. RDO substitutes the terms *columns* for *fields* and *rows* for *records*, in accordance with conventional RDBMS terminology.

◄◄ See "Using Access 97's SQL Pass-Through Queries," p. 940

Microsoft Office Professional Edition includes RDO 2.0 (Msrdo20.dll), which is required for ODBCDirect, but you can use RDO 2.0 only with ODBCDirect. If you set a reference to Microsoft Remote Data Object 2.0 and attempt to use RDO 2.0 with Access 97, you receive an `ActiveX component can't create object` error. Figure 29.19 compares the collection hierarchy of ODBCDirect and RDO 2.0. Visual Basic developers probably will use RDO 2.0, rather than ODBCDirect, because RDO 2.0 offers additional properties and methods for providing more flexible control of the ODBC connection.

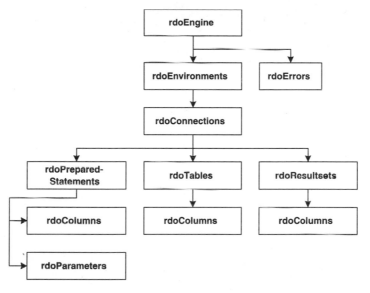

**FIG. 29.18**    The collection hierarchy of the RDO.

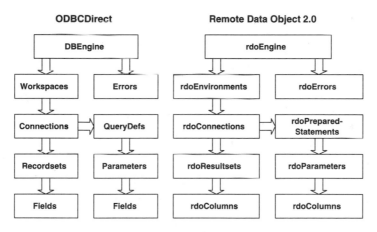

**FIG. 29.19**    A comparison of the collection hierarchy of ODBCDirect and the RDO.

Visual Basic provides the Remote Data Control (RDC) to bind controls, such as grids and combo boxes, to an rdoResultset. Unfortunately, you can't bind Recordsets or QueryDefs created by ODBCDirect or RDO 2.0 rdoResultsets to Access 97 forms, subforms, or controls. This binding limitation, which doesn't apply to QueryDefs generated by Jet SQL pass-through queries, greatly diminishes the utility of ODBCDirect and RDO 2.0 in Access applications. Thus, the two sections that follow provide only brief examples of the VBA syntax for ODBCDirect and the RDO.

> **Note**
>
> ODBCDirect and RDO 2.0 offer other advanced features for client/server front-ends, including *asynchronous queries* and input/output parameters for server *stored procedures*. Asynchronous queries let you continue to execute VBA code while the query executes; you also can terminate an asynchronous query before completion. Stored procedures are precompiled queries that reside on the RDBMS server. You can use Jet's SQL pass-through feature to execute stored procedures and send parameter values to stored procedures. ODBCDirect additionally lets you receive data in the form of output parameter values returned by a stored procedure.

### Experimenting with ODBCDirect

Creating a `Recordset` object from an ODBCDirect data source involves the following steps:

1. Declare object variables of the `Workspace`, `Connection`, and `Recordset` data type, as in

   ```
   Private wsDirect As Workspace
   Private conDirect As Connection
   Private rssDirect As Recordset
   ```

2. Apply the `CreateWorkspace` method to the `DBEngine` object with the `dbUseODBC` constant as the value of the `intType` argument. Specify your SQL Server logon ID and password as the values of the `strUserName` and `strPassword` arguments, as in

   ```
   Set wsDirect = DBEngine.CreateWorkspace("Direct", "sa", "", dbUseODBC)
   ```

3. Apply the `OpenConnection` method to the `Workspace` object with the name of your ODBC data source as the name of the connection and specify the `dbDriverNoPrompt` option to make the connection to the server without prompting, as in

   ```
   Set conDirect = wsDirect.OpenConnection("Nwind", dbDriverNoPrompt)
   ```

4. Apply the `OpenRecordset` method to the `Connection` object to create the `Recordset` object, as in

   ```
   Set rssDirect = conDirect.OpenRecordset("Customers")
   ```

The preceding steps eliminate the need to provide a connection string; ODBCDirect assembles the connection string from the logon ID (`"sa"`) and password (`""`) provided when creating the `Workspace` object, plus the name of the `Connection` object (`"Nwind"`). Your Nwind ODBC data source must specify a database name—nwind, in this example. Invalid entries for any of these three variables result in a run-time error when you use the `dbDriverNoPrompt` option. The default `Recordset` type is a forward-only cursor, which gives the best performance. The `RecordCount` property of a forward-only `Recordset` returns `True` (`-1`) for one or more records and `False` (`0`) if no records are returned. You are limited to the `MoveNext` method to traverse a forward-only `Recordset`.

> **Note**
>
> The online help topics for `CreateWorkspace` and `OpenConnection` provide the full syntax for these methods. Also provided are the names of intrinsic constants for setting the options of the `OpenConnection` method for specifying alternative cursors that let you create bi-directional and updatable `Recordset` objects.

Figure 29.20 illustrates use of the Debug window to experiment with objects based on the ODBCDirect feature of DAO 3.5. The `Connect` property of the `Connection` object returns a complete ODBC connection string, including the database name (`DATABASE=nwind`) obtained from the Nwind ODBC data source. You can use `Recordsets` created over ODBCDirect `Connections` as lookup tables and other operations that don't require binding to Access forms or controls.

**FIG. 29.20**  Using the Debug window to create an ODBCDirect `Workspace`, `Connection`, and `Recordset` object.

# Chapter 30

# Responding to Events with VBA 5.0

All Windows applications are *event-driven*; event-driven means that an event, such as a mouse click on a command button or a change in the position of a record pointer, executes individual blocks of application programming code. Thus the majority of the Access VBA code you write consists of event-handling subprocedures—also called *event procedures*—that are contained within [{**Public**¦**Private**}] **Sub** {Form¦Report}_[ObjectName_]EventName ... **End Sub** structures of *class modules*. Class module is the new VBA term that replaces Access 2.0's and Access 95's use of *code-behind-forms* (CBF) to describe Access Basic or Access VBA code within a Form or Report container. This chapter describes how to write Access VBA event-handling code in Form and Report class modules to automate your Access 97 applications.

Prior versions of Access emphasized the use of Access macros to respond to events. Microsoft promoted Access macros as a simplified programming language for users with little or no programming experience. The repertoire of approximately 40 Access macro actions proved adequate to automate relatively simple applications, and some very large commercial Access applications made extensive use of macros. One of the major drawbacks of Access macros, however, was the inability to handle errors gracefully. Thus, most Access developers abandoned macros in favor of Access 1.x and 2.0, Access Basic, and Access 95 VBA. Now that all of the principal members of Microsoft Office offer VBA, Access macros are on their way to oblivion. There's no guarantee that future versions of Access will continue to support Access macros. Thus, this chapter also shows you how to convert Access macros to VBA code.

## Understanding the Role of Class Modules

Class modules, which were introduced by Visual Basic 4.0, are containers for VBA code that relate to a particular class of objects. Access 97 defines two classes (collections)—Forms and Reports—that contain VBA code for a particular instance of the class: a Form or Report object, respectively. In object-oriented programming terms, class modules encapsulate VBA code within a

Form or Report object. Code encapsulation lets you create reusable objects. For example, when you copy a form from one Access database to another, the copy you make includes the code in the form's class module.

Access's Form and Report class modules differ from *conventional* modules in that a Form or Report object is integral to the code and contributes the object's properties (appearance). Conventional modules, such as Northwind.mdb's Utility Functions, appear in the Modules page of the Database window. Your event-handling code creates a custom set of methods (behavior) that are applicable to the object. When you open a form or report, you create the *default instance* of the corresponding Form or Report object. The default instance of the object appears in the Forms or Reports page of the Database window. VBA 5.0 also lets you create additional temporary, nondefault instances of Form and Report objects with the New reserved word. You need not add an explicit reference to the associated form or report in your code, although in certain expressions you use the Me self-reference to specify the current instance of the Form or Report object.

### Event-Handling Code in the Main Switchboard Form

The Northwind Traders Main Switchboard form is a good starting point for gaining an understanding of class modules and simple event-handling code. The Main Switchboard form contains two event-handling subprocedures: one each for the Display Database Window and Exit Microsoft Access command buttons, plus a single OpenForm function that services the Categories, Suppliers, Products, Orders, and Print Sales Reports command buttons. Figure 30.1 illustrates the relationships between the command buttons and the function or subprocedure that executes when you click the button.

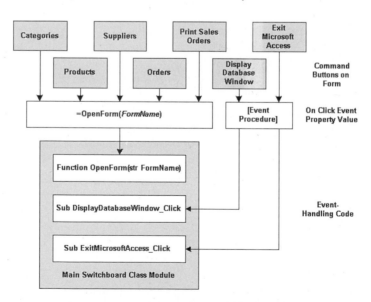

**FIG. 30.1**   Relationships between command buttons and event-handling code in the Main Switchboard form.

To view the event-handling code in the Main Switchboard form, follow these steps:

1. Open the Main Switchboard form in Design view.

2. Click the Code button of the toolbar to open the Class Module window, Form_Main Switchboard, for the Main Switchboard form. By default, the Class Module window opens with the Declarations section at the top of the window.

3. Open the left drop-down list, which Microsoft calls the Object box, to display a list of the control objects of the form, plus the Form object (see Figure 30.2).

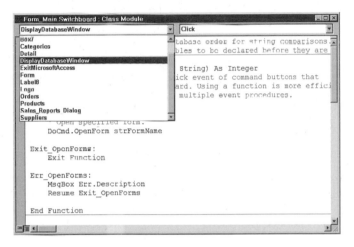

**FIG. 30.2**  Selecting a form control object in the Object list of the Class Module window.

4. Select one of the control buttons, such as DisplayDatabaseWindow, from the Object list to display the subprocedure—**Sub** Form_DisplayDatabaseWindow_Click—for the On Click event of the Display Database Window command button (see Figure 30.3).

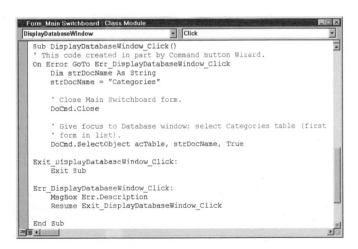

**FIG. 30.3**  VBA code for the Form_DisplayDatabaseWindow_Click event that opens the Database window with the Categories form selected.

5. Open the right drop-down list, which Microsoft calls the Procedure box, to display a list of events applicable to the selection in the Object box. The Click event appears in bold type because the `Form_DisplayDatabaseWindows_Click` event subprocedure contains VBA code. When you select an event, such as `DblClick`, without an existing subprocedure, Access creates a *subprocedure stub*. A procedure stub in a class module consists only of the **Private Sub** `Form_[ObjectName_]` `EventName`...**End Sub** entries (see Figure 30.4).

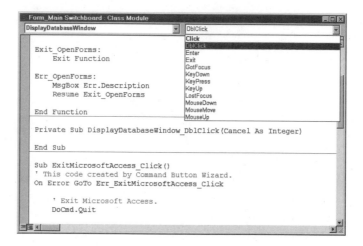

**FIG. 30.4**   A VBA subprocedure stub created by Access for the `DblClick` event.

---

**Note**

All VBA procedures have **Public** scope unless you specify otherwise; procedures that you declare with **Sub** or **Public Sub** are visible to all other class modules and conventional code modules. When you create a procedure stub in a class module, Access adds the **Private** modifier. **Private** subprocedures and functions have slightly less overhead than **Public** subprocedures and function and improve performance in large Access applications. The function and subprocedures of the Form_Main Switchboard class module are declared without the default **Private** modifier.

---

Listing 30.1 shows all of the code contained in the `Form_Main Switchboard` class module. Each of the procedures includes standard error-handling code consisting of **On Error GoTo** `Err_Lable`...**Resume** `Exit_Label`...**Exit** {**Function|Sub**} statements. Adding error-handling to every procedure you write is a generally accepted VBA programming practice. Adding standard error-handling code is one of the subjects of the "Converting Access Macros to VBA Code" section later in the chapter.

  ◀◀  See "Handling Run-Time Errors," p. 1005

**Listing 30.1  Event-Handling Code of the** `Form_Main Switchboard`
**Class Module**

```
Option Compare Database   'Use database order for string comparisons.
Option Explicit 'Requires variables to be declared before they are used.

Function OpenForms(strFormName As String) As Integer
'This function is used in the Click event of command buttons that
'open forms on the Main Switchboard. Using a function is more efficient
'than repeating the same code in multiple event procedures.
On Error GoTo Err_OpenForms

    'Open specified form.
    DoCmd.OpenForm strFormName

Exit_OpenForms:
    Exit Function

Err_OpenForms:
    MsgBox Err.Description
    Resume Exit_OpenForms
End Function

Sub ExitMicrosoftAccess_Click()
'This code created by Command Button Wizard.
On Error GoTo Err_ExitMicrosoftAccess_Click

    'Exit Microsoft Access.
    DoCmd.Quit

Exit_ExitMicrosoftAccess_Click:
    Exit Sub

Err_ExitMicrosoftAccess_Click:
    MsgBox Err.Description
    Resume Exit_ExitMicrosoftAccess_Click
End Sub

Sub DisplayDatabaseWindow_Click()
'This code created in part by Command Button Wizard.
On Error GoTo Err_DisplayDatabaseWindow_Click

    Dim strDocName As String
    strDocName = "Categories"

    'Close Main Switchboard form.
    DoCmd.Close

    'Give focus to Database window; select Categories table (first
    'form in list).
    DoCmd.SelectObject acTable, strDocName, True

Exit_DisplayDatabaseWindow_Click:
    Exit Sub
```

(continues)

**Listing 30.1  Continued**

```
Err_DisplayDatabaseWindow_Click:
    MsgBox Err.Description
    Resume Exit_DisplayDatabaseWindow_Click
End Sub
```

> **Note**
>
> The default Full Module view and Separator Bar settings of the Module page of the Options properties sheet make reading VBA code easier. All of the procedures in the class module appear after the Declarations section of the class module in the alphabetical order of the procedure name, separated by a horizontal gray line. With Full Module view specified, you can use the scroll bars to view all of the procedures within a module.

Access 97's DoCmd object, which replaces the **DoCmd** statement of Access 2.0 and earlier versions, is the key to manipulating Access application objects with Access VBA. The DoCmd statement of Access 1.x and 2.0 used the **DoCmd** *ActionName*[*Argument(s)*] syntax, where *ActionName* was one of approximately 40 predefined macro actions. Application-specific reserved words, such as **DoCmd**, preclude a common version of VBA for all members of Office plus Visual Basic; thus DoCmd is now an Access-specific object, not a reserved word. The macro actions of Access 2.0 and earlier are now called *methods of the DoCmd object*. When you convert an Access 2.0 or earlier database to Access 97, DoCmd.*MethodName* statements automatically replace **DoCmd** *ActionName* statements.

> **Note**
>
> The DoCmd.OpenForm *FormName* statement is the approximate equivalent of Visual Basic's *FormName*.Show [*intStyle*] statement. Access's OpenForm method, however, has several database-related optional arguments that aren't available with Visual Basic's Show method. Some correspondence takes place between Access's DoCmd methods, such as DoCmd.Beep, and Visual Basic statements (Beep). Architectural differences between Access and Visual Basic, however, preclude identical approaches to programming application-specific objects, such as forms.

**Examining Project Class Module Members in the Object Browser.** Each Form and Report object in the current database appears in the Classes list when you select the project name of the current database in the Project/Library (upper) drop-down list Object Browser (see Figure 30.5). By default, the project name for an Access database is the file name of the database without a file extension; thus the project name for Northwind.mdb is Northwind. The default <globals> object displays in the right-hand Members of '<globals>' list all of the procedures in conventional Access modules. These procedures also appear in Members of '*ModuleName*' entries for each module in the project.

> **Note**
>
> To launch the Object Browser, open a form in Design view, and click the Code button of the toolbar to display the class module for the form, then choose View, Object Browser, or press F2.

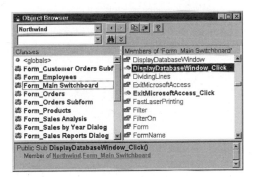

**FIG. 30.5**    The Object Browser displaying objects in the Northwind project (Northwind.mdb).

---

**Note**

You can change the project name of a database by typing a new name in the Project Name text box of the Advanced page of the Options properties sheet.

---

When you select a Form or Report object, items representing properties of the Form or Report object and each of the control objects added to the Form or Report object appear in the Members of '*ObjectName*' list. Each procedure also appears (in bold type) in the list. Figure 30.5 shows list items for the DisplayDatabaseWindow_Click and ExitMicrosoftAccess_Click event handlers. If you double-click a procedure item, the Class Module window displays the procedure's code.

---

**Note**

VBA 5.0 lets you define your own classes and write custom class modules. Custom class modules give you the opportunity to define a set of properties and methods for the object class you create. Custom class modules appear in Object Browser's Classes list, and the properties and methods you define appear in the Members of '*ObjectName*' list.

---

Attached add-in libraries, such as the Access Wizards (Wzmain80.mde and Wztool80. mde), appear in the Available References list of the References dialog. You can make objects of attached add-in libraries visible to the Object Browser by adding references to the libraries (see Figure 30.6). As an example, modules in Wzmain80.mde with the AF_ prefix implement the AutoFormat feature of Access 97 (see Figure 30.7). You can start an instance of the AutoFormat feature by typing **? af_Entry** (the entry point function) in the Debug window and pressing Enter. After clicking OK to bypass a few error messages, the AutoFormat dialog appears with an empty Module AutoFormats list. (Close the dialog by clicking the Cancel button.)

---

**Note**

To open the References dialog, open a form in Design view, and click the Code button of the toolbar to display the class module for the form, then choose Tools, References.

---

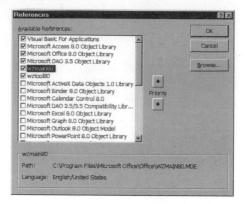

**FIG. 30.6**    Creating references to the Access Wizmain80.mde and Wiztool80.mde libraries.

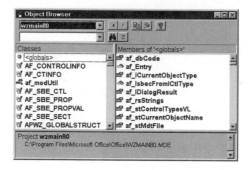

**FIG. 30.7**    Object Browser displaying conventional modules and members of the <globals> object of the Wzmain80 library.

**Adding Event-Handling Code with the Command Button Wizard.** Event-handling subprocedures represent the most common approach to handling events that are generated by control objects and Recordset objects bound to forms and reports. Command buttons are the most common control object to initiate user-generated events. The easiest way to create a simple VBA event-handling subprocedure is to add a command button to a form with the Command Button Wizard. The Command Button Wizard writes most or all of the code for the most commonly used Click event handlers.

To add a command button and its associated event-handling code for opening the Categories form, follow these steps:

1. Open Northwind.mdb, if necessary. Click the Forms tab, and then click the New button to open the New Form dialog.

2. Double-click Design View to open the form in Design view. Click the Toolbox button of the toolbar, if necessary, to display the Toolbox.

3. Make sure that the Control Wizard toggle button is depressed, then click the Command Button tool and add a small button on the form. The first dialog of the Command Button Wizard appears.

4. Select Form Operations in the Categories list and Open Form in the Actions list (see Figure 30.8). Selecting Form Operations displays a sample button with a small form icon. Click Next to continue.

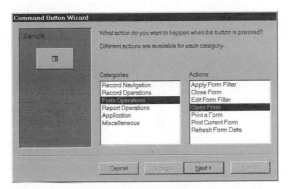

**FIG. 30.8**  Selecting the category and action for the command button in the first Command Button Wizard dialog.

5. Select Categories (or another form) in the What Form Would You Like To Open list (see Figure 30.9), and click Next to continue.

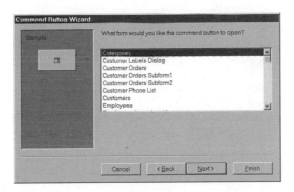

**FIG. 30.9**  Selecting the name of the form to open.

6. If the form to open is bound to a table or query, you can allow the form to display all records or add a filter to display only a single record based on the value of a field in your new form. For this example, select the Open the Form and Show All the Records option (see Figure 30.10), and click Next to continue.

7. You can select from a variety of bitmapped icons for the button by marking the Show All Pictures check box. Alternatively, select the Text option button and type a caption for the command button in the text box (see Figure 30.11). Click Next to continue.

8. Type a name for the command button, such as **cmdOpenCategories**, in the text box (see Figure 30.12). The cmd prefix is the naming convention for command buttons. Click Finish to add the event-handling code to the class module for the new form and close the last Command Button Wizard dialog.

VII

Developing Access

**9.** Click the Code button of the toolbar to display the class module for your new form. Figure 30.13 shows the subprocedure added to the module by the Control Wizard. Close the Class Module window to return to your new form in Design view.

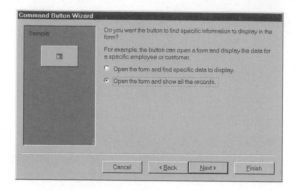

**FIG. 30.10** Selecting whether to apply a record filter or allow the opening form to display all records.

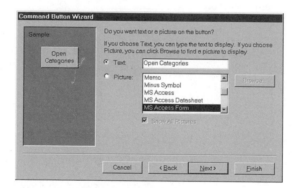

**FIG. 30.11** Adding a text caption to the command button.

The event-handling subprocedure you created in the preceding steps is bound to the On Click event of the cmdOpenCategories button. Select the command button, click the Properties button of the toolbar to display the properties sheet for the button, and click the event tab. The [Event Procedure] entry for the On Click event specifies the `cmdOpenCategories_Click` event handler. When you open the drop-down list for the On Click event, [Event Procedure] and the names of all of the macros, if any, in your database appear (see Figure 30.14).

> **Note**
>
>
>
> You can create a simple event-handling subprocedure stub for any event of an existing control by clicking the builder button for the event and then double-clicking the Code Builder item in the Choose Builder list. In this case, it's up to you to fill in the code to handle the event.

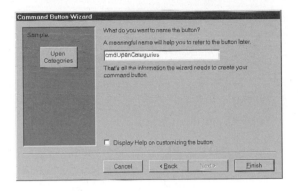

**FIG. 30.12**   Specifying the name of the command button.

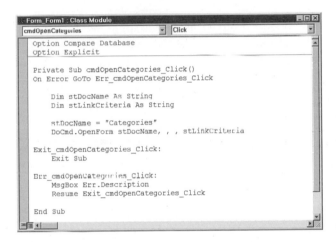

**FIG. 30.13**   The event-handling subprocedure for the Open Categories command button.

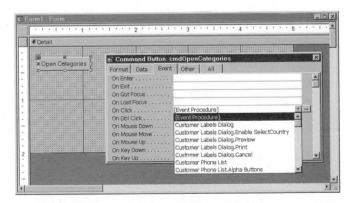

**FIG. 30.14**   Selecting between a subprocedure and an existing Access macro to handle an event.

**Using Functions to Respond to Events.** You can create your own Main Switchboard form by adding additional command buttons to the form in order to open other forms. It's much more efficient, however, to use a single procedure to perform a set of identical tasks in which only the name of the form changes. Minimizing the amount of code in a form speeds opening of the form and minimizes the size of your database file.

Access lets you call a function and pass one or more parameter (argument) values to the function in response to events. A function (not a subprocedure) is required, despite the fact that Access disregards the return value, if any, of the function. Control Wizards won't write the function code for you, nor will the Code Builder create a function stub. You must write the function yourself before calling it from an event. The OpenForms function in preceding Listing 30.1 is an example of using a function as an event handler.

You can easily change code written by the Command Button Wizard to a general-purpose function that opens any form whose name you pass as an argument. Figure 30.15 shows a simple modification of the cmdOpenCategories_Click subprocedure (refer to Figure 30.13), substituting a user-defined function for the event handler. When you substitute **Function** for **Sub** in the first line, the VBA interpreter automatically changes **Exit Sub** to **Exit Function** and **End Sub** to **End Function**. You change the name of the function, add the strFormName parameter, pass the strFormName parameter to the OpenForm action, and eliminate code that's not needed for the function.

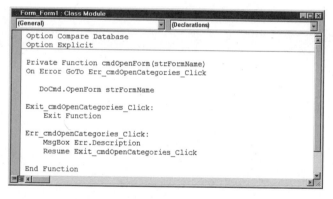

**FIG. 30.15**   A simple modification of the subprocedure in Figure 30.13 for creating an event-handling function.

---

**Note**

If you don't change the name of the subprocedure or pass the caret (insertion point) through the line containing the **Function** reserved word when converting from a subprocedure to a function, you receive a compile error. The VBA interpreter holds the existing subprocedure name in memory until the line is reinterpreted. Thus, creating a function of the same name results in a duplicate procedure name in the same class module if you simply press the Enter key when making the change. Duplicate procedure names aren't permitted within the same module, nor are duplicate names of **Public** procedures permitted within the same project.

---

| Focus | Data and Filter | Print | Error and Timing |
|---|---|---|---|
| GotFocus<br>LostFocus | Change | | |
| GotFocus<br>LostFocus | | | |
| GotFocus<br>LostFocus | | | |
| GotFocus<br>LostFocus | | | |
| GotFocus<br>LostFocus | Change<br>NotInList | | |
| GotFocus<br>LostFocus | | | |
| GotFocus<br>LostFocus | | | |
| Updated | | | |

(continues)

**Table 30.2   Continued**

| Object | Mouse | Keyboard | Window |
|--------|-------|----------|--------|
| Bound Object Frame | Click<br>DblClick<br>MouseDown<br>MouseUp<br>MouseMove | KeyDown<br>KeyUp<br>KeyPress<br>AfterUpdate | Enter<br>Exit<br>BeforeUpdate |
| Subform/<br>Subreport | Enter<br>Exit | | |
| Page Break | | | |
| Line Rectangle | Click<br>DblClick<br>MouseDown<br>MouseUp<br>MouseMove | | |
| Tab Control | Click<br>DblClick<br>MouseDown<br>MouseUp<br>MouseMove | KeyDown<br>KeyUp<br>KeyPress | Enter<br>Exit |
| Form Sections | Click<br>DblClick<br>MouseDown<br>MouseUp<br>MouseMove | | |
| Form | Click<br>DblClick<br>MouseDown<br>MouseUp<br>MouseMove<br>Activate<br>Deactivate<br>Current<br>Delete | KeyDown<br>KeyUp<br>KeyPress<br>Close<br>Resize<br>AfterInsert<br>BeforeDelConfirm<br>AfterDelConfirm | Open<br>Load<br>Unload<br>AfterUpdate<br>BeforeInsert |
| Report Page Header/Footer | Format<br>Print | | |
| Group Header/<br>Footer | Format<br>Print<br>Retreat | | |
| Report Detail section | Format<br>Print<br>Retreat | | |
| Report | Open<br>Close<br>Activate<br>Deactivate | NoData | |

| Focus | Data and Filter | Print | Error and Timing |
|-------|-----------------|-------|------------------|
| GotFocus<br>LostFocus | Updated | | |
| GotFocus<br>LostFocus | Change | | |
| GotFocus<br>LostFocus<br>BeforeUpdate | Filter<br>ApplyFilter | Error<br>Timer | |

Usually the corresponding event property is the event name preceded by the word On; for example, the Click event triggered by a command button becomes the On Click property in the button's property sheet. Figure 30.18 shows the Event page of the property sheet for a text box displaying the 15 events that the text box control can trigger. Notice that all event properties—except the Before Update and After Update data event properties—follow the pattern of preceding the event name with On.

**FIG. 30.18**    The event names that are applicable to a text box control.

# Working with Access 97's *DoCmd* Methods

Some of the DoCmd methods duplicate menu commands, such as Print, Close, and Apply Filter/Sort. Other methods substitute for mouse actions. For example, you can use the SelectObject method to select a database object in the same way that you select an open window by clicking it or select a database object in the Database window by clicking the object's name. Other DoCmd methods provide capabilities that are not available through menu commands, such as Beep, which emits a beep sound, or MsgBox, which displays a custom message.

Table 30.3 lists available DoCmd methods grouped by task. Access 2.0 provided 47 macro actions; Access 95 added two new DoCmd methods: Save and SetMenuItem. Access 97 replaces the DoMenuItem action or method with the RunCommand method, which lets you execute any native menu choice or standard toolbar button. The AddMenu item in the Method column of Table 30.3 is an Access 95 and earlier macro action; it is not a method of the DoCmd object and cannot be executed from Access VBA code.

| Table 30.3 | DoCmd Methods Grouped by Task | |
|---|---|---|
| **Category** | **Task** | **Method** |
| Manipulating | Copy or rename a database object. | CopyObject, Rename |
| | Delete a database object. | DeleteObject |
| | Open a table, query, form, report, or module. | OpenTable, OpenQuery, OpenForm, OpenReport, OpenModule |

| Category | Task | Method |
|----------|------|--------|
| | Close a database object. | Close |
| | Save a database object. | Save |
| | Print a database object. | Print, OpenForm, OpenQuery, OpenReport |
| | Select a database window object. | SelectObject |
| | Copy or rename an object. | CopyObject, Rename |
| | Update data or update the screen. | RepaintObject, Requery, ShowAllRecords |
| | Set the value of a field, control, or property. | SetValue |
| Executing | Carry out a menu command. | RunCommand |
| | Run a query. | OpenQuery, RunSQL |
| | Run a macro or a VBA procedure. | RunMacro, RunCode |
| | Run another Windows or DOS application. | RunApp |
| | Stop execution of a macro. | StopMacro, StopAllMacros |
| | Stop execution of Access. | Quit |
| | Stop execution following an event. | CancelEvent |
| Working with data in forms and reports | Select or sort records Find a record. | ApplyFilter FindRecord, FindNext |
| | Move to a particular location. | GoToControl, GoToRecord, GoToPage |
| Importing and exporting data | Output data from a table, query, form, report, or module in .xls, .rtf, or .txt formats. | OutputAs |
| | Include in an e-mail message data from a table, query, form, report, or module in .xls, .rtf, or .txt format. | SendObject |
| | Transfer data between Access and other data formats. | TransferDatabase, TransferSpreadsheet, TransferText |
| Miscellaneous | Create a custom menubar. | AddMenu, SetMenuItem |
| | Sound a beep. | Beep |
| | Display or hide a toolbar. | ShowToolbar |
| | Send keystrokes to Access or a Windows application. | SendKeys |

(continues)

| Table 30.3   DoCmd **Methods Grouped by Task** | | |
|---|---|---|
| **Category** | **Task** | **Method** |
| | Display an hourglass. | Hourglass |
| | Display or hide system information. | Echo, SetWarnings |
| | Display custom messages. | MsgBox |

> **Note**
>
> Methods applicable to macros—such as RunMacro, RunCode, StopMacro, and StopAllMacros—are obsolete in Access 97; these DoCmd methods are included for backward compatibility only.

### Arguments of *DoCmd* Methods

Most DoCmd methods require additional information as arguments to specify how the method works. For example, when you use the OpenForm method, you must specify the name of the form to open as the strFormName argument. Also, to specify whether you want to display the Form, Design, Print Preview, or Datasheet view, you must use the intView argument. To specify whether you want to allow editing or adding new records, you must use the intDataMode argument. Finally, to specify whether you want the form to be hidden, behave like a dialog, or be in normal mode, you must use the intWindowMode argument. You specify the values of arguments of the **Integer** data type by substituting Access intrinsic constants, which use the ac prefix, as in

```
DoCmd.OpenForm strFormName, acNormal, strFilterName, strCriterion, acEdit,
    acDialog, strOpenArg
```

The acNormal, acEdit, and acDialog argument values are Access intrinsic constant values for the intView, intDataMode, and intWindowMode arguments, respectively. You also can specify the numeric value of the constant, but there is no guarantee that the numeric values of Access constants will remain the same in future versions of Access. Thus using the names of Access intrinsic constants is a better programming practice than supplying numeric values for method arguments. Access 97's online help for DoCmd methods lists the Access constants that are applicable to each argument of the method.

Table 30.4 is an alphabetical list of DoCmd methods, together with the descriptive names of the argument(s) applicable to each method. Methods marked with an asterisk (*) are not recommended for new Access applications and are included for backward compatibility with existing macros.

| Table 30.4   DoCmd **Methods, Argument Names, and Purpose** | | |
|---|---|---|
| **Method** | **Argument Name** | **Purpose** |
| AddMenu* | Menu Name<br>Menu Macro Name | Adds a drop-down menu choice to a custom menubar or adds a custom shortcut menu choice. |
| | Status Bar Text | Replaced by programmable CommandBars in Access 97. |

| Method | Argument Name | Purpose |
|---|---|---|
| ApplyFilter | Filter Name<br>Where Condition | Filters the data available to a form or report using a filter, query, or SQL WHERE clause. |
| Beep | No arguments | Produces a beep tone for use in warnings or alerts. |
| CancelEvent | No arguments | Cancels the normal processing that follows the event. This action is useful if a user enters invalid data in a record; then the macro can cancel the update of the database. See Help on CancelEvent for a list of applicable events. |
| Close | Object Type | Closes the active (default) window or a specified Object Name window. |
| CopyObject | Destination<br>Database<br>New Name | Duplicates the specified database object in another database or the original by using a different name. |
| Delete Object | Object Type<br>Object Name | Deletes the Specified object. Leaves the arguments blank to delete the object selected in the Database window. |
| DoMenuItem | N/A | Replaced by RunCommand. |
| Echo | Echo On<br>Status Bar Text | Turns screen refresh on or off during code execution. Hides results until they are complete and speeds code operation. |
| FindNext | No arguments | Finds the next record specified by the FindRecord or the Find method. |
| FindRecord | Find What<br>Match Case<br>Direction<br>Search As Formatted<br>Search In<br>Find First | Finds the next record after the current record that meets the specified Criteria. Searches through a Table, Form, or Recordset object. |
| GoToControl | Control Name | Moves the focus to the specified field or control in the current record of the open form, form datasheet, table datasheet, or query datasheet. To move the focus to a subform's control, use the GoToControl method twice; first to move to the subform control and then to move to the control on the subform. |
| GoToPage | Page Number<br>Right<br>Down by Tab | Selects the first field in the tab order on the designated page in a multipage form. |

VII

Developing Access

(continues)

**Table 30.4   Continued**

| Method | Argument Name | Purpose |
| --- | --- | --- |
| GoToRecord | Object Type<br>Object Name<br>Record Offset | Displays the specified record in an open table, form, or query datasheet. |
| Hourglass | Hourglass On | Displays an hourglass in place of the mouse pointer during execution. Use this action while running long procedures. |
| Maximize | No arguments | Maximizes the active window. |
| Minimize | No arguments | Minimizes the active window to an icon within the Access window. |
| MoveSize | Right<br>Down<br>Width<br>Height | Moves or changes the size of the active window. |
| MsgBox* | Message<br>Beep<br>Type<br>Title | Displays a warning or informational message box and waits for the user to click the OK button. Replaced by VBA **MsgBox** command. |
| OpenForm | Form Name<br>View<br>Filter Name<br>Where Condition<br>Data Mode<br>Window Mode | Opens or activates a form in one of its views. You can restrict the form to data-matching criteria, different modes of editing, and whether the form acts as a modal or popup dialog. |
| OpenModule | Module Name<br>Procedure Name | Opens the specified module and displays the specified procedure. |
| OpenQuery | Query Name<br>View<br>Data Mode | Opens a select or crosstab query or runs an action query. |
| OpenReport | Report Name<br>View<br>Filter Name<br>Where Condition | Opens a report in the view that you specify and filters the records before printing. |
| OpenTable | Table Name<br>View<br>Data Mode | Opens or activates a table in the view that you specify. You can specify the Data-Entry or Edit mode for tables in Datasheet view. |
| OutputTo | Object Type<br>Object Name<br>Output Format<br>Output File<br>Autostart | Copies the data in the specified object to a Microsoft Excel (.xls), rich-text format (.rtf), or to a DOS text (.txt) file. Autostart = Yes starts the application with the association to the extension. |

| Method | Argument Name | Purpose |
|---|---|---|
| Print | Print Range<br>Page From<br>Page To<br>Print Quality<br>Copies<br>Collate Copies | Prints the active datasheet, report, or form. |
| Quit | Options | Closes Access, saving altered objects according to the command that you specify. |
| Rename | New Name | Renames the object selected in the Database window. |
| RepaintObject | Object Type<br>Object Name | Forces pending recalculations and screen updates for the controls of the specified database object or the active database object if you leave the arguments blank. Does not show new, changed, or deleted records from the object's underlying source. |
| Requery | Control Name | Updates the data in the specified control by repeating the control's query if the control is based on a query or by displaying new, changed, or deleted records if the control is based on a table. Leave the argument blank to requery the source of the active object. |
| Restore | No arguments | Restores a maximized or minimized window to its previous window. |
| RunApp* | Command Line | Runs a Windows- or an MS-DOS-based application. Access 97 uses the VBA Shell function to run other applications. |
| RunCode* | Function Name | Runs a user-defined function written in VBA. Replaced by direct execution of code. |
| RunCommand | Menu Bar<br>Menu Name<br>Command<br>Subcommand | Runs any command on a built-in Access 97 menubar or toolbar if the bar is appropriate for the view when the macro carries out the command. |
| RunMacro* | Macro Name<br>Repeat Count<br>Repeat Expression | Runs the specified macro. Enter the macro name's full syntax to run an individual macro in a macro group. Use the Repeat Count and Repeat Expression arguments to specify how many times to run the macro. Replace macros with VBA procedures in Access 97 applications. |

*(continues)*

| Table 30.4 | Continued | |
|---|---|---|
| **Method** | **Argument Name** | **Purpose** |
| RunSQL* | SQL Statement | Runs an action query as specified by the SQL statement. (To run a select query, use the OpenQuery action instead.) Replaced by the Execute method of a QueryDef object. |
| Save | Object Type<br>Object Name | Saves the specified database object. Leave the arguments blank to save the active window. |
| SelectObject | Object Type<br>Object Name In<br>Database Window | Selects a specified database object. |
| SendKeys | Keystrokes<br>Wait | Sends keystrokes to any active Windows application. |
| SendObject | Object Type<br>Object Name<br>Output Format<br>To<br>Cc<br>Bcc<br>Subject<br>Message Text<br>Edit Message | Sends the specified datasheet, form, report, or module in an electronic mail message. You can't send a macro. This action requires that you have a MAPI-compliant electronic mail application on your computer. |
| SetMenuItem | Menu Index<br>Menu Item<br>Menu Sub Item<br>Flag | Sets the state of a menu item on a custom menu to check a command or make it unavailable (grayed, or disabled). |
| SetValue* | Item<br>Expression | Sets the value of a field, control, or property on a form, form datasheet, or report. Replaced by VBA code to set values. |
| SetWarnings | Warnings On | Turns default warning messages on or off. Does not suppress error messages or system dialogs that require you to input text or select an option. |
| ShowAllRecords | No arguments | Removes any filters and requeries the active object. |
| StopAllMacros* | No arguments | Stops all macros that are currently running. VBA code replaces macros in Access 97. |
| StopMacro* | No arguments | Stops the current macro. VBA code replaces macros in Access 97. |

| Method | Argument Name | Purpose |
| --- | --- | --- |
| TransferDatabase | Transfer Type<br>Database Type<br>Database Name<br>Object Type<br>Source<br>Destination<br>Structure Only | Imports data from another database, exports data to another database, or links a table in another database to the current database. The other database can be an Access or SQL database. |
| TransferSpreadsheet | Transfer Type<br>Spreadsheet Type<br>Table Name<br>File Name<br>Has Field Names<br>Range | Imports data from a spreadsheet file or exports Access data to a spread-sheet file. |
| TransferText | Transfer Type<br>Specification Name<br>Table Name<br>File Name<br>Has Field Names | Imports data from a text file or exports Access data to a text file. |

The OutputTo, TransferDatabase, TransferSpreadsheet, and TransferText methods deserve special attention by application developers. These bulk transfer methods greatly simplify the data interchange between Access and other Office 97 applications, such as Excel and Word. The "Converting Access Macros to VBA Code" section later in this chapter illustrates the power of the TransferText method. The more complex DoCmd methods, together with Access 97's flexible report generation capabilities, are often the deciding factor when choosing between Visual Basic 4+ or Access 97 for developing database front ends. Visual Basic does not offer equivalents of the bulk transfer Access methods.

### Replacing *AddMenu* Macro Actions with *CommandBar* Objects

Prior versions of Access required the use of multiple menu macros with the AddMenu macro action to create custom menu bars. Access 95 included a Menu Builder Add-In, similar to that of Visual Basic, to make creating custom menus easier. All Office 97 applications replace conventional menu bars and toolbars with CommandBar objects. CommandBar objects create menubars, popup menus, toolbar buttons, and combo boxes. To gain VBA programming access to CommandBar objects, your database must include a reference to the Microsoft Office 8.0 Object Library, Mso97.dll (see Figure 30.19). Mso97.dll includes other objects that are common to Office 97, such as the Balloon object of the Office Assistant object and the DocumentProperty object for files. Figure 30.20 shows the Microsoft Office Objects help topic that displays the collections and objects exposed by Mso97.dll. The top-level collections and objects—CommandBars, Assistant, FileSearch, and DocumentProperties—are members of Access 97's Application object.

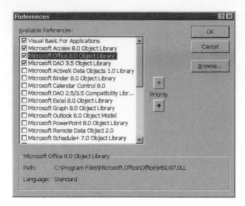

**FIG. 30.19**    Creating a reference to the Microsoft Office 8.0 Object Library.

With a reference to Mso97.dll, Office 97 object classes appear in the Object Browser's window when you select the Office library (see Figure 30.21). Selecting a class or member of the class and then clicking the Object Browser's Help (?) button displays the Microsoft Office Visual Basic help topic for the selection. Using Object Browser's Help button is the easiest way to obtain the VBA syntax for programming specific Office objects.

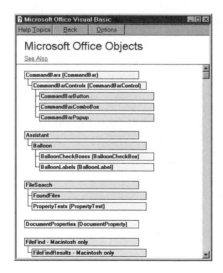

**FIG. 30.20**    The hierarchy of Office 97 collections and objects displayed by the Microsoft Office Objects help topic.

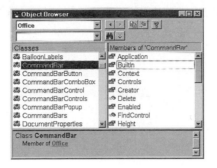

**FIG. 30.21** A few of the Office object classes and members displayed in Object Browser.

The Debug window is useful for gaining familiarity with programming Office objects. Figure 30.22 shows how to obtain property values of the CommandBars collection, CommandBar objects, and the Control objects of CommandBars. Unlike most other Access collections that begin with an index value of 0, the first member of Office collections has an index value of 1. The Application. preface in the first statement of Figure 30.22 is optional; the Application object is assumed when referring to top-level Access objects. To view the members of the Access Application class, open the Access library in Object Browser and select Application in the Classes list.

> **Note**
>
> To open the Debug window, open a form in Design view, and click the Code button of the toolbar to display the class module for the form, then choose View, Debug Window or press Ctrl+G.

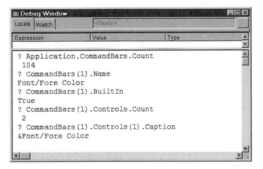

**FIG. 30.22** Using the Debug window to obtain property values of CommandBar and Control.

The following simple VBA subprocedure iterates the CommandBars collection and prints the Name and Visible property values of each CommandBar in the Debug window:

```
Dim msoBar As CommandBar

Sub PrintCommandBars()
   For Each msoBar In CommandBars
      Debug.Print msoBar.Name, msoBar.Visible
   Next msoBar
End Sub
```

Northwind.mdb has a custom command bar that adds the Show Me entry to Access's main menubar. When you run the preceding subprocedure from the Debug window, the last entry in the list is NorthwindCustomMenuBar with its Visible property **True**. Figure 30.23 shows some of the property values of NorthwindCustomMenuBar. The Show Me menu choice is the 15th member of the Controls collection of the menubar, with a Caption property value of "Show Me". The OnAction property value, "=ShowHelpAPI()", uses the ShowHelpAPI function of the Northwind Help Module to open the help file for the Northwind Traders sample database. To display the ShowHelpAPI function, open a module, choose Edit, Find, then search for ShowHelp with the Current Database option selected.

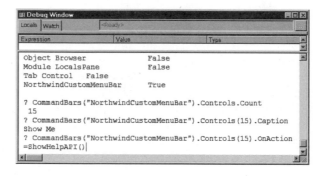

**FIG. 30.23**    Property values of the NorthwindCustomMenuBar and its added Control object, Show Me.

You can change the properties of existing command buttons with VBA code. As an example, typing the following code in the Debug window immediately changes the Show Me menu choice to Show You:

```
CommandBars("NorthwindCustomMenuBar").Controls(15).Caption = "Show &You"
```

You add a new CommandBar object by applying the Add method to the CommandBars collection, setting the properties of the new CommandBar object, and adding members to the CommandBar object's Controls collection. A full exposition of VBA programming of custom CommandBar objects is beyond the scope of this book. Most of the developer-level books for Access 97 listed in the "Bibliography" section of the Introduction to this book cover custom CommandBar programming in detail.

---

**Note**

The Command Bar Browser (CommandBarsForm) form of the Developer Solutions database (Solutions.mdb) in the \Program Files\Microsoft Office\Office folder provides a range of VBA programming examples for the CommandBar object. Solutions.mdb isn't installed when you choose the Typical setup option. If you didn't install Solutions.mdb, run Setup.exe from the Office 97 CD-ROM, click Add/Remove, and then specify installation of the Developer Solutions database in the Sample Databases category of the Access Setup options.

---

### Replacing the AutoExec Macro and Specifying a Custom *CommandBar* with Startup Properties

Access 2.0 and earlier databases required you to write an AutoExec macro to display a specified form automatically upon opening a database with Access. Commencing with Access 95, you replace AutoExec macros with database properties that you specify in the Startup dialog. In addition to a specified opening form, you also can assign an application title to the database and specify the name of a custom CommandBar as Access's main menu bar. To set startup properties, follow these steps:

1. Make the Database window active and choose Tools, Startup to open the Startup dialog. Click the Advanced button to expand the dialog.

2. Type a name for your application in the Application Title text box; the application name replaces Access's default title bar caption. If you have a special icon file (*Filename*.ico), you can specify the icon file in the Application Icon text box.

3. If you've created a custom CommandBar for your application, select the CommandBar in the drop-down Menu Bar list.

4. Open the Display Form list and select the form that you want to appear when you open the database (see Figure 30.24). You can elect to hide the Database window and the status bar by clearing the Display Database Window and Display Status Bar check boxes.

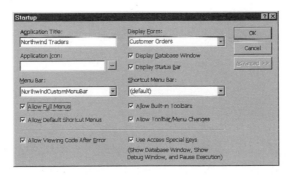

**FIG. 30.24**   Setting the Application Title, Menu Bar, and Display Form properties in the Startup dialog.

5. The remaining check boxes let you limit use of your application's menu bars, shortcut menus, and toolbars. You also can restrict viewing of VBA code when an error occurs and disable Access's special key combinations.

> **Tip**
>
> Don't clear any of the Startup dialog's check boxes until you're ready to release your application to users. Limiting Access's built-in menu, toolbar, and code-viewing feature set is likely to impede your development activities.

6. Click OK to assign the changes you made and close the Startup dialog.

# Converting Access Macros to VBA Code

Many existing Access applications make extensive use of macros to automate form and report operations. You can use Access 97's macro-to-VBA code conversion feature to change all but AutoExec and menu macros to Access VBA procedures. Converting macros to VBA code aids in learning VBA programming in much the same manner as recording Excel 97 or Word 97 macros and then examining the resulting VBA code. The Wildfeeds application (30_wild.mdb), used in this conversion example, began as an Access 2.0 demonstration of the power of Access macros. Wildfeeds imports a fixed-width text file, Wildfeed.txt, that lists unscheduled satellite video programming available to C-band dish owners. Wildfeeds also demonstrates the power of Access's TransferText method.

> **Note**
>
> Wildfeeds is published monthly by Gary Bourgois as "Birdfeed" and is available in text format from **http://www.nmia.com/~roberts/wildfeed** (save the HTML page as Wildfeed.txt). The older version of Wildfeed.txt used with the Wildfeed application described in this section uses 12-hour HH:MM A/P starting time designations. The current version of "Birdfeed" uses 24-hour starting times (HHMM). You might find it an interesting exercise to modify 30_wild.mdb to accommodate the new text format with the 24-hour time field. (The 24-hour time format simplifies the programming considerably.)

The columns of Wildfeed.txt—shown opened in Notepad in Figure 30.25—list the name of the program, the days of the week that the program appears (MF = Monday through Friday), the program starting time (EST), the program's satellite abbreviation (G4 = Galaxy 4) and transponder number, and the classification of the program. 30_wild.mdb includes an import specification that parses the lines of text into designated fields of the tblWildFeed table. Figure 30.26 shows the imported text file opened in the sbfWildFeed subform. Clicking the Yesterday, Today, or Tomorrow button redisplays the subform according to the day of the week.

```
Wildfeed.txt - Notepad
File  Edit  Search  Help
Acting Crazy              FR    2:00 A   E2/08   Game
Acting Crazy              TU    2:30 A   E2/08   Game
Acting Crazy              TH    2:00 A   E2/08   Game
Action Pack Movie         MO   10:00 A   G4/11   Action
Action Pack Movie         TU   10:00 A   G4/14   Action
Action Pack Movie (Reel 1) SU   7:30 A   G4/09   Action
Action Pack Movie (Reel 2) SU   8:45 A   G4/09   Action
Adventures in Wonderland  WE    8:30 P   T1/06   Cartoon
Adventures in Wonderland  TU   12:00 M   T1/06   Cartoon
Agday                     MF    1:00 A   T2/16   Ag News
Aladdin                   MF    4:00 A   T1/06   Cartoon
Aladdin                   MF    1:30 P   T1/06   Cartoon
Aladdin                   SA   12:00 N   T1/06   Cartoon
All American Girl         WE    2:00 P   T1/06   Series
All American Wrestling    SA    4:00 A   G7/01   Wrestling
All My Children           MF    1:00 A   T1/11   Soap Opera
Amazin' Adventures        MO   12:30 P   T1/05   Cartoon
Amazin' Adventures        MO   12:00 N   T1/05   Cartoon
America's Most Wanted      SU    3:00 P   T1/04   Magazine
American Gladiators       WE    1:30 P   T1/05   Sportainment
American Gladiators       TU    8:30 A   T1/05   Sportainment
American Journal          MF    4:30 P   T1/18   Tabloid
Animal Adventures         SU    8:00 A   G4/11   Series
```

**FIG. 30.25**  An early version of the Wildfeeds.txt file opened in Windows Notepad.

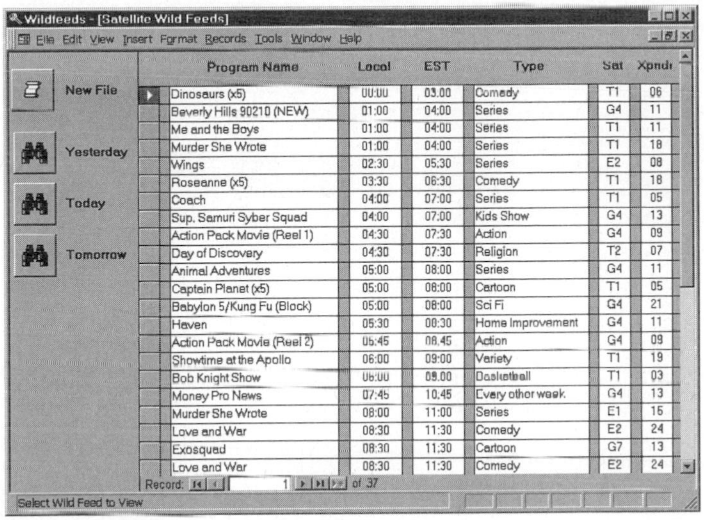

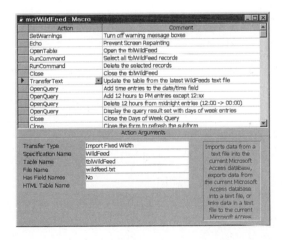

**FIG. 30.26**  The main form and subform of the Wildfeeds application displaying satellite programs sorted by local time (PST or PDT).

The original mcrWildFeed macro, executed by clicking the New File button, consists of a chain of 17 macro actions—13 of which are shown in the mcrWildFeeds macrosheet in Figure 30.27. Converting the Access 95 version of 30_wild.mdb into an Access 97 database changes DoMenuItem actions to RunCommand actions. (DoCmd methods are called actions when executed from macrosheets.) The selected TransferText action imports the Wildfeed.txt file in accordance with the WildFeed import specification. Four queries are required to reformat the time and day-of-the week values for correct sorting. The remainder of the macro actions reopen frmWildFeed and sbfWildFeed to display the newly imported data.

**FIG. 30.27**  The mcrWildFeed macrosheet after converting 30_wild.mdb to an Access 97 database.

> **Note**
>
> The Access 95 version of 30_wild.mdb is included in the Ua97mdb.zip file available for download-ing from **http://www.mcp.com/320336271804569/softlib/database/**. Ua97mdb.zip includes all of the example databases of this book.
>
> You must have the Advanced Wizards installed to convert macros to VBA code. If you used the Typical installation for Office 97 or Access 97, the Advanced Wizards aren't installed. In this case, you must rerun Setup from the distribution CD-ROM or a network installation share. Click the Add/Remove button and specify the Advanced Wizards in the Wizards section of the Access component of Setup.

To convert Access macros in an earlier version database to Access 97 VBA code, follow these steps that use 30_wild.mdb as an example:

1. Open the database in Access 97 and select the Convert Database option. Save the database in the same directory with a new file name, such as **97_wild.mdb**. (Un-like compacting, you can't replace the original version with a converted database.)

2. Open the form whose macros you want to convert in Design view. This action lets the wizard place the generated code for the macros in the class module of the form.

3. Choose <u>T</u>ools, <u>M</u>acro, Convert Form's Macros to <u>V</u>isual Basic to start the conver-sion process.

4. When the Convert Form Macros: *FormName* dialog appears, accept the default Add Error Handling to Generated Functions and Include Macro Comments options (see Figure 30.28). Click Convert to complete the conversion operation, and then click OK when the Conversion Finished message box appears.

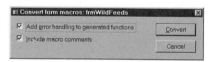

**FIG. 30.28**   Specifying inclusion of standard error-handling code and comments in the code generated by the macro-to-VBA conversion process.

5. Click the Code button of the toolbar to display the class module for the form with the added VBA code. Figure 30.29 shows part of the code generated for the mcrWildFeed macro. Note that converted class modules don't include the standard **Option** Explicit statement in the Declarations section.

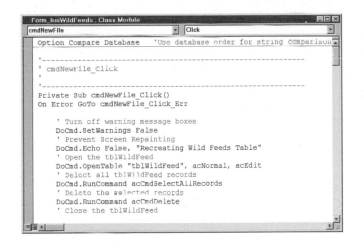

**FIG. 30.29**   VBA code generated for the first five macro actions of the mcrWildFeed macrosheet.

Listing 30.2 contains the event-handling code for each of the converted macros run by the On Click event of the four command buttons: cmdNewFile, cmdYesterday, cmdToday, and cmdTomorrow.

**Listing 30.2   Event-Handling Code for the Four Command Buttons of `frmWildFeed` Created by the Macro Conversion Process**

```
Option Compare Database    'Use database order for string comparisons

'-------------------------------------------------------------
' cmdNewFile_Click
'
'-------------------------------------------------------------
Private Sub cmdNewFile_Click()
On Error GoTo cmdNewFile_Click_Err

    ' Turn off warning message boxes
    DoCmd.SetWarnings False
    ' Prevent Screen Repainting
    DoCmd.Echo False, "Recreating Wild Feeds Table"
    ' Open the tblWildFeed
    DoCmd.OpenTable "tblWildFeed", acNormal, acEdit
    ' Select all tblWildFeed records
    DoCmd.RunCommand acCmdSelectAllRecords
    ' Delete the selected records
    DoCmd.RunCommand acCmdDelete
    ' Close the tblWildFeed
    DoCmd.Close acTable, "tblWildFeed"
    ' Update the table from the latest WildFeeds text file
    DoCmd.TransferText acImportFixed, "WildFeed", "tblWildFeed", _
        "wildfeed.txt", False, ""
    ' Add time entries to the date/time field
    DoCmd.OpenQuery "qryConvertTime", acNormal, acEdit
    ' Add 12 hours to PM entries except 12:xx
```

(continues)

**Listing 30.2 Continued**

```
      DoCmd.OpenQuery "qryFixTimePM", acNormal, acEdit
      ' Delete 12 hours from midnight entries (12:00 -> 00:00)
      DoCmd.OpenQuery "qryFixMidnight", acNormal, acEdit
      ' Display the query result set with days of week entries
      DoCmd.OpenQuery "qryDaysOfWeek", acNormal, acEdit
      ' Close the Days of Week Query
      DoCmd.Close acQuery, "qryDaysOfWeek"
      ' Close the form to refresh the subform
      DoCmd.Close acForm, "frmWildFeeds"
      ' Open the form
      DoCmd.OpenForm "frmWildFeeds", acNormal, "", "", acEdit, acNormal
      ' Maximize the form
      DoCmd.Maximize
      ' Turn screen painting on
      DoCmd.Echo True, "Select Wild Feed"
      ' Turn warnings back on
      DoCmd.SetWarnings True

cmdNewFile_Click_Exit:
      Exit Sub

cmdNewFile_Click_Err:
      MsgBox Error$
      Resume cmdNewFile_Click_Exit

End Sub


' -------------------------------------------------------------
' cmdYesterday_Click
'
' -------------------------------------------------------------
Private Sub cmdYesterday_Click()
On Error GoTo cmdYesterday_Click_Err

      ' Turn off warnings
      DoCmd.SetWarnings False
      ' Turn off screen painting
      DoCmd.Echo False, ""
      ' Close the main and subform
      DoCmd.Close acForm, "frmWildFeeds"
      ' Open the subform
      DoCmd.OpenForm "sbfWildFeeds", acNormal, "", "", acEdit, acNormal
      ' Choose Design View
      DoCmd.RunCommand acCmdDesignView
      ' Set the RecordSource property
      Forms!sbfWildFeeds.RecordSource = "qryYesterdaysWildFeeds"
      ' Close the subform
      DoCmd.Close acForm, "sbfWildFeeds"
      ' Refresh the subform
      DoCmd.OpenForm "frmWildFeeds", acNormal, "", "", acEdit, acNormal
      ' Turn on screen painting
      DoCmd.Echo True, ""
      ' Turn on warnings
      DoCmd.SetWarnings True
```

```
cmdYesterday_Click_Exit:
    Exit Sub

cmdYesterday_Click_Err:
    MsgBox Error$
    Resume cmdYesterday_Click_Exit

End Sub

'----------------------------------------------------------------
' cmdToday_Click
'
'----------------------------------------------------------------
Private Sub cmdToday_Click()
On Error GoTo cmdToday_Click_Err

    ' Turn off warnings
    DoCmd.SetWarnings False
    ' Turn off screen painting
    DoCmd.Echo False, ""
    ' Close the main and subform
    DoCmd.Close acForm, "frmWildFeeds"
    ' Open the subform
    DoCmd.OpenForm "sbfWildFeeds", acNormal, "", "", acEdit, acNormal
    ' Choose Design View
    DoCmd.RunCommand acCmdDesignView
    ' Set the RecordSource property
    Forms!sbfWildFeeds.RecordSource = "qryTodaysWildFeeds"
    ' Close the subform
    DoCmd.Close acForm, "sbfWildFeeds"
    ' Refresh the subform
    DoCmd.OpenForm "frmWildFeeds", acNormal, "", "", acEdit, acNormal
    ' Turn on screen painting
    DoCmd.Echo True, ""
    ' Turn on warnings
    DoCmd.SetWarnings True

cmdToday_Click_Exit:
    Exit Sub

cmdToday_Click_Err:
    MsgBox Error$
    Resume cmdToday_Click_Exit

End Sub

'----------------------------------------------------------------
' cmdTomorrow_Click
'
'----------------------------------------------------------------
Private Sub cmdTomorrow_Click()
On Error GoTo cmdTomorrow_Click_Err

    ' Turn off warnings
    DoCmd.SetWarnings False
```

(continues)

**Listing 30.2   Continued**

```
        ' Turn off screen painting
        DoCmd.Echo False, ""
        ' Close the main and subform
        DoCmd.Close acForm, "frmWildFeeds"
        ' Open the subform
        DoCmd.OpenForm "sbfWildFeeds", acNormal, "", "", acEdit, acNormal
        ' Choose Design View
        DoCmd.RunCommand acCmdDesignView
        ' Set the RecordSource property
        Forms!sbfWildFeeds.RecordSource = "qryTomorrowsWildFeeds"
        ' Close the subform
        DoCmd.Close acForm, "sbfWildFeeds"
        ' Refresh the subform
        DoCmd.OpenForm "frmWildFeeds", acNormal, "", "", acEdit, acNormal
        ' Turn on screen painting
        DoCmd.Echo True, ""
        ' Turn on warnings
        DoCmd.SetWarnings True

cmdTomorrow_Click_Exit:
    Exit Sub

cmdTomorrow_Click_Err:
    MsgBox Error$
    Resume cmdTomorrow_Click_Exit

End Sub
```

Inspecting the code for the three subprocedures that handle the On Click event of cmdToday, cmdYesterday, and cmdTomorrow shows that the only difference between the three procedures is the query name in the Forms!sbfWildFeeds.RecordSource = "qry*QueryName*" line. As discussed in the "Using Functions to Respond to Events" section earlier in the chapter, you can combine the last three subprocedures in Listing 30.2 into a single event-handling function with a parameter to accept the query name. Following are the changes you make to the code of one of the procedures:

```
Private Function cmdDateQuery (strQueryName As String) As Integer
    ...
    Forms!sbfWildFeeds.RecordSource = strQueryName
    ...
End Function
```

The VBA interpreter changes each occurrence of **Sub** to **Function** for you. It's a good programming practice to change the error-handling code to reflect the new name of the function. Once you've tested your code by choosing <u>D</u>ebug, Compile Lo<u>a</u>ded Modules, substitute **=cmdDateQuery("qry*QueryName*")** for [Event Procedure] in the On Click text box for each of the three buttons, where **qry*QueryName*** is **qryYesterdaysWildFeeds**, **qryTodaysWildFeeds**, and **qryTomorrowsWildFeeds** for the cmdYesterday, cmdToday, and cmdTomorrow buttons, respectively.

# Referring to Access Objects with VBA

One of the reasons for using the term *Access VBA* in this book is that Access defines its own set of objects and uses specialized VBA syntax to refer to many Access objects. Although Form objects are common to most Office 97 members as well as Visual Basic, a subform (a form embedded in a form) is unique to Access. You find Report objects and subreports only in Access. The syntax for referring to a subform or subreport and for referring to controls contained in a subform or subreport is unique to Access. Even if you're an experienced Visual Basic programmer, you must become acquainted with the new syntax to write VBA code and refer to objects that are unique to Access.

### Referring to Open Forms or Reports and Their Properties

You can refer to a form or report only if it is open. Access uses the Forms and Reports collections to keep track of which forms and reports are open. The Forms collection is the set of open forms, and the Reports collection is the set of open reports. Because Access lets you use the same name for a form and a report, you must distinguish between the two by specifying the collection. The syntax for the reference is the collection name followed by the *exclamation point operator* (!), more commonly called the *bang operator*, and the name of the form or report:

```
Forms![FormName]
Reports![ReportName]
```

Use the bang operator (!) to separate the collection name from the name of an object in the collection. You only need to use the square brackets ([...]) to enclose object names that include spaces or other punctuation that are illegal in VBA statements.

A Form or Report object has properties that define its characteristics. The general syntax for referring to a property is the object name followed by the dot operator and the name of the property:

```
Forms![FormName].PropertyName
Reports![ReportName].PropertyName
```

Use the dot (.) operator to separate the object's name from the name of one of its properties. For example, Forms!frmProducts.RecordSource refers to the RecordSource property of the open frmProducts form. You can get or set the value of the RecordSource property with the following two VBA statements:

```
strSource = Forms!frmProducts.RecordSource
Forms!frmProducts.RecordSource = strSource
```

To get or set the value of a property of the form in the form's own class module, you use the **Me** self-identifier, as in:

```
strSource = Me.RecordSource
Me.RecordSource = strSource
```

The **Me** self-reference is only valid for the instance of the form open in Form view. Thus, you cannot use the two preceding statements in the Debug window unless you create a breakpoint in your code, open the form in Form view, and then execute the procedure that contains the breakpoint. Figure 30.30 shows the Debug window opened by a breakpoint and set at the first active line of code of the ReviewProducts_Click subprocedure of Northwind.mdb's Suppliers form. In breakpoint mode, typing **?** **Me.RecordSource** returns Suppliers—the name of the table to which the Suppliers form is bound.

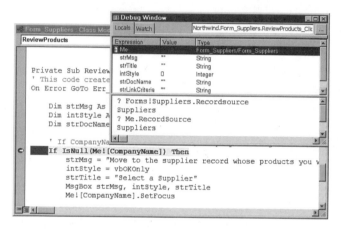

**FIG. 30.30**    The Debug window opened by reaching a breakpoint during VBA code execution.

◀◀ See "Adding a Breakpoint to the IsLoaded( )Function," p. 1015

A form's property sheet lists the form properties that you can set in Design view. Forms also have properties that you can't set in Design view and that do not appear in the property sheet, such as the default Form property. The Form property refers to the collection of controls on a form. Similarly, a report's default Report property refers to the collection of controls in a report.

### Referring to Controls and Their Properties

The following is the general syntax for referring to a control on a form or report:

```
Forms![FormName].Form![ControlName]
```

```
Reports![ReportName].Report![ControlName]
```

As before, the bang operator separates the collection name from the object name. The Form property is the default property that Access assumes for a form; therefore, you need not include the Form property explicitly in the reference. The following expression is the full identifier syntax for a form control:

```
Forms![FormName]![ControlName]
```

Similarly, the following is the full identifier syntax for a report control:

```
Reports![ReportName]![ControlName]
```

For example, `Forms!frmProducts!ProductName` refers to the `ProductName` control on the open `frmProducts` form.

The syntax for referring to a control's property includes the reference to the control, followed by the dot operator, and then followed by the property name:

```
Forms![FormName]![ControlName].[PropertyName]
```

```
Reports![ReportName]![ControlName].[PropertyName]
```

For example, `Forms!frmProducts!ProductName.Visible` refers to the *ProductName* control's `Visible` property.

A control also has a default property. The default property of a text box is the `Text` property. To refer to the value in the `ProductName` text box control in the last example, you could use any of the following equivalent references:

```
Forms!frmProducts.Form!ProductName.Text
```

```
Forms!frmProducts!ProductName.Text
```

```
Forms!frmProducts.Form!ProductName
```

```
Forms!frmProducts!ProductName
```

Notice that the last two expressions refer both to the control's text value and to the control itself.

When you refer to a control on the active form or report, you can use a shorter version of the reference and refer to the control as follows:

```
[ControlName]
```

Likewise, you can refer to the control property as follows:

```
[ControlName].PropertyName
```

Normally, you can use either the short or full syntax to refer to a control on the active form or report. However, in some cases you must use the short syntax. For example, the `GoToControl` action's *ControlName* argument requires the short syntax. You can explicitly refer to a control on the form of the class module with `Me!ControlName` statements. When you refer to a control on a form or report that is not the active object, you usually must use the full identifier syntax.

### Referring to Controls on a Subform or the Main Form

The key to understanding the syntax for referring to a control on a subform is to realize that the subform is a form that is bound to a subform control on the main form. The subform control has the usual attribute properties that control its display behavior, such as size and visibility, as well as linking properties that relate the records in the subform to records in the form, including the `SourceObject`, `LinkChildFields`, and `LinkMasterFields` properties. In addition, the subform control has the Form property. A subform control's Form property refers to the controls contained on the subform.

The following is the syntax for referring to the subform control:

```
Forms![FormName]![SubformControlName]
```

The syntax for referring to a control on a subform bound to a subform control is as follows:

```
Forms![FormName]![SubformControlName].Form![ControlName]
```

When the form is active, the following short syntax refers to a control on a subform of the active form:

```
[SubformControlName].Form![ControlName]
```

The Form property is not the subform control's default property, so you must include it explicitly in the reference. Normally, you use the subform's name as the name of the subform control. For example, if sbfSuppliers is the name of a form bound to a subform control also named sbfSuppliers on the frmProducts form, the following is the full syntax for referring to the SupplierName control on the subform:

```
Forms!frmProducts!sbfSuppliers.Form!SupplierName
```

The short syntax is as follows:

```
sbfSuppliers.Form!SupplierName
```

When the focus is in a subform's control, you can refer to a control on the main form by using the control's Parent property. The Parent property refers to the collection of controls on the main form. In the previous example, to refer to the ProductName control on the main form from VBA code in the class module of a subform, use the following syntax:

```
Parent!ProductName
```

All the preceding syntax examples in this section apply to reports and subreports; just change Forms to Reports and Form to Report.

---

**Note**

The ShowSales_Click subprocedure of the ShowSales form in the Developer Solutions database (Solutions.mdb) provides examples of VBA code that uses references to properties of a subform.

---

# Responding to Data Events

Recordsets underlying forms and reports trigger data events when you move the record pointer or change the value in one or more cells of the Recordset. The most common use of data events is to validate updates to the Recordset; you add validation code to the event-handling subprocedure for the BeforeUpdate event. The use of code, rather than setting field-level or table-level ValidationRule property values, is that VBA provides a much more flexible method of assuring data consistency. Validation rules you write in VBA commonly are called *business rules*. Business rules often are quite complex and require access to multiple lookup tables—some of which may be located in other databases.

◀◀ See "Validating Data Entry," p. 170

Listing 30.3 shows an example of a set of validation rules for postal codes in the Suppliers table of Northwind.mdb, the Recordset of which is bound to the Suppliers form. The BeforeUpdate event, which triggers before a change is made to the Recordset, includes a predefined Cancel argument. If you set Cancel = **True** in your event-handling code, the proposed update to the Recordset does not occur.

---

**Listing 30.3    A VBA Validation Subprocedure for International Postal Codes**

```
Private Sub Form_BeforeUpdate(Cancel As Integer)
' If number of digits entered in PostalCode text box is
' incorrect for value in Country text box, display message
' and undo PostalCode value.

    Select Case Me!Country
       Case IsNull(Me![Country])
          Exit Sub
       Case "France", "Italy", "Spain"
          If Len(Me![PostalCode]) <> 5 Then
             MsgBox "Postal Code must be 5 characters", 0, _
                "Postal Code Error"
             Cancel = True
             Me![PostalCode].SetFocus
          End If
       Case "Australia", "Singapore"
          If Len(Me![PostalCode]) <> 4 Then
             MsgBox "Postal Code must be 4 characters", 0, _
                "Postal Code Error"
             Cancel = True
             Me![PostalCode].SetFocus
          End If
       Case "Canada"
          If Not Me![PostalCode] Like _
             "[A-Z][0-9][A-Z] [0-9][A-Z][0-9]" Then
             MsgBox "Postal Code not valid. " & _
                "Example of Canadian code: H1J 1C3", _
                0, "Postal Code Error"
             Cancel = True
             Me![PostalCode].SetFocus
          End If
    End Select
End Sub
```

---

Data events of combo boxes commonly are used to select a specific record or set of records for display in a form or subform. The EditProducts form of Solutions.mdb, shown in Figure 30.31, displays product and supplier data for selections made consecutively in the Select Category and Select Product drop-down lists. When you make a selection in the Select Category list, the action populates the Select Product list with products. Selecting a product in the Select product list displays product and supplier data in the text boxes of the form.

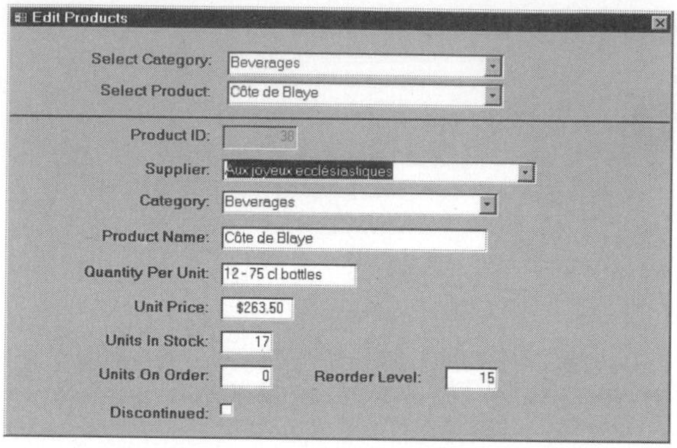

**FIG. 30.31**   The EditProducts form of the Developer Solutions database (Solutions.mdb).

The VBA code of Listing 30.4, from the class module for the EditProducts form of the Developer Solutions database, illustrates extensive use of data events of the Form object and combo box control objects. Making a selection in the Select Category list executes the SelectCategory_AfterUpdate event handler, which requeries the Select Product list to display the products for the selected category. Making a selection in the updated Select Product list executes the SelectProduct_AfterUpdate event handler, which applies a filter to the Recordset of the form to display the product data. In turn, changing the record pointer of the form's Recordset executes the Form_Current event handler, which tests for low product inventory.

**Listing 30.4   Data Event Handlers in the Class Module for the EditProducts Form of Solutions.mdb**

```
Option Compare Database    'Use database order for string comparisons.
Option Explicit

Private Sub Form_AfterUpdate()
   'Requery SelectProduct combo box.
   Me!SelectProduct.Requery
End Sub

Private Sub Form_Current()
'If value in UnitsInStock text box is less than value in ReorderLevel
'text box and value in UnitsOnOrder text box is 0, display
'value in UnitsInStock in red and display LLowStock label.

   If (Me!UnitsInStock + Me!UnitsOnOrder) <= Me!ReorderLevel Then
      Me!UnitsInStock.ForeColor = 255
      Me!LLowStock.Visible = True
   Else
      'Otherwise, display value in UnitsInStock text box in black
```

```
                    'and hide LLowStock label.
            Me!UnitsInStock.ForeColor = 0
            Me!LLowStock.Visible = False
      End If
End Sub


Private Sub GoToSupplierID_Enter()
'Go to SupplierID combo box to prevent advancing
'to another record.

      Me!SupplierID.SetFocus
End Sub


Private Sub ReorderLevel_AfterUpdate()
'Run Form_Current procedure.

      Form_Current
End Sub


Private Sub SelectCategory_AfterUpdate()
'Enable and requery SelectProduct combo box.
'Disable controls in detail section.

      Me!SelectProduct.Enabled = True
      Me!SelectProduct.Requery
      EnableControls Me, acDetail, False
End Sub


Private Sub SelectProduct_AfterUpdate()
'Find record for product selected in SelectProduct combo box.
'Enable controls in detail section and disable ProductID text box.
'Go to SupplierID combo box.

      DoCmd.ApplyFilter , "ProductID = Forms!EditProducts!SelectProduct"
      EnableControls Me, acDetail, True
      Me!ProductID.Enabled = False
      Me!SupplierID.SetFocus
End Sub


Private Sub SelectProduct_BeforeUpdate(Cancel As Integer)
      If IsNull([SelectProduct]) Then
          MsgBox "You must select a product."
          Cancel = True
      End If
End Sub


Private Sub UnitsInStock_AfterUpdate()
'Run Form_Current procedure.

      Form_Current
End Sub


Private Sub UnitsOnOrder_AfterUpdate()
'Run Form_Current procedure.

      Form_Current
End Sub
```

The VBA code examples in this chapter only cover the basics of the use of VBA 5.0 for responding to events triggered by forms, controls, and Recordsets bound to forms or reports. A full course in VBA programming exceeds both the scope and the publishing limitations of this book. Many of the examples of this chapter are drawn from the sample databases supplied with Access 97. You can adapt many of the techniques illustrated in the event-handling subprocedures of the sample databases to custom applications you create. To become an expert in VBA programming requires study, experimentation, and perseverance. Periodicals, books, and Web sites, such as those listed in the "Bibliography" section of the introduction to this book, are likely to satisfy the studious reader. There's no substitute, however, for experimentation. Writing and testing code is the only sure way to become proficient in VBA programming.

# Chapter 31

# Exchanging Data with Automation and ActiveX Controls

Interprocess communication (IPC) has come a long way from its early origins in Windows dynamic data exchange (DDE). DDE made it possible to transfer data between Windows applications by setting up a DDE conversation between the two applications using the Windows Clipboard as an intermediary. Windows 3.1 made Object Linking and Embedding (OLE) 1.0 the preferred method of transferring data between OLE-enabled, 16-bit applications. These transfers are still made via the Clipboard with the Edit, Paste Special menu choice. OLE 2.x, implemented in 16-bit Access 2.0 and 32-bit Access 95, brought drag-and-drop operation to Clipboard-based OLE. OLE 2.x also introduced OLE Automation and programmable objects—the foundation for a Windows component architecture.

Access 2.0 was the first Microsoft application to support 16-bit OLE Controls (OCX), the intended replacement for Visual Basic Extension (VBX) custom controls. OLE Controls let Microsoft and third-party suppliers create special-purpose components to supplement the standard set of native controls offered by Access. Access 95 and Visual Basic 4.0 introduced a common set of 32-bit OLE Controls. Developers found creating OLE Controls with C++ to be a daunting task, and OCXs turned out to be much larger than their VBX counterparts. Despite these hurdles, a wide variety of OLE Controls became available for Access 95 and Visual Basic 4.0.

Microsoft's decision to "embrace and extend the Internet," announced on December 9, 1995, caused Microsoft to rethink its original OLE Control design specification. OLE Controls were much too large to download from the Internet on an as-required basis. Microsoft announced at its Professional Developers Conference on March 12, 1996, the specification for a lightweight version of OLE Controls—called ActiveX Controls—as the major element of a broader ActiveX Technologies program. 32-bit ActiveX Controls are 30 percent to 50 percent smaller than the 16-bit and 32-bit OLE Controls they replace.

This chapter introduces you to (OLE) Automation and ActiveX controls with emphasis on their implementation in Access 97. Automation is the technology that lets you program Jet's Data Access Objects (DAO) with VBA. Automation objects expose only properties and events. ActiveX Controls extend Automation objects with events that connect to VBA event-handling subprocedures.

# Introducing Microsoft's ActiveX Technology

OLE and ActiveX technologies both are built on Microsoft's *Common Object Model* (COM). COM is a specification for designing reusable software components (objects) that you can combine to create useful applications, such as Access database front-ends. The COM specification defines the connection (a set of *interfaces*) between a client, such as Access, and a programmable object—typically the DAO for Access clients. Microsoft's implementation of COM is for Windows; third parties currently are porting COM to the Macintosh and UNIX operating systems. COM objects and their clients must be located on the same computer. *Distributed COM* (DCOM), which is included in Windows NT 4.0, gives clients access to server-based COM objects via a networked connection.

> **Note**
>
> The preliminary specification for COM is available at **http://www.microsoft.com/intdev/ sdk/docs/com/comintro-f.htm**. You can read the first two chapters, which cover the basics of COM, in HTML format or download the entire specification in Word 6.0 format.
>
> Microsoft's ActiveX Web site at **http://www.microsoft.com/activex/default.htm** provides links to a wide variety of information on ActiveX Controls, including many useful controls you can download and use in your Access applications.

Microsoft's goal in developing its ActiveX Technologies is to transform COM and DCOM into public Internet standards. In early October 1996, Microsoft announced that the COM, DCOM, and Automation specifications henceforth are to be managed by the Open Group, an industry standards organization. OLE, which deals primarily with embedding and linking documents, remains Microsoft's proprietary technology. Other COM-based Windows technologies over which Microsoft intends to retain control, such as OLE DB (OLE Databases) and OLE DS (OLE Directory Services) also carry the OLE prefix.

> **Note**
>
> The OLE DB specification defines a generalized method for accessing any data that can be formatted into a row-column structure. ActiveX Data Objects (ADO) is a lightweight Automation interface to OLE DB data providers. The first application for ADO is to support Active Database Components in the new ActiveX Server extensions (code-named Denali) to Microsoft's Internet Information Server. Microsoft says in its Frequently Asked Questions for ODE DB that ADO is an "evolution of our earlier object models," and adds, "Over time, all our products will standardize on ADO and OLE DB." You can get more information on OLE DB and ADO at **http://www. microsoft.com/oledb/**.

In conjunction with the transfer of specifications to the Open Group, Microsoft removed the OLE prefix from the names of Internet-related components. Table 31.1 lists the old and new terms for the affected components and technologies. Microsoft didn't change OLE Automation to ActiveX Automation because COM's Automation interface also is used for programming linked and embedded OLE objects.

| Table 31.1    New COM and DCOM Terminology for OLE Technologies | |
| --- | --- |
| **Old Term** | **New Term** |
| NetworkOLE | Distributed COM (DCOM) |
| OLE Automation | Automation |
| OLE Automation servers | ActiveX components |
| OLE components | ActiveX components |
| OLE Controls | ActiveX Controls |
| OLE Designers | ActiveX Designers |
| OLE document objects | ActiveX documents |
| OLE servers | ActiveX components |
| OLE specification | ActiveX specification |

The Access 97 documentation continues to use the terms *OLE server* and *OLE container*. The name of Jet's OLE Object field data type does not change because OLE Object fields are intended as containers for linked or embedded OLE objects.

# Understanding Automation

Access 97, like Access 95, is an OLE 2.1 client and server application; Access 2.0 was an OLE 2.01 client only. The Jet 3.5 database engine is a programmable Automation object, so VBA-enabled applications, including all members of Office 97, can manipulate the Jet 3.5 DAO with code similar to the Access VBA examples in Chapter 29, "Understanding the Data Access Object Class."

◄◄ See "Writing a Function that Uses Database Objects," 1041

Referencing the Jet 3.5 engine directly in other VBA-enabled applications, rather than using Access 97 as an Automation server, is much faster and uses fewer resources. Therefore, your primary use of Access 97 is likely to be as an Automation client that manipulates various Automation servers, such as Word 97 or Excel 97. The sections that follow describe the types of Automation servers defined by the OLE 2.1 specification and how 16- and 32-bit Automation components interact.

### Categorizing Automation Components
Understanding Automation requires an explanation of the categories of Automation components that you can use in building desktop database applications. Automation components are of five basic types:

- *Full servers* are programs, such as 32-bit Microsoft Excel 97 and Word 97, that are stand-alone productivity applications with Automation capability added. Full servers create insertable objects that you display in Access's bound or unbound object frames. Like Access 97, Excel 97 and Word expose their application objects to their own flavor of VBA through a type library. Full servers also are called *local servers* because the server must reside on the same PC as the Automation client application.

■ *Automation servers* are full (local) servers that are not insertable objects. Access 97 is an Automation server only. Access 97 does not appear in the Object Type list of the Create New page of the Insert Object dialog of Word 97 or Excel 97. If you attempt to specify an .mdb file in the Create From File page, Object Packager attempts to create a package from the .mdb file.

■ *Mini-servers* are applications, such as Microsoft Graph 8.0 (MSGraph8), that can only be executed from within an Automation client application. Mini-servers are similar to the OLE 1.0 applets originally supplied with Word for Windows 2.0 and other early Microsoft OLE 1.0 applications, such as Microsoft Draw. OLE 2.x mini-servers expose objects through a type or object library.

To qualify for mini-server status, the application must be an executable file (.exe) that is capable of displaying a window. Mini-servers that display a particular class of objects, such as video clips, are called *viewers*. Using the Graph Wizard to create MSGraph8 charts is one of the subjects of Chapter 20, "Adding Graphics to Forms and Reports." You also can create custom graphs and charts by programming MSGraph8 with Access VBA code.

■ *ActiveX Controls (OCXs)* are a special type of mini-server. ActiveX Controls, which use the .ocx file extension, expose events in addition to properties and methods. They are the object-oriented equivalent of the VBX custom controls of Visual Basic 3.0 and earlier. Most ActiveX Controls have a visible user interface. Access 97 includes a single ActiveX Control—the Calendar Control (Msacal.ocx). The Office Developer Edition (ODE) includes a variety of useful ActiveX Controls and a license to distribute the Controls with your Access applications.

 ▶▶ See "Examining the Content of the Office 97 Developer Edition," p. 1135

■ *Process servers* are a subclass of automation servers. Process servers are used to perform functions that do not involve interaction at the user interface. Process servers come in two flavors: OutOfProc(ess) and InProc(ess) servers. *OutOfProc* servers are executable files that run in their own process space; that is, they have their own block of allocated memory. (Full servers and mini-servers are OutOfProc servers.) *InProc* servers share memory with the client application. (ActiveX Controls are InProc servers.)

OutOfProc servers communicate with local client applications through Lightweight Remote Procedure Calls (LRPCs), while InProc servers, also called OLE DLLs, use conventional Windows function calls. Thus InProc servers respond considerably faster to client instructions than OutOfProc servers. The advantage of OutOfProc servers is the ability to locate the server on a remote computer and communicate with the server via DCOM. In this case, the OutOfProc server is called a *Remote Automation Object* (RAO). Microsoft's recently announced Viper transaction processing technology lets you create in-process RAOs.

---

**Note**

*Process server* is not an "official" OLE or COM category. The term is used here to distinguish invisible programmable process server objects (that run in the background) from programmable objects with visible representation in Access 97's run or design modes, even if the visible representation is optional.

One of the primary applications for process servers is creating "three-tier" client/server database applications. A three-tier application interposes an RAO between the client front end and the RDBMS back end. The RAO manages connecting to the RDBMS and the processing of queries. The RAO may include code that enforces "business rules" common to all front-end applications. The middle-tier RAO isn't visible to the user.

---

One of the advantages of Automation is that you can manipulate programmable full-server and mini-server objects without creating a visible instance of the OA server. Unlike DDE, which requires that the server application be launched in a window or as an icon, Automation automatically launches the application for you. Unless you instruct the Automation server to activate its window, the server is invisible; the server's name usually does not appear in the Windows Task List.

---

**Note**

Although a full or automation server's window isn't visible, full and automation servers can consume a substantial percentage of the available resources of your computer. This fact is particularly true of mega-apps, such as Excel 97 and Word 97, when used as Automation servers. You can speed the opening of Excel 97 as an OA server and minimize the resources Excel 97 consumes by not loading unneeded add-ins.

If you plan to use Automation extensively in your Windows 95 applications, you should have a minimum of 16M of RAM (preferably 24M or more) and make sure that you have plenty of disk space (30M or more) for the Windows 95's swap file. For Windows NT 4.0 Workstation, 24M of RAM and a paging file of 48M or more is a good starting point.

---

### Interacting with 16-Bit OLE Automation Servers

You can use most 16-bit OLE 1.0 and 2+ OutOfProc servers with 32-bit Automation clients. Many developers supply only a 16-bit version of their OutOfProc servers in order to be compatible with Windows 3.1+, Windows 95, and Windows NT 4.0. The rules for using 16-bit and 32-bit programmable objects in both Windows 95 and Windows NT 4.0 are as follows:

- 32-bit OLE 2+ and Automation clients can employ 16-bit OLE 1.0 and 16-bit and 32-bit OLE 2+ full servers and mini-servers. The conversion to and from 16-bit operations is accomplished by a process called *thunking*, which is implemented by Olethk32.dll.

- 16-bit OLE clients cannot employ 32-bit OLE 2+ or Automation servers.

- 32-bit applications that support ActiveX Controls must use 32-bit OCXs.

- 16-bit applications that support early OLE Controls—only Access 2.0 and 16-bit Visual Basic 4.0—must use 16-bit OCXs. Full support for Visual Basic 16-bit OCXs in Access 2.0 requires installation of several updated files. (ActiveX Controls are 32-bit only.)

- InProc servers (OLE DLLs) must have the same "bitness" as the client application. As an example, you cannot use the 16-bit Jet 2.x database engine with Access 97 or the 32-bit Jet 3.x database engine with Access 2.0.

> **Note**
>
> The thunking process for IPC between 32-bit OLE 2+ clients and 16-bit OLE 1.0 and 2+ servers imposes additional overhead on LRPCs. This process also extracts an application performance toll. If you intend to make extensive use of Automation with Access 95, an investment in 32-bit versions of Automation servers will return substantial performance dividends.

On the whole, the limitations associated with the interoperability of 16-bit and 32-bit OLE Automation components are unlikely to be a problem for Access 97 users running either Windows 95 or Windows NT 4.0. The vast majority of Microsoft and third-party Windows application development has been devoted to 32-bit Windows software since early 1995. It is unlikely that software publishers will make major upgrades to their existing 16-bit applications for use with Windows 3.1+.

# Using Automation Servers with Access 97

To use OLE Automation, you must first write the code to create an instance in your application of the object that you plan to program. Access VBA contains the following four reserved words that you use to create an instance of a programmable object with Access VBA code:

- The **Object** data type is assigned to the programmable object variables you declare with {**Private¦Dim¦Public**} obj*Name* **As Object** statements. The Object property of a programmable Automation object contained in a bound or unbound object frame control points to the instance of the object. You can assign to an **Object** variable a pointer to the Automation object with the general syntax

    **Set** obj*Name* = [Forms!frm*Name*!]uof*Name*.Object

- The CreateObject function assigns a pointer to a new instance of an empty programmable object, such as a blank Excel 97 Worksheet object. The general syntax of the CreateObject function is

    **Set** obj*Name* = CreateObject("*ServerName.ObjectType*")

- The `GetObject` function assigns a pointer to a new instance of a programmable object whose data is contained in an existing file, str*PathFileName*, in the following syntax example:

```
Set objName = GetObject(strPathFileName[, _
    "ServerName.ObjectType"])
```

You can omit the *ServerName.ObjectType* argument if an entry in the Registry associates the file's extension with the object of the application you want to program. In the case of Excel 97, the default object type for .xls files is `Excel.Workbook`. If you substitute an empty string (`""`) for str*PathFileName*, the preceding statement assigns a pointer to an object of *ServerName.ObjectType* if such an object is open. If an object of the specified type is not open when the statement is executed, a trappable error occurs.

- The **New** keyword declares an **Object** variable and assigns in a single command a pointer to a new instance of an empty programmable object, such as an empty Word 97 document. The general syntax for creating an instance of a programmable object with **New** is

```
{Private|Dim|Public|Static} objName As New [ServerName.]ObjectType
```

To use the **New** keyword to create an instance of an **Object** variable, you must add a reference to the Automation server in Access 97's References dialog. Using the **New** keyword to create an object instance is called *early binding*. The advantage of early binding is that the VBA interpreter can check the validity of object references in Design view and the new Auto List Members feature displays candidate objects in a popup list (see Figure 31.1). Auto List Members also displays the syntax for object properties and methods.

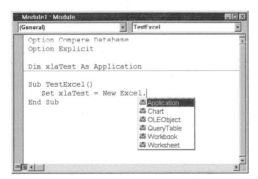

**FIG. 31.1**  The Auto List Members feature displaying the first-tier objects of the Microsoft Excel 8.0 type library.

If the Automation server application is open when you use the `CreateObject` or `GetObject` functions or the **New** reserved word, the type of the Automation server determines whether a new instance of the server is launched or the open instance is used. If the server type is Creatable Single-Instance, as is the case for Word 97, the open instance of Word is used with an empty document (CreateObject) or with a document created from the specified file (GetObject).

> **Note**
>
> Names of programmable objects created by Automation server applications appear in regular (not bold), monospaced type because the names of these objects are not VBA object data types.
>
> This book uses the common lowercase file extensions as the prefix for identifying objects created by full servers (rather than using the object tags specified by the *Leszynski Naming Conventions for Microsoft Access* (*LNC*), incorporated as Appendix A, "Naming Conventions for Access Objects and Variables"). Examples are xlaApp for the Excel application, xlwBook for Excel 5+ workbooks, xlsSheet for worksheets, xlcChart for Excel charts, and xlmModule for Excel VBA modules. (LNC uses xlsa*App*, xlsw*Sheet*, and xlsc*Chart*; LNC does not include a tag for Excel workbooks or VBA modules.) Word 97 Document objects are identified in this book by wdd*Name*, and the Word Application object is wda*Name*.

The four reserved words of the preceding list also are used by VBA to program objects of other applications. To write Automation code, you need to know the server name of the OA server and the names of the object types created by the server. The best way to become familiar with the object hierarchy of an Automation server is to create a reference to the server and explore the object hierarchy with Access 97's Object Browser.

 ◄◄ See "Using the Object Browser," p. 1027

### Manipulating an Excel 97 *Workbook* Object

The hierarchy of Excel 97 programmable objects is at least as complex as that of Access 97. Fortunately, the concepts of addressing objects in all Automation-compatible applications is nearly identical. Thus, the techniques you learned in Chapter 29, "Understanding the Data Access Object Class," stand you in good stead when you encounter Excel 97's Excel.Application object. The following sections describe how to create a test workbook, Customers.xls, with a single worksheet, Customers, and how to transfer data to and from the worksheet using Access VBA and Automation.

**Creating Customers.xls.** The examples that follow use the Customers.xls workbook file with data from the Customers table of Northwind.mdb. The example of OLE Automation with Excel 97 in this chapter uses the GetObject() function to open the Customers.xls file and manipulate the data in the worksheet. To create Customers.xls, follow these steps:

1. Select the Customers table in the Database window, and click the selection arrow of the Office Links button. Choose Analyze It with MS Excel from the drop-down menu to export the data in the table to Customers.xls and open the file in Excel 97 (see Figure 31.2).

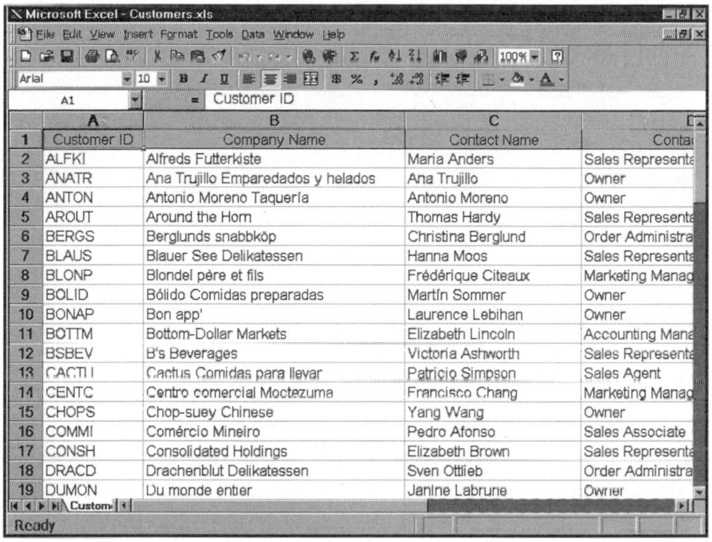

**FIG. 31.2**    The data of the Customers table exported to a Microsoft Excel 97 workbook.

2. Select cells A2 through D9 of the worksheet. Choose Insert, Name, and select Define. Type TestRange in the Names in Workbook text box and click OK. This creates a named range that you use in the examples that follow.

3. Choose File, Save As from Excel's File menu, and select Microsoft Excel Workbook in the Save As Type drop-down list to save the file in the default Microsoft Excel 5.0/95 (.xls) format. Alternatively, you can save the file in Excel 97's default Excel 8.0 format.

4. Change the Save In folder to your \Program Files\Microsoft Office\Office\Samples folder, and accept the default name for the file, Customers.xls, unless you have a reason to do otherwise. Click Save to save the file and close the dialog.

6. Close Microsoft Excel.

**The Hierarchy of VBA Excel 95 Objects.** The following list describes the hierarchy of the most commonly used programmable objects exposed by Excel 97:

■ Application represents an invisible instance of Excel 97. Using the Application object, you can execute almost all of Excel's menu commands by applying methods to the Application object. The Application object has properties such as ActiveWorkbook and ActiveSheet that specify the current Workbook and Worksheet objects. You can specify Excel.Application as the value of the ServerName. ObjectType argument of the CreateObject() and GetObject() functions, plus the **Dim** obj*Name* **As New** Excel.Application statement.

■ Workbook is the primary persistent object of Excel 97. Workbook objects are files that contain the other objects you create with Excel 97: Worksheet and Chart objects. Worksheet and Chart objects are contained in Worksheets and Charts collections, respectively.

- Worksheet objects are elements of the Workbook object that contain data. The primary interaction between Access 97 and Excel 97 takes place with Worksheet objects. You can transfer data contained in rows and columns of an Access Recordset object to cells in an Excel Worksheet object and vice versa. If you specify Excel. Sheet as the value of the *ServerName.ObjectName* argument of the GetObject function or use the **Dim** obj*Name* **As New** Excel.Sheet statement, the first member of the Worksheets collection—the ActiveSheet property of the Workbook object—is opened by default.

- Range objects are groups of cells specified by sets of cell coordinates. You can get or set the values of a single cell or group of cells by specifying the Range object. If the cells are contained in a named range, you can use the range name to refer to the group of cells. (A group of cells is not the same as a collection of cells; no Cells collection exists in Excel 97.)

  The Cells method specifies the coordinates of a Range object. Although no Cell object exists in Excel 97, you can use the Cells method to read or set the value of a single cell or group of cells, specified by coordinate sets.

Excel 97 exposes a variety of other objects. The preceding four objects, however, are those that you use most often in conjunction with Automation operations that are executed with Access VBA code.

**Using Excel's Online Help File for VBA.** If you don't have a printed copy of the *Microsoft Excel Visual Basic for Applications Reference*, you can open the Vbaxl8.hlp online help file to act as a reference for the objects, methods, and properties exposed by Excel 97. To open Vbaxl8.hlp while running Access and to display objects and methods references, follow these steps:

1. Launch Explorer and select your Excel 97 folder (usually C:\Program Files\ Microsoft Office\Office). Double-click Vbaxl8.hlp to open the Help Topics: Microsoft Excel Visual Basic dialog's Contents page (see Figure 31.3).

2. Double-click the Microsoft Excel Visual Basic Reference chapter icon, then double-click the Microsoft Excel Objects icon to display a diagram of the hierarchy of objects exposed by Excel 97 (see Figure 31.4). Objects exposed to Excel VBA are exposed also to Automation client applications.

3. Click the Worksheets (Worksheet) hotspot of the diagram to display the help topic for the Worksheets Collection Object, and click the Worksheet hotspot to display the help topic for the Worksheet Object.

4. Click the Properties hotspot to display the list of proprieties of the Worksheet object in the Topics Found dialog (see Figure 31.5). You can obtain a similar list of methods that apply to the object by clicking the Methods hotspot. (Cells was a method of Excel 95's Worksheet object.)

5. Double-click the Cells Property item hotspot to display the help window for the Cells property (see Figure 31.6).

**FIG. 31.3**   The Contents page of the Vbaxl8.hlp file.

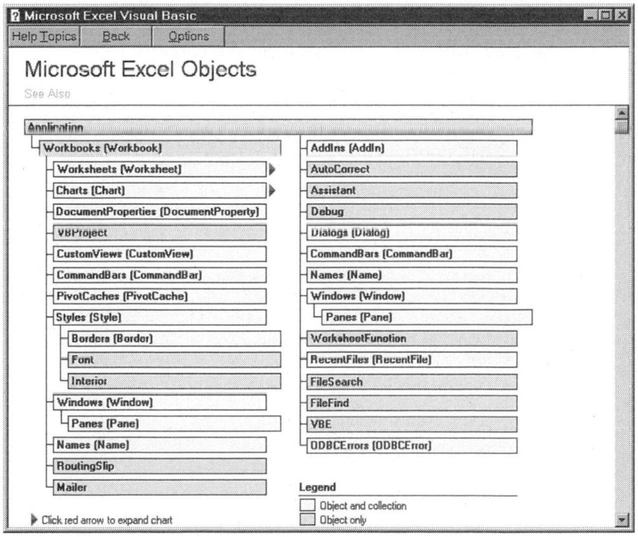

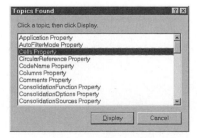

**FIG. 31.4**   The Microsoft Excel Objects hierarchy displayed by the Excel VBA help file.

**FIG. 31.5**   Properties of the Excel `Worksheet` object displayed in the Topics Found window.

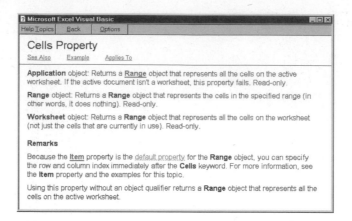

**FIG. 31.6**  The help topic for the `Cells` property of the `Application`, `Range`, and `Workbook` objects.

6. Click the Examples hotspot to display examples of VBA code applicable to the `Cells` property (see Figure 31.7). Most of the Excel VBA code examples are compatible with Access VBA Automation code.

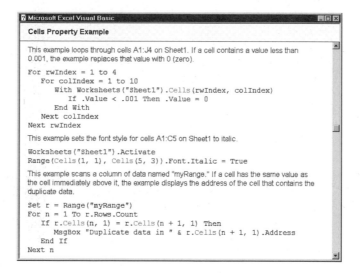

**FIG. 31.7**  VBA example code for the `Cells` property of the `Worksheet` and `Range` objects.

**Creating an Excel Reference and Using Access 97's Object Browser.** Creating a reference to the object or type library of Automation servers offers the following advantages:

- The Access VBA compiler checks the syntax of your Automation code for consistency with the properties and methods of the objects you declare. This test is not made if you don't declare a reference to the Automation server object.

- You can use the Object Browser to determine the proper syntax for object properties and methods.

- You can gain quick access to the help topic for the object, property, or method selected in the Object Browser's lists.

- You gain the advantage of Access 97's Auto List Members feature when writing your Automation code.

- You can use the shorthand **Dim** obj*Name* **As New** *ServerName.ObjectType* statement to instantiate (create an instance of) the server object with early binding.

- You can use the intrinsic constants predefined for the object as argument values. This is especially important for servers, such as Excel, that have many intrinsic constants.

To create a reference to the Microsoft Excel 8.0 object library and explore Excel objects with the Access 97 Object Browser, follow these steps:

1. Launch Access and open Northwind.mdb, if necessary. Open the Utility Functions module and choose Tools, References to display the References dialog.

2. Mark the check box for the Microsoft Excel 8.0 Object Library, Excel8.olb (see Figure 31.8), and then click the OK button to close the References dialog and create the reference.

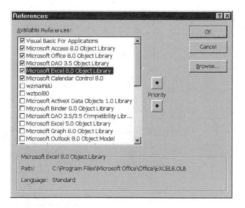

**FIG. 31.8**    Adding an Access VBA reference to the Microsoft Excel 8.0 Object Library.

3. Open Access's Object Browser and choose Excel in the Project/Library list (see Figure 31.9).

4. Select Worksheet in the Classes list and Cells in the Members of 'Worksheet' list. A cryptic syntax example for the Cells property appears in the bottom panel. Clicking the Help button displays the help topic for the Cells property, which is the same topic shown in Figure 31.7.

**FIG. 31.9** Displaying the simplified syntax for the `Cells` property of the `Worksheet` object in Access 95's Object Browser.

5. When you finish exploring properties and methods of the Worksheet object, click the Close button to close Object Browser.

**Registry Entries for Automation Servers.** You can specify any object listed in the Registry that is identified by a *ServerName.ObjectType[.Version]* entry at the HKEY_CLASSES_ROOT level of the Registry, as shown in Figure 31.10. The optional *.Version* suffix, shown in the line below the entry for `Excel.Sheet`, indicates the version number of ServerName. If you have two versions of the same Automation server, you can use the `.Version` suffix to specify one of the two.

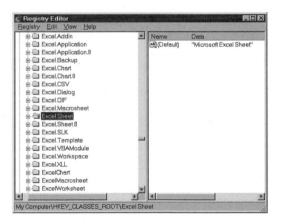

**FIG. 31.10** Registry entries for top-level Excel 97 objects that you can call directly from Automation clients.

In addition to the primary Registry entries for Excel 97 objects that you can open, additional data for creating or opening programmable objects appear in the \HKEY_ LOCAL_MACHINE\Software\CLSID section of the Registry. `CLSID` is the abbreviation for `ClassID`, a globally unique, 32-character (plus hyphens) identifier for each object exposed by any COM object. The additional Registry entries for the `Excel.Sheet.5` object appears in Figure 31.11. These entries provide information required to launch Excel 97 in Automation mode when you create an `Excel.Sheet` object.

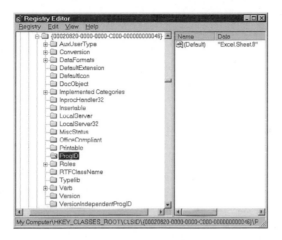

**FIG. 31.11** Additional registration database entries for Excel 95 `Application` and `Worksheet` objects.

**Opening and Manipulating an Existing Excel Worksheet Object.** Learning to write VBA Automation code is a much quicker process if you use the Debug window to try Automation instructions before you begin writing complex Automation code in modules.

> **Note**
>
> In all examples of this chapter in which the Debug window is used, pressing the Enter key after typing **?** *Expression* is implied.

To open the `Worksheet` object of the Customers.xls `Workbook` object, follow these steps:

1. Close Excel if it is running. Open a new module in the Northwind Traders database, and add the following Object variable declarations in the Declarations section:

   ```
   Private xlaCust As Object 'Application object
   Private xlwCust As Object 'Workbook object
   Private xlsCust As Object 'Sheet object
   ```

2. Open the Debug window and type the following statement to create an object of the default `Workbook` class. When you press Enter, Excel 97 is launched in /automation mode.

   ```
   Set xlwCust = GetObject(CurDir & "\customers.xls")
   ```

   `CurDir` returns the well-formed path of your current directory, \Program Files\ Microsoft Office\Office\ \Samples, if you've opened Northwind.mdb in its default location. If you saved Customers.xls elsewhere, add the path to the file name in the preceding statement. Depending on the speed of your computer, opening Excel 97 may take an appreciable period. (When <Running> returns to <Ready> in the status bar of the Debug window, Excel has finished loading.)

3. Customers.xls only includes one Worksheet object, so the Customer worksheet is the ActiveSheet object. To open the Customers worksheet, type

   **Set xlsCust = xlwCust.ActiveSheet**

4. Verify that you have a valid Worksheet object by typing **? xlsCust.Cells(1, 1)**. After a brief interval, the expected result—Customer ID—appears.

5. You can test the ability of the Cells method to return the values of other cells by typing **? xlsCust.Cells(R, C)**, where **R** is the row and **C** is the column of the cell coordinates (see Figure 31.12).

**FIG. 31.12**    The commands to read and set the values of a single cell in the Customers worksheet.

6. You can alter the content of a cell by entering an expression such as xlsCust.Cells(2, 2).Value = "Alfred's Food Store". Like many Access control objects, in which the name of an object returns its value, the Cells method does not require that you explicitly specify the default Value property. Verify that the content changed by typing **? xlsCust.Cells(2, 2)** with and without appending **.Value** (see Figure 31.12).

7. When you are finished using an Automation object, you should close the object to free the memory resources it consumes. To disassociate an object from an object variable, use a **Set** objName = **Nothing** statement (refer to Figure 31.12). Type **Set xlsCust = Nothing**, and **Set xlwCust = Nothing** to close the invisible instance of Excel. Multiple object variables can point to a single object, so the OA object is not closed until all object variables have gone out of scope or **Set** explicitly to **Nothing**.

You also can use the `Formula` property to set the value of a cell. The advantage of the `Formula` property is that you can also use this property to enter a formula using Excel A1 syntax, such as `=A10+B15`.

**Using Named Ranges of Cells.** If you created the named range—TestRange—in Customers.xls, you can return the values of the cells in the range by referring to the `Range` object of the `Worksheet` object. Figure 31.13 shows typical expressions that operate on the `Range` object of a `Worksheet` object and the `Names` collection of a `Workbook` object.

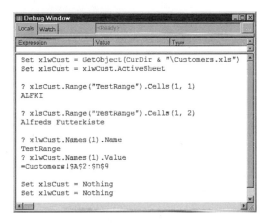

**FIG. 31.13**   Expressions that return the values in `Range` objects and the `Names` collection.

To specify a cell within a named `Range` object, use the following general syntax:

```
wksName.Range(strRangeName).Cells(intRow, intCol)
```

Because named ranges are global for all worksheets in an Excel workbook, the `Names` collection is a member of the `Workbook` object.

You refer to the `Ranges` collection of the `Workbook` object with statements such as

```
strRangeName = xlwName.Names(intIndex).Name
strRangeValue = xlwName.Names(intIndex).Value
```

Unlike Access object collections, which begin with an index value of 0, the first member of a VBA collection has an index value of 1.

**Explicitly Closing a Workbook and the Application Object.** Just as a `Workbook` object is the value of the `Parent` property of a `Worksheet` object, the `Application` object is the `Parent` property of a `Workbook` object. The value of Excel 97's `Application` object is Microsoft Excel. Figure 31.14 illustrates expressions that work their way upward in Excel's object hierarchy, from `Worksheet` to `Application` objects. You can shortcut the process by using `xlsCust.Parent.Parent` to point to the `Application` object from a `Worksheet` object.

You can use the `Close` method to close an Excel `Workbook` object explicitly (you can't close a `Worksheet` object). You can use the `Quit` method of the `Application` object to exit the application. It's a good practice to exit the Application server application to conserve scarce system resources if you have multiple references to the Application server object. (Access 2.0 required brackets around Close and Quit because of conflicts with Access Basic reserved words.) For example, the following statements close the Workbook object and then exit the OA server application, freeing the memory reserved by the server:

```
Set xlaCust = xlsCust.Parent.Parent
xlsCust.Parent.Close(False)
xlaCust.Quit
```

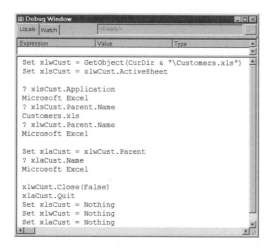

```
Debug Window                                    _□×
Locals  Watch              <Ready>

Expression            Value              Type

Set xlwCust = GetObject(CurDir & "\Customers.xls")
Set xlsCust = xlwCust.ActiveSheet

? xlsCust.Application
Microsoft Excel
? xlsCust.Parent.Name
Customers.xls
? xlwCust.Parent.Name
Microsoft Excel

Set xlaCust = xlwCust.Parent
? xlaCust.Name
Microsoft Excel

xlwCust.Close(False)
xlaCust.Quit
Set xlsCust = Nothing
Set xlwCust = Nothing
Set xlaCust = Nothing
```

**FIG. 31.14**  Assigning objects higher in the hierarchy and closing Workbook and Application objects.

The False argument of the Close method closes the Workbook without displaying the message box that asks if you want to save changes to the Workbook. When using the Quit method to exit the application, you receive that message regardless of whether you modified the worksheet. To avoid this message when reading Excel 95 worksheets, close the worksheet before applying the Quit method. You must create an Application object because you cannot execute the xlsCust.Parent.Parent.Quit statement after closing the xlsCust object. (You receive an Object has no value error message if you try.)

### Creating a New Excel Worksheet with Access VBA Code

You can emulate the Analyze It with MS Excel feature of Access 95 with Access VBA OLE Automation code. The CreateCust function of Listing 31.1 creates a new Workbook object, Cust.xls, and copies the data from the Customers table to a Worksheet named *Customers*. One of the primary incentives for writing your own version of the Analyze It with MS Excel feature is the ability to format the Worksheet object the way that you want. You also can add custom column headers. (The code to add column headers is not included in the CreateCust function.) When you execute the function from the Debug window, you receive a progress report from the Debug.Print statements in the code.

**Listing 31.1    Declarations and Code to Create a New Excel Workbook**

```
Option Compare Database
Option Explicit

Private xlaCust As Object  'Application
Private xlwCust As Object  'Workbook
Private xlsCust As Object  'Worksheet

Function CreateCust() As Integer
'Purpose: Create new Excel 95 worksheet from Customers table

    'Declare local variables (Object variables are module-level)
    Dim dbNWind As Database   'Current database
    Dim rstCust As Recordset  'Table Recordset over Customers
    Dim intRow As Integer     'Row counter
    Dim intCol As Integer     'Column counter

    'Assign DAO pointers
    Set dbNWind = CurrentDb()
    Set rstCust = dbNWind.OpenRecordset("Customers", dbOpenTable)

    DoCmd.Hourglass True

    'Create a new Excel Worksheet object
    Set xlwCust = CreateObject("Excel.Sheet.8")
    Set xlsCust = xlwCust.ActiveSheet
    Debug.Print "Worksheet created"

    'Give the new worksheet a name
    xlsCust.Name = "Customers"

    'Get the Application object for the Quit method
    Set xlaCust = xlsCust.Parent.Parent

    intRow = 1
    intCol = 1

    rstCust.MoveFirst    'Go to the first record (safety)
    Do Until rstCust.EOF
        'Loop through each record
        For intCol = 1 To rstCust.Fields.Count
            'Loop through each field
            If Not IsNull(rstCust.Fields(intCol - 1)) Then
                xlsCust.Cells(intRow, intCol).Value = _
                CStr(rstCust.Fields(intCol - 1))
            End If
        Next intCol
        Debug.Print "Record " & intRow
        rstCust.MoveNext
        intRow = intRow + 1
    Loop

    Debug.Print "Formatting columns"
```

(continues)

**Listing 31.1 Continued**

```
    For intCol = 1 To xlsCust.Columns.Count
      'Format each column of the worksheet
      xlsCust.Columns(intCol).Font.Size = 8
      xlsCust.Columns(intCol).AutoFit
      If intCol = 8 Then
          'Align numeric and alphanumeric postal codes left
          xlsCust.Columns(intCol).HorizontalAlignment = xlLeft
      End If
    Next intCol

    DoCmd.Hourglass False

    Debug.Print "Saving Workbook and exiting"
    xlwCust.SaveAs (CurDir & "\Cust.xls")
    xlaCust.Quit
    Set xlsCust = Nothing
    Set xlwCust = Nothing
    Set xlaCust = Nothing
  End Function
```

> **Note**
>
> The Excel.Sheet object of Excel 97 returns a Workbook, not a Worksheet object, when used as the argument of the CreateObject function. The Excel.Sheet object of Excel 95 returned the expected Worksheet object.

Figure 31.15 shows the Private Object variable declarations in the Declarations section of the module, followed by the first few lines of the preceding code and entries in the Debug window resulting from executing the CreateCust function.

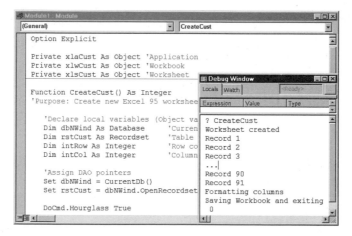

**FIG. 31.15**  The Declarations section and first few lines of code for the CreateCust function.

You must coerce to **String** the data type of the **Variant** values returned by rstCust. Fields(intCol -1) with the **CStr** function. If you omit the **CStr** function, Excel 97 displays #N/A# instead of the proper value. It the `Recordset` contains field data types other than Text, use the appropriate **CType** function to determine the data type for the column.

The `xlLeft` constant, assigned to the value of the `HorizontalAlignment` property of the eighth column, is an Excel intrinsic constant defined when you create a reference to the Microsoft Excel 8.0 Object library. Selecting Constants in the Classes list of the Object Browser with the Excel library active displays the `xlConst` constants. Figure 31.16 shows the numeric value of `xlLeft`, one of the constant values that is valid for the `HorizontalAlignment` property.

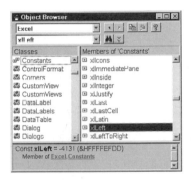

**FIG. 31.16**   Obtaining values of `xlConst` intrinsic constants in Access 95's Object Browser.

Run the function shown in the preceding listing by typing **? CreateCust** in the Debug window. Figure 31.17 shows the Cust.xls workbook with the Customer worksheet created by the `CreateCust()` function opened in Excel 97. Unless you specify a path, Excel saves Cust.xls in the default \My Documents folder.

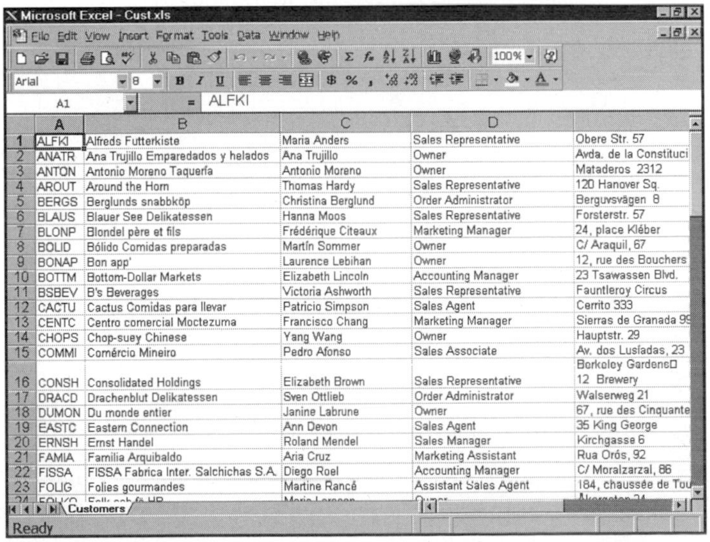

**FIG. 31.17**   Part of the Excel 97 worksheet created from the Customers table.

## Sending Data to Microsoft Word 97 with Automation

Microsoft Word 97 replaces the venerable Word Basic macro language with VBA 5.0. Word 95 exposed the `Word.Basic` object, which gave VBA programmers access to about 800 Word Basic commands, but Word 95 was an Automation server only. Now Word 97 is a full-fledged Automation server and client with programming capabilities similar to Excel 97. You can create references to type libraries and then use Word VBA to program other application's objects, such as Access 97's `Application` object or the DAO.

> **Note**
>
> If you've programmed the `Word.Basic` object and Word 95 menu commands with Access 95 or Visual Basic 4.0, you find that your VBA client code is backwardly compatible with Word 97. Plan to rewrite Automation code that uses the `Word.Basic` object because there's no assurance that future versions of Word will continue to support the `Word.Basic` object and its Word 95 menu commands.

**Using Word 97's Online VBA Help File.** Word 97's object model is even more complex than the object model of Excel 97, so you need the Word VBA help file to guide you when using Word as an Automation server. To display the object model for the Word `Application` and `Document` objects, follow these steps:

1. Launch Explorer and select the Word 97 folder (C:\Program Files\Microsoft Office\Office is the default location). Double-click Vbawrd8.hlp to open the Contents page of the Help Topics: Microsoft Word Visual Basic dialog (see Figure 31.18).

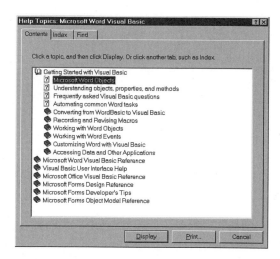

**FIG. 31.18**    The Contents page of the Vbawrd8.hlp file.

2. Double-click the Getting Started with Visual Basic chapter icon, and then double-click the Microsoft Word Objects page icon to display the top-level (`Application`)

objects exposed by Word 97's object library (see Figure 31.19). Objects exposed to Word VBA are available to all Automation client applications.

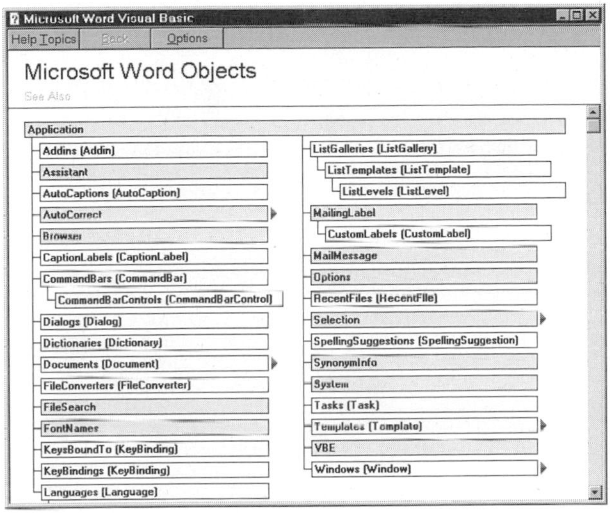

**FIG. 31.19**   Most of the Microsoft Word Objects hierarchy displayed by the Word VBA help file.

3. Click the Documents (Document) triangular hotspot of the diagram to display the Document object model (see Figure 31.20). Document objects are the most common entry point for Automation clients that manipulate existing Word documents.

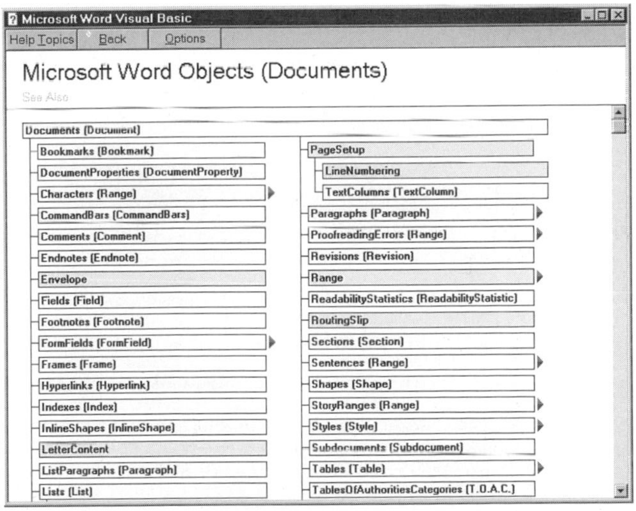

**FIG. 31.20**   Most of the subobjects of Word 97's Document object.

4. Click the Bookmarks (Bookmark) item to display the help topic for the Bookmarks Collection, and then click the Bookmark hotspot to display the help topic for the Bookmark object. A Bookmark object corresponds approximately to a named Range object of Excel.

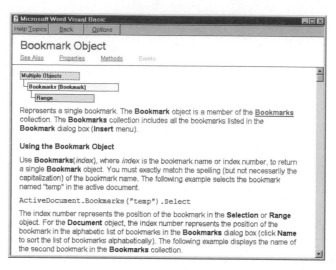

**FIG. 31.21** The Word 97 help topic for the Bookmark object.

> **Note**
>
> The Range object of a Word document defines a temporary contiguous set of characters in a Word Document. Unlike Excel's named Range objects, you can only create a Word Range object with Word VBA code. Word Range objects are not persistent; they exist only for the duration of the procedure that creates the Range.

For quick access to help with Word objects and the syntax for properties and methods, create a reference to the Microsoft Word 8.0 Object Library (see Figure 31.22). When you select Word in the Library/Class drop-down list of the Object Browser, Word 97's objects appear in the Classes list. Figure 31.23 shows the properties and methods for the Bookmark object in the Members of 'Bookmark' list.

**Modifying a Word Document with VBA Code.** The generic code for opening an existing Word 97 Document with VBA and saving any changes made to the file is as follows:

```
Private wdaName As Object 'Word Application object
Private wddName As Object 'Word Document object

Set wddName = GetObject("d:\path\filename.doc")
Set wdaName = wddName.Application

'... Code to manipulate document

wdaName.Save
```

```
wdaName.Quit
Set wddName = Nothing
Set wdaName = Nothing
```

If the document includes bookmarks, you can select and replace the bookmarked text with the following code:

```
wddName.Bookmarks("BookmarkName").Select
wdaName.Selection = "Replacement text"
```

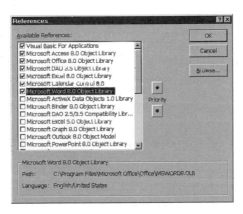

**FIG. 31.22**   Creating a reference to the Microsoft Word 8.0 Object Library.

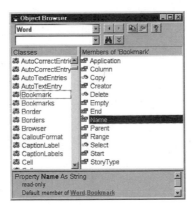

**FIG. 31.23**   Properties and methods of Word 97's `Bookmark` object displayed by Access 97's Object Browser.

One of the most effective methods of using Access 97 to create custom Word 97 documents is to define a set of named bookmarks and replace the bookmarked text with text from an Access Recordset object. In this case, a Word `Bookmark` object corresponds to the `Cells(x, y)` property of an Excel `Worksheet` object, where the `x, y` arguments specify a single cell. Figure 31.24 shows code in the Debug window for reading and writing bookmarked text in the Word file for the manuscript of this chapter (Uaw31rj.doc). `Selection` is a property of the `Application` object, not the `Document` object. Only one `Selection` can be active in an instance of Word, no matter how many `Documents` are open.

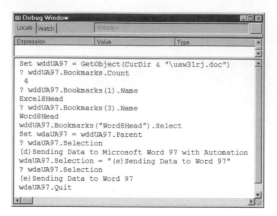

**FIG. 31.24**  Reading and replacing bookmarked text in a Word 97 document.

To create and save a new Word document, use the following generic code:

```
Private wdaName As Object 'Word Application object
Private wddName As Object 'Word Document object

Set wdaName = CreateObject("Word.Application")
wdaName.Documents.Add 'Empty document
Set wddName = wdaName.ActiveDocument

'... Code to manipulate document

wddName.SaveAs FileName:="filename.doc"
wdaName.Quit
Set wddName = Nothing
Set wdaName = Nothing
```

It isn't obvious how to add text to an empty document you create with the `Documents.Add` method. When you add an empty document, it contains a single character (a paragraph marker), which represents the `Content` property of the `Document`. The following code creates a `Range` object representing the entire document and then applies the `InsertBefore` method to add text to the empty document:

```
Private wdrName As Object 'Word Range object

Set wdrName = wddName.Content 'Range = 1 character
wdrName.InsertBefore "Text to insert"
```

Figure 31.25 is an example of using the `InsertBefore` method in the Debug window for adding text to a newly created document. The `Select` method of the `Range` object selects the entire `Range`. With the selection active, you can apply the `Add` method to the `Bookmarks` collection to add a persistent `Bookmark` object to contain the selection.

**Programming a Word Document in an Access Object Frame.** Most people who alter word processing documents want to view the modifications before final acceptance. Thus, the majority of Access applications that use Automation with Word 97 as the server are likely to involve Word documents contained in bound or unbound object frames. Chapter 22, "Using Access with Microsoft Word and Mail Merge," explains how to add a bound object frame containing an embedded Word document.

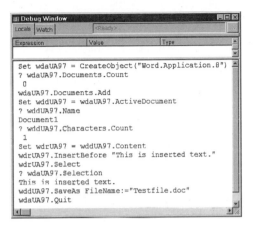

**FIG. 31.25**  Adding text to an empty Word 97 document with the InsertBefore method of the Range object.

◀◀ See "Embedding or Linking Word Documents in Access Tables," p. 778

The following generic code, with a reference to the Microsoft Word 8.0 Object Library, lets you apply Word 97 methods to the embedded document contained in a bound or unbound object frame:

```
Dim wdaName As Word.Application
Dim wddName As Word.Document

[Forms!FormName!]ControlName.Action = acOLEActivate
Set wdaName = [Forms!FormName!]ControlName.Object.Application
Set wddName = wdaName.ActiveDocument

'...Code to manipulate document

[Forms!FormName!]ControlName.Action = acOLEClose
Set wddName = Nothing
Set wdaName = Nothing
```

The *ControlName*.Action = acOLEActivate statement is required if the embedded object has not been activated when you execute the preceding code example, either in the Debug window or a VBA procedure. An embedded object in a frame must be activated before you can refer to its Object.Application.*PropertyName* property. Linked objects in object frames don't support Automation. You receive a "This object does not support OLE Automation" error message when you execute the **Set** wdaName = uofName.Object. Application.WordBasic for a linked file.

Figure 31.26 shows an example of activating an embedded Word 97 object and then reading the value of bookmarked text using the `Selection` object. To execute the code shown in Figure 31.26, you must first insert an unbound Word 97 object created from a file with bookmarks that are named "Excel8Head" and "Word8Head" in a form named `frmWord`. You must also create a reference to the Microsoft Word 8.0 object library and declare the object variables wdaUA97 and wddUA97 in the declarations section of a module.

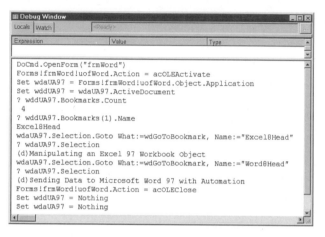

**FIG. 31.26** Reading the text of a bookmark in an embedded OLE object.

By using Automation and code similar to that shown in Figure 31.26, you can create a document that consists of nothing but empty bookmarks. Then you can fill the bookmarks with text contained in Text or Memo fields of tables or from the `Value` property of control objects on forms. Using Automation provides a much more flexible method of creating specialized documents than using Access 95's Merge It feature.

# Adding ActiveX Controls to Your Application

ActiveX Controls (OCXs) are a special class of programmable Automation objects that expose their own events in addition to their properties and methods. You embed the ActiveX Control in a form and program the Control with the same types of statements used with native Access controls, such as a text box or combo box. Some ActiveX Controls are databound, in which case you embed the Control in a form bound to an Access table or query.

ActiveX controls are similar to Visual Basic custom controls (VBXs) in concept and use. VBXs are 16-bit only, while ActiveX controls are 32-bit only. All of the Office 97 applications that support Forms 2.0 let you embed ActiveX controls on forms; Internet Explorer 3.0 also supports ActiveX controls. (Access 2.0 and 16-bit Visual Basic 4.0 use 16-bit OLE Controls, which now are obsolete.)

The sections that follow describe the Calendar ActiveX Control supplied with Access 97; they explain how to register an OCX when necessary, and show you how to insert and program the Microsoft Calendar Control.

> **Note**
>
> Access 2.0 and Access 95 included the Data Outline control, a very large OLE Control that pro-
> vided a form navigation system for Access applications. An ActiveX version of the Data Outline
> control is not included with Access 97.

### Registering OLE Controls

ActiveX Controls must be registered before they appear in the list of Controls available for use with Access 97. Most commercial ActiveX Controls, including those supplied with Access 95 and Visual Basic 5.0, create the required Registry entries during the instal-lation process. Figure 31.27 shows in RegEdit.exe the Registry entries for the Access 97 Calendar Control.

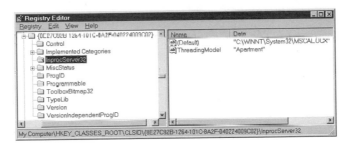

**FIG. 31.27** The Registry hive for the Calendar Control displayed in RegEdit.exe.

Many shareware ActiveX Controls don't come with a Setup application, so you must register the OCXs yourself. If your Windows 95 or Windows NT Registry file becomes corrupted and you cannot solve the problem by restoring the Registry backup file, you must reregister your ActiveX Controls. (If the Registry file becomes irreparably corrupted, you probably will also need to reinstall all of your Windows applications and, perhaps, Windows 95 or Windows NT.)

To register a 32-bit ActiveX Control for Access 97 and for all other applications that use 32-bit OCXs, follow these steps:

1. Choose Tools, ActiveX Controls to open the ActiveX Controls dialog, and then click the Register button to open the Add ActiveX Control dialog.

2. Maneuver to the \Windows\System or the \Winnt\System32 folder, the standard locations for OLE controls, and select the .ocx file you want to register or reregister (see Figure 31.28).

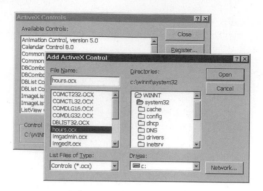

**FIG. 31.28** Selecting an .ocx file to register.

3. Click the Open button to close the Add ActiveX Control dialog and register the Control. You can't register some .ocx files as Access ActiveX controls. If you attempt to register a special-purpose Control, you receive an error message stating that the control cannot be registered.

If you want to delete a custom control from your fixed disk, it is advisable to delete the Registry entry for the control before deleting the control. Select the name of the control in the Available Controls list of the ActiveX Controls dialog, and then click the Unregister button to remove the Registry entry for the control. Then delete the corresponding .ocx file.

### Using the Calendar Control

The Microsoft Calendar Control was one of the three original OLE Controls introduced with Access 2.0. Mscal.ocx, included with Access 97, is an improved, 32-bit ActiveX version of the original Calendar Control. Mscal.ocx is a data-bound control; that is, you can bind the Control to a field of the Date/Time data type. The data-bound Calendar Control displays the date in calendar form.

The following sections describe how to add the Calendar Control to a form and how to program the Calendar Control.

**Adding the Calendar Control to a Form.** To add a Calendar Control in an unbound object frame of a form, follow these steps:

1. Create a new blank (unbound) form about 5 inches wide and 3 inches deep.

2. Choose Insert, ActiveX Control to display the Insert ActiveX Controls dialog.

3. Select the Calendar Control from the Select an ActiveX Control list (see Figure 31.29). Click OK to add the Calendar Control to the form.

4. Size the Calendar Control to about 3×2 inches, position the mouse pointer on the Control, and then click the right mouse button to open the popup menu for the Control.

**5.** Choose Calendar <u>O</u>bject from the floating menu with the left mouse button to open the object's submenu (see Figure 31.30). Choose Properties to open the properties sheet for the Control.

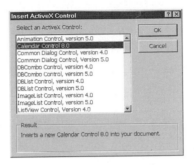

**FIG. 31.29**    Adding the Calendar Control with the Insert ActiveX Controls dialog.

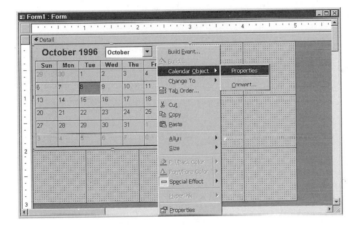

**FIG. 31.30**    The popup menus for an ActiveX Control.

**6.** The tabbed properties sheet opens to let you set a variety of General properties for the Calendar Control. Click the Font tab to open the Fonts properties page.

> **Note**
>
> Technically speaking, the properties dialog of an ActiveX Control is called a *property frame* or, more commonly, *properties sheet*, and the content of the property frame is stored in *property pages*. Entries for the property sheet and property page(s) appear as entries for the ActiveX control in the Registry.

**7.** With DayFont selected in the Property Name list, select Arial from the Font combo list, apply the Bold attribute, set the font size to 10 points, and click the Apply button (see Figure 31.31).

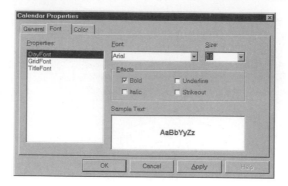

**FIG. 31.31**    The Fonts page of the Calendar Properties sheet.

8. Repeat the font selection process of the preceding step for the GridFont property (10-point Arial bold) and TitleFont property (14-point Arial bold).

9. Click the Colors tab to display the Colors properties page. You can change the color of the background (BackColor), DayFont, GridFont, TitleFont, and GridLines to one of the 16 standard colors or Windows system colors (see Figure 31.32).

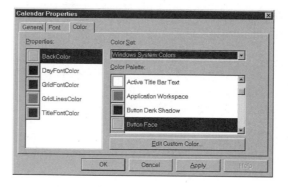

**FIG. 31.32**    The Color page of the Calendar Properties sheet.

10. Click OK to close the properties sheet. Double-click a blank area of the form to display the Form properties window. Then set the Scroll Bars property to Neither and the Record Selectors and Navigation Buttons properties to No. Change the name of the control from ActiveXCtrl1 to **ocxCalendar**. Your Calendar Control appears in Run mode, as shown in Figure 31.33.

11. To eliminate the month and year drop-down lists and change the appearance of the Control, return to Design view and open the properties sheet for ocxCalendar. In the General properties page, clear the Month/Year Selectors check box and select Sunken in the Grid Cell Effect list.

12. Click OK to close the properties sheet. Change to Form view; the modified Calendar Control appears, as shown in Figure 31.34.

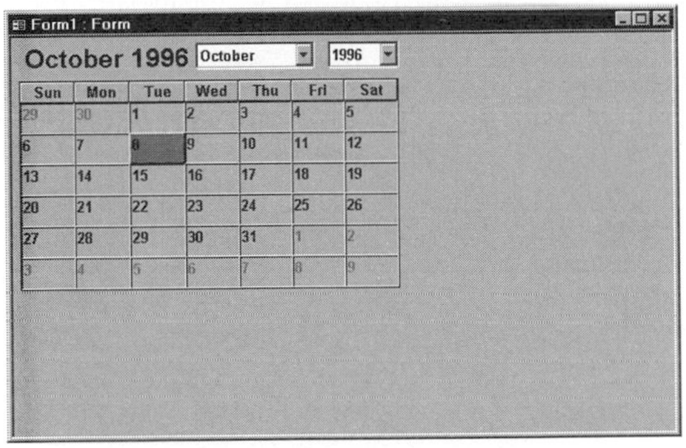

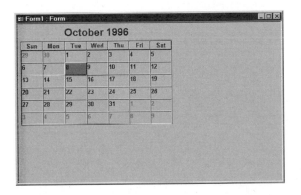

**FIG. 31.33**   The modified Calendar Control in Run mode with month and year drop-down lists.

**FIG. 31.34**   The modified Calendar Control in Run mode without the drop-down lists.

13. Save your form with a descriptive name, such as **frmCalendar**.

**Programming the Calendar Control.** Each ActiveX Control has its own collection of properties, methods, and events. Each of the ActiveX controls supplied with Access 97 and the ODE has an individual online help file to assist you in programming the control. You can open the help file by clicking the Help button of a Control's properties sheet, if present. The Help file for the Calendar Control is integrated with the Access 97 online help file. Another approach is to choose Start, Find, and type **\*.hlp** in the Named text box of the Find: Files Named dialog. Then click the Find button. The help file usually is the file name for the control with an .hlp extension (see Figure 31.35).

Double-click the help file for the ActiveX Control to display the Help Topics dialog for the control (see Figure 31.36). Figure 31.37 shows the help topic for the PreviousMonth method for the Calendar Control.

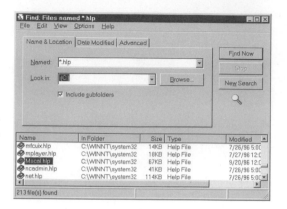

**FIG. 31.35**    Finding help files for OLE Controls in Windows NT 4.0.

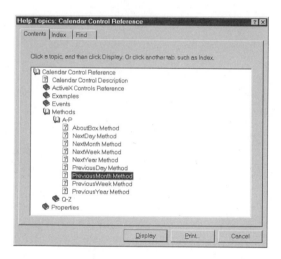

**FIG. 31.36**    The Help Topics dialog for the Calendar Control.

To program the Calendar Control and complete the design of the frmCalendar form, follow these steps:

1. Add six command buttons, stacked vertically to the right of the calendar. Assign **Next Week**, **Last Week**, **Next Month**, **Last Month**, **Next Year**, and **Last Year** as the value of the Caption property for the six buttons in sequence. Name the buttons **cmdNextWeek**, **cmdLastWeek**, and so forth.

2. Add an unbound text box under the calendar. Assign **lblDate** and **txtDate** as the values of the Name property of the label and text box, respectively (see Figure 31.38).

**3.** Click the Calendar Control with the right mouse button and choose Build Event from the floating menu to open the class module for ocxCalendar. Select the `AfterUpdate` event from the events drop-down list to create the **Private Sub** `ocxCalendar_AfterUpdate()`...**End Sub** stub. Note that the events exposed by the Calendar Control, such as `AfterUpdate`, `NewMonth`, and `NewYear`, appear in the list of events for the ocxCalendar control.

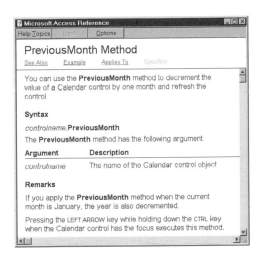

**FIG. 31.37**   The online help topic for the `PreviousMonth` method of the Calendar Control.

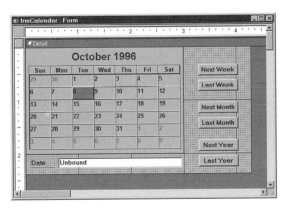

**FIG. 31.38**   The final design of the Calendar Control form.

**4.** Type the following code (see Figure 31.39) for the `AfterUpdate` event to display the date when the form opens and when the date is changed:

```
Private Sub ocxCalendar_AfterUpdate ()
    'Purpose: Update the text boxes
```

```
lblDate.Caption = Format(ocxCalendar.Object.Value, _
    "mm/dd/yy")
txtDate.Value = Format(ocxCalendar.Object.Value, "dddddd")
End Sub
```

> **Note**
>
> Access 97 inserts ActiveX Controls in bound or unbound object frames, so you must specify the `Object` property of the frame to gain access to the properties and methods of the control.

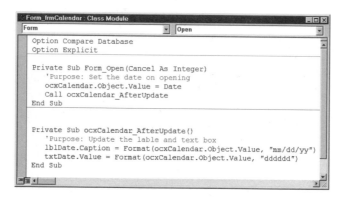

**FIG. 31.39**  Entering the code for the `AfterUpdate` event.

**5.** Enter the following code to set the date explicitly when opening the form:

```
Private Sub Form_Open(Cancel As Integer)
    'Purpose: Set the date on opening
    ocxCalendar.Object.Value = Date 'Explicitly set the date
    Call ocxCalendar_AfterUpdate
End Sub
```

**6.** Mscal.ocx has methods for changing the week, month, and year (refer to Figure 31.37), so you can add the following code to apply the appropriate method to the Calendar Control with each `Click` event for each of the command buttons:

```
Sub cmd{Next¦Previous}{Week¦Month¦Year}_Click ()
    'Purpose: Use the Next or Previous period method
    'to increment or decrement the period
    ocxCalendar.Object.{Next¦Previous}{Week¦Month¦Year}
End Sub
```

**7.** Complete the design of the form by setting the value of the `MinMaxButtons` property to `None`.

**8.** Click the Form View button of the toolbar to open your Calendar Control form (see Figure 31.40). Verify your event-handling procedures by testing the action of each of the six buttons.

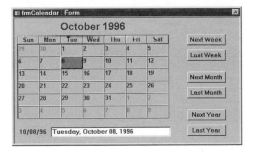

**FIG. 31.40**    The finished Calendar Control in Form view.

# Using Access 97 as an Automation Server

Access 97 exposes all of its application objects to other 32-bit, automation-enabled applications through the `Access.Application.8` object. To use Access as an automation server, you create in a module a reference to the Microsoft Access 97 type library, Msaccess.tlb—which is located in the Access folder, not in \Windows\System. Any member of the Office 97 suite and 32-bit Visual Basic 4+ can manipulate Access 97 `Application` objects, properties, and methods.

The extent to which developers will use Access 95 application objects instead of the Jet 3.5 database engine remains to be seen. Using the Jet 3.5 data access object to manipulate databases is much faster and consumes far fewer resources than launching an instance of Access to perform ordinary database-related operations.

You use the `CreateObject` function to open a minimized instance of Access and then open a database with the `OpenCurrentDatabase` `"DatabasePathName"` method. Alternatively, you can use the `GetObject("path\filename.mdb")` function. From this point on, you program the objects with Access VBA code in the other application. You even can invoke Access VBA's `DoCmd` object from the Automation client with aca*Name*.DoCmd.Action *Argument(s)* statements.

As with using Access to manipulate objects of other applications described earlier in this chapter, the Debug window is the best way to gain familiarity with the Access Application object. To experiment with Access 97's Application object in Excel 97, follow these steps:

1. Close Access if it is open, and launch Excel 97.

2. Choose <u>T</u>ools, <u>M</u>acro, <u>V</u>isual Basic Editor to open an empty Module1 class module.

3. Choose <u>T</u>ools, Re<u>f</u>erences to open Excel's References dialog. In the Available References list, mark the check box for Microsoft Access 95 (see Figure 31.41). Mark the Microsoft DAO 3.5 check box if you want to use database intrinsic constants. Click OK to close the dialog.

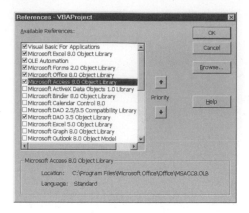

**FIG. 31.41**   Adding a reference to the Microsoft Access 8.0 Object Library to Excel 97.

4. Press F2 or choose <u>V</u>iew, <u>O</u>bject Browser to open Excel's Object Browser. Select Access from the Project/Library list to display the objects exposed by the Microsoft Access 97 Object library (see Figure 31.42). Close Object Browser when you've finished exploring the Access `Application` objects.

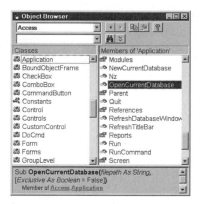

**FIG. 31.42**   Some of the Access Application objects displayed in Excel 97's Object Browser.

5. Add the following object variable declarations to the module:

```
Private acaNwind As Access.Application
Private dbNwind As Database
Private rstNwind As Recordset
```

6. Press Ctrl+G or choose <u>V</u>iew, <u>I</u>mmediate Window to open Excel's Immediate window—the equivalent of Access 97's Debug window.

7. Type **Set acaNwind = CreateObject("Access.Application.8")** in the Immediate window. When you press Enter, the command eventually launches an invisible instance of Access.

8.  When <Ready> appears in the status line, type **acaNwind. OpenCurrentDatabase "northwind.mdb"**. (Add the path if you don't have a copy of Northwind.mdb in the My Documents folder.) Pressing Enter opens Northwind.mdb.

9.  Type **Set dbNwind = acaNwind.CurrentDB( )**. After executing this statement, most of the commands to manipulate database objects are identical to those of Access VBA.

10. Type **Set rstNwind = dbNwind.OpenRecordset("Customers")** to open a Recordset object over the Customers table. Apply typical methods and check some property values of the Recordset object, as shown in Figure 31.43.

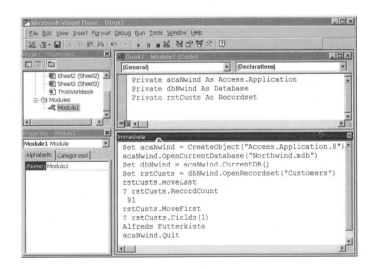

**FIG. 31.43**  Creating and manipulating an Access 97 Recordset object with Excel VBA.

11. When you finish experimenting with Access Application objects, type **acaNwind.Quit** to close the instance of Access.

Experimenting with Access as an Automation server demonstrates that Visual Basic for Applications truly is the *lingua franca* of application programming (also called *macro*) languages. Although the hierarchy of the objects exposed to VBA varies with server applications, the programming language and methodology is independent of the client and server applications. Now that Microsoft Word has adopted Word VBA, Microsoft's Bill Gates has finally achieved his 1989 vision of a "common macro language" for all Microsoft productivity applications.

# Chapter 32

# Using the Office 97 Developer Edition

The Office 97 Developer Edition (ODE) differs greatly from the Access Developer's Toolkit (ADT) of Access 95 and Access 2.0. Earlier versions of Access used a separate run-time executable file, MSARN??0.EXE; like Access 95, Access 97 uses the retail version of Msaccess.exe set to run-time mode for distributing applications. Even if you don't intend to distribute your applications to others, you might want to acquire the ODE because of the additional ActiveX Controls and printed documentation the ODE provides.

This chapter describes what's in the ODE, how to use the Setup Wizard to create run-time distribution disks for your Access 97 applications, and how to use the ODE's API Viewer to add 32-bit Windows (Win32) API function prototype declarations to your Access VBA code.

## Examining the Content of the Office 97 Developer Edition

The new ODE for Office 97 is directed primarily toward the Access developer and Office power-user communities. The ODE contains the following components:

- A royalty-free license to distribute Msaccess.exe for run-time use, the run-time interpreter for VBA 5.0 (Vbrun500.dll), the run-time version of Microsoft Graph 8.0 (Graph8.exe and Graph8rt.srg), and the other distributable components of Access 97, such as the Jet 3.5 database engine, ActiveX Controls used by your application, ODBC files, and ISAM drivers.

- An improved version of the Setup Wizard you use to create images of the distribution disks for your application. The Setup Wizard also writes the Setup.inf and other data files required by Setup.exe.

- A set of three printed manuals: *Microsoft Office 97 Programmers Guide*, *Building Applications with Microsoft Access 97*, and *Microsoft Office 97 Object Model Guide*. The *Programmers Guide* provides an introduction to

VBA 5.0 programming for all of the members of Office 97. *Building Applications* explains how to design database application with Access 97, other Office 97 members, and Jet 3.5. The *Object Model Guide* supplies object model diagrams and lists the properties and methods of application-specific objects.

■ The 32-bit Animation, Common Dialog, FTP, Gopher, HTTP, Imagelist, Listview, Progress Bar, Rich Text, Slider, Status Bar, Tabstrip, Toolbar, Treeview, Up/Down, and Winsock ActiveX controls.

■ The Replication Manager (Replman.exe) to automate Briefcase replication operations between multiple sites. The new Replication Manager lets you replicate Access databases over the Internet and supports partial replication of databases.

■ The Microsoft Help Compiler version 4.0 for Windows (Hcrtf.exe), the graphic front-end for the help compiler (Hcw.exe), and help files for the compiler.

■ A Windows API Viewer application, Apilod.exe, which provides declarations in VBA 5.0 format for all of the Win32 API functions. The API Viewer aids in converting Access 2.0 16-bit Windows API function prototype declarations to the Win32 API.

■ Components necessary to manage multi-developer Access 97 projects with Visual SourceSafe 5.0. You must acquire the Visual SourceSafe 5.0 application to use this feature. (Visual SourceSafe 5.0 is included in the Enterprise Edition of Visual Basic 5.0).

Except for the Help Compiler and API Viewer, all of the preceding components are new or have been significantly upgraded for Access 97 and other Office 97 applications.

> **Note**
>
> The standard version of the ODE includes a copy of Office 97. If you already have the Professional Version of Office 97 or a stand-alone copy of Access 97, you can purchase the ODE as an add-on product.

# Differences Between Run-Time and Retail Access

The behavior of your 32-bit Access applications differs when you execute the applications for use with the run-time, rather than the full (retail), version of Access 97. Following are the principal differences that distinguish run-time execution:

■ All design-related menu choices and corresponding object views are removed. Your run-time applications should use menu macros to create the menubars and menu items your application requires.

■ Built-in toolbars aren't supported, but you can create custom toolbars for your application. (Custom toolbars are stored in the System.mdw file you distribute with your application.)

- The Database window is not visible, and macro and module windows are hidden. You specify the form to open by selecting the form in the Startup dialog opened by choosing <u>T</u>ools, Start<u>u</u>p.

- Special-purpose keys and combinations are disabled. Shift is disabled during the database opening process. Ctrl+Break is disabled so that users cannot halt Access VBA code or macro operation. (Ctrl+Break remains active during query execution so that users can halt a "run-away" query that returns very large numbers of records.)

- Pressing F1 for online help results in an error message if you don't supply a custom online help file for your application and assign the file name to the Help File property of every visible object of your application. (You also must include a valid Help Context ID value.) Supplying even a very simple help file is a better practice than allowing an error to occur when the user presses F1. (You are not allowed to distribute the Access online help files.)

- All errors that occur in the execution of macros, and untrapped errors that occur while executing Access VBA code, result in an instantaneous exit of Access. The user receives no warning of the impending disappearance of your application. You cannot trap macro errors, so you should use Access VBA code with error trapping rather than macros for all event-handling operations. There is no assurance the future versions of Access will support macros.

- If you use separate data and application .mdb files, you need to provide Access VBA code that tests to determine whether the *Data*.mdb file is on the expected drive and in the specified folder. If not, a special form and another routine is required to specify the location of the *Data*.mdb file.

No significant change in the preceding list has occurred with Access 97. Thus, the Access 95 run-time applications you convert to Access 97 are likely to behave identically. Chapter 33, "Migrating Access 2.0 and Access 95 Applications to Access 97," describes the changes you need to make to execute your applications with run-time Access 97. These changes also are necessary for the applications to execute with the retail version of Access 97.

---

**Tip**

You can emulate run-time operation by creating a desktop shortcut that includes the path and file name with the /Runtime command-line switch for Msaccess.exe in the Target text box of the Shortcut page of the Shortcut Name Properties sheet. As an example, type

> **C:\Program Files\Microsoft Office\Office\Msaccess.exe  C:\Program Files\ Microsoft Office\Office\Samples\Nwind.mdb  /Runtime**

in the Target text box to specify the .mdb file used in the following example. It's a good practice to specify the current directory in the Start In text box, **C:\Program Files\Microsoft Office\ Office** for this example.

# Creating Distribution Disks with the Setup Wizard

Microsoft Corporation's standard Setup program changed with the introduction of the Windows 95 round of Microsoft productivity application upgrades. The Setup application for users of your Access 97 run-time applications uses the standard Microsoft Office 97 Setup program, often called *Acme Setup*. The Access 97 Setup Wizard (Wzstp80.mde, an encrypted library) automatically creates the custom .stf and .inf files required by the Acme Setup program.

### Preparing Sample Files to Use the Setup Wizard

The description of using the Setup Wizard that follows assumes that you have created or appropriated an icon file for your application and have an online help and help contents files. The following steps prepare the files necessary to create run-time disk images:

1. The example uses a split version of the Northwind.mdb file (Nwind.mdb as the application file and Nwind_be.mdb as the data file). Compact Northwind.mdb into a copy named Nwind.mdb, open Nwind.mdb, and use the Database Splitter Add-In to move the tables to Nwind_be.mdb in your \Program Files\Microsoft Office\ Office\Samples folder, the default folder for this example.

 ◀◀ See "Splitting Databases for File Sharing," p. 873

> ### Caution
>
> Make sure that you haven't marked the Break on All Errors check box in the Error Trapping Group of the Advanced Page of the Options properties sheet. If Break on All Errors is marked, you receive a `Runtime Error 3025: Item not found in this collection` message when running the Setup Wizard.

2. Copy any icon (*Iconname*.ico) file on your disk to the default folder. (Choose Start, Find, Files or Folders and enter *.ico in the Named text box, then Find Now to locate an icon file to copy.) Rename the icon file copy to **Nwind.ico**.

3. If you don't have your own help files, for this example you can use the Nwind80.hlp and Nwind80.cnt files provided with the Northwind.mdb sample database.

4. Copy \Program Files\Microsoft Office\Office\System.mdw to the default folder. You cannot create a distribution copy of the System.mdw file that Access automatically opens when launched.

### Creating Distribution Disk Images

To create images of the distribution disks for the Northwind Traders (Runtime) application on your fixed disk (or a server drive), follow these steps:

> **Tip**
>
> Make sure you have at least 40M of free disk space on the drive that you use to store the disk images before you start creating distribution disks. The following example requires about 35M to store the compressed disk images and component files.

1. Open Nwind.mdb and choose <u>T</u>ools, Start<u>u</u>p to open the Startup dialog. Type your application's name, such as Northwind (Runtime), in the Application Title text box; click the Builder button and select Nwind.ico in the Icon Browser dialog; and then select Main Switchboard from the Display Form drop-down list (see Figure 32.1). Accept the remaining defaults and click OK to close the dialog.

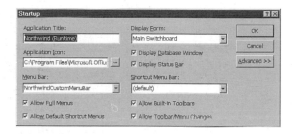

**FIG. 32.1**   Setting the startup parameters for Nwind.mdb.

2. Open the Wzstp80.mde database in your \Program Files\Microsoft Office\ODE Tools\Setup Wizard folder. (If Access isn't running, launch the wizard by choosing Start, Programs, Microsoft ODE Tools, Setup Wizard.) The Setup Wizard displays the opening dialog shown in Figure 32.2. Accept the default Create a New Set of Setup Options choice and click Next to display the second wizard dialog.

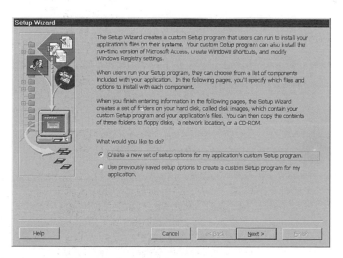

**FIG. 32.2**   The opening dialog of the Setup Wizard.

3. Click the Add button to open the Select Files dialog. Press the Ctrl key and select Nwind.ico, Nwind.mdb, Nwind_be.mdb, Nwind80.cnt, Nwind80.hlp, and System.mdw (see Figure 32.3). Click Add to add the files to List of Files list box of the Setup Wizard's dialog.

**FIG. 32.3**   Selecting the required application files in the \Program Files\Microsoft Office\ Office\Samples folder.

---

**Note**

For a multiuser application, install Nwind_be.mdb and System.mdw on the file server and do not include either of these two files in the List of Files. Create a second Setup program to install the shared database and workgroup files on the server.

---

4. Select Nwind.mdb in the List of Files list box and mark the Set As Application's Main File check box (see Figure 32.4). Accept the default $(AppPath) for the Destination Folder, Older for Overwrite Existing File, and accept Application as the Component Name for the file.

5. Select System.mdw and mark the Set as Workgroup File check box, as shown in Figure 32.5. If you include the workgroup file, this is an important step because marking the Set As Workgroup File check box causes setup to make the appropriate Registry entries for System.mdw.

---

**Note**

For multiuser applications, you must include the Workgroup Administrator application (Wrkgadm.exe from \Program Files\Microsoft Office\Office) so that the user can specify the network location of the workgroup file before launching your application. You add the Workgroup Administrator application, if required, in step 10 of this procedure.

---

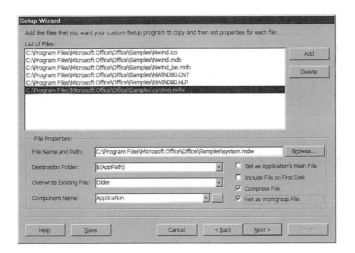

**FIG. 32.4**    Adding the application files to the List of Files list box and setting the application's main file.

**FIG. 32.5**    Specifying System.mdw as the workgroup file for a self-contained application.

6. With System.mdw selected, click the Builder button (to the right of the Component Name drop-down list) to open the Components Builder dialog, then click the Add button. Type Workgroup File in the Name text box and click the Close button to add Workgroup File to the Components list. Optionally, you can add other component names, such as Database and Help Files, before you close the Components Builder (see Figure 32.6). You can change the order of the components with the up and down arrows to the left of the List of Components.

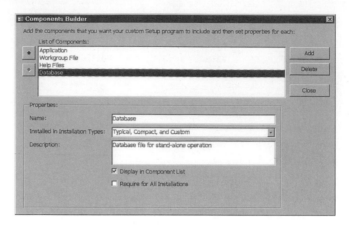

**FIG. 32.6**  Adding new component categories to the List of Components in the Component Builder dialog.

7. With System.mdw selected, open the Component Name drop-down list and select Workgroup File (see Figure 32.7). If you added additional components in the preceding step, select each file and assign the appropriate component name. Click Next to continue.

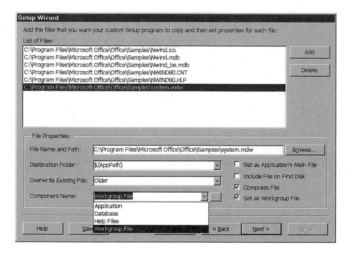

**FIG. 32.7**  Assigning a component name to the workgroup file.

8. The wizard lets you create custom shortcuts and shortcuts to run, compact, and repair your application. To provide a shortcut to launch Nwind.mdb, click the Database Shortcut Properties tab and, with the Open option selected, type **Northwind Runtime** in the Description text box. Mark the Run-Time check box, accept the remaining defaults, and click the Add button. Click Yes when the message box asks if you want to include the Access run-time files on your distribution disks. Repeat this process for Compact Northwind (select the Compact option button) and Repair Northwind (select the Repair and Compact option button).

Figure 31.8 shows the three basic shortcuts added with the Open shortcut selected. You also can add a shortcut for your help file by selecting Nwind.hlp in the File to Open drop-down list and adding a **Northwind Help** description. Click Next to continue.

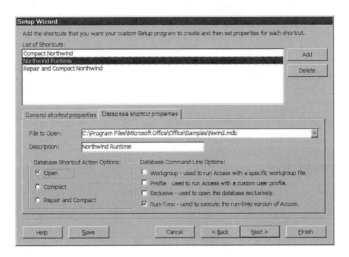

**FIG. 32.8** Creating shortcuts for opening, compacting, and repairing the Nwind.mdb file.

**9.** The Setup Wizard automatically creates all of the Registry keys and values needed to run your application. You can add custom Registry keys, if needed, in the wizard's dialog shown in Figure 32.9. For this example, click Next to continue.

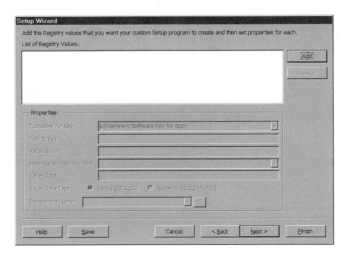

**FIG. 32.9** Adding custom Registry keys, if required, for your run-time application.

**10.** Click the entries in the list box to select additional components to include on your distribution disks or in your network setup directory. An X indicates selected components (see Figure 32.10). If you answered Yes to the message described in step 8, the wizard selects Microsoft Access RunTime for you; if not, make sure to select this component. Also make sure to select Microsoft Graph 8 RunTime, if your application includes graphs or charts. Click Next to continue.

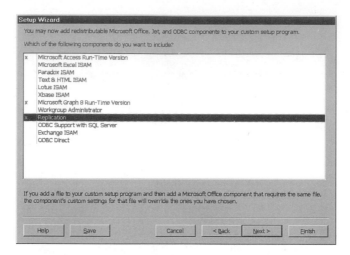

**FIG. 32.10**   Adding required components to the distribution files.

> **Note**
>
> You must include the Workgroup Administrator application with multiuser applications so that users can connect to the workgroup file on the workgroup server.

**11.** Verify that the components required for your application are installed in all three installation types, Compact, Typical, and Custom (see Figure 32.11). Mark the Require for All Installations check box for needed files. (Require for All Installations prevents users from failing to install required files when choosing Custom setup.) If you supply Replication Manager, you can select Custom from the Installed in Installation Types drop-down list so that Replication Manager only is installed when needed. Click Next to continue.

**12.** Type the name and version number of your application, your firm name, and the drive and name of the folder that corresponds to $(AppPath). The wizard provides default values based on previously entered information. Provision is made for a conventional DOS folder name, if your application is installed on a PC that doesn't support long file names, such as Windows 3.1+ and versions of Windows NT earlier than 3.51 (see Figure 32.12). Click Next to continue.

**13.** If you want to run an executable file when the setup operation completes, select the .exe file in the Run the Following File drop-down list. The executable file and any supporting .dll files must have been included in the file list created in preceding step 3, unless the file is known to be on the user's computer. You can include a Readme.wri file and type **Wordpad.exe $(AppPath)\Readme.wri** in the Enter or Edit the Command Line text box to display the file on completion of setup (see Figure 32.13). For a Readme file, be sure to mark the Allow Setup to Complete check box so Setup announces that it has completed successfully before your Readme file appears. Click Next to continue.

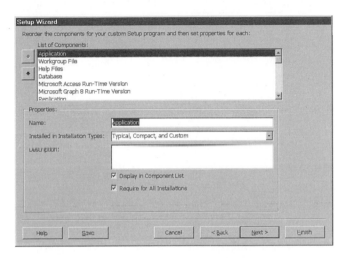

**FIG. 32.11**  Setting the property values of installation components.

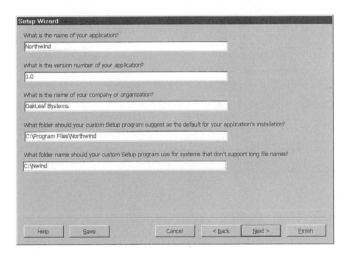

**FIG. 32.12**  Setting the property values for your run-time application.

14. Enter the path and folder name of the directory in which to store the disk images, each of which is stored in a ...\Disks\Disk1...\Disk*n* folder (see Figure 32.14). Alternatively, you can elect to create a single network setup folder in a server share. Compressed network setup files save space on the server, but installation takes slightly longer. Storing a local copy of compressed files makes re-creating your disk images or server files quicker. Click Finish to create your disk or server file images.

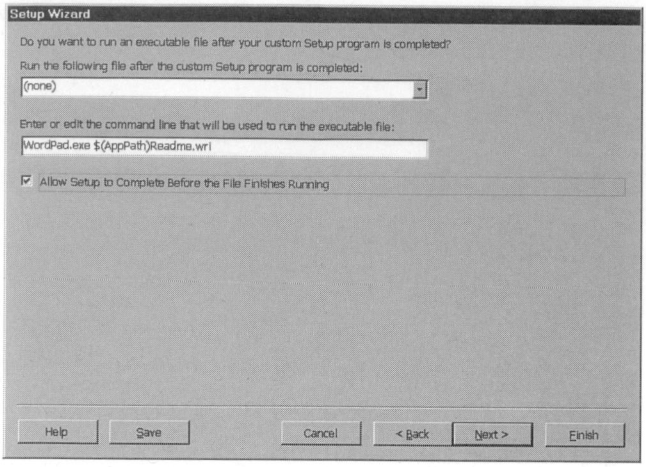

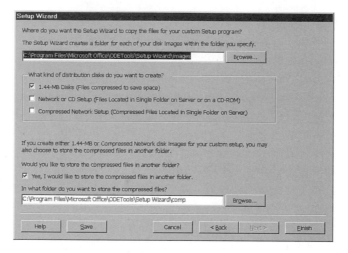

**FIG. 32.13**   Specifying an executable file to run on completion of the setup operation.

**FIG. 32.14**   Specifying the location of network or disk image distribution files and optional compressed files.

**15.** The wizard asks whether you want to save your setup data as a template. Click Yes to open the Save Template dialog (see Figure 32.15). Give your template an appropriate name, such as **Nwind.mdt**, and click the Save button to close the dialog.

**16.** The wizard starts creating the compressed files and disk images and provides a status dialog as shown in Figure 32.16. This is a good time to have a cup of coffee (or lunch), because the process may take five to 30 minutes, depending on the size of your application files, the component options you select, and the speed of your PC and disk drive. When the process completes, you receive the message shown in Figure 32.17.

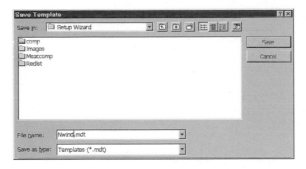

**FIG. 32.15**  Assigning a name to and saving a template for your setup data.

**FIG. 32.16**  The Setup Wizard keeps you informed of the progress of setup file generation.

**FIG. 32.17**  Success at last; the wizard notifies you of the completion of the process.

The setup files that the wizard creates for your application result in an installation process that is very similar to that for Access 97 and other members of the Office 97 suite. You can quickly check your Setup application by executing Setup.exe from your ...\ Images\Disks\Disk1 folder and displaying the first few windows. Figure 32.18 shows the opening Setup window for the example created in the preceding steps. To fully validate your Setup application, however, you need to run Setup.exe from the disks or network file server on a workstation without either the retail or run-time version of Access 97 installed.

# Using the 32-Bit Windows API Viewer

The Win32 API Viewer, which also is included with Visual Basic 4.0 and 5.0, is intended as an aid to converting your existing 16-bit Windows 3.1+ (Win16) API calls to Win32 format. To add Win32 function prototype declarations to your Access VBA code, follow these steps:

1. Launch the API Viewer, Apilod.exe, from your \Program Files\Microsoft Office\ ODE Tools\Win API Viewer folder. You also can run the API Viewer by choosing Start, Programs, ODE Tools, Win32 API Viewer.

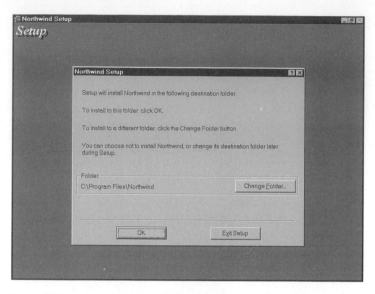

**FIG. 32.18**    The first window of the example Northwind setup program.

2. Choose File, Load Database File to open the Select a Jet Database dialog and select Win32api.mdb (see Figure 32.19). Click the Open button to load the database file and close the dialog.

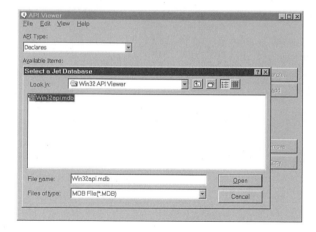

**FIG. 32.19**    Loading the Win32api.mdb file into the API Viewer.

3. With Declares selected in the API Type drop-down list, click the Available Items list box to give it the focus. Type the initial letter(s) of the Windows API function you want to add to your code. The corresponding API function entries appear.

   **4.** Select the API function you want to include in the Declarations section of your Access VBA code and click the Add button to add the entry to the Selected Items list box. Repeat this process for as many API functions as you need (see Figure 32.20).

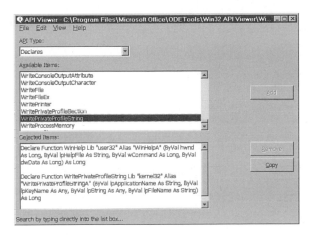

**FIG. 32.20**    Selecting the function prototype declarations to add to your Access VBA code.

> **Note**
>
> The function prototype declarations of Win32api.mdb use C-style naming conventions (variable prefixes), instead of the Leszynski Naming Conventions (LNC) used in this book and described in Appendix B, "Naming Conventions for Access Objects and Variables." As an example, lpHelpFile (long pointer to a string) corresponds to strHelpFile using LNC. Win32api.mdb uses both w (word, usually 16 bits) and dw (double-word, 32 bits) as prefixes for the LNC lng (**Long**) data type prefix.

   **5.** Click the Copy button to copy the function prototype declarations to the Clipboard.

   **6.** Launch Access, if necessary, and open an existing or a new module.

   **7.** Position the cursor at the line below the **Option** Explicit line in the Declarations section of the module and press Ctrl+V to paste the copied declarations.

   **8.** Reformat the function prototype declarations using the line continuation pair (space plus underscore), as shown in Figure 32.21. Reformatting the declarations makes your code easier to read.

You also can use the API Viewer to add Win32 structures (user-defined data types) and constant declarations to your Access VBA code. The API Viewer is capable of using either specially formatted .txt or .mdb files, and can convert .txt files into .mdb files for faster access to a specific function.

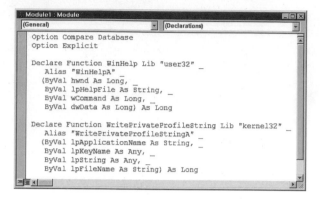

**FIG. 32.21** The function prototype declarations pasted into a module and reformatted for readability.

# Chapter 33

# Migrating Access 2.0 and Access 95 Applications to Access 97

Each version of Access—1.0, 1.1, 2.0, 95, and 97—has a different database file structure at the binary (byte) level. The differences between .MDB files created with versions 1.0 and 1.1 were relatively minor; thus, you could use the Compact feature of Access to convert version 1.0 .MDBs to version 1.1, or vice versa. The file formats of later versions of Jet databases are sufficiently different to require one-way conversion during the upgrade process.

The Convert Database process is not reversible; once you've converted a database to the Access 97 (version 8.0) .mdb structure of Jet 3.5, you can't convert it back to version 7.0 (Jet 3.0) or 2.0 (Jet 2.x). However, you can open and use version 2.0 .MDB and Access 95 .mdb files with Access 97. Many Access 2.0 users were forced to forego the transition to Access 95 because of limited deployment of Windows 95 by large organizations. Consequently, this chapter begins by addressing the ramifications of continuing to use version 2.0 .MDB files with Access 97 and then explains how to convert your existing .MDB files to Access 95's 32-bit .mdb structure. The chapter concludes with a discussion of the relatively minor changes involved in converting Access 95 files to Access 97 format.

## Using Access 2.0 Application .MDB Files with Access 97

Access 97 is designed to be backward compatible with Access 2.0 .MDB files. Nevertheless, the compatibility is not total. The following list describes the principal limitations of running version 2.0 .MDB files with Access 95:

- You cannot save any changes you make to the design of any object contained in a version 2.0 .MDB file.

- You cannot change ownership of, or permissions for, objects contained in a version 2.0 .MDB file.

- DoMenuItem actions that refer to menu choices that have changed in Access 97 produce an unexpected result. Access replaces DoMenuItem action with the RunCommand action in macros and Access VBA code.

- SendKeys operations that execute Access 97 menu choices and make selections in dialogs are likely to fail due to changes in the Access 97 menu structure and the design of Access 97 dialogs.

- Variable names that conflict with the names of new VBA 5.0 reserved words result in failure of Access 97 to compile modules and to execute procedures containing the conflicting variables.

- Access VBA statements that use the dot (.) operator to refer to a field of a Recordset object or a member of a collection fail. Use the bang (!) operator, as in Orders!OrderID or Forms!Orders.

If you don't need to change the design of your Access 2.0 application and the application does not contain any of the specific problem areas in the preceding list, you probably can continue to use the Access 2.0 application with Access 97 and share the application with other users of Access 97 and earlier versions of Access. The message shown in Figure 33.1 appears when you first open an Access 2.0 application in Access 97.

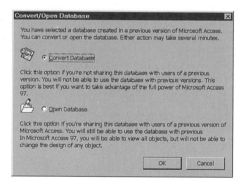

**FIG. 33.1** The dialog that appears when you first open an Access 2.0 .MDB or an Access 95 .mdb file in Access 97.

To attempt to run an Access 2.0 application under Access 97, choose the Open option in the dialog of Figure 33.1. The status bar displays Opening, then Compiling, and finally the message shown in Figure 33.2 appears advising that you can't change the design of objects in the database. The opening and compiling process, which enables Access 2.0 and 95 applications, makes Access Basic modules of Access 2.0 or Access VBA of Access 95 compatible with VBA 5.0. Fortunately, the opening and compiling process only occurs once, but the message box of Figure 33.2 continues to appear each time you open the database.

> **Note**
>
> If you make changes to an Access 2.0 or 95 application, the enabling process reoccurs when you first open the application. Make sure you compile all of the modules in your earlier version .MDB file before opening it in Access 97.

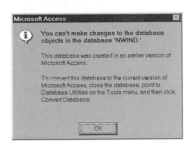

**FIG. 33.2** The recurring message that appears when you open an enabled Access 2.0 or 95 .MDB file in Access 95.

If your application contains code that Access VBA can't handle, you're likely to receive the message shown in Figure 33.3. To find the offending code, open a module and click the Compile Loaded Modules button. As an example, Access 2.0's Nwind.mdb sample database contains a subprocedure, ShowEvents, in the Utility Functions module that the Access 97 VBA interpreter won't compile. Each line that contains the Events variable name is colored red and the message box shown in Figure 33.4 appears. You can't save corrections to Access Basic code in Access 97, so you must make any required changes to the unconverted .MDB file in the appropriate version of Access. In the case of the ShowEvents subprocedure, you change the variable name from Event to strEvent in three locations. You then recompile the code changes in the original version of Access and try opening the .MDB file again in Access 97.

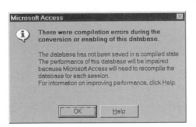

**FIG. 33.3** The message that appears when the VBA 5.0 interpreter can't handle your Access Basic code.

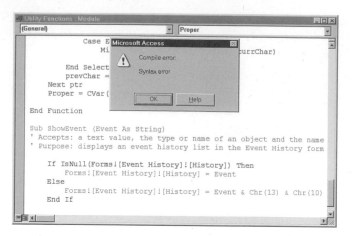

**FIG. 33.4**   The message box that attempts to identify the problem with Access Basic code.

# Using Access 1.x and 2.0 Data
# .MDB Files with Access 97

If you use the recommended split-database method (storing application objects and data objects in two separate .MDB files), you can convert your Access 1.x or 2.0 application .MDB file to Access 97, but leave the data .MDB as a version 1.x or 2.0 .MDB file. Users of 16-bit Access, Access 95, and Visual Basic 3.0, 4.0, or 5.0 can share the linked data .MDB files. When you attach tables contained in Access 1.x, 2.0, or 95 .MDB files, you don't receive a warning message. You cannot use Access 95 features, such as Briefcase replication, with .MDB files created with Access 2.0 or earlier.

> **Note**
>
> It is a relatively easy process to split Access 1.x or 2.0 applications into separate data and application .MDB files. (Access 95 and 97 include the Database Splitter Add-In that automates this process; prior versions of Access do not offer this feature.) In your prior version of Access, create a new .MDB file, then import the tables from your existing .MDB file. Verify that the imported tables contain valid data, then delete the tables from your original .MDB file. Move the table to its final location, such as on a network server. Then attach the tables to the application .MDB file.

 ◀◀ See "Splitting Databases for File Sharing," p. 873

If any of the conditions in the following list apply to your Access applications, maintain your files in their earlier Access format:

■ Some of the users of your Access applications have not upgraded to Windows 95 or Windows NT, so those users are unable to run the Access 97 retail or run-time versions.

■ You are converting a series of different application .MDB files from version 1.x or 2.0 to Access 97 and need to maintain data compatibility with all application .MDBs until the conversion process is complete.

■ You are sharing the database .MDB with a Visual Basic 3.0 application.

If you've developed several workgroup applications using earlier versions of Access, you must maintain the shared data .MDB file in its original format until you have converted all of the application databases to Access 97. There is little or no performance penalty for attaching tables and maintaining the original data .MDB file format.

---

**Caution**

Do not convert existing shared Access 1.x, 2.0, or 95 SYSTEM.MDA or System.mdw files to Access 97 format. If you do, users of prior versions of Access will not even be able to launch Access. (They receive an `Unable to open 'filename.mda'. It may not be an Access database or the file may be corrupt.` message) Access system files are attached, so you can use existing workgroup system files with Access 97.

---

# Converting Access 1.x and 2.0 Files to Access 95

If you elect to convert your earlier versions of Access application .MDB files to Access 95 and all of your users have not converted to Access 95, you need to maintain two versions of the application .MDB file. If the application is mature and does not require significant maintenance, temporarily supplying a 32-bit Access 97 version to users of Windows 95 and Windows NT 4.0, and a 16-bit Access 2.0 or earlier version to users of Windows 3.1+ is not likely to present a problem.

If you're in the development or early roll-out phase, however, consider completion of the application in Access 2.0. Make sure to observe the syntax rules for VBA 5.0 while writing your Access Basic code; doing so minimizes the trauma when converting your Access 2.0 application to Access 97.

### Converting versus Importing .MDB Files

You have the following options for converting version 1.x or 2.0 application, data, or combined application and data .MDB files to Access 97 format:

---

**Tip**

If you encounter problems with permissions to modify objects in your converted .mdb file, try the import method so that you become the owner of the objects in the database.

---

■ Open the file in Access 97 and accept the default Convert Database option. Alternatively, close any open database, then choose <u>T</u>ools, Database <u>U</u>tilities, Conver<u>t</u>. This is the fastest method of performing the conversion. The ownership of objects in the converted database does not change. Access 97 requires you to specify a different file name or directory for the converted .mdb file so you don't overwrite the existing version.

■ Choose File, Get External Data, Import to import all of the objects from the version 1.x or 2.0 .MDB to a newly created Access 97 .mdb file. When you import the objects, you become the owner (Creator) of the objects.

---

**Tip**

When importing an entire database, you can select all of the objects for import at once by clicking each tab (Tables, Queries, Forms, and so on) and clicking the Select All button for each class of object. Once you've selected all of the objects to be imported, click the OK button.

---

The database object permissions assigned to users and groups are not affected by either converting or importing the objects. Only ownership of the objects is affected.

### Handling Conversion and Import Errors

Small Access 1.x and 2.0 applications, especially applications without Access Basic code, are likely to convert to Access 97 without problems. However, large applications that contain substantial amounts of code or use code contained in Access libraries or custom .DLLs, generate errors during the conversion process. The following sections describe the most common conversion errors and how to fix them.

**Converting from Win16 to Win32 Function Calls.** If your application makes use of calls to the Windows API, you must convert the function declarations from the 16-bit (Win16) to the 32-bit (Win32) version. You cannot call 16-bit functions from 32-bit code and vice versa. You receive a `Calls to 16-bit DLLs won't work under Windows 95 or Windows NT` message when the VBA interpreter encounters a 16-bit Windows API declaration.

The Win32 API functions with arguments of the String data type come in two types: ANSI (suffix `A`) and Unicode (suffix `W`, for wide); the ANSI versions are used by Access 97. Most Windows API function arguments that were of the **Integer** data type in the Win16 version must be declared as **Long** in the Win32 version. Examples include all Win32 handles, such as `hWnd` and `hDC`, and values of **Integer** fields in structures. To avoid the need to change all function calls to Win32 API functions in your Access VBA code, you alias the function calls, as shown in the following example:

```
Declare Function OriginalName Lib "lib32" _
Alias "OriginalName[A]" ([ArgumentList]) As Datatype
```

*OriginalName* is the name of the Win16 function in your Access VBA function calls. Win32 libraries, for the most part, have a `32` suffix, as in Kernel32.exe and GDI32.exe. In the majority of cases, you need only include the `A` suffix in the **Alias** name if **As String** appears in *ArgumentList*. For most Win32 functions, *Datatype* is **Long**.

The Win API Viewer, which is included with the Office 97 Developer Edition (ODE) and Visual Basic 4+, lets you copy `Declare` statements for Win32 function calls to the Clipboard, then paste them into the Declarations section of your modules. If you don't have the ODE or Visual Basic 4+, you must either have the Win32 Software Development Kit (SDK) or guess the correct Win32 API function name and data types, then try compiling and executing your code.

◀◀ See "Using the 32-Bit Windows API Viewer," p. 1147

**Converting and Adding References to Libraries and Add-Ins.** In addition to converting your application .MDB file to Access 97, you also must convert any Access 2.0 custom libraries and add-ins used by your application to 32-bit versions. Converting your own libraries and add-ins follows the same process as converting .MDB files. If you use third-party libraries, you'll likely need updated Access 97 versions; the source code of many third-party libraries is password-protected.

> **Note**
>
> If you are using only a few functions in a library, such as the WIZLIB.MDA library included with Access 2.0, consider creating a new library or incorporating the function code in your Access 97 application. Doing so eliminates dealing with problems converting library functions you don't need. Copy the required function(s) to the Clipboard and paste the code into an Access 97 module. (You can run prior versions of Access and Access 97 simultaneously.)

Access 2.0 and earlier use the [Libraries] section of MSACC??0.INI to attach libraries to any application opened in Access. Access 95 and 97 use references to 32-bit libraries in place of entries in MSACC??0.INI. To add a reference to a library, such as Access 97's Utility.mda, follow these steps:

1. Open a module and choose Tools, References to open the References dialog.

2. Click the Browse button to open the Add Reference dialog.

3. Select Add-ins (*.mda) in the Files of Type drop-down list.

4. Maneuver to the folder that contains your library, select the library file, and click the OK button to add the reference at the bottom of the Available References list.

5. When you close and reopen the References dialog, the new reference appears as the last active reference. Figure 33.5 shows Access 97's Utility.mda library added to the Available References list.

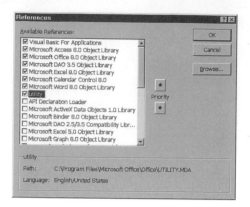

**FIG. 33.5**  References to Access 97 library databases appear below Access 97's default references and any references you added previously.

Access 97 library references are stored in your .mdb file; thus, you must create a reference to a library in each .mdb file that uses the library. Unlike [Libraries] entries in MSACC??0.INI, the full path to the library is hard-coded. You may need to alter the reference for users who don't install your application in the folder specified by the reference in your .mdb file. Access 97 lets you modify references with Access VBA; all members of Office 97 expose a References collection.

Hard-coded reference paths are a compelling reason to move existing library code to your Access application .mdb if you only use a few library functions. If your library code does not contain visible objects, other than message boxes and modal dialogs, an alternative is to convert the library to an in-process Visual Basic 32-bit ActiveX DLL that you manage with Automation code.

> **Note**
>
> Access 97, unlike Access 2.0 and earlier, allows duplicate function names in libraries. If you have duplicate function names in libraries, your application calls the function in the library with the highest priority in the Available References list of the References dialog.

Access 2.0 used the [Menu Add-Ins] section of MSACC20.INI to specify the function name of the entry point for an add-in and the [Libraries] section to attach the .MDA file that contains the add-in. These entries are replaced by the Registry entries in Access 95 and 97. If your Access 97 application uses add-ins, a record in the USysRegInfo table of the add-in is required to make the add-in visible to the Add-In Manager.

You can import the USysRegInfo table of one of the Access 97 wizards into your add-in, then modify the entries as required for your add-in. When you use the Add-In Manager to install the add-in, an entry is appended to the MenuAdd-Ins section of the Registry entries for Access 97. Figure 33.6 shows the data for Access 97's Add-In Manager add-in. Unlike references to library databases, add-ins are available to all databases you open in Access 97.

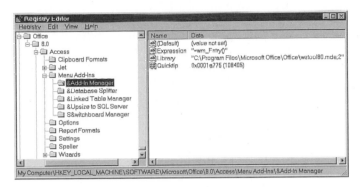

**FIG. 33.6** The Add-In Manager appends entries to the MenuAdd-Ins section of the Registry.

**The 32-Index Limit on Tables.** Access 97 imposes a limit of 32 indexes per table. Each relationship between tables creates an index on the two tables that participate in the relationship, a feature introduced in Access 95. If you have a very complex database with many relationships between tables, you may exceed the 32-index per table limit.

Although your Access 2.0 table may have less than 32 indexes, when you convert the table to Access 97, the additional indexes for relationships may exceed the limit of 32. In this case, you either cannot convert the database or, if the database converts, you lose indexes. Your only option in this situation is to reduce the number of indexes on your table in your prior version of Access, then try the conversion process again.

**Converting 16-bit OLE Controls to 32-bit ActiveX Controls.** If your Access 2.0 application uses 16-bit OLE Controls and you have the 32-bit ActiveX version of the original control, Access 97 automatically updates the control to the 32-bit ActiveX version. The ActiveX control must be registered for the conversion to work. If you don't have a 32-bit ActiveX version of the control, an empty control container appears on your form.

> **Note**
>
> Access 97 does not include a 32-bit ActiveX version of the Data Outline Control provided with Access 95. The 32-bit Data Outline OLE Control of Access 95 works, but is not supported by Microsoft, in Access 97. If the Access 2.0 application you want to convert to Access 97 uses the 16-bit Data Outline (Navigator) Control, you must acquire the Access 95 Developer's Toolkit (ADT) to obtain the 32-bit version and a license to distribute the Data Outline Control.

# Converting Access 95 Databases to Access 97 Format

The binary structures of Access 95 and 97 files are quite similar, so conversion issues between Access 95 and 97 applications are fewer than those between Access 2.0 and 95. Following are the most common issues you might encounter when upgrading your Access 95 .mdbs to Access 97:

- Access 97 converts all `DoCmd.DoMenuItem` statements to `DoCmd.RunCommand` statements. Access 97 also performs this conversion for DoMenuItem actions in macros. Problems may occur in the conversion of custom toolbars and, to a lesser degree, custom menus created in Access 95 to `CommandBar` objects. If conversion problems occur, you must rebuild or repair your custom toolbars and menus in Access 97.

- Access 97 can't open a database replica created in Access 95. You must convert the Design Master and replicas to Access 97 format.

- To improve performance, many optional parameters of Access VBA methods are strongly-typed in Access 97, meaning that use of the **Variant** data type is not allowed. You receive a `Data Type Mismatch` error when the VBA 5.0 interpreter encounters such parameters. Use the Object Browser to determine the required data type.

- A few error codes have changed. If you use numeric error code values in error-handling routines, you might need to change the numeric values.

- Access 95's DAO 3.0 caused SQL statements that modify data to execute as implicit transactions. Using the `dbFailOnError` constant caused failed SQL operations to be rolled back. To improve performance, DAO 3.5 no longer provides implicit transactions. Use the `BeginTrans`, `CommitTrans`, and `Rollback` methods to create explicit transactions in your VBA 5.0 code.

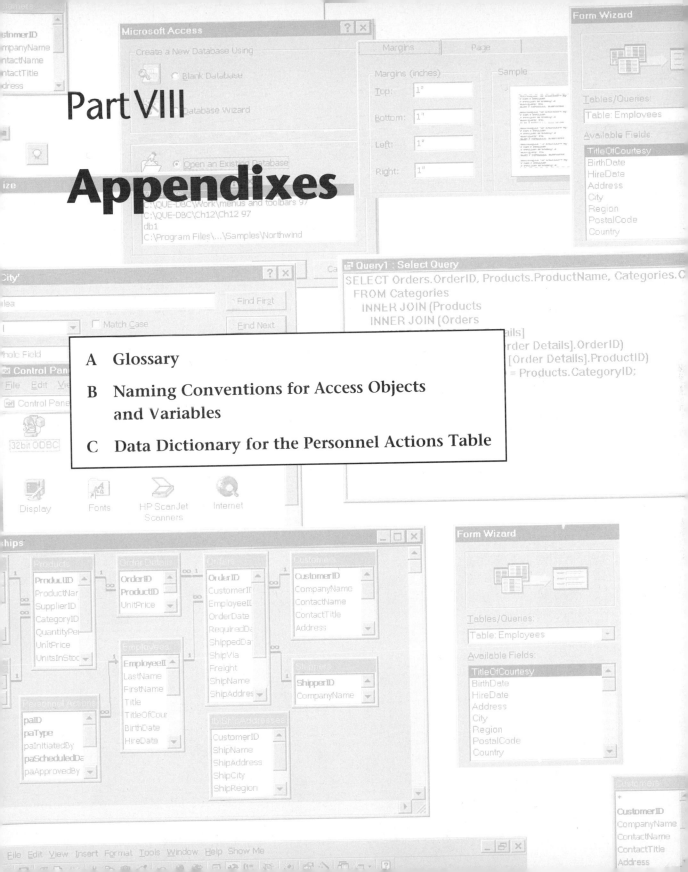

# Part VIII

# Appendixes

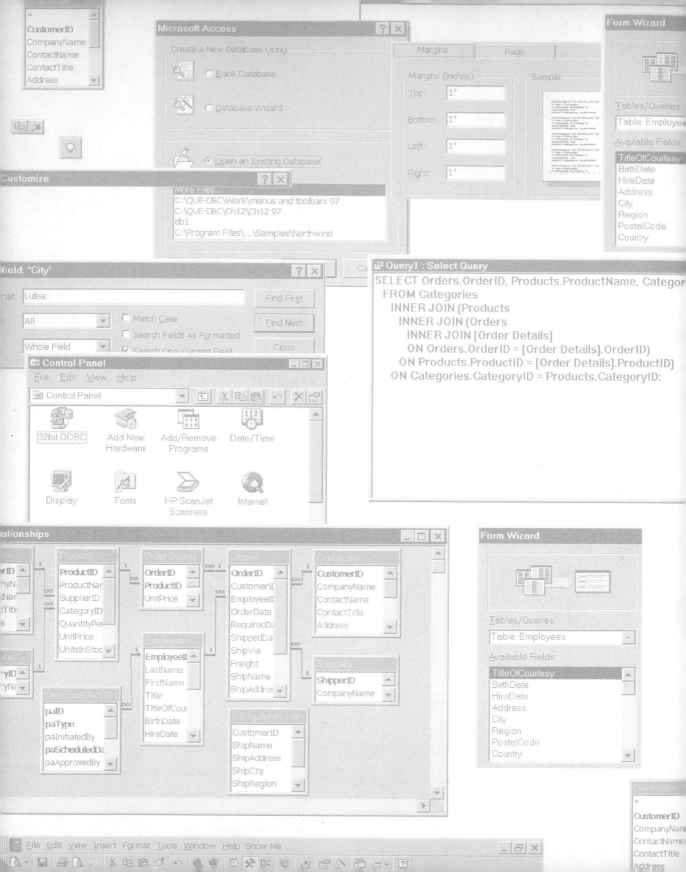

# Appendix A

# Glossary

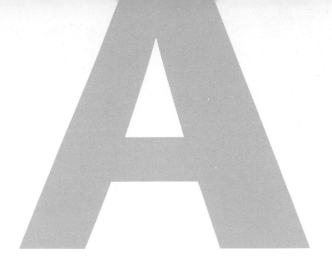

**accelerator key**   A key combination that provides access to a menu choice, macro, or other function of the application in lieu of selection with the mouse, usually by combining Alt+*key*. An accelerator key is identified on menus by an underlined character. It is sometimes (incorrectly) called a *shortcut key*, but shortcut keys usually consist of Ctrl+*key* combinations.

**Access Control List (ACL)**   Part of Windows NT's security description that controls access to a Windows NT object, such as a file. The owner of an object can change access control entries in the list to grant or revoke permissions (access rights) for the object.

**Access Developer's Toolkit**   See *ADT* and *ODK*.

**Access SQL**   The dialect of ANSI SQL used to write queries in all versions of Microsoft Access. For the most part, Access SQL complies with ANSI SQL-92. Access SQL offers additional features, such as including user-defined functions within queries.

**access token**   A Windows NT object that identifies a logged on (authenticated) user. The access token contains the user's security ID (SID), the groups to which the user belongs, and other security information. See *SID*.

**activation**   An OLE 2.0 term meaning to place an object in a running state, which includes binding the object, or to invoke a method of the object. See also *binding*.

**active**   In Windows, the currently running application or the window to which user input is directed; the window with the focus. See also *focus*.

**ActiveMovie**   A Microsoft video technology that provides synchronized images and sound under Windows 95 and Windows NT 4.0, intended as a replacement for 32-bit Video for Windows.

**ActiveX**   A Microsoft trademark for a collection of technologies based on the Common Object Model (COM) and Distributed Common Object Model (DCOM). See *COM* and *DCOM*.

**ActiveX components**    A replacement term for OLE Automation mini-servers and in-process servers, also called *Automation servers*. See *OLE Automation*.

**ActiveX Controls**    Insertable objects supplied in the form of OCX files that, in addition to offering a collection of properties and methods, also fire events. ActiveX Controls are lightweight versions of OLE controls that also use the .OCX file extension. See *OLE controls*.

**ActiveX data objects**    High-level data objects, similar in concept to Access 97's Data Access Object (DAO) and Remote Data Object (RDO), that use Microsoft's new OLE DB (OLE Database) technology to access data from a variety of data sources, including text files and mainframe databases. See *OLE DB*.

**ActiveX documents**    Files that can be inserted into the Microsoft Binder, such as files created by Microsoft Excel 7+ and Word 7+, as well as displayed in their native format in Internet Explorer 3+. ActiveX documents originally were called *Document Objects* or *DocObjects*.

**ActiveX scripting**    Another name for Visual Basic, Scripting Edition (VBScript), a simplified version of VBA designed for client-side automation of Web pages.

**ActiveX server framework**    ActiveX scripting for creating server-side Internet and intranet applications. Unlike ActiveX scripting, the ActiveX Server Framework (code-named Denali) allows file and other low-level operations.

**add-in**    A wizard (such as the Query Wizard) or builder (such as the Menu Builder) that helps users of Access create or run database applications. You use Access 97's Add-In Manager to install wizards and builders (choose Tools, Add-Ins). See also *builder*.

**address**    The numerical value, usually in hexadecimal format, of a particular location in your computer's random-access memory (RAM).

**ADT**    Abbreviation for the Access Developer's Toolkit for Access 2.0 and Access 95 that allowed distribution of files needed to run (but not design) Access 2.0 and Access 95 applications. For Access 97, the ADT is replaced by the Office Developer's Kit (ODK), which provides the same features as the Access 95 ADT, plus developer products for other Office applications. See *ODK*.

**aggregate functions**    The ANSI SQL functions AVG(), SUM(), MIN(), MAX(), and COUNT() and Access SQL functions StDev(), Var(), First(), and Last(). Aggregate functions calculate summary values from a group of values in a specified column. They are usually associated with GROUP BY and HAVING clauses. See also *domain aggregate functions*.

**aggregate object**    An OLE 2.0 term that refers to an object class that contains one or more member objects of another class.

**alias**    A temporary name assigned by Access to a table in a self join, to a column of a query, or to rename a table, implemented by the AS reserved word in ANSI SQL. You can use AS to rename any field or table with Jet SQL. **Alias** is also an embedded keyword option for the VBA **Declare** statement. The **Alias** keyword is used to register prototypes of DLL functions so that the function can be called from programs by another name. Aliasing the ANSI versions of 32-bit Windows API functions to function names without the A suffix is common when converting Access 1.x and 2.0 applications to Access 97, which uses Unicode strings.

**ANSI**   An abbreviation for the American National Standards Institute. ANSI in the Windows context refers to the ANSI character set that Microsoft decided to use for Windows (rather than the IBM PC character set that includes special characters such as those used for line drawing, called the *OEM character set*). The most common character set is *ASCII* (the *American Standard Code for Information Interchange*), which for English alphabetic and numeric characters is the same as ANSI. Windows 95 and Windows NT include both ANSI (suffix A) and Unicode (suffix W) versions of Windows API functions. See *ASCII* and *Unicode*.

**API**   An abbreviation for Application Programming Interface. Generically, a method by which a program can obtain access to or modify the operating system. In 32-bit Windows, the 1,000 or so functions provided by Windows 95 and Windows NT DLLs that allow applications to open and close windows, read the keyboard, interpret mouse movements, and so on. Programmers call them *hooks*. VBA provides access to these functions with the **Declare** statement. See also *DLL*.

**applet**   A Windows application that is supplied as a component of another Windows application, rather than a retail product. The Notepad, WordPad, and Character Map applications supplied with Windows 95 are examples of applets.

**application**   The software product that results from the creation of a program, often used as a synonym for the programming (source) code that creates it. Microsoft Word, Microsoft Excel, WordPerfect for Windows, and Lotus 1-2-3 are called *mainstream Windows productivity applications* in this book. Applications are distinguished by the environment for which they are designed (such as Windows, DOS, Macintosh, and UNIX) and their purpose. Windows applications carry the DOS executable file extension exe.

**Application Close button**   The small, square button with an "X" caption at the extreme right of the title bar of an application running in Windows 95. Clicking the Application Close button closes the running application.

**Application Control menu box**   The small square button with a miniature application icon at the extreme left of the title bar of an application. Clicking the Application Control menu box displays the Application Control menu. Double-clicking the Application Control menu box closes the application.

**argument**   Data supplied to a function and upon which the function acts or uses to perform its task. Arguments are enclosed in parentheses. Additional arguments, if any, are separated by commas. Arguments passed to procedures usually are called *parameters*.

VIII

Appendixes

**array**   An ordered sequence of values (elements) stored within a single named variable, accessed by referring to the variable name with the number of the element (index or subscript) in parentheses, as in `strValue = strArray(3)`. Arrays in VBA may have more than one dimension, in which case access to the value includes indexes for each dimension, as in `strValue = strArray(3,3)`.

**ASCII**   Abbreviation for the American Standard Code for Information Interchange. A set of standard numerical values for printable, control, and special characters used by PCs and most other computers. Other commonly used codes for character sets are ANSI (used by Windows 3.1+), Unicode (used by Windows 95 and Windows NT), and EBCDIC (Extended Binary-Coded Decimal Interchange Code, used by IBM for mainframe computers). See *Unicode*.

**assign**   To give a value to a named variable.

**asynchronous**   A process that can occur at any time, regardless of the status of the operating system or applications that are running.

**attached table**   A table that is not stored in the currently open Access database (native or base table), but which you can manipulate as if the table were a native table. In Access 95 terminology, an attached table is a linked table. See *linked table*.

**authentication**   The process of verifying a user's login ID and password.

**automation**   An ActiveX and OLE 2.0 term that refers to a means of manipulating another application's objects. See also *OLE Automation*.

**automation client**   An ActiveX- or OLE 2-compliant Windows application with an application programming (macro) language, such as VBA, that is capable of referencing and manipulating objects exposed by (OLE) Automation servers.

**automation server**   Technically, any COM- or OLE 2-compliant Windows application that supports Automation operations by exposing a set of objects for manipulation by Automation client applications. This book restricts the term automation server to applications that are not OLE 2+ full servers, but expose application objects. Access 97 is an example of an automation server.

**AutoNumber**   An Access 95 replacement for the Counter field data type of Access 1.x and 2.0. AutoNumber fields may be of the Increment or Random type. Fields of the Increment AutoNumber field data type usually are used to create primary keys in cases where a unique primary key cannot be created from data in the table.

**AutoPlay**   A feature of Windows 95's and Windows NT 4.0's CD-ROM file system (CDFS) that automatically executes a program on the CD-ROM when inserted into the CD-ROM drive.

**back up**   To create a file (backup file) that duplicates data stored in one or more files on a client or server computer.

**background**   In multitasking computer operations, the application or procedure that is not visible on-screen and that does not receive user generated input. In Windows, an application that is minimized and does not have the focus is in the background.

**base date**   A date used as a reference from which other date values are calculated. In the case of VBA and SQL Server, the base date is January 1, 1900.

**base tables**   The permanent tables from which a query is created. A synonym for underlying tables. Each base table in a database is identified by a name unique to the database. Access also uses the term *base table* to refer to a table in the current database in contrast to a linked (attached) table. See *linked table*.

**batch**   A group of statements processed as an entity. Execution of DOS batch files, such as AUTOEXEC.BAT, and SQL statements are examples of a batch process.

**BDC**   An abbreviation for Backup Domain Controller, a Windows NT server that provides an alternative source of authentication for network users. Account and group information from a Primary Domain Controller (PDC) is replicated periodically to each BDC in the domain. See *PDC*.

**binary file**   A file whose content does not consist of lines of text. Executable (.exe), dynamic link library (.dll), and most database files are stored in binary format.

**binary string**   A string consisting of binary, not text, data that contains bytes outside the range of ANSI or ASCII values for printable characters. Access 97 requires that you store binary strings as arrays of the Byte data type to avoid problems with Unicode/ANSI conversion.

**binding**   In Access, attaching a Form or Report object to a table, or a control object to a field of a table or the column of a query result set. The bound Form or Report object determines the current record of the table or the bound control object reflects the value of the data cell or field of the current record or row.

**bit**   The smallest piece of information processed by a computer. A bit, derived from the contraction of BInary digiT (or Binary digIT) has two states: on (1) or off (0). Eight bits make up a *byte*, and 16 bits combined is called a *word*.

**bitmap**   The representation of a screen or printed image, usually graphic, as a series of bytes.

**bitwise**   A process that evaluates each bit of a combination, such as a byte or word, rather than processing the combination as a single element. Logical operations and masks use bitwise procedures.

**blitting**   The process of using the `BitBlt()` function of Windows' GdI32.exe to modify a bitmap using bit block transfer.

**Boolean**   A type of arithmetic in which all digits are bits; that is, the numbers may have only two states: on (true or 1) or off (false or 0). Widely used in set theory and computer programming, Boolean, named after the mathematician George Boole, also is used to describe a VBA data type that may only have two states: true or false. In VBA, True is represented by &HFF (all bits of an 8-bit byte set to 1) and False by &H0 (all bits set to 0).

**bound**    See *Binding and Object frame*.

**break**    To cause an interruption in program operation. Ctrl+C is the standard DOS break key combination, but it seldom halts operation of a Windows application. Esc is more commonly used in Windows to cause an operation to terminate prior to completion.

**breakpoint**    A designated statement that causes program execution to halt after executing the statement preceding it. Breakpoints may be toggled on or off by choosing Run, Toggle Breakpoint in Access, or by pressing the F9 function key.

**BRI**    An abbreviation for Basic Rate Interface, the standard ISDN service for business and residential Internet connections. BRI has two 56Kbps B (bearer) channels and one 16Kbps D (data) channel, providing a maximum bandwidth of 112Kbps. See *ISDN* and *PRI*.

**Briefcase replication**    A feature of Access 97 running under Windows 95 that permits the creation of Access replication sets stored in Windows 95 Briefcase folders, which can be updated by mobile users. Subsequently, the briefcase replicates are used to update the design-master replica to synchronize the design-master replica with the contents of the briefcase replicas. See *design-master replica*.

**buffer**    An area in memory of a designated size (number of bytes or characters) reserved, typically, to hold a portion of a file or the value of a variable. When string variables are passed as arguments of DLL functions, you must create a buffer of sufficient size to hold the returned string. This is accomplished by creating a fixed-length string variable of the necessary size, using the String() function, prior to calling the DLL function.

**builder**    A component of Access that provides assistance in creating expressions (Expression Builder) or controlling objects.

**built-in functions**    Functions that are included in a computer language and need not be created by the programmer as user-defined functions.

**business rules**    A set of rules for entering data in a database that are specific to an enterprise's method of conducting its operations. Business rules are in addition to rules for maintaining the domain and referential integrity of tables in a database. Business rules most commonly are implemented in a three-tier client-server database environment. See *three-tier*.

**cache**    A block of memory reserved for temporary storage. Caches usually store data from disk files in memory to make access to the data faster. By default, Windows 95 caches all disk read and write operations.

**caption**    The title that appears in the title bar of a window. Access calls the text of a label, check box, frame, and command or option button control object the Caption *property*.

**caret**  The term used by Windows to indicate the cursor used when editing a text field, usually shaped as an I-beam. The caret, also called the *insertion point*, can be positioned independently of the mouse pointer.

**Cartesian product**  Named for René Descartes, a French mathematician. Used in JOIN operations to describe all possible combinations of rows and columns from each table in a database. The number of rows in a Cartesian product is equal to the number of rows in table 1 times that in table 2 times that in table 3, and so on. Cartesian rows that do not satisfy the JOIN condition are disregarded.

**cascading deletion**  A trigger that deletes data from one table based on a deletion from another table to maintain referential integrity. Usually used to delete detail data (such as invoice items) when the master record (invoice) is deleted. Access 2+ provides cascading deletion as an optional component of its referential integrity features. See *referential integrity*.

**case sensitivity**  A term used to define whether the interpreter or compiler treats lowercase and uppercase letters as the same character. Most are case-insensitive. C is an exception; it is case-sensitive, and all of its keywords are lowercase. Many interpreters—VBA included—reformat keywords to its standard: a combination of uppercase and lowercase letters. VBA does not distinguish between uppercase and lowercase letters used as names for variables.

**CDFS**  The 32-bit CD-ROM file system shared by Windows NT and Windows 95.

**channel**  In Windows, ordinarily refers to a unique task ID assigned to a dynamic data exchange (DDE) conversation. Channel IDs are Long integers under Windows 95 and Windows NT. Also used to identify an I/O port in mini- and mainframe computers.

**check box**  A windows dialog and Access control object that consists of a square box and an associated caption. A diagonal cross or other mark in the box is created or erased (toggled) by alternate clicks on the box or the label with the mouse or by pressing an assigned hotkey.

**child**  In Windows, usually an abbreviation for an MDI child window. Also used in computer programming in general to describe an object that is related to but lower in hierarchical level than a parent object.

**chunk**  A part of either a RIFF or standard MIDI file that is assigned to a particular function and may be treated as a single element by an application. VBA uses the term *chunk* to refer to a part of any file that you read or write with the GetChunk and AppendChunk methods. See *RIFF*.

**class identifier**  See *CLSID*.

**clause**  The portion of an SQL statement beginning with a keyword that names a basic operation to be performed.

**client**  The device or application that receives data from or manipulates a server device or application. The data may be in the form of a file received from a network file server,

VIII

Appendixes

an object from an ActiveX component or OLE server, or values from a DDE server assigned to client variables. See *automation client*.

**Clipboard**   Windows' temporary storage location for text and graphic objects, as well as Access objects, such as control objects, forms, tables, reports, and so on. The Clipboard is the intermediary in all copy, cut, and paste operations. You can view and save the contents of the Clipboard using the Program Manager's Clipboard applet.

**CLSID**   An identification tag that is associated with an OLE 2.0 object created by a specific server. CLSID values appear in the Registry and must be unique for each ActiveX component or OLE 2.0 server and each type of object that the server can create. See *Registry*.

**clustered index**   An index in which the physical record order and index order of a table are the same.

**clustering**   A server architecture that emulates multiprocessing by interconnecting two or more individual computers in order to share the application processing load. Microsoft's future clustering technology for Windows NT now carries the codename *Wolfpack*. A number of third parties offer proprietary clustering hardware and software for Windows NT 4.0 Server.

**code**   Short for *source code*. The text you enter in your program to create an application. Code consists of instructions and their parameters, functions and their arguments, objects and their events, properties and methods, constants, variable declarations and assignments, and expressions and comments.

**code template**   Self-contained groups of modules and resources that perform a group of standard functions and that may be incorporated within other applications requiring these functions, usually with little or no modification.

**Code window**   In Access, the window that appears when you select Module from the Database window or click the Ellipsis button of an event property to create or edit an event-handling subprocedure. Also called the *code editing window*.

**coercion**   The process of forcing a change from one data type to another, such as Integer to Text.

**collection**   A group of objects of the same class that are contained within another object. Collections are named as the plural of their object class. As an example, the Forms and Reports collections are groups of Form and Report objects contained in the Database object.

**color palette**   A means of establishing a foreground or background color in Windows by selecting a color from those displayed with the mouse. The color palette then converts the selection to the standard Windows RGB (red/green/blue) color format. The color palette provides the set of colors for graphic objects of 256 colors or less. Access 2+ allows you to specify a particular palette for individual forms. Also called *palette* or *Windows palette*.

**COM**    An acronym for Component Object Model, the name of Microsoft's design strategy to implement ActiveX and OLE 2+. Distributed COM (DCOM) allows networked and cross-platform implementation of ActiveX and OLE 2+ operations, and (OLE) Automation. See *DCOM*.

**combo list**    A Windows object that combines text box and list elements into a single object. In Access, combo lists are of the drop-down type by default. The list element of a drop-down combo list appears when a downward-pointing arrow to the right of the text box is clicked.

**command**    A synonym for instruction. Specifies an action to be taken by the computer.

**command button**    A Windows object that causes an event when clicked. Command buttons are ordinarily a gray rectangle containing a caption and surrounded by a border.

**comment**    Explanatory material within source code not designed to be interpreted or compiled into the final application. In VBA, comments are usually preceded by an apostrophe ('), but can also be created by preceding them with the Rem keyword.

**common dialog**    A standardized dialog box, provided by Windows 95 and Windows NT, that may be created by a Windows API function call to functions contained in Cmdlg32.dll. Common dialogs include FileOpen, FileSave, Print and Printer Setup, ColorPalette, Font, and Search and Replace. Using the common dialogs in Access applications requires that you use the Declare statement to create function prototypes for the functions in Comdlg32.dll that you plan to use. The Comdlg32.ocx control, included with the Office Developer's Kit, lets you implement most of the common dialogs without the necessity of calling Comdlg32.dll functions.

**Common User Access**    See *CUA*.

**comparison operators**    See *operator*.

**compile**    To create an executable or object (machine-language) file from source (readable) code. In Access, *compile* means to create pseudo-code (tokenized code) from the VBA source code you write in the code editing windows.

**Component Object Model**    See *COM*.

**composite key or index**    A key or index based on the values in two or more columns. See also *key* and *index*.

**composite menu**    A menu that includes menu choices from an OLE 2.0 server application that uses in-place (in-situ) activation (editing). Creating a composite menu also is called *grafting a menu*.

**composite moniker**    The location within a container document or object where the compound document is located.

**compound**    In computer programming, a set of instructions or statements that requires more than one keyword or group of related keywords to complete. `Select Case…Case…End Select` is an example of a compound statement in VBA.

**compound document**    A document that contains OLE objects created by an application other than the application that originally created or is managing the document.

**concatenation**    Combining two expressions, usually strings, to form a longer expression. The concatenation operator is `&` in SQL and VBA, although VBA also permits the + symbol to be used to concatenate strings.

**concurrency**    The condition when more than one user has access to a specific set of records or files at the same time. Concurrency is also used to describe the ability of a database management system to handle simultaneous queries against a single set of tables.

**container**    An object or application that can create or manipulate compound documents.

**context switching**    The process of saving an executing thread or process and transferring control to another thread or process. Windows NT 4.0's context switching—one of the major bottlenecks in COM operations—is substantially faster than in Window NT 3.x.

**control**    A synonym for a dialog object in Access. Controls include labels, text boxes, lists, combo lists, option buttons, and command buttons. Access 97 also provides compatibility with ActiveX Controls (formerly OLE Controls).

**control array**    In Visual Basic, the term given to multiple controls on a single form with the same `Name` property. (Access does not support control arrays.) Individual controls (elements) of a control array are designated by their index, starting with 0, up to one less than the number of controls with the same name.

**Control menu box**    See *Application Control menu box* and *Document Control menu box*.

**conversation**    In DDE operations, the collection of Windows messages that are passed between two different applications—the client and server—during an interprocess communication.

**correlated subquery**    A subquery that cannot be independently evaluated. Subqueries depend on an outer query for their result. See also *subquery* and *nested query*.

**counter**    A special field data type of Access 1.x and 2.0 tables that numbers each new record consecutively; called an *AutoNumber field* in Access 95 and 97. See *AutoNumber*.

**CUA**    An abbreviation for Common User Access, an element of IBM's SAA (Systems Application Architecture) specification, which establishes a set of standards for user interaction with menus, dialogs, and other user-interactive portions of an application. The CUA was first implemented in Windows and OS/2 and has been an integral part of these GUIs since their inception.

**current database**   The database opened in Access by choosing File, Open Database (or the equivalent) that contains the objects of an Access application.

**current record**   The record in a Table or Recordset object whose values you modify. The current record supplies values of the current record's data cells to control objects that are bound to the table's fields.

**current statement**   The statement or instruction being executed at a particular instance in time. In debugging or stepwise operation of interpreted applications such as Access, it is the next statement that will be executed by the interpreter when program operation is resumed.

**custom control**   The former name for a control object not native to the application. Access 97 supports 32-bit ActiveX and OLE Controls (OCXs). Visual Basic 3.0 and Visual C++ 3.0 use 16-bit Visual Basic Extension custom controls (VBXs). Visual Basic 4.0 supports 16-bit VBXs and OCXs, plus 32-bit OCXs. See *ActiveX Control* and *OLE Control*.

**data access object**   The container for all of the objects that can be embodied in an Access application, often abbreviated *DAO*. The top member of the data access object hierarchy of Access is the DBEngine object, which contains Workspace, User, and Group objects in collections. Database objects are contained in Workspace objects. See also *ActiveX Data Object*.

**data definition**   The process of describing databases and database objects such as tables, indexes, views, procedures, rules, default values, triggers, and other characteristics.

**data dictionary**   The result of the data definition process. Also used to describe a set of database system tables that contain the data definitions of database objects, often called *metadata*.

**data element**   The value contained in a data cell, also called a *data item*, or simply an *element*. A piece of data that describes a single property of a data entity, such as a person's first name, last name, Social Security number, age, sex, or hair color. In this case, the person is the data entity.

**data entity**   A distinguishable set of objects that is the subject of a data table and usually has at least one unique data element. A data entity might be a person (unique Social Security number), an invoice (unique invoice number), or a vehicle (unique vehicle ID number, because license plates are not necessarily unique across state lines).

**data integrity**   The maintenance of rules that prevent inadvertent or intentional modifications to the content of a database that would be deleterious to its accuracy or reliability. See *domain integrity* and *referential integrity*.

**data modification**   Changing the content of one or more tables in a database. Data modification includes adding, deleting, or changing information with the INSERT, DELETE, and UPDATE SQL statements. Data modification often is called *updating*.

**data sharing**   The ability to allow more than one user to access information stored in a database from the same or a different application.

**data type**    The description of how the computer is to interpret a particular item of data. Data types are generally divided into two families: strings that usually have text or readable content, and numeric data. The types of numeric data supported vary with the compiler or interpreter used. Most programming languages support a user-defined record or structure data type that can contain multiple data types within it. Field data types, which define the data types of database tables, are distinguished from Access table data types in this book.

**database**    A set of related data tables and other database objects, such as a data dictionary, which are organized as a group.

**database administrator**    The individual(s) responsible for the administrative functions of client-server databases. The database administrator (DBA) has privileges (permissions) for all commands that may be executed by the RDBMS and is ordinarily responsible for maintaining system security, including access by users to the RDBMS itself and performing backup and restoration functions.

**database device**    A file in which databases and related information, such as transaction logs, are stored. Database devices usually have physical names (such as a file name) and a logical name (the parameter of the USE statement). In SQL Server, database devices use the DAT file extension.

**database object**    A component of a database. Database objects include tables, views, indexes, procedures, columns, rules, triggers, and defaults. The DBEngine object in Access VBA is the topmost member of the class of Access objects. All objects within a single database are subclasses of the Database object.

**database owner**    The user who originally created a database. The database owner has control over all of the objects in the database, but may delegate control to other users. Access calls the database owner the *creator*. The database owner is identified by the prefix dbo in SQL Server.

**Database window**    The window that appears when you open an Access database and lists the objects (tables, queries, forms, reports, macros, and modules) that are contained in the Database object.

**date function**    A function that provides date and time information or manipulates date and time values.

**DCOM**    An acronym for Distributed Common Object Model that allows communication and manipulation of objects over a network connection. Windows NT 4.0 is the first Microsoft operating system to support DCOM (formerly called NetworkOLE). Microsoft is expected to release a DCOM update for Windows 95 in late 1996. See *COM*.

**DDE**    An abbreviation for dynamic data exchange. DDE is an Interprocess Communication (IPC) method used by Windows and OS/2 to transfer data between different applications. Automation (formerly OLE Automation) provides a more robust IPC method.

**deadlock**   A condition that occurs when two users with a lock on one data item attempt to lock the other's data item. Most RDBMSes detect this condition, prevent its occurrence, and advise both users of the potential deadlock situation.

**debug**   The act of removing errors in the source code for an application.

**Debug window**   A non-modal dialog in which you may enter VBA expressions and view results without writing code in a code editing window. You may also direct information to be displayed in the Debug window by use of the Debug object. The appearance of the Debug window varies slightly between VBA-enabled applications.

**declaration**   A statement that creates a user-defined data type, names a variable, creates a symbolic constant, or registers the prototypes of functions incorporated within dynamic link libraries.

**declaration section**   A section of a VBA module reserved for statements containing declarations.

**declare**   In text and not as a keyword, to create a user-defined data type, data holder for a variable or constant. As a VBA keyword, to register a function contained in a dynamic link library in the declarations section of a module.

**default**   A value assigned or an option chosen when no value is specified by the user or assigned by a program statement.

**default database**   The logical name of the database assigned to a user when he or she logs in to the database application.

**demand lock**   Precludes more shared locks from being set on a data resource. Successive requests for shared locks must wait for the demand lock to be cleared.

**dependent**   A condition in which master data in a table (such as invoices) is associated with detail data in a subsidiary table (invoice items). In this case, invoice items are dependent upon invoices.

**design-master replica**   The member of an Access replica set that allows changes in the design of objects, such as tables. The design-master replica usually (but not necessarily) is the .mbd file that is updated by briefcase replicas of the .mbd. See *Briefcase replication*.

**Design mode**   One of three modes of operation of Access, also called *Design view*. Design mode allows you to create and modify tables, queries, forms, reports, and control objects, enter macro actions, and write VBA code. The other two modes are Run mode, also called *run-time* (when the application is executing), and Startup mode (before you open an Access database).

**destination document**   A term used by OLE 1.0 to refer to a compound document.

VIII

Appendixes

**detail data**   Data in a subsidiary table that depends on data in a master table to have meaning or intrinsic value. If a user deletes the master invoice records, the subsidiary table's detail data for items included in the invoice lose their reference in the database—they become *orphan data*.

**detail table**   A table that depends on a master table. Detail tables usually have a many-to-one relationship with the master table. See also *detail data*.

**device**   A computer system component that is capable of sending or receiving data, such as a keyboard, display, printer, disk drive, or modem. Windows uses device drivers to connect applications to devices.

**device context**   A Windows term that describes a record (struct) containing a complete definition of all of the variables required to fully describe a window containing a graphic object. These include the dimensions of the graphic area (viewport), drawing tools in use (pen, brush), fonts, colors, Drawing mode, and so on. Windows provides a handle (hDC) for each device context.

**DHCP**   Abbreviation for Dynamic Host Configuration Protocol, an Internet standard protocol that allows IP addresses to be pooled and assigned as needed to clients. Windows NT 4.0 includes DHCP Manager, a graphical DHCP configuration tool. See *IP* and *IP address*.

**dialog**   A popup modal child window, also called a *dialog box*, that requests information from the user. Dialogs include message boxes, input boxes, and user-defined dialogs for applications, such as choosing files to open.

**DIB**   An acronym for Device-Independent Bitmap, a Windows-specific bitmap format designed to display graphic information. DIB files take the extension .dip and use a format similar to the .bmp format.

**difference**   In data tables, data elements that are contained in one table but not in another.

**directory list**   An element of a file selection dialog that selectively lists the subfolders of the designated folder of a specified logical drive.

**distributed database**   A database, usually of the client/server type, that is located on more than one database server, often at widely separated locations. Synchronization of data contained in distributed databases is most commonly accomplished by the two-phase commit or replication methods. See *replication* and *two-phase commit*.

**disk mirroring**   Creating on two or more physical disk drives exact duplicates of a disk volume to make files accessible in case of failure of one drive of the mirror set. See *RAID*.

**disk striping**   Distributing the data for a single logical disk volume across two or more physical disk drives. Simple disk striping (RAID 0) provides faster I/O operation. Disk striping with parity (RAID 5) provides faster I/O and protection from failure of a physical disk in a stripe set. See *RAID*.

**DLL**   An abbreviation for dynamic link library, a file containing a collection of Windows functions designed to perform a specific class of operations. Most DLLs carry the .dll extension, but some Windows DLLs, such as Gdi32.exe, use the .exe extension. Functions within DLLs are called (*invoked*) by applications, as necessary, to perform the desired operation.

**docfile**   The file format for creating persistent OLE objects, now called ActiveX documents. Docfiles usually have the extension .ole. Applications that are fully OLE 2-compliant create docfiles with specific extensions, such as .doc (Word) and .xls (Excel). Access 95 .mbd files also are OLE 2 docfiles. OLE 2.1 requires that docfiles include file property values derived from choosing File, Properties. See also *ActiveX documents*.

**document**   A programming object that contains information that originates with the user of the application, rather than being created by the application itself. The data for documents usually is stored in disk files. Access tables, forms, and reports are documents, as are Excel or Lotus 1-2-3 worksheets. In Windows 95 and Windows NT 4.0, a document is a file with an association to an application that can display or manipulate the file.

**Document Control menu box**   The small, square button at the upper-left corner of the menubar of an application that uses the multiple document interface (MDI). Clicking the Document Control menu box displays the Document Control menu. Double-clicking the Document Control menu box closes the document (but not the application). See also *MDI server*.

**domain**   A group of workstations and servers that share a common security account manager (SAM) database and that allow a user to log on to any resource in the domain with a single user ID and password. See also *BDC* and *PDC*. In Access, a domain is a set of records defined by a table or query.

**domain aggregate functions**   A set of functions, identical to the SQL aggregate functions, that you can apply to a specified domain, rather than to one or more Table objects. See also *aggregate functions*.

**domain integrity**   The process of assuring that values added to fields of a table comply with a set of rules for reasonableness and other constraints. As an example, domain integrity is violated if you enter a ship date value that is earlier than an order date. In Access, domain integrity is maintained by field-level and table-level validation rules. See *business rules*.

**drag-and-drop**   A Windows process whereby an icon representing an object, such as a file, can be moved (dragged) by the mouse to another location (such as a different directory) and placed (dropped) in it. You can use drag-and-drop techniques in Access 97's Design mode. Access does not provide the same drag-and-drop capabilities for control objects that are available with Visual Basic.

**drive**   The logical identifier of a disk drive, usually specified as a letter. When used as a component of a path, the drive letter must be followed by a colon and backslash, as in **C:\**.

VIII

Appendixes

**dynamic data exchange**   See *DDE*.

**dynamic link library**   See *DLL*.

**dynaset**   A set of rows and columns in your computer's memory that represent the values in an attached table, a table with a filter applied, or a query result set. You can update the values of the fields of the underlying table(s) by changing the values of the data cells of an updatable Dynaset object. In Access 2+, Dynaset is a type of Recordset object. See also *recordset*.

**embedded object**   A source document stored as an OLE object in a compound or container document.

**empty**   A condition of a VBA variable that has been declared but has not been assigned a value. Empty is not the same as the Null value nor is it equal to the empty or zero-length string ("").

**enabled**   The ability of a control object to respond to user actions such as a mouse click, expressed as the True or False value of the Enabled property of the control.

**environment**   A combination of the computer hardware, operating system, and user interface. A complete statement of an environment follows: a 166MHz Pentium computer with a VGA display and two-button mouse, using the Windows 95 operating system.

**environmental variable**   A DOS term for variables that are declared by PATH and SET statements, usually made in an AUTOEXEC.BAT file, and stored in a reserved memory location by DOS. In Windows 95 and Windows NT, required environmental variables are stored in the Registry, although Windows 95 accepts environmental variables in the AUTOEXEC.BAT file for backward compatibility with 16-bit Windows applications. The environmental variables may be used by applications to adjust their operation for compatibility with user-specific hardware elements or folder structures.

**equi-join**   A JOIN in which the values in the columns being joined are compared for equality and all columns in both tables are displayed. This results in two identical columns in the result.

**error trapping**   A procedure by which errors generated during the execution of an application are rerouted to a designated group of lines of code (called an *error handler*) that performs a predefined operation, such as ignoring the error. If errors are not trapped in VBA, the standard modal message dialog with the text message for the error that occurred appears.

**event**   The occurrence of an action taken by the user and recognized by one of Access's event properties, such as On Click or On DblClick, corresponding to VBA's Click and DblClick event handlers. Events are usually related to mouse movements and keyboard actions; however, events also can be generated by code using the Timer control object, for example.

**event-driven**    The property of an operating system or environment, such as Windows, that implies the existence of an idle loop. When an event occurs, the idle loop is exited and event-handler code, specific to the event, is executed. After the event handler has completed its operation, execution returns to the idle loop, awaiting the next event.

**exclusive lock**    A lock that prevents others from locking data items until the exclusive lock is cleared. Exclusive locks are placed on data items by update operations, such as SQL's INSERT, UPDATE, and DELETE. In Access and SQL Server, page locking is used; SQL Server 6.5 provides row locking for INSERT operations.

**executable**    Code, usually in the form of a disk file, that can be run by the operating system in use to perform a particular set of functions. Executable files in Windows carry the extension .exe and may obtain assistance from dynamic link libraries (DLLs) in performing their tasks.

**exponent**    The second element of a number expressed in scientific notation, the power of 10 by which the first element, the *mantissa*, is multiplied to obtain the actual number. For +1.23E3, the exponent is 3, so you multiply 1.23 by 1,000 (10 to the third power) to obtain the result, 1,230.

**expression**    A combination of variable names, values, functions, and operators that return a result, usually assigned to a variable name. Result = 1 + 1 is an expression that returns 2 to the variable named Result. DiffVar = LargeVar  SmallVar returns the difference between the two variables to DiffVar. Functions may be used in expressions, and the expression may return the value determined by the function to the same variable as that of the argument. strVar = **Mid$**(strVar, 2, 3) replaces the value of strVar with three of its characters, starting at the second character.

**failover**    A fault-tolerant clustering architecture in which two servers share a common set of fault-tolerant fixed disk drives. In the event of failure of one of the servers, the other transparently assumes all server processing operations. See *clustering* and *fault tolerance*.

**FAT**    An acronym for file allocation table, the disk file system used by MS-DOS, Windows 95, and (optionally) Windows NT. Windows NT is compatible with the 16-bit FAT system, but not the optional 32-bit FAT (FAT32) for Windows 95 that Microsoft announced in mid-1996. See *HPFS* and *NTFS*.

**fault tolerance**    A computer system's capability to maintain operability, despite failure of a major hardware component such as a power supply, microprocessor, or fixed-disk drive. Fault tolerance requires redundant hardware and modifications to the operating system. Windows NT Server includes fault tolerance for a failed disk drive by disk mirroring (RAID 1) or disk striping with parity (RAID 5). Clustering provides fault tolerance for individual computers. See *clustering* and *RAID*.

**fiber**    A lightweight thread, introduced in Windows NT 4.0, that makes it easier for developers to optimize scheduling within multithreaded applications. See *thread*.

**VIII**

**Appendixes**

**field**   Synonym for a column that contains attribute values. Also, a single item of information in a record or row.

**fifth normal form**   The rule for relational databases that requires that a table that has been divided into multiple tables must be capable of being reconstructed to its exact original structure by one or more JOIN statements.

**file**   The logical equivalent of a table. In dBASE, for instance, each table is a single .dbf file.

**file moniker**   The location of the well-formed path to a persistent OLE 2+ object.

**first normal form**   The rule for relational databases that dictates that tables must be flat. Flat tables can contain only one data value set per row. Members of the data value set, called *data cells*, are contained in one column of the row, and must have only one value.

**flag**   A variable, usually Boolean (True/False), that is used to determine the status of a particular condition within an application. The term set is often used to indicate turning a flag from False to True, and reset for the reverse.

**flow control**   In general usage, conditional expressions that control the sequence of execution of instructions or statements in the source code of an application. If... Then...End If is a flow control statement. The term is also used to describe diagrams that describe the mode of operation of an application.

**focus**   A Windows term indicating the currently selected application, or one of its windows, to which all user-generated input (keyboard and mouse operations) is directed. The object with the focus is said to be the *active object*. The title bar of a window with the focus is colored blue for the default Windows color scheme.

**font**   A typeface in a single size, usually expressed in points, of a single style or having a common set of attributes. Font often is misused to indicate a typeface family or style.

**foreground**   In multitasking operations, the application or procedure that is visible on-screen and to which user-generated input is directed. In Windows, the application that has the focus is in the foreground.

**foreign key**   A column or combination of columns whose value must match a primary key in another table when joined with it. Foreign keys need not be unique for each record or row. See also *primary key*.

**form**   A synonym for a user-defined MDI child window in Access. A Form object contains the control objects that appear on its surface and the code associated with the events, methods, and properties applicable to the form and its control objects.

**form-level**   Variables that are declared in the Declarations section of an Access form. These variables are said to have *form-level scope*, and are not visible to procedures outside the Form object in which the variables are declared, unless declared with the Public reserved word.

**fourth normal form**   The rule for relational databases that requires that only related data entities be included in a single table and that tables may not contain data related to more than one data entity when many-to-one relationships exist among the entities.

**frame**   In Windows, a rectangle, usually with a single-pixel-wide border, that encloses a group of objects, usually of the dialog class. When referring to SMPTE timing with MIDI files, it is one image of a motion picture film (1/24 seconds) or one complete occurrence of a television image (approximately 1/30 seconds in NTSC, 1/25 seconds in PAL).

**front-end**   When used in conjunction with database management systems, an application, window, or set of windows by which the user may access and view database records, as well as add to or edit them.

**full server**   An OLE 2-compliant executable application capable of providing embeddable or linked documents for insertion into OLE 2+ container documents. Excel 95, Word 95, Project 4.1, and Wordpad are examples of OLE 2.1 full server applications. Access 97 is not a full server, because you cannot embed or link an Access .mdb file in an OLE 2.1 container application.

**function**   A subprogram called from within an expression in which a value is computed and returned to the program that called it through its name. Functions are classified as internal to the application language when their names are keywords. You may create your own user-defined functions in VBA by adding code between Function FunctionName...End Function statements.

**global**   Pertaining to the program as a whole. Global variables and constants are accessible to, and global variables may be modified by, code at the form, module, and procedure level. VBA uses the reserved word Public to create or refer to global variables.

**global module**   A code module (container) in which all global variables and constants are declared and in which the prototypes of any external functions contained in DLLs are declared. Use of a global module in Access applications is common, but not required.

**grid**   A preset group of visible or imaginary vertical and horizontal lines used to assist in aligning the position of graphic objects. In Access, the intersection of the imaginary lines is shown as dots on forms and reports in Design mode. Control objects automatically align their outlines to these dots if the Snap To Grid option is enabled. In Access Datasheet view, a set of lines that establish the demarcation of columns and rows.

**group**   In reports, one or more records that are collected into a single category, usually for the purpose of totaling. Database security systems use the term *group* to identify a collection of database users with common permissions. See also *permissions*.

**HAL**   An acronym for Hardware Abstraction Layer, a Windows NT DLL that links specific computer hardware implementations with the Windows NT kernel. Windows NT 4.0 includes HALs for 80x86, Alpha, MIPS, and PowerPC hardware platforms.

**handle**   An unsigned Long integer assigned by Windows 95 and Windows NT to uniquely identify an instance (occurrence) of a module (application, hModule), task

**VIII**

**Appendixes**

(hTask), window (hWnd), or device context (hDC) of a graphic object. Handles in 32-bit Windows applications, including applications for Windows 95 and Windows NT, are 32-bit unsigned long integers (dw or double-words). Also used to identify the sizing elements of control objects in Design mode. See also *sizing handle*.

**header file**   A file type used by C and C++ programs to assign data types and names to variables and to declare prototypes of the functions used in the application. C header files usually carry the extension .h.

**hierarchical menu**   A menu with multiple levels, consisting of a main menubar that leads to one or more levels of submenus from which choices of actions are made. Almost all Windows applications use hierarchical menu structures.

**host**   Any computer on a network using the Internet Protocol (IP). See *IP* and *IP address*.

**hotlink**   A term used to describe a DDE (dynamic data exchange) operation in which a change in the source of the DDE data (the server) is immediately reflected in the object of the destination application (the client) which has requested it.

**HPFS**   An abbreviation for the High-Performance File System used by OS/2 and (optionally) Windows NT 3.x. Windows NT 4.0 doesn't support HPFS but can connect via a network to files on HPFS volumes of Windows NT 3.x PCs.

**HTML**   An abbreviation for HyperText Markup Language, a variant of SGML (Standardized General Markup Language), a page-description language for creating files that can be formatted and displayed by World Wide Web browsers.

**icon**   A 32×32-pixel graphic image used to identify the application in the program manager window when the application is minimized, and in other locations in the application chosen by the programmer (such as the Help About dialog). Windows 95 also uses 16×16-pixel icons to identify the application in the title bar.

**identifier**   A synonym for *name* or *symbol*, usually applied to variable and constant names.

**idle**   In Windows, the condition or state in which both Windows and the application have processed all pending messages in the queue from user- or hardware-initiated events and are waiting for the next to occur. The idle state is entered in VBA when the interpreter reaches the End Sub statement of the outermost nesting level of procedures for a form or control object.

**immediate window**   Replaced in Access 95 and other VBA-enabled applications by the Debug window. See *Debug window*.

**in-place activation**   The ability to activate an object (launch another application) and have the container application take on the capabilities of the other application. The primary feature of in-place activation (also called *in-situ activation*) is that the other application's menu choices merge with or replace the container application's menu choices in the active window.

**in-process**   A term applied to (OLE) Automation servers, also called *OLE DLLs*, that operate within the same process space (memory allocation) of the (OLE) Automation client using the server. In-process servers commonly are called *InProc servers*. See *out-of-process*.

**index**   For arrays, the position of the particular element with respect to others, usually beginning with 0 as the first element. When used in conjunction with database files or tables, index refers to a lookup table, usually in the form of a file or component of a file, that relates the value of a field in the indexed file to its record or page number and location in the page (if pages are used).

**infinite loop**   A Do While...Loop, For...Next, or similar program flow control structure in which the condition to exit the loop and continue with succeeding statements is never fulfilled. In For...Next loops, infinite looping occurs when the loop counter is set to a value less than that assigned to the To embedded keyword within the structure.

**initialize**   In programming, setting all variables to their default values and resetting the point of execution to the first executable line of code. Initialization is accomplished automatically in VBA when you start an application.

**inner query**   Synonym for subquery. See *subquery*.

**insertion point**   The position of the cursor within a block of text. When the cursor is in a text field, it is called the *caret* in Windows.

**instance**   A term used by Windows to describe the temporal existence of a loaded application or one or more of its windows.

**instantiate**   The process of creating an instance of an object in memory.

**integer**   A whole number. In most programming languages, an integer is a data type that occupies two bytes (16 bits). Integers may have signs (as in the VBA Integer data type), taking on values from –32,768 to +32,767, or be unsigned. In the latter case, integers can represent numbers up to 65,535.

**interface**   A noun describing a connection between two dissimilar COM objects or (OLE) Automation clients and servers. Another common phrase is *user interface*, meaning the "connection" between the display-keyboard combination and the user. Adapter cards constitute the interface between the PC data bus and peripheral devices such as displays, modems, CD-ROMs, and the like. Drivers act as a software interface between Windows and the adapter cards. A *bridge* is an interface between two dissimilar networks. (OLE) Automation uses Iole_ interfaces for inter-process communication. Use of *interface* as a verb is jargon.

**intersection**   The group of data elements that are included in both tables that participate in a JOIN operation.

**invocation path**   The route through which an object or routine is invoked. If the routine is deeply nested, the path may be quite circuitous.

VIII

Appendixes

**intranet**   A private network that uses Internet protocols and common Internet applications (such as Web browsers) to emulate the public Internet. Intranets on LANs and high-speed WANs provide increased privacy and improved performance compared with today's Internet.

**invoke**   To cause execution of a block of code, particularly a procedure or sub-procedure. Also used to indicate application of a method to an object.

**IP**   An abbreviation for Internet Protocol, the basic network transmission protocol of the Internet.

**IP address**   The 32-bit hexadecimal address of a host, gateway, or router on an IP network. For convenience, IP addresses are specified as the decimal value of the four address bytes, separated by periods, as in **124.33.15.1**. Addresses are classified as types A, B, and C, depending on the subnet mask applied. See *subnet mask*.

**IPX/SPX**   Abbreviation for Internetwork Packet Exchange/Sequenced Packet Exchange, the transport protocol of Novell NetWare, supported by Windows NT's NWLink service. See *NWLink*.

**ISDN**   An abbreviation for *Integrated Services Digital Network*, a switched telephone service that provides mid-band digital communication capabilities used for Internet connections and for remote access to LANs, as well as voice communication. Windows NT 4.0 has built-in support for ISDN modems, more properly called *network terminators*.

**item**   The name given to the elements contained in a list or the list component of a combo box.

**Jet**   The name given by Microsoft to the database engine native to Access and Visual Basic. The name *Jet* came from an acronym for Joint Engine Technology, the predecessor of Jet 3.5 used by Access and Visual Basic 5.0.

**join**   A basic operation, initiated by the SQL JOIN statement, that links the rows or records of two or more tables by one or more columns in each table.

**jump**   In programming, execution of code in a sequence that is not the same as the sequence in which the code appears in the source code. In most cases, a jump skips over a number of lines of code, the result of evaluation of a conditional expression. In some cases, a jump causes another subroutine to be executed.

**key or key field**   A field that identifies a record by its value. Tables are usually indexed on key fields. For a field to be a key field, each data item in the field must possess a unique value. See also *primary key* and *foreign key*.

**key value**   A value of a key field included in an index.

**keyword**   A word that has specific meaning to the interpreter or compiler in use and causes predefined events to occur when encountered in source code. Keywords differ from reserved words because you can use keywords as variable, procedure, or function names. Using keywords for this purpose, however, is not a good programming practice. You cannot use a reserved word as a variable or constant name.

**label**   In VBA programming, a name given to a target line in the source code at which execution results upon the prior execution of a GoTo *LabelName* instruction. A label also is an Access control object that displays, but cannot update, text values.

**LAN**   An acronym for local area network. A LAN is a system comprising multiple computers that are physically interconnected through network adapter cards and cabling. LANs allow one computer to share specified resources, such as disk drives, printers, and modems, with other computers on the LAN.

**launch**   To start a Windows application.

**leaf level**   The lowest level of an index. Indexes are "botmorphic" and derive the names of their elements from the objects found on trees, such as trunks, limbs, and leaves.

**library**   A collection of functions, compiled as a group and accessible to applications by calling the function name, together with any required arguments. DLLs are one type of library; those used by compilers to provide built-in functions are another type.

**library database**   An Access database that is automatically attached to Access when you launch it. Access library databases usually have the extension .mda; encrypted libraries use the extension .mde. Attachment of library databases to Access is controlled by entries in the Registry.

**linked object**   A source document in a compound document that is included by reference to a file that contains the object's data, rather than by embedding the source document in the compound document.

**linked table**   A table that is not stored in the currently open Access database (native or base table), but which you can manipulate as if the table were a native table. Linked tables were called *attached tables* in Access 1.x and 2.0.

**list**   A Windows control object that provides a list of items that the user can choose from with the mouse or the cursor keys.

**livelock**   A request for an exclusive lock on a data item that is repeatedly denied because of shared locks imposed by other users.

**local**   The scope of a variable declared within a procedure, rather than at the form, module, or global level. Local variables are visible (defined) only within the procedure in which they were declared. VBA uses the prefix Private to define functions, subprocedures, and variable of local scope.

**local area network**   See *LAN*.

**lock**   A restriction of access to a table, portion of a table, or data item imposed to maintain data integrity of a database. Locks may be *shared*, in which case more than one user can access the locked element(s), or *exclusive*, where the user with the exclusive lock prevents other users from creating simultaneous shared or exclusive locks on the element(s). Access uses *page locks* (2K of the .mdb file), which may lock several adjacent records. Some RDBMSs provide *row locks* that only lock a single record. SQL Server 6.5

**VIII**

**Appendixes**

uses row locking for INSERT operations and page locking for UPDATE and DELETE operations.

**logical**    A synonym for Boolean. Logical is a data type that may have true or false values only. Logical is also used to define a class of operators whose result is only True or False. VBA includes a Boolean data type.

**loop**    A compound program flow control structure that causes statements contained between the instructions that designate the beginning and end of the structure to be repeatedly executed until a given condition is satisfied. When the condition is satisfied, program execution continues at the source code line after the loop termination statement.

**LRPC**    An acronym for lightweight remote procedure call used for OLE 2+ and some ActiveX operations between OLE clients and OLE full servers on a single computer. LRPC requires that both applications involved in the procedure call be resident on the same computer. See *RPC*.

**machine language**    Program code in the form of instructions that have meaning to and can be acted upon by the computer hardware and operating system employed. Object files compiled from source code are in machine language, as are executable files that consist of object files linked with library files.

**macro**    A set of one or more instructions, called *actions* by Access, that respond to events. Macros and VBA code, which can substitute for Access macros, are used to automate Access applications. Although Access 97 supports macros for backward compatibility with earlier versions, VBA is the preferred method of programming responses to events. Future version of Access may not support macros.

**mantissa**    The first element of a number expressed in scientific notation that is multiplied by the power of 10 given in the exponent to obtain the actual number. For +1.23E3, the exponent is 3, so you multiply the mantissa, 1.23, by 1,000 (10 to the third power) to obtain the result: 1,230.

**MAPI**    Acronym for the Windows Messaging API created by Microsoft for use with Microsoft Mail, which implements Simple MAPI. Microsoft Exchange Server implements MAPI 1.0 (also called *Extended MAPI*).

**master database**    A database that controls user access to other databases, usually in a client-server system.

**master table**    A table containing data on which detail data in another table is dependent. Master tables have a primary key that is matched to a foreign key in a detail table. Master tables often have a one-to-many relationship with detail tables. They sometimes are called *base tables*.

**MDI server**    An OLE 2+ server that supports multiple compound documents within a single running instance of the application.

**memo**   An Access field data type that can store text with a length of up to about 64,000 bytes. (The length of the Text field data type is limited to 255 bytes.)

**menu**   A set of choices from which the user determines the next set action to take. The design of menus in Windows is governed by the CUA or Common User Access specification developed by IBM.

**metafile**   A type of graphics file, used by Windows and other applications, that stores the objects displayed in the form of mathematical descriptions of lines and surfaces. Windows metafiles, which use the extension .wmf, are a special form of metafiles. Windows 95 and Windows NT 4.0 also supports enhanced metafiles (EMF).

**method**   One of the characteristics of an object and a classification of keywords in VBA. Methods are the procedures that are applicable to an Access object. Methods that are applicable to a class of objects are inherited by other objects of the same class and may be modified to suit the requirements of the object by a characteristic of an object, called *polymorphism*.

**mini-server**   An applet with OLE server capabilities that you cannot run as a stand-alone application.

**mirroring**   See *disk mirroring*.

**MISF**   An abbreviation for *Microsoft Internet Security Framework*, a set of high-level security services that rely on CryptoAPI 2.0 functions to provide certificate- and password-based authentication. MISF also incorporates secure channel communication using SSL (Secure Sockets Layer) 2.0 and 3.0, plus PCT (Personal Communications Technology), SET (Secure Electronic Transactions) for credit-card purchases, and the Microsoft Certificate Server for issuing authentication certificates.

**mission-critical**   A cliché used in software and hardware advertising to describe the necessity of use of the promoted product if one wants to create a reliable database system.

**modal**   A dialog that must be closed before further action can be taken by the user within the application.

**modeless**   A window or dialog that may be closed or minimized by the user without taking any other action; the opposite of *modal*.

**module**   A block of code, consisting of one or more procedures, for which the source code is stored in a single location (a Form or Module object in Access). In a compiled language, a code module is compiled to a single object file.

**module level**   Variables and constants that are declared in the Declarations section of a module. These variables have module-level scope and are visible (defined) to all procedures that are contained within the module, unless declared Public, in which case the variables are visible to all procedures.

**moniker**   A handle to the source of a compound document object.

**monitor**   A name often used in place of the more proper terms, display or video display unit (VDU).

**multimedia**   The combination of sound and graphic images within a single application for the purpose of selling new computer hardware and software. Related outcomes are the creation of animated presentations that incorporate sound effects and graphics, as well as expansion of the market for PCs in the music industry.

**multiprocessing**   The ability of a computer with two or more CPUs to allocate tasks (threads) to a specific CPU. Symmetrical multitasking (SMP), implemented in Windows NT, distributes tasks among CPUs using a load-sharing methodology. Applications must be multithreaded to take advantage of SMP.

**multitasking**   The ability of a computer with a single CPU to simulate the processing of more than one task at a time. Multitasking is effective when one or more of the applications spends most of its time in an idle state waiting for a user-initiated event, such as a keystroke or mouse click.

**multithreaded**   An application that contains more than one thread of execution; a task or set of tasks that executes semi-independently of other task(s). The Jet 3.0 database engine is multithreaded (three threads); Access 95 and VBA are each single-threaded. See *thread*.

**multiuser**   Concurrent use of a single computer by more than one user, usually through the use of remote terminals. UNIX is inherently a multiuser operating system. Access uses the term *multiuser* to refer to Access applications that share a common .mdb file on a network file server.

**named pipes**   A method of interprocess communication, originally developed for OS/2, that provides a secure channel for network communication.

**natural join**   A SQL JOIN operation in which the values of the columns engaged in the join are compared, with all columns of each table in the join that do not duplicate other columns being included in the result. Same as an equi-join except that the joined columns are not duplicated in the result.

**NBF**   An abbreviation for NetBEUI Frame, the transport packet structure used by NetBEUI.

**nested**   An expression applied to procedures that call other procedures within an application. The called procedures are said to be *nested* within the calling procedure. When many calls to subprocedures and sub-subprocedures are made, the last one in the sequence is said to be *deeply nested*.

**nested object**   An OLE 2+ compound document incorporated in another OLE 2+ compound document. You can nest OLE 2+ documents as deeply as you like. OLE 1.0 does not supported nested objects.

**nested query**   A SQL SELECT statement that contains subqueries. See *subquery*.

**NetBEUI**    An acronym for NetBIOS Extended User Interface, the transport protocol of Microsoft Networking. NetBEUI isn't a routable network, so its popularity is declining in comparison with TCP/IP.

**NetBIOS**    An acronym for Network Basic Input/Output System, the original network API for MS-DOS and the foundation for NetBEUI.

**newline pair**    A combination of a carriage return, the Enter key (CR or `Chr$`(13)), and line feed (LF or `Chr$`(10)) used to terminate a line of text on-screen or within a text file. Other characters or combinations may be substituted for the CR/LF pair to indicate the type of newline character (soft, hard, deletable, and so on). The VBA newline constant is VbCrLf.

**NFS**    An abbreviation for Network File Server; a file format and set of drivers, created by Sun Microsystems, that allows DOS/Windows and UNIX applications to share a single server disk drive running under UNIX.

**non-clustered index**    An index that stores key values and pointers to data based on these values. In this case, the leaf level points to data pages rather than to the data itself, as is the case for a clustered index. Equivalent to SET INDEX TO field_name in xBase.

**normal forms**    A set of five rules, the first three of which originally were defined by Dr. E.F. Cobb, that are used to design relational databases. Five normal forms are generally accepted in the creation of relational databases. See *first normal form*, *second normal form*, *third normal form*, *fourth normal form*, and *fifth normal form*.

**normalization**    Creation of a database according to the five generally accepted rules of normal forms. See also *normal forms*.

**not-equal join**    A JOIN statement that specifies that the columns engaged in the join do not equal one another. In Access, you must specify a not-equal join using the SQL WHERE *field1* <> *field2* clause.

**NT**    An abbreviation for New Technology used by Windows NT.

**NTFS**    An abbreviation for New Technology File System; Windows NT's replacement for the DOS FAT (file allocation table) and OS/2's HPFS (high-performance file system). NTFS offers many advantages over other file systems, including improved security and the ability to reconstruct files in the event of hardware failures. Windows 3.1+ and Windows 95 can access files stored on NTFS volumes via a network connection, but cannot open NTFS files directly.

**null**    A variable of no value or of unknown value. The default values, 0 for numeric variables and an empty string (`""`) for string variables, are not the same as the Null value. The NULL value in SQL statements specifies a data cell with no value assigned to the cell.

**object**    In programming, elements that combine data (properties) and behavior (methods) in a single container of code called an *object*. An Access Form or Report object is a member of the class of Access Database objects; a particular control object is a subclass of the control objects class. Objects inherit their properties and methods from the classes above them in the hierarchy and can modify the properties and methods to suit their own purposes. The code container may be part of the language itself, or you may define your own objects in source code.

**object code**   Code in machine-readable form that can be executed by your computer's CPU and operating system, usually linked with libraries to create an executable file.

**object frame**   An Access control object that contains and displays or plays an OLE object. Bound object frames display or play OLE objects contained in OLE Object fields of Access tables. Unbound object frames display or play objects that are either embedded in a Form or Report object or are linked to a file that supplies the object's data. ActiveX Controls (formerly OLE Controls) are inserted into bound or unbound object frames, depending upon whether or not the ActiveX Control is classified as a data-bound control.

**object library**   A file with the extension .olb that contains information on the objects, properties, and methods exposed by an .exe or .dll file of the same file name that supports OLE Automation.

**object permissions**   Permissions granted by the database administrator for others to view and modify the values of database objects, including data in tables. See also *statement permissions*.

**ODBC**   An abbreviation for the Microsoft Open Database Connectivity API, a set of functions that provides access to client-server RDBMSs, desktop database files, text files, and Excel worksheet files through ODBC drivers. Access 95 uses 32-bit ODBC 3.0 and requires 32-bit ODBC drivers. ODBC most commonly is used to connect to client-server databases, such as Microsoft SQL Server, Sybase System 10+, Informix, and Oracle 7. Access 95 includes a 32-bit ODBC driver for Microsoft SQL Server 4.2+.

**ODBCDirect**   A new feature of the Jet 3.5 database engine that lets you use ODBC to access client/server databases without the necessity to load all of Jet 3.5. ODBCDirect conserves client resources if you only need to connect to SQL Server or another client/server RDBMS. You create an ODBCDirect workspace by using the dbUseODBC constant as the value of the *Type* argument of the CreateWorkspace method. ODBCDirect is closely related to the Remote Data Object (RDO). See also *RDO*.

**offset**   The number of bytes from a reference point, usually the beginning of a file, to the particular byte of interest. The first byte in a file, when offset is used to specify location, is always 0.

**OLE Automation**   An extension of OLE 2+ that provides the framework (interfaces) for applications and libraries to expose programmable objects that can be manipulated by client applications. Applications that expose programmable objects are called (OLE) Automation servers. See *automation* and *programmable object*.

**OLE Control**   An in-process OLE Automation server with the extension .ocx that exposes a single object, plus the properties, methods, and events of the object. Exposing events differentiates OLE Controls from other types of (OLE) Automation servers. Access

95 referred to OLE Controls (the first Microsoft term) as *Custom Controls*; the term *Custom Control* is more commonly used for 16-bit Visual Basic Extensions, VBXs. OLE Controls have been superseded by 32-bit ActiveX Controls. *See ActiveX Controls.*

**OLE DB**  A new Microsoft framework for providing a uniform interface to data from a variety of sources, including text files and mainframe databases. OLE DB doesn't replace ODBC, but includes an ODBC provider that takes the place of the ODBC driver manager. See also *ActiveX Data Objects* and *ODBC.*

**OLE DLL**  A synonym for an in-process OLE Automation server implemented as a Windows DLL. See *in-process.*

**OpenDoc**  A standard proposed by Apple Computer, Borland International, Lotus Development, Novell, and other competitors of Microsoft to supplant or replace OLE 2+.

**operand**  One of the variables or constants upon which an operator acts. In 1 + 2 = 3, both 1 and 2 are operands; + and = are the operators. See *operator.*

**operating system**  Applications that translate basic instructions, such as keyboard input, to language understood by the computer. The most common operating systems used with personal computers are MS-DOS (Microsoft Disk Operating System), Windows 95, Windows NT, UNIX, and OS/2.

**operator**  A keyword or reserved symbol that, in its unary form, acts on a single variable, or otherwise acts on two variables, to give a result. Operators may be of the conventional mathematics type such as + (add), – (subtract), / (divide), and * (multiply), as well as logical, such as **And** or **Not**. The unary minus (–), when applied to a single variable in a statement such as intVar = – intVar, inverts the sign of intVar from – to + or from + to –.

**optimistic locking**  A method of locking a record or page of a table that makes the assumption that the probability of other users locking the same record or page is low. With optimistic locking, the record or page is locked only when the data is updated, not during the editing process (LockEdits property set to False).

**option button**  A synonym for *radio button*, the original terminology in the CUA specification. Option buttons are circular control objects whose center is filled when selected. If grouped, only one option button of a group can be selected. If placed directly on a form, the form becomes the group and only one option button can be selected.

**outer join**  An SQL JOIN operation in which all rows of the joined tables are returned, whether or not a match is made between columns. SQL database managers that do not support the OUTER JOIN reserved words use the *= (LEFT JOIN) operator to specify that all of the rows in the preceding table return, and =* (RIGHT JOIN) to return all of the rows in the succeeding table.

**outer query**  A synonym for the primary query in a statement that includes a subquery. See also *subquery.*

**out-of-process**  An (OLE) Automation server in the form of an executable (.exe) file that operates in its own process space (memory allocation) and uses LRPCs (lightweight remote procedure calls) to communicate with the Automation client. The term *OutOfProc* often is used as shorthand for *out-of-process*.

**page**    In tables of client-server RDBMSs, such as Microsoft SQL Server and Access databases, a 2K block that contains records of tables. Client-server and Access databases lock pages, while DOS desktop databases usually lock individual records. Page-locking is required by most RDBMSs when variable-length records are used in tables.

**parameter**    The equivalent of an argument, but associated with the procedure that receives the value of an argument from the calling function. The terms *parameter* and *argument*, however, are often used interchangeably.

**parse**    The process of determining if a particular expression is contained within another expression. Parsing breaks program statements into keywords, operators, operands, arguments, and parameters for subsequent processing of each by the computer. Parsing string variables involves searching for the occurrence of a particular character or set of characters in the string, and then taking a specified set of actions when found or not found.

**PDC**    An abbreviation for Primary Domain Controller, the Windows NT server in a domain that's responsible for maintaining user and group accounts for a domain. Primary and Backup Domain Controllers authenticate domain users during the logon process. See *BDC*.

**permissions**    Authority given by the system administrator, database administrator, or database owner to perform operations on a network or upon data objects in a database.

**persistent (graphics)**    A Windows graphic image that survives movement, resizing, or overwriting of the window in which it appears. Persistent images are stored in global memory blocks and are not released until the window containing them is destroyed.

**persistent (objects)**    An object that is stored in the form of a file or an element of a file, rather than only in memory. Table and QueryDef objects are persistent because these objects are stored in .mdb files. Recordset objects, on the other hand, are stored in memory. Such objects are called *temporal* or *impersistent objects*.

**pessimistic locking**    A method of locking a record or page of a table that makes the assumption that the probability of other users locking the same record or page is high. With pessimistic locking, the record or page is locked during the editing and updating process (LockEdits property set to True).

**point**    In typography, the unit of measurement of the vertical dimension of a font, about 1/72 of an inch. The point is also a unit of measurement in Windows, where it represents exactly 1/72 of a logical inch or 20 twips. Unless otherwise specified, all distance measurements in VBA are in twips.

**pointer**    A data type that comprises a number representing a memory location. Near pointers are constrained to the 64K default local data segment. Far pointers can access any location in the computer's memory. Pointers are used extensively in C-language applications to access elements of arrays, strings, structures, and the like. VBA has only one pointer data type—to a zero-terminated string when the `ByVal...As String` keywords are applied to a VBA string passed to an external function contained in a dynamic link library.

**poke**  In DDE terminology, the transmission of an unrequested data item to a DDE server by the DDE client. In BASIC language terminology, placing a byte of data in a specific memory location. VBA does not support the BASIC `POKE` keyword and uses the `DDEPoke` method for DDE operations.

**PPP**  An abbreviation for Point-to-Point Protocol, the most common Internet protocol for connection to TCP/IP networks via conventional and ISDN modems.

**PPTP**  An abbreviation for Point-to-Point Tunneling Protocol, a Microsoft-sponsored protocol, included with Windows NT 4.0, that uses encryption to assure privacy of communication over the Internet. See *VPN*.

**precedence**  The sequence of execution of operators in statements that contain more than one operator.

**primary key**  The column or columns whose individual or combined values (in the case of a composite primary key) uniquely identify a row in a table.

**primary verb**  The default verb for activating an OLE 2+ object. `Edit` is the default verb for most OLE objects, except multimedia objects, whose default verb is usually `Play`.

**print zone**  The area of a sheet of paper upon which a printer can create an image. For most laser printers and standard dot-matrix printers, this is 8 inches in width. The vertical dimension is unlimited for dot-matrix printers and usually is 13.5 inches for a laser printer with legal-size paper capabilities.

**printer object**  A VBA object representing the printer chosen as the default by the Control Panel Printers function's Set Default choice.

**procedure**  A self-contained collection of source code statements, executable as an entity. All VBA procedures begin either with the reserved word `Sub` or `Function`, which may be preceded by the `Public`, `Private`, or `Static` reserved words, and terminate with `End Sub` or `End Function`.

**process server**  An "unofficial" term used in this book to specify an (OLE) Automation server, either in-process or out-of-process, that does not provide user-interface components, such as dialogs or windows. Process servers often are used in three-tier client-server applications to implement business rules. See *business rules* and *three-tier*.

**program**  All of the code required to create an application, consisting basically of declarations, statements, and in Windows, resource definition and help files.

**programmable object**  An object exposed by an (OLE) Automation server, together with a set of properties and methods applicable to the object. The exposed object can be manipulated by the application programming language of an (OLE) Automation client application.

**projection**    Identifies the desired subset of the columns contained in a table. You create a projection with a query that defines the fields of the table you want to display, but without criteria that limit the records that are displayed.

**Properties window**    A window that displays the names and properties of Access `Table`, `Form`, `Report`, and `Control` objects.

**property**    One of the two principal characteristics of objects (the other is methods). Properties define the manifestation of the object, for example, its appearance. Properties may be defined for an object or for the class of objects to which the particular object belongs, in which case they are said to be *inherited*.

**protocol**    A description of the method by which networked computers communicate. Windows NT and Windows 95 allow the simultaneous use of multiple network protocols, including TCP/IP, NetBEUI, and IPX/SPX.

**protocol stack**    Network protocol software that implements a specific protocol, such as TCP/IP.

**pseudo-object**    Objects that are contained within other OLE 2+ objects, such as the cells of a spreadsheet object.

**qualification**    A search condition that data values must meet to be included in the result of the search.

**qualified**    To precede the name of a database object with the name of the database and the object's owner, or to precede the name of a file with its drive designator and the path to the directory in which the file is stored. The terms *well-qualified path* and *well-formed path* to a file appear often in documentation.

**query**    A request to retrieve data from a database with the SQL SELECT instruction or to manipulate data in the database, called an *action query* by Access.

**QueryDef**    A persistent Access object that stores the Access SQL statements that define a query. `QueryDef` objects are optimized, when applicable, by the Jet database engine's query optimizer and stored in a special optimized format.

**RAID**    An acronym for redundant array of inexpensive disks, a method of connecting multiple disk drives to a single controller card to achieve faster data throughput, data storage redundancy for fault tolerance, or both. See *disk mirroring, disk striping,* and *fault tolerance*.

**RDBMS**    An abbreviation for relational database management system. An RDBMS is an application that is capable of creating, organizing, and editing databases; displaying data through user-selected views; and printing formatted reports. Most RDBMSs include at least a macro or macro language, and most provide a system programming language. dBASE, Paradox, and FoxPro are desktop RDBMSs.

**record**    A synonym for a user-defined data type, called a *structure* in C and C++. Record also is used in database applications to define a single element of a relational database file that contains each of the fields defined for the file. Records need not contain data to exist, but Jet does not append a record without a value in at least one field. A record is the logical equivalent of the row of a table. A set of related fields or columns of information that are treated as a unit by an RDBMS application.

**recursion**    A condition in which a procedure or function calls itself. As a general rule, you should avoid recursive procedures and functions in VBA unless you are an experienced programmer.

**redirector**    Software that intercepts requests for remotely provided services, such as files in server shares, and sends the request to the appropriate computer on the network.

**reference**    In VBA, the incorporation of pointers to specific sets of programmable objects exposed by Automation servers and manipulated by VBA code in the Automation client. You create a VBA reference to a set of objects exposed by an Automation server, such as Microsoft Excel 97, in the References dialog that is accessible by choosing Tools, References when a module is the active Access object. Once you declare a reference to the set of objects, the VBA pseudo-compiler checks the syntax of your code against the syntax specified for the referenced object. You also can use predefined intrinsic constants for the referenced objects in your VBA code.

**referential integrity**    Rules governing the relationships between primary keys and foreign keys of tables within a relational database that determine data consistency. Referential integrity requires that the values of every foreign key in every table be matched by the value of a primary key in another table. Access 2+ includes features for maintaining referential integrity, such as cascading updates and cascading deletions.

**refresh**    To redisplay records in Access's datasheet views or in a form or report so as to reflect changes others in a multiuser environment have made to the records.

**Registry**    A database that contains information required for the operation of Windows 95 and Windows NT, plus applications installed under Windows 95 and Windows NT. The Windows Registry takes the place of Windows 3.1+'s REG.DAT, WIN.INI, and SYSTEM.INI files, plus *PROFILE*.INI files installed by Windows 3.1 applications. The Registry also includes user information, such as user IDs, encrypted passwords, and permissions. Windows 95 and Windows NT include Rwgedit.exe for editing the Registry. ActiveX Components and OLE 2+ servers add entries to the Registry to specify the location of their exe files. Automation servers add Registry entries for each of the objects they expose. The Windows NT and Windows 95 registries differ in structure and thus are incompatible.

**relation**    Synonym for a table or a data table in an RDBMS.

**relational database**    See *RDBMS*.

**relational operators**    Consist of operators such as >, <, <>, and = that compare the values of two operands and return True or False depending on the values compared. They are sometimes called *comparative operators*.

**Remote Automation Object**    An out-of-process (OLE) Automation server, usually called an RAO, that resides on a server and is accessible to RAO-compliant applications that connect to the server with DCOM. See also *DCOM*.

**Remote Data Object**    A substitute for the Jet 3.5 Data Access Object that provides a more direct connection to the ODBC API. Access 97 offers ODBCDirect as an alternative to RDO. You can reference the RDO 2.0 type library in Access 97 applications and write VBA code for the RDO to speed queries against client-server databases. Like ODBCDirect, RDO also offers additional RDBMS connection management features. See also *ODBCDirect*.

**remote procedure call (RPC)**    An interprocess communication method that allows an application to run specific parts of the application on more than one computer in a distributed computing environment. Visual Basic 5.0 is capable of creating Remote Automation Objects (RAOs) that use RPCs for communication over a network.

**replication**    The process of duplicating database objects (usually tables) in more than one location, including a method of periodically rationalizing (synchronizing) updates to the objects. Unlike Access 95, Access 97 supports partial replication. Database replication is an alternative to the two-phase commit process. Microsoft SQL Server 6.5 supports replication of databases across multiple Windows NT servers. Access 97 includes a mini-replication feature designed for mobile users of Access databases running Windows 95. See *Briefcase replication* and *two-phase commit*.

**reserved word**    A word that comprises the vocabulary of a programming language and that is reserved for specific use by the programming language. You cannot assign a reserved word as the name of a constant, variable, function, or subprocedure. Although the terms *reserved word* and *keyword* often are used interchangeably, they do not describe an identical set of words. See also *keyword*.

**restriction**    A query statement that defines a subset of the rows of a table based on the value of one or more of its columns.

**RGB**    A method of specifying colors by using numbers to specify the individual intensities of its red, green, and blue components, the colors created by the three "guns" of the cathode-ray tube (CRT) of a color display.

**RIFF**    An acronym for the Windows Resource Interchange File Format used in conjunction with the Multimedia Extensions to Windows. Depending upon their definition, these files may contain MIDI sequence, sample dump or system exclusive data, waveform files, or data to create graphic images. RIFF is the preferred file format, at least by Microsoft Corporation, for multimedia files.

**rollback**    A term used in transaction processing that cancels a proposed transaction that modifies one or more tables and undoes changes, if any, made by the transaction prior to a COMMIT or COMMIT TRANSACTION SQL statement.

**routine**    A synonym for *procedure*.

**row** A set of related columns that describes a specific data entity. A synonym for *record*.

**row aggregation functions** See *aggregate functions*.

**rule** A specification that determines the type of data and value of data that may be entered in a column of a table. Rules are classified as validation rules and business rules. See *business rules*.

**Run mode** The mode of Access operation when Access is executing your database application. Run mode is called *run-time* by Microsoft; however, the term *run-time* normally refers to errors that occur when running the executable version of an application.

**running state** An OLE 2+ object is in the running state when the application that created the object is launched and has control of the object.

**SAM** An acronym for Security Accounts Manager, a Windows NT subsystem that maintains a database of user account names and passwords for authentication.

**scalable** The property of a multiprocessing computer that defines the extent to which addition of more processors increases aggregate computing capability. Windows NT 4.0 Server is generally considered to be scalable to eight Intel processors.

**scope** In programming terminology, the extent of visibility (definition) of a variable. VBA has global (`Public`, visible to all objects and procedures in the application), form/report (visible to all objects and procedures within a single form or report), module (visible to all procedures in a single module file), and local (`Private`, visible only within the procedure in which declared) scope. The scope of a variable depends upon where it is declared. See also *global*, *form-level*, *module level*, and *local*.

**screen object** An Access VBA object and object class defined as the entire usable area of the video display unit. All visible form and control objects are members of subclasses of the `Screen` object.

**scroll bar** Vertical and horizontal bars at the right side and bottom, respectively, of a multiline text box that allow the user to scroll the window to expose otherwise hidden text. Access also provides scroll bars for tables and queries in Run mode (Datasheet view) and for forms or reports that exceed the limits of the display.

**SDI server** An OLE 2+ server that supports only a single compound document (Single Document Interface) within an instance of the application. SDI is the preferred design of applications for Windows 95; however, all Microsoft Office 95 productivity applications are multiple-document interface (MDI) applications. Windows 95's Explorer and Exchange client are examples of SDI applications.

**second normal form** The rule for relational databases requiring columns that are not key fields each be related to the key field. That is, a row may not contain values in data cells that do not pertain to the value of the key field. In an invoice item table, for instance, the columns of each row must pertain solely to the value of the invoice number key field.

**seek**    To locate a specific byte, record, or chunk within a disk file. The Seek method of Access VBA can only be used in conjunction with Recordset objects of the Table type and requires that the table be indexed.

**select list**    The list of column names, separated by commas, that specify the columns to be included in the result of a SELECT statement.

**selection**    In Windows, one or more objects that have been chosen by clicking the surface of the object with the mouse or otherwise assigning the focus to the object. When used in conjunction with text, selection means the highlighted text that appears in a text box or window. See also *restriction*.

**self-join**    A SQL JOIN operation used to compare values within the columns of one table. Self-joins join a table with itself, requiring that the table be assigned two different names, one of which must be an alias.

**separator**    A reserved symbol used to distinguish one item from another, as exemplified by the use of the exclamation point (!, bang character) in Access to separate the name of an object class from a specific object of the class, and an object contained within a specified object. The period separator (., dot) separates the names of objects and their methods or properties.

**sequential access file**    A file in which one record follows another in the sequence applicable to the application. Text files, for the most part, are sequential.

**server**    A computer on a LAN that provides services or resources to client computers by sharing its resources. Servers may be *dedicated*, in which case they share their resources but do not use them themselves except in performing administrative tasks. Servers in client-server databases are ordinarily dedicated to making database resources available to client computers. Servers may also be used to run applications for users, in which case, the server is called an *application server*. Peer-to-peer or workgroup servers, such as servers created by using Windows 95 and Windows NT to share disk folders, are another class of server.

**session**    In Access 97, an instance of the Jet 3.5 database engine for a single user, represented by the Workspace object. You can establish multiple sessions which become members of the Workspaces collection. In RDBMS terminology, the period between the time that a user opens a connection to a database and the time that the connection to the database is closed.

**shared application memory**    Memory that is allocated between processes involved in an LRPC call. See also *LRPC*.

**shared lock**    A lock created by read-only operations that does not enable the user who creates the shared lock to modify the data. Other users can place shared locks on data so they can read it, but no user may apply an exclusive lock on the data while any shared locks are in effect.

**shortcut key**    A Ctrl+*key* combination that provides access to a menu choice, macro, or other function of the application in lieu of selection with the mouse.

**SID**    An acronym for security ID, a numeric value that identifies a logged-on user who has been authenticated by Windows NT or a user group.

**single-stepping**    A debugging process by which the source code is executed one line at a time to allow you to inspect the value of variables, find infinite loops, or remove other types of bugs.

**sizing handle**    The small black rectangles on the perimeter of Access control objects that appear on the surface of the form or report in Design mode when the object is selected. You drag the handles of the rectangles to shrink or enlarge the size of control objects.

**SMB**    An abbreviation for Server Message Block, a networking protocol used by NetBEUI to implement Microsoft Networking.

**source code**    The readable form of code that you create in a high-level language. Source code is converted to machine-language object code by a compiler or interpreter.

**source document**    A term used by OLE 1.0 to refer to a compound object in a container document.

**SQL**    An acronym, pronounced either as "sequel" or "seekel," for Structured Query Language, a language developed by IBM Corporation for processing data contained in mainframe computer databases. (Sequel is the name of a language, similar to SQL, developed by IBM but no longer in use.) SQL has now been institutionalized by the creation of an ANSI standard for the language.

**SQL aggregate functions**    See *aggregate functions*.

**statement**    A syntactically acceptable (to the interpreter or compiler of the chosen language) combination of instructions or keywords and symbols, constants, and variables that must appear on a single line or use the line continuation pair (a space followed by an underscore) to use multiple lines.

**static**    When applied to a variable, a variable that retains its last value until another is assigned, even though the procedure in which it is defined has completed execution. All global variables are static. Variables declared as `Static` are similar to global variables; however, their visibility is limited to their declared scope. Static is also used to distinguish between statically linked (conventional) executable files and those that use DLLs.

**stored procedure**    A set of SQL statements (and with those RDBMSs that support them, flow control statements) that are stored under a procedure name so that the statements can be executed as a group by the database server. Some RDBMSs, such as Microsoft and Sybase SQL Server, precompile stored procedures so that they execute more rapidly.

**string**   A data type used to contain textual material, such as alphabetic characters and punctuation symbols. Numbers may be included in or constitute the value of string variables, but cannot be manipulated by mathematical operators.

**stripe set**   See *disk striping* and *fault tolerance*.

**structure**   Two or more keywords that are used together to create an instruction, which is usually conditional in nature. In C and C++ programming, a user-defined data type. See also *compound*.

**Structured Query Language**   See *SQL*.

**stub**   A procedure or user-defined function that, in VBA, consists only of `Sub` `SubName...End Sub` or `Function` `FnName...End Function` lines with no intervening code. Stubs for subprocedures are created automatically by Access for event-handling code stored in `Form` and `Report` objects. Stubs are used to block out the procedures required by the application that can be called by the Main program. The intervening code statements are filled in during the programming process.

**style**   In typography, a characteristic or set of attributes of a member of a family of typefaces created by an outline or bitmap designed specifically to implement it. Styles include bold, italic, bold-italic, bold-italic-condensed, and so forth. Styles may contain attributes for weight (bold, demi-bold, black), form (italic, roman), and spacing (compressed or extended) in various combinations.

**subform**   A form contained within another form.

**submenu**   A set of choices presented when a main menu choice is made. In Windows, the first-level submenus are similar to drop-down dialogs. Second-level submenus usually appear horizontally at the point of the first submenu choice.

**subnet mask**   A local bit mask (set of flags) that specifies which bits of the IP address specify a particular IP network or a host within a subnetwork. An IP address of 128.66.12.1 with a subnet mask of 255.255.255.0 specifies host 1 on subnet 128.66.12.0. The subnet mask determines the maximum number of hosts on a subnetwork.

**subprocedure**   A procedure called by another procedure other than the main procedure (WinMain in Windows). In Access, all procedures except functions are subprocedures because Msaccess.exe contains the WinMain function.

**subquery**   A SQL `SELECT` statement that is included (nested) within another `SELECT`, `INSERT`, `UPDATE`, or `DELETE` statement, or nested within another subquery.

**subreport**   A report contained within another report.

**syntax**   The rules governing the expression of a language. As with English, Spanish, Esperanto, or Swahili, programming languages each have their own syntax. Some languages allow much more latitude (irregular forms) in their syntax. VBA has a relatively rigid syntax, while C provides more flexibility at the expense of complexity.

**system administrator** The individual(s) responsible for the administrative functions for all applications on a LAN or users of a UNIX cluster or network, usually including supervision of all databases on servers attached to the LAN. If the system administrator's (SA's) responsibility is limited to databases, the term *database administrator* (DBA) is ordinarily assigned.

**system colors** The 20 standard colors used by Windows for elements of its predefined objects such as backgrounds, scroll bars, borders, and title bars. You may change the system colors from the defaults through Control Panel's Color and Desktop functions.

**system databases** Databases that control access to databases on a server or across a LAN. Microsoft SQL Server has three system databases: the master database, which controls user databases; tempdb, which holds temporary tables; and model, which is used as the skeleton to create new user databases. Any database that is not a user database is a system database.

**system function** Functions that return data about the database rather than from the content of the database.

**system object** An object defined by Access rather than by the user. Examples of system objects are the Screen and Debug objects.

**system table** A data dictionary table that maintains information on users of the database manager and each database under the control by the system. Access system tables carry the prefix MSys.

**T-1** The most common moderate-speed telecommunication connection between LANs to create WAN. Dedicated T-1 lines provide 1.544Mbps of bandwidth. T-1 lines also are the most common method of connecting servers to the Internet.

**tab order** The order in which the focus is assigned to multiple control objects within a form or dialog with successive pressing of the Tab key.

**table** A database object consisting of a group of rows (records) divided into columns (fields) that contain data or Null values. A table is treated as a database device or object.

**TCP/IP** Abbreviation for Transport Control Protocol/Internet Protocol, the networking protocol of the Internet, UNIX networks, and the preferred protocol for Windows NT networks. TCP/IP is a routable network that supports subnetworks. See *IP*.

**TDI** An abbreviation for Transport Driver Interface, used by Windows NT to implement multiple network protocols by using various network interface cards.

**text box** A Windows object designed to receive printable characters typed from the keyboard. Access provides two basic types: single and multiline. Entries in single-line text boxes are terminated with an Enter keystroke. Multiline text boxes accept more than one line of text, either by a self-contained word-wrap feature (if a horizontal scroll bar is not present) or by a Ctrl+Enter key combination.

VIII

Appendixes

**text file**   A disk file containing characters with values ordinarily ranging from `Chr$`(1) through `Chr$`(127) in which lines of text are separated from one another with newline pairs (`Chr$`(13) & `Chr$`(10)).

**theta join**   A SQL `JOIN` operation that uses comparison or relational operators in the `JOIN` statement. See also *operator*.

**third normal form**   The rule for relational databases that imposes the requirement that a column that is not a key column may not be dependent upon another column that is not a key column. The third normal form is generally considered the most important because it is the first in the series that is not intuitive.

**thread**   A part of a process, such as an executing application, that can run as an object or an entity.

**three-tier**   The architecture of a database application, usually involving a client-server RDBMs, where the front-end application is separated from the back-end RDBMS by a middle tier application. In Access and Visual Basic applications, the middle tier usually is implemented as an OLE Automation process server, which implements the database connection, enforces business rules, and handles transfer of data to and from databases of the RDBMS. See *business rules* and *process server*.

**time stamp**   The date and time data attributes applied to a disk file when created or edited. SQL Server and the ODBC API support the timestamp field, which resolves concurrency issues when updating tables.

**timer**   An Access control object that is invisible in Run mode and that is used to trigger a `Timer` event at preselected intervals.

**title bar**   The heading area of a window, usually blue, in which the title of the window appears, usually in bright white (reverse).

**toggle**   A property of an object, such as a check box, that alternates its state when repeatedly clicked with the mouse or activated by a shortcut key combination.

**toolbar**   A group of command button icons, usually arranged horizontally across the top of a window, that perform functions that would ordinarily require one or more menu choices. *Floating toolbars* can be located anywhere on your display.

**toolbox**   A collection of command buttons designated as tools, usually with icons substituted for the default appearance of a command button, that choose a method applicable to an object (usually graphic) until another tool is selected. An example is the Access Toolbox.

**topic**   In DDE conversations, the name of the file or other identifying title of a collection of data. When used in conjunction with help files, the name of the subject matter of a single help screen display.

**TRANSACT-SQL**   A superset of ANSI SQL used by Microsoft and Sybase SQL Server. TRANSACT-SQL includes flow control instructions and the capability to define and use stored procedures that include conditional execution and looping.

**transaction**   A group of processing steps that are treated as a single activity to perform a desired result. A transaction might entail all of the steps necessary to modify the values in or add records to each table involved when a new invoice is created. RDBMSs that are capable of transaction processing usually include the capability to cancel the transaction by a rollback instruction or to cause it to become a permanent part of the tables with the COMMIT or COMMIT TRANSACTION statement. See *rollback*.

**trigger**   A stored procedure that occurs when a user executes an instruction that may affect the referential integrity of a database. Triggers usually occur prior to the execution of INSERT, DELETE, or UPDATE statements so that the effect of the statement on referential integrity can be examined by a stored procedure prior to execution. See also *stored procedure*.

**trust**   In Windows NT domain terminology, a relationship between domain controllers in which users who are members of the trusted domain can access services on another trusting domain without the need to log onto the trusting domain.

**twip**   The smallest unit of measurement in Windows and the default unit of measurement of VBA. The twip is 1/20 of a point, or 1/1440 of a logical inch.

**two-phase commit**   A process applicable to updates to multiple (distributed) databases that prevents a transaction from completing until all of the distributed databases acknowledge that the transaction can be completed. The replication process has supplanted two-phase commit in most of today's distributed client-server RDBMSs. See *replication*.

**type**   See *data type*.

**type library**   A file with the extension .tlb that provides information about the types of objects exposed by an ActiveX component or (OLE) Automation server. The type library for Msaccess.exe is Msaccess.tlb. See *object library*.

**typeface**   Synonym for face. A set of fonts of a single family in any available size possessing an identical style or set of attributes.

**unary**   See *operator*.

**UNC**   An abbreviation for Uniform Naming Convention, the method of identifying the location of files on a remote server. UNC names begin with \\. Windows 95 and Windows NT support UNC; 32-bit Windows applications must support UNC to qualify for application of Microsoft's "Designed for Windows 95" logo. All Microsoft Office 95 applications support UNC.

**VIII**

**Appendixes**

**Unicode**    A replacement for the 7-bit or 8-bit ASCII and ANSI representations of characters with a 16-bit model that allows a wider variety of characters to be used. Windows 95 and Windows NT support Unicode. Access 95 automatically converts Unicode to ANSI and vice-versa.

**uniform data transfer (UDT)**    The interprocess communication (IPC) method used by OLE 2+. OLE 1.0 uses DDE for IPC.

**unique index**    An index in which no two key fields or combinations of key fields upon which the index is created may have the same value.

**UNIX**    Registered trademark of Novell Incorporated (formerly of AT&T) for its multi-user operating system, now administered by the Open Systems Foundation (OSF). Extensions and modifications of UNIX include DEC Ultrix, SCO UNIX, IBM AIX, and similar products.

**update**    A permanent change to data values in one or more data tables. An update occurs when the INSERT, DELETE, UPDATE, or TRUNCATE TABLE SQL commands are executed.

**user-defined**    A data type, also called a record, that is specified in your VBA source code by a `Type...End Type` declaration statement in the Declarations section of a module. The elements of the user-defined record type can be any data type valid for the language and may include other user-defined types.

**user-defined transaction**    A group of instructions combined under a single name and executed as a block when the name is invoked in a statement executed by the user.

**validation**    The process of determining if an update to a value in a table's data cell is within a preestablished range or is a member of a set of allowable values. Validation rules establish the range or set of allowable values. Access 2+ supports validation rules at the field and table levels.

**variable**    The name given to a symbol that represents or substitutes for a number (numeric), letter, or combination of letters (string).

**VBA**    An abbreviation for Visual Basic for Applications, the official name of which is "Visual Basic, Applications Edition." VBA is Microsoft's common application programming (macro) language for Access 97, Excel 5+, Project 4+, Word 8, and Visual Basic 4+. Each application has its own "flavor" of VBA as a result of automatically created references to the application's object hierarchy in VBA code. Thus, this book uses the terms *Excel VBA* and *Project VBA* when referring to a particular flavor of VBA. VBA alone is used when the subject matter is applicable to all current flavors of VBA.

**view**    The method by which the data is presented for review by the user, usually on the computer display. Views can be created from subsets of columns from one or more tables by implementing the SQL CREATE VIEW instruction.

**Visual Basic for Applications**    See *VBA*.

**VM**   Abbreviation for virtual memory, a method of mapping a combination of RAM and images of RAM stored in a paging file to provide an address space larger than that available from the RAM installed in the computer.

**VM manager**   The Windows NT executive service that loads memory images stored in a paging file on demand, as well as saving memory images in the paging file when no longer needed by a thread.

**VPN**   An abbreviation for Virtual Private Network, a means of establishing secure communication channels on the Internet using various forms of encryption. See *PPTP*.

**WAN**   An acronym for wide area network. A WAN is a system for connecting multiple computers in different geographical locations through the use of the switched telephone network or leased data lines, by optical or other long-distance cabling, or by infrared, radio, or satellite links.

**WAVE file**   A file containing waveform audio data, usually with a .wav extension.

**Waveform audio**   A data type standard of the Windows Multimedia Extensions that defines how digitally sampled sounds are stored in files and processed by Windows API functions calls.

**WDM**   An abbreviation of Windows Driver Model, a 32-bit architecture for creating device drivers that run under both Windows NT and Windows 95.

**wild card**   A character that substitutes for and allows a match by any character or set of characters in its place. The DOS ? and * wild cards are similarly used in Windows applications.

**Win32**   An API for creating 32-bit applications that run under Windows 95 and Windows NT. Applications that are written to the Win32 API are purported to provide substantially improved performance when run under Windows 95 and Windows NT.

**Win32s**   A subset of the Win32 API designed to add limited 32-bit capabilities to Windows 3.1+. Very few applications have been written to the Win32s API, which appears to have become obsolete.

**WinHelp32**   A contraction used to describe the Windows help engine of Windows 95 and the files that are used in the creation of Windows 95 help systems. WinHelp 32 offers many useful built-in features not available in 16-bit WinHelp, including full-text indexing and search capability.

**Winsock**   An abbreviation for Windows Sockets, a networking API for implementing Windows applications that use TCP/IP, such as FTP and Telnet.

**workstation**   A client computer on a LAN or WAN that is used to run applications and is connected to a server from which it obtains data shared with other computers. It is possible, but not common, for some network servers to be used as both a server and a workstation. Microsoft Windows NT, for instance, permits this. Workstation is also used to describe a high-priced PC that uses a proprietary microprocessor and proprietary architecture to create what some call an *open system*.

VIII

Appendixes

**WOSA**    Acronym for the Windows Open Services Architecture that is the foundation for such APIs as ODBC, MAPI, and TAPI. Microsoft also develops special vertical-market WOSA APIs for the banking, financial, and other industries.

**WOW**    An acronym for Windows on Win32, a subsystem of Windows NT that allows 16-bit Windows applications to run in protected memory spaces called *virtual DOS machines* (VDMs).

**xBase**    Any language interpreter or compiler or a database manager built upon the dBASE III+ model and incorporating all dBASE III+ commands and functions. Microsoft's FoxPro and Computer Associates' Clipper are xBase dialects.

**Yes/No field**    A term used by Access to describe a field of a table whose allowable values are Yes (True) or No (False). Yes/No fields are called *logical* or *Boolean fields* by Access 95.

# Appendix B

# Naming Conventions for Access Objects and Variables

*by Stan Leszynski, Leszynski Company, Inc., and Kwery Corporation*

This appendix describes the Leszynski Naming Conventions (LNC), a set of standardized approaches to naming objects during Access development. These naming conventions were born of necessity, because some members of the staff of my firm spend all day in Access development, year after year. They were also born of a different need—a void that existed in the marketplace due to a lack of consensus about development styles among leading Access developers.

I am grateful to Greg Reddick, a former contractor with one of my companies, for jointly authoring the Access 1.x and 2.0 versions of our Access naming conventions with me (referred to as *L/R* for *Leszynski/Reddick*). The L/R conventions were distributed broadly, with more than 500,000 copies in print, and have become the most widely used such conventions in the Access community. During the last few years, we have received feedback about L/R from hundreds of developers and companies, and have tried to accommodate some of their input—as well as our ongoing experiences—into LNC.

LNC improves upon the previous Access style by considering developers who work with multiple Microsoft development tools. Access, Visual Basic, Excel, and other Microsoft products such as Visual Basic Script (VBScript) have more in common in their Windows 95 and Windows NT 4.0 versions than in any previous iterations. Consequently, this Access style dovetails with the LNC development style for all of VBA and FoxPro.

The prefixes, tags, and qualifiers in the naming conventions described in this appendix that are derived from L/R are underlined. If you are a user of the Access 2.0 version of L/R, new additions for you to note are those conventions that are not underlined. I use the terms *naming conventions*, *style*, and LNC interchangeably throughout this chapter.

> **Note**
>
> Publishing limitations preclude reprinting of the complete text of LNC in this appendix. To obtain the unabridged version of the LNCs, see the section "How to Get the Complete Text of the LNCs" at the end of this appendix.

# The Leszynski Naming Conventions for Microsoft Access: A Primer

Naming conventions are one of the foundation elements of your overall development style. The naming conventions were developed primarily to achieve four objectives:

- To enable you to quickly understand an application's structure and code by making object names more informative.

- To simplify team development of applications by creating a standardized vocabulary for all team members.

- To improve your ability to work with Access objects, including enforcing object name sort orders, creating self-documenting program code, and enhancing find and replace capabilities.

- To increase your ability to create tools for our Access development work, and to create code libraries across various VBA platforms.

To meet these objectives, you create and apply consistent naming conventions to the following Access objects:

| | | |
|---|---|---|
| Tables | Reports | Variables |
| Table fields | Report controls | Constants |
| Queries | Macros | User-defined types |
| Forms | Modules | |
| Form controls | Procedures | |

Object names are the foundation upon which your entire application is built, so they are almost impossible to change once development has begun in earnest. Therefore, you will probably not find it cost- or time-efficient to retrofit these conventions into your existing applications. For new applications, however, you should apply these naming conventions consistently from the moment you create your first object in a new Access database file.

Your naming conventions rely primarily on *leading tags*—several characters placed before an object's name (for example, `qryOrderByMonth`). This approach is sometimes referred to as *Hungarian Notation*. Leading tags provide several benefits:

- The first item you observe about an object when you see its name is the leading type tag, which is often more important than the name itself.

- Leading tags drive the ordering of object names in Access lists, sorting by type and then by base name.

- Leading tags are consistently located in the same place in an object's name, making them easier to find by parsers and other tools.

> **Note**
>
> The term *Hungarian* refers to the nationality of Charles Simonyi, a programmer at Microsoft who wrote a doctoral thesis titled "Program Identifier Naming Conventions," in the 1980s.

If you are averse to Hungarian Notation for some reason and prefer trailing tags, LNC can still work for you. However, LNC prescribes no standard for locating and punctuating trailing tags. You have to decide if they are offset with an underscore (OrderByMonth_qry), capitalization (OrderByMonthQry), or some other technique.

Using trailing tags on database objects is problematic for you when your application also contains Visual Basic for Applications (VBA) code. The primary justification given by developers who prefer trailing tags on database objects is that it allows the objects to sort by base names rather than tags in ordered lists. However, such developers often still use leading tags and prefixes in their VBA code, because there seems to be no compelling argument that can be made for trailing tags on VBA objects such as variables. If you mix your styles like this, be prepared to justify your lack of consistency.

Because some developers, especially newer ones, prefer to minimize the complexity of a naming convention, LNC provides the following two levels for Access users:

- Level One has the minimum realistic subset of tags, but consequently provides lesser detail about the application. It is intended for users whose work is centered around the Database window and who do not develop applications but only database objects.

- Level Two provides greater detail and the flexibility to create your own extensions. It is intended for application developers.

# Access Object Types

For purposes of this appendix, the standardized terminology for grouping objects was created. These group names are used when discussing naming conventions:

- Database objects:

| | | |
|---|---|---|
| Tables | Queries forms | Macros |
| Table fields | Reports | Modules |

**VIII**

**Appendixes**

- Control objects:

    Form controls          Report controls

- VBA objects:

    Procedures          Constants

    Variables          User-defined types

# Structuring Object Names

In *LNC*, object names are constructed using this syntax for Level One:

    [*prefix(es)*] [*tag*] *BaseName* [*Qualifier*] [*Suffix*]

For Level Two, the syntax varies slightly:

    [*prefix(es)*] *tag* [*BaseName*] [*Qualifier*] [*Suffix*]

The brackets indicate optional syntax elements. Notice that, for Level One, the `BaseName` element is required and the `tag` is optional in some cases. At Level Two, the `tag` element is required even though the `BaseName` is not in some cases. These options are explained in the sections "What is a Tag?" and "Creating Database Object Base Names" later in this appendix.

> **Note**
>
> In the syntax diagrams, the case of each element reflects its case in actual use. The element `tag` is lowercased because the tags themselves are always found in lowercase.

Table B.1 shows sample object names using these constructions.

| Table B.1    Object Names Constructed in LNC Format | | | | | |
|---|---|---|---|---|---|
| **Object Name** | **Prefix** | **Tag** | **Base Name** | **Qualifier** | **Suffix** |
| tblCust | | tbl | Cust | | |
| qsumSalesPerfBest_WA | | qsum | SalesPerf | Best | _WA |
| plngRecNumMax | p | lng | RecNum | Max | |
| ialngPartNum | ia | lng | PartNum | | |

### What Is a Prefix?

A *prefix* is an identifier that precedes a tag and clarifies it narrowly. Prefixes describe one or more important properties of an object. For example, a `Long` variable that is public in scope (declared `Public`) has a prefix p, as in `plngRecNumMax`. Prefixes are one or two characters long and lowercased. Multiple prefixes can be used together on one object.

### What Is a Tag?

A *tag* is a multi-character phrase placed against an object base name to characterize it. In object-oriented programming terms, the tag is basically an identifier for the class. At Level One, you could say that tags define an object's general class; for example, qry for a query of any type. At Level Two, the tag defines the specific class; for example, qdel defines a delete query.

> **Note**
>
> The word *class* here refers to a naming convention construction, not an exact object model construction. For example, there is only one Query (or QueryDef) class object in Access, and the data action (delete, update, and so on) is determined by its SQL statement, not its class. LNC prescribes several tags for this one Access class.

Tags are three or four characters long for readability purposes and to allow for the hundreds of combinations necessary as the Office object model grows over time. They are always to the left of the base name and lowercased, so that your eye reads past them to the beginning of the base name.

A tag is created to mnemonically represent the word it abbreviates, such as frm for form. However, some tags may not seem fully mnemonic for two reasons:

- The perfect (or obvious) tag for a particular object may already be assigned to another object.

- Where common objects (objects with similar properties and usage) exist in multiple Microsoft applications, the tag for one may be used to represent similar objects in other products, even if the names are different. For example, an Access Rectangle object is almost identical in structure and purpose to a Visual Basic Shape object. Because the Visual Basic conventions have existed longer than your Access conventions, you use the Visual Basic Shape object tag you were already using, —shp—to represent Access rectangles.

### What Is a Base Name?

The *base name* is the starting point when you name a particular object—the name you would use anyway if you had no naming conventions. The LNC guidelines for creating base names are driven by a set of rules stated in the following sections.

### What Is a Qualifier?

A *qualifier* is an extension following the base name that provides context to the specific use of an object. Unlike prefixes, which detail properties of the object (for example, that the variable has public scope), qualifiers describe how the object is being used in a context. For example, plngRecNumMax is obviously the maximum record number in an application that could also have variables for the minimum (plngRecNumMin) and current (plngRecNumCur) record numbers. Qualifiers are short and written with mixed upper- and lowercase (see Table B.2).

**Table B.2    Standard LNC Qualifiers**

| Qualifier | Usage | Qualifier | Usage |
| --- | --- | --- | --- |
| Cur | Current element of a set | Next | Next element of a set |
| Dest | Destination | New | New instance or value |
| First | First element of a set | Old | Prior instance or value |
| Hold | Hold a value for later | Prev | Previous element re-use of a set |
| Last | Last element of a set | Src | Source |
| Max | Maximum item in a set | Temp | Temporary value |
| Min | Minimum item in a set | | |

### What Is a Suffix?

*Suffix elements* provide specific information about the object and are only used as "tie-breakers" when more detail is required to differentiate one object name from another. These are the only elements in the syntax where your naming conventions do not specify standardized values. You will create suffix items as needed by your company, development team, or application. For example, a series of queries that summarized the best sales performance by state would need the state name in each object name to properly qualify it, as in qsumSalesPerfBest_AK. Placing the state name at the very end of the name as a suffix item allows the entire collection of related queries to sort together, like this:

```
qsumSalesPerfBest_AK
qsumSalesPerfBest_AL
...
qsumSalesPerfBest_WY
```

Because the suffix is the last piece of information on a name, it can be easier for you to find if delimited from the rest of the object name with an underscore, as shown here. Use of the underscore is optional, not required.

# Creating Database Object Base Names

The building blocks of your Access application are its database objects. When creating base names for these objects, you should give careful consideration to the purpose of the object, the approaches used to name associated objects, and the rules of thumb that follow for naming database objects.

### Rules for Base Names

Follow these rules when developing a base name for a new database object:

- Spaces are not allowed in any object name. Spaces create a multitude of problems with consistency, readability, and documentation. Where the readability of a space is required, use an underscore instead.

- Object names begin with a letter and should only include letters, digits, and underscores. The use of special characters in object names is disallowed to comply with the naming rules of both VBA and Microsoft SQL Server. This allows your Basic variable names to include database object base names, and your entire Access schema to be easily upsized to the more powerful Microsoft SQL Server platform.

- Object names use mixed upper- and lowercase to add readability to the name. (Previously, some developers used all lowercased names to allow for upsizing to Microsoft SQL Server. Starting with SQL Server Version 6.0, that product is now installed case-insensitive and allows you to maintain upper and lower case in object names that are moved to the server from Access.)

- The only syntax element that can have multiple capital letters is the base name. A qualifier or suffix begins with a single capital letter and then contains only lowercased letters, unless it is an abbreviation, as in qsumSalesPerfBestUSA. If you need to clearly see the elements of a name (prefixes, tag, base name, qualifier, and suffix), LNC permits—but does not require—underscores as separators, as in qsum_SalesPerf_Best_USA.

- Object names are usually singular (Widget) rather than plural (Widgets). By implication, tables, queries, forms, and reports are plural; they usually work with more than one record, so why restate the obvious?

- An object's base name should include the base names of any table objects it is built on, if practical. This rule is explained later in this section.

The first and second bullets also apply to the other naming convention elements: prefixes, tags, qualifiers, and suffixes. These elements should never include spaces or special characters.

You should abbreviate object base name elements wherever possible using a standardized abbreviation table. You can extend LNC with your own standard abbreviations as well. You should create and use standardized terminology in your applications wherever possible.

### Base Name Length Limits

LNC includes some constraints and suggestions for object name lengths. You should target table name lengths at a 15-character maximum, for two reasons:

- Short names (15 characters or less) fully display within the default column width of the Access query design grid.

- Query, form, and report names usually include the base name(s) of the primary table object(s) they relate to, and will be unusably long if the table base names are long.

Beyond the 15-character target, you should absolutely limit table name lengths to 30 characters, which maintains compatibility with the table name length limit in SQL Server. For other objects, you should target a 30-character limit as well, because Access shows no more than the first 30 characters of object names in the default width of any of its lists or property grids.

VIII

Appendixes

### Compound Base Names

The name of an object that is driven by a table must include the base name of the table. Thus, for the tblCust table, the primary query would be qryCust, the primary form frmCust, and so forth. Queries, forms, and reports that are sourced from multiple tables should reflect the base names of all the tables if it is practical. If not, you must decide which tables are the primary tables and list as many as possible in the name.

Generally, in a multitable query, form, or report, the most important tables are not necessarily the first and second, but more often the first and last. So, a query joining tblCust to tblAddr to tblPhone to get the phone numbers for customers would be named qryCustAddrPhone if the address information is included in the query result, or simply qryCustPhone if the address information is used to join to the phone numbers and is not displayed.

Bound control base names on forms and reports are always equivalent to the base name of the bound field (the ControlSource). For example, a text box tied to the LastName field is named txtLastName.

### Field Base Names

As a part of standardizing terminology, you should adhere to the concept of a centralized data dictionary. This principle dictates that any fields in the data structure that have the same name must have the same properties and data purpose. For example, if the LastName field in tblCust is of type Text 30, and holds the customer last name, any other field named LastName in the same application must have the same type, length, properties, and purpose. If your application needs last name fields for both customers and dealers, this philosophy dictates that you name them differently (such as CustLastName and DlrLastName).

Applying the centralized data dictionary principle also means that table fields do not get leading prefixes or tags, because your data dictionaries should be platform-neutral. That way, a field does not have to be renamed if data is upsized or ported to a platform with different data types. A table is still called a table in SQL Server, so moving tblCust there from Access would require no rename. However, if tblCust had a field lngCustID defined as a Long Integer in Access, moving the database to SQL Server would require a field rename to intCustID, because SQL Server uses the data type name Integer to mean the same as Access's Long Integer. Renaming fields affects all dependent objects and code, so should be avoided at all costs. You would call the field simply CustID.

Qualifiers and suffixes are acceptable in field names, however, because they describe the object's data purpose and not its type.

### Ordering Base Name Elements

Object base name elements should be ordered from left to right with respect to their importance, readability, and desired sort order. In the example from the previous paragraph, CustLastName is a better name than LastNameCust, because the group name portion (Cust or Dlr) carries greater weight in an object's name than the specific item name (LastName or PhoneNum). Think of Cust as the name of a collection of customer-related items and this rule becomes clear—what you are really saying is that CustLastName is analogous to `Cust(LastName)` or `Cust.LastName` in `Collection.Object` terminology.

You can naturally carry this example to its extreme and say that the `Customers` collection really has a `Names` collection with multiple elements, including Last, thus the representation of that idea as `Cust.Name(Last)` would lead to the field name CustNameLast instead. Such a construction model still fits within the rules of LNC, and there's no reason not to use it. In practice, however, such names often become fairly unreadable, even if they are accurate.

# Naming Conventions for Database Objects

In Level Two of LNC, tags are required for all of the Access (and Jet) database objects listed in Tables B.1 and B.2. Level One also recommends that you place tags on every object name, but recognizes that non-developers may prefer to save time, effort, and complexity by leaving tags off of objects where the context is obvious while viewing the Database window. Thus, Level One users are required only to place the `qry` tag on queries in order to differentiate them from tables in any combined lists, such as the "Choose the table or query…" combo box on Form and Report Wizards. Placing tags on the other objects listed is recommended, but optional.

> **Caution**
>
> It can be difficult to propagate name changes throughout a database, so if you are a casual user now but expect to become a developer later—and thus migrate from Level One of LNC to Level Two—you would be unwise to leave tags off of any object names. Use the Level One tags now on all objects.

### Tags for Database Window Objects

Table B.3 lists the Level One tags for Database window objects. Note that only one tag exists for each object type.

**Table B.3   Level One Database Window Object Tags**

| Object | Tag | Object | Tag |
|--------|-----|--------|-----|
| Class | cls | | |
| Form | frm | Report | rpt |
| Macro | mcr | Subform | fsub |
| Module | bas or mdl | Subreport | rsub |
| Query | qry | Table | tbl |

Though Level One is the simplified naming model, you provide tags to identify subform and subreport objects specifically. The distinction between objects and subobjects is critical for non-developers who navigate using the Database window. Because it is not appropriate to open subforms and subreports directly from the Database window, they must be clearly identified and grouped using tags.

Table B.4 lists the Level Two tags for Database window objects.

| Object | Tag | Object | Tag |
|--------|-----|--------|-----|
| **Table B.4   Level Two Database Window Object Tags** | | | |
| Class module | cls | | |
| Form | frm | Query (select) | qsel |
| Form (class module)[1] | fcls | Query (SQL pass-through) | qspt |
| Form (dialog) | fdlg | Query (union) | quni |
| Form (lookup table)[2] | flkp | Query (update) | qupd |
| Form (menu/switchboard) | fmnu | Report | rpt |
| Form (message/alert) | fmsg | Report (detail) | rdet |
| Form (subform)[3] | fsub | Report (sub)[4] | rsub |
| Form (wizard main) | fwzm | | |
| Form (wizard subform) | fwzs | | |
| Macro | mcr | Report (summary) | rsum |
| Macro (for form/report) | m[*obj*] | Table | tbl |
| Macro (bar menu) | mmbr | Table (attached Btrieve) | tbtv |
| Macro (general menu) | mmnu | Table (attached dBASE) | tdbf |
| Macro (shortcut menu) | mmct | Table (attached Excel) | txls |
| Macro (submenu/dropdown) | mmsb | Table (attached Fox) | tfox |
| Module[4] | bas | Table (attached Lotus) | twks |
| Query | qry | Table (attached ODBC) | todb |
| Query (form/report source) | q[obj] | Table (attached Paradox) | tpdx |
| Query (append) | qapp | Table (attached SQL Server) | tsql |
| Query (crosstab) | qxtb | Table (attached text) | ttxt |
| Query (data definition) | qddl | Table (audit log) | tlog |
| Query (delete) | qdel | Table (lookup)[3] | tlkp |
| Query (form filter) | qflt | Table (many-to-many relation) | trel |
| Query (lookup table)[2] | qlkp | Table (summary information) | tsum |
| Query (make table) | quak | | |

*1. Access does not implement class modules formally as an object type, as Visual Basic does.*

*2. A lookup table has records that map short codes to full text values, like state abbreviations to states, and is used to populate combo and list boxes, validate fields, and so forth.*

*3. A single subform or subreport may be used in several different parent objects, thus naming subobjects is not as simple as just adding **_Sub** to the end of the parent's base name (or some similar technique).*

*4. You use the module tag bas to maintain consistency with the file name extension used by Visual Basic modules.*

The tags for Level Two provide rich detail about the objects and sort objects with similar attributes together. For example, lookup tables and their maintenance forms are often used over and over in multiple applications. The tags `tlkp`, `qlkp`, and `flkp` clearly identify these objects, making it easy for you to import them from an existing database into a new one when using the object list in Access's Import dialog. However, if a particular database does not warrant rich detail, you have generic tags to use as well (for example, `qry` instead of `qsel`).

In two special cases, the conventions prescribe a single character tag added to the front of the full object name (including the tag) of the related object. This situation occurs where a macro is created solely for a particular form or report, as in `mfrmCust`, and a query is created solely to serve as the `RecordSource` property for one particular form or report, as in `qfrmCust`.

### Tags for Form and Report Control Objects

Table B.5 lists the Level One tags for control objects on forms and reports.

| Table B.5   Level One Form and Report Control Object Tags | |
| --- | --- |
| **Control** | **Tag** |
| Label | lbl |
| Other types | ctl |

These Level One control tags provide no differentiation of control type other than to distinguish labels (which do not interact with the user) from controls that can display or modify data. This level of detail is not adequate for applications where VBA code will be written behind forms or reports, but can be a convenience with macro-centric applications.

Table B.6 lists the Level Two tags for control objects on forms and reports. A different tag is provided for each built-in control type. Tags also can be created for standard OLE controls. VBA code written behind forms and reports using this convention will reflect a control's type in its event procedure names (for example, `cboState_AfterUpdate`). The automatic sorting provided by this notation in the Access module design window can be very helpful during development. The value returned by the `TypeOf()` function for an Access control is a reflection of its class.

> **Tip**
>
> Make sure all control tags are three characters long so objects sort correctly.

| Table B.6   Level Two Form and Report Control Object Tags | | |
| --- | --- | --- |
| **Control** | **Tag** | **TypeOf** |
| Bound object frame | frb | BoundObjectFrame |
| Chart (graph) | cht | ObjectFrame |
| Check Box | chk | CheckBox |
| Combo box | cbo | ComboBox |

*(continues)*

**VIII**

**Appendixes**

| Table B.6   Continued | | |
|---|---|---|
| **Control** | **Tag** | **TypeOf** |
| Command button | cmd | CommandButton |
| Custom control | ocx | CustomControl |
| Hyperlink | hlk | Hyperlink |
| Image | img | Image |
| Label | lbl | Label |
| Line | lin | Line |
| List box | lst | ListBox |
| Option button | opt | OptionButton |
| Option group | grp | OptionGroup |
| Page break | brk | PageBreak |
| Rectangle | shp | Rectangle |
| Section | sec | Section |
| Subform/Subreport | sub | Subform |
| Tab | tab | TabControl |
| Text box | txt | TextBox |
| Toggle button | tgl | ToggleButton |
| Unbound object frame | fru | ObjectFrame |

## Using Menu Macros

Access 97 replaces menu macros used by previous versions of Access with command bars. Thus, this section applies only to existing Access applications that you upgrade to Access 97 and retain their menu macros.

Menu macros behave differently than standard macros; thus, they fall under separate guidelines when creating their names. Menu macros are either used for bar menus or for shortcut menus.

If you use the Menu Builder Add-In, your custom menu macros are assigned names when the builder saves your menu design. You have little control over anything but the tag and base name for the primary (bar) menu. If you use the LNC convention of mmnuname for your menu macro, the builder creates an entire tree of macros beginning with the string you enter, for example:

```
mmnuMain
mmnuMain_File
mmnuMain_File_Print
```

If you prefer to create and name menus yourself, you can use a similar convention, but with more explicit tags. Bar menus should be prefixed with mmbr, sub (drop-down) menus with mmsb, and shortcut menus with mmct. Detailed tags like this help greatly when you are selecting from a list of menus to assign to the MenuBar or ShortcutMenuBar properties of a form. This convention also sorts menus by type in the Database window. The macro listing shown here, if produced manually rather than with the builder, would look like this:

```
mmbrMain
mmctMain_File
mmsbMain_File
mmsbMain_File_Print
```

Any saved submenu macro can be selected as the primary object in a shortcut menu, so this convention gives you the flexibility shown here to create component submenus, which can be called from both multiple bar menus and multiple shortcut menus, and thus reused.

# Creating VBA Object Base Names

When creating VBA object base names, remember that the base name must be descriptive even in the absence of its tag. For some programmers, the syntax `Dim I As Integer` for a loop variable is quite acceptable. Within LNC, however, the variable `I` would become `iintLoop`. Single-character variable names, especially without tags, are not allowed. Instead, create a list of short and standardized work variables to handle common daily needs. The following sections describe the LNC rules for creating VBA object base names.

### Rules for Base Names

Creating VBA object base names involves following the same rules listed earlier for creating database object base names:

- Spaces are not allowed in any object name.

- Object names begin with a letter and should only include letters, digits, and underscores.

- Object names use mixed upper and lowercase to add readability to the name.

- The only non-abbreviated syntax element that can have multiple capital letters is the base name.

- Object names are usually singular rather than plural.

- An object's base name should include the base names of any objects it is built on, if practical.

> **Note**
>
> The final rule is an expanded version of the corresponding rule for database objects, which stated that table base names should propagate into names of dependent objects. In Visual Basic, that rule expands to require a reference in variable names to objects of any type that they relate to. For example, a Recordset variable created on `tblCust` should be named `rstCust`. Also, if a string array variable of part numbers `astrPartNum` had an Integer index variable, it should include the array's base name in its own: `iaintPartNum`.

### Base Name Lengths

There is no LNC rule limiting variable name length, but common sense dictates that variable names longer than 15 or 20 characters waste a lot of keystrokes at each use.

For procedure names, the VBA Module Editor by default shows the first 30 characters of a procedure name, so this number is suggested as the target maximum procedure name length.

> **Tip**
>
> Abbreviate VBA object base name elements wherever possible using a standardized abbreviation table. You can extend LNC by creating your own standard abbreviations as well. You should create and use standardized terminology in your applications wherever possible.

### Compound Base Names

Procedure base names should follow the construction `ObjectVerb`, where the `Object` portion describes the primary object type affected (often the same as the primary argument), and `Verb` describes the action. This style sorts functions and subs by their target object when shown in ordered lists:

```
FormCtlHide
FormCtlShow
FormPropAdd
FormPropGet
FormPropSet
```

This sort order is much more appealing than the more common alternative with `VerbObject` construction:

```
AddFormProp
GetFormProp
HideFormCtl
SetFormProp
ShowFormCtl
```

### Naming Conventions for VBA Objects

In Level Two of LNC, tags are required for the following VBA objects:

- Variables
- Type structures
- Constants

Optional tags are also available for some types of procedures. By definition, if you are a Level One user, LNC assumes that you are not writing VBA code. If you are creating procedures, you are a Level Two user and should always apply Level Two tags and prefixes to database objects as well as VBA objects.

In the syntax diagram earlier, you saw that base names are optional in some Level Two constructions. When programming in VBA in Level Two, the tag element is always required, but the base name is optional for local variables only. For example, a procedure that declared only one form object variable could legitimately use the variable name `frm`, which is a tag without a base name. Type structures, constants, and variables that have module-level or public scope must have both a tag and base name.

## Tags for Variables

Visual Basic variable tags are noted in Tables B.7–B.9, grouped by type of variable.

**Table B.7  Tags for VBA Data Variables**

| Variable Type | Tag | Variable Type | Tag |
|---|---|---|---|
| Boolean | bln | Integer | int |
| Byte | byt | Long | lng |
| Conditional Compilation Constant | ccc | Object | obj |
| Currency | cur | Single | sng |
| Date | dtm | String | str |
| Double | dbl | User-Defined Type | typ |
| Error | err | Variant | var |

**Note**

Many developers use dat as a tag for date objects, but this conflicts for us with the tag for Visual Basic's Data control.

In the preceding table, note that Conditional Compilation Constant, Error, and User-Defined Type are not true data types (created with `Dim Name As Datatype`), but rather programming concepts. A Conditional Compilation Constant variable is a flag of type `Boolean`, an Error variable is a `Variant` created with the `CVErr()` function, and user-defined types are unique constructs. Table B.8 lists examples of tabs for VBA object variables.

**Table B.8  Tags for VBA Object Variables**

| Object | Tag | Object | Tag |
|---|---|---|---|
| Access.Application | acca | Graph.Application | gpha |
| Assistant | ast | | |
| Application | app | Graph.Chart | gphc |
| Collection | col | GroupLevel | lvl |
| Control | ctl | MSProject.Application | prja |
| Controls | ctls | MSProject.Project | prjp |
| CommandBar | cbr | Module | bas or mdl |
| CommandBars | cbrs | Modules | bass or mdls |
| | | Page | pge |
| | | Pages | pges |
| CustomControl | ocx | PowerPoint.Application | ppta |
| | | Reference | ref |
| | | References | refs |

(continues)

| Table B.8 | Continued | | |
|---|---|---|---|
| **Object** | **Tag** | **Object** | **Tag** |
| CustomControlInReport | ocx | Report | rpt |
| Excel.Application | xlsa | Reports | rpts |
| Excel.Chart | xlsc | SchedulePlus.Application | scda |
| Excel.Sheet | xlsw | Word.Application | wrda |
| Form | frm | Word.Basic | wrdb |
| Forms | frms | | |

Table B.8 mixes entry points for OLE automation server objects, such as Excel worksheets and Project projects, with objects internal to Access, such as collections. While all of these items are objects, the two object types are treated differently in code.

Variables for objects in the Access object hierarchy can be dimensioned directly by class, as in this line:

```
Dim colFrmBldr As Collection
```

OLE Automation variables are created and used with a different syntax, as in this example:

```
Dim oxlsa As Object
Set oxlsa = CreateObject("Excel.Application")
```

The naming convention for entry points into OLE Automation server applications follows this syntax:

```
applicationtag entrypoint
```

where *applicationtag* is three characters and *entrypoint* is a single character. See the section "Creating Your Own Tags" later in this appendix for a complete explanation of this syntax. Note also that OLE Automation object variables are prefixed with o, as described in the "Prefixes for Variables" section that follows.

Table B.9 lists the LNC tags for Access DAO (data access object) variables.

| Table B.9 | Tags for Data Access Object Variables | | |
|---|---|---|---|
| **Object** | **Tag** | **Object** | **Tag** |
| Connection | cnc | QueryDef (Paradox) | qpdx |
| Connections | cncs | QueryDef (SQL Server) | qsql |
| Container | con | QueryDef (Text) | qtxt |
| Containers | cons | QueryDefs | qdfs |
| DBEngine | dbe | Recordset (Any type) | rst |
| Database (Any type) | dbs | Recordset (Btrieve) | rbtv |
| Database (Btrieve) | dbtv | Database (Excel) | dxls |
| Database (dBASE) | ddbf | Recordset (dBASE) | rdbf |

| Object | Tag | Object | Tag |
|--------|-----|--------|-----|
| Database (FoxPro) | dfox | Recordset (Dynaset) | rdyn |
| Database (Jet) | djet | Recordset (Excel) | rxls |
| Database (Lotus) | dwks | Recordset (FoxPro) | rfox |
| Database (ODBC) | dodb | Recordset (Lotus) | rwks |
| Database (Paradox) | dpdx | Recordset (ODBC) | rodb |
| Database (SQL Server) | dsql | Recordset (Paradox) | rpdx |
| Database (Text) | dtxt | Recordset (Snapshot) | rsnp |
| Databases | dbss | Recordset (SQL Server) | rsql |
| Document | doc | Recordset (Table) | rtbl |
| Documents | docs | Recordset (Text) | rtxt |
| Dynaset | dyn | Recordsets | rsts |
| Error | err | Relation | rel |
| Errors | errs | Relations | rels |
| Field | fld | Snapshot | snp |
| Fields | flds | Table | tbl |
| Group | gru | TableDef (Any type) | tdf |
| Groups | grus | TableDef (Btrieve) | tbtv |
| Index | idx | TableDef (dBASE) | tdbf |
| Indexes | idxs | TableDef (Excel) | txls |
| Parameter | prm | TableDef (FoxPro) | tfox |
| Parameters | prms | TableDef (Jet) | tjet |
| Property | prp | TableDef (Lotus) | twks |
| Properties | prps | TableDef (ODBC) | todb |
| QueryDef (any type) | qdf | TableDef (Paradox) | tpdx |
| QueryDef (Btrieve) | qbtv | TableDef (SQL Server) | tsql |
| QueryDef (dBASE) | qdbf | TableDef (Text) | ttxt |
| QueryDef (Excel) | qxls | TableDefs | tdfs |
| QueryDef (FoxPro) | qfox | User | usr |
| QueryDef (Jet) | qjet | Users | usrs |
| QueryDef (Lotus) | qwks | Workspace | wsp |
| QueryDef (ODBC) | qodb | Workspaces | wsps |

In Tables B.8 and B.9, tags for collection variables are made by adding s after the tag for the object type stored in the collection. The tags dyn, snp, and tbl above for Dynaset, Snapshot, and Table objects are directly relevant to users of Access 1.x and Access 2.0. Starting with Access 95, these object types are allowed only as a subtype of recordset variables, thus the recordset tags rdyn, rsnp, and rtbl.

> **Note**
>
> Although you saw earlier that a tag by itself is a legitimate variable name, a few variable tags shown (such as int) are VBA reserved words and will not compile in your procedures. Such tags require a base name.

## Prefixes for Variables

The prefixes for Visual Basic variables can be categorized into two groups: prefixes for scope, and all other prefixes. Because the model for variable scope has changed somewhat in Access 95, you examine scope prefixes first. The prefixes in the following list are ordered by increasing (broader) scope:

- *No Prefix*. Use no prefix for variables that are local to a procedure.

- s. Place this prefix before variables that are declared locally to a procedure with a Static statement.

- m. Use this prefix for module-level variables that are declared with **Dim** or **Private** statements in the Declarations section of a module.

- p. Use this prefix to denote variables declared as **Public** in the Declarations section of a form or report module. Such variables are publicly available to other procedures in the same database only.

- g. Use this prefix to denote variables declared as **Public** in the Declarations section of a standard module. Such variables are truly global and may be referenced from procedures in the current or other databases.

When used, scope prefixes always begin a variable name and precede any other prefixes.

In addition to scope, there are other characteristics of variables that can be identified by prefixes, as in the following list:

- a. Use this prefix to denote a variable that is declared as an array, including a ParamArray argument to a function.

- c. This prefix is placed before constants defined by the user.

- e. Use this prefix for a variable that is an element of a collection. Such variables are usually part of a **For Each...Next** loop structure.

- i. Use this prefix to denote a variable (usually of type **Integer**) that serves as an index into an array or an index counter in a **For...Next** loop.

- o. This prefix is placed before object variables that reference OLE Automation servers, where the tag denotes the type of server.

- r. Use this prefix for variables that are arguments (parameters) passed in to a procedure and declared **ByRef**, or not declared as either **ByRef** or **ByVal** (including a ParamArray), which implies **ByRef**.

■ t. Use this prefix to describe a variable that is declared as a user-defined **Type** structure.

■ v. Use this prefix for variables that are arguments (parameters) passed in to a procedure and declared **ByVal**.

A prefix provides a very detailed description of a variable, so the number of allowable prefix combinations is limited, as shown in Table B.10.

| Table B.10 Allowable Prefix Combinations | |
| --- | --- |
| **Any One of These...** | **...Can Come Before This** |
| s, m, p, g, r, v | a |
| m, p, g | c |
| s, m, p, g, r, v | e |
| s, m, p, g, r, v | i |
| s, m, p, g, r, v | ia |
| s, m, p, g, r, v | o |
| m, p, g | t |

Variables require a unique prefix when declared **Public** in a widely distributed application to prevent name contentions. See the section "Tags and Prefixes for Procedures" later in this chapter for more information.

### Naming Constants

Access 95 introduced sweeping changes in the area of constants. The changes most relevant to naming conventions include these:

■ A constant can now be assigned a data type when it is defined.

■ All Access constants have been renamed and carry a tag of ac, db, or vb to identify their primary functional area, Access, Jet, or VBA, respectively.

■ Constants can now be created with the **Variant** data type.

When creating constants, use a scope prefix (if appropriate), the prefix c, and the suitable tag for the constant's data type. To properly synchronize the tag and the data type, do not let Access assign the type; always use the full **Const** *Name* **As** *Datatype* syntax.

Constants require a unique prefix when declared **Public** in a widely distributed application to prevent name contention. See the following sections for more information on name contention.

### Tags and Prefixes for Procedures

Whether and how to prefix and tag procedure names is a debatable subject. In general, this style neither requires nor encourages placing characters before a procedure name except in the following situations.

**Prefixes for Procedures**   Procedures can have scope similar to that of variables:

- s (**Static**)
- p (**Public**)
- m (**Private**)
- g (global **Public**)

LNC supports the use of these scope prefixes on function names if they solve a particular need and are used consistently throughout an application.

If you are creating software for retail sale, for inclusion in the public domain, or that will be broadly distributed in some other manner, LNC requires that you prefix **Public** variables, constants, and procedures with a unique author prefix identifying you or your company. The prefix consists of two or three unique characters and an underscore, and prevents your object names from conflicting with object names in other referenced or referencing databases on a user's machine.

To create an author prefix, use your personal or company initials. For example, author prefixes for my companies are lci for Leszynski Company, Inc., and kwc for Kwery Corporation. Before using your selected prefix, make an effort to determine if the prefix is already widely in use. Kwery Corporation maintains a registry of VBA prefixes for Office add-in vendors.

**Tags for Procedures**   The LNC style prescribes the following naming convention tags for procedures:

- cbf. Use this tag on procedure names for code behind a form or report. This tag clearly differentiates such procedures from `Property` procedures and event procedures.

- prp. Use this tag on `Property` procedure names defined with `Property Get`, `Property Let`, and `Property Set` statements. This tag clearly differentiates such procedures from functions, subprocedures, and event procedures.

LNC does not require or suggest assigning a data type tag to functions to reflect their return value. However, if you have a specific need to tag procedures to reflect their return value type, use the appropriate tags from the preceding section "Tags for Variables" and apply the tags consistently to all procedures in an application.

### Using Macros Instead of VBA

If you use Access macros, apply the rules previously described for VBA procedure base names to your macro base names. Macro groups in the Database window should also utilize the macro prefixes and tags noted earlier in this appendix. Individual macros within a macro group do not have prefixes or tags, except for event macros as noted later on.

All macros for a specific form or report should be placed into one macro group, with the form or report name as the macro base name. Within the macro group, create standard macros and event macros for the form or report. If a macro is tied to a form or report event, show the event name or an abbreviation in the macro name. For example, you would store macros related to frmCust in macro group mfrmCust. Event macro names in the group might include `Form_Current` and `txtLastName_Change`.

Macros that are not specific to a form or report should hold actions that have some common functionality or purpose. Use the same grouping methodology (related items together) that you would apply to locate procedures in standard VBA modules.

### VBA Object Name Examples

Table B.11 shows examples of VBA variables applying the various conventions in this section.

| Table B.11 VBA Variable Name Examples | |
| --- | --- |
| **Declaration** | **Description** |
| **Dim** oxlsaBudget **As Object** | Excel.Application |
| **Function** lci_ArraySum (ParamArray _ <br> ravarNum() **As Variant**) **As Double** | Company identifier |
| **Public** giaintPartNum **As Integer** | Global index into array |
| **Const** clngCustNumMax **As Long** = 10000 | **Const** for maximum value of CustID |
| **Function** FileLock(**ByVal** vstrFile **As** _ <br> **String**) **As Integer** | **ByVal** argument |

# Creating Your Own Tags

What do you do when LNC doesn't address a particular object naming need?

- First, contact Kwery Corporation with an explanation of your need, so that the LNC style can be improved for the benefit of all users.

- Second, consider if what you are trying to do is covered by the style in some other way. For example, in your development team you call tables that link two other tables in a many-to-many relationship linking tables, and you want to create a new table tag tlnk as a result. However, on examination of all table tags, you would find trel already exists, defined as "Table (many-to-many relation)," which is the correct tag for what you need. Even though the nomenclature is not exactly what you require, it is better to use an existing tag than create another one.

When other options are exhausted, you can create a custom tag to address your need. When creating a custom tag, these should be your guidelines:

- Do not redefine an existing tag. No matter how badly you really want the three- or four-character combination for your own purpose, never reuse a defined tag.

- Do not change the rule for tags. Stay within the three- to four-character range followed by LNC.

- Use the conventions in existing tags as your guide for the new one. For example, all table tags start with t, all query tags with q, and so forth. Any new tags you make for these objects should begin with the correct letter. See Table B.12 for guidelines on standard tag components.

---

> **Note**
>
> Some of the examples are from the Microsoft Office version of LNC. Tag components that can be easily inferred from the preceding tags are not listed in the table (for example, the component fox for FoxPro can be inferred from the tags tfox and dfox.)

---

When creating a new tag, it should be mnemonic enough to uniquely shorten the word it represents, and should only use characters from the root word or a generally accepted shorthand.

**Table B.12   Some Standard Tag Components**

| Item | Segment | Examples | Location |
|------|---------|----------|----------|
| bar | br | mmbr, pbr, tbr | anywhere |
| data/databound | d | dout | leading |
| database | db | dbe | leading |
| form | f | fdlg | leading |
| macro | m | mmnu | leading |
| MAPI | mp | mpm | leading |
| module | b | bas | leading |
| query | q | qsel | leading |
| report | r | rdet | leading |
| set | st | rst | anywhere |
| table | t | tdf | leading |
| view | vw | lvw, tvw | anywhere |

To create tags for object variables pointing to (OLE) Automation server applications, start with the three-character DOS file extension for the files created by the server application, if unique and applicable. If not unique, create a meaningful abbreviation of the application name. Add to the three-character abbreviation a single character for the actual object that serves as the entry point for the application, such as Basic in Word.Basic.

For example, to create a tag for OLE Automation with Shapeware's Visio program, which is an OLE server, use either vsd (the data file extension) or vis (a mnemonic for Visio) as the basis for the tag, then add a for Application, because the entry point to Visio's automation engine is a call to Visio.Application. Thus the tag and its use in variable declarations would appear as:

```
Dim ovisa As Object
Dim ovisaDoc As Object
Set ovisa = CreateObject("Visio.Application")
Set ovisaDoc = ovisa.Documents.Open("C:\VISIO\HOUSE.VSD")
```

# How to Get the Complete Text of the LNCs

The full text of the Leszynski Naming Conventions for Microsoft Access and an expanded discussion of the naming convention philosophy appears in Que's *Access Expert Solutions* by Stan Leszynski. You also can obtain the full text of the Leszynski Naming Conventions for Microsoft Access, on which this abridged appendix is based, from Kwery Corporation. The following additional information is also available:

- The Leszynski Naming Conventions for Microsoft Solution Developers paper

- The Leszynski Naming Conventions for Microsoft Visual Basic paper

- Windows Help file versions of each LNC document

- LNC programmers' tools

Contact Kwery via the order line at 1-800-ATKWERY, or on the product information line at 206-644-7830. Kwery also can be reached on CompuServe at **71573,3261** or by fax at 206-644-8409. ●

# Appendix C

# Data Dictionary for the Personnel Actions Table

You use the Personnel Actions table in examples in the following chapters:

| | |
|---|---|
| 4 | "Working with Access Databases and Tables" |
| 5 | "Entering, Editing, and Validating Data in Tables" |
| 9 | "Understanding Operators and Expressions in Access" |
| 10 | "Creating Multitable and Crosstab Queries" |
| 12 | "Creating and Using Forms" |
| 13 | "Designing Custom Multitable Forms" |
| 17 | "Exporting Data to World Wide Web Pages" |
| 20 | "Adding Graphics to Forms and Reports" |
| 24 | "Working with Structured Query Language" |

The step-by-step procedures for creating the Personnel Actions table and adding the first nine records to the table are included in Chapter 4, "Working with Access Databases and Tables."

Tables C.1 through C.5 provide a tabular data dictionary for the Personnel Actions table.

Table C.1 lists the values of the Field Name, Caption, Data Type, Field Size, and Format properties of the Personnel Actions table. These values are entered in the Properties text boxes for each field.

| Table C.1 Field Properties for the Personnel Actions Table | | | | |
| --- | --- | --- | --- | --- |
| **Field Name** | **Caption** | **Data Type** | **Field Size** | **Format** |
| paID | ID | Number | Long Integer | General Number |
| paType | Type | Text | 1 | @> (all caps) |
| paInitiatedBy | Initiated By | Number | Integer | General Number |
| paScheduledDate | Scheduled | Date/Time | N/A | Short Date |
| paApprovedBy | Approved By | Number | Integer | General Number |
| paEffectiveDate | Effective | Date/Time | N/A | Short Date |
| paRating | Rating | Number | Integer | General Number |
| paAmount | Amount | Currency | N/A | ##,##0.00# |
| paComments | Comments | Memo | N/A | None |

Table C.2 lists the entries you make to assign default values to each field for which default values are required. You enter these values in the Default Values text box of the indicated field.

| Table C.2 Default Field Values for the Personnel Actions Table | | |
| --- | --- | --- |
| **Field Name** | **Default Value** | **Comments** |
| paType | Q | Quarterly performance reviews are the most common personnel action. |
| paScheduledDate | =Date() | The expression to enter today's (DOS) date. |
| paEffectiveDate | =Date() +28 | Four weeks from today's date. |

Table C.3 lists the values you enter as Validation Rules and the accompanying Validation text that is displayed in the status bar if an entry violates one of the rules. Only those fields with validation rules are shown in Table C.3.

| Table C.3 Validation Criteria for Fields of the Personnel Actions Table | | |
| --- | --- | --- |
| **Field Name** | **Validation Rule** | **Validation Text** |
| paID | >0 | Please enter a valid employee ID number. |
| paType | "H" Or "S" Or "Q" or "C" Or "Y" Or "B" | Only H, S, Q, Y, B, and C codes may be entered. |
| paInitiatedBy | >0 | Please enter a valid supervisor ID number. |
| paScheduledDate | Between Date()—3650 And Date()+365more | Scheduled dates cannot be than 10 years ago nor more than one year from now. |

| Field Name | Validation Rule | Validation Text |
|---|---|---|
| paApprovedBy | >0 Or Is Null | Please enter a valid manager ID number or leave blank if not approved. |
| paRating | Between 0 And 9 or Is Null | Rating range is 0 for terminated employees, 1 to 9, or blank. |

Table C.4 lists the key fields, indexes, and relationships for the Personnel Actions table. A composite key field is used so that duplication of an entry of a record for an employee is precluded. The default index that Access creates on the primary key field is shown for completeness; you do not add this index because Access creates indexes on key fields automatically. You establish the relationship with the Employees table by opening the Database window, choosing Tools, Relationships, and making the selections that are listed for the Relationships property in Table C.4 in the Relationships dialog.

**Table C.4   Key Fields, Indexes, and Relationships for the Personnel Actions Table**

| Property | Value |
|---|---|
| Primary Key Fields | paID;paType;paScheduledDate |
| Primary Key Index | paID;paType;paScheduledDate |
| Relationships | Primary table: Employees<br>Related table: Personnel Actions<br>Enforce Referential Integrity: True (checked)<br>Cascade Deletions: True (checked)<br>Cascade Updates: True (checked) |

Table C.5 lists the first nine entries in the Personnel Actions table that are used to demonstrate use of the table. The Scheduled and Effective entries are based on the HiredDate information in the Employees table. Enter these values after you have created the composite primary key for the table. Assigning performance ratings (except 0, terminated) to the records is optional.

**Table C.5   First Nine Entries for the Personnel Actions Table**

| ID | Type | Initiated By | Scheduled | By | Approved Date | Effective Amount | New Comments |
|---|---|---|---|---|---|---|---|
| 1 | H | 1 | 01-May-92 | | 01-May-92 | 2,000 | Hired |
| 2 | H | 1 | 14-Aug-92 | | 14-Aug-92 | 3,500 | Hired |
| 3 | H | 1 | 01-Apr-92 | | 01-Apr-92 | 2,250 | Hired |
| 4 | H | 2 | 03-May-93 | 2 | 03-May-93 | 2,250 | Hired |
| 5 | H | 2 | 17-Oct-93 | 2 | 17-Oct-93 | 2,500 | Hired |
| 6 | H | 5 | 17-Oct-93 | 2 | 17-Oct-93 | 4,000 | Hired |
| 7 | H | 5 | 02-Jan-94 | 2 | 02-Jan-94 | 3,000 | Hired |
| 8 | H | 2 | 05-Mar-94 | 2 | 05-Mar-94 | 2,500 | Hired |
| 9 | H | 5 | 15-Nov-94 | 2 | 15-Nov-94 | 3,000 | Hired |

VIII

Appendixes

# Index

**M**

# Microsoft® FrontPage™ 97
## Web Authoring and Management Tool
### with Bonus Pack

## Professional Web Site Publishing Without Programming

Microsoft FrontPage 97 with Bonus Pack is the ideal way to get professional-quality Internet or intranet sites up and running fast. It offers all the best new Web technologies, plus powerful tools for all your Web creation and management tasks.

## Easy for everyone.

Microsoft FrontPage 97 with Bonus Pack can quickly turn you into a Webmaster. Use more than 30 built-in templates and wizards to build entire Web sites and individual pages easily. And with the WYSIWYG FrontPage Editor, there's no need to know HTML! Insert hyperlinks and add information from Microsoft Office and other sources with drag-and-drop simplicity. And manage your Web sites easily with the graphical tools in the FrontPage Explorer.

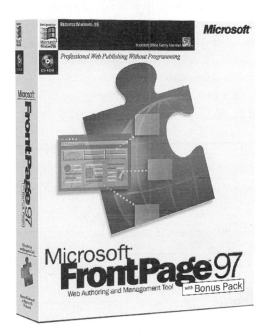

FrontPage 97 with Bonus Pack makes creating professional-quality Web sites effortless with powerful new functionality, support for the latest Web technologies, and seamless integration with Microsoft Office. It's never been easier!

## The best of the Web.

The latest Web technologies are at your fingertips. Drop WebBot™ components onto your pages to add such advanced functionality as full-text searching and forms. Customize your Web sites with JavaScript™ and Microsoft Visual Basic®, Scripting Edition, using an intuitive user interface. Or easily connect to databases or add ActiveX™ controls, Java applets™, and Netscape™ plug-ins for interactive, compelling Web pages.

# Professional Web site publishing is no longer just for experts!

## The complete Web suite.

FrontPage 97 with Bonus Pack gives you powerful tools to create rich content and manage your Web sites effectively. Enliven your Web pages with images designed in Microsoft Image Composer, included in FrontPage 97 with Bonus Pack, or incorporate professional photographs from the Microsoft Image Composer stock photo library. Edit HTML code directly in the FrontPage Editor and preview your Web pages in any browser – without leaving FrontPage. And use advanced tools to remotely author and edit your Web sites.

## Office integration.

FrontPage 97 with Bonus Pack has a familiar environment that allows you to use any document created with Microsoft Office 97 easily because it works like other Office 97 applications. Use the shared spelling checker, global Find and Replace, and the Microsoft Thesaurus to guarantee your Web sites remain accurate and compelling.

The future of Web publishing is here today! Create and manage your Web sites the fast and easy way with Microsoft FrontPage 97 with Bonus Pack.

**Visit the Microsoft Office 97 World Wide Web site at http://www.microsoft.com/office/**